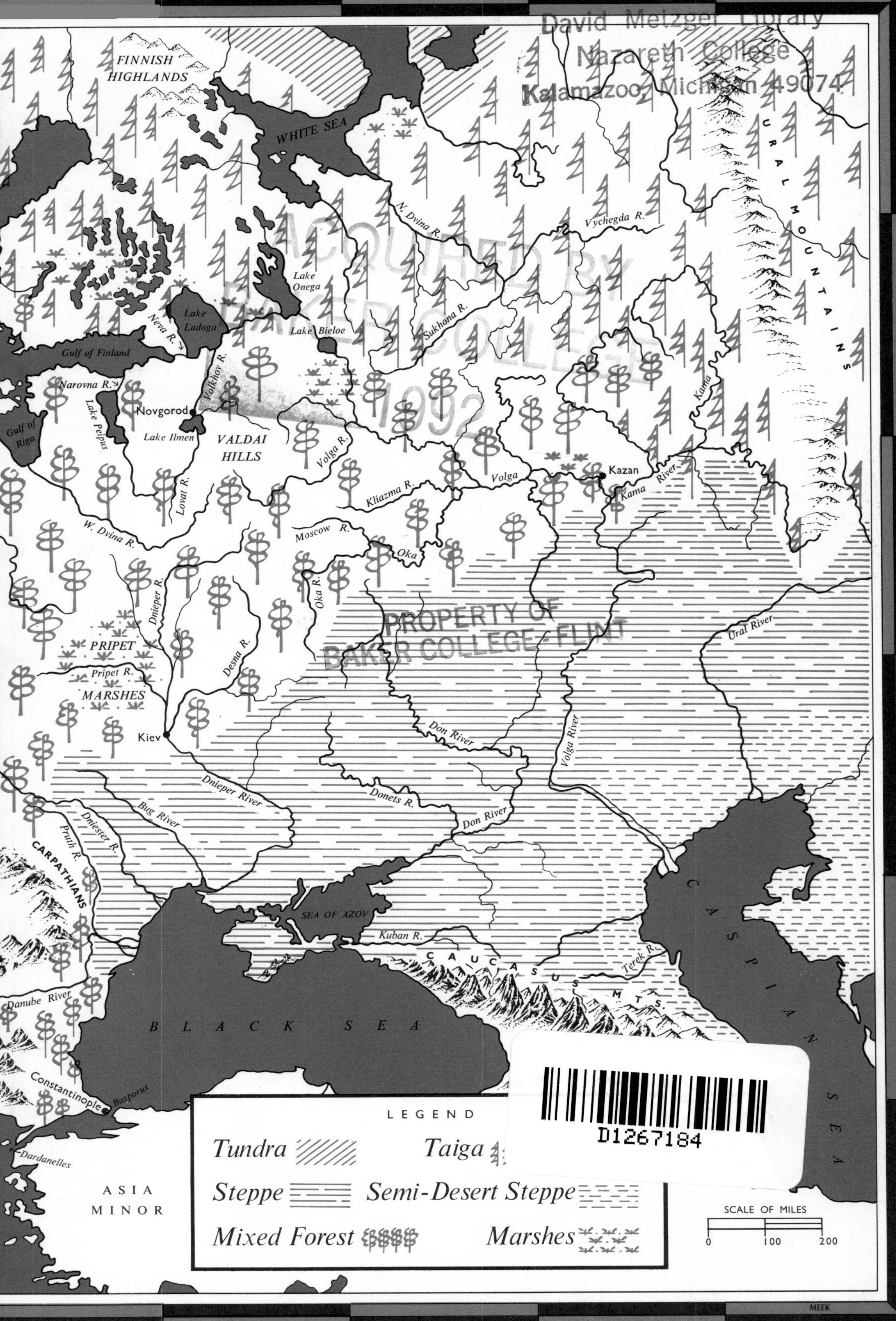
FINNISH HIGHLANDS
WHITE SEA
N. Dvina R.
Vychegda R.
URAL MOUNTAINS
Lake Onega
Lake Ladoga
Neva R.
Gulf of Finland
Lake Bieloe
Sukhona R.
Kama
Narovna R.
Volkhov R.
Gulf of Riga
Lake Peipus
Novgorod
Lake Ilmen
VALDAI HILLS
Volga R.
Volga
Kazan
Kama River
Kliazma R.
Lovat R.
W. Dvina R.
Moscow R.
Oka
Oka R.
Dnieper R.
Desna R.
PRIPET
Pripet R.
MARSHES
Kiev
Ural River
Don River
Volga River
Dnieper River
Donets R.
Bug River
Dniester R.
Pruth R.
CARPATHIANS
SEA OF AZOV
Kuban R.
CAUCASUS MTS.
Terek R.
CASPIAN SEA
Danube River
BLACK SEA
Constantinople
Bosporus
Dardanelles
ASIA MINOR
LEGEND
Tundra
Taiga
Steppe
Semi-Desert Steppe
Mixed Forest
Marshes
SCALE OF MILES
0
100
200
MEEK

A HISTORY OF RUSSIA

A HISTORY OF RUSSIA

By JESSE D. CLARKSON

SECOND EDITION

RANDOM HOUSE • NEW YORK

9876543

Library of Congress Catalog Card Number: 69–11101

Manufactured in the United States of America
by The Haddon Craftsmen, Inc., Scranton, Pa.

Published 1961 Second Edition 1969

To VANWY *and* KEM

Preface to the First Edition

The purposes of history are many, and sometimes in conflict with each other. Some think of history as a story to amuse; some expect to find in the past lessons useful in the present and for the future. History has been defined as simply the record of past politics; it has been conceived as the complex product of the operation of material forces, scarcely subject to control by man's will. Some think of history as the conscious result of human thought; others have seen in it the working of an inscrutable divine power. At one pole are those who maintain that history should be presented *wie es eigentlich gewesen,* without reference to the sequel; at the other are those who believe that the past, on the whole, is dead, and that consideration should be given only to what has survived from the past into the living present.

However one thinks of history, it is obvious that within the confines of a single volume—or, for that matter, of a dozen or a hundred volumes—it is not possible to present the whole history of even one country or its people. There must be a process of deliberate selection of facts and of ruthless exclusion of an infinitely greater number of facts, to say nothing of the still vaster body of data of which any individual writer is necessarily ignorant.

Limits of space forbid any attempt here at careful analysis or exposition of the principles that have guided the writing of the present book. Suffice it, then, to say that history is here viewed as a continuum, in which any given "present moment" is but the algebraic sum of the cumulative past, immediately itself becoming part of the past and contributing to condition the new present throughout all future time. Historically viewed, the distinctions between past, present, and future are shifting and fundamentally meaningless. However "present-minded" one may be, there is much truth in the saying that there is nothing new under the sun.

This, of course, does not mean that there is no change. Change is, indeed, one of the most continuous things about history; without change there would be no point in the study of history. Yet, however radically different from the old the new pattern may be, it can never be more than a recombination and outgrowth of existing elements. It is not merely a question of conservative survival of traditional habits of human thought and action; it is a matter also of the effect of the accumulation, conscious or subconscious, of the life-experience of mankind. Human physiology and human psychology persist basically unchanged; great as are the differences between the relationship of man to nature a thousand—or even a hundred—years ago and now, Nature is still Nature and man is still man, not God.

This book is the product of more than thirty years of teaching Russian history. It is an attempt to distill from studies made by many others, tempered by the writer's own thinking and partial investigations, what it is hoped may be a coherent account of the development of Russia and of the Russian people from the earliest times to the moment of writing. Whatever merit it may have must be assigned in the first instance to the reactions of many academic generations of college students who have helped to shape this presentation.

Columbia University Library, the New York Public Library, and the Library of Congress have been of inestimable value. The Ukrainian Academy of Arts and Sciences in the United States and the Yivo Institute for Jewish Research, in New York City, have also been most coöperative, while Brooklyn College Library has freely supplemented its resources through interlibrary loans. Courtesies extended at the British Museum and at the Bodleian Library at Oxford University also merit acknowledgment, as does assistance from the Inter-University Committee on Travel Grants (for research in the Soviet Union).

The author is deeply indebted also to innumerable colleagues in Departments of History and in other disciplines throughout the country and abroad, who in most cases have perhaps been unaware of the services they have rendered. Particular mention must be made of three Brooklyn College colleagues, Dr. Madeline R. Robinton, Dr. Samuel J. Hurwitz, and Dr. Abraham S. Eisenstadt, and of the Rev. Prebendary Eley, who by their peculiarly patient yet acid criticisms have eroded some of the imperfections in the manuscript. Among members of the Random House staff special mention should be made of the work of David Wolfe Biller, and in particular of Leonore C. Hauck, whose unflaggingly painstaking collaboration has been invaluable in very many ways. Jane Alles worked ably on much of the auxiliary material, while the index was prepared by Bernice Zelditch and the maps by Bill Meek. Especially, also, must be mentioned the self-denying patience of my wife, Mary Griffiths Clarkson, which has left in the shade even the extensive work she has put in on various phases of the task.

J.D.C.

Preface to the Second Edition

Since the publication of the first edition, many excellent studies have appeared, both in the Soviet Union and in the Western world, especially in the United States. So far as these have affected the interpretative analysis offered in the first edition, the text has been altered to incorporate these findings of subsequent research. In addition, the concluding chapters have been revised to bring the story down to date, and the Suggestions for Further Reading at the end of each chapter have been revised to call attention to the best of the many new studies of particular aspects of Russia's history.

The author wishes to express his appreciation for the helpful assistance of the editorial staff of Random House, particularly of Mrs. Leonore C. Hauck and of Mrs. Sybil Elman Maimin, as well as of those colleagues in the profession who have in many cases offered valuable comments.

A Note on Russian Dates and Names

In presenting Russian history in the English language, special problems arise from the persistence of use of the Julian calendar ("Old Style") in Russia until shortly after the Bolshevik seizure of power and from the differences between the alphabets.

In general, dates are here given according to whatever calendar prevailed in Russia at the time. To avoid chronological confusion with related Western events, however, an exception is made for the twentieth century: even before the Bolshevik's adoption of the Gregorian calendar ("New Style") in February, 1918, dates have been converted to their Western equivalents. In the eighteenth century, the O.S. lag was 11 days; in the nineteenth, it was 12 days; in the twentieth, it was 13 days. Thus, the following correspondence may be made:

	Julian (O.S.)	*Gregorian* (N.S.)
Death of Empress Elizabeth	December 25, 1761	January 5, 1762
Decembrist uprising	December 14, 1825	December 26, 1825
Bolshevik seizure of power	October 25, 1917	November 7, 1917

In bibliographic references to Russian newspapers, the O.S. date as it appeared on the newspaper has been followed with the N.S. equivalent.

In transliterating from Cyrillic into Roman characters, the Library of Congress system has been in general adhered to. The principal departures, some of which conform to the usage of the Russian Translation Project of the American Council of Learned Societies, have been that final-*ii* has been rendered as *y*, final-*oi* has been rendered as *-oy*, and initial *Ia, Ie,* and *Iu* have been rendered as *Ya, Ye,* and *Yu.* (Normally *y* has been used only to render a Russian vowel that does not exist in English.) The "soft sign" (often represented in English by an apostrophe) has been omitted.

Exceptions have been made in rendering into English the names of some Russian persons or places. Since many well-known Russian names have come into English prominence through French or other European languages, their popular spellings (e.g., Tchaikovsky) often conform to no acceptable or consistent transliteration system; for the reader's convenience, however, the familiar spellings have been retained. Similarly, many other names which have become Anglicized are given in their popular form rather than transliterated: Moscow (for Moskva), Alexander (for Aleksandr), Nicholas (for Nikolai), etc.

To facilitate library research, however, the Library of Congress system has been retained more fully in the Notes and Suggestions for Further Reading (following each chapter) and in the more complete Bibliography (at the end of the volume).

CONTENTS

MAPS*

PHOTOGRAPHS*

PICTURE ACKNOWLEDGMENTS

Sovfoto Pictures on plates ii, vi, x (bottom), xi, xii (top, middle), xiv, xvi (top [right] and bottom), xvii, xviii (bottom), xxii (top), xxiii, xxiv

Brown Brothers vii, xix (bottom), xxi

Bettmann Archive xix (top)

Wide World xxii (bottom)

* plates i-xii follow page 266
plates xiii-xxiv follow page 586

A HISTORY OF RUSSIA

Chapter

1

Introductory

PERSPECTIVES

In approaching the study of any country's history, it is well to give some attention to the perspective in which it should be viewed. Mankind, at bottom the same the world over, has at different times and in different areas produced a variety of civilizations fundamentally different one from the other. Cultural borrowings have not been uncommon, but basic differences remain. For any given civilization, it is possible to develop a standard terminology and a conventional periodization, but an attempt to carry this frame of reference over to the study of the history of some other civilization only leads to confusion, since each has followed a distinctly different course of development. Explanation of the history of any country can therefore be successful only in terms of the peculiar civilization of which it is a part.

Within the covering envelope of any general type of civilization there have been developed many variants; the histories of Spain and Sweden, of England and Italy, of Ireland and Hungary, differ widely from each other. Yet it is possible in all of these and in all others that constitute the "Western" world, including its offshoots in such lands as the United States and Canada, Australia and New Zealand, Brazil and Argentina, to perceive significant factors that supply a common denominator in their genesis and development. In the broadest sense, of course, all mankind is affected by the same fundamental human attributes, but the form of their expression and the differing emphases placed on basic human values have over the centuries—in some cases over millenniums—created vital differences in patterns which the student of human relations cannot intelligently ignore.

In the case of Russia, the fundamental question is whether that country historically forms an integral part of Western civilization or whether, as many have argued, her history can only be explained in terms of "Asia." The term "Asia," of course, requires definition. Asia can be understood in terms of a distinct land mass on the map, but not in terms of a specific civilization. That huge and widely diversified area has given birth to a number of separate civilizations as distinct from one another as any of them is from that of the much smaller peninsula of Europe. Among them, those of the river valleys of China, of India, and of Mesopotamia have been the most important, but with none of these three civilizations has Russia, at least in the formative centuries of her history, had any meaningful contact. If one is to speak at all of Asia as influencing Russian development, it is only Central Asia, often called "Turkestan" or "Tatary" that is involved. A homely formulation of the theory that Russia is Asia is the old saying, "Scratch a Russian, and you'll catch a Tatar."

The concept that Russia is "Asiatic" is an old one, which may perhaps be traced as far back as Herodotus' description of "Scythia." In the nineteenth century it had a great vogue. The West's picture of Russia was largely in terms of Siberia and wolves, of the knout and the nagaika wielded by presumably Oriental Cossacks; nursemaids were wont to frighten children with lurid but familiar tales of the land of "the bear that walks like a man." In the 1920's the *New York Times* correspondent in Moscow regularly interpreted Russia in the light of her "Asiatic" character, and even today there are many who think of Stalin as essentially an "Oriental" despot. In Russia itself a prolonged and acrimonious intellectual controversy was waged over the question whether the reforming energy of Peter the Great had or had not rescued Russia from her dark "Asiatic" past.

Gradually an opposite point of view has come to prevail. As Russians set themselves seriously to the study of their own history, they began to see matters in a different light. The importance of the "Tatar yoke" diminished as the history of Russia before the Mongol conquest came to be better understood. In many quarters, both in Russia and among Continental scholars who began to be interested in her history, the idea that Russia had an "Oriental" rather than an "Occidental" flavor lingered on, but it tended to be expressed merely in terms of the influence of Byzantium on Rus as contrasted with that of Rome over the West.

One of the sharpest and most extreme statements of the close relation of Russia to the West was penned by the Czech scholar-statesman, T. G. Masaryk, in his admirable study, *The Spirit of Russia.* The Czechs, fighting to assert their ethnic integrity under German rule, have long been attracted, as the more independent Poles and Yugoslavs have not, by the idea of Pan-Slavism. Partly, no doubt, under the influence of the feeling of Czechs that they constitute the Slav link between civilized Europe and backward Russia, Masaryk described the situation by noting that

> it must be remembered that the Russian crossing the Western frontier speaks of "going to Europe." . . . The further eastward we go, the further do we find ourselves from Europe, until at length Europe is represented only by the railway, the refreshment rooms at the station, and isolated hotels furnished and managed in European style.

Yet his conclusion was:

> Russia is of our own kind, exhibits our own quality, is what Europe has been. . . . When, therefore, I contrast Russia and Europe, I contrast two epochs. Russia does not differ essentially from Europe; but Russia is not yet essentially one with Europe.[1]

The concept that Russia is merely a retarded Europe is, however, an oversimplification. The cultural relationship of Russia to Western Europe is a complicated one. On the one side, many of the phenomena characteristic of the history of Western Europe were not duplicated in Russian experience. The customary periodization of Western history, with its oversharp division into "the Middle Ages" and "Modern Europe," is very difficult to fit into Russian history. Russia never formed, as did most of the West, part of the Roman Empire. Russia never acknowledged the spiritual, much less the temporal, supremacy of the Roman pope. In Russian history the term "Renaissance" has no meaning. Russia never underwent the tremendous upheaval of the "Reformation." The "Enlightenment" came to Russia from outside, and only as the thinnest veneer on an upper crust of her society. Russia was not shaken by the internal commotions that attended the growth of liberal thought in England, in France, and in other areas of the West. She was not transformed by the rise of individual economic initiative that accompanied the growth of trade and industry in the West. Nor did Russia pass through that evolution of representative institutions which in the West underlay the rise of democracy.

On the other hand, Russia had experiences that the West did not share. The most spectacular of these was the "Tatar yoke," which rested on Russia for more than two centuries. Partly on this account, but for other reasons as well, Russia lived for a number of centuries in a near-isolation from other Christian communities that implanted a virulent xenophobia deep in the Russian consciousness. Unlike Western Europe, Russia developed to the south and east a frontier in something of the American sense, which had a profound effect on the older settled regions, though not on the lines of the Turner hypothesis concerning the influence of the frontier on the growth of American democracy. Although Western Europe produced personalities not too unlike Ivan the Terrible and Peter the Great, it would be hard to match the impact they had under the peculiar conditions of Russian life. Finally, the West never developed any counterpart of the Bolsheviks, who, despite the fact that they drew their official ideology ready-made from the West, so completely transmogrified it that their actions emphasized the uniqueness of Russia.

Nevertheless, there are many basic threads running through Russian history which make evident the close relationship of Russia to the West. The course of Russian development has in many respects diverged from that of the rest of the Western world. Yet the original equipment of the Russians—their religious beliefs, their way of making a living, their political practices, and the basic principles of their language—was one with that of early Western Europeans. The late appearance of Russia on the historical scene and the conditions of the environment in which Russians lived profoundly affected Russia's evolution, but the main lines of her history were the same as those of the West. Strongly individual as Russia's history has been, Russia's kinship is to Europe, not to "Asia."

Since the problem of the light in which Russia should be viewed is not a simple one, this book will attempt not to treat Russia in a vacuum, but instead, by cross-reference, to compare her history with that of the more familiar West. It is to be hoped that, by constantly calling attention to phases of development parallel to those of the West considered as a whole and by pointing out significant differences, this account will the better enable the reader to form his own judgment of the true place of Russian history in the development of world civilization and thus arrive at a juster understanding of its present state and even of the prospects for the future.

GEOGRAPHY

One of the most powerful conditioning forces in the history of any country is its geographic setting. This is particularly true in the earlier period of its history, before the advance of technology has begun to enable man to bend nature to his will. Under modern conditions, the influence of geography on history has been much reduced; it is now largely a question of available natural resources, particularly minerals which in earlier centuries were of no consequence. Yet, even today, latitude, topography, climate, and soil conditions play a very vital role. Before embarking, therefore, on consideration of the human factor in history, it is necessary to summarize the principal features of the natural environment in which man has played his role. In considering the influence of geography on Russian history, it is important to note that it is the geography of the area in which Russians lived in the early centuries, not of the whole Soviet Union today, that exercised a formative influence on Russian ideas and institutions.

The largest part of the Union of Soviet Socialist Republics, as of its predecessor, the Empire of All the Russias, is Siberia. Siberia is an area larger than the lighted surface of the moon at its full, but its population per square mile is less than one person more than as yet are known to live on the moon.

Granted that a fraction of a human being is infinitely more important than nobody at all, it should nevertheless be fairly evident that Siberia has not been of great significance in a world of people. One may in fact doubt whether Siberia has been at all comparable in historic importance to the moon; after all, without human aid the moon does govern the tides throughout the world.

In any case, until the late sixteenth century, i.e., a period later than the conventional date for the beginning of modern as distinct from medieval history, Siberia meant nothing at all to Russia. The first Russians to penetrate Siberia were, like the French *coureurs de bois* in Canada, simply in quest of furs; moving from river basin to river basin, all of which drained northward into the frozen Arctic, Russian fur traders gradually worked their way eastward until, shortly before the middle of the seventeenth century, they found themselves on the bleak shores of the Sea of Okhotsk. Initially they were disappointed at having reached the apparent limit of hunting and trapping, but realization that fur-bearing animals were to be found also in the sea led them, early in the eighteenth century, to island-hop from Kamchatka to Alaska and so down the Pacific coast of North America until they established advanced posts in what is now California, whence, under pressure of the Monroe Doctrine, they withdrew northward. The main point is that Siberia and what lay beyond it were of no importance to Russia except as a source of furs and, much later, as a suitable site for penal settlements. It should be further noted that the Amur country and the coastal province, with its "warm-water" port of Vladivostok, were acquired by Russia only a hundred years ago (1858); from the late seventeenth to the late nineteenth century China had easily held Russia back. Until quite recent times, therefore, the vast expanse of Siberia can be wholly dismissed from the study of Russian history.

Central Asia was brought under Russian control only in the second half of the nineteenth century. Nevertheless it exercised a very powerful, though external and negative, influence on the early centuries of Russian history. Unlike Siberia, most of which was covered by forest interspersed with swamps, Central Asia was open grassland, with very little water. Without irrigation works—wholly beyond the power of its early inhabitants—the region was unsuited for agriculture. On the other hand, the open spaces and the natural grass cover lent themselves to the far easier occupation of pastoral nomadism. These nomads, periodically spilling over into the Russian plain, were a formidable destructive force. Apart from these incursions, however, Central Asia in itself had no significance for the course of Russian history until quite recent times.

The Caucasus area offered no natural advantages, save as a place of refuge for peoples broken in struggle on a wider scene. For centuries, the principal interest of this area, apart from its striking scenery, was as an ethnographic museum, sheltering in its divided valleys remnants of all sorts of peoples, from the south as well as from the north, who eked out a precarious and generally savage existence in their isolation. The Caucasus region therefore has little bearing on Russian history until the beginning of the nineteenth century, when Imperial Russia began to take it under its protection.

The portion of the territory of the Soviet Union that merits attention at this point is therefore that area sometimes defined as "Russia in Europe." It is the geography of this area that was capable of vitally affecting the course of Russian history. Though considerable stretches of it, including the coastlines of the Baltic and Black seas, became Russian much later than the establishment of English colonies on the Atlantic coast of North America, their inhabitants had for centuries intimate contact with the Russians and were therefore able in some measure to influence their development. The geographic factors that made these non-Russian parts of "Russia in Europe" important, even in the early centuries of Russian history, cannot here be ignored. The whole area under consideration, though only a fraction of the Empire of All the Russias and of its successor, the Soviet Union, is a huge one: about two-thirds the area of the continental United States and considerably exceeding the total area of Western Europe.

If, with reference to a physical map, one compares "Russia in Europe" with the rest of Europe, one cannot fail to be impressed with certain considerations.* For one thing, "Russia in Europe" presents an enormous area with relatively little coastline: Western Europe is peninsular, allowing strong interaction of land and sea; Russia is continental, the sea playing a very slight role. Secondly, Russia is almost flat; from the Valdai Hills, rising little more than a thousand feet above sea level, the land gradually shelves off, uninterrupted by any mountain barriers. Russia's mountains—the Urals, the Caucasus, the Carpathians, and the Finnish highlands—are located at the extreme corners of the plain, leaving the four sides and the interior unprotected. In contrast, Western Europe slopes rapidly down in all directions from the huge central upsurge of the Alps and the mountain chains radiating from it. In both respects "Russia in Europe" certainly bears far more resemblance to the vast area of Central Asia than it does to Western Europe. If topography were the whole story, the answer to the question "Is Russia Europe or Asia?" would have to be "Asia."

The radical geographical difference between Russia and Europe is magnified when one considers climatic conditions. Here latitude is of major significance. Western Europe does lie in rather northerly latitudes, but its center of gravity is considerably farther south than is Russia's. Western Europe enjoys also the inestimable advantage of proximity to the Atlantic Ocean, warmed by the Gulf Stream. Although the Gulf Stream, curling around Scandinavia, does lap the northern shores of Russia, with the par-

* See the map on the inside front cover of this book.

adoxical result that her most northerly seaport is also the most ice-free, the fact that this part of Russia lies within the Arctic Circle nullifies any advantage to her agriculture. It should not be forgotten that almost the whole of Russia lies farther north than any part of the continental United States, a fact of fundamental significance in terms of the growing season and one of the major reasons for the relative agricultural poverty of Russia. The portion of Russia that lies far enough south to permit the raising of crops is so remote from the sea that precipitation is often inadequate. As one crosses the Russian plain from west to east, the threat of drought increases.

In Western Europe, at any given season of the year, there is considerable variation of climate north and south of its mountain ranges, but nowhere are there tremendous differences of temperature at different seasons. On the other hand, the Russian plain shows little variation from one point to another, but it suffers from an extreme seasonal range of temperature, much as do the Great Plains of the American West. In Russia, such local variation in mean temperatures as exists is in summer between north and south; at Archangel the average July mean is 57 degrees Fahrenheit, at Moscow 66, at Kiev 68, and at Rostov nearly 75. Winter variation is slightly greater, and changes from east to west; the average January means are 21 degrees Fahrenheit at Kiev, 14 at Moscow, about 7 at Kazan. The average annual range in mean temperatures is therefore greater as one goes east and especially away from the coast: at Leningrad it is only 45 degrees Fahrenheit; at Archangel and Kiev 47; rising to 52 at Moscow, Kharkov, or Rostov; and to an extreme 59 degrees at Kazan or Astrakhan. These figures may be contrasted with an average seasonal variation of less than 25 degrees on the western shores of Europe.

Since most of the Russian plain is made up of the basin of the Volga and its tributaries, it is an easy temptation to draw a parallel between Russia and the American Middle West. It should not be forgotten, however, that the Mississippi empties into the Gulf of Mexico and so communicates with the open sea, whereas the Volga empties into the completely landlocked Caspian Sea. Furthermore, even the southernmost tip of the Crimean peninsula, jutting out into the Black Sea, lies far north of Iowa. Most of the Middle West is a land of almost unparalleled richness, with successive belts ideally suited for growing wheat, corn, and cotton or sugar cane. For all that one hears nowadays of the vast mineral resources of Russia, it is well to remember that historic Russia was an agricultural country, and that few portions of the earth have been less blessed by nature than most of the Russian plain. Unable to support a population of a density approaching that of Western Europe or of the inhabited portion of the continental United States, Russia has demanded of her people extraordinary effort and extraordinary fortitude merely to maintain existence.

Topographically and meteorologically the Russian plain presents a striking uniformity, more conducive to ethnic and political unity than are the physical conditions of Western Europe. These factors are strongly reinforced by the existence of a remarkable river network, which has from the earliest times made communication easy from one end of the plain to the other. The flatness of the plain makes for innumerable lakes and marshes, facilitating communication by small boats from one river system to another. The Valdai Plateau, not far southeast of present-day Leningrad, is the sole significant eminence in the whole expanse of the plain and gives rise to most of European Russia's important rivers.

From the source of the Volga in the Valdai Hills to its mouth in the Caspian is, as the crow flies, little over a thousand miles. Thanks to the slight drop (633 feet) from source to mouth, the river turns and twists at the slightest obstacle, stretching its length to over twenty-five hundred miles. Therefore, though frozen over almost half the year, it is for shallow-draft vessels more easily navigable in either direction than even the Mississippi. Among the many tributaries of the Volga, the most significant is the Oka. Rising considerably south of the Valdai Plateau and flowing first northward and then eastward, it and the Volga almost enclose an area similar in shape to ancient Mesopotamia; this area, therefore known in Russian history as *mezhduriechie* ("between the rivers") occupies the very center of the plain, with Moscow at its heart.

Rivaling the Volga in historic importance is the Dnieper, which takes over twelve hundred miles to cover less than half that distance from its source, near that of the Volga, to its mouth in the Black Sea; its course is interrupted by rapids (in modern times of great value for generating hydroelectric power) which did not, however, prevent this river from becoming Russia's main artery of communication with Constantinople, for centuries the center of Christian civilization. The other major river flowing to the Black Sea is the Don. Though its headwaters are not far from the upper Oka and from the Desna, one of the chief tributaries of the Dnieper, the Don was too remote from the early areas of Slav settlement to equal other rivers in importance; the coal deposits in the basin of its tributary, the Donets, were later to make the "Donbas" the chief center of heavy industry in Russia, but this was a nineteenth-century development.

Other rivers rising in the Valdai Hills lead, by shorter courses, to the Baltic Sea. The Dvina flows into the Gulf of Riga; a more complex, but historically more important, route runs, by way of Lake Ladoga and the Neva, into the Gulf of Finland. From Lake Ladoga it was possible to make all but direct communication with the northern river system, which drains, by the Northern Dvina, into the White Sea. The rivers of the plain were of such immense significance to Russia, particularly in the early formative centuries, that much of the course of her history cannot be understood without a clear understanding of their location on the map.

Emphasis on the aspects of physical uniformity, which provides such a striking contrast to the variegated landscapes of Western Europe and makes

"Russia in Europe" so strongly resemble the Central Asian "heartland," should not obscure the equally important, if seemingly contradictory, fact that the Russian plain is divided by nature into distinct zones. These zones, largely created by the long process of the emergence of the land from under the sea that in remote ages linked the Arctic Ocean with the Black and Caspian seas, run roughly east and west; they are prolonged into Asia and, to a lesser extent, into Europe. Under primitive conditions they were of paramount importance in shaping the mode of life of their inhabitants and gave rise to a long and bitter struggle for mastery between their respective inhabitants.

The most northern portion of the plain, roughly about one-third of the total area, is separated from the rest by a low watershed (*volok,* whence the term *Zavoloche,* "the region beyond the watershed") and drains into the White Sea and Arctic Ocean. Across it run two zones. Its northern rim is a continuation of the great Siberian tundra, habitable only by a handful of Lapps and Samoyeds, whose chief domestic animal is the reindeer. Most of this region, however, lies south of the Arctic Circle and was in its natural state covered by coniferous forests, intermingled with swamp, rich in fur-bearing animals but unsuited to agriculture. This zone, the *taiga,* was Russia's equivalent of the Mackenzie River country, farther north than the outposts of the Hudson's Bay Company, and of a piece with most of Siberia.

South of the watershed, though marked off from each other by no topographical barrier, lie the two major zones of the Russian plain—the forest and the steppe. The area of forest, shading gradually from coniferous to deciduous, extends southward to a line running northeasterly from the angle of the Carpathians to the southern end of the Urals, roughly from just south of Kiev to Kazan. Throughout this area the soil is either clay or sand, of low fertility, and the latitudes are such (even Kiev lies north of Winnipeg) that rye, rather than wheat, is the principal crop. The forests were interspersed with swamps and dotted with natural clearings. This zone, which does not extend into Siberia, is continued westward by the lowlands of Poland, Germany, and northern France. Though more deficient in rainfall than its westward extension, it is this forested portion of the Russian plain that, in its ecology, most closely resembles conditions to be found in a large part of Western Europe.

The remaining triangular portion of the plain, lying between the Kiev-Kazan line and the Black Sea, is the steppe, famed in song and story. Along its northern border lies the "black earth" (*chernozem*), a belt of extremely rich soil in the latitudes of Manitoba and Dakota, admirably suited for wheat-growing. Except for its southernmost semi-desert fringe, the steppe was by nature covered with tall grass; under primitive conditions, it invited, as did Central Asia, pastoral rather than agricultural pursuits. Stretching westward beyond the barrier of the Carpathians into the plain of Hungary, the steppe was wide open at its eastward end—the four-hundred-mile wide "gateway" between the foothills of the Urals and the Caspian Sea—to the broad plains of Central Asia.

This juxtaposition of two zones—the forest and the steppe—so dissimilar in their natural attributes, gave rise in the earliest times to two distinct cultures. One was based on agriculture, carried on under difficult conditions in clearings in the midst of forests and swamps; the other was based on the grazing of livestock in the open plains. Each sought to trespass on the domain of the other: the forest-dwellers were tempted by the rich soil of the south but were driven back by the superior military power of the horsemen of the steppe, constantly reinforced from the heart of Central Asia; the steppe-dwellers took repeated advantage of the frozen rivers as ready-made roads by which to penetrate into the depths of the forests, seeking to impose tribute on its scattered denizens. The steppe was Asia, in the sense of the pastoral nomad culture of Turkestan. The forest was Russia, slowly and painfully gathering strength in the gloom of her forests and swamps.

SUCCESSIVE PEOPLES OF THE STEPPE

The early inhabitants of the Russian plain were of origins as different as the zones they inhabited. Though the forest zone remained in obscurity until long after the break-up of the Roman Empire in the West, the history of the open steppe has been traced back to a respectable antiquity.

About 1000 B.C., when King David sat on the throne of Judah and Israel, the use of iron began to penetrate from the ancient land of the Hittites across the Caucasus, spreading slowly northward and westward among the early inhabitants of the steppe. In the seventh century B.C., Greek colonies began to be founded along the northern shore of the Black Sea and particularly on the coasts of the Crimea. For some time they acknowledged the hegemony of the Persian empire and carried on an active trade, exchanging the metal goods of the Caucasus area for fish and grain. Later, in the fifth century B.C., they were drawn more closely into the orbit of Athenian activity. One of the earliest among them was Olbia, at the mouth of the Bug. Another, which had to recognize the dominance of native kings, was Panticapaeum (later Kerch) on the Crimean Bosporus, the strait connecting the Sea of Azov with the Black Sea. For centuries these Greek outposts maintained a precarious and checkered existence, serving as the chief commercial and cultural intermediaries between the successive civilizations of Persia, Athens, Macedon, Rome, and Byzantium, on the one hand, and the barbarians of the steppe and even of the remote forest, on the other.

About the same time that the first Greek colonies were planted along the shore line, and when the Aryan Medes, an Iranian people, were beginning their pressure on Semitic civilization in the Fertile Crescent, another Iranian people, the Scythians, occupied the Russian steppe, formerly known to the Greeks as the land of the Cimmerians. The ruling element among them may well have been Turco-Tatar or Mongol, swept in from the heart of Asia, though the mass of their subjects were evidently Iranian in language. In contact with the scattered Greek colonies along the northern shore of the Black Sea, they developed a certain degree of civilization, which endured throughout the great period of Hellenic history, when Athens reigned supreme.

The Scythians remained, however, mainly a pastoral people, who, as Herodotus affirmed, "have an extreme hatred of all foreign customs"; their neighbors he described as "more unpolished than those of any other region that we know of." The customs of the Scythians, in which Herodotus found little to admire, seem strikingly similar to those of their nomadic successors in later centuries. Almost constantly on the move with their herds of horses and cattle, they lived most of the year in felt-covered wagons and consumed quantities of mares' milk. They made drinking cups of foemen's skulls and buried their kings in remote tombs with their favorite horses and attendants, male and female, together with an abundance of gold and jewels of Assyrian and, later, Grecian handiwork. Their mobility stood them in good stead in evading Darius' invading army (512 B.C.):

> They resolved, as the neighboring nations refused their alliance, that they would not openly venture on any pitched battle with the enemy, but would retire before them, driving off their herds, choking up all the wells and springs as they retreated, and leaving the whole country bare of forage.[2]

In the fourth century B.C., about the time when the rising power of Macedon began to threaten the Greek world, the Scythian power was broken by nomads dwelling further to the east. These Sarmatians, Herodotus relates, were sprung from a remnant of the Amazons, seduced by heroic young Scyths to abate their attacks. Although modern scholarship questions this noble story, it seems certain that the Sarmatians were also Iranian in language. Nature-worshipers like their predecessors, the Sarmatians never attained so high a cultural level as had the Scythians. Though they established no unified state, their military pressure was felt as far west as the Roman province of Dacia along the Danube. In the Russian steppe, their leading tribe was that of the Alans, described as tall and blond, excelling in horsemanship and in metalwork. Professor Vernadsky advances the theory that the term "Rhos" (or "Rus") derives from the name of one of the Alan clans, the *Rukhs-As* ("Light Alans").

As the great period of mass migration, familiar in the West as the *Völkerwanderung* (when the German barbarians invaded the Roman Empire), drew near, the Alans lost control of the western portion of the steppe, which was in the third century of the Christian era occupied by the Teutonic Goths. Although the Goths made the arduous trek from the Baltic to the Black Sea on foot, they speedily adapted themselves to the ways of the steppe-dwellers; their aristocracy, unlike that of most of the other barbarian Germans, was mounted. In two ways the Goths proved unique on the long list of steppe nomads; in both respects they foreshadowed their Scandinavian relatives who, some five centuries later, were to become the masters of the forest zone. For one thing, they accepted Christianity, though in the Arian form later condemned as heretical. For another thing, they took to the sea, marauding along the shores of the Black Sea and even of the Aegean, attacking Athens in 267 A.D.

Relatively soon, however, both Goths and Alans were swept away by the impact of the Huns, whose name has in Western Europe become symbolic of the utmost in ferocity. The Goths, in two principal successive waves—the Visigoths and the Ostrogoths—secured admission behind the Roman defenses along the Danube, moving on to play a significant role in Spain and Italy. Many of the Alans joined the Germans in their descent on the old domains of the Roman Empire in the West; a remnant still survive in the fastnesses of the Caucasus as the Ossetes.

The Huns themselves represented one of the most formidable waves of those nomads of other than Iranian stock from the open though remote recesses of Central Asia who, throughout the European "Middle Ages" and until pushed back by the power of Moscow, were to control the steppe. Under their greatest leader, Attila, they imperiled Constantinople itself (447), invaded Frankish Gaul (451), and menaced Italy (452). Almost immediately after Attila's death (453), the far-flung power of the Huns disintegrated in fratricidal strife.

Hard on its heels arose the rule of the Bulgars, another swarm of Asiatic nomads, compounded in part of remnants of the Huns. In the sixth century (*c.* 560) they were succeeded by the Avars. A broken remnant of the Bulgars was in the seventh century still formidable enough to induce the Byzantine emperor to cede them a province south of the Danube, where, in the region that still bears their name, they became absorbed into the local population, by then predominantly Slav. Another remnant retained its independence around Kazan, at the great bend of the middle Volga, until the thirteenth century.

The conquering Avars were the most dreaded military force of their time. Though they did not penetrate quite as far west as had the Huns, their kingdom stretched from the Volga to the Elbe and endured considerably longer than that of their more famous predecessors. In the sixth century they levied heavy tribute on the Byzantine emperors; in the eighth they were still formidable foes of Charlemagne. Yet they have left no monument to attest their greatness. Their very name vanished, even from the plains of the Danube and the Theiss, where their power centered. In what was later to be southern Russia, their empire was so speedily and completely extinguished as to give rise to the proverbial saying, "as dead as the Obri," the name under which they appear in the earliest Russian chronicle.

Out of the welter of divers Asiatic peoples—remnants of Hunnic Bulgars and of Altaic Turks who had pushed in on the heels of the Avars—arose a new and curiously pacific military despotism along the northern shores of the Black and Caspian seas. In the seventh century the Khazars pushed their control westward from the Volga across the Don to the Dnieper and the Dniester. The area subject to their tribute extended far northward into the forest zone, and they entered into close relations with Byzantium, which they aided militarily against its ancient Persian foe. The simultaneous rise of Mohammedanism and the wide extension of Arab empire precipitated a severe struggle for control of Armenia and the Caucasus, in which the Khazars suffered defeat. They were able, however, to prevent the penetration of conquering Islam across the Caucasus. Though they continued to assist Byzantium against its external enemies, they refused to accept Christianity. When the Jews were expelled from Constantinople, the Khazars harbored them, as they did various other imperial exiles. About 740 (some prefer the year 865, or even a later date) the Khazar ruler and his court were converted to Judaism but made no attempt to enforce this or any other religion upon the subject population. With the active participation of Jews, who benefited materially, if not spiritually, from the conversion, the Khazars carried on lively trade both with Constantinople, the imperial center of Christianity, and with Baghdad, which had become the seat of the Moslem Caliphate.

The Khazar capital, Itil, on the lower Volga, developed from a winter city of skin tents into a great commercial town, well provided with baths and market places. Its trade was of vital importance to Byzantium. When, in the ninth century, the Khazars were threatened by fresh Turkish inroads from the east, the emperor sent them artisans and materials to erect at Sarkel, on the Don, the first stone fortress in the steppe. The Khakan (or Kagan) of the Khazars was, in Byzantine diplomatic exchanges, rated higher than the pope or the Frankish rulers. Indeed, as early as the eighth century, the son of a Khazar princess, Leo IV (775-80), had sat on the throne of the Roman emperors.

It was the Khazars who controlled the steppe when Russia first emerged into the light of history; further reference to their relations with the Russians must be made in later pages. Here, however, it should be noted that they were not the last Asiatic nomads to occupy that area. As already remarked, they were in the ninth century subjected to heavy pressure from another Turkish group, the Pechenegs (or Patzinaks). The Khazars succeeded in ousting the Pechenegs from their then home between the Volga and the Urals. The result, however, was merely that the Pechenegs moved westward, driving before them the Magyars, who had been subject to the Khazars. By a series of thrusts, the Pechenegs pushed the Magyars across the Carpathians, where, in the former haunts of the Avars, they founded the kingdom of Hungary. The Pechenegs settled along the lower Dnieper, whence they inflicted much damage on all their neighbors.

In the eleventh century a still wilder Turkish horde, the Polovtsy (known to the Greeks as Cumans, to the Chinese and Arabs as Kipchak) wiped out the remnant of the Khazars and the Pechenegs as well. The new masters of the steppe were to be a constant scourge to the Russians. The Russian Ancient Chronicle, composed about 1113 A.D., records that

> even in our own day, the [Polovtsy] maintain the customs of their ancestors in the shedding of blood and in glorifying themselves for such deeds, as well as in eating every dead or unclean thing, even hamsters and marmots. They marry their mothers-in-law and their sisters-in-law, and observe other usages of their ancestors. . . .[3]

In their turn the Polovtsy—and the Russians as well—were in the thirteenth century overwhelmed by the mightiest of all the invaders from Asia. Led by the Mongols, welded by the genius of Jinghis Khan into the world's most formidable fighting force, the Turco-Tatar peoples of Central Asia were for the first time in history united into a single power, which no neighboring people could withstand. Though its most striking manifestation was the Mongol conquest of China, the rise of Mongol power had consequences also for Russian history. The Mongols were the first to establish a relatively stable political organization, ruling all the peoples from the Baltic to the China Sea, with a rather highly developed system of taxation. Their direct influence, however, was limited to the areas physically occupied by the various Turco-Tatar elements who fought under their banners. Since they continued to be pastoral nomads, like all their predecessors, they could not settle in the forest zone. In the grassy steppe, until the sixteenth century, they reigned supreme in the manner of the long line of their precursors, but the history of the steppe, so long as the nomads had the mastery, formed no integral part of the history of Russia.

The reader will doubtless have perceived that the history of the steppe zone, despite the long succession of surface changes, remained essentially changeless throughout what, with reference to Western European history, are known as ancient and medieval times. Its rulers were indeed of the most diverse ethnic stocks; but, by whatever name they were known, it is probable that each successive horde was itself of mixed origin. The predominant language of its population might in different periods be Iranian, Finno-Ugric, or Turco-Tatar. Yet the way of life of the steppe-dwellers remained constant; one group after another of marauding pastoral nomads lived mainly on the produce of its flocks and herds. Some might develop greater commercial activity than others. Some, under peripheral influence, might show greater artistic progress. Some might earn greater reputation for bestial ferocity. Yet none of these peoples showed permanent progression in the development of their economy, their political organization, or their general cultural level. As on the ocean, waves succeeded waves, presenting temporary new configurations, rapidly wiped out and reconstituted by their successors.

EARLY PEOPLES OF THE FOREST

Far different was the story of the forest zone. More forbidding than the open steppe and much longer in emerging into the light of history, the area of forest and swamp was nevertheless ultimately to produce a complex, ordered society and a state organization capable of permanently subjecting a vast area, including the steppe.

Even Herodotus could not credit what he had heard of this distant region, alleged to be inhabited by "the one-eyed race of men and the gold-guarding griffins." He could record detailed accounts of the dwellers in the steppe as remote as the baldheaded men in the foothills of the Urals, who "are well known to us," but "it does not seem to me credible, that the people who live in these mountains have feet like goats; and that after passing them you find another race of men, who sleep during one half of the year." He had no doubt that Scythia and the region beyond had

> winters of exceeding rigour. During eight months the frost is so intense that water poured upon the ground does not form mud, but if a fire be lighted on it mud is produced. The sea freezes. . . . Above, to the northward of the farthest dwellers in Scythia, the country is said to be concealed from sight and made impassable by reason of the feathers which are shed abroad abundantly.

Herodotus' zeal for sober truth led him to explain that "snow when it falls looks like feathers. . . . These northern regions, therefore, are uninhabitable, by reason of the severity of the winter." [4]

Modern scholarship, however, has peopled the extensive forested plain with three distinct categories of inhabitants. Least significant of these, in a cultural sense, were the Finns. Although linguistically closely related to the Magyars, these early denizens of the northern forests on both sides of the Urals were never militarily formidable. Drifting westward along the river courses, they subsisted mainly on fish and clothed themselves in the skins of the wild animals in which the forest abounded. Furs served also as a commodity of trade for their neighbors to the southward; this commodity was so valuable that their stronger neighbors, especially the Volga Bulgars, who engaged in punishing winter raids along the frozen rivers, were tempted to subject the Finns to tribute and, in the process, to carry off many of them to be sold as slaves in the markets of the Near East. Today only remnants of these aborigines remain as distinct ethnic units, principally in modern Finland and in Estonia, in both of which they were subjected to strong Swedish influence. There are also isolated linguistic islands, protected by such natural phenomena as the marshes along the Volga between Nizhny Novgorod (now Gorky) and Kazan; such are the Mordva and the Cheremis (or Marii).

Though, so far as written records go, it took place in obscurity, the process of the absorption of the Finns by the Slavs in the area between the upper Volga and the Oka may have somewhat resembled the replacement of the

Britons by the Anglo-Saxons. To be sure, the Britons had in Caesar's time a certain warlike renown. Tacitus in his *Germania* (first century) says:

> The Fenni are strangely beastlike and squalidly poor; neither arms nor homes have they; their food is herbs, their clothing skins, their bed the earth. They trust wholly to their arrows, which, for want of iron, are pointed with bone. . . . Heedless of men, heedless of gods, they have attained that hardest of results, the not needing so much as a wish.[5]

Jordanes (or Jornandes), in his *History of the Goths* (sixth century), barely mentions "the most gentle Finns, milder than all the inhabitants of Scandza." [6]

Tangible survivals of Finnish influence have been discerned in certain distinctive features of the "Great Russian" language—i.e., "Russian," as distinct from Ukrainian ("Little Russian") and Byelorussian ("White Russian"). Central Russia abounds in Finnish place names, especially names of rivers, which frequently end in "*-va,*" the Finnish word for "water" (e.g., Moskva, or Moscow). The last and greatest historian of tsarist times, V. O. Kliuchevsky, commented that the Finnish stock had contributed to

> the formation of the Great Russian anthropological type . . . the high cheekbones of the Great Russian, the predominance of dark complexion and hair, and especially the typical Great Russian nose, resting on a broad base. . . .[7]

The same thought was more crudely expressed by the founder of Russian Marxist historiography, M. N. Pokrovsky; his statement that "Great Russia was built on the bones of people of 'alien' stock, and the latter could hardly find much comfort in the fact that in the veins of Great Russians flows more than 80 percent of their [Finnish] blood" [8] was to become one of the most telling accusations against his memory when, in the 1930's, Russian historiography veered abruptly from internationalism to chauvinism.

A second category of early inhabitants of the forested plain, the Lithuanians, belonged to the Indo-European language group. The territory they at one time occupied extended along the Baltic from the mouth of the Vistula to the Gulf of Finland, and stretched eastward into the upper Dnieper basin and beyond, almost as far as present-day Moscow. They were agriculturists of a very primitive type, apparently living on isolated farmsteads rather than in village communities. Dwelling in a remote area with no natural advantages, they long remained politically as well as economically backward and unorganized. For the most part, they, like the Finns, were subjected by more powerful neighbors.

At the very end of the twelfth century, the Germans undertook, from their trading base at Riga, to convert these natives to Christianity. A military-monastic order, the Swordbearing Knights, carved out a wide domain embracing the territory later known as the Baltic provinces of Imperial Russia. Only during the interval between the First and Second World Wars were these provinces to enjoy a precarious existence as independent states. A similar, but older, crusading order, the Teutonic Knights, abandoned the futile struggle in the Holy Land to undertake, in coöperation with Roman Catholic Poland, the reduction of the heathen Prussians; these original Lithuanian inhabitants of the sandy and marshy southern shore of the Baltic became so thoroughly Germanized that the Lithuanian-speaking area was much contracted.

On the east, also, but at a much earlier date, it was narrowed, by a process that can only be guessed at. All that seems certain is that the Finns spread westward, occupying both shores of the gulf that now bears their name, while the third category of early inhabitants of the forest and swamps, the Slavs, moved up from the south, establishing Novgorod (i.e., "Newtown") as their principal outpost near the head of the Gulf of Finland. Only a remnant of Lithuanians, sheltering in the barren marshy region back of the coast, survived as an independent people. Welded together by pressures from the seacoast and from the interior, they were to form, late in the thirteenth century, a powerful principality, which played a great role in subsequent Russian history.

It is the third category of peoples, the Indo-European Slavs, who form the principal subject of Russian history, just as they constitute the great and preponderant majority of the inhabitants of the Soviet Union. The Slavs with whom this history is concerned are, however, only a fraction of the whole. According to the Ancient Chronicle, the earliest Russian source, "Over a long period the Slavs settled beside the Danube. . . . From among these Slavs, parties scattered throughout the country and were known by appropriate names, according to the places where they settled." The Chronicle gives a list of such Slavs, including Moravians, Czechs, White Croats, Serbs, Carinthians, Liakhs (i.e., Poles), as well as of the various tribes settled along the Dnieper and Dvina and their tributaries, adding "the Slavs also dwelt about Lake Ilmen, and were known there by their characteristic name. They built a city [which they] called Novgorod." [9]

The term "Slav" cannot be traced further back than the sixth century, when it first appears in a Greek source. Yet there is no doubt that the Veneti (Venedi or Venedae) of Pliny and Tacitus, who wrote in the first century of the Christian era, were a people of the sort later called Slavs. Tacitus was not the best of ethnographers, but he could at least distinguish between Germans and Sarmatians; the Veneti he found hard to classify:

> In their plundering expeditions they roam over the whole extent of forest and mountain between the Peucini [Lithuanians] and Fenni. They are however rather to be referred to the German race, for they have fixed habitations, carry shields, and delight in strength and fleetness of foot, thus presenting a complete contrast to the Sarmatae, who live in waggons and on horseback.[10]

Indeed, there is some reason to believe that even the Neuri of the fifth century B.C. were Slavs; of them Herodotus incredulously records a story suggestive of Slav werewolf mythology that "both the Scythians and the Greeks who dwell in Scythia say, that every Neurian once a year becomes a wolf for a few days, at the end of which time he is restored to his proper shape."[11] Vernadsky makes out a good case for his belief that the Antes, who seem to have inhabited the Dnieper basin even before the Goths invaded the steppe in the third century, and who were finally destroyed as a political entity by the Avars in the sixth century, were Slavs led by Alan chiefs. All in all, despite the version given by the Ancient Chronicle, it seems probable that, before the Christian era, the Slavs inhabited the forested area north and east of the Carpathians, from the middle Vistula to the middle Dnieper.

During the great period of migration in the early centuries of the Christian era, the Slavs expanded in various directions. Many of them early drifted to the Danube, though mass penetration of the Balkan Peninsula by the Southern Slavs did not come until the sixth century, possibly largely under pressure of the Avars. As already mentioned, a portion of them there accepted the leadership of a Bulgar khan; others became the Serbs, Croats, and Slovenes. When many Germanic tribes moved into Italy and Gaul, Slavs pushed westward to the Elbe. Though the reversal of the tide with the German *Drang nach Osten* from the tenth century overwhelmed many of these Western Slavs, the Czechs behind the mountain walls of Bohemia, and especially the Poles in the remote ancient homeland of the Slavs, successfully resisted political extinction, paying only the price of acceptance of Roman Catholicism and thus becoming integrated into Western Europe.

The greatest and most permanent expansion was that of the Eastern Slavs, though they had no united political organization. A constant tendency to move downstream into the steppe, somewhat successful in the time of the Khazars, was on the whole prevented by the counterpressure of the steppe nomads, who repeatedly drove the Slavs back into the protecting forests. No such formidable enemies, however, blocked Slav expansion northward and northeastward, into the lands of the Lithuanians and the Finns.

It should not be supposed that the process of Slav dispersion necessarily implies common descent of all Slavs from a common parent stock. There is some anthropological evidence to indicate that the earliest Slavs were of the long-headed "Nordic" type, but even prior to the sixth century, it is clear that the Slavs possessed no racial unity. What was common to them all was the bond of speaking kindred languages and, to some extent, community of social institutions and religious concepts. In these latter respects, however, the Slavs show many close similarities with the Germans and members of other linguistic groups.

In subsequent chapters attention will be focused on the Eastern Slavs. The history of the Western Slavs belongs to that of the West; the Southern Slavs early fell, more or less completely, under the rule of the Ottoman Turks. The Eastern Slavs, dwelling in the basin of the Dnieper and adjacent areas, from Kiev to Novgorod and from the Pripet marshes to the confluence of the

Oka with the Volga, were not initially differentiated into Great Russians, Little Russians (Ukrainians), and White Russians (Byelorus). It is with their common history that the narrative must begin.

NOTES

(*For more complete bibliographic data on titles referred to in the Notes, see the alphabetical Bibliography beginning on page 781.*

As explained in the "Note on Russian Dates and Names," page xi, the Library of Congress system of transliterating Russian names has been used in the Notes and Suggestions for Further Reading.)

1. Masaryk, *Spirit of Russia,* I, 1, 6.
2. Herodotus, *History,* Rawlinson translation, Everyman edition, I, 305-333 *passim.*
3. Cross (ed.), *The Russian Primary Chronicle,* revised edition, p. 58. Quoted here and elsewhere in this book by courtesy of the Mediaeval Academy of America.
4. Herodotus, *op. cit.,* pp. 289-299 *passim.*
5. Tacitus, *Complete Works,* Modern Library edition, p. 732.
6. Jordanes, *Gothic History,* Mierow translation, p. 56.
7. Kliuchevskii, *Kurs russkoi istorii,* 3rd edition, I, 367.
8. M. N. Pokrovskii, in *Istorik Marksist,* 1930, No. 18-19, p. 28.
9. Cross, *op. cit.,* pp. 52-53.
10. Tacitus, *op. cit.,* p. 732.
11. Herodotus, *op. cit.,* p. 329.

SUGGESTIONS FOR FURTHER READING

(*For more complete bibliographic data on titles referred to in these Suggestions at the end of each chapter, see the alphabetical Bibliography beginning on page 781.*)

The most important general treatment of Russian history is still the classic *Course of Russian History,* in five volumes, based on the university lecture notes of Professor V. O. Kliuchevskii (d. 1909); the first four volumes, to 1762, were carefully edited by Kliuchevskii himself. Although in many respects now antiquated, its comprehensive organization and the beauty of its style have not yet been surpassed; unfortunately, the English translation is seriously defective; the German translation is better. Since the lectures were addressed to Russian university students already familiar with the basic facts, much in them is somewhat obscure for the foreign student making an initial approach to Russian history.

Another general treatment of the subject is M. N. Pokrovskii's *Russkaia istoriia . . .* , in four volumes, also written before World War I. Pokrovskii was a trained historical scholar, who, however, deliberately forced his interpretation into a Marxist mold. After his death in 1932, this work was condemned in the Soviet Union as a sociological outline, lacking the warmth and color of history; under Khrushchev, Pokrovskii's memory was officially rehabilitated and his works republished. The first two volumes, compressed into one and ending with 1730, were translated into English with the collaboration of the author as *History of Russia from the Earliest Times to the Rise of Commercial Capitalism.* Also addressed to students with some knowledge of Russian history, it is not to be confused with his two-volume *Brief History of Russia . . .* , written after the Revolution; the first volume of the *Brief History* is a frankly political tract, while the second was conceived as a fifth volume to continue his major work from 1900 to 1907.

A partial translation of P. N. Miliukov's famous *Essais sur l'histoire de la civilisation russe* (translated from the Russian) is available as *Outlines of Russian Culture.* Among general accounts originally written in languages other than Russian, the only one deserving special attention is T. G. Masaryk, *The Spirit of Russia,* ably translated from the German; although sometimes inaccurate in factual details, the sketch of Russian history in the first half of the first of its two volumes is very suggestive.

For the beginner, A. G. Mazour, *Modern Russian Historiography,* may be a useful summary of the development of historical writing in Russia. Two invaluable bibliographic guides are Horecky's *Basic Russian Publications* and *Russia and the Soviet Union;* both are topically arranged, the one for works in Russian, the other for books in Western languages. Even more comprehensive is Karel Maichel and J. S. G. Simmons' *Guide to Russian Reference Books.* The *Guide* is planned for six volumes, of which only the first two had been published by 1968. For the nineteenth century, see also David Shapiro's *A Select Bibliography of Works in English on Russian History, 1801-1917.* Confined to the Soviet period are P. Grierson's *Books on Soviet Russia, 1917-1942* and its continuation as Carew Hunt's *Books on Communism,* more recently revised by W. Kolarz. On a special topic T. T. Hammond's *Soviet Foreign Relations and World Communism* is an excellent annotated bibliography.

As a narrative outline, George Vernadsky's *Political and Diplomatic History of Russia* is a useful manual, with sketch maps and helpful appendixes, though without adequate bibliography. The pioneer work of Alfred N. Rambaud is still very readable, though of little analytical value.

Among economic histories, special mention must be made of G. T. Robinson, *Rural Russia Under the Old Regime;* although confined to the development of agrarian relations, it covers the whole period to 1917 and offers the most careful and masterful analysis of the most fundamental aspect of Russia's history available in any language. Jerome Blum's *Lord and Peasant in Russia . . .* is more recent but can be used only with great caution. The best general account of Russian economic history through the seventeenth century is J. Kulisher, *Russische Wirtschaftsgeschichte,* translated from the Russian. James Mavor's *Economic History of Russia* is merely an assemblage of materials relating to the subject, with serious gaps. Tugan-Baranovskii, *Geschichte der russischen Fabrik,* is still valuable for the eighteenth- and nineteenth-century growth of industry. Of much less value is P. I. Liashchenko, *History of the National Economy of Russia to the 1917 Revolution,* translated from an edition widely acclaimed in the Soviet Union at the height of the Stalin regime.

Among cultural histories, I. Grabar's *Istoriia russkago iskusstva* is admirably illustrated; L. Réau's two books on *L'art russe . . .* provide a good general treatment. The Tretiakov Gallery in Moscow has published an illustrated *Short Guide* to its collection of Russian paintings and sculpture of the late nineteenth and early twentieth centuries. R. A. Leonard's *History of Russian Music* is a very good study. D. S. Mirsky's *History of Russian Literature* is the best general discussion; M. L.

Slonim's *Epic of Russian Literature* and *Modern Russian Literature,* and Gleb Struve's *Soviet Russian Literature* are good more recent accounts. William K. Matthews' *Structure and Development of Russian* is a helpful outline.

For Russian geography, the first volume of the very old Leroy-Beaulieu, *L'empire des tsars et les russes* (available also in English translation) is still extremely valuable. Two fairly recent Soviet works are available in English translation: Lev S. Berg, *Natural Regions of the U.S.S.R.,* is highly technical and does not deal with mineral resources; S. S. Balzak, *et al., Economic Geography of the Soviet Union,* sandwiches much valuable material between passages obviously intended only for the censorship. G. B. Cressey, *Soviet Potentials: A Geographic Appraisal,* is an excellent brief treatment by a well-informed American geographer, with emphasis on natural resources realistically appraised. It may be supplemented by his *Asia's Lands and Peoples.* R. C. Kingsbury and R. M. Taaffe's *An Atlas of Soviet Affairs,* G. Kish's *Economic Atlas of the Soviet Union,* and P. E. Lydolph's *Geography of the U.S.S.R.* are also very useful. G. Goodall's *Soviet Union in Maps* (earlier editions were styled *Soviet Russia in Maps*) is inexpensive and contains an extraordinarily useful assortment of historical, physical, meteorological, ethnic, economic, and political maps; it is an indispensable companion volume for any history of Russia.

The ancient civilizations of the steppe, and particularly of the littoral, have been best treated by M. Rostovtzeff, *Iranians and Greeks in Southern Russia,* which largely supersedes E. H. Minns, *Scythians and Greeks.* For background, consult A. A. Vasiliev's *Byzantine Empire;* his *Goths in the Crimea* is more specialized. The chief Greek and Latin sources have been cited in the Notes. For the steppe nomads in their homeland, see W. M. McGovern, *The Early Empires of Central Asia.*

For the peoples of the forest, the most comprehensive treatment is George Vernadsky's *Ancient Russia,* which is of great general value for detail and bibliography. F. Dvornik's *The Slavs in European History and Civilization* develops further the theme of his earlier works.

S. H. Billington's *The Icon and the Axe* and M. Cherniavsky's *Tsar and People* are interesting novel approaches to the history of Russian culture and political ideas, respectively.

Chapter

2

The Emergence of Russia: 9th to 11th Centuries

THE EARLY DNIEPER SLAVS

At the opening of the historic period, in the ninth century of our era, the Eastern Slavs had no central organization. Whatever the nature of the earlier confederation dominated by the Antes may have been, it had been definitely disrupted by the onslaught of the Avars in the sixth century. Nothing had taken its place, unless one considers the tribute imposed on many of the Dnieper Slavs by the Khazars as affording a bond of unity. According to the Ancient Chronicle, the Eastern Slavs were divided into a number of tribes, the names and habitats of which it lists. The Ancient Chronicle was composed at Kiev not earlier than the end of the eleventh or beginning of the twelfth century, and its account of the early Slavs must of course be received with great reserve; yet on this point it may be taken as accurate.

The prejudices of its monkish compilers probably account for the ascription to the Polyanians, whose chief center was Kiev, of all the virtues, while the other tribes of Slavs are represented to have lived in the fashion of the Polovtsy, with whom the annalists were only too well acquainted:

> For the Polyanians retained the mild and peaceful customs of their ancestors, and showed respect for their daughters-in-law and their sisters, as well as for their mothers and fathers. . . . They observed a fixed [marriage] custom, under which the groom's brother did not fetch the bride, but she was brought to the bridegroom in the evening, and on the next morning her dowry was turned over. The Derevlians, on the other hand, existed in bestial fashion, and lived like cattle. They killed one another, ate every impure thing, and there was no marriage among them, but instead they seized upon maidens by capture. The Radimichians, the Vyatichians, and the Severians had the same customs. They

> lived in the forest like any wild beast, and ate every unclean thing. They spoke obscenely before their fathers and their daughters-in-law.[1]

The organization of the various tribes was evidently very loose. Notwithstanding the patronymic endings of most of the tribal names, their structure would seem to have had but little relationship to blood affinity. Apparently control, such as it was, was exercised by an aristocracy operating from the widely scattered towns; these towns must be understood in the sense of military centers, protected by wooden or earthen palisades, rather than in any economic sense. Despite the reputation of the early Slavs as a peaceful people—a reputation perhaps not unconnected with the circumstance that until the ninth century they seem to have known no weapons but bows and spears—the several tribes appear to have been engaged in frequent struggles with each other and with their still weaker neighbors, the Lithuanians and the Finns. Based in the "towns," of which Kiev was to become the greatest, bands of marauders levied tribute on adjacent areas and plundered remoter regions, using furs, honey, wax, and slaves thus acquired as commodities of exchange with the neighboring nomads of the steppe, to whom they themselves also often paid tribute.

The more basic unit of Slav organization, which would appear to have varied little from tribe to tribe, was the village community. It was evidently common, not only to the Eastern Slavs, but to all the Slavs in general, and indeed, at a more remote epoch, to the other peoples of Europe. The resemblances between the manner of life of the eighth-century Slavs in the Dnieper area and that of the Germans as described by Tacitus, or for that matter, of the Greeks of the time of Homer, are very strong. Whatever the subsequent divergences of Russian and Western history, there can be no question but that, at the starting point of Russian history, its institutional equipment was of a piece with that of the West. This starting point, however, is centuries later than is the case of the West; consequently it does not follow that Russian history was bound to reproduce the characteristic course of Western history, even if one leaves out of account the special nature of added influences, such as geography and historical contacts with other peoples.

The village community was basically a family community, which, however, often absorbed outside elements. By family must be understood the complex family, including not merely children and grandchildren but also more remote relatives, or even dependents without any blood or even marriage relationship. Such a community might be housed in one dwelling or might include more than a score of households. Property, if we may apply this term at all in that period, was collective. This collectivity extended not merely to the holding of land but to its utilization and may, in early times, have included even the fruits of common labor. Leadership in these communities by no means always depended on paternity or seniority. Frequently village chiefs were chosen by election; occasionally the widow of a chief succeeded him. Social stratification was simple: a bottom stratum of slaves, for the most part captives, was largely absorbed into the structure of the complex family; the mass of the members were legally free; among them there are strong signs of the differentiation of an aristocracy, from the members of which the chief was normally chosen.

The principal economic occupation was agriculture, with subsidiary cattle-raising. The principal crops were grain, mainly rye and barley, and flax. The implements were crude. The ground was usually turned over with the aid of a forked stick, sometimes drawn by animals. Genuine plows seem to have been introduced not before the ninth century, under the influence of more technically advanced agricultural peoples with whom the Eastern Slavs then came into contact. To describe the Eastern Slavs as agricultural nomads would be to exaggerate somewhat. Yet the primitive character of their agricultural techniques, permitting no recovery of fertility by land kept too long under cultivation, and the vast extent of available land impelled a considerable part of the population to move on at frequent intervals, abandoning outworn soil in favor of fresh areas. On the other hand, the rarity of natural clearings and the inevitable difficulties in the way of making artificial clearings were undoubtedly a restraining factor. Nor is it probable that the new settlement was usually far removed from the old. Kliuchevsky's emphasis on the mobility of the agricultural population was grossly exaggerated by the Marxist Pokrovsky when he wrote that "it was rare for a Russian peasant to die where his grandfather was born."[2] Slavs undoubtedly filtered in across the Danube in very considerable numbers and at times found it possible to settle in the open steppe as far east as the Don. They also advanced northeastward into the region between the upper Volga and the Oka, but the Slavicization of the Finns there appears to have been due more to military and ecclesiastical pressure than to substantial peasant colonization.

Since the products of agriculture in the forest zone scarcely exceeded the subsistence needs of the population, the chief surplus commodities available for exchange were the natural products of the forest. The sparsely inhabited forests still abounded in fur-bearing animals and in wild bees. Furs, honey, and wax were therefore the principal export goods, and it was in them that tribute to the steppe nomads was normally reckoned. Coins were not unknown, but they were of foreign origin. Such trade as existed was largely carried on by the neighboring nomads—Khazars, Volga Bulgars, and even the more remote Arabs.

The economy of the Slavs, resembling that of the early inhabitants of the West European forests, is not the only respect in which they differed sharply from the pastoral nomads of the steppe. Their living conditions, their laws, and their religious beliefs also stamp them as "European" rather than "Asiatic." In place of felt-covered wagons and skin tents, the abodes of the Slavs were of earth and wood; basically holes in the ground, the sides of which were built up with logs, they were covered with timber, thatch, or reeds. The dress of the Slavs consisted of shirts and tight trousers (or skirts), covered with a long cloak (*kaftan*) lined with fur or with the skins of bear, wolf, or sheep; their footgear was leather or, more usually, bast. Even in later centuries only a select minority were able to afford horses; the bulk of the armed population (the "children") fought on foot and without armor.

The laws of the Eastern Slavs were based on custom and were not recorded before the eleventh century. The earliest code, the *Russkaia Pravda,* so strongly reflects Byzantine influence, especially in its ecclesiastical aspects, that it cannot be taken as fully representative of old Russian law. Yet, if due allowance be made, not only for emendations obviously incorporated in extant texts by later copyists, but also for the social development of Russia prior to this first effort at recording its law, it would appear that early Slav concepts of proper conduct did not differ radically from those of the Germans before their irruption into the territories of the Roman Empire or, for that matter, of the Italians and Greeks in much earlier times. The primitive Mosaic concepts of "an eye for an eye and a tooth for a tooth" had apparently been reduced into a fairly elaborate system of tariffs, with penalties payable in terms of furs and graded both according to the severity of the injury and the status of the persons involved. The obligation of exacting the penalty apparently rested on the relatives of the injured party; a survival of this practice is found (though not mentioned in the *Pravda*) in the judicial duel (*polie*) of the later period.

The religious concepts of the Eastern Slavs also strongly resembled those of other early Indo-European peoples. Their loose hierarchy of gods, representing the forces of nature, may roughly be compared with the early denizens of the Grecian Olympus and with Roman or Teutonic counterparts. It is difficult to define with precision the attributes of the gods of the pagan Slavs; the Eastern Slavs had no knowledge of writing prior to the introduction of Christianity, and the monks had no interest in preserving pagan mythology. Dazhbog was the god of the sun, but Perun, the god of thunder and lightning, seems to have outweighed him in importance. Of lesser stature was Volos, later confused by monkish chroniclers with St. Blasius, patron of flocks and herds, but apparently originally a sort of Pluto. A second strain in Slav religious beliefs was a veneration of ancestors, regarded as the protectors of their descendants.

THE VARANGIANS

The "European" character of Russian history is not diminished by Russia's experience with a "Norman conquest." In somewhat the same way as the Anglo-Saxons submitted to the leadership of the Normans while absorbing them into their own mores, the Eastern Slavs in the ninth century accepted the rule of the Varangians (Northmen) from across the Baltic and speedily Slavicized them. The Varangians were closely akin to, and in individual instances quite possibly identical with, those "swift Danes" who, from the eighth and ninth centuries, harried all the coasts of Western Europe, carried their raids up the rivers far into the interior, and ultimately established their rule over considerable areas—notably the Danelaw in Saxon England and Normandy in Carolingian France.

Lured by possibilities of plunder and of trade rooted in plunder similar to those that brought the Viking swarms down on the West, the Scandinavians fully developed the potentialities of the great river waterways from the Baltic to the Black and Caspian seas. These pagan barbarians gathered tribute from the Slav, Lithuanian, and Finnish populations, mainly in the familiar form of furs, wax, and honey; to these forest commodities they often added the persons of their victims, as well as more specifically Baltic products, such as amber. They exchanged their loot for precious metals and articles of luxury derived from Christian Byzantium and Moslem Baghdad. In this enterprise these masters of the waterways possessed superior weapons and showed greater organizing ability than their Slav predecessors.

The details of the process by which the Northmen established themselves among the Slavs along the Dnieper are not well substantiated and have given rise to many ingenious and controversial interpretations. Archaeological evidence makes it certain that Scandinavians traded with the Arabs by way of the Volga as early as the seventh century. It is doubtful whether, as Professor Vernadsky argues, Swedes had in the eighth century established a "kaganate," independent of the Khazar Kagan, near the mouth of the Don; it is in accordance with this theory that he traces the term "Rus" back to the Alans. Modern Soviet scholarship, infused by patriotism even more than by Marxism, strives to leave intact no shred of the "Normanist theory" of the "origin of the Russian state"; their battle-cry, relying on Ibn-Khordadbei (a ninth-century Persian who described an attack on Constantinople by the "Rus" in 860), is: "The Rus are a tribe of Slavs." They connect the term "Rus" (Greek *Hros*) with the river Ros, a tributary of the Dnieper near Kiev, and scornfully reject the older derivation of the term from the Finnish *ruotsi* (rowers).

In the ninth century, the period of greatest Norse activity in the West, their visits to "Gardarik"—"the land of towns" (*goroda*), as the Scandinavian sagas call the country of the Slavs—increased in intensity. This was not an organized movement, supported by a central authority in the homeland. Rather was it a matter of small armed bands, warring with each other as well as preying on the native population; these bands established themselves in the already existing Slav towns. That these Norsemen at this time carried on active trade with Constantinople is attested by the hoards of Byzantine coins of this period that have been found in Scandinavia. An odd entry in a Frankish annal under the year 839 records that in that year a Byzantine embassy to the Carolingian emperor was accompanied by some

"Rus," whose way home by the Dnieper had been blocked by the Pechenegs; recognizing the "Rus" as Swedes, the suspicious emperor, Louis the German, detained them. That at home the Rus were by no means peaceful merchants is attested by their attack on Amastris, a Byzantine outpost on the south shore of the Black Sea, in 840.

So long as the Khazars remained in effective control of the steppe, they evidently did not interfere with the trade of the Slavs and the Rus by way of the Dnieper with Constantinople, but were content with exaction of a mild tribute. With the decline of Khazar power and the growing menace of the Pechenegs on the lower Dnieper, the Rus were constrained to form a tighter organization if they were to keep open the waterway to Constantinople. In the early part of the ninth century, the Rus had still developed no central authority; each band was a law unto itself in its own "town" and in the surrounding province on which it levied tribute. Rurik (more properly Riurik, the Slavicized form of the Norse Hrörekr), the traditional founder of the Russian state, had held sway only in the northwestern corner of the plain. The story in the Ancient Chronicle that Rurik and his brothers were in 862 called in by the Slavs to put an end to their constant strife and to "rule over them" cannot be taken seriously; it strongly resembles the story of the "invitation" to Hengest and Horsa to come to Britain after its abandonment by Roman troops. Quite independently of Rurik, who finally settled in Novgorod, other leaders established themselves at various strong points in the Dnieper basin. As early as 860, Askold and Dir, the chieftains at Kiev, were able to organize a force sufficiently formidable to make an attack on Constantinople, at a time when most of the imperial forces were involved in a war on the eastern frontier of the Byzantine Empire.

Oleg, who succeeded Rurik at Novgorod, killed Askold and Dir and established his residence at Kiev (879). He levied tribute on most of the Slav population of the Dnieper area and warred with the Magyars, who then controlled the lower course of the river. In 907 he apparently made another serious attack on Constantinople. The terms of treaties with the Greeks, stated to have been concluded in 907 and 911, are given in the Russian Chronicle; they define with care the terms under which the Rus were to be admitted to Constantinople and the provision to be made for them by the imperial authorities. The regularity and nature of the Russian contacts with the metropolis of Christendom are amply confirmed by a tenth-century description incorporated in *De Administrando Imperio* of the Emperor Constantine Porphyrogenitus. Oleg's successor, Igor, alleged to be a son of Rurik, made a fresh attack on Constantinople in 944; the resultant treaty of 945 confirms the impression that the "grand prince" of Kiev was but one of a number of rulers who simultaneously levied tribute on the agricultural population of their respective principalities. Apparently the ascendancy of the prince of Kiev rested mainly on the situation of his city, the last fortified point in the forest zone before the Dnieper emerged into the open steppe; as host to his fellow princes, assembled for the annual spring visit to Constantinople, he quite naturally served also as the leader of the expedition, without being able to assume any regular authority over the territories and populations subject to the other princes. The most he could hope to do was to install his sons or loyal followers in the other "towns" whenever he was strong enough.

In the Kievan period there was at no time a "Russian state." Each prince had his following, the *druzhina,* the Russian counterpart of the Latin *comitatus* and Teutonic *Gefolge.* The leadership of the war band passed by no regular system of succession. When Igor was killed while collecting tribute (945), it was his widow Olga who organized the exaction of vengeance. Apparently in her time the practice of making annual winter expeditions to gather tribute was replaced, in the areas under her control, by a system of local agents of the princes, responsible for the regular collection of dues. When her son Sviatoslav was grown, he became the war leader:

> Upon his expeditions he carried with him neither wagons nor kettles, and boiled no meat, but cut off small strips of horseflesh, game, or beef, and ate it after roasting it on the coals. Nor did he have a tent, but he spread out a horse-blanket under him, and set his saddle under his head.[3]

He warred mightily against the Khazars, taking their famous stone fortress at Sarkel on the Don (963), and against the Volga Bulgars, whose capital he plundered (965). He succeeded in destroying the power of the Khazars, sacking their capital, Itil, on the lower Volga (968), and thereby assisting the rise of a stronger and fiercer horde of steppe nomads, the Pechenegs. He was a willing tool of the Byzantine emperors in their struggle against the Bulgars of the Danube. His effort to destroy the Balkan Bulgars after they had made peace with the emperor led to hostilities with the Greeks, which were terminated by a fresh treaty with Constantinople (971). In the end, he met death at the hands of the Pechenegs, whose chief had Sviatoslav's skull made into a gold-encrusted drinking cup (972).

Among the agents left by Sviatoslav in charge of his domains were three of his sons. The problem of succession was settled by fratricidal wars. The sole survivor, Vladimir, installed himself at Kiev (977), whence, by savage campaigns, he collected wives and tribute from most of the Dnieper basin. Vladimir's chief fame rests on his forced conversion of the Russian Slavs to Christianity, a topic to be discussed later. During his reign, Kiev was repeatedly harassed by the Pechenegs; to hold them off, Vladimir built a sort of fortified line of new towns along the steppe frontier. At his death (1015) he left seven sons—of four or five different mothers—each ruling as prince in a portion of the Russian land; one of them, Yaroslav of Novgorod, was in open rebellion, having refused to pay tribute to his father. Sviatopolk, who seized Kiev, promptly murdered three of his brothers, but was defeated in a four-year struggle by Yaroslav, who succeeded to the title of grand prince. Yaroslav, however, was forced to share the territory with another brother, Mstislav, who took the opportunity to move his residence from outlying Tmutorakan, beyond the Sea of Azov, to Chernigov, near Kiev. Not until Mstislav's death (1036) did Yaroslav "the Wise" venture to remove his seat from Novgorod to Kiev.

The fact that for a dozen years no prince sat at Kiev, the "mother of Russian towns," betokens the early decline of the paramount importance of the trade with Byzantium and, with it, of such significance as the title of grand prince had. After Yaroslav's death (1054), no "grand prince" even pretended to exercise direct authority over the whole of Rus; at most, he acted *in loco parentis* toward his younger brothers; Yaroslav's sons had been enjoined by their dying father to "remain at peace, brother heeding brother." For another century, however, Kiev remained the chief prize, the throne on which each prince aspired to sit.

By agreement among the princes, a "rota" system of succession developed. Under it each brother was recognized as having the right to succeed to the throne of Kiev on the death of his next older brother. When the turn of the next generation came, each oldest son was deemed to have the right to sit on whatever throne his father had occupied. On each of these thrones, brother was to succeed elder brother, and they in their turns were to be succeeded by their cousins, sons of their father's next younger brother. Thus, if each prince died in order of his genealogical (not necessarily chronological) seniority, each in his turn would before his death sit on the throne of Kiev. If, however, any prince died prematurely, his progeny became *izgoi;* they had the right to succeed in their proper turn to whatever thrones their fathers had sat on, but were excluded from the general system of rotation.

The various towns were ranked in order—Kiev, Chernigov, Pereiaslav, Smolensk, Vladimir-Volynsk, and the rest. Each of them had other towns junior to it, which were to be the temporary portion of the younger brothers of their respective princes. Could the rota system have worked perfectly, no branch of the family could have established its particular hereditary authority in any portion of the plain. Rather, the theory of collective family authority over the whole area of settlement would have become a living fact.

Actually, nothing of the kind developed. Brothers did not die in the order of their birth, giving each his turn to sit at Kiev. The sons of those who died prematurely would not reconcile themselves to exclusion from rota computations. Sons of older brothers might be older than some of their uncles, creating conflict between genealogical seniority and actual age. Inevitably, there were incessant disputes, and all the thrones of Rus changed hands frequently in defiance of rota principles. As a disheartened grand prince admitted (1151), "A place does not go to a head, but a head to a place."[4] Particularly was this true of the most strategic thrones, such as those of Kiev and Novgorod. In lesser principalities, branches of the family frequently established themselves on a hereditary basis, though also subject to the principle of local rotation.

In short, each prince—like the kings, dukes, counts, and barons of the West—strove to subject to himself as much territory as he could militarily control. In his own domains he collected dues and administered justice; in his relations with other princes he was guided by his own self-interest, sometimes joining other Russian princes in campaigns against the Pechenegs (or their successors, the Polovtsy) or the Poles, sometimes allying himself with the alien foe against his own kinsmen. There is little use in tracing these constant internecine feuds; attention may better be centered on the influence exerted by Byzantium on Rus.

CHRISTIANITY AND THE ROLE OF THE CHURCH

By reason of her geographical remoteness Russia had never formed part of the Roman Empire. Not only did Roman legions never tramp on Russian soil; Roman civilization could leave no monuments in the form of roads and buildings, no skeleton political and ecclesastical structure such as that which had aided the German barbarians painfully to rebuild civilization in the West. On the other hand, the annual visits to Constantinople gave the Russians a more direct contact with the living remains of Greco-Roman civilization than was enjoyed by the Western world, particularly after the rise of Arab power in the Mediterranean. Moreover, it was the eastern end of the Mediterranean where antique civilization had reached its greatest heights; even the Roman law, so influential in the later development of Europe, was codified at Byzantium, not at old Rome. Throughout the Kievan period Constantinople was the metropolis of Christendom, the political, ecclesiastical, and economic center of the Occidental world, rivaled only by Moslem Baghdad.

The impact of the imperial city, considered in its physical aspects alone, on the senses of the rude barbarians from the forests and swamps of the north, must have been tremendous. The solemn services in the magnificent cathedral of St. Sophia, the impressive singing and the overpowering incense, could not fail to sway the minds of the Rus. Coupled with the wealth and splendor of the imperial court, they proved irresistible to many a Scandinavian warrior, the more so as the emperors welcomed these doughty fighters into their service. Apparently, it was not uncommon for men to move back and forth between the emperor's service and membership in the *druzhina* of a Kievan prince. Thus gradually there grew up in Kiev a Christian element among the pagans. The treaty of 945 refers to a Russian church (St. Elias) and distinguishes between Christian Rus and pagan Rus. Princess Olga herself was baptized under the name of Helen in 955, two years before she paid an official visit to Constantinople. Although she was not able to persuade her snub-nosed son, Sviatoslav, to follow her example, and although Constantinople showed little of the missionary zeal that characterized Rome, it was not long before the official conversion of all Rus to Christianity was effected (c. 988).

Vladimir, son of Sviatoslav, who had won the throne of Kiev by the murder of his older brother, was the last major European ruler to abandon paganism. Within the preceding quarter of a century, the kings of Poland, Denmark, Norway, and Hungary had accepted Christianity from Rome. The Khazars had been Jewish for at least a century; more recently Russia's other neighbors, the Volga Bulgars, had embraced Islam. According to the Chronicle, Vladimir invited envoys of all the major faiths to discuss their beliefs for the benefit of himself and his followers. The Bulgars explained

> . . . that they believed in God, and that Mahomet instructed them to practice circumcision, to eat no pork, to drink no wine, and, after death, promised them complete fulfilment of their carnal desires. [They added details, some of] which out of modesty may not be written down. Vladimir listened to them, for he was fond of women and indulgence, regarding which he heard with pleasure. But circumcision and abstinence from pork and wine were disagreeable to him. "Drinking," said he, "is the joy of the Russes. We cannot exist without that pleasure."

The pope's emissaries said

> . . . their teaching was . . . "Fasting according to one's strength. But whatever one eats or drinks is all to the glory of God, as our teacher Paul has said." Then Vladimir answered, "Depart hence; our fathers accepted no such principle."

The Khazars' envoys had to repeat unpleasant things about pork and circumcision and had further to admit that though their native land was Jerusalem,

> "God was angry at our forefathers, and scattered us among the gentiles on account of our sins. . . ." [Vladimir scornfully demanded,] "How can you hope to teach others while you yourselves are cast out and scattered abroad by the hand of God? If God loved you and your faith, you would not be thus dispersed in foreign lands. Do you expect us to accept that fate also?"

Then the Greeks, according to the Chronicle, gave Vladimir an extended account of the history of the world since the creation, not forgetting to run down their competitors. Vladimir, who punctuated this exposition with his naïve questions, was apparently more impressed with a canvas depicting the Day of Judgment than with the Greek scholars' explanations; evidently he continued to be troubled "why God should have descended to earth and should have endured such pain."

It is not surprising that Vladimir and his simple warriors should have been unable to make up their minds in this war of words. Their final decision was based on empirical investigation. Russian emissaries visited the temples of the Bulgars, the "Germans," and the Greeks; only with the Jews they did not bother further. These envoys reported the mosques were unclean: "Their religion is not good." Western Catholic worship was tolerable, "but we beheld no glory there." Then, however,

> the Greeks led us to the edifices where they worship their God, and we knew not whether we were in heaven or on earth. For on earth there is no such splendor or such beauty, and we are at a loss how to describe it. We only know that God dwells there among men, and their service is fairer than the ceremonies of other nations. . . .[5]

On the practical side, the Byzantine emperor at the time found himself hard pressed both by the Balkan Bulgars and by revolt in Anatolia. In despair he sought military aid from Vladimir, promising him the hand of his sister Anna, a princess "born in the purple," who had previously been refused to the chief western ruler, the Holy Roman Emperor Otto II. Vladimir permitted himself to be baptized at Kherson and sent some six thousand warriors to aid the emperor. Though victory cooled the latter's ardor for the bargain, military pressure by Vladimir on Byzantine holdings in the Crimea effected its consummation (988). In 990 Vladimir returned to Kiev with his imperial bride and a retinue of priests. Throughout his dominions the population was compulsorily baptized wholesale, and construction of the Tithe Church, entitled to receive one-tenth of all the prince's revenues, was begun at Kiev. Bishops were established in all the major centers of Rus, although it was not until about 1037 that the first metropolitan arrived from Constantinople to head the new Russian branch of the Greek Orthodox Church.

As in the West, the Church was destined to play an enormous role, but with far-reaching differences. Russia was to know no Cluniac reform, which in the eleventh century West, along with its effect in freeing the clergy from lay control and in strengthening the power of the papacy, insisted on the rule of celibacy for the secular clergy (priests) as well as for the regular clergy (monks). By the same token, Russia experienced no Investiture Conflict, that great battle between the Church and the temporal rulers over the right to appoint ecclesiastics. It is true that for almost five hundred years the successive metropolitans were, with two brief exceptions, Greeks, chosen not by the grand princes but by the ecclesiastical authorities at Constantinople. On the other hand, a good half of the bishops were Russians, and in their selection the local authorities exerted great influence. The patriarchs of Constantinople, moreover, never advanced claims to spiritual supremacy, even in the eastern part of the empire, comparable to those of the bishops of Rome. The Ecumenical Patriarch was only one of four patriarchs (five if Rome be included) all of equal spiritual weight, and ecclesiastical questions were settled, not by them, but by general councils of the church. It is interesting to recall that the Council of Nicaea (325), which definitely committed the church to the acceptance of Trinitarian doctrine, later enshrined in the Athanasian creed, was presided over, not by a patriarch but by the emperor (himself a pagan). Lord Bryce exaggerated when he wrote that "the Teutonic Emperor was the shadow of the Pope, cast on the secular world. The Eastern Patriarch was the shadow of the Emperor, cast on the spiritual world."[6] Yet there was a very large element of truth in his dictum, and the whole spirit of the Orthodox Church, in Russia as in the Byzantine Empire, was dominated by a caesaropapism unknown in the West.

However doubtful one may be of the spiritual significance of Christianity in Kievan Russia—for the mass of the population, Christian ritual was evidently but a thin veneer on pagan superstition, while the rulers honored Christian precepts mainly in the breach—there can be no question of the immense cultural influence of the Church. Russian architecture was profoundly influenced by Byzantine models; the arts and crafts, largely in the service of the Church, flourished in Kievan Rus after the conversion, particularly several schools of icon-painting. The canon law provided precedents for developing the legislative activity of the Kievan princes and thus constituted an early channel for the penetration of the principles of the Roman law into primitive Slavonic legal concepts. It would seem to be an exaggeration to suggest that the influence of the Church extended so far as to eliminate the death penalty in Kievan Rus; its absence in extant copies of the *Russkaia Pravda* may be accounted for by the fact that these were ecclesiastical versions to be applied in Church courts, not the code that prevailed in the prince's tribunals. In Russia, as in the West, "church people" were subject to trial and punishment only by the Church itself. These included, not only the clergy proper, but also those in one way or another serving, whether in the churches or in the eleemosynary institutions it maintained (hospitals, inns, etc.), and various categories of people (*izgoi*) who had somehow lost their proper social status and had been taken under the wing of the Church. Education, of course, was monopolized by the Church, and the clergy constituted the bulk of the literate population. For priests' sons, education was compulsory; those of them who remained illiterate were—along with bankrupt merchants and slaves who had bought their freedom—classed among the *izgoi*. The character of the instruction in the Kievan schools is perhaps suggested by a passage in one of the few Russian translations of Greek lay thought to the effect that there are three woes—grammar school, poverty, and a vicious wife. Formal education was, however, not wholly confined to the clergy; a few of the leading sons of ruling families even studied at Constantinople; and cases of educated women are not unknown, especially in convents. Although the penalty for murder of a woman was only half that of a man, Kievan women enjoyed extensive property rights.

The Church in Russia was inferior to the Roman Church in its preservation and transmission of the culture of the ancient world. The renowned missionaries to the Slavs, Cyril and Methodius, had devised a modification of the Greek alphabet suited to the tongue of the Slavicized Bulgars of the Danube. Instead of requiring the Russian clergy to learn Greek, the necessary ritual books were translated for their benefit into Old Church Slavonic. Although practically all the metropolitans of Kiev and many of the Russian bishops were themselves Greeks, they were too few in number, and their interest in the barbarians among whom they were stationed was too slight, for them to exert any profound influence. Portions of the Bible and certain other religious or canonical writings were translated into Slavonic and served as models for a considerable body of native literature, heavily hagiographic. However, the philosophic and scientific lore, as well as other secular literature of antiquity, remained almost a closed book to most of the Russian literati, however "saturated with the sweetness of book learning" an exceptional figure such as the Metropolitan Ilarion (1051-53) may have been.

Finally, it should be observed that Russian asceticism, at least in the Kievan period, was far more passive than its Western counterpart. The most outstanding monasteries in the West—Monte Cassino, Cluny, Fulda, Iona—were founded on the initiative of men who withdrew from the world in quest of eternal salvation; their renown for piety attracted settlers —and endowments—but their original impetus had carried them out into the wilderness. In Kievan Rus, monasteries were almost without exception founded on the initiative, or closely under the wing of, princes. The greatest of them all, the Monastery of the Caves (*Pecherskaia Lavra*) at Kiev, which down to the twentieth century continued annually to attract pilgrims by the million, owed its rapid rise to wealth and fame mainly to the favor of the princes. Founded late in the reign of Yaroslav the Wise by St. Antonii, who had visited the great Greek monastery of Mt. Athos, its first few inmates lived in caves hollowed out of the clay bank of the Dnieper below Kiev. The tunnel under the river, lined with the sealed cells in which the most enthusiastic monks lived and died and were buried, has remained one of the showplaces of the history of asceticism, but the monastery itself was soon moved to more comfortable quarters on the hilltop by its third abbot, the humble aristocrat St. Feodosii, the third person to be canonized by the Russian Church. It is perhaps characteristic that the first two Russians to be recognized as saints were not ascetics or even ecclesiastics but princes, Boris and Gleb, two of the younger sons of Vladimir, whose meekness in tamely submitting to their murders by the agents of their brother Sviatopolk is curiously suggestive of the attitude which so many Soviet leaders were to show in the purge trials of the 1930's.

Though monks. unlike the secular clergy, were required to be celibate, and though they spent most of their time in prayer and literary activities, with some fasting and occasionally even more severe mortification of the flesh, the monasteries of the Kievan period were generally princely foundations. The piety of their members was highly regarded as of vicarious service to the princes and their men, whose consciences, secure in the knowledge of their gifts to these holy men, need not be further troubled by their own conduct. It was, of course, from the monks that the higher clergy, so far as they were native-born Russians, were drawn. Trained to obedience and but little interested in secular matters, the Russian prelates in Kievan times, with scarcely a murmur, followed the Byzantine tradition of rendering unto Caesar the things that are Caesar's. Only when their extensive wealth was threatened, as at the time of the "democratic revolution" in Kiev in 1113, did they exert themselves in a political sense.

Perhaps because of this attitude that men of God need not be troubled about political arrangements in this ephemeral life, the Church showed no hostility to dynastic interchanges between the Orthodox East and the Latin West. The long ecclesiastical controversy between Greek Orthodoxy and Roman Catholicism resulted in 1054 in permanent schism and mutual anathema by both parts of the Church Universal. Yet the Russian Church did not, in the days of Kiev, manifest the virulent hatred of the "Latin heresy" that was later to become so marked and was to find classic expression in the doctrine of Moscow as the third and final Rome. Especially in the earlier part of the Kievan period, the dynasty of Rurik enjoyed high prestige among the ruling families of Europe. The relative wealth and grandeur of the towns in the Dnieper basin—Bishop Dietmar of Merseburg was profoundly impressed by the report that Kiev in 1018 was a city of 400 churches and eight markets—put Russian brides at a premium in the West. Three daughters of the great Yaroslav, whose wife was herself a daughter of the king of Sweden, married the kings of France, of Hungary, and of Norway; a granddaughter, widowed at sixteen, became at eighteen the unhappy second wife of the Emperor Henry IV, of Canossa fame. The process was a two-way one; among the many Western brides of Russian rulers may be mentioned the refugee daughter of Harold of England, who married Vladimir Monomakh, who was to sit as grand prince of Kiev from 1113 to 1125. It was only later that Russia, her trade fallen away to insignificant proportions and her land overrun by the nomads of Asia, was to disappear for a time from the consciousness of Western Europe.

NOTES

1. Cross (ed.), *The Russian Primary Chronicle,* revised edition, p. 56.
2. Pokrovskii, *Brief History,* I, 52.

3. Cross, *op. cit.*, p. 84.
4. *Polnoe sobranie russkikh lietopisei*, II, 65 (Ipatievskii version).
5. Cross, *op. cit.*, pp. 96-111 *passim*. The dates in the chronicles are somewhat confusing at this point.
6. James (Viscount) Bryce, *Holy Roman Empire* (new edition, London, 1920), p. 334.

SUGGESTIONS FOR FURTHER READING

For general treatments, see the Suggestions for Chapter 1. The best detailed account of this period is to be found in Vernadsky, *Ancient Russia* and *Kievan Russia*. A still more recent study by the same author is *The Origins of Russia*, with emphasis on cultural factors; Professor Vernadsky adds fresh arguments, drawn particularly from religious beliefs, in support of his concept of the influence of nomadic Asia on the Russian Slavs.

Cross (ed.), *The Russian Primary Chronicle*, provides an English translation of this most important source, with an excellent introduction. Useful sidelights may be found in Masudi, *Meadows of Gold and Mines of Gems*, and in Frähn, *Ibn-Foszlan's und anderer Araber Berichte über die Russen älterer Zeit*.

A general history of the Scandinavians, with a careful chapter devoted to their activities in Russia, is Kendrick's *History of the Vikings*. An earlier, path-breaking discussion is Thomsen, *Relations Between Ancient Russia and Scandinavia and the Origins of the Russian State*. For an unusual "anti-Slav" argument, largely philological, by an *émigré* Pole, see Paskiewicz, *Making of the Russian Nation* and *Origin of Russia*, which are bitterly condemned by all patriotic, "anti-Normanist," Russians, whether Soviet or *émigré*.

The most thorough account of the Church in ancient Rus is Golubinskii, *Istoriia russkoi tserkvi;* a study in English is Fedotov, *The Russian Religious Mind: Kievan Christianity*. Meyendorff, *The Orthodox Church*, is a good introduction, continued to recent times.

Buxton's *Russian Mediaeval Architecture*, Kondakov's *Russian Icon*, Gudzy's *History of Early Russian Literature*, Magnus' *Heroic Ballads of Russia*, and Afanas′ev's *Russian Fairy Tales* deal with certain aspects of early Russian culture. Zenkovsky's *Medieval Russia's Epics, Chronicles, and Tales* contains a number of useful source items.

Chapter

3

The Kievan Period: 11th to 13th Centuries

In the course of the Kievan period—the quarter of a millennium stretching approximately from the adoption of Christianity (988) to the Mongol conquest (1238-40)—the early forms of robber-trade evolved to produce a complex, roughly ordered social structure, able to support a fairly advanced urban culture. The area of settlement of the Eastern Slavs of this period* was roughly a parallelogram: its southern boundary ran irregularly from the northeastern slopes of the Carpathians to the headwaters of the Donets; its most rugged edge ran northeasterly from the Dnieper near the confluence of the Psel to the confluence of the Oka and the Volga, and thence northerly to the watershed; its northern limit followed the watershed westward, reaching northward to touch the southern shores of Lakes Onega and Ladoga and the southeastern coast of the Gulf of Finland; its westward boundary slanted southwestward to the Carpathians. Otherwise expressed, the territory occupied by the Russian Slavs was bounded on the south and east by the open steppe, which was then the domain of the nomadic and pagan Pechenegs and, from the eleventh century, of the still more formidable Polovtsy (or Cumans); in the northeast the principal obstacle to further expansion into the area still inhabited by unslavicized Finns was the malarial marshes of the middle Volga below Nizhny Novgorod (now Gorky), beyond which, around modern Kazan, lay the powerful principality of the Moslem Bulgars; to the north, climatic difficulties rather than the watershed or formidable enemies restricted expansion; in the north-

* See Map II.

west, the remnants of Lithuanian peoples in the Baltic provinces and in Prussia almost completely barred the Slavs from the sea; to the west, beyond the Pripet marshes and the Carpathians, lay the two kingdoms of Poland and Hungary, which had received Christianity from Rome and were attached to the Romano-German rather than to the Byzantine orbit.

Politically, authority remained locally centered, but economically, socially, culturally, and ethnically there would seem to have been no wide differences from one part of the forested plain to another. To be sure, in the northeast, where absorption of the Finns by the Slavs was still taking place, a special ethnic type, later to be known as the "Great Russian," was in the early stages of formation. In the southwest, the original homeland of the Slav "Rus" and in closest contact both with Byzantine civilization and with Turkish nomads of the steppe, was to develop a different type, later known as "Little Russians" or "Ukrainians" (i.e., frontiersmen); neither appellation was used or could have had any meaning in Kievan times. In the northwest, in contact with Lithuanian influences, was to emerge a third type of Eastern Slav, the "White Russian." Such differentiation, however, at the period now under discussion still lay far in the future.

ECONOMIC AND SOCIAL STRUCTURE

The Russian portion of the plain was an area of over half a million square miles, covered by forest, and interspersed, thanks to its extreme flatness, by frequent swamps. The population can only be roughly guessed at; Vernadsky reckons it at about seven and a half million, a figure more likely to be too high than too low. The bulk of this certainly sparse population was forced to live by agriculture, under extremely unfavorable conditions of soil and climate. Land, of course, existed in abundance, but cultivable land was relatively scarce. Individual effort was hopeless in the struggle with the harsh natural conditions, which encouraged the survival of the communal complex "large family." Not agricultural villages, but scattered settlements, of one or a few dwellings, inhabited by a group of individual families, were therefore the rule. Methods of cultivation were still quite primitive, only the crudest of plows gradually coming into use. The land could be used only for a very few years at a time, necessitating a constant clearing of fresh ground; it has been well said that the axe was the principal tool of Russian agriculture. In these northerly latitudes, rye, barley, and oats were the principal crops. Flax could be raised to supply clothing, and there was some slight growing of vegetables, though practically none of fruit. Sheep, cattle, and horses, though indispensable, could not be raised in large numbers. Bog-iron could be worked in quantity sufficient to supply minimum needs for tools and weapons, but genuine mining was virtually unknown. Apart from iron, all metals had to be imported, as, indeed, were the better quality weapons.

Such an economy could produce little or no surplus beyond the actual minimum physical needs of the toiling population. The surrounding forests, however, still afforded valuable products in considerable abundance. Chief among them were furs—ranging from ermine, sable, and beaver, down through lynx, marten, and squirrel, to the coarser pelts of bear and wolf. Also of high value in those days were the wild bees, which supplied important quantities of honey and wax. It was in terms of furs, honey, and wax that Russian wealth was then measured; slaves, originally a prime commodity of Russian export, steadily diminished in significance. It was, then, on the by-products of the forest rather than on the basic agricultural economy that Russia's trade with her neighbors rested. Internal trade remained of little account.

This peculiar situation has given rise in Russian historiography to extended disputes as to how Kievan economy should be characterized. Apart from the fact that much of the controversy is semantic—the meaning that should be attached to the word "feudal," for example—the controversy has largely been kept alive by partisan efforts to prove the validity of opposing theoretical preconceptions as to the place of Russia in world history and especially as to its relation to the history of Western Europe. It would be futile in a book of this kind to devote any space to the explication of these disputes. What seems beyond dispute is that the economy of Kievan Rus existed at two levels, connected by the political structure rather than by direct economic factors.

The lower level, by which the bulk of the population existed, was a sustenance agriculture, with subsidiary stockbreeding, almost untouched by the necessities of exchange. The higher level, which gave the towns their economic *raison d'être,* was foreign trade. The commodities of this trade were acquired by the urban population, not through economic services rendered by the town to the countryside, but by the use of the political authority (*vlast*) of the towns to extract from the rural inhabitants of the town's province (*volost*) surplus forest products in demand at Constantinople or at Baghdad or in the Baltic ports. Which of these two levels should be taken as the essential characteristic of Kievan Rus is the whole substance of the controversy between the followers of Kliuchevsky, who stressed the foreign trade, and of the neo-Marxist Grekov, who stressed sustenance agriculture. Soviet scholars now stress internal trade.

The rural population were not all on the same legal footing, though the material conditions under which they lived probably varied more by virtue of local conditions than because of their legal status. There is no way of knowing what proportion the various categories bore to one another. Yet it is generally assumed that the normal condition was that of the free peasant, generally referred to as *smerd* (in modern Russian, the verb *smerdiat* means "to stink"). His freedom found expression in the fact that in case a *smerd* was murdered, the murderer must pay compensation to his family as well as pay five grivna (the value of which cannot be certainly determined) to the prince; it found further expression in the fact that a *smerd* might be fined by the prince for certain offenses, whereas slaves, "because they are not free,"[1] could not be so fined. The *smerd* was free also to move about at will, although, in view of the scarcity of available clearings, it was probably more important to him that he could not be deprived of the right to use the lands he tilled; this right passed by inheritance to his sons and, in part, to his daughters. Ownership of the land, however, did not vest in him but in the town, and this, throughout most of Russia, meant the prince. It was one of the prince's chief duties to protect the *smerd,* as appears, for instance, from Prince Vladimir Monomakh's expostulation, in 1103, at a conference with his older cousin, Sviatopolk II, then Grand Prince of Kiev:

> The retainers of Sviatopolk began the discussion, and remarked that it was not advisable to open hostilities in the spring, since they would ruin the peasants and their fields. Vladimir then replied, "I am surprised, comrades, that you concern yourselves with the beasts with which the peasant plows. Why do you not bear in mind that as soon as the peasant begins his plowing, the Polovcian will come, shoot him down with his bolt, seize his horse, ride on into his village, and carry off his wife, his children, and all his property? Are you concerned for the horses and not for the peasant himself?" [2]

In protecting the *smerd,* the prince was, of course, protecting his own chief source of income, the *dan* ("tribute"), to which the *smerd* continued to be subject. Gradually, the right to collect tribute over a given area merged imperceptibly into the right of ownership, which might be alienated by the prince to his men, or even to the Church.

The rights of the prince—or of the landholders to whom in some part he alienated them—whether considered as preponderantly economic or preponderantly juridical, were not exercised over the individual peasant. The peasants were organized in communes, which were collectively responsible both for payment of tribute and for apprehension of malefactors or, at least, for a share of the judicial penalties for crime. In the old code, the *Russkaia Pravda,* the *verv* ("rope") was held financially responsible for cases of murder or robbery occurring in its jurisdiction. Whatever the precise etymology of the term—it may be noted that cognate terms ("rope," *"Seil,"* *"ligne"*) occur in a similar connection in Western Europe—it is clear that the *verv* was a territorial unit, possibly originally a kinship unit. In later times it appears under the name of *volost,* with elected elders (*starosty*). The *volost,* not the prince's officials, apportioned and collected all taxes imposed on it. It was the *volost* also which made representations to the prince and his officials about the peasants' right to use plowland, meadows, woods, and fisheries. This did not at this early period signify collective property rights vested in the commune. So long as land existed in relative abundance, each peasant could put under cultivation as much as he was able, without specific authorization from his fellows.

Beside the free peasants, there existed various classes of temporarily or permanently unfree. Chief among them were the *zakupy,* who were obligated to work off debts they had incurred while free. The *zakup* was in effect an indentured servant, who recovered his full freedom at the termination of a specified term of service. In addition to this and other categories of half-free persons, there were also chattel slaves (*cheliadin, rab,* or *kholop*), who had no civil and few personal rights. Cases are, indeed, not unknown in which slaves were allowed to use property as though it were their own; anyone who knowingly did business with such a man took a certain risk, for neither the slave nor his owner could be held liable in case of default on an obligation. The chief sources of permanent slavery were voluntary self-sale, marriage to a female slave, or acceptance of certain positions in a lord's household. Another common source of slaves was capture in war, but such slavery was temporary, for war prisoners were regarded as subject to ransom; pending payment, the captive was a slave, whose work was credited toward the ransom. In case of the murder of an unfree man, compensation was payable, not to his family, but to his owner. Escape, even from permanent slavery, was possible not only by running away or, in rare cases, by self-redemption, but more commonly by manumission, frequently testamentary. How relatively little these legal differentiations mattered is suggested by the fact that the murderer (if he were not also the owner) of a slave had to pay the prince the same five-grivna blood fine as if he had murdered a free *smerd.* What mattered most was that *smerd, zakup,* and *kholop* all had to work to earn their own livelihood and to make a payment, whether regarded as a tax or as a rent, to the holder of the land on which they lived.

In the towns—and it should not be forgotten that "town" means primarily a fortified center—lived the masters of Russia, the princes and their men. Since members of these war bands early withdrew from personal negotiation of the sale of their booty, there grew up in the towns also a population of traders (*kuptsy,* from the verb *kupit,* "to buy") and of artisans who served the increasingly specialized needs of their betters, whether as carpenters, masons, smiths, tanners, or a number of other types of handicraftsmen. Many of them were free, but many also were in debt-bondage as *zakupy* or even in full slavery, particularly in the households of the great.

The top social stratum, after the twelfth century called boyars, whose ranks were never by any means closed to intrusion from below, had originally been composed of the members of the prince's *druzhina,* his personal armed followers and domestics. In the course of time they had become also great landowners. The blood fine payable for the murder of an ordinary free man (*muzh* or *liudin*) was forty grivna, eight times the price of the murder of a *smerd;* for murder of a member of the prince's retinue, the fine was eighty grivna. Whether or not they belonged to the charmed innermost circle, the members of the upper minority of the urban population constituted a well-to-do creditor class, which furnished the traders and artisans with the wherewithal to carry on their activities. The existence side by side of these two classes—creditors and debtors—gave rise to frequent disturbances in the Kievan towns, strongly suggestive of the *tumolto dei ciompi* in medieval Florence.

POLITICAL STRUCTURE

The basis of the power—and of the wealth—of the boyars, and of the princes who stood at their head, never rested, however, on economic services performed by them. It was nakedly political, rooted in their military power. The princes and their boyars were the successors of those marauding bands of Vikings who, sheltering their booty behind the fortifications of the towns, had subjected to tribute the mass of the Slavs, Finns, and other earlier inhabitants of the forested portion of the Russian plain. This tribute, gradually regularized in the course of successive generations, had come to be supplemented by other sources of revenue. Prominent among them were the proceeds from the administration of justice, for the interests of the population and of the rulers were alike served by the assumption, on the part of the latter, of the function of enforcing the penalties for crime customary under early Slav (as also under early Teutonic) law. The princes' interest was guaranteed by providing a scale of extra payments to be made by criminals to the enforcing authority. The princes and the boyars deputized by them had thus come to exercise judicial authority over the tributary population. As society became more complex and cases not adequately covered by existing law arose, it was inevitable that (as in the West also) judges should make rulings to cover future cases as well as the immediately pending ones, and thus the judicial function was naturally extended into the field of legislation. In this process the Church, with its knowledge of the Roman (Byzantine) law, was of inestimable value to the extension of princely power. Executive power remained, of course, in the hands of the rulers, who wielded the military force necessary both to ensure the continued submission of their subjects (*poddannye,* "those under tribute") and defense against alien enemies and rival princes.

The increasing concentration of power in the hands of the rulers of the towns did not, however, betoken the growth of autocratic monarchy. Princes whose right to rule theoretically depended on the complicated "rota" system of succession, constantly tempered by the vagaries of individual enterprise, could not afford to dispense with the support of their personal following. When a prince moved up (or down) from one throne to another, he took his own boyars with him. As in the earlier days when the prince was but the leader of a war band, he continued to require their coöperation and their assent to his enterprises. The boyars therefore were not merely his household officers and his territorial deputies for purposes of judicial administration and tax collection; the topmost stratum constituted his council, the boyar duma, which shared in policy decisions. Its composition was determined by no fixed rules, but the reality of its power is apparent. The "Testament" (*Pouchenie*) of Vladimir Monomakh, one of the greatest and most powerful princes of the period, specifies that his children should "sit and deliberate" each morning, presumably with a small innermost circle of *muzhie perednie* ("foremost men"). Major decisions required wider deliberation by the whole duma.

The prince and his boyars were constantly ready for warfare; their numbers were, however, too small to take the field alone. A supplementary force was the town militia, organized—as in ancient Rome, in Saxon England, among the nomads of Asia, and in many other instances—on the decimal principle; the supreme commander of the town militia, the *tysiatsky* ("thousand-man"), ranked as one of the prince's most intimate advisers. Only a portion of the townsmen could afford war horses; the poorer citizens, the "children," fought afoot. Though qualitatively inferior to the boyars, the numbers of the armed townsmen sometimes made them a formidable opponent even for the prince and his men.

Organized as the *vieche* (a word derived from the same root as *soviet*), the town population occasionally rose in revolt against a prince and even expelled him from the town. More frequently, on the death of a prince, the *vieche,* assembled in the market place, decided to reject his prospective successor in favor of some other prince the populace preferred. The most famous, but by no means the only, case of such intervention by the "democratic" element occurred at Kiev in 1113 on the death of Grand Prince Sviatopolk II. Sviatopolk had coöperated in the formation of a salt monopoly and was hated as the friend of the chief moneylenders, the monasteries, and the Jews. The populace, assembled in a *vieche,* appealed to Vladimir Monomakh, than a junior prince in another town, not in regular line of succession. His reluctance to accept the irregular invitation led to riots: "The men of Kiev plundered the home of Putiata, the thousand-man, and attacked and robbed the Jews." In the emergency, the leading prelates and lay magnates joined in the appeal for salvation, stressing that the rioters would soon attack the boyars and the monasteries, "and if they plunder the monasteries, O prince, you will be responsible for it."[3] Vladimir overcame his scruples and took the throne, calming the disorders by sweeping legislative measures in the interest of the debtor population; these measures, reminiscent of the reforms of Solon, were adopted on the advice of a conference of his most highly placed officers (none of whom, probably, knew anything of ancient Athens).

In some ways, to be sure, this was an exceptional case. Vladimir was outstanding both as a statesman and as a human being, and his often quoted

"Testament," faintly suggestive of *Poor Richard's Almanac,* finds no parallel in the utterances of other princes of the period. The high principles with which it is infused cannot be taken as representative of the governing ideas of the times, nor were his practices emulated by other rulers. It was far more usual for an expelled or excluded prince to resort to foreign enemies, whether Poles or Polovtsy, for armed assistance, a device not scorned by intruding princes either. Nevertheless, the "democratic" principle made considerable headway in the major Kievan towns in the twelfth century. On the one hand, the "children" were admitted to full participation in the *vieche*. On the other, a number of town officials became "elective" by the *vieche,* though by acclamation rather than by voting. The status of the rural population, however, remained unaffected by "democratization" within the towns. The *vieche,* moreover, never became a permanent, regularly functioning institution; it remained a mass meeting, assembled at irregular intervals, which interfered with but did not replace the regular organs of government.

It would serve little purpose to attempt to unravel here the tangled political narrative history of Kievan Rus. Although the princes who "sat" at Kiev bore the distinctive title of "grand prince," there was no centralization of authority in their hands. Rus was made up of ten or a dozen "lands"—the *volosti* of Kiev, Novgorod, Chernigov, Pereiaslav, Smolensk, Rostov-Suzdal, Murom-Ryazan, Polotsk, Volhynia, and Galicia were chief among them—corresponding more or less to the old tribal divisions, and in each of which a branch of the family of Rurik made itself, after a fashion, hereditary. Almost constantly, though in ever shifting combinations, feuding with each other and frequently torn by internal strife, the major principalities often found it impossible to co-operate even against the ever-present menace of the raiding nomads of the steppe.

DECLINE OF KIEVAN RUS

So long as the importance of Kiev, the "mother of Russian towns," was buttressed by the continuing significance of the trade with Constantinople and of the transit trade from western Europe along the "route from the Varangians to the Greeks," that city continued to be the chief prize in the feuds among the princes. With the reopening of the Mediterranean sea route, of which the Crusades were the most dramatic facet, and the decline of the Russian export trade, Kiev rapidly lost all but prestige value. Significant of its declining status were the unemotional words of Andrei Bogoliubsky to his weeping father, Yury Dolgoruky, a prince of Suzdal who had successfully asserted his rights to the throne of Kiev, only to be almost immediately expelled: "Here, father, in the land of Rus [near Kiev] we have neither an army nor anything; let us depart [to Suzdal] while it is still warm." [4]

Yury later succeeded in recovering the throne of Kiev and in retaining it for the last three years of his life. His more practical son, Andrei, did not bother to repeat his father's exploits. For a dozen years Kiev was ruled by a succession of minor princes, each of whom, however, duly boasted the title of grand prince. Then, in 1169, Andrei sent an army, the command of which he entrusted to junior kinsmen, against Kiev. Kiev was taken and sacked, not by a foreign foe but by a Russian force. Contemptuously Andrei assigned the principality to a younger brother, assuming for himself, however, the title of grand prince without stirring from his remote province in the northeast. As if to point up the declining value to be placed on the old commercial centers—and to avoid conflicts with the *vieche* to which they had given rise—Andrei refused to reside even in his father's capital, the town of Suzdal, continuing to dwell in the new and minor fortified point, Vladimir-on-the-Kliazma, where he had ruled in his father's lifetime.

Even before the murder of Andrei in 1174, Kiev had been lost to the house of Suzdal, but Andrei's successors at Vladimir continued to bear the title of grand prince. In the southwest a new center of power rose in the principality of Galicia-Volhynia, whose rulers also boasted the grand-princely title. Thus even the symbol of the political unity of the Russian land disintegrated. Although the future development of the main stream of Russian history was to belong to the northeast—the land of the "Great Russians"—at the close of the twelfth century it was the southwestern rulers, in close contact with Poland and Hungary, who seemed to have the brighter future. It was the southwestern grand princes who appear in Western European records under the style of *rex russorum,* "king of the Russians."

The decline of Kievan Rus did not adversely affect what has been referred to above as the lower level of Kievan economy—the near-sustenance economy of the countryside. Indeed, it may perhaps be safely assumed that, despite recurrent famines and plagues, despite the constant raiding of the nomads and feuding of the princes, the population increased fairly steadily. With the thickening, as well as widening, of the settled area, it is probable that the economy was moving gradually ever farther from the sustenance level, with increasing specialization of labor function and slowly improving techniques of production. Whatever additional surplus above its own basic needs the peasant population was able to produce did not, however, outstrip the consumption needs of the growing ruling military portion of the population, which was evidently spreading from the old commercial towns into new and relatively unimportant strong points scattered over the face of the countryside. The rise in the level of rural economy did not therefore lead to an important growth of trade. Rather, it reflected a decline in the availability of forest products, the only commodities this backward agricultural land could hope to export. In a relative sense, furs, wax, and honey figured less and less in Russian production; grain, flax, meat, hides, and wool, locally consumed, came more and more to be the measure of the wealth of the Russian landed magnate, lav or ecclesiastical.

It was the higher level of the Kievan economy—the foreign trade that had supported the great towns—that was clearly in decline. This trade had been principally, though not exclusively, with Constantinople, and the new situation of Rus was dramatically emphasized by the spiritual catastrophe of 1204. In that year the Fourth (Venetian) Crusade, abandoning its purpose of fighting the infidel Turk in the Holy Land, turned its arms against the Byzantine Empire at Constantinople; overthrowing the Greek Orthodox "Emperor of the Romans," whom they had come to assist, the crusaders established for a time a Latin Empire of the East. The fall of the metropolis and the victory of the Latin Church, which since 1054 had been in permanent schism from Greek Orthodoxy and consequently under anathema to the true believers of Rus, seemed the most dire of calamities, than which nothing could be more fatal.

THE MONGOL CONQUEST

For the materially minded, however, still worse things were in store. Almost at the same moment that the Byzantine Empire was overthrown (1204), a Mongol chieftain, Temuchin, was proclaimed supreme ruler of that fierce, nomadic people (1206). Although this event occurred thousands of miles away in the dim recesses of eastern Asia, it was soon to have important repercussions for Russia and to bring panic even to western Europe. A brief nine years later (1215), as Jinghis Khan (or "Genghis Khan" of story-book and movie), Temuchin overthrew the mighty Chinese empire, taking Peking. After such a victory it was but child's play to overthrow (1219-20) the sprawling Moslem power of Khorezm and to enlist under the banners of the pagan Mongols all the Turco-Tatar populations of Central Asia. Shortly afterward, a reconnoitering expedition penetrated across the Caucasus from the south, subjugating the mountaineers, Georgians and Ossetians, as it passed. The terrified Polovtsy appealed for assistance to their wonted victims, the Russian princes (with whose families, incidentally, they had often intermarried). Under the leadership of Mstislav the Bold, prince of Galicia, most of the chief Russian princes—those of Kiev, Chernigov, and Volhynia, among others—responded; Suzdal sent a force, though its prince, notwithstanding his claim to be grand prince of all Rus, himself remained at home. Pushing far out into the steppe, the ill-disciplined Russians and their pagan allies met and attacked the Mongols on the banks of the Kalka, a tributary of the Don (1223).

The result was a crushing defeat at the hands of the Mongols. The prince of Kiev, taken prisoner by treachery after the battle, proved of some slight embarrassment to the Mongols, whose tradition forbade them to shed the blood of a ruler; the difficulty was resolved by simply using him and two other captive princes as the foundation for a platform of boards, "and themselves took seat on the top to have dinner." Other princes, more fortunate, fell in the fighting; a handful, including Mstislav the Bold, saved themselves by headlong flight. The Mongols, however, made little use of their victory, ravaging the country only as far as the Dnieper; on their return, they suffered a check at the hands of the Volga Bulgars. They vanished into Asia as suddenly as they had come, leading a Russian chronicler to remark: "We know not whence they came, nor where they hid themselves again; God knows whence he fetched them against us for our sins." [5]

Unfortunately for the people of Rus, the Tatars, under their Mongol overlordship, returned little more than a dozen years later. No preparation had been made against such an eventuality, nor is it easy to see what could have been effectively done. In the winter of 1237-1238, when the frozen rivers supplied ready roads for the Asiatic horsemen, Batu Khan, a grandson of the great Jinghis, with a force of little over one hundred thousand men, struck at the Bulgars of the Volga. Characteristically, the Russian princes had persisted in regarding the Moslem Bulgars as more to be dreaded than any pagans; concentrating on his enmity with them, the grand prince of Vladimir, another Yury, was therefore busy building a new fortress, Nizhny Novgorod, at the eastern edge of his domain, where the Oka flows into the Volga; from this outpost he hoped to subjugate the Mordva, a backward Finnish people on the middle Volga, and thus be in a position to attack the Bulgars beyond them. Unassisted by their Russian neighbors, the Volga Bulgars paid heavily for the shame they had inflicted on the Mongols fourteen years before; their very name vanished from history.

After the Bulgars came the turn of the Russians. The whole land of Suzdal was speedily overrun. Unable to muster the full forces even of the area over which he was nominally grand prince, Yury made no effort to save his neighbor, the prince of Ryazan. Yury himself was overtaken in flight and slain in battle. One after another the towns of northeastern Rus succumbed. Those that offered serious resistance suffered cruel reprisals; those that submitted were relatively spared. Yury's brother, Yaroslav, was permitted to succeed as grand prince, but at the price of making the long trip to the Mongol capital, Karakorum, and accepting a tributary relationship. By the spring of 1238 the Mongols had penetrated within sixty miles of Novgorod; fearing the thaws, which would destroy their freedom of movement, they withdrew from the forest area to the open steppe, leaving behind them this time not merely impressions of terror but scenes of savage desolation and lasting fiscal subjection.

After a year's pause, they returned again in the winter of 1239-1240 to complete the subjugation of Rus by overrunning the Dnieper area as they had first swarmed, "like locusts," over the Oka-Volga mesopotamia. Kiev itself, after determined resistance, was punishingly sacked (1240) and for long after remained desolate. None of the Russian principalities long escaped submission; "they numbered themselves for tribute." [6] The last to be taken into "the Tartar number" was Novgorod, which avoided ruin under the guidance of its young prince, Alexander, son of Grand Prince Yaroslav of Vladimir-Suzdal, by accepting the "Tatar yoke" before the city was attacked (1259).

With all Russia under tribute, the Mongol warriors, whose original numbers must have been considerably reduced, turned their horses still further west (1240). To the aid of Hungary, their next chosen victim, rallied the kingdoms of Poland and Bohemia, the Holy Roman Empire itself, and the great crusading orders of the Knights Templars and Knights Hospitalers. Keeping his enemies divided by masterly strategy, the Mongol general divided his own army into two parts; one crushed the pride of Poland at Szydlov and pushed rapidly on to destroy the forces of the Germans and of the crusading orders at Liegnitz before the Czechs could join them; the main force, under Subutai, the victor on the banks of the Kalka in 1223, wiped out the forces of Bela of Hungary. Suddenly, on receipt of news of the death of the grand khan at far Karakorum, Batu abandoned his designs on Vienna to take part in the struggle over the succession.

Violent as the blow had been, the shock to Western Europe was more psychological than physical. The problem of peaceful coexistence seemed acute. In dismay and wonderment the pope in 1246 selected a Franciscan friar, Giovanni de Piano Carpini, who, at the age of 65, had already behind him a lifetime of eminent service in various parts of Europe. Traveling with one fellow Franciscan, Piano Carpini made the long journey overland from Bohemia across Poland to Kiev and thence, though "feeble unto death," across the wintry steppe to the headquarters of Batu Khan on the lower Volga, only to be sent on to the court of the grand khan at Karakorum in Mongolia. Under "strait commaundement from the Pope" to "diligently searche out all things that concerned the state of the Tartars," the friars suffered not only from the rigors of the long and difficult journey but also from the embarrassing hospitality of the Mongols, who gave them very little nourishing food, but "gave us of their ale, because we could not drink their mares' milk. And this they did unto us in token of great honour. But they compelled us to drink so much, that in regard to our customary diet, wee could by no means endure it." From the beginning the emissaries of Christendom took a high but charitable tone, explaining:

> We are the legates of our lord the Pope, who is the father and lord of the Christians. . . . it is his pleasure, that all Christians should be in league [i.e., friends] with the Tartars, and should have peace with them. It is his desire also that they should become great or in favour with God in heaven, therefore he admonisheth them aswel by us, as by his own letters, to become Christians, and to embrace the faith of our Lord Jesu Christ, because they could not otherwise be saved. . . . he much marveilith at their monstrous slaughters and massacres of mankind. . . . he adviseth them from henceforth to beware of such dealing and to repemt them of that which they had done. . . .

To their dismay, however, the friars learned that even during their months of sojourning at the headquarters of the new grand khan,

> the Emperor new elect . . . erected a flag of defiance against the Church of God and the Romane empire, and against al Christian kingdomes and nations of the west. . . . For, except Christendom, there is no land under heaven, which they stande in feare of, and for that cause they prepare themselves to battel against us.

The pope's envoys were therefore careful not to ask that Mongol envoys be sent back with them:

> First, because we feared, least they, seeing the dissentions and warres which are among us, should be the more encouraged to make warre against us. Secondly, we feared that they would be insteade of spies and intelligencers in our dominions. . . .[7]

No better success attended a further effort at appeasement undertaken two years later by Friar Andrew of Longjumeau, sent from the Holy Land by the king of France (St. Louis of crusading fame), or the more famous journey, another five years later, of another Franciscan, Guillaume de Rubriquis, who, to avoid another rebuff to his royal patron, was careful to travel unofficially. On his return in 1255, Rubriquis wrote a detailed and sober account of his observations, which, despite the untrustworthiness of the interpreter who accompanied him, stands as the best account of the Asiatic "heartland" and its then masters. Although it proved impossible to establish friendly relations between the East and the West, no further dire consequences ensued. The worst that Western Europe was to experience at the hands of Asia came a century later in the form of the Black Death, but the bubonic plague came in the wake of peaceful commerce with Western Europe (1352), not of military conquest.

Only Russia had prolonged experience of contact with nomad Asia. For over two centuries the Russian forest zone, which from time immemorial had been plagued with the constant menace of the steppe raiders, was to remain under tribute to the Mongols and their Tatar subjects. The nature of the regime in "appanage Rus," as the next period of Russian history is conventionally called, must be reserved for later examination. Here it may be noted that the area of Russian history proper contracted during that period to the confines of the Oka-Volga mesopotamia. The historic scene of early Russian history, the Dnieper basin, fell under the control of non-Russian powers—Poland and Lithuania. Novgorod, too, though she continued to be under the authority of Orthodox and Russian princes, developed on lines quite different from those that governed in the northeast. Before continuing, then, with discussion of the aftermath of the Mongol conquest, it will be well to turn attention briefly to the fate of western Rus and of Lord Novgorod the Great.

NOTES

1. *Russkaia Pravda,* Article 46 (cf. also Article 121).
2. Cross (ed.), *The Russian Primary Chronicle,* revised edition, p. 200.
3. *Polnoe sobranie russkikh lietopisei,* II, 4 (Ipatievskii version).
4. *Ibid.,* II, 65.
5. Michell and Forbes, *The Chronicle of Novgorod,* p. 66.
6. *Ibid.,* p. 97.
7. Richard Hakluyt, *The Principal Navigations, Voyages, Traffique and Discoveries of the English Nation,* 1903 edition, I, 134, 170, 161, 173, 177.

SUGGESTIONS FOR FURTHER READING

For general treatments, see the Suggestions for Chapter 1. Among other works mentioned under Chapter 2 (page 38), see especially Vernadsky's *Kievan Russia* and the Cross edition of *The Russian Primary Chronicle.* B. D. Grekov, *The Culture of Kiev Rus* (in English), should be consulted for a curtailed version of the views of one of the ablest of Soviet historians. The most comprehensive study of variant texts of the *Russkaia Pravda,* edited by Grekov, has been published (in Russian) by the Academy of Sciences of the U.S.S.R.; a convenient English translation of one of the long and one of the short versions has been made by Vernadsky.

H. H. Howorth, *History of the Mongols,* is a standard encyclopedic account of that people. Vladimirtsov's *Life of Chingis-Khan* is available in English translation. Slightly divergent translations of the reports of Plano de Carpini and of Guillaume de Rubriquis may be found in *Travels* of Sir John Mandeville and in M. Komroff (ed.), *The Contemporaries of Marco Polo.*

Chapter

4

Western Rus and Novgorod: Through the 16th Century

In this chapter the narrative of the main line of development of Russian history is interrupted in order to explain how large parts of the "Russian land" were detached from it and for some centuries subjected to alien rule. There will also be included an account of the Novgorod area which, although it remained part of the "Russian land," experienced for a time an evolution distinctly different from that of the central "mesopotamia."

RUSSIA'S ROMAN CATHOLIC NEIGHBORS

To understand the process by which the Dnieper basin, which was the central area of Rus in the Kievan period, came to be politically separated from the more recently settled area between the upper Volga and the Oka, it is necessary to give some attention to Russia's neighbors on the west. These were: the kingdoms of Poland and Hungary; the great crusading orders of German knights on the Baltic shore; and of less importance, the new kingdoms of Denmark and Sweden. Later arose also a new power, the Grand Principality of Lithuania, which played the most significant part of all in relation to the western portion of what had been Rus.

With the exception of Lithuania, all of these powers in the Kievan period were Roman Catholic. In 1054, when the Roman Catholic and Greek Orthodox Churches finally fell into lasting schism, their respective ecclesiastical authorities, at Rome and at Constantinople, pronounced anathema on each other and on each other's followers. This did not in itself prevent friendly relations between the adherents of the two main branches of the

Christian Church, any more than submission to a common ecclesastical jurisdiction ensured peaceful relations either among the Russian princes or among the various Roman Catholic states. A certain amount of overland trade existed between the Russians and their western neighbors, and dynastic intermarriages were fairly frequent. On the other hand, neighborly relations could not prevent recurrent hostilities, the character of which, initially at least, was a shifting dynastic or personal one rather than one of deeply ingrained national or religious hostility.

Thus, in the middle of the twelfth century, Hungary was threatened by joint action of the Holy Roman and Byzantine emperors; some of the Russian princes, including Hungary's nearest neighbor, the prince of Galicia, joined enthusiastically in the chase; but the grand prince then "sitting" at Kiev allied himself with the king of France in defense of the Magyar ruler. Again, toward the end of the twelfth century, the Hungarian king succeeded for a time in establishing his son as ruler in Galicia, but the Carpathian Mountain barrier, the support of some other Russian princes, and the jealousy of Poland combined to thwart Hungarian ambitions. Despite repeated efforts by Hungary, the grand prince of Volhynia-Galicia was able to maintain his style of *rex russorum,* a title formally conferred by the pope in 1253, until the extinction of the dynasty in the fourteenth century; the precarious nature of his authority was, however, marked by the special strength of the southwestern boyar aristocracy, reflecting the position of the feudal magnates of encroaching Poland and Hungary.

Poland played a more active part than did Hungary in intervening in Russian affairs. Twice in the eleventh century a Polish army occupied Kiev: in 1018, Boleslaw I, who did so much to check the German *Drang nach Osten,* aided Sviatopolk briefly in recovering his throne from his brother, Yaroslav the Wise; fifty years later, Boleslaw II helped Grand Prince Iziaslav recover the throne from which he had been driven by a *vieche* following a defeat by the Polovtsy. In the twelfth and thirteenth centuries, however, Poland, itself torn by internal strife, confined its activities to intervention in bordering Russian principalities, usually to check—though sometimes to assist—Hungary. It was Poland that inherited Galicia (1340) and (until 1366) Volhynia.

The greatest menace to the independence of the western Russian princes came, though indirectly, from a more remote source in the West. The German *Drang nach Osten,* in the proper sense of the phrase, was mainly an affair of the tenth century. At the time when the Eastern Slavs, under Scandinavian leadership, were emerging into the light of history through contacts with Byzantium, the Western Slavs were being swamped under the military, ecclesiastical, and economic pressures that were building a *Kolonialdeutschland* eastward from the Elbe. This German pressure on the Slavs was largely checked by the rise of the kingdom of Poland, which in the year 1000 succeeded in having the see of Gnesen (Gniezno) made directly dependent on Rome; thus Poland avoided further ecclesiastical dependence on Germany and was able to escape even the degree of Germanization undergone by Bohemia, which retained its Slavic dynasty and language but was incorporated into the political and ecclesiastical structure of the "Holy Roman Empire of the German Nation."

Late in the twelfth century, commercial and missionary zeal combined to renew the eastward pressure of the Germans; they were, however, compelled to bypass their immediate Slav neighbors, Poland and Bohemia, and direct their attention against the still pagan and politically unorganized Lithuanian and Finnish peoples on the sandy shores of the Baltic. These peoples had long been subject to exploitation by the neighboring Russian principalities. Princes of Novgorod had frequently campaigned against them; as early as the eleventh century the Russian town of Yuriev (later renamed Dorpat by the Germans) had been established among the Estonians. The princes of Polotsk had subjected the Livonians (now called Letts or Latvians) to tribute as far as the mouth of the Dvina, and the princes of Volhynia had exerted strong pressure on the Lithuanians proper to the south of them.

Far more intensive was to be the activity of the Germans and of their allies, the kings of Denmark and Sweden. Following in the wake of German traders, a German missionary from Bremen, Meinhardt, secured permission from the prince of Polotsk to build a church, enclosed by fortifications, on the lower Dvina (*c.* 1186). Soon one of his successors, Bishop Albert, founded the city of Riga, an essentially German town (1201). In 1202 he founded also the military crusading Order of Swordbearing Knights (later better known as the Livonian Order), intent on the forcible conversion of the heathen natives. The prince of Polotsk, preferring appeasement to resistance, was induced to surrender his claims to tribute along the course of the Dvina for about 150 miles from its mouth. Mstislav the Bold, then prince of Novgorod, showed fight, thus bringing added misery to the hapless Livonians. In the year after Mstislav's defeat by the Mongols on the banks of the Kalka, Yuriev fell to the Livonian Knights (1224). Meanwhile the Danes had established a foothold at Reval (1219), whence they had extended their power over all Estonia by 1237. The Swedes were at the same time engaged in the reduction of the Finns to the north of the Gulf, pushing their power almost to the mouth of the Neva.

Still more formidable were the results of the transfer to the Baltic region of the activities of the Teutonic Order, which like the Knights Templars and Knights Hospitalers, had been originally organized for campaigns against the Moslems in the Holy Land. Unsuccessful there, they gladly accepted (1226) an invitation from a Polish prince to relieve him from the marauding operations of the Prussians, a heathen Lithuanian people on the southern shore of the Baltic. Beginning operations in 1229, the Teutonic Knights so thoroughly organized their campaign of conquest and colonization that within half a century the very name of the province had become a thoroughly

German word. In 1237, the year in which the Mongols began their serious onslaught on Rus, the Teutonic and Livonian orders were merged, though the latter retained a measure of autonomy under its own *Landmeister*.

The power of the Knights, mighty as it was, was yet not invincible; still less formidable were the two Scandinavian kingdoms. It was one thing to subjugate and Christianize the backward Letto-Lithuanian peoples of the shore line; it was quite another to press on against the organized Russian principalities in the interior. First to suffer a severe check were the Swedes, who sought to move around the head of the Gulf of Finland into the territory of Novgorod; Novgorod's prince, Alexander, the twenty-year-old son of the new Grand Prince Yaroslav, who in 1238, as we have seen, had been allowed by the victorious Mongols to succeed his slain brother Yury, won undying fame by his resounding victory over the Swedes on the banks of the Neva (1240). Two years later Alexander Nevsky ("of the Neva") scored an even greater triumph by his crushing defeat of the German Knights on the ice of Lake Peipus.

LITHUANIA AND THE UKRAINE

Thus it was not by direct attack that the Teutons were destined to cause a serious shrinkage of the area under Russian control. Rather was it the by-product of their pressure on the remnants of the Lithuanian peoples that was to give rise to a new and formidable political power. Caught between the German hammer and the Slav anvil, the denizens of the swampy Baltic hinterland, like the Poles at an earlier day, ultimately became welded into a single strong military principality, whose principal architects were Mindovg (d. 1263) and Gedimin (1316-41). By force and fraud, by conquest and by marriage, they extended their hegemony southward and eastward into the basins of the Pripet and the upper Dnieper.* Remaining pagan, the Lithuanian rulers showed complete tolerance toward the Orthodox Russians. Though unable to recover the lost coastal regions from the Knights, Gedimin's son, Keistut (1340-82), proved able to check their further expansion, while Gedimin's more famous son, Olgerd (1340-77), as co-ruler with his brother, extended his military leadership ever further southward, absorbing the old principalities of Kiev, Volhynia, Chernigov, Novgorod-Seversk, and Pereiaslav, and even making his power felt as far as the Black Sea coast between the mouths of the Dniester and the Dnieper. Keistut's son, Vitovt (1392-1430), added Smolensk to his dominions. Thus, as under the Varangians in the ninth century, a foreign and pagan leadership effected a high degree of superficial unity throughout the basin of the Dnieper and its tributaries. It was with good reason that, until the Revolution in 1917, the male descendants of Gedimin ranked with those of Rurik in retaining the

* See Map III.

right, whatever their material fortunes, to the honorary style of "Prince" (*kniaz*).

A factor of the highest importance in this southeastward expansion of Lithuania was the waning of the power of the Mongol-Tatar overlords of Rus. Quarrels over succession and the extreme difficulty of maintaining anything like centralized authority over far-flung nomadic tribes had led to the rapid disintegration of the grand khanate of Karakorum into a number of "hordes." Inevitably their local khans were immeasurably weaker than the combined forces of nomadic Asia, and their title was often contested by dynastic rivals.

The only one of these local khanates of concern here was the Golden Horde, which had established its "capital" (or winter city) at Sarai on the lower Volga, near that Itil from which the Khazars had once ruled the steppe and imposed tribute on the forest zone. The Golden Horde, not unassisted by some of the Russian princes, remained until the middle of the fifteenth century strong enough to maintain its grip on the Oka-Volga mesopotamia, but was unable to exact tribute from the newly risen Lithuanian rulers or from their Russian protégés. For the Russian princes of the Dnieper basin submission to Gedimin and Olgerd therefore meant escape from the burden of the Tatar tribute. Vassalage to pagan Lithuania seemed a lighter yoke than continued subjection to the steppe nomads, who early in the fourteenth century had somewhat tepidly embraced Islam.

It might have been expected that the consequences of such rapid Lithuanian expansion would have been the conversion of Lithuania into a genuine Russian state. The bulk of the population of the expanded grand principality were, of course, Russian in speech and Orthodox in religion, and they had attained a far higher economic and cultural level than their protectors. Under such conditions, over and over again, history has witnessed the absorption of the rulers by the ruled. This process was however checked by a dynastic accident.

Olgerd's son and successor, Yagailo (Jagellon), who in 1382 murdered his uncle Keistut, was in 1386 offered the hand of Yadwiga (Hedwig), heiress of the original Polish dynasty of the Piasts. As a condition of the offer, Yagailo had to be baptized as a Roman Catholic (under the name of Ladislas) and had to remove his residence from Vilna to Cracow. No attempt was made to fuse the kingdom of Poland and the grand principality of Lithuania into a single state; they remained under separate administrations and separate laws and customs. Yet the example of the grand prince sufficed to effect the conversion of most of the pagan Lithuanian nobles to Roman Catholicism. Even many of the Orthodox Russian boyars followed suit.

Thus a deep rift developed within Lithuania. Although Yagailo was forced to recognize his cousin Vitovt, son of Keistut, as grand prince of Lithuania (1392) and although, even after Vitovt's death in 1430, Poland and Lithuania for the most part had separate rulers, the Roman Catholic, Polonizing party continued to have strong influence. Even Vitovt, faced with the rising menace of Moscow to the east and with the still ever-present dangers of the Golden Horde and the Teutonic Order, had to depend on Poland for military support. Only so was it possible for him to inflict crushing defeat on the Knights at the great battle of Tannenberg (1410). Vitovt—and still more his successors—were all the less able to throw their weight on the side of the Orthodox, Russian party because at a joint diet in 1413 it had been agreed that Roman Catholics in Lithuania were to enjoy the same rights as their co-religionists in Poland. Since Poland then lived under a highly developed form of feudal system, and since the Polish nobility enjoyed wide powers over their peasants as well as much independence toward their king, this agreement provided a powerful magnet attracting the Russo-Lithuanian nobility to embrace Roman Catholicism and thus to acquire the peculiarly privileged position of the Polish nobility. Increasingly, religious and linguistic differentiation tended to be associated with class distinction.

The bulk of the Lithuanian-Russian aristocracy gravitated more and more in the direction of closer union with Poland, a drift that kept pace with the rising strength of Muscovite autocracy. In 1501 the Polish and Lithuanian diets agreed that thenceforth they would always choose the same individual as joint ruler. In 1569, in the midst of a long and difficult war with Moscow, the Lithuanian diet, by the Union of Lublin, even more definitely accepted the principle of a single realm—the *Rzeczpospolita* (Republic)—with a common ruler, common diet, and common senate, though with separate laws and customs, separate administrative and military officers. In return for the promise of more constant support from Poland, Lithuania was induced to surrender the southern half of her territory to Poland proper.

Particularly in this transferred territory, henceforth known as Poland's *ukraine* (frontier), the penetration of Polish usages and Polish institutions proceeded rapidly. Polish magnates (*pani*) organized huge landed estates, reducing the "Little Russian" peasants to Polish serfdom. The towns were increasingly peopled with Jews and other German-speaking elements, who had long served agricultural Poland as traders and artisans; as early as the thirteenth century, these immigrant townsmen were put under a special code of laws, the Ius Magdeburgicum, adapted from the law under which they had lived in their homeland. The new order of things found spiritual symbolization in the fate of the Orthodox Church. Over a century earlier, in the face of the advancing Ottoman Turks, Rome and Byzantium had made a desperate effort to heal the schism by the Union of Florence (1438); after its rejection by Moscow, the Greek Orthodox clergy of Lithuania had broken with the Russian metropolitan, then resident at Moscow, and had restored the metropolitanate of Kiev, dependent directly on Constantinople, as a rival leadership of the Russian Church. Thus, cut off ecclesiastically as well as politically from the rest of the Russians, the Orthodox population of Lithuania was subjected by the Roman Catholic rulers and magnates to increasing persecution. In the sixteenth century, the position was complicated by the Protestant Reformation, against which the Jesuits speedily developed a vigorous and, in Lithuania, almost wholly successful, counterattack. Encouraged by the Union of Lublin (1569), the Jesuits turned their attention to winning over the Orthodox. The Orthodox bishops, who owed their positions to the king rather than to the faithful, petitioned the pope to take them under his protection. In 1596, at Brest, a church council formally accepted union with Rome. Although a substantial number of the members refused to accept the verdict, the ruler proclaimed the decision to accept the Uniate Church as binding on the whole Orthodox population. Lay "fraternities" continued to resist and successfully, though illegally, kept their Church in existence, despite vigorous persecution and deprivation of political rights. An important by-product of the situation was the work of many monks, including the inmates of the great Pechersky Monastery at Kiev, in promoting the study of Orthodox theology and in spreading, by sermons and books, the fruits of their work. This intellectual movement, centering in Kiev, was later to have important results at Moscow as well.

Along the edges of the ukraine, the Poles were confronted with a special problem. From time immemorial the steppe had tempted a certain number of wild and adventurous people, known in Kievan times as *brodniki.* They lived a precarious existence along the main watercourses, subsisting by fishing, horse-trading, and assorted forms of thievery, as well as by casual agriculture. In constant peril of their lives from the steppe nomads, they could count on no regular assistance from the Russian princes, toward whom, indeed, they felt no love. The *brodniki* had been the first to welcome the Mongol force that penetrated across the Caucasus in 1221 and had offered to serve the Mongols even before their great victory on the Kalka (1223).

Their successors came to be known as cossacks (*kazaki*—not to be confused with the Kazakhi, a branch of the Asiatic nomads who have given their name to one of the member states of the Soviet Union). The cossacks were Russian in speech, Orthodox (at least nominally) in religion. Though they were found along all the rivers that crossed the edge of the steppe—on the Don and the Volga as well as on the Dnieper—it was the cossacks of the Dnieper who were the most formidably organized and who played the greatest role in history. On islands in that river "below the rapids" (*za porogi*), the "Zaporogian" cossacks had their stronghold and winter headquarters, whence they ranged afield as farmers, fishermen, warriors, or robbers. The more well-to-do, the cossack "elders" (*starosty*), owned boats or even landed estates; the rest worked for them but shared politically in a rude "democratic" society. At the head of each group stood an elected *ataman;* over all, chosen by the general assembly (*rada*) was the *hetman.*

Not only did they bitterly resent and resist all efforts of Polish landlords to reduce them to subjection. The khanate of the Crimea had accepted the protection of the Turkish sultan; the fierce raids of the cossacks into its territories, and their attacks on Turkish towns along the coast of the Black Sea, provoked reprisals, the brunt of which had to be borne by the Polish ukraine rather than by the elusive cossacks. The Poles made vigorous efforts to curb the wild independence of the cossacks: they forbade them to bear arms, save for those who were permitted to register in the king's military service; they built forts and stationed German artillerymen to impede the cossacks' movements. It was all in vain. Particularly drastic measures, such as burning the cossacks' boats, regularly led to savage uprisings, which often were combined with peasant revolts. Most famous of Ukrainian heroes in the sixteenth century were the cossack leaders Loboda and Nalivaiko, who threatened the continuance of Polish rule in the middle Dnieper basin.

Such, in summary outline, was the fate of the western Russian lands, and such were the conditions under which, under Lithuanian rule, the White Russian and, under Polish rule, Little Russian (Ukrainian) national types began to develop. This is not meant to suggest that the Great Russian was the true Russian, from which the others diverged. It should never be forgotten that the Ukraine was originally not the frontier, but the very center of Russian settlement, and that the Great Russian type developed in what had been the remote northeast, perhaps the least Slavicized portion of the forested plain. What is meant by reserving the Great Russian area for more extended discussion is that the direct line of economic and institutional development is there most readily to be observed, relatively free from external influences, and that it was in this area that the Muscovite state, later the core of the Russian empire, had its rise.

NOVGOROD

It remains, however, to consider the history of one other portion of Rus which, for a period of some centuries, was not subject to the same influences that shaped the rise of Moscow. This embraced Novgorod and her "younger brother," Pskov. Their development was not, indeed, under the control of a non-Russian power, as was that of the Dnieper basin, nor yet did it take place in total isolation from what was to become known as Great Russia. Nevertheless, continuing more strictly in the Kievan tradition, they boasted until the late fifteenth century forms of society and government unknown elsewhere in Russian history.

The geographical situation of Novgorod had from the earliest times given the city a special role in the economy and politics of Kievan Rus. Standing on both banks of the Volkhov, where that river emerges from Lake Ilmen, it had unimpeded water communication with the Gulf of Finland and the Baltic by way of Lake Ladoga and the Neva; yet it was far enough inland to be secure against casual raids by sea-roving marauders. By easy portages

Novgorod also enjoyed access both to the upper Dnieper, the main waterway to the Black Sea and Constantinople, and to the upper Volga, the subsidiary route to the land of the Volga Bulgars and, beyond, to the Caspian and the Moslem lands. Thus, the advantages of Novgorod for purposes of trade were second only to those of Kiev, and second only so long as trade with Constantinople was dominant. For these reasons, it was at Novgorod that Rurik had established himself. Similarly, his successors, after their removal to Kiev, constantly sought to retain control of the upper end of the water route "from the Varangians to the Greeks"; they had assigned its governance to their eldest sons, not sharing it with brothers or more remote relations as they were content to do with other portions of the territory they subjected to tribute.

A further and vital advantage of Novgorod's geographical location was that it was possible, by almost continuous water transport, to round the western end of the great northern watershed (*volok*) and reach the basin of the northern Dvina. The huge area of the *zavoloche,* little fit for agriculture but largely covered with pine forest, was an ideal source of supply for furs, the chief commodity of trade. Although this region was for a long time not occupied by Slav settlers, it constituted a sort of "colonial empire"; regular expeditions from Novgorod collected a rich annual tribute, with little possibility of competition from the principalities lying south of the watershed. From the shores of the White Sea, the men of Novgorod acquired walrus tusks. Penetrating eastward to the Urals and the headwaters of the Kama, they were able to tap rich resources of silver, which contributed enormously to their commercial prosperity.

Novgorod thus remained in possession of an abundant stock of goods in demand in foreign lands. The loss of contact with Constantinople did not destroy Novgorod's market. As early as the middle of the twelfth century, Swedish merchants based at Wisby in the Baltic built a trading establishment, including, of course, a Roman Catholic church, on the right bank of the Volkhov near the great market square, the Court of Yaroslav. Before that century was over, German merchants had added their own place of business, the "German temple" of St. Peter, competing with the "Varangian temple" of St. Olaf. Before long, the rising Hanseatic League, centered at Lübeck, had ousted the Wisby merchants and established their own monopoly of the westward foreign trade of Novgorod; there they maintained a well-fortified depot (*Hof*) on much the same lines as their "Steelyard" (*Stahlhof*) in London.

Novgorod also maintained a thriving trade by way of the Volga to the Caspian. The Mongol conquest, which bore so heavily on the other commercial centers of Rus, brought Novgorod unparalleled opportunities. The establishment, from the Baltic to the Pacific, of a *pax Mongolica,* relatively short-lived though it was, enormously stimulated overland caravan trade from China to the Caspian. Secure of easy access, thanks to the removal of the Bulgar power, to that landlocked sea, the merchants of Novgorod multiplied their activities.

A disadvantage of her position, ultimately to prove fatal to Novgorod's independence, was the increasing impossibility of supporting a growing urban population from the meager agricultural resources of the surrounding countryside. More and more Novgorod became dependent for her grain supply on other parts of Rus. The readiest source of supply was from the Oka-Volga mesopotamia, ruled by the princes of the Suzdal branch of the descendants of Vladimir Monomakh, and frequently called, by reason of its downstream position from Novgorod, the "Low Country." Need of grain forced Novgorod to maintain specially close political relations with the princes of this area and, when power there had become sufficiently centralized in the hands of the princes of Moscow, made the threat of "economic sanctions" so powerful as to make military action against her almost superfluous.

Yet for some three centuries, while the Russian land was still divided among a number of princes, none of whom could wield more than psychological dominance over his fellows, Novgorod was able to live an independent and flourishing life as a republican city-state. Her political institutions were, to be sure, the same as those of other principalities in the Kievan period—the prince and his *druzhina,* balanced by the irregularly asserted authority of the *vieche.* In Novgorod, however, for reasons suggested above, no branch of the princely family established itself as a permanent fixture; there could be no question of a prince claiming Novgorod as his patrimony (*otchina*). Nor could the personal following of any temporary prince have time to establish itself as a ruling oligarchy. As a result, there grew up in Novgorod a specially powerful class of wealthy men—permanent landowners and capitalists who financed the activities of the trading and artisan population.

The "democratic revolution" of the twelfth century therefore produced results even more striking than in the other commercial towns of Kievan Rus. From 1126—the year after the death of the great Grand Prince Vladimir Monomakh—the office of *posadnik* (mayor) was recognized as elective. Soon the *tysiatsky* (head of the town militia) also was elected by the *vieche.* From 1156 the bishop (*vladyka*) was locally chosen, only the right of consecration being reserved to the metropolitan. Before the close of the Kievan period, even the office of prince had been officially admitted to be subject to the will of the men of Novgorod. Although Andrei Bogoliubsky, who had been responsible for the sack of Kiev in 1169, had ultimately succeeded in forcing a prince of his choice on Novgorod, his brother and successor, Vsevolod "Big-Nest" of Suzdal, had to agree with the other princes of Rus that Novgorod was free "where it pleased them, there they might take to themselves [a prince]." [1]

Throughout the thirteenth century Novgorod used its powers to compel its successive princes to accept sworn and written agreements before admitting them to the throne. The city felt the need of a military protector—in later times 5,000 of the Novgorod militia, though mounted, were routed by 200 footsoldiers of Moscow, and a mob of 40,000 townsmen, who "had never from birth been on horseback," were beaten by a force of 4,500 Muscovites, with a loss of 12,000 slain—but it watched jealously lest the prince use his position to gain real control of the city and its dominions. The prince was expected to administer justice, in person and on the spot, but was to make no decisions without the assent of the *posadnik;* very often the *vieche* itself undertook to interfere with his administration. The prince and his family were strictly forbidden to acquire any property in Novgorod, whether in the form of real estate or of loans to citizens of the city-state; he had to fix his residence outside the city proper, and even his hunting and fishing rights were narrowly circumscribed by the treaties. At the slightest sign of dereliction in his military duties, the "kept" prince was liable to expulsion; it is small wonder that even in the twelfth century an impatient prince, on being invited to take its throne, indignantly exclaimed: "Talk not of Novgorod; let the men of Novgorod worry as they like, and get themselves a prince where they like." [2]

In form, Novgorod evolved into a democratic republic, in which the assembly of all the citizens, the *vieche,* was sovereign. In actuality, power was vested in a small group of capitalist families, the boyars of Novgorod and other less eminent but prosperous landowners and suppliers of capital goods. In the course of the thirteenth century there were twenty-three elections of a *posadnik* by the *vieche;* since several men held the office more than once, only fifteen individuals were involved, ten of whom belonged to one or another of the two leading boyar families. A local aristocracy, known to the Germans as *Herrenrath,* directed the affairs of the city; its internecine quarrels, rather than the activities of the princes, account for most of the turbulence that characterized the history of "Lord Novgorod the Great."

In the later period of Novgorod's independent existence, the rivalries among her magnates faded in importance before the rising clash of class interests. Partly because of her relative release from external dangers after Alexander Nevsky's decisive victories over the Swedes (1240) and the German Knights (1242) and his successful persuasion of the Novgorodans to submit to the Tatar "number" for tribute (1259), the significance of the prince steadily declined. It has been said that in the period from the death of Yaroslav the Wise (1054) to the Tatar conquest there were at least twelve disturbances in Novgorod, all but two of which involved a change of ruler; from the Tatar conquest to the treaty imposed by Vasily the Dark (1456), there were more than twenty disturbances, but not more than four of them were connected with a change of prince.

The social structure of the republic became much more complex than that of Kiev, of which, however, it was the logical outgrowth. As everywhere else in Rus, the countryside, in the *volost* of Novgorod itself as well as in her "colonial" territories stretching north of the watershed to the Urals and the White Sea, remained subject to the town, whether directly to the metropolis itself or to one of its subordinate towns (*prigorody*). The land was for the most part owned by wealthy individuals resident in the towns or by the state itself—which here did not mean the prince. It was worked, as elsewhere in Rus, by free peasants (*smerdy*) or by bondsmen (*kholopy*). In the later centuries a portion of the free peasants, known as *polovniki* (sharecroppers), increasingly lost their mobility; in successive treaties with princes they were more and more assimilated to the *kholopy*. A unique category were the *svoezemtsy* ("own-landers"), who owned land as small individual proprietors. Apparently they were townsmen who had acquired land in the countryside, either for agricultural or commercial exploitation. As men of relatively small means, however, they seldom held the land as individuals but combined into formal associations. Although it was scarcely possible to distinguish them economically from the upper strata of the peasantry, they retained their special juridical position, which associated them with the urban rather than with the rural population.

In the town, though all free citizens had a right to participate equally in its political life, socio-economic distinctions were very pronounced. The highest category, the boyars (i.e., the boyars of Novgorod, not the personal followers of the temporary prince) monopolized all the important governmental positions. Close to them ranked the "men of substance" (*zhitie liudi*). Boyars and "men of substance" alike were landowners and capitalists, drawing from their rural estates, worked by *polovniki* and *kholopy,* the wealth which was the basis of Novgorod's commerce. Taking little active part in trade or even in the regulation of trade, they financed the merchant and artisan population. The actual traders (*kuptsy*) were for the most part debtors or agents of the boyars and "men of substance," in which respect they resembled the *chernye liudi* ("black," i.e. common, "people") who supplied the necessary manual labor. They boasted, however, of important distinctions, being organized in guilds. The chief of these guilds, which had as its headquarters the Orthodox Church of St. John the Baptist, had what was for those times a high admission fee—fifty silver grivnas, more than double the fine to be paid for the murder of a princely retainer. The organization was privileged to maintain a court controlling all commercial litigation, with jurisdiction independent of the *posadnik* and presided over by the thousand-man (*tysiatsky*).

The division of the urban population into two basic classes increasingly became the source of Novgorod's internal factional disputes. The creditor minority resided on the left bank of the Volkhov—the *Sophiskaia storona,* around the cathedral of St. Sophia. Most of the debtor population lived on the opposite bank—the *torgovaia storona,* where was situated the great market place (*torg*) on which the *vieche* normally assembled; there stood also the specially fortified Hansa *Hof.* This physical arrangement lent a touch of picturesqueness to the drab tumultuousness of uprisings of the *vieche*. The main connecting bridge occasionally became the scene of fierce combats, at least once (1418) dramatically terminated by the intervention of the clergy, headed by the archbishop, who in full sacramental vestments and with crucifix in hand pushed his way out onto the Great Bridge and stilled both parties with his blessing. A legend, recorded by Baron Herberstein, who visited Russia as the envoy of the Holy Roman Emperor early in the sixteenth century, assigned the origin of these fights to the vengeance of Perun, the early pagan Slav god of thunder, whose idol had been hurled from the bridge at the time of the Christianization of Rus by St. Vladimir.

Significantly, the riotous *vieche* never sought to replace the real authority exercised by the oligarchic magnates with a regular constitutional structure. The riots were directed at individual boyars, in the face of resistance spilling over into wild general looting. They might result, as in 1359, in the replacement of one *posadnik* by another, but the new incumbent was chosen from the same boyar aristocracy. "God did not suffer the devil utterly to exult, but Christianity was exalted to generation and generation," complacently records the monk-chronicler.[3]

The dependent towns (*prigorody*) often had a prince and *vieche* of their own. Their citizens did not participate in the conduct of the government and polity of the metropolis, to which they were fiscally and administratively subordinate. One of them, Pskov, in 1347 was granted by Novgorod the right to choose its own *posadnik,* while the archbishop agreed to name a native of Pskov to preside over the ecclesiastical court in Novgorod's "younger brother." Though other *prigorody* occasionally revolted, Lord Novgorod the Great retained the right to appoint their chief officers, to hear appeals from their courts, and to demand money and troops.

In the fifteenth century the rising power of Moscow made steadily increasing encroachments on Novgorod's independence, culminating in the full acceptance of Moscow's appellate jurisdiction following the "crusade" of Ivan III in 1471. The republican institutions of the great city-state were not at once destroyed, but in 1478 the principality was formally annexed, the *vieche* bell being sent to Moscow. Thither, and to more remote parts of the realm, were soon to follow the boyars and "men of substance," deported by the thousands by the Muscovite conqueror. With the expulsion of the Hansa (1494), the special relations of Novgorod to the West also came to an end. The circumstances which led to the fall of Novgorod and what this meant for the further history of Rus may best be discussed, however, in a later chapter on the formation of the Muscovite state. It is time now to turn back to "appanage Rus" and to consider the state of affairs in the Oka-Volga mesopotamia under the "Tatar yoke."

NOTES

1. Michell and Forbes, *The Chronicle of Novgorod,* p. 39.
2. *Polnoe sobranie russkikh lietopisei,* IX, 165 (Patriarchal or Nikonovskii version).
3. Michell and Forbes, *op. cit.,* p. 148.

SUGGESTIONS FOR FURTHER READING

For general treatments, see Suggestions for Chapter 1; for treatments of early Rus in general, see Suggestions for Chapters 2 and 3. On Russia's western neighbors, there is no satisfactory work in English; Gimbutas' *The Balts,* though somewhat prejudiced, is, however, useful. More valuable are Schiemann, *Russland, Polen, und Livland bis ins 17. Jahrhundert,* and Wittram, *Baltische Geschichte.* Forskreuter, *Preussen und Russland,* includes a good outline of relations with the Teutonic Order. Kirchner's *Rise of the Baltic Question* is the best study of the general problem; Hill's *Danish Sound Dues* merely suggests its significance.

For the Ukraine, see Allen, *The Ukraine;* the nationalist Hrushevsky, *A History of the Ukraine;* and Doroshenko, *History of the Ukraine.* Kubijovyc's *Ukraine: A Concise Encyclopedia* is a revised version of an earlier work.

For Novgorod, the chief source is *The Chronicle of Novgorod,* translated by Michell and Forbes. See also Winckler, *Die deutsche Hanse in Russland,* and Goetz, *Deutsch-russische Handelsgeschichte.*

Chapter

5

Appanage Rus and the Rise of Moscow: 13th to 15th Centuries

It is conventional in Russian history to refer to the thirteenth to fifteenth centuries either as the "period of the Tatar yoke" or as the "appanage period." The reason for the former term is obvious; from 1238 to 1480 Russia was subject to tribute to the Mongol-led Tatars. Yet, as will be indicated, this was a superficial phenomenon, not profoundly influencing the course of Russian development. The other term, the "appanage period," is a mistranslation of *udielnoe vremia,* which has become standard in Russian historiography; the reason for it can best be discussed in its place later. A more appropriate title for the chapter might be "The Feudal Period and the Rise of Moscow." However, pending discussion below of the problem of feudalism in Russia, it seems best to retain here the conventional term. The reader is again reminded that the area now under discussion is not the whole forested area of the Russian plain but only the central mesopotamia between the upper Volga and the Oka.

THE TATAR YOKE

The "Tatar yoke," catastrophic though the term sounds, made remarkably little difference to the history of Russia. It must be remembered that the conquest of Rus by the Asiatic nomads, complete as it seemed, was neither accompanied nor followed by a process of colonization. The Tatars remained, as their predecessors—the Khazars, Pechenegs, and Polovtsy—had been, essentially an external force brought to bear on the forest zone from without, from the steppe. The Tatars did not give up their pastoral way of life, suited only to the open grasslands, nor did they expect the Russians to abandon their accustomed occupations, so long as they paid tribute punctually. It is perhaps symptomatic of the total situation that the Black Death, the bubonic plague from Asia, was transmitted to Rus, not directly through the nomads, but by way of Novgorod, coming from Western Europe (1352).

Economically, it may be true that the Mongol-led Tatars, anxious to destroy the most likely foci of resistance, bore most hardly on the old urban centers of Rus (Novgorod excepted), administering the coup de grâce to Russia's dying foreign trade. Yet for the agricultural countryside the substitution of the Tatar tribute for the old levies imposed by the commercial towns had its compensations; it resulted in virtual cessation of those inter-princely feuds which, even more than the raids of steppe nomads, had scourged the population. Under pressure of the Tatars, anxious for the regular dispatch of their tribute, the princes had perforce to keep the peace or reckon with the vengeance of their Tatar overlords.

Politically, the Tatars showed no interest in remodeling the existing order in Rus. In the region of the middle Dnieper, to be sure, they substituted the rule of their own agents for some of the old principalities. Yet in the northeast, where the commercial town and its *vieche* had been weakly developed, they had readily accepted the intermediary role of the native Russian princes and had been well content to permit the survival of old Russian customs, including the rota system of succession on the grand princely throne. In this sphere, the principal contributions of the Tatars were twofold. For one thing, they introduced a more efficient system of taxation, both direct and indirect; the first registers of taxable population date from the thirteenth century. For another, the Tatars treated city and country alike, wiping out the duality of the Kievan period and strengthening the basis for common subordination of all subjects to their ruler. It is in the area of fiscal administration that the adoption of Tatar terms into the Russian language most clearly reflects their continuing influence.

Generally speaking, the princes coöperated loyally with their new masters. Yaroslav, who had succeeded his fallen brother Yury as grand prince of Vladimir-Suzdal (1238), was duly confirmed by Batu Khan on his victorious return from Hungary (1243); one of his sons was sent to Karakorum for ratification. In 1246 Yaroslav was himself sent to Mongolia, where he died, as Batu's representative at the selection of a new grand khan. He was succeeded in accordance with ancient rota custom by his surviving brother and, in due course, by his sons in turn. The last to have to make the long trip across Asia were Andrew and Alexander "Nevsky," who received the Mongol *yarlyk* (charter), the one to Vladimir, the other to Novgorod and desolate Kiev. Andrew, an exception to the general rule, conspired against the Mongols with another ambitious prince, Daniel of Galicia-Volhynia (who in 1253 was to be honored, but not assisted, by the gift of a royal crown from the pope). Andrew had to flee (1252), and his brother Alexander—since celebrated as a national hero for his defense of Novgorod against the Teutons (1240-42)—was confirmed in his stead. After his death (1263), the title successively passed in regular order and without further incident to his brothers and later to his sons and nephews until, in the early fourteenth century, Moscow advanced its unwarranted pretensions to the title.

Such resistance as there was to the Tatar yoke came principally from the lower strata of the population, notably in Novgorod. In 1257 Kublai Khan, preparing to undertake the conquest of southern China, summoned recruits from all his dominions. At Novgorod, relates the chronicler, "There was a sign in the moon; such as no sign had ever been." When the Tatar *baskaki* arrived to count the houses,

> the common people would not give their numbers for tribute but said: "Let us die honourably for St. Sophia and for the angelic houses [the churches]." Then the people were divided; the wealthy feared that "for our sins God has brought wild beasts out of the desert to eat the flesh of the strong, and to drink the blood of *Boyars*." [1]

The riots were checked by the firm intervention of Grand Prince Alexander Nevsky, later canonized by the Church. "Christ's might" triumphed, and Novgorod escaped Tatar vengeance by timely submission. Alexander's last service to the Russian land was to intervene with Berke Khan, an early convert to Islam, to win forgiveness for the rebellious men of Rostov and other towns in the Suzdal region, who in 1262 had "willed a *vieche*" and expelled the Tatar tribute-takers. A subsequent outbreak at Rostov in 1289 was similarly quelled by its prince. Such princely intervention doubtless saved the population from frightful bloodshed, although at the cost of strengthening the autocratic principle.

The Tatars welcomed the military aid of the Russian princes and boyars in maintaining popular submission to the Tatar yoke. They also valued highly the spiritual services of the Russian Church in protecting the lives of the khans against magic and witchcraft. Themselves pagans, they showed customary pagan tolerance toward the faith of their subjects, whether Christian (Nestorian in Central Asia and Orthodox in Russia), Moslem, or Buddhist. Accustomed to use the services of their own witch-doctors ("shamans"), they evidently regarded the Russian clergy in a similar light, as persons able to appease an admittedly jealous, though little understood, deity. To the arguments of Guillaume de Rubriquis, who ventured the fearsome journey across Asia as envoy of St. Louis of France, Mangu Khan replied:

> We Mongols believe that there is one God [for all peoples], by whom we live and by whom we die, and toward Him we have a loyal heart; but as God gave the hand many fingers, so He gave men many roads; to you God gave

the Scriptures and you Christians do not keep them, while to us He gave diviners and we do all that they tell us and we live in peace.[2]

In the first shock of conquest, the clergy, together with other conspicuous personages, suffered heavily. The Russian chroniclers, themselves monks, may have exaggerated in emphasizing the slaughter or enslavement of "monks and nuns," "priests and priests' wives," [3] but there can be little doubt but that the Church fully shared in the horrible suffering of the first wave of invasion.

Within a few years, however, as the new position was stabilized, the Orthodox Church was able to win a series of *yarlyki* not merely confirming, but extending, its powers and privileges. The Church, planted in Russia by the will of the princes, had remained dependent on them, despite the fact that metropolitans were appointed by Constantinople. The Tatars confirmed the special jurisdiction of the Church over those categories of the population classified as "Church folk" and, in what may be called moral questions, over the whole population. They further exempted "priests, monks, and all men of God" from all fiscal obligations to the secular power, and even from the Tatar tribute. They enjoined on their agents respect for the Church and obedience to the metropolitan. Paradoxically, in later centuries the Church rested its claims against the growing exactions of the princes of Moscow on these grants of privileges derived from the infidel overlords of Rus. In return for such favors, the clergy regularly said public prayers for the khans and established a diocese at the seat of the Golden Horde (1261). Even more pointedly, when Pskov sheltered a prince who had put the khan's envoys to death, the metropolitan excommunicated its population. Like Alexander Nevsky, the Church performed the double duty of securing the submission of the Orthodox and of protecting them against the wrath of their Tatar masters.

For some decades the metropolitans continued to maintain their official residence in ruined Kiev; actually, however, they showed an increasing tendency to be peregrinatory, affixing themselves to the throne of whatever grand prince seemed best to them, which usually meant at the court of the grand prince of Vladimir. In 1305, however, on the death of Metropolitan Maxim, who for the preceding six years had been residing at Vladimir, the powerful southwestern rival for leadership in Rus endeavored to have Maxim's successor instructed to fix his residence in Galicia. The authorities at Constantinople honored his request, but within a few years the new metropolitan, Peter, though himself born in Volhynia, had moved to Vladimir and thence to Moscow, with results of great importance for the further rise of that new magnitude.

ECONOMIC CONDITIONS

The bulk of the population, now exclusively rural, continued peacefully to cultivate the land in much the same way and under much the same conditions as their ancestors of the Kievan period. The majority of the peasants, retaining their legal freedom, had now come to be known as *krestiane* (not to be confused with *khristiane,* i.e., Christians), but it is by no means certain how numerous they were compared to *zakupy, kholopy,* and other categories of bondsmen. The classic concept of the free peasant, constantly shifting his abode and thus exchanging one landlord for another, has undergone considerable revision. Kliuchevsky's denial that feudalism ever existed in Russia was based fundamentally on his conviction that "feudalism [in the West] rested upon an altogether different social basis than [the appanage system in Rus], namely, upon a fixed rural population."[4] The Marxist Pokrovsky, though impelled by his philosophy to accept the existence of feudalism in Russia, still took it for granted that "it was seldom that the grandson of a peasant died where his grandfather had been born. Even in the course of a single life a peasant might have to change his field dozens of times."[5]

More recent investigation, however, has cast great doubt on the validity of the antithesis between Russia, with its free, mobile peasantry and Western Europe, with its serfs fixed to the soil (*servi adscripti glebae*). On the one hand, it is evident that, whatever their legal status might be, the Russian *krestiane* were prevented by the natural conditions of the land and by their lack of material wherewithal from undertaking cultivation of the soil without some assistance from above. It may be specifically noted that among the free (and supposedly mobile) peasants there was legally recognized a special category of "old-dwellers" (*starozhiltsy*); the term is nowhere legally defined, save that their testimony might be admitted as evidence in case of boundary disputes since boundaries were generally defined in terms of trees and other perishable landmarks; prejudice in favor of the concept of a constantly roving peasantry seems, indeed, the only evidence that the "old-dwellers" were not in fact the majority of the free peasant population.

On the other hand, the notion embedded in old textbooks of a Western European peasantry fixed to the soil does not comport well with the known facts of vigorous colonization, both internal and external (in the German marches, in the still Celtic portions of the British Isles, in Spain—to say nothing of the displacement of population attendant on the Crusades), in that variegated entity known as Western Europe.

That migration of free peasants did constitute a problem for Russian princes is attested by the increasing number of treaties by which they obligated themselves not to receive emigrants from the domains of others. Yet the sum of the evidence strongly suggests that in Russia of the appanage period, there was a substratum of peasants, legally either free or bond, sufficiently permanently fixed to the soil to enable us to dismiss the *a priori* concept that there did not exist "a fixed rural population" adequate to support a feudal superstructure.

Though individual peasants might come and go, there remained the permanent territorial commune (later known as *mir*). The commune continued to exercise authority at the lowest level through its own elected officials; it continued to be responsible for the collection of taxes and for judicial liabilities; it continued to act collectively in disputes over the right to use lands in its territory. There are even indications that, with the growth of population and the beginnings of relative land scarcity, the commune began to assume the right of assigning particular lands to its members, though still without asserting communal rights to the point of depriving any peasant of land he was actually utilizing. Grant of permission to a newcomer to settle on virgin or abandoned land was still far from communal redistribution of the land.

In this period there are observable, in addition to the *zakupy* and *kholopy* of the Kievan period, a significant category of *zakladchiki,* men who, though technically free, had put themselves under the special protection of powerful landholders and performed for them services not unlike those of the villeins of the West. They could leave their patron only within a brief period after the harvest was in (St. George's Day, November 25) and, if they exercised their right, must surrender at least half their property to the patron.

Even those peasants who retained their full technical freedom were subject to a wide variety of obligations. Those who owned plows and cattle had to plow, sow, and harvest their lord's grain, as well as bring in his hay; they were obligated also to assist in building and fencing, in cleaning fishponds and in hunting, as well as to bring presents on Easter Sunday and on St. Peter's Day of "whatever they had in their hands." [6] The poorer peasants, unable to discharge obligations so onerous, aided in threshing, baking, brewing, fishing, and retting flax; they, too, had to pay dues in kind and to provide food, fodder, and lodging for their lords and their lords' servitors.

In sum, allowing for the difference in geographic conditions—and these varied from one part of Western Europe to another—there seems little reason to suppose that the actual condition of the Russian peasantry, free and unfree, in the "appanage period" differed substantially from that of the Western European peasantry in the "feudal period," some three centuries earlier in time. The basic socio-economic situation in appanage Rus further resembled that of feudal Europe in the insignificant role played by production for the market. Some trade there was in both cases, and in both cases there existed a small fraction of the total population which earned its living by artisan activities. Yet, both in feudal Europe and in appanage Rus, production was predominantly for local consumption and, correspondingly, political authority was organized on a local basis.

THE QUESTION OF FEUDALISM

Thus, the possibility that Russia, like Western Europe, though more belatedly, experienced a feudal regime is by no means excluded. There remains a stumbling block in that in Russia "sovereign" authority (with one solitary exception), no matter how subdivided, never passed into the hands of anyone not descended from Rurik. In Western Europe innumerable dukes, margraves, counts, and even simple barons usurped powers which in Russia were always reserved to the princes. This is, however, quite obviously a historical accident, arising rather from the male fecundity of the dynasty of Rurik (as contrasted with the descendants of Charlemagne) than from anything inherent in the nature of the feudal structure. The domain of many a Russian prince in the appanage period consisted of no more than his residence, a church, and a single hamlet, whereas many a boyar, with no princely pretensions, held sway over hundreds, and even thousands, of peasant homesteads. Such petty "princes" did not, of course, in any real sense enjoy "sovereign" powers, while the wide immunities enjoyed by boyars, monasteries, and bishops made them almost rulers over their estates. The fact of descent from Rurik could not in itself confer real power. The relevant fact is that there were always males of the stock of Rurik to inherit the more important principalities. This was largely due to the partial survival of rota principles, which obviated the danger that extinction of the ruling dynasty on any particular throne might open the way to usurpation from below. It is these circumstances which caused the striking but superficial difference between appanage Rus and feudal Europe.

A further and apparently more substantial stumbling block is the fact that grants of land by princes to their boyars and to the Church were usually in *otchina,* i.e., unconditional, hereditary tenure (*otets* = "father"). The prevalence of "allodial" over strictly "feudal" tenure has often been cited as evidence that landholding in Russia was independent of service obligations and was therefore not truly feudal. In reality, however, the boyars regularly served the prince from whom they held their land "unconditionally." There are many cases on record in which boyars who attempted to exercise their theoretical right of free transfer of service to another prince lost their estates and even their lives as the price of their exercise of juridical freedom. On the other side, it must be remembered that the Western fief, though theoretically a personal holding, speedily became in practice hereditary. There is little use in stressing legal concepts in the face of practical realities.

In appanage Russia, as in the feudal West, the practical correlation of military force outweighed any legal theory. The customary phrase, "our boyars and servitors shall be at liberty to come and to go," seems to have been little more than a formula handed down from Kievan days. Powerful princes were able to inflict condign punishment on boyars or servitors who attempted to quit them for a weaker master. On the other hand, boyars of a prince threatened by superior military force, as was Boris of Nizhny Novgorod in 1391, freely exercised their right to renounce their fealty (the Russian term *otkazatsia* is etymologically the same as the French *se désavouer*) and enter the service of a mightier lord (in the cited case, Vasily I of Moscow).

Pavlov-Silvansky, who first seriously argued the close similarity between feudalism and appanage practice, pointed out that even the ceremonial rites attendant on acceptance of service relationship in Russia closely paralleled the ceremony of homage. Whereas in the West the vassal knelt before his suzerain, the Russian boyar beat his forehead (to this day the Russian word for "to petition" is *chelobit*—to beat the forehead) on the ground in token of submission. In both cases a religious ceremony came to be added, which in Russia took the form of kissing the Cross.

Also as in the feudal West, the boyars and lesser military servitors of the princes, as well as their household officials, took into their own service military and other retainers whom in their turn they provided with land; the monasteries and the prelates similarly made grants of land and received military and other service from the holders. Thus, there developed in Russia a hierarchy of military landholders, the lesser depending on and performing military service to the greater, though members of any rank might, as in the West, be in direct relationship to the prince. At the top stood the boyars, roughly comparable to English barons. Below them came the more numerous, but both individually and collectively much less significant, "sons of boyars"; this term has no physiological significance but merely betokens inferior rank (a usage similar to the later English distinction between "baronets," who were not peers, and barons, who were). Normally, both boyars and "sons of boyars" held their land in unconditional hereditary tenure (*otchina*). In the later portion of this period there developed another type of tenure (*pomestie*), under which landholding was theoretically conditioned on performance of specified service, whether domestic (as falconers, huntsmen, and the like) or military; these military servitors, rapidly increasing in numbers, supplied the bulk of the *dvoriane,* a term which may be translated either as (untitled) "nobles" or "gentry."

The distinction, however, should not be exaggerated. Just as the hereditary landholder (*otchinnik*) risked losing his holding by an imprudent attempt to exercise his legal rights, so the conditional landholder (*pomeshchik*) was generally permitted to retain his land even when unable to perform his service; thus, an infant son was normally permitted to inherit his father's land "until he shall ripen into service." Whatever the legal phrases might say, both kinds of tenants (*otchinniki* and *pomeshchiki*) tended in practice to be assimilated to the feudal type as holders of land on condition of (or in prospect of) military or other service to some lord, whether he be prince, boyar, abbot, bishop, or even of some lesser condition.

Theoretically, in each principality the land belonged to the prince, to whom belonged also sovereign authority. It is, of course, virtually impossible to distinguish between the two forms of princely power, the economic and the political. In any case, the prince's relation to the tenants took three principal forms. A portion of the land, comparable to the Western demesne, was set apart for the service of the prince's court (*dvor*). It was worked either by the obligatory labor of bondsmen or by free peasants; in the latter case a specified portion of the produce (*izdielie*) went into the prince's storehouses. Normally, the larger portion of the principality consisted of the "black [i.e., common] lands" (*chernye zemli*), occupied ordinarily by free peasants (*krestiane*), who paid stated dues (*obrok*) for their use.

The third category of lands was made up of those granted by the prince to lay or ecclesiastical proprietors—boyars, "sons of boyars," *dvoriane,* or the Church. Over such lands and their occupants the prince retained rights of jurisdiction; some of them might enjoy "immunities," though with what frequency cannot be stated with certainty. Church lands, apparently as early as the eleventh century, enjoyed such privileges; documentary evidence of grants of "immunity" to lay holders is rather scanty (none have survived of earlier date than the fifteenth century), but it is quite probable that the practice was fairly general, for the Church naturally had facilities for preserving archives not available to boyars and lesser nobles.

The outstanding aspect of such "immunities," in Russia as in the West, was surrender to the tenant of jurisdiction over the inhabitants, a privilege of enormous direct economic value, even though the prince usually retained the most lucrative cases, such as murder and robbery caught red-handed, commonly known as "high justice." Indirectly, immunities may have meant for the dwellers on the estate escape from the unbridled rapacity of the prince's officials, for a local landlord, who must live permanently with his peasants, would be less likely to exploit immediate opportunities for squeezing litigants and malefactors. Furthermore, immunities carried exemption from the obligation to supply food, fodder, and lodging to the prince's servants on all sorts of occasions, for the prince's people were forbidden even to enter lands over which immunities were granted. Such considerations doubtless affected the apparent preference of peasants to live on privileged estates rather than on "black lands."

Since land without peasants was of no value, and since the free peasant—though not the bondsman and slave—had at least a theoretical right to move from one estate to another in accordance with his own advantage, there developed a certain struggle to retain one's own tenants while luring away those of other landlords. Consequently, grants of land to privileged holders usually specified that the landlord might settle people from other principalities on his lands, but not those from the estates of his own prince. Frequently, however, treaties between princes specified that they would not receive each other's peasants in their principalities. As early as the thirteenth century, restrictions on the mobility even of the free peasant began to take form, ultimately to develop into general serfdom.

In the increasingly complex agrarian society of the Russian mesopotamia, relations between the princes underwent profound changes. The notion of their collective right, as members of one family, to rule all the land steadily gave way to the concept of their individual and hereditary proprietorship over portions of the land. Only the title of grand prince of Vladimir continued, until the fourteenth century, to pass in accordance with rota principles, and this circumstance became the more meaningless, partly because princes inheriting this title preferred to remain in their own principalities and partly because, as a secondary development, several of the leading princes arrogated to themselves the style of grand prince, without pretending to be rulers of all Rus.

Each prince, claiming hereditary authority over his own principality, divided it among his sons. Each son's "portion" (*udiel*) became hereditary and was subject, in the next generation, to a further subdivision. In the days when political, and especially dynastic, relationships were the main concern of historians, this splitting up of princely authority was thought of as the main characteristic of the period. Consequently, Russian historians gave it the name of *udielnoe vremia* ("the period of portions"); first translated by French historians, who thought they saw a resemblance to their own historic *apanages,* the term "appanage period," though a mistranslation, has become generally accepted as a convention.

It did not, of course, follow that all the sons shared equally in such divisions. Juridically, they might have equal rights, each in his own share (*udiel*), but if the oldest son received a larger territory than his brothers, his power was obviously greater than theirs. Thus emerged—or, perhaps, survived—among the welter of principalities a relatively small number of "suzerain" thrones. The majority of the princes, despite their "sovereignty," had to accept dependence on the more powerful. Such "serving princes" were forced by circumstances into what amounted to feudal relations with "suzerain" princes, becoming in effect their boyars. Thus, despite the multiplication of princes, there was an obvious tendency toward concentration of power; the principal problem was which of the suzerain princes would be able to reduce the others into his service and thus emerge as the real overlord of all Rus.

TENDENCY TO CENTRALIZATION

A similar struggle for ascendancy had characterized the feudal period in Western Europe, where the centrifugal force had been represented by dukes, counts, and barons rather than by "sovereign" princes. Reasoning by analogy, one might have been tempted to suppose that Russia, whose social, political, and economic structure in the thirteenth century seems so similar to that of the West in the tenth century, was fated to go through the same historic evolution, emerging, with corresponding retardation, as a national monarchy.

Such expectations, however, would have reckoned without certain essential differences, for "appanage" Rus was not merely a delayed repetition of Western Europe. Western Europe went through a protracted period of economic growth, marked by a significant rise of trade and towns, which underlay the growth of monarchy—national, provincial, or merely urban—in her several parts. Central Russia, largely by virtue of her geographical uniformity and ethnic homogeneity, but also by virtue of certain other special factors, attained unity under a monarchy at a much lower stage of economic growth than did the countries of Western Europe, with results that have continued to make themselves felt to the present time.

The towns of appanage Rus remained essentially fortified residences of princes, important as centers of consumption, not of trade and industry. Trade was principally in the hands of the visiting men (*gosti*) of Novgorod, supplemented chiefly by Tatar horse dealers and the activities of some monasteries—especially Troitsa-Sergievo—which specialized mainly in salt and fish. No "bourgeoisie" developed to facilitate, by its leavening activity, the mobilization of the prince's revenue, so largely collected in kind. As a political consequence, no institutions developed in this period comparable to parliament, estates-general, cortes, or diet, which served as such powerful props to the centralizing efforts of Western rulers in the High Middle Ages. In the flat Russian plain, well provided with internal water communication, the absence of a thriving middle class did not, however, hinder the strong centripetal tendency to "gather" the land into the hands of a few suzerain princes by way of taking the lesser princes into service.

At the end of the thirteenth century the princes of Tver, on the upper Volga and therefore in closest proximity to commercial Novgorod, might have seemed the most likely to emerge successful in the process of "gathering" the land. To them belonged the genealogical seniority among the princes, and they held the title of grand prince of Vladimir, which since the time of Andrew Bogoliubsky had been the symbolic center of northeastern Rus. Fate, however, determined otherwise. The then insignificant principality of Moscow was, with surprising rapidity, to expand its power at the expense of the other principalities.

First mentioned as a border meeting place in 1147, and fortified nine years later, Moscow long remained of so little account that its successive princes made haste to abandon it at the first opportunity to move to other and more promising thrones. Not until 1263 was a permanent local dynasty founded there, and it owed its permanence largely to the accidental fact that Prince Daniel of Moscow, youngest son of Alexander Nevsky and still a minor when he inherited his throne from his father, died before his older brother. Daniel's children were therefore *izgoi,* able to inherit their father's possessions, but ineligible to succeed to the grand-princely title, which passed in 1304 to Daniel's cousin, Michael of Tver. Daniel's son Yury did indeed seek the title, but his claim was rejected by the khan of the Golden Horde.

In the carefully considered opinion of Kliuchevsky, the greatest historian of tsarist times, this circumstance of their lack of seniority among the princes was of primary importance. It permitted them

> to depart earlier and more decisively than others from the wonted rut of princely relationships and to follow new paths without thinking . . . of political traditions and customs. . . . They were keen observers of what was going on around them. . . . The first princes of Moscow were bold robbers.[7]

Their outlook was indeed not far removed from the shrewd petty acquisitiveness of an enterprising peasant. They were not rulers of a powerful independent state, with their eyes fixed on distant political goals; they were concerned rather with appropriating to themselves everything of immediate economic value, whether it was land or fur coats or the lucrative official position of grand prince. As Kliuchevsky phrased it,

> Displaying neither great talents nor striking valor, these princes were likewise not distinguished by great vices or passions. This made them in many respects models of moderation and regularity; even their inclination to drink too much at dinner was not carried to such a notorious passion of the Old Russian as was put [by the Chronicle] in the mouth of St. Vladimir. These average men of Old Rus were, so to speak, chronological marks rather than historical persons.[8]

Apart from the character of the princes and independently of their subjective will, there were however several factors making for the steady rise of Moscow's influence among the principalities of the Russian mesopotamia. Perhaps most important of these were certain natural advantages arising from its geographical situation. Almost in the very center of the mesopotamia, Moscow was better protected against punishing raids by the Tatars or by the grand princes of Lithuania than were principalities situated on the Upper Volga or on the Oka. Yet it had good water connections, direct or by relatively easy portages, with all points in the land; at the same time, it lay at the intersection of the chief overland routes in this area. In consequence, Moscow seems to have attracted deposit of a denser population than did other principalities, with obvious benefit to the treasury and hence to the power of its ruler.

The Moscow dynasty was fortunate, too, as had been the early Capetians in France, in that either younger brothers died first or deceased rulers left no sons. At Moscow the rota system of succession therefore early merged with the principle of inheritance in the direct descending male line; until well into the fifteenth century—until the feud of Shemiaka—no dispute over the succession could arise between uncle and nephew. In successive generations, also, each prince willed a larger proportion of his estate, whether measured in villages or in sheepskin coats, to a single one among his heirs. Thus, while the possessions of the family were being steadily extended at the expense of other branches of the stock of Rurik, there proceeded within the family a rapidly increasing concentration of the wealth and power of a single member. In such a situation, the usual pious admonitions of dying princes, such as the oft-quoted testament of Simeon the Proud (d. 1353)—"This word of our grandfather do I write unto you, that the memory of our parents shall not cease and our own candle shall not be extinguished" [9]—could take on real meaning.

THE TRIUMPH OF MOSCOW

It would serve little purpose to reproduce here the drab narrative of the process by which the original "appanage" of Prince Daniel, which cannot have exceeded five hundred square miles in area, was within a century and a half expanded to over fifteen thousand square miles, embracing much the greater part of the basin of the Upper Volga and the Oka.* The methods employed were diverse, as circumstances might dictate. Especially in the early stages, the princes of Moscow frequently used guile, as when Daniel invited a neighboring prince to dinner and threw him into prison. From the time of Daniel's younger son, Ivan I—nicknamed *Kalita* ("Money-bags")—purchase, either outright or by way of a preliminary mortgage, became the preferred method. Yet, whenever the "peace-loving" Muscovite princes were sure of their overwhelming military preponderance, they openly employed the cheaper method of armed force, as in the case of Nizhny Novgorod (1391). Many lands, also, Moscow acquired by treaty; their former sovereign princes retained their lands and their rights over them but, as "serving princes," entered the ranks of the Muscovite boyars as military servitors and advisers of the suzerain prince of Moscow.

To a certain degree all that has been said here might be applied to the simultaneous concentration of power in the hands of other rival princes. To understand Moscow's meteoric rise it is necessary not only to consider such vital though humdrum factors, but to give some attention to the sphere of high politics. Moscow had, throughout this century and a half, three strangely assorted but extremely powerful and fairly steadfast allies. These were the khans of the Golden Horde, the metropolitans of the Russian church, and the great commercial republic of Novgorod.

In 1304 Yury of Moscow did not succeed in persuading the khan to interfere with the normal order of succession on the grand-princely throne of Vladimir; that throne, which carried the right of being the intermediary between the other Russian princes and the khan, had then been permitted to pass under regular rota principles to Michael, prince of Tver. Yury, however, watched every opportunity to do injury to his successful rival. By heavy bribes Yury won the hand of the sister of Uzbek Khan; she was escorted to Moscow by a Tatar chieftain who used the occasion to ravage Michael's lands. In self-defense, that prince attacked the Tatar force and had the mis-

* See Map IV.

fortune to capture Yury's bride, who was taken to Tver, where she died. The khan summoned Michael to his headquarters and, after some hesitation, executed him, conferring the title of grand prince on Yury (1319). However, Michael's son Dmitry was allowed to succeed at Tver and soon was even also recognized as grand prince (1322). While the rival grand princes were both visiting the Horde, Dmitry of Tver murdered Yury of Moscow (1325); the khan executed the murderer but confirmed his brother Alexander, not only as prince of Tver, but as grand prince of Vladimir as well. Only two years later, however, the new grand prince proved unable to check an uprising in his own capital against the Tatar tax collectors. Ivan "Kalita" of Moscow was given command of an avenging army, and from that time on the princes of Moscow, with Tatar support, regularly held the title of grand prince of Vladimir. In that capacity they were responsible for the collection of the Tatar tribute throughout northern Rus and for its punctual remittance to the Horde. Their faithful performance of this duty, which gave them alone the right to "know the Horde," proved invaluable in securing them Tatar support in making some of their major territorial acquisitions.

Only once did a prince of Moscow dare raise his hand against the Tatars. Grand Prince Dmitry, grandson and third successor of Kalita, attempted to take advantage of the internal strife that then plagued the Golden Horde. In 1380 Dmitry met Mamai Khan in open battle at Kulikovo on the upper Don and completely routed the dreaded Tatars. Though the victorious Dmitry has ever since been known as "Donskoy," his triumph was less long-lasting than that of his grandfather's grandfather, Alexander "Nevsky," over the Teutons. Two years later a new khan, Tokhtamysh, sought vengeance; the heroic Dmitry sought safety in the remote north; Moscow, tricked into opening its gates, was ruthlessly sacked. Tver put itself under the direct protection of the Horde, and the further growth of Moscow's power was temporarily checked. Nevertheless, the complete submission of Dmitry and his boyars gradually restored the Horde's confidence. On Dmitry's death (1389), his son Vasily I was not merely allowed to succeed him as grand prince but was given support in the subjugation of Nizhny Novgorod.

Even the overthrow of Tokhtamysh by the dreaded Timur the Lame (Tamerlane), ruler of Persia and soon (1398) to be conqueror of India, did not long threaten Moscow's power. The city had to undergo another punishing attack by the Tatars (1408) but, though the grand prince was again absent, Moscow was not taken. Good relations were soon restored (1411). Tatar intervention was of great value to Vasily II (1425-62) against the claims of his uncle Yury and his cousins Shemiaka and Vasily "Squint-Eye." The rapid internal disintegration of the Golden Horde prevented it from exercising its wonted authority as decisively as in earlier days. At one stage of the long feud (1430-50), Vasily II was taken prisoner and blinded by his kinsmen (1446)—hence he is known as Vasily "the Dark"—but Tatar contingents contributed importantly to Vasily's ultimate victory. One of their leaders was rewarded by recognition as "tsar" of a new buffer khanate of Kasimov, a vassal principality of Moscow (1452).

Even more constant than the Tatar khans were the metropolitans. As already noted, these dignitaries had removed their seat from Kiev to Vladimir. Metropolitan Peter, who after a few years residence in his native southwest had transferred to Vladimir (1309), soon found himself at loggerheads with the then grand prince, Michael of Tver. Michael, unable to overcome his resentment that the candidate of the prince of Galicia-Volhynia had been chosen to head the whole Russian Church, soon accused Peter of the sin of simony. The Greek dignitaries sent from Constantinople to investigate this grave charge found Peter guiltless: he had not been selling the office of priest; he had merely been charging newly ordained priests fees to cover his expenses, a practice common among the Greeks. The charge therefore boomeranged on the grand prince, for it might be suspected that it was his proximity to the lands of the Latin heresy that had led him to fall into such a serious error. The indignant Peter found a ready welcome at the court of Yury of Moscow, who had his own grievances against Michael.

Thus it happened that the seat of the leading official of the Russian Church came to be permanently established at Moscow. A close working alliance developed between the grand prince and the metropolitan; the latter apparently acted as regent for the infant Dmitry (the future Donskoy), who came to the throne at the age of nine. In 1368 "Grand Prince Dmitry Ivanovich and the Metropolitan Alexis lovingly invited to Moscow Michael Alexandrovich of Tver" (grandson of the earlier Michael of Tver), where they "seized him and all his boyars";[10] when Michael escaped and summoned Olgerd of Lithuania to his aid, the metropolitan excommunicated Moscow's enemies. How much this spiritual aid contributed to saving the citadel from Olgerd's onset and how much the successful defense was due to the new brick walls erected in 1367 may be a matter of doubt. What is certain is that the Church, with all its moral and economic power, remained the staunch ally of the princes of Moscow against all their foes throughout this whole period.

The third of Moscow's great allies, Novgorod, was more fickle, as she well might be, for the complete triumph of Moscow over the other princes of the "Low Country" could not fail to spell doom to Novgorod's freedom. Yet, in the earlier part of the fourteenth century, the financial assistance of the great commercial town was of enormous importance; it was Novgorod's money with which Yury won the Tatar bride whose death at Tver was to gain him the title of grand prince of Vladimir (1319). Novgorod's immediate interest in the politics of the area was twofold: (1) Novgorod depended for her bread supply on regular access to the grain-raising area of the "Low Country"; (2) Novgorod's "colonial empire" was vulnerable to raids coming from the towns of the Upper Volga across the watershed. In both respects it was Tver, by reason of her geographical situation, that posed the greatest immediate danger to Novgorod's interests. Moscow, as the chief rival of Tver, was Novgorod's obvious ally. By way of Volokolamsk and Moscow the men of Novgorod could reach the lowland—and the lower Volga beyond—without passing under the walls of Tver, and Moscow lay too far from the watershed for her young men often to attempt piratical attacks on Novgorod's tribute-gatherers.

Of course, in proportion to the expansion of Moscow's power, the number of Russian princes with whom the great republic could negotiate as necessary defenders diminished, forcing her ever more into the position of having to choose between the two evils of a Muscovite or a Lithuanian candidate. The inability of the Novgorod militia to fight its own battles without a princely protector was, perhaps, less serious than her continuing dependence for her food supply on Moscow-controlled territory. When Moscow sought to recoup herself for the damage done by Tokhtamysh's pillage, Novgorod at first successfully resisted; within two years, however, she was constrained to submit to the "black levy," which became a precedent for further forced exactions. In 1397-98 Moscow made a still more drastic aggression, invading Novgorod's "colonial empire" in force and seeking to detach the Dvina region. This first attempt failed, but the effort was twice repeated. The story of the final subjugation of Novgorod may be reserved for later telling.

By the time of the death of Vasily the Dark (1462), Moscow had taken under her control the whole basin of the upper Volga and the Oka, save for such (by now) relatively small principalities as Tver, Rostov, Yaroslavl, and Ryazan.* Novgorod and Pskov maintained an ever more precarious independence. The rest of the Russian land was under the rule of the grand princes of Lithuania, dynastically linked with Poland. On the Baltic seaboard was entrenched the Teutonic Order, still formidable in spite of its defeat at Tannenberg (1410), while Swedes ruled the Finns to the north. In the southeast, the Golden Horde still survived in tottering fashion. A separate Crimean Horde had been formed about 1420, an independent Tatar khanate at Kazan a score of years later. Distant Constantinople, whence Russia had borrowed so many institutions and ideas, had finally succumbed to the Ottoman Turks (1453).

All these factors in the situation presented new problems or radically altered the light in which old ones must be viewed. The next century and a half was to be perhaps the most critical period in the formation of the lasting characteristics of the nascent Russian state.

* See Map IV.

NOTES

1. Michell and Forbes, *The Chronicle of Novgorod,* pp. 96-97.
2. Golubinskii, *Istoriia russkoi tserkvi,* II, i, 18.
3. Troitskii, *Tserkov i gosudarstvo v Rossii . . . ,* p. 30.
4. Kliuchevskii, *Kurs russkoi istorii,* 3rd edition, I, 451.
5. Pokrovskii, *Brief History,* I, 52. See also Borzakovskii, *Istoriia Tverskago Kniazhestva.*
6. Kulisher, *Russische Wirtschaftsgeschichte,* p. 77.
7. Kliuchevskii, *op. cit.,* II, 13.
8. *Ibid.,* pp. 59-60.
9. *Dukhovnye i dogovornye gramoty velikikh i udielnikh kniazei XIV-XVI v.,* p. 14.
10. *Polnoe sobranie russkikh lietopisei,* VIII, 15.

SUGGESTIONS FOR FURTHER READING

In addition to works previously mentioned, Vernadsky, *The Mongols and Russia,* should be consulted for detail. Rambaud, *History of Russia,* and Curtin, *The Mongols in Russia,* supply a narrative ignored in these chapters.

The posthumous second volume of Fedotov's *Russian Religious Mind: The Middle Ages* is flawed but still useful for this period. Howes' *Testaments of the Grand Princes of Moscow* contains valuable source material for this and the next two chapters.

Chapter

6

The Formation of the Muscovite State: 1462-1533

NEW SYMBOLISM AND SELF-CONFIDENCE

The fall of Constantinople in 1453 was for so long taken by Western historians as marking the dividing line between "medieval" and "modern" history that it is at first a little startling to realize with what equanimity that event was received in fifteenth-century Moscow. Instead of being regarded, as had the capture of the city by the Crusaders in 1204, as a world-shaking catastrophe, the triumph of the infidels was philosophically accepted as the just judgment of a righteous God.

The reasons for this attitude are deeply embedded in the altered condition of Rus and in its rising self-consciousness. The immediate background was the despairing effort of the shrinking Byzantine Empire to win military support by spiritual compromise with the Catholic West. At Florence in 1439 a joint council of the Latin and Greek churches had worked out a scheme of union, the essential point of which, from the Russian viewpoint, was acceptance by the Orthodox Church of the headship of the Roman pope. Moscow therefore rejected the union. The "Latin heresy" had become only too well known to the Russians through the unremitting pressure on their western borders of the Teutonic Knights and still more through the rising power of Lithuania, increasingly penetrated by Catholic influences from Poland.

One of the chief architects of the Union of Florence was the Greek Isidor, who had been sent to Moscow as metropolitan a few years earlier. On his return to Russia, he was promptly shut up in a monastery by order of Vasily (not yet "the Dark"). Allowed to escape, he fled to Lithuania and ended his days as a Roman cardinal. After some hesitation, the outraged Russians in

1448 installed as his successor a Russian bishop, Iona, whose nomination as metropolitan had been rejected at Constantinople in 1431; the new metropolitan did not even seek confirmation from Constantinople.

Ecclesiastically, Russia had at last become autocephalous, free to choose its own head. Twice before a Russian had been raised to the office of metropolitan, but both—Ilarion and Clement—had been compelled to withdraw by pressure from the patriarch. The gain was marred by the fact that, as noted in Chapter 4, the western provinces, controlled by Lithuania, accepted a separate metropolitanate at Kiev (1458), in continued direct dependence on Constantinople. The Greek Church soon abandoned its futile union with Rome, but the Russians persisted in remembering the sin of Constantinople and saw the conquest of the old center of Orthodoxy by the "unclean Turks" as a proper fate for heretics.

This new-found ecclesiastical autonomy found its supreme expression in the doctrine of "the third Rome." Filofei, a monk writing a few decades after the fall of Constantinople, explained that the first Rome on the Tiber had lost its world supremacy and succumbed to the barbarian Germans because of its lapse into heresy, expressed in the rise of papal claims and powers; a second Rome had risen on the shore of the Bosporus, only to fall similarly into heresy and to be overthrown by the infidel instrument of God; now their place was taken by the new and pure center of Orthodoxy, the new capital of the world: "for two Romes have fallen, and the third stands, and a fourth will not be." [1] Other monks, with creative imagination as great as that of their Frankish predecessors who had traced the ancestry of the Carolingians, not merely to the Merovingians, but back to Trojan Aeneas and thus to Aphrodite, gave a more secular twist to the matter. It was alleged that Augustus Caesar had had a brother Prus, to whom he had assigned dominion over the region of the Vistula; "from Prus the fourteenth generation was Rurik." [2] All this, of course, was fantasy, confined to religious circles.

Yet similar ideas appeared in the thinking and practice of the rulers. Ivan III, son and successor of Vasily the Dark, took as his second bride a niece—though not the heiress—of the last Byzantine "Emperor of the Romans," Constantine Palaeologus, who had fallen fighting in the final heroic defense of "Tsargrad" ("the City of the Caesars"). Zoe (rechristened Sophia) Palaeologa had been brought up as a refugee at Rome. Though she had been nurtured in the spirit of the Florentine Union and though she was accompanied to Moscow by a cardinal, there was no taint of heresy that could not be removed by the waters of the baptismal font, and the prestige value of the marriage was enormous. Her Catholic escorts were hurried back to Rome, but the Byzantine ceremonial to which she had been accustomed was retained. The bicapitate eagle—the Eastern version of the symbol of the Roman legions—was adopted for use on Moscow's seal of state. Within a few years, once the Tatar yoke had been formally ended, Ivan could subscribe himself "Ioann, by the Grace of God, Sovereign [*Gosudar*] of all Rus, and grand prince of Vladimir and of Moscow and of Novgorod and of Pskov and of Tver and of Yugria and of Viatka and of Perm and of Bolgary and of others." [3] Ivan did not have himself recrowned in his new capacity, but in 1498, at a solemn ceremony in the new Cathedral of the Assumption (the work of the Italian architect, Aristotle Fioraventi), Ivan placed on the head of his infant grandson Dmitry the "cap of Monomakh," while the metropolitan saluted Ivan as "Orthodox tsar Ioan, grand prince and autocrat of all Rus." [4] Further embroidery developed an official legend that the "cap of Monomakh" had been bestowed by an earlier Byzantine Emperor, Constantine Monomachus (1042-54), on his daughter's son, Vladimir Monomakh, grand prince of Kiev (1113-25), in token of the fact that they shared the power of the Caesars.

Examples of the new outlook, as expressed in assumption of titles, rationalization of their use, or elaboration of court ceremonial, might be multiplied a hundredfold. Mention may be made also of a negative aspect of the same attitude—rejection of titles proffered by those not deemed to have sufficient authority to confer them. In 1486 the Holy Roman Emperor, Frederick III, was informed by a wandering German knight of the strange Rus of Moscow that lay behind the familiar and often hostile Rus of Poland-Lithuania. He sent the knight, Poppel, back to Moscow with the request that Ivan give one of his daughters in marriage to Frederick's nephew. The Emperor accompanied this proposal with an offer to honor the Muscovite with the title of king, a privilege which the emperors were very chary of bestowing. Ivan replied with due civility, but added:

> As to what thou hast said to us of kingship, whether we should like to be ordained by the Kaiser as King over our land, we by the grace of God have been Sovereigns over our land from the beginning, from our first forefathers, and we have our ordination from God, as did our forefathers, so also we, and we pray God that God grant us and our children forever to be as we now are Sovereigns over our land, and as we have not heretofore wished ordination from anyone, so now we do not wish it.[5]

EXTENSION OF MUSCOVITE POWER

Even more potent than symbolism, however, was the further progress of Ivan in extending and stabilizing his new dignity. All but one of the remaining independent principalities accepted Muscovite hegemony; even Ryazan, however, was ruled under wardship by Ivan's nephews and was definitely annexed by Ivan's son, Vasily III, in 1517. The last prince of Tver made a despairing effort to put himself under Lithuanian protection but lost his throne completely and forever (1485).

Not content with absorbing the remnants of the Great Russian land, Ivan began the process of winning back the Russian lands that had long since passed under the control of Lithuania. A number of Orthodox Russian princes along the southern border seized opportunities to transfer their allegiance to Moscow, with whose assistance they retained their estates as vassals of Grand Prince Ivan III. Others, abandoning their old estates, came over as refugees and were provided with new lands as Muscovite boyars.

In this piecemeal process of disintegrating the grand principality of Lithuania, Ivan did not neglect to advance far-reaching claims. In 1501, when the pope's envoy to Moscow—himself the older brother of Grand Prince Alexander of Lithuania, who had just been elected also to the Polish throne, and of Ladislas, King of Hungary and of Bohemia—protested that Ivan was seizing territories to which he had no right, the Muscovite replied:

> We have been told by the Pope that [Ladislas and Alexander] have declared to the Pope that they wish to stand against us for their patrimony: do these kings call their patrimony the towns and provinces and lands from which Russian princes and boyars and other men have come to serve us? . . . We think it is well known to the Pope that Kings Ladislas and Alexander have inherited the Polish kingdom and the Lithuanian land from their ancestors; but the Russian land from our ancestors since antiquity has been our patrimony.[6]

In the name of this concept of all the Russian land—not merely its Great Russian corner—as the proper patrimony of the princes of Moscow, was begun the long intermittent westward push of Russia. The appetite growing with eating, this reverse *Drang nach Osten* was to be for centuries—and into the present century—one of the characteristic features of Russian foreign policy.

Of greater immediate significance was Ivan's completion of the conquest of Novgorod, already alluded to. His father, Vasily the Dark, failing to secure from Novgorod a pledge that she would take no prince hostile to him, had marched against her, sacked the city, and imposed a treaty (1456), by which the proud republic had to surrender the right to use her own seal on diplomatic documents. The Novgorod aristocracy, however, dreaded further encroachments on its position and privileges; it had succeeded in overcoming the resistance of the popular *vieche,* which feared Orthodox, Russian Moscow less than it did Catholic, alien Lithuania; in 1470, accordingly, the republic was formally put under the protection of Grand Prince Casimir of Lithuania, who was also king of Poland.

It might be difficult to determine whether the Muscovite grand prince or the metropolitan was the more dismayed. The metropolitan and the whole synod of the Russian church promptly proclaimed a crusade, blessing the grand prince and his warriors "as Samuel did David against Goliath." As the Moscow chronicler went on to explain:

An infidel knows not God from the beginning, nor has he learned the true faith from anyone, holding to his first custom of idol-worship, but these men so many years were in Christendom and finally began to desert to Latinism. And so the grand prince went upon them, not as upon Christians, but as upon aliens and upon apostates from the true faith. [With exceptional ferocity the Muscovites] visited them with the wrath of God for their iniquity and for their desertion not only of their sovereign but of the Lord God himself.[7]

Another version of the Chronicle more romantically adds:

As in former times his Orthodox great-grandfather Grand Prince Dmitry Ivanovich [went] upon the godless Mamai and upon his impious Tatar host, so did this Orthodox Grand Prince Ivan [go] upon these apostates.[8]

The terms of the resultant treaty of 1471—the last the free republic was ever to make—were, under the circumstances, surprisingly lenient. At the price of a heavy indemnity, confirmation of the treaty of 1456, severance of all relations with Lithuania (which had not moved to Novgorod's rescue), and full acceptance of the right of appeal from the courts of Novgorod and its archbishop to those of the grand prince and the metropolitan, Novgorod was allowed to retain its peculiar institutions. The respite was but brief. In 1478, Ivan, who had already put some of the leading men of the ostensibly free republic on trial, marched against Novgorod. This time the city and all its extensive domains were integrated into the grand principality of Moscow; even the *vieche* bell was removed.

This rounding-out of the territory of the Muscovite state was almost immediately followed by formal repudiation of the overlordship of the Tatar khans. The Golden Horde had long been crumbling; some Tatar chieftains had actually entered the service of Moscow; others had set up independent khanates, one of which, in the Crimea, was a frequent ally of Moscow, while another, at Kazan—the ancient haunt of the Volga Bulgars—was alternately in dependence on and at war with the grand prince. In 1480, encouraged by Lithuania's offer of alliance, the khan of the Golden Horde made a last effort to force Ivan to resume payment of the tribute. Circling around his enemy, the khan took up a position on the banks of the Ugra, then the boundary between Muscovy and Lithuania; Ivan's army encamped on the opposite bank. Soon the grand prince, remembering that his great-grandfather Grand Prince Dmitry, after his victory at Kulikovo in 1380, had not dared again to offer battle to the Tatars, caused his subjects consternation and chagrin by leaving his forces and returning to his capital:

Hardly hadst thou, o lord grand prince, begun to reign over us in times of peace, then didst thou squeeze us immoderately; and now, having offended the tsar [i.e., the khan] by not paying him the tribute, dost thou hand us over to the tsar and the Tatar.[9]

Archbishop Vassian of Rostov vigorously upbraided Ivan, warning him that "all the Christian blood will flow on thy account, since thou hast let them come so close, without offering the Tatars battle and fighting with them; why dost thou fear death?" Ivan (sometimes called "the Great") was afraid to enter angry Moscow, though he did not dare return to his army either. The khan, however, dared not attack, his Lithuanian ally being distracted to the south by a raid of the Crimean Tatars. Finally, in the autumn, both armies in mutual panic went their separate ways. Without a battle, the "Tatar yoke," which had already lapsed in fact, was ended in form as well.

The end of the Tatar yoke did not mean the end of Russia's troubles with the Tatars. The Golden Horde did not long linger on, and its successors—the khanates of the Crimea, of Kazan, and of Astrakhan, to say nothing of lesser and more ephemeral bands—were of course not nearly so formidable on the field of battle. Yet in some ways the disorganized activities of the Tatars were a worse plague than had been the might of the Horde. In the old days disobedience on the part of the Russians had brought down decisive but occasional wrath. Now there were constant friction and ceaseless frittering of energy in protecting the frontier against elusive marauding bands. The old days of the Pechenegs and the Polovtsy had returned, with no central Mongol power to maintain some sort of peace and order. True, the Tatars could more easily be defeated if caught, for the balance of strength was turning heavily in favor of the forest against the steppe. Yet it was never possible for the lords of the forest to relax their vigilance. Only gradually, and in large part by the efforts of unruly cossacks, was the steppe to be tamed.

In Muscovy itself, the disappearance of Tatar power had a curious repercussion on relations of Church and state. It will be recalled that the extended privileges of the Russian Church were supported by Mongol *yarlyki*. Now there was no longer a shred of physical force behind these documents, a circumstance that inevitably raised some question of their validity. Grand prince and metropolitan had too many interests in common to permit of a serious breach between them at this stage. Nevertheless, a subsidiary question soon arose—that of monasterial landholding—which held grave danger for the economic position of the Church. Some Church property had been confiscated at the time of the subjection of Novgorod in 1478.

A more dangerous sequel of this event was the transportation of a number of persons from Novgorod to Moscow and other places. Among them were adherents of the "Judaizing heresy," which spread alarmingly. The "Judaizers" denied some of the most sacred Christian doctrines—the Holy Trinity and the divinity of Christ; they refused to venerate the Virgin Mary and the saints or to show respect for the Cross and for icons; they lived by the law of Moses and celebrated the Sabbath on Saturday. In addition, they rejected the idea of ecclesiastical ownership of property. For a time their influence penetrated even Ivan's court; his daughter-in-law Helena of Moldavia became a convert, and her influence was momentarily in the ascendant. It was at this point that Ivan ordered the coronation of her fifteen-year-old son Dmitry as grand prince (1498). She was able even to cause the execution of one of Ivan's officials, Vladimir Gusev, despite the great service he had done his master in consolidating the laws of all Ivan's domains into a single code (the *Sudebnik* of 1497).

The danger to the monasteries was heightened by the rise of a group of ascetic monks, of whom Nil Sorsky was the most eminent. Though otherwise perfectly orthodox, Nil insisted that the monks should have no worldly wealth; in all her history this was Russia's nearest approach to the friars of the thirteenth-century West.

The other side of the argument was presented chiefly by Joseph Sanin, the exceedingly able and well-rounded abbot of Volokolamsk. Among his most telling arguments was the probably indisputable fact that unless the monasteries were well endowed with villages, nobles would be unlikely to take monastic vows; there would therefore be among the monks none suitable for high ecclesiastical offices, and the faith would suffer. It was the function of the Church to care for souls, not to meddle by offering to the grand prince officious political advice; relieved from manual labor by rich endowments, the monks and higher clergy could best perform their holy offices, with no thought of interfering in affairs of state.

Tempting as was the prospect of enriching himself and his lay servants by confiscation of monasterial lands, Ivan—who in no way resembled Henry VIII of England—was not the man to look for unaccustomed trouble. Only a year after the coronation of his grandson, Ivan associated twenty-year-old Vasily, his son by Sophia, with Dmitry as his prospective successor; in 1502 Dmitry was deposed and Vasily named sole heir. A Church Council in 1503 decided for the "Josephites," and Nil Sorsky and his associates were banished beyond the watershed, there to lead the type of life they preached but without effective influence on the world they had chosen to renounce. The following year another Church Council condemned the "Judaizers," many of whom were handed over to be burned at the stake.

EFFECT ON POSITION OF BOYARS

Much more acute became the strife between the new power of the grand prince and the old power of the landlord aristocracy, the *boiarstvo*. The scale of aggressive expansion was such that the ruler was ceasing to be merely the first among equals. The disparity between the military force that he could raise and that which any individual vassal—or temporary combination of vassals—could raise had become so great that the grand prince could act with an arbitrariness unknown in the "appanage period."

Yet by tradition the grand prince shared his authority with the council of his vassals, the boyar duma. The tradition had proved its worth in critical times, such as the minorities of Dmitry "Donskoy" and of Vasily "the Dark," when the collective force of the Muscovite boyars had preserved the power of the nominal ruler.

The new titles assumed by the ruler did not directly challenge the established theory and practice. It is not without significance that they were employed chiefly in diplomatic documents, for they represented claims against external powers rather than a new concept of domestic authority. The word "autocrat," as then used, did not signify that the grand prince was not bound to consult with his associates at home; it was merely the token of the fact that he no longer recognized the superior authority of any external mortal ruler, whether Roman emperor or Tatar khan.

In fact, the old concept of the right of the boyars to share the grand prince's authority was being simultaneously strengthened by the existence of "serving princes." For the most part, when Great Russian princes submitted to the suzerainty of Moscow, they retained their old inherited lands and their juridical authority over them. They remained conscious of the fact —and on occasion reminded the grand prince of it—that they, too, were descended from Rurik. Though more dimly than of old, they still thought of the Russian land as their collective patrimony (*otchina*). Constituting an upper stratum of the feudal, boyar aristocracy, they persisted in asserting their rights, which the grand princes dared not openly challenge.

Ivan III did on occasion strike down arbitrarily an individual boyar who was offensive to him; particularly in the dispute between his wife and his daughter-in-law as to who should succeed him, he even went so far as to order the execution of one boyar who had supported Dmitry. The monarchical idea was strengthened by Ivan's will, under which Sophia's son, Vasily III (or "Basil III") succeeded him in 1505. Not only did Ivan leave to Vasily more than two-thirds of his material possessions, he specified that Vasily alone should exercise "sovereign" powers: the right to coin money, to have relations with foreign princes, and to inherit lands of any childless relatives.

Vasily incorporated the remaining free areas—Pskov (1510) and Ryazan (1517)—in his domains and took strategically situated Smolensk from Lithuania (1514). At home he acted even more highhandedly than had his father. Many high-placed persons, both lay and ecclesiastic, felt the full weight of his hand. Among them was Vassian "Squint-Eye," a boyar who had been forced into a monastery by Ivan III for opposing the deposition of the tsarevich Dmitry. As a monk, and later an abbot of the ascetic school, Vassian had been one of the principal outspoken critics of "Josephism" and of monasterial landholding, even after the Council of 1503. Now he attacked Vasily III for putting his childless wife in a convent in order to remarry; Vassian was imprisoned, along with the learned but impolitic

Maxim the Greek, who had been invited from Mount Athos to put the grand prince's library in order.

In addition to psychological factors, the domestic power of the grand prince was steadily being strengthened by the growth of a bureaucratic, military, and fiscal apparatus, made necessary by the growing extent of the state territory and by recurrent wars with Moscow's neighbors. In older, simpler times, the ruler had simply entrusted any specific executive function to one or another of his boyars by a special command (*prikaz*). As record-keeping increased in importance, there arose a category of officials—secretaries (*diaki*) and clerks (*podiachie*)—to assist the "*prikaznye*" boyars. Under Ivan III and Vasily III the *prikazy* began to harden into permanent administrative institutions. The most important of the secretaries were given seats in the boyar duma, as were also a certain number of military servitors (*dumnye dvoriane*).

Just as the boyars were no longer adequate by themselves to staff the increasingly complex administrative apparatus, so they played an ever smaller independent role in putting armed forces into the field. The "serving princes" and other boyars continued to lead their own armed forces and in addition monopolized the chief commands in the grand prince's armies. Yet the mass of the military servitors was made up of "sons of boyars," who of old had held small hereditary estates (*votchiny*), and of *dvoriane*—originally servants, free or unfree, of the prince's household (*dvor*), most of whom held their lands conditionally (as *pomestiya*). These distinctions rapidly became blurred: many "sons of boyars" were provided with *pomestiya,* either as a supplement to their holdings or in exchange for exhausted *votchiny;* additional *dvoriane* were recruited from all sorts of able-bodied elements. At the same time, further limitations were imposed on the right of holders of *votchiny* to refuse service, while *pomestiya* became in practice hereditary.

A subsidiary force, chiefly for frontier service, was recruited from the cossacks, persons who for one reason or another had broken away from their social origins as artisans, peasants, or traders. These hired "serving cossacks," who were generally placed under the command of "sons of boyars," should not be confused with the "free cossacks" who, living on the lower reaches of the rivers crossing the steppe, were not brought under any sort of state control until after the middle of the sixteenth century.

The mounted forces, which made up the bulk of the field armies, were supplemented by infantry conscripted from the taxpaying population. Most of the foot soldiers were used principally for garrison duty, but a special force of harquebusiers was formed about the turn of the century. This unit, the forerunner of the *strieltsy* (shooters), along with detachments of *pushkary* (cannoneers) were the special pride of the Russian forces and performed important service at the taking of Smolensk (1514).

Attempts to systematize the state revenues were not wholly successful.

The unit of assessment of direct taxes (*sokha*—"plow") was partially standardized in terms both of land and of industrial enterprises, and careful registers of taxable property (*pistsovye knigi*) were compiled. The hopeless confusion of local customs and tolls inherited from feudal times was simplified by farming out their collection locally for fixed total sums. Monopoly of the right to coin money enabled the government to profit, even without resorting to debasement. Although many persons engaged in trade or industry escaped taxation by "whitening" themselves under the protection of monasteries or powerful boyars or in government service as harquebusiers or cannoneers, the government forbade further extension of private fiscal immunities. Taken in conjunction with codification of the laws of the whole realm by the *Sudebnik* of 1497, the general tendency of fiscal, as well as military and administrative, practice was strongly in the direction of centralization.

Yet the position of the boyar aristocracy as the ruling element remained unchallenged, and the curious practice of *miestnichestvo* was hardened. In Russia, high offices of state, civil and military, never became hereditary in particular families, as was the case with Western feudalism; nevertheless, feudal considerations had to be taken into account in selecting their incumbents. Each boyar was deemed to have his own place (*miesto*) in his family in accordance with a system of reckoning somewhat resembling the old rota principle of princely succession. If the oldest brother be counted as number one, each of the younger brothers had a place one behind, in order of seniority; after the brothers ranked the next generation. For convenience of reckoning, it came to be assumed that the normal number of brothers was three; the oldest son of the oldest brother, coming next after his two uncles, therefore ranked as number four; in case there was a fourth brother in the older generation, he thus ranked on a par with his senior nephew. On this principle, every oldest son ranked three places behind his father and might outrank some uncles. To keep track of the relative order of the members of ramifying boyar families—an order which determined both social and official precedence—the Moscow War Office (*Razriadny Prikaz*) was ultimately charged with keeping a sort of stud book, the *Rodoslovets*.

All official positions—whether a seat at table on a ceremonial occasion or a command in an army in the field—similarly bore a rank order of precedence. If two members of any boyar family carried on the genealogical register were appointed to the same command, care must be taken that their "places" in the family bore the same relation to each other as did the offices to which they were to be appointed.

What is more, the rank of each boyar family in relation to any other could be determined by consulting old lists of appointments (*razriady*). It could thus be established that certain members of different families had in the past held posts separated by a given number of "places." All that remained was for the War Office clerks to compute the number of "places" from these earlier appointees that the living boyars stood in their respective families and thus to determine their eligibility, relative to each other, for current appointment. Naturally it was necessary for boyars to check these computations carefully, lest by accidentally accepting a "place" below their dignity, they establish a precedent for future appointments. Indeed, it behooved their kinsmen also to be alert, for loss of inherited standing (*otechestvo*) might, if not caught in time, permanently debase the whole family.

Miestnichestvo did not guarantee any individual boyar appointment to any particular post—or to any post at all—but it did severely restrict the grand prince's freedom in choosing his agents. It gave a corporate solidarity to the *boiarstvo* as against the grand prince. Yet it also tended to divide the *boiarstvo,* for there inevitably resulted endless jealous wrangles between families and even between members of the same family. This new version of the old princely feuds might not work as much havoc on the hapless peasant population, but it did often offer the grand prince opportunity for violent and arbitrary action against individual boyars, for their fellows might frequently be more concerned with their personal advantage than with the corporate position of their class. *Miestnichestvo* therefore was an exceedingly imperfect instrument for maintaining the power of the boyars against the ruler.

CHANGING POSITION OF THE PEASANTRY

The boyars were not the only element in the population to feel the adverse effects of the rising state power; the freedom of the peasantry was even more imperiled. For the most part, to be sure, the peasants continued into the sixteenth century to be juridically free tenants on a sort of sharecropping basis. Since most agreements between peasants and landlords were oral, it is not possible to define their obligations with great precision; especially is this true since most of the surviving documents pertain to ecclesiastical rather than lay landholding. It is, however, clear that money economy made rapid strides in the course of the sixteenth century. Most of the dues in kind were converted into money payments; grain seems to have been the commonest exception. Not only dues (*obrok*) but labor services (*barshchina*), which often supplemented and sometimes replaced them, came to be computed in terms of money. Labor services seem rarely to have been specifically limited in peasant agreements with their landlords, a circumstance which of course held grave danger for the economic freedom of the peasants, but does not necessarily mean that they were excessive; otherwise the resistance of a still free peasantry might have been expected to find expression in insistence on some stipulation as to their extent. The prevalence of immunities, though apparently lightening the fiscal burdens resting on the peasants of the great estates which enjoyed them, also threatened their juridical rights by leaving them largely at the mercy of their landlords; the landlords' responsibility to the state for payment of taxes by their peasants tended in the same direction.

So rapidly and imperceptibly did the free peasants become subject to the will of the landlords that there can be instanced, from the second half of the sixteenth century, a whole series of cases in which transfers of land, with the peasants on it, are recorded as normal; sometimes, in splitting up an estate, peasants were compelled to move from one portion of it to another in order to maintain a desired ratio between acreage and peasant population. Transactions of this kind were effected by private agreements as well as by official orders. Sometimes, indeed, private individuals transferred peasants without any transfer of land. Such disposition of "free" peasants, without consulting their wishes, can hardly have developed overnight; it must be assumed that it was the result of a long process, and that it became customary before it began to find expression in legal documents. As early as 1553, there is documentary evidence that peasants were expected to be obedient to their lords, who might at their pleasure require payment of dues either in money or in kind and in any amount they saw fit, provided they did not ruin their peasants and force abandonment of their holdings to the fiscal detriment of the ruler.

Yet there was in this period no general establishment of serfdom in its full sense. There were multiplying legal restrictions on the freedom of movement of the peasants, but they were only partial limitations. In the middle of the fifteenth century a number of monasteries were formally granted the right to forbid all their peasants to move except during a three-week period around St. George's Day (November 25); the right seems to have become general by custom. No such specific power appears in any extant privilege extended to the Troitsa monastery; yet when it appealed to Ivan III, complaining that its peasants had left at another time of the year, the grand prince sent a bailiff to fetch them back, whether he found them in villages belonging to Ivan or on estates belonging to boyars. In the code (*Sudebnik*) of 1497, this temporal limitation of the right of peasants to leave any landlord's land was made generally applicable, and the open season was reduced to a two-week period.

Another type of restriction on freedom of movement was the increasingly common legal provision that "old-dwellers" (*starozhiltsy*) might under no circumstances leave. Disuse is ever the surest road to loss of a right; why the "old-dwellers" had so little valued their freedom of movement must remain disputable. Some investigators believe that they were the most comfortably fixed peasants, having the least incentive to roam; others, on the contrary, believe that the more hopeless and unenterprising peasants were the most settled, succumbing to the psychological attraction of the land of their fathers and forefathers and unable to envision the possibility of improvement of their material lot.

Undoubtedly the major factor leading to the enserfment of the peasants is not to be found in any such legal regulations, which could only reflect but not initiate the general tendency toward the growth of serfdom. Indebtedness of peasants to their landlords was evidently on the increase. In the circumstances of a transition from sustenance economy to exchange economy and of the rapidly mounting demands of landlords for the produce of their labor, the peasants were faced with ever more difficulty in making ends meet. Apparently, migrating peasants normally presented themselves to landlords with no possessions other than the clothes on their backs—"merely with body and soul," as the phrase ran.

This was all the more true because of the rapid extension of private landholding. Despite the agitation for the abolition of monasterial landholding, the acreage in the hands of the Church continued to grow. By the end of the sixteenth century the Troitsa monastery owned some twenty-five hundred villages, two-thirds of which it had acquired in the course of that century. Far more rapid, however, was the growth of lay landholding on condition of military service (*pomestie*). With amazing rapidity the ruler found it necessary to make over to his military servitors (who, in their political aspect, are usually styled *dvoriane*) the lands that were directly at his disposal. Thus, in connection with the conquest of Novgorod, Ivan III confiscated about 80 percent of the lands, whether belonging to the "boyars" of Novgorod or to its "Latinizing" clergy; three-fourths of the confiscated lands passed almost immediately into the hands of *pomeshchiki*.

The main source of land for such grants was, however, found in the "black lands," where the peasants had previously known no overlord save the tribute-taking prince. "Black lands" almost completely disappeared in the central provinces, the old settled area of Muscovy between the upper Volga and the Oka. Only in the inhospitable regions north of the watershed, to which after the fall of Novgorod there was a certain amount of emigration, did "black lands" continue to constitute a significant proportion of the available land. Even here, in the region to which the ascetic partisans of Nil Sorsky had been banished, monasterial landholding also throve.

Thus the peasant had virtually no place to go without settling on the lands of some lord. The lords, to whom land was valueless without peasant labor, for their part generally took it for granted that the peasant must be provided with the wherewithal to carry on his economy. Even the peasant who had the necessary means of production could be attracted to the lands of those lords who were most generous in advancing loans or in extending temporary exemption from state taxes and other obligations. Until such loans were repaid, the peasant of course could not legally leave his benefactor. As rates of interest often ran to 33 percent, the free peasant's chances of escape were not great, even if he desired it. Those peasants who did not fall into debt bondage were also subject to prohibitive penalties if they chose to leave. In addition to fines for leaving before expiration of an agreed term of years, there was the normal obligation to pay for the use of the homestead they had occupied; according to the code of 1550 this amounted to one-quarter of its capital value annually.

While the free peasantry was thus drawn ever further down toward the formal level of serfdom, the older bondaged categories became more and more assimilated to them. Although full slavery continued to exist into the sixteenth century, the sources of its recruitment tended to dry up. The "gathering" of the land left only foreign captives, if unransomed, to be enslaved; this meant mostly Tatars, who were, however, regularly emancipated on accepting Orthodox baptism. The older forms of slavery, both full and partial, were being largely replaced by *kabala* bondage. Since service under *kabala* (a Tatar and Arab word for a certificate of indebtedness) was credited only toward payment of interest on the debt, *kabala* bondage (unlike that of Kievan *zakupy*) was for life unless—as frequently happened on the death of his creditor—he was emancipated. *Kabala* bondsmen supplied most of the labor in the boyars' households; some of them rose to positions of affluence as stewards or business agents and even acquired estates, though their position remained precarious, for their possessions were legally the property of their masters.

The multiplying signs of the progress of enserfment did not of themselves adversely affect the material condition of the peasantry, nor did they betoken destruction of the communal structure. The commune, in fact, took on new functions. Still operating through elected elders, it retained its responsibility for payment of state taxes and its financial liability for crime committed in its territory. To its power to assign pieces of land to its members, it began in this period to add occasionally redistribution of holdings, a process which entailed depriving some of its members of part of their land for the benefit of others. This last operation was evidently not unconnected with pressure from the landlords, who in their own interest were concerned with rough equalization of peasant holdings. Certainly, the cases of which there is documentary evidence in this period all are represented as occurring on the initiative of the lord. Yet, in view of observed developments in latter-day Siberia, it may be surmised that, with increasing scarcity of land, the peasant communes might of their own initiative have moved in the same direction.

Although the population of Muscovy at this time is an unknown quantity —estimates have ranged from four to eleven or more million—there is every reason to believe that in the first half of the sixteenth century the population of the old central provinces had reached a much higher point than ever previously, and, for that matter, than it was to maintain for a long time to come. With increased population had proceeded a vast amount of clearing of forests and even draining of swamps. The forest products that had so long supported Russia's foreign trade were no longer to be procured in any quantity, even in outlying territories. Even such areas could no longer produce more wax and honey than Russia herself consumed.

Agriculture, on the other hand, developed not merely quantitatively but qualitatively in the improvement of techniques. In the provinces around Moscow and also in the old territories around Novgorod and Pskov, grain-raising on the basis of the three-field system predominated. Here the cultivated area (one-third of which, of course, was left fallow each year) is reported to have reached 95 percent of the whole. Implements also showed marked improvement, and iron plows began to come into use. Manuring is frequently mentioned among the obligations resting on the peasants. Since the climate remained unchanged, rye, oats, and flax continued to be the principal crops; the northwestern provinces had already attained clear predominance in the production of linen. Cultivation of vegetables, and even of fruit, developed strongly; cabbage and cucumbers were already staples, and foreign visitors, accustomed at home to exotic, subtle spices, frequently complained of the free use of garlic and onions. Stockraising remained somewhat backward, the normal ratio of meadow to arable land apparently being 1:9; horses were generally purchased from the Tatars rather than bred at home.

Fishing in rivers and lakes continued to be an important occupation, closely interwoven with the extraction of salt, though salt-boiling was chiefly carried on along the northern coasts. In both enterprises the lion's share of the business was absorbed by the monasteries; many monasteries not themselves located in the salt-producing region were at pains to acquire extensive holdings there. Among lay lords, Anika Stroganov, a boyar of Novgorod, took by far the first place, developing a network of enterprises that left even his monasterial competitors far behind. Establishing himself in 1515 at Solvychegodsk, near the point where the confluence of the Vychegda and the Sukhona gives rise to the Northern Dvina, he not only built up a monopoly in that area, but the family extended its operations southeastward toward the Urals. Combining with salt-production extensive fisheries and hunting of furbearing animals, the Stroganovs were soon to launch the expedition that overthrew the weak khanate of Sibir and thus start the march toward the Pacific.

TRADE AND INDUSTRY

Simple forms of manufacture and a considerable amount of internal trade also developed, as is attested by the growth of money economy. The towns, however, remained largely undifferentiated, in an economic sense, from the countryside. The rural population, especially during the long winter months, very largely engaged in industrial production—almost all spinning and weaving was done in the countryside—and in commercial activity; the "urban" population was still largely engaged in agricultural pursuits.

A considerable part of the "town" population, running perhaps as high as one-half, was of an official character, including large numbers of military men in the state service and watchmen (*dvorniki*) in private households of absentee magnates; the bulk of these, however, engaged also in handicraft trade and industry. In any case, at a generous estimate, the whole town population can hardly have been more than 2 or 3 percent of the total; most of it, apparently, was concentrated in the overgrown village of Moscow. To what extent this concentration was the result of a favorable central and geographical position, already alluded to above in connection with the rise of Moscow to supremacy, and to what extent it was the political result of Moscow's rise, is a question that need not detain us here.

Russian industry and Russian trade were carried on at this time on an exceedingly small scale and displayed a minimum of organizational development. In general, the economy of Russia in the early sixteenth century may be compared roughly to that of Western Europe in the thirteenth century, though in certain respects, notably in the absence of those practices which crystallized in the guild system, it was more backward. There was in some occupations development of a system of apprenticeship and of accrediting of new craftsmen by senior masters, but there was little of the spirit of local association by free and independent artisans that contributed so much to the development of the Western bourgeoisie. The place of guilds was only partly filled by "artels," more or less temporary associations, such as had been known in Kievan Rus, the members of which pooled their resources and made a collective contract with a prospective employer. Wage laborers existed in large numbers, but were engaged mostly in common ("black") labor, and their freedom was constantly in jeopardy. Many of the artisans and petty traders stood in some sort of bondage relationship. In few trades was there any advanced specialization of function; the icon-makers were the principal exception to the rule.

Perhaps the most conspicuous role was played by foreign craftsmen—chiefly Italian, though Germans excelled as doctors—who, from the fifteenth century, began to be invited to Moscow in significant numbers. When Ivan III married Sophia Palaeologa (1472), he ordered the erection of a new cathedral, which, however, collapsed while being built. In the emergency he entrusted to the sexagenarian artisan, Rodolfo ("Aristotle") Fioraventi, the construction at Moscow of a replica of the famous Cathedral of the Assumption (Uspensky Sobor) at Vladimir. Successfully mastering the principles of this Russian version of Byzantine architecture, Fioraventi brought to completion the beautiful Cathedral of the Assumption in the Kremlin. Other Italian architects built the famous *Granovitaia Palata* and the present brick walls of the Kremlin, as well as the Cathedral of the Archangel. Most of the construction of the period, however—including the Cathedral of the Annunciation and the *Teremnyi Dvorets* (upper apartments) in the Kremlin, as well as many fortresses throughout the land—was the work of native architects, who evolved a distinctive style representing as profound a modification of Byzantine tradition as is represented in the West by the evolution of Roman architecture, through Romanesque, into the Gothic style.

In foreign commerce the principal role was played by foreign visitors (*gosti*), for the suppression of the Novgorod *Hof* of the Hansa (1494) could not check the appearance of alien merchants either there or in other border towns. Their activities, however—even their very presence—were viewed with suspicion by the Muscovite state. Even local, independent principalities had throughout the fifteenth century forbidden foreigners to engage in retail trade. The grand princes regularly required offer of imported goods to themselves before they could be put on public sale. As intermediaries in this traffic, there gradually emerged a specially privileged category of native Russian merchants, also called *gosti;* they alone were permitted to trade with outlanders, who, as was later remarked of the Dutch, "pay no town dues and perform no services to the tsar."

Despite the very considerable development of trade, the governing principle of the Russian economy remained that each landlord strove to cover his own consumption directly from his own estates. Only the fact that, for local and special reasons, some landlords—particularly the monasteries—found themselves with more of a particular product on their hands than they could themselves use, led them to offer it for sale on the market and thus become able to satisfy wants they could not otherwise indulge. For the peasants the reverse was apparently true; pressure of the landlords forced the peasant to dispose of products he might himself have used. Internal trade was principally in salt and fish and furs; animal products (such as hides, tallow, meat, and wool), flax, hemp, and to a lesser extent, grain virtually complete the list of commodities. A considerable interregional trade was necessary to cover deficiencies of local production in some areas.

In early Muscovy there is—apart from the Stroganovs and the monasteries—no indication of any capitalistic spirit, of rational calculation of economic activity for the sake of long-time gain. If the foreign observers who have recorded their impressions of the Muscovites in the sixteenth (and seventeenth) centuries are in almost universal agreement that the Russians loved to trade—and to cheat in a thousand petty ways—this may (as Kulisher, the leading Russian economic historian, has put it) be more properly compared to the rapid assimilation by an economically backward people of the more obvious habits of traders from the West than to any peculiarity of the "Russian soul." It may equally well be a result of the innate greed of human beings: "According to Stanley the natives of Maniema in Central Africa overprice their wares just as much as do the dealers of London, Paris, or New York."[10]

SUMMARY

The main economic problem of Muscovy in the sixteenth century had no direct connection with trade and industry, which, whatever their dynamic implications for the future, were at that time of very secondary importance. The real problem was the problem of how to attract peasants to one's lands and how to keep them there. The chief means to that end was the granting of loans and tax exemptions, for the lure of economic advantage is ever more potent than juridical compulsion. In the struggle for peasants, therefore, the advantage lay with the rich—the monasteries and the boyars.

The mass of the military servitors, the "sons of boyars" and the *dvoriane,* not only lacked the financial resources of the old-established feudal magnates; they were obligated, by the conditions of their tenure (as *pomeshchiki*) to spend an undue part of their time in the military service of the grand prince. Though they might receive money grants to aid them in such service, during their absence from their estates peasants were very likely to take advantage of them, even to slip away to estates of boyars who could offer them easier terms. To be sure, any landholder might appeal to the grand prince for assistance in recovering runaway peasants who were in debt bondage. If, however, a boyar advanced the "silver" owing from the peasants and thus transferred their obligations to himself, there was no legal redress. Moreover, many of the boyars were powerful enough, in defiance of all law, to carry off peasants by force from the lands of a weaker or absent neighbor and to settle them on their own estates.

It was this struggle over labor force (not in any capitalistic sense) that, becoming inextricably intertwined with the sharpening conflict between the old feudal aristocratic principle and the new monarchical autocratic principle, is the principal key to understanding of the critical reign of Ivan IV, "the Terrible," and of the ensuing "Time of Troubles." The crisis was complicated by other factors—the gradual opening of the steppe to agricultural settlement, which intensified the struggle for peasants and at the same time endangered the fiscal interests of the state, and the opening of direct and active commercial intercourse through the White Sea with the nascent capitalism of the West. The solution worked out to this complex of problems was in fundamental ways to determine the whole future development of Russia. Here, rather than in the reign of Peter the Great, came the decisive transformation that was to shape the subsequent course of Russian history.

NOTES

1. Kapterev, *Kharakter otnoshenii Russii k pravoslavnomu Vostoki v XVI i XVII stolietiiakh,* p. 15.
2. *Polnoe sobranie russkikh lietopisei,* VII, 231, 268 (Voskresenskii chronicle).

3. *Sobranie gosudarstvennykh gramot i dogovorov . . .* , V, 16.
4. *Polnoe sobranie russkikh lietopisei,* VI, 242 (Sofiiskaia second chronicle).
5. *Pamiatniki diplomaticheskikh snoshenii drevnei Rossii s derzhavami inostrannymi,* I, col. 12.
6. *Akty otnosiashchiesia k istorii Zapadnoi Rossii . . .* , I, 260.
7. *Polnoe sobranie russkikh lietopisei,* VIII, 163 (Voskresenskii chronicle).
8. *Ibid.,* XII, 132 (Patriarchal or Nikonovskii chronicle).
9. *Ibid.,* VI, 230-231 (Sofiiskaia second chronicle).
10. Kulisher, *Russische Wirtschaftsgeschichte,* p. 334.

SUGGESTIONS FOR FURTHER READING

In addition to works previously noted, particularly at the close of Chapters 1 and 5, the most thorough study of this period in English is Vernadsky's *Russia at the Dawn of the Modern Age.* See also Chapter 16 (by J. B. Bury), "Russia 1462-1682," in the *Cambridge Modern History,* Volume V. An older narrative is Bain's *Slavonic Europe . . . from 1447 to 1796.*

Studies in English of special problems of this period include Koncevicius' *Russia's Attitudes Towards Union with Rome, Ninth to Sixteenth Centuries,* Zernov's *Moscow, the Third Rome,* Fennell's *Ivan the Great of Moscow* (which tries to make a hero of Ivan III), and Backus' *Motives of Russian Nobles in Deserting Lithuania for Moscow, 1377-1514.* See also Denisoff's *Maxime le Grec.*

Baron Herberstein's account of his visits to Muscovy in 1486-1506 is the earliest attempt at a serious description of this strange land, then scarcely known in the West, but it is not of the greatest value.

Chapter

7

Ivan the Terrible: 1533-1584

It is always a temptation to write history in terms of outstanding personalities. The mass of legend that has arisen around the curious, not to say fantastic, figure of Ivan the Terrible has a special allure. Ivan's reign overlaps those of Henry VIII of England and of Good Queen Bess, of Francis "Big Nose" of France and the regency of Catherine de' Medici, of Emperor Charles V and of Philip II of Spain, of Suleiman the Magnificent and of Gustavus Vasa, as well as the activities of Martin Luther and of John Calvin.

IVAN AND THE BOYARS

Succeeding his father, Vasily III, at the age of three, Ivan IV was the first grand prince formally to assume the title of tsar (1547). Thoroughly educated in Biblical and classical lore, he was well acquainted with the original meaning of the phrase "anointed of God" and fully conscious of the centuries-long secular power of the Roman Caesars. On state occasions he was accustomed to the formal ritual of neo-Byzantine court ceremonial. Yet in his childhood he was normally treated with contempt by the boyars who during his minority actually controlled affairs of state. Throughout his life he retained bitter memories of how a Prince Shuisky had lolled in the grand prince's bedchamber, with his elbow propped on the bed in which the sovereign's father had died. He could not forget the scenes of violence in the palace, when boyars in factional fights had chased each other through his private apartments, jostled and torn the robes of the metropolitan, and made free with the grand prince's personal valuables. He did indeed marry the daughter of a boyar—Anastasia, of an old boyar family later to be known as Romanov—but for reasons quite unconnected with any such consideration as *miestnichestvo*. He chose his "beloved heifer" for purely personal reasons. After her death in 1560, Ivan assumed that she had been poisoned by jealous boyars and could find no consolation in the other six wives he successively married.

According to his chief opponent—Prince Kurbsky, a prominent boyar who, although commander of Ivan's field forces, deserted to the enemy in the midst of war with Lithuania—Ivan later degenerated into a madman, passing easily from prayer to dissipation while torturing and executing "traitors" right and left without reason. One of his victims was the Metropolitan Philip, who tried to curb his excesses. Another was his own son Ivan; as (Sir) Jerome Horsey, an English agent frequently at Ivan's court, records:

> Strake him in his furie a box on the ear; whoe toke it so tenderly, fell into a burninge feavour, and died within three daies after. Wherat the Emperor tore his hear and byrd like a madd man, lamentinge and morninge for the loss of his sonn.[1]

Out of such materials and much more, it would be easy to construct an interpretation of Ivan's reign that would be no more than a case study in abnormal psychology, with no meaning for broad historical movements. Such presentations, some of them strongly empathetic, have been numerous enough. The most graphic was a Sovkino film dealing with his reign, made when bygone rulers were still in disrepute and emphasizing the cruelties, the bloodshed, and the orgies. Perhaps to correct this error, a second film on the same topic, made in the era of Stalin's rehabilitation of Russia's great past, presented Ivan as a national hero who had wisely struck down the overweening boyars (including Kurbsky, whose beard was pictured as cut like Trotsky's).

There is also the famous story of how Ivan engaged an Italian architect to build for him the Cathedral of the Blessed Vasily, which still dominates the Red Square in Moscow, across from the Kremlin wall; it is related that Ivan, proud of this remarkable structure and dreading lest it be reproduced elsewhere, had the builder blinded. Official records, however, show that this edifice was planned and built by two native Russian architects, who seem to have suffered no pains for their work. The story is as fantastic as is one's first impression of the apparently bizarre and gingerbread building, an impression corrected when one comes to appreciate the essential symmetry of its structure. Foreshadowed by the much simpler church built by Vasily III at Diakovo in 1529, the *Sobor Vasiliia Blazhennago,* built in the Red Square in 1555-60 to celebrate Ivan's conquest of Kazan, is a genuine *sobor* (assembly) of nine separate churches clustered together in a honeycomb pattern. The most significant feature of these two buildings is the success achieved by their architects in converting into bulbous brick the wooden steeple (somewhat suggestive of New England) and other features of Russian village churches which the natural conditions and convenient building materials of the Russian plain had caused to be evolved. Though capped with the usual onion cupolas so suited to Russian winters, their basis in traditional Russian village architecture embodied features totally unknown to the Byzantine style and sets them apart sharply from the Kremlin cathedrals.

Unfortunately—or fortunately for more objective history—any attempt to interpret these critical years in terms of Ivan as a person breaks down from sheer lack of trustworthy data: by reason of the frequent fires that plagued wooden Moscow, "the burning city," it cannot be established even where Ivan was for whole series of years, much less what he was doing or thinking; the standard delineation of his personality rests mainly on accounts of émigrés who had private reason to hate him. One nineteenth-century Russian scholar, N. P. Likachev, devoted virtually his whole career to attempting to establish what extant documents can be assigned to Ivan's personal composition; he found only two possibilities, mutually exclusive, although Ivan was unquestionably a literate and an educated man.

Apart from Ivan's personal activity, however, there is a wealth of information about less subjective aspects of his reign. It is undoubtedly true that much of the deep-seated bitterness of the period reflects the ferocity of personal enmities and individual ambitions. Yet the story is meaningless unless understood in terms of a struggle of whole classes and primarily of the rising mass of the military landholders ("sons of boyars" and *dvoriane*) against the entrenched feudal power of the boyars.

In that light, the conflict between Ivan and the boyar aristocracy—a conflict in which the bulk of the lesser landholders necessarily and instinctively supported the centralizing monarch—is strongly reminiscent, though with tremendous differences in detail and in final outcome, of the long-drawn struggle of the Angevins of England, who rallied the "knights of the shire" against the feudal baronage.

One of the obvious divergences is the difference in the role played by the Church, for the normal dependence of the Russian Church on the lay power and its lack of any external point of support prevented the development of anything comparable to the controversy between Henry II and Thomas à Becket; the murder in 1570 of the Metropolitan Philip by Maliuta Skuratov, the notorious henchman of Ivan and himself a relative of a previous metropolitan, was in reaction to a moral protest by Philip, not to a political one. In fact, one of the chief influences on the mind of the young Ivan had been the scholarly Metropolitan Macarius, who particularly impressed on his pupil the concept of Moscow as the third and final Rome.

The viewpoint of the boyar opposition had been clearly expressed, even before Ivan's birth, by the boyar Bersen ("Gooseberry") Beklemishev; this reactionary curmudgeon had been expelled from the duma by Vasily III, and had hobnobbed with the learned Maxim the Greek, whom he berated for not making more widely known the perils of deserting old customs. The boyars had no recipe for improvement of the state structure, with its inherent contradiction between the rising power of the ruler and the ancient custom of boyar participation in the formulation of policy. From his refuge in Lithuania, Prince Kurbsky, Ivan's most articulate opponent, wrote four letters (1564-79) to his sovereign, who was provoked to write two long replies. Yet even Kurbsky had no remedial prescription save return to time-hallowed practices, which under Ivan III, Vasily III, and Ivan IV were progressively violated. In his "History of the Grand Princes of Moscow," which he composed in exile, Kurbsky wrote:

> If I were to recount from the beginning and in sequence, I should have to write much of how in the worthy house of Russian princes the devil sowed evil customs, especially through their evil sorceress wives, as happened also with the kings of Israel, and most of all by those who were taken from among strangers.[2]

Kurbsky did not, however, blame everything on Sophia, Greek wife of Ivan III, and on Helena Glinskaia, Lithuanian wife of Vasily III, who had induced her husband to shave off his beard. Himself sprung from the stock of Rurik, Kurbsky resented the ascendancy of one alone of its branches: "It is the custom of old of the princes of Moscow to desire their brothers' blood and to destroy the poor wretches for the sake of their accursed estates, on account of their greed."

It was part of the weakness of the boyars' position that the "gathering of the land" in the hands of the princes of Moscow had deprived them of even the theoretical possibility of renouncing their service and transferring their allegiance to another prince. To take service under Lithuania was obviously an act of desperation; if an increasing number of boyars did desert Moscow, it was clearly treason and, by the standards of the time, justified the most severe penalties. The only other way to change one's service was to try to influence the succession.

It will be recalled that a dispute of this kind had disturbed the court of Ivan III toward the end of his reign. During the infancy of Ivan IV, his uncle, Prince Andrew of Staritsa, attempted to persuade the military-serving landholders of the Novgorod region to abandon in his favor their allegiance to the boy-ruler; the boyars who then held the reins had ordered the rebels hanged "along the Novgorod highway, not together, but all along the road to Novgorod." [3] It was to the son of this Prince Andrew, Ivan's cousin Vladimir, that Kurbsky and other boyars wished to swear allegiance during what was expected to be the fatal illness of Ivan in 1553.

To do without a ruler altogether, or even to devise organs that could impose effective restraints on the growth of his power, was of course unthinkable to these medieval-minded men, whose strength lay in their traditional political and economic status, just as their weakness lay in the negativeness of their conservatism. Their traditional power, however, reflected mainly their position as individuals in a feudal order. They proved even more unable than the English baronage to develop a solid corporate structure. The most that the boyars, torn by personal and family quarrels, were able to accomplish was an apparent stabilization, about 1550, of *miestnichestvo,* expressed in the composition of the *Rodoslovets* (Genealogical Register) and of an official abstract of *razriady* (lists of past appointments) for the last eighty years; at the same time, however, some posts were exempted from *miestnichestvo* rules.

In one other respect the role of the boyars remained unassailable, at least by frontal assault. The boyar duma continued to be a body with which the ruler had to reckon in making major decisions. Ivan's father and grandfather had provoked bitter complaints because they tried to rule with their own secretaries (*diaki*); also, like some earlier princes, they had sometimes consulted with members of the duma of their own choosing rather than with the whole boyar duma.

In Ivan's youth, after a protracted period of murderous personal and family squabbles, power had come to be concentrated in a small inner circle, known as the "Select Council" (*izbrannaia rada*). Not all of its members were of boyar families. One of them, Silvester, archpriest of the Cathedral of the Assumption, had not merely ecclesiastical standing but was an active merchant, engaged in foreign as well as domestic trade; his *Domostroi* (*Housekeeping*) is a classic manual of economical management. Another, Alexis Adashev, was a man of modest origin, who served as Ivan's valet and was in 1550 put in charge of receiving petitions to the throne. Most of them were, however, like Prince Kurbsky, boyars descended from former ruling princes, and the newcomers to the ranks seem quickly to have been assimilated.

Who selected these men—whether the young Ivan or whether, as Kurbsky suggests, the duma itself—is not altogether clear. In later days an embittered Ivan reviled the "churlish priest" Silvester and the "dog" Adashev whom he "had taken from the dunghill and ranked with the magnates." [4] In action, certainly, this inner group sought to guide affairs in the general interests of the boyars as a class, though with statesmanship enough to offer sops to the discontented "sons of boyars." Among other things, they restored to the princes hereditary estates confiscated by Ivan III and Vasily III.

PERESVIETOV AND THE SELECT COUNCIL

The broad challenge to boyar ascendancy came initially not from above, not from the tsar, but from below, from the "public." Its principal mouthpiece, who wrote under the name of "Ivashko, son of Simeon Peresvietov," is so difficult to trace in extant records that he was long supposed to have been using a pseudonym; the internal evidence of his petitions to Tsar Ivan, however, is completely reconcilable with known facts. Peresvietov represented himself as a descendant of a hero of the same family name who had fallen fighting on the field of Kulikovo under Dmitry Donskoy; born under Lithuanian rule, he had apparently ignored the prohibition of the Polish king and in 1528 had been a member of a detachment of three hundred Polish *szliachta* who took service under Szapolya Ianos in his successful bid, backed by the Turks, for the crown of Hungary. Later, during an armistice with the Hapsburgs, Peresvietov had transferred to the service of Emperor Ferdinand I, king of Bohemia; in 1535 he had served under Peter, the duke of Walachia, an ally of Moscow. After a few years at home in Lithuania, he had in 1538 or 1539 entered the service of Moscow, with a commission to manufacture shields of his own devising, "of Macedonian pattern." The death of the boyar under whom he was working ended this project, and Peresvietov had a difficult time in the Muscovite service; as an immigrant and therefore unwelcome, he seems even to have lost the estate (*pomestie*) he had initially been assigned. In 1549 he succeeded in presenting his "Little Petition" and some other writings to the young Tsar Ivan; though there is some indication that he was somehow connected with Adashev, he won no redress. His "Great Petition," in which he leaned heavily on the sayings of his former chief, Peter of Walachia, was less personal, addressing itself to what he regarded as the chief problems of statecraft. The last reference to him is an obscure note in the archives which suggests that he may have shared the fate of Matvei Bashkin, a "son of a boyar" associated with the Archpriest Silvester and prosecuted for heresy in the middle 1550's.

Peresvietov's ideas were in line with the reforms undertaken by the Select Council but went so far beyond them that he has been acclaimed as a "progressive" thinker. Among them was his reiterated condemnation of slavery (*kholopstvo*) and even of partial (*kabala*) bondage. In this respect he did not go as far as other "heretics" of the time. Like Silvester when he proudly wrote in his *Domostroi,* "And now our domestics [*domochadtsy*] are all free and live with us of their free will," Peresvietov was merely expressing his approval of the gradual process, already referred to, of the upgrading of various categories of bondsmen to merge with the legally free, but economically still inferior, class of peasants (*krestiane*). Silvester's explanation was that servants kept by force, though furnished with food and drink and clothing, whether "men, women, or children, if unfree, weep and lie and steal . . . and commit all sorts of evil. And their lord and lady sin against God and are a laughing-stock for men." [5] The exclamation which Peresvietov attributed to his hero, the Turkish ruler whom he calls Makhmet-Saltan (Mohammed II, 1451-81), "We are all sons of Adam," related to the equality that should exist among warriors, not between warriors and tillers of the soil.

Peresvietov's concept of equality was rooted in the jealousy of the general body of military servitors, the "sons of boyars" and *dvoriane,* toward the aristocratic feudal boyars. Quoting Peter, Peresvietov wrote:[6]

> The magnates of the Russian tsar themselves grow rich and grow lazy, and impoverish his realm, and call themselves his servitors because they go forth on his service in full panoply, on horseback, and followed by their men, yet do not stand firmly for the Christian faith and do not fiercely play the game of death against the foe, and thus betray God and their sovereign.

In Turkey, Peresvietov had asserted,

> Whoever stands firmly for the tsar [sultan] against the foe, plays the game of death, breaks up the regiments of the foe, faithfully serves the tsar, though he be of lesser degree, him he raises up to greatness and gives him a great name [i.e., raises him to high office] and adds much to his pay, so that he raises the hearts of his warriors. . . . And though it be unknown of what father they are the sons, the tsar for their wisdom gave them a great name, so that others likewise may turn out to serve the tsar loyally.

Peresvietov freely criticized certain aspects of the Muscovite political order, from which he himself suffered, in the guise of explaining how justly the Turkish "tsar" ruled his dominions. His principal theme was that the Greeks "for their sins" had been justly visited by the wrath of a righteous God, but in his view the "Latin heresy" played no role. It was true, as a "voice from Heaven" had replied to the lamentations of Patriarch Anastasius after the fall of Constantinople in 1453, that

> if I unleashed on you, as on Sodom and Gomorrah, My everlasting wrath of fire and flood, and as a lesson unleashed on you the alien Turks, [it was because] you in everything transgressed against My holy commandments.

The "heresy" into which Constantine Palaeologus had fallen was that, under the influence of his magnates, he had abstained from wars, had neglected his warriors, and had not made justice prevail in his realm. Pointedly, though most inaccurately, Peresvietov asserted that Constantine had ascended the throne at the age of three (as Ivan had actually done) and that his magnates had succeeded in curbing his will, for "the wealthy never think of the military, they think of meekness and gentleness and peace." Under their influence, "the tsar departed from righteous judgment," leaving control to "cunning judges and their unrighteous judgment."

> The tsar's dignitaries in the towns and in the townships in their double-dealing and diabolical practices went so far as to exhume newly buried corpses, reinterring the empty coffins; they leave the dead man, pierced with a boarspear or hacked with a sabre, and smeared with blood, in the house of some rich man; then they find an informer who knows not God, and having condemned the rich man by an unjust trial, they plunder all his household and his wealth. [In contrast,] Makhmet-Saltan introduced true justice into his realm and removed false, and gave God heartfelt joy, and spake thus: "God loves justice

> best of all; it is not possible for a ruler to keep his realm without terror. . . ." And the Lord God was incensed at Tsar Constantine and at his magnates and at the whole Greek realm, because they disdained justice and did not know that God loves justice above all.

The main burden of Peresvietov's argument was the need for reform of judicial administration:

> If there is not justice, there is nothing at all. . . . And in whatever realm there is justice, there God abides and gives it his great aid, and God's wrath is not visited on that realm.

On the strength of this conviction, which relied only minimally on ecclesiastical authority, Peresvietov has been characterized as a "humanist," though Soviet scholars are emphatic in denying that he was indebted to Western influences. In one passage of his "Great Petition" he does go so far as to put in the mouth of his favorite Peter the words: "God loves, not faith, but justice." Peresvietov's concept of justice, however, was peculiarly suited to the nascent Muscovite autocracy:

> Justice brings heartfelt joy to God: to maintain justice in his realm and to introduce justice into his realm, a ruler must not spare his favorite, if he be found guilty. There cannot be a ruler without terror; like a steed under the ruler without a bridle, so is a realm without terror.

The essence of Peresvietov's "progressive" thought was contained in his humble salutation to Ivan: "Thou art a sovereign terrible and wise."

Complaints against the prevailing system of local administration had long been multiplying. Governors vested with fiscal and judicial authority were not salaried officers but enjoyed the right to pocket most of the fees and fines they collected. Their interest was therefore in the punishment, not the prevention, of crime; the more numerous and the more heinous the offenses in their territory, the larger their revenues. Their posts were frankly known as "feedings" (*kormleniia*) and were assigned, not on the basis of the official's abilities and the interests of the local population, but as rewards for service to the grand prince. The most lucrative of these appointments were monopolized by boyars. Hesitating attempts had been made, as early as the fifteenth century, to limit the powers of the holders of *kormleniia* by associating with them locally elected subordinate officials and by subjecting the appointed officials to closer responsibility to the tsar and the duma.

While Ivan IV was still a minor, more drastic measures were taken by occasionally establishing a new police-judicial unit (*guba*), headed by a small number of elected landholders. The first charter relieving the appointed "feeder" of his authority was granted in 1539; in 1541 the chronicle of Pskov records great rejoicing because the "evil men"—one of whom was Prince Andrew Shuisky—had been replaced there also. In 1549 the tsar publicly promised that the old officials, the "feeders," should not judge without the assistance of communal officials, "save for murder, robbery, and theft taken redhanded"; the new law code (*Sudebnik*) of 1550 formally embodied the new principle of transferring judicial authority to the community, already charged with collective responsibility for direct taxes. If the administrative unit included military-serving nobles as well as taxpayers, the police-judicial powers were vested in officials elected from among these local "sons of boyars." In 1556, the reorganization of local government known as the "zemsky reform" was completed by granting general permission to all towns and townships to substitute locally elected officials for the hated appointees from the center; at the same time, special taxes were imposed, to be collected by the community and transmitted to the capital, thus solving the problem of providing a suitable substitute for the value of the "feedings." Only the collection of indirect taxes was withheld; this privilege was farmed out "on faith" to groups of merchants, some of the members usually being from Moscow.

It does not, of course, follow that the local population had no cause to regret this reform. Although the new officials were elected by the whole free population, including the taxpayers, the "heads" were always drawn from the noble landholding class. Furthermore, they were vested with arbitrary powers of holding inquisitions without waiting for accusations to lead to trials and had the authority to administer summary punishments as under a reign of terror. As Peresvietov had written: "And for a thief or a robber under the Turkish tsar there is no prison; on the third day they execute him, that iniquity shall not multiply; only for suspects is there prison until the royal inquest."

Also under the guidance of the Select Council, fresh effort was made to increase the amount of land available for distribution to the "sons of boyars," by restricting ecclesiastical landholding. In 1551, a Church Council adopted a revised manual, prescribing the correct ritual for religious services, and providing for the better governance of the manners of the clergy and the morals of the laity. Known as the "Hundred Chapters" (*Stoglav*), these articles included prohibition of acquisition of new lands by the Church, while explicitly confirming the Church in its existing possessions. The new limitations were frequently evaded and proved impotent to do more than slacken the pace of extension of monasterial and episcopal landholding. A simultaneous attempt to abolish lay immunities was also nullified by a whole series of fresh grants.

In anticipation of the addition of new crown lands, a select group of a thousand favored nobles, the young Prince Kurbsky among them, were in 1550 given lands around Moscow itself. It was to prove a dangerous precedent, ominous for the continuance of boyar ascendancy.

About the same time a new corps, the *strieltsy,* was established. Conscripted for life chiefly from the urban taxable population, armed with handguns, halberds, and sabers, and officered by "sons of boyars," the *strieltsy* were originally intended as a special bodyguard for the tsar. In 1550 their number was set at three thousand; by the end of the reign there were some twenty thousand of them, stationed as garrisons in towns throughout the realm. Like the artillerymen and other conscripted elements (*pribornye*) they were permitted in peacetime to engage in trade and industry; quartered in special tax-exempt "liberties" (*slobody*), they had a serious depressing effect on the growth of a civilian bourgeoisie.

The bulk of the armed forces, which amounted in all to over one hundred thousand men, was still made up of the boyars, "sons of boyars," and *dvoriane,* who were obligated to serve on horseback, followed by their retainers and armed at their own expense with swords and bows and arrows. The extent of their service was theoretically scaled to the size of the land grant (*pomestie*) they received, but the standard norms could not be maintained, and hereditary estates (*otchiny*) were also taken into account. By law the military landholders became liable to service at the age of fifteen, but absenteeism (*nietstvo*) and flight increased steadily despite the most severe penalties the ruler dared apply.

Because of the technological backwardness of these feudal levies, the *strieltsy* and the artillerymen became ever more important in a qualitative sense and constituted the nearest approach to a standing army. Employment of cossacks, now including also the "free cossacks," especially those living along the Don, became more usual; cossacks recruited as individuals served under officers appointed by the government, but many, enlisted as detachments, served under their own elected *atamans.*

WAR AND TRADE WITH THE WEST

It was not only in domestic matters that the ideas championed by Peresvietov triumphed. He also urged the expansion of the state's territory into richer lands, where the "warriors" might be more amply rewarded with land grants. To him the Tatar khanate of Kazan seemed "a heavenly land, fit for all," which should be conquered even if it "were in friendship" with Moscow.[7] In a carefully planned two-year campaign, Kazan was conquered by the Muscovites. Pressing on down the Volga, Ivan's armies entered Astrakhan. With the formal annexation of that khanate (1556), Moscow's territory officially extended from the Gulf of Finland and the White Sea to the Caspian. Even the southern steppe began to be penetrated by Russian colonists, although the Tatar khanate of the Crimea, since 1475 an autonomous vassal state of Ottoman Turkey, continued to be a constant menace. As a buffer, there developed the democratic community of the Don cossacks, whose loyalty to Moscow was no greater than their current self-interest. In fact, the acquisition of the lower Volga country did not for some time reduce Moscow's troubles with the Tatars. Although a Russian population was planted in the heart of Kazan, and although Astrakhan was fortified, the open stretches in between continued to be plagued by restless and rebellious Tatars, constituting a constant drain on Moscow's military resources.

Nevertheless, the appetite of the land-hungry (and peasant-hungry) service nobility was not satisfied. Defying the resistance of the conservative boyar aristocracy, which would have preferred to live in peace on its hereditary estates, Ivan in 1558 picked a quarrel with the Livonian Knights, the remnant of the Teutonic Knights who still ruled the Baltic shoreline. Expansion in this direction promised the possibility of developing Russian trade by securing control of Baltic seaports; Narva was speedily taken, and a number of captured merchantmen were turned into a war fleet, officered by foreigners. This threatening development speedily brought on the intervention of Lithuania, Denmark, and Sweden. The Livonian Knights followed their Prussian brethren in becoming converts to Protestantism and in secularizing their estates; Estonia passed to Sweden, Ösel to Denmark, Livonia to Lithuania, while Courland became a hereditary fief of the former Master, as a vassal of Poland (1561).

Despairing of direct conquest, Ivan offered (1570) to support a Danish prince as king of Livonia and Estonia in a relation of vassalage to Moscow, a proposal unacceptable to Poland and Sweden. The war, in which the Crimean Tatars also participated, sacking Moscow in 1571, dragged on through almost all of the remaining years of Ivan's life. It ended only in armistices (with Poland in 1582, with Sweden in 1583). Sweden remained in firm control of Livonia as well as of Estonia, Poland retaining only suzerainty over Courland. Moscow not only gained no territory; she lost to Sweden even her ancient foothold at the head of the Gulf of Finland. What is more, the alarm engendered by the desperate struggle threw Lithuania definitely into the arms of Poland by the Union of Lublin (1569).

Nevertheless, it was the first time that Moscow, the Third Rome, had seriously challenged the West. An appeal of the Polish king to Elizabeth of England has an oddly prophetic ring:

> . . . as we have written afore, so now we write againe to your ma-ty that we know and feele of a surety, the Moscouite, enemy to all liberty vnder the heauens, dayly to grow mightier by the increase of such things as be brought to the Narue [Narva], while not onely wares but also weapons heretofore unknowen to him, and artificers and arts be brought vnto him: by meane whereof he maketh himself strong to vanquish all others. Which things, as long as this voyage to Narue is vsed, can not be stopped. And we perfectly know your ma-ty can not be ignorant how great the cruelty is of the said enemy, of what force he is, what tyranny he vseth on his subiects, and in what seruile sort they be vnder him. We seemed hitherto to vanquish him onely in this, that he was rude of arts, and ignorant of policies. If so be that this nauigation to the Narue continue, what shall be unknowen to him? Therefore we that know best, and border vpon him, do admonish other Christian princes in

> time, that they do not betray their dignity, liberty and life of them and their subiects to a most barbarous and cruell enemy, as we can no lesse do by the duty of a Christian prince. For now we do foresee, except other princes take this admonition, the Moscouite puffed vp in pride with those things that be brought to the Narue, and made more perfect in warlike affaieres with engines of warre and shippes, will make assault this way on Christendome, to slay or make bound all that shall withstand them: which God defend. . . .[8]

Elizabeth was not impressed, but continued to develop the friendly trade relations that she had, by a curious quirk of fate, inherited along with the crown from her predecessor, "Bloody Mary." In 1553, Edward VII had sent out an expedition under Sir Hugh Willoughby to discover a northeastern passage to the Orient. Most of the ships were lost, but Richard Chancellor, the "pilot-general," successfully followed a track known to the Norwegians and made port at the mouth of the Northern Dvina. Thence he was assisted by the local authorities to reach Moscow, where he was cordially received. Soon after his return to England the next year, the Muscovy Company was chartered. Its vigorous commercial activities—together with those of the Dutch rivals who soon adopted the new trade route—were to have great importance for the development of economic policy in Russia. A chain of commercial towns, including Ustiug and Vologda, came to connect the new port of Archangel with the old central portion of the state. The English were particularly interested in the possibilities of trade by the Volga with the Caspian area; as early as 1558 one of the agents of the Muscovy Company, Jenkinson, made a bold visit to Khiva and Bukhara, deep in the heart of Central Asia.

Soviet historians are prone to insist that it was Russia that "discovered" Western Europe, not the other way around. In fact, negotiations with Rome concerning the marriage of Ivan III and Zoe (Sophia) Palaeologa had been opened in 1468. After the marriage, Ivan had sent repeated embassies to Italy, at irregular intervals. The interest of the Hapsburgs in using Russia as a counterpoise to Poland and their hope of embroiling Muscovy with the Turks had involved many visits, including that of Baron Herberstein, whose account of Russia was for long the West's chief source of knowledge of that remote land. For her part, Moscow had sent several embassies to visit Emperor Charles V in Spain; one of these had traveled by way of England (1524), another by way of the Netherlands (1527). With Denmark, Ivan III had coöperated against the Hansa. Yet Chancellor's visit was of revolutionary importance in opening direct and constant communication between Russia and the West.

To Russia the active interest of the English was an important compensation for the failure to secure control of the Baltic coast. Ivan also had a keen appreciation of the political aspects of the question. In 1567 he proposed an offensive-defensive alliance and a mutual promise of asylum in case either he or Elizabeth should have need of it. Elizabeth's reluctance to go beyond trade relations led the quick-tempered Ivan to reproach her for being ruled by merchants, "like a poor lady," not like a mighty sovereign. His disappointment did not prevent him from sending a formal embassy in 1581 with secret instructions, to be divulged only to Elizabeth, to inspect Lady Mary Hastings, "daughter of the appanage prince of Tintun" (Earl of Huntingdon), with a view to a marriage offer if the report pleased the tsar and if the girl would accept "baptism into the Christian faith."

The terrific strain of the great Livonian War had meanwhile naturally intensified the domestic crisis. The boyars, who had opposed the war, felt themselves more and more driven into resistance and even into treason. In 1562, the tsar forbade the princes in his service to "sell or exchange" their hereditary estates; at the same time he ordered confiscation of estates which, in defiance of earlier similar decrees, had changed hands without his license even years before. Increasingly suspicious of the most eminent boyars, Ivan more and more often required them to go bail for each other's loyalty. The crowning blow to him was the desertion in 1564 of Prince Kurbsky, who—abandoning his family as well as his army—sought personal salvation as a refugee in the enemy camp. A few months later Ivan struck decisively, but in a unique way. Still not daring to make a frontal assault on the powers and privileges of the boyars as a class, he intensified and multiplied his blows at them as individuals. His principal instrument was the *oprichnina.*

THE *OPRICHNINA*

Shortly before Christmas, 1564, Ivan left his capital for his favorite residence at Alexandrovsk. He took with him all his most precious movable possessions and also his chosen bodyguard. On January 3, 1565, messengers from him arrived at Moscow with the tidings that the tsar, weary of the treasons of his boyars—and of the clergy and officials who had connived with them—had "from the great compassion of his heart" [9] abandoned his throne; the specific offenses with which he charged the boyars had, oddly enough, for the most part been committed during his childhood. Simultaneously, a second proclamation was read in the Red Square, assuring the merchantry and common people that Ivan had no grievance against them.

The coup had obviously been elaborately prepared, and Ivan had with him a military force adequate to overcome any possible resistance. No time therefore was lost in sending a deputation, headed by a few of the higher clergy and some boyars and accompanied by a number of the excited lower orders, to beseech the ruler to reconsider. Ivan promptly and graciously consented to "take his state anew," but on carefully defined terms; he was thenceforth to have the right to ban those he deemed disloyal to him and to execute some of them, confiscating their estates, all without any interference by the clergy, the boyars, or the officials. The confiscated lands became the nucleus of the *oprichnina,* in which, as will be discussed presently, Ivan was absolute master. "The tsar as it were asked the state council for a police dictatorship—a unique form of contract between a sovereign and his people!"[10] On the day after Ivan's return to Moscow, one eminent boyar was impaled upon a stake, while six others were simply beheaded.

Peresvietov had written approvingly of the Turkish sultan's treatment of unjust judges:

> The ruler did not accuse them, he only ordered them flayed alive, saying "if they grow new skins, their fault shall be forgiven them." And their skins he bade to be peeled off . . . and bade them to be affixed in the law courts with an iron nail, and bade to be inscribed on their skins: "without such terrors justice cannot be brought into the realm."[11]

If the *guba* authorities had been given the right to subject persons of ill repute to torture, it was not unreasonable that the tsar should have corresponding powers even over the boyars. As Ivan wrote to Kurbsky, if the ruler could not mete out summary punishment to traitors, "then all realms are in disorder, and all are corrupted with internecine quarrels."[12]

Whatever discount one allows for exaggerations by outraged émigrés, there can be no doubt that from this time on Muscovy was subjected to a reign of systematic terror. Torture, banishment, and execution were, of course, not new phenomena. At the age of thirteen, Ivan had suddenly arrested the most eminent of the boyars, Prince Andrew Shuisky, and "ordered him handed over to the huntsmen, and the huntsmen took him and killed him," leaving his body in the gutter for hours. Of this incident in 1544, one of the chroniclers remarks calmly: "And from those times the boyars began to have great fear of the tsar and [showed] obedience."[13] Innumerable hapless lesser folk suffered horribly along with boyars. Kurbsky, perhaps thinking only of his fellow magnates, estimated the number of victims at over four hundred; foreigners' estimates ran up to ten thousand. A macabre feature of the terror was Ivan's practice of sending to monasteries lists of the executed, together with a donation to defray the cost of prayers for these "departed Orthodox Christians of man's, woman's, and child's degree who . . . are here written down by name, degree, and surname: grant them, O Lord, eternal remembrance!" Sometimes, in place of a list, occurs the phrase "their names, O Lord, Thou thyself dost know," or simply "their names God knows."[14]

Those who felt the weight of Ivan's therapeutic measures were not by any means all political opponents or their adherents. Jerome Horsey, an agent of the Muscovy Company during the reign of Ivan the Terrible, relates how the tsar remedied poverty:

> One deed of charitie I maie not omytte, one memorable act, to shutt up his devocion with. In anno 1575 a great famine followed the pestilence of the better sortt of people. The towns, streets, and waies swarmed with the rogs, idell beggers and counterfeit crippells; no riddence could be made of them in the time of scarsetie. Proclamacion was made they should resortt to receav the

> Emperors great almes upon such a day at Slobida. Owt of som thowsands that came, 700 of the most villest and counterfeits wear all knockt in the heads and cast into the great lake, for the fish to receav their doll ther: the rest most febliest wear disperst to monnestaries and hospitalls to be relived.[15]

Such techniques should, however, be viewed in the perspective of their times. It will suffice, perhaps, to recall the treatment of "sturdy vagabonds" in Elizabethan England, contemporary with but economically, politically, and culturally far more advanced than Ivan's Muscovy.

What was most significant for the further development of Russian institutions was Ivan's establishment of the *oprichnina,* itself only a temporary phenomenon but one which had enduring consequences. *Oprichnina* was not a new term in Russian law; it was the name given to the portion of a man's estate set apart (*oprich*) for his widow. In demanding that the confiscated estates be set apart for him personally, Ivan was merely giving a novel twist to an ancient custom. In the portion of his domains not included in the *oprichnina* no revolutionary change was effected. In the remainder of the realm, known as the *zemshchina,* the tsar continued to rule by time-hallowed custom, in association with the boyar duma.

In the *oprichnina,* on the contrary, Ivan was absolute master, not as tsar but as proprietor. The distinction, and the oddly low value that Ivan was capable of setting on the office of tsar, are emphasized by the fact that for a time (1575-76) Ivan even invested a baptized Tatar, Semen Bekbulatovich, with the title of "lord grand prince of all Rus" and was content to bow before this pseudo-tsar, while calling himself simple "little Ivan, son of Vasily, prince of Moscow."

The original territory "set apart" in the *oprichnina* was not compact. It was made up of certain streets and wards in the capital and of a number of towns and townships—or parts of them—scattered over the central provinces. These holdings were distributed, at Ivan's pleasure, among the members of a picked corps, the *oprichniki* and their dependents. The former tenants were summarily evicted; in the dead of winter some twelve thousand persons and their families were driven from their homes to find their way, often on foot, to the new, undeveloped holdings assigned to them. The area embraced in the *oprichnina*—after 1572 renamed the "Great Court" (*Bolshoi dvor*)—was steadily extended by fresh confiscations. On their own petition, the towns along the new northern trade route, developed under the pressure of English capital, were also included. By the time of Ivan's death, about half of the territory of the Muscovite realm was under this peculiar special regime. Although lands in the *zemshchina* and in the *oprichnina* continued to be intermingled in a crazy-quilt fashion, most of the latter lay within an inverted triangle, with the Arctic Sea as its base and Moscow near its apex. Thus, the lands which remained under normal *zemshchina* jurisdiction were chiefly those along the western, southern, and eastern frontiers, where constant warfare made life and property most insecure. The old-settled central provinces were subjected to an almost complete revolution in landholding.

The *oprichniki,* who, without counting their dependents, came to number six thousand, were of diverse origins. Most of them came from the ranks of the *dvoriane* and "sons of boyars," the military-serving landholding nobility. Among them also were a number of boyars, including Nikita Romanov, brother-in-law of Ivan, and Boris Godunov, whose sister married Ivan's younger son and successor; some of them, such as Vasily Shuisky and Athanasius Viazemsky, were even princes of the stock of Rurik. All of them were chosen for their personal devotion to Ivan; *miestnichestvo* and *otechestvo* meant nothing in the *oprichnina.*

Ivan himself dwelt no longer in the Kremlin, but in a new fortified palace at Alexandrovsk, surrounded by his followers, whom he is alleged to have organized into a wild parody of a monastic brotherhood. Like the political police of the Soviet Union, the *oprichniki* wore a special black uniform—the effect being enhanced by their black horses and the emblems of a dog's head and a broom (to sweep treason from the land) which they carried on their saddlebags. Exempt from all normal state authority, they interfered freely and with impunity in the affairs of the *zemshchina,* evoking widespread dismay and deep hatred.

As one observer expressed it, Ivan had "cut his whole realm in two as though with an ax, playing with God's people. . . ." [16] In those days of sudden violence, the *oprichnina* itself did not escape internal purges: conservative boyars and men like the Metropolitan Philip were by no means its only victims. Prince Viazemsky, "cellarer" of Alexandrovsk; the Basmanovs, chief intimates of Ivan; and the dreaded Maliuta Skuratov, who had personally strangled Metropolitan Philip—all themselves in due course met sudden death at the hands of their fellows in the *oprichnina.*

It must be emphasized that the *oprichnina* was not a state institution. Its establishment did not mean that Ivan had solved the political contradictions by replacing old institutions with a streamlined autocracy. Only in the *oprichnina,* which never embraced much more than half the state territory (including the relatively uninhabited northern regions), was Ivan undisputed master. Side by side with the *oprichnina,* however temporarily overshadowed by it, continued the *zemshchina,* in which the tsar made no direct attempt to challenge old usages.

The principal new development in the *zemshchina* was the appearance of the zemsky sobor (assembly of the land), an institution basically similar in composition and in function to the early medieval "representative" bodies in the West (Parliament, Estates-General, Cortes, Diet). Like its Western counterparts, it evolved gradually from informal consultations, such as one held in 1471 before marching on Novgorod, with various elements of his subjects in addition to his regular advisers, the Holy Synod and the boyar duma; not until 1566 did such a meeting take a form that can properly be characterized as a zemsky sobor. In that year, only a year after the establishment of the *oprichnina,* the tsar "spoke" with his people about the desirability of concluding the Livonian War. In addition to the members of the Holy Synod, leading boyars, and officials, there were assembled representatives of the *dvoriane* and of the trading population; these latter two "estates" supplied three-fourths of the membership of the sobor (*dvoriane* 55 percent, merchantry 20 percent). Apparently these "representatives" were not elected by their constituents; leading men, already in government service, were summoned by virtue of their position.

By analogy to Western history, the zemsky sobor might have been expected to become a major instrument in the hands of the monarch for curbing the traditional power of feudal lords, an instrument more effective in the long run and less revolutionary than the drastic and bizarre *oprichnina.* However, the institution underwent no further development during the reign of Ivan, though it was to play a short-lived role in and after the "Time of the Troubles" (1598-1613).

Institutionally the tsar developed no device for curbing boyar power in the normal governance of the realm. Thus he failed to resolve the fundamental political contradiction in sixteenth-century Muscovy and prepared the way for the shattering catastrophe of the Time of the Troubles, for which the extinction of the dynasty was only the immediate occasion. Yet the *oprichnina* did, in an indirect way, permanently undermine the position of the boyars and open the door for the consolidation, in the next century, of the autocracy. The confiscations of hereditary estates which attended the execution and banishment of so many individual boyars gradually and progressively stripped the class of the real basis of its power.

Even though a boyar was assigned new lands in compensation for old estates taken into the *oprichnina,* a diminution of his status was inevitable. The new lands might be fully as extensive, even better lands than those he had held. The fact remained that—like the boyars of Novgorod under Ivan III—he had been uprooted and transplanted into a new region where traditionally he meant nothing, and tradition had lain at the very core of his authority. Particularly was this true of the princes, whose ancestors had for generations ruled over the estates now lost or exchanged. It was in this way, rather than by the torture chamber or the executioner's ax, that the *oprichnina* proved ultimately deadly to the *boiarstvo.*

AGRARIAN CRISIS AND CONTROLLED ECONOMY

Whatever satisfaction Ivan might have derived from this humbling of the mighty, the unanticipated but attendant consequences for the rest of the population and for the state itself were ruinous. When a boyar fell under the tsar's ban, his whole establishment was disrupted: his household usually shared his personal fate. His bondsmen were set free but forbidden to enter another's service; "condemned to a free but hungry existence,"[17] they became homeless vagrants and drifted in large numbers to the southern frontiers, often joining the lawless cossack "brigands."

The bulk of the tenants, the "free" peasants, were transferred to the new landlords to whom the confiscated estates were doled out in small parcels. The result, as in the case also of distribution of "black" lands to private landlords, was the destruction of the autonomous peasant commune and the subjection of its members to the direct exploitation of the new masters, whose lack of capital and onerous conditions of military service made them ruthless plunderers. The peasant, formerly protected by the immunities enjoyed by the great estates, sought salvation in a mass exodus from the central provinces. Few of them could hope to eke out existence in the climatically harsh regions north of the watershed, where alone "black" land (i.e., land without landlords) continued to predominate. Most of them therefore fled to the steppe.

This process was intensified by the interests of the state itself, which needed colonists for the new lands being brought under its control along the middle and lower Volga and in the "wild field" (the unoccupied steppe) south of the Oka. In the early stages, therefore, the state pulled peasants away from the center to the frontier at the same time that the effects of the *oprichnina* were pushing them from their old homes. By the 1570's, the reports of local tax assessors had become genuinely alarming, and throughout the life of the *oprichnina* the desolation of the old provinces became ever more terrifying. By 1584, according to tax registers for an area near Moscow itself, out of 50,000 dessiatines of arable land—a dessiatine equals 2.7 acres—16,000 had been completely abandoned and 4,000 more had been leased out for lack of tenants; worse still, of the remaining 30,000, some 18,500 belonged to monasteries; only 23 percent of the land was still cultivated for the support of men who were obligated to perform military service. In the Novgorod area, the least fertile region and subject also to devastation from the war, the desolation was extreme; 92.5 percent of the arable land had been abandoned.

Without peasants to work for them, even the chief beneficiaries of Ivan's attack on the boyars could derive no comfort from his large-scale distribution of land to them. Without peasants to pay taxes and without military servitors economically capable of supporting their service, Ivan's armies dwindled away, and all the sacrifices of the Russian population promised to be vain. Yet the state could find no effective remedy. The crux of the problem was the need for peasant labor. The wealth and privileges of the boyars had given them an economic advantage over the *dvoriane* in the struggle to attract peasants to their estates. Although this was largely canceled by the wholesale violent destruction of the old feudal aristocracy, the mass flight of the peasantry to new lands prevented the lesser landholders from benefiting by it. The prevalence of ecclesiastical landholding also continued to invite the hostility of the *dvoriane*. In 1580, the tsar abolished the tax exemption of church lands but did not venture to proceed to confiscation or even to total prohibition of new acquisitions.

In these circumstances, Ivan resorted to the desperate expedient of the "forbidden years," depriving the peasantry in particular areas, under any and all conditions and for periods of years together, of their legal right to move. Such prohibitions first appear in the Novgorod area, spreading southeastward. Thus the tsar put his power, however fitfully, behind the growth of serfdom. Herein lies the basic connection between the Russian autocracy and peasant bondage, a tie that was to be strengthened in subsequent generations and to endure into modern times. A strong and unfettered state power was to prove itself as the only means to effect the enslavement of the agricultural masses, the surest guarantee of the economic stability and prosperity of the noble ruling class, itself content not to share in the power so long as it derived the benefits from its exercise.

In Western Europe the rising power of the centralized monarchies had been rooted in the rise of trade; the growth of state power had proceeded almost *pari passu* with the growing wealth and influence of the bourgeoisie; even before the great revolutions of the seventeenth and eighteenth centuries, this new class was able, by virtue of its economic independence, to set limits to the growth of the power of even the most absolute monarchs. In Russia, at the time of the violent birth of the autocracy, there was virtually no bourgeoisie. The bulk of the traders and artisans were of extremely petty stature, a mob able occasionally to exert some pressure—as after the Moscow fires which in 1547 destroyed the Kitai Gorod (the walled traders' quarter along the Red Square) and later swept through the Kremlin itself. Yet such riots of petty townsmen could have no more effect than to serve the manipulations of the great and powerful. The emergence of a special class of capitalist merchants, the *gosti*—bitterly hated by the townspeople in general—was chiefly the work of the state itself, which employed them as its subordinate agents.

A special factor tending to keep Muscovite commerce and industry as dependent on the state as were the mass of the military-serving nobility was the direct pressure exerted by the nascent capitalism of the West. The English had been welcomed when they first found their way to the mouth of the Dvina and had been showered with special trading privileges, without having to pay tariffs, throughout the Muscovite realm; they were accorded the special honor of being taken into the *oprichnina*. Angered by Elizabeth's evasive response to his political proposals, Ivan soon put the English merchants under his ban. Although he speedily restored their franchise (1572), Ivan imposed a 50 percent duty. Moreover, he persisted in encouraging the trade of Narva so long as he was able to retain that Baltic port. When he lost Narva to the Swedes (1581), Ivan decided to encourage the trade of

England's competitors—especially the Dutch—by the northern route. He therefore ordered the transfer of all foreign trading establishments to the new town of Archangel.

The old jealousy of foreigners and desire for maximum gain to the tsar's treasury continued to operate against the free development of commercial relations with the West and at the same time indirectly to promote the rise of the importance of the *gosti*. A new charter to the English (1584) withheld even from them the right—never accorded to their competitors—to engage in retail trade. The prohibition was of course evaded in all sorts of ways, but the Muscovite government strove hard to prevent free intercourse with the foreigners. They were forbidden to operate save at specific points, and the commodities they were most interested in were declared state monopolies. Thus early, to cope with foreign capital, Russia embarked on an effort to establish a regime of controlled—if not planned—economy in the sphere of trade.

Dread of foreigners did not prevent Ivan from inviting to Russia considerable numbers of foreign specialists, a tendency which evoked much criticism in wide circles. Ivan sought the most advanced military techniques and encouraged also the settlement of civilian artisans. He was particularly fond of German doctors, whence many thought he suffered "injury to his soul, and bodily harm," putting his head "into the mouth of the asp." [18]

SUMMARY

No amount of selected borrowings from the more advanced West could enable Russia to overcome the time lag in her development. The striking fact that Russia laid the foundations of absolute monarchy almost simultaneously with Valois France and Tudor England did not mean that she had found a short cut to overtake the rest of Europe. Nor did it at all mean that, after centuries of lapse and by some mystical process, she had reverted to "Oriental" Byzantine tradition. Russia had begun her history centuries before with much the same human and institutional equipment as had the West. In the course of her history, however, she had not simply passed through the same evolution as had the West, but had struck out on unfamiliar paths, a divergence from the historical pattern developed in the West that was to have lasting and far-reaching significance.

Absolute monarchy in Russia bore no inner relation to Byzantinism or to Mongol-Tatar despotism. It was more closely akin to the contemporary national monarchies of the West but with the vital distinction that it rested on a wholly different socio-economic basis. In the West, by the sixteenth century, the rising economic power of the bourgeoisie, though not as yet expressed in acquisition of a major share of political power, had enabled the ruler to liquefy and mobilize his revenues and to dispense with the services of a landed nobility; it had been attended also by the dissolution of serfdom.

In Russia, peculiar features of geography—a huge, almost level, plain, knit together by a mesh of natural river-roads—had been a principal factor in permitting political unification in the hands of a single prince while the economy remained at a "sustenance" level. At the corresponding stage of its economic history, some three or four centuries earlier, the West had witnessed the successful struggle of its principal kings to beat down the political independence of the most powerful feudal lords by allying themselves with the lesser nobility and with the Church. It was essentially this earlier process which in Russia culminated in the reign of Ivan the Terrible.

Imposing as was the power of the Russian monarch, it was a power that rested on the active support, as well as the submission, of the lesser landed nobility; it entailed the consolidation of serfdom and impeded, rather than promoted, the development of the bourgeois relationships so characteristic of the West. The further course of Russian history, for some centuries, was therefore to center around the dual fact of tsarist absolutism and of noble power over the serf. Before the new relationships could become stabilized, the struggle between the old order and the new gave rise to violent convulsions.

NOTES

1. Bond (ed.), *Russia at the Close of the Sixteenth Century,* p. 195.
2. Kurbskii, *Istoriia o velikom kniazie Moskovskom,* pp. 1-2, 166 (see also pp. 125, 135, 138, 160).
3. *Polnoe sobranie russkikh lietopisei,* VIII, 295 (Voskresenskii chronicle).
4. Fennell, J. L. I. (ed.), *The Correspondence Between Prince A. M. Kurbsky and Tsar Ivan IV of Russia, 1564-1579,* p. 84.
5. Silvester, *Domostroi* (Glazunov edition), pp. 67, 27.
6. Zimin and Likhachev (eds.), *Sochineniia I. S. Peresvetova.* The several quotations are from pp. 148-181 *passim.*
7. *Ibid.,* pp. 182-183.
8. George Tolstoy, *The First Forty Years of Intercourse Between England and Russia, 1553-1593,* p. 30.
9. *Polnoe sobranie russkikh lietopisei,* Vol. XIII, Part II, p. 392 (supplement to Nikonovskii chronicle).
10. Kliuchevskii, *Kurs russkoi istorii,* 3rd edition, II, 215.
11. Zimin and Likhachev, *op. cit.,* p. 153.
12. Fennell, *op. cit.,* p. 36.
13. *Polnoe sobranie russkikh lietopisei,* XIII, 444 (so-called Royal Book).
14. *"Tetrad'"* . . . in *Chteniia,* 1859, III, v (*Smies*), pp. 89-100 *passim.*
15. Bond, *op. cit.,* p. 208.
16. *"Vremennik d'iaka Ivana Timofeeva,"* in *Pamiatniki drevnei russkoi pis'mennosti otnosiaschchiesia k smutnomu vremeni,* 3rd edition, Vol. XIII, Part I, p. 271.

17. Platonov, *Ivan Groznyi,* p. 134.
18. "*Vremennik . . . ,*" *loc. cit.*, pp. 271-272.

SUGGESTIONS FOR FURTHER READING

For general accounts and narratives, see the suggestions for Chapters 1 and 6. The best studies of the sixteenth and seventeenth centuries, by Platonov, have not been translated into English. Among biographies of Ivan in English, one of the most readable is the translation of that by Waliszewski, an excellent raconteur. For a Stalinist interpretation, see the English translation of Vipper, *Ivan Grozny.* A. K. Tolstoi's historical novel, *Kniaz Serebrianyi* (translated as *A Prince of Outlaws*), should be read for fictional color. Fennell's *Correspondence between Prince A. M. Kurbsky and Tsar Ivan IV of Russia, 1564-1579* and his *Prince A. M. Kurbsky's History of Ivan IV* are very valuable as source material.

Very useful contemporary accounts by English observers are: (1) the report of Queen Elizabeth's envoy, Dr. Giles Fletcher, who visited Moscow in 1591; (2) the memoirs of Sir Jerome Horsey, long an agent of the Muscovy Company; and (3) the detailed account of the travels of Anthony Jenkinson (the first two were edited by Sir E. H. Bond as *Russia at the Close of the Sixteenth Century,* the third will be found in the Bibliography as Jenkinson, *Early Voyages and Travels to Russia and Persia*). Staden, *The Land and Government of Muscovy,* is a somewhat unreliable account of a German *oprichnik.*

Among modern studies of English activities in Russia are Sir William Foster's *England's Quest of Eastern Trade,* George Tolstoy's *First Forty Years of Intercourse Between England and Russia,* and Thomas S. Willan's *Early History of the Russia Company, 1553-1603.*

Chapter

8

Boris Godunov and the Troubles: 1584-1613

THE HERITAGE OF THE *OPRICHNINA*

Queen Elizabeth's ambassador, Dr. Giles Fletcher, visited Moscow five years after the death of Ivan the Terrible. His report is extraordinarily well-informed and coincides amazingly well with the extant documentary evidence as to conditions in Muscovy toward the end of the sixteenth century and as to then current political trends. It was his opinion that

> this wicked pollicy and tyrannous practise . . . hath so troubled that countrey, and filled it so full of grudge and mortall hatred ever since, that it will not be quenched (as it seemeth now) till it burne againe into a civill flame.[1]

If realization of his prophecy was delayed a few years, it speaks highly for the statesmanlike qualities of Ivan's successor, Boris Godunov, so often represented as a cruel and conniving murderer or—through the medium of poetry and music—as a sort of Russian Macbeth.

Ivan the Terrible died suddenly on March 18, 1584. He had succeeded in his immediate objective of freeing himself from the control of the boyars, who had been the colleagues of the grand princes in the building of the Muscovite state. He had not succeeded in freeing himself from his own panic terror and narcissistic hatred directed against those who did not appreciate him—the factors that had motivated his revolutionary experiment, the *oprichnina*. Nor had he succeeded in establishing a well-ordered state. On the contrary, he had destroyed the old collaborative functioning of the boyar aristocracy and had developed in its stead only a group of toadying assistants, most of whom could think of nothing but palace intrigue and conspiracy as a means of enhancing their personal fortunes. By contributing to the ruin and depopulation of the central provinces, he had undermined the fiscal and military strength of the state. At no time, not even as an immediate aftermath of the Mongol conquest, had the future of the Russian land looked so black.

The imminent crisis was all the more threatening by reason of the extinction of the dynasty. The only functioning institution Ivan bequeathed was the nascent autocracy, and autocracy requires a person capable of wielding it. Ivan had himself slain his own eldest son and heir. There remained a younger son by Anastasia Romanovna, Fedor, then twenty-seven years of age. Yet Fedor was obviously weak-minded; he was noted for his piety, but clearly incompetent to rule. There was one other son, the two-year-old Dmitry, child of Ivan's seventh wife and therefore canonically ineligible to succeed. The possibility could not, however, be excluded that some powerful personage might attempt to use the infant as a lever to establish his own authority over the state. The widow was therefore promptly packed off—and Dmitry with her—to Uglich, a remote provincial town. The only remaining problem was: who was to guide Tsar Fedor?

Most of the old princely families of the stock of Rurik and Gedimin, who had been the chief target of the *oprichnina,* were extinct or broken. Those who survived, like the Princes Shuisky, had done so only because they had tamely submitted to Ivan's will; they were not able—though they were willing—immediately to resume their old primacy. First place among the "princes" now belonged to Prince Ivan Mstislavsky, but principally for the collateral reason that he was a grandson of the sister of Vasily III. Among old families, as among new ones, the ascendancy had passed to those who could claim kinship with the dynasty.

Palace position, rather than ancient lineage, had become decisive. Fortunately for Russia—though only temporarily—the two closest kinsmen of the new tsar were mutually friendly. One of them, Nikita Romanov, Tsar Fedor's maternal uncle, was dying; the other, Boris Godunov, was left to lead the field. Sprung from a family of Tatar origin which since early in the fourteenth century had been in the service of the princes of Moscow, Boris Godunov owed his position largely to two fortunate marriages: his own to the daughter of Maliuta Skuratov, one of the most notorious of the *oprichniki;* and that of his sister Irene to Ivan's son Fedor, the new tsar.

It was a most unlikely source from which to expect a desirable ruler. Yet Boris soon proved his worth. Skillfully outmaneuvering his rivals, who sought to rouse to mob action the townspeople whose trading booths lined the Red Square, Boris avoided executions of his peers and was content to banish his opponents from the capital. Ivan's special regime lapsed, and Boris quietly ruled the whole realm through the boyar duma, now largely filled, however, with new men. The work of the *oprichnina* was not undone. The eminent boyars, who had ruled their hereditary estates and claimed to share the central power with the tsar, never recovered their traditional position. If Napoleon was the "Son of the Revolution," Boris was the heir of the *oprichnina.*

In 1584, Prince Belsky, personal favorite of Ivan the Terrible and closely connected with young Dmitry's mother's family, had been involved in the street disturbances at Moscow; he was banished to the provinces, but in a position of high local authority. In 1587, Mstislavsky and the senior members of the Shuisky family attempted to arouse the Moscow mob in support of a demand for the divorce of Tsar Fedor, for, despite the importation from England in 1586 of a skilled obstetrician, Boris' sister had not yet succeeded in giving birth to an heir to the throne. The riots were quelled, and the leading "princes" were exiled from Moscow. Boris' position seemed impregnable.

Gradually his role was elevated from that of the tsar's brother-in-law to that of actual regent (as early as 1586 the English referred to him as "Lord Protector of Russia"). Though he amassed vast wealth in the process, he impressed all by his constant readiness to share his possessions with the poor and the needy. Of these there was abundance, for the heir of Ivan the Terrible inherited a severe economic crisis. Lack of money—and lack of men—had constrained Ivan to accept truces with Sweden (1583) and with Poland (1582). The "human sea" with which Muscovy had won its victories in the early part of the long Livonian War (1558-83) had ebbed; the peasant tide flowed off to the border provinces to the south and east, where it was not easily controlled by the state.

It was now not Moscow, the third Rome, that threatened the West, but the West that threatened to engulf all Russia if the war should break out again. The victorious king of Poland, Stephan Báthory, meditated the overthrow of the infidel Turks and, as a first step, the subjection of Russia in order to permit of a comprehensive encircling movement by way of Persia and Asia Minor against Constantinople. Through the Jesuit, Possevinus, Báthory won the blessing of the pope. However, by skillful diplomacy, taking advantage of the resistance of the Polish nobility to any strong ruler, the Muscovites secured extensions of the truce until after Báthory's death in 1586. They failed in an ambitious countermove to secure the election of Tsar Fedor as Báthory's successor; a Swedish prince was chosen to succeed as King Sigismund of Poland (1587), but the truce was extended for fifteen years. Sweden itself was a less formidable enemy, and after brief and intermittent fighting (1590-1593) was persuaded to restore to Moscow (1595) that small portion of the coastline, except Narva, which had of old belonged to Novgorod. In relations with the Holy Roman Emperor, who desired Moscow's aid against both the Poles and the Turks, Boris' government was careful to insist on full recognition of the parity of the "dear and loving brothers," the Moscow tsar and the Roman Kaiser.

Thus Boris' regime from the outset redressed the balance disturbed by Ivan's defeat and gave promise of early resumption of Russian expansion. Platonov, the chief student of the period, wrote:

> After surviving a series of grievous military and diplomatic failures, after losing the conquests of many years, weakened by internal disorders, the Moscow government did not lose its vigor of spirit and its will power. It showed itself ready for a new struggle immediately on the conclusion of the old one; it vigilantly watched and rightly appraised the domestic difficulties of its neighbors and well understood when to give way and when it was permissible to strike the enemy. Unable to convert its healthy instinct and keen sagacity into a norm and a principle, it nevertheless was firm and perseverant in its methods and actions, and thanks to its unique suspicious caution did not permit anyone to make game of it.[2]

To the south and east, also, Moscow continued to make advances. The last serious attack of the Crimean Tatars on Moscow occurred in 1591 and was seriously punished, the khan escaping with only a third of his forces. The line of fortified posts which were making the open steppe habitable for agriculturists was pushed steadily southward into the "wild field" and southeastward down the Volga, where a number of strong fortresses, including Tsaritsyn (later Stalingrad), were established. Remnants of the Tatars, such as the Nogais, were forced to submit, and from Astrakhan Russian power began to reach out toward the Caucasus, whence it was to be thrown back disastrously in the Time of the Troubles (1605). More permanent was the penetration of Siberia. In the last years of Ivan, a cossack, Yermak, in the employ of the Stroganovs, had overthrown the Tatar khanate of Sibir in a raiding expedition, but by 1584 Yermak had been killed and his followers expelled. Boris acted vigorously, sending an army in 1586 which established fortresses at Tiumen and Tobolsk. In succeeding years Moscow's authority was extended steadily eastward from the Ob toward the Yenisei; Tomsk was established in 1604.

To these successes abroad corresponded what was to the Orthodox an even more resounding triumph, the elevation of the Moscow metropolitan to the rank of patriarch. Since the fall of Constantinople in 1453, the Russian Church had had almost no relations with Greek Orthodoxy save through the secular authorities. Yet the idea of the importance of the patriarchs had survived. It was a cause of concern that the coronation of Ivan as tsar in 1547 had not been performed by an ecclesiastic of the highest rank. Despite its confirmation in writing by the Ecumenical Patriarch in 1561, there remained a blemish on the position of Moscow as the third and final Rome. Taking advantage of the visit to Moscow of the patriarch of Antioch in 1586—the first time any one of the four Orthodox patriarchs had ever visited Rus—Boris opened negotiations for the recognition of Moscow as an additional patriarchate. Although they were dependent on Moscow for financial favors and for friendly representations to the sultan in their behalf, the Eastern patriarchs were still unwilling to admit Moscow's claims. In 1588, however, an ill-advised visit by the Ecumenical Patriarch permitted Boris to hold him virtually as a hostage until, in a formal ceremony, he had consecrated the

Moscow metropolitan as patriarch and two archbishops as metropolitans (1589). His action was reluctantly confirmed by the four patriarchs.

Foreigners who had their own troubles at home were easier to deal with than were Moscow's own subjects. The survivors of the old boyar aristocracy were sulkily watching for an opportunity to overthrow Boris, and even among the new palace aristocracy there were envious rivals. Boris' political policy necessarily represented a continuation, though in infinitely milder form, of the purposes of the *oprichnina* in which he had grown to manhood. He did not continue the violent oppression that had characterized the rule of Ivan the Terrible and, to a lesser extent, of his immediate predecessors, but so far as possible he substituted "ill-born" men for members of the old families in positions of responsibility. As a Polish envoy reported in 1608, under Boris "it was hard for the boyars." [3]

Still more important, the socio-economic crisis showed no signs of abating. It was in the interest of the state to support by all possible means the interests of the lesser nobility and of the peasantry, who supplied it, the one with the bulk of its fighting forces, the other with the bulk of its revenues. Without further intervention of the state power, the position of these classes threatened to grow ever worse. Only the remaining wealthy landlords and the Church had the inherent economic strength to stabilize—even to improve—their situation. *Kabala* bondage therefore spread rapidly, especially with the development of "voluntary" servitude (bondage without formal indenture), which flourished under a variety of names and could be adapted equally well to agricultural labor or to all sorts of other service. The state thus lost taxpayers and even military servitors, who found protection under the wing of the rich, who alone could afford to assist them. At the same time, the monasteries engaged widely in the practice of receiving lands "on mortgage" from impoverished *dvoriane* to whom they gave economic assistance and who remained in actual possession of their lands, but without service obligations to the state.

Boris' efforts to deal with the crisis were not of course motivated by humanitarian desire to rescue the oppressed. Many of his contemporaries, and even of his enemies, have indeed testified to a kindly streak—with a firm belief in abstract justice—in his personal character, but considerations of state interest were necessarily paramount. In this aspect of his activity, however, Boris did not blindly continue the policies of Ivan but modified, without abandoning, the principle of the "forbidden years."

His major innovations were embodied in his famous decree of 1597, once interpreted as effecting the legal consolidation of serfdom. By this decree Boris ordered continuance of the practice of returning "fugitive peasants," after judicial action, "back where they lived," but only in case they had fled within the five years preceding their apprehension. If they had fled "six or seven or ten or more years" before they were caught, they were to be allowed to remain in their new homes unless suit for their recovery had been begun within a five-year period.[4] This statute of limitations was to become a sore point with the service nobility, who naturally showed a strong preference for an unrestricted right of recapture of "free" peasants who had fled from their estates.

More to the liking of the *dvoriane* was the permission given to them, but not to the large landholders, to take peasants at the usual time (a two-week period around St. George's Day) from other landholders. This right, granted in 1601 and 1602, was, however, strictly limited to "one peasant or two, but three or four no one may take from another." [5] The state, in the interest of the stability of tax payments, would clearly have preferred to bind all peasants to their established place of residence but was unwilling simply to abolish the legal fiction of their freedom, on which the tax obligation rested. It was content, therefore, by an arbitrary and presumably temporary decree to "forbid" peasants to exercise their legal right save under conditions favorable to the small landholders whose military service it needed.

Toward bondsmen it took a more definite position. In 1586 Boris ordered that all future *kabala* agreements must be registered. A decree of 1597 ordered a general registration of such indentures. At the same time it abolished "voluntary" servitude: all who had been giving "free" service for six months or more were to be inscribed as bondsmen (*kholopy*); the others were to go free. *Kabala* servitude was no longer to be redeemable during the lifetime of the master, though it was to lose all effect on his death. The chief interest of the state was in the stability of economic relationships.

For this reason Boris took a very hostile attitude toward the cossacks. Unable to control them in their abodes beyond the fortified frontier, he strictly forbade relationships between them and his more amenable subjects. These "brigands" were not to be permitted to enter the confines of Muscovy, "and buying and selling is everywhere forbidden." [6] As the area under the control of the state pushed ever farther southward, he set aside portions of the arable to be worked by the local population, whatever their former status, for the benefit of local state granaries. For obvious reasons, however, the power of the state was weaker the nearer one approached to the frontier (*ukraine*), and serfdom could not develop in the "wild field" as fully as in the old settled area of the central provinces. A special problem in frontier organization was created by the habit of Ivan the Terrible, continued under Boris, of exiling politically unreliable persons to this ever-disturbed area. The southern provinces, where large landholding on the basis of peasant labor had not yet had time to develop, were for all these reasons continually in a state of ferment, with a considerable movement back and forth between state service and free cossackdom.

Boris' care for the interests of the state found expression not only in measures for the protection of the smaller landholder against the wiles of the greater but also in his treatment of ecclesiastical landholding. The new patriarch remained a firm friend of his patron, and Boris' support of the

Church was constant; he even restored to the Church the tax exemption of which Ivan, in his last years, had deprived it. Yet he forbade the practice of taking lands "on mortgage" as injurious to the military strength of the state, and carried through a careful revision of ecclesiastical land titles, resuming for the state many properties illegally acquired by the Church. Nor did he permit the monasteries and the prelates to take peasants from the estates of other landholders.

Platonov, the outstanding student of sixteenth- and seventeenth-century Russia, concluded that "Boris did not serve any private or class interest." He modified this judgment by the further opinion that "he acted in favor of the middle classes of Muscovite society and against the aristocracy and the peasant masses," whose combined action was responsible for "the tragedy of Boris." By "middle classes" must be here understood, not the bourgeoisie, but the general run of *dvoriane* and "sons of boyars," with whose interests, as the class chiefly owing military service, the interests of the state most closely coincided. Actually, no great love was lost between the service nobility and Boris; Platonov also remarks: "Of the serving men he demanded service in full measure and watched lest their land exceed their service as strictly as ever did the Muscovite authorities." [7]

If Boris ever erred as a *Realpolitiker,* it was on the side of the poor and needy, a trait which earned him the sobriquet of "bright-souled." In 1601-03, Russia suffered from one of her most severe famines, allegedly reducing some of her people to cannibalism; speculation in grain was rife, and landholders were often tempted to set adrift their bondsmen, expecting to reclaim their services when there were once more harvests to be reaped; Boris issued a series of stringent decrees against speculators, forbade the recovery of peasants turned loose to shift for themselves, and furnished a considerable amount of famine relief from his own funds. It was a far cry from Ivan's method of dealing with destitution as recorded by Jerome Horsey. There was reason—at least by the standards of those times—why the peasantry "looked upon him as upon God" and were glad to "act uprightly" and serve him. Unfortunately for Boris and for Russia, the peasantry could not muster the organized strength necessary in time of crisis to uphold his "just and firm rule," his "perceptive intelligence and justice," which even hostile contemporaries recognized. Boris' policy could not prevent much peasant unrest, manifested in a long series of local disturbances, involving acts of resistance, including murder and other forms of violence, against landlords. The most serious outbreak, widespread in the central provinces, was the revolt in 1603, headed by Khlopko, which was suppressed only with great difficulty.

Throughout his reign, both as regent and later as tsar, Boris was a great builder, both of fortresses and of churches. He encompassed the suburbs of Moscow with a whitewashed brick wall (hence the "White City"), fortified Astrakhan and many towns in the *ukraine,* and—a measure soon to prove its value—strengthened Smolensk. He rebuilt the old trading quarter of Moscow (the "Kitai Gorod") of brick, erected the Kremlin bell tower "named Ivan the Great" and many other edifices. Much of this building activity was undertaken to provide employment in times of stress—a forerunner of "public works programs." At the same time he managed to effect tax reduction (which entailed, however, increased reliance on indirect imposts), to reinstate immunities, and to stimulate trade, so that, despite the unkindness of nature in 1601 and 1602, Muscovy knew a brief and unparalleled period of tranquillity and prosperity.

A respect in which Boris, to the chagrin of many of his subjects, continued the interests of Ivan—and anticipated what is often attributed wholly to Peter—was his promotion of European influences on Russia.

> Boris dreamed of introducing into Russia European schools (even, perhaps, a university); he ordered scholars sought out abroad and brought to Moscow; he showed exceptional favor to those foreigners who from need or free will chanced to enter Moscow's service, whether for industry or with the purpose of trade; he conversed much and frequently with his foreign physicians; he ordered the construction of a Lutheran church in one of Moscow's suburbs; finally, he earnestly [though futilely] desired to give his daughter Xenia in marriage to some reigning European prince.[8]

His boldest experiment was to send abroad a number of young nobles to study in England, France, and Germany; as luck would have it, none of them returned. (One of them became an Anglican clergyman; he lost his parish during the "Puritan Revolution.") Despite the best efforts of Moscow's diplomats, no foreign country was willing to extradite these students.

THE SUCCESSION CRISIS

So long as Tsar Fedor lived, Boris' unprecedented power was secure. With the death of Fedor in January, 1598, everything became uncertain. Fedor's only child, Feodosia, had died as an infant in 1594. His brother Dmitry, Ivan's child by "his unlawful, his seventh wife," had been reported dead at Uglich in 1591. With Fedor's death the dynasty of Rurik—or its ruling branch—was extinct. It was a situation that might well have shaken a better ordered state than existed in Russia. A temporary solution of the crisis was arrived at in a way that can only be guessed at, for the violent partisanship of contemporaries hampers agreement on essential facts, much more on their interpretation. The most fantastic legends, ramifying with the years, became hallowed by repetition and even received the permanent blessing of the Church.

According to the original official version, which itself is of course also partisan, Boris promptly ordered the boyars, in the presence of the patriarch and his council, to take oath to his sister Irene, Fedor's widow. Unprecedented as it was for a woman to sit on the throne of Moscow, there was much justification in the equally unprecedented fact that she had in her husband's lifetime sat regularly with him in council, dealing with domestic, foreign, and even ecclesiastical questions. The ailing Irene, however, promptly renounced the throne and entered a convent. The patriarch, taking temporary charge of affairs much as Metropolitan Alexis had done on the accession of Dmitry Donskoy, summoned a zemsky sobor to "elect" a tsar.

Despite later bitter accusations against this "comedy," it has been established by the painstaking work of Professor Kliuchevsky that this zemsky sobor was perfectly normal and regular in its composition and functioning. As in 1566, the members were not elected to sit in the sobor; in this case, however, the leading members of the lesser estates (military servitors and merchantry) were men who had been elected to perform local services for the government in the towns and provinces. Sitting with the older elements (high clergy and boyars) with whom the ruler traditionally consulted, they could be considered "representative" of all the land. On the nomination of the patriarch, Boris was unanimously "elected," the malcontent boyars finding it prudent to hold their tongues. Even so, according to the official version, Boris was reluctant, ultimately yielding only to the prayers and threats of the clergy and the urgings of the mass of "simple people" who thronged to his cell in the Novodevichy Monastery.

This version undoubtedly obscures skillful maneuvering by the regent to seat himself on the throne with a minimum of difficulty in the face of a number of ambitious and powerful rivals, for the extinction of the traditional dynasty obviously opened the road "to the talents." The government had attempted to throw a curtain of secrecy around Russia, closing the frontiers and imposing a careful watch over all foreigners. Yet a Lithuanian border governor, Andrew Sapieha, managed to gather much information through spies. According to their reports, the leading contender for the throne was Fedor Nikitich Romanov, nephew of Ivan's "heifer" and therefore first cousin of Tsar Fedor; Sapieha was somewhat surprised at the victory of Boris, "for he is not of high birth." [9] From Sapieha's spies it further appears that, in the event he could not win the throne for himself, Boris was prepared to put forward an impostor, pretending that he was Dmitry, youngest child of Ivan the Terrible. In the light of later events, this is decidedly paradoxical, for Boris' undoing was to come precisely from a "False Dmitry." Officially—and probably—Dmitry had died in 1591 of a self-inflicted injury during an epileptic seizure. The riot (*pogrom*) at Uglich incited by his hysterical mother had led to official investigations, first by an ecclesiastical inquiry, later by a commission of boyars headed by Prince Vasily Shuisky, and their reports seemed conclusive.

Apparently, even after the oath had been taken to Boris, his rivals continued to plot to cheat him of his victory, seeking to drag from obscurity the baptized Tatar, Semen Bekbulatovich, whom Ivan had briefly seated on the tsar's throne. Semen was now old and blind, without power or ambition, but still a possible figurehead to oppose to Boris. This, at least, seems the only possible explanation of the curious fact that Boris insisted on the taking of a second oath, with the specific promise not to "wish" Semen or his children as tsar.

On the throne Boris found himself in a very fluid and slippery situation. Against him were now arrayed not only the old boyar aristocracy which Ivan had combated but also the new palace aristocracy that Ivan had raised up. In his uncertainty Boris soon returned to some extent to the practices of the *oprichnina.* Relying heavily on informers—contemporaries were most shocked by a case in which a bondsman (*kholop*) was rewarded "with land and freedom," becoming a "son of a boyar"—the "slave tsar" belatedly struck down a number of leading figures and their aristocratic satellites, usually on charges of "witchcraft." In 1600 he ordered the arrest and exile of Bogdan Belsky, who on Ivan's death in 1584 had seized the Kremlin in an effort to induce the new tsar to restore the *oprichnina.* Indeed, Belsky had, on Fedor's death in 1598, appeared at Moscow with a formidable following of retainers, doubtless with the thought of seizing the throne by a coup, and he was now lording it as viceroy in the ukraine, reputedly saying that at Moscow Boris was tsar but that at Tsarevo-Borisovo he, Bogdan, was tsar.

About the same time Boris banished from Moscow the Shuiskys and other leading persons; among them were the Nikitichi (as the Romanovs were then known) and a number of their highborn kinsmen, who were sent to various remote parts of the country; the oldest of the five brothers, the Fedor Nikitich who had seemed so close to the throne in 1598, was given the tonsure under the name of Philaret and immured in a northern monastery. Three of the brothers died in their prisons, perhaps not without the assistance of their jailers, but Boris himself displayed none of Ivan's savage ferocity. Ivan Nikitich and Prince Vasily Shuisky were allowed to return to service in the capital in Boris' lifetime; Belsky survived to hold high office under his successor. Boris' chief rival, Fedor Nikitich, under his monastic name of Philaret, later became patriarch and was associated as co-tsar with his son Michael, whose election in 1613 was to bring the Time of the Troubles officially to an end.

All Boris' efforts, however—whether his "just and firm rule" and his labors to restore the ruined economy of Muscovy or his efforts by highhanded action to strike down his personal foes—were of no avail in averting the Time of the Troubles, a worse disaster for Russia than the Thirty Years' War was to be for Germany. The situation was complicated by the extremely severe famine of 1601-03, already referred to, which put a heavy drain, almost as great as that of a war, on the financial resources of the state. Even before the famine, however, and apparently before Boris' belated action against the Nikitichi, ominous rumors were current that the "Tsarevich Dmitry" was actually alive, and in Poland.

By 1603 the rumors were given countenance by the Polish government.

Boris replied by denouncing the pretender—probably correctly—as an apostate Russian monk, Gregory Otrepiev, who had been brought up under the patronage of the Nikitichi. In 1604 the pretender, who under Jesuit influences in Poland had accepted Roman Catholicism, left Kiev with less than four thousand adventurous followers, both Polish and Russian, and crossed into the Russian *ukraine*. That inflammable area, thronged with political exiles and with refugees from the economic crisis in the central provinces, was filled also with resentment against Boris' attempts to organize it in the service of the state. The local military servitors, required to supply labor for the state granaries, made common cause with the free cossacks, whom Boris had been striving to reduce to regular service. The whole *ukraine* flared up in revolt; thousands of cossacks joined "Dmitry's" forces, while one fortress garrison after another declared itself for him, and independently led forces struck northward against Moscow.

Thus what had begun as an intrigue of one faction of palace favorites against another suddenly took on the proportions of a great socio-political movement, threatening to reinstate in full force, under the alleged son of Ivan the Terrible, the regime of that dreaded despot. The princely boyar aristocracy—Mstislavskys, Shuiskys, Golitsyns—who had no more to hope from a Romanov version of a restored *oprichnina* than from Godunov, at first served faithfully against the uprising; under boyar leadership Boris' armies checked the pretender's advance and almost captured him.

The death of Boris (April 13, 1605), who although only fifty-three had for some years been suffering from heart trouble, removed the strong rallying point of the loyal forces and also tempted the boyars with the thought of turning the succession in their favor. The Princes Golitsyn, commanding in the field, promptly went over to "Dmitry," easily carrying with them an army exhausted and discouraged by the hardships of a winter campaign. One of them, the renowned Prince V. V. Golitsyn, personally supervised the murder of Boris' widow and son. Prince Vasily Shuisky, who had been recalled to Moscow, produced a new version of the affair at Uglich in 1591. After Boris' death, but before the defection of the army, he announced that Dmitry had not died by accident fourteen years before but had been murdered by agents sent for the purpose by Godunov. In public he asserted that the pretender was an impostor, but apparently privately confirmed the widespread popular belief that the murderers had killed the wrong child, and that the alleged Dmitry was really the tsarevich. Prince Belsky turned up in enthusiastic support of the son of Ivan the Terrible. Ivan's widow was brought back to Moscow to receive with joy her long-lost son, who entered Moscow on June 30, 1605.

"Dmitry," triumphantly installed on the Kremlin throne, promptly distributed all available funds with a lavish hand. The general orgy of spending was at first not unwelcome to the Moscow townsmen, but the nature of the new tsar's most active supporters had its unpleasant side. Undisciplined cossacks and fortune-hunting Poles thronged the streets, and no man's property was safe. Especially to the old feudal aristocracy, who had resented Boris' regime as essentially a continuation of Ivan's autocratic policy, the accession of "Dmitry" was unacceptable. He gathered around him that portion of the new court aristocracy that had quarreled with Boris—the surviving Romanovs, Belsky, and lesser creatures of the *oprichnina;* he banished the Shuiskys and ignored the other "princes," even the Golitsyns. The Shuiskys, allowed to return to Moscow, made common cause with the Golitsyns in opening secret negotiations with King Sigismund of Poland, suggesting that they would support the candidacy of his son Vladislav (Wladyslaw or Ladislas) for the throne of Moscow.

Ideologically, too, "Dmitry's" Jesuit sympathies and his marriage at Moscow to a Polish bride, Marina Mniszek, outraged Orthodox susceptibilities. The jubilant "Dmitry" made a further blunder, to the delight of his followers from the *ukraine* but to the consternation of the more staid *dvoriane* of the central provinces; he deliberately sent to the Moslem khan of the Crimea the present of a pigskin. The indignant khan set his forces in motion, and the new regime was embarked on a difficult war, entailing severe hardships on the *dvoriane* and "sons of boyars" of the old portion of the state, for whom expansion in the steppe threatened only increased difficulty in restraining the flow of their peasants to the more fertile "black earth."

It was not difficult for the boyars, nursing their ancient grudges against Ivan, to organize fresh conspiracies. On May 27, 1606, less than a year after "Dmitry's" triumphant accession, he was murdered by the mob, and his body dragged through the streets. Taking advantage of the confusion, Prince Vasily Shuisky, the most supple and quick-witted survivor of the boyar aristocracy, organized a riotous parody of a zemsky sobor, which hailed him as tsar. His fellow boyars, however jealous of his sudden ascendancy, had to be content with vague promises that he would share power with them. Maria Nagaia, Ivan's widow, repudiated her recognition of "Dmitry." Tsar Vasily recurred to one of his earlier versions of what had happened at Uglich, asserting positively that Boris had sent murderers and that they had carried out their mission successfully. To strengthen this story, he caused the real Dmitry's remains (though there was much difficulty in finding suitable ones at Uglich) to be ceremonially brought to Moscow. Like Boris and Gleb, the murdered sons of St. Vladimir, the martyred Dmitry was canonized, thus making it forever after impossible for any dutiful son of the Church—and for the Church itself—to admit any serious doubt of what had actually transpired in 1591.

To consolidate his position at Moscow was not difficult for Vasily Shuisky, whose forebears had had primacy among all the descendants of Rurik who had entered Moscow's service. To the boyars, Vasily's accession seemed to promise some hope of an oligarchic reaction, a real restoration of the old order as it had existed before the *oprichnina*. To be sure, individual ambitions and rivalries continued, as of old, to divide the boyars, and Shuisky therefore could not weld them into a body of solid supporters of his authority. The Moscow mob had strong economic reasons to remain quiet, for Shuisky, the *shubnik* ("fur-coat maker"), gave many of them employment, but its active share in overthrowing both the Godunovs and "Dmitry" had given it a taste for riotous exertion of its power; the mob continued to be a restless threat to the stability of any regime.

Somewhat more reliable, rather paradoxically, were the *dvoriane* and "sons of boyars" in the central provinces, which had formerly been part of the *oprichnina*. It might have been expected that they would have rallied to the support of tsars who continued in the tradition of Ivan the Terrible, refusing to accept the oligarchic reaction headed by Shuisky. Yet the fact that they were unaccustomed to take the initiative, that the benefits they had derived from Ivan and from Boris had been the gifts of autocratic leadership, tended to leave them passive under Shuisky's regime. Nor did they share the aggressive desires of the dwellers in the *ukraine*. The trading towns of the north and along the Volga, interested mainly in the maintenance of order, also accepted the new tsar.

Yet Vasily was unable to secure general submission. The *ukraine* immediately rejected him, and within a few months Bolotnikov, a former household bondsman who had been captured by the Tatars and sold into galley slavery, from which he had escaped to Venice, was leading a new army from Kaluga to the gates of the capital. The elements that made up his forces were basically the same as those which had supported "Dmitry" in 1604-05 and avowedly were acting in his support, for it was alleged that he had again miraculously survived. Yet in the absence of a physical dynastic symbol, since no fresh impersonator had appeared, the rebels were more prone to think of their own interests instead of being content blindly to support an abstract concept.

SOCIAL REVOLT AND POLISH INTERVENTION

With Bolotnikov's revolt, the Troubles therefore entered a new phase, for he preached not merely a change of ruler but a general uprising of bondsmen against their masters. His was not, of course, an attempt at social revolution in the nineteenth- and twentieth-century sense. The objective was not to reconstruct the social system on a new basis but to turn its personnel upside down, simply reversing the position of lord and serf. Yet it had significance as the first of a long series of elemental, haphazardly organized peasant revolts, which, when linked with the rise of capitalistic industry, were ultimately—three centuries later—to complete the ruin of autocracy and aristocracy alike.

At this stage, however, a number of landlords—including Bolotnikov's former master, Prince Teliatevsky—were not above serving in the rebel forces. Along with cossacks and fugitive peasants were organized forces of *dvoriane* and "sons of boyars." The latter groups, however, were animated not by ideas of social revolution but by desire to preserve the existing order against the aristocratic reaction. When, under the walls of Moscow, they became convinced that their comrades-in-arms actually constituted a graver threat to the social order than did the boyar tsar, they subordinated their political hostility to him to their socio-economic fear of Bolotnikov and made their peace with the forces of law and order. Bolotnikov was defeated in battle and driven back to Tula, where in the following year he was captured by the tsar's forces. The execution of Bolotnikov and his chief associates (1608) did not, however, signify the restoration of order.

It had been relatively easy to put an end to "Dmitry" as a person. It was not easy to put an end to him as an idea. Despite the public exhibition of the pretender's corpse at Moscow, a new impersonator appeared shortly before the surrender of Tula. Marina Mniszek, who had been allowed to go home to Poland, reappeared in the Russian *ukraine* and with open arms welcomed the Second False Dmitry as the very husband she had wed—and lost—in Moscow. Her testimony—and it ought to have been impregnable—was scarcely needed to rally the remnants of Bolotnikov's forces, the cossacks, the frontier service nobility, and the Polish free lances to his cause. The Poles, indeed, gave the Second False Dmitry more effective support than they had given the first. Refugees from an unsuccessful anti-royalist uprising in Poland—such as the dreaded Lisovski—and Polish aristocrats working in King Sigismund's interest—such as Ian Peter Sapieha—led well-trained cavalry, estimated to have reached the number of forty thousand; against such experienced warriors the disorderly and unreliable levies of Tsar Vasily Shuisky could make no headway.

By the summer of 1608, the new pretender had firmly established himself at Tushino, a village only a few miles from Moscow. Among his Russian followers were not only the anarchic forces of the *ukraine*. A considerable number of *dvoriane,* hostile to the "boyar tsar," now flocked to the standards of the new "Dmitry." High-placed patrons of the First False Dmitry also joined him. Philaret (Fedor Nikitich Romanov), who had been released from his monastery and promoted to high ecclesiastical office, was proclaimed patriarch at Tushino. Around the "brigand of Tushino" there thus developed a rival court, with its own tsar, patriarch, and boyar duma, paralleling and challenging the authority of Shuisky's government.

Under Polish leadership, detachments from Tushino ranged over all the central provinces, besieging even the holy—and well-fortified—monastery of Troitsa and receiving the submission of such leading towns on and beyond the upper Volga as Yaroslavl and Vologda. On the middle Volga, revolts broke out afresh, involving the subject Finnish and Tatar peoples as well as the Russian serfs and threatening even Nizhny Novgorod and Kazan. In despair Tsar Vasily accepted the aid of the Swedes (1609), ceding some territory in return for the dispatch of a small but efficient auxiliary force.

Fortunately for Shuisky, the local population of the upper Volga region reacted vigorously against the uninhibited plundering by the alien enemy. The local artisans, traders, and peasants, unassisted by mounted military-serving men, were of course no match for Polish cavalry in the field, but—assisted by money and volunteers from the remoter northern region—developed tactics of erecting temporary fortifications which enabled them to check the Polish offensive. Operating from Novgorod, the tsar's nephew, Prince Skopin-Shuisky, was enabled to utilize the successes of the northern townsmen and peasants and, recovering Yaroslavl, to launch a drive to relieve beleaguered Moscow. Meanwhile the boyar Sheremetev cleared the towns of the lower and middle Volga.

The intervention of Sweden and the successes of Skopin-Shuisky and Sheremetev, however, brought about a change in the attitude of Poland. King Sigismund, urged on by his Catholic advisers, now abandoned the policy of giving disguised support to Tushino. The royal army itself laid siege to Smolensk, so recently fortified by Boris Godunov. This move naturally was not welcomed by the Polish freebooters in the camp at Tushino, which was, however, increasingly torn by the conflicting social interests of the diverse Russian elements attracted thither. The "brigand" himself, who had been little better than a puppet in the hands of his Polish advisers, now feared that they might after all obey Sigismund's summons to join him before Smolensk. In December, 1609, he fled from Tushino to Bolotnikov's old headquarters at Kaluga, where he again rallied the lower orders of the population. Deprived of their symbol, the Russian *dvoriane* at Tushino, unable to make their peace with Shuisky on satisfactory terms, bethought themselves of the earlier mooted idea of asking Sigismund to allow his son Vladislav to ascend the throne of Moscow as an Orthodox tsar.

A deputation, headed by Michael Saltykov, sought out the Polish king in his camp under the walls of Smolensk. The result was an agreement in February, 1610, though Sigismund rejected several of the major conditions suggested by the self-constituted spokesmen of the Russian *dvoriane*.

In his version of the Treaty of Smolensk, Sigismund blandly ignored the proposal that Vladislav "adopt the Greek faith," but he unhesitatingly agreed that his son was to be "crowned at Moscow with the tsar's crown with the diadem by the hands of the patriarch of Moscow, according to former ceremony" (Article 1).[10] He promised also that "the Holy Orthodox faith of the Greek law and the Holy Apostolic Church shall retain their integrity and beauty and shall be inviolate in the learning and tradition of the apostolic and ecumenical teachers" (Article 2). At the same time, he inserted provisions that a Roman Catholic chapel should be established in Moscow and that Russians should be free to go abroad for study. He also added (Article 2) that no one should be converted "from the Greek faith to the Roman nor to any other . . . for faith is a gift of God, and it is not fitting to lead anyone to a faith by force or to compel them." To please the Russians, he agreed (in the same article) that "Jews shall not be permitted in the realm of Moscow for trade or for any business and shall be forbidden altogether."

An enumeration of the duties of the new ruler was summed up with the statement: "And all this his grace the sovereign shall do with the advice and consent of the boyars of the duma, and without the counsel and consent of the boyars of the duma his grace the sovereign shall make no decision"; significantly, Sigismund here curtailed the proposed phrase "boyars and men of the duma" (Article 11). Still more significantly, he substituted a specific promise not to raise taxes without the advice of "the boyars and men of the duma" for a proposal that he consult with "the boyars and with the land [the zemsky sobor]" (Article 14). Similarly, he omitted the phrase "with all the land" from a concluding general promise that any matters not covered in the treaty would be discussed "with the patriarch and the whole Holy Synod, and with the boyars," though in this case he substituted for it "and the *dvoriane* and men of all stations." Only in connection with supplements to Ivan's *Sudebnik* did he specifically agree that the matter "shall be free to the boyars and to all the land, that all shall be just" (Article 8).

In guarantees of the economic interests of the *dvoriane,* Sigismund was more generous. Neither they nor the boyars were to be dismissed from their offices, and no Poles or Lithuanians were to be appointed to high posts. Men in service were to be paid regularly, and at rates not less than were customary, the ruler reserving the right to raise men "according to their worth" (Article 5). Trade between the two realms and within Muscovy itself was to continue to be "free," subject to payment of old-established tolls (Article 15). Peasants, however, were not to be permitted to cross the Muscovite-Lithuanian border, nor were they to receive freedom of movement within Russia (Article 16). Bondsmen were not to be set at liberty (Article 17), and the status of the cossacks "on the Volga, on the Don, on the Yaik, and on the Terek" was to be discussed "with the boyars and with the men of the duma" (Article 18).

On the basis of this treaty the camp at Tushino was abandoned. Most of the Poles joined the king, though a few—like Lisovski—continued to support the "brigand," and others—led by Sapieha—drew apart to await further developments. Most of the Russian *dvoriane* and "sons of boyars," hating the boyar reaction represented by Shuisky, joined the Poles under beleaguered Smolensk, though their example did not persuade the heroic garrison to surrender. Unfortunately for Shuisky, Philaret, who had accepted the candidacy of Vladislav, was intercepted and brought to Moscow, where his prestige made him a dangerous focus for the opposition to Tsar Vasily. The cossacks, on the other hand, followed the "good tsar" to Kaluga and continued to harass the countryside.

The breakup of the "brigand's" army at Tushino, which resulted both from the pressure of King Sigismund and from the successes on the Volga of Skopin-Shuisky and Sheremetev, supported by local townsmen and peasants, did not help Tsar Vasily to stabilize his position. Skopin-Shuisky, the hero of the hour, died suddenly at Moscow in April, 1610; it was widely believed that the Shuiskys, fearing his popularity, had poisoned him. Without leadership, the efforts of the Volga population slackened. An army sent to relieve Smolensk was badly beaten at Klushino (June 24, 1610). Tsar Vasily was left "a featherless eagle, without bread and nourishment." The victorious Poles, led by Hetman (General) Zolkiewski, advanced on Moscow. Even the "brigand" made a fresh effort and again encamped under the walls of the capital.

In this desperate situation, an influential *dvorianin,* Prokopy Liapunov, who was serving as *voevoda* (governor) in his native Ryazan, organized a coup d'état. His brother Zakhar led a mob attack on the Kremlin; Tsar Vasily was deposed (July 17) and forcibly given the tonsure. Liapunov was, however, unable to seat his own candidate, Prince V. V. Golitsyn, on the vacant throne. Instead, authority passed to the boyar duma or rather, to seven of its members, representing both the old feudal aristocracy and the new court aristocracy created by Ivan the Terrible. The "rule of the seven boyars," though formally accepted as a provisional government by most of the towns which served as centers of local administration, could not muster the strength to fight off the imminent dual threat posed by the Poles and by the "brigand's" cossacks. A choice had to be made, and quickly. Despite the military weakness of the anarchic cossack forces, there was grave danger that the Moscow mob, craving a "good tsar," might riotously open the gates to the social enemy of the Muscovite order. Repugnant as it might be to accept Polish rule, with all its peril to the Orthodox faith, the boyars and *dvoriane* alike felt constrained to open negotiations with Zolkiewski.

On August 17, a slightly revised form of the treaty of Smolensk was accepted by the boyars at Moscow. There was still no promise that Vladislav would be baptized into the Orthodox faith. Hetman Zolkiewski simply spelled out that "the Christian Orthodox faith of the Greek law shall in no way be destroyed or dishonored, and no other faiths shall be introduced"; he repeated also the prohibition of conversion from Orthodoxy and of the admission of Jews into Muscovy.

In the provisions guaranteeing the preservation of the status and material rewards of the various ranks of military servitors was inserted a special concession to the boyars: "and Muscovite princely and boyar families shall not be oppressed and abased in standing [*otechestvo*] and in honor by foreign newcomers." No similar special protection was given to the general body of *dvoriane,* save repetition of a promise that Poles and Lithuanians would not be appointed governors of Russian provinces. Though no specific guarantee was given that old boyar families would not be "abased" by preferment of more pliable *dvoriane,* presumably the general guarantee of old customs was deemed sufficient to preserve what remained of boyar ascendancy under established *miestnichestvo* practices.

The provisions about "free" trade, the restrictions imposed on freedom of movement of "trading and plowing" peasants, and the doubts about the future status of the cossacks remained unchanged. The hetman added emphatic promises to "take or kill" the "brigand" alleging himself to be Dmitry Ivanovich, and to send Marina back to Poland to avoid further troubles.

A concluding provision expressed confidence that all other questions, specifically including the conversion of Vladislav to Orthodoxy, would be easily disposed of because "love, grace, and good will on both sides will increase and grow stronger forever." [11]

The worried boyars were content to echo the hetman's statement of the understanding. Zolkiewski acted promptly, and the "brigand" fled back to Kaluga. A delegation of over twelve hundred persons, in which the hetman was able to secure inclusion of all who might have led resistance to his power, including Prince V. V. Golitsyn and the Tushino patriarch, Philaret, was sent off to Sigismund. Without waiting for ratification of the new treaty, the Poles were admitted to the Kremlin (September 20). Though the "rule of the seven boyars" nominally continued, Sigismund now felt himself master of Muscovy. He sent a number of former Tushino men to staff the administrative departments and began to distribute estates to his most loyal supporters. The siege of Smolensk was not raised, and only the stubborn resistance of its defenders enabled it to hold out until June, 1611.

RESTORATION

Muscovy could not, however, be held down by a handful of Polish troops and German mercenaries in the Kremlin. The aged Moscow patriarch, Hermogen, issued eloquent appeals to the Russian people to rise in the name of the Orthodox faith. Although he was speedily put under house arrest, a number of towns had promptly entered into a correspondence, in which Prokopy Liapunov at Ryazan played the leading role. The middle elements in Russian society—the provincial *dvoriane* and "sons of boyars," supported by the propertied townsmen—took up the task of resistance to the Poles that the boyars had abandoned. Liapunov even effected an alliance with the forces of the "brigand" (who had been murdered in December, 1610, leaving an infant son by Marina) under the leadership of Prince Trubetskoy at Kaluga and even with more lawless cossacks who had gathered around ataman Zarutsky at Tula. In the spring of 1611, a sort of national militia advanced on Moscow. On the eve of its arrival, the restless populace of Moscow rioted against the hated Polish garrison (March 19); the rising was bloodily repressed, and most of the city was destroyed by fire.

Encamped outside the capital, the rebel forces established a triumvirate composed of the leaders of its three elements. Liapunov led the remnants of the troops that had fought for Tsar Vasily Shuisky—the *dvoriane* of Ryazan and adjacent areas, the *muzhiks* ("common people") of the Volga towns, and the forces gathered by Skopin-Shuisky. Trubetskoy had the support of the remainder of the "Brigand's" army. Zarutsky led the free cossack detachments, made up largely of runaway peasants and bondsmen.

This triumvirate, on Liapunov's urging, secured the acceptance (June 30) of a decree which attempted to provide for the orderly administration of the army and of the country on the basis of old Muscovite custom. However, it subordinated the temporary executive authorities to the will of the "council [soviet] of all the land." It included detailed regulations for distribution of land according to specified norms and subject to forfeiture for failure to perform the holder's duty to the realm. "Old" cossacks might be granted lands, but in the mass the cossacks were to receive only money wages for state service and were to be subjected to strict discipline. Fugitive peasants were to be returned to their owners.

Instead of stabilizing the situation, this decree provoked an acute crisis in the camp. Cossacks, offended at its essentially conservative character, murdered Liapunov (July 22) and threatened to attack their propertied allies instead of the Poles. The vast majority of the *dvoriane* and "sons of boyars" withdrew and scattered to their homes. The cossacks remained around Moscow, though now unable to maintain more than a loose blockade of the city. Meanwhile, Sigismund rejected the treaty of August, 1610, and openly claimed Moscow as his own. The Swedes, disappointed in their hope that the leaders of the militia would accept a Swedish prince in the place of Vladislav, seized Novgorod for themselves (July 16).

Before the year was out, however, the combination of forces which had kept Shuisky on the throne was in process of being reconstituted. Threatened with ruin by the almost total cessation of trade on the Volga, the capitalist merchants began to organize in an effort to check disorder and plundering. Under the leadership of Kuzma Minin, a wholesale cattle-dealer of Nizhny Novgorod, they organized committees in the commercial towns and raised funds with which to finance a new military effort by the *dvoriane*. In 1612, a *dvorianin,* Prince Pozharsky, with the blessing of a zemsky sobor assembled at Yaroslavl, took command of a new army. The approach of this force to Moscow overawed the cossack besiegers: the more lawless part, under Zarutsky—now protector of Marina, widow of the first "Dmitry" and by the second "Dmitry" mother of a third—withdrew to Astrakhan; the rest, under Prince Trubetskoy, accepted Pozharsky's leadership. Beating off a Polish relief force, the combined armies took the Kremlin after a three-months' siege, during which the cossacks had the honor of storming the Kitai Gorod.

Prince Pozharsky proved to be the Cincinnatus rather than the George Washington of Russia. The monarchical habits of mind of the Muscovites required a tsar of higher degree than a petty scion of the house of Rurik. A statue of Minin and Pozharsky still occupies an honored place at the edge of the Red Square, but these national heroes were not eligible to take command of the restored Muscovite state. The problem of choosing a ruler was exceptionally difficult. It was not thought impossible to work out an arrangement by which Polish Vladislav might still assume the throne. Sweden, in possession of Novgorod, had a spare prince to offer. The Hapsburgs were not without partisans. There were also several possibilities among the leading boyars, though the most eminent of them, Prince V. V. Golitsyn, was being held as a hostage in Poland. Of less significance were the numerous alleged sons of Ivan IV who mushroomed all over the country; nothing was easier than to manufacture a "tsarevich."

The question was referred to a new zemsky sobor, assembled at Moscow early in 1613. This assembly was somewhat more representative, in the modern sense, of "all the land" than had been the custom earlier. The practice of holding local assemblies to choose their "best men" had been stimulated by the weakness of the central authority during the years of disorder. The elective principle, though in no democratic sense, had therefore made much progress. Furthermore, this zemsky sobor included representatives of elements not summoned in the early years; cossacks and "black" peasants (i.e., peasants who had no landlord over them) took part. The outcome was naturally extreme division of opinion as to who should be chosen tsar. Agreement was fairly easily reached not to take any ruler who was not Orthodox; all foreign princes and "the son of Marina" (the preferred candidate of the cossacks) thus seemed ruled out. However, it was only after much pulling and hauling that a name was found on which, though partly for negative reasons, all could agree. Finally a *dvorianin* submitted a written opinion that the candidate nearest to the dynasty was Michael, son of Fedor Nikitich Romanov. A storm of protest was stilled when a Don cossack ataman supported the "born tsar."

Michael was then a boy of sixteen, with no reputation for force of character; his very physical whereabouts at the moment seem to have been unknown. His father was the nephew of Ivan's first wife and might be regarded as the heir of the *oprichnina,* which had struck down the boyars to the advantage of the lesser nobility; as Philaret, he had served as patriarch at Tushino and thus stood close to the cossacks' hearts; at the moment of his son's election, he was a helpless prisoner of the Poles. Combining traditions that made him acceptable to the two partners in the military enterprise that had freed the Kremlin—the *dvoriane* and the cossacks—Michael's personal insignificance made him not wholly unacceptable to the quarreling boyar factions. Above all, he embodied the idea of a "born tsar," whose right to rule could not be successfully challenged. Thus, the election of Michael—and of the wife and child he did not yet have—was rather a recognition of restored continuity than free choice of a new course.

NOTES

1. Bond (ed.), *Russia at the Close of the Sixteenth Century,* p. 34.
2. Platonov, *Boris Godunov,* p. 98.
3. *Ibid.,* p. 147.
4. *Ibid.,* p. 139.
5. *Akty sobrannye . . . Arkheograficheskoiu ekspeditsieiu . . . ,* II, 70-71.
6. Platonov, *op. cit.,* p. 144.
7. *Ibid.,* pp. 150-166 *passim.*
8. *Ibid.,* p. 162.
9. *Ibid.,* p. 224.
10. The quotations in this and the next two paragraphs are translated from Russkoe Istoricheskoe Obshchestvo, *Sbornik . . . ,* CXLII; Saltykov's proposals are there stated on pp. 64-69; Sigismund's version on pp. 69-73.
11. *Ibid.,* pp. 93-112 *passim.*

SUGGESTIONS FOR FURTHER READING

In addition to works previously cited, Platonov's *Boris Godunov,* one of this scholar's masterly biographies, is available in a French translation. Waliszewski's *Les origines de la Russia moderne: La crise révolutionnaire* is less satisfactory than his *Ivan le Terrible.* Barbour's *Dmitry, Called the Pretender . . .* may be a helpful account for beginners.

A somewhat useful contemporary Dutch narrative is available in Isaac Massa, *Histoire des guerres de la Muscovie (1601-1610).* More valuable is Zolkiewski's *Expedition to Moscow.*

Cresson, *The Cossacks,* is a popular account.

Chapter

9

The First Romanovs and Old Muscovy: 1613-1689

The reigns of the first few Romanovs—almost equal in their lack of striking personal qualities—may conveniently be considered as a unit. Though troubled by numerous disorders, there is no one dramatic event that may be singled out as dividing the seventeenth century—or so much of it as lies between the official end of the Time of the Troubles in 1613 and the coming of age of Peter the Great in 1689—into well-marked chronological periods.

Tsar Michael (1613-45), weak and suffering from foot trouble, preferred to divert himself with clocks and German trumpeters rather than with affairs of state. From 1619 to 1633 he was dominated by his father, Philaret, who on his release from captivity in Poland assumed the vacant throne of the patriarch and was recognized as co-sovereign with the tsar. On Michael's death in 1645, at the age of forty-seven, he was succeeded, in accordance with the decision of the zemsky sobor of 1613, by his son Alexis, then sixteen years old. Tsar Alexis (1645-76), the "most pacific tsar," was a man of great piety and no force of character, capable of outbursts of petty violence but much too devoted to the comforts and amenities of life to give consistent guidance to state affairs. Through his indulgence rather than through his will, Muscovy experienced in his reign a considerable amount of "Europeanization"; directly against his will, Muscovite foreign policy underwent an abrupt about-face in its fundamental orientation; and his role in the development of the church schism was that of following the path of least resistance. On his death in 1676, also at the age of forty-seven, he was succeeded by his son, Fedor, whose accession it was deemed unnecessary to ratify by convoking a zemsky sobor. Fedor, who was fourteen at the time he became tsar, proved as incompetent as his namesake of a century earlier. His brief reign of six years was disturbed by the feud of the relatives of his father's two wives, the Miloslavskys and the Naryshkins, until both were pushed aside by a neutral clique. On Fedor's early death in 1682, this clique effected the succession of Peter, ten-year-old but vigorous son of Alexis' second wife, in preference to Ivan, his older but half-witted half-brother. However, Ivan's unprepossessing but able and energetic sister Sophia, aided by her uncles, the Miloslavskys, succeeded in stirring up a riot of the *strieltsy,* who slaughtered the brothers and friends of Peter's mother. Using the form—but not the substance—of a zemsky sobor, Ivan and Peter were proclaimed co-tsars, with Sophia as regent. Peter and his mother were sent into comfortable exile at the suburban village of Preobrazhensk. Only in 1689 was the regency of Sophia overthrown.

Rather than follow in detail this dreary succession of reigns, it seems more serviceable to treat the whole period topically, considering first those aspects which represent the greatest continuity with Muscovy's past and reserving until later those which reflected newer tendencies, ultimately to effect serious modification of the long-term characteristics of Russian society and of the Russian state. Under the first heading fall: consolidation of the autocracy, consolidation of serfdom, resumption of an aggressive foreign policy, and formalization of the subordination of Church to state. Under the second, more dynamic, heading will be considered: the impact of the West on Russia's economy, innovations in military and industrial techniques and in manners and habits, and the beginning of the long-drawn-out ideological struggle between those who felt Russia should hasten to overtake Europe and those who believed in a special mission Russia was called on to play in the world.

CONSOLIDATION OF AUTOCRACY

Russia at the close of the Time of the Troubles was in essential ways already a very different Russia from that of a century before. The autocratic power of the tsar was, to be sure, not yet fully recognized. Michael was proclaimed ruler on the basis of a charter which explicitly recognized limitation of his authority by the boyar duma. *Miestnichestvo,* with its basic principle that the tsar "can reward with money and land but not with inherited standing (*otechestvo*)," remained in force and produced even more wrangles in the seventeenth century than in the sixteenth. This very fact, however, reflected its decline as a protection to a generally recognized position. Most of the old families recorded in the *Rodoslovets* and whose names had filled the *razriady* were extinct or had lost much or all of their wealth and power. The boyar duma was filled with members of new families, "accidental" men who owed their position to service or, more importantly, to the favor of the tsar. They might fill the air with the noise of their pretensions to outrank each other; even Pozharsky might be compelled to make amends by walking on foot from the tsar's palace to the home of a disgruntled aristocrat whose claims to precedence he had ignored. Yet a change of family personnel inexorably proceeded, and the idea grew ever stronger that "great and small live by the sovereign's favor." Long before the formal abolition of *miestnichestvo* in 1682, the system had lost its historic significance.

Steadily losing ground in relation to the ruler, the boyar duma had to face also encroachment from below—from the zemsky sobor which briefly played something of the role of medieval Western parliaments in strengthening the monarch against his peerage. Tsar Vasily Shuisky in 1606 had sought to rid himself of the influence of his fellow boyars by resting his authority on the support of a zemsky sobor, though a partial and local one. Saltykov, in negotiating the treaty of Smolensk with Sigismund of Poland, had included reference to it as the ultimate source of new legislation. In 1612, a zemsky sobor had endorsed Pozharsky's campaign against the Poles, and it was a zemsky sobor that in 1613 had sanctioned the elevation of Michael Romanov to the throne. It was only natural that he, or his advisers, should continue annually to summon the zemsky sobor in order to secure the widest possible measure of support in the continuing wars with Poland and with Sweden and in the no less desperate effort to suppress the marauding bands of cossacks, fugitive peasants, and freebooting Poles who continued to ravage the whole length and breadth of Muscovy. Not until 1617 was peace made with Sweden at Stolbovo; under the terms of the treaty the Swedes evacuated Novgorod but remained in possession of the coastline lost by Ivan the Terrible and partially recovered by Boris Godunov. The following year, a fifteen-year truce with Poland, concluded at Deulino, confirmed the enemy in possession of strategic Smolensk; Vladislav did not renounce his claims to the Russian throne; but the hostages were released, and the young tsar's father returned to Moscow to be enthroned as patriarch and co-tsar. Gradually the prevalence of rapine, looting, and murder was brought under control. By 1623, the Troubles, officially ended with the accession of Michael ten years earlier, were practically over—though their effects endured much longer—and no zemsky sobor was summoned that year.

Thereafter, the zemsky sobor met only at irregular intervals, whenever the tsar chose to seek ratification of his will by the "assembly of all the land." The institution never developed a well-defined organization. The social elements included in its composition continued to fluctuate widely. No regular system of selection of deputies was ever arrived at; in some cases the spokesmen of the nobility and of the townsmen were elected, in others they were called into consultation because they happened to be in the capital. The procedures by which it responded to the questions laid before it varied from time to time, nor was it usual for the several estates to give collective answers.

The attitude of the ruler toward the opinions garnered at these meetings was also subject to change. In 1632, a zemsky sobor recommended that the tsar renew the war with Poland; he did so, but with humiliating results, and the attempt to recover Smolensk had to be abandoned in 1634. In 1642, another sobor was assembled to advise the tsar whether to accept from the Don cossacks the gift of Azov, which they had seized in 1637 and which the Turks were trying to recover. The seven answers given by the various elements in the sobor ranged from the clergy's comment that "we thy Sovereign's prayer-sayers are bound to pray to God for the ordering of all peace, and for the well-being of the holy churches of God, and for thy Tsar's long-lived health, and for all thy Sovereign's house; but this matter is military consideration for thy Tsar's Majesty and for thy Sovereign's boyars and men of the duma, but for us, O Sovereign, all this is not customary," [1] through the statement of the higher-ranking *dvoriane* that they would leave the question of war and mobilization to the tsar if he ordered the cossacks to keep Azov, down to the vigorous, though separately composed, protests of provincial *dvoriane* and of the commercial groups, who suggested that graft and corruption on the part of the tsar's officials were more dangerous than the Turks. Though all elements in the sobor promised their assistance to the best of their ability, the tsar deemed it unwise to accept the cossacks' offer.

The total lack of positive unity regularly manifested by the chief social classes represented in the zemsky sobor—the tax-eating nobility and the tax-paying merchantry—to say nothing of the very deep mutual grievances cherished by the metropolitan nobility and the provincial nobility, by the Moscow *gosti* and the inferior commercial groups—made it impossible for the sobor to develop into an independently functioning body, capable of opposing community resistance to the will of the ruler. Accordingly, the early Romanov tsars, despite their personal incapacity and indolence, emerged more and more as autocrats in the modern sense, unfettered either by a boyar duma, now largely made up of new "accidental" men, or by the zemsky sobor which ceased to function after the middle of the seventeenth century; only occasionally thereafter did the tsar continue to sound the thoughts of special categories of the population, without convening a full zemsky sobor. The last significant zemsky sobor was held in 1649 to confirm the codification of the laws known as the *Ulozhenie*.

The *dvoriane* had become the ruling social class, and it was in their interests that state measures were for the most part taken. They had no need of a representative organ. They monopolized the administrative positions in the muddled system of bureaus (*prikazy*) that had grown up with the development of the tsar's household into the machinery of state. They controlled the local administration of justice and collection of direct taxes. Above all, they were secure, with the powerful backing of a tsar wielding the collective military and police power, in mastery over the peasants on their estates. In accepting the role of humble slaves of the tsar, they were enabled to extend and consolidate their dominion over the mass of the population.

CONSOLIDATION OF SERFDOM

Economically and socially the tendencies in evidence before the *oprichnina* and the Time of the Troubles continued their apparently inexorable development. Gradually, the shattered economy of Muscovy was restored, though not on any basis of individual or corporate freedom. Progress was reflected in the extension of the cultivated area, not in a more intensified agriculture. As population began once more slowly to increase, the area of land under cultivation grew with it.

The rising power of the central administration was ever more able to bring the steppe, once the "wild field," also under control. Only in the lower reaches of the rivers did there survive free cossack communities; unable to check the advance of cultivation and of enserfment into the black-soil zone, they clung to some measure of independence only in the less fertile southern fringe of the steppe. The continuing drift of population toward the south no longer spelled total loss, for this area began in the course of the century to be assimilated to the social and political conditions of the center. Settlement of the western portion of Siberia also proceeded slowly; in 1662, the total population of Siberia was officially recorded as 288,000, less than a quarter of whom were Russians. In 1678, the tax registers showed over ten thousand homesteads in the Siberian towns, which were, however, principally a byproduct of the fur trade.

Private landholding had by the seventeenth century definitely triumphed. Except in the far north, beyond the watershed, what little "black" land had survived the Time of the Troubles almost wholly disappeared. Fresh attempts were made to curb ecclesiastical landholding, and in 1649 a zemsky sobor even demanded that the clergy surrender all lands acquired since the edict of 1580. A special Bureau of Investigation (*Prikaz sysknyx diel*), charged with the task of strengthening the tax-paying ability of the townsmen (*posadskie*) by recovering for the tax-rolls "whitened" homesteads (i.e., trading establishments maintained by clergy, boyars, *dvoriane, strieltsy,* cannoneers, and other privileged elements), bore most heavily (59%) on Church properties. If acquisition of land by the monasteries did slacken in the second half of the century, it was not, however, the result of adverse legislation. The now predominant small landowners could not afford to make endowments as well as their wealthier predecessors had been able to, while the monasteries, for their part, showed a marked tendency to prefer investment of their surplus wealth in trade and moneylending rather than in land.

For some reason, as yet unsatisfactorily explained, the legal form of service landholding showed a tendency to revert to the hereditary *votchina* rather than the temporary *pomestie.* In any case, the legal distinction between the two forms had become very blurred. It is probable that the more inefficient economy observable on *pomestie* holdings was the result, not directly of the type of legal tenure, but of the fact that small landholding, by men often absent on military service, was inherently less efficient than large-scale holding, and that the smaller estates were more frequently granted on *pomestie* terms. Money payments by peasants continued to become more common, but wide variation remained in the economic obligations resting on the peasants. Obligatory labor (*barshchina*), sometimes in specified amounts, was normally included; of thirteen hundred extant agreements pertaining to lands of two monasteries in the north, about eleven hundred provide that the peasant "has to perform every task according to the bidding of the monks." [2]

The combined operation of peasant indebtedness, fines, and house-rent were still the main forces in destroying the remnants of peasant freedom of movement. They were increasingly reinforced by state action. In the state's interest rather than in that of the landholders as individuals, the zemsky sobor of 1619 ordered registration of all persons liable to direct taxes, directing that all evaders be compelled to reassume their obligations, whether they had run away physically or had mortgaged their persons to tax-exempt protectors. The records were destroyed in the great fire of 1626, but a new and more careful registration was carried out in 1627-28. In the *Ulozhenie,* a general codification of the law endorsed by a zemsky sobor in 1649, this register was made the basis on which fugitive peasants might be returned to their landlords.

At the same time, a desperate effort was made to check the forbidden practice of escaping tax liability by mortgaging one's person; it was provided that the estates of boyars and ecclesiastics who accepted such *zakladchiki* were to be confiscated. Furthermore, the statute of limitations on suits for recovery of fugitive peasants, which after the Troubles had been again set at five years, was abolished altogether. A novel legal principle was that the whole peasant household—the "big family"—was made subject to recovery. Thus, peasant attachment, for life, by means of a freely negotiated loan-contract was broadened into hereditary family attachment on the basis of legal registration.

It is worth emphasizing that the principles of the *Ulozhenie* were regarded, not as new legislation, but as codification of existing law. So far had peasant bondage developed in actual practice that the *Ulozhenie* contained no provision for peasants not in debt-bondage. Yet there were still in fact categories of peasants whose freedom of movement remained unaffected by the threat of being returned to a landholder. In the north, where natural conditions made landholding less attractive, "black" lands still exceeded privately held estates. Even on the latter, the seventeenth-century monastery records regularly show agreements with sharecroppers whose freedom of movement is explicitly recognized.

In the rest of the country, too, there was a category of peasants known as *bobyly,* a term of somewhat indefinite meaning which first appears in the middle of the sixteenth century. In general, *bobyly* appear to have been landless (or relatively landless) cottagers, most often referred to as wayfarers and therefore not subject to regular taxation. They seem, however, frequently to have remained settled for years on particular estates and even to have been set up as regular peasants, the lightening of the tax burden compensating the landlord for his lack of right to interfere if they chose to leave. This practice, regarded by the state as an evasion, caused alarm when in some districts the numbers of *bobyly* came to exceed the number of regular peasants (*krestiane*) and apparently was an important factor in the substitution, late in the century, of a homestead tax for the old "plow" tax. There were also free wage-workers, paid either in money or in kind, who were subject to barbarous abuses at the hands of overseers, who for their part complained that "we are continually troubled by them as by dogs." [3]

In other ways, too, there was a great lack of correspondence between the law and the fact. Peasants continued to flee, and in large numbers. As an example, Kulisher cites the fact that in a single town for the one year 1664 the official records show 177 cases of fugitive peasants, involving in each case from four to eight individuals. An edict of 1658 had established special officials to hunt down fugitive peasants. It was, however, impossible to check wholesale movement, especially into the newly opened "black-soil" steppe. For that matter, the movement was, as of old, encouraged by the rich and powerful, like the boyar Ivan Romanov, who, to secure settlers for his estates in the "wild field," organized bands to burn down his neighbors' establishments and forcibly carry their peasants off to his own estates. A series of edicts sharply increased the penalties even for more peaceful methods; in 1661, for instance, it was ordered that landlords harboring strange peasants be flogged and forced to surrender their own peasants in numbers equal to their contraband acquisitions.

Yet the general tendency continued to be a drift of an ever-increasing proportion of the peasantry into legal serfdom. As in earlier periods, the downward movement of the free peasantry was balanced by an upward movement of the slaves. The old possibility of selling oneself into full slavery had been replaced by the milder form of *kabala* servitude, which terminated on the death of the master. A number of intermediate categories grew up. Since in the eyes of the government there was no desirable distinction between the peasants (*krestiane*) and *bobyly,* on the one hand, and the several categories of bondsmen, on the other, save that the latter were tax-exempt, all those settled on the land were in 1679 equated by the expedient of introducing the household tax, which rested equally on all. Only bondsmen in the master's household (*dvorovye liudi*) remained for a time tax-free.

The rights which the landlord enjoyed over his peasants were not merely economic. He was charged by the state with judicial, police, and fiscal authority over them, whatever their legal status. The break-up of large estates and the resettlement of much of the population during the reign of Ivan IV and during the Troubles had tended to destroy the old communal structure. Yet the institution survived, both on the "black" lands of the north and on many privately held estates. Indeed, in this period it acquired—or had imposed on it—a larger measure of power, by way of periodic redistribution, over the holdings of individual peasant households.

Underneath the dominance of the landlord and subject to his intervention, the rural community stubbornly persisted, for in the last analysis it was peasant action, not landlord regulation, on which life depended. Whether the developing practice of redistribution of strips of arable land reflected peasant reactions to a developing land scarcity, or whether it arose from pressure of the landlord and the state in the interest of assuring the capacity of all to pay dues and taxes may be a disputable point. In this period, there would seem to have been no contradiction between these pressures, which tended to obstruct the development of any sense of individual proprietorship in land on the part of the peasant.

RESUMPTION OF AN AGGRESSIVE FOREIGN POLICY*

While autocracy and serfdom were thus developing in interlaced fashion, other aspects of state life observable a century earlier continued to operate. One of the characteristics of seventeenth-century Muscovy was the resumption, midway in the century, of that expansionist movement which economic ruin and political disorder had temporarily checked. From the defensive, Russia passed again to the offensive, and in a way curiously related to the growth of serfdom. In the reign of Tsar Michael (1613-45)—from 1619 to 1633 the real ruler was his father, Patriarch Philaret—Russia remained militarily weak and therefore diplomatically passive. She did expand rapidly eastward across Siberia, as fur traders found their way from one river basin to the next (the cossacks playing the role of the *coureurs de bois* of Canada) without serious resistance from the thinly spread aborigines. In 1639 they reached the inhospitable coast of the Sea of Okhotsk, an arm of the Pacific Ocean. Under Michael's successor, southward penetration into the Amur basin brought on hostilities with China, which were not terminated until 1689, when the Chinese, using the diplomacy of Jesuits (who in their desire to convert China had made themselves invaluable agents of its state power) and mythical armies, convinced the cossacks that they must abandon the Amur area. The position was officially stabilized by the Treaty of Nerchinsk, which provided for the admission of state-organized merchant caravans into China.

In the west, where expansion entailed fighting, Michael made no headway. After a brief war (1632-34), "permanent" peace replaced the long truce with Poland; Vladislav—now having succeeded to the Polish throne as Ladislas IV—renounced his claim to the Russian throne, while Michael abandoned Smolensk and paid an indemnity. After this check, the tsar did not dare, de-

* See Maps V and VI.

spite the loyal expressions of the groups represented in the zemsky sobor of 1642, to risk war with Turkey over Azov; that Black Sea port was accordingly restored to the Crimean Tatars by the indignant Don cossacks.

It was under the rule of Michael's son Alexis (1645-76), "the most pacific tsar," that Russia again resorted to arms, this time on behalf of her "little brothers," the cossacks of the Dnieper. The lower Dnieper basin had been surrendered by Lithuania to Poland under the Union of Lublin (1569), but the progress of Polonization and enserfment of the Polish *ukraine* was much hampered by the existence of the Zaporogian *Siech,* the winter headquarters of the Dnieper cossacks below the rapids (*za porogi*). Frequent conflicts between the Poles and the cossacks culminated in a particularly violent explosion in the spring of 1649. Under the leadership of Bogdan Khmelnitsky, a cossack of noble origin, the Zaporogian "host," aided by the khan of the Crimea, defeated the royal armies of Poland in pitched battle. A general uprising of the Little Russian peasants against the Polish landlords threatened to engulf Poland itself. The death of King Ladislas IV and the limited character of Bogdan's ambitions permitted the conclusion of a peace treaty (August, 1649): Khmelnitsky was recognized as "hetman," and allowed to retain an armed force of forty thousand "registered" cossacks; Polish troops, Jesuits, and Jews were not to be tolerated in Little Russia; but no provision was made for the revolted peasantry, thousands of whom emigrated to the Donets basin under Russian protection. War broke out again in the next year; Khmelnitsky, now deserted by the Crimean Tatars, was compelled to accept reduction of the number of registered cossacks to twenty thousand.

At this point Bogdan offered to put the "host" under the protection of Moscow. After two years of hesitation and consultation with two successive zemsky sobors, the tsar consented (1653) to play the role initially played by the khan of the Crimea. He required, however, an agreement, though a somewhat vague one, on terms. In 1654, on the formal proposal of Hetman Khmelnitsky, the cossack assembly (*rada*) unanimously accepted the arrangement. Although the tsar's agent refused to swear to preserve cossack rights and privileges, the cossacks took an oath of allegiance to the tsar. The "registered" cossacks were to number sixty thousand; Khmelnitsky was to remain hetman for life, and his successor was to be elected by the *rada;* all existing privileges of the cossacks were to be preserved, as were also the rights of the Little Russian nobility, while the towns were to continue to enjoy their special status under the fourteenth-century *Ius Magdeburgicum.* In general, the cossacks proposed to become vassals rather than subjects of Moscow; they might have relations with other powers, save that negotiations with Poland and Turkey were to be directed from Moscow.

In extending its protection to the Zaporogian cossacks, Moscow well knew that war with Poland must follow. Justification for breach of the "permanent" peace of 1634 was found both in a Polish failure to address the tsar by his correct title and in oppression of the Orthodox who refused to accept the

Union of Brest of 1596. Partly due to the reorganization of Russian military forces under Michael and to the wide extension of the practice of regimenting nobles and their followers on Western patterns, partly due to the internal weakness of Poland, Alexis speedily won great successes. Not merely did he take Smolensk, but he seized a number of other towns deeper in Polish territory. The war seemed to promise even greater things; in 1656 the ruler of distant but Orthodox Moldavia (then, like Walachia, under Turkish control) was, at his own request, taken under the tsar's protection.

In 1656, however, Sweden, whose king had claims to the crown of Poland, also entered the war; the Swedes swiftly took both Warsaw and Cracow. Acceptance of Swedish rule by part of her aristocracy paralyzed Poland, and the Russo-Polish war was temporarily superseded by a Russo-Swedish one. Riga was besieged, and Russian arms won successes around the head of the Gulf of Finland. Sweden's victory over Poland was short-lived; the other Baltic powers were alarmed, and the Dutch joined the hard-pressed Danes. The Peace of Oliva (1660) released a resurgent Poland to pursue the war with Russia, which was constrained to abandon the war with Sweden; by the Treaty of Kardis (1661), Moscow relinquished her gains in the north.

In 1657, the death of Bogdan Khmelnitsky had opened the way for the succession of a series of hetmans, who thought of Poland as a lesser danger than their new protector. Their policy split the *ukraine;* the left bank of the Dnieper tended to support the Moscow connection and carried on a civil war with the Polish sympathizers. Finally, in 1667, the Truce of Andrusovo between Poland and Russia confirmed this division. The right bank of the Dnieper, except the city of Kiev, remained Polish; Kiev, nominally for two years only, and the whole left bank were recognized as under the control of Moscow. Moscow also kept Smolensk, though surrendering her conquests in "White Russia" to the west of it. In 1686, this tremendous gain was confirmed by a "permanent" peace; the Regent Sophia and the Polish hero-king, Jan Sobieski, who in 1683 had turned the Turks back from the gates of Vienna, concluded an alliance against the infidel Turk, thus initiating Russia's serious desire for control of the Black Sea coast.

A still more important implication of the new policy of a working partnership with Poland was the freedom thus won to prepare for an attack on a weakening Sweden, the power which blocked Russian access to the Baltic. Riga—no longer merely Narva—became increasingly the chief goal of Russian foreign policy. Its realization, however, had to await settlement of the struggle with Turkey to which peace with Poland committed Russia and in which Sophia's chief minister, Prince V. V. Golitsyn, won not even glory.

Acquisition of half the Polish *ukraine* was not an unmixed blessing. Successive hetmans, conspiring with the Turks, the Crimean Tatars, and the virtually independent hetmans of the Polish right bank, prevented realization of Moscow's control of Little Russia. In the midst of her troubles on the Dnieper, Moscow was faced with a revolt of the Don cossacks, who roused the flames of peasant revolt almost as far as the capital itself. Although frowned on by the more well-to-do Don "elders" (*starosty*), the cossack "youth," themselves propertyless and addicted to plunder, found an energetic leader in Stenka (Little Stepan) Razin. Crossing to the Volga and joined by the cossacks along the Ural River, Razin's raiders looted the Persian coast of the Caspian Sea (1669). Returning to the Don with rich booty, they were emboldened to strike again (1670) and this time directly at Russian authority, taking Astrakhan and Tsaritsyn (modern Stalingrad) on the lower Volga. Inciting the peasants and the non-Russian tribes to wild revolt, Razin assembled a force far more threatening than Bolotnikov's bands had been in 1607. As he moved up the Volga, however, Razin was met and driven back by the disciplined army of the tsar. In the course of 1671, the peasant revolts in areas far north of any that Razin had reached were, with whatever difficulty, stamped out. The Don cossack elders, moving against a rebel who defied their authority as well as that of the tsar, seized Razin's headquarters and handed him over to the government. Brought to Moscow in a cage, Razin was beheaded in the "Place of Execution" in the shadow of the Vasily Cathedral in the Red Square. Despite the failure of the revolt, its memory lingered on among both the lawless and the oppressed; it was later emulated on a number of occasions and on a vaster scale.

With Razin out of the way, and with quiet restored on the Don and Volga, Moscow was able in the last years of Alexis' reign and under his son Fedor (1676-82) to strengthen her grip on the left bank of the Dnieper, though making no serious attempts to seize the right bank, over which Poland and Turkey waged a protracted struggle. Under Sophia's regency (1682-89), on the basis of her alliance with Sobieski, two attempts were made to seize the Crimea. Although supported by Mazepa, the hetman who was later to lure his Teutonic ally, Charles XII of Sweden, to defeat at Poltava at the hands of Peter the Great, nothing resulted from this premature attempt to push the Turks back.

RELATIONS OF CHURCH AND STATE

Closely related to annexation of a portion of Little Russia was the church schism, the most dramatic domestic development under the early Romanovs. The establishment under Polish auspices of the Uniate Church (1596) had intensified interest in recalcitrant circles in Kiev in the foundations of Orthodoxy and in seeking contacts with its spiritual home in the Near East. The activities of learned Kievan monks, centering around the Ecclesiastical Academy founded there in 1631, were well known, although generally unfavorably viewed, in Moscow. The Kievan clergy looked to Greece, not to "the third Rome," for inspiration and enlightenment; they were extremely critical of many ritualistic practices—such as the use of only two fingers in making the sign of the Cross or the serving of six wafers at mass—which over the centuries had grown up in Russia. The fathers assembled at the Stoglav Sobor in 1551 had been largely oblivious of the divergences between Greek and Russian ritual and had officially sanctioned current local practice on some of the very points the Kievans now raised. Hesitating attempts to make some corrections even in Michael's reign had raised much protest and had not been pressed.

In 1652, however, there was consecrated to the patriarchate a man of great vigor, already forty-seven years old. Nikon, son of a peasant family, who had been a village priest before he renounced the world and his wife, accepted his elevation only after being assured by Tsar Alexis that he would be permitted to share in the guidance of the realm. Like Philaret in the early days of Michael, Patriarch Nikon was accorded the title of "Great Sovereign" (*veliky gosudar*) and recognized as coadjutor of the tsar. Unlike most of the Muscovite clergy, Nikon was not impressed by the concept of Moscow as the third and final Rome, at least in its usual narrow interpretation. Rather, he was imbued with the concept of the Church Universal and with the necessity that Moscow fit herself for the role of protector of all Orthodoxy. Tsar Alexis, profoundly influenced by Nikon's views and meditating extension of his power over Little Russia, was quite prepared, in an effort at preliminary appeasement, to heed the criticism of the Kievan scholars.

Accordingly, at the moment Alexis made his decision to accept Khmelnitsky's offer (1653), Nikon ordered the Muscovite clergy to change the number of prostrations during the reading of a certain prayer as well as the number of fingers to be used in making the sign of the Cross. While thus conciliating the Little Russian clergy in the matter of ritual, Alexis insisted that the metropolitanate of Kiev admit the jurisdiction of the Moscow patriarchate instead of continuing in dependence directly on Constantinople. Thus, Church and state continued to work harmoniously together in pursuit of common ends. In Russia itself, Nikon forced through a Church Council a whole program of ritual revision. As regent in the tsar's absence, he vigorously pressed the reform, though many of the clergy and large numbers of merchants and peasants stubbornly resisted. Despite vigorous persecution, the Old Ritualists (sometimes called Old Believers) clung persistently to the old ways. Besides the intangible consequences of this great schism (*raskol*) in the ranks of the Orthodox, Nikon's activity produced an odd by-product.

Returning from his first successful campaign, Tsar Alexis showed himself less amenable to the patriarch's dictatorial ways. Reacting warmly to the tsar's coolness, Nikon suddenly withdrew from Moscow to his favorite monastery (1658). Refusing to renounce his office, he refused also to perform its duties. His attempted coup was less successful than had been that of Ivan the Terrible in 1565. The "most pacific tsar" hesitated to take drastic steps but stubbornly refused to make amends. In 1660, another Russian Church Council recommended the deposition of the patriarch, but Alexis waited until he was able to secure the attendance of all the other Orthodox patriarchs—two of them in person, two by proxy—at an Ecumenical Council in Moscow. This council (1666-67) endorsed Nikon's ritual reforms but condemned his insistence that "the clergy is greater than the realm; the clergy is from God and from the clergy is the anointment of the realm. . . . The authority of the clergy is superior to the civil as the sky is to the earth, only much greater." [4] The Church, Nikon had argued, is the soul, the temporal realm merely the body; the tsar must therefore in all things submit to the guidance of the patriarch. By unanimous vote of the council, Nikon was reduced to the rank of a simple monk and banished to a remote monastery in the north.

Not content with settlement of this specific question, at the urging of Tsar Alexis the patriarchs attempted, though with imperfect success, to define the relationship between Church and state. The Russian prelates, though they had joined in the condemnation of Nikon, had not been able to reconcile themselves to some of the provisions of the *Ulozhenie* of 1649; they resented the encroachments of the lay power on the independence of ecclesiastical courts, as well as the administration of all Church lands (except those of the patriarch) by the Monastery Bureau (*Monastyrsky Prikaz*), a government office which had been set up in 1650. They therefore favored Nikon's concept of the Church as the sun, the state as the moon. The Greek patriarchs, however, true to Byzantine tradition, criticized this view: "Those who seek to abase the tsar's power and raise the clergy to the heights resemble Nikon and the pope." Their threats of anathema finally secured adoption of a compromise formula: "The tsar has preëminence in civil matters, the patriarch in ecclesiastical ones, so that thus shall be preserved intact and firm forever the harmony of the Church establishment." [5]

Alexis did in practice give ground somewhat on the question of the independent jurisdiction of Church courts, and in 1677 even abolished the Monastery Bureau. On the other hand, in the election of a new patriarch the Council submitted to the tsar a panel of three candidates, from which Alexis made his own choice. No subsequent patriarch revived Nikon's claims to supremacy; only in the brief interval between the overthrow of Sophia in 1689 and Peter's personal assumption of authority on his return from the West in 1698 did the patriarchs carry any weight in secular matters.

Thus the solution arrived at was not unlike that reached by the Church of England a century earlier, as recorded in the Thirty-nine Articles adopted by the Anglican bishops in 1571 (foreshadowed by a Latin version in 1563) and ratified by Parliament in 1572:

> . . . We geue not to our princes the ministring either of God's word, or of Sacraments. . . . But that only prerogatiue which we see to haue ben geuen alwayes to all godly Princes in holy Scriptures by God him selfe, that is, that they should rule all estates and degrees committed to their charge by God, whether they be Ecclesiasticall or Temporall, and restraine with the ciuill sworde the stubberne and euyll doers.[6]

It is true that the Moscow settlement did not, as had the English one, involve repudiation of foreign authority. Far from being directed against an alien pope, the council of 1666-67 relied heavily on the authority of the Greek patriarchs to confirm the ancient Byzantine principle, rooted in the notion of caesaropapism, that in all governmental matters the authority of the secular ruler is superior to that of the Church.

The victory of the tsar over the patriarch did not produce any relaxation of enforcement of the reforms, which had served the interests of the state perhaps more than those of the Church. The bulk of the "Old Ritualist" schismatics (*raskolniki*) were folk too humble to attract much attention as individuals, but this Russian parody of the Protestant Reformation found its martyrs, particularly among the resistant clergy. The great Solovetsky Monastery on an island in the White Sea had to be subjected to an eight-year siege by the tsar's forces before it would submit. The most outspoken opponent of the reforms was the Archpriest Avvakum, who defied the council of 1666-67 with all the fervor of a Luther at Worms:

> Although I am a man not clever and unlearned, yet I know that everything handed down by the holy fathers of the Church is sacred and inviolable; I will maintain unto death, as is meet . . . : on us it is enjoined, keep it thus for all eternity.[7]

For his unrelenting intransigence, following another Church Council in 1681, Avvakum was in 1682, during a vigorous and protracted period of repression, burned at the stake, others suffering with him.

FISCAL AND ADMINISTRATIVE PROBLEMS

The troubles attendant on the schism and on the revolt of Razin were by no means the only domestic disturbances in seventeenth-century Moscow. In 1648, for example, there were violent riots in the capital against the excessive corruption encouraged by the young tsar's tutor, B. I. Morozov. It was from this tumult that there resulted the decision to attempt to introduce some order into administrative, judicial, and fiscal chaos by recodifying the laws. In the preparation of the new code, the *Ulozhenie* of 1649, a zemsky sobor played an active role. The benefits of its work were felt mainly by the classes thus represented, the *dvorianstvo* and the privileged urban classes; the peasantry and the lesser elements in the town population were thought of only as sources of state revenues.

Enormous as the tsar's income seemed to foreigners (who then as now were prolific in producing "eyewitness" accounts, not always of the greatest reliability, of conditions in Russia), it was always a terrific struggle to make revenue cover the tremendous expenditure, principally for military purposes. The usual remedy in time of difficulty was simply to devise new taxes, to increase old ones, or to resort to a crude sort of capital levy; such was the imposition of "fifth money" on everyone engaged in trade or industry, in connection with the first resumption of war with Poland (1632). The costs of the struggle over Little Russia inspired the government to try a new device; instead of striking coins of silver, the supply of which was short, it began in 1656 to make them of copper, of the same size and nominal value, but at less than one-sixtieth the cost to the mint. To cope with the inevitable counterfeiting, the tsar removed from office the heads of the mint and had the hands and feet of a number of their subordinates cut off. When these measures proved inadequate, the state refused to accept copper coins in payments to the treasury, while insisting that they be received at face value in payments out of the treasury. In 1662, violent outbreaks were bloodily repressed; a contemporary (Kotoshikhin) said over seven thousand persons were executed and over fifteen thousand subjected to amputation of hands and feet, followed by exile, with confiscation of their property ("and there perished many honorable and eminent and wealthy men").[8] A year later, the government abandoned the technique of token currency, withdrawing the copper coins and redeeming them at 1 percent of their face value.

Before turning attention to those aspects of Russian life which were more subject to foreign influences, it may be well to note in summary fashion the fiscal and governmental organization of the Muscovite autocracy at this time. The medieval concept that the ruler should "live of his own," i.e., from the revenues of his own estates, had long since given way to the concept that he was entitled to support by his subjects, at least by that portion of them who did not serve in his armies.

The basic direct taxes were of several kinds—some of great antiquity—and were paid, not into one central treasury, but into a variety of central offices according to the purposes for which they were officially intended. The amount to be paid by each community—urban or rural—was, as in the days of the Tatar yoke, determined by the central authorities. For this purpose were used the registers of 1627-28, modified by subsequent partial corrections; these registers had carefully enumerated all homesteads, with the names of their holders (if any), and the amount of arable land, meadows, pastures, and woodlands attached, together with all shops, smithies, saltworks, tanneries, mills, or other industrial equipment. The lump sum thus assessed was left to each community—or private landholder—to collect in varying amounts from the local taxpayers on the basis of a "circular guarantee" (i.e., collective responsibility of the community for payment of the whole amount).

In 1677, an order to prepare new registers (*pistsovye knigi*) was not carried out. Instead census records (*perepisnye knigi*) were compiled, listing all homesteads with careful enumeration of their male inhabitants but without reference to property values. Such a listing had been made in 1646 for the purpose of facilitating recovery of fugitives. Now, in the absence of other data, the new listing was used also as the basis for assessing taxes; thus was accomplished (1679) the transition to the "homestead" tax. Since the registers included all sorts of bondsmen as well as taxable peasants, the establishment of the homestead tax was a significant step toward completion of the process of fusing the whole non-noble rural population into one general mass with a minimum of rights and a maximum of obligations; only bondsmen in a noble's household (*dvorovye liudi*) remained tax-exempt.

In addition to these "assessed taxes" there were also more irregularly levied "non-assessed imposts." On rare occasions, especially in the days immediately after the Troubles, these might take the form of a specific authorization by a zemsky sobor to enforce a "loan," as on the Stroganovs or on the Troitsa Monastery. More customary, as noted above, was the grant by a sobor of a special assessment, known as "fifth money," resting sometimes on the privileged classes as well as on those normally subject to tax; the rates varied and were often somewhat vaguely defined. These extraordinary levies apparently were intended to rest principally on the commercial population, whose profits, to judge by the fact that 20 percent was the usual rate of interest, must normally have exceeded the "fifth money." They were collected with such increasing frequency (though sometimes at lower rates) as to come to be regarded as almost a regular impost on all those engaged in trade and industry, whatever their legal status otherwise. Thus, members of the "white" (tax-exempt) elements of the population—nobles, *strieltsy,* cannoneers, etc.—as well as the normally taxable townsmen and peasants were subjected to these taxes. By reason of the weak development of the tax-collecting apparatus, however, these "non-assessed" levies were often collected in the same manner as the older "assessed" taxes.

The larger part of the state's revenues came from indirect taxes, not because of fiscal theories then current in Western Europe, but rather because the government apparently felt that a tax in connection with which the individual acquired something of real value (not merely a tax quittance) was more palatable to the population. It is not possible to distinguish the relative amounts derived from customs duties and from tolls of various kinds (which were in 1653 consolidated at one standard rate of 5 percent *ad valorem*) and from the state liquor monopoly. These revenues were farmed out or, in the absence of voluntary collectors, imposed "on trust" upon locally elected officials, who were held liable, on punishment of death, for punctual payment. In 1652, at Nikon's instance and in an effort to combat drunkenness, the taverns were abolished; spirits were to be sold only in bulk or through "package stores"; these stores were to be closed on Sundays, were to extend no credit, and were not to sell to ecclesiastics. The state's loss of revenue was so great that the experiment was abandoned after ten years.

Some experiments in increasing the revenue by imposing new indirect taxes also proved disastrous. In 1646, the tax on salt was raised from 5 to 20 kopecks a pood (36 pounds); in consequence, quantities of fish were left to rot, and in 1648 the official held responsible for the new rate was murdered by a rioting mob. Similarly, the government established a tobacco monopoly, offering the "accursed and impious poison" for practically its weight in gold; after the riots of 1648, an earlier law of 1634 was reinstated, making use or sale of tobacco punishable by death.

Seigniorage and judicial revenues were not unimportant; fines for failure to register horse trades alone brought in ten thousand rubles a year. More important were the state enterprises and state participation in trade, which supplied a large share of the state's revenues. By far the major source was the fur monopoly, the yield of which was estimated by Kotoshikhin, a foreign-office clerk who fled abroad in 1664, to have been almost half as great as the income from all taxes. Yet revenues could only with the greatest difficulty be made to keep pace with rising expenditures, chiefly military. The number of men in treasury pay by a muster-roll of 1631 was some 70,000, not counting irregular auxiliaries; a list of 1681 shows 164,000. The cost of the army, largely due to its reorganization on foreign models, had risen even more rapidly—from 3 million rubles in 1631 to 10 million in 1680.

The civil administration, on the other hand, had changed but little. In the confused state of affairs arising from the Troubles, the system of elected local officials had broken down. First in the border provinces, later in many of the old central provinces, the *gubnoi starosta* had been replaced by an appointed governor (*voevoda*). In theory, this was not a restoration of the old system of "feedings," for the *voevoda* was forbidden to receive fees unless offered voluntarily, "for honor." It was of course not long before candidates for such posts were frankly asking for specific towns "to feed themselves." The powers of the *voevoda* were ill defined; their instructions were festooned with red tape, but the sum and substance of them was to act "as is fitting, in view of the business there, as God teaches." The arbitrary power of the *voevoda* was sometimes tempered by the continued existence, side by side with him, of one or more elected *gubnye starosty,* usually subordinate to him but occasionally substituting for him altogether. Absorption of local judicial and police authority by the *voevoda* did not disturb the old "zemsky" institutions for collection of taxes, direct and indirect; their work was merely aggravated by the added exactions of the *voevoda* and his staff.

The tendency to centralization reflected in the establishment of an appointed *voevoda* was carried further by a grouping of their counties (*uiezdy*) into larger units (*razriady*) for purposes of more efficient military organization. Beginning along the frontiers, by the time of Fedor the whole country had been thus organized into nine military districts, which provided the basis for Peter's later organization of provinces (*guberniyas*).

At the capital, power was still officially exercised by the boyar duma. The term "boyar," as applied to an individual, retained its old significance of an official of the highest rank, and *miestnichestvo* considerations were still operative. It had, however, as already noted, lost its more general significance of membership in a closed class apart from temporary official position. Kotoshikhin, a minor official who went into voluntary exile as a sequel to punishments stemming from a mistake he made in writing the tsar's proper title, may be suspected of some prejudice; he sketches sittings of the duma at which some of the boyars, "ordering their beards," gave no reply to the tsar's questions; they were unable to give him good advice "because the tsar makes many to be boyars, not for their intelligence but for their great birth, and many of them are not learned in writing and have not studied." [9] The real power lay, of course, not with such men, but with the secretaries (*diaki*) who concentrated the actual business in their hands. How little decisive were the opinions of the boyars in the duma is suggested by an extant set of notes made by Tsar Alexis in preparation for a meeting of the duma. In it appear not only the questions he intended to submit but the answers he expected to receive. Only on two matters did he express uncertainty and the intention to be guided by what the boyars might say.

The administrative organs under the duma were known as "commands" (*prikazy*) because they had gradually evolved from commands to individual boyars to take charge of specific duties in connection with the tsar's household and with the evolving state apparatus. They had grown up in most haphazard fashion and had the sanction of many decades for their confused structure. For that matter, attempts to recombine their functions were rarely carried out on any logical principle. They numbered about fifty, several of which might be administered by the same individual.

One of Alexis' innovations was the establishment of an Office of Privy Affairs (*Prikaz tainykh diel*), which, like the *oprichnina* of Ivan the Terrible, was personal to him. Its primary purpose was to provide for the tsar's pleasures, among which falconry was foremost; at its height it was said to maintain some one hundred thousand broods of pigeons to feed and train over three thousand falcons, gerfalcons, and buzzards. It handled also his personal correspondence and his private charities; it acted also as his "private eye" in watching the whole administrative apparatus of the state. No one of duma rank was employed, and the whole personnel of the office numbered less than a dozen officials. Yet it contained the germ of an idea which was later to become, in one form or another, a permanent feature of Russian governmental practice. Though the "most peaceful tsar" lacked consistent force of will, he insisted on attaching to embassies sent abroad and to the staffs of armies serving in the field members of this forerunner of the political police, "to the end that his, the tsar's, thought and acts be fulfilled all according to his wish." [10]

NOTES

1. Got′e [Gautier], *"Akty otnosiashchiesia k istorii Zemskikh Soborov,"* in *Pamiatniki russkoi istorii,* No. 3, p. 46; cf. also Platonov, *K istorii moskovskikh zemskikh soborov.*
2. Kulisher, *Russische Wirtschaftsgeschichte,* p. 203.
3. *Ibid.,* p. 234.
4. Kapterev, *Patriarkh Nikon i Tsar′ Aleksiei Mikhailovich,* II, 183.
5. *Ibid.,* p. 244.
6. Hardwick, *A History of the Articles of Religion,* 3rd edition, pp. 343-345.
7. Gudzy (ed.), *Zhitie protopopa Avvakuma im simim napisannoe i drugie ego sochineniia,* pp. 138-139.
8. Kotoshikhin, *O Rossii . . . : Sochinenie Grigorii Kotoshikhina,* 4th edition, p. 118.
9. *Ibid.,* pp. 26-27.
10. *Ibid.,* p. 95.

SUGGESTIONS FOR FURTHER READING

In addition to general works previously cited, Bain's *The First Romanovs* is a conventional discussion of seventeenth-century Russia. Among many studies of Russian relations with the Orient, a pioneer work is Golder's *Russian Expansion on the Pacific, 1641-1850.* This has been followed by Lobanov-Rostovsky's *Russia and Asia;* the more specialized administrative study by Lantzeff, *Siberia in the Seventeenth Century;* R. H. Fisher's *The Russian Fur Trade, 1550-1700;* and M. N. Pavlovsky's *Chinese-Russian Relations.* Sebes' *The Jesuits and the Sino-Russian Treaty of Nerchinsk (1689): The Diary of Thomas Pereira, S. J.,* provides interesting sidelights. On the struggle for the Ukraine, see, in addition to works cited in Chapter 4, Vernadsky's *Bohdan, Hetman of Ukraine* and O'Brien's *Muscovy and the Ukraine.* For fictional flavor, see Sienkiewicz' historical trilogy, *With Fire and Sword, The Deluge,* and *Pan Michael.* A contemporary account of Razin's uprising may be found in *Relation des particularités de la rébellion de Stenko Razin. . . .* The classic study in English of the Nikon episode is W. Palmer, *The Patriarch and the Tsar.* There is an English translation of the life of Avvakum by Harrison and Mirlees; a more general work is Conybeare's *Russian Dissenters.* A non-Russian account of fiscal difficulties is Brückner's *Das Kupfergeld 1656-1663 in Russland.*

Chapter

10

The First Romanovs and the Impact of the West: 1613-1689

One of the tsar's dearest wishes was to make Russia militarily strong, and it was in the pursuit of this goal that Western influences first made themselves strongly felt. It had soon become as obvious to the Russians as to their foes the Poles that the victories of the latter resulted only from the pitting of brains against brawn. The ill-organized feudal militia of Muscovy was no match for much smaller forces arrayed in disciplined regiments that could be maneuvered on the battlefield. Weight of numbers might seem to sweep all before it in the early stages of a war, but the weakness of Russia's economy deprived her of staying power. It had not sufficed to introduce firearms, although the *strieltsy,* whose arquebuses were now replaced by muskets, had become the most effective part of the Russian forces. The small bands of mercenaries recruited abroad by such "Germans" (i.e., foreigners) as Leslie and Vendome were far too expensive a luxury.

Remedy was sought in organizing the *dvoriane,* often under foreign officers, in regiments patterned on Western models. The army that moved against Smolensk in 1632 totaled 32,000 men, with 158 cannon. Included in this corps were six regiments of infantry, trained and armed in European fashion; 1,500 were hired foreigners, and some 13,000 were Russians. Smolensk was not taken, but the effort to press military reorganization became only the more vigorous. By 1681 only the *dvoriane* of the capital retained their medieval organization; they numbered 2,624 men, making, with their bondsmen and conscripts, a force of about 22,000. In the other eight military districts (*razriady*) the *dvoriane* were assigned to one or another of the 63 regiments of horse and foot; together with the sixteen "commands" of *strieltsy,* they constituted a force of about 90,000 somewhat disciplined troops. At the same time the practice of conscripting peasant soldiers (*datochnye*) was extended and regularized.

Alexis undertook construction of a regular navy for service on the Caspian Sea, commanded by foreign officers. It fell prey, however, to Razin, and the effort was not renewed.

GROWTH OF INDUSTRY

Although fully conscious of the importance of improved military techniques, the Muscovites of the seventeenth century were only dimly aware of the need of developing Russia's economy in order that it might sustain the burden of an ever-increasing military establishment. Yet even minds untutored in political economy could not fail to perceive the importance of protecting, even stimulating, trade and industry. In the quest for methods of promoting commercial activity, the Muscovite authorities stumbled along the same mercantilist paths that Western Europe had followed. If they led Russia to less successful results, it was in part the result of Russia's unfavorable geography, in part the product of the fact that Russia, unlike the West in its earlier development, was suddenly confronted with the aggressive and far superior economic force of the English and the Dutch. The task of developing her economic potential was much complicated by the need of taking special measures of defense against the foreigners, to whom in the first flush of enthusiasm Ivan the Terrible had accorded extensive privileges. Far more than in the West, the organized power of the state was required to redress the balance of economic strength, and it was thus that the Russian state entered on the path of active participation in commerce and industry on a scale not reached even by Colbertist practices in the West. Not only peasant serfdom but commercial submissiveness was to be one of the enduring hallmarks of the Muscovite autocracy.

Russian traders continued to amaze foreigners by their multitude and by their sharp practices, but it was only in the course of the seventeenth century, and under pressure from the state, that some concentration of handicraft trade and industry in the towns took place. Russian towns had never developed, as did Western towns in the Middle Ages, into economically specialized centers of trade and industry. They had remained administrative and military centers, around which often grew up a subordinate walled *posad,* whose inhabitants—artisans and small traders—had to compete with the "white" (i.e., tax-exempt) members of the garrison and with landholders' bondsmen. In view of their relative insignificance, the townsmen had never been able to develop a corporate unity, even on a local basis; Russia knew no counterpart of the Western guilds, save among the icon-painters and among the handful of specially privileged traders who ranked as *gosti* or as members of the "*gost* hundred" and the "cloth hundred."

The economic dislocation attendant on the political convulsions in the reign of Ivan IV and during the Troubles had seriously affected the urban population no less than the rural. Before the crisis, Novgorod, despite her decline under Muscovite rule, had still boasted over two thousand craftsmen; as late as 1638 Moscow, despite the practice of compulsorily transporting thither the ablest workers from all over the realm, had only 2,367 (not including "white" categories) on the official tax registers. No other town—except Nizhny Novgorod—could show more than 55, and few towns reached any such numbers; Pskov, which succeeded Novgorod as the chief town near the western border, had 180 registered craftsmen at the end of the century. These figures are to some extent misleading, for they do not include the *strieltsy* and other tax-exempt garrison elements, who made up a substantial proportion of the urban population and who freely engaged in trade and industry.

To protect its revenues, the state, in the *Ulozhenie,* attempted to make trade and industry a monopoly of the townsmen (*posadskie*) whom it sought to bind, like the peasants, to a fixed place of residence. *Posadskie* were forbidden to move out into "liberties" (*slobody*), and all who did not live in the *posad* were ordered to sell their booths there; only the soldiers were exempted from this restriction, but they too were subjected to taxation on their business activities. The existing urban and suburban commercial and industrial "liberties" were simultaneously incorporated into the *posady,* thus artificially effecting a sharp increase in the numbers of the urban population, at least as taxpayers. A special effort was made to recover for the treasury those who had mortgaged themselves to patrons (*zakladchiki*); those who had harbored them were to be flogged and sent to Siberia. Even household domestics (*dvorniki*) of boyars and monasteries, who also frequently engaged in trade or industry, as well as relatives and lodgers in taxable households, were subjected to the urban tax. Just as the various categories of the peasant population were gradually being assimilated into one mass of taxable bondsmen, so were all those engaged in petty trade and handicraft industry being reduced, so far as possible, to the uniform status of immobilized taxpayers, living at an almost incredibly low level of material comfort.

Despite this general tendency toward freezing occupational relationships, there existed a considerable number of free wage-workers. These were naturally the poorest of the poor, whether urban or rural, and therefore had to be distinguished in the registers from the taxable ("has neither house nor yard," "has nothing," "has only one cow, otherwise nothing at all").[1] They were engaged mainly in common labor, in hauling barges on the rivers, and in building. They furnished also the bulk of the labor in new, relatively large-scale industrial enterprises, such as Tsar Alexis' potash-works at Arzamas, which in 1680 employed 103 bondsmen from the tsar's estates and 394 peasants freely hired on the basis of wage contracts. Their freedom remained precarious, not only economically but legally, for their service was often performed for a long period of years, and it was difficult for poor men to insist on their rights, even if, as was not always the case, they had taken the precaution to specify a time limit.

Maskiewicz, a Pole who had been with the force that during the Troubles for a time occupied the Kremlin, wrote:

> All the Russian artisans are excellent, very skillful and so intelligent that a thing they have never made or even seen before they understand at the first glance and execute as well as though they were accustomed to it from infancy. . . .[2]

A later foreign observer added:

> Tradesmen . . . are very handy, and easily imitate anything they see done, though they are not so rich in inventions as the Germans and other Europeans. . . . So that strangers who are not willing to have the secret of their professions discovered, must take heed of Muscovites.[3]

Tsar Alexis was ambitious to realize the dream of producing in Russia all sorts of "curiosities, which formerly did not exist in the Muscovite realm." As part of this phantasy he attempted to introduce on his estates cultivation of melons from Bukhara, of almonds, figs, Hungarian pears, Astrakhan pepper, cotton, and mulberries to feed silkworms. For this purpose he diligently sought out seeds and proper soil and engaged skilled gardeners, both Russian monks and foreign apothecaries. Of equally impractical consequence was his importation of "masters, so skilled that they can make birds that sing and walk and speak as in a playhouse." [4] Incidental also were the German coach in which he took his wife driving, the picture books on which his son Peter was brought up, or the brass bands he so dearly loved.

More importantly, Alexis continued and widely expanded the practice, begun in the fifteenth century and steadily developed, of encouraging the immigration into Russia of all sorts of foreigners, skilled in military pursuits or in the industrial arts. In Russian parlance all non-Slavs were called *nemtsy* (from *nemets,* "dumb"—a usage analogous to the Greek "barbarous"); in modern Russian, *nemtsy* means specifically Germans and is therefore so translated here. Even in 1649, their number in Moscow was so great—and the quarrels of their wives over precedence in church so disturbing to the patriarch—that it was deemed expedient to expel the "German" churches from the city of Moscow proper; in 1652 the tsar assigned to foreigners a special settlement, the "German Liberty" (*nemetskaia sloboda*), from which, of course, they easily overflowed into the capital itself.

Under the guidance of foreign technicians and organizers, a number of industries were introduced or developed in the deliberate effort, inherited from the Romanovs' predecessors, to make Russia independent of the outside world. In first place came naturally the manufacture of weapons, which had in the main been imported from Holland. As early as 1547, Swedish and

English iron miners had been recruited. Under Michael was established at Tula (1632) the first Russian ironworks to use water power. It was directed by a Dutchman, Andrew Vinnius, to whom were assigned as laborers some of the tsar's peasants; his contract called for production, not only of instruments of war, but of iron for peaceful uses as well. Among his successors were several other foreigners (including the Dane Marselis, who incidentally first introduced the cultivated rose into Russia), also employing serf labor and producing for peaceful consumption as well as for the tsar's arsenals.

Under the direction of the tsars were established also potash-works, limekilns, saltworks, glassworks, paper mills, and workshops for the manufacture of silk, velvet, and other goods; production of more prosaic stuffs—hemp and linen—was not neglected. Special attention was given to the quest for supplies of iron, copper, gold, and silver; though Tula remained the chief seat of iron production, a beginning was made at exploitation of the Ural area. All these enterprises suffered considerably from the naïve enthusiasm of the Russians, from the tendency of the ablest foreigners to return home as soon as they could afford to, and from a constant sacrifice of quality to quantity. Yet, small as was industrial progress, a serious beginning was made, and valuable experience acquired for later development.

CAPITALISM, NATIVE AND FOREIGN

It is, however, in connection with trade rather than with industry that one may find the beginnings of Russian capitalist enterprise. The industrial workshops were small and somewhat ephemeral. Handicraft industry, except certain branches especially connected with the export trade (like the manufacture of leather), remained free from control by entrepreneurs operating under a putting-out system. Yet a number of merchants, chiefly ranking as *gosti,* operated with what was for those times exceedingly substantial capital. They traded mainly in salt and fish or engaged in the transport of goods on the Volga; Nizhny Novgorod, where later the fair of St. Macarius was held, became the greatest purely commercial center in Muscovy. The chief seat of capitalist activity was, of course, Moscow, for its *gosti* acted largely as agents of the tsars and exercised the right of preëmption on all wares offered for sale. The *gosti* managed all sorts of state enterprises throughout the realm, from the collection of customs to the fur trade of Siberia.

By far the most outstanding capitalists of the period were the Stroganovs, who controlled vast saltworks, operated iron mines and ironworks, sold Siberian sables and other furs through their own agents in Holland and Flanders, supplied Astrakhan with grain and brought thence silk and caviar for export. They maintained depots in a number of towns, even in the steppe. Yet their enterprises differed only in magnitude, not in variety, from those of a number of other humbler yet overbearing men, whose economic power excited the envy and hatred of the handicraft traders. "It is to be feared," wrote a

German observer in 1674, "that in case of a disturbance all the *gosti* would have their necks broken by the mob." [5] In 1681 "this selfish and pernicious college" declined an opportunity to take over the collection of all indirect taxes on the ground there were no men in the provinces they could trust; it has been suggested that what the *gosti* meant was that they feared overstraining the patience of the local population.

In the growth of capitalism, as in so many other ways, Russia showed a substantial lag behind Western Europe. By the seventeenth century, the time had long since gone by when Western rulers and nobles, churches and monasteries, had participated actively in the conduct of trade; a specialized merchant population had replaced them. If foreigners attributed the amazingly large number of tiny trading booths in Moscow to the fact that the inhabitants "from the highest to the least, love commerce," [6] the fact reflects the essentially precapitalistic character of the Muscovite economy, in which wholesale and retail trade and traffic in the widest variety of wares were combined in the same hands. Even for the capitalists, salt-extraction, fishing, trapping, and leasing of government monopolies—all combined with large landholding—far outweighed in importance trade itself. The conduct of trade on capitalist lines was severely handicapped by the absence of banking, of payment by bills of exchange, of a bourse. Debts weighed heavily, not only on the peasants but even on the tsars; yet there was no development of a system of public credit. The chief moneylenders were, as of old, the monasteries. Rates of interest, normally 20 percent, sometimes ran to 33⅓ percent even on loans to merchants; short-term loans might run at 1 percent per diem.

Foreign traders, on the other hand, employed far more advanced capitalist techniques, even securing the establishment of a postal system, both for travelers and for correspondence. The latter was first organized about 1665 by a Dutchman, John of Sweden, who about the middle of the century had founded the first cloth "factory" in Russia. The system was later extended to include a route via Smolensk to Vilna and Prussia, letters taking about four weeks from Moscow to Hamburg. In consonance with the spirit of the times, incoming letters were immediately taken to the Foreign Office (*Posolsky Prikaz*) and there "opened, so that no private person should learn what is happening within or without the land before the court knows it." [7] Russian merchants did not share in the government's knowledge. Ivan Pososhkov (1652-1726), a small trader of rural artisan stock who differed from thousands of his fellows only in his articulateness, complained bitterly to young Tsar Peter in 1701 about this ruinous "hole," which should be stopped up: "If there were no foreign post, trade would be equal; as our Russian men do not know of their wares, so they would not know of our wares, and trade would be without injury." [8]

Most of the foreign trade of Russia went through the White Sea, not directly overland or through the ports of Riga and Narva, then controlled by the Swedes. Baltic trade with England, Holland, and other countries of the Atlantic seaboard suffered, not only by alien control of the whole shoreline, but also by the fact that Denmark imposed heavy tolls on all ships passing in and out of that sea. The Danish kings, indeed, claimed the right to take toll of all vessels trading with Russia by way of the Arctic, asserting that the waters between Norway and Iceland were a Danish "strait." Even in the time of Ivan the Terrible their cruisers had done so much damage to foreign traders who rounded the North Cape and to their Russian hosts that all trade had been ordered concentrated under the walls of the monastery of St. Michael the Archangel, at a safe distance up the Dvina River.

The English were the earliest and the most favored visitors, but Moscow was keenly aware of the possibility of raising export prices by encouraging competition and consequently constantly altered the rules. For example, until 1649 the English in theory enjoyed the exclusive right to trade in the interior of Muscovy. Yet traders of many other nationalities exercised the privilege under special licenses, which on one occasion were summarily canceled to please an insistent English agent; shortly afterward, however, the right was accorded to the Dutch and English in equal numbers.

Through all such shifts nevertheless ran a fairly consistent pattern. The English and especially the Dutch persistently cherished the hope of treating Russia as a colony. Toward the end of the sixteenth century it was urged on the Dutch States-General that "God Almighty . . . shows us a new path, which is just as lucrative as sailing to Spain [i.e., to America], and this is the path to Moscow." [9] The Dutch were particularly interested in the grain trade. In 1630 they formally asked, not only for a monopoly of grain exports, but for the right to organize cultivation in Muscovy. Tsar Michael's reply was discouraging: "If Dutch traders are permitted to engage in agriculture in the realm of Moscow, it will be grievous for Russians." [10] The tsar was willing to have his agents buy grain and sell it to the Dutch, at a profit to the treasury ranging from 60 to 75 percent. However, still more profitable uses were found for it, and by 1674 it was reported that "now all the grain remains in the country, and the distilleries consume much of it." [11] The Dutch did secure a monopoly of the export of caviar, but notwithstanding the most energetic efforts, none of Moscow's foreign suitors was able to secure the grand prize, the right to monopolize the trade in silk and other Oriental goods through Astrakhan.

The superior organization, experience, and capital of Western merchants, whether operating through Archangel or through the Baltic, bore heavily on Russian traders. A typical complaint is one of 1646, signed by a number of merchants as spokesmen for all the principal trading towns:

> . . . The English Germans . . . wishing to get control of all the trade, bribed the duma secretary Peter Tretiakov with many promises. . . . And they [i.e., the foreigners] living in Moscow and in the [provincial] towns go through Novgorod and Pskov five, six, and ten times a year with news of what

> is being done in the Moscow realm, what prices are being paid for wares, and whatever wares sell dear in Muscovy, those they begin to prepare, and they all act according to their private information and according to letters, agreeing in concert. . . .[12]

In this case the specific grievance was that the Moscow merchants had bought up all the available silk in the tsar's warehouses, only to be caught by a decline in price on the European market; the foreign traders laughed at what the Russians thought a fair price. The complaint continued:

> Gracious Sovereign Tsar and Grand Prince Alexis Mikhailovich of all Rus, have mercy upon us, thy bondsmen and orphans, the traders of all the realm; look, O Sovereign, upon us poor people and do not permit us, thy born bondsmen and orphans, on account of these heretics to be in eternal misery and poverty; forbid that our trades, O Sovereign, ours from time immemorial, be snatched from us poor people. Command, O Sovereign, that the English and the Hamburg and the Bavarian and the Dutch and the Danish Germans, merchants and traders, trade at the wharf in Archangel and do not permit, O Sovereign, that they be admitted to Moscow and to the other towns of all the realm of Moscow.

There was little that the tsar's government could do in a positive way, but what could be accomplished by prohibitions, short of expelling the foreigners altogether, it did. Sometimes it took specific action to curtail the advantages of foreigners. Thus, in 1649 Tsar Alexis deprived the English Russia Company of its privilege of trading without paying customs duties, on the ground that he had

> heard that the English by [action of] all the land [i.e., Parliament] have done a most evil deed: their Sovereign King Charles they have done to death, for which evil deed you will not be admitted in the realm of Moscow.[13]

In 1650, when Culpeper came to Moscow to ask aid for Prince Charles, the tsar ordered him given furs to the value of 20,000 rubles; though Culpeper would have preferred half the amount in grain, he was forced to sign a receipt for 5,000 rubles in grain and 15,000 in furs. In 1654 an envoy from Cromwell was coldly received and lectured for showing resentment. Restoration of the Stuarts in 1660 resulted in repayment of the loan, but the tsar's effort to convert his brief experience as creditor into the pleasanter role of debtor was rebuffed; accordingly the special privileges of the English were never restored.

At other times the government acted in a narrow mercantilist spirit against all comers. In the first place, it tried to strengthen and make general in its application the prohibition of retail trade by foreigners in Muscovy. Secondly, it forbade any direct trade with the rural population. Further, trade among foreigners resident in Russia was outlawed, as well as trade between foreigners and Russian merchants not resident in the towns where trade was permitted; an exception was made only for traders from the capital. The length of time foreigners might remain in Russia and the places where they might live and store their wares were also elaborately circumscribed. All these provisions, reflecting ingrained attitudes, though consistently violated or evaded, were incorporated into a new commercial code in 1667.

More important was the frequent resort to establishment of government monopolies, a practice dear to the Muscovite treasury for domestic fiscal reasons also. The spirit monopoly, though impossible to enforce completely, had long been one of the chief and most constant sources of state revenue; together with customs duties it brought in far more than all the direct taxes, in the interest of which the state was so vigorously promoting the enserfment of the peasantry. Monopolies gave the state the highest possible prices that could be extracted from foreigners and at the same time gave encouragement to Russian traders, but they also tended to keep the volume of exports to a minimum.

The commodity most eagerly sought after by foreigners was Persian silk, which could be carried by water to Astrakhan for little more than a third of the cost of overland transport to the Persian Gulf. By river from Astrakhan to Archangel and thence by sea to Western Europe, transportation was much cheaper than by the long passage around the Cape of Good Hope. Yet the Muscovites refused to allow foreigners to buy in Astrakhan and themselves delivered silk only once in three years, and at exorbitant prices, at Archangel. The export of silk, as shown by customs entries, therefore amounted to less than 1 percent of Archangel exports. Hides and leather, with which the Russian government did not bother, constituted a third of the total; together with tallow, potash, and monopolized furs they accounted for three-fifths of the value of shipments through Archangel.

TECHNICAL AND IDEOLOGICAL BORROWINGS FROM THE WEST

Russian exports, however highly valued in the West and however vital currently to the tsar's treasury, were of course far less significant for the development of Russian history than were her imports. Here it is not a question of the cloth, wine, buttons, paper, and the like which foreigners so eagerly vended. Rather, it was a matter of introducing into backward Russia, torn and confused by the commotions attendant on the *oprichnina* and the extinction of the old dynasty, of new ways of thinking inspired by the wholesale importation of techniques and technicians from the relatively advanced lands of Western Europe.

It is possible to distinguish the beginnings of the struggle for mastery between the two great schools of Russian thought, which, though manifested at different times under a wide variety of forms, may be most conveniently thought of as "Westerners" and "Slavophiles" (the names under which the antagonists were known in the early nineteenth century).

On the one hand were men impressed by the superior material advantages of certain aspects of life in the West, attracted by the amenities of other aspects, and at the same time oppressed by a sense of the backwardness, the crudity, the hopelessness of Russian customs, manners, and institutions. They therefore went far beyond the men of the fifteenth and sixteenth centuries, who had welcomed—and at the same time been suspicious of—foreign artisans and doctors. They sought to acquire not only the practical results of foreign learning and foreign skills; they desired also to master the knowledge and the thought that produced those practical results. They enjoyed also the more frivolous sides of life in the West. Muscovite envoys brought home detailed reports of court entertainments. Clothing, furnishings, mechanical devices, music—all were imported for the delectation of the tsar and of his intimates.

The bulk of the population, of course, remained unaffected or even reacted hostilely. When opportunity offered, the mob riotously destroyed such examples of Western craftsmanship as the wedding coach, upholstered in gold brocade and sables and equipped with silver tires, which Alexis had presented to his unpopular brother-in-law Morozov (1648). Less boisterous, though hardly less energetic, was the reaction of some highly placed persons to the intellectual dominance of the West. As early as 1618, Ivan Timotheiev, secretary of one of the *prikazy,* who had lived through the Time of the Troubles, wrote a "Chronicle of the Times" (*Vremennik*) beginning with the reign of Ivan the Terrible. To him Godunov and Shuisky were usurpers, who had happily been succeeded by another "born tsar," Michael Romanov. Old Russia, he thought, had lost faith in herself; "there is no certainty in anything, no responsibility in words or deeds, but everything is turning like a wheel." [14] In their confusion, men did not know where to look for leadership.

Conservative as the precursors of the Slavophiles necessarily were and much as they insisted on the need to preserve Russian ways, they were as conscious as were the would-be imitators of the West that change and reform were necessary. Since what they desired to conserve were the principles, not the forms, of old Russia, they worked together with their opponents in carrying through the reform of Nikon. Tending to cling to the concept of Moscow as the third and final Rome, they looked not only to the past but to the future. In the Church reform their difference with the "Westerners" found its expression in the controversy as to whether or not Latin should be studied along with Greek. The "Latin heresy," as a peril to Orthodoxy, must be scrupulously avoided, but they welcomed development of old Byzantine tradition. Nor were they averse to the borrowing of material aspects of "Latin" culture, so far as they were not allowed to influence the thought of Muscovy.

It was, of course, a difficult matter to limit borrowings from the West. Introduction of new weapons from the West had led inevitably to importation of men capable of teaching their use, to efforts to reproduce them and ammunition for them in Russia, and so in turn to importation of artisans capable of making them and of teaching Russians how to make them. Even in the sixteenth century all sorts of persons possessing—or professing to possess—all sorts of special skills had found their way to Moscow; in the seventeenth century the floodgates opened wide, for foreign residents in Russia did not willingly abandon the comforts and pleasures they had known at home and at the earliest opportunity introduced ways of life in which the Russians had at first been scarcely interested. For example, Johann Gottfried Gregory, pastor of the Lutheran church in the "German Liberty," organized among his young parishioners a group of actors to celebrate the birth of Tsarevich Peter and subsequently presented for the tsar's edification and enjoyment a number of Biblical (and secular) dramas with burlesque features. Troubled by criticisms of this "devil's game, defilement of the soul," Alexis consulted his confessor, who was also his companion in his cups, and was reassured to learn that he was only following the example of Byzantine emperors.

Not content to be admiring spectators of imported amusements, some Russians inquired more deeply into the customs and ideas that lay behind them. Some simply began to adopt foreign manners of dress, others began to study foreign languages and acquire foreign books. One, Matveev, who was appointed by Alexis as boyar in charge of the Foreign Office, became so un-Russian as to hold "at homes" in his house, which was furnished in European style; these social occasions, devoted to conversation and discussion of the latest new ideas, were even graced with the attendance of the mistress of the house and without that heavy drinking which St. Vladimir had called "the joy of the Russes."

Naturally, it was chiefly through Poland, Moscow's nearest neighbor, that European manners entered the country. Particularly important was the surviving Orthodox community in Poland, for the Kievan Academy played a wider role than merely promoting the ritual reform of Nikon. Even before Nikon became patriarch, three Kievan monks were imported, at a much lower rate of pay than German military officers but with free accommodations in a monastery and with liberal extra rations of beer from the tsar's palace. Their principal task was to make the first complete translation of the Bible from Greek into Russian, but they also translated, in more or less condensed form, a number of scientific works, ranging from geography and a *Book of Medical Anatomy* to *Citizenship and the Teaching of Children's Manners*. About the same time, Rtishchev, one of the tsar's closest advisers, founded a special monastery, which he tenanted with more than thirty learned Little Russian monks, charged with making translations from foreign languages—including Western chivalric romances—and also with giving free instruction in the classical tongues, in rhetoric, and in philosophy. A number of attempts were made to establish schools under other imported pedants; since material knowledge was what the educated Russian most craved, a number of officials were ordered to take instruction in Latin, the language in which was recorded the scientific progress of the West. The Office of Ambassadors was particularly active in securing copies of foreign works and effecting their translation into Slavonic, the literary language of the time, now known as Old Church Slavonic, from which in the next century, under the influence of the Great Russian vernacular, was to develop the modern Russian language.

The great schism in the Church was not directly the product of specifically Western influences. There did arise heresies, such as that of the "Bread-Worshippers" (who were influenced by the Roman doctrine of transubstantiation), stemming directly from "Latin" influences and often attributed to Simeon Polotsky, a Kievan monk employed as tutor for Alexis' children, who distinguished himself by open denunciation, *ex cathedra,* of the general ignorance of the Muscovite clergy. Yet Nikon's activity, which ruthlessly drove a large proportion of the faithful into the status of anathematized Old Ritualists, had not been concerned with questions of theology; Nikon was interested in correcting ritual practices, with the objective of fitting the Russian Church to play its role as the standard-bearer of universal orthodoxy. A backward and provincial Church, treated with tolerant contempt by the Eastern patriarchs and with more strenuous scorn by the monks of Mount Athos, could not well be counted on to withstand the insidious penetration of Catholic and Protestant ideas. On the other hand, a Moscow patriarchate, strong in its ancient inherited faith and untainted by ritual debasements and corruptions, could claim leadership of the whole Orthodox world and give richer meaning to the concept of Moscow as the third and final Rome. In this sense it was the protagonists of a "Slavophile" view who were chiefly responsible for the reforms.

At the same time the abrupt and high-handed manner—so reminiscent of Ivan the Terrible—in which Nikon set about the work played unconsciously into the hands of the "Westerners." Unable to win the active support either of the clergy or of the laity, Nikon relied on his position as "great sovereign" to break his more outspoken opponents and to bend the more pliable to his will. The result was that when he challenged the authority of the tsar, he found no support from the Church. After his fall, the state continued to support his revisions of the ritual, for they had received the blessing of an Ecumenical Council, but the hierarchy which had assisted him in creating the schism was viewed with suspicion. What little influence the Church had possessed over the state in secular matters was irretrievably gone, and its moral influence was reduced to so low an ebb that, for all its reactionary instincts, it was impotent to offer any resistance to the increasingly rapid westernization, not merely of techniques, but of manners and of habits of thought.

CRITICISMS OF OLD MUSCOVY

Prince Kurbsky, the chief critic of Ivan the Terrible, has sometimes been cited as an early example of the "Western" point of view. He did, to be sure, flee to the West and under Polish-Lithuanian protection formulate a vigorous indictment of the tsar. His attack, however, was based on the thought that Ivan was doing violence to the sound and time-honored principles of government by refusing to share his power effectively with his boyars. Kurbsky, though a refugee in the West, did not advocate adoption of new ideas but simply stood for the reinvigoration of what had always been. Nor can Peresvietov, despite his recommendation of concepts new in Muscovy, be considered a "Westernizer." What he argued for and presented as practices prevailing in the well-ordered lands of the Ottoman Turk were in no way importations from the West.

It is not until well into the seventeenth century that far-reaching criticisms of Russian realities were presented, not in the spirit of a craving for return to a golden age, but in wholesale rejection of the inherited bases of Muscovite life. Very soberly presented was *Concerning Russia in the Reign of Aleksiei Mikhailovich* by Gregory Kotoshikhin, whom his Swedish biographer called "a man of great intellect." To be sure, as noted earlier, Kotoshikhin had personal grievances: when an undersecretary in the Office of Ambassadors, he had been cudgeled for making a mistake in the tsar's title (1660); attached to an army operating against Poland, he had deserted, as he said, rather than slander the commander to whom he had been attached (1664). After a period of wandering in Poland and Germany, he had settled in Sweden under the name of Selitsky and had become a Protestant; there he was ultimately beheaded for stabbing with a Spanish dagger the suspicious husband of his landlady. In the meantime, however, with the encouragement of the Swedish chancellor, he had written a description of Muscovy as viewed in the light of his acquired knowledge of the West.

Most of Kotoshikhin's memoir is devoted to a detailed description of the diplomatic protocol and court etiquette that had been his professional concern; in addition, he lists the social ranks and describes the possibility of recruiting various categories of government personnel from the several social strata; he gives great attention to an extended catalogue of Muscovite administrative organs (*prikazy*) and their revenues; he is at pains to indicate the rates of compensation of various grades of officials and the nature of the presents which "it is fitting to give." [15] Occasionally he inserts explanatory remarks that betray his feelings:

> The men of the Russian realm are puffed up and unused to any kind of business, since in their realm they have no good instruction at all and acquire nothing but haughtiness and shamelessness and hatred and falsehood; . . . for learning and breeding they do not send their sons into other realms, fearing

that, on learning of the faith and manners and blessed freedom of realms there, they might begin to cast off their faith and adhere to others and would have no care or thought to return to their homes and kindred. . . . Any man, be he prince or boyar or anyone whatever, whether himself or whether he sent his son or his brother for any reason at all into another realm without permission of the sovereign, such a man for such an act would be accounted guilty of treason, and his estates hereditary [*votchinas*] and conditional [*pomesties*] and his chattels would be taken by the tsar; and if anyone went himself, and his relatives remained behind, they would be put to torture to see if they had knowledge of their kinsman's thoughts; or if anyone sent his son, or brother or nephew, he would be put to torture. . . .[16]

In sharp contrast to Kotoshikhin's views were the opinions of an "emigrant Serb Yury Ivanovich" Krizhanich. Whereas Kotoshikhin, a Russian who fled abroad, offered no hope for improvement of his native land save by emulation of the West, Krizhanich, an immigrant Slav, viewed Russia as a separate cultural world, which could indeed benefit by limited borrowings from the West, but only in order to strengthen the native potential. Orphaned as a child, Krizhanich had been educated at various Catholic ecclesiastical seminaries. To complete his education as a missionary to the Orthodox Slavs, he was sent to a college in Rome maintained by the Congregation of the Sacred Propaganda. In 1659, he left for the land of his dreams, which he had come to think of as the future center of all Slavdom. At Moscow he managed to become the tsar's librarian but was soon banished (1661) to Tobolsk, where his salary and ample leisure enabled him to write until he himself was bored. He buttressed his arguments by authorities ranging from Aristotle, through the Bible, to Machiavelli. On the death of Alexis he was recalled to Moscow, but he left Russia the following year.

Krizhanich was as well aware as was Kotoshikhin of the shortcomings of the Muscovites, and he dwelt on them at infinitely greater length. He attributed Russia's economic backwardness primarily to the faults of the Slavs themselves. He did not envy Araby and Hungary their precious metals, nor even other lands their abundant products that could be used for personal adornment or for food and drink. His ideal of a prosperous country was to be found in England or in Brabant, where men had good minds, "wherefore all sorts of handicrafts and agriculture flourish, and great maritime trade";[17] most fortunate of all were kingdoms that had "good laws," as had France. Peoples that lived by war could never be rich, as witness the Crimean Tatars, the Turks, and the Kalmucks.

He did recognize that Russia was handicapped by the fact that she was shut off from foreign trade by the Arctic Ocean, by desert wastes, by the wild peoples of Siberia. He was well aware that internal communication was made difficult by the lack of good roads, by great distances, by forests and swamps, and by fear of Tatar marauders of various sorts. He was distressed because Russia's products—chiefly honey, wax, caviar, wheat, rye, flax, and hides—were exported "not by reason of abundance but by reason of need and foreigners' double-dealing."

What was worse, however, was that "the minds of our people are stupid and sluggish; and men have no skill in trade or in agriculture or in housebuilding." Merchants did not even learn arithmetic, and foreigners were able to cheat them without mercy. Russians invented nothing and must be shown everything; they were lazy, unindustrious, did not want to do things good for themselves unless compelled to by force; they had no books about either agriculture or industry.

Russians knew nothing of history or of antiquity and could not carry on political conversations, so that foreigners despised them. Their personal appearance, their poverty-stricken language, their clothes, their houses and furnishings, their carts and implements—all were ridiculously unattractive. Krizhanich duly reported the saying abroad that when a Russian envoy visited a shop, a whole hour must pass before anyone could go in because of the stench; the king of Denmark said that the lodgings he assigned to Russian ambassadors were unusable for a year afterward. Russians were constant drunkards: "you might travel the whole world round, nowhere would you find such abominable, hideous, terrible drunkenness as here in Russia." Russians lacked all personal pride and dignity. Another great evil was lack of moderation on the part of the authorities.

Unsparing as he was in his strictures, Krizhanich nevertheless firmly believed in the future of Russia and, through her, of the whole Slav world. Russia's deficiencies were not wholly of her own making:

> Not one nation under the sun from the beginning of time has ever been so outraged and disgraced by foreigners as have we Slavs by the Germans. . . . Foreigners sit on our backs and ride us and beat us like cattle, they call us swine and hounds . . . they lead us like bears with a ring through the nose . . . they make themselves out Gods and us fools. . . .

Slavs were not by nature inferior; Russia's boorishness was a manifestation of her youth as a nation. With peoples as with individuals, the power of reason, which alone makes men superior to dumb animals, develops only gradually; it was not so long since Western Europeans had learned not to eat with their fingers. Protestant heretics, such as Adam Olearius, exaggerated the faults of Russians in the same spirit in which Luther had magnified the sins of the popes. Slavs, and especially Russians, should cease to cringe before foreigners: they should not fall into foolish admiration of the superior good looks of the Germans; they should not be tempted by their comfortable clothes, by their wines, by their music; they should not be overawed by the eloquence and articulateness that Western languages made possible.

Slavs could benefit, as they had in the past, by judicious borrowings. Russia was ideally situated between the East and the West. "The Germans and the Greeks though in much contradictory, yet agree perfectly in a deliberate plan of seduction, as though it were a sworn conspiracy for our ruin." The Germans offered novelty, heresy, science, luxury; the Greeks urged ancient tradition, orthodoxy, ignorance, superstition. Reason dictated that Russia should choose with care; Russia had taken the true faith—and the alphabet—from Greece, but had wisely taken bells and compasses from Italy; cannon, printing, and clocks from Germany.

Russia was right in her old policy of closing her borders; her people were wrong in their "xenomania." No one who might ever aspire to political power should be admitted; no foreigner should ever be permitted to become a citizen; astrologers, alchemists, and magicians, as well as players and entertainers, should be rigidly excluded; traders should be admitted only to border towns, and for periods not exceeding four weeks; embassies should be received only when strictly necessary; doctors, translators, and artisans might be freely admitted for purposes of instruction, but only if their special crafts were not already known in Russia; warriors should be hired only as needed, not permanently retained; needy ecclesiastics should be free to come and go; refugees and traitors might be entertained as occasion indicated; under no circumstances were rootless people—Scots, Jews, Armenians, and Gypsies—to be allowed to reside in Russia.

Krizhanich had no faith in the doctrine of Moscow as "the third Rome"; this was a delusion, for Christ had destroyed Rome, and man could not restore it. Royal authority came directly from God, and no earthly ruler has claim to power over other realms. The fate of Nebuchadnezzar, of Alexander, of Justinian attests the folly of such pretenses; for all his vain claims, the Holy Roman Emperor cannot keep his own country in subjection. "When [Emperor Constantine] Monomachus sent the royal insignia to our Vladimir and made him King, Vladimir would have done best if he had returned those insignia to Monomachus and replied, 'Thou makest me king of the Russians, and I make thee king of the Greeks!' " The very assumption of the title of "tsar," implying continuity with Roman power, was an error. Granted that Russia was backward, her hope lay in no slavish imitation of the West.

To transform Russia from the condition in which he pictured her into a state fit to lead in a pan-Slav world might seem to require a miracle. Russia's great advantage over any Western state and over those Slav realms like Poland, Bohemia, and Croatia, which had fallen into subjection to the West, was the fact that her ruler had unlimited power. "O Tsar, thou dost hold in thy hands the miracle-working rod of Moses, and with it thou mayst work amazing miracles in the realm. Thou holdest full Autocracy. . . ."

Rulers are only mortal and are prone to false opinions; they must take counsel with age; but living counselors too often are guided by their own selfish interests:

> Therefore . . . inanimate counselors are the very best friends; these are books. Books are not led astray by greed, neither by hatred nor by love; they are not flatterers; they do not fear to tell the truth. . . . For kings there is need to learn wisdom from good teachers, books and counselors, and not from trial and error. . . . Thus there is need for us to learn, for under the honored rule of the Most Pious Tsar and Great Sovereign Alexis Mikhailovich, we may hope to rub off the mould of our old savagery, learn how to do things, acquire a more attractive form of society, and attain a more prosperous condition.

To this end the tsar, without divesting himself of a jot of his authority, should cause to be carefully defined the liberties of each of the several estates, from the boyars down. Artisans, whom Krizhanich regarded as the chief source of a country's wealth, should be organized into self-governing guilds, patterned on the German model. He even proposed that "everyone shall be free to play music, and to smoke, and to arrange his beard and hair as he likes, only not in the Tatar fashion." Steps must be taken so that the whole taxpaying population, free from arbitrary exactions and malpractices, would pay their just obligations gladly:

> Let it be known to all that in our kingdom the peasant is much better treated than under any neighboring powers. . . . Let no one make bold in any way to offend or injure the country people or to impose work or burdens beyond our edict.

Throughout his work Krizhanich recurs constantly to the need for technical instruction, and for this specific purpose skilled instructors—and still more, books—should be brought from abroad, under rigid control by the beneficent state; the government should organize a network of technical schools, including special ones for women, and every prospective husband should be required by law to ask his bride for evidence of what she had learned. All in all, it is perhaps Krizhanich, rather than Peter the Great, who should be hailed as "the first Bolshevik."

Krizhanich was by no means the only man dissatisfied with the way society was ordered—or disordered—in seventeenth-century Muscovy. Others also looked to the autocrat for remedy. The replies of various groups represented at zemsky sobors and at partial meetings are replete with complaints of ruinous maladministration and with guarded, unsystematic pleas that the autocrat curb his officials' greed. Yet these latter grumblings did not reach the ideological level. The tsar's subjects, in expressing their opinions to his face, could not dare do more than ask for redress of fairly specific grievances; they could not utter—and perhaps did not have in mind—any views on sweeping reconstitution of the Muscovite order. Under the circumstances the problem of westernization versus reform on unique Slav principles was one that could be effectively weighed only by the most highly placed and secure personages, the tsar and his most intimate advisers.

PARTIAL WESTERNIZATION OF THE COURT

Their tendency, consciously or unconsciously, moved strongly in the direction of imitating the West. Alexis was a simple, kindly, though frequently irascible soul, brought up in the best traditions of Orthodoxy. Strongly religious and well informed in godly matters, he was eminently satisfactory in terms of old Russian customs, scrupulously observing all the rules of the Church with respect to prayer and fasting and capable of out-arguing any monk at sessions that lasted far into the night until even his confessor slipped under the table. At the same time, the benign indulgence which he regularly showed to others (especially if he had first been moved to berate and revile them) he extended also to himself. Apparently without thought of the possible significance of his actions, he welcomed all sorts of Western luxuries that pleased his fancy—gilded coaches, brass bands, a troupe of actors, German toys, German pictures, and even German clothes for his children. In short, without deliberate intention—an exception must perhaps be made in connection with his expectation of preparing himself for the throne of Poland—he created by his whims an atmosphere conducive to the rapid spread of foreign manners which later generations were prone erroneously to attribute to the reign of his son Peter.

One of Alexis' closest associates was F. M. Rtishchev (1625-73), noted for his self-effacing, conciliatory work as a minister of state. Outstanding in his honesty, he was noted also for his rare and genuine humility as a practicing Christian, alert to intervene, at the expense of his personal comfort and advantage, for the needy and the suffering, whether in a physical or in a moral sense. Like Boris Godunov, he expended his own wealth freely in times of famine and assisted the establishment of hospitals and asylums, with special attention to drunkards, incurables, and the aged. Refusing for himself the rank of boyar, Rtishchev was active in almost every department of the administration. A strong champion of the Kievan scholars, he was one of the strongest positive influences in spreading a more civilized viewpoint in a land which Europeans of the time regarded as generally barbarian.

More outspoken than Rtishchev was another of Alexis' ministers, A. L. Ordin-Nashchokin. Of relatively humble origin as the son of a *dvorianin* from the provinces, he nevertheless held a long succession of important military, diplomatic, and administrative posts and was rewarded for his work in negotiating the Truce of Andrusovo (1667) by being raised to the exalted rank of boyar. Ordin-Nashchokin owed his phenomenal rise, not to the accident of birth or wealth, but to unusual diplomatic talent, backed by an excellent education, with especially good grounding in mathematics and languages. Both in his ruthless foresight in the despatch of state business and in his skillful handling of his master, for whose judgment he had little respect, Ordin-Nashchokin strongly resembled Bismarck. It was ever his thought to sacrifice lesser or temporary advantage for the sake of greater and more permanent gain. He did not share Alexis' anxiety for acquisition of Little Russia; in particular, he recommended the restoration of Kiev to consolidate the peace with Poland, for his gaze was fixed on Sweden as Russia's greatest enemy and on the port of Riga as the chief objective of Russian foreign policy. His goals were not accomplished until the next generation, and he himself (unlike Bismarck) chose to retire into a monastery in 1671 rather than endanger his work by carrying out his master's more obvious policy.

Ordin-Nashchokin had a far-ranging eye; he sought to promote trade with Khiva and Bukhara, as well as with Persia; he tried to open relations with India and proposed to establish cossack settlements on the Amur. The central theme of his foreign policy was, however, to put an end to the traditional Muscovite enmity toward Poland, even to renounce portions of the historic "patrimony" of Rus, to which Ivan III had so emphatically asserted his claims two centuries earlier, and thus to free all Russia's forces for a drive toward the Baltic. If a dynastic union of Russia and Poland could be effected by securing the Polish throne for the tsar, so much the better. If not, the cossacks were certainly not worth expenditure of Muscovite efforts; it was only Smolensk and the upper reaches of the Dnieper, not Little Russia, that Moscow needed to control.

In full consonance with his attempt to revolutionize Russian foreign policy was his repudiation of old Muscovite attitudes toward the outside world in general. "It is not shameful," he wrote while on a campaign against the Poles in 1659, "to practice what is good from abroad, and from our enemies we may all the more accept evidence." [18] He became an ardent and outspoken Westernizer, though not at all in the same superficial sense as did Tsar Alexis: "What have we to do with the customs of other nations? Their clothes will not fit us, nor our clothes them." [19] He was deeply hurt and thought of retiring when, in 1660, his own son ran away to Western Europe. On the other hand, in the conduct of state administration everything should be done "from the example of outside, alien lands." [20] Reform of the army, by getting rid entirely of the *dvoriane,* who served, even in foreign-model regiments, only in times of emergency, and by replacing them with a permanent standing army, recruited from all classes, was in the forefront of his thoughts. A professional army, under leaders free to act without specific orders from the ruler in his capital and without considerations of custom and routine, would really be intelligently modeled on the West:

> Where the eyes see and the ear hears, there must initiative be kept without fail. . . . Better than any force is initiative; the point is in initiative and not in having many men; . . . of all neighboring realms the Swedes have the fewest men, but by initiative they have the upper hand over all; . . . sell half the army and buy one man of initiative—that would be the most advantageous.[21]

Ordin-Nashchokin was the first Russian minister clearly to see the need of building up the economy of the country to support its military strength. He recognized that the interests of trade and industry were being regularly subordinated to the convenience of the treasury. He believed also that Russians should learn to treat each other in friendly fashion and to avoid becoming dependent on foreigners. In remedy of these conditions he attempted, when *voevoda* of his native Pskov in 1665, to introduce there a system of local self-government and commercial organization deliberately patterned after his understanding of Western practices. To curb the power of the "best men" and to rescue the majority of the traders from the clutches of the "Germans," Ordin-Nashchokin worked out, in consultation with the town elders, a charter under which the whole conduct of the town's fiscal, administrative, and judicial business (except for reserved powers in cases of treason, robbery, and murder) was entrusted to a board of fifteen members; they were to be elected by all the citizens, and five were to serve each year. The poorer traders were to be put under the wardship of individual capitalists and to be assisted by public loans. The small traders were to purchase export goods and deliver them to the capitalists, who, besides paying their wards enough extra "for their feeding," were, after disposing of the goods to the foreigners, to hand over "full profit" to these junior associates. Thus only the strong would have dealings with the "Germans," but the rank-and-file traders would be assured of a decent livelihood.

The charter was promptly revoked by Nashchokin's successor (a man whom, as even Alexis admitted, "everyone called a fool"), but its principles were preserved in the "New-Trade Statute" (*Novotorgovyi Ustav*) of 1667, which proposed also to establish at Moscow a single office for dealing with all administrative aspects of the life of Russian traders. Although most of Ordin-Nashchokin's domestic projects—ranging from the establishment of fleets on the Baltic and Caspian to, as was alleged, decentralization of the cumbersome bureaucratic apparatus—were not accomplished in his lifetime, he was the statesman who laid the groundwork for the reign of Peter and left a ready-made assortment of carefully laid plans to which Alexis was not decisive enough to give his support.

Far more Western in his outlook than any of Alexis' associates was Prince V. V. Golitsyn, who became prominent in the brief reign of Tsar Fedor and served as the right-hand man of the Regent Sophia. Although a member of a very old boyar family, Golitsyn broke completely in his personal manner of life with old Russian tradition and did not hesitate to receive even Jesuits in his home or to give employment to Jews. By the grandeur and scope of his dreams he roused the limitless admiration of a French envoy (though for security reasons traveling with Polish credentials), who wrote: "He wished to people deserts, to enrich beggars, to turn savages into men, cowards into heroes, shepherds' huts into stone palaces."[22] In fact, he did carry forward the ideas of Ordin-Nashchokin: in 1686 permanent peace with Poland and a quadripartite alliance of Moscow, Warsaw, Vienna, and Venice against the Turks brought Russia recognition as a full-fledged member of the European state system; *miestnichestvo,* which had so plagued Ordin-Nashchokin, was abolished in 1682; he urgently pressed the boyars to send their sons abroad to study; although he won no glory by his personal efforts as a commander in the field, he brought the army and the state's finances to a condition of exceptional efficiency. Even Peter's brother-in-law, who had no reason to love Peter's domineering half-sister, recorded in his memoirs:

> The reign of the Tsarevna Sophia Alekseevna began with all diligence and all justice and to the satisfaction of the nation, so that never had there been such a wise reign in the Russian realm. And the whole realm came during her reign in the course of seven years into the flower of great wealth. So much were augmented commerce and all sorts of crafts, and the learning began to be restored of the Latin and Greek tongues, and also *politesse* was established among the great nobility and the other courtiers in the Polish manner—as well in carriages, and in housebuilding, and in attire, and in dining. And there triumphed then the great contentment of the nation.[23]

Less practical, perhaps, than Ordin-Nashchokin's, Golitsyn's plans for reforms went far beyond administrative and economic matters to embrace the dream of the spread of education and tolerance, of freedom of conscience and free movement across the borders, of improvement of the social structure and of moral life.

This dream was not to be realized. Instead, there came the reign of Peter I, who, heedless of the warning of Krizhanich that a nation that lives by war can never prosper, was to devote his magnificent energy, not to amelioration of Russia's own life, but to foreign conquest. On the fall of Sophia in 1689, Golitsyn was exiled to the Arctic. To men who had regarded him as an exceptionally enlightened statesman,

> Golitsyn's catastrophe was bound to seem a misfortune that had befallen the world. With him, it had seemed, a period of reform was being ushered in even in Russia; after him one could expect a reaction, a return to Asiaticism.[24]

NOTES

1. Kulisher, *Russische Wirtschaftsgeschichte,* p. 305.
2. Maskiewicz's diary, in *Skazaniia sovremennikov Dimitrii Samozvantse* [Contemporaries' Accounts of the Pretender Dmitry], 3rd edition, II, 147; cited in Fal′ kovskii, *Moskva v istorii tekniki,* p. 442.
3. Adam Olearius, *The Voyages and Travels . . . ,* p. 89.
4. Kulisher, *op. cit.,* pp. 395-396.
5. *"Kilburgers Unterricht von dem russischen Handel . . . ,"* in *Büshings Magazin für die neue Historie und Geographie,* III, 1769, p. 323.
6. *Ibid.,* p. 248.

7. *Ibid.*, p. 320.
8. Pososhkov, *"O ratnom povedenii,"* in *Kniga o skudosti i bogatstve . . .*, pp. 255-256.
9. Kordt (ed.), *"Otchet Al'berta i Iogana van Feltdrilia . . .*, in Russkoe Istoricheskoe Obshchestvo, *Sbornik,* CXVI, p. lxxi.
10. *Ibid.*, p. 80.
11. *"Kilburgers Unterricht . . . ,"* *loc. cit.*, p. 269.
12. *Akty sobrannye . . . Arkheograficheskoiu ekspeditsieiu,* IV, No. 13, pp. 15-20 *passim.*
13. Martens, *Sobranie Traktatov i Konventsii zakliuchennykh Rossieiu s inostrannami derzhavami,* IX (X), xciv.
14. *"Vremennik d'iaka Ivana Timofeeva,"* in *Pamiatniki drevnei russkoi pis'mennosti otnosiashchiesia k smutnomu vremeni,* 3rd edition, Vol. XIII, Part I, 263.
15. Kotoshikhin, *O Rossii . . . : Sochinenie Grigorii Kotoshikhina,* 4th edition, p. 100.
16. *Ibid.*, p. 59.
17. Krizhanich, *Russkoe gosudarstvo v polovinie XVII vieka,* I, 7. The quotations in the remainder of the section are from the same work, respectively, I, pp. 9, 8, 176, 182-183; II, pp. 174, 295, 5; I, pp. 107-110, 326, 329.
18. Solov'ev, *Istoriia Rossii . . .*, 2nd edition, Book III, 43.
19. Collins, *The Present State of Russia . . .*, p. 110.
20. Ikonnikov, "Blizhnyi boiarin A. L. Ordin-Nashchokin," in *Russkaia Starina,* XL, 1883, p. 55.
21. Solov'ev, *op. cit.*, pp. 43, 60.
22. Foy de la Neuville, *Relation curieuse, et nouvelle de Moscovie . . .*, pp. 177-178.
23. Kurakin, *"Gistoriia o tsarie Petrie Aleksievichie, 1682-1694,"* in *Arkhiv kn. Th. A. Kurakina,* I, 50.
24. Brückner, *"Fürst W. W. Golizyn . . . ,"* in *Russische Revue,* XIII, 1878, pp. 207-208.

SUGGESTIONS FOR FURTHER READING

In addition to works previously cited, the account of Russia by Adam Olearius, secretary of two Holstein embassies (in 1634 and 1636), has been translated into English. Collins was a physician attendant at the Russian court from 1659 to 1666. Kilburger's account is available in the original German. Among a number of articles, those of Wrett-Smith and of Liubimenko on the English and the Dutch in Russia are of particular interest (see Bibliography for full data).

For a general account of the impact of the West on Russia, Kliuchevskii's account in the third volume of his *Kurs* has not been surpassed.

Chapter

11

Peter the Great: 1682-1725

Once upon a time it was customary to regard as the major turning point of Russian history, if not actually its real beginning, the reign of Peter the Great. Many saw in him the great reformer, who had inherited the throne of an essentially Asiatic country and who, by Europeanizing it, had set it on the road to a great and enlightened future. An opposite school of thought saw in him only a destructive force, which had shattered the Russian spirit and had set back the progress of Slavdom. On one point only was there complete agreement: Russia before Peter had had only a dark past, with no history worth recording. The great controversy whether to continue the work of Peter or to undo it and make a fresh start raged hotly far into the nineteenth century. Out of its heat gradually came light, and this, paradoxically enough, largely through the work of German scholars who took over the study of chronicles begun by the amateur Tatistchev.

Although for propaganda purposes the legendary figure of Peter I has been kept alive, costumed anew as "the first Bolshevik," it has long since become obvious that the continuity of Russian history was unbroken by the reign of Peter. Irresistible forces, which owed little or nothing to the efforts of outstanding individuals, had before Peter's birth given form to an autocracy rooted in peasant bondage, to a Church wholly subordinate to the state, to a state-directed economy struggling to make headway against unfavorable geographic conditions, to the problem of progressive expansion of the limits of Russian power, and to the steady permeation of Russian life by the manners and customs of the more civilized West.

All these fundamental tendencies continued their development through and long after the reign of Peter, without change of direction. The impress that Peter left on Russia was the result, not of his initiative or sagacity, but of that boundless and untrammeled energy, displayed also by Ivan the Terrible, by Patriarch Nikon, and later by Bakunin, which tends to distract attention from the steady course of historical evolution. Peter's personal qualities kicked up a terrific dust storm, focused men's attention on things seen obscurely and without reference to their background, and satisfied the deep subjective human craving to find shelter behind a leader or to fix blame on a scapegoat. Although Peter's individual attributes have very little meaning for objective understanding of the lasting significance of the events of his reign, it is yet necessary to examine his own life history in order to comprehend how tremendous was the impression made, both on contemporaries and on subsequent generations, by his brief tenure of power.

PETER'S EARLY LIFE

Peter was born in 1672 of Alexis' second marriage, when the tsar had already reached the advanced age of forty-three. The death of his father in 1676, the simplemindedness of young Tsar Fedor, and the court rivalries of the relatives of Alexis' wives, combined to enable Peter in his most formative years to escape the normal education of a tsarevich. The tutor to whom he was entrusted, Nikita Zotov, in whom some might see a pioneer in progressive education, was content to leave the child to his German picture books and German toys rather than struggle with formal instruction. In later years a grateful Peter made Zotov "All-rowdiest and Most Mock Patriarch of Moscow, Cuckoo, and of all the Yauza," presiding over a formally organized "maddest, most mock, and most drunken Synod," composed of twelve "cardinals" and a host of other pseudo-ecclesiastical dignitaries, including "abbesses," amongst whom Peter himself was content with the rank of archdeacon.

On Tsar Fedor's death (1682), the boyars passed over his half-witted brother Ivan in favor of the healthy ten-year-old half-brother Peter. The Miloslavskys, relatives of Alexis' first wife, seized on the pretext that Peter's accession had not been ratified by a zemsky sobor and stirred up the Moscow *strieltsy* with tales of the alleged cruel treatment of the tsarevich Ivan. There ensued riotous scenes in the Kremlin, surpassing anything that the young Ivan the Terrible had had to witness. The brothers and friends of Peter's mother were brutally murdered; Peter himself watched while the enlightened Matveev was torn from the tsaritsa's protecting arms and hacked in pieces. One of Peter's uncles managed to hide in a wardrobe but had ultimately to be handed over to the *strieltsy* before their drunken looting could be checked. Ivan was proclaimed co-tsar under the regency of his able sister Sophia.

On the heels of this bloody brawl came an outbreak by the Old Ritualists, who staged a violent demonstration, harshly suppressed, in the Granovitaia Palata itself. The events of 1682 could not fail to leave a deep impression on the child, whose ingrained hatred of everything traditional in Muscovy may well have stemmed in large part from this association of turbulent *strieltsy,* defiant Old Ritualists, and the bloodstained Kremlin.

The immediate sequel was that Peter and his mother were removed from the Kremlin to the suburban village of Preobrazhensk. Here, while Natalia Naryshkina dreamed of vengeance, the boy was allowed to run wild. As co-tsar he was admittedly entitled to indulgence and, although his half-sister Sophia, as Regent, firmly monopolized the reins of power, Peter was provided with a company of playmates and servants, of all ranks, among whom the child made no distinctions save on the basis of his personal favor. It was here that began his lifelong friendship with Alexander Menshikov, of very humble birth though not, as widely reported, the son of a pastry cook, yet by Peter's interest ultimately raised to the style of Prince.

Interested, as any normal boy might be, in playing soldiers, Peter had the abnormal opportunity of organizing play regiments, the nucleus of the later Imperial Guard, and of equipping them with real instruments of war, from swords and guns to drums and bugles—to say nothing of many other strangely assorted items—issued from the government arsenals. Unburdened with serious schooling, Peter spent a glorious seven-year vacation, not studying statecraft but staging sham battles, with real casualties, among his playmates.

The nearby "German Liberty" exercised a profound fascination on the inquisitive and undisciplined youth, physically developed beyond his years. There he made the acquaintance of François Lefort, a Swiss officer, who, as Prince Kurakin, an admirer of the Italian Renaissance, regretfully recorded,

> was an amusing and luxury-loving man, what you might call a French *débauché.* And ceaselessly he gave dinners, suppers, and balls at his house. And in this house it began to come to pass that His Majesty the Tsar consorted with foreign ladies, and his first amour was with a merchant's daughter named Anna Ivanova Mons. True, the girl was passable and intelligent. Here in this house began debauchery and drunkenness so great as cannot be described; for three days, shut up in that house, they were drunk, and it befell many to die therefrom. And from that time to this date and till now drunkenness continues and has become the fashion among great houses.[1]

It was another of Peter's "German" friends, Patrick Gordon—who had allegedly "fought in seven hosts, and under seven kings"—who gave Peter his most valuable military lessons and helped him make his "play" troops fully the equals of any soldiers in the Russian service. Not all of his time went into military pursuits. When a Russian envoy, returning from Paris, brought him an instrument with which "can be taken distances or ranges without going to the place," Peter found a Dutchman, Timmermann, able to explain the practical workings of the astrolabe. Though scarcely literate, Peter went on with an assiduous study of mathematics and military engineering. Timmermann also reconditioned for him an old English boat, which Peter later fondly (though extremely inaccurately) referred to as "the grandfather of the Russian fleet."

As the boy neared the age of seventeen, his mother took a desperate measure to prepare him for the solemn tasks that official manhood should bring; she found him an aristocratic wife in the person of Eudocia Lopukhina. The Regent Sophia, uncertain what to expect from the young boor who was her half-brother but positive of the intentions of her stepmother, attempted to inspire the *strieltsy* with the idea of converting her regency into permanent rule. Rumors reached Preobrazhensk that the troops were coming. Peter, abandoning his mother and pregnant wife, fled by night and found sanctuary in the holy Monastery of the Trinity, some forty miles from the capital. There his mother and her friends soon gathered round him, together with his "play" companies. Thither, too, came the patriarch Ioakim, who, sent to make peace, championed Peter's cause. The *strieltsy* similarly deserted to him. Sophia's regime, weakened by Golitsyn's failures in the Crimea, collapsed without a blow.

On Peter, the turn of events seemed to make little impression. His fright left him forever after with a nervously twitching face, but his victory simply permitted him to develop more fully his juvenile tastes. Leaving court ceremonial to his weak-minded brother and the business of state to his small-minded mother and to the patriarch, Peter returned to his playmates at Preobrazhensk and to the delights of the "German Liberty." His activities merely became more extensive: now he could visit Archangel and go sailing on the White Sea; he could maneuver his "play" troops (which became the Preobrazhensk and Semenovsk Regiments) far to the south and make a sudden attack on the Turkish town of Azov, briefly held by the cossacks in Michael's reign. Peter chose to serve as a bombardier but interfered constantly with his commanders. Failing to take the town in a siege that dragged on throughout the summer of 1695, he fitted out a flotilla of river craft, with the aid of which Azov was successfully blockaded and starved out in the following year. Paying slight heed to the death of his mother early in 1694 or of his brother in 1696, Peter left all matters of state in the hands of an incompetent and greedy clique of upstart relatives, who robbed the state treasury and outdid each other in scandalous conduct.

Peter's triumphant return to his capital in 1697 did nothing to restore confidence in the administration. Instead of attempting to put his house in order, he dreamed only of a great crusade in which, with the aid of Western Europe, the Turks were to be completely overwhelmed. To this end he immediately dispatched a "grand embassy," charged with winning the collaboration of the pope and the Holy Roman Emperor. The tsar himself proposed to go abroad, traveling "incognito" as simple "Peter Mikhailov."

The astounding notion that a Muscovite tsar should leave his own land and risk personal contamination by the "Latin heresy" excited widespread consternation. The rumor began to spread—and was to grow throughout the years—that this hulking giant with the rolling blue eyes was not the true son of Alexis but a German changeling. It was the story of Tsarevich Dmitry Ivanovich in reverse, and its credibility was aided by recollection of Alexis' "full, almost fat, figure, with his low forehead, white face, clipped red beard, with his puffy, reddened cheeks, his flaxen hair, with his benign face and mild eyes."[2] Peter, on the other hand, was an unusually handsome man to whom all must look up; nearly seven feet tall, he was of proportionate build, with flowing locks and saucer-like eyes; with an obvious birthmark on his cheek and a variety of disconcerting nervous habits, he was all in all a sight that might easily cause "an involuntary shudder in any man of weak nerves."[3]

A conspiracy was detected, and the ringleaders were beheaded in the "place of execution" in the Red Square. To solemnize the occasion, a long-dead uncle of Sophia was disinterred, in order that the dripping blood of the victims might return to its presumed source.

At Riga, Peter met with a rebuff from the Swedish governor, who deemed it unwise to permit the Russian tsar to inspect the fortifications. Traveling by sea to Königsberg, the tsar was tempted by his Hohenzollern host, soon to be the first "king in Prussia," to abandon his plans against the Turks and to join in a coalition to drive the Swedes back across the Baltic. Unmoved by this scheme, Peter parted company with his envoys and set off in personal quest of positive knowledge, especially of shipbuilding and navigation. As his party danced and feasted its way through the various German courts, frequent difficulties arose, as when the Russians trod too heavily on the toes of their partners or mistook corset stays for ribs. Nevertheless, German academicians fell to debating the possibility that Peter's trip might lead to the enlightenment of Russia, and the mathematician-philosopher Leibnitz even composed plans for its reform.

In Holland the tsar was warmly greeted by William of Orange, then also king of England, who arranged for Peter to satisfy his curiosity to the full. A week's work in a shipyard—surrounded by a gaping crowd of onlookers—earned Peter the sobriquet of "the carpenter of Saardam." On visits to mills and workshops, Peter was allowed himself to operate the levers, for it was only through his fingertips that the tsar seemed capable of intellectual apprehension. Museums and scientific institutes were not overlooked. In an anatomical theater at Leyden, Peter gave his hesitant suite their first genuine taste of European culture, ordering them to step forward one by one and with their teeth sever a muscle of the corpse on the dissecting table.

Ultimately concluding that he had absorbed all the practical knowledge available in Holland, Peter was conveyed to England by Admiral Mitchell. There is a story traditional in the English navy that Peter, who was passionately interested in all things nautical, was fascinated by a description of "keelhauling" and asked to be given a demonstration. When the English admiral demurred, pointing out that none of his sailors at the moment deserved this drastic punishment, Peter promptly offered one of his own men for the purpose.

Ostensibly, Peter had crossed the Channel because he believed the English understood the theory of shipbuilding better than did the Dutch. He was accordingly housed near the government dockyard at Deptford. While in England, he did not altogether neglect his opportunity to study English achievements in the field of political science: he visited the mint and the dungeons in the Tower; he was impressed by a "stealthy" visit to the House of Lords. He reviewed the fleet at Portsmouth, "tried the casting of bombs" at Woolwich, saw "all sorts of wonderful things" at the Royal Society. He attended the theater and conversed with bishops. Only occasionally, he recorded, "we were at home and made sufficiently merry."[4] The gentleman whose house had been leased for Peter's accommodation later submitted a curious bill for damages: his flower beds had been used as drill grounds, his ancestors' portraits for target practice of various sorts. Bishop Burnet recorded:

> I waited often on him. . . . I had good interpreters, so I had much free discourse with him; he is a man of a very hot temper, soon inflamed, and very brutal in his passion; he raises his natural heat, by drinking much brandy, which he rectifies himself with great application: he is subject to convulsive motions all over his body, and his head seems to be affected with these; he wants not capacity, and has a larger measure of knowledge, than might be expected from his education, which was very indifferent; a want of judgment, with an instability of temper, appear in him too often and too evidently; he is mechanically turned, and seems designed by nature rather to be a ship-carpenter, than a great prince.[5]

The bishop apparently uttered a general English sentiment when, impressed with the thought that "God moves in a mysterious way His wonders to perform," he added:

> After I had seen him often, and had conversed much with him, I could not but adore the depth of the providence of God, that had raised up such a furious man to so absolute an authority over so great a part of the world. . . . Man seems a very contemptible thing in the sight of God, while such a person as the czar has such multitudes put as it were under his feet, exposed to his restless jealousy and savage temper.

Returning to the Continent in 1698, intent on visiting Venice, Peter learned at Vienna that in his absence the *strieltsy* had rioted again. Though order had been restored, he cut short his tour, mainly because of the disturbing news that instead of coöperating in the idea of a crusade, the Hapsburgs were negotiating a separate peace with the Turks. In this mood,

Peter readily succumbed to the suggestion of the new king of Poland, Augustus of Saxony, that they join forces in a war against Sweden. Two sets of envoys were promptly dispatched: one to inform the Swedes of Moscow's undying love; the other to negotiate a peace with the Turks.

PETER AT THE HELM*

Arrived at Moscow, Peter went, not to the Kremlin, but to Preobrazhensk. Sophia, who had been imprisoned in a convent, was now forced to become a nun. Tsaritsa Eudocia was informed by messenger that her wish also to enter a convent would be granted. When she replied that she preferred to continue as Peter's wife, an armed escort was sent to carry out what Peter persisted in representing as her inflexible will. Thus, the result of one of Peter's first conscious actions as ruler was that the two most prominent women in Muscovy went into permanent seclusion.

Though impatient with the undisciplined nature of the *strieltsy,* Peter continued to employ them as garrison and communication troops. A number of them, however, were executed; it is said that Peter organized competitions, in which he personally participated, to see who could strike off the most heads with one blow. More startling to contemporaries than the treatment of the necks of the *strieltsy* was Peter's simultaneous shaving of the faces of his courtiers and his compulsory "Europeanization" of their clothing. Only a little less disturbing was his decree that henceforth the New Year should be celebrated on January 1 instead of September 1, and that January 1 of "the year 7208 since the creation of the world"[6] should be counted as the first day of the year 1700 since the birth of Christ. Perhaps unaware that Roman Catholic countries had in 1582-83 accepted the "New Style" (Gregorian) calendar, Peter adopted the "Old Style" (Julian) calendar, which most of the Protestant countries of the West were then on the point of abandoning (though Great Britain retained it until the middle of the eighteenth century). Thus Peter created an eleven-day time lag behind the West, which was not corrected until 1918, when the Bolsheviks closed what was by then a thirteen-day gap by adopting the system of Pope Gregory XIII. Another innovation reflecting the dreaded "Latinization" was his approval of new forms of the letters of the alphabet somewhat more similar to Roman characters than the old had been; devised in 1708 and endorsed by Peter personally in 1710, the new type was ordered used in all non-ecclesiastical printing.

Peace with Turkey was not concluded until 1700; Russia retained Azov under a thirty-year truce but abandoned her new Black Sea fleet. Immediately, in accordance with a secret treaty of 1699 with Poland and Denmark, Peter ordered his army of thirty-five thousand men to move against Narva.

* See Maps V and VI.

Charles XII, the child prodigy who then ruled Sweden, swiftly knocked Denmark out of the war and moved to the relief of his beleaguered fortress on the Gulf of Finland. Peter, remembering—as had so many of his predecessors—that it is the ruler's prime duty to organize the rear, left his army only the night before it was cut to pieces by eight thousand Swedes. At Narva, Peter lost the whole of his artillery, and a Swedish council of war advised an immediate march on Moscow. Instead of following up his victory against a thoroughly demoralized and almost disarmed foe, Charles turned his attention to his more immediately formidable opponent, Augustus of Saxony, whom he pushed back from Riga. It took seven years of fighting before Augustus was forced to make peace (1707), abandoning the Polish throne in favor of Stanislas Leczynski.

Tsar Peter, unable to persuade any Western power to mediate for him, had conscripted fresh thousands of recruits and commandeered one-fourth of all the church bells in Russia to be cast into new cannon. The stubbornness of Saxony's resistance had accorded him seven years in which to organize his new armies and to blood them in persistent skirmishes with the Swedish rear guard along the Baltic and the Gulf of Finland. It was during this breathing space that the indefatigable Peter began (1703) construction in the marshes at the mouth of the Neva of the Peter-and-Paul Fortress, the nucleus of "the city built on bones," to which characteristically he gave the un-Russian name of St. Petersburg.

Yet even in 1707 the Russian tsar was sufficiently chastened to be willing to make peace on the basis of cession by Sweden of a single harbor on the Baltic. Charles, however, contemptuous of his lumbering enemy, determined to deal decisively with Peter despite his new armies and his new Russian commanders, amongst whom were Menshikov, Sheremetev, and "Admiral-General" Apraxin. Tempted by the food-rich resources of the poorly fortified area today known as the Ukraine and by his alliance with the cossack hetman, Mazepa, Charles neglected the opportunity to drive straight at Moscow; instead he struck southeastward without providing adequately for the security of his supply trains. Menshikov seized the opportunity and destroyed Loewenhaupt at Lesna (1708). Mazepa proved unable to bring more than a small detachment of cossacks into Charles's camp, and his capital was stormed by Menshikov; the clergy anathematized him, and the majority of the Dnieper cossacks accepted the pro-Russian Skoropadski as their new hetman, while the Little Russian peasantry waged guerilla war on the advancing alien Swedes. Peter was thus enabled, with an army of one hundred thousand men, to surround and overwhelm the thirty thousand Swedes, exhausted and half-starved, under the walls of Poltava (1709); only the military skill of Charles XII enabled him to cut his way out and, with a small following, escape over the border into Turkey. In his absence the Russian forces overran the whole Baltic shoreline from Riga to Vyborg (1710).

Intoxicated by victory, Peter, leaving administration of Russia in charge of a new "Senate," made a headlong dash across the Pruth and thus brought the Turks into the war. This time it was the Russians who were cut off by overwhelming forces, but they escaped military disaster by judicious and generous presents to the vizier and by the diplomatic skill of Shafirov. Peter had been ready to promise surrender of all his Baltic conquests and even to cede Pskov to Sweden if the Turks insisted, but the peace treaty merely restored Azov and the adjacent fortifications to Turkey and gave Charles free passage home.

After Poltava, Denmark and several small German principalities had joined Peter in a new alliance against Sweden. Peter sent troops to support them, married one of his nieces to the duke of Mecklenburg, and even made brief personal appearances among them. However, their mutual jealousies and their fear of Peter's own ambitions—which also brought English fleets annually to the Baltic—prevented an invasion of southern Sweden and disgusted the tsar. He therefore concentrated his efforts on the military reduction of the Swedish province of Finland. Peter also paid another visit to Western Europe—one of the most curious episodes in his whole career—in the ambitious effort to marry one of his daughters to Louis XV and thus detach France from its friendship with Sweden.

A fleet was got together by purchase of a number of foreign vessels as well as by construction of new ones (which did not last long in service), and a horde of galleys won the mastery of the narrow waters of the Gulfs of Finland and Bothnia. An exhausted Charles agreed to the opening of a peace congress in the Åland Islands (1718), at which the Russian delegation was headed by two of Peter's "Germans," Bruce and Osterman. Charles's death at an obscure battle in Norway speedily gave power in Sweden to the party of resistance, but repeated raids on the Swedish coast by Russian galleys, which in those waters were able to elude the more cumbersome British warships, finally induced even the most stubborn Swedes to accept the Peace of Nystadt (August 30, 1721).

By this treaty, Russia was confirmed in possession of Livonia, Estonia, and Ingria, though Finland and part of Karelia were restored to Sweden, and a substantial indemnity was paid by Russia (2 million yefimki, i.e., Dutch thalers). Russia's allies were left to make the best terms they could without assistance from her. Tsar Peter celebrated the peace—despite his gout—by dancing on the banquet table, and soon after, at a solemn ceremony in the cathedral, formally accepted the new title of Emperor (*Imperator*), as well as the no less formally conferred appellation of "the Great." [7]

The Great Northern War conditioned most of Peter's domestic policies, but it did not exhaust his expansionist energies. Peter, "the first Bolshevik," was much interested in diverting the course of the Amu Darya, hoping to make it empty into the Caspian instead of the Aral Sea and thus give Russian traders easier access to the ancient crossroads of East-West trade in Turkestan. Even while the war with Sweden was still in progress he sent four thousand men to serve as a "guard" for the khan of Khiva; unfortunately, the khan slaughtered them all one night (1717). Peter's firmest progress toward Central Asia was the fortification of Omsk (1716) and Semipalatinsk (1718). He reopened negotiations with China (1719), though he failed to make direct contact with Korea (1721), and he ordered Captain Bering to explore the North Pacific and find where "Asia joined America" (1724).[8] Two ships which Peter sent out under secret orders to visit Madagascar and proceed to India had to turn back, their green timbers proving unsafe in the Atlantic (1723).

By war with Persia, begun immediately on the close of the war with Sweden, he acquired the western and southern shores of the Caspian (1723). The cost of this victory was high. Louis XV's envoy reported:

> As the Russians are extremely distrustful, I have not thought it fitting to press further the necessity of entirely abandoning the Persian campaign. . . . I think in the meantime I can assure [Your Majesty] that however good countenance they keep here and whatever firmness they pretend, they are scarcely in condition to sustain a war against the Turks. . . . The finances of Russia are in bad condition. The grain shortage is beginning to be felt very keenly. The cavalry is dismounted by the loss of all the horses that served the preceding campaign, and the troops in general have not been paid for seventeen months, something that did not happen in the last war, which has almost depopulated the provinces around Moscow, where most of the best lands in Europe are untilled, for lack of peasants and because of the ill-treatment they receive from their masters.[9]

Within a decade after Peter's rather sudden death in January, 1725, the new provinces taken from Persia were abandoned.

Thus, practically all of Peter's active reign was spent in aggressive warfare, to which he gave almost constant personal supervision, and it is only in this light that Peter's "Reforms" can be understood. At no time did Peter evince any clearly formulated long-range program for the reordering of Muscovite society or even of its state administration. To trace his measures chronologically could give only a haphazard picture, faithfully reflecting, perhaps, the state of Peter's own mind but leaving no coherent concept of the net effect of his reign on the development of Russian history.

MILITARY REFORMS

Peter's prime need, directly imposed by the Great Northern War, was to create efficient armed forces. This entailed measures to secure a supply of the needed manpower and to improve the economic condition of the country so that it might furnish the "sinews of war." It further became necessary to make more efficient the fiscal and administrative apparatus to ensure a fuller flow of revenue and to supervise enforcement of the tsar's edicts. Incidental to these changes and in large part dependent on Peter's personal whims were further changes in the cultural outlook of at least the ruling circles.

Simplest as well as most pressing were Peter's military reforms. In essence they amounted to reviving and extending the regimenting, on foreign models, of the army, which had fallen sadly into neglect in the interval between the overthrow of Sophia and the outbreak of the war with Sweden, and to increasing the recruitment of conscripts from all classes of the population. Service was for life, not for a campaign; the military life thus became a special form of dedication—not exactly monastic—separated from the home and private business interests that had confused the *strieltsy* and, to a lesser extent, the regimented "soldiers" of the seventeenth century. The ratio of recruits to homesteads was fixed (in the hardest years of the war it was one from each twenty homesteads, but a Senate decree of 1715 reduced the figure to one from every seventy-five peasant homesteads) in an effort to build up reserves beyond current battle needs. Losses by disease and desertion were exceedingly heavy; it has been estimated that in the ten years needed to build up the army of over one hundred thousand men that Peter commanded in the year of Poltava, some three hundred thousand had been enlisted, out of a total population of perhaps 14 million. A German official stationed in Moscow from 1714 to 1719 reported that more recruits died of hunger and cold while being trained than were subsequently killed in battle. Peter's efforts to extend regular military discipline to the cossacks, whether of the Don or of the Dnieper, were more intensive but scarcely more successful than had been those of his predecessors. Yet by the end of his reign Peter had under arms about two hundred thousand regular troops, besides over one hundred thousand cossacks and other auxiliaries.

The navy required special attention and helped raise military expenditures to embrace two-thirds of the whole budget. Even before Peter thought of war with Sweden, he had signed on nearly a thousand Dutch officers and seamen. The first Russian frigates were launched in 1703; at Peter's death the Russian navy boasted forty-eight ships-of-the-line, though they were soon afterward dismantled as unfit for sea service. The great naval victory of Hangud fought in the Finnish fiords in 1714 was, however, won not by sailing ships but by swarms of rowboats (galleys) filled with soldiers. An English sea captain long in the tsar's service has left an extended commentary on Peter's most expensive and useless toy:

> It being about twenty years since the Tsar began to build and rig his ships, he has a sufficient number of people tolerably skilled in fixing the rigging and going through all parts of a seaman's duty to be done ashore, or whilst the ship is in the haven, and yet are good for little at sea. . . . [As for officers,] there are also some men of capacity amongst the Russians, but as to the generality of these, in quality of lieutenants, foreigners ever desire to leave 'em ashore; seeing in good weather their pride is insupportable, taking great state upon them, and arrogating much attendance; but in bad weather, or any extremity,

> are sick abed, when they should be serviceable. . . . [True,] few if any ships in the world are able to wrong the Russian [ships] especially those built at St. Petersburg, if well manned, in the qualification of excellent sailing . . . [but] experience confirms that his best fir-built ships will not last above seven years; and even some of oak timber might want rebuilding at the expiration of eight.[10]

As for the land forces, the *dvoriane* no longer constituted the bulk of Moscow's fighting men, but their importance to the military establishment was increased rather than diminished under Peter. In the seventeenth century, their service had not been of the highest quality, though Pososhkov, himself of peasant origin, doubtless exaggerated when he wrote in 1701:

> They have no care to slay the foe; they care only how to stay at home. And so they pray to God that they may suffer a slight wound, that they may not be much hurt by it but may receive for it compensation from the tsar. And they look on service in such a way that in time of battle they hide behind a bush. And some are so shameless that they hide by whole companies in the woods or in a ravine, and watch until the fighting men leave off the battle and they too may return to camp. And I have heard many *dvoriane* say: "May God grant that I may serve the great sovereign and never take my sword from its scabbard." [11]

Pososhkov was convinced that fifty or sixty thousand men, well armed, well equipped, well trained, and well paid, would be far more valuable than a force of three hundred thousand such as Golitsyn had led against the Crimea. He submitted careful calculations to prove that it would be truly economical and emphasized the importance of developing iron works, arms factories, and other industrial establishments in Russia; only thus could the tsar escape dependence on foreigners, who always cheated and supplied inferior muskets and unserviceable gunpowder. Peter paid no heed, if indeed he ever saw this treatise "On the Conduct of War" composed by a man who was then a technician in the Mint.

Peter did not dispense with the services of the *dvoriane* but tried, as had his predecessors, to get the most efficient service from them. He ordered compilation of registers of all sons of *dvoriane* and of other kinsmen resident in their households and required that, if over ten years old, they present themselves for periodic inspection. Until the age of fifteen they were under obligation to study elementary mathematics; at fifteen they were to be assigned to some branch of the state service. For failure to pursue their studies satisfactorily, edicts of 1714 imposed penalties, of which prohibition of marriage was not the most drastic. Under no circumstances, under a confirmatory decree of 1723, were they to remain in schools beyond the specified age, "even though they themselves might wish it, lest in the name of that learning they hide themselves from reviews and assignment to service." [12] On one occasion, a group of youngsters, seeking to avoid mathematics by entering an ecclesiastical school, were seized and put to work driving piles in connection with the building of a canal; among them was a relative of "Admiral-General" Apraxin, who registered his protest by stripping off his uniform and his decorations and himself joining in the work of pile-driving.

The *dvoriane* were the only possible source from which effective officers could be drawn, though as far as edicts went, promotion was open to any soldier. To fit them for their careers, the young nobles were required to serve for a time in the ranks. The more influential managed to be posted to the Guard regiments, which became the chief road to all commands in the army. The fact that these regiments, regularly stationed in the capital, were made up from top to bottom of nobles was to give them a special significance, under Peter's less forceful successors, as an instrument through which the nobility could decisively guide state policy in the narrow interests of the ruling class.

Peter himself in 1714 made an unfortunate effort to guarantee the serviceability of the *dvoriane* by decreeing that their real estate must pass undivided to a single heir; the testator might choose any one of his sons (or, in default of children, some other relative) to inherit to the exclusion of the others. In the absence of a will, the oldest son was to inherit; hence, incorrectly, this edict has become known as the law of primogeniture (*majorat*). Thus was legally completed that fusion of hereditary tenure (*votchina*) and service tenure (*pomestie*) that had gradually been developing in fact. Although the rule of indivisibility of inheritance of real estate was abolished in 1730, the obsolescent legal distinction between the two basic forms of "immovable property" was not restored; the word *votchinnik* soon disappeared from the language while the word *pomeshchik* survived with the simple significance of "landlord."

It should not be supposed that Peter's attempt to utilize the full force of the nobility in the military and naval service was as successful as he desired. Many nobles had to be used in the ever-growing civilian services, a fact recognized by Peter himself in 1722, when he ordered that not more than one-third of the male members of any noble family be thus allowed to escape from the fighting services. All sorts of abuses developed, such as the entry of newborn babies into service, to the end that seniority might give them respectable rank by the time that they actually appeared on the drill ground. "No-ism" (*nietstvo*) was so common that an edict of 1714 ordered that informers, even servants, were entitled to receive all the property of a culprit; an edict of 1722 made evaders outlaws. As Pososhkov put it in his *Book on Poverty and Wealth* (1724):

> The healthy and wealthy who are in the very prime of manhood live at home, while the poor and sickly are in the service, and from the weak and the hungry there is only bad service.[13]

Miestnichestvo had been abolished under Peter's older brother, Tsar Fedor, and Peter strove to ignore its survivals. Nevertheless, hereditary standing (*otechestvo*) continued somehow to assert its prerogatives. Peter in 1722 established a new order of precedence, the "Table of Ranks," with military, naval, and civilian service carefully equated in fourteen parallel grades. Although service, rather than birth, was ostensibly made the basic principle of the new system, the Table of Ranks actually strengthened the essential principle of *miestnichestvo,* though on a broader base. It did not restore the special hereditary status of the old *boiarstvo;* instead, it reinforced the rise of the whole body of the service nobility, swallowing within itself the old inner feudal élite. This was a development that had been proceeding since the sixteenth century; the case of Adashev (who Ivan said had been "taken from the dunghill and ranked with the magnates") will be remembered as an early instance of what had become common in the seventeenth century.

At the same time, the special privileges of nobles were specifically recognized, even though they had no service record, if they could prove noble ancestry of not less than a hundred years. Foreigners need only give documentary proof that their families had been noble in their own country. Special articles dealt with the status of wives and daughters of nobles, as well as of women holding court positions. In true *miestnichestvo* spirit, severe fines were imposed for claiming higher rank than was warranted; the same fines were imposed for neglecting to claim the precedence to which one's rank entitled one.

The main distinctive feature of the Table of Ranks was that what had long been true in practice now became a formal matter of legal right. Henceforth membership in the "best senior nobility (*dvorianstvo*) in all its dignities and advantages, even though they be of low birth,"[14] was automatically accorded to anyone who had succeeded in rising into the first eight ranks. It did not, however, follow that those of high birth would not continue almost to monopolize positions in these higher grades. In effect, the "Table of Ranks" served to confirm the rise of the *dvorianstvo* at the expense of the remnant of the old feudal *boiarstvo*.

Peter also introduced purely honorary hereditary titles—*Graf* (Count), and Baron—borrowed from Germany; like the ancient Russian title of *kniaz* (Prince), borne by all male descendants of old ruling families, and conferred by Peter also on special favorites such as Menshikov, these designations had only prestige value. Most of the Russian nobility—into which baptized Tatar and Caucasian chieftains, cossack elders, and the German and Swedish nobility of the new Baltic provinces were absorbed—continued to be untitled.

FINANCIAL MEASURES

The expenses of Peter's wars substantially exceeded his revenues. So long as there remained in the treasury an accumulation from the prewar years, current deficits caused no serious difficulty. When, however, in 1710, his officials had to inform Peter that there remained no funds with which to meet the anticipated annual deficit, Peter was forced to give thought to the problem of finance. His immediate remedy was the old device of ordering increase in the existing rates of taxation; new, special direct taxes were also superimposed on the old. The fact that taxes were still being assessed on an enumeration of homesteads made in 1678 gave hope that a new count would show substantial increase of the taxpaying population in the last generation and would therefore permit reduction of excessive rates. The result of the new census of 1710 was bitterly disappointing. Even though the estimate made by the Senate in 1714 that one-fourth of the taxpayers had disappeared may have been exaggerated, there was no possibility of blinking the fact that Peter's wholesale recruitment of taxpayers into the armed forces, complicated by his enrollment of additional tens of thousands of forced laborers for the building of St. Petersburg (forty thousand a year, for lifetime service), of canals, and of other grandiose projects, had done grave damage to the taxpaying capacity of the population. A fresh count in 1716-1717—to remedy the supposed inefficiency of the original census-takers—merely disclosed a further heavy decline in the number of taxable homesteads; in one province it showed a loss of one-third even since 1710.

In the emergency, Peter resorted to imposition of an amazing variety of new taxes. In devising them, he welcomed and liberally rewarded schemes proposed by persons in all ranks of life, from aristocrats and army officers down to petty traders and peasants. Whenever he deemed a proposed new tax practicable, he set up a new administrative department, headed by a *pribylshchik,* ("revenueman") to collect it. Outstanding among these "contrivers," most of whom had been household serfs of nobles, was Nesterov, who rose to be *oberfiscal,* a sort of comptroller-general of the finances, and who, after earning a dreaded reputation for ferreting out grafters, was himself at last broken on the wheel following his own conviction for corruption.

Sometimes business enterprises were taken over by the state, as were fisheries; sometimes they were subjected to heavy treasury participation in the profits, up to 25 percent as in the case of lodging houses. Luxuries, from baths and honey to oak coffins, were made to contribute to Peter's revenues. In Kliuchevsky's words,

> As from an evil sieve new taxes were strewn on the heads of the Russian taxpayers. . . . Not only possessions and occupations were subjected to taxation, but even religious beliefs as well—not merely property but conscience.[15]

The Old Ritualists were tolerated, but on payment of a double tax. Weddings of non-Christians—Mordva, Cheremis, Tatars, and other alien subjects of the Russian tsar—entailed payment of special fees, collected by a chancellory originally established to levy a tax on beekeepers. Most famous—though not most lucrative—was the tax on beards, those evidences that man is made in the image of God. This tax was established as early as 1705 at rates graduated to the social importance of the wearer and, in the case of peasants, contingent on whether they brought their beards to town or were content to remain at home; ten years later these complicated provisions were simplified and replaced by a flat annual license fee. In 1722, Peter himself solemnly proposed to the Senate that thenceforth anyone with a beard (or any schismatic) be required to wear a specified costume; if he did not, he must pay again for each offense; if he could not pay, he was to be sent to the galleys; anyone effecting his arrest was to receive half the fine.

Elaborate as these numerous and annoying levies were, they scarcely justified the ingenuity expended on them. For instance, the beard tax, which was officially estimated to yield 2,148 rubles 87 kopecks in 1720, actually produced only 297 rubles 20 kopecks that year. In 1724, even Peter ordered a number of these taxes abolished. More reliable sources of income were found by resuming control of Church revenues and by extending the practice of state monopolies. The Monastery Bureau, set up in 1649 by Alexis and abolished in 1677, was revived by Peter in 1701. Peter's alleged reason—to combat corruption among the monks—somewhat resembled that of Henry VIII of England; Peter in 1724 added the thought that most monks took the tonsure "from laziness and from taxes, in order to eat their bread for nothing." [16] The lands of the monasteries, and later also those of the patriarch and the members of the hierarchy, were to be administered by the state: a fixed sum per inmate was to be paid to the monasteries, rich or poor, and the eleemosynary functions of the Church were to be provided for from the balance. A substantial sum remained, however, in the hands of the treasury until, toward the end of the war with Sweden, the administration of Church lands was turned over to the Holy Synod, as reorganized in 1722.

To existing state monopolies, such as pitch, potash, rhubarb, and glue, were added others, including salt, tobacco, chalk, tar, cod-liver oil, playing cards, dice, chessmen, and vodka. The salt monopoly gave the state 100 percent profit on its purchases from the salt-boilers, but created an alarming scarcity, with widespread disease and death. A special form of monopoly—the minting of coins—was vigorously exploited, on the theory that the tsar had but to give an order and a kopeck (one-hundredth of a ruble) would become a grivna (one-tenth of a ruble). One cautious adviser urged that the currency be debased by 10 percent, but secretly, with prohibition of its export. The nominal profits of the mint rose to equal 10 percent of what had in 1710 been the whole revenue, but the purchasing power of the coinage fell by nearly 50 percent.

Peter's major fiscal innovation was the "soul tax." The fact that, under the old system of assessment by households, the taxable population had been crowding into fewer homesteads was made very obvious by the censuses of 1710 and 1717, the average number of males being five and one-half per homestead as against three or four in 1678. Under Sophia the idea of shifting assessment of direct taxation to a per capita basis had been considered. Peter, however, stumbled on this solution by a different route, hitting on the idea of quartering his soldiers directly on the peasant population. In 1718, the Senate therefore ordered an enumeration of the whole male agricultural population, "without overlooking from the old to the very latest infant," [17] to be completed within a year. When the lists were not forthcoming, the Guards were ordered to put the enumerating officials in fetters, in order to encourage prompter execution of their task. By the beginning of 1722, five million "souls" had been counted, and generals were appointed to supervise the distribution of the troops in the new barracks that had been ordered. In desperate but vain efforts to carry out the original program, the military superseded the normal jurisdiction of the local authorities and imposed a frightful burden on the peasantry. "To create the victorious army of Poltava and in the end to convert it into 126 unbridled police commands, scattered over the ten provinces amongst the terrified population," remarked Kliuchevsky, "in all this you will not recognize a reformer." [18]

Nevertheless, in 1724, the direct taxes were collected by the military on the new per capita basis; arrears amounted to 18 percent. Ultimately the new system was to be a contributing factor in the recovery of agriculture, for the old system of basing direct taxation on acreage under cultivation had encouraged contraction of tillage. This beneficial consequence, which made itself felt in the course of the eighteenth century, was wholly unanticipated in Peter's time. Apart from the psychological shock of imposing a material value on such an intangible and spiritual phenomenon as the human soul, the rough methods by which the new tax was brought into being, and the additional sums thus extracted from the toiling population, undoubtedly produced a very real lowering of Russia's material prosperity. The state, unable to develop trade and industry, which might have permitted a continued preponderance of indirect taxation, now drew 53 percent of its revenues directly from the peasantry.

In the process of registering the taxpaying population, though obviously without deliberate design, Peter completed the tendency, implicit in the *Ulozhenie* of Tsar Alexis and quickened by Fedor's introduction of the household tax, of reducing the mass of the population to one common fiscal denominator, the "bound people" (*krepostnye liudi*)—bound not to the land but to the person of a master. The old legal distinctions between "free" (taxpaying) peasants, *kholopy* (some of whom had been subjected to taxation before Peter), and various types of tax-exempt "wandering" people and Church people were ignored in compilation of the new tax registers, as they had been ignored in Peter's early military recruitments. In this respect, without introducing a new tendency, Peter went far beyond his predecessors. Peter did not initiate serfdom in Russia; he did unwittingly give it a tremendous, almost revolutionary, extension.

Economically as well as socially, Peter's financial measures, forced on him by the exigencies of the war and by his own lack of ability to anticipate consequences, had an extremely depressing result. To quote once more from Kliuchevsky:

> Peter left behind him not a kopeck of state debt [for the reason that he could not persuade anyone, not even John Law of Mississippi Bubble fame, to lend him anything]. The decline of the exhausted taxpaying and moral forces of the people amounted to an enormous loan and could scarcely have been redeemed if Peter had conquered, not only Ingria and Livonia, but the whole of Sweden or even five Swedens.[19]

NOTES

1. Kurakin, *"Gistoriia o tsarie Petrie Aleksievichie 1682-1694,"* in *Arkhiv kn. Th. A. Kurakina,* I, 66.
2. Kliuchevskii, *Kurs russkoi istorii,* 3rd edition, III, 415.
3. *Ibid.,* IV, 3.
4. *"Zhurnal,"* in Ustrialov, *Istoriia tsarstvovaniia Petra Velikogo,* III, *Prilozhenie,* pp. 602, 603. See also Tumanskii (ed.), *Sobranie raznykh zapisok . . . ,* III, 56-59.
5. *Bishop Burnet's History of His Own Time . . . ,* IV, 407-408.
6. *Polnoe sobranie zakonov . . .* (First collection), No. 1735 (December 19, 1699), III, 681.
7. *Ibid.,* No. 3840 (October 22, 1721), VI, 444.
8. *Ibid.,* No. 4649 (February 5, 1725), VII, 413.
9. Campredon dispatch (April 16, 1723), in Russkoe Istoricheskoe Obshchestvo, *Sbornik,* XLIX, 335-336.
10. Bridge (ed.), "History of the Russian Fleet During the Reign of Peter the Great," in *Publications of the Navy Record Society,* XV, 102ff.
11. Pososhkov, *"O ratnom povedenii,"* in *Kniga o skudosti i bogatsvie . . . ,* p. 268.
12. *Polnoe sobranie zakonov . . .* (First collection), No. 4326 (October 17, 1723), VII, 134.
13. Pososhkov, *Kniga o skudosti i bogatstvie . . . ,* p. 96.
14. *Polnoe sobranie zakonov . . .* (First collection), No. 3890 (January 24, 1722), VI, 486-493.
15. Kliuchevskii, *op. cit.,* IV, 165.
16. Peter, *"Obiavlenie o monashestvie,"* in *Polnoe sobranie zakonov . . .* (First collection), No. 4450 (January 31, 1724), VII, 230.
17. *Polnoe sobranie zakonov . . .* (First collection), No. 3287 (January 22, 1719), V, 618.
18. Kliuchevskii, *op. cit.,* IV, 124.
19. *Ibid.,* pp. 184-185.

SUGGESTIONS FOR FURTHER READING

It should be noted that, among the works on economic history cited at the end of Chapter 1, Kulisher is not serviceable for this and subsequent periods and there is no other comparable study to replace it. Liashchenko's work is frankly Marxist, and Blum's is careless.

The startling phenomenon of Peter's personality long made the significance of his reign extremely controversial and has continued to occasion a great deal of writing, mostly without the benefit of any perspective. Most of the literature on Peter available in English is therefore of doubtful value. The most sober and complete personal and political study is still Schuyler's *Peter the Great.*

The relevant portion of Kliuchevskii's fourth volume has been published in a new translation as *Peter the Great*. Among many accounts by contemporary foreigners, one of the most interesting is Perry's *State of Russia Under the Present Czar*. Admiral Bridge's "History of the Russian Fleet During the Reign of Peter the Great", in *Publications of the Navy Records Society,* contains very detailed information. Price's *The Tobacco Adventure to Russia* gives fascinating sidelights.

Chapter

12

The Petrine Reform: 1698-1725

The aspects of Peter's reign reviewed in the preceding chapter reflect in the main activities which required little in the way of conscious deliberation on the part of the tsar. The military and financial reforms were little more than instinctive reaction by a vigorous and untutored personality to the overshadowing fact of the Great Northern War; the war itself was more the product of impulse than of deliberate rational thought. In the matter of economic, administrative, and cultural reform there was freer scope for such creative talent as Peter possessed, though here, too, the reformer's work was conditioned by the war and by the inherent poverty and consequent backwardness of the country as well as by Peter's personal idiosyncrasies, by his susceptibility to alien impressions, and by his lack of training and self-discipline.

ATTEMPTS AT ECONOMIC REFORM

Peter was himself well aware that commercial matters were beyond his understanding. It was, of course, clear to him, as it had been to his predecessors, that the power of the state must rest on its economic prosperity. Yet he had no clear idea of how to promote economic activity. In accordance with the crassest mercantilist concepts of the times, he was anxious that Russia should become industrially self-sufficient, and he was confident that to the size of his realm must correspond a wealth of resources, as yet untapped, even unexplored. How to unlock Russia's abundance, how to make the strength of her economy consonant with the military might she appeared to be developing, seemed to him a simple problem of technology, an aspect of economics he himself could well understand. Of the importance of motivation—contemptuous as he was of others—he had not the slightest inkling.

His decrees accordingly often went into the pettiest minutiae of technological detail. This habit of leaving nothing to the imagination of subordinates more than once led to disastrous waste. For instance, in 1717 enormous piles of precious oak, collected at great cost for the Baltic fleet, were left to become buried in the sands on the shores of Lake Ladoga because Peter had neglected to order that he be reminded when the oak was ready. Peter's only concept of how to get things done was to issue commands, sugar-coated with financial benefits not made contingent on successful execution.

It was no doubt true that little or nothing could be expected from the initiative of the Russian merchantry, mostly petty folk of restricted outlook, ground down by the weight of obligations to the state, and oppressed by the competition, in a limited and impoverished market, of the tax-exempt nobility and clergy. One of the most difficult aspects of the matter was the energy and skill with which foreign traders, with vastly superior capital resources, carried on trade in Russia, aided by the venality of Russian officialdom. As one of Peter's would-be advisers, the peasant-trader Pososhkov, put it: before Peter, foreigners

> thrust on powerful personages a gift of a hundred rubles or so, and for the hundred rubles these foreigners made a profit of a million because the boyars rated the merchantry as but an eggshell; they would trade the whole merchantry for two kopecks.[1]

To continue and to expand, as Peter did, the practice of his predecessors of inviting foreign technicians into Russia was not enough. Too many foreigners, liberally paid to spend a term of years teaching the industrial arts to Russians, went home leaving their tasks unfinished. The greatest solicitude for their happiness while in Russia seemed unavailing, and it was suspected that their loyalty to organizations at home was making them deliberately sabotage their mission in Russia. Hence the intensification of another old practice, that of sending young Russians abroad to study; though in Peter's day a larger proportion returned home than had formerly been the case, the practical results were not encouraging. As the sea captain already quoted remarked:

> Upon their recall, undergoing a strict examination, they were found instead of attaining the rudiments of a seaman, to have acquired only the insignificant accomplishments of fine gentlemen.[2]

Always dazzled by the obvious superiority of Western Europe, Peter sought to transplant to Russia the forms to which he attributed its success, without seriously considering their adaptability; nor did he weigh the problem of whether these forms were the result rather than the cause of the economic activity he sought to stimulate. Mistrusting the family business of the type developed by the Stroganovs in the time of Ivan the Terrible or by the Demidovs in the Ural iron mines of Peter's own time, and unimpressed by the type of business organization which Ordin-Nashchokin had encouraged at Pskov, Peter put all his faith in the commercial capitalist company of Western type. Combining tax-exemptions and subsidies with compulsion, Peter ordered the establishment of a number of enterprises, carefully supervised by state administrative departments. In the sequel, most of these companies, to which he granted monopolies, fell into the hands of court favorites such as Menshikov, Apraxin, Shafirov, and Tolstoy.

Such Russian capital as there was took fright. Rather than venture their funds in business enterprises, at the risk of having them commandeered at the whim of the tsar, men took to hoarding gold and silver; those who could, including Peter's closest collaborators, deposited large sums abroad for safekeeping. Those who simply hid their wealth in their homes or buried it in the ground ran, to be sure, the risk of having it confiscated; informers were rewarded with one-third of the hoard. Yet the effect of Peter's policy of compulsory investment was something in the nature of a strike of capital, a paralysis of the unfolding free industrial development that had marked the latter half of the seventeenth century.

The policy of subsidizing industrial development was powerless to promote healthy economic growth. No private initiative could possibly compete with the privileged state-supervised enterprises, though the encouragement given to manufacturers violated even some of the privileges extended to the landholding nobility. Thus, an edict of 1721 gave factory-owners the right to buy serf-villages, with the sole restriction that the peasants so acquired could not be alienated by the manufacturer. By an edict of 1722 Peter ordered that fugitive serfs, if found working in a factory, were not to be recoverable by their masters. In this way, non-noble manufacturers were permitted to share the nobles' privilege of owning serfs and were given an additional privilege that no noble enjoyed, the right to harbor runaway serfs. Compulsion was Peter's remedy, not only for securing the capital needed to found a factory, but also for providing the labor necessary to work it.

It was in mining, the branch of industry in which serf labor could be most effectively employed, that Peter's reign scored its main advance. It may, of course, be a question whether similar results would not have been obtained regardless of Peter's efforts. The combination in close proximity of abundant forests to supply charcoal and of rich deposits of iron ore was bound further to promote the production of iron in Russia, as it had in Sweden from the sixteenth century. No doubt Peter's wars, like those of Sweden's House of Vasa, were both made possible by the existence of an iron industry and immensely stimulated its further growth. The seventeenth-century ironworks near Tula became a great government arsenal, and Petrozavodsk rose on the shores of Lake Ladoga. To Peter's initiative in ordering the exploitation of the Urals and to the successful management of the Demidovs, who had learned the business at Tula when Peter was a child, was due the rise of the iron industry near Perm and, later, at Yekaterinburg also. Russia took third place as producer of iron, being surpassed only by Sweden and England. Copper production, though much less, was also significant, but the quest for silver yielded no satisfactory results.

Much less successful were Peter's efforts to develop a cloth industry, intended to make Russia self-sustaining in the provision of uniforms. Disastrous was Peter's attempt to improve the linen industry: advised by an agent abroad that Russian linen was woven in too narrow strips, Peter forbade the production of linen cloth of less than the desired width; the hasty order did not take into account that Russian linen was woven in peasant huts throughout the northern regions and that it was utterly impossible to replace existing looms with larger ones.

Perhaps Peter's favorite project, inspired by his observations in France on his second trip to the West, was the promotion of a Russian silk manufacture. The task was entrusted to his vice-chancellor, "Baron" Shafirov and to "Count" Tolstoy; with them became associated the greatest of Peter's cronies, "Prince" Menshikov, though he was soon replaced by the admiral-general, "Count" Apraxin. Although Peter's purpose was to establish silk manufacture in Russia, the company soon won, in addition to other privileges, the right of free importation of silk manufactured abroad. Despite—or perhaps because of—the favors showered on the company, the original idea was soon abandoned.

It is in the light of the realities of production, not of the optimistic and monitory edicts issued by Peter, that one must comprehend the fact that by the time of Peter's death there were 191 "factories" in Russia, only thirteen of which antedated his accession. The word "factory" is, of course, anachronistic, for at that time it meant a trading agency, such as those maintained by Western Europeans on the Indian or African coasts. By "factory" in Petrine Russia should be understood only a more or less centralized workshop, with hand-operated machines or none at all; only a few operations in heavy metallurgy employed water power. These enterprises had to compete with the "putting-out system," something the importance of which Peter does not seem to have understood at all, for Peter's comprehension was narrowly limited to the physically tangible. It must be further remembered that Peter's "factories," unlike the beginnings of large-scale industrial enterprise in seventeenth-century Russia, were supported almost wholly by serf labor and were kept going by the grant of extensive tax exemptions and direct subsidies. Shortly after Peter's death, a large proportion of his "factories" were closed down, for it was obvious that many of them, while producing nothing, were consuming state revenues.

A special feature of Peter's effort to promote industrial and commercial development was his heroic effort to improve means of communication. In large measure this resulted directly from military considerations. Before the loss of Azov, Peter imposed measureless sacrifices on the population of the south in the endeavor to build highways to permit the swift movement of troops. He constructed also a five-hundred-mile highway to connect St. Petersburg with Moscow; by reason of the unconquerable mud and unreliable bridges, complicated by delays of as much as eight days at a time in waiting for relays of post horses, even the swiftest traveler might take five weeks to traverse the distance between the two capitals. Peter therefore attempted a new and shorter route which, however, became hopelessly bogged down in the morasses near Novgorod.

Peter had perforce to fall back on an effort to improve Russia's ready-made system of communications, the river network. At various times he attempted to build six canals, one of which was completed in his lifetime. Canal-digging then involved expenditure of an inconceivable amount of human labor, a consideration which never seriously bothered Peter. His first projects, to protect his beloved Azov, were a canal to connect tributaries in the lower reaches of the Volga and the Don and another canal to connect the source of the Don with a tributary of the Oka near Tula. Despite stupendous expenditure of human lives and of material wealth, both had to be abandoned after the loss of Azov. In the meantime, Peter had set himself the task of providing direct water communication between Moscow and St. Petersburg. This, with the labor of twenty thousand men for four years, he achieved by the Vyshnevolotsky Canal, connecting a tributary of the upper Volga with a stream flowing into Lake Ilmen. Officially completed in 1708, it became truly useful only after a Novgorod merchant had built a reservoir to maintain the necessary water level (1720). Even so, the shallow-draft vessels, which alone could negotiate the new canal, were wrecked with frightening regularity in stormy Lake Ladoga. Peter in 1718 personally surveyed a route for a new canal to skirt that open expanse. After Menshikov had wasted over 2 million rubles without achieving anything, the project was entrusted to a German engineer, Münnich, who completed it (1732) after Peter's death. Two other grand projects—one to provide an alternate water route from the Volga to the Neva by connecting Lakes Onega and Beloe (built over a hundred years later as the Mariinsk Canal) and another to link the White Sea with the Baltic—did not get beyond the dreaming stage.

Despite the slight results of Peter's tremendous plans, he did succeed, by persistent prohibitions, in forcing virtual abandonment of the Archangel trade route, opened in the days of Ivan the Terrible, in favor of his newly won Baltic outlets. His hope of establishing a Russian merchant marine came to nothing, as did his struggles to construct a safe and satisfactory harbor for his navy, but his desire for a "favorable" balance of trade was easily gratified. Since Russia, without credit, had no means of making purchases abroad without paying for them in exports, Russia showed a heavy positive balance, though on a light total volume.

ADMINISTRATIVE REORGANIZATIONS

Like his attempts to better Russia's economy, Peter's measures to improve the old Muscovite administrative system partook of a hit-or-miss character and reflected the influence of the financial requirements of the Great Northern War. In the field of political science, Peter was no better grounded than in the field of economics. His concepts of government were in terms, not of institutions, but of men, and unfortunately his judgment of individuals was based, not on their fitness or honesty, but on the zeal with which they seemed to do his bidding.

When, on the eve of his first trip abroad, he personally assumed the reins, he showed no signs of wishing to alter the existing boyar duma, the complicated confusion of central bureaus (*prikazy*), or the rapacious provincial governors (*voevody*). After his return, however, Peter's personal vigor and his obsession with the military problem and its financial implications gradually resulted in an increased tendency to dispense with deliberations in the duma. The process was hastened by the establishment (1699) of the Privy Chancellery, an organ of administrative and financial control nominally headed by Peter's old tutor, Zotov. The duma, reduced in numbers, became a mere executive committee, implementing the will of an often absent monarch. This development was, of course, not novel; it was at most an acceleration of the whole tendency of Russian history in the seventeenth century.

The bureaucratic apparatus had always suffered from the complex confusion of the *prikazy,* some of which were charged with certain types of business throughout the realm, while others dealt with all types of business in certain areas; many of them were statewide for some of their functions, territorially limited for others; and no clear line of demarcation existed between their administrative, financial, and judicial duties. In the early years of Peter's personal administration, the situation was worsened by creation of several new *prikazy* and of a number of independent "chancelleries." Most significant of the new organs was the *Preobrazhensky Prikaz*; founded in 1689 to administer the "play" regiments, it was in 1697 assigned universal jurisdiction, superior to the authority of any other *prikaz,* over all "political" prosecutions.

Peter's first major administrative reform was the imposition on urban communities of a measure of self-government, strongly reminiscent of the *guba* reform of Ivan the Terrible. At the beginning of 1699 the commercial population of Moscow was granted the right annually to elect *burmistry,* "good and true men, as many as they wish," [3] to be responsible for the collection of taxes and to enjoy judicial autonomy. The other towns, as well as communes of the "black-plow" and court peasants, were, "if they wish," also to be relieved of the vexatious exactions of the admittedly greedy and unscrupulous *voevody* hitherto appointed by the central authority; the catch was that they were to pay double the rate of the old assessments. Only eleven of seventy towns were willing thus to ransom themselves; the rest replied that they could not afford it, and that anyway there was no one they could elect. As a result, in 1699 they were given the privilege without paying the price and were made subject to the supervisory authority of the *Ratusha* (a Polish version of German *Rathaus,* "council chamber"); the *burmistry* were to be elected mainly by the great merchants of the capital. In this way the government was able to provide for the more efficient collection of taxes then amounting to more than one-third of its whole estimated revenue. It was the old story of devising new means to circumvent the corruption of its own officials. At the head of the new apparatus was placed Kurbatov, a "revenue-man" whose humble origin did not hinder him in ferreting out peculations by the most highly placed courtiers (save for his patron Menshikov).

The authority of the *Ratusha* cut across and further confused the authority of the *prikazy*. Matters were worse confounded in 1708, when Peter attempted administrative decentralization. The realm was divided into eight (later twelve) *guberniyas,* each under a governor (*gubernator*) or governor-general, assisted by a vice-governor and staff of subordinate agents. The new local rulers, suggestive of the satraps of ancient Persia, were all chosen from the tsar's intimate circle of friends. In 1712, the unwieldy *guberniyas* were subdivided into "provinces," each of which included a number of the old *uiezdy*. These "provinces" were destined to survive the recentralization of 1718 and ultimately were rechristened *"guberniyas,"* though without the local autonomy originally intended. The forty-five (later fifty) *voevody* appointed to the new "provinces" were charged with numerous duties, as the *gubernators* had been, but under closer central supervision. They were responsible for the details of quartering troops, administering justice, collecting taxes, organizing police, promoting commerce, and supervising the hospitals, orphanages, and schools which, however, did not exist outside the larger cities.

In 1718, after some pains to collect information about the administrative structure of foreign lands (especially of Sweden), the direct authority of central organs of the government was restored. "Colleges" (*Collegia*), ultimately numbering sixteen and with fairly precisely defined jurisdictions, replaced the forty-odd *prikazy* whose authority had been almost wholly destroyed by the experiment at reform of the local government. Each "college" (*Collegium*) was provided with its own *reglament;* under the general Reglament of 1720 each was to consist of a president, a vice-president, four councilors, and four "assessors," who were to arrive at decisions by majority vote. Actually, of course, they became in practice, like the old *prikazy,* virtually one-man ministries. Unlike the old *prikazy,* however, their functions were reasonably coherent, and their competence was statewide. At the head of each stood one of Peter's trusted intimates.

In 1720, Peter established a new organ to replace the *Ratusha* of 1699. In the *reglament* of this new "Chief Magistracy," the tsar attempted to impose a carefully devised organization on the whole urban population, which he divided into two classes, "regular" and "base." The latter, made up of day-laborers, were given no share in municipal self-government; they were permitted only to elect elders (*starosty*) to represent their interests before the "magistracy." In each town the "regular" citizens were divided into two "guilds": the upper one was to be made up of bankers, merchants, professional men, and artists; the other, comprised of petty traders and artisans, was to be organized in crafts (*tsekhi*) according to their occupation. The "regular" citizens elected the local "magistracy," which was subordinate to the "Chief Magistracy" at St. Petersburg. All citizens of the town were to be subject to the soul tax, but "regular" citizens were exempted from military conscription and, after 1722, from labor services for the treasury; in addition, any burgher who operated a factory or mill might purchase land and peasants to guarantee it a labor supply. This novel form of municipal organization was impotent to change the condition of the burghers in any fundamental way.

According to the "first revision," as the count for the new soul tax was called, the taxable urban population numbered 169,426 (male) souls, or 3.1 percent of the total; about one-fourth of them were accounted merchants, the rest being artisans or common laborers. Moscow remained economically preëminent, despite the official establishment of St. Petersburg as the capital (1712); politically, also, Moscow retained much of its importance, though its further architectural development was sacrificed for the sake of the "window to the West." Many towns, particularly in the south, remained merely centers of military concentration; the population of Kiev, for example, was 74 percent military in 1710.

A curious by-product of Peter's systematization of the central administrative organs in the form of "colleges" was the new institution to direct the affairs of the Church. Patriarch Ioakim, offended by the protection Sophia's regime had extended to the heretical "Bread-Worshipers" and even to the Jesuits, had supported the young Peter in the critical year 1689. However, Peter could scarcely fail to be aware that his successor, Patriarch Adrian, and the Muscovite clergy generally, did not look with favor on the essentially irreverent trend of Peter's initial actions on his return from Europe. On Adrian's death (1700), the tsar therefore blocked the election of a successor.

The ecclesiastic whom he regarded with most favor was Stefan Yavorsky, metropolitan of Ryazan. In his youth Yavorsky, a Little Russian, had pretended conversion to Roman Catholicism and had thus secured admission to a Jesuit college in the West. There he had acquired a favorable inclination toward Western innovations, so long as they were not in the spirit of Protestantism. A supple man, he was fairly successful in concealing from the tsar his Romanist convictions on the score of spiritual authority; he was thus able to serve as a useful instrument of a master with whom he was in fundamental disagreement. Yavorsky belonged to the Kievan school, and his elevation to the exalted position of patriarch would have given great offense to the Muscovite hierarchy. The office was therefore left vacant. Yavorsky was named *miestobliustitel* (the nearest English equivalent is Vicar-General), with the administrative but not the spiritual authority of the patriarchate.

Financial control, however, was not left in the hands of this substitute for a patriarch; it was entrusted to the Monastery Bureau (re-created in 1701). Edicts of 1696 and 1697 had required the monasteries to send their account books to Moscow for inspection. A careful census of monasterial real estate and peasants was now undertaken by lay officials: the number of inmates permissible in each monastery was fixed, and excess monks and servants were drafted into the army or other service; nuns, if not of noble birth, were to be set to work at spinning or other useful occupations; no paper or ink was to be allowed in the cells of monks; and the control of schools, printing presses, and almshouses was taken over by the secular authorities. So far did the practical authority of the Monastery Prikaz extend that it even ordered corrections made in the Bible without consulting the Vicar-General.

This dual regime endured until 1720, when the office of patriarch and the Monastery Prikaz were both abolished. In their stead was established a Collegium similar to the newly formed organs of secular administration. The *reglament* for the new "college," speedily renamed the Holy Governing Synod, was written by Feofan Prokopovich, bishop of Pskov, a slavish admirer of Peter, and—under Lutheran influences—a devout believer in the principle of absolute monarchy. Yavorsky was translated to the titular headship of the new institution, but Prokopovich was its guiding spirit. Like the other *collegia,* the Synod was in 1722 put under even more direct control of the monarch by the appointment of a lay *Ober-Prokuror,* assisted by a staff of "inquisitors," who controlled appointments of prelates, decided points of dogma, combated heresies, and exercised judicial authority in all cases involving faith and morals.

The progressive deterioration of the boyar duma left the administrative structure of the state without an adequate supervising organ. The Privy Chancellery, established at Moscow in 1699 and transferred to St. Petersburg in 1714, served as a coördinating instrument for the executive departments but was not adapted to function well as a policy-determining organ in the absence of the tsar. When Peter left for the Pruth campaign in 1711, he therefore entrusted power to a body of nine "senators." After his return the Senate continued to function as the highest judicial and administrative organ, sometimes exercising virtually legislative authority. In composition it varied from time to time; when the Collegia were set up in 1718, their presidents were added to the Senate, but in 1722 all but three of them were excluded. What the Senate thus lost in efficiency as an organ of direct administration, it gained in increased power of guidance and control.

Peter, however, was never able to trust his subordinates, intimate with them as he might be. As early as 1711, he appointed "fiscals" charged with maintaining a vigilant, if secret, watch for violations of law, for peculation, and for bribery, either in the local or in the central organs of government. At their head stood the *oberfiscal* of the Senate, a post long held by the redoubtable Nesterov. The system of inspectors grew ever more complex. In 1722, it reached its full development in the appointment of a procurator-general, theoretically elected by the Senate but actually chosen by the emperor. All business to be transacted by the Senate was channeled through him, and under him functioned a whole network of procurators and fiscals supervising all government organs, from the highest to the lowest.

It was easier to introduce some order into the organization of the bureaucracy than it was to cope with the enormous confusion of the laws. Three separate attempts—in 1700, 1714, and 1720—to recodify the law broke down completely, as did halting efforts to separate administrative and judicial functions. Crime, as an offense against the state, continued to be subject to savage punishment; inquisitorial torture was normally employed; hanging and beheading were the mildest forms of execution, which included also running the gantlet, breaking on the wheel, and suspension by a rib from a hook. Publicity of punishment was heavily relied on as a deterrent, and for bribery especially, a new form of punishment was devised—public proclamation as a "rogue" (a Russian version of "sending to Coventry"). Military offenses were ruthlessly punished: if a garrison surrendered a fortress to the enemy, every tenth man was to be hanged. Political offenses, including oral criticism of the tsar, were treated with peculiar severity. While the Preobrazhensky Prikaz continued to function at Moscow, a parallel organ, the Secret Chancellery, was established at St. Petersburg; its first, but not its last, assignment was to try the tsar's only son, Alexis, on charges of treason (1718).

"WESTERNIZATION"

The aspect of Peter's reforms that most clearly bears the imprint of Peter's personal interest is his "Westernization" of Muscovy. The term is misleading, for what Peter was attempting was not to get rid of nonexistent "Asiatic" influences but rather to quicken the pace of Russian development, to enable her to catch up to a Western Europe which had in the past experienced but had long outgrown the rude customs, manners, and ways of thinking which still lingered on at Moscow. By "Westernization" one should understand modernization, not reorientation.

It was impossible to effect rapid changes in the way of life of the mass of the people. It was only a thin upper stratum that was at all capable of responding to Peter's efforts, thus driving a deep wedge between the roughly polished "Europeanized" elite and the masses over whom they ruled. Only far-reaching changes in the economy of Russia, opening up opportunities for men to advance themselves by their own efforts, could really have Europeanized Russia, and this was far beyond the capacity of Peter. The net effect of his desperate effort to "write edicts with the knout" was to harden class lines, to stifle initiative, and thus to thwart the tendency still manifest in the seventeenth century to progress along the lines that Western Europe had traveled.

Even his educational reforms clearly reflected Peter's limited aims and his failure to comprehend the bases of the intellectual superiority of the West. Peter, indeed, showed no interest in encouraging the free play of the human intellect; the schools he founded were intended to serve only specific technical objectives. The interest of the state in the training of specialists, not the interests of society in free intellectual exploration—much less the interests and curiosity of the individual—determined the choice of students and the subjects of study. First of his foundations (1701) was the Navigation School at Moscow; under the guidance of Leonid Magnitsky it succeeded in producing a number of sailors, engineers, hydrographers, topographers, bombardiers, and architects, but made no effort to produce educated men. A more advanced school was the Naval Academy founded at St. Petersburg in 1715; its curriculum emphasized shipbuilding, with the strictest discipline. In 1701 also was founded at Moscow the Artillery School, with 180 pupils, drawn largely from sons of cannoneers: many entered active service before finishing the course; a few of the best were sent abroad to complete their studies; but its graduates numbered barely a dozen a year.

At a higher level was founded in 1712 an engineering school, intended to train 100 to 150 students, two-thirds of whom were to be nobles; as only 23 presented themselves voluntarily, the rest had to be drafted. In 1707, under the direction of a Dutchman, a medical school was opened, where, on a diet of bread and water, sometimes in chains, and under constant threat of being made soldiers, fifty draftees "of all ranks" were taught anatomy, surgery, and "apothecary science."

In the seventeenth century, much effort had been devoted to teaching officials the necessary foreign tongues. In 1702, Peter's troops captured at Marienburg in Livonia a Saxon missionary named Glück, who had been trained in philosophy and theology at German universities. This Lutheran pastor had taught himself the Latvian and Russian languages and had dreamed of translating the Bible into them. Because of the shortage of interpreters, Glück was promptly assigned to teach in an existing school in the German Liberty. When word of Glück's wider potentialities reached Peter, he was entrusted with the organization of a "Gymnasium" to teach geography, ethics, politics, Latin rhetoric, Cartesian philosophy, and a number of languages—French, German, Latin, Greek, Hebrew, Syriac, and Chaldean—as well as dancing and horseback-riding. Glück himself died in 1705 but the school was continued under one of his pupils, with Glück's widow as housemistress. The Gymnasium, however, failed to flourish, and in 1715 the remnant of its pupils were transferred to the Naval Academy; in the years of its existence it trained about 250 students in foreign languages.

A small number of pupils, recruited from the poorest nobles' children and from the sons of minor officials and artisans, were subjected to instruction in mining. The old Slav-Greek-Latin Academy at Moscow continued to give instruction, mainly ecclesiastical, though under Yavorsky's influence Greek was dropped. A fairly vigorous effort was made to force archbishops to establish schools in the provinces; by the time of Peter's death, there were forty-six episcopal schools, attended by the sons of priests and deacons who would otherwise have had to pay the soul tax. Elementary "ciphering schools" were established under an edict of 1714, which ordered that two graduates of the Moscow Navigation School be sent to each *guberniya* to teach the sons of nobles and of officials between the ages of ten and fifteen; these proved very difficult to establish, though some energetic governors sent troops to round up the necessary pupils; of forty-seven teachers sent out from Moscow, eighteen found no students. Nevertheless, at Peter's death there were forty-two such schools, with two thousand pupils (of whom only five hundred remained two years later).

The first Russian multiplication table had been published in 1682; the first using Arabic numerals appeared in 1714. The first Russian textbook in arithmetic was published at Amsterdam in 1699; Magnitsky's *Arithmetic* (1703), with examples to serve navigation and trade, was issued in 2,400 copies. Under Peter, many translations were published in Russia, ranging from the learned works of Pufendorf and Baronius to Aesop's *Fables,* Ovid's *Metamorphoses,* and Varenius' *Geography;* a variety of foreign dictionaries also appeared. Newspapers, which had begun to be prepared for the information of seventeenth-century tsars, now took the form of Peter's *Vedomosti* ("News"), a propaganda sheet which appeared irregularly from 1703 on in issues of anywhere from one hundred to twenty-five hundred copies.

Peter had a certain interest also in Russia's past. By edicts of 1720 and 1722, it was ordered that copies of records kept in monasteries should be made at Moscow. In 1708, a certain Polikarpov was instructed to write a history of Muscovy from the time of Vasily III, but his work was adjudged unsatisfactory in 1716. In 1722, Peter ordered the writing of a history of the Great Northern War in the fullest detail; indeed, as early as 1713 he had ordered the collection of narratives and engravings of battles.

Peter was deeply interested in the promotion of science, especially of geography and geology, with their immediately practical implications. He ordered the establishment of herb gardens and chemical laboratories at St. Petersburg, Moscow, and elsewhere. He had been fascinated by a visit to the Royal Society at London and was assiduous in fostering the development of applied science in arms manufacture, coinage, and spinning. In 1718, he took seriously the idea of founding a Russian Academy of Sciences, which was established on paper in 1724, though its first meeting took place only after his death. Its predecessor was a library and *Kunstkammer,* established in 1714 to house his father's books, with later accessions, as well as a collection of "curiosities" in the form of bones, stones, and other natural phenomena.

In other fields, too, Peter was much attracted by curiosities, and in none, perhaps, more than by what many Russians found the peculiarities of social intercourse in the West. Mention has already been made of Peter's establishment of the "All-rowdiest Most Mock, and Most Drunken Synod," composed of his personal cronies, which was wont to carouse in the streets of Moscow. Singing bawdy ditties instead of Christmas carols, Peter and his friends gave great offense to grave and relatively sober citizens. The parody of Church ritual was carried even to the length of having his "Prince-Pope" give a public blessing at Shrovetide, with tobacco pipes arranged in such fashion as to resemble the candlesticks used at sacred rites. It does not appear that Peter had any deliberate intention of mocking religion—or even the hierarchy; indeed, he frequently insisted on strict observance of Orthodox practices, and his toleration of the schismatic Old Ritualists was conditioned on their payment of double taxation. Rather it seems to have been a matter of uninhibited animal spirits, coupled with his impressions of conduct he understood to be *de rigueur* in the West. For that matter, the drunkenness associated with Peter's intimate circle was not novel in Russia; indeed, visiting foreign Protestant ministers remarked that it was the Orthodox prelates who seemed best to survive Peter's parties.

What was new was the way in which Peter flaunted his social activities and the emphasis he placed on Western manners. Along with the shaving of beards, Peter insisted on the wearing of wigs and of Western-style clothing. He hired a troop of German actors, not for his private delectation, but to give public performances in the Red Square. Their repertory, translated into Russian, ranged from *Scipio Africanus, Don Pedro and Don Juan,* and *Bajazet and Tamerlane* to *Le Médecin malgré lui* of Molière. His chief of police for St. Petersburg decreed (1718) that "assemblies" should be held in the homes of aristocrats, merchants, and leading craftsmen; they might take the form of receptions or dances, with unrestricted conversation, gambling, drinking, and eating: for violation of decorum it was ordered that the culprit must drain an "eagle" (a big goblet of strong spirits stamped with the sovereign's coat of arms). In 1717 Peter caused to be issued a translation of a German pamphlet, *The Honorable Mirror of Youth,* in which were set forth in detail the proper rules of conduct for anyone seeking preferment: youths must doff their hats to acquaintances at three paces' distance; they must not pick their noses or clean their teeth with a knife; they should spit to one side and not in the midst of a group; they must not wolf their food, put their elbows on the table, or scratch their heads; nor must they wear heavy boots when dancing. In short, those who would be rated as members of the ruling class, whatever their own origin, must sharply mark themselves off from peasants.

Peter himself sought to set his subjects a good example by giving formal parties. At these functions strong liquor flowed freely, and guests were not permitted to plead that they had had enough. Many an unfortunate was made the subject of practical jokes or given a lesson in Western etiquette. As a mild example might be cited the occasion on which a boyar, evincing distaste for salad, was held by Guardsmen while Peter stuffed lettuce into his mouth and poured in vinegar until the boyar's nose began to bleed. Peter's cudgel was much in evidence and was freely applied, even to his favorite Menshikov. When the tsar himself tired of his parties, he withdrew for a nap, ordering his guests to continue their festivities until his return. It is not difficult to understand why it was frequently necessary for the tsar to send Guardsmen to enforce his invitations and to post them at the gates to prevent early departures.

OPPOSITION AND THE PROBLEM OF THE SUCCESSION

The heavy fiscal, military, and labor burdens which the tsar imposed on his subjects inevitably bred discontent and led to wholesale flights of peasants. Peter's reign also was troubled by several uprisings, the most notable of which occurred in Siberia, at Astrakhan, among the Bashkirs, and—most serious of all—among the cossacks of the Don, led by Bulavin. Bulavin's appeals to revolt did not attack the tsar personally; they were directed, as usual, against those around him who were "bad men, princes, and boyars, revenue-men, and Germans." Yet a different note was frequently sounded by malcontents. The records of the Preobrazhensky Prikaz are filled with reports that men and women had been heard to exclaim: "How could God have sent him to us as tsar? We have never seen such burdens on the community [*mir*] . . . there is no rest for our brethren, the peasantry. . . ." "What kind of a tsar is he? He has driven the peasants from their homes, taken our husbands as soldiers, and orphaned us and our children and made us to weep forever. . . ."[4]

To the suffering of the population, the offensive traits of Peter's personality added insult. A tsar who did not look like his predecessors, who did not stay at home, who did not dress like a Russian and did not comport himself with the decorum expected of an Orthodox ruler, had raised grave doubt and question whether he was the rightful tsar. The story that Peter was no true son of Tsar Alexis but a German changeling foisted on his unhappy subjects became ever more widespread. One of many variants was that the true Peter, on his trip abroad, had been seized in Sweden, nailed up in a chest, and set adrift.

A related myth arose in ecclesiastical circles. Even in 1700 it was deemed necessary to execute Archdeacon Telitsky and to exile the bishop of Tambov for circulating stories that Peter was Antichrist. The idea could not be got rid of. Although no general mass revolt could develop, Peter was well aware, through the reports of his secret investigators, of mass hostility to him. He was well aware also that among the reasons that discontent did not burst into open rebellion was the fact that powerful opposition circles were waiting only for his death, confident that his son and heir would make all things right again.

The marriage into which Peter's mother had inveigled him in 1689 had not been a happy one. A son, Alexis, had been born in 1690 (a second one a year later, died almost immediately), but Peter had already deserted his wife for a succession of more attractive partners. In those carefree days between the fall of Sophia and Peter's return from the West, the young tsar had found no time to give thought to his son or to his upbringing. Alexis therefore grew up in the care of his mother, living in the traditional Kremlin palace, educated in piety and idleness, until the age of nine, when Peter, on his return from Europe, retired his wife to a convent. All Peter's subsequent efforts to bend the twig in another direction and to make the child take an active interest in the business and pleasures that absorbed his father were doomed to failure. The boy found the time he had to spend with Peter "worse than penal servitude," and Peter's resort to beatings proved futile. No more successful was Peter's adoption of the method tried by his own mother; in 1711, Peter found his son a German wife, Sophia-Charlotte of Brunswick-Wölfenbüttel; Alexis treated her better than Peter had treated his mother Eudocia, but showed no signs of changing his attitude toward his father. Peter was tormented by the obvious fact that his heir would not continue his work.

In the meantime, however, Peter had found hope in another quarter. When his armies invaded Livonia, one of the prizes of war had been the Lutheran pastor Glück, whose Gymnasium has already been mentioned. A still greater prize was Glück's maidservant, a robust peasant girl named Catherine, who found rapid promotion among the military until she found herself established in the St. Petersburg palace of no less a person than Peter's intimate subordinate, Menshikov. There Peter became acquainted with her; he soon removed her to his own residence. With satisfactory rapidity she bore a series of children, whom Peter gladly accepted as his own. By 1712, appreciating her careful study of his every whim, he formally took her as his wife. From this source might come an alternate heir.

Alexis' fate was sealed when, in 1715, Alexis' wife, at the cost of her own life, presented him with a son, Peter. Whatever difficulty might be raised about the validity of the tsar's relations with Catherine, there now existed an unquestionably legitimate grandson, and the tsarevich Alexis had become superfluous. Tsar Peter promptly demanded that his son renounce his right of succession; however hypocritically, Alexis agreed. Peter thereupon further demanded that Alexis clinch the matter by taking the tonsure as a monk;

Alexis did not refuse, nor did he immediately comply. Giving his son six months in which to make an irrevocable decision, Peter set off again for the West (1716). From Denmark he incautiously summoned Alexis to join him. Thus enabled to leave Russia, the tsarevich slipped away to Vienna and threw himself on the mercy of his wife's brother-in-law, the Holy Roman Emperor, who sent him to St. Elmo, near Naples, for safety. Peter dispatched Tolstoy and Rumiantsev to Vienna with threats; finally permitted to visit Alexis, they succeeded in persuading him that if he returned to Russia voluntarily, he would be freely forgiven; alternatively, his protector, the Emperor, would be forced to return him unconditionally.

On his return, early in 1718, Alexis received a full and public pardon. His mother's friends, however, were carefully investigated; some were broken on the wheel, and Eudocia herself was more strictly confined. It was soon announced that Alexis, after his pardon, had expressed his delight at news of a mutiny of Russian auxiliary troops in Mecklenburg. A special court of 127 dignitaries, lay and ecclesiastical, and including 39 Guard officers, tried the tsarevich on charges of high treason; with the aid of torture, it found him guilty and sentenced him to death. "So that our conscience should be clear on the Day of the Last Judgment and our fatherland be unharmed," [5] Peter empaneled a new court, which confirmed the sentence. The sentence was not carried out, for, after a night-time visit by his father, it was announced that Alexis had died in the fortress of Peter and Paul on June 26, 1718.

To Peter's chagrin, Catherine's two sons, Peter and Paul, died in infancy of natural causes. There remained only one male heir, the infant grandson Peter. Of possible female heirs there were four: Catherine's daughters Anna and Elizabeth, and Peter's nieces Catherine and Anna, daughters of his half-brother and predecessor, Ivan. Three of them had been successfully exported as brides of princes, though of petty ones; all Peter's efforts to find more desirable husbands by peddling his daughters' portraits in France, Spain, and Italy had come to nothing. Catherine Ivanovna was married to Peter's good ally, the duke of Mecklenburg. Anna Ivanovna had been married to the duke of Courland. Anna Petrovna was married to the duke of Schleswig-Holstein-Gottorp. Elizabeth Petrovna remained at home, unmarried.

The disappointing state of his family decided Peter to arrogate to himself (1722) the right of freely choosing a successor as Emperor. Mindful of the uncertainties of life, Peter never took the dangerous step of naming his successor. He merely complicated the problem by formal coronation of his peasant wife as Empress (1724). On his deathbed in January, 1725, Peter was at last persuaded to express his wishes but got no further than the words "Give everything——." As events were to prove, the new law on the succession, the confused state of his family, and the existence of the Guard regiments, which were made up from top to bottom of nobles, were in their consequences to be the most lasting of the Petrine reforms.

APPRAISALS OF PETER'S SIGNIFICANCE

As Platonov, the last of the great historians of tsarist days, phrased it: "Peter's reforms in their essence and in their results did not constitute a revolution." [6] The class structure, the political institutions, the economic practices of Russia—all remained basically unchanged. New forms for old relationships were reflected in new names, but in little else. The nobility, though called by the Polish term *shliakhetstvo* instead of old Russian *dvorianstvo,* remained the ruling class, though its old and always blurred internal subdivisions, the Muscovite "grades" (*chiny*), were replaced by the clear-cut Table of Ranks. The obsolescent distinction between *votchinniki* and *pomeshchiki* was retained to signify the origin of their rights to their lands, but no further distinction remained in their practical rights. The peasants retained their theoretical legal personality as "free" taxpayers, but in practice were ever more firmly bound, not to the land, but to the landholders, who were held responsible for collection of the soul tax. The legal distinction between *krestiane* (free peasants), *kholopy* (bondsmen), and *guliashchie* (wanderers) was in effect wiped out by common subjection to taxation. The continuing efforts of the state, for fiscal reasons, to treat the *kholopy* as *krestiane* and of the landholder, for economic reasons, to treat the *krestiane* as *kholopy* combined to further the development of a gray mass of "bound people" (*krepostnye liudi*).

Economic differentiation, however, was great, especially where *obrok* payments prevailed, and alongside the 4 million landowners' peasants there existed also about a million and a half others, including: (1) the old category of "black-plow" peasants, chiefly in the north, who retained their communal autonomy; (2) the monasterial peasants taken over by the state and later known, from the name of the bureaucratic organ that administered them, as "economic" peasants; (3) "court" peasants serving the tsar's personal household; (4) a new category, later known as "possessional" peasants, purchased by or given to owners of factories (whether noble or non-noble) and attached, not to their owners, but to the factories; and (5) a curious relic of frontier days, the "single-householders" (*odnodvortsy*), formerly classed as service-nobles and still, though themselves subject to soul tax, permitted personally to hold land and peasants. The existence of these groups did not, however, affect the general picture of that simplification of class relationships which is one of the chief results of Peter's highhanded methods. Prince Menshikov, speaking in the Senate in 1725, summed up the significance for the peasantry of Peter's reign:

> Now there are over the peasants ten and more commanders where formerly there was one, and of the military, from the soldier to the staff and to the generals, and of the civilians, from the fiscals, commissars, waldmeisters, and the rest to the voevodas, there are none who can be called shepherds, but wolves ravishing the flock.[7]

Nor did Peter's vigorous efforts to alter the status of the Russian traders and craftsmen, by imposing by decree new forms of organization on the town population, result in any serious change in their condition. It was to this class that belonged one of Peter's admirers and would-be advisers, Ivan Pososhkov. Pososhkov was the author of several treatises. His major literary effort, *A Book on Poverty and Wealth,* was composed in his old age; it is improbable that Peter ever saw it, written as it was less than a year before the emperor's death; a few months later, however, the author of this piece of what may be called "Bolshevik self-criticism" was arrested and imprisoned in the Peter-and-Paul Fortress, where he died early in 1726.

Pososhkov wrote in the spirit of Krizhanich, though at a much lower intellectual level. Like Krizhanich, he accepted as right and just the principles of unfettered autocracy under God, of serfdom, and of minute regulation of every phase of the life of the tsar's subjects; he, too, while profoundly mistrusting foreigners, advocated cautious borrowings, for purposes of technical instruction, from the West.

Pososhkov condemned the ignorance of the priests, which played into the hands of the schismatic Old Ritualists, the Lutherans, and the Romans; he wanted the clergy to abandon agriculture and trade; supported by a tithe, they should concentrate on achieving piety, cleanliness, and sobriety. He condemned the inefficiency of the military classes, who could not even shoot straight; they should be better paid and better disciplined. He condemned the delays and injustices of the courts and urged the compilation of a new code of laws, to be prepared by elected representatives of all classes; he even added: "It seems to me that it would not be bad to elect also from the peasants. . . . I have seen that even among the Mordva [a Finnish remnant on the middle Volga] there are intelligent men, then why should there not be among the peasants intelligent men?" [8] There should be a special chancellery to supervise the judges, who should be put on regular fixed salaries; too many men were detained in prison, for "no men should lose their days for nothing and eat their bread for nothing."

"And it is not meet to reduce the merchantry to nought. . . . For as the soul cannot be without the body, so the military cannot survive without the merchantry." There should be "freedom of trade," but only for those registered as traders; professional merchants should be protected, both against foreigners and against unfair competition, whether from nobles or from free peasants. As for the artisans, "if they do not have good supervision and proper regulation, they cannot possibly flourish . . ."; they should be organized into guilds.

"In all the Christian and Musulman realms there are not so many robbers as there are in Rus . . ."; they must be dealt with summarily, as in other lands; a complete system of internal passports would be of great assistance. "The life of the peasants is poverty-stricken for no other reason than their own laziness. . . . If any peasant begins to lie abed, he must be severely punished. . . ." They must be made to work both summer and winter, but the practice of many landlords of fleecing them like sheep should be checked, for "their true possessor is the all-Russian autocrat, and [the landlords] possess them temporarily."

In a concluding chapter, Pososhkov enumerates his suggested remedies for a variety of fiscal abuses. There is little that is original in his detailed examination of matters that needed attention in his beloved Russia, and his sole hope was in the tsar, "Who is like unto God. . . . And so I offer [my writing] for the consideration only of the one high-soaring white eagle, the manifest lover of truth, the all-Russian emperor, Peter the Great, true autocrat and unshakeable pillar." Yet even this devoted and earnest soul had his doubts:

> The great sovereign has no upright zealots, but all the judges walk crookedly. . . . We all see how our great monarch labors, and nothing succeeds, because he has not many assistants to do his will . . . how can his cause succeed? . . . and if he cannot change the old order, strive as he will, the business must be abandoned.

It is only in the field of cultural change that Peter's reign produced striking results. Even here, his intensification of the influence the West had been exerting on manners, customs, and ways of thinking affected only a thin upper crust of Russian society. What is more, in Peter's own time, even this superficial "Westernization" produced a parody on, rather than a genuine emulation of, the West.

NOTES

1. Pososhkov, *Kniga o skudosti i bogatstve* . . . , p. 123.
2. Bridge (ed.), "History of the Russian Fleet . . . ," p. 102.
3. *Polnoe sobranie zakonov* . . . (First collection), No. 1675 (January 30, 1699), III, 600.
4. Solov'ev, *Istoriia Rossii* . . . , 2nd edition, Book XV, col. 1368-1369.
5. Ustrialov, *Istoriia tsarstvovaniia Petra Velikogo,* VI, 516.
6. Platonov, *Lektsii* . . . , p. 540.
7. Bogoslovskii, *Oblastnaia reforma Petra Velikago,* p. 490.
8. Pososhkov, *op. cit.,* p. 82. The quotations in the remainder of the chapter are from the same work, pp. 96-99, 107-244 *passim.*

SUGGESTIONS FOR FURTHER READING

See the suggestions cited under Chapter 11.

Chapter

13

Triumph of the Nobility: 1725-1762

THE SUCCESSION PROBLEM

The death of Peter, like the deaths of Lenin and of Stalin in a later era, necessarily precipitated a series of struggles for power. Different as were the circumstances, there is basic resemblance in the conflict between the two principles of "the cult of the individual" and of "collective leadership."

In Imperial Russia, of course, the "cult of the individual" might seem implicit, but there was no possible successor to Peter who had the force of personality to become the real wielder of power. Whoever might sit on the throne, the real question was who would guide that ruler's actions, and here was advanced the principle of "collective leadership." Peter's associates in ruling Russia, the "supreme lords," were not locked in the tight bonds of Communist Party discipline; their only common denominator was their relationship to Peter. In the absence of a Party, also, it was inevitable that the active force manipulated by rivals among the "supreme lords" should take some other form than this instrument of power in Soviet Russia. This force was supplied by the Guard regiments, whose personnel made them, however blindly, the instrument of the nobility as a class. The history of the eighteenth century is therefore essentially the story of the rise of the nobility to a pinnacle of power it had not previously achieved.

Among the "supreme lords," first place was held by Menshikov, ever Peter's chief collaborator, whether on the battlefield, in the council chamber, or in the palace. Of obscure origin, he owed his preëminence primarily to the favor of Peter, whose playmate he had been—and of Catherine, whom he had discovered—but also to the fact that he possessed undoubted talents. However marred by an inordinate pride and by a penchant for wholesale peculation, Menshikov had fully earned his position as head of the War Collegium, an office which gave him also a prominent place in the Senate. Though frequently subjected to cudgelings at the hands of his irate master and, toward the end of Peter's reign, subjected to financial investigation, Menshikov had remained an outstanding figure.

One of Menshikov's former bondsmen, Kurbatov, became for a time virtual head of Peter's financial administration. Of similarly "base" origin among Peter's entourage were Shafirov, a baptized Jew who became a "Baron," and Yaguzhinsky, who in Peter's last years held the key post of Procurator-General (*General-Prokuror*) of the Senate. Both were foreign-born and both had entered Russian service by being taken prisoner in war. Shafirov, after a period of service as a domestic in a boyar's household and later as shop attendant for a Moscow merchant, had begun his official career as a foreign-office translator with the Grand Embassy in 1697 and had risen to be Vice-Chancellor; an extraordinarily able diplomat, his services at Constantinople in 1711 and later at Paris had not sufficed to save him from condemnation to death as an outstanding grafter, though he had been reprieved on the scaffold. Yaguzhinsky, "boisterous and often tipsy," said to have been the son of a Lutheran organist in Livonia and a swineherd in his childhood, incurred the fear—and hatred—of his colleagues by being put over them, in Peter's last years, as the intermediary between the emperor and the Governing Senate.

A number of Peter's other co-workers were nobly, though humbly born; Chancellor "Count" Golovkin, Admiral-General "Count" Apraxin, "Count" Tolstoy, and many others had—like Ordin-Nashchokin under Tsar Alexis—been raised from the ranks of the provincial nobility. A few among the "supreme lords" were descended from ancient boyar families, but their position, too, reflected Peter's appreciation of their service to him rather than the past glory of their families. Among these latter were several field marshals—Sheremetev, Prince Michael M. Golitsyn, and Prince Repnin; several of them belonged to the Dolgoruky family, including a senator, Prince Yakov Fedorovich—renowned as one of the very few men who dared mix criticism with praise of Peter. Ablest of these relics of the old *boiarstvo* was the senator, Prince Dmitry M. Golitsyn. Sent abroad for study by Peter in 1697, when he was already thirty years old, Golitsyn assembled one of the finest collections of Western books to be found in Russia; while governor at Kiev, he caused many of them to be translated into Russian, including Pufendorf and Grotius, but neither Hobbes nor Locke.

Some of Peter's creatures were frankly aliens, "Germans" imported for their technical ability. Such was "Count" Bruce, the only "German" to be made president of a Collegium; an able diplomat, Bruce did not however push himself forward in the ranks of the "supreme lords." More active were "Baron" Osterman, son of a Westphalian pastor who had served as valet to a Dutch vice-admiral and whose diplomatic talents and administrative zeal made him a special favorite of Peter; though he held no top office in Peter's reign, his career was to last longer under Peter's successors than that of any of his colleagues. A latecomer was the engineer Münnich, subsequently to find a brief moment in the sun.

Such were some of the "supreme lords" who assembled on the night of January 28, 1725, to determine the succession to the imperial throne. Officially advised by the cabinet-secretary that Peter had left no will, his orphaned collaborators fell into a stubborn debate. Those whose origin inclined them to the preservation of traditional forms—the Golitsyns and the Dolgorukys—argued for the late ruler's nine-year-old grandson Peter. Those who had been too closely connected with the fate of the child's father, Tsarevich Alexis, or who saw personal advantages for themselves—Tolstoy, Menshikov, Yaguzhinsky—argued for the widowed Catherine. The debate was heavily influenced by the presence in the hall of a number of Guard officers, whose preference for their honorary colonel was obvious. By morning the arrival outside the palace of the two Guard regiments—the Preobrazhensky and the Semenovsky—decided the issue. Catherine was proclaimed empress in the name not only of the Senate but also of the Synod and of the "generality," neither of which had had any part in the selection.

THE SUPREME PRIVY COUNCIL

Catherine, uneducated and unaccustomed to public business, concentrated her attention on maintaining the favor of the Guardsmen and left the conduct of state affairs wholly to Menshikov. The "cult of the individual" was not, however, to triumph so easily. Menshikov's haughty attitude toward his fellow-senators and the obvious fact that Catherine's life expectancy was short combined to effect the victory of the principle of "collective leadership." In February, 1726, largely through the efforts of the wily Tolstoy, a Supreme Privy Council (*Verkhovnyi Tainyi Soviet*) was established. The Senate, reduced from "Governing" to "High," was made subject to the edicts of the new organ, the competence of which was even greater than had been that of the procurator-general, an office now abolished.

Despite the abolition of Yaguzhinsky's office, his reports that bad harvests, famines, and heavy taxes were responsible for continuing mass flights of peasants to Poland, to the Don, and even to the Bashkirs, were heeded. The official estimate was that, between 1719 and 1727, two hundred thousand peasants had become fugitives; Menshikov formulated the fear that soon, without peasants, there would be no soldiers. In January, 1727, the Supreme Privy Council decreed reduction of the rates of soul tax, abolition of collections by the army, and suppression of a number of expensive offices created by Peter.

The Supreme Privy Council at first consisted of Menshikov, Apraxin, Golovkin, Tolstoy, D. M. Golitsyn, and Osterman. Though Menshikov retained the leadership, Golitsyn steadily came to the fore as a most influential member of the new regime. As Catherine's health rapidly decayed, Menshikov and Golitsyn struck a bargain: Menshikov persuaded a reluctant Catherine to pass over her own daughters and name young Peter as her successor; Peter was to marry Menshikov's daughter. Tolstoy, who desperately tried to block the arrangement, was exiled to Solovki. On the empress' death (May 6, 1727) the child, then eleven years old, was proclaimed Emperor Peter II and removed to the home of his prospective father-in-law, with Osterman as his tutor.

The artificiality and instability of the situation was clear. The boy hated both Menshikov and his daughter, and through his friendship with a young Prince Dolgoruky, two of whose relatives had been admitted to membership in the Supreme Privy Council, the new emperor was soon persuaded to sign a decree exiling his grandfather's favorite to Berezov, in Siberia.

"Collective leadership" had triumphed. The Supreme Privy Council ruled in the name of Peter II, who shifted his residence to Moscow. This return to the pre-Petrine capital was not as symbolic as might seem. It is true that some of the reforms dear to Peter's heart were sacrificed in the light of experience. The Senate was never to recover the guiding place it had held in Peter's scheme of administration. Even in Catherine's brief reign, in the interests of economy, many of Peter's special chancelleries and even some of his Collegia had been abolished; superfluous local offices, vainly designed by Peter to separate justice from administration, had been suppressed; the city "magistracies" had been placed under the local governors. Under Peter II the Chief Magistracy, on which Peter had set such high hopes of improving the status of the trading and artisan population, and his dreaded Preobrazhensky Prikaz were also abolished; the navy was neglected. Many of Peter's industrial enterprises were closed down as wasteful of government funds, and many of his regulatory measures, including his closing of the port of Archangel, were repealed; a number of monopolies, including salt and tobacco, were abandoned.

To consolidate the position, the emperor was, late in 1729, affianced to a Princess Dolgorukaia, but his death, at the age of fourteen, on January 18, 1730, radically altered the situation. The dying Catherine had provided that in the event Peter II died childless, the title was to pass to her daughters or their offspring, but this was in violation of Peter's law of 1722 on the succession. Peter II himself had named no successor.

The Supreme Privy Council therefore felt free to make its own choice of a ruler who would guarantee the continuity of its power. The Dolgorukys proposed that Peter's unwed fiancée, who nevertheless might be with child by him, should be declared empress, but the idea was rejected. At the suggestion of Golitsyn, supported by Osterman, the collective leadership decided on Anna Ivanovna, a middle-aged niece of Peter the Great and widowed duchess of Courland. The choice made, the Supreme Privy Council accepted a further suggestion by Golitsyn that the letter of invitation to the new empress be accompanied by a document for her signature, embodying "points" limiting her power. Anna was asked to promise that she would not remarry or name a successor, that she would take no governmental action without the approval of the Supreme Privy Council, then consisting of eight members, and that the Guard was to be subject to its orders.

This ingenious covert attempt to achieve a sort of "Glorious Revolution" reckoned without the realities of power, which made any "collective leadership" perilous in the extreme. Too many powerful personages were excluded from the inner circle, and the interests of the Guard were ignored. Yaguzhinsky, who had never been included in the Supreme Privy Council, sent a messenger to Anna at Mitau, advising her "not to believe everything she would be told." Though forewarned, Anna signed the "points."

Feofan Prokopovich, who had been Peter's chief ecclesiastical adviser, exerted all his spiritual influence also against the scheme. When the "points" were published at Moscow (February 3, 1730), a Prince Cherkassky demanded that the nobility be given opportunity to submit to the Supreme Privy Council, Anna agreed. Seizing the opportunity, the Guard officers in the crowd loudly demanded that the empress assume autocratic power. ture historian Tatishchev, who had served well, though not conspicuously, under Peter the Great) were signed by over eleven hundred nobles. Though contradictory on many points, their general tenor demanded election of members of an enlarged Council by the nobility at large, limitation of the period of obligatory service of nobles to twenty years, establishment of schools that would enable nobles to enter on service as officers without serving in the ranks, and abolition of Peter's 1714 law of *majorat,* which forbade division of real estate among heirs.

THE GUARD AND THE RESTORATION OF AUTOCRACY

On Anna's arrival at Moscow (February 15), it was evident that all was not well. The Preobrazhensky Regiment refused to take the oath of allegiance in the prescribed form, and Anna refused to honor the Supreme Privy Council with her presence at its meetings. On February 25, a mob of about eight hundred nobles appeared at the palace to beg the empress to review the projects they had submitted; over the protest of the Supreme Privy Council, Anna agreed. Seizing the opportunity, the Guard officers in the crowd loudly demanded that the empress assume autocratic power. Professing to be amazed that the "points" had not represented the will of the "generality," Anna sent for the casket containing the document she had signed and dramatically tore up the "points." Two Dolgorukys were beheaded, the rest exiled; the Golitsyns suffered also.

The Supreme Privy Council was abolished, the Senate apparently restored to its old role. In fact, however, in November, 1731, a new governing organ, the "Cabinet," was interposed between the sovereign and the Senate. Its first members were Golovkin and Osterman, who had survived the fate of their colleagues, and Prince Cherkassky, who had contributed to the downfall of Golitsyn, Osterman's old rival in the Supreme Privy Council.

Anna's reign is conventionally known to Russian historians as the period of the "German yoke." The new empress, extraordinarily self-indulgent—the "Ice Palace" was one of her whims—had brought with her from Courland her personal favorite, Bühren; Bühren's greed brought great hardship on the taxpaying population, which was stricken also with plague and famine; it was said that the grain would not grow because a woman sat on the throne. The chief role in state administration was left to the Westphalian Osterman, while the army was entrusted to two other "Germans," Münnich and Lacy. Yet, apart from Osterman, the principal men later brought into the Cabinet, such as Volynsky and Bestuzhev-Riumin, were genuine products of the lesser Russian nobility. The court returned to St. Petersburg, but the significance of Anna's reign lay not in its "German" flavor. Nor did it lie in the activity of the Secret Chancellery, which revived the terroristic traditions of Peter's Preobrazhensky Prikaz; it was estimated that in Anna's reign more than twenty thousand persons were exiled to Siberia. The evil memory of Anna's regime was chiefly the fruit of her failure fully to appreciate the significance of the palace revolution of 1730.

The nobility had in its projects confusedly put forward demands for recognition of its own aspirations; the Guard, itself noble in personnel, had been the active force in the coup d'état of February 25. Despite her promises, Anna gave no adequate recognition to the interest of the Guard and of the nobles generally. She created a third Guard regiment, the Izmailovsky, which might have given opportunity for more nobles to avoid service in the ranks of ordinary regiments; but she had let it be officered by her favorites, the nobles of the Baltic provinces, German or Swedish in ancestry. She did repeal Peter's hated law of *majorat* in 1731. In the same year she established the *Shliakhetsky Korpus,* a school for noble children whose graduates became officers immediately; at first limited to two hundred pupils, it was later enlarged to provide for three hundred and sixty. Not until 1736 did she move to lighten the burden of obligatory service for nobles by setting the term at twenty-five years. At the same time she conceded that one brother in each family might be released from service to manage the family estates; even in 1727, nobles had been offered some release from service to put their estates in order and to protect their peasants against the "wolves," as the local officials were frequently styled. The number of applications for retirement was, however, so great that the provisions of the law of 1736 were not always observed.

Anna also continued the whittling down of the remaining rights of the peasantry to the advantage of their noble landlords. In this she acted contrary to the advice of Anisy Maslov, whom she had appointed to the restored office of procurator of the Senate, though without the wide powers his predecessors had enjoyed under Peter the Great; in the interests of state tax collections, Maslov in 1734 recommended establishment of a tariff of peasant obligations to their landlords, an idea which died with him in 1735, not to be resurrected until the nineteenth century. Under Peter II, landholders' peasants had been forbidden to escape their obligations by voluntarily enlisting in the army. In 1730 peasants were forbidden to buy real estate, in 1734 to operate cloth factories. In 1726, they had lost the right to go into industry without the permission of the landlord; in 1731 they were forbidden to make contracts. The right of landlords to transfer peasants from one estate to another, even in a different district, was legally recognized. Above all, in 1731, after a brief return to Peter's system of military collections, the responsibility for payment of taxes and arrears was permanently imposed on the landlords, who were empowered to call on the authorities to help constrain the peasants.

Thus the nobility made some gains, both in the lightening of their obligations to the state and in the firmer riveting of bondage on their peasants. Yet these gains were slight as compared to the growing appetite of the nobles, and it was obvious that the Guard needed only opportunity and leadership to make a fresh bid for influence.

Anna died in 1740, bequeathing the throne to her newborn grandnephew, Ioann Antonovich of Brunswick (Ivan VI), under the regency of the generally detested and thoroughly frightened Bühren. The new emperor's mother, Anna Leopoldovna (herself a grandniece of Peter the Great), persuaded Field Marshal Münnich to organize a conspiracy. With the aid of a company of the Preobrazhensky Regiment on guard duty in the palace, Bühren and his chief supporter, Bestuzhev-Riumin, were arrested. The regent was banished to Pelym, in Siberia, and his place was taken by Anna Leopoldovna.

The change, however, was insignificant; the administration remained in the hands of the old triumvirate, headed by Osterman and including both Chancellor Golovkin and Prince Cherkassky. Münnich briefly became "first minister" but was soon removed from office. The malcontent Guardsmen therefore had to look elsewhere for leadership; increasingly they appealed to Elizabeth, Peter's unmarried daughter, who, by prudent abstention from the public eye, had managed to survive through these sixteen kaleidoscopic years.

The position was complicated by the international situation. Friendship with Austria, which had its own troubles with two of Russia's frequently hostile neighbors, Poland and Turkey, had become the cornerstone of Russia's foreign policy. When the anti-Austrian Stanislas Leczynski was elected to the Polish throne in 1733, fifty thousand Russian troops drove him out in favor of the Saxon candidate, Augustus III; at the same time Lacy, an Irish general in Russian service, led twenty thousand men to aid the Austrians on the Rhine. From 1735 to 1739 as Austria's ally, Russia waged war on the Turks, Lacy even retaking Azov; but despite expenditure of a hundred thousand Russian soldiers, the Treaty of Belgrade (1739) yielded Russia only insignificant territorial gains and did not even win her the right to maintain fortresses or shipping (even commercial) on the Black Sea.

Russia also endorsed the Pragmatic Sanction of Emperor Charles VI, intended to secure inheritance of the diverse Hapsburg domains intact by his daughter Maria Theresa. Anxious to prevent Russia from coming to Austria's aid in the War of the Austrian Succession, France succeeded in inciting her old ally, Sweden, to attempt recovery of the lands taken from her by Peter. At the same time, the French envoy at St. Petersburg, the Marquis de la Chetardie, aided by Elizabeth's personal physician, Lestocq, sought to encourage Elizabeth to attempt overthrow of the pro-Austrian Russian government. Well aware, from other sources, that the Guardsmen would support her initiative, and herself threatened by the rattled regent, Elizabeth appeared at the barracks of the grenadier company of the Preobrazhensky Regiment. On the night of November 24, 1741, a torchlight parade to the Winter Palace resulted in the unopposed arrest of the baby emperor, of the regent, and of all their chief ministers. One of the first to appear to congratulate the new empress was Bestuzhev-Riumin, sometime trusted minister of Bühren, but now on his way to becoming Elizabeth's chancellor.

ELIZABETH AND THE NOBILITY

Under the new empress, most administrative posts were held by native-born Russians; the "German yoke" was at an end. The coarseness that had characterized the courts of Peter and of Anna was replaced by a new atmosphere, perhaps basically no less gross, but disclosing more of that veneer of Western refinement that was steadily strengthening its influence over the upper stratum of Russian society. French comedies, Italian light opera, the minuet, and the elegancies of a gourmet's table were the empress' chief preoccupations. Lazy and intelligent, capricious and good-natured, Elizabeth undertook no major enterprises. While earnestly professing her intention to rule as her father had done, in practice she relaxed rather than created tensions; early in her reign (May 17, 1744) she decreed the abolition of the death penalty. Elizabeth's personal popularity enabled the Secret Chancellery, from 1746 headed by Alexander Shuvalov, to relax its vigilance; he was therefore overshadowed by his brother Peter, an able and skillful entrepreneur who amassed an enormous personal fortune and earned tremendous hatred by ruthless exploitation of the fiscal monopolies showered on him by the doting empress, and by his cousin Ivan, whose love of learning laid the basis for the development of higher education in Russia.

At the instance of Ivan Shuvalov, an Academy of Arts was separated from the Academy of Sciences (1758). Previously, students "unfit" for the latter had been assigned to the arts. The new institution, with forty students under French teachers, proved just as unsatisfactory. Its president, I. I. Betskoy, had been chiefly interested in the education of well-born maidens and carried over the comfortable conviction that "not all children can be of equal keenness." Its slipshod method of instruction consequently tended to produce pupils with a modicum of theoretical knowledge, without developing potential talent.

In token of her intention to return to the regime of her illustrious father, Elizabeth promptly restored, in outward form at least, the Collegia and the "Chief Magistracy" that her predecessors had suppressed. Also she abolished Anna's "Cabinet" and announced the restoration of the Senate to its old role; in actuality, of course, this merely meant the dominance of Elizabeth's favorites. In addition to the Shuvalovs, these included the Razumovskys: the elder, Alexis, was Elizabeth's handsome cossack intimate; the younger, Cyril, was the boy-wonder of his time—at sixteen Count, at eighteen President of the (Russian) Academy of Sciences, at twenty-two Field-marshal-General and Hetman of Little Russia. There was also Bestuzhev-Riumin, survivor from the Bühren regime, who until his fall in 1757 was the chief architect of Russian policy.

Yet the general character of Elizabeth's reign was a direct continuation of the period of favorites and of the period of the "German yoke," which had successively replaced the military tension of Peter's times. Elizabeth was well aware that she owed her throne to the Guard, and the rise of the power of the nobility continued. Not only did the empress create a fourth unit, the Bodyguard Regiment, whose nucleus was the grenadier company of the Preobrazhensky Regiment; not only did she lavish her personal favors on Guardsmen. In 1746, she forbade any persons other than nobles to purchase "men and peasants without lands or with lands."[1] In 1754, she ordered a general official measurement and rectification of boundaries of all privately held lands and required that anyone not entitled to own land and peasants dispose of them at once; the geodetic work, however, proceeded very slowly. In 1758, the empress forbade those who had acquired personal nobility by service in lower categories of the Table of Ranks to acquire estates, "since their children are not nobles and cannot have and purchase villages."[2] By these and a number of other decrees Elizabeth guaranteed to the hereditary nobility the exclusive right of owning real property and peasants.

At the same time, without reducing the term of obligatory service, she took a number of steps to lighten its burdensomeness on the nobles. The Academy of Sciences, founded by Catherine I on the basis of Peter's notions, had been mainly the preserve of German scholars, against whom occasional Russian members, such as the famed Lomonosov (to be met in a later chapter) had waged seemingly futile war. Under the presidency of the young cossack, Cyril Razumovsky, the Academy had been divided (1747) into (1) a group of ten Academicians, representing the best of Russian scholarship; (2) a separate teaching institution, and (3) a preparatory Gymnasium for twenty young men drawn from the non-taxpaying elements of the population. In 1754, at the instance of Ivan Shuvalov, the university of Moscow was founded; it began to function in 1755 with ten professors constituting three faculties—law, medicine, philosophy. Under it were founded two Gymnasia, one exclusively for nobles, the other for non-nobles who were, however, also non-taxpayers (*raznochintsy,* men of mixed status). Inevitably these institutions of higher learning, like the older Shliakhetsky Korpus, the Artillery School, and other specialized institutions, served chiefly the interests of the nobility.

On the economic side, too, the interests of the nobility were specially favored. In 1753, when private credit was not available at less than 20 percent interest, Elizabeth decreed establishment of a state-operated Nobles' Bank, which was opened the following year with power to extend mortgage loans to individual nobles in amounts up to ten thousand rubles at 6 percent interest. The interests of the merchants were not overlooked but were less generously treated than were those of the hereditary nobility. A separate Merchants' Bank, which supplied a limited amount of commercial credit, also was founded at St. Petersburg (1754). Its operation, however, was subject to great abuses; by 1764, it was found that more than half the outstanding loans were overdue; one-sixth of the total was owed by a former director of the bank. In 1770, it ceased to make loans; in 1782, it was formally liquidated. Of more importance for traders was the abolition (1754) of internal tolls; the consequent loss of state revenue was made up by raising import and export duties.

The question of how far to recognize the merchantry as a specially privileged class created difficulties. At the instance of the Shuvalovs, it was proposed in 1760 that merchants, as a distinct category, be given freedom to "establish and maintain manufactures and factories, except distilleries, glassworks and any other metal and mineral works, all of which appertain to the nobles." [3] Merchants were to be judged, except in criminal cases, by their own courts and to be released from payment of the soul tax and from liability to military conscription. They were even to be permitted to send their sons abroad to study "commerce and credit." The highest group were to be permitted to inherit villages as well as to wear swords and, like the nobles, to be exempt from corporal punishment.

A counter project aimed at consolidating the exclusive rights of the nobles to own lands and peasants, to exploit mines, and to open distilleries. It proposed also to relieve the nobles of any service obligations to the state. The balance of forces at the court of the ailing Elizabeth was too delicate to permit the complete triumph of either view.

With respect to the peasants there was not even any such question. By a series of decrees throughout Elizabeth's reign, she extended the legal power of the nobles over their peasants, going so far as to grant to landlords (1760) the right to send recalcitrant peasants to Siberia at government expense and to count the exiles as recruits supplied to the army.

In practice, though not explicitly in law, the peasants were rapidly becoming chattel slaves. "Serfdom," as it was developing in Russia, was a very different thing from what had existed in Western Europe in the Middle Ages. The Russian "serf" was not bound to the land; he was bound to his master. Serfs could be freely shifted from one estate to another. They were subject to sale, like animals, with or without their families, and they might be assigned to any kind of employment at the whim of their owners. If the bulk of the peasants continued to be exploited, as medieval serfs in the West had been, on the basis of some combination of *obrok* (dues paid in money or in kind) and of *barshchina* (obligatory labor on the lord's land) instead of on the basis of plantation economy, it was for reasons of geography, not of their legal social status.

The extent of the change in the light in which the peasants were viewed is attested by the fact that—perhaps simply by oversight but for the first time in Russian history—the peasants were not included with the rest of her subjects required to take the oath of loyalty on Elizabeth's accession. As yet, the law did not define peasants as slaves, but the confusion of laws was such that, as Elizabeth herself phrased it, it would be impossible to understand them in detail "unless one had the abilities of angels." [4] Ivan Shuvalov, the most enlightened of Elizabeth's close advisers, urged her to renew her father's vain efforts to establish "fundamental laws." As a sequel, in 1754 at a meeting of the Senate attended also by officials of the Collegia and chancelleries, Count Peter Shuvalov formally proposed codification of the laws; Elizabeth in person gave the project her urgent blessing. A commission was set up, headed by a professor from the Academy of Sciences; it worked for a year, but without ultimate success.

It is significant that its draft, though never completed, did formulate a basic attitude on the peasant question. Whereas the *Ulozhenie* of 1649 had carefully defined a number of categories of the rural population, the new draft, without distinguishing even between bondaged peasants and household domestics, simply provided: "The nobility has over its people and its peasants male and female and over their property full authority without exception, save the taking of life and punishment with the knout and infliction of torture on them." The noble landlord might dispose freely of their persons and their labor, might even control their marriages, and "inflict any except the aforementioned punishments." [5] For violation even of these restrictions, the draft provided no specific punishments. On the other hand, the portion of the draft dealing with the right of recovery of fugitives was most carefully worked out. Although at this time the governments of Austria and Prussia were showing concern to give their peasants some protection against arbitrary treatment by their landlords, Elizabeth's government, which evinced great anxiety to ameliorate the severities of the ordinary law, was ready to abandon the Russian peasantry almost completely to the mercies of the nobles. No longer was there any suggestion, such as that of Maslov in 1734, that the obligations of peasants to their masters be limited by law. Under Elizabeth the government was content to impose on the landlords full responsibility and full authority to provide for the welfare of their property, nor was any legal distinction made between landowners' peasants and the various categories of state peasants who made up almost half the subject population.

ARCHITECTURE

The chief way in which Elizabeth emulated her father was in the further embellishment of the new capital. In his usual style, Peter had had no faith in private initiative; in 1709, he had entrusted to an official Chancellery of Buildings control of all construction in his infant city. The man finally hired as "architect-general," Jean Baptiste Leblon (died 1719), was, Peter thought, "a real wonder"; he drew the plans for the city, laid out gardens, raised sunken ships, organized foundry and metalwork, and opened the first school of architecture in Russia. A talented technician, he was not a gifted architect but was content to copy, on a more modest scale and in crude fashion, the Late Renaissance architecture of his native France. Although in 1718 he secured the establishment of a special police department to force Russian nobles to build according to his plans, complete with mansard roofs, little of his work has survived. The principal exception is the Peter-and-Paul Cathedral, whose Protestant spire still dominates the river skyline.

Little progress was made after his death, for Russian architects, trained in a different tradition, could make nothing out of the new and alien forms save barrack-like imitations of the seventeenth-century West. Under Elizabeth, however, there returned to Russia Bartolomeo Rastrelli (1700-71), whose father, a sculptor, had been brought to Russia by Peter to cast cannon. Rastrelli, no longer young, brought back from his studies in France a strong taste for rococo architecture and found his services in great demand. He was made a "Count" and allowed to increase the state debt by 17 million rubles. Like "Aristotle" Fioraventi of the fifteenth century, Rastrelli was able to combine Russian architectural traditions with the current taste of the West. His supreme effort was the plan of the Smolny Monastery, a structure not completed until the reign of Nicholas I. In his model (1748), he combined the Russian baroque of the seventeenth century with new forms; its bell tower, never erected, owed its inspiration to the Moscow Kremlin bell tower named "Ivan the Great"; its main building is one of a number of striking examples of Rastrelli's power of adapting old Russian characteristics to the new ideas. In civil architecture also, Rastrelli, the most important builder of the city now known as Leningrad, gave free reign to the extravagant craving for lavish ornamentation and display that characterized the Russian court of his time. His chief monument is the Winter Palace, though its reconstruction after the fire of 1837 did not do full justice to his concepts. Rastrelli also profoundly modified the suburban palace erected at Peterhof and began the construction of the more elaborate Tsarskoye Selo. His work was not confined to the new capital, many structures at Moscow and in lesser centers, including the bell tower of the Troitsa Monastery, also bore his imprint.

The rococo period was of short duration. After Elizabeth's death, a new empress, Catherine II, was to be passionately addicted to building; she wrote to her epistolary friend Grimm, "This disease is like intoxication." Catherine's interest in building projects, often far beyond her means, may well have been connected with her desire to impress the West with the solvency of her regime by erection of monumental structures. It was a technique which she welcomed when used on her by Potemkin, a Guardsman who was for a time her personal favorite but survived to be a trusted minister and was in 1787 given the title of "Prince of Tauris" (i.e., of the Crimea); the "Potemkin villages," which he allegedly caused to be erected on riverbanks and moved overnight to the next stopping-place for his mistress' delectation have become a classic of Madison Avenue techniques. Some of her commissions were fortunately not carried out; such was the project to tear down the walls of the Moscow Kremlin and construct in their place an all-embracing mammoth palace; abandonment of this scheme almost broke the heart of its architect, V. I. Bazhenov (1737-99), who had studied in the West and was highly thought of there.

In Catherine's reign, Russian architecture veered sharply, in harmony with Western tendencies, toward classicism, restoring the simple straight line and effective use of colonnades. It was influenced originally by imported Italians, who made the mistake, as in the case of Quarengi's "Hermitage," of building as though they were in their native land; marble structures and niches for statuary were ill adapted for Russian winters. Among the best examples of the new "Empire" style, as it shook off the superficial influences of the West, was the Tavrichesky Dvorets, built by I. E. Starov (1741-1808) for Catherine's favorite Potemkin and later used to house the Imperial Duma.

At Moscow, and in the provinces, architecture had been only minimally affected by the West. The distinctive Russian style introduced in the sixteenth century had undergone uninterrupted development; importation of many German and French architects in the seventeenth century had contributed to ever more complicated ornamentation in Western style but had not affected the basic peculiarities of Russian architecture. By the end of that century, Italian baroque, substantially modified by Polish and Little Russian influences, had become predominant; perhaps the best-known example of distinctively Russian baroque is the Pokrovsky church in the village of Fili, built in 1693. Late in the eighteenth century, however, even Moscow was affected by the swing to classicism, the finest specimen of which is the *Dom Pashkova,* later the Rumiantsev Museum and destined to be devoted to one of the most important libraries in the Soviet Union. It was designed by a Russian architect, M. F. Kazakov (1733-1812), who never left Russia but is regarded as the man who best seized the spirit of the ancient Greeks.

CULMINATION OF THE RISE OF THE NOBILITY

In international affairs, as in domestic, Elizabeth's reign was a continuation, without the necessity of conscious thought on her part, of established policies. Despite the size of her standing army and the hope which it inspired in the contestants on both sides in the War of the Austrian Succession (1740-48), Elizabeth made no attempt to capitalize on her strength. At her accession, she was sufficiently under the influence of her French physician, Lestocq, and of the French ambassador, La Chetardie, not to honor Anna's endorsement of the Pragmatic Sanction; on the other hand, inheriting the war to which France had incited Sweden, she was not inclined to join in the Franco-Prussian effort to despoil the Hapsburgs. In 1742, she appointed as chancellor Bestuzhev-Riumin, who had been sent abroad in 1708 by Peter and was well schooled in the diplomatic principle of the balance of power. The war with Sweden was terminated in 1743, with some slight territorial gains, including Vyborg, for Russia. Yet Bestuzhev, though stimulated by liberal English bribes as well as by his avowed concept of not deserting one's allies, was unable to effect the expulsion of La Chetardie and the exile of Lestocq until the War of the Austrian Succession was over (1748).

The "diplomatic revolution" engineered by Kaunitz, the Austrian chancellor, was welcome to Bestuzhev. When the struggle between Hohenzollern and Hapsburg broke out again in the Seven Years' War and when France and Austria momentarily overcame their inveterate mutual enmity, Russia abandoned Peter's principle of friendship with England and made common cause with these strange allies against the newly rising power of Prussia, now supported by Great Britain. The misogynist Frederick the Great had cause to rue that which, two centuries earlier and in a different setting, John Knox had termed "the Monstrous Regiment of Women"; Maria Theresa and Madame de Pompadour were joined by Elizabeth of Russia. The die once cast, Bestuzhev's fall from grace (1757) made no difference. Long years of peace and of employment as mere gendarmes at first hampered the Russian armies, but by 1760 Berlin was firmly occupied by Russian troops. Russia's armed might, which had alarmed the Poles in the time of Ivan the Terrible and which had been felt in the northern Germanies under Peter, now for the first time seemed on the verge of decisively determining the balance of power in the West.

The death of Elizabeth on December 25, 1761 (January 5, 1762 N.S.) saved Prussia and altered the whole situation. Elizabeth, last of the Romanovs, had as early as 1742 been gravely concerned to provide for the succession. She had had little choice, for there remained only one descendant of Peter, her nephew Karl-Peter-Ulrich, orphaned duke of Schleswig-Holstein-Gottorp. This boy—fourteen years old in 1742—was, however, not only a grandson of Peter; he was also a grandson of the sister and successor of Peter's arch-enemy, Charles XII of Sweden. In the expectation that he might succeed to the Swedish throne, the child was being brought up in the Lutheran faith and made to study Swedish and Latin. Nevertheless, the desperate Elizabeth sent an envoy to Kiel with instructions to bring her only nephew to Russia, cost what it might (1742).

At St. Petersburg the new heir was rebaptized into the Orthodox faith and set to learning the Russian language and Russian customs. Whatever capacities of mind and body he may originally have possessed had long since been undermined by the brutal and stupid methods of instruction to which he had been subjected in Holstein. In St. Petersburg, the methods of reëducation were no more successful, and the passively resistant youth acquired only one new knowledge, the pleasure (though not the art) of drinking heavily. Hating and fearing his new surroundings, he displayed his grandfather's love for playing with soldiers, though, by reason of his bodily and moral weakness, he was content with lead soldiers and paper fortresses. The famous story of how the heir to the throne held a solemn courtmartial on a rat and hanged it for interfering with his military arrangements may be apocryphal, for his unloved wife is not the best source of testimony in his case. Yet the picture she drew in her *Memoirs,* intended for the eye of her grandson Alexander, in general rings true. Although a slavish admirer of Frederick of Prussia, the young Peter understood military achievement mainly in terms of beer and tobacco.

Further to ensure the succession, Elizabeth accepted for him a bride recommended by her early French advisers. In 1745, Peter, then seventeen, was formally married to the sixteen-year-old Sophia-Augusta-Frederika of Anhalt-Zerbst, whose father was a minor general in the service of Frederick the Great. Rebaptized as Catherine, this petty German princess was to display great acumen. In 1754, she fulfilled her expected function, giving birth to a son, Paul; whatever his actual paternity, it is virtually certain that Peter, who had his own amusements, was not involved. The Empress Elizabeth, who had abundant cause to exclaim against the cruel fate that had given her no possible heir but her nephew, considered transferring the succession to Paul, but her native inertia and the fears of the court to offend the recognized successor prevented her from taking remedial action. Catherine's position was clearly one of extreme danger, and she had been working energetically, though secretly, to form a strong party in her own interests.

Looking back on the period when she feared that Elizabeth no longer had need of her, Catherine later wrote:

> My natural pride and temper made the idea of being miserable unbearable to me. . . . This was the disposition of mind with which I had been born; I was endowed with great sensibility and a face that was at least interesting and pleasing at the first glance, without any artifice or pretence. My spirit was so conciliatory that no one ever spent a quarter of an hour with me without being at their ease and conversing as though they had known me for a long time.
>
> Naturally tolerant, I easily attracted the confidence of those who had anything to do with me, because they felt that meticulous honesty and goodwill were the qualities that I evinced most readily. If I may venture to be frank, I would say about myself that I was every inch a gentleman with a mind much more male than female; but together with this I was anything but masculine and combined, with the mind and temperament of a man, the attractions of a lovable woman. . . .

With equal frankness she added:

> I have just said that I was attractive. Consequently one-half of the road to temptation was already covered and it is only human in such situations that one should not stop half-way. . . . in spite of all the finest moral maxims buried in the mind, when emotion interferes, when feeling makes its appearance, one is already much further involved than one realizes, and I have still not learnt how to prevent its appearance. . . . One cannot hold one's heart in one's hand, forcing it or releasing it, tightening or relaxing one's grip at will.[6]

Peter's first act after assuming the throne was to recall the Russian troops from Prussia, even ordering them to turn over their stores to their late enemy. Asking nothing for Russia in return for her five-year expenditure of blood and treasure, Peter III insisted only that Frederick sanction Peter's new war against Denmark to secure Schleswig for his native duchy of Holstein.

In a still more important way, Peter III scrapped the advantages to the state which Elizabeth's policy toward the nobility had derived. While strengthening its position in every possible way, Elizabeth had still insisted on performance by each noble of twenty-five years of service. Peter lost no time in announcing (January 17, 1762) his intention to release the nobility from their service obligations. The consequent manifesto of February 18, 1762, was in a sense only the climax of the long evolution of noble privilege since the death of Peter the Great; only by its abrupt and sweeping character did it constitute a departure from the historic trend. Explaining that in the past compulsory service and compulsory education for service had been necessary because of the bygone "roughness" and "ignorance" of the nobility,[7] the manifesto provided that henceforth any noble might at his pleasure continue in state service, but with the right of retirement at any time; only for military officers actually engaged in a campaign was this right to be suspended. In a bid for still wider popularity, the new administration also abolished the Secret Chancellery, which had, however, not been very active under Elizabeth.

Such a beginning might have provided a sure basis for the stability of Peter's reign, had he possessed the personality and strength of character to profit by it. Peter III, however, could not restrain himself, and his petty absurdities brought him to a speedy end. He preferred Prussian uniforms to the traditional Russian ones. He forbade the maintenance of private chapels. He ordered the clergy to remove all icons from the churches and prescribed that ecclesiastics should wear secular costumes. Far more serious was the fact that he referred to the Guardsmen as "Janissaries," and that he was openly considering sending them to Holstein to fight his private war.

These accumulated resentments speedily led to the formation of conspiracies designed to replace him on the throne either with his official son, Paul, or with Catherine. Catherine, openly threatened with seclusion in a monastery, skillfully maneuvered the excited young Guardsmen. Taking advantage of Peter's absence from the capital at Oranienbaum, a suburban palace built by Menshikov, Catherine inspired a sudden nocturnal seizure of power by the Guard regiments (June 28, 1762) and had herself crowned empress in the Kazan Cathedral before the advocates of Paul's accession knew what was happening. Within a few days Peter died in a brawl under the supervision of Alexis Orlov, elder brother of Catherine's favorite Guardsman, Gregory Orlov.

To outward appearances the triumph of the nobility was complete. Not only had the nobles, while retaining all their privileges, secured exemption from all service obligations. They had also put on the throne a ruler of their own choice, whose right to rule depended entirely on their continued support. Yet the essence of the position remained unchanged: to remain masters of their serfs, the nobles themselves had to remain slavish toward the autocrat. Much as the immediate sequel was conditioned by the adroitness of Catherine the Great, even after her death the nobility were to prove quite unable to prevent the development of a bureaucratic machine which enabled the autocracy to survive without actually sharing supreme power with the aristocracy.

NOTES

1. *Polnoe sobranie zakonov* . . . (First collection), No. 9267 (March 14, 1746), XII, 528.
2. *Ibid.,* No. 10,796 (February 6, 1758), XV, 159.
3. *Ocherki istorii SSSR,* VII, 263.
4. Solov'ev *Istoriia Rossii* . . . , 2nd edition, Book V, col. 786.
5. Latkin (ed.), *Proekt novago ulozheniia* . . . , Chapter XIX, p. 119.
6. Catherine II, *Memoirs* . . . (Maroger edition), pp. 300-301.
7. *Polnoe sobranie zakonov* . . . (First collection), No. 11,444 (February 18, 1762), XV, 912.

SUGGESTIONS FOR FURTHER READING

Among general works cited in Chapter 1, the English translation of Pokrovskii ends with 1730. The portion of Kliuchevskii's *Kurs* edited by himself continues only to 1762. For the remaining portion of the tsarist regime, a good general narrative is Kornilov, *Modern Russian History;* Karpovich, *Imperial Russia, 1801-1917,* is a brief outline; more recent and complete is Pushkarev, *Emergence of Modern Russia, 1801-1917.*

Standard conventional narratives may be found in Bain's *Pupils of Peter the Great,* his *Daughter of Peter the Great,* and his *Peter III, Emperor of Russia.* There are also biographies by Waliszewski, including *L'Héritage de Pierre le Grand: règne des femmes* . . . and *La Dernière des Romanovs: Élisabeth . . . de Russie,* as well as two books devoted to Catherine II. A specialized study of the major development in Russian foreign policy of this period is Kaplan, *Russia and the Outbreak of the Seven Years' War.*

Catherine's *Memoirs,* covering the period up to her accession to the throne, are available in several English translations, among which the best are those of Katherine Anthony and Dominique Maroger.

Raeff's *Origins of the Russian Intelligentsia* is a thoughtful study of an unduly neglected topic. His *Plans for Political Reform in Russia, 1730-1905* contains valuable documents for this and the next seven chapters. Rogger's *National Consciousness in Eighteenth-Century Russia* is an important study of a largely unexplored field. Confino's *Domaines et seigneurs en Russie* . . . is a significant work on noble landholding at the end of Catherine's reign.

Chapter

14

Aristocracy or Bureaucracy: 1762-1815

The period of time from the death of Peter I to the accession of Catherine II was only a fraction over thirty-seven years, but it had witnessed eight transfers of the supreme power, five of them by highly irregular proceedings. The nobility, acting through the pivotal Guard regiments, had secured a position of extraordinary special privilege. Yet it had established no claim to share in the day-to-day control of state power. Some sort of oligarchic constitution might have seemed a logical sequel to the growth of the nobles' influence.

This process was not consummated, for a variety of reasons. For one thing, emancipation of the nobility by Peter III from service obligations soon destroyed the special character of the Guard regiments; since nobles did not choose to serve except as officers, the rank and file now had to be recruited from the peasantry. For another thing, the nobility lacked a developed class-consciousness; the Guardsmen had acted instinctively as spokesmen of noble interests, but not as deliberately chosen representatives of a corporate entity. Again, the historic basis of the Russian autocracy was the linkage between the power of the landlord over his bondsmen and the power of the ruler over all his subjects; the nobility still needed a strong state power to repress frequent, and often serious, manifestations of peasant discontent. There was therefore no real basis for revolutionary change in the political structure of Russia, save by the time-honored method of replacing one wielder of autocratic power with a less objectionable one.

CATHERINE THE GREAT (1762-1796)

Catherine's position on the throne was obviously insecure. Most of Elizabeth's counselors, including the astute Nikita Panin, would have preferred that the young Paul succeed. There was also the possibility of resuscitating the claims of Ioann Antonovich (Ivan VI), who, since his deposition from the Imperial cradle in 1741, had been kept prisoner in the fortress of Schlüsselburg. This latter danger was eliminated in 1764 when, during an attempt to release him, he was beaten to death by his guards.

Catherine, though she had spent seventeen years in Russia, was a German, and she had been excluded from state business by her husband's aunt. She had the ardent support of enthusiastic young Guardsmen, but they had no experience of affairs of state. Elizabeth's former advisers, such as Panin and Bestuzhev-Riumin, were inclined to despise Catherine and certainly were not men in whom she could repose genuine confidence. The new empress, imbued from books and correspondence with the ideas of the French Enlightenment, had to move warily in this strange land, listening with studious patience to the advice and the requests of all sorts of potentially powerful elements in Russia. She was well aware that her position only partly resembled that of Elizabeth in 1741, who had also been enthroned by the Guard; Catherine lacked the prestige that Elizabeth had enjoyed as a daughter of Peter the Great. What was more, the nobility was now more conscious of its power, and Catherine had therefore to exert herself as Elizabeth had not in order to control the situation.

Catherine's first success was attained covertly. She had no group of dependable favorites who could guide the Senate; she therefore had to deprive it of the position it had enjoyed under Elizabeth. This she accomplished by dividing it into six departments (1763), each with a special function, and by once more channeling its activities through a procurator-general, whom she secretly instructed to prevent the Senate from exercising any legislative function. By exercising extreme caution, she managed to withdraw administrative control from the Senate without creating in its stead any new central organ, such as the Supreme Privy Council and the Cabinet had been; Panin's suggestion of an Imperial Council (1762), which would have substituted oligarchic for autocratic power, she declined to accept.

To counter the obvious ambitions of many of the nobility for some sort of constitution, Catherine professed great interest in the concepts of the *philosophes* and undertook a sweeping revision and codification of the law. It was a task at which both Peter and Elizabeth had totally failed. Catherine therefore proposed a new approach, not a systematization of existing laws, but a reconstruction of the law on the basis of new principles. She herself in 1765 undertook the formulation of a set of principles, embodying the ideas she had derived from the reading of Montesquieu, Beccaria, and other Western writers. She submitted portions of her final draft to various persons, made substantial changes, and summoned a conference of men of differing opinions to help her put the text in final form. The result was the famous "Instruction" (*Nakaz*), which at the end of 1766 she presented to a special Commission charged with preparation of the new code of laws.

The Commission was made up of deputies representing various elements in the population and various state organs. One deputy was to be sent by the nobility of each county (*uiezd*), one from each town, one from the lower strata (not including landowners' peasants) of each province (*guberniya*), and one from each non-nomadic non-Russian people; the Senate, the Synod, the various Collegia, and certain other administrative bodies were also to send one deputy each. The total number was 565, and the deputies were provided with salaries and various special privileges.

It soon proved that Catherine was right when she wrote to Voltaire (May 29, 1767): "It is easy to find general principles, but the details? . . . This is almost the same as creating a whole world." [1] The deputies had been asked to bring instructions from their constituents; they brought almost a thousand of them. They were also told to study all decrees issued since the composition of the *Ulozhenie* in 1649; of these there were well over ten thousand. Out of all this material the Commission was expected to select the laws that would both fit the abstract principles stated in Catherine's own *Nakaz* and would be practicable in the light of the conditions of Russian life.

An elaborate system of committees was set up to deal with specific portions of the task, but no preliminary work had been done. The whole Commission listened patiently to public reading of much of the material but skipped from one topic to another without finishing any of them. Finally, at the end of 1768, after holding more than two hundred sessions, first at Moscow, later at St. Petersburg, the Commission was adjourned, though not dissolved. Its committees continued to toil on until 1774, when Catherine was effectively relieved of further fear that the nobility might seriously claim a real share in active control of the state power. In that year the ever-present menace of mass peasant revolt, which so often in the past had produced a rally round the throne, found its most formidable expression in the "Pugachevshchina."

The emancipation of the nobility from obligations to the state under Peter III had excited many peasant disturbances. Catherine had acted vigorously to suppress them, but fresh outbreaks continued to occur; Moscow itself was seriously threatened in 1771. Worst of all was an uprising which began in 1773 among the cossacks of the Ural. Its leader, Emilian Pugachev, professed to be Peter III, the rightful emperor fighting for his rights against his wicked wife and her evil advisers. Unimportant in itself as a border cossack revolt might be, this one took on proportions even greater than the seventeenth-century movement headed by Stenka Razin. It became a fierce peasant uprising against the landlords. Pugachev moved up the Volga and was enthroned at Kazan; his forces lapped at the gates of Nizhny Novgorod and threatened an advance on Moscow. Catherine adroitly used the opportunity to identify her autocracy with the interests of the nobility, signing her proclamations "Catherine, a landlord of Kazan." In a series of battles her generals—including the renowned Suvorov, whose name is now attached to the highest military decoration in the Soviet Union—defeated the ill-organized rebels. In January, 1775, Pugachev was publicly quartered in the Red Square. A by-product of his defeat, facilitated by peace with Turkey, was definitive subordination of all cossackdom to the central authorities. Reorganized as "Hosts," the cossacks, particularly those of the Don, retained a considerable measure of local autonomy and fiscal privileges in return for a larger measure of military service in special Cossack regiments.

Gradually the embers of peasant rebellion were stamped out. Yet the dread of its recurrence remained. The committees of the Commission wound up their work; no codification resulted from the *Nakaz,* but the empress' personal power had been much enhanced. Catherine made no further pretense of reforming the central government of Russia, but she realized that the obvious weakness of the local authorities offered an opportunity to consolidate the relations of the autocracy and the nobility.

In 1775, she accordingly revised the structure of the local government, inviting the nobility—as Ivan IV and Peter I had done—to coöperate actively at the local level with the central autocracy. She broke up Peter's overly large *guberniyas* and suppressed his "provinces." By the end of her reign, the empire was divided into fifty-one *guberniyas.* In each she provided for clear separation of administrative, judicial, and fiscal functions, under bureaucratic officials. However, under the supreme *guberniya* authority she established judicial bodies on a class basis, separating the nobles, the townsmen, and the state peasants (with no provision for landowners' peasants); these bodies were elected by the class concerned, though headed by appointive officials. To these she added an organ for supervision of educational and eleemosynary functions, composed of members elected on an all-class basis (again excluding landowners' peasants) but headed by appointed officials. The boundaries of the *guberniyas* were drawn with the idea that each would include from three hundred thousand to four hundred thousand inhabitants; no provision was made, however, for differences arising from varying densities of population.

Each *guberniya* was subdivided, as of old, into *uiezdy,* now redrawn to have each from twenty thousand to thirty thousand inhabitants. Unlike the higher administrative divisions, the local governance of the *uiezdy* was entrusted to elected officials, in the main representing the local nobility. Thus, unintentionally perhaps, Catherine filled the gap left by the emancipation decree of Peter III. Release of nobles from service had tended to destroy the unity of political action that this service obligation had imposed on them. Now, in the interest of more efficient state administration, Catherine was imposing on the nobles, who had been scattering to their individual estates, a sort of local corporate unity.

The process was completed in 1785 by Catherine's "Charter to the Nobility." There was little that could be added to the then-existing rights of the nobility; the principal novel provision was the creation, and at *guberniya* level, of autonomous corporations of the nobility, endowed with legal personality. The chief significance of the Charter, however, was that its systematic exposition of the rights of the nobility was not, as had been the case in 1775, tied to the interest of the state in securing a local bureaucratic personnel. The Charter frankly recognized the position of the nobility as a specially privileged ruling class.

A simultaneously issued "Charter to the Towns" created no such corporate privileges for the townspeople. It did confirm the existing autonomy of organs of municipal government, but the burghers remained subject to the soul tax and continued to be deprived of the right to own estates or peasants. Catherine's economic policy, in the new spirit of Adam Smith, departed radically from Peter's ideas of strict supervision of trade and industry; she once more abolished his regulatory Collegia of Mines and of Manufacturing. Favoring the policies of laissez faire, she attempted also to facilitate mercantile credit by founding a new State Loan Bank.

Catherine's interest in the liberal philosophy of eighteenth-century France and England also conditioned her ideas on the "peasant question." This problem was forced on the consciousness of intellectual Russia by Peter III's emancipation of the nobility, which upset the theoretical concept that the peasant had to be bound to the landowner because the landowner was himself bound to the service of the state. Under the auspices of the Free Economic Society, founded at St. Petersburg in 1765, the peasant question was widely aired. Catherine herself evinced great interest in the idea of peasant emancipation. She forbade the extension of serfdom to freemen or to freedmen; in building new fortified towns, she ransomed the local serfs and made them burghers; she took the ecclesiastical peasants from the private control of the Church (1763) and converted them, as noted before, into a new category of state peasants, known, from the name of the state organ administering their affairs, as "economic peasants."

On the other hand, she handed over vast numbers of state peasants to her intimates; the number of privately owned serfs, even in Great Russia, did not diminish in her reign. Indeed, her legal confirmation of serfdom in Little Russia (1783) widely extended the geographical area affected by peasant bondage. What is more, the rights of the peasant were steadily whittled down even further by emergency decrees. During peasant disturbances in 1765-66, the right of the owner to send a serf as a settler to Siberia was broadened; the landlord might sentence a peasant to penal servitude "for impudence" or send him into the army at any time. In 1767, Catherine forbade peasants to file complaints against landlords under any circumstances. Her *Nakaz* to the codifying Commission in 1766 contained many suggestions about ameliorating the condition of the "slaves" but also said: "It is not meet suddenly and through general legislation to make a large number of freedmen." [2] With a woman's wisdom, Catherine did not let her dreams interfere with her life. The "landowners' peasants" were the only class not represented in the Commission of 1766-68 and not drawn into the elective structure of the bureaucracy at the local level in 1775; the Charter to the Nobility of 1785 implicitly recognized the peasants' status as chattel slaves.

The area in which Catherine gave freest reign to her dreams was in connection with her faith in education as a sovereign remedy, capable of regenerating human nature. Not content with Peter's emphasis on vocational education, Catherine tried to extend the progress that more liberal education had begun to make in Elizabeth's reign. Although unable to carry out her scheme of founding additional universities, she did succeed in establishing a network of provincial schools with special emphasis on the training of future mothers. Interested in the health of the body no less than in that of the mind, Catherine gave great added impetus to the spread of medical care and medical education. Catherine's often professed devotion to education and to liberalism did not, however, prevent her from stifling intellectual criticism of her regime. *A Journey from St. Petersburg to Moscow,* a vigorous protest against serfdom by Radishchev, won him transportation to Siberia (1790). At the other extreme, Novikov's criticism of court morals, inspired by his Rosicrucian mysticism, resulted in his imprisonment (1792).

IMPERIAL EXPANSION*

It is the wont of Russian historians to say that Peter the Great solved only one of the three problems of Russian foreign policy, the Swedish one, and that it remained for Catherine the Great to solve the remaining two, the Polish and the Turkish problems. In fact, Catherine, abstaining from involvement in problems of the Western balance of power, warred with all three of her neighbors and made immense territorial acquisitions from Poland and Turkey, creating huge new problems for the Russian state.

Catherine did not reënter the war against Prussia. On the contrary, she allowed her minister, Count Panin, to try to effect an understanding with England, Prussia, Poland, and the Scandinavian states to balance the power of France and Austria. The "Northern Accord," however, came to nothing. In 1763, on the death of the third Saxon king of Poland, Russia and Prussia jointly exercised pressure to secure the election of Stanislas Poniatowski, a former favorite of Catherine. When, however, he attempted to strengthen the monarchy by trying to secure the abolition of the *liberum veto* (which permitted a single negative vote to block any action by the Polish Diet), Catherine seized on the pretext of oppression of the Orthodox minority in Poland; by armed force she established a virtual protectorate over moribund

* See Map VII.

Poland, guaranteeing the maintenance of its loose aristocratic constitution (1767).

At this point, there broke out in the Polish *ukraine* a new fierce uprising of the peasantry and the cossacks, in part directed to the same end of protecting the rights of the Orthodox. Fearful of a peasant revolt that might spread into Russia, Catherine again sent troops into Poland. Failing to show proper gratitude for Russian suppression of their peasants, the Roman Catholic nobility soon demanded withdrawal of their protectors. Their resistance was beaten down by Suvorov, but Prussia and Austria also took the opportunity of occupying parts of the country. Catherine had to forgo her protectorate over the whole of Poland-Lithuania and agree to Frederick's proposal of a partition (1772). The Hohenzollerns, consolidating their kingdom by the acquisition of West Prussia, were the chief gainers, while the Hapsburgs, by acquiring Galicia, became the rulers of a considerable number of Little Russians. Russia had to content herself with the portion of the old grand principality of Lithuania lying east of the Dnieper and north of the Dvina.

While this fiasco was developing, Turkey had been incited by France to declare war on Russia (1770). Despite brilliant Russian victories on the lower Danube and the operations of a Russian fleet in the Aegean, the domestic difficulties which built up into the Pugachev revolt led to the conclusion of a compromise peace. By the Treaty of Kuchuk-Kainardji (1774), Russia restored to Turkey the captured islands in the Aegean and the rich trans-Danubian provinces of Walachia and Moldavia; she even agreed to Austrian annexation of another Little Russian province, Bukovina. On the other hand, Russia acquired the whole northern shore line of the Black Sea, except the Crimea, which was, however, detached from Turkish control. Pregnant for the future was a provision somewhat vaguely authorizing Russia to intervene in the internal affairs of Turkey in the interest of the Orthodox population.

Suppression of the Pugachev uprising permitted Catherine to destroy the remnant of Little Russian (Ukrainian) autonomy, which had already been gravely impaired under the hetmanship of Elizabeth's appointee, Cyril Razumovsky. By a series of measures, the freedom of movement of the Ukrainian peasantry had been curtailed; by 1783, serfdom was as firmly established in Little Russia as in Great Russia. Inclusion of the Little Russian nobility in the provisions of the Charter of 1785 virtually entailed total incorporation of the Ukraine into Russia. The Zaporozhian "cossack host" had been broken up immediately after the defeat of Pugachev (1775); its place was taken by Cossack cavalry regiments incorporated into the regular army.

To the Far East Catherine paid no more attention than had other Russian rulers since Peter. Relations with China continued to be governed by the Treaty of Kiakhta, negotiated after Peter's death by an agent he had sent for the purpose. This treaty, ratified in 1728, had provided for limited commercial contacts through that one frontier point and for maintenance of a Russian ecclesiastical mission, with some diplomatic functions, at Peking. Peter's passion for geographical knowledge had led him, in 1724, to send one of his Danish naval officers, Captain Vitus Bering, on a voyage of exploration from the Sea of Okhotsk around Kamchatka, from which he returned in 1730. A second government-sponsored expedition had lasted from 1733 to 1743. The rich furs brought back from the Aleutian Islands had stimulated fresh expeditions by private traders. In Catherine's reign, a Russian fur merchant, Gregory Shelekhov, sometimes called the "Russian Columbus," visited the Kurile Islands and undertook serious exploration of Alaska.

Catherine successfully avoided participation in the European war that grew out of the American War of Independence, but her formation of the Armed Neutrality of the North (1780), directed against England, destroyed Panin's system and threw Russia back into the arms of Austria. Catherine's dreams now centered on the Turkish problem, left unsolved by the Treaty of Kuchuk-Kainardji. They took the form of the "Greek project." European Turkey was to be partitioned: Walachia, Moldavia, and Bessarabia were to become a Russian protectorate, under the ancient Roman name of "Dacia"; the Yugoslavs were to pass under Austrian control; Constantinople was to be restored as an imperial city, ruling over Thrace and Macedonia. Catherine's second grandson, born in 1779, was significantly christened Constantine.

These dreams came to nothing, but Potemkin, one of Catherine's most businesslike favorites, was entrusted with the organization of "New Russia," and in 1783 the Crimea also was annexed. In 1785, the year of the Charters, Catherine issued one guaranteeing freedom to Moslems in Russia, but in 1787 Turkey declared war; Sweden joined her in 1788. Suvorov added fresh laurels to those he had already won in fighting the Poles, the Turks, and the cossacks. Sweden made peace in 1790, and in 1792 Turkey, by the Treaty of Jassy, confirmed Russian control of the Black Sea steppes and of the Crimea. At the same time, Russia moved the remnant of the Dnieper cossacks to new homes along the Kuban River, where they became a spearhead for later Russian penetration of the Caucasus.

In the meantime, Poniatowski had made a fresh effort to save Poland by securing the adoption of a new and more centralized constitution (1791). Seizing the first pretext, Catherine again threw her armies into Poland at a moment when Austria and Prussia were entangled with France. In 1793, Poland was compelled to submit to the Second Partition, in which Austria did not share. Russia annexed a huge territory, including White Russia and most of the remaining Polish *ukraine*. The new Polish constitution was annulled, and Poland again became virtually a Russian protectorate. The desperate effort led by Thaddeus Kosciuszko was defeated by Suvorov; and in 1795, the Third Partition wiped Poland from the map. Austria and Prussia were allowed to divide between them the purely Polish parts of the kingdom, but Russia again took the lion's share, including the rest of the *ukraine,* Lithuania, and Courland. After a lapse of centuries, all the territory that had once formed part of Kievan Rus, save some provinces now held by Austria, was once again Russian soil.

THE JEWISH PROBLEM

The apparent disappearance of the Polish problem was not to be permanent. It created also for Russia a new internal difficulty, the Jewish problem, for Catherine had guaranteed their existing rights to all the inhabitants in the annexed territories. Among them were perhaps a million Jews. In Muscovite Russia, Jews had not been tolerated; occasional Jewish physicians had risked their lives in the service of the rulers, and Jewish merchants had been permitted to make brief visits, but permanent residence of Jews in the Russian realm was strictly forbidden. Vigorous efforts had been made to root out the few thousands of Jews who had become Russian subjects by virtue of the annexation of Smolensk and part of Little Russia in 1667. Even Catherine the Great, in her most "liberal" phase, aware that "it was only eight days since Catherine had come to the throne" and that "she had to deal with a pious people," had not dared to act contrary to the sentiment expressed by Empress Elizabeth—"From the enemies of Christ I desire neither gain nor profit." [3] Despite the advice of the Senate that Russia's economy would benefit from the admission of Jews, Catherine's edict of December 4, 1762, permitting foreigners to settle in Russia, specifically excluded Jews. The Empress consoled herself in her *Memoirs* by adding: "Thus often it is not sufficient to be enlightened, to have the best intentions and the power to bring them into execution. But how often rash judgments are expressed about wise decisions." [4]

Quite opposite had been the policy of Poland and, consequently, of Lithuania also. When persecution drove the Jews from the Germanies, they were welcomed by kings and nobles who, with no native bourgeoisie, gladly employed them as efficient business agents. The Jews had not been integrated into Polish society but, as in other Western lands in an earlier age, had been given a special status under royal protection. They were not subject to the ordinary judicial and administrative authorities; in each major town they were authorized to elect their own officials; their *kahal* (community) was given wide jurisdiction over religious and economic matters, governed by the law of Moses. In cases of dispute between a Jew and a Christian, the case was tried before a special Christian officer, the "Jewish judge," appointed by the king or his representatives from nominees of the Jewish elders. The *kahal* organization was dominated by the rabbinate and by the small minority of wealthy Jews who farmed the taxes and performed other fiscal services for the crown and the landed magnates (*pani*).

Thus, Polish-Lithuanian Jewry had lived among, but distinct from, the general population. They were set apart, not only by their religion and by the special judicial and fiscal regime, but by language, dress, and cultural traditions. They spoke the dialectic German they had brought from their own homes, which became the basis of Yiddish. They were generally restricted to special streets (ghettos), and the Church insisted on their wearing a special costume; they themselves, in their religious orthodoxy, chose to wear distinctive beards and earlocks. They had also their own schools, the elementary heder and the more advanced academy, the yeshiva; these schools, which were for boys only, concentrated strictly on Biblical and Talmudic studies. Secular learning was rare; even the renowned Solomon Luria (*c.* 1510-73) had condemned as useless to Jews the teachings of "the uncircumcised Aristotle." The Jewish physicians of the Polish kings were therefore drawn mainly from the refugee Sephardic Jews of Spain and Italy; the local Ashkenazi Jews lived in a closed world of tradition, in which philosophy was condemned as "the harlot."

Still more importantly, perhaps, the Jews performed special economic roles. Although they constituted about one-eighth of the total population of the country, a Polish census in the late eighteenth century found only fourteen Jewish families engaged in agriculture. On the other hand, they controlled three-fourths of the export trade. Nowhere a majority, they formed a good third of the population of the towns, large and small. A great many of them were artisans, but it has been estimated that about one-half of them lived, in whole or in part, by leasing from the landlords the right to sell liquor. Most of the village tavernkeepers were themselves desperately poor, but they were widely regarded as exploiters of the peasantry; in conjunction with the sale of spirits, they vended other goods, bought up agricultural produce, and leased meadows, woodlots, and fishponds (hence the term *arendar,* from the Latin word for "rent," which became almost a synonym for the rural Jew).

The peasantry had always reacted hostilely, when opportunity offered, to this alien element in their midst. With the gradual growth of a gentile bourgeoisie, living under the "Magdeburg Law" but feeling the competition of the Jews, bitterness increased, as in earlier centuries it had in the West. The Polish masses were prone to give credence to wild stories of ritual murders. The best efforts of the kings and nobles were not always able to keep anti-Semitism in check; the city magistracies frequently failed to give the necessary protection against mob violence. Particularly in the Polish *ukraine,* the Jews suffered frightfully, along with the Polish nobility and their retainers, at the hands of rebellious cossacks and peasant *haidamaks* (a term derived from a Turkish word for "bandits"). One of the most notable instances was the massacre of Uman, near Kiev (1762), in which some twenty thousand Poles and Jews, who had fled thither from the surrounding area, were slaughtered in a vast pogrom.

Precarious as was the position of the Jews in the Rzecz Pospolita, it was a golden age compared to what was in store for them when suddenly plunged into "Holy Russia." Catherine's promise at the time of the First

Partition to preserve "the free exercise of religion and the inviolability of property for one and all" was initially implemented by confirmation of the *kahal* structure in White Russia (1776). In 1783, however, an edict deprived the *kahals* of all but their spiritual jurisdiction and fiscal responsibilities; thenceforth the Jews of White Russia were to be subject to the jurisdiction of the town magistracies, in the election of which they were supposed to share on an equal basis with Christian merchants and burghers. In 1786, they were guaranteed proportionate representation on the basis of the new Charter to the Towns of 1785.

The effort of Jewish merchants to extend their activities from White Russia to Smolensk and Moscow evoked loud protest; as a result, a decree of 1791 initiated formally the policy of the Pale of Settlement; Jews might reside only in the newly annexed provinces or in New Russia, the sparsely settled provinces that had recently been taken from Turkey. Following the Second Partition of Poland, the area of the Pale was extended to include, not only Russia's new acquisitions, but the whole of Little Russia, including even Kiev (1794). At the same time, Jews throughout the Pale were required to enroll in the merchant or burgher classes, on penalty of total expulsion, and to pay double the rate of normal taxation. It was small consolation that by the end of Catherine's reign official documents were using the term *Yevrei* (Hebrews) instead of the original pejorative *Zhid*.

From her triumphs in the West and South, Catherine, like Peter the Great, turned promptly eastward. Derbent and Baku were again snatched from Persia, but the war was abruptly ended by Catherine's death on November 6, 1796 (November 17 N.S.).

PAUL (1796-1801) AND THE YOUNG ALEXANDER

The death of Catherine, like that of any other Russian autocrat, necessarily threatened the beneficiaries of the deceased ruler. In 1796, the question of the way in which the new ruler would use the power was peculiarly significant, for Catherine had left only one recognized son, and his right to the throne depended on the theory that he was actually the son of Peter III. The situation was especially complicated because Catherine had in 1762 seized power at the expense of this son, then eight years old. Fully conscious that the Tsarevich Paul might be used as a symbol to overthrow her authority, Catherine had carefully excluded him from any contact with either the civil or military authority. At the time of Catherine's death, Paul was already forty-two years old, but he had resided in his suburban palace at Gatchina in constant fear that he would be set aside in favor of his own son Alexander, who early developed remarkable talent at ingratiating himself equally with his unfortunate father and with his magnificent grandmother, the empress.

Dominated by fear and hatred of all his mother had stood for, Paul failed to realize the essential facts of power in Russia. His first step was harmless enough, but highly significant. It was to repeal Peter's law of 1722 on the succession and to establish inheritance of the throne in the direct descending male line (April 5, 1797). This confirmation of his own right to the throne was, however, accompanied with an assertion that ran counter to the whole tendency of the seventeenth and especially of the eighteenth centuries. Paul reputedly maintained that in his Empire "no one is great except the one to whom I speak and only while I am speaking to him." [5]

Denying in principle the class privilege of the nobility, Paul threatened it also in detail. Apparently deliberately, Paul aped his alleged father, adding idiosyncrasies of his own. Constantly reviewing his troops on the parade ground, Paul punished unshined buttons, not by ordering the careless soldier beaten, but by slapping his officer in the face in the presence of his delighted men. With perhaps unconscious demagoguery Paul encouraged the submission, for his private perusal, of petitions from anonymous citizens. Paul released Novikov from prison and recalled Radishchev from exile; he set Kosciuszko free. Yet he reëstablished the political police and had thousands punished for offenses such as wearing French-style clothing or failing to kneel when the emperor's carriage was passing. Russian students abroad were peremptorily summoned home. Though Paul gave no evidence of being motivated by any serious consideration for the welfare of the serfs, he issued an edict setting the optimal limit of obligatory labor (*barshchina*) as three days a week; by another edict, applying only to Little Russia, he forbade the sale of serfs without land. Yet it was Paul who authorized the introduction of serfdom into New Russia, from which Potemkin had tried to exclude it; in five years he handed over to private owners more than half a million peasants, whereas even Catherine had in thirty-six years turned over only some eight hundred thousand. Peasant mutinies were punished with extreme severity.

Paul's foreign policy was as contradictory as was his domestic policy. At the end of her reign, Catherine had committed herself to an alliance with England, Austria, and Prussia against France. Without repudiating it, Paul announced that Russia, exhausted by ceaseless war since 1756, needed a breathing spell. Speedily, however, Paul was outraged by French diplomatic blunders, of which not the least was Bonaparte's seizure, en route to Egypt, of the island of Malta from the Knights Hospitalers of St. John. Paul, accepting the honorary grand-mastership of this Roman Catholic order, promptly declared war on France and arranged with Turkey, for the first time in history, to permit the Russian Black Sea fleet to pass through the Straits into the Mediterranean.

Suvorov was sent to Italy, where in short order he undid the work of the absent Bonaparte. In Switzerland, however, the noncoöperation of Austria threatened Suvorov with disaster, from which only his unparalleled military genius extricated him. Annoyed at Austria—and also at England, which had not sufficiently appreciated the assistance of a Russian army in Holland

—Paul withdrew from the war and, together with Prussia, Denmark, and Sweden, menaced his former allies. The Don cossacks were started on an impossible overland march across Central Asia against India.

The offense Paul gave to the nobility, the ruling class in Russia, combined with the money furnished by English representatives and with family troubles to put a swift end to Paul's regime. Shortly after he moved for safety into his new residence, the "Michael Castle," Paul was visited at night by a group of officers who demanded his abdication in favor of his son Alexander. While the argument was in progress, the conspirators were alarmed by the sound of approaching footsteps; lest the emperor be rescued by the plebeian rank-and-file, he was hastily garroted.

Paul's brief reign—which was thus ended on March 23, 1801—was not, however, merely a fantastic episode in the history of the Russian autocracy. Paul was the first, but not the last, Russian emperor to challenge the position that the Russian nobility had won in the course of the eighteenth century. In the nineteenth century, the autocracy was to grope for a new basis of support to replace the serf-holding nobility on which it had rested in its formative period. Russia was gradually to be transformed from an aristocratic into a bureaucratic mold. Having outlived its original function and unable either to adapt itself to new needs or to resist their pressures, the autocracy itself was ultimately doomed to total collapse.

Alexander, who was twenty-four years old at the time, professed great contrition over his father's death but took no action to punish the conspirators. With the play-acting skill he had learned in his childhood, he restored Catherine's old associates to administrative offices and confirmed her charters, which Paul had infringed. Only Count Pahlen, the chief figure behind the scenes in the removal of the late emperor, was gently maneuvered into honorable retirement. Yet Alexander neither trusted nor respected his grandmother's system or her courtiers. Influenced by his chief tutor, the "Jacobin" La Harpe, he had dreamed of imposing on Russia a free constitution and of abandoning his throne for private life on the banks of the Rhine; at one time, when Catherine had suggested making him her heir, he had maundered about "saving himself in America." [6] In this mood he gathered round him in the early years of his reign four "young friends"—Novosiltsev, Kochubei, Stroganov, and the Pole Czartoryski—who referred to themselves as the "committee of public safety."

The fruit of their deliberations about the "best model of revolution" was very wizened. In 1802, the remainder of Peter's "colleges" were replaced and supplemented by "ministries." The new executive organs were grouped under a Council of Ministers (*Soviet Ministrov*), collectively responsible to the emperor, but without impairing their individual responsibility. The Senate was reorganized as the supreme judicial and administrative organ, with the right to demand accounts even from the ministers. It was given also the power, like that of the pre-revolutionary French *Parlements,* to remonstrate even against imperial edicts; however, the first time it attempted to use this right (1803), it was told that the right of protest did not apply to new laws.

The contempt felt by the emperor's intimate circle for the general run of the landed nobility and a sense of the injustice of leaving the peasantry in virtual slavery to these despised nobles produced in 1803 the decree on the "free agriculturists." Under this law, by mutual agreement between individual landlords and their serfs, but on terms set by the state, peasants might be permitted to buy their individual freedom. Naturally it produced almost no practical results; in the remaining twenty-two years of Alexander's reign only some forty-seven thousand peasants were liberated, including seven thousand set free without land by the bequest of a single owner. For Livonia and Estonia, at the initiative of the local landowners, certain restrictions were imposed on the exploitation of the serfs there (1804-05). Alexander's doubtful attitude toward the noble monopoly of social power was reflected also in an edict of 1801 authorizing non-nobles to buy real estate, though not with serfs, and in an injunction to the Academy of Sciences to cease advertising the sale of serfs in its journal. Such "liberalism" could not seriously frighten the Russian nobility, able to draw breath again after Paul's severities; the Secret Chancellery, which had been active again under Paul, was again abolished at the opening of Alexander's reign.

In 1799, Emperor Paul had appointed the poet Derzhavin, who was also a Senator, to investigate the complaint of some Jews in White Russia that a local landlord was treating them as serfs; the following year, during a famine, he was sent again to prevent the landlords and their Jewish *arendars* from converting their grain into alcohol. After extended study of Holy Writ and consultation with the provincial governors, Derzhavin submitted an "Opinion" embodying detailed recommendations which became the basis of government policy toward the Jews. On the premise that "the best institutions are borrowed from the mores of the peoples for whom they are instituted," he attempted to answer the question: "Can the Jews be advantageous for the state?" His conclusion was that

> since Divine Providence, in fulfillment of its inscrutable designs, has left this people, dangerous because of its mores, on the surface of the earth and has not exterminated it, the governments under whose scepter it has taken refuge must suffer it [and] extend over the Jews its tutelage, to the end that they may be advantageous for the society amidst which they dwell.
>
> In a word, if in general their mores and conduct cannot be approved, the only correct conclusion is that the Jews, in their present condition, are not good people and therefore cannot be accounted good subjects of the Russian state.

Therefore, "to weaken their fanaticism," their autonomous communities (*kahals*) must be abolished, their excessive numbers in White Russia must be reduced, and they must be "set in order politically and morally, similarly to enlightened peoples." To avoid "disturbances, flights, or even the slightest grumbling" and "to inspire in them themselves a desire for a new pattern of life," an Imperial Manifesto should assure them of direct guardianship, of the most abundant means of livelihood, and "in every respect toleration of their faith and privileges" under the promise of 1772, "with a certain cancellation only of old ordinances incompatible with the pattern of well-ordered Christian monarchical governance and onerous for the people itself." [7]

In 1802, Alexander I accordingly appointed a five-man "Committee for the Amelioration of the Jews," including, along with Derzhavin, now Minister of Justice, two of Alexander's intimate young friends, Kochubei and Czartoryski. The alarm created among the Jews persuaded the committee, from which Derzhavin soon resigned, to invite deputies from the provincial *kahals* to advise the committee in St. Petersburg; incidentally, the transitory Jewish community in the capital was granted the right to establish its own cemetery there.

The outcome was the "Statute on the Ordering of the Jews" (1804), intended to bring about complete reformation of the Jewish manner of life and to encourage assimilation of Jews into the general population. Alexander himself was well pleased:

> We find the principles adopted by the Committee very just and all its articles conformable as well to moderation and solicitude for the true welfare of the Jews as founded on the basic welfare of the inhabitants of the *guberniyas* where these people are permitted to live.[8]

Jews were not required to abandon their religion, and they were to be freely admitted to all public educational institutions, at any level. They might open their own secular schools, providing they gave compulsory instruction in Russian, Polish, or German. They were encouraged to conform their attire to that of Christians. They were, nevertheless, to retain their communal autonomy for religion and taxpaying.

They were, however, to be excluded from their time-honored rural occupations:

> No one among the Jews, beginning with January 1, 1807 [in some *guberniyas;* 1808 in others], in any hamlet or village may hold any leases, pot-houses, taverns, and lodging-houses either in his own or in another's name, nor sell liquor in them or even live in them, under any pretext whatever save in passing through.[9]

For good measure, the prohibition was made applicable to "other establishments, situated on a highway, to whomever they may belong, whether to a company or to individuals." In compensation, Jewish manufacturers and artisans in the towns were to be relieved of the burden of double taxation; they were to be assisted to found factories and might be given permission to reside temporarily anywhere in Russia. Most important of all, they were to be assisted to engage in agriculture anywhere in the Pale, which was extended to include Astrakhan and the Caucasus.

Transplantation of the rural Jews, originally designed for 1807-08, was delayed on account of fear of the effect of Napoleon's flirtation with the Jews, ultimately reflected in his calling of the "Grand Sanhedrin" (1807). When the transplantation was finally undertaken in 1808, it caused such obvious mass suffering that even the provincial governors reported it was more likely to cause the ruin, rather than the reformation, of the Jews. At the same time, the supply of land in New Russia available for settlement even of the few thousands of Jews desperate enough to attempt agriculture was so short that the whole program was suspended. After three years of further study by a new committee, the idea was, at least temporarily, abandoned on the eve of the Napoleonic invasion (1812).

RUSSIA AND EUROPE

Alexander had promptly proclaimed Russia's neutrality in the European wars and had abandoned all preparations for war with England, thus escaping a threatened bombardment of St. Petersburg by Nelson. Gradually, however, Napoleon's high-handed actions in reorganizing Germany and Italy and his proclamation of a French Empire so offended Alexander's vanity that it became possible for Great Britain to organize a fresh coalition against France. At Austerlitz (1805), the Austro-Russian army was risked, contrary to the advice of Suvorov's pupil, Kutuzov, in disastrous open battle, and Austria was forced out of the war.

Prussia's belated entry into the coalition resulted in her crushing defeat at Jena (1806). In defeat, Alexander showed signs of that obscurantist mysticism that was later to become his most marked characteristic; he even went so far as to permit the Holy Synod officially to denounce the promised "new Grand Sanhedrin of the Hebrews" as designed "to proclaim a false messiah in the person of Napoleon." [10] Although the retreating Russian and Prussian armies in a series of exceptionally bloody battles made Napoleon pay dearly for further victories, Alexander was forced to withdraw across the Niemen. However, meeting Napoleon face to face on a raft in midstream, Alexander was captivated by his enemy.

The resultant peace-treaty of Tilsit (1807) largely anticipated the Hitler-Stalin pact of 1939. In effect, the two dictators agreed not to interfere with each other's activities on their respective sides of a line running from the Baltic to the Aegean. Napoleon was dissuaded from totally destroying Prussia but was allowed to reconstitute Poland, under the style of the Grand Duchy of Warsaw, out of most of Prussia's shares in the three partitions; Russia was given a few additional crumbs. In 1809, Austria's premature resumption of war with France caused her share of the Polish booty in the Third Partition to be added to the Grand Duchy. Above all, Napoleon gained at Tilsit a free hand against England and was promised Russia's participation in the Continental System, designed to weaken England economically. For her part, Russia once more made war on Sweden and Turkey, thus acquiring Finland (1809) and Bessarabia (1812), respectively.

The war with France had completed the process of Alexander's cooling toward his "young friends." Into the gap in the Emperor's affections moved Michael M. Speransky, an exceptionally talented and versatile administrator of non-noble origin. Speransky's major task was the preparation of a project for the social and administrative reconstruction of the empire. As the basis of his system, he distinguished three kinds of rights: (1) general civil rights, to be enjoyed by every subject; (2) special civil rights, extended only to the nobility; and (3) political rights, to be enjoyed by the nobility and the middle classes on the basis of a property qualification. Speransky's concept of civil liberty to be enjoyed by the peasants equally with other classes of the population did not prevent him from referring to them as "bondsmen" excluded from his representative system. Nor did he conceive of the creation of representative bodies as necessarily impairing the essence of autocracy; to Alexander, Speransky pointed out that maintenance of the representative principle in France affected the form but not the reality of the ruler's power. The project called for a four-level legislative structure: in the smallest unit of local government (*volost*) all landowners were to elect a duma; at the next higher level of administration (*okrug*) the duma was to be composed of deputies of these local dumas; and so on up to the State Duma composed of deputies of the *guberniya* dumas, themselves composed of deputies of the *okrug* dumas. A corresponding hierarchy of courts was to be headed by the Senate, while executive power was to be delegated downward from the Council of Ministers. Over the whole was to be set up a State Council (*Gosudarstvenny Soviet*), whose members were to be appointed by the emperor. The State Council began to function on New Year's Day, 1810, and the ministries were again reorganized in 1811. The rest of the project remained on paper.

As Minister of Justice, Speransky had also undertaken the oft-attempted task of codifying the laws, this time using the Code Napoléon as a model. This effort also produced no immediate results, but it did lay the groundwork for reform in the next reign. More directly fruitful were Speransky's efforts to reform the finances. His report at the beginning of 1810 had showed a revenue of 125 million rubles, expenditures of 230 million, and an accumulated state debt of 577 million. Although his dismissal in March, 1812, prevented execution of his full program of financial reform, Speransky's ideas, developed by his successors, saved Russia from financial collapse. A decree making promotions in the higher grades of state service dependent on examinations to test educational qualifications (1809) played a conspicuous part in his fall, but the basic reason was identification of his policies with the French connection.

The Continental System played havoc with the economic interests of the Russian ruling class. Economically, Great Britain was the only possible consumer of Russian exports and the only source of imports at reasonable prices. As in the time of Paul, murmuring against the regime became widespread; Napoleon's spies received much evidence of the growing possibility that Alexander might share his father's fate. Increasingly disturbed—and dissatisfied with the obvious advantages accruing to France—Alexander began to prepare for war and toyed with the idea of joining Great Britain in a new coalition. Not daring to leave the initiative to Russia, lest the Germanies rise in support of a Russian invasion, Napoleon struck in June, 1812, with a Grand Army almost six hundred thousand strong.

The Russian commander, Barclay de Tolly, adopted Scythian tactics, falling back to Smolensk without offering battle. The emperor, yielding to loudly voiced public opinion, ordered Barclay replaced with Kutuzov, who, hampered by Alexander's personal directions, had lost the battle of Austerlitz. Barclay, after attempting a stand at Smolensk, resumed his retreat and handed over his command. Kutuzov made a desperate effort to check the Grand Army near Borodino; he succeeded in inflicting more losses on the enemy than his own forces suffered but, fearing total destruction of his smaller force, again fell back. Refusing to attempt a defense of Moscow, he turned south, interposing his still undefeated army between Napoleon and the food-rich Ukraine. Moscow was burned, and the French army, worn down by the rigors of its long march, became thoroughly demoralized. With an intact army in his rear, Napoleon could not venture to turn against St. Petersburg, defended by a fresh army. Failing in an effort to fight his way south, he had to beat an ignominious and harrowing retreat by the road he had already traveled, harassed at every step by the unorganized resistance of the peasant population, instinctively patriotic, and by partisan bands detached from Kutuzov's army, which followed the French at a respectful distance to the south.

Evacuation of Russia brought Napoleon no relief. The Russians followed him into Germany, where they were joined, promptly by the Prussian army, after some hesitation by Austria. A series of battles culminated in the four-day "Battle of the Nations" at Leipzig (1813), in which the half-million men engaged suffered over one hundred thousand casualties. Unrelentingly the allies pursued into France, and on March 31, 1814, Emperor Alexander made a triumphal entry into Paris. At the Congress of Vienna (1814-15) Russia was able to play a dominant role in the work of resettling Europe on the basis of "legitimacy" and "compensations." Although Russian forces had no immediate part in the episode of the "Hundred Days," they formed part of the garrison subsequently established in France.

Russia had begun to play her new role as the "gendarme of Europe," the chief guarantor of internal order and the preserver of international peace. It is true that Alexander's proposal of a Holy Alliance was received with more or less open derision in Western Europe but, transmuted into the Quadruple (later Quintuple) Alliance, Alexander's policy, if not his rationale, became the bulwark of the Restoration.

NOTES

1. Reddaway (ed.), *Documents of Catherine the Great,* p. 18.
2. *Polnoe sobranie zakonov . . .* (First collection), No. 12,949—*Nakaz,* Chapter XI, Article 260—(July 30, 1767), XVIII, 239.
3. *Ibid.,* No. 8840 (December 16, 1743), XI, 983.
4. Catherine II, *Memoirs . . .* (Maroger edition), p. 362.
5. De Sanglen, *Zapiski,* in *Russkaia Starina,* 1882, XXXVI, 497.
6. Sementkowski-Kurilo, *Alexander I,* p. 38.
7. Derzhavin, "*Mnienie . . .* ," in *Sochineniia,* VII, 261-331 *passim,* especially 275-277 and 290-292.
8. *Polnoe sobranie zakonov . . . , op. cit.,* No. 21,547 (December 9, 1804), XXVIII, 731.
9. *Ibid.,* Article 34, pp. 734-735.
10. *Ibid.,* No. 22,394 (December 13, 1806), XXIX, 928-929.

SUGGESTIONS FOR FURTHER READING

Among general works cited in Chapter 1, Kliuchevskii is at this era no longer serviceable. The best general narrative of the remaining portion of the tsarist regime is Kornilov's *Modern Russian History*. Karpovich, *Imperial Russia, 1801-1917,* is a brief but excellent outline.

In addition to biographies of Catherine, of which Katherine Anthony's edition of the *Memoirs of Catherine the Great* is still the best, those of Potemkin by Soloveytchik and of Suvorov by Blease may be consulted. Reddaway's *Documents of Catherine the Great* translates much valuable material. McConnell's *A Russian Philosophe: Alexander Radishchev* is an excellent study. Radishchev's *Journey from St. Petersburg to Moscow* is now available in English translation.

For Catherine's foreign policy, see Gladys S. Thomson, *Catherine the Great and the Expansion of Russia;* on special aspects, Kaplan's *First Partition of Poland* and Lord's *Second Partition of Poland* are especially valuable, as is de Madariaga's *Britain, Russia, and the Armed Neutrality of 1780.*

For the Jewish problem from this point on, Dubnow's *History of the Jews in Russia and Poland* is the most comprehensive; Greenberg's *The Jews in Russia* is a more recent account; Levitats' *The Jewish Community in Russia, 1772-1844,* is a specialized study of *kahal* organization and functioning.

On the early Alexander I, see Choiseul-Gouffier, *Historical Memoirs . . . ; Memoirs of Prince Adam Czartoryski*; and Maurice Paléologue, *The Enigmatic Tsar. . . .* For the classic account of Alexander's foreign relations, see Vandal, *Napoléon et Alexandre Ier*; a study which became controversial in the Soviet Union is Tarle, *Napoleon's Invasion of Russia, 1812.*

Chapter

15

Reaction and Intellectual Ferment: 1815-1855

Alexander himself underwent a profound psychological change as a result of the stirring phenomena of the burning of Moscow, the national upsurge of the Russian peasantry in the "Fatherland War," and the acclaim with which he was initially greeted in the West. Perhaps also due to his relations with Madame de Krüdener, he settled down from the charming, if undecided, Deistic liberal he had seemed in his youth into an occasionally irascible, but normally calm, Romantic mystic.

THE NEW RUSSIAN EMPIRE AND REACTION

In his proposal for a "Holy Alliance," the rationalistic accents of the eighteenth-century *philosophes* were replaced by a language which scandalized or amused the practical statesmen of the West. In the name of "the Most Holy and Indivisible Trinity," inspired by "the eternal Law of God the Saviour," it was proposed that the contracting monarchs, "united by bonds of true and indissoluble brotherhood and considering Themselves as fellow-countrymen," who ruled their respective subjects "as fathers of families," promised to "lend each other on every occasion and in every place aid, succor, and assistance." [1] In Metternich's version, the idea became a powerful instrument for suppressing revolutions in Italy, Spain, and the Germanies by action of the "Concert of Europe," determined on in international conferences of the great powers. Yet, though the period from 1815 to 1848 is conventionally known as the Era of Metternich, it should not be forgotten that the inspiration and the chief supporting arm were supplied by Russia, to whom the hegemony over the Continent now clearly belonged.

To use the terms of the Hegelian dialectic, this situation contained within itself the seeds of its own destruction. Russia might dominate the Continent, but the leading world power was clearly the United Kingdom. France, Austria, and Prussia might claim rank as great powers, but primacy clearly belonged to Russia by land, to England by sea. As has happened throughout history, there inevitably developed a polarity between the two giants, which no conference at the summit could possibly have avoided.

Great Britain and Russia had been the two powers which at the Congress of Vienna had chiefly insisted on compensations to rectify the general principle of legitimacy. Russia's claims had taken the form of demand for confirmation of her conquest of Finland and for annexation to Russia of the Grand Duchy of Warsaw. Finland caused little trouble, for Sweden could be compensated by transfer of Norway from Denmark, and Denmark had been driven by Nelson so deep into Napoleon's arms that she commanded no sympathy from the victors.

The Grand Duchy of Warsaw was a different matter, for it raised questions more serious than mere territorial compensation. Prussia was quite willing to forgo restoration to her of her share in the Partitions of Poland, provided she be allowed to annex Saxony, whose ruler had also been Grand Duke of Warsaw. Thus Prussia would acquire as subjects a number of German "souls" equal in number to the Polish souls she would give up—and, in her estimation, superior both in quality and in location. Austria, however, apart from the problem of suitable compensation to her, was wholly unwilling to witness such a westward extension of the paw of the Russian bear. Great Britain, especially, fearing permanent intrusion of Russian power into the affairs of the West, negotiated an alliance (January, 1815) with Austria and France, menacing her recent allies, Russia and Prussia, with war if they would not yield. The matter was compromised, Alexander contenting himself with approximately the territories annexed by Prussia and Austria in the Third Partition; Cracow, the old Polish capital, was withheld, and the new provinces, except for Bialystok, were not incorporated into the Russian empire; an "independent" kingdom of Poland was again set up (the "Congress kingdom") with the Russian emperor as ruler. The Concert was therefore able to act unitedly against Napoleon in the Hundred Days.

Yet the "cold war" continued. The harmonious working of the Alliance soon broke down over a Greek rebellion against Turkey and over the question of the Latin-American colonies. The début of the United States in world politics, by the issue of the Monroe Doctrine, represented basically her alignment with Great Britain against Russia in the rivalry that was to be the chief thread of world politics throughout the nineteenth century.

Russia's new position in the world was reflected in the continuing and more rapid expansion of her territory.* This expansion was rapidly altering also the internal character of the Russian empire. The new territories added by Catherine, and still more those added by Alexander, were not inhabited by Russians, at least not by "Great Russians." The Partitions of Poland had "restored" areas that had indeed formed part of historic Rus, but Little Russia and White Russia had been under an alien regime for too many centuries to permit of easy assimilation to Great Russian ideas and institutions. "New Russia" and the Crimea, though vigorously colonized by settlers from the more densely populated older provinces, contained also a considerable Tatar population. Throughout the Pale, Jews proved to be a peculiarly indigestible, though easily oppressed, minority. Alexander's acceptance of a protectorate over Georgia (1801) led to fresh wars with Persia and with the mountaineers of the Caucasus; the consequent extension of Russian authority along the shores of the Black and Caspian seas resulted in long-drawn-out efforts to subjugate the whole Caucasian area. The annexation of the enormous Kirghiz region prepared the way for later Russian absorption of the whole of Central Asia, which was neither Slavic nor Christian. The "Congress kingdom" of Poland, though both Slavic and Christian, was non-Russian and non-Orthodox, and the Poles remained unreconciled to the loss of the frontiers of 1772; although nominally independent of Russia under its own constitution, Poland was treated much like a subject province of the Empire. Finland, annexed only for the protection of St. Petersburg, was more fortunate in its existence as a separate grand duchy, with a promise of the same measure of autonomy its population had enjoyed under Swedish rule. In the Baltic provinces, added by Peter, time had been given the German ruling class, which had suppressed the native peasantry, to adjust to membership in the Russian ruling class, without regrets for the days of government by Sweden.

Thus the Russian Empire was no longer purely Russian. Its polyglot character had not, however, made it cosmopolitan, despite the superficial influences of the French "Enlightenment" on the upper circles of society. Rather, Russia had acquired a very grave problem of ruling over a number of subject nationalities, whose individual weakness did not prevent them from constituting a constant danger to internal state order.

In Russia proper, in the very early years of Alexander's reign, the vocal portion of the public, reacting from Paul's police crudities, had welcomed the emperor's intention, announced in his accession manifesto, of reigning in the spirit of his grandmother Catherine. Regardless of the fact that Catherine had never allowed her professions of liberalism to impose any fetters on her autocratic will, even enlightened men, like Academician Storch, had thought that Alexander would introduce a liberal constitution. A rash of intellectual

* See Map VII.

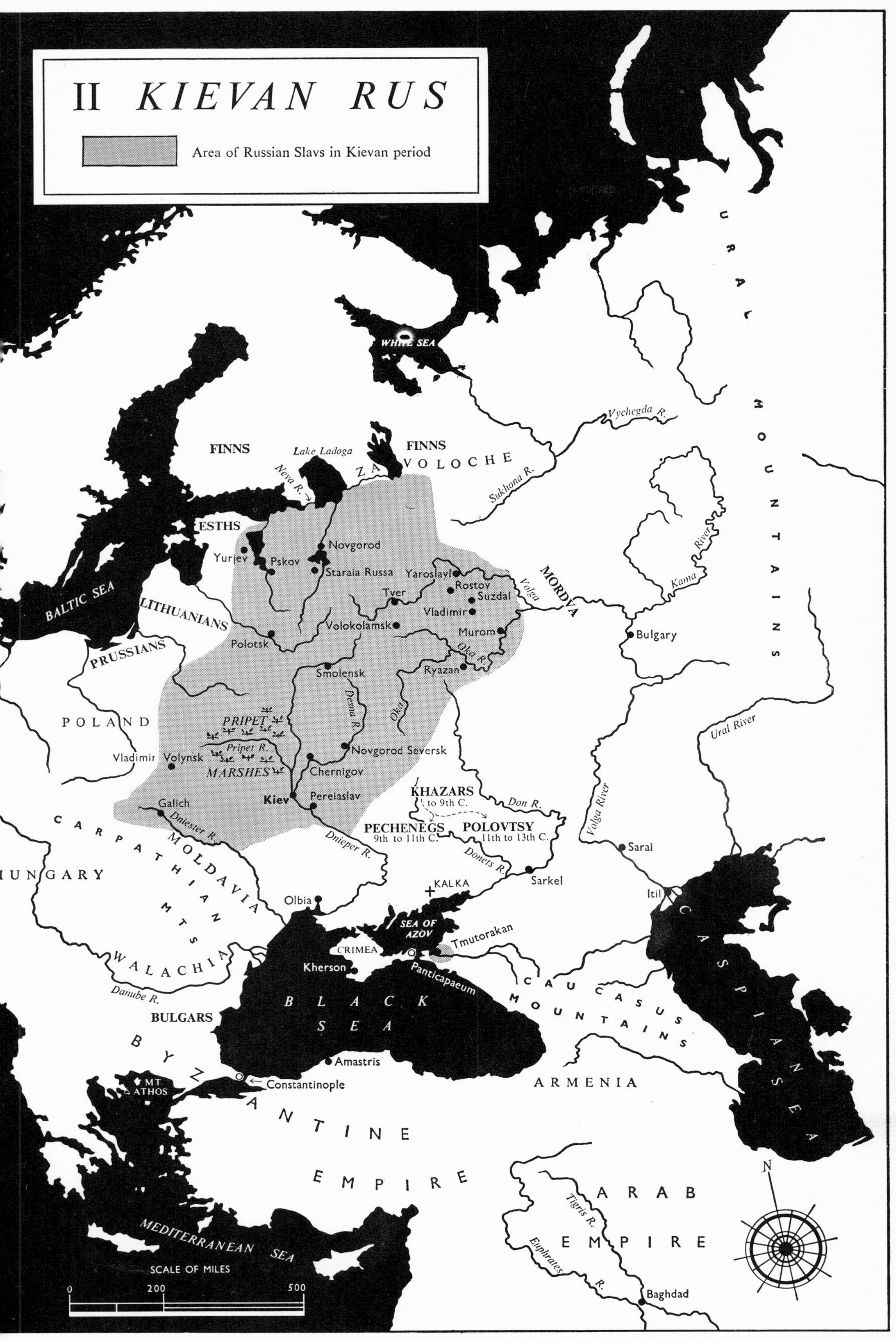
II KIEVAN RUS
Area of Russian Slavs in Kievan period
WHITE SEA
URAL MOUNTAINS
FINNS
Lake Ladoga
FINNS
ZAVOLOCHE
Neva R.
Vychegda R.
Sukhona R.
ESTHS
Novgorod
Yurjev
Pskov
Staraia Russa
Yaroslavl
Rostov
Suzdal
Volga
MORDVA
Kama
River
BALTIC SEA
LITHUANIANS
Tver
Vladimir
Volokolamsk
Murom
Bulgary
PRUSSIANS
Polotsk
Oka R.
Ryazan
Smolensk
Desna R.
Oka
POLAND
PRIPET
Pripet R.
MARSHES
Novgorod Seversk
Ural River
Vladimir Volynsk
Chernigov
Kiev
Pereiaslav
Galich
KHAZARS
to 9th C.
Don R.
Volga River
PECHENEGS
9th to 11th C.
POLOVTSY
11th to 13th C.
Dniester R.
Dnieper R.
CARPATHIAN MTS
MOLDAVIA
HUNGARY
Donets R.
Sarai
Sarkel
KALKA
Itil
Olbia
CASPIAN SEA
SEA OF AZOV
CRIMEA
Tmutorakan
WALACHIA
Kherson
Panticapaeum
Danube R.
CAUCASUS MOUNTAINS
BULGARS
BLACK SEA
Amastris
MT. ATHOS
Constantinople
ARMENIA
BYZANTINE EMPIRE
N
ARAB EMPIRE
Tigris R.
Euphrates R.
Baghdad
MEDITERRANEAN SEA
SCALE OF MILES
0
200
500

LEFT
Pecherskaia Lavra
(Monastery of the Caves) at Kiev, so called because the cells of the eleventh-century monks lined a tunnel dug in the clay hillside, extending under the Dnieper River, shown in the background. The buildings in the foreground, ruined by the German invasion in 1941, date only from the seventeenth century. (See page 36.)

Cathedral of St. Sophia
at Novgorod. A fine example, from the middle of the eleventh century, of Byzantine architecture in Russia.

Uspensky Sobor
(Cathedral of the Assumption) at Vladimir-on-the-Kliazma. Representing considerable modification and embellishment of the original Byzantine type, this late twelfth-century cathedral served as the model for the one of the same name built by "Aristotle" Fioraventi for Ivan III in the Kremlin at Moscow (1479). (See page 99.)

Andrei Bogoliubsky
twelfth-century Prince of Vladimir Suzdal, marching against Novgorod, as depicted in a Novgorod icon of the period.

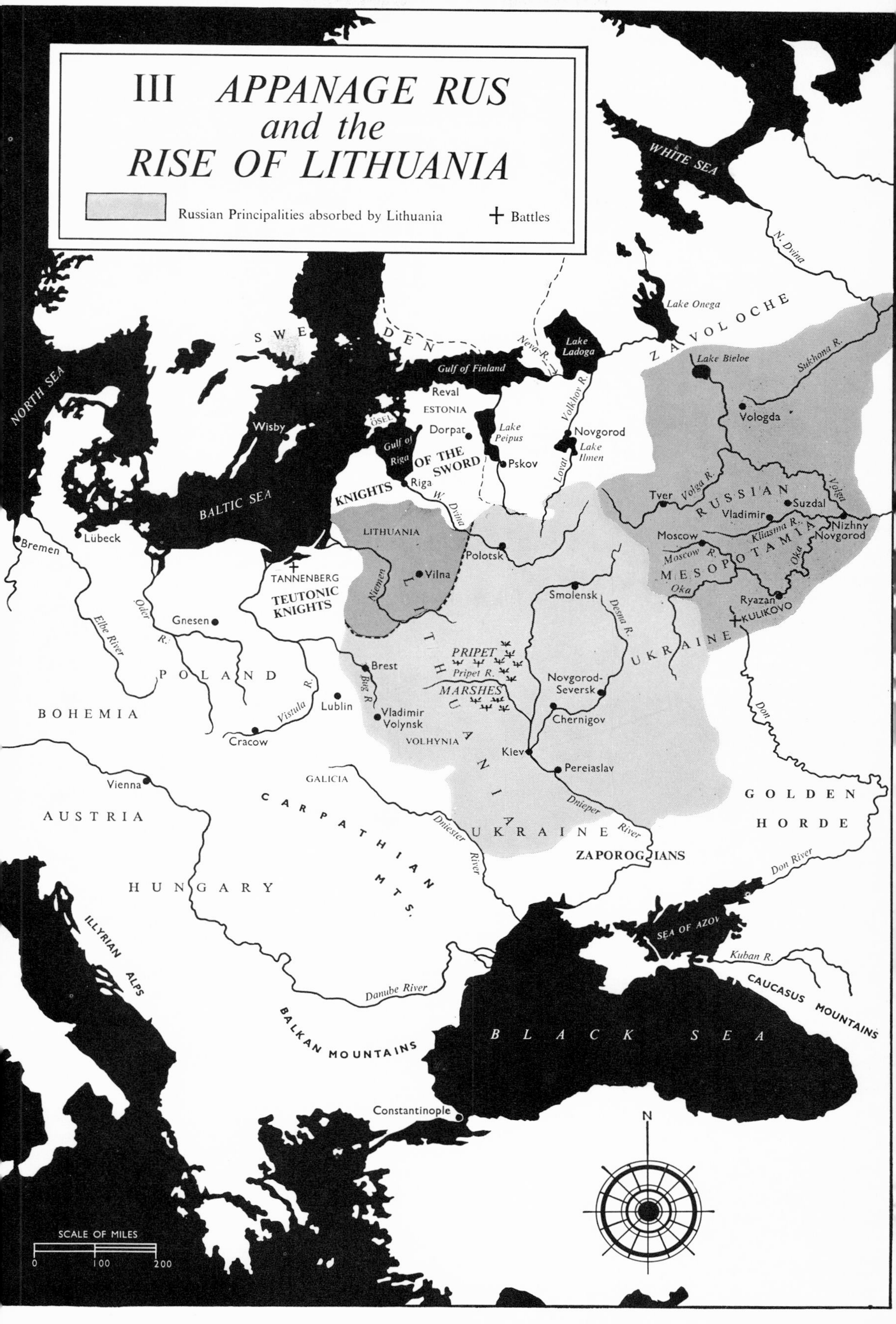

III APPANAGE RUS and the RISE OF LITHUANIA
Russian Principalities absorbed by Lithuania
Battles
WHITE SEA
N. Dvina
Lake Onega
ZAVOLOCHE
SWEDEN
Neva R.
Lake Ladoga
Gulf of Finland
Lake Bieloe
Sukhona R.
NORTH SEA
Reval
ESTONIA
ÖSEL
Wisby
Dorpat
Lake Peipus
Volkhov R.
Novgorod
Lake Ilmen
Vologda
Gulf of Riga
OF THE SWORD
Pskov
Lovat
Riga
KNIGHTS
BALTIC SEA
W. Dvina
Tver
Volga R.
RUSSIAN
Suzdal
Volga
Vladimir
Nizhny Novgorod
Kliasma R.
Moscow
Moscow R.
MESOPOTAMIA
Oka
LITHUANIA
Polotsk
Lübeck
Bremen
TANNENBERG
TEUTONIC KNIGHTS
Niemen
Vilna
Smolensk
Desna R.
Ryazan
KULIKOVO
Oder R.
Gnesen
Elbe River
PRIPET
Pripet R.
MARSHES
UKRAINE
Brest
Bug R.
POLAND
Vistula R.
Lublin
Novgorod-Seversk
BOHEMIA
Vladimir Volynsk
Chernigov
Cracow
VOLHYNIA
Kiev
Don
Pereiaslav
Vienna
GALICIA
GOLDEN HORDE
AUSTRIA
CARPATHIAN MTS.
Dniester River
Dnieper River
ZAPOROGIANS
Don River
HUNGARY
ILLYRIAN ALPS
SEA OF AZOV
Kuban R.
CAUCASUS MOUNTAINS
Danube River
BALKAN MOUNTAINS
BLACK SEA
Constantinople
N
SCALE OF MILES
0
100
200

The Shock of the Mongol Conquest (1238) as depicted in an illuminated chronicle. The new Grand Prince, Yaroslav (father of Alexander Nevsky) returns to ruined Vladimir, a scene of slaughter.

The Battle of Kulikovo (1380), a painting by Vasnetsov, a nineteenth-century Russian artist particularly famous for his historical scenes. The Russian champion (at left) is the hero claimed by Peresvietov as his ancestor.

Monastery of Troitsa-Sergievo, named for St. Sergius and founded in the fourteenth century, was the holiest, richest, and best-fortified monastery in the Russian mesopotamia. It contains many famous icons, including the best of Rublev. The bell tower is a late addition by Rastrelli, the chief architect of St. Petersburg.

Cathedral of Vasily the Blessed in the Red Square at Moscow. Built to celebrate the conquest of Kazan by Ivan the Terrible, it is the most striking example of specifically Russian architecture, representing the translation into brick of the honeycomb structure, with a central steeple, developed by Russian carpenters. At the left is the heroic statue of Minin and Pozharsky, moved from its original site near the place of execution. (See pages 104–105.)

IV GROWTH OF MUSCOVY TO 1584
Principality of Moscow, c. 1300
Acquisitions to 1462
Acquisitions, 1462-1533
Acquisitions of Ivan the Terrible, 1533-1584
SCALE OF MILES
100
200
N
NORTH CAPE
ARCTIC OCEAN
SIBIR
URAL MOUNTAINS
YUGRIA
WHITE SEA
Archangel
N. Dvina R.
Vychegda R.
Lake Onega
KARELIA
Lake Ladoga
FINLAND
SWEDEN
Gulf of Bothnia
ALAND ISLANDS
Gulf of Finland
INGRIA
Narva
ESTONIA
OSEL
LIVONIA
BALTIC SEA
COURLAND
Riga
Pskov
Novgorod
Lake Beloe
Sukhona R.
Ustiug
Vologda
Yaroslavl
Tver
Alexandrovsk
Troitsa
Vladimir
Volga R.
MORDVA
Kazan
Nizhny Novgorod
Moscow
Oka R.
Ryazan
Smolensk
Vilna
PRUSSIA
LITHUANIA
Vistula R.
Warsaw
POLAND
Cracow
Kiev
LITTLE RUSSIA
Dnieper River
Don River
Donets R.
Volga R.
Ural River
KIRGHIZ
Astrakhan
CARPATHIAN MTS
HUNGARY
MOLDAVIA
Pruth R.
WALACHIA
ZAPOROZHE
KHANATE OF CRIMEA
Kuban R.
BLACK SEA
CAUCASUS MOUNTAINS
DAGHESTAN
CASPIAN SEA
GEORGIA
ARMENIA
Constantinople
Bosporus
OTTOMAN EMPIRE

V GROWTH OF MUSCOVY 1584 to 1725
Muscovy in 1584
Acquisitions of Alexis, 1645-1676
Acquisitions of Peter the Great, 1689-1725
+ Battles
SCALE OF MILES
100
200
NORTH CAPE
ARCTIC OCEAN
WHITE SEA
SIBIR
YUGRIA
URAL MOUNTAINS
Archangel
N. Dvina R.
Vychegda R.
Solvychegodsk
Ustiug
Sukhona R.
Tiumen
Perm
Yekaterinburg
Vologda
Lake Beloe
Lake Onega
Petrazavodsk
Lake Ladoga
KARELIA
SWEDEN
FINLAND
Gulf of Bothnia
Nystadt
Vyborg
ALAND ISLANDS
HANGUD
Gulf of Finland
St. Petersburg
INGRIA
Reval
OSEL
ESTONIA
Narva
LIVONIA
Pskov
Riga
Novgorod
BALTIC SEA
COURLAND
W. Dvina R.
Königsberg
PRUSSIA
Vilna
Smolensk
LESNA
KLUSHINO
Uglich
Tver
Troitsa
Tushino
Moscow
Kaluga
Tula
Volga R.
Vladimir
Nizhny Novgorod
MORDVA
Kazan
Arzamas
BASHKIRS
Ural River
KIRGHIZ
Warsaw
POLAND-LITHUANIA
Cracow
Kiev
LITTLE RUSSIA
POLTAVA
ZAPOROZHE
Voronezh
Don River
DON COSSACKS
Tsarevo-Borisovo
Volga River
Tsaritsyn
VOLGA COSSACKS
Astrakhan
CARPATHIAN MTS.
HUNGARY
MOLDAVIA
Jassy
WALACHIA
KHANATE OF CRIMEA
Azov
Kuban R.
TEREK COSSACKS
CHERKESSES
CAUCASUS MOUNTAINS
DAGHESTAN
CASPIAN SEA
BLACK SEA
GEORGIA
ARMENIA
OTTOMAN EMPIRE
Constantinople
Bosporus
N

LEFT **Muscovite warriors** of the early sixteenth century, as depicted by Baron Herberstein, author of one of the earliest descriptions of Russia by a foreign visitor.

BELOW
St. George slaying the Dragon from a sixteenth-century icon originally in the Church of St. George at Kostroma.

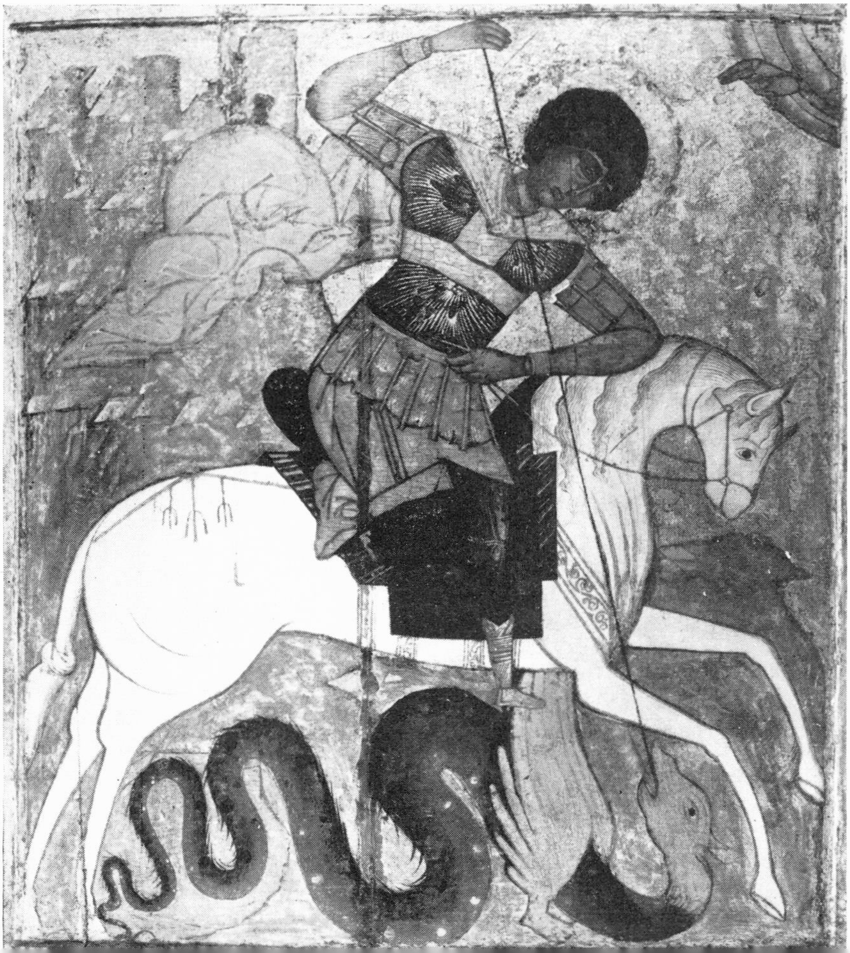

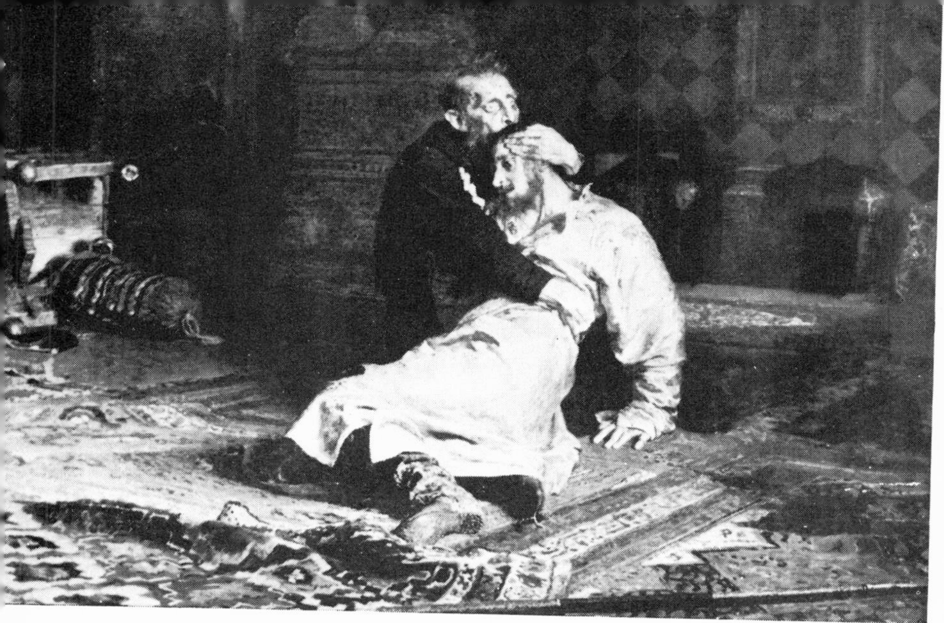

"Fathers and Sons"

ABOVE *Ivan the Terrible* holding his son to whom he has just dealt a mortal blow with his staff, as painted by Repin (1885), the most renowned of the Russian realist school.

BELOW *Peter and Alexis* a painting by Gué (1871) depicting the character of the struggle between the vigorous father and his obstinate son.

The Battle of Hangud (1714), Peter's sole naval victory, won by the Russian galleys against the Swedish vessels helpless in the narrow Finnish fjords.

Fortress of Peter-and-Paul, the essential core of the new city of St. Petersburg (1703). The Emperors and Empresses are buried in the Cathedral of Peter-and-Paul, remarkable for its Protestant spire. The bastions jutting into the river were used as dungeons.

The Mice Bury the Cat an example of eighteenth-century popular caricature. This particular version reflects the sentiments of Old Ritualists toward Peter the Great.

periodicals had broken out, of which the most successful was the *European Messenger,* edited by Karamzin. Karamzin was later to become renowned as an arch-conservative historian, a Russian Carlyle, but in 1802 he put great hope in the anticipated development of free education. The new Ministry of Education, provided with a generous budget and staffed by a number of able and enthusiastic men, did indeed seem to promise great things. By 1804, the University of Moscow, founded by Elizabeth, had been supplemented by new universities at Kharkov and Kazan; there were also the older Polish university at Vilna and the German one at Dorpat; at St. Petersburg was founded a Pedagogical Institute, in 1819 converted into a sixth university. A University Statute, guaranteeing academic freedom, gave autonomy to university councils.

In the later years of his reign, however, most of this program was undone. In 1812, there was imported from England a branch of the Bible Society. Innocuous in England, this organization came in Russia under the control of Prince A. N. Golitsyn, a friend and admirer of Joseph de Maistre and *Oberprokuror* of the Holy Synod. In 1817, "desiring to have Christian piety as ever the basis of true enlightenment," [2] Alexander combined the Ministries of Spiritual Matters and of Popular Education into one, and entrusted it to Golitsyn. His subordinates soon reduced university education to the level of that of barracks-schools, dismissing professors and revising textbooks. At St. Petersburg, Uvarov, personally an earnest conservative, managed for a short time to resist the reaction but was soon himself forced out as curator. The censorship of books and periodicals, tightened as early as 1807, grew ever more severe. Similar abandonment of liberal pretenses was manifest in Alexander's treatment of the "Congress kingdom" of Poland, where the constitution granted in 1815 was prevented from ever functioning.

For later generations, the growing reaction came to be symbolized by Arakcheiev, who, without holding any official position of the highest consequence, was so trusted by Alexander that his influence was felt in almost every government institution. Arakcheiev was not, however, the evil genius of the emperor, inspiring him with reactionary designs; he was merely a personally upright man—an extraordinarily rare phenomenon among Russian officials of the time—willing faithfully and ruthlessly to carry out his master's wishes, regardless of his own estimate of their wisdom.

The principal "reform" with which his name is associated was not his idea but the casual result of a French book the emperor read in 1810. In that year, Alexander ordered the settlement of an infantry regiment in a district on the southwest frontier; the original population was resettled in New Russia, and their houses and lands were assigned to the married soldiers, whose families were transferred to the new settlement. The unmarried soldiers were quartered on their married confrères as farm laborers, to be fed in lieu of wages. The whole "military colony" was exempted from taxation, the idea being that the regiment, somewhat after the fashion of the *strieltsy* of old, would maintain itself in peacetime without cost to the government.

The experiment was interrupted by the campaign of 1812, but after the war the idea was revived, first near Novgorod, later also in parts of Little Russia. In the new version, the existing inhabitants were not evicted but arbitrarily declared "military colonists," bound to support the troops distributed among them. Although provided at government expense with needed equipment and livestock, the "military colonists" had cause bitterly to resent the strict disciplinary supervision of the authorities, which, with its strict regulation of marriages and its barracks education of children ("cantonists"), constituted a peculiarly onerous form of serfdom. Arakcheiev prided himself on the saving of very substantial sums of money, and the system won the approval even of men like Speransky, recalled from exile after the war, and of Karamzin. Yet the estimated saving did not take account of the colonists' tax exemption, while those subjected to this special regime reacted even more violently than did other bondsmen.

The general "peasant question" continued to be agitated, and by imperial decrees the peasants of Estonia (1816), Courland (1817), and Livonia (1819) were emancipated. Their freedom, however, was purely personal; allotted no land, the peasants of the Baltic provinces, like the Polish peasants emancipated by Napoleon, became helpless objects of economic exploitation by their former owners. Alexander personally subsidized a French edition of Academician Storch's lectures condemning any form of bondage labor, but a Russian edition was forbidden by the censor. Similar was the fate of Pushkin's poem, *The Village;* the emperor thanked the author for the ideas expressed in it, while the censor forbade publication. An effort by a group of liberal nobles to form an all-Russian society to prepare the elimination of serfdom was blocked by Alexander, who was willing only that gradual liquidation of the institution be effected by individual landowners; they were authorized to sell strictly limited amounts of land to the peasants they might choose to release from bondage.

THE DECEMBRISTS

The drift of the autocracy into reaction intensified certain tendencies in the opposite direction and gave rise to what may be called, if not the first revolution in Russian history, at least Russia's first conscious revolutionary movement, deliberately planning a reconstruction of the Russian social and political system. The "Fatherland War" had called into military service large numbers of young aristocrats, and their prolonged experiences in Germany and France had left them with a great admiration for the ideas and institutions of the West. It was the first time that a significant number of highly placed young men had had revealed to them, and by first-hand observation, the glaring differences between the West, which they had been told was groaning under despotism, and the backwardness of their own beloved native land. Continuing in service after their return to Russia, many of them joined Masonic societies, which became in Arakcheiev's Russia the principal milieu for the discussion of social and political problems.

By the time Masonry was banned in 1822, these officers, including a disproportionate number of colonels, had formed the inveterate habit of forming secret societies. The "Union of Salvation," founded as early as 1816, soon came under the domination of Paul Pestel; he was the son of a governor-general of Siberia, himself a war hero, aide-de-camp to General Wittgenstein, and an ardent devotee of Jacobin republicanism. In the absence of Pestel on duty outside the capital, the society was reorganized as the "Union of Welfare" (1817), which was more influenced by the ideas of the German Tugendbund than by the notions of the Italian Carbonari. Its "Green Book" outlined four chief fields of activity—philanthropy, education, justice, and economy—in which the members were to participate. By reason of internal dissensions the society was formally dissolved in 1821.

There survived, however, several conspiratorial organizations, of which the most extreme was the "Southern Society," headed by Pestel, then twenty-seven years old and colonel commanding a regiment at southern headquarters. More strategically situated in the capital was the "Northern Society," in which the chief figure was Nikita Muraviev, a Guards officer. Muraviev felt it would be necessary, in introducing a new constitution, to preserve the monarchy, but many of his associates shared the republican views of Pestel. The point of difference came down to the question whether it was necessary to assassinate only Alexander, or whether the whole dynasty must share his fate. Another, more academic, disagreement came over the "peasant question." All the conspirators anticipated that serfdom must be abolished, but few shared Pestel's conviction that private property in land must also be regulated and that the peasants must be guaranteed the usufruct, though not the ownership, of land. The socio-economic ideas of the revolutionaries were for the most part very vague and scarcely went beyond allotment to the emancipated peasants of some dozen acres.

Even Pestel was neither a socialist nor a democrat. Perhaps unjustly accused by many of his fellow-conspirators of a tendency toward Bonapartism, he envisioned a period of aristocratic-military dictatorship following the overthrow of the autocracy. For ethnic aspirations Pestel had no sympathy: Poland might have independence only if it abandoned the idea of the frontiers of 1772, and if it modeled its internal order on the new Russian one; the Mohammedans must abandon their special attitudes, particularly toward women; the Jews, as exploiters of the Russian peasantry, were to be forcibly transplanted to "Asia Minor."

How long these conspiracies might have gone on is a matter of speculation. Various abortive plans were laid to assassinate Alexander. For his part, the emperor, though aware of the work of the societies, had refused to take action against young men for sharing, as he said, ideas he had nourished in his youth. However, on December 9, 1825 (N.S.), it became known in St. Petersburg that the emperor had died of natural causes eight days earlier at Taganrog. By an agreement known only to a handful of contemporary functionaries, his next brother, Constantine, had in 1823 for personal reasons been induced to renounce his right of succession in favor of a third brother, Nicholas. Nicholas, though aware of the renunciation, was unwilling publicly to assume the power without further voluntary confirmation by his older brother. The oath of allegiance was therefore taken to Constantine, then serving as Commander-in-Chief at Warsaw. Not until December 26 (December 14 O.S.) could Nicholas, whose narrowly military education had given him the appearance of decisiveness without the ability to make decisions, be persuaded to agree to proclamation of his own accession.

This period of hesitation forced on the revolutionary conspirators the opportunity they had been discussing for years. Though unprepared to act and uncertain of their objectives, the colonels led a couple of regiments out into the Senate Square in the name of "Constantine and Constitution," although the latter was something he would have been the last man to grant. Legend has it that the soldiers assumed "Constitution" (*Konstitutsiia*) to be Constantine's wife. Only the fact that the confusion of the insurgents was almost matched by the hesitation of Nicholas allowed the revolt to last most of the day. In the end, a "whiff of grapeshot," kept up for an hour, dispersed the soldiers on that bleak December day.

The *opéra bouffe* "Decembrist Revolution" was over. In the south, Pestel had been arrested the day before, and a military rising led by Sergei Muraviev-Apostol lasted only from January 11 to January 15. It remained only for a penitent Nicholas, ruing the fate that had compelled him to begin his reign with bloodshed (*"au prix du sang de mes sujets,"* as he phrased it), to moderate the sentences imposed by a special court. The five men sentenced to be quartered were hanged instead; thirty-one sentenced to decapitation were merely exiled to hard labor in Siberia for life, along with eighty-five others for various terms of years.

NICHOLAS I (1825-1855)

The new emperor, Nicholas I, had not been educated with the thought that he would some day rule, nor had he been drawn into the conduct of state affairs by Alexander I. Yet he was far more serious-minded, far more conscious of the burden of his duties, than his more spectacular brother had been. Unable to forget that he had come to the throne *"au prix du sang de mes sujets,"* Nicholas made a conscientious effort to understand the factors that had produced the December uprising and was honestly shocked to find how widely spread was discontent with the existing reactionary regime. He promptly dismissed Arakcheiev, though he did not abolish the "military colonies." He called into his service some of the ablest men to be found in Russia and took into his own hands far more state business than any emperor had been accustomed to bother with. This required expansion of his personal chancellery; in the first year of his reign he added to it a "second section," under Speransky, charged with the task of codifying the law, and a "third section," which was officially intended

> to take care lest the peace and the rights of citizens be violated by any authority of an individual or by the dominance of powerful persons or by the pernicious aims of evil-minded men.[3]

Subsequently, other sections were added, of which only the "fourth section," inheriting the eleemosynary interests of his deceased mother, became permanent.

Above all, Nicholas set up, under the chairmanship of one of Alexander's "young friends," the erstwhile "Jacobin" Prince Kochubei, a secret committee to study the bases of the state organization. This "committee of December 6, 1826" drafted sweeping proposals for reorganization both of governmental institutions and of class relationships, but the outbreak of revolution in France in July, 1830, so frightened Nicholas that no major reforms were actually instituted.

The "third section" of the Imperial chancellery acquired an evil reputation as the successor of the political police institutions which had existed under so many earlier rulers. Russia remained "frozen," and the quest for subversive thinkers was vigorously pursued. Chaadaev (1794-1856), a nobleman and war hero who had been associated with the Decembrists but had been abroad in December, 1825, was officially declared insane and forbidden to write after publication in 1836 of the first of his *Philosophical Letters,* in which he had taken sharp issue with the ideological slogans of the autocracy. The "Petrashevtsy," a group of young men who after 1845 met in the home of an admirer of the Utopian Socialist Fourier to discuss a variety of intellectual problems, were in 1849 sentenced to execution; the sentence was commuted, when they were already on the scaffold, to exile at hard labor; among those subjected to this experience, deliberately designed "to frighten them," was the twenty-eight-year-old Dostoevsky. Innumerable other literary men were arrested, especially after 1848, that flaming year of revolution in Western Europe; among them was Turgenev, detained in a police station in 1852 for an obituary notice of Gogol. The spirit of the repressive regime is perhaps best expressed in Masaryk's anecdote of the two Jews condemned to death by a military court at Odessa in 1837 for violating quarantine regulations during an outbreak of plague:

> Nicholas commuted the death penalty as follows: "The convicts are to run the gauntlet—a thousand men—twelve times. God be thanked, with us the death penalty has been abolished, and I will not reintroduce it." [4]

Toward the Jews as an entity, Nicholas' attitude was much like that of his brother Alexander, though without the latter's "liberal" ruthlessness. In 1827, Nicholas extended to the Jews the obligation of military service, from which they had previously been excluded; since the well-to-do were permitted to buy substitutes, the burden rested only on the impoverished Jewish masses. Nicholas fitfully continued the policy of Alexander—initiated in 1804, formally abandoned in 1812, but resumed in 1823—of expelling Jews from rural areas in the Pale into the towns; in inducing Jews to become agriculturists, he had no more success than his brother had achieved. A new "Statute Concerning the Jews" (1835) similarly failed to achieve assimilation; baffled by their "religious fanaticism and separatism," Nicholas took the drastic step of abolishing the *kahals* (1844), save as a fiscal agency of the government. Subsequent ridiculous efforts to promote assimilation by inspecting Jewish brides to see if they had shaved their heads or by forcibly cutting off earlocks and shortening the long coats of men had of course no useful effect. Nor did the government know how to make use of tendencies beginning to stir within the narrow confines of Jewish orthodoxy: Max Lilienthal, a German-born Jew who attempted to coöperate with Uvarov, abandoned the effort and left for America; Isaac Baer Levinsohn (1788-1860), "the Russian [Moses] Mendelssohn," failed to impress his fellow-Jews by his appeals for a more tolerant attitude toward an alien government, which, for that matter, was becoming constantly more alien in the eyes of all its subjects.

Yet Nicolaitan Russia had another aspect. Speransky did succeed in the task that had defeated Peter, Catherine, and Alexander alike. In 1833 was published the *Full Collection of the Laws of the Russian Empire,* arranged in chronological order from the *Ulozhenie* of 1649 to the accession of Nicholas, in forty-five big volumes. From this mass Speransky excerpted and arranged in systematic order, in fifteen volumes, a *Digest of the Laws of the Russian Empire.* His work not merely classified and systematized then existing law but provided a basis for maintaining orderly knowledge of later changes. Similarly, Kankrin, as Minister of Finance, succeeded in bringing the finances out of chaos, eliminating the "assignats" with their wildly fluctuating course and substituting a sound paper money with a stable relationship to the metallic currency.

The "peasant question" was assiduously studied by a series of secret committees. In this matter, Nicholas relied mainly on the advice of General Kiselev, who, as Chief of Staff of the Southern Army, had been on friendly terms with Pestel and other Decembrists, though he had cleared himself to Nicholas' entire satisfaction of any suspicion of active involvement in the conspiracy. In 1837 Nicholas created for him the office of Minister of State Domains. Kiselev established for the state peasants an autonomous communal structure, which later served as a model at the time of general emancipation; though they remained serfs of the state, the fiscal peasants elected their own headmen and elders and were given agronomical assistance and advice.

So far as "landowners' peasants" were concerned, negligible progress was made: an edict prohibited the sale of peasants without their wives and minor children; another forbade purchase of peasants without land or sale of land without peasants unless the transaction would leave the owner in possession of a defined acreage for each peasant he owned; landowners were authorized to emancipate peasants, provided they were assigned hereditary land allotments in return for which they must discharge fixed economic obligations (1842). But all such laws, however benevolent the intention they evinced, remained dead letters.

In 1847, Bibikov, Governor-General of Kiev and a disciple of General Kiselev, was permitted to prescribe the minimum land allotment owners must make to their peasants and the maximum of obligations they could exact; these "Inventory Regulations," reminiscent of Maslov's proposals in 1734, applied only to Kiev, Volhynia, and Podolia. A later attempt (1852) by Bibikov, who had become Minister of the Interior, to apply similar regulations to Lithuania and White Russia, though approved by Nicholas, was blocked by the vigorous opposition of his son and heir, soon to be Emperor Alexander II.

The dual character of the Nicolaitan regime was most clearly displayed in the field of education, which from 1833 to 1849 was directed by Count Uvarov. In earlier days, Uvarov had spoken of political freedom as "the latest fair gift of a god" and had criticized those who wished to make education "a fire which should not scald." Now, as Minister of Education under Nicholas, Uvarov formulated the famous slogan "Orthodoxy, Autocracy, Nationality" as the summary of the basic principles on which to build the educational system. Much was done for the extension and improvement of specialized military and technical instruction. The number of classical gymnasia also was much increased; their student enrollment rose from seven thousand in 1825 to eighteen thousand in 1855. Every effort was made to limit attendance to the sons of nobles and officials, but it proved impossible to keep out a flood of *raznochintsy* (those who had been freed from membership in the "tributary orders" without attaining noble rank), described as "hovering 'twixt heaven and hell." The result was a rather abrupt change in the character of the intelligentsia, formerly made up almost exclusively of nobles.

Despite Uvarov's conservatism, the universities, under his regulations of 1835, enjoyed substantial autonomy. The shock of the Western revolutions of 1848-49, however, brought a number of repressive measures: the teaching of some subjects, such as philosophy, was forbidden; a halt was put to foreign study for aspirants to professorships; the number of students in any university was restricted to three hundred; and all students were subjected to military training and discipline. Uvarov himself was dismissed in favor of Shikhmatov, popularly known as "Shakhmatov" (Checkmate). Against the new intelligentsia, largely brought into being by his own educational reforms, Nicholas waged ceaseless and bitter war.

THE INTELLECTUALS

The intellectuals, for their part, replied with a negatively hostile attitude, refusing to believe in the sincerity of the autocracy's desire for reform. The situation was complicated by the dominance in the West of German philosophy, and especially of the ideas of Schelling and Hegel. Particularly fascinating to Russian students was the idea that man had gone through a sort of evolution in the realm of ideas, and that certain nations—such as Babylonia, Egypt, Greece, and Rome—had been fated to play special historic roles, successively dominating the world in order to fulfill their historic mission of transmitting the ideas they embodied to all mankind. Slavs could not, of course, accept Hegel's conclusion that this process had reached its ultimate stage in the rise of Protestant German *Kultur,* but the effort to prove that Slavdom also had a contribution yet to make ran into baffling difficulties.

Some Russian thinkers, ill-informed about Russia's history, jumped to the conclusion that Russia had had only a dark Asiatic past until Peter the Great had pointed the way to Westernization, to enlightenment. For these "Westerners," therefore, the task was to press on the work of Peter. Condemning the backwardness of contemporary Russia, they advocated sweeping reform and thus were driven to criticize the cautious, seemingly immobile, autocracy.

An opposite school of thought, likewise accepting Hegelian principles but not Hegel's application of them, reacted against the notion that Russia should follow the road already traveled by the West, that vast cemetery where beneath marble monuments slept the spirits of the departed great. These "Slavophiles" felt no need of the road to a cemetery: they were convinced that there must be in Russia's dark past, however difficult to unearth, some ideal principle the nurturing of which would put Russia in the forefront of world development. They believed in orthodoxy, autocracy, and nationalism, but not at all in the bureaucratic sense of the Uvarov formula. They, too, like the "Westerners," displayed a severely critical attitude toward the regime, and they, too, were subjected to repression and even persecution. In the days of the great intellectual controversy between Slavophiles and Westerners, coöperation between either wing of the intellectuals and the government was unthinkable. Yet their attitude of opposition did not go so far as to qualify them for the epithet of revolutionaries. They were not the heirs of the Decembrists.

Russian literature is more deeply indebted to the Decembrists than was Russian political or social thought. It is true that the beginnings of the greatness of Russian poetry, of Russian drama, and of Russian prose long antedate the Decembrists. The first significant figure in Russian literature, Michael V. Lomonosov (1711-65), was born in the reign of Peter the Great. The son of a peasant-fisherman, he entered the Slav-Greek-Latin Academy at Moscow in 1730 and was sent to German universities for further study; in 1741 he was appointed to the staff of the Academy of Sciences, which he dominated after 1758. Like so many outstanding figures in the eighteenth-century West, his fame rests both on his contributions to physical chemistry and on his work in the world of letters. In this latter field, he was chiefly distinguished by his work in standardizing and enriching the Russian literary language, as distinct from the Old Church Slavonic from which it was confusedly emerging. His contemporaries hailed him as "the Russian Pindar" for his odes to Peter the Great and the Empress Elizabeth.

The reigns of Catherine II and Alexander I had produced also the poet Derzhavin (1743-1816), the playwright Fonvizin (1745-92), the historian Karamzin (1766-1826), and the fabulist Krylov (1769-1844), all but the last of whom were of noble origin.

The great age of Russian letters, however, was ushered in by Alexander S. Pushkin (1799-1837). Pushkin was proud of the fact that he came of an old and prominent *dvorianin* family. He was no less proud of the fact that his mother was a granddaughter of Ibrahim, an Ethiopian slave presented when a child to Peter the Great; his first effort to write a novel was therefore *The Negro of Peter the Great,* begun in 1828 but never finished. His family life was unhappy, and for years the young aristocrat lived in dissolute idleness. A chance approving reference to atheism sent him into exile on his mother's estate in the provinces (1824), thus saving him from active participation in the Decembrist uprising. Though Pushkin did not deny his revolutionary sympathies, Nicholas granted him a full pardon; the penalty he had to pay was the subsequent stifling "protection" extended to him by the emperor, from which he escaped only by death in a duel over his too-beautiful wife.

Of Pushkin's voluminous poetic output, the most outstanding was his "novel in verse," *Eugen Onegin* (begun in 1823, finished in 1831), sometimes unfairly compared to Byron's *Don Juan;* it was to have a profound influence on later Russian writers, notably Lermontov, Goncharov, and Turgenev, and, in a negative sense, Dostoevsky. Perhaps even more deserving of fame was his *Bronze Horseman* (1833). His first and perhaps best-known play, *Boris Godunov* (1825), was less happy; much of its fame is due to Mussorgsky's music. Though best known as a poet, Pushkin in his later period proved himself the first master of Russian prose; *The Captain's Daughter* (1836), dealing with the Pugachev uprising, and especially *The Queen of Spades* (*Pikovaia Dama,* 1834) were in themselves enough to make the reputation of any writer.

Among his literary contemporaries were two other Decembrists. One was K. F. Ryleiev (1795-1826), hanged for his active share in the revolt. The other was Alexander S. Griboyedov (1795-1829); narrowly escaping punishment, he soon gave his life on a mission for the emperor to the shah of Persia. Thus were cut short the witty comedies which, despite official opposition, circulated widely among the Russian intelligentsia.

Pushkin's successor as the leading Russian poet was Michael I. Lermontov (1814-41). A nobleman and a cavalry officer, Lermontov was frequently in trouble with the authorities before the duel that cut short his life. In his youth he modeled himself on Byron; cured of this pose by his life in cadet school, he developed in his later poems a blend of romanticism and realism that approached the level of Pushkin. Like Pushkin, Lermontov was also a distinguished prose writer; his *Hero of Our Times* (1840) has been regarded as anticipating—even as surpassing—Leo Tolstoy's *War and Peace.*

The most important writer in "frozen Russia" was, however, Nicholas V. Gogol (1809-52), of an upper-class cossack family. A failure as a professor of history at St. Petersburg (1834-35), he achieved his first major success with *The Inspector General* (1836), a satiric comedy which delighted Emperor Nicholas. During the next twelve years, most of which he spent in Rome, Gogol completed his masterpiece, *Dead Souls,* published at Moscow in 1842. His subsequent work, suffused with a dull religiosity, suggests that Nicholas was more right in regarding Gogol's writings as "self-criticism" than were those who hailed him as a supreme social satirist. Nonetheless, the public effect of Gogol's masterly comedies was such that Turgenev was punished for writing a laudatory obituary notice of him.

Notwithstanding the repressive attitude of Nicholas' regime toward any manifestations of political or social criticism, his reign witnessed the rise of the great Russian novelists, whose work reached its fullest flower under the reign of his son Alexander II. Fedor M. Dostoevsky (1821-81), son of a Ukrainian doctor in Moscow, was at first hailed by the radical "Western" intelligentsia as a "new Gogol." He already exhibited the morbid tendencies which, enhanced by his experience on the scaffold in 1849 and by his four years in a Siberian convict prison, were nevertheless later to be sublimated in *Crime and Punishment* (1866), *The Idiot* (1868), and *The Brothers Karamazov* (1880); always intensely subjective, fascinated by "proud women," the young Dostoevsky had not yet developed the essentially hopeless and reactionary spirit that infused his greatest works.

More characteristic was Ivan A. Goncharov (1812-91), whose *Oblomov,* with its heavy-handed satire of the slothfulness of provincial nobility, was to be one of Lenin's favorites; although not completed until 1859, the ideas were clearly outlined in 1849.

From the standpoint of influence on the thinking of his contemporaries, as well as from the viewpoint of style, the most important of the Russian novelists was Ivan S. Turgenev (1818-83), son of a poor noble serf-owner and of his unloved and domineering wealthy wife. As a student, Turgenev had some personal contacts with Pushkin, of whom he was to be the truest successor in Russian literature (especially in his delineation of women). Always moderate and objective, his writings had an enormous impact; of chief importance in his early work was *A Sportsman's Sketches* (1847-51), which exposed, far more effectively than had the bitterness of Radishchev half a century earlier (or than the melodrama of *Uncle Tom's Cabin,* publication of which was prohibited in Russia), the shocking injustices of serfdom. His other major works of social significance—*Rudin* (1856) and *Fathers and Sons* (1862)—belong to the early years of the reign of Nicholas' successor.

Few of Russia's great writers can be regarded as revolutionaries. Men of revolutionary bent turned to journalism rather than to literature. Tightly bridled in the reign of Nicholas I, the protest of the intelligentsia broke loose only in the era of reform ushered in by Emancipation in the next reign. Thus, the revolutionary movement, to be discussed in a later chapter, was the product rather than the cause of change in Russia.

In every Museum of the Revolution in the Soviet Union, the Decembrists are given the place of honor as the first Russian revolutionaries. In point of fact, the Decembrists in some ways represented a mere continuation of the palace revolutions of the eighteenth century, which had depended on succession to the throne and had been carried out by military action of the nobility, without popular participation. On the other hand, eighteenth-century palace revolutions had not been preceded, as had the Decembrist revolt of 1825, by any intellectual weighing of the sort of regime that was to result from the coup d'état. Cloudy and confused as were the ideas of the Decembrists, they do merit the honor of being the first revolutionaries in Russian history seriously to consider changes in the Russian socio-political structure. Essentially conservative in their "liberalism," the surviving Decembrists from their Siberian exile sent to Nicholas sincere protests against the ideas of a subsequent generation of revolutionaries. The Decembrists nevertheless had dreamed of a really new sort of society in their beloved Russia.

Emperor Nicholas I was not wrong in the conclusions he drew from the Decembrist episode. Stupid as he personally was, his advisers could not fail to see that the foundations of the autocracy were in danger. The emperor might be hesitant to change anything, but it had been made clear to thinking statesmen—and they existed even in the midst of the grafting bureaucracy—that Russia could not continue on the basis of serfdom, that codification of the laws was imperative, and that any further attempt passively to rest autocratic power on the supremacy of a privileged nobility was doomed to disaster.

Granted that the rebellious Decembrists had been only a small minority among a slave-minded nobility, it was clear enough that the privileged landowning nobility, so far as it permitted itself to think, would no longer be content with the rule of an arbitrary and capricious master. If the nobles were not to be permitted to take power into their own hands, the autocracy must find a new point of support. In this sense, the reign of Alexander I—and that of Nicholas I—were a continuation of the new course foreshadowed in the reign of the "mad" Paul.

NOTES

1. Martens, *Sobranie Traktatov i Konventsii* . . . , IV, i, 4-7 *passim*.
2. *Polnoe sobranie zakonov* . . . (First collection), No. 27,106 (October 24, 1817), XXXIV, 814.
3. Adjutant-General Benckendorff's instructions to an official of the Third Section, by direction of Emperor Nicholas, in *Russkii Arkhiv*, No. 7 (1889), p. 396.
4. Masaryk, *The Spirit of Russia*, I, 107.

SUGGESTIONS FOR FURTHER READING

Among works previously mentioned, those of the greatest value for this period are Kornilov's *Modern Russian History*, Pushkarev's *Emergence of Modern Russia*, Masaryk's *Spirit of Russia*, Dubnow's *History of the Jews of Russia and Poland*, and Mirsky's *History of Russian Literature*.

Nechkina's *Russia in the Nineteenth Century* is a Soviet high-school text available in English translation. Lobanov-Rostovsky's *Russia and Europe, 1789-1825* is helpful for international relations. Baddeley's *Russian Conquest of the Caucasus* is a specialized study extending into a later period.

The most extensive study is Schiemann's *Geschichte Ruszlands unter Kaiser Nikolaus I*, on which the now somewhat outmoded conventional picture is largely based. Mazour's *The First Russian Revolution* is an early study of the Decembrists. Raeff's *The Decembrist Movement* makes excellent use of documents. Four excellent studies of aspects of Nicholas' reign are: Monas, *The Third Section*; Riasanovsky, *Nicholas I and Official Nationalism*; Curtiss, *Russian Army under Nicholas I*; and McGrew, *Russia and the Cholera*. For the "Slavophiles," see especially Riasanovsky, *Russia and the West in the Teaching of the Slavophiles*, and Christoff, *Introduction to Nineteenth-Century Slavophilism* (Vol. I, A. S. Xomjakov). Hans' *History of Russian Educational Policy, 1701-1917* and *Russian Tradition in Education* contain some material of value for this and other chapters. An additional study of Russian letters is Slonim's *Epic of Russian Literature* . . . ; Wiener's *Anthology of Russian Literature* is also convenient.

Chapter

16

Forces of Change: 1750-1856

The most revolutionary force in nineteenth-century Russia was not the romantic effort of the Decembrists nor yet the more orderly thinking of their successors, but the growing strength of capitalist industry, to which the continuation of serfdom was anathema.

GROWTH OF INDUSTRY

Large-scale industry had had its small beginnings in the seventeenth century; under Peter's pressure it had had an apparent rapid flowering. Peter's "factories," however, had not been capitalist enterprises, motivated by rational calculation of the possibility of profit and exploiting free wage labor. Peter had been interested in promoting the production in Russia of the industrial goods needed by the state; therefore he had sought to induce or force merchants to invest their capital, accumulated by trade, in iron mines, ironworks, arms factories, or woolen, linen, and canvas mills. Sometimes he had granted direct subsidies; more generally he had guaranteed a market for their products, had exempted both the owners and their workers from all forms of fiscal and military obligation to the state, and had placed them under a special jurisdiction designed to foster their administrative interests. The greatest problem had been the provision of an adequate labor supply; since free wage labor was scarce, Peter had resorted to assignment to the factories of bondage labor and had permitted factory-owners to buy villages for their enterprises and even to retain fugitive peasants in their service.

Under Peter's successors, the "hothouse" aspects of Petrine policy had been largely abandoned, and in the eighteenth century large-scale industry had slowly increased in volume without special assistance from the state. Yet the prevalence of the employment of compulsory labor continued to keep it inefficient and to block progress in technique. The state, alarmed by the poor quality of the goods supplied to it by Russian factories, made sporadic and ineffective attempts to regulate working conditions in them; such was the official limitation of the working day to fourteen hours (1740).

More importantly, the rising influence of the nobility had made itself felt in restrictions placed on non-noble factory-owners. In 1736, Anna had decreed that all skilled wageworkers then in the factories were to be permanently bound, together with their dependents, to their enterprises; the factory-owner had only to pay compensation to the former owner of any fugitives among them; at the same time, however, the non-noble factory-owner temporarily lost his treasured right to buy additional peasant villages. Under Elizabeth the number of peasants a factory-owner might acquire was made dependent on the number of looms or other items of capital equipment he possessed (1752). Under Peter III the non-noble factory-owner was forbidden to buy any peasants, with or without land, and Catherine II promptly confirmed the nobles' monopoly (1762).

The consequences were twofold. On the one hand, nobles, who alone possessed an inexhaustible supply of bondage labor, began to set up factories of their own in competition with the older merchant-owned enterprises. As far as available statistics go, it appears that by 1773 almost one-third of all factories, including one-half of the cloth factories, belonged to nobles; by the beginning of the nineteenth century, out of ninety-eight cloth factories supplying goods to the government, seventy-four belonged to nobles and only twelve to merchants. The other consequence was a sharp increase in the proportion of hired workers employed in merchant factories; increasing numbers of peasants, abandoning agriculture to their womenfolk, secured permission to spend the summer in the towns in all sorts of industrial operations. One German observer compared the phenomenon to the annual migration of birds. This development was closely connected with the growing incidence of *obrok* (dues) in place of *barshchina* (obligatory labor) in the central provinces of Russia. According to Semevsky, at the end of the eighteenth century 74 percent of the peasants in the Great Russian "black-soil" provinces owed *barshchina,* but in the non-black-soil provinces the figure was only 45 percent. For the serf-owner in this area it was increasingly advantageous to transfer his peasants to an *obrok* basis and let them earn the money they must pay him in some sort of industrial employment.

The increasing employment of free hired workers was particularly marked in newer branches of industry, such as the printing of cotton cloth, which arose, not to serve the needs of the state, but to sell to private consumers. The cotton industry, established in Russia toward the close of the eighteenth century, grew with special rapidity throughout the first half of the nineteenth century. It owed nothing to government protection, not even to the widely oscillating tariff policy. Spinning, to be sure, could not compete with the cheap product of ever-improving machinery in England, but weaving and printing made rapid headway. Genuinely capitalistic, as Petrine and most eighteenth-century industry in Russia had not been, the cotton industry almost wholly dispensed with compulsory labor. It could not, of course, do without the labor of the serfs, but, while obligated to their owners, these serf laborers were, in relation to their industrial employers, free wageworkers.

According to the calculations of Tugan-Baranovsky, the leading student of economics in the last decades of tsarist Russia, the number of "free" workers in all branches of Russian industry (excluding mines and ironworks) was, even as early as 1804, 48 percent of the total employed; by 1825, it had reached 54 percent and apparently rose more sharply thereafter. The distribution of such "free" workers was, however, very uneven in different branches. In the old woolen industry, free workers were in 1804 less than 10 percent of the total, in linen manufacture a little over 50 percent, in cotton over 80 percent. By 1825, these percentages had risen to 18, 61, and 95, respectively.

This phenomenon was largely the consequence of a development which at first sight might seem contradictory. The newer industries, with their relatively simple technique, overflowed easily from factories into peasant homes. Especially in consequence of the difficulties in securing labor for factories, their owners resorted widely to the practice of "putting-out" work to be done by peasants. The first half of the nineteenth century therefore witnessed a rapid increase in "independent" household (*kustarny*) industry. Among many villages affected by this development was Ivanovo-Voznesensk, a village not far from Moscow, owned together with all its inhabitants by Count Sheremetev; it became such an outstanding center of the cotton industry as to acquire the sobriquet of the "Russian Manchester."

Among these *kustarny* workers emerged a number of men who subordinated their fellow-workers and made fortunes for themselves. Personally serfs, and therefore legally owning nothing, they were such important sources of revenue to their owners that they were given a free hand in their operations. In some cases, these new capitalists were able to ransom themselves from their owners and attain rank as free merchants. A notable early instance was that of Savva Morozov, a privately owned serf who in 1797 founded a small ribbon factory, which he later expanded, producing nankeen as well as silk; in 1820, he purchased freedom for himself and his family at the price of 17,000 rubles; his descendants were to be the most prominent industrial capitalists in Russia in the late nineteenth century. In many cases, however, such peasant capitalists were unable to achieve personal freedom, even though they might be able to bequeath whole villages of serfs to their children. At Ivanovo, according to Tugan-Baranovsky, prior to Emancipation, only fifty peasant families were permitted to redeem themselves, and at an average price of 20,000 rubles. Similar conditions were observable in other industries, notably in the production of cutlery and other ironwares for the open market.

In older industries, whose market was still largely guaranteed by the needs of the state and in which the size of the enterprises was greatest, compulsory labor continued to predominate. The largest part of this bondage industry rested on direct employment by nobles of the obligatory labor (*barshchina*) of their own serfs, often without payment of any money wages. A substantial portion, however, particularly in the manufacture of woolen and linen cloth and of iron, was still supplied by the "possessional peasants," bound to the factories, not to their owners.

In view of the near-monopoly of serf ownership by the nobles, "possessional" peasants had been a necessary adjunct of most merchant factories in the eighteenth century. In the nineteenth century, however, in the face of the growing competition of more efficient "free" hired labor, the "possessional" peasants became increasingly a burden to the owners of the factories to which they were ascribed. As government property, the conditions of their employment were circumscribed by the government as those of freely hired workers were not. While the wages of "free" labor fluctuated with conditions of supply and demand, those of "possessional" peasants were fixed by law; nor was the employer legally free to dismiss "possessional" peasants in hard times. No alteration in the method of manufacture in "possessional" factories could be made without government permission.

Factory-owners began to bombard the government with petitions to release them from these conditions. The government, as usual, responded slowly and cautiously. In 1824, owners of possessional factories were authorized to release their workers provided they secured the specific sanction of the government. In 1835, they were permitted, subject to certain conditions, to give leave of absence to superfluous workers. Finally, by an edict of 1840, it was left to the free choice of the owner of an operating possessional factory to emancipate his workers. If the owner had originally paid for the "revision-soul," he was to receive 36 silver rubles from the government; if the worker had been ascribed to the factory gratis, the owner received no compensation. The emancipated worker might choose to be enrolled either as a "burgher" or as a state peasant; in the latter case, he was to be given by the factory-owner 50 paper rubles (20 for females), plus 20 paper rubles to cover the cost of resettlement. Apparently, only a minority of the workers thus set free chose to become state peasants, partly because they had become unaccustomed to agricultural pursuits, partly because they would have to accept any place of residence, even in western Siberia, that the government might assign them.

In consequence of these laws, it has been estimated, more than half the "possessional" peasants were released from bondage before Emancipation in 1861. Statistics are not available to indicate with any precision what happened to the landowners' serfs compelled to work in factories, but there seems every reason to accept Tugan-Baranovsky's thesis that, especially with the rapid introduction of imported machinery from the 1840's, "the first half of the nineteenth century was characterized by the growth of industrial capitalism and by the conversion of the former bondage factory into a capitalistic one." [1] In their official statements of reasons for availing themselves of the law of 1840, factory-owners rang the changes on the same themes: the relative inefficiency of compulsory labor, the introduction of machinery, the general change in the structure and character of industrial enterprises. A contributing factor may also have been the frequent disturbances that characterized the bondage factories, and particularly the "possessional" factories.

The progress of new industries was largely counterbalanced by the decline or slow growth of old ones. In particular, the introduction of cotton goods caused a serious fall in the prices of linen; the Russian linen industry had depended very largely on the export market and in the nineteenth century suffered heavily in consequence of the general cheapening of textile production abroad. Inability to compete on the Russian market with cheaper cotton goods resulted in grave crisis and the ruin of most linen factories. The manufacture of woolen cloth, needed in large quantities by the Russian armies, had been carefully nurtured by the government but, stifled by regulation, had made little or no progress until removal of restrictions on free public sale in 1816. Thereafter the industry began to thrive and by 1822 was for the first time able to meet government demand. However, failure to make technological progress exposed it to successful competition by household (*kustarny*) industry, and in the late 1840's the number of factories and of factory-workers showed decline.

Most striking were the vicissitudes of the iron industry, then concentrated in the Urals and almost wholly dependent on serf labor. At the end of the eighteenth century, Russia had been producing about the same amount of pig iron as Great Britain. As late as the 1830's, Russia still produced about 12 percent of the world's total, but by 1859 this figure had fallen to 4 percent. In absolute terms, Russian production by the eve of Emancipation had about doubled as against the end of the eighteenth century, while British production had increased almost thirty-fold. The increasing relative economic backwardness of Russia was emphasized by the fact that in an age of rapidly expanding world trade her exports of manufactured or partly manufactured goods declined absolutely in value and, in relation to total Russian exports, dropped from 32 percent to 9 percent of their value.

It was therefore not in any direct sense that the growth of industrial capitalism led to the revolutionary decision to emancipate the peasantry. The total weight of industry in the economy of Russia was still too small, and the upstart capitalist manufacturers were of too little social and political consequence, for the needs of industry to sway the government in any major sense.

If the "golden age of the nobility" had ended with the death of Catherine "the Great," the nobility still remained the ruling class in Russia, and its interests, real or imagined, were still ultimately decisive.

THE QUESTION OF EMANCIPATION

In this upper realm, however, conclusions were increasingly being drawn similar to those so vigorously urged by the manufacturers. In the 1820's and 1830's, many noble landlords were caught up by a wave of enthusiasm for "English" farming. It was hoped that by spreading knowledge of advanced agricultural techniques and of improved implements, the noble could rent his estates to capitalist farmers, thus simultaneously increasing his income and his freedom from care. There was, however, the difficulty that the Russian peasant neither showed the inclination nor possessed the capital necessary to become an "English" farmer. Nor did the Prussian type of estate-management by a capitalist landlord, the development of which was much stimulated by the emancipation of the serfs in Prussia, hold hope of solution for the difficulties of Russian agriculture; the Russian noble generally possessed neither the capital nor the initiative to imitate the Prussian Junker. The development of "industrial" crops, notably sugar beets, did make some headway, but only in areas such as New Russia, where the percentage of serfs was relatively small and where there was a considerable population of immigrants, mainly Germans. On the whole, the disillusioned Russian landlord fell back on expanding grain cultivation, despite the shockingly low yields attainable from inefficient serf labor.

Thinking noble landlords were therefore beginning to doubt the value of compulsory labor even in agriculture. This was particularly true of the black-soil provinces, where landlords were developing an interest in growing wheat for export to Western markets. In the absence of an adequate supply of free wage labor, the landlords of the agricultural zone necessarily clung to obligatory labor (*barshchina*). It was obvious that for any individual owner to emancipate his own serfs would not guarantee that he could induce them to work on a wage basis for him rather than for someone else; only in the event of general emancipation could any landlord count on a sufficient supply of wage laborers.

Action by any individual landlord was the more impracticable because the decree of 1803 forbade the emancipation by whole villages without land; in the highly fertile black-soil belt, the landlord was naturally anxious to recover from his peasants use of that part of the land which they cultivated for their own subsistence. The landlords of the agricultural zone therefore were beginning to be willing to contemplate general emancipation, even without compensation, so long as it was without land.

The situation was quite otherwise in the older central provinces, ill adapted for modern commercial agriculture. Here the serf-owner derived his revenue less from the land than from the industrial occupations of his peasants, whether in their own homes (*kustarny*) or in factories, and whether they worked by their own choice or on the basis of a contract the landowner made with a factory-owner. This circumstance accounted for the growing prevalence in this area of dues payment (*obrok*) in place of obligatory labor (*barshchina*), a growth particularly rapid from the closing decades of the eighteenth century. Here those landlords who thought favorably of emancipation did so in terms of emancipation with land but for compensation.

Two other considerations tending to breed sentiment in favor of emancipation were more general in character. One was the increasingly obvious fact that under serfdom the economy of the nobles was not prospering. It has been computed that by mid-century two-thirds of the privately owned serfs had been mortgaged, and that the consequent debts of their owners amounted to more than half the market value of the serfs they owned. The other consideration was the continuing restlessness of the serfs themselves, which kept alive memories of the Pugachev revolt. In this respect, however, there was no new factor in the situation, and one may doubt the real motive power of the sentiment expressed in the classic words of Alexander II, "better that this reform be effected from above than from below."

Had it not been for the growth among the ruling class of ideas favorable to emancipation, it seems highly improbable that the autocracy, rooted in the support of the landowning and serf-owning nobility, could ever have essayed emancipation of the peasantry. Yet the main force leading in this direction would seem to have been the growth—and still more the retardation—of capitalist industry. Industry, far more than the effects that the changing world economy was producing on Russian agriculture, was the chief dynamic factor in revolutionizing Russia. Capitalist industrialists might safely be ignored so long as it was only a question of their personal advantage, but in the new world conditions created by the so-called "Industrial Revolution," it was clear that no state could hope to rank as a great power unless it developed a viable industry. The interest of the Russian state—and therefore, at least indirectly, of its ruling class—demanded the growth of industry in Russia. The growth of industry, however, demanded an abundant supply of free labor and thus required the abolition of serfdom.

On the other hand, the growth of capitalist industry threatened the introduction into Holy Mother Russia of such social plague centers as Manchester or Lyons—or even Paris in the "June Days" of 1848. This might mean the development of new forms of social disorder which would leave peasant disturbances—even those led by Razin and Pugachev—in the shade. Nor could partisans of the autocracy be unaware that its historic roots lay, not in the activity of a bourgeoisie, but in the interests of a serf-owning nobility. To emancipate the serfs might also mean to emancipate the nobility from subservience to an autocracy that had begun to come into existence in the sixteenth century to serve the nobility. For the autocracy now to turn to promotion of the interests of a nascent bourgeoisie would in itself constitute a social revolution of major dimensions.

Thus, the arguments for and against state action in emancipation of the peasantry were so nicely balanced that it would have required a man of strong will to take the step. Nicholas I, who had ascended the throne in the shadow of the Decembrist revolt and of the consequently necessary executions and exiles of nobles to Siberia, was not such a man. Repeatedly appointing secret commissions to study the "peasant question," the Emperor consistently avoided any decisive steps. In consequence, Nicolaitan Russia acquired the name of "Frozen Russia." Only a severe external shock could break up the ice and set Old Russia swirling in a modern current.

THE CONCERT OF EUROPE *vs.* THE NEAR EASTERN QUESTION

The foreign policy of Russia in the first half of the nineteenth century was characterized by a not unnatural ambivalence. Unresolved problems of national interest, arising from earlier territorial gains, necessarily continued to drive her to further expansion. Nowhere is the truth of the saying, "The appetite grows with eating," more clearly exemplified than in Russia's relations with Turkey. Originally purely defensive, directed at checking the destructive raids of the Crimean Tatars, Russian policy and Russian arms had under Catherine given her a wholly defensible frontier, the northern shore line of the Black Sea. The natural sequel had been her "Greek project," designed to seat her grandson on the throne of a re-created Christian empire at Constantinople. Such futile dreams apart, the consolidation of Russian power over Little Russia and the acquisition of New Russia had laid the basis for a new national Russian interest. The possibility of growing wheat, and the mounting demand for wheat in the West, made control of the Straits, the narrow outlet from the Black Sea to the Mediterranean, of paramount importance to Russia. It was not sufficient to secure guarantees for peaceful commerce; in an uncertain world, in which "international law" remains a fiction, only military control of the essential passage could really satisfy Russian national interests.

Yet this Russian craving, natural though it might be, seemed to threaten to disturb the balance of the world. It was naturally regarded by the mistress of the seas as a special menace to her predominance. If Russia was determined to secure control of the Straits—the Bosporus and Dardanelles—Great Britain was no less determined to prevent it. Thus was brought into focus the dominant theme of nineteenth-century diplomacy, the "cold war" waged between Britain and Russia, in which Britain persistently pursued a policy of "containment" of any Russian expansion in any quarter which England could effectively reach. The quarrel had, of course, still wider implications. Britain had played the lion's role in destroying the power of France and in tumbling the European dictatorship of Napoleon, but this tremendous victory had not been attained single-handed. Much as Russia had owed to British subsidies, the fact remained that without the massed military might of Russia the Battle of Leipzig and the campaign around Paris in 1814 would have been impossible. There was no question that, next to Great Britain, Russia was the leading world power.

It was inevitable, then, that in the very moment of triumph there should develop a strong polarity between Great Britain and Russia. Inevitable is a word at which every historian shies, but it is the inevitability of specific events, not of general trends, that chiefly gives him pause. There was no reason to be surprised that, less than six months after the abdication of Napoleon, the victorious allies, led on opposite sides by Great Britain and by Russia, should be threatening each other with war over the Polish question. Temporary community of larger interests momentarily prevented open conflict. Though Alexander's mystically conceived "Holy Alliance" was sidetracked, the Concert of Europe found expression in the Quadruple (later Quintuple) Alliance.

Stronger than Russia's native expansionist tendencies was Russia's desire to preserve the status quo arrived at by the Treaty of Paris (1814) and by the Final Act of the Congress of Vienna (1815). Determined to preserve intact the existing regime in Russia itself, it had been only natural for Alexander I and, in large measure, for his brother Nicholas I, to wish to preserve also the existing international regime. This was the basis for Russia's role as "the gendarme of Europe," ready to stamp out anywhere any movement threatening the established order. From the standpoint of the Western liberal, then necessarily a revolutionary, the situation was not inaptly described by Herzen, a Russian exile who hated the Russian autocracy but fervently loved his native Russia. In 1851, from his precarious perch in Paris, he wrote of "this uncomfortable neighbor, who is making himself felt throughout Europe —here by bayonets, there by spies. The Russian government is reaching out to the Mediterranean Sea through its protection of the Ottoman Porte, to the Rhine through its protection of its German brothers-in-law and uncles, to the Atlantic Ocean through its protection of order in France." Herzen challenged "this universal protector," questioned "the negative role adopted by the Petersburg government, the role of an obstacle ceaselessly cropping up on the path of mankind." [2]

Underneath the ecumenical conservatism of the Russian government, however, lay the continuing pressure of specific Russian national interests, and it was this factor that caused the ambivalence of Russian policy. Early in 1821, Prince Ypsilanti, a Phanariot Greek whose father and grandfather had served the Turks as *hospodars* (governors) in Moldavia and Walachia and who himself was a Russian major-general, led a small band across the Russo-Turkish frontier and seized Jassy, the capital of Moldavia. His fantastic conduct there led to his prompt repudiation by Emperor Alexander. The hatred of the Rumanian nobles for their Greek oppressors also played into the hands of the Turks. Ypsilanti's enterprise fizzled out; by 1822 Turkish suzerainty was restored, local authority as *hospodars* being now vested in Rumanian nobles instead of Phanariot Greeks.

In the meantime, however, news of Ypsilanti's venture had touched off savage risings among the Greeks in Morea, the ancient Peloponnesus, whence the revolt spread to the other Greek provinces and to the islands, including Crete. Though the Turks replied with a ferocity that even exceeded that of the rebels, they could gain no decisive military advantage. Alexander I was sorely troubled by this outbreak. On the one hand was the temptation to go to the rescue of his strategically situated fellow Orthodox Christians; on the other, there was the conviction that revolt was inherently wrong. In his dilemma, he accepted the advice of Metternich to let the uprising burn itself out beyond the pale of civilization. It therefore remained for his less gifted successor Nicholas to drift into a war against the Turks which, though it aided the disruption of the Concert of Europe, had the advantage of serving Russian national interests.

At that time Egypt, though nominally part of the Turkish Empire, was actually a far more powerful state than was its suzerain. It was ruled by Mehemet Ali, a former Albanian tobacco-dealer who had, by an extensive system of monopolies, built up in Egypt a formidable sort of state socialism and, with the aid of French advisers, had modernized his army and his navy. A few months before the death of Alexander, Mehemet Ali had accepted the sultan's invitation to give aid against the Greeks in return for major territorial cessions by Turkey to Egypt. His son, Ibrahim, appointed pasha of the Morea, turned the tide decisively against the Greeks. Their defeats, however, forced them to agree on a single leader; in 1827, a national assembly elected as president Count Capo d'Istria, who had represented Russia at the Congress of Vienna in 1815. Shortly afterward, an Anglo-French-Russian demand for an immediate armistice led to a collision between their fleets and those of Turkey and Egypt in the bay of Navarino, in the Morea, at which the latter were completely destroyed.

In Great Britain, Navarino was officially described as an "untoward event," but Emperor Nicholas was no longer to be deterred. On April 26, 1828, Russia declared war on Turkey. Despite initial difficulties, a small Russian force crossed the Balkans and occupied Adrianople, while a more formidable army advanced from the Caucasus toward Trebizond. The Turks' power of resistance was by no means broken, and the Russians were weakened by an outbreak of plague. Nevertheless, by a successful bluff, the "Sublime Porte" was persuaded to accept the Treaty of Adrianople (September 14, 1829). Turkey lost little territorially, for Russia restored all her conquests in Europe and part of those in Asia. But in other ways she had to pay heavily: the independence of Greece, though severely truncated, was recognized; formal autonomy was conceded to Rumania and to Serbia; the Straits were declared open to Russian merchantmen and to those of other nations at peace with

Turkey; and the provisions of the treaty of Kuchuk-Kainardji relating to protection of the Christian subjects of Turkey were confirmed. In addition, Turkey was forced to agree to pay an indemnity far beyond her actual capacity.

Thus Russia, while implicitly sanctioning the right of revolution, had made great gains. Her chief waterfront, the Black Sea, had been made open to free commerce; she had acquired a virtual protectorate over the provinces of Moldavia and Walachia, which her troops continued to occupy and on which she imposed a form of constitution under which the powers of the Rumanian princes and boyars were nicely balanced to the advantage of their protector; she had confirmed her special interest in the Orthodox subjects of Turkey; and she had a means of extorting further concessions by offering to waive instalments of the indemnity.

Scarcely had Nicholas achieved this diplomatic triumph when his complacency suffered a rude shock because of the outbreak of revolutions in Christian Europe. The July Revolution of 1830 in France was speedily followed by the defeat of the Tories by the Whigs in England, by the revolt of the Belgians against the work of the Congress of Vienna, by disturbances in some of the smaller German and Italian states, and by Polish defiance of Russian rule. The established system of order, to the maintenance of which Russia was so deeply committed, seemed to be everywhere crumbling. Nicholas would have liked to act but, unable to induce even Austria or Prussia to coöperate, had ultimately to content himself with stubborn refusal to address Louis Philippe as "brother."

Only in Poland could Nicholas actively assert himself. The Polish aristocracy were willing to coöperate by upholding the tsar's authority as constitutional king, but Nicholas insisted on unconditional submission. Though outnumbered almost three to one, the Polish forces resisted gallantly for nearly a year. In the end, the constitution was replaced by the arbitrary authority of a viceroy, who maintained what was virtually a reign of terror. In addition, a Russian university at Kiev replaced the Polish university at Vilna (1834); heavy pressure was put on the Uniates to force their return to the Orthodox Church. In the Ukraine, the Magdeburg Law, which had given special privileges to the townsmen, was revoked; even the Lithuanian Statute lost its validity, though some of its special provisions were carried forward as Russian law, applicable only in two of the Ukrainian provinces. In 1835, the emperor himself issued a solemn oral warning to a delegation of Poles whom he received privately in Warsaw:

> If you obstinately cherish the dream of separate nationality, of an independent Poland, and all these chimeras, you will only bring great misfortunes on yourselves.[3]

Even Russian gains by the Treaty of Adrianople soon seemed endangered. Mehemet Ali of Egypt, encouraged by the new French regime, claimed Syria as a reward for his aid against the Greeks. In 1832, he forcibly seized the area and advanced into Asia Minor as far as Brusa, the ancient cradle of Ottoman power. The sultan, finding no support from either Great Britain or France, admitted a Russian fleet to the Bosporus; a Russian army was landed on the Asiatic shore ready to check the advancing army of Egypt.

The Western powers, more alarmed by the threat of Russian power in the Straits than by the gains of Mehemet Ali, successfully exerted diplomatic pressure on the sultan to confirm the loss of Syria and thus save Asia Minor. Yet Russia, though her troops had not engaged the Egyptian forces, was able to persuade the terrified sultan to accept the Treaty of Unkiar-Skelessi (1833); under its terms Russia promised military assistance to Turkey in any further emergency in return for the virtual control of passage of warships through the Dardanelles. By diplomacy rather than by war, Russia had at length secured the long-coveted position of protector, not merely of certain provinces or even of Orthodox subjects, but of the Ottoman Empire as a whole.

The solution was not long lasting. Ibrahim, governing Syria for his father and attempting to use his father's methods of monopolies and military conscription, speedily provoked revolt in the Lebanon (1834). Encouraged by a series of further revolts, the Turkish sultan made an attempt to recover Syria from Egypt (1839). His army was annihilated, and his fleet deserted to the enemy. A new sultan offered peace, but Great Britain was anxious to undermine the exclusive position of Russia at Constantinople; she therefore engineered a four-power demand by England, Austria, Prussia, and Russia that the Egyptians evacuate northern Syria, Crete, and the Moslem holy places in Arabia. Ignoring the threats of France, which supported Egypt, a British squadron, coöperating with the Lebanese mountaineers, took Beirut and Acre. Mehemet Ali was forced back into Egypt and stripped of his military and naval power.

THE SICK MAN OF EUROPE AND THE CRIMEAN WAR

Turkey had been saved by international action, and Russia had lost her protectorate. A new international Straits Convention (1841) closed the Bosporus and the Dardanelles to the warships of all foreign powers, including Russia, when Turkey was at peace. The Liberal Palmerston's diplomacy had driven Russia back to her earlier policy of destroying Turkey. In 1844, Nicholas revisited London; in earnest and frank conversations with the Conservative Lord Aberdeen, then Foreign Secretary, the Russian emperor began to develop the concept of "The Sick Man of Europe." Turkey's mortal illness was of such a pestilential nature that it was prudent to arrange the funeral in advance. Nicholas went so far as to draw up a memorandum covering what he understood to have been agreed on as representing the mutual interests of

England and Russia; he apparently felt that Aberdeen had committed the British ministry permanently to a policy of Anglo-Russian coöperation.

Once more the broader interests of Russian policy pushed aside her more specific interest in the Straits question. The revolutions of 1848 were far more serious and wider in scope than those of 1830 had been; this time the governments of Austria and Prussia were also involved. Although Russia remained internally unaffected, she could not venture to counter England's policy of assisting liberals wherever her maritime arm could reach. The shadow of Russian intervention, however, hung over the Frankfurt Assembly, contributing not a little to its failure to achieve German national unity by peaceful democratic action. In 1849, the Hungarian Republic was destroyed by a Russian army, and that country was handed back to the Hapsburgs.

In 1850, Russian threats deterred Prussia from risking war with a renascent Austria; Frederick William abandoned the idea of unifying Germany under Prussian leadership and at Olmütz accepted total humiliation. Though badly shaken, the European order seemed to be in process of reëstablishment. In Central Europe, the primacy of Austria had been restored, and within Austria, Schwarzenberg promised a reactionary policy more vigorous than that of Metternich. In France, the Second Republic was eliminated by the coup d'état of Louis Napoleon Bonaparte; if the new monarch was not one who could officially be called "brother," he was at least a monarch. In England, the bogy of Chartism had been definitely laid.

For Russia in 1852, the time seemed opportune to press her claims on Turkey. A quirk of British politics had forced the bellicose Palmerston out of the Foreign Office and had seated Lord Aberdeen as prime minister; Aberdeen was the president of an apparently powerful peace society and a longtime personal friend of Emperor Nicholas; the air at Westminster was full of the idea of international free trade and international peace, so vigorously urged by Cobden and Bright, and echoed by Russell, who was at the Foreign Office. Napoleon III, for purposes of the plebiscite which overwhelmingly ratified his assumption of the imperial title, had vigorously insisted "the Empire means peace." Austria was doubly indebted to Russia, and Prussia seemed innocuous.

It was small wonder that Nicholas thought the demise of Turkey was impending. To the British ambassador at St. Petersburg, the emperor remarked:

> We have on our hands a sick man—a very sick man; it will be, I tell you frankly, a great misfortune if, one of these days, he should slip away from us, especially before all necessary arrangements were made.[4]

Nicholas denied that he had any ambition to realize his grandmother's dream of reconstituting the Byzantine Empire, though he emphasized his duty toward his fellow-Christians under Turkish rule. Specifically, he suggested that the Serbs and Bulgars should be put under a regime similar to that already in effect for Moldavia and Walachia, that Egypt and Crete should be given to

Great Britain, and that Constantinople might be "temporarily" occupied by Russia. Great Britain did not take the bait but stood on the position that a sick man needs a physician, not a firm of undertakers. Unfortunately for Russia, Great Britain chose this moment to send back as her ambassador to the Porte Lord Stratford de Redcliffe (formerly Stratford Canning), an inveterate foe of Russian ambitions in the Near East and independent enough to ignore instructions from London.

Obstinately determined to take advantage of the apparently favorable international conjuncture, Russia had hoped to use a Turkish attack on Montenegro as a *casus belli* but was foiled by Austria's prompt and successful diplomatic intervention in Montenegro's behalf. Cheated of this pretext, the tsar sent Prince A. S. Menshikov, great-grandson of Peter's favorite, as a special envoy to Constantinople with a peremptory demand that a dispute between Roman Catholic and Greek Orthodox monks over the custody of the keys to the Holy Sepulcher be decided in favor of the latter. The envoy was charged also to offer Turkey military and naval protection against any Western power in return for a clarification of the Treaty of Kuchuk-Kainardji in Russia's favor. Although France, on the basis of a series of treaties dating back to 1535, supported the Latin Catholics, Stratford de Redcliffe was able to secure a mutually satisfactory solution of the narrower issue.

Russia, however, confident that she did not have to fear war with the West, persisted in pressing the broader question. Finding the Turks stubborn, Nicholas sent his troops to reoccupy Moldavia and Walachia (July 2, 1853). To his dismay, Great Britain and France promptly sent fleets to the Dardanelles. At the same time, in consultation with Austria and Prussia, they arrived at a formula, which Russia accepted, for solution of the difficulty. On the advice of the British ambassador, however, the Turks modified the formula in a way which Russia rejected. On October 22, 1853, the British fleet entered the Straits; the following day Turkey declared war on Russia.

Desultory fighting along the Danube was followed by the destruction of the Turkish fleet by the Russian at Sinope (November 30). Nicholas apparently still hoped for peace, an illusion strengthened by an ill-timed and effusive visit to St. Petersburg by a delegation of English Quakers. In both Great Britain and France, war fever rose quickly. On February 27, 1854, a British ultimatum, closely followed by a French one, demanded prompt promise that the Russians would evacuate the Danubian principalities by April 30; in the absence of a satisfactory reply, war was declared on March 28. A British squadron operated ineffectually in the Baltic, and British and French troops were sent to defend Constantinople. In the face of Austrian threats, the Russian troops were withdrawn during the summer, and the principalities were occupied by neutral Austrian troops. The avowed purpose of the war had been achieved without fighting. Yet it was now impossible to make peace without bloodshed and glory.

In September, 1854, some seventy thousand French, British, and Turkish troops were landed in the Crimea, intent on the siege of Sevastopol; there they were joined by a handful of Sardinians. The allies had had no experience of serious war for over a generation; they had no single commander-in-chief; they were besieging a fortress generally regarded as impregnable; their military blunders, including the famous "Charge of the Light Brigade," fully justified the remark "It's magnificent, but it is not war"; the crews of the wooden ships suffered horribly from the Russian explosive shells (a French invention, which, rather than the later battle between the *Monitor* and the *Merrimac,* led to the development of the armor-clad battleship). Storms and cholera took frightful toll; the logistical problems, difficult at best, were complicated by remarkable inefficiency and corruption; the deficiencies of the hospital service have made the name of Florence Nightingale renowned. The Russians had all the advantages of unitary command, of numerically superior forces available, and of fighting on their own soil. Yet, after protracted siege, during which Emperor Nicholas died, Sebastopol fell (September 9, 1855). Honor was satisfied, and on both sides, for the Russians took the fortress of Kars in Armenia (November 28).

An international Congress at Paris, early in 1856, arranged terms of peace. All conquests were restored, but Russia ceded a portion of Bessarabia, acquired in 1812, and relinquished control of the mouths of the Danube. Russian pretensions to any special role in Moldavia and Walachia were destroyed. The Black Sea was neutralized and demilitarized, save for minimal coastguard forces; the Straits Convention of 1841 was reaffirmed. For his part, the sultan promised religious freedom and civil rights to his Christian subjects. These terms proved to have but slight importance. The Black Sea clauses were repudiated by Russia in 1870, during the Franco-Prussian War, and Russia speedily resumed her pressure on Turkey.

The significance of the Crimean War lay not in the peace terms, but in the complete destruction of Russian hegemony over the Continent. Released from fear of Russian military intervention, the Western powers were free to embark on that series of wars among themselves which resulted in the political unification of Italy and Germany. Vastly more important were the internal consequences in Russia itself. That which the secret commissions of Nicholas I had failed to achieve was made manifestly necessary by the humiliating defeat of Russia at the hands of the West, operating at its lowest level of efficiency. The superiority of an industrial economy, the ingrained incompetence of a serf-ridden country, could no longer be denied.

NOTES

1. Tugan-Baranovskii, *Geschichte der russischen Fabrik,* p. 119.
2. Herzen, *Sobranie sochinenii v tridsati tomakh,* VII, 308.
3. There are several versions of the emperor's remarks; the one given here is

from *Journal de St. Petersbourg,* November 21 [December 3] 1835, published by order of Nicholas after it had appeared at Paris in *Journal des Débats* (November 11, 1835); cf. Ya. V. Fomin, *"Imperator Nikolai Pavlovich v Varshavie. 1835 g.,"* in *Russkaia starina . . . ,* VII (May, 1873), 676-690; cf. also D. V. Davydov, *"Riech' imperatora Nikolaia deputatam goroda Varshavy pri priemie ikh vo dvortsie Lazenki,"* in *loc. cit.,* VI (October, 1872), 391-393, and Baron F. A. Bühler, *"O napechatanii riechi imperatora Nikolaia Varshavskim deputatam. 1835 g.,"* in *loc. cit.* (December, 1872), 679-683. The account given in Schiemann, *Geschichte Ruszlands unter Kaiser Nikolaus I,* III, 277-278, is quite unreliable.

4. Official translation, as later submitted to Parliament, of dispatch dated January 11, 1853, from Sir G. H. Seymour, ambassador at St. Petersburg, to Lord John Russell, H. M. Secretary of State for Foreign Affairs, in *Accounts and Papers,* 1854, LXXI, 836. Temperley notes that in the actual dispatch, the phrase "sick man" does not occur; Seymour reported that Nicholas' remark was "the bear is dying."

SUGGESTIONS FOR FURTHER READING

Among books previously mentioned, the most valuable here is Robinson. Tugan-Baranovskii, though old, is still more valuable than Liashchenko (cf. p. 22 *supra*).

A general account of Russian foreign relations in this period may be found in Lobanov-Rostovsky, *Russia and Europe, 1825-1878.* A study of the hardening of English sentiment against Russia is Gleason's *Genesis of Russophobia in Great Britain.* Among many studies of the Near Eastern question, Moseley's *Russian Diplomacy and the Opening of the Near Eastern Question in 1838 and 1839,* Puryear's *France and the Levant,* and his *England, Russia, and the Straits Question* are most useful; Miller's *Ottoman Empire* is still serviceable for general background; a more detailed narrative of the whole problem, principally from the standpoint of Turkey and of the British Cabinet, is *The Crimea,* the first volume of Temperley's *England and the Near East.* Jelavich's *A Century of Russian Foriegn Policy, 1814-1914,* may also be consulted.

Leo Tolstoy's *Sevastopol Stories* were written while he was in service there during the siege.

Chapter

17

The Great Reforms: 1857-1875

The new emperor, Alexander II (1855-81), had given no promise of becoming "the Liberator." He had been carefully educated for his duties as the future ruler and had been entrusted with responsibility by his devoted father. As heir, he had exercised his influence to restrain Nicholas I from imposing even mild restrictions on the power of the nobles over their serfs. One of his first acts as emperor was to dismiss Bibikov, who in 1847 had imposed the "Inventory Regulations" in the Kiev area and who later as Minister of the Interior had attempted to extend them to the Lithuanian and White Russian provinces.

The radical intelligentsia hoped for little from him; the most they ventured to propose in the early months following his accession were promotion of education, relaxation (not abolition) of censorship, and railway construction. In Russia no publication presumed to raise openly the question of the abolition of serfdom; it was merely hinted at in terms of "a rational distribution of the economic forces." It was with pleased surprise that the opposition welcomed Alexander's cancellation of university restrictions imposed after 1848 and the grant of permission to travel abroad.

EMANCIPATION AND ITS SIGNIFICANCE

Yet Alexander understood very well the significance of Russia's defeat and, with whatever distaste, set resolutely about the task of finding a solution for the crippling burden of serfdom. His new Minister of the Interior, Lanskoy, was quite sympathetic to the general principle of emancipation but hesitated over the means. Immediate emancipation of the peasants without land —the method soon to be adopted for American slaves—would obviously have produced enormous disorders, perhaps another "Pugachevshchina"; unless the unthinkable idea of requiring payment for personal freedom were adopted, it would also have threatened the nobles of the central provinces with loss of the revenues earned by their serfs apart from cultivation of the land. Emancipation with land would require compensation to the landowners, and this, unless the burden could be placed on the peasants, must entail state expenditures on a scale seemingly impossible in view of the frightening disorder of the state finances caused by the war; especially in the "nonagricultural" provinces, it would be necessary to price the land to be transferred, not in terms of its intrinsic value, but in terms of the possibilities its holders had of earning money in industry.

In this dilemma, Alexander preferred to invite the views of the nobility, whose elected "marshals" assembled at Moscow in August, 1856, for the coronation. Even earlier, in March, 1856, in a speech to the local nobility of Moscow, Alexander had thrown out the famous propaganda warning "that serfdom cannot be continued forever, and that it would therefore be better that this reform be effected from above than from below." [1] It was not a new thought, but merely a pointed echo of a suggestion that Emperor Nicholas I, speaking "not as Sovereign, but as the first noble in the Empire," had made to the nobility of Smolensk in 1847:

> It would be better for us to give it up voluntarily than to permit that they [the peasants] take it away from us. Serfdom is the reason that we have no trade or industry.[2]

The nobles, however, declined to take the initiative; only a few submitted projects, and only as individuals. The emperor therefore had no recourse but to appoint, in January, 1857, still another secret committee. This committee, despite the urgings of the Ministry of the Interior, dragged its feet. Not until the end of the year did Alexander venture to order the nobles to set up in each province an elected committee to discuss the question. At the beginning of 1858, an imperial Rescript was published, announcing the August intention to emancipate the landowners' peasants on the basis of communal purchase of stated amounts of land. Critical as the nobles in general might be, there could no longer be any turning back. Once the intention to emancipate had been publicly announced, it remained only to choose the method.

The work of the local committees in 1858 brought out very clearly the sharp conflict of interests between the nobility of the central "non-agricultural" provinces, where the industrial earnings of the serfs were the chief source of their owners' income, and the nobility of the "black-soil" provinces, where the labor of the peasants on the land itself produced the revenue. The chief spokesman of the former, and therefore the chief critic of the solution indicated by the government, was Unkovsky, marshal of the nobility of Tver. His proposal was for immediate emancipation with land, and with compensation to the owner both for the land and for the person of the serf. Granted that it was unjust to expect the peasant to redeem his own person, he was to be required only to pay for the land; since, however, the original assignment to the noble of power over the labor-strength of the peasant had been made in the interests of the state, it was held to be just that the state, out of its general revenues, should now compensate the noble for the impending withdrawal from him of the right to exploit the labor of the peasant.

To counterbalance this idea, the government entrusted to Posen, an alleged liberal, formulation of a program which it hoped to persuade the provincial committees of the nobles to accept. Posen's program, expressing the interests of the black-soil landlords, proposed that, after a temporary obligatory period to ease the transition, the peasants should be given personal freedom without compensation and without land. Thus the landlord would recover at his own disposal the land formerly allotted to the peasants for their sustenance; able to hire the labor of landless peasants, he would receive his compensation in the increase of his commercial acreage. The answer of the Tver committee was a vigorous threat to resign and leave the work entirely to government officials.

Early in 1859, an "Editing Commission," divided into four sections, set to work. It was composed mainly of representatives of the ministries concerned, supplemented by "expert-members" whose work in the provincial committees of nobles had attracted favorable attention. The chairmanship was given to Rostovtsev, who in 1825 had given the first warning of the impending Decembrist rising and who had since become chief of the military schools; his appointment in 1857 as a member of the secret committee had provoked dismay among the advocates of reform, but he proved to be a serious and loyal servant of Alexander's purpose.

The guiding spirit, however, was N. A. Miliutin, an exceptionally able and energetic man, still only forty years of age but with a distinguished record of twenty-three years of service as an official in the Ministry of the Interior. Originally prominent because he was a nephew of Count Kiselev, whom Nicholas had called his "chief of staff for peasant affairs," Miliutin had proved his own worth. In 1857, he had almost been dismissed as a holder of radical political opinions but had been protected by powerful supporters, including the Minister and even the Chancellor, Prince Gorchakov. He now became Deputy Minister of the Interior and the soul of the new line taken by the government. To guide the work of the Editing Commission, both the original ideas of the Rescript of 1857 and the Posen program of 1858 were set aside; the new directions proposed emancipation with land, subject to government-assisted redemption, with a brief transition period, during which the peasants would pay the landlords a fixed *obrok* (money payment) for land temporarily assigned to them; *barshchina* (obligatory labor) was to be converted into *obrok;* the peasants, organized in communes, were to have autonomy.

The work of the Editing Commission required over a year and a half; its published records fill twenty-seven large volumes. The original chairman, Rostovtsev, died of overwork and was replaced by Count Panin, personally hostile to the reform but also a loyal servant of the emperor. Despite sharp conflicts, Miliutin was able to salvage the main features of the project. An important factor in the delay was that the nobles were permitted to send delegates to review the work in progress and to submit their criticisms.

The first such delegation represented chiefly the relatively non-agricultural provinces: most of its members accepted the general principle of emancipation with land, but they feared the consequences of permanent fixation of *obrok;* they also objected strenuously to the projected surrender of the nobles' administrative power over the peasants and sharply criticized the anticipated bureaucratic supervision of "autonomous" peasant-communes. Fortunately for the scheme under consideration, a high-ranking aristocrat who was not a member of the delegation gave personal offense to Alexander by the sharpness of his criticism of the existing bureaucratic system and by his demand that elective organs of the nobility should share in state authority. The second delegation, representing mainly black-soil provinces, had vainly hoped to swing Panin to their view favoring landless emancipation and with no provision for peasant autonomy. In the final stages of the struggle, the utmost that Miliutin's opponents could win was some downward revision of the size of land allotments and upward revision of the *obrok* in the black-soil areas, together with the promise, never realized, that the temporary *obroks* would be revised after twenty years.

In the Main Committee, to which the draft scheme was submitted in October, 1860, it proved exceedingly difficult to secure a majority. Only after two months of stubborn argument, and at the price of further reduction in the size of allotments, was the project endorsed. The draft was subjected to final review by the Council of State, the members of which were personally instructed by the emperor that "laying aside all personal interests, you should act as state officials invested with my confidence."[3] Only one significant change was made: the addition of a provision that by mutual agreement between peasants and landlord a "beggarly," "gratuitous" allotment, one-quarter of the normal size, might be transferred to the peasants without compensation. On February 19 (March 3 N.S.), 1861, Alexander celebrated the sixth anniversary of his accession by signing the necessary covering manifesto, which after appropriate military precautions had been taken, was published two weeks later (March 17).

The tsar had become the emancipator and, as events were to prove, had cut from under his feet the historic basis of the autocracy. Every precaution had been taken to protect the economic interests of the nobility, but the fact remained that they had been converted from "gratuitous chiefs of police" in the villages into state pensioners. The power they had once dreamed of wielding in affairs of state had passed irrevocably into the hands of the bureaucracy. The personnel of the state apparatus was still staffed principally from the ranks of the nobility, but the nobility, losing their direct economic and administrative power, were no longer to be capable of playing the role of a ruling class on which the monarch could solidly base his power. It remained to be seen whether the ruler could find another social element, economically strong enough to replace the old land-owning, serf-owning nobility, or whether the autocrat and his bureaucrats would find themselves suspended in a vacuum, isolated from any significant social support.

It was, of course, theoretically possible that the regime, which since Catherine had viewed the nobility with suspicion, might succeed in finding the necessary replacement. That it was necessary, in view of the desperate hostility nurtured in the peasantry by the terms of Emancipation, was to be made clear in the course of the revolution in the twentieth century. Why the peasants had no cause to be grateful for Emancipation requires summary examination of its immensely complicated, often confusing, and sometimes contradictory provisions. Some of the statutes applied generally; others applied to special portions of the empire or to special categories of landlords' peasants. Here only the main features of the reform will be noted in generalized form. A clear distinction must be observed between the juridical and the economic powers of the nobles, both before and after the reform.

TERMS OF EMANCIPATION AND REDEMPTION

In the first place, the juridical authority of the noble over the persons of his peasants was terminated, without compensation to the former owner; the peasant ceased to be a chattel at the mercy of the whims of another human being. The peasant, however, acquired neither complete individual freedom nor legal equality with his former master. He remained a member of the "tributary" orders, subject to capitation ("soul") tax and to military conscription; he became a member of a legally recognized group, the commune, which controlled his freedom of movement.

The commune (*selskoe obshchestvo* or "village community," which in practice did not always coincide with the actually functioning *krestianskaia obshchina* or "peasant-commune") was of course not wholly new. The old practice of communal landholding, or at least of communal control exercised over land held by individual peasant households, had never died out in Russia, as it long since had in most of the West. A factor of great importance in keeping it alive had been its use, even on lands privately held by the nobles, as a means of imposing collective responsibility on the peasants for discharge of their obligations both to the state and to their owners. It had of course been perfectly possible for a noble landowner to interfere with the autonomy of the pre-Emancipation peasant-commune, popularly known as *mir* ("world"), but in general the old institution had proved normally serviceable. The new legal commune did not necessarily coincide with the old *mir,* but there was a strong tendency for the law, which at best was confused, to be largely ignored in practical operation by the tradition-bound peasantry.

The official commune, with which the former serf-owner had no right to interfere, was a local class institution, composed of peasant householders; it elected its own officials and enjoyed a limited autonomy in the control of its property and in the distribution among its members of the obligations which, under the "circular guarantee," rested on it as a collective unit. No member of the commune could escape membership in it, or even leave its territory temporarily, without an official document issued by his commune. Over the commune was established a higher organ of peasant autonomy, the *volost,* similarly governed by officials elected by the peasants themselves and vested with low-level judicial and punitive authority. Both *volost* and commune were to be under the jurisdiction, not of the local nobility, but of the bureaucratic authority of the local apparatus of the state power. This arrangement was essentially similar to that worked out by Kiselev for the state peasants under Nicholas I.

Thus the new "freedom" of the peasants bore no relationship to the principles of the Declaration of Independence, the Declaration of the Rights of Man and of the Citizen, or John Stuart Mill's *On Liberty*. However well disposed the authors of Emancipation were toward the peasants, they could not shake off the traditional Russian concepts of corporate status or rise above the thought of imposing a measure of welfare on wards of the Orthodox state. The ideology of Emancipation was a fitting prelude to the ideology of the Soviet Union.

On the economic side, the changes wrought by Emancipation were less sweeping than the juridical provisions. The peasants did not immediately become proprietors of their land, either as individuals or as communes, nor were they released from their economic obligations to their former masters. Instead, they became "temporary obligatory peasants" for an indefinite term; the only change was that the amount of land they must be assigned for their own use and the corresponding payments, in money or in labor, they must make to the landlords were officially regulated within narrowly flexible limits. For every part of the country, there was officially determined the normal land allotment per "revision soul" which must be temporarily assigned by the landowner for the peasants' use; except in the non-black-soil parts of the steppe, where land was relatively more plentiful, the landlord and the peasant commune were given the option of agreeing on an allotment ranging downward in size to not less than one-third of the statutory norm.

These provisions were hedged about with innumerable reservations, such as that the allotment per emancipated male must not be smaller than the pre-reform holding unless the latter had exceeded half the new statutory norm, or that allotments above the maxima or below the minima might be made with corresponding adjustment of the peasants' obligations, or that landlords might arbitrarily reduce allotments to the minimum in order to keep a permitted proportion of the arable land in their own hands. In addition to the right of landlords under certain circumstances to make such "cut-offs" from the pre-reform holdings of the peasants, they had the right to insist on an unscrambling of the land retained by them for their own use from the lands temporarily allotted to the peasants. This frequently resulted in loss of access by peasants to essential streams or meadows.

The obligations which the "temporary obligatory peasants" were to owe to the landlords were equally carefully defined, so far as possible in *obrok* (money dues) rather than *barshchina* (obligatory labor). To the maximum allotment in each district corresponded a maximum annual charge, which did not diminish in proportion to reduction in the size of the allotment; acceptance of a minimum allotment (one-third of the maximum) might entail payment of one-half the maximum annual rate.

Still more importantly, the principle of fixing annual obligations in terms of opportunities for industrial earnings resulted in higher annual charges per acre in the non-agricultural provinces than in the rich black-soil provinces. Despite the theory that the peasant was being emancipated without compensation for his personal freedom, the actual fixing of obligations took careful account of his earning power apart from the land. It was not the intention of Emancipation that the noble should suffer in his pocketbook.

For some areas there were departures from these general terms. In the parts of Little Russia affected by the Inventory Regulations and in the Lithuanian and White Russian provinces which had been threatened with them, the elaborate new calculations were not necessary for the temporary obligatory peasants. In those western provinces where Polish influences had been strong among the landlords, and still more in the "Congress kingdom" of Poland itself, where serfdom had been legally, though not economically, abolished by Napoleon, the impact of the Polish revolt of 1863-64, to be referred to below, soon resulted in specially favorable conditions for the peasants.

Household peasants, who had not held land when serfs, were emancipated, like the American Negro slave, without compensation and without land. If they could not enroll in some commune—where, being landless, they were not likely to be welcome—they were permitted to enroll as members of the burgher population. Most of those who did not stay on as servants in their old homes joined the small but growing army of wageworkers in industry.

To complete the emancipatory process it was necessary that the peasants "redeem" themselves from their status as "temporary obligatory peasants." The basic principle of redemption was that, by mutually voluntary agreements, the peasants, organized in communes, were to redeem the land (not their persons) from the owner; conclusion of a redemption agreement would not merely transfer legal title to the land thus redeemed to the commune; it would also terminate forever, and without further compensation, the economic obligations of the peasants to their former owners.

It should be obvious that this theoretical redemption was not merely a matter of selling land to peasants (who already had the use of it) but a device to make them pay compensation for their former obligations. It is not surprising that the overwhelming majority of redemption agreements were concluded on the initiative of the landowners, and that peasant refusal to accept such agreements was the chief impediment to swift implementation of the reform.

Cash redemption by the peasants was clearly impossible. Only with government assistance could the peasants raise the necessary sums, for the official redemption price was arrived at by capitalizing at 6 percent the current obligations of the peasants involved. The government therefore undertook to issue to the landlords interest-bearing bonds covering 80 percent of the redemption price (75 percent if the temporary allotments were reduced in size at the time of redemption); the balance had to be arranged with the peasant commune. The landlord had the right to force conclusion of a redemption agreement, though in such case he was to forgo any compensation beyond the government's share. Whether redemption was forced or voluntary, the commune was to reimburse the government through a special tax in the form of redemption payments spread over forty-nine years.

Since it was to be anticipated that landlords and peasants would not readily agree on details, it was provided that supervision of the working out of the reform should be entrusted to special officials, who were to discuss general and specially difficult particular problems among themselves at county and provincial congresses. These "peace mediators" were to be appointed by the provincial governors from among the local nobility. Lanskoy, as Minister of the Interior, instructed the governors to choose men with a sense of justice and fairness, whose word would command the confidence of the peasants.

Lanskoy, however, was promptly removed from office, as was his deputy, Miliutin. The new Minister, Valuiev, had been the chief opponent of the reform when it was in the hands of the Main Committee. He now attempted unsuccessfully to browbeat the peace mediators and force them to interpret their duties in the way desired by influential landlords. When, however, he attempted to get rid of the most honest among them by proposing, on grounds of economy, to reduce the total number, the peace mediators defeated him by announcing their willingness, if necessary, to accept reduction of as much as half their salaries provided there were no dismissals. In the early stages, therefore, the reform was carried out with somewhat surprising fairness.

However carried out, the reform inevitably produced bitter disappointment among the peasantry, who, from the publication of the original Rescript in 1857 to the publication of the final terms, had been unusually quiescent. In the months following Emancipation, unable to believe that the officials were not betraying the intentions of the tsar, the peasants reacted with unusual violence. These peasant disturbances, far more numerous than at any time even in the reign of Nicholas I, were ruthlessly suppressed by the military; in one case, in which university students had a requiem mass celebrated for the dead, the officiating monks were exiled to Solovki.

CONSEQUENTIAL REFORMS AND THE ALL-CLASS PRINCIPLE

The atmosphere of reaction on the part of the government could not, however, stop further reforms. The hopes of greater state efficiency which had inspired Emancipation required additional measures, and the abolition of the nobles' control over the peasants created a situation with which the existing structure of the bureaucratic apparatus could not cope. The special position the nobility had occupied had been shaken at its base, and it became progressively necessary to make provision for other classes somehow to share in the conduct of public affairs.

The most direct consequence of Emancipation was its extension to the numerous categories of fiscal peasants, for the reform of 1861 had applied only to privately owned peasants. The latter, in 1858, had numbered almost eleven million "souls" (males of all ages registered for capitation tax purposes); there remained almost thirteen million "souls," most of whom, since Kiselev's reforms, had enjoyed much the same sort of communal autonomy imposed on the landowners' peasants in 1861, without owning the land they cultivated. In 1863, serfs on the lands of the imperial family, who had been granted communal autonomy only in 1858, were freed with allotments close to the maximal norms of the landowners' peasants. In 1866 and 1867, most of the state peasants were also granted as permanent allotments the lands they already cultivated; though their annual payments to the state were at the same time increased, the burden resting on them was substantially less than that on the former landowners' peasants.

The position of the peasants renting state lands in Siberia and Transcaucasia was not seriously affected. In the Cossack areas, where the peasants had long enjoyed a special regime of collective local autonomy in return for a heavier burden of military service, the land had been held in the name of the Cossack "army." By decree of 1869, some two-thirds of this land was distributed among the individual villages or among the "*stanitsas*" into which they were grouped. The individual Cossack received no inalienable rights in land, which was held communally.

Specially favorable treatment was accorded in 1864 to the former serfs in the western provinces, where a number of the landlords were Polish and had shown sympathy for the Polish insurrection of 1863-64. In Poland itself, as a frankly propagandistic measure, the peasants, who had been "free" but landless since the time of the Grand Duchy of Warsaw, were in 1864 granted at least the land they were then cultivating; the landlords were compensated on the same basis as in Russia, but the value of the dues and services they had levied on their tenants was underestimated instead of overestimated, and the redemption dues to the state were collected, not alone from the recipients of the land, but from all landholders. Manorial jurisdiction, which had survived the Napoleonic abolition of serfdom, was replaced by communal autonomy; the Polish *gmina,* however, was not a purely peasant organ like the Russian commune but an all-class organ based on landholding.

Another immediately pressing reform was financial. Even without the load of redemption bonds, the state treasury was in grave difficulties. Despite foreign loans at high interest and internal lottery loans, it had been necessary to cover wartime and postwar deficits with heavy emissions of paper money, which speedily declined in value. The operation Kankrin had performed on the old "assignats" in Nicholas' time was again necessary, and this time the circumstances were more unfavorable. Once again, however, the emperor was able to find a competent Minister of Finance. Reitern, appointed in 1862, began badly with an ill-conceived and nearly disastrous scheme to redeem government paper with the aid of a large foreign loan. Not until the middle of the next decade was he able to eliminate deficit financing, and his successes in this respect were almost immediately canceled by a fresh war with Turkey. He did, however, succeed in introducing more systematic management of the state's economy. Beginning in 1863, he introduced the practice of annual publication of a statement of all revenues and expenditures; he also established unification of the treasury by securing abolition of the old practice of allowing each ministry to manage its own revenues and expenditures. By a series of other measures, he vastly improved receipts and reduced the prevalence of corruption; for Catherine's practice of farming out the liquor revenues he substituted a fixed excise, a system which was applied also to tobacco, salt, and sugar. Above all, he contributed to the growth of industrial and commercial activity by assisting railroad construction and by the development of a system of public credit. In 1865, there were little more than three thousand miles of railway in all Russia; a decade later mileage had been more than trebled, and at least the chief agricultural regions and the Donets coal basin had been linked with Moscow and with the seaports. The State Bank had been founded in 1860; Reitern encouraged the opening of private joint-stock banks, the first of which was founded in 1864.

The deficiencies of the local bureaucratic machinery and its inadequacy to fill the gap left by the destruction of seignorial authority over the peasants precipitated the most important of the administrative reforms of Alexander's reign. In 1864, it was decreed that a new organ of government, the zemstvo, was to be established at two levels, the county (*uiezd*) and the province (*guberniya*). To the county zemstvo delegates were to be elected for three-year terms by landholders, businessmen owning sufficient property, and peasant communes. These three categories of electors voted separately, each curia being entitled to a number of delegates depending on the total amount of land held by its members. Significantly, and as a matter of principle, no distinction in this respect was made between the noble curia and the peasant curia, though of course the larger size of his holdings gave the individual noble many times the electoral weight of the individual peasant; the representation of urban businessmen naturally had to rest on the worth of their business assets rather than on the acreage they owned. The delegates to the higher-level zemstvo were elected by and from the lower-level bodies. Each zemstvo, county or provincial, elected a small administrative board.

The new organ was given a limited power of taxation of real estate and business undertakings in its territory. It was charged with construction and maintenance of roads and bridges, primary schools, hospitals, clinics, orphanages, and other social services; it hired teachers, doctors, nurses, engineers, agronomists, veterinarians, and other professionals; it also gave assistance to peasant cultivators by providing crop and other insurance, tested seeds, breeding stock, agricultural equipment, and advice.

Zemstvo institutions were not at once introduced everywhere; in the first three years (1865-67), they were established in only thirty of the provinces. After 1866, when reaction was intensified, their activity was hedged around by all sorts of restrictions. They were subjected to interference by provincial governors and by lesser bureaucrats, but they were better able than the peasant communes and *volosti* to offer resistance in defense of their rights.

Not the least significant fact about the zemstvo was that it was a representative body cutting across class lines. The old form of local participation in discussion of any political questions had been a purely class organ, the local corporation of the nobility established by Catherine. The zemstvo was, to be sure, elected on the basis of weighted class representation, and in it the nobility remained dominant. Yet the participation of the nobility was no longer exclusive; in the new institutions, the nobles had to work side by side with representatives of other classes. Under the new order the nobility, which retained also its old class organization under elected marshals, might be *primus inter pares,* but it was no longer the sole class with any voice in public affairs.

The same principle was applied in 1870 when the existing city administration was overhauled. Although the old division into merchants and artisans, organized in "guilds" and "crafts," remained, the government of the city was put in the hands of a city duma, analogous to the rural zemstvo. The city duma was elected for four years by all who paid a certain amount in taxes on real estate, trade, or industry.

Almost simultaneously with the zemstvo reform there was an attempt made, under the guidance of Zarudnyi, a reform adviser, to modernize the judicial system and to guarantee the independence and integrity of the judges. The judicial reform of 1864 was also based on the new principle of equality for all subjects irrespective of class. Petty cases, whether criminal or civil, were to be tried by "justices of the peace," who were to be chosen by the county zemstvo or the city duma; in civil cases, they were charged with the duty of seeking amicably to effect an agreed decision. Justices of the peace had jurisdiction over the whole population without distinction, save that peasants were to be tried in their own *volost* courts. More serious cases were to be tried by regional courts, composed of judges appointed for life. In criminal cases, the question of guilt or innocence was to be decided by jurors chosen by lot from the local population. In both civil and criminal cases, the accused was to have the right of being represented by a qualified attorney. The courtroom was to be open to the public. Appeals might be taken to the Senate. At the same time the severity of the penal laws was mitigated, and most forms of corporal punishment—beating with rods, whips, or cudgels; running the gauntlet; and branding—were abolished.

Thus, a great leap forward had been taken. In addition to the principle of equality before the law, there was established complete separation of the judiciary from the administration. Reduction of the number of judicial instances expedited justice and reduced its cost. The judges were made permanent and independent. The reform was, however, marred by the fact that the judges were of several grades, with salary differentials, so that hope of promotion could be used as a lever by the Minister of Justice. There was the further fact that certain types of cases, including press cases as well as high treason, were not subject to decision by a jury. These weaknesses, inherent from the beginning, were freely exploited by the intensified reaction that set in from 1866. In addition to further narrowing of the competence of juries, there developed the practice of appointing as judges temporary substitutes, thus wholly destroying in fact the theoretical independence of the judiciary.

Magnificent as this reform was in concept, its real significance in practice boiled down to a restatement and amplification of the words of Emperor Paul: "In Russia only he is great with whom I speak and only while I speak with him." Equality of subjects before the law did not and was not intended to establish a distinction between the law and the will of the autocrat; it represented rather another step in the course marked out since the end of the eighteenth century, the reduction of the erstwhile highly privileged and therefore overambitious nobility to the level of subjects governed by a bureaucracy responsible to the ruler alone. By the same token, though like the other reforms designed to increase state efficiency, it contributed to that mounting isolation of the autocrat that led to revolution.

Since the basic purpose of all the reforms of the 1860's was improvement of state efficiency, it was inevitable that the army also should be subjected to sweeping reforms. These were carried out by General D. A. Miliutin, brother of the man who had been the guiding spirit of peasant emancipation. Unlike his brother or the other ministers who planned the major reforms, D. A. Miliutin enjoyed the full confidence of the emperor and was not dismissed when the immediately necessary work had been done. Prior to his appointment in 1861 as Minister of War, he had had experience as a professor in the General Staff Academy and as chief of staff of the Army of the Caucasus.

For some years his reforming activity, though important, was not spectacular. He reduced the term of military service from twenty-five years to sixteen. He strove to reduce the brutality of military discipline and to inculcate self-respect in the rank and file. He introduced economies in military administration without affecting the quality of rations or of barracks. He applied to military justice the principles of Zarudnyi's judiciary reforms. He overhauled the military schools, destroying their class exclusiveness and establishing several "Junker" (cadet) schools for special purposes.

The culminating item in his program had, however, to wait until significant progress had been made toward the construction of a railway network. Western Europe had long since adopted the rotating principle of universal military service devised by Scharnhorst after 1807, which permitted of the maintenance of a relatively small standing army backed by a trained reserve. The advantages of the Prussian system had long been obvious, but the vastness of Russia and the weak development of the transport service had made it impracticable to dream of mobilizing trained reserves. Hence Russia had felt the need of keeping up a huge standing army.

On January 1, 1874, however, Miliutin's plan for transition to the Prussian system became law. Henceforth, in the year of their twenty-first birthday all Russian males, without distinction of class, became liable to a six-year period of service, followed by nine more in the reserve. Exemptions of varying degrees were granted to only sons and to others needed for the support of their families, the degree of exemption depending on the degree of need. From the remainder, the number of recruits required from each district were chosen by lot; only if sufficient recruits were not forthcoming could those exempted be called up, in order of degree of exemption.

Apart from the system of exemptions, the only privileges accorded were based on education. University students had to serve only six months; those with secondary education served only two years; those with primary education four years. As a result of the new system, literacy in the army rose sharply. Prior to 1874, only 13 percent of the soldiers were able to read and write; in that year, this figure jumped to 20 percent. A further reform in 1875 made literacy one of the objectives of military training, and army service thus became an important substitute for an adequate system of primary instruction in Russia.

The army reform was perhaps the most revolutionary of all the Great

Reforms, though it obviously could not have been accomplished without antecedent Emancipation; it was in full consonance with the non-class principles of the administrative and judicial reforms. It was also perhaps the most successful, the only one carried through in the spirit of its planners. It is a curious commentary that in the midst of reaction the Minister of War had to struggle against his colleagues, the Ministers of Education and Justice, to attain his objective of putting the army on a basis that might make it able to contend with the armies of the West.

The army reforms were not, of course, the only changes in the field of education, which, like every other branch of the state power, badly needed refurbishing. In this area, reforms were, however, much more limited and even shorter lived than in the case of the judicial reforms. The initial measures of Alexander II had in essence meant a return from the extreme repression after 1848 to Uvarov's university statute of 1835. They had not sufficed to prevent pugnacious student demonstrations, whether against old-fashioned professors or in sympathy with the peasantry.

Early in 1861, soon after the publication of the Emancipation Manifesto, a new Minister of Education secured the emperor's sanction for new rules forbidding any corporate activity by university students. Their application in the fall led to large-scale student riots; in St. Petersburg alone, three hundred university students had to be lodged in the fortress. Alexander, disturbed, appointed a new Minister, Golovnin, who took the road of conciliation; professors who had been dismissed for their protests were reinstated. In 1863, a new university statute restored a large measure of autonomy to the faculties. Though it made no provision for student control of their own affairs, its liberal administration went far to quell unrest among them.

In 1864, the secondary schools were reorganized. Admission to the Gymnasia was thrown open to children "of all conditions without distinction of calling or faith." [4] In the "classical" Gymnasia, the study of Greek was added to that of Latin. In the *Real* Gymnasia, instruction was to be mainly in science. Gymnasia for women, with a slightly shorter course, had already been added in 1859.

An effort was made also in the direction of establishing some sort of system of primary instruction. This had previously been the monopoly of parochial schools or of individuals. "Sunday schools," established after 1859 by public-spirited citizens, had become hotbeds of propaganda and were closed by the government in 1862. Finally, however, a project of Golovnin's for systematic primary instruction was handed over to the zemstvos, for implementation.

This limited progress toward improvement of public education in Russia was brought to an abrupt halt by the attempt of Karakozov, a deranged young noble, to assassinate the emperor on April 14, 1866. Karakozov's attempt was purely individual but had a profound effect, the more so as his hand had been jogged at the crucial moment by a non-noble (who was promptly given noble rank as a reward). Golovnin was immediately replaced by Count Dmitry A. Tolstoy, who found it necessary to be tutored in Greek in order to make a satisfactory impression as Minister of Education.

This Tolstoy had in 1859 published a sharp criticism of the work of the Editing Commission on the problem of emancipation; even the emperor had commented that its author either did not understand anything about the peasant question or was a person of evil intentions. Nevertheless, in 1864, Tolstoy was appointed *Oberprokuror* of the Holy Synod and in 1866 was given the opportunity to correct the reform tendencies in the field of education.

Tolstoy was the most determined opponent of all the reforms of the period and a firm believer in the social ascendancy of the nobility. He admired the then English system of education because of its aristocratic character, though he had no sympathy for pitting aristocracy, as a political principle, against the autocracy to which he was devoted. An ardent reactionary, Tolstoy was by no means devoid of faith in education. His concept of education, however, allowed no scope for independent thinking on the part of the student; the function of education as he saw it was to impart exact information and to discipline the mind. In his opinion, rigorous study of classical languages, supplemented by mathematics, should constitute the core of the curriculum. Natural science led to materialism; it should only be taught "technologically." History, which stimulated thought, was particularly dangerous.

So extreme were Tolstoy's views that he met with determined opposition from many of his ministerial colleagues; he therefore found it necessary to move slowly and was unable to realize all his ideas. He did not succeed in fundamentally altering Golovnin's university statute of 1863, but by issue of supplementary restrictive rules and by the general character of his administration he provoked a series of disturbances among the students; these he tried to use, though unsuccessfully, to sway Alexander in the direction of more sweeping educational reaction. He was also unable to prevent establishment of lectures which women could attend; even Tolstoy had to admit that the alternative was that Russian girls would attend universities in Switzerland, and that this held even greater dangers than their receiving higher education at home. He resolutely refused to admit women to the study of medicine, but in 1872 his chief opponent, the Minister of War, opened medical courses for women at an army hospital.

At the other end of the educational scale, Tolstoy also fought a losing battle to prevent the zemstvo institutions from establishing a network of primary schools under lay auspices, with tens of thousands of pupils. Despite the Ministry of Education, a serious beginning was made in the opening phases of the fight against illiteracy.

It was only in the matter of secondary education that Tolstoy succeeded in realizing his ideas. In 1871, despite the opposition of a majority of members of the Council of State, Alexander gave his approval to Tolstoy's new statute to govern the classical Gymnasia. Most of the students' time was thenceforth to be devoted to the study of Latin and Greek, taught in the most formal way. The hours allotted to instruction in mathematics were also increased. Science disappeared from the curriculum altogether, while history and modern languages were severely cut back. The Gymnasia thus reformed were the sole avenue of admission to the universities. The *Real* Gymnasia were reduced to *Real* schools, designed to give merely technical education, with emphasis on drawing, mathematics, and applied science. The Gymnasia for women were treated in a similar spirit, and their chief inspiration, the eminent Vyshnegradsky, was forced out.

REALISM IN RUSSIAN CULTURE

The official reforms were not the only major development in the reign of Alexander II. The cultural flowering that had characterized the Russia of Nicholas I continued in full swing. This period witnessed the rise of a distinctive Russian school of "realist" painters. A favorite theme in the decade following Emancipation was the injustice of serfdom; clergy, nobles, and merchants were generally displayed in a strongly unfavorable light. Among the earliest and most bitter of these painters were V. G. Perov (1833-82) and N. V. Nevrev (1830-1904). N. N. Gué (1831-94) was particularly noted for his portraiture, both contemporary and historic. Vasily V. Vereshchagin (1842-1904), who exhibited his first work in 1866, acquired a special reputation as a painter of war scenes; though their grimness caused considerable consternation in military circles, their emphasis on heroic courage kept him in official favor; Vereshchagin was to lose his life in the sinking of the Russian flagship in a sally from Port Arthur. Ilya Y. Repin (1844-1918), son of a poor military colonist, achieved the greatest reputation of all; his works ranged from depiction of contemporary life, through portraits, to the historical paintings for which he is best known; the best of his earlier works included his *Bargemen Wading the River* (1872), his peculiarly impressive *Religious Procession in Kursk Guberniya* (1880-83), his *Portrait of Mussorgsky* (1881), and his *Unexpected Arrival* (1884). In sculpture this was the period when M. M. Antokolsky (1843-1902) produced his windswept bronze of a pedestrian Peter I (1872), perhaps inspired by Pushkin's *Bronze Horseman,* and his careful marble of Ivan the Terrible (1875) which profoundly moved Turgenev.

This was also the beginning of the great age of Russian music. Its precursor had been Michael I. Glinka (1803-57). In the eighteenth century, successive empresses had been patrons of all the arts, but especially of music. Anna had introduced Italian opera and the ballet. Elizabeth had continued this interest, combining it with her favorite masked balls. Under Catherine,

Italian opera had become thoroughly acclimatized; one of her importations, Giuseppe Sarti, even composed operas to Russian librettos; some of these were written by Russian serfs who, through the road of musical ability, rose to prominence at Catherine's court.

Despite the strong Italian tradition in which he grew up, Glinka, the son of a wealthy landowner, drew his material largely from Russian folklore. *A Life for the Tsar,* performed under Nicholas I in 1836, merits the honor of being the first Russian musical composition to be taken seriously; basically, however, it was still dominated by his own musical training in Italy. His *Russlan and Ludmilla,* though a disastrous failure when presented in 1842, was far more distinctively Russian and clearly pointed the way to the subsequent development of a school of Russian national music, using Russian rhythms and folk themes, blended with musical principles eclectically drawn from Western models.

In striking contrast was Anton Rubinstein (1829-94) who, a prodigy at ten, studied in Germany and became a world-famous pianist. Rubinstein was a conservative in music, a devotee of Felix Mendelssohn, and fought a losing battle alike against the rising tide of Wagnerism and against the Russian nationalist composers. As a composer himself he achieved nothing of note, but in the era of the Great Reforms he performed an important service by founding the Russian Musical Society (1859) and the St. Petersburg Conservatory of Music (1862), which his brother Nicholas matched at Moscow (1866).

Those who carried on Glinka's work were, compared even to Glinka, amateurs. Known as "The Five," their leading figure was Milii Balakirev (1837-1910). Balakirev was the son of a poor noble but was befriended by a rich one, who made him, at the age of fourteen, conductor of his private orchestra in Nizhny Novgorod. He was inspired by meetings with Glinka and in 1857 began to gather around himself a small company of friends and piano pupils, consciously dedicated to the idea of creating a new, distinctively Russian, music. In opposition to Rubinstein's "den of professors," with "not a Russian in the whole lot," Balakirev founded a Free Music School, which neither charged tuition nor imposed a strict course of instruction. As another of "The Five" later recalled: "Balakirev, who had never had any systematic course in harmony and counterpoint and had not even superficially applied himself to it, evidently thought such studies quite unnecessary." [5] Although his songs were the first Russian compositions to be worthy of comparison with Schubert's or Schumann's, Balakirev's chief significance was, through his dominant influence over his associates, the development of Russian instrumental music.

Another of "The Five," Modest P. Mussorgsky (1839-81), made the earliest and most significant contributions to the new Russian music. Of a wealthy provincial noble family, Mussorgsky became at seventeen an officer in the crack Preobrazhensky Guard regiment. Although he resigned two years later, he there acquired the habit of heavy drinking that brought him to an early grave. In 1863, his family lost its money; the young Mussorgsky was forced to support himself as a government clerk but persisted in finding solace as a member of Balakirev's circle, which he had joined in 1857. His main successes were in the composition of songs, though his unconventional rhythms and heavy reliance on folk music puzzled contemporary critics. His greatest single achievement was his opera, *Boris Godunov,* completed in 1870 but not produced till 1874, when it found a very mixed reception. Based on Pushkin, *Boris Godunov* reflected received tradition rather than historical fact; nevertheless it must be classed as representing an important step toward operatic "realism," breaking with historical romanticism and almost dispensing with a star. Strongly nationalist, drawing freely on Russian folk and ecclesiastical music, its definitely pioneer character made its acceptance difficult. Only posthumously and as a sequel to reworking by Rimsky-Korsakov—at whatever temporary cost to its own merits—did *Boris* and *Khovanshchina* (incomplete at the time of his death) receive their due.

Another of "The Five" was Alexander P. Borodin (1834-87), illegitimate son of a Caucasian prince, who was intended for the medical profession. He did indeed have a distinguished career as a professor of chemistry, especially in the newly-founded school of medicine for women (1872-87). As a "Sunday composer," however, despite the lack of any systematic musical training, he became one of Russia's leading musicians. Though little known, his *Second Symphony* (1876), notwithstanding its nationalist originality, was the first of the genre to be well received outside Russia. Borodin was, for a Russian, exceptionally successful in composing polyphonic music in the German style; yet, encouraged by Franz Liszt, Borodin did not hesitate to break with convention. Much of his music was infused with an Oriental cast. The finest example of his work was *Prince Igor,* based on a twelfth-century Russian epic; begun in 1869, it was still incomplete at the time of his death. Posthumously, its Polovtsian Dances were most effectively used by Diaghilev.

Youngest of "The Five" was Nicholai A. Rimsky-Korsakov (1844-1908), who broke with the tradition of his aristocratic family by resigning from an active career in the navy to accept a professorship in the St. Petersburg Conservatory of Music (1873). As a member of the Balakirev circle since 1860, he had acquired an intense love of music, with no knowledge of its technique; only by the most energetic efforts was he able to keep ahead of his pupils. Despite this break with the nationalist "Five," Rimsky-Korsakov never succeeded in adapting himself to classical traditions; symphonies and chamber music were beyond his powers. His successes lay in the field of music for entertainment, picture-music inspired by fairy tales and fantasy, rooted in Russian folk music. His symphonic poem *Sadko* (1867) set the tone for all his significant later work. It was in the 1880's that he composed his opera *The Snow Maiden,* his universally successful symphonic suite *Scheherezade,* and his pagan-inspired overture *Russian Easter.*

Quite unlike "The Five," Peter Ilyich Chaikovsky—or, to use the familiar French spelling, Tchaikovsky—(1840-93) was trained in the classical Western school. He was one of seven children of a thrice-married mining engineer. Throughout his life he was afflicted by an extreme morbid sensibility, which was reflected in much of his work. At nineteen he found himself, with a training in law which he hated, a clerk in the Ministry of Justice; two years later, after his first trip abroad, he began the study of music. He was in the first class to enter Anton Rubinstein's Conservatory (1862). Although his master did not appreciate his pupil's modernist leanings, he nevertheless recommended the youth to his brother as a member of the faculty of his new Conservatory at Moscow (1866). In this post, remote from the advanced center of Russian aesthetic life, Tchaikovsky remained until released (1878) by a pension from the neurotic widow, Madame von Meck, who conditioned her support on confining their acquaintanceship to correspondence. This queer relationship lasted to the end of 1890; the composer survived its abrupt termination for less than three years.

Tchaikovsky's work corresponded closely to the ambivalence of his personal life. His first real success was his *Romeo and Juliet Overture* (1870), which was deeply indebted to his close personal association with Balakirev but also to his own keen dramatic flair. The best of his work was always infused with a striking juxtaposition of his mastery of lyric, if sometimes exceedingly sentimental, melody and of a driving force that often degenerated toward melodrama. Although he early abandoned the conscious use of folk tunes that was so characteristic of "The Five" and was heavily influenced by Western operatic techniques, his music somehow remained, though not nationalist, profoundly Russian. His *Piano Concerto No. 1* (1874), bitterly denounced by Nicholas Rubinstein as vulgar, has survived as one of his dramatic masterpieces. His *Violin Concerto* (1878), also roundly condemned by the professional critics, became a favorite of Leopold Auer, who from 1868 to 1917 trained at the St. Petersburg Conservatory a whole generation of violinists. One of his strongest likes was for ballet music, at which, despite the initial failure of *Swan Lake* when performed at Moscow in 1877, he proved himself a past master. In this field his culminating triumph was to be the *Nutcracker Suite* (1892).

Tchaikovsky was, in addition, the only Russian composer of his time to achieve success with symphonies. In 1877, when his brief but disastrous marriage led him to a fantastic effort at suicide, he composed his first immediately successful Symphony, the *Fourth*. In the same year he composed his most successful opera, *Eugen Onegin,* in which he converted Pushkin's satirical "novel in verse" into a basically Western romance. His *Fifth Symphony* was not composed until 1888; aesthetically subject to more criticism than its predecessor, as reflecting the composer's persisting personal immaturity of spirit, it has continued to command the affection of a vast audience. His greatest symphony, the *Sixth,* was completed only shortly before his death from cholera, that disease of a backward country.

In literature, the emphasis shifted from poetry and the short story to the novel. The Russian novelist of outstanding importance for his ability to portray social problems photographically was Ivan S. Turgenev (1818-83). His *Sportsman's Sketches* (1847-51) had produced a startling impression. *Rudin* (1856) was enthusiastically welcomed by the progressive elements in Russian society as a candid portrayal of the ineffective idealism of the older generation. Responding to the criticism that, while a master in his delineation of women, he was unable to depict a Russian man of action, Turgenev offered a young hero in *Fathers and Sons* (1862). The result was to Turgenev a great disappointment; Russian radicals rejected his "nihilist" hero Bazarov as a caricature. Subsequently Pisarev was to adopt Turgenev's "nihilist" as the archetype of the militant revolutionary materialist; the term is still loosely applied to the then rising generation of *narodniki,* who developed a peculiarly Russian form of socialism focused on their concept of the peasantry as the "people" (*narod*). Yet Turgenev's reputation in Russia never recovered, and he spent most of the rest of his life abroad. His subsequent attempts at social novels, including *Virgin Soil* (1877), did not achieve the social veracity of his earlier work. Turgenev's style and subtle portrayal of individual character endeared him to Western Europe. Himself profoundly influenced by the West, as Pushkin had been, Turgenev was the first Russian writer to achieve an international reputation.

Quite different was the work of Ivan A. Goncharov (1812-91), who, like most other literary men of this period, had begun to write under Nicholas I. The flat mediocrity of his style was in striking contrast to the grace and beauty of Turgenev's. Like many other Russian writers, Goncharov dispensed with narrative interest. Nor could he indicate any character development. Yet his *Oblomov* (1859) had a powerful impact by its presentation of the fatalistic degeneration, physically and morally, of a rural landowning noble. It was widely accepted as a realistic portrayal of the "Russian soul," at least as embodied in the ruling class. It was as a symbol of indolence and uselessness that *Oblomov* later became one of Lenin's favorite literary characters.

A later variant on the theme of the dehumanization of the provincial nobility, this time stressing animal rather than vegetable traits, was *The Golovlev Family* (1871-73) by Michael E. Saltykov (1826-89), who wrote under the name of "Shchedrin." Saltykov was himself sprung from the lesser provincial nobility and spent nearly a quarter of a century in a variety of official posts, mainly in the provinces. The deep gloom of his novel was matched only by the biting sarcasm of his journalistic work. His satirical attacks on post-reform officialdom, on unregenerate landowners, and on rising capitalists made him a favorite of the radical intelligentsia. Yet neither Goncharov nor Saltykov could rival Gogol's "How Ivan Ivanovich Quarreled with Ivan Nikiforovich."

In 1859, Fedor M. Dostoevsky (1821-81) was allowed to return from Siberia, where after his release from prison he had been compelled to serve in the army. He was no longer a "Westerner" or a "new Gogol." In 1861-62 he completed *Memoirs from the House of Death,* an autobiographical novel based on his experiences in prison at Omsk (1850-54). Although it was the book on which his fame chiefly rested during his own lifetime, it was also one of the most uncharacteristic of his writings. Notwithstanding its tragic undertone—the rejection of educated men even by fellow-sufferers from "the people"—this novel was filled with optimistic faith in human nature. For some years, Dostoevsky suffered from a love affair with an "infernal" woman and from heavy gambling losses; in 1864, his review (*Vremia*) was closed. In 1867, he married his secretary and went abroad to escape his creditors. Under his wife's devoted guidance, he rehabilitated his finances and was able to return to Russia in 1871.

It was during this period of troubles that he wrote most of his greatest novels. *Memoirs from Underground* (1864), the least-read of his major works, perhaps displays most forcefully his psychopathological mysticism, his paradoxical blend of faith in individual values with an intuitive sense of the "cruelty" of an irrational universe. In his four supreme novels—*Crime and Punishment* (1866), *The Idiot* (1868), *The Possessed* (1871-72), and *The Brothers Karamazov* (1880)—Dostoevsky evinced his strong journalistic interest in social problems. Yet all of them are essentially studies of human individuality, with no meaning for the realities of the Russian social life about him. They are strongly imaginative and strongly ideological, but the imaginative concepts were personal to the author and the ideology did not reflect that of the movements he sought to portray. In his own time, Dostoevsky's work was more acceptable to conservatives, who saw truth in his depiction of the morbid traits of revolutionary individuals. Efforts to understand Dostoevsky as revealing a new Christianity inevitably break down; his God, whose essential characteristics are indeed pity and charity, is never able to provide a basic solution for Dostoevsky's tragedies.

However lacking in penetrating understanding of social problems, however remote from the psychology of the "normal" individual, Dostoevsky was undoubtedly a past master of mystery and suspense, qualities that seem to assure his novels survival long after the demise of any notion that he typified the Russian soul. Strangely enough, his last success—and one of his most resounding—was his address at the unveiling of a memorial to Pushkin (1880). Although Pushkin and Dostoevsky were poles apart, both in style and in outlook, it was this tribute by the plebeian and "realistic" Dostoevsky that laid the basis for the modern cult of the aristocratic and romantic Pushkin, who had been so little appreciated in his own time.

Strikingly similar to, and strikingly contrary to, Dostoevsky was a newly risen star, Count Leo N. Tolstoy (1828-1910), the most massive and perhaps the most revered figure in Russian literature. It has, and with some reason, been sometimes questioned whether Tolstoy can properly be classified as a figure in Russian literature, whether it is not more appropriate to speak of him in connection with world literature. Tolstoy's forte was the dissection and depiction of individual character, not in its specific Russian manifestations, but in terms of universal values.

He himself was a member of the Russian aristocracy, and at its very highest level. It was a fact of which he was ever conscious, even in later life when, after his "conversion" (1880), he sought to reject its manifestations. He found it difficult to tolerate contacts with the literary intelligentsia and at one time even challenged Turgenev to a duel. His own use of the Russian language was superb, combining impeccable grammatical construction with free use of aristocratically colloquial words.

By virtue of his education he was exceptionally well acquainted with Western culture. Among the most profound influences on his thinking were a number of Western writers; chief among them were Rousseau, de Maistre, Stendhal, and Proudhon—an ill-assorted quartet to whom he was in some ways strongly antipathetic, yet in others strikingly akin. For all his contact with the West, Tolstoy consistently and flatly rejected its ideas of progress; nor had he ever any respect for the trained specialist, the "expert," in any walk of life.

His distaste for Western materialism did not, however, throw him into the arms of mystical Slavophilism. Tolstoy was always a rationalist, a keen observer of life and of sentient human individuals. Constantly in quest of ultimate answers, he turned his magnificent powers of critical analysis against all efforts of others to explain the ultimate reason of things. Yet he was deeply troubled by his own inability to supply a viable solution for the problems of the universe.

His outstandingly great novels, *War and Peace* (1869) and *Anna Karenina* (1877), were masterpieces of character analysis, penetrating beneath the surface of the individual as Turgenev was incapable of doing. It was a result achieved by Gogol's method of "superfluous detail," but with infinitely greater insight into human psychology. It was a method which Tolstoy himself was later to condemn, in the days when he denounced Shakespeare (whom he considered a bad craftsman anyway) and Homer (whom he hailed as an artist) as "immoral writers" and sang—in *What Is Art?*—the praises of a small number of works, including *Uncle Tom's Cabin,* as "examples of the highest [art] flowing from the love of God and one's neighbor." [6]

What Tolstoy was disappointed with himself for not achieving was reconciliation of his belief in the reality of the individual personality with his conviction that there must be some identifiable principle controlling all individual differences. What Tolstoy refused to be interested in were contemporary socio-political issues; his writing therefore lacks the value as social analysis at which Turgenev excelled. In consequence, Tolstoy in this period was not highly regarded by the contemporary revolutionary thinkers. The ingrained egoism of his aristocratic anarchism was repellent to a socialist-minded intellectual generation.

The literature of this period, the greatest in Russian history, had little connection with the "great reforms." Nor had the social philosophies of the leading novelists much in common with each other. Among them, only Turgenev can be thought of as a liberal in a Western sense.

For that matter, the "great reforms" owed their inspiration to no spirit of liberalism. The curious combination of extensive reforms and of simultaneous harsh reaction reflected the ambivalence of the government's situation. On the one hand, the need for reordering many aspects of Russian life in the interest of strengthening the power of the state was obvious. At the same time, the autocracy could hardly be expected to be willing to cease to be an autocracy. While altering in its own interest the status of its subjects, the autocracy refused to contemplate the possibility that in their changed status they might become less willing to remain subject to its will.

NOTES

1. There are many variant versions of this well-known phrase; the one given here is as Alexander repeated it in the State Council on February 9, 1861. *Russkaia Starina,* XXVII (1880), 377.
2. Semevskii, *Krest'ianskii vopros v Rossii . . .* , II, 165*n.*
3. *Russkaia Starina,* XXVII (1880), 378.
4. *Polnoe sobranie zakonov . . .* (Second collection), No. 41,472, ¶53 (November 19, 1864), XXXIX, 172.
5. Rimsky-Korsakov, *My Musical Life,* p. 24.
6. Tolstoi, *Chto takoe iskusstvo?,* p. 151.

SUGGESTIONS FOR FURTHER READING

Among books previously mentioned, Robinson is here indispensable for emancipation, Kornilov and Pushkarev extremely useful for general narrative, and Mirsky very valuable for literature.

Among additional titles, Pares' chapter on "Reaction and Revolution in Russia" in the *Cambridge Modern History,* Vol. XII, contains much material useful for this and the following chapter. Mosse's *Alexander II and the Modernization of Russia,* though overdrawn, is a well-organized presentation. Two old works, Kovalevsky's *Russian Political Institutions* and Vinogradoff's *Self-Government in Russia,* treat certain aspects of the Great Reforms. For the light in which Alexander wished his motives to be viewed, see Rieber, *Politics of Autocracy: Letters of Alexander II to Prince A. I. Bariatinskii, 1857-1864.*

Montagu-Nathan's *History of Russian Music* is the standard work; a more recent perceptive analysis is Leonard's *History of Russian Music*. Newmarch's *Russian Opera* and Hofmann's *Un Siècle d'opéra russe* are more specialized. A broader treatment is Newmarch, *The Russian Arts.* For fiction throwing light on social conditions, read especially the works of Turgenev mentioned in the text.

Chapter

18

Revolutionary Thought and Official Reaction: 1860-1900

The Great Reforms—both in themselves and in their incompleteness—alienated many elements and failed to win new friends for the autocracy. Instead of stabilizing the government's position, they brought into being for the first time strong currents of revolutionary thought.

BACKGROUND OF THE REVOLUTIONARY MOVEMENT

The peasants reacted with great violence to the announcement of the terms of Emancipation. Peasant disturbances, to be sure, were local and were suppressed without too great difficulty. The peasantry remained, however, a discontented mass, eternally restless and constituting a great temptation for would-be organizers of revolution. University students were more vocal and uninhibited, but they were too few in number to constitute any great danger or to be able to exercise serious pressure. A series of university disturbances merely annoyed the government and intensified its repressive attitude.

What was far more threatening than peasant or student outbreaks was the patent fact that hardly any element in society refrained from open criticism of government policy. The nobles, despite the government's solicitude for their economic welfare, nourished their own grievances. Many of them were unable to reconcile themselves to the loss of their exclusive position of privilege; they tended to resent particularly the loss of their seignorial jurisdiction over the peasantry. In this mood, they tended to think that they should receive compensation in the form of the right to participate in the formulation of state policy at the highest level.

Thus, once again there were developing within the ranks of the most privileged group constitutional aspirations such as had been dimly foreshadowed at the time of the accession of Anna, more consciously formulated in the early days of Catherine, and reaching revolutionary proportions in the minds of the Decembrists. In the atmosphere of the period of the Great Reforms, these ambitions constituted a more serious danger to the principle of autocracy than at any previous time. Even the ruling class could no longer be relied on for slavish submission. It was pure accident that Karakozov, the crank who attempted to assassinate the emperor in 1866, was a noble, but Alexander had some reason to make a parade of the fact.

Some, for whom the term "repentant nobles" was coined, went much farther in their criticism of the government. Among them, the nobility of Tver, who had taken the most advanced position with respect to emancipation, again took the lead. These men were willing to make even greater sacrifices than had been demanded of them; they offered to renounce their exemption from taxation and from military conscription. Yet, while they thus proposed broader and more thoroughgoing reforms than were actually being made, they denied the competence—even the right—of the autocracy and its bureaucrats to make any reforms whatever. They insisted on the right of the people—the whole people, not merely the nobility—to determine what should be done and how it should be done. In 1862, the Tver nobility published a formal address to the emperor, openly and emphatically stating these views. Their "peace mediators," assembled in provincial congress, went further and specifically refused any longer to be governed by directions from above, asserting that their responsibility was to the public. This challenge was squarely met; the thirteen nobles in official position who had signed the defiant document were imprisoned for five months and narrowly escaped serving two-year sentences. Yet the government could not proceed against the Tver nobility as a whole and had to ignore the corporate address, which evoked sympathetic echoes elsewhere.

The attitude of the nobles was most dangerous and largely accounts for the emphasis on the all-class principle in the subsequent bureaucratic reforms of local government and of the judiciary. The oppositional mood, however, was by no means confined to the nobility. The non-noble intelligentsia, though less powerful, was more extreme.

In Russia, even more than in the West, revolutionary thought naturally developed most strongly among those elements of the population which, while well-educated, had the least secure status in society. In Russia particularly, this element, while standing above the masses, found itself excluded also from the topmost stratum. Known as *raznochintsy* ("men of no set rank"), they "hovered 'twixt heaven and hell.'" Generally full of magnanimous idealism, they inevitably tended to project their own interests upon their view of society as a whole and threw themselves zealously into the effort to reconstitute the social, political, and economic structure.

They had begun to be numerous in the first half of the nineteenth century. Unlike their noble precursors, down to and including the Decembrists, the new intelligentsia did not draw its inspiration from French Rationalism; they were subject to the powerful influence of post-Kantian German Idealism. Sometimes at first hand, more often at second or even third hand, they absorbed in more or less distorted form the ideas of Fichte, Schelling, and Hegel. For the most part, they spent their energies in abstract metaphysical disputes about moral problems, dividing roughly into the two great camps of Westerners and Slavophiles already alluded to.

Among them the leading figure was the "Westerner" Bielinsky (1811-48), who, perhaps because he did not know German, was able to shake off his early imperfect understanding of Hegel and throw himself in the 1840's into vigorous positive criticism of the backwardness of Russian life. Though his attacks on the more mystical Slavophiles were quite as sharp as his comments on the official ideology, their leaders recognized his honesty and courage. As the Slavophile Ivan Aksakov wrote to his parents in 1856:

> I have traveled much throughout Russia: the name of Bielinsky is known to every youth who does any thinking at all, to everyone who craves fresh air amidst the stinking bog of provincial life. . . . "We are indebted to Bielinsky as our savior," young men of integrity tell me everywhere in the provinces. . . . And if you need a man of integrity, capable of having compassion for the illnesses and misfortunes of the oppressed, an honest doctor or an honest inspector fit for a fight, in the provinces seek them among the followers of Bielinsky. Of Slavophilism here in the provinces you hear not a sound, or if you do hear one, it is from men of a hostile trend.[1]

Bielinsky's main activity was literary criticism, which under the conditions of the times was also the chief channel for social and political criticism. Hostile to autocracy, he became a partisan of the ideas of the French utopian socialists. In his famous *Letter to Gogol,* written while abroad and therefore uncensored, he burst out:

> Only as an artist do you know Russia deeply, not as a man of thought. . . . Therefore you have not perceived that Russia sees her salvation not in mysticism, not in asceticism, not in humility, but in the progress of civilization, education, humanity. She needs no sermons (she has heard enough of them!) nor prayers (she has repeated enough of them!), but an awakening among the people of a sense of human dignity, for so many centuries lost in mud and filth; she needs rights and laws conforming, not to the teachings of the Church, but to common sense and justice, and the strictest possible implementation of them.[2]

Although never involved in any revolutionary activity, Bielinsky profoundly influenced the later revolutionary generation. In the crackdown that was the government's answer to the revolutions of 1848 in the West, he was saved from arrest only by his death.

His most eminent successor was Alexander Herzen (1812-70), illegitimate son of a Russian aristocrat. His conscience-smitten father gave him education and money but could not give him the sense of having these advantages as a matter of right. In 1833, he was one of a number arrested for celebrating their graduation from the university by singing revolutionary songs; in consequence he spent five years in administrative exile in various provinces. The embittered Herzen became an émigré in 1847 and spent the rest of his life consorting with a strange assortment of Western intellectuals of the most diverse opinions. In 1857, he founded in London a Russian-language paper, *Kolokol* ("The Bell"), which exercised an enormous influence on Russian thinkers and was said to have been read by men like Rostovtsev, chairman of the Editing Commission. Herzen may be regarded as the first representative of that current of Russian thought loosely known as *narodnichestvo*. Though the term may be translated as "populism" (*narod* means "the people"), the result is likely to be confusion with American Populism, a totally different movement; *narodnichestvo* was a form of socialist thought peculiar to Russia and therefore sometimes called "Russian socialism."

Essentially a "Westerner," but with strong Slavophile undertones, Herzen's constant stress was on the virtues of the Russian peasant and of the unofficial pre-Emancipation Russian commune (*mir*). In a letter to his friend, the French historian Michelet (1851), subsequently published as *Russia and Socialism,* he wrote:

> Apart from the tsar and the clergy, all other elements of the society and of the administration are completely alien, essentially hostile to the people. The peasant is placed literally outside the law; justice sees to it that it does not protect him, and his whole participation in the existing order is limited to the twofold tax that crushes him: the tax in blood and the tax in sweat. Thus, poor outcast, he understands instinctively that he is ruled not for his benefit but to his disadvantage, that the whole problem of the government and of the landlords consists only in extorting from him as much labor and as much money as possible. Understanding this, and endowed with a shrewd and cunning mind, he deceives them all and in every way. It could not be otherwise, for if he told them the truth, it would be a confirmation by him, an acceptance of their authority, and if he did not rob them (take note that they accuse the peasant of robbery when he hides a part of the product of his labor), he would inevitably be recognizing the justice of their demands, the rights of the proprietors, and the fairness of the judges. . . .
>
> The Russian people has never lived anything but a communal life; it understands its rights and its duties only in relation to the communes and their members. Apart from them, it recognizes no duties and sees nothing but violence. . . . There is much more freedom in lying before a judge whom one knows to be the agent of an unjust power than in pretending respect for the verdict of a

jury impaneled by a prefect whose revolting lack of justice is clear as day. . . .

The Russian peasant has no morality save that which flows instinctively, naturally, from his communism; it is profoundly of the people; the little he knows of the Gospels nourishes it; the flagrant injustice of the government and of the landlords binds him all the more to his customs and to his commune. . . .

. . . ; the communal organism, though it has been vigorously attacked, has resisted the encroachments of power; happily it has been preserved until the development of socialism in Europe. . . .

The man of the future in Russia is the *muzhik* [peasant—literally "little man"], as the man of regenerated France will be the *worker.*[3]

. . . "Unfortunately, in Russia free speech is still regarded with astonishment, even with horror. I have tried to raise only an edge of the heavy curtain that conceals us from Europe."

Despite the normal vigor of his pronouncements, Herzen's attitude toward the government oscillated from extreme adulation when he thought it was about to realize his ideas to severe criticism when it disappointed him. Although in 1862 he endorsed the constitutionalist aspirations of the nobility, his most insistent arguments, apart from the "peasant question," were for mitigation, rather than for abolition, of autocratic techniques. His newspaper, *Kolokol,* itself chided the younger generation of revolutionaries in Russia for their extremism, much as the surviving Decembrists in Siberia condemned Herzen for "washing Russia's dirty linen with the eyes of the world fixed upon him." His own influence, which had been paramount in Russian intellectual circles in the 1850's, suffered rapid eclipse because of his support of the Polish insurrection of 1863-64.

NARODNICHESTVO IN THEORY

The obvious imminence of reform after publication of Alexander's Rescript in 1857 and the attendant moderate relaxation of the censorship invited the emergence in Russia itself of revolutionary intellectual criticism in the spirit of *narodnichestvo*. Its chief exponent was Nikolai G. Chernyshevsky (1828-89), the highly educated and extremely verbose son of a provincial ecclesiastical family, officially regarded in the Soviet Union as the greatest of the "pre-Marxist" Russian thinkers. In view of his humble origin and his great personal talents, the only career open to him was in journalism and literature. In 1858, he became economic editor of the *Contemporary,* once the chief vehicle for the expression of Bielinsky's thought, and with which Chernyshevsky had been connected since 1854; with him was associated, at the head of the department of literary criticism, the brilliant young Dobroliubov (1836-61), son of a provincial priest, who was to become renowned for his appreciation of Goncharov's *Oblomov* and for his concept of the "superfluous man." Chernyshevky soon went beyond his agitation for more education and less censorship; he dropped his praise of Alexander as greater than Peter. His acerbity alienated the liberal novelists, such as Turgenev (whose *Sportsman's Sketches* were said to have influenced Alexander in favor of emancipation), Goncharov, and Leo Tolstoy, then only a rising star. Despite the fact that he was living and writing in Russia and therefore, unlike Herzen, had to face the censorship, Chernyshevsky became the advocate of the most radical solution of the peasant question.

Constantly stressing materialist—and at the same time, ethical—views, Chernyshevsky did not share Herzen's exalted views of the peasant and of the commune. More in the spirit of Marx, but without any reference to him, Chernyshevsky tried to argue for the scientific necessity of radical action. Rejecting in general the philosophy of Hegel, he nevertheless applied the "triadic law," which he used to demonstrate the alleged inevitability of the transition from the primitive peasant commune, through its antithesis, the regime of individual private property and capitalism, to the ultimate synthesis, the advanced communism of the future. He was convinced that Russia was fortunate in that this transition could be accomplished practically immediately. without going through a long intermediate period of capitalist development. "History, like a grandmother, passionately loves the youngest grandchildren"; backward Russia could skip whole stages of social evolution.[4]

Chernyshevsky's activity, though of profound importance for the development of the revolutionary movement, in its *narodnik* form, was short-lived. In 1862 he was arrested and, after months of imprisonment, sentenced to fourteen years at hard labor in Siberia. While in prison he wrote his famous novel, *What Is to Be Done?* In it Chernyshevsky picked up the challenge to "the new man" that Turgenev had posed in *Fathers and Sons* by his delineation of Bazarov. Whereas Turgenev had presented an accurate but coldly dispassionate analysis of his young hero, Chernyshevsky supplied a warm appreciation of the "sons," with their high standards of work, not for themselves but for the good of society, dominated by the shade of Robert Owen. Though the novel was of scant literary merit, the circumstances under which it was written and the communist views long-windedly expressed by its characters made it a sort of Bible for would-be revolutionaries of all shades in the next generation. After twenty years in Siberia, during which he produced nothing more of note, Chernyshevsky was allowed to go to Astrakhan; he was allowed to return to his native Saratov only in 1889, when he had but a few months left to live.

Publication of the Emancipation proclamation and its attendant statutes provoked, besides peasant revolts and student disorders, a spate of revolutionary proclamations. Among them, "To the Young Generation" (1861) and "Young Russia" (1862) were especially distinguished by their ferocious tone; they threatened the dynasty, the police, and all enemies of "the people" with wholesale annihilation. "Young Russia," in particular, called for the immediate establishment of a federated communal republic, to be achieved by the voluntary coöperation of Russians with the Poles and the Lithuanians, of Orthodox believers with the persecuted schismatics and sectarians. It appealed to youth as "our main hope" and advocated the emancipation of women by the abolition of marriage. A number of secret societies were formed, including "Land and Freedom" and "Great Russia." The government replied by arresting and punishing all its prominent critics, including Chernyshevsky, and by ruthlessly ferreting out their followers.

For a time the rising tide of Russian socialism seemed threatened by an intellectual withdrawal from social and political problems. In *Fathers and Sons* (1862), Turgenev had put in Bazarov's mouth the phrase "I am a nihilist." Dmitry I. Pisarev (1840-68), a brilliant young literary critic just out of the university, proudly seized on this epithet as truly descriptive of himself. Pisarev was an extreme individualist, so radical that he even asserted:

> It is impossible to regard woman as an instrument to be employed in family life and useful in bringing up [children]: it must not be forgotten that a woman is an independent individual, with her own spiritual needs and with a right to her independent development.[5]

Occasionally on the verge of mental breakdown and sometimes compared to Nietzsche, Pisarev laid about him with a characteristically heavy hand:

> Here is the ultimatum of our camp: what can be smashed, must be smashed; whatever survives a blow has value, whatever flies to smithereens is rubbish; in any case, smash right and left, it will and can do no harm.[6]

Among those he regarded as fit for the rubbish heap were Pushkin and Lermontov, Chaadaev and Bielinsky, even Chernyshevsky and Dobroliubov.

Three and a half years in prison (1862-66) did not break his spirit but perhaps helped to tone down his concept of the individual as the center and meaning of the universe. In "Realists," written in 1864 "to my best friend, my mother," he took the position:

> For a realist the idea of human solidarity is simply one of the basic laws of nature, one of those laws which are violated every minute by our ignorance and which by their violation give birth to all the chronic sufferings of our nature. The human organism, the realist argues, is so constructed that it can develop in a human way and satisfy all our needs only if it is in constant and varied relationships with other similar organisms. Simply and shortly expressed, a man needs for his own well-being the society of other men.[7]

Yet, for the masses, whether workers or peasants, Pisarev had only contempt; poverty bred stupidity, and stupidity bred poverty. Such "proletarian realism" could have no profound social significance. The concept of "nihilism," developed by Pisarev, had only a tangential effect on the growth of *narodnichestvo,* providing some of its adherents with a sort of intellectual rationalization of terrorism.

More potent in this respect, however, were the contributions of an older man, Michael Bakunin (1814-76), a contemporary and close friend of Herzen. In a sense, Bakunin was a misfit among the revolutionary intelligentsia, themselves misfits in society. Of a very well-to-do family, decidedly aristocratic on his mother's side, Bakunin was utterly unable to get along with his father. A graduate of the Artillery School, his personality blocked his career; he resigned his commission in 1834. Bielinsky, in his last personal letter to Bakunin (1838), tried to hold up a mirror for his formerly intimate friend:

> Strength, savage power, restless, uneasy, deep stirring of the spirit, ceaseless onward striving, lack of satisfaction with the present moment, even hatred for the present moment and for yourself at the present moment, rushing from details to the general—there are your characteristics; there must also be added a lack of cordiality (of *Gemütlichkeit*), of delicacy, so to speak, in your relations with persons close to you. . . . I do not know how to express my feeling toward you except *as love which is like hatred and hatred which is like love.* . . .
>
> Farewell. One way or another, *forever* yours.[8]

Bakunin's knowledge of German enabled him to study Hegel at first hand. His voluntary emigration, however, brought him into direct contact with a wide assortment of Western radicals. He was particularly attracted by the ideas of the anarchist Proudhon, though he had no sympathy for the latter's faith in peaceful propaganda. In 1848, the Paris revolutionaries succeeded in diverting Bakunin's energies to the plight of the Germans; he was one of the triumvirate—which included also Richard Wagner—that unsuccessfully defended Dresden against the Prussian army in 1849. Condemned to death by court-martial, he was handed over to Austria, which reassumed the presidency of the German Confederation in 1850; again condemned to death, he was surrendered to his native Russia (1851). Without a new trial, he was incarcerated, first in Peter and Paul, later in Schlüsselburg; in 1857 he was released to permanent Siberian exile. There he married a Polish merchant's daughter but escaped to China. He entered America by the Golden Gate, was entertained by the Brahmins of Boston, and fled back to Western Europe (1861), where he spent the balance of his days in plotting the establishment of a completely free society by way of "destruction—terrible, total, universal, and inexorable." [9] He preached

> destruction of all the religious, political, juridical, economic, and social institutions that constitute the present bourgeois order of things.
>
> We have complete faith in the instincts of the masses and understand Revolution as *an organized outburst* of what is called *revolutionary passion* and as a destruction of that which in bourgeois language is called *social order.*

> We acknowledge ANARCHISM as the expression of the people's life and aspirations. . . .[10]

Since he was totally opposed to any "system of authority" whatever, he rejected a "so-called revolutionary dictatorship or provisional government. . . ." Specifically, for his own country,

> we want radical destruction, complete annihilation of that empire of Russia which is a menace for the freedom of the world, a shameful prison for all the peoples subject to it, a violent and systematic negation of everything called human right, justice, humanity.[11]

Bakunin did not attempt to return to Russia; instead, he became a thorn in the side of Karl Marx, who secured Bakunin's expulsion from the First International in 1872. His teachings penetrated Russia, but without producing substantial results. A *narodnik* in the sense that he put all his faith in a peasant uprising, Bakunin scorned as "stupid" the idea of "teaching the People":

> What can we do for them? . . . Only one thing, but an extremely important thing: we can give them what they have hitherto lacked and the lack of which was the chief cause of all their defeats—*the unity of a universal movement. . . .*[12]

Plan, system, organization—this would enable a revolt to succeed. This is the same Bakunin who in 1862 had written that he would rather put his faith in Alexander II than in a new Pugachev or Pestel.

The absurdity of his recurrent dream of a mass peasant uprising reduced his practical significance to that of an advocate, though a hesitating one, of acts of individual terrorism. The most direct consequence of his teaching was the formation, in 1869, of a secret society with the magniloquent title of "The People's Assize." It was absolutely controlled, on the basis of a cellular structure, by Nechaiev, a protégé of Bakunin with winning personal manners; its sole achievement was the murder in 1870 of one of its own members, a student whom Nechaiev suspected of independence of mind.

Bakunin was the last man capable of standing at the head of a "general staff of revolution." As his friend Herzen wrote to him in 1863:

> Cut off from life, steeped from your youth in German Idealism, from which time, *dem Schema nach,* made a Realist philosophy, not knowing Russia either before your imprisonment or after Siberia, but full of broad and passionate inclinations to noble activity—you have lasted to the age of 50 in a world of phantoms . . . of great aspirations and petty faults. . . . After 10 years of confinement, you have shown yourself the same theorist, with all the uncertainty *du vague* [of the void], a windbag . . . unscrupulous in money matters, with a share of mild but persistent epicureanism, and with an itch for revolutionary activity that falls short of revolution.[13]

Yet, notwithstanding the obviously aristocratic nature of his concept of an elite of "forty or even fifty thousand men" to direct "the irresistible but still latent power of the people,"[14] Bakunin's teachings found many disciples among Russian revolutionaries, though largely in the Blanquist version of Tkachev.

Peter N. Tkachev (1844-85) was one of the most earnest believers among Russians in the doctrine of economic materialism. Yet his thinking was highly subjective. He anticipated Lenin's fierce concentration on the seizure of political power as the necessary preliminary to any serious revolutionary achievement. In Tkachev's view, accomplishment of this goal could not be effected by educating the masses; what was needed was "a disciplined organization of revolutionary forces . . . based on centralized authority and decentralized revolutionary functions . . . seizure of power from above . . . a popular uprising from below."[15] It was a formula which, under more favorable circumstances, Lenin was to apply. In Tkachev's time, however, this program, translated into working terms, could mean only systematic assassination of persons vested with state authority.

Similar to Bakunin in his concept of the role of the intelligentsia as the general staff of revolution, though wholly dissimilar in tactics, was Peter L. Lavrov (1823-1900), who was perhaps the foremost systematizer of *narodnik* thought. Son of a retired colonel who was also a wealthy landowner, Lavrov was himself a teacher of mathematics in the Artillery School. Despite the conservatism of his background, Lavrov became implicated in the fringes of the revolutionary movement and was sent into administrative exile in the north. There he wrote his *Historical Letters,* published in 1868-69; in 1870 he escaped abroad and from 1873 to 1876 edited in Switzerland the anti-Bakuninist journal *Forward.*

Although on better terms with Marx than was Bakunin, Lavrov could not accept the "scientific" aspects of the idea of class struggle. As Lavrov phrased the general opinion of the *narodniki,* "however small the progress of mankind, whatever there is rests exclusively on critically thinking individuals; without them it is unconditionally impossible." [16] The majority of men are condemned "to monotonous, exhausting, and incessant commonplace toil for the advantage of others, with no leisure for the work of thinking . . . and therefore they have remained incapable of using their enormous power for the conquest of the right to education, to truly human life." [17]

Realizing the debt they owe to the suffering masses, "critically thinking individuals" are obligated to devote all their intellectual energies to improvement of the condition of the people. Lavrov explained at length how, through successive stages, this handful of individuals could become a significant social force:

> For victory the organization of a party is necessary. . . . Its kernel is a small number of cultivated, reflective, energetic men, for whom critical thought is inseparable from action. Around them are the less cultivated men of the intelligentsia. The real soil of the party is in its inevitable allies, in the social groups suffering from the evil to combat which the party has been organized.

> Establishing the distinction between the essential and the non-essential in individual opinions defines alike the freedom of action within the party and its outward tolerance. . . . Any member of the party who passes these bounds is no longer a member but an enemy. Any person outside it who differs from it on essential questions is likewise an enemy. . . .[18]

NARODNICHESTVO IN ACTION

Thus by Lavrov was formulated the distinctive tactic of Russian socialism, the strictly disciplined party of the elite. Grafted onto Marxian concepts of class struggle and proletarian action, the idea was destined to enable a handful of men to ride to power in the crisis of 1917. *Narodnichestvo* itself, however, was to fail, not because it was unsuccessful in attracting the support of the masses, but because its devotion to subjective principles made it impossible, as it was for Lavrov himself, to subject its followers to rigid discipline and ruthless concerted action. The *narodniki* proved to be too obviously conscious of their own intellectual superiority to the masses, too unwilling to abandon, even momentarily, their own cherished programs of what they deemed to be right, to be able to take advantage of fleeting opportunities and to seat themselves firmly in power. Their fault was shared by all of the revolutionaries in 1917, except the Bolsheviks.

It was reform that had first brought revolutionary zeal to the boil. The reactionary trend that so soon set in and the nascent revolutionary movement had a mutually stimulating effect on each other. The constitutionalist aspirations of the more sober portion of society became obscured by the urge for social revolution that grew more widespread and active among the intelligentsia. Its direction was chiefly determined by the ideas that Lavrov had expounded in his *Historical Letters.* The first of a number of groups that sought to implement these ideas was the circle formed around young N. V. Chaikovsky in 1871.

Large numbers of young men and young women began to throw themselves into the "Go to the People" (*v narod*) phase of the *narodnik* movement. Taking jobs as doctors, nurses, teachers, clerks, or sometimes as migratory laborers, they flocked by the hundreds to the villages. Their purposes were often vague, and not always revolutionary in any direct sense. They tried to distribute the writings of Chernyshevsky, Dobroliubov, Lavrov, and even the first volume of Marx's *Capital,* translated into Russian in 1872. They soon found it more effective to fall back on their own secretly printed pamphlets. Among these revolutionary idealists was Prince Peter Kropotkin (1842-1921), a lineal descendant of Rurik, who had abandoned his military career to devote himself to the study of natural science; he shared Bakunin's anarchist ideals, though not his notions of flaming revolt; from 1872 until his arrest in 1874 he carried on agitation among the workers of St. Petersburg.

The "Go to the People" movement was of short duration and bore no fruits. On the one hand, the police had no difficulty in finding and arresting these inexperienced and naïve agitators. On the other hand, the peasantry evinced a natural rural mistrust of city slickers, whose teachings seemed calculated, if they could have any effect at all, to get the peasants into trouble with the authorities. A series of mass trials, culminating in "the trial of the 193" in 1877, disheartened the participants in this sort of haphazard agitation.

Returning to the idea of organization, *narodnik* enthusiasts reconstructed "Land and Freedom" (*Zemlia i volia*) in 1877. Its constitution was quite elaborate, its aims quite simple. Its principal purpose was still to make propaganda among the "people," i.e., the peasantry, in preparation for the ultimate goal of a Bakuninist general uprising. For the most part, the society conducted itself quite peacefully; on occasion its members might encourage the peasants to demonstrate by a petition, a strike, or a refusal to pay taxes. Only in one case did the society attempt to foment a local armed uprising; at Chigirin in 1877, they distributed a forged document purporting to be a summons to action issued by the tsar himself. The agitators were to try to make contact with other focuses of resistance to the government, such as oppressed religious groups; students and workers were not to be neglected.

The harder the *narodniki* tried to rouse the peasantry, the more they were driven to the belief that "the people" were too backward to be able to reorganize society from below under existing conditions. Unwilling to give up in despair, they turned impatiently toward the idea of reversing their efforts; instead of seeking reform from below, they chose to seek it by "disorganizing" the state through a campaign of deliberate terrorism. A special small group within "Land and Freedom" was charged with this specific task.

The earliest such attempt was made by Vera Zasulich, a girl who shot at General Trepov, chief of police of St. Petersburg; the occasion was his order that an imprisoned student, with whom she was not even acquainted, be flogged for having refused to remove his hat while being questioned (1878). To the dismay of the government, she was acquitted by a jury; when the police tried to take "administrative" action against her, she was rescued by a crowd outside the courtroom. Several assassinations of officials followed; more successful in their immediate purpose, they however contributed less to the broader objective of rousing public sympathy and brought swift retaliation from the government.

Nevertheless, a firmer terrorist organization was founded by Zheliabov, an ex-student of peasant origin, within the framework of "Land and Freedom." The older or cooler members, including George V. Plekhanov (1857-1918), son of a small landlord, who had first attracted attention as speaker at a demonstration before the Kazan Cathedral in St. Petersburg

(December 6, 1876), formed in 1879 a new, non-terrorist organization known as "General Redistribution" (*Chernyi Perediel*). The majority, however, supported Zheliabov's "The People's Will" (*Narodnaia Volia*), which soon resolved to concentrate all its attention on the emperor himself. There followed two years of feverish activity, romanticized as "the hunt of the wild beast." Streets were mined, trains derailed; a carpenter, Khalturin, employed in the Winter Palace, took the opportunity to set a bomb timed to blow up the emperor at dinner. It seemed all to no avail, especially when Zheliabov himself was captured, allowing the authorities to breathe more easily.

However, very shortly after his arrest, his fellow-conspirators, guided by Sophia Perovskaia, succeeded in assassinating the "Tsar-Liberator" as he was driving through the streets of his capital; though a first bomb failed to injure him, a second caught Alexander as he was commiserating with the wounded victims of the first bomb; it shredded the lower half of his body (March 1, 1881). The enormous revulsion of public feeling against such a deliberate and brutal murder helped to discourage even the most devoted terrorists; in addition, the rate of executions—one per lunar month during the "hunt of the wild beast"—suggested that the supply of revolutionists would be exhausted before the supply of Grand Dukes. In a few years, terrorism had subsided, and with it the *narodnik* movement of which it had been the most spectacular aspect seemed to be a thing of the past. Even "General Redistribution" was dissolved.

In exile in Switzerland, Plekhanov and a handful of associates underwent intellectual conversion, abandoning the subjective concept of "the critically thinking individual" for the more comfortable "scientific socialism" of Karl Marx. The ideological transition was tremendously assisted by dawning realization of the falsity of the cherished notion—so stressed by Chernyshevsky—that Russia could escape the development of industrial capitalism. In view of the rapid and increasingly obvious growth in the midst of agrarian Russia of significant capitalist industry, Russian thinkers had to find some other basis for a millennial future than the old agrarian commune. In 1883 four men and one woman founded at Geneva the first Russian social-democratic group, styled "Emancipation of Labor" (*Osvobozhdenie Truda*). In the course of the 1890's, similar groups began to be formed in Russia itself; they waged a vigorous war of words against survivals of *narodnik* thought.

Marxism had a profound effect on the university generation of the 1890's, though less as a revolutionary doctrine than as a climate of opinion, generating the most various practical conclusions. "Legal Marxism," accepting Marxist philosophical concepts stripped of any revolutionary content, became widespread and was even encouraged by manufacturers who found in it a rational justification for the growth of capitalism and the ascendancy of the bourgeoisie. Others, more concerned with its avowed implications for proletarian welfare, sought to use Marxism, in the "revised" sense already being popularized in the West by Eduard Bernstein, to advance the material interests of the workers; the attitude of these "Economists" entailed illegal work but did not emphasize the necessity of immediate overthrow of the autocracy.

Still others, including the young V. I. Lenin, whose older brother, Alexander Ulianov, had been hanged for participation in *narodnik* terrorism, stood with the exiled Plekhanov in favor of concentration on the political struggle against the government. A special-interest group, the "Bund," was formed in 1897 among the discontented Jewish workers. In 1898, an effort was made to weld the scattered Marxist "circles" into a single organization. Only nine intellectuals, secretly assembled at Minsk, formally founded the Russian Social-Democratic Workers' Party. Though no workers were in attendance, police informers were; most of the "apparatus" of the new party was promptly put under lock and key.

RUSSIFICATION AND THE JEWS

To the weakness of the revolutionary movement corresponded the strength of the reactionary repression. Throughout the later years of Alexander II, under Alexander III, and in the early years of the reign of Nicholas II, it was the policy of the government, with minor vacillations, to whittle away any bits of liberalism that had more or less accidentally been embedded in the "Great Reforms." Not a whit less than in the reign of Nicholas I, the purpose of the ruler was clear—to maintain the principle of autocracy and, along with it, the principles of orthodoxy and nationalism.

The schismatics and the numerous dissenting sects were vigorously persecuted. At the same time was undertaken a policy of "Russification" of the heterogeneous ethnic elements that the expansion of the empire had been bringing under the sway of "Great Russia." The leaders of the Little Russian (Ukrainian) literary movement were for the most part driven abroad; after 1889, the deliberate conciliatory policy of the Austrian government toward its "Ruthenian" subjects in Galicia made this question an added source of international friction. The Poles continued to be a special target of Russian repression, especially after the defeat of the insurrection of 1863-64. From the end of the 1880's, a similar policy was directed at the dominant German middle-class element in the Baltic provinces, despite the fact that the descendants of the Baltic barons had become loyal members of the Russian aristocracy; among other measures, the university town of Dorpat was rechristened Yuriev. Even Finland, despite its special status as an autonomous grand duchy, found its liberties curtailed at the end of the 1890's. In Central Asia, Buddhists and Moslems were subjected to severe restrictions.

Especially drastic were the measures taken against the Jews, who by mid-century numbered over three million. Early in his reign, Alexander II had announced (March 31, 1856) his intention

> to review all existing decrees on the Jews in order to make them agree with the general aims of fusing this people with the native inhabitants as far as the moral condition of the Jews may permit.[19]

The measures actually taken were small, but eagerly welcomed by the wealthy portion of the Jews.

In 1859, Jewish merchants of the first rank were permitted to establish permanent residence outside the Pale. In 1861, this permission was extended to Jews with university degrees who entered the government civil service, except in the two capitals; only in 1879 was it applied to all Jews with certificates of higher education. In 1865, artisans with special qualifications were also permitted to remove from the Pale; in their wake a considerable number of proletarian Jews were able to escape, illegally and precariously, from the area in which the mass remained pent up. As a further step toward peaceful Russification, as early as 1844 a number of officially directed elementary schools had been established for Jewish children in the Pale; those who attended them were exempted from military conscription. The resistance of most Jews to exposing their children to these official schools had led Alexander to announce in 1855 that the traditional *heders* and *yeshivas* were to be eliminated in twenty years; this intention was ultimately abandoned (1879). Another cherished device for combating the "separatism" of the Jews, the policy of encouraging their resettlement in agricultural colonies, was also scrapped (1866).

The hope of the government was now centered on chipping off from the Jewish masses the educated and prosperous elements in Russian Jewry. It seemed largely on the way to realization. Jewish financiers transferred their investments from farming the liquor traffic (a system abolished in 1861) into the building of railways and related large-scale business enterprises. A new Jewish intelligentsia, made up of graduates of Russian universities and Gymnasia, condemned the narrow backwardness of traditional Hasidism and threw themselves into the arms of *Haskalah* (Enlightenment). Some of these intellectually emancipated young Jews, reacting against the obscurantism of their cultural background, became allies of the government in its fight against separatism. Others, accepting the Russian intelligentsia as the bearers of true cosmopolitanism, took active part in the *narodnik* movement. Others again, despising the "medievalism" of the orthodox Jews, still had no desire to cease to be distinctive as Jews; such was Moses Lilienblum (1843-1910), who evolved into an active proponent of political Zionism.

In the years of general reaction that characterized the latter portion of the reign of the "Liberator," anti-Semitism began to grow both in official circles and among the Russian masses. In 1870, after a visit to Poland, the emperor ordered stricter enforcement of the laws against the attire obstinately affected by the Jewish rank and file. In 1871, a frightful pogrom occurred in Odessa; for three days the troops did not interfere with rioting and looting mobs. After the assassination of Alexander II, anti-Semitism was given free rein. In 1881, violent pogroms took place in Yelizavetgrad in New Russia, at Kiev, and in a number of other towns and villages; Odessa suffered again. The one at Warsaw was the most conspicuous, for Catholic Poland had long been free from such excesses of barbarism.

The pogroms provoked a storm of protest abroad. In Great Britain, the Bishop of London, speaking for the Archbishop of Canterbury, joined with a number of eminent laymen, including the aged Earl of Shaftesbury and Lord Bryce, and with Cardinal Manning in expressing their horror. The Gladstone government did not feel it had the right to make official representations about an internal matter, but the government of the United States officially registered its distress. In Russia most literary figures, including Leo Tolstoy, refrained from joining in the chorus of condemnation raised abroad by men such as Tennyson, Renan, and Victor Hugo; Shchedrin-Saltykov, the satirist, was almost alone in voicing his denunciation.

The government attempted to explain the pogroms as the work of revolutionaries. It was a notion that was given only a very faint color by an appeal issued, late in the summer of 1881, in the name of the Executive Committee of the "People's Will," calling on the Ukrainians to rise against the landlords, the Jews, and the tsar's officials. Apparently convinced that the Jews, by their economic "exploitation" of the Christian masses, had merely incurred the righteous resentment of the loyal Orthodox people, the authorities at first took no drastic action. Instead, Ignatiev, Minister of the Interior, publicly announced that "The Western border is open to them. . . . They have already made use of this opportunity and nobody has put obstacles in the way of their emigration." [20]

Ignatiev succeeded in imposing on the Jews new "Temporary Rules" (May 3, 1882); under them, in the future no Jew might settle or acquire real estate in any rural community, even in the Pale; Jews were forbidden to do business on Sundays or on Christian holidays. Ignatiev was, however, overruled by his ministerial colleagues in the handling of pogroms; an edict of May 13 warned the governors of provinces that they would be held responsible for failure to check pogroms. Ignatiev resigned soon after; his successor, Count Dmitry Tolstoy, famous for his reactionary conduct of the Ministry of Education under Alexander II, emphasized that any disorders would lead to prompt prosecution of the responsible local officials. Pogroms became relatively rare occurrences for the next score of years.

The virtual cessation of major pogroms did not signify the adoption of a more liberal policy toward the Jews. On the contrary, enforcement of special legislation against them became more energetic. Large numbers of Jews were expelled, on one pretext or another, from villages in the Pale. Illegal residents outside the Pale were rounded up and returned; on one occasion, Sir

Samuel Montagu, a British M.P., was given twenty-four hours to get out of Moscow. The employment of Jews in the army medical service was sharply curtailed (1882), and the Ministry of Justice was given authority to veto the promotion of Jewish attorneys to the rank of barrister (1889). In 1887, a quota system for admission of Jews to universities was established: in the Pale, where anywhere from 30 to 80 percent of the urban population was Jewish, the figure was set at 10 percent of the Christian population; outside the Pale, the quota was only 5 percent, in the two capitals 3 percent.

The chief reply of the Jews was the growth of the notion of physical escape from Russia. Largely under the influence of Leon Pinsker, the idea of Jewish "auto-emancipation" took shape. Although only a few dozens risked the hardships of life in Palestine, then under Turkish rule, there set in a flood of emigration to the West, and particularly to the United States. By 1890, over two hundred thousand Jews had already established themselves in America, while the financial resources of the French branch of the Rothschilds had been put behind the dribble of emigration to Palestine.

In 1888 a special High Commission, presided over by Count K. I. Pahlen, a former Minister of Justice, seriously challenged the policy of the government.[21] Appointed in 1883, it had been engaged in conscientious review of the laws relating to the Jews, from Catherine's time on, and in evaluating, "wholly dispassionately and objectively," the accusations brought against the Jews by the advocates of special legislation. The Commission found that the long-established objectives of "gradual rapprochement" and "fusion of the Jews with the general Christian population" were sound, and it strongly criticized a number of lapses into discriminatory regulations, particularly after 1865. It praised the efforts that had been made to assimilate the Jews through developing the educational system but acknowledged that admission of all, without distinction of status, to secondary schools and to institutions of higher learning had permitted entry of masses of Jews "from the market place and from the street." They were badly prepared and frequently morally depraved, and these students, "for the most part receiving no regular religious instruction, were naturally more subject than others to the influences of nihilistic and revolutionary propaganda."

The Commission recognized that "a considerable influence creating dislike of Jews is still the secret feeling against non-Christians on religious grounds," particularly among the common people. The policy of complete religious toleration consistently pursued by the Orthodox Church and by the Russian state had, however, been quite correct. Although "religious difference is one of the chief reasons for the impossibility of permitting immediately rapprochement of the native Russian population with the Jews," this prejudice—as well as differences in social customs—could be overcome with time and with the spread of education.

A far greater danger, thought the Commission, was abandonment by Jews of their traditional faith. The high percentage of Jews addicted to anarchistic and revolutionary doctrines was the result of the large number of the "half-educated who have managed to leave one shore without reaching the other." The altruism professed by revolutionaries was quite contrary to the natural egotistic and selfish conservatism of the Jewish religious communities. The "masses of students from the lower strata of the Jewish population, without means of subsistence and without any religious beliefs, embittered by their difficult personal situation and by the oppression of the special laws" were merely a symptom of the wider problem.

The charges against the Jews that the High Commission found to be really valid were four in number:

> (a) Jewish isolation and exclusiveness; (b) a tendency to get control of the economic strength of the population; (c) a tendency to shirk state obligations [in this respect the Jews had shown so much improvement that there was no further cause for worry]; and (d) avoidance of physical, muscular labor.

This last fault had blocked all efforts to settle Jews on the land (or in Palestine); there was little hope of overcoming it, for "the Jew lives by his head, he is proud, and he will not stoop to physical heavy labor."

It was the first two criticisms of the Jews which, in the opinion of the Commission, the government should strive to correct. Unfortunately, many Jews, particularly in the lower strata, "regarding themselves, as of old, as the chosen people . . . consider the world about them as the world of the despised 'goy,' " with whom they want only business contacts. "It must be admitted that our government itself, by creating for Jews a whole labyrinth of special rules . . . has in the highest degree strengthened and reinforced this isolation . . . has concentrated the strength of Jewry, strengthened its bad influence and has thus attained absolutely negative results; it has not made over the Jews into good citizens, it has not schooled them to 'useful labor,' . . ." There was, remarked the Commission, no solidarity among the Jews except in their common resistance to oppression.

"The passion for acquisition and money-grubbing is inherent in the Jew from the day of his birth; it is a characteristic of the Semitic race, manifest from almost the first pages of the Bible." It was especially strong among the uneducated and was "stimulated also by the helplessness and insecurity of his family, by the desire to protect himself and his relatives from poverty, hunger, and all sorts of oppression." It found expression chiefly in usury and liquor-selling, but "in justice it must be admitted that for the most part the Jewish usurer is no worse and no more merciless than are professional usurers of other nationalities (Greeks, Armenians, and sometimes even Russians)." Moreover, "the peasants would not so frequently fall into the toils of the Jews if it were not for their habit of drinking liquor . . . passing so often into *intoxication.*"

All the efforts to improve the Jews by punitive and regulatory laws had failed, in the Commission's judgment. "Given the flexibility of the Jewish mind, their skill at evasion and concealment, and with the help of hundreds of other devices," the Jew constantly got round all such laws. The policy of repression by discriminatory legislation had consistently led to results contrary to its purposes and must be abandoned.

It was foolish, the Commission remarked, even to ask whether the Jews were of any use to society. Besides aiding trade, they had produced numbers of gifted scholars, technicians, artists, and physicians. "The purity of their morals, their high respect for learning, their absolute sobriety, their thrift and constant activity . . . deserve all praise."

In addition to reasons of state, the Commission advanced "considerations of a humanitarian character" pointing to the same conclusions. "About 90 percent of the whole Jewish population forms a mass totally lacking in material security, somewhat resembling a proletariat; a mass living from day to day, in poverty, and under the most grievous sanitary and everyday conditions." To say that they could be earning their living by muscular labor was absurd in view both of their own aversion to it and of the physical weakness bred in them by their manner of life for generations. In addition, "the mass lives in dread of pogroms, in dread of violence. . . ." The Jews were fully justified in complaining of their condition; they could not be expected to show the same patriotism as their fellow-subjects.

The Jewish question, the Commission concluded, was a Russian, not merely a Jewish, problem. Its solution demanded, not palliative measures, but organic reform. Though it was imperative to proceed gradually and cautiously, discriminatory legislation must give way to the enlightened policy envisaged when the problem first arose in the reign of the great Catherine.

In the midst of a general policy of enforced Russification, these opinions were ignored. Instead, there was a continuation of the policy of persecution; one of its striking manifestations was a sudden nocturnal expulsion of Jews from Moscow (1891). Baron Hirsch, a wealthy German Jew, proposed to transfer half of the Russian Jews, now numbering about six million, to Argentina. The failure of this scheme merely contributed to the rapid growth of the idea of founding somewhere a Jewish state, as eloquently advocated in the West by Theodore Herzl; the first Zionist Congress met at Basel in 1897. Simultaneously an alternative remedy took shape in the *Bund,* which attempted to coördinate the activities of the Jewish labor organizations that had begun to be formed in Russia in the 1880's. Not entirely disconnected from the nascent organization of political and social activism among the Jews was a renaissance of specifically Jewish literature; outstanding among Yiddish writers was the humorist who called himself Shalom Aleichem.

REJECTION OF LIBERALISM

Intensified persecution of ethnic and religious minorities was not counterbalanced by any extension of liberty to Orthodox Great Russians. Under all three rulers—Alexander II (1855-81), Alexander III (1881-94), Nicholas II (1894-1917)—the censorship, relaxed prior to Emancipation, grew ever more drastic; if press prosecutions diminished in number, it was chiefly because the opposition had been silenced or driven underground. There were even cases of conversion from liberalism to reaction. The outstanding instance of the tendency of journalists to drift to the right was Michael Katkov (1818-87). In his youth an associate of Bielinsky and Bakunin, in 1850 he had been dismissed from his post as professor of philosophy. A great admirer of England, Katkov won the reputation of being the leading liberal publicist in Russia; in the 1860's he enthused over the new all-class principle embodied in the reforms, particularly of the judiciary. It was in his *Russian Messenger* that Turgenev's *Fathers and Sons* first appeared, but so did the more reactionary novels of Dostoevsky.

Even in the sixties, Katkov had begun to show signs of anti-liberal tendencies, particularly in his bitter hostility to the Polish uprising. He began to develop a leaning toward a special type of Russification, not unlike the principle which, a little more than half a century later, the Bolsheviks were to apply:

> Whoever knows Russian history, whoever has not altogether lost his sense of understanding his environment, can have no doubt of the virtues of the Russian nationality, at least in relation to the state order and to the supreme power by which it is maintained.

Extolling the fertilizing advantage that Russia derived from having incorporated ethnically diverse peoples, Katkov could "only wish . . . that the great nationality which composed its true center of gravity and conditioned its state activity should become ever more a moral force and an element of enlightenment and citizenship." Highly as he valued the Orthodox Church as a traditional national institution, he was glad that "the Russian government, free from any narrow and deadening doctrinairism, is to be Russian, and only Russian, offering to everyone without distinction of faith or of ethnic origin the possibility of being an honorable *Russian* citizen." While he had no objection to the instruction, secular or religious, of the scattered subject nationalities in their own languages, he stressed the importance of Russian as "the general language of the Empire." What troubled him was the government's failure to recognize that alien elements could really be Russified:

> Russia by law recognizes religious toleration; she contains, as do all other [states], alien populations; but her peculiarity consists in the fact that the aliens who were at various times brought into the composition of the Russian state and granted all the rights of Russian citizenship, are required to consider themselves foreigners and to be natural foes of the nationality to which they belong. They are Russian subjects, children of the same fatherland, they live

> with us, are linked with us by a thousand interests . . . but they are compelled to remain non-Russians.[22]

Thus he remained quite distinct from the Slavophiles, among whom at this time the chief figure was Ivan Aksakov (1823-86). The Slavophiles in general, and Aksakov in particular, had never been friendly to the Western concept of liberalism. Their emphasis on mystically conceived theocratic ideas, their refusal to accept Orthodoxy in the Uvarov sense, and the sharp criticisms their notion of Russia's messianic role had led them to make of bureaucratic policy had often attracted the unfavorable attention of the censorship. Yet the Slavophiles, though they nourished wholehearted hatred for St. Petersburg as alien, never challenged the autocratic principle. Constantine Aksakov (1817-60), who had been compelled to shave off his beard in 1848, had indeed proposed, at the accession of Alexander II, the summoning of a zemsky sobor; he had not, however, proposed that such a body, which in past ages had been a consultative body, should now be given legislative authority.

Early in 1880, following Khalturin's unsuccessful bomb explosion in the Winter Palace, Alexander II, after slight hesitation, accepted a suggestion by his son and heir that a new investigating commission be appointed with wide punitive powers. The task was entrusted to General Loris-Melikov, who had distinguished himself by the capture of Kars and who, as Governor-General of Kharkov, had been combining a policy of vigorous repression of revolutionaries with an effort to effect reconciliation between the government and the public. Under his "dictatorship of the heart," the inefficient "Third Section" was reorganized as a department in the Ministry of the Interior; at its head was placed V. K. Pleve, later to be regarded as an organizer of pogroms. Its vigorous activity was not directed only against terrorists. Among others, the most outspoken of the zemstvo liberals, Petrunkevich, was kept in administrative exile from his home province. On the other hand, many ministers were shifted, Dmitry Tolstoy being among those dismissed; reform of burdensome taxes was undertaken. The press censorship was relaxed, though Loris-Melikov personally warned editors that they were not to mention any ideas of a constitution.

After six months of apparent success, the special commission was abolished. Loris-Melikov continued in office as Minister of the Interior. While he advised the emperor against any idea of granting a constitution, he recommended adoption of the principle employed in preparing for Emancipation, when the Editing Commission had consulted with elected representatives of the nobles. His proposal was to permit the zemstvos and the city dumas to elect delegates to advise the Council of State, without themselves being members of that body. When it is remembered that the Council of State was in itself only an advisory—not a legislative—body, the absurdity of any notion that Alexander II was on the point of granting a constitution is apparent.

The project, approved by the emperor on the morning of the day on which he was assassinated (March 13, 1881), died with him. Alexander III (1881-94), despite his filial reluctance to depart from his father's principles, soon dropped both Loris-Melikov and his ideas. Instead, he fell under the influence of his former tutor, Constantine Pobiedonostsev, who in 1880 had been appointed Procurator of the Holy Synod. Pobiedonostsev called in Katkov and Ivan Aksakov to advise the emperor, who accepted their views as representative of those of the public. Tolstoy was recalled to office (1882), this time in the key post of Minister of the Interior. Thenceforth the autocracy pursued a wholly reactionary policy.

On the death of Alexander III, the zemstvo of Tver respectfully petitioned his son and successor, Nicholas II (1894-1917), to allow those local representative bodies "to express their opinion on questions of concern to them, in order that expression of the need and thoughts, not only of spokesmen of the administration, but also of the Russian people might reach the height of the throne. . . ." Nicholas' unpublished comment was: "I am extremely astonished and displeased with this inappropriate *démarche*. . . ." When other zemstvos followed with even less guarded requests for "open access to the throne for the voice of the zemstvo" and for admission "of representatives of all the zemstvos of Russia to meetings of the highest government institutions when questions of concern to the zemstvos are under discussion," the emperor decided to call a halt to these "senseless dreams about participation of representatives of the zemstvos in matters of internal administration" by a flat announcement that, "in dedicating all my powers to the people's welfare, I shall preserve the principle of autocracy just as firmly and unflinchingly as my late unforgettable Parent preserved it." [23]

Thus, it was not the thought of Karl Marx, nor yet that of John Locke, that prevailed in Russia. The dominant tone was set by Pobiedonostev in his *Reflections of a Russian Statesman:*

> What is this freedom by which so many minds are agitated, which inspires so many insensate actions, so many wild speeches, which leads the people so often to misfortune? . . . Among the falsest of political principles is the principle of the sovereignty of the people. . . . The press is one of the falsest institutions of our time. . . . The man in the street may establish [a newspaper] and exercise the concomitant authority with an irresponsibility enjoyed by no other power in the world. . . . There can be no question that learning is light, and that ignorance is darkness, . . . [yet] the school is a deceptive formality when its roots have taken no hold among the people. . . . There are periods when reform is the ripe fruit of social evolution . . . then the reformer appears to be a prophet who speaks with the voice of the public conscience. . . . But when his work is done, sometimes arise after him legions of false prophets. . . . Wealth sets in motion a multitude of the basest impulses of human

nature. . . . It becomes the object of exploitation, and is surrounded by a web of falsehoods of every kind. . . .[24]

It was a challenge that Russian capitalists were about to take up. If the sequel was their own destruction, they at least pulled down also the pillars of autocracy.

NOTES

1. *Aksakov v ego pis'makh,* III, 290-291.
2. Bielinskii, *Polnoe sobranie sochinenii,* X, 213.
3. Herzen, *Le peuple russe et le socialisme,* in *Sobranie sochinenii v tridsati tomakh,* VII, 285-302 *passim.*
4. Chernyshevskii, *"Kritika filosofskikh predubezhdenii protiv obshchinnogo vladeniia"* [Critique of philosophic prejudices against communal landholding], in *Polnoe sobranie sochinenii,* V, 387.
5. Pisarev, review article (1857), *"O vospitanii dievoshek. Sochinenie Fenelona"* [Of the education of girls. A work of Fenelon], in *Sochineniia,* 1894 edition, I, 167.
6. Pisarev, *"Skholastika XIX veka"* [Scholasticism of the nineteenth century], in *Sochineniia,* 1955 edition, I, 135.
7. Pisarev, *"Realisty"* [Realists], *loc. cit.,* III, 164.
8. Bielinskii, *op. cit.,* XI, 345.
9. Bakunin, *"Pravila, kotorymi dolzhny rukovodstvovat'sia revoliutsionery"* [Rules by which revolutionaries should be guided], No. 24, included in *"Katekhizisa revoliutsionera"* [Catechism of a revolutionary], 1869, in Steklov, *Mikhail Aleksandrovich Bakunin,* III, 472 (full text, 468-473).
10. Bakunin, *"K russkim revoliutsioneram"* [To Russian revolutionaries], No. 1, September, 1873, in Dragomanov, *M. A. Bakunin,* pp. 274-275.
11. Bakunin, *Discours prononcés au Congrès de la Paix et de la Liberté à Berne (1868)* . . . , p. 5.
12. Bakunin, *"Postanovka revoliutsionnago voprosa"* [Formulation of the question of revolution], a proclamation issued in 1869, in appendix to Dragomanov, *Pis'ma M. A. Bakunina,* 1896 edition, p. 471.
13. Herzen, *Polnoe sobranie sochinenii i pisem,* XVI, 491-492.
14. Bakunin, *Discours* . . . , *op. cit.,* pp. 15-16.
15. Tkachev, *"Nabat"* [The Tocsin] in *Izbrannye sochineniia na sotsial'no-politicheskie temy,* III, 227-229 *passim.*
16. Lavrov, *Istoricheskiia pis'ma,* p. 95.
17. *Ibid.,* p. 84.
18. *Ibid.,* pp. 147-151 *passim.*
19. *"Zapiska Ministra Vnutrennykh Diel"* [Memorandum of the Minister of the Interior], in *Polnoe sobranie zakonov* . . . (Second collection), No. 42,264 (June 28, 1865), XL, i, 692-703.
20. Wischnitzer, *To Dwell in Safety,* pp. 38-39.
21. Following ten paragraphs (to p. 335) quoted or paraphrased from *"Obshchiia*

soobrazheniia Vysshei Kommisii po sushchestvu vozlozhennoi na nee zadachi" [General observations of the High Commission on the essence of the task imposed on it], Section XXXIV of "Pahlen Report," pp. 252-294 *passim.*

22. Katkov, *Sobranie peredovykh statei Moskovskikh Viedomostei, 1867,* pp. 201, 202, 237, 698, 477.
23. Veselovskii, *Istoriia zemstva . . . ,* III, 498-500.
24. Pobiedonostsev, *Reflections of a Russian Statesman,* pp. 26, 32, 62, 67, 76, 114, 121.

SUGGESTIONS FOR FURTHER READING

Among books previously mentioned, Masaryk is invaluable, though not wholly reliable, for analysis of intellectual currents; Kornilov and Pushkarev give the best general discussions of the period.

Kulczycki's *Geschichte der russischen Revolution* contains a wealth of detail on the development of the Russian revolutionary movement. Yarmolinsky's *Road to Revolution: A Century of Russian Radicalism* is a careful and interesting summary restatement of a familiar topic. Venturi's *Roots of Revolution* is a translation of an excellent Italian study.

The careers of several *narodnik* theorists and activists are examined in Lampert's *Sons Against Fathers* and Wortman's *Crisis of Russian Populism,* respectively. Lavrov's *Historical Letters* are now available in English translation. Herzen's *My Past and Thoughts,* the *Memoirs* of Figner and of Kropotkin, and Stepniak's *Underground Russia* reflect various phases of the movement through the eyes of active participants. Malia's *Alexander Herzen and the Birth of Russian Socialism* is an interesting account of Herzen's earlier career through 1855. Carr's *Michael Bakunin* is the best biography on Bakunin in English but is much inferior to Kaminski's *Michel Bakounine.* Baron's *Plekhanov: The Father of Russian Marxism* is a pioneer study. Mendel's *Dilemmas of Progress in Tsarist Russia: Legal Marxism and Legal Populism* and Kindersley's *The First Russian Revisionists* deal with an important and neglected fringe of radical thought. A significant contrast to the revolutionaries is provided by Thaden's *Conservative Nationalism in Nineteenth-Century Russia.*

On special topics, see Salo Baron's *The Russian Jew under Tsars and Soviets* and Zenkovsky's *Pan-Turkism and Islam in Russia.* Berdiaev's *Origins of Russian Communism,* Hare's *Pioneers of Russian Social Thought,* and Hecker's *Russian Sociology* are attempts at philosophical treatment. Lossky's *History of Russian Philosophy* and Zenkovsky's *History of Russian Philosophy* essay a broader treatment of Russian thought.

Chapter

19

The Autocracy at the Close of the Century: 1860-1900

As the end of the century approached, Russia in her own way showed many of the signs of what in the West has come to be known as *"la fin du siècle."* This was particularly true of domestic developments.

IMPERIAL EXPANSION AND CONSOLIDATION*

In international developments, Russia at this time showed less clearly the stigmata of approaching catastrophe. Internal tension did not prevent Russia from continuing the expansion of her territory. Throughout the centuries, Russia has somewhat resembled an amoeba, pushing out pseudopodia less in response to internal stimuli than to absence of external resistance.

In the remote Far East, so long as China remained powerful, she had been able to throw back the advance of Russian fur traders and cossacks, even despite the ambitions of Peter. In the nineteenth century, however, China's weakness was made manifest by the easy military successes of the English and the French in their imperialist pressure on the hidebound Celestial Kingdom. Taking advantage of the situation created by their threat to Peking (1858), the Russian governor-general of Eastern Siberia, N. N. Muraviev, with a few hundred men, annexed the enormous area of the left bank of the Amur. China's attempt to repudiate the treaties of Tientsin with England and France not only cost her further concessions to those powers but enabled Muraviev "Amursky" ("of the Amur") to secure

* See Maps VI and VII.

treaty confirmation of his conquest and cession as well of the extensive coastal province as far south as the port of Vladivostok, already founded by Muraviev (1860).

Russia further strengthened her position in the Far East by ceding to Japan the distant Kurile Islands in exchange for the southern half of Sakhalin, close offshore (1875). In the meantime (1867), she had successfully negotiated the sale to the United States of Alaska and the Aleutian Islands, for the seemingly enormous sum of $7 million, then desperately needed by the Russian treasury. Defense of these overseas territories would have required that Russia have naval power in the Pacific.

Closer to home, the period of the "Great Reforms" had also witnessed the firm establishment of Russian power over defenseless neighbors. As early as Paul's reign, some of the chieftains in the Caucasus, caught between the rival pressures of Turkey and Persia, had appealed to Russia for aid. Alexander I, in a ten-year war with Persia (1804-13), had won suzerainty over part of Georgia (the coastline was held by Turkey), Daghestan, and Azerbaijan (once briefly won by Peter). Russia's grip on the Caucasus had been strengthened by Turkey's forced cession of most of the Black Sea shore line (but not including Batum) in 1829 and by Persia's surrender of a part of Armenia (1828).

The hardy mountaineers of the Caucasus, however, long gave the Russians much trouble, although their own ethnic differences, emphasized by the rugged and broken character of the region, made it difficult for them to coöperate harmoniously with each other. In 1857, the Russian viceroy, Prince Bariatinsky, launched a determined attack on Shamil, a Moslem imam who had become the soul of resistance in Daghestan; by 1859, Shamil had been forced to surrender and was deported to Russia. In connection with Emancipation, the Russian government sought to bind the native chiefs, the natural leaders of the local population, to the interests of the Russian state by giving them and their principal followers specially favorable terms. The last focus of active resistance was dealt with by enforced emigration of the Cherkesses (or Circassians) from their mountain homes to assigned areas in the plains or on the seacoast; some two hundred thousand of them availed themselves of the alternative of emigrating to Turkey (1864), where numbers of them served as irregulars in the Ottoman forces under the name of bashi-bazouks.

In still another contiguous area, Russia pushed out her effective frontiers. The Turco-Tatar pastoral nomads of Central Asia had once been the terror of the agricultural population of the forest zone. For centuries they had barred the steppe to Russian settlement; until 1480 they had levied tribute on Muscovy. As late as 1717, they had still been able to destroy the army sent against them by Peter the Great, although authority in Turkestan was shared by several Moslem rulers.

In the nineteenth century, however, the ill-organized nomads were no match for Russia's disciplined armies, which had seriously to contend only with the rigors of the climate and with miles of arid desert. Consequently the power vacuum was gradually filled in, on much the same principle that has made it necessary for other countries constantly to expand the frontier in order to protect their existing territories. In the reigns of Alexander I and Nicholas I, the Kirghiz had been firmly subjected by establishment of chains of fortified posts as far as the Syr-Daria. Conquest of the three major khanates of Khiva, Bukhara, and Kokand was effected on the initiative of the local Russian military governors, provoked by fanatical raids of these Moslems. Tashkent, the chief commercial center of the region, was occupied in 1865; Samarkand, the sacred burial place of Timur the Lame, in 1868.

In 1866 was established the office of governor-general of Turkestan; further local collisions followed. In the end, the emir of Bukhara (1868) and the khan of Khiva (1873) agreed to accept dependent status as the price of not losing their thrones altogether; the khanate of Kokand, more stubborn, was totally eliminated (1876). It remained only to reduce the semi-independent Turkmen and Uzbek tribesmen. By 1885, the Russian frontier marched with that of Afghanistan, a development which further embittered diplomatic relations with Great Britain. Particularly in 1884, when the Russian annexation of Merv provoked in London a "fit of Mervousness," England made warlike preparations for the defense of the Khyber Pass into India, which the British navy alone could not hope to protect.

In addition to the new problems created by Russian advances in the Middle and Far East, two old problems, supposedly settled by Catherine the Great, reasserted themselves. One was the eternal Polish question. Alexander II, on a visit to Warsaw in 1856, had bidden the Poles forget their "senseless dreams" of national independence. Yet, in the reform atmosphere, he had permitted Polish émigrés in the West and Polish exiles in Siberia to return home. The actual administration of Poland, under the authority of the viceroy, was entrusted to a Pole, Marquis Wielopolski. The Poles' hopes were so raised that they staged numerous peaceful but dramatic demonstrations.

In 1861, Alexander took the further and, as it proved, fatally provocative, step of again separating the government of the "Congress kingdom" from that of Russia: central authority was entrusted to a state council made up of Poles appointed by the ruler; local government was put in the hands of elected provincial councils. Instead of satisfying the Poles, these concessions whetted their appetite; at the same time, it divided them into two parties, the "Whites" and the "Reds." The Whites, strong among the nobility, objected to Wielopolski's obvious intention of seeking the support of the middle class; the Reds were dissatisfied with the inadequately democratic character of the governmental organs. Both parties refused to be content with anything less than restoration of the frontiers of 1772, before the First Partition.

Wielopolski's effort to persist in his middle course led to attempts at his assassination. In 1863, his unsuccessful effort to ease the tension by conscripting the restless urban youth proved catastrophic. On a January night, at many points in Poland and also in the Lithuanian provinces, armed bands slaughtered the Russian soldiers in their barracks.

Thus was begun the second Polish rebellion. Unlike 1830, Poland had in 1863 no army, no government, no system of finance. Instead of war, the Poles could wage only a guerilla struggle, which was ruthlessly repressed. Repeated attempts of France and other Western powers (not including Prussia) to intervene diplomatically were flatly rejected; publication of Chancellor Gorchakov's note asserting Russia's rights produced a flood of enthusiastically patriotic addresses from virtually every element in Russia, even from the persecuted schismatics. In 1864, order was restored. The very name of Poland was wiped from the map; the "Congress kingdom" was converted into "the Vistula region" and administratively integrated into the Empire of All the Russias. Use of the Russian language was made obligatory in the schools, the courts, and for all public business. A Russian university was founded in Warsaw. The Uniate Church was ordered reunited with the Orthodox Church. To drive deeper the wedge between the Polish classes, the peasants were, even while the revolt was still burning, given specially favorable treatment in the matter of land allotments. In the Lithuanian provinces of Russia, specially vigorous efforts were made to root out the Polonizing influences that had involved western Russia also in the uprising.

In the southwestern provinces of Russia, somewhat similar measures were applied. Here the victims were not Poles but Little Russians (now called Ukrainians). Since the eighteenth century, there had begun to develop a literature in the distinctive Little Russian language. This movement, like other nationalist manifestations throughout the empire, had suffered from the repressive activities of Nicholas I; the poet Shevchenko (1814-61) had been drafted into the army and sent as a private soldier to serve in the Urals. The Little Russian movement, though it refused to sympathize with the Poles, the former oppressors of the Ukraine, had links with Great Russian *narodnichestvo*. In 1863, the Minister of the Interior (the same Valuiev who had attempted to sabotage Emancipation) forbade the publication in Little Russian of "books for popular reading." His reason was that

> there has not been and cannot be any special Little Russian language, and that their dialect, used by the common people, is the Russian language, corrupted by Polish influence. . . .[1]

In 1876, more severe measures were taken, with the consequence that the Little Russian protest tended to become political instead of merely cultural.

FOREIGN RELATIONS

The second old problem which vexed the empire in the post-reform period was necessarily the most central problem of foreign relations for almost land-locked Russia. This was the problem of Turkey and the Straits. The way for resumption of a forward policy in this direction was opened during the Franco-Prussian War of 1870-71; during that crisis, no Western power was in a position to oppose Russia's unilateral repudiation of the Black Sea clauses of the Treaty of Paris of 1856. Once again Russian fortresses were to line the northern and eastern shores of the Black Sea; once again a Russian fleet, in uncontested control of that sea, might enable Russia to strike at Turkey and to support land attacks from both ends, across the Balkans and through the Caucasus.

Unfortunately for Russia, the opportunity—even the necessity—for action arose before she was ready, and in a way that impeded decisive action. The army reform of 1874 could not immediately bear the fruit of heightened military efficiency, while construction of a new Black Sea fleet, hampered by financial difficulties, had been delayed. Moreover, the situation that arose in Turkey invited action in terms of rescuing "little brother" Slavs, but the Russian government could not vigorously embrace a Pan-Slav policy, not only because it would endanger her relations with Austria but because of her own attitude toward Poles and Little Russians.

In 1875, the Serbs in Herzegovina rose against the Turkish tax system. While the European powers jointly urged reform on the Turkish government, the revolt spread among the Bulgar peasants (1876). Threatened also with a "Young Turk" revolt, the Porte in its despair unleashed on the Christian Bulgars the irregulars, the bashi-bazouks. The civilized world was shocked at what Gladstone dubbed the "Bulgarian atrocities"; the Powers agreed to impose reforms on Turkey, although England's dread of Russian expansion led her to dissent. Meanwhile, the Serbs and the Montenegrins attacked the Turks; Russian volunteers rushed to aid them, while in Russia itself a ferment developed similar to that directed against the West in the Polish matter. The sultan published a Western-style constitution and informed the Powers that for him now to decree the reforms they demanded would be unconstitutional. A fresh international conference at Constantinople (January, 1877) nevertheless threatened joint intervention, in which even England expressed willingness to join.

Turkey remained obdurate, and Russia declared war (April, 1877). There seemed reason to believe that this war would be no repetition of the disastrous Crimean War. England was committed to drastic reforms in Turkey; France was impotent; Austria was neutralized, this time not by gratitude, but by her secret Reichstadt agreement (1873) with Russia; Germany's position was clearly what Bismarck later formulated in his assertion (1885) that the Balkans were "not worth the bones of a single Pomeranian grenadier."

Russia was promptly joined by Rumania; thus the way was open for a direct attack across the Danube.

Only the deficiencies of the Russian high command and the incompleteness of her military reforms protracted the struggle. Nevertheless, by the end of the year, the Russian armies had forced their way through the Shipka Pass across the Balkans and once more stood under the walls of Constantinople; in Asia, Kars had for the third time been taken, and Erzerum was threatened. As in the past, Russian successes alarmed England: a fleet was sent into the Sea of Marmora; as Bismarck phrased it, the conflict between the whale and the elephant seemed imminent.

The Turks, however, felt constrained to accept the Russian terms, and the preliminaries of peace were signed at San Stefano early in 1878. The principal point of this treaty that was vital for Russia provided for the establishment of an autonomous Bulgaria, extending from the Danube to the Aegean and from the Black Sea westward to include Macedonia. This was in direct violation of the Reichstadt agreement with Austria. The new principality, expected to be a Russian protectorate, would give Russia her long-sought preponderance of power in the region of the Straits. England openly, Austria more cautiously, threatened Russia with war. The situation was saved by Bismarck's offer to serve as an "honest broker." An international congress was assembled at Berlin to consider the whole problem.

The upshot was humiliating disappointment for Russia. To be sure, Russia retained some of the fruits of her victory. She recovered from her Rumanian ally the part of Bessarabia surrendered in 1856, Rumania being given the Turkish Dobrudja in exchange. Kars this time remained in the hands of Russia, which received also the seaport of Batum, though as an open, not a military, port. Bulgaria did indeed receive autonomy, but it was not the "Big" Bulgaria of which Russia had dreamed. Instead of the Bulgaria of San Stefano, the autonomous principality fronted only on the Black Sea; moreover, the autonomy of the zone south of the Balkans, known as Eastern Rumelia, was to be on a more restricted basis than that of Bulgaria proper.

The furious reaction of the frustrated Russian public boded no good for the future of relations between the government and the people. Particularly distressing was the paradoxical fact that Bulgaria was given a constitution, while her protector remained an autocracy. Nor was it only in Russia that the empire's prestige was diminished. Bulgaria soon evicted her Russian advisers (1885), while Serbia and Rumania turned for support to Austria-Hungary.

In the international field, Russia was left isolated; her sullen resentment at Bismarck's "betrayal" of her interests led that statesman to conclude a formal alliance with the Hapsburgs (1879). Bismarck's genius did enable him to succeed in partially restoring the *Dreikaiserbund* (1881), that pale ghost of the one-time Concert of Europe. The agreement between Germany, Austria-

Hungary, and Russia was, however, an unstable one. Russia did not become a member of the Triple Alliance (1882), and in 1887 Bismarck was able to secure, not a renewal of the tripartite agreement, but only a separate "reinsurance" treaty with Russia. In 1889, Alexander III made his famous toast to the prince of Montenegro: "To Russia's only sincere and faithful friend."

This steadily growing isolation of Russia gradually drove her onto a new path. As normally happens when two countries are treated as pariahs by a dominant third power, France and Russia moved into ever closer relations. France could supply the capital which Russia so badly needed for industrial and especially for railway expansion; Russia had the manpower which could be poured across the German border in case of a fresh outbreak of hostilities between Germany and France. Democratic, anti-clerical, and republican France, glad to be able to sleep at night without worrying about noises along the Rhine, unquestioningly accepted the ideologically strange, politically quite natural, alliance with autocratic, Orthodox, and anti-liberal Russia.

As so often before, Russia was quite willing to receive the material benefits of Western civilization without being asked to participate spiritually; Holy Russia seemed to have less to fear from atheist French money than from the abrupt termination of the career of Bismarck, who had so firmly believed in the necessity to "keep open the wire to St. Petersburg." By 1894, the Dual Alliance was an accomplished fact, and the balance of power on the Continent had become uneasy.

It was, however, obvious both to the Russian government and to its French military mentors that, pending reëquipment of its artillery, the Russian army could not face the realities of war. Accordingly, the Russian government launched in 1898 a movement for world peace and disarmament. An international Peace Congress met at The Hague for two months in 1899 and discussed various problems. It even recommended the establishment of an international court of arbitration; its major practical consequence was to be the saving of Russia from English wrath as a result of the Dogger Bank incident of 1905.

Professed addiction to world peace did not prevent Russia from approaching the brink of limited war. In 1891, with the aid of French loans already contracted, construction of the long-planned Trans-Siberian railway was begun. In 1895, with the backing of both France and Germany, Russia exerted diplomatic pressure to force Japan to renounce the Liaotung Peninsula in southern Manchuria, which she had won in war with China. In 1896, China agreed to allow construction of a railway across Manchuria, immensely shortening the mileage from Irkutsk to Vladivostok. The Chinese Eastern Railway and the Russo-Chinese Bank which financed it were the first fruits of French imperialism operating under the cloak of Russian power. In 1896-97, Russian attention was briefly diverted to the Straits; Russia even concluded with Austria-Hungary a secret agreement, never implemented, for division of the remaining Turkish spoils. In 1898, however, Germany's enforced "lease" of the Kiaochow territory in the Shantung Peninsula precipitated a similar Russian lease of the Liaotung Peninsula. In her turn, ever watchful against Russian expansion, Great Britain leased Wei-Hai-Wei across the Strait from Port Arthur.

Despite very considerable extension of territory and the beating down of nationalist movements within the empire, Russia's external policies failed to restore the earlier international position of the autocracy. Internally, the post-reform developments did not work out in a way favorable to maintenance of the autocratic regime. If Emancipation was not the inevitable prelude to Revolution, it did fail to solve "the peasant question" and permitted the rapid rise of a new force incompatible with the historic autocracy.

THE PEASANTRY AFTER EMANCIPATION

It is impossible to arrive at a satisfactory general judgment of the consequences for the peasantry of Emancipation and Redemption. Despite the inadequacy of available statistics, some things are however clear. Robinson's careful calculations show that in 1877 in the forty-nine provinces of European Russia (not including Finland, Poland, the Caucasus, or the Don region) the peasants owned, as allotment land, 111.6 million dessiatines as against 113 million they had held as serfs prior to Emancipation.[2] In addition, individual peasants, voluntary associations of peasants, and peasant communes had acquired title to a further 6.5 million dessiatines. As against this total of 118 million dessiatines owned by the peasants, the nobles retained 73 million. Townsmen had acquired 11.7 million, while churches, monasteries, and municipalities owned 4.3 million. By far the largest acreage —157.8 million dessiatines—remained in the hands of the state and the imperial family, but almost all these fiscally held lands, together with a substantial proportion of privately owned lands other than those of the peasants, were non-agricultural; most of the arable land already belonged to the peasantry.

By 1905, peasant holdings had increased to 146.9 million dessiatines; those of nobles had fallen to 52.1 million. This sharp decline in noble landholding, accompanied by a smaller decline in fiscal holdings, more than outbalanced increases in other non-peasant holdings, such as the rise in holdings of townsmen to 16.2 million dessiatines. At the same time, however, the population, which had been growing rapidly before Emancipation, continued to multiply at a rate beyond any possible increase of land under cultivation. It is true that over-all population increase was attended by a very significant redistribution among the provinces, as had also been true before Emancipation. Furthermore, growth of urban population, concentrating especially in St. Petersburg and Moscow and in a few industrial or commercial cities such as Kharkov or Odessa, was somewhat reducing the proportion of the population engaged in agriculture. Yet, when all allowances have been made, there still remains the fact, as computed by Robinson, "of the shrinkage in the average size of the household allotments from 13.2 desiatinas in 1877 to 10.4 in 1905."[3] There can be no doubt that after Emancipation—but not because of it—the peasantry in general did increasingly suffer from land shortage.

In remedy, the peasants tried several expedients. There was continuing wholesale migration from thickly settled areas to new lands, chiefly to the south and southeast or into western Siberia. It is estimated that in the first quarter-century after Emancipation some three hundred thousand emigrated to Siberia and Turkestan, and that after the building of the Trans-Siberian railway, government assistance raised this emigration to about 115,000 a year. Yet the great concentration of population remained in the older areas. Though the percentage increase was less, in provinces such as Tula and Kursk the population density per square mile rose from 1600 and 1400 to 2400 and 2800, respectively.

For the stay-at-homes there was another possibility, that of buying or renting additional land. The acreage owned by peasants, individually or collectively, in addition to the communally owned allotment lands, by 1905 totaled 23.6 million dessiatines. Yet these acquisitions, though assisted by a Peasant Bank founded in 1881, had been quite unable to keep pace with the growth of population. Rented lands apparently amounted to nearly as much again, though estimates vary enormously. Rents, however, were so excessive that "in a great many instances after payment of the rent 'there did not remain for the renter even so much as the customary wage for the labor he had expended in the cultivation' of the rented plot."[4] Wagework for landlords or for fellow-peasants was always a possibility, though frequently entailing a long and often fruitless trek for employment. In any case, in the 1890's, according to Robinson's calculations, "the average wage paid to male workers hired for the entire year was sixty-one and one half *rubls* with subsistence."[5]

A more satisfactory solution for the problem of "the hungry village" would undoubtedly have been an increase in yields per acre, together with supplementary livestock breeding. Many of the zemstvo boards—which did not exist in all provinces—strove, and with some success, to make progress in this direction. Yet collective ownership of allotment lands by the commune was a deadweight against change. As earlier in Western Europe, open-field cultivation tied the ablest and most ambitious down to the level of the ignorant tradition-bound majority. In Russia in those decades, the three-field system, leaving one-third of the arable land idle, represented an advanced technique. Scientific crop rotation or upgrading of livestock was impossible in view of scattered intermingled strips and common pastures. Poverty had a severe depressing effect; although chiefly engaged in the heavy labor of growing grain, the Russian peasant at the turn of the century had, on the average, only a single work horse per household. Notwithstanding the best efforts of zemstvo agronomists, the yield per acre of intensively cultivated land in Russia, even on the eve of the war of 1914, was only about the same as that on extensively cultivated mechanized farms in the United States (wasteful of land though saving labor), or little more than half what even the French peasant won from his petty holdings.

The only other recourse for the land-hungry peasant was to steel himself against his craving for land and to take industrial employment. For the Russian peasant, particularly in the old thickly settled central provinces, this was, of course, nothing new. Home handicraft (*kustarny*), whether independently carried on or using materials and even tools supplied by a city merchant, and whether individual or through the collective medium of the artel, had long been the financial mainstay of the "non-agricultural" zone, where the fields supplied barely enough rye for subsistence. The return for a long winter's labor of the whole family might be meager, but it spelled the difference between existence and non-existence.

After Emancipation, though not immediately, there came into existence the necessary preconditions for a phenomenal growth of factories, a development to be discussed more fully presently. Here it need only be observed that the factory workers were necessarily recruited from the peasantry. The working conditions in the factories were evil; the reports of government factory inspectors in the 1880's leave in the shade the famous Parliamentary investigations into the status of workers in English factories in the early part of the nineteenth century. Yet, as in late eighteenth-century England, the advantages of factory employment over agricultural misery were a powerful magnet in pulling labor from the soil. The average money wage of workers in Russian mills and factories in 1900 might be only eighteen rubles a month, but this was a fantastic figure compared to what was being earned in wage labor in the countryside.

In Russia, therefore, whenever business prosperity increased the demand for factory hands, peasants flooded in so rapidly that the figures of industrial unemployment rose sharply; conversely, in times of depression unemployment statistics showed a great decline. This phenomenon, so contrary to conditions in Western Europe and at first sight so paradoxical, reflected the fact that the Russian peasant, in taking factory employment, did not sever his connection with the village. Only to a relatively slight extent did Russia develop a genuine proletariat. For the most part, the Russian worker remained a peasant, still involved in its communal structure, contributing out of his wages to its communal obligations, and often receiving at least part of his food supply direct from his fellow-villagers.

It remains to be emphasized that the foregoing summary discussion has been in generalized terms; in reality the condition of the peasants varied widely from one region to another, varied also from commune to commune, and from household to household within one and the same commune. In the "black-earth" provinces, the peasants had lost relatively more of the land they had cultivated before Emancipation, even as much as one-quarter of their holdings. In this region, the landlord had strong incentive to continue cultivation of the rich wheatlands on the basis of employment of the wage labor of peasants whose landholdings were hopelessly inadequate.

Particularly significant were the differences within any given commune, though statistics are of little help in determining their extent. Most of the peasants belonged to "repartitional" communes; these had the right, though they did not always exercise it, from time to time to redistribute "allotment" land among their members. The peasants themselves might refer to this process as taking land from the dead to give it to the living, but it could theoretically have resulted in a tendency to equalize holdings. In practice the peasants seem rather to have been guided by the Biblical principle: "To him that hath shall be given, and from him that hath not shall be taken away even that which he hath." [6]

It was only natural that a peasant who—whether by luck, thrift, industry, or intelligence—was able to acquire somewhat more of this world's goods—whether in the shape of grain or potatoes, cattle or sons—than did his fellow-villagers, would be in a position to exercise a certain leverage on them in the matter of land redistribution. This practical consideration could only be enhanced by the rationalization that, if God cursed one peasant by giving him a succession of daughters ("useless mouths to feed") while he blessed another with additional "souls" in the family, it was not for a bearded and devout Christian to treat his fellow-man otherwise than as God did. According to figures later used by Lenin, the differentiation within the village went so far that 17 percent of the peasantry might be classed as well-to-do, with adequate provision of land, several head of livestock, and money in the savings bank; 11 percent lived "in Christ's name," holding no arable land, owning no livestock, perhaps helping to keep a fortunate fellow-villager's cattle warm by sleeping in his cow-barn; the remaining 72 percent stood on various intermediary levels.

Whatever judgment one may form of the value of Emancipation to the Russian peasantry, whatever significance one may attach to the intangibles involved in the facts that the Russian peasant ceased to be a chattel and that he acquired by law a limited and collective control over his life as an individual, there can be no doubt that the economic burden resting on him as a sequel to Emancipation and Redemption was almost unbearable. Despite the most vigorous efforts to enforce payment of redemption obligations on the basis of the "circular guarantee," arrears piled up enormously. By the end of the nineteenth century,

> the total accumulation of arrears (118,695,000 *rubls*) in payments due to the State had finally come to exceed by a substantial margin the average amount of the current assessments (99,341,000 per year in the period 1896-1900) which the State was attempting to collect.[7]

The state, indeed, was forced to face the question squarely: twice in the 1880's, the amount of the redemption debt due from former landowners' peasants was reduced; twice in the 1890's partial moratoriums were granted. In 1886, the soul tax was abolished, throwing onto indirect taxation, which already yielded the great bulk of state revenues and which inevitably rested mainly on the poorer elements of the population, a still greater share of the burden of keeping the state afloat. Recurrent crop failures brought frequent local famines, the most widespread and severe of which occurred in 1891. After the first violent wave of peasant outbreaks in the months immediately following Emancipation, the peasantry did indeed relapse into a state of relative quiescence. Yet no thinking person could altogether exclude the possibility of a fresh outbreak like those led by Razin and by Pugachev. It might well be that a third such rising, despite the seeming docility of the long-suffering peasantry, would be more terrible and more conclusive than its predecessors. Here lurked one of the major possibilities of revolution.

INDUSTRY AND LABOR

Nevertheless, notwithstanding the fact that the peasantry continued to be the overwhelming mass of the Russian population, Emancipation had opened the door to the development of a still more dynamic force, which perhaps did make inevitable the end of the autocracy, either by the road of revolution or by the road of reform. This was the rapid rise of capitalist, "bourgeois" industry.

The immediate effect of Emancipation on the growth of factory industry was very depressing. Insofar as industry had relied on the obligatory labor of serfs, it was sharply set back. The noble factory, which had been giving way before the encroachment of the capitalist factory prior to Emancipation, now suffered rapid collapse. The iron industry, concentrated in the Urals and resting almost wholly on the labor of serfs, was extremely hard hit. To some extent it suffered from the liberalization of tariffs which had been decreed in 1857 and again in 1868 in order to facilitate the construction of railways. This factor, however, was insignificant compared to the mass flight of emancipated peasants from the ironworks, which cut Russian production of iron by one-fifth in the years 1860-67. Some ironworks, unable to adjust quickly to new conditions of free hired labor, had to close down completely. While the iron industry, the pampered child of the state, suffered most acutely, other branches of industry also experienced a grave crisis in the 1860's. The nobles' woolen factories virtually disappeared. Simultaneously, though for a quite different reason, the cotton industry, which in the main already employed free labor, was depressed by the cotton famine incidental to the American Civil War; in consequence, the linen industry was temporarily stimulated.

The immediate adverse consequence of Emancipation was, however, not of long duration. The cotton industry, quickly recovering, advanced with remarkable rapidity in the new, relatively free, capitalistic atmosphere. It experienced, to be sure, approximately the same cyclical booms and depressions that affected the whole world, but the general trend was rapidly upward. From the end of the 1860's, the iron industry also, though more slowly, showed a steady increase, accompanied by marked improvements in technique, without state protection. After the middle 1880's, indeed, the production of pig iron in Russia increased at a rate unparalleled in the Western world. Between 1886 and 1895, American production of pig iron increased 69 percent, passing that of Great Britain, while German output, rising 55 percent, came within measurable distance; Russian production, however, increased 178 percent, moving up from eighth to fifth place in the world.

Of vital importance in this connection were the transition in Russia from the smelting of ore with charcoal to the use of coke and the construction of railways which made it possible to bring the ore and the coke together. In this same period, coal production in Russia doubled. Partly because of the difficulty of luring free workers to the remote and scantily populated Ural area, partly because of the richness of the local coal deposits, the Donets basin shot into prominence while the Ural ironworks declined. In 1884, a railway was completed connecting the iron mines of Krivoi Rog, in the bend of the Dnieper, with Donets coal; as in the case of the Ruhr-Lorraine nexus, the chief centers of heavy industry sprang into existence near the coal mines. Kharkov, Yekaterinoslav, Rostov, and other industrial cities mushroomed at a rate usually associated with Pittsburgh, Chicago, and Detroit. A secondary center of heavy industry developed at St. Petersburg, which could avail itself of coal and iron imported, without too great transportation cost, by water.

Russian heavy industry earned enormous profits, in part because of the reintroduction of protective tariffs in the 1880's but principally on account of the demand for rails and other equipment arising from the tremendously rapid expansion of the railway network. Magnificent as was the achievement of the opening of the single-track Trans-Siberian railway, it represented but a small proportion of Russian railway construction in the closing decades of the century. Had it not been for government protection and subsidies, the profits of the Russian ironmasters might have been less exorbitant—40 percent net profit was not exceptional—but the industry might easily have won itself an even more solid economic foundation by developing the production of iron for commercial purposes instead of concentrating on state business.

In backward Russia, capital was scarce. It was inevitable therefore that the bulk of the capital invested in the phenomenal growth of Russian industry came from abroad, chiefly from England, France, and Belgium. This fact was to have marked significance in many ways, not least of all, perhaps, in helping to lay the groundwork for chaotic revolution. Economically, the consequent heavy indebtedness of Russia to the West forced her to maintain a positive balance of trade and made her economy peculiarly susceptible to the consequences of cyclical price movements. Politically, it handicapped Russian industrialists in developing an independent attitude toward the autocracy. In view of the low state of Russian credit on the international money market, the Russian manufacturer was largely dependent on government intervention to attract the necessary funds; needing capital for the development of his enterprises, he could therefore not afford to be an active force in demanding political rights; only in the twentieth century, when he had become financially independent of government assistance in borrowing, could he indulge in constitutional aspirations. Socially, the fact that the capital invested in Russian industry was mostly owned abroad prevented the formation within Russia of a significantly large *rentier* class, interested in the profits of capitalist industry and capable of giving serious support to the industrialists in a moment of crisis; there was therefore the great danger that the industrialists, by pressing their own constitutional demands and withholding support from the autocracy, might sign their own death warrant.

There was also the consideration that, because Russian industry so largely owed its inception to foreign capital, it tended to come into existence on an initially large scale instead of developing gradually from small beginnings. A computation made early in the twentieth century showed that if Russian industrial enterprises were classified on the basis of the number of workers employed, the percentage of large-scale enterprises was far higher than in Germany, and the percentage of small enterprises strikingly low. This tabulation has been cited as proving that in Marxist terms Russia, with a greater degree of concentration of capital, was more ready for proletarian revolution than was Germany.

The fallacies are fairly obvious: the number of workers, without reference to the degree of technological advance and the ratio of labor to mechanical equipment, shows nothing with respect to concentration of capital; the percentage of enterprises in the highest category meant little, for the absolute number of large-scale enterprises (even on the indicated basis) in Germany was much greater than in Russia. Moreover, the computation overlooks the role of proletarian class consciousness in Marxist thinking; the Russian worker was in the main not a proletarian, to say nothing of the fact that his total numbers were in any case insignificant in the midst of the peasant ocean. The one prophecy that could safely be made—a prophecy borne out by the event—was that if Russia were to experience a revolution, it would not be a proletarian one.

In the long run, the government had more to fear from the manufacturers than from the workers. If it deliberately created the conditions which would permit the rapid growth of industrial capitalism, it did so only because a thriving industry was necessary in the interests of state power. As cannot be overemphasized, the "Great Reforms" had been undertaken in no liberal spirit. The government's attitude toward the problems of industrial labor was affected in part by the paternalistic humanitarianism characteristic of so many English and Prussian landlords in the nineteenth century. In part also it was influenced by the desire, as in the matter of land reform in Poland and in western Russia, for propaganda reasons to protect the interests of the lower orders against their masters, who might become too powerful for the security of the autocracy. The state had no intention of granting to the workers freedom of action; it did feel it desirable to try to provide for a certain degree of welfare in the factories.

As early as 1859, a project was worked out at the instance of the Governor-General of St. Petersburg, to require the installation of safety devices in the factories and to insist on certain hygienic and sanitary measures. It was also proposed to forbid employment of children under twelve and to limit to ten hours per day that of children from twelve to fourteen; night work was to be forbidden for all under sixteen. Enforcement was to be entrusted to a staff of factory inspectors, empowered also to investigate wage payments.

The project was well received by most of the Petersburg manufacturers but met with violent criticism when submitted to the factory owners of the central industrial area, headed by those of Moscow. The arguments they advanced for "freedom of contract" strongly resembled those of the liberal economist Nassau Senior in the England of the 1830's: idleness would ruin the health and morals of the children, for the factories were far more hygienic and wholesome than the huts in which they lived; unable to contribute to the family income, children would be neglected by their parents; the children would be deprived of the essential early opportunity to learn their trade; productivity would be reduced; and profits would be eliminated. Moscow manufacturers expressed special resentment at the shameful lack of confidence in them implied in the appointment of government factory inspectors.

The government, concerned lest the project might really ruin the factories to the advantage of petty *kustarny* (household) industry, submitted the idea to a special committee in the Ministry of Finance, presided over by Stackelberg. This committee elaborated a project of far wider scope than the original, providing for abolition of Peter's guilds and complete reorganization of industrial legislation. The new arrangement was to apply to all industrial establishments, great and small, including handicrafts and *kustarny* workshops. Among much else, it retained the provisions forbidding the employment of children under twelve, raised the age bracket limited to a ten-hour day to eighteen, and prohibited night work for all under eighteen. In addition to factory inspectors, it provided for the establishment of labor courts. They were to be composed of judges elected in equal numbers by workers and employers and with power to impose penalties for both strikes and lockouts, for uncompensated physical injuries, and for illegal fining of workers, as well as for violation of safety and child-labor regulations. Strikers were to be subject to imprisonment for from one to three weeks, instigators of strikes for periods up to three months, while employers might be fined for combining to reduce wages.

The idea of state intervention between capitalists and workers proved to be premature. In the face of the vociferous and emphatic objections of the Moscow manufacturers, the project was shelved. In 1866, to be sure, a section of the old law, which equated disobedience of workers with revolt against the government and which had been criticized by the Stackelberg committee as outmoded once serfdom had been abolished, was repealed. From time to time, new bureaucratic proposals were drawn up, going even beyond the earlier ones in some respects. Repeatedly, the manufacturers of St. Petersburg and of some other industrial centers, such as Lodz in Poland, recommended the enactment of legislative restrictions; they were unable to overcome the government's unwillingness to override the objections of the employers in the central industrial region.

The difference in opinion between the Petersburg and Moscow employers, like the difference of opinion about the terms of Emancipation between the black-soil landlords and those of the older central provinces, stemmed from a difference in local economic conditions. St. Petersburg, set in a thinly peopled area, had to draw its industrial workers from remote provinces; Moscow was in the heart of the most overpopulated rural area, where the quest for industrial employment was greatest. The result was a significant wage differential. The fact of wage rates one-third higher in St. Petersburg than in the central provinces had compelled greater attention to the productivity of labor and so had led to great advances in mechanical technique. The Petersburg manufacturers pointed out to the government that night work was difficult to supervise properly, with consequent reduction in the quantity and especially the quality of the output per worker; they argued that the expenditure for extra heat and light at night was ruinous and that machinery in constant use wore out too quickly. In their own interest, they found it desirable not to employ children, to eliminate night work, and to limit the hours of work even of adults in the daytime. Since, however, they were in competition with the backward factories of the Moscow area, which relied on extracting the utmost in manual labor rather than on investing in machine production, they were ardently convinced that there ought to be a law.

In 1882, twenty-three years after the idea had been first considered but shortly after the accession of a new emperor, Alexander III, the St. Petersburg manufacturers won a limited victory. The law of June 1, 1882, approved at the instance of Bunge, the Minister of Finance, officially forbade the employment in factories of children under twelve and limited the work hours of those under fifteen to eight hours. Night work and work on Sundays and holidays were also forbidden, and employers were instructed to make school attendance possible. Inspectors, though in glaringly insufficient numbers, were appointed to supervise enforcement. In order to minimize the shock of this first government intrusion in the field of labor relations, the Ministers of Finance and of the Interior were given joint power to grant exemptions.

The handful of factory inspectors, though personally devoted men, could not possibly visit more than a small fraction of the establishments for supervision of which they were responsible. Yet their reports shed immense light on conditions in the factories and contributed to further rapid extension of government intervention. They found a fourteen-hour working day normal—sometimes even one of sixteen hours; Sunday labor was widespread. They found sanitary and hygienic conditions unspeakable, with men, women, and children often bedded down for their few free hours in the workrooms themselves. The workers were generally paid in truck, sometimes never seeing any cash; their necessary contributions for taxes were often sent by the employer direct to the communes. From their nominal wages, large amounts were subtracted for all sorts of infractions of factory rules. They could be severely punished for quitting their jobs but were subject to arbitrary dismissal before the end of the agreed term of employment. In short, they were virtually serfs, bound to "blind obedience," save that, under the principle of freedom of contract, the employer was not liable for their maintenance when he had no need of their work.

Under such conditions, violent blind spontaneous outbreaks were even more frequent in the factories than in the countryside, and it was chiefly out of considerations of police security that the government, despite the objections of most of the manufacturers, proceeded to enact further measures. In the early 1880's, a severe depression of trade compelled the dismissal of thousands of workers. In 1883, the mayor of St. Petersburg, fearing riots, invited the master cotton-spinners to advise him; they replied that the industrial crisis could only be overcome by general prohibition of night work. The Moscow manufacturers disagreed strongly, and only minor action was taken until after the outbreak of extremely violent disturbances in the Morozov works and other factories in Moscow, Ivanovo-Voznesensk, and Vladimir; to suppress the disorders it was necessary to call out troops.

Early in 1885, Count Dmitry Tolstoy, then Minister of the Interior, officially urged on his colleague Bunge, Minister of Finance, that the chief cause of the disturbances was the absence of properly regulative laws:

> Excessively high fines . . . have often served factory-owners as a means of artificially reducing wages. . . . High prices in factory stores . . . have roused dissatisfaction among the workers. Inexactness in fixing wage conditions with people who are scarcely literate has evoked constant disputes in the settlement of weekly pay. . . . The impossibility of settling these [disturbances] except by force of arms is sufficient proof of the inescapable necessity of working out rules to bridle in some degree the arbitrariness of factory owners. . . .[8]

By a law of June 3, 1885, night work of women and boys under seventeen was forbidden in the chief textile industries; opposition was unusually weak, apparently because it was widely realized that in the highly competitive conditions of the depression, it would do the survivors little harm if marginal firms were forced out of business. In 1886, a more sweeping decree regulated the conditions under which wage agreements might be negotiated: wages must be paid in cash, and at least once a month; no deductions might be made and no interest charged on alleged advances; the factory inspectors were given a considerable measure of authority in regulating the internal organization of the factory. Simultaneously, the penalty for striking was increased to a maximum sentence of four months (double for instigators), while the fines on employers for violation of the law were set at a maximum of three hundred rubles.

The new law was difficult to enforce, especially because there was nothing to prevent management from arbitrarily dismissing any workers who complained to the inspectors and from effectively blacklisting these troublemakers throughout the industry. Bunge, the chief author of the law of 1886, was dismissed in 1887, and factory reforms suffered much the same fate as had the earlier reforms of local government, of the judiciary, and in the field of education. To be sure, in the next period of industrial depression, a further law of June 2, 1897, restricted the working day, even for adult males, to eleven and one-half hours (ten if they were employed between 9 P.M. and 5 A.M.); no work was to be allowed on Sundays or on the fourteen chief holidays, unless by agreement between the workers and management such time was substituted for other employment. By this time, a number of manufacturers, even in the Moscow area, had come to realize that curtailment of working hours raised the productivity of labor to such a degree that their enterprises were not adversely affected, especially when business was slack. A modifying law of 1898, however, permitted overtime under a wide variety of conditions.

SPIRIT OF REACTION

It should be obvious that government intervention in labor questions was no sign of liberalism. Rather, it reflected the same swing away from liberalism that motivated Bismarck's social legislation. The very fact that Dmitry Tolstoy was the prime mover in the law of 1885 is the best proof of the fundamentally reactionary character of the government's policy. The fact that in the 1890's Witte, in the Ministry of Finance, did everything in his power by railway construction, by tariffs, and by direct government subsidy—as duly recorded at length in his *Memoirs*—to promote the more rapid industrialization of Russia does not alter the fact that, though personally despised by the emperor, he was an ardent partisan of autocratic power.

In other respects, too, the regime showed itself in the closing decades of the nineteenth century fully as reactionary as in the days of "frozen Russia." In 1881, as part of the "dictatorship of the heart," land redemption had been made compulsory, though many nobles felt it an infringement on their property rights. In the early 1880's, too, Bunge had been allowed to continue tax reforms, including abolition of the soul tax (1886). On the other hand, a new university statute in 1884 destroyed the autonomy of the faculties; students were threatened with enrollment in the army as private soldiers if they offered any protest against government regulations. A fresh attempt was made to exclude non-nobles from the Gymnasia, and only the factor of cost prevented the government from taking the primary schools out of the hands of the zemstvos.

Earlier in the century, there had been "repentant nobles." Now it was the government's turn openly to repent its efforts to downgrade the nobility. The regime of Alexander III (1881-94) made every effort, both in theory and in practice, to restore the special privileges of the old ruling class. In founding a special Nobles' Bank (1885), the government announced its purpose that

> the Russian nobles, in the present as in the past, should preserve a place of primacy in leadership of the armed forces, in matters of local government and justice, in unselfish care for the needs of the people, in spreading by their own example the principles of faith and loyalty and of the healthy fundamentals of popular education.[9]

In 1889 was established the new office of *zemsky nachalnik,* generally translated as "land captain." This official was to be appointed from the ranks of the local nobility and was given wide authority over peasant communes and *volosti.* The transfer to him of the functions of the justice of the peace also dealt a heavy blow to a basic principle of the judiciary reform of 1864, the separation of judicial and administrative functions. By a law of 1890, the structure of the zemstvos was drastically revised; the number of peasant delegates was reduced and, instead of being elected, they were henceforth to be appointed from a panel of elected candidates. At the same time, the autonomy of the zemstvos was cut down in an effort to make them subordinate elements in the local bureaucracy. The press was so harshly treated that scarcely any papers of even moderately liberal tendencies survived. In the borderlands, the work of Russification was vigorously pressed.

Nor did these policies change with the death of Alexander III in 1894; reference has already been made to the attitude of Nicholas II (1894-1917) toward zemstvo addresses. If anything, the alienation of the autocracy from the people was emphasized by a tragic incident connected with the coronation of Nicholas at Moscow in 1896. Through the stupidity of the arrangements for mass festivities on the Khodynka Field and the brutal efforts of the mounted police to keep the crowds in order, an estimated two thousand men, women, and children lost their lives by falling into deep ditches; the horror of the affair was enhanced by the callousness with which the imperial party attended a ball that night at the French embassy.

RUSSIAN CULTURE AT THE END OF THE CENTURY

The approach to the end of the century, which witnessed the growing weakness of the position of the autocracy, brought also a certain cultural decline, somewhat similar to the *fin de siècle* atmosphere in the West. In painting, to be sure, Repin and Vereshchagin were at the height of their powers. They had been joined by Vasily I. Surikov (1848-1916), famed for his historical scenes, such as *The Execution of the Strieltsy* (1881) and *The Boiarinia Morozova* (1887), and by Valentin A. Serov (1865-1911), particularly distinguished for his portraits, notably his *Girl with Peaches* (1887). Victor M. Vasnetsov (1848-1926) had progressed from sympathetic depiction of local scenes to his poignant *Alionushka* (1881), which reflected his deep interest in Russian folk art and poetry, and his best-known *Bogatyri* (1881-98), which blended his nationalist hero-worship with national folk tales. To this period belong such famous works of Repin as *Ivan the Terrible and His Son Ivan, November 16, 1581* (1885) and his *Zaporogian Cossacks* (1891). This period also witnessed the rise of a swarm of "decadents," such as Mikhail A. Vrubel (1856-1910), whose *Spain* (1890) is his best-known product. The stylized work of the *Mir Iskusstva* ("World of Art") school also achieved a certain popularity; least characteristic, but perhaps most appreciated, was the *Lady in Blue* (1897-1900) of Konstantin A. Somov (1869-1939).

In music, Tchaikovsky passed from the scene the year before the accession of Nicholas II; his *Sixth* (*Pathétique*) *Symphony* was long mistakenly construed as a deliberate requiem for himself. Rimsky-Korsakov, despite a severe nervous breakdown in 1892, remained the dominant figure; most of his creative effort, however, was squandered on operas in an alternating struggle to emulate Wagner and to free himself from his influence. Only when his penchant for colorful fantasy won the upper hand, as in *Sadko* (1894-96) and *Tsar Saltan* (1899-1900), did he achieve notable successes.

By this time, largely through the influence of the Rubinsteins' Conservatories, musicians were coming to be regarded in Russia not as aberrant eccentrics but as normal members of society. Piano and violin teaching were respected professions, and musical scholarship flourished. At the same time, and largely as a consequence, the new generation of musicians, whether pupils of Rimsky-Korsakov at St. Petersburg or of the originally more conservative Moscow Conservatory, produced no creative giants such as the men of the first musical generation. The emphatic drive for a national Russian music was spent. The chief rising star seemed to be young Alexander Scriabin (1872-1915). Always an abnormal mystic, his sanity was to become increasingly questionable. At first an imitator of Chopin, Scriabin passed through a brief period of Wagnerian sensualism and ultimately emerged as a pioneer of the "modern" music of dissonance.

A fellow-pupil of Scriabin at the Moscow Conservatory, one equally devoted to the piano, was Sergei V. Rachmaninoff (1873-1943). A member of an aristocratic landholding family with musical traditions, the boy was given an excellent training in the Rubinstein convention. He came very strongly under the influence of Tchaikovsky; his *C-sharp Minor Prelude* was composed in the year of Tchaikovsky's death (1893). His work was seriously interrupted by an access of characteristic self-depreciation, from which he was rescued by a hypnotic psychologist (1900). Throughout his life, Rachmaninoff remained a conservative; his music was in the nineteenth-century romanticist tradition and played no part in the "modernist" movement.

Unnoticeable at the end of the century was Igor F. Stravinsky (b. 1882), who was to precipitate a fresh revolution in Russian music. His father was a noted opera singer who planned a legal career for his son. Thus, like the older generation and unlike his leading contemporaries, Stravinsky lacked early careful training in musical techniques. Only in 1905 did Rimsky-Korsakov accept him as a pupil, and only in the years between the revolution of 1905 and World War I was he able to make his profound impression on the musical world.

In literature, too, there was a certain carry-over. Though Turgenev and Dostoevsky had left the scene almost simultaneously with the Tsar-Liberator, Tolstoy still displayed his vast creative powers. However, following his self-conversion in 1880 to an ethical religion of his own devising—a sort of untheological Christianity—Tolstoy deliberately turned against his own earlier style of writing. As much a rationalist as ever, his continued quest for an ultimate meaning now led him into the field of religious, propagandistic writing. He thundered against alcohol and tobacco as well as against the "immorality" of all forms of violence. His inherent anarchism now caused him vigorously to reject the authority of both church and state as agencies of compulsion repugnant to Christ's teaching of "resist not evil." Although he disapproved also of revolutionary terrorism, he most strongly condemned all executions by the government. In this period, therefore, Tolstoy became the sainted darling of the discontented.

A Confession (1880-82) ushered in Tolstoy's new period, in which he sought to keep his special brand of mysticism subordinate to reason. Avoiding preaching and endeavoring to "infect" the reader with the truth of his revelation, *A Confession* has been called "in some ways his greatest artistic work." In addition to a number of other essentially religious works, Tolstoy in this period wrote a number of moralistic short stories centering on the themes of the fear of death and the power of sex. Such were *The Death of Ivan Ilyich* (1886), *Master and Man* (1895), and *The Kreutzer Sonata*

(1889); some of the best, including *The Memoirs of a Madman* and *The Devil,* as well as the novel *Hajji Murad,* were published only posthumously. His most popular play, *The Power of Darkness* (1887), was a throwback to his older technique of "superfluous detail" and was therefore condemned by its author as in the "bad manner." Of least intrinsic merit was his third long novel, *Resurrection* (1899), rushed to completion to raise money to finance the emigration to Canada of the persecuted sect of the Dukhobors.

Apart from Tolstoy, however, the end of the century could boast no writers to compare with the earlier giants. Nicholas K. Mikhailovsky (1842-1904), a "repentant noble," had in the post-Reform era exercised an influence on Russian radicalism second only to that of Lavrov. His *What Is Progress?* (1869-1870) strongly attacked the "devil-take-the-hindmost" aspects of English liberal economics; to "social Darwinism," Mikhailovsky had opposed the concept of "subjective" socialism, designed to achieve the maximum of human happiness. In this later period, while retaining intellectual preëminence among the neo-*narodnik* intelligentsia, he continued also as a journalist and critic to display the extraordinary perception that had characterized his analysis of Tolstoy (1873) and of Dostoevsky (1882).

Vladimir S. Soloviev (1853-1900), son of the great historian, had early attracted attention by his doctoral dissertation, *The Crisis of Western Philosophy* (1875). After profoundly mystical experiences in the British Museum and in the Egyptian desert, he had entered on an academic career; it was cut short by his open appeal to Alexander III not to execute the assassins of his father (1881). In 1889, he created a sensation by the strongly Romanist position he took in *La Russie et l'Église Universelle,* publication of which was forbidden in Russia. Soloviev had an unusually excellent training in philosophy and was the first Russian to make a serious name as a philosopher of religion. All his writings display a brilliant wit and ironic humor, combined with precise logic and informed theological scholarship. Yet, unable either to reconcile Plato and Kant or to choose between them, he was not destined to make significant contributions of his own.

His chief intellectual preoccupation was the need for a union of Christian faiths, in which Orthodoxy was to take the lead; Judaism, the basic principles of which he identified with those of Christianity, was to be included in this general renovation. Significant in this connection was his *Three Conversations on War, Progress, and the End of Human History, to Which Is Added a Short History of Antichrist* (1899-1900). In this work he depicted a tremendous and successful military onslaught on Europe by the "yellow peril"; Europe's subjugation would lead, however, to a victorious resurgence of the West and the formation of a United States of Europe. The president, a caricature of Leo Tolstoy, would prove to be Antichrist and would proclaim himself emperor. Only after reconciliation of the leaders of Orthodoxy, Catholicism, and Protestantism—whose faithful adherents would by this time have been reduced to forty-five million—would the thirty million Jews then settled in Palestine rise against the emperor, who had transferred his residence from Rome to Jerusalem. With the appearance of Christ for the Last Judgment, the millennium would be ushered in.

Another mystic writer who briefly had a great vogue was Dmitry S. Merezhkovsky (1865-1941). Beginning as a Symbolist poet, he soon became a champion of "new ideas" in opposition to orthodox positivist radicalism. His best-known work was his trilogy of historical novels, *Christ and Anti-christ,* made up of *Julian the Apostate* (1896), *Leonardo da Vinci* (1901), and *Peter and Alexis* (1905). Its central theme was the carefully stressed "polar" opposition of the Hellenic worship of the flesh, with its Christian reflection in God the Father, and the concept of the sanctity of the spirit, reflected in God the Son; the antithesis was to be resolved by messianic Russia in a neo-Christian religion of the Holy Ghost.

Though its literary merit was not great, Merezhkovsky's work undoubtedly had great significance in reopening for the Russian reading public the reality of ancient Greece and of medieval Italy, which had previously remained closed books. Even before the appearance of the third novel of the trilogy, Merezhkovsky had begun to publish his more enduring *Tolstoy and Dostoevsky* (1901). In it, persisting in his sharp emphasis on ideological antitheses, he represented Tolstoy as "the seer of the flesh" and Dostoevsky as "the seer of the spirit." Although much inferior to Isaiah Berlin's recent *The Hedgehog and the Fox,* it remains the most penetrating of Merezhkovsky's writings.

The principal new writers in this period were Chekhov and Gorky. Anton P. Chekhov (1860-1904) was the grandson of a serf whose money, made in trade, had enabled him to buy his freedom. The family had lost its money, and young Chekhov, as a medical student at Moscow, was forced to support himself and his family by writing stories for the comic papers; his success proved so great that, though he took his degree in 1884, he never had to practice his profession. Despite, or perhaps because of, the crudity and coarseness of tone of his early writings, Chekhov quickly acquired an immense popularity in Russia. As he turned his craftsmanship to more serious work, including *Sakhalin Island* (1891), and as he simultaneously drifted leftward, Chekhov's reputation did not diminish, though in Russia he long continued to be considered as a writer for the vulgar. Easily translatable, when freed from local allusions, abroad, he became the symbol of the esoteric highbrow.

Entirely characteristic was *A Dreary Story* (1889). Uninterested in individual personality, Chekhov used the old technique of "superfluous detail" to convey an atmosphere of disillusionment and hopelessness, in which his characters, singularly alike in their colorlessness, reacted to trivial pinpricks. Perfect as works of art, his numerous short stories of the 1890's totally lacked the psychological penetrative power of Tolstoy or Dostoevsky and offered nothing of the social analysis of Turgenev at his best. The same characteristics were reflected in his plays. *The Sea-Gull,* written in 1895, was a total failure at the St. Petersburg State Theater (1896). Only when taken up by Stanislavsky and the Moscow Art Theater did Chekhov score a success (1898). In rapid succession, *Uncle Vanya* (1899), *The Three Sisters* (1901), and *The Cherry Orchard* (1904) also proved well adapted to Stanislavsky's method of dispensing with individual stars and staging "undramatic drama."

"Maxim Gorky" (A. M. Peshkov, 1868-1936) was a pure proletarian, whose youth was spent in a succession of humble and laborious jobs, punctuated with grim unemployment. The first story to appear over his famous pseudonym (which means "Bitter") was printed in a provincial paper; by 1898, a collection of his stories had been published as a book. Financial success came quickly but did not enrich him, for he was steadily milked by the Marxist organizations he had joined. The story of greatest merit was "Twenty-six Men and a Girl" (1899); it was also the last of any great worth until in 1913 Gorky turned to autobiographical writing. His novels were little more than presentations of the dark backwardness of provincial life. Of his plays, only *The Lower Depths* (1903) was a success, and largely thanks to Stanislavsky's casting rather than to its author.

In large measure, Gorky's popularity reflected appreciation of the brutal vigor of his writing, coming so close on the heels of Chekhovian anemia. Abroad, Gorky's fame rested largely on the strange notion that his social outcasts, engaged in deep metaphysical discussion, constituted a realistic portrayal of life in mysterious Russia, "a riddle wrapped in an enigma." In 1902, Gorky was accorded the signal honor of election as an honorary member of the Russian Academy of Sciences; the election was quashed because Gorky was under police surveillance, whereupon Chekhov indignantly resigned his own membership. Gorky's reputation owed far more to the strength of social and political protest than to his literary merits. His prestige was of great value to Russian Social Democrats, but he was also to be a thorn in their sides by virtue of his frequent lapses from Marxist orthodoxy into "revisionism" and even into *narodnichestvo*.

Thus, contemporary criticism of the autocratic regime, no matter what sentimentally oppositional chords it might strike, had nothing to offer but negative programs. It is a truism of politics that you cannot beat somebody with nobody. Herein lay the weakness of the radical opposition: if the old order had been losing inner strength, the most vocal partisans of a new order seemed to have no viable alternative to offer.

NOTES

1. Efremov, *Istoriia ukrains'kogo pis'menstva,* I, 47.
2. Robinson, *Rural Russia Under the Old Regime,* p. 268.
3. *Ibid.,* p. 94.

4. *Ibid.*, p. 100.
5. *Ibid.*, p. 105.
6. *Matthew* 13:12.
7. Robinson, *op. cit.*, p. 96.
8. Tugan-Baranovskii, *Geschichte der russischen Fabrik,* p. 471.
9. *Polnoe sobranie zakonov* . . . (Third collection), No. 2882 (April 21, 1885), V, 169.

SUGGESTIONS FOR FURTHER READING

Among books previously mentioned, Kornilov, Pushkarev, Robinson, and Tugan-Baranovskii are most valuable.

Von Laue's *Sergei Witte and the Industrialization of Russia* is immensely helpful, and Gerschenkron's *Economic Backwardness in Historical Perspective* is extremely thoughtful. Mavor's *Economic History of Russia* contains much useful, but disjointed material. Pipes' *Social Democracy and the St. Petersburg Labor Movement* is helpful in understanding the difference between socialism and the labor movement; see also Wildman's *Making of a Workers' Revolution.* Wallace's *Russia* is still helpful to understanding the period.

For Russia's Asian empire, Lobanov-Rostovsky's *Russia and Asia* should be consulted. Skrine and Ross, *The Heart of Asia,* reviews the whole history of Turkestan; Pierce, *Russian Central Asia, 1867-1917,* is a more advanced study. Lensen's *The Russian Push Toward Japan* is a good summary of Russo-Japanese relations from the time of Peter the Great to 1875. Wheeler's *Modern History of Soviet Central Asia* contains a competent summary of earlier days. An excellent account of imperial diplomacy is contained in Langer's *Franco-Russian Alliance.* Garthoff's *Soviet Military Policy* harks back to these days. For Finland, the histories by Jutikkala and Wuorinen are complementary.

Yarmolinsky's *Memoirs of Count Witte* and Pobiedonostsev's *Reflections of a Russian Statesman* give first-hand portrayal of the viewpoints of those two leading figures of the era.

In addition to other works previously cited on Russian culture, Rice's *A Concise History of Russian Art,* Varneke's *History of the Russian Theatre,* and Slonim's *Russian Theatre: From the Empire to the Soviets* should be consulted.

Chapter

20

The Revolution of 1905: 1900-1905

THE AUTOCRACY AND THE ORGANIZED OPPOSITION

As the present century opened, the autocracy in Russia remained intact. Major reforms had been carried out, but their character had in large measure been canceled by subsequent constrictions. Even at the peak of reforming activity no concession had ever been made offering the slightest modification in the essential principle of autocracy. Notwithstanding grant of partial autonomy in limited and local respects, the theory—and the fact—had been retained that the will of the autocrat was still absolute.

Such a theory, for its effective realization, might seem to require that there stand at the helm a being capable of withstanding pressures and deciding questions on an independent basis. There had been few, if any, rulers with such qualifications. Certainly the ruler of the moment, Nicholas II, was not a person capable of properly wielding autocratic power. Good-natured, weak-willed—characterize him as one may—Nicholas II obviously did not possess the attributes of character expected of an autocrat such as the Russian ruler was supposed to be.

This fact in itself need not have mattered. There have been many instances in history of fainéant rulers, themselves overshadowed by a major-domo or other "servant," who actually wielded the power in the name of the ruler. It was perhaps Holy Mother Russia's misfortune that at this critical time there did not exist any such person, combining administrative ability, strength of will, and personal ascendancy over his "master," who might have guided the autocracy in the days ahead. The subjection of Nicholas to his wife, a woman of narrow mind and imperious will, with whom subjective considerations were ever paramount, was a poor substitute for the absence of a consummate statesman who might have successfully piloted the ship of state.

The organs through which the autocracy exercised power were relatively simple. The Senate, since Catherine's time, had served as the supreme judicial authority under the ruler. The emperor had an advisory body, the State Council (*Gosudarstvennyi Soviet*), made up of his own appointees, whose advice he was in no sense bound to respect. He had also an executive body, the Council of Ministers (*Soviet Ministrov*), the members of which were appointed for indefinite terms. Though technically collectively responsible, each minister held office individually at the emperor's pleasure; rivalry, rather than coöperation, was normal among them, and it had often proved possible for ministers to be working, each in his respective department, in contradictory directions.

The autocracy had powerful supports. Its chief reliance, developed principally in the nineteenth century, was the enormous bureaucratic apparatus. This consisted not only of officials in the capitals but of the local regime as well. Governors or Governors-General, appointed by the central authority, lorded it over the provinces in much the same way as the emperor did at the center, always with the reservation that these governors derived their powers from the central authority, which was itself independent of any earthly control, lay or ecclesiastic. The bureaucracy, central and local, though in some respects it might seem an inert weight, without initiative, nevertheless had an inner life of its own, not always subject even to the direction of the autocrat, and deriving no impetus from any class interest in the country, not even that of the nobility.

The nobility had its own local class organs of representation, dating from Catherine's time, and headed by elected provincial "marshals of nobility." These organs, however, had no share in determining the policies of the central government, nor did they have any direct share in the work of the local government, exclusively controlled on the bureaucratic principle.

The sole significant exception to the rule that the governance of Russia, centrally and locally, rested in the autocracy and the bureaucracy, was the existence of the zemstvos and of the city dumas. These bodies, as has been remarked, had been set up or reorganized in the period of the "Great Reforms" on the "all-class" principle, which had not prevented in fact the dominance of the noble or the wealthy. Their powers had been narrowly circumscribed at the outset and, by laws of 1890 and subsequent years, had been even further contracted. Though some of the leaders in these organs of partial local self-government had persistently asked for a larger role in the conduct of state affairs, their requests had been regularly and emphatically denied. The functioning of these organs, however important in certain respects, did not alter the general picture of the integral character of the autocracy. Much less did the extremely limited autonomy at the lowest level of peasant commune and *volost,* especially after the establishment in 1889 of the "land captains," affect the reality of bureaucratic autocracy.

The autocracy had also other supports. Some of them were intangible: centuries of tradition of authority; the ritual, if not spiritual, authority of the Orthodox Church, which was no more than a subdivision of state power; the absence of any vital liberal movement, deeply rooted in a free economy. Other sources of support were quite tangible: a carefully organized and centrally controlled system of police; an enormously powerful army, subjected to rigid discipline and cut off from any continuing contact with the civil population. There were, of course, also elements of weakness, such as the easily disorganized state of the finances or the incorrigible graft and corruption with which the whole official machinery was shot through. Yet, on the whole, the position of the autocracy—resting not only on Cossacks, the knout, the nagaika, and Siberia, but also on the cumulative forces of Russian history—seemed impregnable.

Arrayed against it were various determined and implacable organized foes, but they were puny compared to the vast forces at the disposal of the autocracy. Several "parties" were formed to combat the power of the government. It should, of course, always be borne in mind that Russian "parties" are not to be understood in the sense that term conveys in a democratic or even a liberal country. They could not be organizations to "get out the vote"; they existed only to make propaganda, by word or by deed, in the hope that somehow, sometime, the autocracy would be brought to an end. Their membership was secret; their chief leaders spent most of their time in foreign exile, while the lesser lights who remained in Russia were frequently in jail or in Siberia.

Among these groups, the oldest in point of time and the most formidable in point of numbers was the reconstituted force of peculiarly Russian socialism. The *narodnik* movement had, after the assassination of Alexander II in 1881, fallen on evil days. Yet at the turn of the century it was undergoing a significant revival, with some modification of its original views. Out of it rose the revolutionary party which doubtless had the largest measure of support that the Russian people was capable of extending to any politically active group.

As earlier noted, Russian intellectuals no longer felt they could pass over with slight notice—as Herzen, Chernyshevsky, and Lavrov had done—the role of the industrial proletariat. Yet, while borrowing some elements from Marx, the new tendency persisted in stressing the two main concepts of *narodnichestvo:* the paramount role of the "critically thinking individual" as opposed to the concept of "class consciousness"; and the predominance of the peasant and the peasant commune as the essential kernel of the approaching revolution. By 1901, this modified form of "Russian socialism" had launched a new revolutionary organization, the Socialist Revolutionary Party; the name, suggested by Catherine Breshkovskaia, the aristocratic "grandmother of the Russian Revolution," was soon shortened to its initials, and its members are generally referred to as SR's (or, using the Russian pronunciation of these letters, *esers*).

The SR party did not become a tight-knit organization. Its members believed too strongly in the overriding ascendancy of the popular will for it to be possible for them to submit to any sort of strict party discipline. It is therefore extraordinarily difficult to characterize this party in terms more precise than those already stated. In general, the SR's were committed to "socialization" of production, thinking primarily in terms of the land. This "socialization" did not initially go beyond community of landholding, without entailing any communalization of production.

What they were in practice striving for was maintenance and development of the existing structure of peasant agrarian relations, which was essentially non-Marxist. They demanded transfer of all privately held land to the communes, which they wished to preserve. They desired to strengthen the commune by extending and enlivening "repartitional" tenure, but this inevitably involved them in support of the holding of land by individual peasants within the communal structure. Thus it was not the very poorest peasants, the germ of an agricultural proletariat, whose interests they were likely to promote. Rather, they put their faith in landholding (not landowning) peasants, and this opened the way for support of the SR Party by the well-to-do peasants who were actually dominant within the existing commune.

This curious paradox, which made these "socialists" the spokesmen, not of peasant egalitarianism, but of the mass of peasants who were, or aspired to be, individual landholders (not necessarily landowners), was paralleled by the curious position of the Party with respect to methods. The chief intellectual figure among the SR's, Victor Chernov, was a devout believer in peaceful democracy, but there was tolerated within the Party a conspicuous minority which preferred the alternative road of oligarchic terrorism. This wing, the "Fighting Organization," though not in control of the Party, naturally impressed itself, by virtue of its activity, on the public and on the official mind as the most significant element in the Party.

In retrospect, one may be convinced that the long series of assassinations of governors, ministers, and police chiefs—and also of grand dukes, though avoiding the mistake of 1881—impeded, rather than aided, the attainment of the Party's objectives. Certainly, however, the government regarded these activities as more seriously dangerous than those of any other variety of socialists and accorded them the honor of the most careful attention of the political police. Their activity is reflected in the currency among Russian chess-players of the older generation of the phrase *polozhenie khuzhe gubernatorskoe* ("the position is worse than that of a governor"). Among the most striking achievements of the new outbreak of terrorism were the murder of Bogolepov, Minister of Education (1900), of Sipiagin, Minister of the Interior (1902), and of Pleve, his successor (1904). Yet terrorist activity, though perhaps just as effective—or ineffective—as any other form of propaganda in affecting the mind of the masses, played into the hands of the government by lending it an appearance of righteousness in vigorously repressing manifestations of revolutionary sentiment.

The other main tendency of extremist sentiment was therefore perhaps right in frowning on terrorist activity. While fulminating just as vigorously against tsarist rule, it insisted that destruction of classes, not of individuals, was its objective. This current was that of Social Democracy, whose origin in the disillusionment of Plekhanov and some other *narodniki* has already been referred to. The failure of the Minsk Congress in 1898 had not checked the agitational energies of isolated Marxist groups, both in Russia and in emigration.

In 1903 a fresh attempt was made to bring together Russia's true believers in the revolutionary Marxist philosophy. In preparation for a new congress, Lenin in 1902 advanced his rigidly disciplinarian views of the role and structure of the Party in *What Is to Be Done?*, a title borrowed from Chernyshevsky's famous novel:

> We have said that *there could not be* social-democratic consciousness among the workers. This could only be introduced from outside. The history of all countries attests that, if left entirely to its own efforts, the working class is in a position to develop only trade-union consciousness, i.e., a conviction of the necessity for combining in unions, of fighting against the employers, and of striving to win from the government the labor legislation they need, etc.
>
> The doctrine of socialism, however, grew out of the philosophical, historical, and economic theories worked out by educated representatives of the propertied classes, the intellectuals. The founders of modern scientific socialism, Marx and Engels, themselves belonged by virtue of their social position to the bourgeois intelligentsia. In just the same way, in Russia the theoretical doctrine of social-democracy arose absolutely independently of the spontaneous growth of the labor movement. . . .[1]
>
> . . . The spontaneous labor movement is trade-unionism. . . . Therefore our task, the task of social-democracy, consists in a *struggle against spontaneity,* to *divert* the labor movement, with its spontaneous trade-union effort, from under the wing of the bourgeoisie, and to bring it under the wing of revolutionary social-democracy. . . .[2]
>
> . . . Is it conceivable for us [in Russia] for all "who accept the principles of the Party program and support the Party as far as they are able" to control every step of the revolutionary-conspirator? Is it conceivable that these all elect one or another of their number when, in the interest of his work, the revolutionary must conceal from nine out of ten of these "all" who he is?
>
> . . . The only serious organizational principle for men in our movement must be the strictest secrecy, the strictest selection of members, and the training of professional revolutionists. . . .[3]

In order to minimize the dangers of the attendance of police informers, the Second Congress was held abroad, at Brussels. To be sure, it attracted local police attention, but the Belgian police merely stressed the broadening effects of travel. The upshot was that the Congress adjourned to the possibly foggier, but less inhibited, air of London. There, in the atmosphere of the physical, though not the spiritual, home of Karl Marx, his Russian disciples strove to re-found the Russian Social Democratic Workers Party.

From the outset, it was clear that predominance belonged, not to any group or combination of groups functioning within the Empire of all the Russias, but to a group of émigrés clustering around a Russian-language newspaper, *Iskra* (*The Spark*), published in Switzerland; among its six editors, primacy rested with the veteran Plekhanov, Martov (Y. O. Tsederbaum), and Lenin (V. I. Ulianov). In a series of hard-fought battles, the *Iskra* group triumphed, at the expense of the secession of defeated groups and of a split in its own ranks.

Its most important and easiest victory was over the "Economists," the Russian counterpart of "Revisionists" or "Reformists" in Western Europe. In the absence of trade-union organization and in view of the weak participation of proletarians in the Russian Marxist groups, it was relatively easy to lay down the principle of the paramount importance of political revolution as the primary goal of the Party. After all, improvement of the material condition of the working class might hamper the growth of its class consciousness, and thus concentration on economic struggle in behalf of the proletariat might postpone proletarian revolution. Conversely, every failure of workers to achieve material betterment of their condition by strikes and negotiations might even seem valuable propaganda against capitalism.

The Party Program drafted by Lenin, with stress on reviving the concept of the "dictatorship of the proletariat," was triumphantly adopted, despite the vigorous opposition of the two "Economists" present. However, trouble developed in debate on the Party Statute (*Ustav*). Lenin's draft of Article 1, defining membership in the Party, was rejected by a vote of 28-23, despite the backing of Plekhanov. In its stead was approved a slightly different formulation by Martov, by a vote of 28-22 with one abstention; slight as seemed the difference in wording, it was highly significant, for it subjected Party members to less rigid discipline than Lenin had wished. With other lesser changes, the revised Statute was adopted.

Lenin watched for a more favorable opportunity to take control, successfully opposing a proposal to proceed at once to election of the Party's three governing bodies. The Bund attempted to secure a guarantee of its continued autonomy in a federal structure; defeated by a vote of 41-5, its five delegates left the Congress. The "Economists," anticipating a similar defeat, followed them. It was next announced that the Polish Social Democrats (thinking along the lines of Rosa Luxemburg, later a leader of the German Sparticists), unlike the Polish Socialist Party (of which Pilsudski was the leader), preferred fraternal relations with socialists of a nationality other than their own rather than with uncongenial elements of their ethnic group, and were therefore dismayed by Lenin's insistence on Poland's right of self-determination and were not to become affiliated with the Congress.

In the elections to *Iskra*'s editorial board the winning candidates were Plekhanov with 23 votes, Martov with 22, and Lenin trailing with 20. Lenin's slate of members for the Central Executive Committee won by 24-0, with 20 abstentions. The fifth member of the Party Council was elected by 22-21, with one abstention. It is the outcome of these elections that enabled Lenin's partisans to style themselves *Bolsheviki* ("majority men"). Though defeated on the question of the definition of Party membership, Lenin had won control of the Party "apparatus."

Lenin, though accepting the outward Marxist paraphernalia of class struggle, proletarian revolution, and the rest, had never succeeded in shaking off the fundamental *narodnik* concept of the role of the "critically thinking individual," organized, as Lavrov had advocated, in a tightly governed Party of the elite. He never assimilated the distinctive notion of "scientific socialism," the achievement of which depended on the working out of objective material forces stemming from a given organization of production. Lenin regarded the Party as the essential general staff of revolution, with himself as commander-in-chief.

For Lenin, the words of Marx and Engels were never more than "dead dogma." Socialists whose knowledge was confined to books were fit only for the museum. Marxism was a doctrine that had been formulated in Western Europe; it could not be taken over bodily but must be adapted to the specific conditions of life in Russia under an autocracy and in the presence of the fact that the "masses" were not proletarians but peasants. "Leninism" therefore entailed a revision of Marxism even more fundamental than the "Revisionism" of Eduard Bernstein. Since Lenin, for all his apparent dogmatism, was a keen observer of real conditions and constantly had an eye for ever-shifting power relationships, it would be futile to try to pinpoint his permanent theoretical ideas. Lenin was a Russian Bismarck rather than a Russian Marx; his forte was not abstract thought but opportunistic political acumen.

His victory at London, won by skillful timing, was not lasting. Plekhanov soon became convinced that Lenin was too dictatorial; he therefore switched his powerful support to Martov and the Mensheviks (the "minority men" at the 1903 Congress). Lenin, thus deprived of control over the Party newspaper organ, went into a fit of sulks. Lashing out bitterly against all rival socialist groups—and especially against the "Economists"—he for a time lost serious influence over the revolutionary movement.

The Menshevik fraction of the Russian Social-Democratic Workers' Party was no less revolutionary in spirit than were Lenin's Bolsheviks. Martov, too, condemned the "Economists," even more rigorously than Karl Kautsky in Germany waged the struggle against their counterpart, the "Revisionists." The Mensheviks, no less than the Bolsheviks, wanted to use the Russian proletariat, not in a struggle to improve its material condition within the framework of capitalism, but to destroy capitalism along with autocracy. Whereas Bolshevism was rooted in the traditional *narodnik* belief in the subjective role of an intellectual elite (Lenin's concept of the Party as the revolutionary "vanguard"), the Mensheviks deemed revolution to be the task of the whole proletariat as a class. More confident than the Bolsheviks of the universal truth of Marxist teachings, they were the Russian counterpart of Western left-wing "orthodox" revolutionary Marxism. This fact was to prove an immense handicap to them in effecting a working alliance with the peasantry or with any significant portion of it. Marxist theory did not allow for the psychology of the Russian peasant, a circumstance to which even Lenin was somewhat slow to adjust.

The Social-Democratic land program of 1903, then supported by the Bolsheviks as well as by the Mensheviks, called only for restoration to the peasants of "cutoffs" from allotments in connection with Emancipation, for the refunding to them of all redemption payments, and complete freedom in disposal of communal lands. This program, conceived "in the interest of the free development of the class struggle in the village," [4] could only mean anticipation of a growing differentiation between a small minority of capitalist peasants and a growing landless agricultural proletariat. It could hardly be expected that peasants would welcome an idea that would require them to lose what little land they had in order to attain the blessing of Marxist support as proletarians. Neither in the village nor in the factory were the Social Democrats able to make any appreciable headway. Both halves of the Party necessarily were almost wholly confined to a small number of petty-bourgeois intellectuals, waging a violent war of words with each other and with their SR rivals.

More formidable, if more restrained, was the attitude of more highly placed individuals who, for lack of a more precise word, may be called "liberals." Reference has already been made to the repeated mild efforts of the zemstvo men to induce the government to convert itself from an autocracy into a constitutional, perhaps even a democratic, monarchy. As early as 1878, zemstvo liberals had taken the lead in the formation of a "League of Opposition Elements," into which they had invited also such *narodniki* as would repudiate terrorism. Soon evolving into the "Zemstvo Union," this group asked for civil liberties and decentralized representative government. Though sternly rebuffed by Nicholas II at his accession in 1894, leading zemstvo figures, such as Shipov and Petrunkevich, contrived in the 1890's to hold informal meetings in an effort to counteract the restrictive attitude of the government which so severely hampered their ameliorative work in the provinces.

Despite all handicaps, many of the zemstvos had done excellent practical work in raising the material and cultural level of the peasantry. Particularly outstanding had been the work of the Moscow provincial zemstvo, which succeeded in bringing the free hospital within five, and the free elementary school within two, miles of any peasant hut. In 1903, the reëlection of Shipov, who had been its president since 1893, was vetoed by V. K. Pleve, the Minister of the Interior. Shipov's successor, however, was even less interested in restraining the anti-autocratic tendencies of his fellow zemstvo workers; the most progressive of them promptly formed a group known as "Zemstvo Constitutionalists."

Meanwhile, eminent zemstvo men had been joining forces with academic figures such as Professors Vinogradov and Miliukov. In 1902, they founded at Stuttgart a new organ, *Osvobozhdenie'* ("Liberation"), edited by Peter Struve, who had prepared the draft of the manifesto for the Minsk Congress of the Social Democrats in 1898 but had become an advocate of constitutional democracy. In Russia itself was organized, in January, 1904, the underground "Union of Liberation," which attracted capitalist as well as academic support. This group was more extreme than were the majority of the zemstvo men in its endorsement of the principle of the establishment of a central representative assembly. Less than a month after its formation, war with Japan began, under circumstances which at first deprived the Liberators of popular support. Yet from them was to come the most serious agitation for putting an end to the autocracy.

IMMEDIATE BACKGROUND OF THE REVOLUTION

Taken all together, the organized and vocal opposition to the autocracy was weak in numbers and hopelessly divided. There was little possibility of effective coöperation between the Socialist Revolutionary Party, the Russian Social Democratic Workers' Party (itself split into Mensheviks and Bolsheviks), the Union of Liberation, and the Zemstvo Constitutionalists, to say nothing of minor groups, organized chiefly on nationalist lines. Neither their objectives nor their methods agreed, and the influence of many of the leaders was further weakened by the inevitable fact that they were of necessity in emigration. Under such circumstances there was no great chance of the autocracy being overthrown. There remained the possibility that under certain circumstances it might collapse of its own weakness and from the lack of support from any significant element outside bureaucratic circles.

The class with the most reason to support the autocracy was the nobility. But, despite the pains the government had been at to protect the nobles from injury to their economic interests, the nobility had suffered irreparable loss. In 1885, the state had established a Nobles' Land Bank, set up

> in consideration of the needs of noble landholding, which in many localities has been ruined by the scantiness of economic resources and by the tightness of credit . . . in order that the nobles may thereby be more attracted to permanent residence on their estates, where it behooves them primarily to devote themselves to the work required of them as an obligation of their rank.[5]

Notwithstanding specially favorable interest rates, the result had been that by 1904 more than one-third of the land still in noble hands was mortgaged to this bank, to say nothing of other credit institutions, and arrears in payments were rising. Moreover, the total landholdings of the nobles had been decreasing with mounting rapidity; by 1905 they retained only 52 million of the 73 million dessiatines they had still owned in 1877.

In the black-soil region, a relatively small number of nobles had successfully adapted themselves to capitalist agricultural techniques and had produced a disproportionate share (about one-fifth) of the grain put on the market. Yet the role of the nobility in organizing economic activity was no longer able to support their surviving political privileges. Even had they not shown a marked tendency to sulk at home and leave the government to its own devices, they no longer had the strength to play their old role as the ruling class. A number of them, indeed, were conspicuous among the advocates of political reform and of a constitution.

The place the nobles had once held in the economic life of the country had, with the rapid rise of large-scale industry, passed to the capitalist entrepreneurs. This class was totally excluded from the formulation of government policy. So long as Serge Witte held the post of Minister of Finance (1892-1903), they had little reason to complain. Witte's protective tariff policy, his emphasis on indirect taxation (including the spirit monopoly), his promotion of railway construction (with minimal attention to merely strategic needs), his sound-money policy, his encouragement of the investment of foreign capital, his government loans and subsidies, his soft-pedaling of labor legislation—these policies were everything that the industrialists could ask for. The insecurity of their position was, however, made clear by Witte's "promotion" in 1903 to the supernumerary post of President of the Council of Ministers and by the rise of Pleve, appointed Minister of the Interior in 1902, to dominance in ministerial counsels.

Particularly annoying to industrialists was a police scheme, launched in 1901, to play off the workers against the employers and at the same time to smoke out members of the revolutionary parties. Under the guidance of Zubatov, a Moscow public official who had himself been a revolutionary, were organized a number of pseudo trade unions, which even conducted strikes. At Odessa, in 1903, a police-inspired strike got so far out of hand that the troops had to be called out. Zubatov was rebuked, but his idea was not abandoned. In 1904 a "police-socialist" organization was founded at St. Petersburg, under the direction of a young priest, Father Gapon.

Even without benefit of police inspiration, the workers had in the 1890's engaged in a number of major strikes, which the socialists had tried to use for propaganda purposes. A strike simultaneously affecting nineteen cotton factories in St. Petersburg in 1896 for a twelve-hour day had so alarmed Witte that he had carried through legal establishment of an eleven-and-a-half-hour day. Despite the vigorous efforts of the socialists, the strike movement remained almost wholly confined to economic purposes. Although they were engaging in illegal activities, the workers were concerned with improvement of their material condition, not with remote political objectives. Nor was the movement more than sporadic: only in 1898 did it affect more than 1 percent of the factories; only in 1897 and 1899 did the number of strikers approach 4 percent of the total number of factory workers.

Yet, although trade unions remained illegal, both the degree of organization and the demonstrative character of the strikes steadily increased; it would be hard to determine whether "police-socialism" or "social democracy" had the greater influence in these respects, insofar as either one was involved at all. In 1903, a wave of violent strikes, starting at Rostov, swept across southern Russia from Odessa to Baku. It was said that over five hundred factories (over 3 percent of the total number in Russia) and 225,000 workers (over 5 percent of the total) were affected; the slogans of the strikers ranged from demand for an eight-hour day to demands for political freedoms. The movement was crushed by employment of Cossacks; large numbers of participants were subjected to punishment. In 1904, the strike movement dropped off to the lowest figures in the reign of Nicholas II, but it had become obvious enough that the proletarian workers constituted a volatile mass, as capable of exploding as was the peasantry from which it was not too clearly differentiable. It was evident also that, though the primary impulse must be given in terms of economic motivations, the Russian workers, once excited, would accept also political objectives.

The peasantry itself remained the chief conundrum. It had shown little response to the provocative appeals of revolutionaries; yet it had not remained quiescent under the pressure of ever-present economic distress. Every year there were scores of sporadic disturbances, including arson and murder, on the part of the peasants. In 1902, in two southern provinces, these took especially serious form, though they were quickly and rigorously suppressed by the troops. The fact that the 1902 troubles occurred in an area where the "repartitional" commune prevailed caused much disquiet. Witte began to veer away from his former faith in the commune; in 1903, the remnant of the "circular guarantee" (collective responsibility for payment of taxes and redemption dues) was abolished. Witte, however, was engaged in a bitter and losing quarrel with his colleagues in the ministry, and the government remained uncertain and hesitant.

On the very eve of revolution, the situation somewhat resembled that of France in 1789. A monarchy which had largely lost the confidence of its subjects and was beginning to feel unsure even of itself, a nobility with little more than decorative functions, a rising bourgeoisie, a restless lower class in the towns, and an oppressed peasantry were elements of instability that added up, not to a united revolutionary urge, but to several disparate and uncoördinated currents. In fundamental ways, however, there was no parallelism between the France of 1789 and the Russia of 1905—or of 1917. Among many differences were the existence in Russia of large-scale capitalist industry and of a peasantry with no ingrained sense of individual property rights in land.

A special, if relatively minor, peculiarity of the Russian situation was the restlessness of the peoples of the borderlands, who violently resented some of the stupidities of the official policy of Russification. The Little Russians were showing increasing consciousness of themselves as distinct from the Great Russians; the influx of the latter into the rising industrial area of the Donets coal basin created added friction. In White Russia, the complexities of ethnic differentiation were further embroiled by the stubborn struggle for survival of the Uniate Church. Both in White Russia and in the Little Russian Ukraine, the continuing oppression of the Jewish minority, crowded into the towns, remained a source of trouble. The revival of major pogroms, not discouraged by the government, could not fail to drive a disproportionate number of Jews into revolutionary activity; the Kishinev massacre (1903) was to cost Pleve his life in the following year.

Poland remained hostile. Here the rigidity of the policy of Russification had been carried even to the point of allowing the teaching of Polish literature only in the Russian language. The exclusion of Poles from all government posts in their native country turned many of them to business activity; the rapid rise of factory industry, in such new centers as Lodz, also stimulated the growth of a Polish middle class and of a Polish socialist movement as well. The influence of the landed nobility was diminished, and a National Democratic Party was organized (1897); its chief spokesman was Roman Dmowski, who openly worked for autonomy rather than independence.

In the Baltic provinces, the official drive against the traditional German culture of the middle class played into the hands of the submerged aboriginal Letto-Lithuanian and Estonian population; but these peoples, however glad to be relieved of German dominance, had no desire to accept Russification in its stead; they contributed to the troubles of the Russian government by endeavoring to assert their own right to national existence. Particularly grave was the situation in Finland. Despite the fact that on his accession Nicholas II had confirmed its historic constitutional liberties and privileges, Finland was forcibly converted into a military district of the Russian Empire, and the powers of the Finnish Diet were curtailed (1899). A period of passive resistance was met with further measures of Russification. In despair a Finn assassinated the Russian Governor-General (1904).

In the east, as in the west, Russia was faced with increasing nationalist resistance. In the Caucasus, the three principal peoples were the Georgians, dominated by their native nobility; the Armenians, largely middle-class; and the Moslem Tatars, who supplied most of the industrial workers. Russia's Armenians had been much stimulated by emigrants from Turkey, fleeing massacre by the Kurds in 1894-95. In 1903, Pleve turned them violently against the Russian government by taking over control of their church funds. Ethnic and religious difficulties were much exacerbated by the rapid growth of the Caspian oil industry; Baku became one of the chief centers of labor disturbances in the whole empire.

In Central Asia, too, Russia's efforts to "civilize" the Moslem population, so recently brought under imperial control, bred serious hostility. Though the peoples of that region were deeply divided among themselves, they tended to make common cause against the centralizing efforts of the autocracy.

Still farther to the east, the effort to extend Russian power, this time beyond the limits of her acknowledged territory, brought on foreign war. Combined with humiliating defeat, this episode was to be the decisive factor in precipitating revolt in Russia itself.

WAR AND REVOLUTION

The forward policy of Russia in the Far East under Nicholas II had, as earlier noted, owed its drive to the interests of French investment rather than of business opportunities for Russian capitalists. Russian acquisition of Port Arthur had, however, alarmed Great Britain and offended Japan; their answer was the Anglo-Japanese alliance of 1902. Faced with this development, Russia made an agreement with China, promising to withdraw from Manchuria the troops she had poured in during the Boxer Rebellion (1900). It was at this juncture that the experienced policeman, Pleve, succeeded to the Ministry of the Interior, in which post he soon was able to overreach the influence of the cautious Witte. Pleve was not averse to a "little war," in the hope that some glorious bloodletting would relieve tensions at home. In addition, a powerful court clique, influenced by the spectacular Bezobrazov, was tempted by the possibilities of lucrative return by exploiting the resources of the area. Not content with Manchuria, which Japan was willing to concede as a Russian sphere of interest, an attempt was made to extend operations to the timber and mineral potentialities of Korea, which Japan regarded as definitely within her sphere of expansion.

After almost a year of negotiations, failing to receive a satisfactory reply to her proposals, Japan broke off diplomatic relations with Russia (February 5, 1904) and launched a sudden attack on Russian warships at Chemulpo and Port Arthur (February 9). Though the physical damage done by Japanese torpedoes was not very great, the psychological effect paralyzed the Russian navy, despite the courage of some of its admirals. For Russia, the war in the main resolved itself into the problem of maintaining and supplying an army at the end of over 5,500 miles (Moscow to Vladivostok) of single-track railway, still not quite completed.

The initiative could not be denied to the Japanese. General Kuropatkin's land forces, badly served by military intelligence, suffered repeated defeats in detail. The Japanese fleet suffered heavily from mines, but efforts of successive Russian admirals to use their superior fighting strength were foiled by their own deaths in battles. Besieged by land, Port Arthur was surrendered (January 1, 1905). The ill-assorted Russian Baltic fleet had been sent in October, 1904, to make the long voyage around Africa, without possibilities of adequate refueling or of cleaning the ships' bottoms before going into action. In its passage across the North Sea, it opened fire on the English Dogger Bank fishing fleet, which it mistook for Japanese torpedo boats (October 21), and war with Great Britain was narrowly averted by international arbitration. The fleet reached the China Sea seven months later, in no condition either for fight or for flight; intercepted by Admiral Togo in the Strait of Tsushima (May 27-28, 1905), it was annihilated. Meanwhile, Kuropatkin had been defeated, though not routed, in a fifteen-day battle before Mukden.

Japan's victories were won at the price of financial exhaustion and extremely heavy sacrifice of lives. Russia, financed by French loans, might have continued the struggle, but the alarming state of affairs at home boded ill for the success of even the most heroic efforts. Both sides therefore accepted an American invitation, issued June 8, to discuss peace at Portsmouth, New Hampshire; the idea had been suggested to the tsar by the German Kaiser on June 3. After three weeks of negotiations, during which Witte obdurately refused to consider payment of an indemnity, the Japanese suddenly accepted his offer (August 29) of half the island of Sakhalin in lieu of cash. The terms of the treaty signed at Portsmouth (September 5) surrendered to Japan the Liaotung Peninsula, with Port Arthur and Dalny. Russia agreed to evacuate Manchuria and recognized Japan's special position in Korea. Witte was rewarded by being made a Count; despite general relief at escape from this foolish war, Witte was frequently referred to thereafter as "Count of Portsmouth" or "Count Half-Sakhalin."

The war had enhanced political discontent in Russia and had tended to paralyze the government's repression of its manifestations. Pleve, the arch-practitioner of reaction, was assassinated (July 28, 1904). His successor, Prince Sviatopolk-Mirsky, seemed the herald of a "Russian spring," inviting the confidence of the press and public. In conference with Shipov, a meeting of zemstvo members was permitted to discuss reform at St. Petersburg (November 19-22). Anxious to avert revolution, they recommended proclamation of amnesty and of civil liberties for all, even including the peasants. Among their proposals were freedom of conscience; freedom of speech, assembly, and association; freedom of the press; and inviolability of the person and of domicile. Though all agreed on the need for establishment of an elected national assembly, a very considerable minority, including Shipov, favored the grant to it of advisory functions only.

Some of the "Liberators," who had been sounding out the Poles and the

SR's on the possibility of concerted action, attempted to anticipate grant of the proposed reforms by founding outspoken newspapers; the government replied by intensifying the censorship. In December, 1904, various categories of professional people—writers, lawyers, professors, journalists, engineers, doctors—had imitated the French revolutionists of 1848 by holding a series of "banquets" in support of the reform program. Disturbances occurred in connection with the dispatch of recruits and reservists to the Far East. A vaguely worded edict of December 25 instructed the ministers to prepare drafts of a number of suggested reforms but ignored the idea of a representative assembly. Another edict condemned the reformers as willful disturbers of the peace.

This gentlemanly game of announcing the imperial intention to "initiate" reforms while repressing those who were asking for them was brought to an abrupt halt by "Bloody Sunday" (January 22, 1905, frequently referred to by its date in the Russian calendar, January 9). Gapon's organization of workers, licensed by the police, was tending to act like a bona-fide trade union. The employers' demand that the government dissolve the organization was refused. When they attempted a lockout, the workers decided to present to the "Little Father" a petition setting forth their grievances against the employers; in the excitement, a number of the political demands of the intellectuals were incorporated. Monster peaceful demonstrations, carrying pictures of the tsar, converged toward the Winter Palace; they were fired on by troops, Gapon being among the first to fall, unhurt.

This panicky and savage action of the government had been intended to prevent repetition of the scenes at Versailles in 1789. It provoked a wave of strikes; the movement was spread over the country by workers hastily expelled from the capital by General Trepov, newly appointed Governor-General of St. Petersburg. An appeal early in February by Kokovtsov, Minister of Finance, to the employers to make concessions that would quiet the workers was met by the firm answer, both in St. Petersburg and in Moscow, that only general political reforms, including civil rights for all, could remedy the situation. The intellectuals intensified their agitation; throughout Russia the universities closed down in protest. There was a wave also of murders of police officials, especially in the Jewish Pale and in the Caucasus. The assassination of Grand Duke Serge, Governor-General of Moscow (February 17) provoked in the general public only a slight feeling of revulsion against revolutionary terrorism. In Poland, where the National Democrats organized a successful boycott of the Russian language, and in the Caucasus, where Christian Armenians and Tatar Moslems waged a sort of civil war, martial law was proclaimed.

A new Minister of the Interior, Bulygin, attempted appeasement. General Trepov had tried to stage a reconciliation by admitting a selected group of workmen to the emperor's presence to beg his pardon for having forced his troops to fire on the unarmed workers. A special commission was set up to hear the grievances of the workers; no appeals were brought before it. On March 3, it was announced that, while

> preserving inviolate the Fundamental Law of the Russian Empire on the essence of the Autocratic Power, [the Emperor held] the conviction that men elected by the confidence of the whole population and summoned by us for joint legislative work with the Government will in the face of all Russia prove themselves worthy of the Tsar's trust by virtue of which they are called to this great work.[6]

In the following months there followed a series of ameliorative amendments of existing legislation; under the circumstances, these measures commanded little respect.

The Liberators, at their March Congress, replied with a demand for a constituent assembly, to be elected by universal, direct, equal, and secret suffrage, to which they added endorsement of an eight-hour day and of the principle of compulsory expropriation of privately owned land in favor of the peasantry. Although they coupled this last point with a promise of fair compensation to the landowners, they alienated moderate upper-class opinion, as represented by men like Shipov. At successive congresses, the zemstvo-constitutionalists went only part way with the Liberators. They indicated serious limitation of the circumstances under which private land might be expropriated, and they proposed a bicameral legislature, accepting the "four-point [suffrage] formula" only for the lower house. At the other extreme of the liberal movement, the professional men, whose vociferousness obscured the quiet support of the Liberators by industrialists, formed "unions" of their several occupations. In May, 1905, these groups formed a Union of Unions, of which Professor Paul N. Miliukov, who had proved himself an adroit politician, became president.

Throughout the spring and early summer of 1905, while the war dragged on, matters grew steadily worse for the autocracy. At the beginning of March came the great defeat at Mukden, in May the catastrophe of Tsushima. Strikes were numerous and widespread. Though scarcely noticed at the time, the first Soviet of Workers' Deputies was formed as a strike committee at Ivanovo-Voznesensk, the great center of the cotton industry, at the end of May. Worse still, as early as the end of February the peasants began to come into action; most significant was the fact that they used the legal communal organization for violent attacks on landlords' property. These disturbances, beginning in the south, spread rapidly throughout the land. The peasants' demands, almost ignoring constitutional questions, centered around the SR slogan of "the land for the people."

Most ominous of all were occasional local mutinies in the armed forces, though they were provoked by maggoty meat rather than by any revolutionary ideology. In June, the crew of the armored cruiser *Potemkin,* the pride of the Black Sea fleet, threw its officers overboard; in this case, the sailors demonstrated their sympathy with the workers by bombarding Odessa in support of a strike; in order to prevent the spread of the infection the rest of the Black Sea fleet was ordered to avoid the mutinous vessel, which ultimately had to put into a Rumanian port, where it was interned.

On August 19, while the peace negotiations at Portsmouth were still in progress, the government published its complicated ideas about the Imperial Duma promised by Bulygin more than five months earlier. The Duma was to be purely consultative. Its members were to be elected indirectly, on the basis of heavily weighted class representation. Many categories were, by various provisions, excluded from the franchise altogether; among them were the proletarian workers and the Jews. President Roosevelt, inhibited by the terms of the American Constitution, could not validly protest the disfranchisement of men of no property. He did offer friendly objections, which were ignored, in the case of the Jews. The latter had only the more cause to throw themselves enthusiastically into revolutionary work.

Whether to accept the government's concessions posed a grave problem for Russia's revolutionary liberals. The Liberators had to balance between the more conservative zemstvo element and the more radical Union of Unions. A midsummer (July) congress of the zemstvo men had pronounced in favor of the organization of an open political party to participate in the elections. Early in September, a congress of the Union of Liberators took similar action. The commissions appointed by these two congresses formed the temporary committee of the nascent Constitutional Democratic Party. A congress of the Union of Unions, on the other hand, voted for boycott of the elections. This decision, however, was not regarded as final because of doubts expressed by the newly formed Peasants' Union. The Union of Liberators accordingly recommended that the new political party enter into relations with the local organs of the Peasants' Union.

The peasants themselves did not give full support to the position of the Liberators. The Peasants' Union, which held its first congress in Moscow on August 13-14, affiliated with the Union of Unions; it still showed, however, far more interest in the land question than in the constitutional problem. Throughout the country, the peasants were active in burning down manor houses, expelling landlords, and seizing the land. They showed, however, little hostility to the tsar as such; to them the Duma apparently meant only direct access to the "Little Father" without "land captains."

The workers displayed more interest in political slogans. Toward the end of October, a local rail strike began in Moscow in the name of civil liberties and an amnesty. It spread rapidly throughout the country and swept factory workers along with it. On October 27, a Council (*Soviet*) of Workers' Deputies met at St. Petersburg as a committee to organize the strikes; at its head stood Khrustalev-Nosar, a radical lawyer of no specific party affiliation.

Professional men and industrialists alike seized the opportunity to put maximum pressure on the hesitant government. The former refused to perform their normal services; doctors and bankers refused to operate, teachers to teach, even lawyers refused to argue. Many businessmen shut down their plants to increase the number of "strikers"; some, like the management of the great Putilov metallurgical works in St. Petersburg, paid their employees for attending meetings of the Soviet. Russia experienced perhaps the nearest approach any country has ever made to the ideal of the general strike. In the midst of it was launched a new party, the Constitutional Democrats (better known from their initials as "Cadets"). The Cadets were committed to the English principle of government by a ministry responsible to an elected legislature; insistently they demanded that this body be elected on the basis of universal, direct, equal, and secret suffrage.

The October strike was a sort of national passive resistance. Men like General Trepov, who would not have feared an armed uprising, felt themselves helpless. Unwilling to entrust power to the leaders of the popular movement, Nicholas II had no other recourse than to put himself wholly in the hands of Count Witte; much as the emperor disliked this upstart bourgeois, there was no doubt of his ability or loyalty.

Witte's remedy was the Manifesto of October 30 (in the Russian calendar, October 17). The essential part of this brief document read:

> We impose upon the Government the duty of executing Our unchangeable will:
>
> 1. To grant to the population the unshakable foundations of civil liberty on the principles of inviolability of the person and freedom of conscience, speech, assembly, and union.
>
> 2. Without postponing the appointed elections to the State Duma, to draw into participation in the Duma, so far as is possible in view of the short time that remains before the convocation of the Duma, those classes of the population which have hitherto been altogether deprived of electoral rights, leaving the further development of the principle of universal suffrage to the newly established legislative procedure.
>
> 3. To establish as an immutable rule that no law shall take effect without the approval of the State Duma and that to those elected by the people shall be guaranteed the possibility of real participation in supervision of the legality of the acts decreed by Us.

On paper the Russian Revolution was accomplished. The country was stunned by its sudden success. It remained to see how far life could affect the "unchangeable will" of the Russian sovereign, "Given at Peterhof . . . in the eleventh year of Our Reign." [7]

NOTES

1. Lenin, *Sochineniia,* 3rd edition, V, 384-385 (II A—Beginning of the Spontaneous Movement).
2. *Ibid.,* p. 392 (II B—Bowing to Spontaneity).
3. *Ibid.,* pp. 468-469 (IV E—Conspirative Organization and "Democracy").
4. *Kommunisticheskaia Partiia . . . v rezoliutsiiakh . . . ,* 7th edition, p. 42.
5. *Polnoe sobranie zakonov . . .* (Third collection), No. 2882 (April 21, 1885), V, 169.
6. *Ibid.,* No. 26,656 (August 6, 1905), XXV, 637-638.
7. *Ibid.,* No. 26,805 (October 17, 1905), XXV, 754-755.

SUGGESTIONS FOR FURTHER READING

In addition to works previously cited, Miliukov's *Russia and Its Crisis* is a contemporary work by the leading liberal politician. Kokovtsov's *Out of My Past* is the later recollections of a prominent tsarist minister. Curtiss' *Church and State in Russia* is a valuable specialized study. Sir Bernard Pares' chapter on the "Reform Movement in Russia" in the *Cambridge Modern History,* Vol. XII, contains much detail, as does Major Maurice's chapter on "The Russo-Japanese War." See also White's *Diplomacy of the Russo-Japanese War.* Boris A. Romanov's *Russia in Manchuria, 1892-1906* and M. N. Pavlovsky's *Chinese-Russian Relations* give background on Russian policy in Asia.

Recent accounts of the revolution include Harcave's *First Blood* and Solomon Schwartz's *The Russian Revolution of 1905,* the latter by a participant. Wolfe's *Three Who Made a Revolution* is a fascinating biographical and ideological study of men soon to become famous. There is no adequate biography of Lenin; the best available is Fischer's *Life of Lenin.* Getzler's *Martov* is a valuable portrait.

A more careful study of Russian communism, from its origins to 1958, is Schapiro's *Communist Party of the Soviet Union.* A volume of great supplementary value is Daniels' *Documentary History of Communism.* Another study, from the standpoint of political theory, is Meyer's brief *Communism.* Haimson, *The Russian Marxists and the Origins of Bolshevism,* Keep's *Rise of Social Democracy in Russia,* Treadgold's *Lenin and his Rivals,* and Radkey, *The Agrarian Foes of the Bolsheviks,* give thorough accounts of the rise of the main competing schools of socialist thought. Dan's *Origins of Bolshevism* is an interpretation by a prominent Menshevik: See also Avrich, *Russian Anarchists.* Savinkov's *Memoirs of a Terrorist* and Steinberg's *Spiridonova* are personalized accounts of the dramatic side of the SR's.

Serge's *Memoirs of a Revolutionary, 1901-1914* and Woytinsky's *Stormy Passage* contain much of interest for 1905 and later. Interesting sidelights on Lenin are contained in Zetkin's *Reminiscences* and Balabanoff's *Impressions.*

Chapter

21

Reaction, Reform, or Revolution? 1905-1907

The October Manifesto might seem to mark the triumph of revolution. Actually it marked the success of Witte in securing a reprieve for autocracy. The forces arrayed against the old regime were far weaker and more disorganized than the government had supposed. Its sudden promise to capitulate confused and divided its enemies, thus allowing it to regain its self-confidence and to begin all over again to exercise its power. The most influential and best-organized elements in the opposition, represented by the Union of Liberation, had never wished a revolution. They had not perceived that the reforms for which they had pressed inevitably meant revolution, that transition from autocracy to constitutionalism meant more than a "reform." Suddenly confronted with reality, the professional intelligentsia and its capitalist allies turned away from agitation that could evoke continued mass action.

SUBSIDENCE OF THE REVOLUTION

In November, 1905, there began to be formed a new political group, which took the name of the "Union of October 17" (the Russian date of the Manifesto). The basic principle of the "Octobrists" was that the government had made adequate concessions, which should be accepted in a spirit of reconciliation between government and people. Prominent in the new grouping were Shipov, long a leading zemstvo worker; Count Heiden, who had presided over the zemstvo congress in July; and Alexander Guchkov, an industrialist. A new and final zemstvo congress, with some hesitation, asked that the Duma be given constituent functions. It also endorsed universal suffrage and demanded both a general amnesty and abolition of the death penalty. At the same time, it proposed support for Witte so long as he adhered to his newly announced policy. Even the Cadets, under Miliukov's guidance, abandoned the verbally more radical Union of Unions and showed signs of willingness to work with the government.

Negotiations with Witte, however, broke down. Witte had suggested to Shipov that he form a cabinet; it was indicated that Cadets, such as Muromtsev and Petrunkevich—though not the sharp-tongued Miliukov—might be included. Miliukov, however, insisted on formal recognition of the principle of ministerial responsibility to the Duma, which Witte was not prepared to grant. Witte's only further concession to the bourgeois opposition was promise of a new press law, duly issued on December 7; by that time, while confirming abolition of preliminary censorship, it was possible again to clamp down by including, not only incitement to strikes, mutinies, and assassinations, but even printing of false news, as criminal offenses, heavily punishable. Instead of going further on the path of conciliation, Witte in November accepted appointment of another experienced policeman, Durnovo, as Minister of the Interior.

The reactionary forces had already been heartened by the success of the policy of pogroms. A number of organizations, popularly known as "Black Hundreds" and evidently supplied with funds by the secret police, openly incited mob action against the revolutionaries. Most successful was the "Union of the Russian People," which concentrated attention on the Jews. Whether or not active in revolutionary work, Jews had seemingly most cause publicly to celebrate the grant of civil liberties. They were, however, also the easiest target against which to direct the violent passions of street mobs, only too eager for blood and plunder. Beginning the very day after the issue of the October Manifesto, pogroms were unleashed in over a hundred cities; conspicuously, St. Petersburg and Moscow were exempt. For the most part, these riots affected the Pale; in Odessa alone several hundred lives were lost in a brutal four-day massacre before the troops even attempted to restore order. The effect of the pogroms was to steady the nerves of reactionary ministers and to encourage them to refrain from hasty implementation of the promised constitution.

The changing atmosphere did not immediately affect the workers. Now that they were politically aroused, they were naturally less willing to compromise than were the bourgeois elements. The St. Petersburg Soviet, in which the Mensheviks exercised considerable influence, promptly (November 1) called off the general strike as of noon on November 3, but it simultaneously announced its intention to prepare for "the final struggle to obtain convocation of a Constituent Assembly on the basis of universal, equal, direct, and secret suffrage for the purpose of establishing a Democratic Republic"; the Soviet also adopted, unanimously, a Bolshevik resolution in favor of "preparing fighting units for the purpose of a more imposing and majestic attack on the tottering monarchy, which can be definitely overthrown only by a victorious popular uprising." [1]

The Soviet was not, however, primarily interested in political objectives. On November 11, the rank and file rejected a proposal by their leaders that they consider affiliating with the Social-Democratic Party; instead, at the instance of workers without party connections, the Soviet took upon itself to legislate an eight-hour day for workers and called a strike for the thirteenth to enforce compliance. In the meantime an abortive mutiny of sailors had occurred at the Kronstadt naval base; on November 14 the Soviet responded to the threatened execution of the ringleaders by converting the strike, as of November 15, into a protest against martial law. Witte's advice to his "brother-workers" to remain at work was ignored, but his submission to an ordinary court-martial of the problem of punishing the mutineers was accepted. The strike reverted (November 18) to the economic question of an eight-hour day; by the twenty-first, for lack of adequate support, it was abandoned. The shift of emphasis on the part of labor from political to economic demands of course played into the hands of the autocracy; the industrialists were given added reason to think twice before further challenging the authority of the government.

Additional mutinies occurred in the armed forces. Outstanding among them was another disturbance in the Black Sea fleet, this time at Sevastopol (November 27-28). Its leader, Lieutenant Schmidt, sent a loyal telegram to the emperor asking immediate convocation of a constituent assembly; although he neglected to give the signal for armed insurrection until it was too late, he was executed. Despite other mutinies and other strikes, despite the formation (December 5) of a Moscow Soviet of Workers' Deputies, the government plucked up its courage: the committee of the Peasants' Union was arrested (November 29); on December 9, Khrustalev-Nosar, chairman of the St. Petersburg Soviet, was also arrested. The Petersburg Soviet retorted by electing as chairman a Menshevik then known as Yanovsky, later to be famous as Trotsky; it also joined with the remnant of the Central Committee of the Peasants' Union and with the executives of the SR's and the Social Democrats in calling on the people to refuse payment of taxes and redemption dues and to withdraw their money from the savings banks (December 15). The government replied by arresting almost the whole Executive Committee of the Petersburg Soviet (December 16). An attempt to call a fresh general strike failed dismally.

The center of interest shifted briefly to Moscow, the "First Capital." On December 15, a regiment of the garrison mutinied. On the seventeenth, the Moscow Soviet called a general strike. It was already too late to secure the coöperation of the garrison; although barricades were thrown up on the twenty-third, the mutiny had been quelled, and Admiral Dubasov, the Governor-General, had received reinforcements. In three days of street fighting (December 30-January 1), the government artillery and machine guns crushed the handful of workers, armed mainly with revolvers. The chief problem confronting the government forces was to round up enough suspects to justify the panic of the admiral who, after all, was as far from the sea as he could well be. The December armed uprising at Moscow was principally the work of the Bolshevik fraction of the Social Democrats, who had not been strong enough to influence the course of the revolution elsewhere. Its principal effect was to make all moderate elements turn even more sharply against any form of violent action and thus further to strengthen the hands of the autocracy.

In the midst of the Moscow disturbance, the electoral law for the Duma had been published (December 24). Its provisions were extremely complicated. At their base lay the principles adopted for the election of zemstvos in the 1860's—indirect election and weighted class representation. Notwithstanding the wave of peasant disturbances in 1905, it was still the official theory that the mass of the peasantry were loyal. The peasants, of course, were regarded as of less account than were the noble landowners, but it was the urban classes, both propertied and proletarian, that were still regarded as the most suspect.

During the winter, the revolution seemed to have reached a low ebb. Even the enthusiasm of the workers declined sharply, although in November, 1905, the number of factory workers on strike was still two-thirds that recorded in October, rising in December to seven-eighths of that figure. As a result, the number of industrial strikers in 1905 was recorded as one and two-thirds the number of workers; though many workers had not gone on strike at all, others had struck several times during the year. In the first half of 1906, though the number of strikes was still nearly nine times as great as in any year prior to 1905, the average monthly number was much lower than in 1905. Peasant disturbances also slacked off substantially. This result was definitely not the outcome of the October Manifesto, which had stimulated, rather than calmed, peasant unrest. Nor was it the result of Witte's effort (November 16, 1905) to conciliate the masses by halving the redemption dues for 1906 and canceling all payments of redemption dues thereafter. Rather, it must be attributed to the climate; in the spring of 1906, peasant disturbances were resumed and on a very wide scale.

During this breathing spell, the autocracy retracted or seriously modified most of the concessions granted by the October Manifesto. On March 5, 1906, a new Imperial manifesto redefined the role of the legislative Duma. The old Council of State, set up by Alexander I as an advisory body, was made a coördinate upper house of the new legislature. Henceforth only half its members were to be appointive; the others were to be elected by special bodies, such as the noble corporations, learned organizations, and the Church. Even jointly, the Council (*Soviet*) and the Duma could not alter the budget as objectively determined under existing laws, nor could they change these laws without the emperor's assent. If they rejected the budget, taxes remained at the level of the preceding year; if they disagreed on appropriations, the government could choose the figures that suited it best. The ministers were given the power of interim legislation. Further modification of the "Fundamental Laws" imposed additional restrictions on the authority of the new legislature. The culminating point was an imperial rescript of May 6; while it repeated the promises of the October Manifesto, it summarized their implementation in the words: "To the Emperor of All the Russias belongs supreme autocratic power." [2]

A spate of other legislation, not of "fundamental" character but seriously limiting civil liberties, was enacted. Most important were two edicts of March 17 which practically canceled the right of free assembly and seriously crippled the operation of the newly emancipated trade unions and political parties. It is even quite possible that the government might have taken the further step of altogether canceling the promise of a Duma, had it not been for the insistence of its indispensable French ally. The French government, concerned over the possibility of repudiation of its loans by a victorious revolution, had threatened, unless the Duma endorsed the loan, to withhold payment of the last and largest installment of its advances toward the cost of the Russo-Japanese War. The imminence of the Algeciras Conference, at which France badly needed Russian support against Germany, persuaded the French government to honor its commitments without waiting for approval by the Duma. By that time, however, preparations for the opening of the Duma were so far advanced that it seemed scarcely worth while to abandon them. The Duma was allowed to meet (May 10, 1906).

THE DUMA

The situation in the Duma was very confused. The socialist parties had declared a boycott of the elections. A number of constitutionalist parties had entered the field, but only the Cadets manifested any talent at all for political organization. The idea of open political agitation, of competing for votes, was too new a phenomenon in Russia for the results to resemble the outcome of an election in countries accustomed to any degree of popular participation in the formulation of public policy. Russian intellectuals, dreaming of a new regime, lost their heads in clouds of hairsplitting programs even while they remained uneasily conscious that their feet were mired in the mud of anarchic mass revolutionary sentiment. Votes were therefore cast less for party labels than on the basis of specific promises made by individuals. These individuals, finding themselves in the Duma, formed shifting alliances with the various "fractions" organized in that body. It is therefore impossible to give with any approach to precision figures reflecting the partisan composition of the First Duma. More than one-fifth of the nearly five hundred members remained officially "non-party."

Some things were clear. The Cadets, with well over 150 deputies, occupied the leading position. Supported by other groups, they were able to put Muromtsev in the chair, while Petrunkevich served as floor leader; Miliukov had been disqualified as a candidate on technical grounds, but in the lobbies he was in effect the dominant figure.

At their Second Party Congress, held at the end of January, 1906, the Cadets had declared definitely for establishment of a constitutional and parliamentary monarchy, dismissing the idea of a republic without clarifying the question whether a republic was undesirable or merely impracticable. They had again affirmed their support of the principle of compulsory alienation, for just compensation, of privately held land; they emphasized that inflated rents should not be taken as establishing fair value. They had also indicated their sympathy with the strike movement. At the same time, they had condemned the tactics of armed uprising and even of financial boycott. On the other hand, they had announced their refusal at this moment to enter into negotiations with the ministry. In return, they had been refused legalization as a party. The government's obvious distrust of the Cadets and its effort to hamper their campaign had stood them in good stead with the voters.

Most of their deputies were elected from the towns; they were supported by 1,468 of the 1,761 electors allotted to the urban propertied class. In St. Petersburg, they won all 160 electors, though somewhere between 20 percent and 40 percent of the voters there had preferred candidates further to the right. These circumstances reflected the fact that the Cadets' electoral strength lay mainly in the literate middle classes; two-thirds of their deputies had had the benefit of higher education, and only 7 percent of them had not graduated from secondary school; among Duma deputies as a whole, only a shade over two-fifths were university men. A substantial number of Cadet deputies were returned also both by noble electors (especially of the middling landed category) and by the peasants.

The peasantry on the whole did not accept direct Cadet leadership. Some peasant constituencies even returned "dark" forces, which remained unorganized in the Duma, but most of the deputies elected by the peasants adhered to a new political group, the *Trudovik* (Laborite) fraction. This new "party" originally numbered over a hundred deputies, who realized their community of views only after their arrival at the capital. At the elections they had presented themselves as "non-party" or under the vague label "left of the Cadets." Among them were nine members of the Peasants' Union, two SR's, and ten Social Democrats, who had been unable to run as such because their organizations had boycotted the elections. These extreme elements had to refrain from attempting leadership in the new group lest their undisciplined associates gravitate toward the organized Cadet fraction. On this uneasy basis, the Trudoviks remained "left of the Cadets" instead of becoming the left wing of that party.

The main interest of the Trudoviks was in the agrarian problem. Many of them realized the hopelessness of doing more than air the views of the peasantry, but the practical need to satisfy their constituents led them to formulate a program not widely divergent from the position of the Cadets, though somewhat colored by SR utopianism. Compulsory alienation of privately held land in favor of the peasants was their principal demand. Since there were among them fourteen deputies returned by the separate workers' curia, they included also demands for an eight-hour day, for state insurance, and for more extensive labor and factory laws, with participation of workers in their enforcement. They demanded also, in full agreement with the Cadets, abolition of capital punishment and of "exceptional regimes" (arbitrary suspensions of normal legal procedures), legally enforceable definition of promised civil rights, ministerial responsibility, and democratization of the franchise, both for the Imperial Duma and for local bodies, on the basis of the four-point formula (universal, equal, direct, and secret suffrage).

To the left of the Trudoviks, there were only a handful of deputies in the First Duma. The SR's had remained resolutely self-excluded, but the Social Democrats had wavered. In November, 1905, even Lenin had favored participation in the elections. After the December uprising, however, Lenin and his fellow Bolsheviks had swung violently to the position that the workers must, by boycott of the Duma, emphasize the gulf between them and the whole of bourgeois society. The Mensheviks, in the interest of Party unity, suggested that the first stages of the elections should be contested for propaganda purposes, though still refusing ultimate election. This idea was submitted to the lower Party organizations, in which Bolsheviks and Mensheviks were still undifferentiated; the rank and file endorsed the less subtle plan of the Bolsheviks. Nevertheless, in April, 1906, when it had become clear that the masses were not boycotting the elections but were voting for non-party candidates, a "unity Congress" of the SD Party was held at Stockholm. It agreed to full-scale participation in those constituencies, mainly in the Caucasus, where the elections were not yet complete. The eight Social-Democratic deputies thus elected were soon joined by ten members of the "workers' group," who seceded from the Trudoviks to help form a separate SD fraction. Small as were its numbers, the very fact of its irresponsibility gave its members the possibility of spreading propaganda under the protection of their immunity as members of the Duma. Their immediate efforts were devoted to a struggle to drive a wedge between the Cadets and the Trudoviks and thus to attract the latter into the camp of the extreme revolutionary Left.

The Cadets were not wholly dependent on the Trudoviks. To their right stood a number of groups with grievances of their own, mainly ethnic, against the existing autocratic regime. Chief among them was the Polish "Kolo," with thirty-odd deputies. Only ten days after the October Manifesto, Poland had been subjected to martial law. The moderate bourgeois party, Dmowski's National Democrats, had completely swamped all varieties of Polish socialists, who had toyed with the notion of a national boycott. Similar results were attained in the Baltic provinces and in Central Asia. All the groups representing the interests of subject nationalities normally supported the Cadets.

Most distressing to the autocracy was the poor showing of the parties of the Right. The "black hundreds" elected none of their candidates. Most of the "Rightists" who were elected preferred to remain unidentified and listed themselves as "non-party." The only significant group to the right of the Cadets was therefore the "Union of October 17"; because Shipov was defeated in Moscow, leadership devolved on his fellow zemstvo workers, Count Heiden and Stakhovich. The Octobrists numbered only sixteen, but they were the core of a group of about thirty closely allied deputies.

Such a Duma could not be satisfactory to anyone, least of all to the government. Ministerial hostility to the Duma was unconcealed. Witte's gamble that the electoral law might after all produce a submissive legislative body had not paid off; with the French loan in hand, he was no longer necessary and was allowed to resign from office on the eve of the meeting of the Duma. His real successor was the new Minister of the Interior, Peter Stolypin, though the latter did not nominally become the head of the ministry until July. Yet the government, remembering the divided but almost universal revolutionary opposition of the previous year, at first moved warily. There was at least the possibility that the Cadets might be able to cement their alliance with the Trudoviks and with the national autonomist groups, and that they might even win the loyal support of both the socialists and the Octobrists in a fight for a real measure of civil freedom and political responsibility.

The Cadets, however, were in a scarcely happier position than was the government. They led the opposition, but they did not control it and could not consolidate it. Only by skillful tactical maneuvers could they maintain their ascendancy. To appease the Trudoviks, they must seem to be more radical on the agrarian question than they actually were, and this would make impossible coöperation with the openly conservative constitutionalists to their right. To go too far in advocacy of national self-determination was bound to destroy them as a Great Russian party. Nor could they hope to satisfy the socialists by a mere program of social reform, such as gradual introduction of an eight-hour day or legalization of peaceful picketing. They were reduced therefore to an effort to insist on a minimum program, stressing constitutional and legal demands, such as establishment of ministerial responsibility, grant of general amnesty, and abolition of "exceptional" courts. Above all, they dreaded any premature conflict with the government before they had opportunity to develop their program for the next appeal to the electorate.

Miliukov's parliamentary skill did succeed in winning the Cadets several tactical victories, which helped to hold the Duma opposition together. On May 26, the Duma even adopted, with only eleven votes in opposition, a motion of censure of the ministry for refusing to submit to interpellation. The government made a fresh effort at compromise. Shipov was again approached to form a ministry. His unwillingness to do so without including a majority of Cadets, Miliukov's unwillingness to break with the Trudoviks by issuing an open condemnation of revolutionary violence, and Stolypin's distrust of the whole idea combined to delay any concessions.

In the prolonged jockeying for mastery between the Duma and the government, the key problem was the land question, on which the Cadets had to support the Trudoviks. Disaster for the Cadets' policy came, however, from a side issue, a brutal pogrom at Bialystok, the causes of which the Duma undertook to investigate. Prince Urusov, the only liberal whom Witte had persuaded to accept office, had soon resigned in disgust at the government's toleration, not to say encouragement, of pogroms. He now led an attack on the ministers, charging them with responsibility for the Bialystok affair. Following the lead of the Social Democrats, the Trudoviks supported a downright condemnation; the Cadets, engaged in negotiations for the formation of a new ministry, carried a motion condemning the officials who had instigated the pogrom but not the ministry itself (July 5). This first open rift in the ranks of the opposition was soon followed by a still more serious one. When the government announced that land reform would under no circumstances provide for compulsory alienation of privately owned land (July 9), the Cadets led in carrying a vote of condemnation (July 19). Their resolution was, however, not forceful enough to satisfy the Trudoviks, who walked out in protest; the Octobrists, for their part, abstained from voting.

The government promptly seized the opportunity offered by such disunity. On July 21, without formal notice, it declared the Duma dissolved. That night almost half the members of the Duma met at Vyborg, in Finland, just across the Russian border. A resolution was adopted calling on the Russian people to refuse to pay taxes or to supply recruits to the army unless the Duma was restored. It was an empty gesture; the government had already announced that the Second Duma would meet the following March.

Nor did the Vyborg Manifesto evoke any popular response. The Menshevik leadership called for a general political strike, but the number of strikers rose only briefly and unspectacularly. For the whole year 1906, the number of strikers was not much more than a third the number in 1905, and the great majority of these were recorded in the first half of the year, before the dissolution of the Duma. The Bolsheviks, though still harping on the need for "open struggle [of "the revolutionary people"] against the forces of the autocracy," yet accepted the caution of the majority at the Fourth (Unity) Congress of the Russian Social-Democratic Party, held at Stockholm in April, 1906. This Unity Congress, while admitting the imminent "necessity of an armed uprising," held that "the Party, as an organization, cannot take upon itself a commitment to an uprising of the people that would inspire false hopes" and that it was obligated to discourage "an armed conflict under unfavorable circumstances." [3]

Though the Socialist Revolutionaries appealed for a general peasant uprising, even the peasants showed a marked decline in willingness to participate in agrarian disorders. They were faced with a vigorous and ruthless repression. The number of formal executions, with or without trial (but not including those killed without being arrested), has been placed at 386 in 1905 and 1,008 in 1906. In addition, 21,000 persons were exiled to Siberia or to the North, along with other thousands subjected to lesser punishments. It is small wonder that the peasantry lapsed into sullen hostility to the government's efforts to appease them by intensifying purchases of land by the Peasants' Bank from private holders. Although the bank offered land, both public and private, at startlingly low prices, far below its own costs, and although interest rates were sharply reduced, the peasants showed no eagerness to buy.

The classes showed even less enthusiasm for continuance of the revolution than did the masses. During 1906, a "righting of the zemstvos" took place; in thirty-four *guberniyas,* the Cadets lost all but one of their board presidencies; the Octobrists raised their total from thirteen to nineteen, while the Right, which had held none of these offices, won eleven. There took place also a considerable realignment of parties and of party attitudes toward the Duma. At the extreme Left, the Socialist Revolutionaries and the Social Democrats, despairing of the utility of their previous intransigent attitude, abandoned their boycott of elections. The left wing of the Octobrists, led by Stakhovich and Shipov, joined some of the Cadets in forming a new grouping, which called itself "Peaceful Renovation"; although they recognized the legitimacy of the dissolution of the First Duma, they praised its work and wished to carry it forward. The Octobrists proper, slipping toward the Right, fused with the "Party of Commerce and Industry." Although they refused affiliation to the violently nationalist "Party of Right Order," they saw no difficulty in working with Stolypin.

The Second Duma, which met on March 2, 1907, was, mainly because of the abandonment of political boycotts, more "leftist" than the First Duma had been. Yet as an instrument of opposition to the government it was far weaker. The Cadets, still not legally recognized as a party, were reduced to less than a hundred deputies; they continued to play the leading role, but they were in no position to exercise any sort of control over the majority. The Trudoviks, unaffected in numbers, were still unable to develop independent leadership, nor did they any longer monopolize the role of the only significant group "left of the Cadets." The socialists had experienced the most startling growth; the Social Democrats of various colors now numbered sixty-five, the Socialist Revolutionaries thirty-six. The extremeness of their views, their socialist convictions, and their innate hostility to a "bourgeois" regime made it impossible that they should exercise anything but a negative and disrupting influence.

Similar was the position of the extreme "rightist" parties. Unrepresented in the First Duma by any organized group, their recovery of self-confidence had rewarded their energetic participation in this electoral campaign and had won them almost as many seats as the Social Democrats held. Although divided in their views, the majority of them, as "Bolsheviks of the Right," had entered the Duma only with the purpose of destroying it.

The Octobrists and affiliated groups had slightly increased their strength (to over forty). Their sincere desire to secure the establishment of a genuinely constitutional regime made them fear their new neighbors to the Right and tended to drive them, under the leadership of Guchkov, somewhat closer to the Cadets. Yet the land question prevented whole-hearted coöperation between the two leading constitutionalist groups. The representation of subject nationalities was also more confused than in the First Duma. In Poland, where the nationalist Polish Socialist Party had persisted in its boycott, the National Democrats still maintained their preponderance; so did the petty-bourgeois Ukrainian Revolutionary Democratic Party in Little Russia. In Armenia, however, the terrorist *Dashnaktsiutiun,* which had boycotted the First Duma, now brought added support to the Socialist Revolutionaries.

This Duma was obviously even more unsatisfactory than the First. Prime Minister Stolypin, who, though he consistently rejected the principle of ministerial responsibility, professed to respect the constitution of 1905, found it impossible to work with such a legislature. Following announcement of an alleged plot to assassinate the emperor, Stolypin demanded of the Duma authority to arrest the Social-Democratic members. When the Duma insisted on going through the motions of investigating the evidence, it was unceremoniously dissolved (June 16, 1907). In violation of the Fundamental Laws, Stolypin promptly issued a new electoral law.

THE STOLYPIN REFORM

In the interval between the first two Dumas, Stolypin had already violated the October promises by decreeing a radical change in the state's agrarian policy. By edicts of October 18 and November 22, 1906, the prime minister had embarked on a sweeping social revolution of his own, designed to evade the threat of political revolution. Subsequently, in 1910-11, the Third Duma was to endorse this legislation and, on the government's initiative, still further extend its application.

At the time of Emancipation, official theory had regarded the peasant commune, an ancient institution, as a stabilizing force and had built the whole structure of agrarian relationships on it. In the years of reaction, government policy, while subjecting the commune to the authority of the "land captains," had further strengthened its control over the individual peasant and his landholding. However, peasant unrest, rising to a climax in 1902, and the obvious fact of economic distress, attested by huge accumulations of arrears, had impelled some reconsideration. By 1903, Witte had reached the conclusion: "Woe to the country that has not nurtured in its population a sense of law and of property, but on the contrary has established different forms of collective possession. . . ."[4] Witte was, however, losing influence in the ministry, and no action was taken beyond general abolition of the "circular guarantee" for payment of taxes and redemption dues; for communes in which land was held by hereditary tenure, this action had been taken in 1899.

It remained for the experience of 1905 and 1906, in which the peasant commune itself served as an instrument for organizing seizure of landlord land, to produce a complete about-face by the government. The edict of October 18, 1906, somewhat strengthened the juridical position of the peasants; it restored to them their right to choose their own representatives to the zemstvos and restricted the authority of the "land captain" over the commune. Still more importantly, it diminished the authority of the commune to limit the freedom of movement of its own members by destroying its control over the issue of peasant passports and even over the peasants' right permanently to withdraw from a particular commune. At the same time, it reduced the difficulty in the way of disposing of his landholding.

The edict of November 22, 1906, went much further. It was aimed at the total dissolution of the commune as an economic unit. The problem was so broad and the provisions of the law necessarily so complex that all that can be attempted here is a very summary statement. Any peasant householder must, on demand, be given individual hereditary title to the arable land he then held, together with the right to retain the use of his accustomed share of other lands, such as meadows. In addition, the commune as a whole might by two-thirds vote decide on permanent hereditary distribution of its lands. The later law of 1910 further provided that in any commune where there had been no general redistribution since the original allotment, repartitional tenure was to be considered as automatically converted into hereditary tenure, even without request by a single peasant.

The results seemed very substantial. By the end of 1915, there were in fifty provinces some 13 or 14 million peasant households with allotment lands. Of these it may be estimated that more than 3 million had held their lands by hereditary tenure before 1905 or had arisen by subsequent subdivision of such communes. To these the Stolypin legislation had added 4.3 million hereditary holdings: 2 million on the initiative of individuals, about 130,000 by general dissolution, and 2.2 million (of which only 470,000 had actually received documentary confirmation) on the basis of automatic dissolution in the absence of general repartition. Since a large number of additional households might, without their suspecting it, have been found to be included in this wholesale transformation of title, it is clear that substantially more than half of all the allotment-holding peasant households then held their arable lands by hereditary tenure; the proportion would be further somewhat increased if non-allotment holdings were added to the reckoning.

It should be noted also that these hereditary holdings, whether old or new, were now, with minor reservations, the property not of the household collectively, but of the individual head of the household; so also were the homesteads, even in communes where repartitional tenure legally survived. Thus the household as well as the commune was subjected to a disintegrating process. There remained collective responsibility of all members of the family for payment of taxes, but the control of the peasant over his children and other relatives was undermined.

Sweeping and rapid as the success of the reform seemed, it was so mainly on paper. So long as the open-field system survived, it mattered relatively little whether an individual owned particular scattered strips or whether the household simply had the right to an appropriate share in collectively owned fields. Collective control of agricultural techniques—the decision how to utilize any given field, the times of plowing and harvesting, and all the other factors affecting the efficiency of agriculture—necessarily remained subject to the will of the commune. This had been clearly realized, and therefore every effort was made by the government to match the change in paper titles with a recasting of the physical arrangements of the peasant villages. In cases where the individual initiative of a peasant rather than the will of a two-thirds majority—and they were the rule—determined separation of title, the other villagers naturally resisted actual consolidation of holdings, which must necessarily entail reorganization of their own economy.

The law of 1906 had merely provided that the separating peasant must be given a consolidated holding "in so far as possible." [5] The laws of 1910 and 1911 imposed on "Land-Organization Commissions" the task of carrying through consolidation, not only of arable holdings but of shares of meadows, pastures, and woodland. These commissions, set up in 1906, included a minority representation of peasants but were dominated by officials and landed nobles. The official instructions given them were to encourage consolidation by every means possible. The preferred form was that in which the peasant quit the village and established a new homestead on an enclosed farm (*khutor*); as an alternative the peasant might continue to live in the midst of his fellows but be provided with a separated farm (*otrub*).

Essentially, what Stolypin was aiming to accomplish was equivalent to the so-called "agricultural revolution" that had taken place in England in the late eighteenth and early nineteenth centuries. It was attended by all the same problems—the difficulty of matching a strip surrendered with land of equal natural fertility, equivalent in drainage, or at a similar distance from the homestead. Even granted the most earnest efforts at equitable re-allocation, it was inevitable that there should be an enormous amount of social dislocation and hardship. To the hostility of a tradition-bound, yet shrewd, peasantry there was added in Russia the hesitation of minor officialdom, no less tradition-bound. It could hardly be expected that an inefficient and corrupt bureaucracy would share the statesmanship of Stolypin. Too many ministers had risen and fallen for their subordinates to reorient themselves quickly in a new direction; an excess of zeal in prosecuting the reform might easily bring trouble if a new minister were suddenly to order reversal of this revolutionary policy.

It is then not surprising that the real progress of the reform was slow. Rather, it is surprising that within the single decade between the initiation of the reform and the revolution, about one-tenth of the peasant households were provided with individual consolidated farms. It was true that probably more than half of these farms were still economically more or less enmeshed with the open-field system, particularly in the matter of use-rights in, rather than outright ownership of, such lands as meadows, pastures, and woodlots. Moreover, less than half of all these individual farms were of the completely separated type (*khutor*), and even these were not always wholly independent of collective ownership. If the English "agricultural revolution" took decades for its completion, the Russian could hardly have taken less. Given a long period of peace, Stolypin's "wager on the strong" might well have been won.

The question of what sort of peasants took advantage of the Stolypin reform is an important but very difficult one. The evidence is scant and contradictory. The purpose of the reform had been twofold. Economically, it had been intended to promote the economic welfare of the Russian state by enabling the peasant with initiative to manage his lands as he saw fit; it was hoped that, freed from the dead weight of traditional inefficient methods imposed by the ignorant majority in the village, he would adopt modern techniques and thus increase yields per acre, concentrating on the crops best suited to the locality and escaping from the trammels of a backward sustenance economy. Politically, it was expected that the peasant, acquiring a deep sense of individual property rights in his own land, would become a partisan of law and order in general; the difference in the socio-political outlook of the proprietary peasants of Western Europe and the communal peasants of Russia had finally impressed itself on the minds of the advisers of the Russian autocrat. It was in both these senses that Stolypin, in his own phrase, was placing the "wager on the strong."

It does not, however, appear clearly that it was the well-to-do peasant who was most inclined to separate his economy from that of the village. Statistics on the size of separated holdings as compared to the average of communal allotments and returns received to an official questionnaire suggest, however hazily, that the separators may have been "on the average, in an inferior economic position."[6] This idea is borne out by the speculative consideration that under the old system, taken by and large, the well-to-do peasants tended to dominate the commune and therefore had perhaps the least to gain by a change of system. Their chief interest may well have been revolutionary acquisition by the commune of the remaining privately owned land, for, if it were distributed on the established principle of "to whom that hath shall be given," the lion's share would have fallen to them. Certainly the other half of this formula, "from him that hath not shall be taken away even that which he hath," was apparently honored. Facilitated by the Stolypin reform, an active process of land transfer seems to have been proceeding within the peasantry itself; the more prosperous peasants seem in these years to have been engaged in buying up the allotments of their less fortunate fellows; this did not necessarily involve consolidation into compact holdings.

In any case, there seems little doubt that economic differentiation within the peasantry was proceeding rapidly. The door to this development had been thrown open by Emancipation, which had destroyed the power of the nobles to force their serfs to maintain an equality of landholding which the latter had never found equitable. In the years following the revolution of 1905, transfer of privately owned land to the peasantry proceeded at an accelerated rate. The nobles sold about one-fifth of the land they had still retained in 1905, though much of it, because of peasant reluctance to pay for it, stuck in the hands of the Peasants' Land Bank. Most of this non-allotment land evidently went into the hands of the already well-to-do peasantry.

The nobles' loss of land was by no means pure gain to the peasants. It could not keep pace with the increase in peasant population and outstripped also the peasants' financial strength; almost half of the non-allotment land held by the peasants was mortgaged to the bank for a total amounting to more than three-fourths of its official value. Here, too, arrears were accumulating. Nevertheless, by 1914 the peasants held, in forty-seven provinces, about 40 percent of all the land; since much of the remainder was forest or waste land, and more than two-thirds of it belonged to the state, the age-old class struggle between nobles and peasants had objectively been reduced to relatively small proportions. Subjectively, however, it persisted strongly, and all the more so since the appetite grows with eating.

Thus the autocracy, striving to resist change, found itself forced to accept, even to initiate, reforms that held promise of being of far-reaching significance. The grant of a Duma, in however niggardly a spirit and narrowly circumscribed though its powers were, had opened the door for persistent agitation without the necessity of resort to illegal methods of struggle. Whether its slow pressure would be able to drive the autocracy further on the path of constitutional reform, whether resumption of rapid economic progress would simultaneously bring alleviation of the economic woes of the lower strata of the population, and whether general social advance would relax tensions remained to be seen. Certainly the autocracy had no intention of dying tamely; it might still prefer, like Samson, to bring destruction down on its opponents if they should triumph over it. There was also the riddle of the other major reform, Stolypin's policy toward the peasantry. If successful, it would inevitably change the socio-political role of the "dark" masses; but whether a reformed peasantry would become the bulwark of a "bourgeois" constitutionalist regime or whether, as Stolypin hoped, it would serve as the mainstay of an otherwise unreformed autocracy, remained an enigma.

NOTES

1. *Tysiacha deviat' sot piatyi god v Peterburge,* II, 13-14 *passim.*
2. *Polnoe sobranie zakonov . . .* (Third collection), No. 27,805 (April 23, 1906), XXVI, 456-461.
3. *Kommunisticheskaia Partiia . . . v rezoliutsiiakh . . . ,* 7th edition, II, 107, 129.
4. Robinson, *Rural Russia Under the Old Regime,* pp. 145-146.
5. *Polnoe sobranie zakonov . . . , op. cit.,* No. 28,528 (November 9, 1906), XXVI, 970-974 *passim.*
6. Robinson, *op. cit.,* p. 233.

SUGGESTIONS FOR FURTHER READING

Robinson is still of supreme importance, especially the chapter entitled "The Wager on the Strong." In addition to other books previously mentioned, Pares' *Russia and Reform* may be consulted for a sympathetic study. On the Duma, see especially Levin's *The Second Duma* and Harper's *New Electoral Law for the Russian Duma;* Badaev's *The Bolsheviks in the Tsarist Duma* deals with a minor theme. Treadgold's *Twentieth-Century Russia* is a comprehensive general treatment, which becomes increasingly valuable for the period in which Soviet power was firmly established. Von Laue's *Why Lenin? Why Stalin?* is a thoughtful essay.

Chapter

22

The Balance of Forces: 1907-1914

In the last few years of peace before World War I, there was a striking contrast between the forces making for progress and the reaction apparent on the surface. The former were most evident in the field of economics, the latter in politics and in the realm of art and letters. After surveying these factors of development and of inertia, and before considering the impact of the war, it may be well to essay also a summary analysis of the sort of future that peace might have held in store for Russia.

ECONOMIC PROGRESS AND GOVERNMENT INTERVENTION

It would be rash to attribute to the Stolypin reform any radical influence on changes in Russian agricultural production in the years before the war. These depended in far greater degree on vicissitudes of the weather, on international market conditions, and on the growth of internal communications by canal and railway construction. In any case, Russian agriculture continued to be mainly on a sustenance basis; of the total grain produced, barely more than one-quarter was put on the market. In 1913, cultivation under the direction of landlords is estimated to have accounted for less than one-eighth of the total product, but for more than one-fifth of the grain marketed. Production by peasants was also very uneven; it is roughly estimated that the poorer peasants, while they produced half of all the grain, supplied little more than one-quarter of what was sold.

Grain production was, however, increasingly supplemented by cultivation of industrial crops. Beet sugar, specially encouraged by the government, had put Russia far ahead of any other country in the area devoted to this crop. It is true that gross inefficiencies in production and handling left her far behind Germany and Austria-Hungary in total yield, but sugar had become an important article of Russian export. To be sure, this result was achieved at the expense of leaving her domestic per-capita consumption of sugar less than one-sixth of the English or American level, but the development of beet production was a very significant factor in promoting the progress of Russian agriculture by stimulating rotation of crops and the practice of fertilizing the soil. In Central Asia, cotton production increased more than fourfold in the score of years before the war. Despite rapidly increasing consumption in Russia, her dependence on imports of cotton from abroad had dropped from 75 percent in 1890 to less than 50 percent by 1910.

Agriculture was still the main occupation, engaging the labor of about 80 percent of the population and supplying almost half of the total income of the population. Yet it was manufacturing industry that represented the chief dynamic force. Although in 1913 it still supplied less than one-fourth of the national income, and although the factories employed only about three million workers, this represented a doubling since 1890.

The cotton industry had trebled its output, and Russia had taken fourth place in the world in production of manufactured cotton. The industry was almost wholly concentrated in the old central provinces, centering around Moscow, Vladimir, and Ivanovo-Voznesensk. Here density of population and relative unsuitability for modern agriculture combined to keep wage rates low. This area produced two-thirds of the yarn and three-fourths of the cloth. Secondary centers were Poland and the Baltic region, which, taken together, produced almost all the remainder. High tariff protection contributed to keeping imports of cotton goods at the insignificant proportion of one-eighteenth the volume (though not the value) of Russian production, both of yarn and of cloth. Exports, though they slightly exceeded imports, were very small; half of them went to Persia.

The iron and steel industry also showed enormous growth after its recovery, by 1908, from world depression, which for Russia had been compounded by the revolution. Although still heavily dependent on the government's requirements for railway construction and on fluctuations in agricultural production, the metallurgical industries in this period showed great progress in basing themselves increasingly on the general Russian market. Output of iron ore increased tenfold in the three decades before the war. Progress in production of steel was even more rapid than the growth of pig-iron output; by 1913, Russia had already passed France and had taken fourth place in world production. The industry was located principally in the south, where the reasonably close juxtaposition of Donets coking coal and the ore of Krivoi Rog created a situation similar to the Ruhr-

Lorraine nexus in Western Europe. In this area, the output of ore shot up from 7 million poods—a pood equals 36.1 pounds—in 1885 to 402 million in 1913; thus, the Ukraine, already the breadbasket of Russia, supplied also two-thirds of her ferrous metal. Output in the Ural area, where ore production merely doubled, was hampered by lack of available fuel, other than charcoal, and by the difficulty of attracting voluntary wage labor to such a remote and forbidding region. Despite increase in absolute production of metal, the Ural area had by 1913 declined relatively to barely one-fifth of the total. A third, though less significant, seat of heavy industry was the Baltic region, which depended mainly on the possibility of cheap water transport of coal from Germany and England and of ore from Sweden.

Coal-mining progressed less rapidly; output had merely quadrupled in the last twenty years before the war, and Russian production still lagged behind that of France. Almost three-quarters of Russia's coal was mined in the Donets basin; most of the rest was produced in Poland. Siberia, though blessed with the most extensive deposits and increasing her output most rapidly (sixty-fold in twenty years), still supplied only 5 percent of Russia's total. In view of these circumstances and particularly in view of the enormous difficulty and tremendous cost of transporting coal over the vast land distances entailed by the remoteness of her most extensive coal deposits from her centers of population, it is not surprising that imports of coal grew more than twice as fast as did her own production. In 1913, the tonnage of coal imported into Russia was one-quarter of the amount consumed in the whole empire.

Russian oil production had lost its early world primacy and had been dwarfed by the United States. The original Baku field showed a decreasing yield, not yet compensated for by the newer Grozny and Maikop wells. Serious labor troubles arising from a state of near civil war between Tatars and Armenians, especially in the Baku area, helped to dash the hope that petroleum, chiefly controlled by German financial interests, would become an important export commodity. Among other significant natural resources, however, were platinum, of which Russia had a virtual monopoly; manganese and other vital steel alloys, in which Russia had a preponderant position; and gold and copper, in which Russia played a very significant role.

Russian industry and mining, vital as they were to her prosperity, also contributed in large measure to the wealth of foreigners. Their exceedingly rapid growth in Russia (surpassed only by that in Japan) had in the main been made possible by heavy investment of foreign capital. It seems probable that the proportion of new capital being invested in further industrial development was shifting in favor of Russian ownership. This has been denied by Liashchenko, who in the Stalin period dominated the writing of economic history in the Soviet Union.[1] It is not possible in America to check all the references he gives for his attempt to bolster Lenin's theory of the increasing subjection of tsarist Russia to "imperialism," but the balance of available evidence seems to be against him. In any case, whether the role of foreign capital was waxing or waning, there is no doubt that as matters stood in 1914 about one-third of all joint-stock capital in Russia was owned abroad. In mining and metallurgical industries, the proportion was apparently one-half, in the electrical industry even two-thirds.

Capital investment was the most important link between Russian and world economy. Although the value of her imports more than doubled in the years from the revolution of 1905 to World War I, and the value of her exports increased by 50 percent, the total foreign trade of Russia remained insignificant for so vast a country. Substantially more than half her exports were naturally foodstuffs, principally wheat and barley. A good deal more than one-third of the remainder was made up of industrial raw materials, in which timber figured very prominently. Manufactures supplied little more than 5 percent of the value of her exports. Conversely, manufactures made up one-third of her imports; industrial raw materials, including cotton and coal, represented almost half. Heavily indebted as she was, Russia necessarily had to show a "favorable" balance of trade, though the excess in value of exports over imports was not great. An inevitable consequence was depression of the Russian standard of living, for exports were encouraged at the expense of Russian consumption.

The economy of Russia had always been exceptionally subject to government interference and control. As early as the sixteenth century, when the activities of foreign capital had through Archangel first seriously impinged on Russia, the autocracy had interfered in the business life of its subjects in a paternalistic effort to protect them and to defend its own interests. In early twentieth-century Russia, government intervention in economic life was very pronounced and took many forms. These included high protective tariffs, subsidies in the guise of monopoly of government orders to the exclusion of cheaper or better foreign products, a carefully managed currency, assistance in floating loans on foreign exchanges, heavy expenditure on the system of transportation, and promotion of cartels and other restrictive practices. Government intervention also went to the extreme of direct participation in many commercial and industrial enterprises.

This was particularly marked in forestry, transportation, and banking. Russia could boast of forest lands estimated as amounting to one-fourth of the world's total; somewhat more than half of them lay in Siberia. About two-thirds of the forests in European Russia and all of the Siberian forests belonged to the state. To check ruthless exploitation of private forest lands after Emancipation, the government had imposed rigid controls. An ambitious program of reforestation of the northern and central regions was accompanied by still more daring projects of afforestation of the steppe, in the hope of extending the area of cultivation without creating a dangerous "dust bowl."

The economic interdependence of various regions of the empire, physically separated by great distances and needing many things they could not themselves produce, had always posed a special problem for Russia; it was a problem that had grown steadily greater with expansion of colonial control over enormous areas, particularly in Asia. The difficulty had in large part been counteracted, especially for European Russia, by the flatness of the country and by the consequent existence of a huge network of navigable rivers. The value of the rivers had in the last century been much enhanced by construction of a number of interconnecting canals, which made it possible to carry goods by water from Astrakhan to St. Petersburg or Archangel and from the eastern foothills of the Urals to Kiakhta on the Chinese frontier. Yet the rivers were frozen a large part of the year and tended to become unduly shallow in the summer. Although the central government maintained some 20 million miles of paved roads, the great bulk of Russian land communication was still supplied by "natural" roads, amounting to over 450 million miles.

For Russia, much more than for any country of Western Europe or even the United States, an adequate system of railways was a necessity. Yet, in 1913, her total length of railways was approximately equal only to that of Germany; in proportion to area, it was less than that of any Western country and less than a tenth that of the United Kingdom, France, or Germany. Even this utterly inadequate system was maintained only at the price of outright state ownership of two-thirds of the whole and of heavy state participation in the remaining private lines. Only partly because of gross official incompetence and corruption, the Russian railways were operated out of the pockets of the Russian taxpayer. An investigation by a Duma committee in 1908 established that more than half of the state debt at that time was assignable to government expenditures on the railways.

The banking system was almost completely dominated by the government. The State Bank had been founded in 1860 to replace the state credit institutions dating from the eighteenth century; only after 1897, when the transition to the gold standard was begun, did it become truly a bank of issue. In the main, it served as a "bankers' bank" financing and controlling the operations of the very rapidly growing private banks, which were closely interconnected with the growth of industry. However, the State Bank itself was intimately bound up with the coal, iron, sugar, and oil industries, even participating in their management by placing its officials on their boards of directors. Like other government organs, the State Bank did not escape grave suspicion both of corruption and of mismanagement. It was also widely accused of neglecting the interests of agriculture for the sake of rapid industrialization.

The State Savings Banks, authorized in 1862, had served largely to channel the savings of the population, not into small businesses but into the government securities in which they principally invested. In these last years of tsarism, their importance was lessened by the rise of official Petty Credit Institutions and of coöperative societies. The Nobles' Land Bank, founded in 1885, and the Peasants' Land Bank, founded in 1883, served mainly the special interest of these two classes; the former, by advancing mortgage money on easy terms, strove vainly to retard the economic decline of the old landholding class; the latter strove to assist peasant communes and, in this period, individual peasants, to increase their holdings.

The housekeeping of the government itself had grave difficulty in making income cover expenditures, but from 1910 it succeeded in effecting some reduction of the national debt. Direct taxes brought in less than 10 percent of all revenues. Excises and customs duties were far more important; although they constituted about the same proportion of the budget as in Great Britain and France, their impact on the poorer classes was much heavier in a country relatively so impoverished as Russia. Most striking was the yield of the spirit monopoly, which, without including liquor excises, produced more than one-quarter of the whole state revenue apart from loans; after the abolition of redemption dues, this proportion approached one-third. Notwithstanding well-founded official distress at the alarming increase in drunkenness, the fear of bankruptcy made it impossible to abandon this inexhaustible cruse. An effort to check the evil by restricting the amount a customer might buy at any one time failed to achieve the ideal of continuous moderate drinking; the peasant merely went sober until he had saved up alcohol enough for a worth-while carouse.

POLITICAL REACTION AND CULTURAL RECESSION

Politically, the years from 1907 to 1914 were relatively quiet. The electoral law that had accompanied the dissolution of the Second Duma had radically changed the weights assigned to various classes of electors; it had heavily reduced the voting strength of the peasantry while increasing that of the nobility; to a smaller extent, it had made similar transfer from the industrial workers to the propertied classes in the towns. In the majority of provinces, the system of curias was now so arranged as to give the noble landowners an absolute majority over all other classes combined; this group was to elect a majority of members of the Duma. The law had also cut down the number of seats allotted to nationalistically restless areas and had disfranchised some of them altogether. In addition, the government took severe punitive measures against its opponents. Of the Social-Democratic members of the Second Duma, thirty-one were sent, after a secret trial, to Siberia. Even the moderates who, under Cadet leadership, had signed the Vyborg Manifesto were sentenced to three months imprisonment. Penalties were provided in case at electoral assemblies "opinions are expressed arousing the hostility of one part of the population against another." [2]

The resultant Third Duma, elected in October, 1907, was of course a more coöperative assembly than its predecessors. It was not, however, a wholly submissive body. On the Right, it included about fifty extremists, among whom Purishkevich openly announced that he had entered the Duma in order to effect the restoration of undiluted autocracy. There were nearly a hundred other monarchists, known as "Nationalists," who accepted the Duma for what it was but wished no broadening of the constitutional regime. At the opposite pole were a handful of Social Democrats; the Socialist Revolutionaries had again boycotted the elections. The only other group "left of the Cadets," the Trudoviks, had also shrunk to insignificance. The various nationality groups, even all lumped together, were no more numerous than the Left. The constitutionalist groups in the middle were now divided into three main factions: the former leaders of the Duma opposition, the Cadets, were now reduced to about fifty; the less intransigent Progressives numbered almost forty; the commanding strategic position was held by the Octobrists, about 150 strong. The Octobrists could form a majority either by combining with the Nationalists on their right or with the Progressives and Cadets on their left, as circumstances might dictate. Leadership had passed from Miliukov, the professor, to Guchkov, the industrialist. He was backed by the larger portion of the provincial nobility, whose financial interests had become increasingly involved in capitalist development and whose political sentiments had been alienated by the bureaucratic autocracy.

The history of the Third Duma was therefore not remarkable. The policy of the Octobrists was in general to work loyally with the prime minister, Stolypin, while at the same time exerting pressure as occasion offered to secure correction of bureaucratic abuses and gradually to give more reality to the powers of the Duma. The Duma endorsed the Stolypin land reform and approved its further extension. A scheme to provide for universal primary education, to be completed by 1922, was similarly approved. Other useful, though not startling, legislative reforms were made, and particular attention was paid to investigation of the government's financial status and fiscal techniques.

This slow progress toward a more genuine constitutionalism was hampered by Stolypin's own difficulties with his colleagues and even with his master. Extreme reactionaries, assisted by secret police funds and operating under the cloak of anti-Semitism, became increasingly active, winning some support among the urban masses. The State Council (*Soviet*), which Witte had strengthened in 1906, offered resistance to measures which, at Stolypin's instance, the Dumas had approved. In September, 1911, Stolypin was assassinated; the chief of the secret police was put on trial for negligence but was released by special order of the emperor. Under a puppet premier, relations with the Duma worsened. A demand by the Duma (April, 1912) for explanation of the shooting of some hundreds of strikers in the Lena goldfields was met with the words of the Minister of the Interior:

> You don't joke with troops. . . . When, losing its reason under the influence of malicious agitators, the crowd assailed the troops, there was nothing else left for the troops to do but to shoot. Thus it has been and thus it will be in future.[3]

In the fall of 1912, the term of the Third Duma having expired, a Fourth Duma was elected; it was still sitting when revolution broke out in 1917. Its party composition differed somewhat from that of the Third in that the middle elements, including the Octobrists, lost ground to the advantage both of the extreme Right and of the Left. The Social Democrats numbered thirteen: seven of them were "minority men" (Mensheviks), six "majority men" (Bolsheviks); the rabid leader of the "Bolshevik six," Malinovsky, was later discovered to have been on the police payroll.

In the stirring years of political and social ferment after the subsidence of the revolution of 1905, Russian arts and letters went through the doldrums. Tolstoy lived on as the grand old man of Russian literature until 1910, but his output in those last years was not specially remarkable. Gorky was prolific, but until the appearance in 1913 of *My Childhood,* the first of his autobiographical works, the aesthetic quality of his writing was very low. In 1905, Merezhkovsky swung violently leftward, with the result that he emigrated to Paris. His refusal to accept Lenin's "defeatism" was to result in a fresh flight (1919) to the West and to alliance with Boris Savinkov, an SR terrorist who directed his energies to underhand struggle against the Bolsheviks. In his remaining decades Merezhkovsky, who has been characterized as "a good novelist for boys," [4] produced little of value after his first withdrawal from Russia.

Of the new writers of the period, A. I. Kuprin (1870-1938), I. A. Bunin (1870-1953), and Leonid Andreev (1871-1919) were the most significant, while M. P. Artsybashev (1878-1927) was the most sensational. Of them only Bunin perhaps compared to the writers of the nineteenth century. There were also the Symbolists, of whom Alexander Blok (1880-1921) was the greatest, and the Futurists, including Vladimir Maiakovsky (1894-1930), who was to become the chief Bolshevik literary figure. In painting, despite the decline of the old "realist" tradition, Repin continued to hold his dominant position.

Only in music did Russia continue to be distinguished in this period. Balakirev lingered on till 1910, but, in the shadow of the greater composers to whom he had rendered invaluable assistance, he was fighting a losing battle for Russian nationalism in music. Rimsky-Korsakov was almost at the end of his career and did not even live to see the production in 1908 of his last and greatest achievement. In 1905, his open sympathy for his revolutionary students had led to his dismissal from the St. Petersburg Conservatory. Yet, after a brief trip to Italy, he composed (1906-07) *Le Coq d'Or,* using an Arab story which Pushkin had borrowed from Washington Irving. Its satiric caricature of an outworn political regime could not be mistaken, and the composer had given it his brilliant best.

Rachmaninoff also had gone into temporary, and more prolonged, exile, spending three years in Germany, followed by an immense success in America. There he declined the post of conductor of the Boston Symphony Orchestra, later to be accepted by Serge Koussevitzky, at this time champion of the Scriabin school of music. From his return to Russia in 1910 until the revolution of 1917, which he strove to ignore, Rachmaninoff continued to be one of the most productive of Russian composers, mainly in the form of piano concertos. After his flight from Moscow late in 1917, he was to embark in America on a new career; he became one of the world's leading concert pianists, but his work as a composer was virtually at an end.

Scriabin's return to Russia in 1909 from a five-year sojourn in the West heralded a brief period of enthusiasm for his new dissonant techniques. He was ably assisted by the eminent conductor Koussevitzky, but was disappointed in his attempt to combine his music mechanically with a play of colored lights. Though clearly the forerunner of "modern" music, Scriabin lacked the creative ability to give it a form of its own. Even his most ardent admirers, such as Aaron Copland, acknowledge that the ten piano sonatas present "musical ideas of genius . . . strait-jacketed" in an old classical form.

Even before his death in 1915, Scriabin had been eclipsed by Stravinsky, the most outstanding Russian composer of the current century. The making of this ardent disciple of Rimsky-Korsakov was Serge Diaghilev, who was impressed by some of Stravinsky's early short pieces played in St. Petersburg in 1908. Following the fabulous success of Diaghilev's Ballet Russe at Paris in 1909, Diaghilev enlisted the young composer's services for the next season. The result was *The Firebird.* The scenario, prepared by Diaghilev's master-choreographer, Michael Fokine, was based on old Russian mythology; Leon Bakst supplied the setting and costuming, Nijinsky the dancing; Stravinsky's music was distilled from Rimsky-Korsakov. Its brilliant success led to an even greater triumph, *Petrouchka,* which broke sharply with nineteenth-century techniques of orchestration. In 1913, still under Diaghilev's auspices, Stravinsky plunged even further into the new unromantic realism. *Le Sacre du Printemps* far outdid *Petrouchka* in what many found its shocking, nerve-wracking dissonance. A fourth work of the same type, *Les Noces,* was composed during the war, though not presented till 1923, again in Paris; its extreme of ear-splitting rhythms caused it to find less favor than its predecessors. All of these earlier ballets, despite the revolutionary character of their "modernism," were strongly in the Russian nationalist tradition and constituted transfiguration of essentially Russian folk themes.

Stravinsky, who happened to be abroad at the outbreak of war in 1914, never returned to Russia. In 1934, he became a French citizen, in 1945, an American. The nationalism of his earlier music gave way to a broad cosmopolitanism, an eclecticism that had also been characteristic of the great Russian composers of the preceding century, who, like Stravinsky, had lacked systematic early musical training. He made no return, however, to their emotional romanticism. Rather, he represented a return to the intellectualism of classical music. He displayed a strong tendency to evoke bygone styles, ranging from Bach to Debussy and from Russian folk music to American modernism. The variety of forms he gave his music, his passion for the woodwinds, for which at times he neglected the strings, his violent antipathy for Wagner, his articulate expression of his own ideas—all have combined to make him one of the most striking figures in world artistry, but without tearing him loose from his Russian roots despite the completeness of his physical break with his homeland.

One other composer in the new style was just emerging in this period. Serge Prokofiev (1891-1953) was the son of an estate manager in the Ukraine; as a child, he was inspired by his mother's playing of Beethoven and Chopin. In contrast to Stravinsky, he was early in life given an excellent musical education; like Stravinsky, he later numbered Rimsky-Korsakov among his teachers. Although he was graduated from the St. Petersburg Conservatory with the highest honors, he had already created much annoyance by his youthful brash assertiveness regarding the supreme merits of the new school of music. His *First Piano Concerto,* composed in 1911, was greeted by the critics as "football music." His early association with Diaghilev was less happy than was that of Stravinsky; the impresario rejected Prokofiev's *Scythian Suite* (1915) as too close to *Le Sacre du Printemps.* His burlesque *Buffoon,* based on Russian folk music, was not performed till 1921. During the war Prokofiev composed a number of other satirical and realistic works, among which the *Classical Symphony* (1917) represented an amusing employment of older techniques, with his own distinctive stamp. Unhappy in Soviet Russia, the young composer early in 1918 secured permission to leave by way of Siberia. En route he began composition of an opera, *Love for Three Oranges,* which found great favor in Chicago; in New York, however, this work of the expatriate composer was rejected as "Bolshevism in Art." Prokofiev was indeed the only product of prerevolutionary musical genius to return to the land of the soviets, where—partly under pressure, partly from patriotism—he was to accommodate his original musical views to the dictates of expedient conformity.

SUMMARY

To sum up, there can be no doubt that at the beginning of 1914 a revolutionary situation existed in Russia. It is, however, necessary to consider carefully the nature of this situation, for it would be a grave error to attribute the revolution in any important sense to the agitation carried on by a few handfuls of professional revolutionaries. The objective situation was very grave, and the crisis was not precipitated by the subjective programs of any of the competing groups, whether liberal or socialist.

The primary fact was that the autocracy had outlived the forces that had produced it. The only questions were how long it could still survive and whether it would be swept away by revolution or transmuted by reform into some other kind of regime. Historically the autocracy had rested on the support of a land-owning and serf-owning nobility. At times, particularly in the eighteenth century and in 1825, some of the nobility had shown signs of aspiring to a direct share in power. The autocracy had countered these efforts, not necessarily consciously, by shifting its weight to rest on a bureaucratic apparatus and ultimately, in its own interest, had abolished serfdom. In doing so, it had tried to protect the economic interests of the nobility, and in the last decades before 1914 it had even been trying to strengthen also the political prerogatives of the nobility as the most reliable social support for autocracy. Emancipation and Redemption had, however, dealt an irreparable blow to the economic role of the nobility. Not only had noble monopoly of landholding been broken, but the amount of arable land controlled by the nobles had shrunken to a small proportion of the total. Most of the nobles had proven quite incompetent to organize production without serf labor and, becoming essentially pensioners of the state, had ceased to have great significance in the productive life of the country. A class economically impotent, despite all the political rights and privileges that might be conferred upon it, could not possibly provide the necessary social basis for continuance of autocracy.

The gap left by the decline of the nobility as owners of the means of production could not be filled by the peasantry. Even apart from the survival of communal organization, the land in the hands of the peasants was necessarily too minutely subdivided to make them a possible alternative as conscious supporters of the government. In Western Europe, a proprietary peasantry did indeed exercise a stabilizing influence and was repeatedly used to support governments against revolution. But its organization depended on the existence of "bourgeois" relationships, even in the monarchies of Central Europe. In economically backward Russia, it would not have been possible to organize the peasantry in support of a government against revolution, any more than it was possible for the peasantry to initiate and carry through a revolution on its own. The most that could be expected was that the land-hungry Russian peasantry would prove itself an anarchic "dark" force, compounding and confounding any socio-political disturbance that might occur in Russia.

Nor could the industrial workers, still not overclearly differentiated from the peasant masses from which they were recruited, play the role of an independent force, either for or against the autocracy. The years immediately preceding World War I were boom years and consequently were marked by great labor activity. Strikes had again become numerous, though only in St. Petersburg in 1913 did the number of strikers exceed the number of workers; even so they remained far below the level of 1905, and elsewhere they lagged far behind. This labor activity strengthened, as Lenin had feared it would, trade-union consciousness rather than socialist consciousness. Though under the existing electoral law it was a foregone conclusion that the workers' curias would elect socialists to the Duma, the main interest of the workers was obviously in improvement of their own material condition, even within the framework of capitalism.

The tsarist government had not abandoned its limited commitment to protective labor legislation. In the twentieth century, it had been carried further. A workmen's compensation act of 1903, which had proved very inadequate in practice, had been supplemented in 1912 by imposition on employers of a system of accident insurance, with no contributions required of the workers. In the same year (1912), a national health-insurance system had been enacted; it provided for contributions by both workers and employers, but the administration of the insurance funds was largely left to the workers themselves.

Even more important was implementation in 1906, on the eve of the meeting of the First Duma, of the promise made in October, 1905, of freedom of association. This legalization of the formation of trade unions was, to be sure, framed in an ungenerous spirit. The role of the trade union was conceived mainly in the spirit of the "friendly society" authorized by English Liberals in the nineteenth century. Yet in addition to mutual self-help and educational activity, it had for the first time in Russia authorized trade unions as legal entities to study the economic relations between workers and employers and to make collective representations to the latter. On the other hand, it restricted labor organization to a craft basis and stipulated official registration. Above all, it denied the right to strike, in the sense that deliberate stoppage of work before a labor contract had expired, even without resort to violence, was made a punishable offense. Strikes did, however, frequently occur, particularly in the metal trades, where the workers were both more highly paid and more conscious of their desires. Most strikes lasted less than two days. A significant proportion of them were officially classed as political, again particularly in the metal trades (583 out of 954 in 1913).

The government's attitude toward the strike movement was also largely political. The shooting of some hundreds of striking workers in the Lena goldfields (1912) did not mean that the autocracy had become the obedient tool of a predatory capitalism. Nor was it a mere repetition of "Bloody Sunday." It reflected rather a denial by the government of the principle of free association conceded in 1905. That it occurred in the midst of the boom years, 1911-13, when labor activity was naturally at a peak, emphasized its significance. The government was challenging the growth of an independent labor movement, just as it was seeking to limit also its antithesis and counterpart, the rise of industrial capitalism.

As in other countries, however, the interest of the workers was primarily in the improvement of their own condition, not in the reconstitution of society in the interests of all mankind. Lenin was completely right in his position that the working class, left to itself, would never develop "proletarian class consciousness," that it would merely become "trade-union conscious," raising no challenge to capitalism as such. It was this radical departure from Marx's prediction that was to embark Lenin, the consummate political strategist, on his effort to adapt Marxist theory to the actual conditions of life. The Bolshevik revolution was not to be, and objectively could not be, the outcome of the growth of "proletarian class consciousness," which could not arise in Russia any more than it did in the West.

There remains to consider the class which Marx himself had singled out as the most revolutionary class in history—the class which, perhaps against its own interests, was also the most revolutionary in Russia. The rising industrial bourgeoisie, as already indicated, could not permanently support the authority of an autocracy which had been rooted in the dominance, now outmoded, of a landlord class controlling every phase of the life of the peasant masses. The various forms of assistance that the government had given to the rise of industry did not at all mean that the autocracy was putting itself in the service of rising industrial capitalism. The situation was by no means so simple. The autocracy, while fighting against manifestations of independence by industrial labor, was fighting also against what it regarded as the more serious challenge of autonomous industrial capital.

It is this confusion in the official attitude that largely accounts for its sudden collapse in 1917. The autocracy represented a survival from economic conditions that no longer existed and, like a dinosaur, it demonstrated total inability to adjust to the changed conditions of life. Although the monarchy had, by Emancipation, destroyed the economic dominance of the landlords, it continued to refuse to accept as an alternative basis of power the rule of the only class economically strong enough to replace them. By fighting against the rising influence of the industrialists and by refusing them any significant share in the formulation of political policy, the autocracy was signing its own death warrant.

Nevertheless, granted that a revolutionary situation existed in 1914, it was not a foregone conclusion that Russia would experience a violent revolution. There were in the situation elements that might have suggested ultimate transition to a regime not dissimilar to what prevailed in Western Europe. In this respect, the two principal factors were the Duma and the Stolypin reform. In order to have significance, both of these would have required a long period of peaceful development. If given this precondition, however, it would not have been unreasonable to suppose that the Duma might gradually have been able to develop into something similar to a Western parliament. It is of course true that the Duma, as it existed in 1914, did not have powers at all comparable to those of any Western parliament, not even to those of the German Reichstag, often cavalierly though inaccurately dismissed as a mere "debating society." Yet, despite the apparent legal impotence of the Duma, the history of the West, England included, strongly supported the possibility that the Duma in course of time might by degrees—under certain circumstances by leaps and bounds—expand its sphere of competence.

If one may again suggest what was not fated to happen—that Russia might have had a long period of development uninterrupted by events in the outside world—the policy of the Octobrists might have proved itself right. Against such a peaceful evolution, of course, might be cited a number of factors, not the least among them the fact that the reigning emperor, weak-willed as he undoubtedly was, was also an extremely obstinate person. Backed by his neurasthenic wife, he undoubtedly would have continued to oppose that protozoan resistance to change which was surely one of the chief factors in the way of fundamental reform.

Reform, if it could have any meaning at all, must have amounted to revolution, in the sense that autocracy must have given way to constitutional monarchy. Nicholas II in no way resembled the Iron Duke of Wellington, whose military experience had convinced him that strategic retreat, as in the matter of Catholic Emancipation or the Reform Bill of 1832, was needed to preserve the essence of what he stood for. Yet Nicholas II, already forty-six years old, could not have lived forever. There is no reason to believe that, sooner or later, the establishment of the Duma might not have led, without violent revolution, to the conversion of the Russian political system into something similar to what prevailed in the West.

The possibility that Russia might have escaped anything resembling the revolution of 1917 is immeasurably increased by the fact of the Stolypin reform. If it had had time to effect the change from a peasantry committed to spasmodic violent disorder to a peasantry of Western type with an interest in supporting the social order, the revolution of 1917 could never have taken the form it did.

NOTES

1. Liashchenko, *History of the National Economy of Russia to the 1917 Revolution,* Chapter XXXIV, esp. pp. 712-719.
2. *Polnoe sobranie zakonov . . .* (Third collection), No. 29,242, V, 81 (June 3, 1907), XXVII, 321-335 *passim.*

3. *Gosudarstvennaia Duma . . . Stenograficheskie otchety, 1912 g., chast'* III, col. 1953.
4. Mirsky, *History of Russian Literature . . .* , p. 417.

SUGGESTIONS FOR FURTHER READING

In addition to works previously cited, Margaret S. Miller, *Economic Development of Russia, 1905-1914,* and G. Pavlovsky, *Agricultural Russia on the Eve of the Revolution,* are very useful. Maynard's *Russia in Flux, Before October* contains thoughtful suggestions by a former British civil servant in India. H. W. Williams' *Russia of the Russians* is also worth consulting. Suggestive discussions of special problems include articles by Halmson, "The Problem of Social Stability in Urban Russia, 1905-1917," and Mosse's "Stolypin's Villages." The volumes in the *Carnegie Series on the Economic and Social History of the World War* contain summaries useful for the preceding years.

Chapter

23

War and Revolution: 1914-1917

THE ALLIANCES AND THE OUTBREAK OF WAR

The suggestions just advanced are "might-have-beens." The facts of history are far different. Russia was committed by the Dual Alliance of 1894 and the Triple Entente of 1907 to a foreign policy which, combined with her own Balkan interests, brought her into war in 1914. Thorough examination of the development of the international situation in Europe does not properly fall within the scope of this book, but it may be well here to recall some of the salient points in connection with Russia's involvement.

The role that Russia had played as "the gendarme of Europe" after the Napoleonic wars has been discussed in earlier chapters. The triumph of liberal forces in France in 1830 and 1848 and their evanescent victory in Central Europe in 1848-49 had shaken but had not destroyed Russian ascendancy over a large part of the Continent. The Crimean War, however, which precipitated the "Great Reforms" within Russia, had also relegated Russia to a secondary position in the international scheme. Freed from dread of her intervention, Prussia had effected the unification of Germany.

After 1871 it was the chief goal of Bismarck's policy to preserve his country's new position in the world by keeping the peace. To this end he had sought to keep France, irreconcilable because of the loss of Alsace-Lorraine, diplomatically isolated by tying the other Continental powers into a web of alliances centering in Berlin. Although the keystone of his policy was a firm alliance with Austria-Hungary, he had succeeded in knitting both Russia and Italy into the pattern, in the one case by reviving the Three Emperors' League in 1881, in the other by forming the Triple Alliance of 1882. When friction between his Austro-Hungarian ally and Russia over the Balkans had become too great to make possible continuance of his system, Bismarck had still managed, by the "Reinsurance Treaty" of 1887, to prevent a total break between Germany and Russia.

The impatience of William II with this ramshackle arrangement had expedited French courting of Russia. As earlier noted, the Franco-Russian Dual Alliance of 1894 had confirmed to Russia the flow of economic assistance from France but had also opened the possibility of Russian entanglement in a potential Franco-German war. Imperialist rivalries indicated the alternative possibility, equally remote from Russian national interests, that France and Germany might make common cause against the United Kingdom, dragging Russia along with them.

To avert this danger, England abandoned her Shakespearean policy of "glorious isolation" ("Come the three corners of the world in arms, and we shall shock them")[1] and negotiated the Entente Cordiale with France. Inveterate lingering British suspicions of Russia's policy in the Far, Middle, and Near East at first made it impossible to extend this Anglo-French understanding to include Russia. However, Russia's defeat by Japan (1904-05), together with German bluster over Morocco (1905-06), facilitated the formation in 1907 of the Triple Entente to balance German power. A belated effort by the Kaiser, through the "Willie-Nickie" correspondence, to regain lost ground in Russo-German relations, did achieve the Treaty of Björkö (July 24, 1905), from which, however, the tsar, on the advice of his ministers, quickly withdrew; Russia remained the ally of France and entered the partnership with England in the Entente of 1907. Ironically, it was Russia, the pawn in this international game played for quite other stakes, that dragged the world into war over a Balkan issue.

Russia's Balkan interests, which centered in the problem of control of the Straits, have already been outlined. Russia's hope that an "autonomous" Bulgaria would serve as a *point d'appui* for Russian interests had been disappointed. The inconclusive Serbo-Bulgarian War of 1885 had been regarded as a dress rehearsal for a grander conflict between their respective protectors, Austria-Hungary and Russia, but the subsequent development of Bulgarian polity had steadily undermined the influence of Russia. Early in the new century, Serbia, partly in connection with a change of dynasty, had also shifted her orientation from a pro-Austrian to a Russophile policy. This substitution had helped to create a serious international crisis in 1908. Austria-Hungary had taken advantage of the "Young Turk" revolution to convert her military occupation of Bosnia-Herzegovina, internationally sanctioned in 1878, into outright annexation of these provinces, which were inhabited principally by Serbs. Russia's protest had not been supported by France and England; the 1905 revolution was still too recent and the military and naval rejuvenation of Russia, under French auspices, was still too incomplete for the Western powers to risk support to Russia in a war that must clearly involve Germany. The Balkan Wars of 1912 and 1913, fought without overt assistance from the great powers, resulted in a situation further deleterious to Russian interests in that area.

In 1914, the murder at Sarajevo in Bosnia—with fairly obvious Serbian connivance—of the heir to the Austro-Hungarian throne provoked a new crisis. In this situation, Russia felt she dared not permit the complete humiliation of Serbia by Austria-Hungary. France and England, however reluctant to engage in a general war, did not find it possible to withhold support from Russia. Accordingly, Russia ordered general mobilization, not merely against Austria-Hungary but also along the frontier of the latter's necessarily staunch ally, Germany. Such mobilization had long been recognized in what is euphemistically called international law as tantamount to a declaration of war. This forced Germany immediately into the struggle. The existence of the Dual Alliance of 1894 made it certain that France would come to Russia's aid. To Germany, faced with the dreaded bogy of a two-front war, it was clear that the only hope of victory must depend on knocking France out of the war before Russia could begin serious operations. It was therefore inevitable that Germany should declare war also on France. Britain's concept of her own interests, expressed in the Entente Cordiale of 1904 and the Triple Entente of 1907 and implemented by a long series of technically unratified and unpublished agreements, made it necessary for her, on whatever pretext came to hand, to declare war on Germany. Thus, against the conscious will for peace of all the participating governments, the war of 1914 was touched off much after the fashion of a Greek tragedy.

The possibility of such a development had been clearly foreseen, in Russia no less than in other countries. In Russia, however, this clairvoyance had been largely confined to reactionary individuals who were not in control of affairs at the time. This is no contradiction of the fact that the Russian autocracy of 1914 was reactionary; it suggests only that the Russian government was not then intelligently reactionary. The most expressive description of the situation, from a narrowly Russian viewpoint, is that embodied in a private memorandum of Durnovo to Emperor Nicholas in February, 1914. Durnovo, whose role as Witte's Minister of the Interior in 1905-06 has already been referred to, was at this time in retirement, and his warning was not heeded.

As Durnovo saw the international position, it was basically a question of rivalry between England and Germany. He was convinced that the brunt of the inevitable conflict would, given the existing structure of military potential and of international relations, fall on Russia. He therefore urged that Russia reorient her foreign policy, reverting to the days of the *Dreikaiserbund* of Bismarck's time, if not to the reëstablishment of a Concert of Europe in the spirit of the Age of Metternich. What is here of particular concern, however, is Durnovo's appraisal of what would happen to Russia, if, contrary to what he regarded as her true interests, she became involved in war against Germany. He anticipated that such a war might entail military defeat, and that defeat would bring revolution. He warned:

> Things will begin with all reverses being attributed to the government. In the legislature a violent campaign will be begun against it, as a result of which revolutionary speeches will begin throughout the country. These latter will at once advance socialist slogans, the only ones that can rouse and rally wide strata of the population; at first the slogan will be general redistribution [of the land], later general division of all valuables and possessions. The defeated army, which in addition will during the war have lost its most reliable personnel, and for the most part instinctively gripped by the general peasant yearning for land, will prove too demoralized to serve as a bulwark of law and order. The legislature and the opposition parties of the intelligentsia, devoid of real authority in the eyes of the people, will not be able to control the divergent popular waves they themselves have raised, and Russia will be plunged into hopeless anarchy, the issue of which cannot even be foreseen.[2]

It was a remarkably accurate preview of what actually did happen.

When war came, no serious opposition was offered within Russia. Regardless of the facts, the war was practically universally accepted as a war of defense against centuries-old Teutonic aggression. At a special meeting of the Duma on August 8, 1914, not a single vote was cast against a resolution endorsing the policy of the government. To be sure, no *Burgfrieden* (civil peace) was proclaimed, although Miliukov did plead:

> Whatever our attitude toward the domestic policy of the government, our first duty is to preserve our country one and undivided [stormy applause]. Let us lay aside our domestic controversies, let us not give the foe the slightest cause to hope for differences that may divide us [stormy applause in the center, on the right, and on the left]. . . .

The only denunciatory speech was made by the Trudovik leader, Kerensky, who was the first to ascend the rostrum:

> Inexpiable is the responsibility of the governments of all the European states which, in the interests of their ruling classes are pushing their peoples into a fratricidal war. The socialists of all the countries now at war . . . tried to protest against the war now breaking out. We, the Russian democracy, were unable even in this last dreadful hour to raise our voice freely and in time against the imminent war. But, deeply believing in the unity of all the toiling classes of all countries, we send our fraternal greeting to all those who are protesting against the devouring fratricidal war of peoples.

Stressing that the Russian people had no enemies among the toiling classes, but only among their governments, he denounced the Russian government for not granting an amnesty to "fighters for the liberty and happiness of our country," for refusing reconciliation with the non-Russian nationalities, and for burdening the toilers by increasing indirect taxation. He called on the "peasants and workers, all who wish the happiness and welfare of Russia" to "steel your souls, save all your strength and, while defending the country, set it free." The only point at which he evoked applause (not "stormy," at that, and only "in spots" on the right) was in his peroration: "To you, our brothers, who are shedding your blood for your native land, a deep bow and fraternal greeting."

With only one exception, all other speakers were enthusiastic. For the Social Democrats, Khaustov only palely echoed Kerensky's rhetoric:

> The proletariat, the constant defender of the liberty and interests of the people, will at every moment defend the cultural welfare of the people against any encroachments, wherever they come from. . . .

Not daring to oppose the prevailing climate of opinion, he promised only that the Social Democrats would work for an early peace, on terms dictated, not by diplomats, but by the people itself; then "the present outburst of barbarism will at the same time be the last."

A series of spokesmen of subject nationalities hastened to pledge their loyalty. Among them, Friedman, while stressing "the exceptionally burdensome legal conditions" under which Jews lived, promised that "the Jews will go forth to the battlefield shoulder to shoulder with all the peoples" of Russia. He evoked not only stormy applause on all sides but shouts of "Bravo" by his assertion:

> In the present hour of trial, pursuant to the call sounded from the height of the Throne, we Russian Jews will as one man stand under the Russian banners and will devote all our strength to repelling the foe.

Even Miliukov and a series of spokesmen much further to the right could evoke no greater response from the receptive Duma.[3]

The Russian press of course did not lag behind the Duma deputies. Perhaps specially impressive, however, was a letter to the London *Times* from a Russian exile, Vladimir Burtsev, who had been an active Socialist Revolutionary for some thirty years: "Even we, the adherents of the parties of the Extreme Left, and hitherto ardent anti-militarists and pacifists, even we believe in the necessity of *this* war."[4] How insignificant seemed Lenin's suggested thesis, penned a month later, after his arrest in Austrian Galicia as a potential spy and his expulsion to neutral Switzerland, that "by far the lesser evil would be the defeat of the Tsar's monarchy and the Tsar's armies. . . ."[5]

This rally around the throne was by no means confined to the Duma. To the public at large, the change of the name of the capital from St. Petersburg to Petrograd seemed long overdue, and was generally welcomed. Resentment was directed at the Germans and contributed to reinforce the remarkable stolid courage which Russian infantry normally display. Although military preparations had been incompetent and wastefully managed, Russian soldiers initially did not on occasion hesitate to go into battle literally barehanded, waiting for opportunity to pick up the rifles of their fallen comrades. Russian workers, except during the original mobilization largely exempted from service at the front, similarly showed good spirit in the factories. Strikes fell to a very low ebb, and strikes of political character were almost unknown.

It cannot be said that the war was ever popular among the peasant masses; rather, it was frankly received as an overwhelming misfortune, but not as a misfortune imposed by the tsar, or even by the landlord nobles. One is reminded of the Novgorod populace in 1257 when the Tatars insisted on subjecting that city to tribute: "Who were good stood by St. Sophia and by the True Faith; and they made opposition."

DEFEAT AND DISCOURAGEMENT

Despite delays in mobilization caused by the economic weakness of the country as well as by incompetence and corruption in high places, the Russian "steamroller" did indeed roll into East Prussia and into Galicia while the Germans were busy with their drive in the west. Before the war was a month old, however, the Russian invasion of Germany was overwhelmed in the battle of the Mazurian Lakes, which incidentally created the Hindenburg legend. Thenceforth, the war brought Russia an almost unbroken series of defeats. In the summer of 1915, the Russians not only were expelled from Galicia but lost all Poland and considerable additional territory, as far as the gates of Riga. In 1916, when the Germans again concentrated their efforts in the west, the eastern front, despite desperate Russian efforts, remained virtually unchanged; Rumania's entry into the war on the side of the Allies merely gave the Central Powers a fresh area of conquest.

The causes of Russia's unhappy military record were numerous, and not all purely Russian. One of the major difficulties, a shortage of ammunition, was fully shared by the English and the French, well into 1915. Russia, however, proved completely unable to overcome it until, by the end of 1916, Allied shipments through Murmansk and Archangel, supplemented by the long haul from Vladivostok, gave hope of launching a really successful Russian offensive in the spring of 1917. To make matters worse, the Russian Artillery Department was administratively independent of the Ministry of War and was headed by a wholly incompetent grand duke, surrounded by corrupt subordinates. The civilian Ministry of War was itself poorly coördinated with the Supreme Command of the army, and both complained bitterly of lack of coöperation from the other. Although nominally the Council of Ministers was collectively responsible to the emperor, each minister, who owed his place to intrigue and personal favor rather than to administrative ability, frequently acted independently of his colleagues. All attempts to improve matters, whether made by the few conscientious ministers or by leading members of the Duma, were foiled by the jelly-like character of the emperor, in whom all authority theoretically resided. Again and again, men such as Rodzianko, the president of the Duma, whose personal loyalty to the monarchy is beyond all question, had the experience of receiving a courteous and apparently sympathetic audience with Nicholas, only to find later that in fact they had made no impression. Ministers who offered critical suggestions were given warm thanks and soon after relieved of their posts.

Nicholas' decisions—if one can use the term in connection with a man of so weak a will—were determined by his wife, a woman chiefly distinguished for the vindictive rancor she continually displayed toward all who did not show adequate appreciation of her husband's august majesty and her own infallible wisdom. She, in her turn, was subject to the control of all sorts of ambitious adventurers and particularly of faith-healers. Outstanding among them was Rasputin, who professed to be a monk and who, in his career of debauchery, was protected against the ecclesiastical authorities by powerful friends at court. His apparent success, based on low cunning, in contributing to the survival of the hemophilic heir to the throne had since 1907 given him increasingly complete ascendancy over the neurotic empress and therefore gave him access to all state and military secrets. Though there is no indication of deliberately treasonable activities on his part, his greed and craving for sensual indulgence made him an easy mark for contractors anxious to make financial profit by knowledge of the government's military plans. There is no doubt that, indirectly, he more than once enabled the Germans to penetrate Russian strategic intentions even before they were divulged to the Russian generals who were to carry them out. In many other ways, too, Rasputin became a symbol for all the evils that affected Russia's conduct of the war. A word from "Our Friend," passed on by the empress to the emperor, was the surest way of effecting another move in the constant replacement of officials, the game of "ministerial leapfrog," in which genuine devotion to Russia seemed to be the surest road to disgrace.

It would, however, be a mistake to overemphasize the inadequacy of the emperor, the ill-advised interference of the empress, and the shame of influences such as that of Rasputin. Even had the core of the autocratic regime been sounder, it is difficult to see how the progressive degeneration of a country too weak to support the frightful stresses of the war could have been checked. It should not be forgotten that all the other major belligerents, though economically, socially, and politically far healthier and stronger than was Russia, suffered frightfully from internal exhaustion. Toward the end of 1916, all of them seemed at the point of cracking: Germany's suffering in the "turnip winter" found compensation only in the Russian revolution; France had to jail many a prominent politician for "defeatism"; even in England, Lord Lansdowne, architect of the Entente Cordiale in 1904, officially urged a negotiated peace. In the case of Russia, it is not surprising that similar stresses produced far greater strains. The early defeats and the inability of the Russian commanders to repair the damage had been prepared by conditions that have little to do with the personalities in the capital.

The mood of general devotion was of very short duration. Discouragement seized the peasant rank and file and rapidly affected even the generals. The vast superiority of the German artillery fire-power wiped out whole Russian regiments without any assistance from the German infantry. Baffled and humiliated, the Russian sea of gray coats had to draw back before an almost unseen enemy. Even in 1914, General Yanushkevich, chief of staff to the Supreme Commander-in-Chief, Grand Duke Nicholas Nicholaevich, had become, as he himself acknowledged, "hysterical." In November, 1914, he reported that General Ruzsky, one of the most successful of the Russian leaders, had "suddenly lost faith in the troops." In December, he reported that five hundred Russian prisoners, rescued by Cossacks, had rounded on their deliverers: "Who the devil asked you to do that? We don't want to starve and freeze again." [6] The Russian peasant did not have the positive nationalist urge of so many Austro-Hungarian subjects, particularly the Czechs, that induced them often to surrender *en masse,* but, torn from his fields and his family for purposes he little comprehended, he could not withstand the shortages, not only of guns and ammunition, but of food and clothing as well. The French ambassador to Russia, who commented frequently on the "enormous losses" suffered by the Russian army, "the fatigue of its troops and the exhaustion of its munitions," and its "frightful sacrifices," was pleased to record General Joffre's message of "admiration for the magnificent effort of the Russian armies [which] thanks to their bravery and tenacity, have succeeded . . . in thus rendering the greatest service to the general cause." It was small wonder that Joffre felt it to be "a question of honor as well as interest" to launch an offensive to relieve the pressure on the Russians.[7] Many a Russian general found it difficult whole-heartedly to condemn even "disgusting cases" of troops who were "weary of the hardships of war" and depressed by "the enemy's obvious superiority." [8] There was a rapid growth of a spirit that has been described as Tolstoyan, of meeting the enemy with offerings of bread and salt, and which curiously presages Trotsky's later theory of "no war, no peace."

If the front was profoundly troubled by the spectacle of mass surrenders, of self-infliction of "finger-wounds," and of wholesale desertions, beginning as early as 1914 and constantly increasing, the rear was in even worse condition. It was notorious that the morale of units in reserve, which frequently had to drill with broomsticks instead of rifles, was normally lower than that of those at the front, so much so that front commanders viewed reinforcements with the greatest mistrust. Recruiting of conscripts presented extraordinary difficulties. In the summer of 1915, the Minister of the Interior privately admitted to his colleagues:

> The police are unable to cope with the mass of slackers. . . . If it becomes known that the calling up of soldiers of the second category is being carried out without the sanction of the State Duma, I fear that in the present humor we shall not get a single man.

This secret meeting had been opened with a disheartening report from the Minister of War, General Polivanov, who painted a picture of utter defeat and confusion, concluding with the words: "I place my hopes on the impassable distances, on the deep mud, and on the grace of St. Nicholas of Mirlikia, the protector of Holy Russia." [9]

The marvel is not that the regime collapsed but rather that it survived so long. It is an extraordinary tribute to the capacity for endurance of suffering, perhaps also to the "darkness" of the Russian people. It is worth noting that the steady deterioration of the power and prestige of the monarchy owed extraordinarily little to any "light" cast by revolutionary propaganda. It was not propaganda that made an officer, wounded and decorated for heroism, say to his father, the president of the Duma, "We are ready to die for Russia, for our Mother country, but not for the caprice of the generals. . . ." [10] The commanders of the several fronts, in conference with the Minister of War, all urged that the material conditions under which the soldiers existed were the basic cause of demoralization. Ironically enough, the War-Censorship Section of the Twelfth Army at the beginning of February, 1917, confidently reported that "the excellent and timely supply of warm clothing" had more than counteracted the effect of German peace proposals, of Wilson's speeches, and of the bad influence of Czech prisoners of war.[11]

THE WAR, THE PEOPLE, AND POLITICS

After all, despite the worry of the generals, it was not the front army that precipitated the revolution. The significance of the army for the revolution was not that it led but that, due to its demoralization, it could not be used, as it had been in 1905, to suppress the revolution.

Nor was the revolution initiated by the peasantry, on which nineteenth-century revolutionists had staked their faith. Of the approximately 15.5 million who served in the armed forces, at least 80 percent were drawn from the peasantry, of whom, it was estimated, there were some 27 million of military age. Labor shortage, rather than land shortage, was the prevalent condition, which bore more hardly on landlord agriculture than on peasant. The acreage sown to grain by peasants seems actually to have increased substantially during the war years, while the area under the more commercial, and more efficient, supervision of landlords declined sharply. Temporary cessation of peasant land-hunger tended to produce quiescence in the countryside, though the progress of the Stolypin reform was seriously slowed.

The workers naturally gave more trouble than did the peasants. As also in Western belligerent countries, the demand for industrial labor and the rapidly rising cost of living resulted in a revival of strike activity. As early as the summer of 1915, at a secret meeting of the Council of Ministers,

> General Ruzsky referred to the condition of the workers in the Petrograd plants, pointing out that they were performing extremely intensive labor and feeling the full burden of the high cost of living; the factories had not set new rates of wages, and the workers, to avoid starvation, had to resort to overtime, which was definitely exhausting them; most serious attention must be given to the matter and speedy measures taken, since strikes and accompanying disorders were possible. Then, remarked General Ruzsky, the war would be absolutely hopeless.[12]

In 1915, the number of strikers was, to be sure, little more than half the figure for the pre-war boom years 1912 and 1913. In 1916, however, it reached new heights, while workers participating in strikes of "political or non-economic" character made up one-third of the total; "political" strikes, however, lost an average of less than two days per striker, "economic" strikes nearly five days. It should also be noted that "political" strikes were not by any means always revolutionary in spirit; they could be set off by an incident such as the arrest of a street orator for falsely reporting Russian victories. Although the government was at times seriously worried whether it had the force it was accustomed to use to suppress "disorders," the Russian labor movement during the war showed less conscious ambition to take matters into its own hands than did, for instance, the shop-steward movement in wartime Glasgow. After all, despite the fact that prices rose in some cases as much as ten times the increase in wages, the factories were, after the initial mobilization, recognized as reasonably safe refuges against the rigors of the front.

The Marxist socialists, whose chief purpose it was to lead the workers in the direction of revolution, were in no position to give any guidance. Their only legal leadership lay with the thirteen Duma deputies elected in 1912. Of these, the six Bolsheviks ("majority-men") had in 1913 been induced by the police-agent Malinovsky—under the dual urging of Lenin and of his police employers—to break with the seven Mensheviks ("minority-men") led by Chkheidze. Malinovsky's sudden resignation from the Duma in May, 1914—which failed to open Lenin's eyes to the realities of the position—had left the Bolsheviks in the Duma without effective leadership; the five, together with Kamenev, editor of the Bolshevik newspaper *Pravda,* had been arrested in November, 1914, and after a public trial in February, 1915, had been exiled to Siberia. On the spot there remained no one of more consequence than young Molotov—that "incurable dumbbell," as Lenin is said to have called him[13]—to represent the ideas of Bolshevism. Social Democracy, therefore, was represented only by the Mensheviks, who, like their counterparts, the left-wing socialists of Western Europe, saw "defensism" (or "social-patriotism") as the crying need of the moment. They advocated peace, but not defeat. Under Chkheidze's leadership, the Mensheviks opposed further grants of war credits and worked for an early peace by international socialist effort. They accepted the Zimmerwald condemnation of the "capitalist" war, which their spokesmen in emigration, Martov and Axelrod, helped frame in September, 1915, but they were deaf to the imprecations which the "Zimmerwald Left," led by Lenin in Switzerland, heaped on them and on the "phrase-lover," Trotsky.[14] They were resolutely opposed to all efforts to scrap the old Socialist International for a new, Third International and simply did not envisage the possibility of proletarian revolution during the war.

The non-Marxian socialists were also divided. The Socialist Revolutionaries, by virtue of their boycott of Duma elections, could operate only underground. Their propaganda, especially among workers drafted into the army, gave special alarm to the police, but they themselves had not thought out their ideas to the stage of making any preparations for insurrection. In the Duma, the Trudoviks joined the Mensheviks in "Zimmerwald" opposition to continuance of the war. As early as August, 1915, Kerensky and Chkheidze advanced in the Duma the idea of a "democratic" peace, without annexations and without indemnities. Yet they, too, refused to accept the slogan of "defeat" and showed no conscious desire for revolution.

It was the "bourgeois" Cadets in the Duma who became once more the focus of opposition to the autocracy, centering now on the autocracy's conduct of the war. Not only the Cadets, but other groupings well to the Right of them, permitted themselves ever increasingly open criticism of the way things were going in Russia, going so far as to charge treason. By September, 1915, there had definitely taken form a "Progressive Bloc"; its chief architect was Professor Miliukov, veteran leader of the Cadets, but it extended so far to the Right as to include even Count Bobrinsky, the immensely wealthy spokesman of the "progressive group of Nationalists." Its program centered around the establishment of a "ministry of confidence" (not of a responsible ministry) and insisted on "strict observance of the principles of legality in administration"; it demanded political and religious amnesty, recognition of the rights of Poles, Jews, Finns, Ukrainians, and trade unionists; it urged that the peasants be placed on a footing of legal equality with other classes; and it pressed for many other reforms, including permanent prohibition of the sale of alcoholic liquor. It did not allude to radical solution of the agrarian problem, much less advocate any measure which could be deemed socialistic.[15]

The formation of the bloc—into which the leftist parties, the Trudoviks and Mensheviks, were not invited—posed a grave problem for the ministers. The majority of them, though conceding the desirability of adjourning the Duma, advocated coming to some understanding with the Duma majority. As Sazonov, who still retained his office as Foreign Minister, put it: "I find that for interests of state we have to support this bloc, which is essentially moderate. If it falls apart, we will have one far more to the left. . . . Who will benefit? In no case Russia." Another minister, less perturbed, also advised preliminary conversations with representatives of the bloc about their program and agreement to whatever was acceptable in it: "Thus we would open a way out for the Duma people, who crave adjournment because they feel the hopelessness of their position and are afraid that in the end they will become a plaything in the hands of left elements." The Minister of the Interior agreed, remarking that such procedure

> will raise the credit of the government in the country, for we shall be acting in agreement with the Duma people. It will be easier for us to govern. . . . If we succeed in attracting to our side against the Kerenskys even two hundred of the bloc, it will give us great strength, which will play an enormous political role.

A report from the Minister of the Interior that "in general the program of the Progressive Bloc is in significant degree acceptable and differs only in details from the government's viewpoint" evoked from another minister the proposal that they should suggest to the emperor that he let the Duma "form a cabinet corresponding to the expectations of the country." Most of the ministers enthusiastically endorsed this proposed leap in the direction of genuinely responsible government, but the prime minister, stubbornly admitting that he was "archaic," consented only to report their sentiment to the emperor.

On his return from Headquarters, he announced the emperor's decision to adjourn the Duma without more ado. Although the Ministers of Foreign Affairs and of War (the latter expressing his fear of the consequences on the morale even of officers at the front) accused him of having failed properly to represent the views of his colleagues, and although the Minister of the Interior emphasized that he could not rely on the forces at his disposal, even in Moscow, to suppress popular disturbances, in which the thirty thousand convalescent soldiers there would certainly join, Prime Minister Goremykin could not be budged: "The Duma will be adjourned on the appointed day, and nowhere will there be any bloodshed." [16]

For the moment, indeed, no disastrous consequences ensued, but the credit for the outcome must be given to the bloc, not to Goremykin. A few weeks later, a new prime minister, Stürmer, reconvened the Duma, and the Progressive Bloc peacefully continued its agitation, though with mounting bitterness and vehemence. Yet its intentions were by no means revolutionary. Miliukov stubbornly and successfully resisted the efforts of left-wing members of his own fraction to shift its orientation. The chief of the Moscow Security Division in the Department of Police, Colonel Martynov, turned in what he represented as an "almost verbatim report" of a speech made by Miliukov at a Cadet party conference in June, 1915, expressing his dread of a popular outbreak:

> It would not be a revolution, it would be that awful "Russian revolt, senseless and merciless," that made even Pushkin tremble. . . . It would be a new wave of those dregs rising from the depths that ruined the beautiful shoots of the revolution in 1905. No matter what the authority be, bad or good, a firm authority is more necessary now than ever.[17]

At the other end of the bloc, Shulgin, a Nationalist deputy, argued the need

> to replace the discontent of the masses, which might easily lead to revolution, with the discontent of the Duma. . . . It seemed to me as if we were a chain such as soldiers form when they link hands. . . . We hold each other's hands and do not let the mob break through.[18]

Nevertheless, the agitation carried on by the Duma undoubtedly contributed in the long run, not only to inspire and inflame uneasiness among the masses, but, what was perhaps more important, to hasten the undermining of the self-confidence of the most devoted servants of the autocracy, civilian and military alike. As Shulgin recorded in his diary,

> There are moments when I begin to doubt . . . where we had agreed not to fan the fire but to extinguish the fire—are we fulfilling our intention? Are we extinguishing the revolution? [19]

Before the eyes of the ministers hovered the specter, not merely of violent mass revolution, but of quiet, and possibly permanent, supersession of their authority by elected bodies, whether national, such as the Duma, or local, such as the zemstvos and the city dumas. As Maklakov, Minister of the Interior at the beginning of the war, had phrased it: "According to my secret information, this conference, under cover of the needs of the army, will discuss the political situation and demand a constitution." [20] In the face of an indignant Rodzianko, anxious only that the soldiers should be supplied with boots, even the "archaic" Goremykin overruled his colleague. Under pressure of the German advance in the summer of 1915, the government, unable to provide the army with food and clothing, sanctioned the formation of self-constituted War Industry Committees to discharge, on a voluntary and non-profit basis, functions which properly belonged to the state itself. Had it not been for the work of the public-spirited citizens who threw themselves into the task of organizing victory in the rear, Russia could not long have continued in the war.

ECONOMIC CONSEQUENCES OF THE WAR

The initial shock of losing practically all her foreign trade had threatened to have a severe depressing effect on Russian industry. This had soon passed, for the government's war needs resulted in shortages of supply. At first, consequent rising prices were taken as encouraging signs of the recovery of economic health. As time went on, however, the impossibility of matching demand with supply became alarming. This was particularly true of Russia because of the prewar scarcity of skilled labor, of reserves of capital, of transport facilities, and of fuel and raw materials.

Before the war, Russia had imported, mainly by way of the Baltic, a quarter of the coal she consumed; now, when she needed far more coal than in peacetime, the only import routes open were the Arctic and the Pacific. No adequate means of transportation connected these routes with the centers of consumption, and the enormous distances would in any case have made hauling of heavy or bulky goods prohibitive. The deficiency was not made good at home; output of coal in 1916 was only half what it had been in 1913. Wood, which Russia had in abundance, was a poor substitute for industrial purposes, and the supply of petroleum, though increased by one-third, did not keep pace with the appetite of the railways.

Production of iron, the most important of all raw materials for war purposes, also dropped absolutely, though less sharply; excluding occupied Poland, output of pig-iron was off by one-tenth in 1916 as against 1913. The textile industries, too, suffered from lack of raw materials. The cutting off of the export trade might have been expected to result in increase of the supply for Russian consumption, but the general decline in agricultural production, resulting largely from shortage of labor and work animals, left even the army far short of its requirements. Even in cotton goods, supply lagged far behind rising demand; though increased production of raw cotton in Central Asia balanced the fall in imports, virtual suspension of imports of cotton yarn aggravated the situation. Still worse was the situation with wool, for which Russia had before the war depended mainly on imports; as early as 1915, in the face of greatly increased demand, it had to be admitted officially that the supply was only about one-half of the pre-war consumption. In sole leather, the shortage was particularly bad; while the demand for boots for the army shot up to be almost equal to total pre-war consumption, the wartime deficit averaged about twenty million pairs of boots a year.

Russia's railway system had never been adequate for the country's rapidly expanding needs. In wartime, mobilization of the army and its continuous reinforcement and supply were a necessary first charge on its capacities. Even with the most intensive use of locomotives and cars, normal traffic had to be heavily curtailed, aggravating the shortages of fuel and raw material available for industry. In its turn, intensive use of rolling stock resulted in sharp decline, particularly in the number of locomotives, which fell from twenty thousand in 1914 to under seventeen thousand by 1916. Under war conditions in Russia, it was not possible to maintain, much less to increase, the serviceability of the railways.

One of the gravest aspects of the industrial picture in wartime Russia was an incorrigible labor shortage. Although the government fairly early in the war had granted exemption from conscription to most factory workers, much damage had already been done by loss of skilled workers in the haste of initial mobilization. The usual supply of new recruits to industry was surplus labor in the village, but this was now drawn off into the armed forces. Money wages increased substantially, but the gain in real wages was not impressive. In efforts to increase the labor force in the factories and mines, large numbers of prisoners of war and of refugees from occupied areas were assigned as workers; women and children were also employed. The result was a serious progressive decline in average output per worker; proclamation of total prohibition of alcoholic liquor, which dealt a terrific blow to government revenue, was not enough to restore labor efficiency.

The crux of the problem was that of food supply, which was closely connected with the impossibility of maintaining the transport system and of preventing the decline of industrial production for the civilian market. Weakened by absorption into the army of so large a proportion of its manpower, the peasantry could be offered no incentive to struggle to maintain production, while the surplus it still did produce could not be effectively conveyed to places so remote from the source of supply as was Petrograd.

Left to its own devices, the government could not have seriously combated this complex of retrograde tendencies in the Russian economy. However grudgingly, it was forced to accept a substantial measure of coöperation from Russian industrialists, who were the real architects of the system of state controls imposed in the effort to stave off total collapse of Russian industry and transport. In the long run, the task was hopeless.

Under pressure of the Union of Cities, of the Union of Zemstvos, and of the War Industry Committees, the government allowed itself to be guided in the task of organizing the economic front. It would perhaps have preferred to attack war profiteering, although wholly unable to root out peculation among its own officials. In any case, the autocracy could not permit itself to feel gratitude for the work of private volunteers from the ranks of businessmen. To have done so would have been to confess its own inutility and to provide overwhelming argument for revolution, in the sense of the establishment of a genuinely constitutional, perhaps even a democratic, regime. Prince G. E. Lvov, leading figure in the work of the zemstvos and later to be first prime minister after the Revolution, well summarized the position in September, 1915:

> The Government itself intends to organize for victory, and considers it unnecessary for the popular representatives to take part. . . . We have to manifest civic courage of a high order, bearing in mind that it is not the Government, but the people, that is fighting the war. The Government may hold itself aloof from the people, but we shall be only still more confirmed in our conviction that the organization of victory is possible only through full union of the Government and the people. . . . Let the purely formal responsibility for . . . the fate of our country rest with the Government. . . . We shall continue unflaggingly to work and to perform our national duty.[21]

Even so humble an attitude could not prevent the War Industry Committees and the Unions of Cities and of Zemstvos from supporting the agitation led by the Progressive Bloc in the Duma and from urging formation of a government of confidence.

In the fall of 1915, another element was introduced by organization of a labor section of the Central War Industry Committee. The representatives, elected in the factories by the workers, were not anti-war; they proved themselves quite willing to coöperate with the capitalists in its more vigorous prosecution. The Bolsheviks, who attempted to elect their own candidates with the idea of boycotting meetings of the Committee, suffered defeat at the hands of the combined forces of "social-patriot" Mensheviks and of "Narodnik" Socialist Revolutionists. Nevertheless, the Workers' Group of the War Industry Committee became naturally more outspoken than their more cautious "bourgeois" colleagues in pressing for "resolute elimination of the autocratic regime and complete democratization of the country." [22] It was from this group that the call came, on February 6, 1917, for a mass demonstration to greet the Duma on February 27 and urge it to take over the reins of government. The demonstration, sabotaged by the Bolsheviks, who tried to steal the show by staging a demonstration of their own—which was wretchedly unsuccessful—four days earlier, caused little disturbance.

COLLAPSE

The tsarist government was not destined to be overthrown by deliberate intent but to collapse of its own ineptitude, having alienated the active support of all strata of society as well as of the army. In Shulgin's words,

> The trouble was that in all that huge city [Petrograd] it was not possible to find a few hundred people sympathetic toward the Government. Even that's not all. The trouble was the Government didn't feel sympathetic toward itself. In fact there was not a single minister who believed in himself and in what he was doing. Not one of them was capable of banging his fist on the table.[23]

Among the colossal blunders of the moribund autocracy was the decision, in September, 1915, that Emperor Nicholas should himself assume supreme command in place of his father's cousin, Grand Duke Nicholas Nicholaevich. The step was energetically protested by the devoted Rodzianko, by the empress dowager, and by many others; eight of the ablest ministers tendered their collective resignation. The harm lay not only in the fact that the military position did not improve, save on the Caucasus front, to which the grand duke had been transferred. At Headquarters the emperor was almost completely isolated from any competent civilian advice. Direction of the state was more than ever concentrated in the hands of the empress, who began to be called, however unjustly, "the German." The countervailing influence of the "chatterbox," "that fat Rodzianko," was reduced to a minimum, and only the thought that all ills were assignable to the "dark" influence of Rasputin consoled those who strove to maintain their faith in autocracy.

By the end of 1916 the most extreme reactionaries were reduced to despair. On December 2, Purishkevich, a Duma deputy associated with the notorious "Black Hundreds," launched in the Duma a long, vitriolic attack on Rasputin, concluding with a ringing demand that the ministers "overcome their cowardice and use their access to Headquarters to plead with the Sovereign to deliver Russia from this filthy, vicious, and venal peasant." He was startled by the number of congratulations he received from "an infinite number of people . . . known and unknown." [24] Among those who congratulated him was a Prince Yusupov, well-known as a wealthy art connoisseur, closely connected with the ruler by marriage. Yusupov, however, emphasized the futility of such an appeal. The upshot was that Purishkevich, Yusupov, a Grand Duke, and a few other extreme monarchists prepared a careful plan. On the night of December 29, Rasputin accepted an invitation to Prince Yusupov's home to meet his wife. The prince greeted Rasputin cordially and left him in an apartment liberally provided with poisoned wine and poisoned cakes. On his return, Yusupov was dumbfounded to find Rasputin still greedily consuming the refreshments, without visible effect. A shot from Yusupov's revolver brought the victim to all fours, but he managed to scrabble up the stairs and, despite severe clubbing by the conspirators, to escape into the courtyard. There more shots brought inquiring policemen, who were quieted by being told that a dog was being shot. The supposed corpse was hastily bundled over the parapet of one of the Neva bridges; an autopsy is said to have found water in the lungs. By reason of their own high station and of widespread sympathy for their act in influential circles, the murderers escaped serious punishment.

Rasputin had been "removed," but all went on as before. The disappearance of the scapegoat merely forced criticism to focus on the emperor himself, or at least on the empress. For the remaining two and a half months of the tsarist regime, the possibility of assassinating the empress or of incarcerating her in a convent, and perhaps even of deposing the emperor himself, in order to save the monarchy, was bruited in the salons of the capital and even at the tables of the generals at Headquarters. One of the most determined fighting generals, Krymov, later distinguished by his energetic hostility to the socialist revolution, met, in January, 1917, with a group of Duma deputies at Rodzianko's apartment in Petrograd. "The spirit of the army," said Krymov, "is such that the news of a *coup d'état* would be welcomed with joy. A revolution is imminent, and we at the front feel it to be so. If you decide on such an extreme step, we will support you." Dr. Shingarev, a Cadet deputy, exclaimed: "The General is right. . . . But who will have the courage to undertake it?" [25] To Rodzianko's dismay, other deputies chimed in with vigorous words, but it was clear that the civilians hoped the generals would take the initiative. Such an Alphonse-and-Gaston situation, in which the military and the civilians each offered the other the honor of initiating the palace revolution, could of course lead to nothing. Revolution was indeed close at hand, but it was to come not through the conscious planning of any individuals or groups but by spontaneous action and reaction.

The initial impetus came neither from professional revolutionaries nor from malcontent patriots, nor yet from workers or soldiers, but from women and boys, who, after standing in long lines before the bakeshops on March 8, 1917, were told there was no bread. Largely unbelieving, and suspecting hoarding for speculative profit, they became disorderly. When the police intervened, the cry of "bread" was naturally supplemented with the cry of "Down with the police," which, reverberating throughout the city, grew into the cry of "Down with the autocracy," "Down with the war." On succeeding days, rioting multiplied under the triple slogan of "Bread, Peace, and Freedom." The bread riots evoked sympathetic response from overdriven factory workers. Strikes spread rapidly. Some employers responded with lockouts, but the more usual result was that factory managements abandoned their property. Disorders so elemental, so unorganized, by unarmed mobs, could doubtless have been suppressed with ease, had the Petrograd garrison consisted of well-disciplined troops of pre-war caliber. Actually, despite the renowned historic names of some of the regiments, the garrison consisted only of training cadres, which had not yet been reduced by incessant drill in the manual of arms and in barrack-square evolutions to the level of semi-automatons. When ordered to fire on the mobs, such raw troops were still capable of hesitation, of reflecting whether they should shoot down fellow-Russians, who, after all, were asking only for bread and peace, the desirability of which was quite comprehensible to any human being.

In streets where the soldiers fired into the crowd, as most of them did in the first days, the mass of survivors fled down side streets; but in those cases in which hesitant soldiers fumbled with the bolts of their rifles or fired into the air, the crowds rushed forward, embraced the soldiers, and the process—somewhat erroneously called "fraternization"—absorbed the troops into the riotous mob. News of such incidents spread by the military grapevine, and more and more of the soldiers became infected by a holiday mood, scarcely affected by ideological considerations. Efforts to recall the disobedient units to their barracks and to have them disarmed by more sober-minded forces were of little avail. Relaxation of discipline grew like a snowball, and the authorities soon found themselves without any reliable forces. By March 12, it was clear that the Revolution had taken place. Even the Cossacks made common cause with their fellow-conscripts in gray. The police, a professional, mercenary, and therefore more reliable force, were joyously slaughtered by the troops who had joined the rioters. Without obedient armed forces, the discredited government was utterly powerless.

NOTES

1. Shakespeare, *King John,* Act V, Scene 7.
2. *Krasnaia Nov,* VI: Nov.-Dec. 1922, 197; for a nearly complete translation, see Golder, *Documents of Russian History, 1914-1917,* pp. 3-23.
3. *Gosudarstvennaia Duma . . . Stenograficheskie otchety, 1914 g.,* July 26 [August 8], pp. 18-25 *passim.*
4. London *Times,* September 18, 1914, p. 9.
5. Lenin, "The Tasks of Revolutionary Social-Democracy in the European War," No. 6, in *Sochineniia,* 3rd edition, XVIII, 46.
6. *"Perepiska V. A. Sukhomlinova s N. N. Yanushkevichem,"* in *Krasnyi Arkhiv,* I, 215-262; II, 130-174; III, 29-74 *passim.*
7. Paléologue, *La Russie des tsars . . . ,* I, 361; II, 25.
8. Yakovlev, *Razlozhenie armii v 1917 gody,* pp. 1-5.
9. Yakhontov, "Notes on meetings of the Council of Ministers," in *Arkhiv russkoi revoliutsii,* XVIII, 38, 37.
10. Rodzianko, *Reign of Rasputin,* p. 206.
11. Golder, *Documents of Russian History, 1914-1917,* pp. 223-224.
12. Yakhontov, *loc. cit.,* p. 66.
13. Wolfe, *Three Who Made a Revolution,* p. 563.
14. Lenin, "On evaluation of the slogan 'Peace,' " in *Sochineniia,* 3rd edition, XVIII, 225.
15. Golder, *op. cit.,* p. 134; for full text, cf. pp. 134-136.
16. Yakhontov, *loc. cit.,* pp. 107-136 *passim.*
17. Grave, *"Burzhuaziia nakanune fevral'skoi revoliutsii,"* pp. 62-63, in *Tysiacha deviat'sot semnadtsatyi god . . . ,* No. 6.
18. Shulgin, *Dni,* pp. 113-114.
19. *Ibid.,* p. 67.
20. Rodzianko, *op. cit.,* p. 120.
21. Golder, *op. cit.,* p. 149; for full text, cf. pp. 146-149.
22. Chernov, *Great Russian Revolution,* p. 65.
23. Shulgin, *op. cit.,* p. 127.
24. Purishkevich, *Comment j'ai tué Raspoutine,* pp. 39, 43.
25. Rodzianko, *op. cit.,* pp. 244-245.

SUGGESTIONS FOR FURTHER READING

Golder's *Documents of Russian History, 1914-1917* is of exceptional value, though a work to be consulted rather than read. Chernov's *Great Russian Revolution* provides a penetrating introductory analysis from the standpoint of a revolutionary intellectual who played a significant, if not helpful, role in the Revolution. For the contemporary reactions of Lenin in exile, see his *Imperialist War* (Vols. XVIII and XIX of the English translation of his *Collected Works,* revised edition).

Most of the monographs in the Carnegie series on *Economic and Social History of the War* are well worth examination. Rodzianko's *Reign of Rasputin* is the memoirs of the president of the Duma, loyally trying to serve the emperor and yet to save Russia.

A helpful study of Russia's diplomatic position in the Balkans is Thaden's *Russia and the Balkan Alliance of 1912*. Sazonov's *Fateful Years*, Izvolsky's *Recollections of a Foreign Minister*, Buchanan's *My Mission to Russia*, and Paléologue's *An Ambassador's Memoirs* deal principally with diplomatic aspects from the standpoint of leading participants; C. J. Smith, *The Russian Struggle for Power, 1914-1917*, is a study of tsarist diplomacy during the war.

On the military side, see General Brusilov's *Mémoires* and especially General Golovin's *The Russian Army in the World War*.

Cherniavsky's *Prologue to Revolution* is a translation of Yakhontov's revealing notes on the meetings of the Council of Ministers during August, 1915. Katkov's *Russia 1917: The February Revolution* contains an account of Russian society during the war, although a doubtful importance is attributed to German subversion.

Chapter

24

Revolution: March to June, 1917

Rarely has history witnessed such a sudden and total collapse of power as occurred in those March days of 1917. Even to the Duma intellectuals, the immensity of what was happening was none too clear. The Progressive Bloc had since 1915 been pressing hard for concessions that would, it thought, save the regime by taking the Duma into real partnership with the ruler. It had never willed overthrow of the monarchy. Its most insistent demand had been for the appointment of a "ministry of confidence," to be headed by the president of the Duma, Rodzianko, and to include, along with Cadet and Octobrist leaders such as Miliukov and Guchkov, the most honest of the old conservative bureaucrats, such as Krivoshein, General Polivanov, and Count Ignatiev. The Bloc had not requested formal recognition of the principle of ministerial responsibility.

THE DUMA AND THE SOVIET

In the midst of the rioting in Petrograd, it was stunned by an Imperial edict proroguing the Duma (March 11). News of the edict, released by the prime minister on March 12, swung the rioters and the defecting troops of the garrison into a mood suggestive of that of the Paris mob of 1789, when it had tumultuously rallied to the cause of the National Assembly. On March 12, 1917, tens of thousands of unorganized and leaderless people—workers, soldiers, housewives—swarmed to the Tauride Palace to hail the Duma. Their support was no more welcome than that of the rioters who had stormed the Bastille or carried out the march to Versailles. Shulgin, one of the most articulate and conservative members of the Progressive Bloc, recorded his impressions in his diary:

> The endless, inexhaustible current of the human flood poured into the Duma [building] ever new faces. . . . But no matter how many there were, they all had the one face: villainous, brutish, stupid . . . God, how ugly it was! So ugly that, clenching my teeth, I felt within myself a melancholy, helpless, and therefore all the more spiteful rage. Machine guns! Machine guns, that's what I wanted. For I felt that only the tongues of machine guns could be understood by the street rabble and that only lead could drive back into its lair the terrible beast that was escaping. Alas, this beast was His Majesty the Russian people. What we had so dreaded, what we had wanted to avoid at all costs, was already a fact. The revolution had begun.[1]

Rodzianko had assembled in his office the leaders of all the fractions in the Duma. They decided loyally to obey the order of prorogation. A meeting of members of the Duma was convened; to emphasize that this gathering was only an "informal conference," not a meeting of the Duma, it was not held in the usual hall. In the confusion, all that could be done was to agree to the formation of a "Provisional Committee" of Duma members, on which Kerensky, leader of the Trudoviks, and Chkheidze, leader of the Mensheviks, were invited to serve along with the leaders of the Progressive Bloc.* Rodzianko, its chairman, bombarded Headquarters with telegraphic appeals that the emperor immediately appoint the long-craved "ministry of confidence." For the rest, he and his colleagues wore themselves out in efforts to greet the street crowds in the name of "Holy Mother Russia" and to achieve at least some semblance of a return to order.

The situation was very much complicated by the simultaneous formation

*The reader is cautioned to distinguish carefully between

(1) The *Provisional Committee* of the Duma (set up March 12);
(2) The *Provisional Governments:*
  (a) headed by Prince Lvov (March 15-May 18)
  (b) the coalition with the Soviet also headed by Lvov (May 18-July 20)
  (c) the several successive governments headed by Kerensky (July 20-Nov. 7);
(3) The *Executive Committee* of the Petrograd Soviet of Workers' and Soldiers' Deputies (March 12 to the Bolshevik seizure of power);
(4) The *Central Executive Committee* of the (First) All-Russian Congress of Soviets of Workers' and Soldiers' Deputies (set up in June);
(5) The Executive Committee of the All-Russian Soviets of Peasants' Deputies set up in May (which generally acted jointly with the Central Executive Committee);
(6) The *Central Committee* of the Bolshevik Party;
(7) and other bodies with confusingly similar names occasionally mentioned in the text.

The terms in italics have generally been used as short titles, sometimes prefaced with Duma, Soviet, or Party, where greater clarity seems to be indicated. Where not otherwise indicated "Soviet" means the Petrograd Soviet until June, and the All-Russian Congress of Soviets thereafter.

of another potential power center. This was the Petrograd Soviet of Workers' Deputies, speedily restyled Soviet of Workers' and Soldiers' Deputies. Yet it would be quite wrong to think of the Duma Committee and the Soviet as rival aspirants for power. Neither had the slightest intention of forming a revolutionary government. The socialist leadership in Russia was as much taken by surprise and as devoid of ideas how to cope with the fact of revolution as was the liberal leadership of the "bourgeois" parties. This was not merely due to the fact that none of the outstanding leaders of the socialists, whether Social Democrats or Socialist Revolutionaries, were on the spot. The first-string socialists, even less in touch with developing realities, were no less caught unprepared. The actual course of events simply did not coincide with the preconceived ideas of any of the schools of professional revolutionists.

Just as the rioting crowds, the striking workers, and the mutinous soldiers had acted without premeditation and without guidance, so the Soviet began to be elected, as early as March 9, by blindly spontaneous action of factory workers who remembered the days of 1905 but did not even know where the delegates they were acclaiming were to meet. It was only on March 12 that the members of the Workers' Group of the War Industry Committee, released from arrest by mob action, met in the Tauride Palace with socialist members of the Duma and organized a "Provisional Executive Committee of the Soviet of Workers' Deputies." This body took measures to organize the food supply and established a sort of revolutionary general staff to control the holiday-making soldiery. It also immediately issued a proclamation addressed "to the citizens":

> Meeting in the State Duma, representatives of the workers, soldiers, and inhabitants of Petrograd announce that the first meeting of their representatives will be held at 7 o'clock tonight in the premises of the State Duma. All the troops that have gone over to the side of the people are immediately to elect their representatives, one for each company. The factories are immediately to elect their deputies, one for each thousand. Factories with less than a thousand workers will elect one deputy each.[2]

The resultant mass meeting that jammed into the Tauride Palace, crowding the Duma members out into committee rooms, unquestionably better reflected public sentiment than did the Duma members. Yet the method of election had not been systematic; the deputies were hastily named by acclamation or, at best, by show of hands in response to a shouted nomination. It was impossible to check the credentials of those in attendance, who soon numbered nearly three thousand; the organizers of the Soviet had no list of the factories and military units entitled to membership. It was even recognized that some men were entitled to membership merely on the strength of their records and organizational connections. The absence of a well-developed trade-union organization, the consequent lack of well-known labor leaders, the preponderance of ignorant peasant-soldiers, the necessary secrecy and pseudonyms that shrouded the identity of members of the relatively tiny socialist parties—all contributed to the difficulty of finding appropriate leadership for the Soviet.

It was no accident that Duma deputies, whose names had become familiar as spokesmen of opposition, should play the leading role in the Petrograd Soviet. The only organized groups representing the masses in the Duma were the Mensheviks and the Trudoviks; the Bolshevik deputies had been sent to Siberia in 1915, and the Socialist Revolutionaries had boycotted the election in 1912. Consequently, the Georgian Chkheidze, leader of the Mensheviks in the Duma, was installed as president of the Soviet; as vice-presidents were chosen Skobelev, another Duma Menshevik, and Kerensky, leader of the Trudoviks. The latter now announced that he was actually a Socialist Revolutionary, an assertion which, to the later regret of the old party leadership, was not repudiated. A large Executive Committee, composed of persons imbued with the most diverse ideologies, was also chosen. The Soviet itself could not possibly initiate anything; it remained a huge sounding board, receiving reports of the action of its Executive Committee and ratifying them with varying degrees of enthusiasm.

From March 12 to March 15 there was a sort of vacuum of power. Nominally, the autocracy still existed; actually, it had no functioning agencies in the capital. The Duma existed only in the form of the unofficial Provisional Committee, still hoping that the emperor would vest with authority a ministry of confidence. The Petrograd Soviet, or its Executive Committee, was, by virtue of its psychological influence over the masses, in truth the government; yet it refrained from openly assuming power.

On March 14 the Soviet issued to the Petrograd garrison the widely misunderstood Order No. 1, which provided (#6) that "In formation and in discharge of service obligations soldiers must observe the strictest military discipline." [3] The order, however, permitted complete relaxation of discipline when the soldiers were off duty, emphasized the right of the soldier to participate in elections to the Soviet and to army committees, and forbade the surrender of weapons to officers. This last point, startling as it seems, was even more emphatically incorporated in a simultaneous order by the military commission of the Provisional Government set up by the Duma members. As soon as it became clear that some soldiers were interpreting Order No. 1 as meaning that they could elect their own officers, the Soviet issued a clarifying Order No. 2, making it plain that the political rights of a soldier as a citizen did not alter the authority of his military superiors over him as a soldier.

The damage to military morale often attributed to Order No. 1 in reality had already been done by the fact of revolution, which had opened wide the gulf between the old officer caste and the bulk of the revolutionary army. Shulgin tells a pointed story of how he was approached in the crowded corridors of the Tauride Palace by a soldier who asked if there were "any good ones" here. To Shulgin's proffer of cigarettes the soldier indignantly explained that he meant officers, adding that his regiment had officers but that they were no good. Among the first duties of the Provisional Committee was the task of dissuading regiments from shooting their officers. For its part, the high command of the army, though quite willing to accept the downfall of an inept autocrat, bowed to the revolution only in the hope that it would facilitate the task of defeating the enemy. Fearful of the consequences of relaxing the harsh discipline to which they were accustomed, the generals perhaps unnecessarily alienated the rank and file by frequently rejecting reasonable requests simply because they were made by subordinates.

It was very difficult for most men to adjust to the new conditions of life and to act decisively in unaccustomed ways. Shulgin's recollections of those confused days serve to illuminate the situation. He pictures most of the Duma men, himself included, wandering around picking up rumors, watching the mob thronging through the Tauride Palace, or holding endless futile discussions in committee rooms. In striking contrast is his story of what happened to Shcheglovitov, the first of the tsar's former ministers to be dragged to the Duma by a threatening mob, of how Kerensky pushed his way through the crowd, announced that Shcheglovitov was under arrest, adding loudly, "The Duma does not shed blood." Similar is his story of how Protopopov, Minister of the Interior and perhaps the most hated of all Rasputin's creatures, came in panic to surrender himself to the Duma; it was Kerensky who, commandeering the services of two soldiers with fixed bayonets and repeating with emphasis, "Do not dare touch this man," escorted the quaking Protopopov through the midst of the milling, hostile crowd to safety in a committee room. In similar vein is Shulgin's story of how Kerensky, accompanied by two soldiers bearing a bundle of papers, interrupted a committee meeting of his colleagues; dismissing the soldiers, he announced that the papers were the secret treaties with the Allies, which their fearful custodian had turned over to him. Leaving his irritated and dumbfounded colleagues to put the precious documents in the only place of safekeeping they could think of—under the cloth-draped committee table—he soon returned to add to the cache two million rubles he had found in some government office.

Thus early in the Revolution, the young Kerensky, a man of tremendous physical energy and an impassioned orator, began to move into the limelight. While others mourned and conspired, Kerensky manifested a bustling activity, though to what end no one knew. "He grew on the mud of the Revolution," sourly noted Shulgin, "mud on which he was already accustomed to run and jump when we did not even know how to walk." [4]

At the moment, however, Kerensky was not a phenomenon of primary importance. The chief question of the moment concerned the relationship between the Duma Provisional Committee and the Executive Committee of the Petrograd Soviet. In Kerensky's own phrase, he, although a member of both, "took no part whatever in these academic, dogmatic discussions. I was entirely taken up by the whirlwind of revolution."[5] It was Miliukov, who had amply proved his capacity, if not as a statesman, at least as a politician, who played the chief role in hammering out an agreement.

PARTY ATTITUDES

The leaders of the Progressive Bloc, now organized as the Provisional Committee, were loath to abandon hope that the emperor could still be persuaded to legalize the overturn by appointing a ministry of confidence, which might yet enable them to still the commotion and canalize the revolution into the course they had always wished for. The emperor, however, remained obdurate; on March 12 he had set in motion a picked force, which on the fourteenth reached the suburban palace-town of Tsarskoye Selo, only to melt away in peaceful contact with the mutinous garrison. The emperor himself left Headquarters by train to join his wife and children at Tsarskoye Selo, but was forcibly diverted to Pskov, headquarters of the Northern Front. There, on March 14, he reluctantly agreed to appoint Rodzianko prime minister; the latter, however, advised the generals by telephone that it was already too late. On the morning of the fifteenth, after telegraphic consultation of the generals commanding the various fronts, the stunned emperor was persuaded to abdicate in favor of his son. Unaware of this, Guchkov and Shulgin had set out for Pskov; on their arrival, they were shocked at the passivity with which Nicholas II confirmed his abdication, substituting his brother Michael as his successor. They had no trouble in securing his signature, predated, to the appointment of the ministers they proposed. The list was headed by Prince George E. Lvov, an ardent zemstvo worker whose party affiliation had shifted from the Cadets closer to the Octobrists.

It was all in vain. On their return to Petrograd, the delegates were roughly received by hostile crowds. The following morning (March 16), Grand Duke Michael, on being bluntly informed by Rodzianko that his personal safety could not be guaranteed, declined to assume the crown unless it were tendered him by the promised Constituent Assembly. Nor was it deemed prudent for the Provisional Committee of the Duma to flaunt the emperor's consent to the appointment of Prince Lvov as prime minister. Legal continuity of the executive authority had come to seem less important than forestalling assumption of the reins by the "scoundrels" in the Soviet. The Provisional Government established at Petrograd on March 15 with Lvov at its head thus represented, to its own regret, a revolutionary break with traditional authority.

The fear that the "scoundrels" would wish to set up a revolutionary government of their own was as baseless as the hope that the Provisional Government established by the Provisional Committee of the Duma could carry out the policies of the Progressive Bloc. The theory of soviet government, as formalized by the Bolsheviks after their seizure of power in November, was no part of the thinking of the original Petrograd Soviet. Its purposes were negative rather than consciously positive; it simply sprang into existence to defend the cause of revolution, whatever that might prove to mean. It was based on no previous organizational experience on the part of the masses and was therefore constrained to follow the lead of the small socialist intelligentsia.

Yet the socialists were hopelessly divided among themselves. The leading role was initially played by the Mensheviks. Their whole theory was based on the Marxist concept that proletarian-socialist revolution must be preceded by bourgeois-democratic revolution. Until the victory of the liberal bourgeoisie over the autocracy was complete, it was the duty of socialists to abstain from taking power. The Bolsheviks, as professed Marxists, shared this basic view, though Lenin had been developing a corrective idea: since the Russian bourgeoisie was not itself democratic, in Russia the bourgeois-democratic revolution could be accomplished only by an alliance between the working class and the peasantry; admittedly, the proletarian-peasant dictatorship could not even attempt to achieve socialism until it had completed the bourgeois-democratic revolution. The Mensheviks retorted that to proclaim the dictatorship of the proletariat at a stage when only liberal and democratic reforms could be achieved, when there was as yet no possibility of a transition to socialism, could bring only stultification and frustration of the masses.

At this time, the Bolsheviks had no clear-cut policy to offer. During the interregnum, on March 13, *Pravda* had urged the workers and soldiers to "elect representatives to a Provisional Revolutionary Government," but the appeal was ignored by the Soviet. After the return from Siberia (March 25) of Kamenev and Stalin, who promptly took over the direction of Bolshevik tactics, the Bolsheviks on the spot drew closer to the Mensheviks. In *Pravda* (March 28), Kamenev attacked the "empty" slogan of "Down with the War," while Stalin apparently worked for organizational unity with the Mensheviks. On April 9, he told his colleagues that "the Provisional Government has in fact undertaken to entrench the conquests of the revolutionary people," adding that "it is not advantageous for us to force events and thus hasten the secession of the bourgeois strata, which later must inevitably break with us." [6]

The Socialist Revolutionaries, unhampered by commitment to Marxist dogma, could not rationalize their desire to avoid taking power on the same grounds as did the Social Democrats. The SR's had always rejected the concept of a "bourgeois" revolution to be followed by a "proletarian" one. They argued in terms of a transitional period of "labor democracy," during which, without the aid of government edicts, the socialist mode of production would in free competition with individualist economy prove its superiority and peacefully emerge triumphant.

There were also sharp differences of opinion, which cut across socio-economic ideologies, on the question of the proper attitude toward the war. The great majority of socialists rejected the notion of turning foreign war into civil war. The main argument was whether, since victory over the foreign aggressor was of paramount importance, the war must take precedence over class and party struggles (the "defensist" position) or whether it was first necessary to effect a change in war aims in the interest of a "democratic" peace (the "revolutionary defensist" position).

To the confusion of purposes there was added the obvious fact that the socialist intelligentsia, adept at underground activity and at formulation of hairsplitting theoretical programs, had absolutely no experience in the practical handling of administrative tasks. The "bourgeois" leaders had had considerable experience, through practical work in the Duma and its commissions, as well as through direction of zemstvos and city dumas. The socialists had spent too much of their time in prison, in Siberia, or in exile, troubled mainly with the problems of their own private affairs; their parliamentary activity had been confined to irresponsible denunciation of the autocracy and of capitalism, without the need to work out practicable solutions for day-to-day problems. In addition, they now found themselves swamped with a flood of new recruits, inspired by revolutionary enthusiasm but difficult for the old party leadership to control and educate.

Only on the surface was Soviet abstention from taking power motivated by doctrinal considerations. At bottom there was the sheer realization of the inadequacy of their preparation for the immense task of guiding the revolutionary monster. The Soviet therefore adopted the attitude that the task of government belonged to the "bourgeois." The role reserved for the Soviet was to exert pressure on the Provisional Government to guarantee that it would pursue a democratic course. The bourgeoisie must not, however, be alienated, lest it throw itself into the arms of whatever reactionary forces might still survive. Consequently, the Soviet did not raise demands for socialization of industry or for transfer of privately owned land to the peasants. It did advance the idea of a "democratic" peace without annexations or indemnities and with self-determination for all peoples, but it did not press for immediate forthright clearing of the air with Russia's allies, much less for a separate peace. It confined itself in the main to insistence on the grant of civil liberties and accepted the idea that all other major questions should be determined by a Constituent Assembly, to be elected as soon as possible by universal, direct, equal, and secret suffrage. In the meantime, the Soviet, at least by implication, took the position that the Provisional Government was to carry out the legislative wishes of the Soviet, as though it were a cabinet responsible to the Soviet. Yet the Soviet refused point-blank to interest itself in the personnel of the Provisional Government, beyond refusing to send representatives into it. In this contradictory attitude lurked the seeds of that "paralysis from without" that plagued the first Provisional Government.

THE PROVISIONAL GOVERNMENT AND THE SOVIET

On this basis, the Petrograd Soviet on March 15 ratified the agreement between its Executive Committee and the Provisional Committee of the Duma. The points stipulated by the Soviet were: (1) amnesty; (2) freedom of speech, press, assembly, association, and strikes; (3) subjection of the soldier to "strict military discipline" while on duty, with preservation of all the rights of other citizens when off duty; (4) a citizen militia subject to democratically elected local authorities; (5) abolition of class, nationality, and religious restrictions; (6) guarantee of non-interference with the Petrograd garrison. The question of republic or monarchy was specifically reserved for the Constituent Assembly. The Soviet announced that

> we propose that, to the extent that the nascent authority takes action toward realizing these duties and decisively fighting against the old authority, the democracy must lend it its support.[7]

A curious addendum added by the general meeting required that the Manifesto of the Provisional Government be signed, not only by its members but also by Rodzianko, president of the Duma and chairman of the Provisional Committee.

The Lvov government, installed in the Mariinsky Palace, loyally lived up to these terms. It was made up almost entirely of Cadets and Octobrists; its two strongest men were Miliukov, Minister of Foreign Affairs, and Guchkov, Minister of War. Minor posts had been offered to Chkheidze and Kerensky; Chkheidze, obeying the Soviet, declined, but Kerensky accepted the office of Minister of Justice. His explanation to the Soviet that he would be its "eye," watching the ministers without committing the Soviet, was applauded but not endorsed; however, he was not deprived of his vice-presidency.

The regime has often been characterized as the "dual power." It would be more accurate to say that this was the period of soviet rule in Russia, for the Provisional Government had no independent means of enforcing its decrees. Workers and soldiers habitually checked every order of the ministers to be sure the Petrograd Soviet approved. Ultimately Guchkov, physically exhausted and nervously worn out by the necessity of constant speechmaking to secure compliance with the simplest directions, quit his office in disgust. All sorts of people brought their personal problems to the Soviet rather than to the ministries; even the banks applied to the Soviet rather than to the Provisional Government for permission to reopen (March 16). Only under pressure of the Soviet did the Provisional Government order (March 20) arrest of Nicholas II and his immediate family, who were to be detained at Tsarskoye Selo; a commissar of the Soviet was to assist in guarding them, and any further arrangements for their safekeeping were to be undertaken only with the consent of the Soviet. Similarly, Soviet insistence forced Prince Lvov

(March 25) to relieve Grand Duke Nicholas Nicholaevich of his post as Commander-in-Chief, to which he had been elevated at the time of the emperor's abdication. As Sukhanov, a left-wing Social Democrat, recalled, "We had to . . . take over various functions of 'administration,' while creating and maintaining the fiction that the Mariinsky Palace was 'governing.' "[8]

Nor was this true only in the capital. The Petrograd Soviet had only a local basis; the Provisional Government theoretically governed the whole empire. Yet it was to the Petrograd Soviet that other soviets of workers' and soldiers' deputies, speedily elected all over the country and in the army, looked for leadership. On April 11, an All-Russian Conference of Soviets was opened at Petrograd; by 325 votes to 57, with 20 abstentions, it endorsed the "revolutionary defensist" position on the war of the Menshevik leader, Tsereteli, against Kamenev's call for international revolution. Not until June was provision made for more formal participation of other soviets by convening the First All-Russian Congress of Soviets of Workers' and Soldiers' Deputies. Organization of the peasants remained separate, though an All-Russian Congress of Peasants' Deputies assembled at Petrograd in May.

Occasionally, as at the naval base of Kronstadt, at the industrial town of Tsaritsyn (later famous as Stalingrad) on the lower Volga, or at the textile center of Ivanovo-Voznesensk near Moscow, local soviets asserted their total supremacy. Even where they nominally accepted the authority of the Provisional Government, the soviets almost always were the real center of power. The Provisional Government, for its part, took no steps toward creating a new system of local government, either by attempting to set up a centralized network of revolutionary commissars or by developing new, democratically elected, autonomous organs. Absorbed by the immensity of its own problems and lulled by the flood of congratulatory messages from the provinces, it left matters there to take their course. Prince Lvov simply replaced the tsarist governors with the zemstvo presidents, leaving them to act according to their best judgment.

Equally serious was the failure of the Provisional Government to take account of nationalist aspirations. In the case of Poland, wholly occupied by the Germans, Russia's new rulers promptly conceded independence; at the same time, in Pan-Slav spirit, they made it clear that they expected Poland to accept a binding military alliance against the Teutons. The Finnish constitution was restored, but without recognition of Finland's right to independence. Other subject nationalities, not then significant from the military point of view, were not encouraged in their aspirations, even for limited cultural autonomy. The natural consequence was increased restlessness, with rapidly mounting demands.

The leading part was of course played by the largest of the ethnic minorities, the "Little Russians," who preferred to be known as Ukrainians. At Kiev, the initial reaction to the revolution had been the formation of organizations similar to those of the capital. Soon, however, Ukrainian intellectuals formed a rival organization, which took the historic name of "Rada." Within a month, the Rada had rallied the support of the rural Ukrainian masses and, under the presidency of the historian Hrushevski, was putting forward demands for "a free Ukraine in a free Russia." The Rada's concept of autonomy included a separate Constituent Assembly for the Ukraine and, so far as practicable without disorganizing the front, formation of a separate Ukrainian army. Although the Ukrainians showed no signs of desire to break away from a Russia reconstituted on federal lines, the reaction of the Great Russian minority in the Ukraine, sparked by the local Bolsheviks, was extremely hostile to them. For Petrograd, however, despite increasing friction, the question did not become acute until July.

The one field in which the Provisional Government acted with some energy was in the implementation of civil liberties. This point had been the chief common denominator of the Duma members who had sponsored the government and it had been the core of the agreement under which the Petrograd Soviet had initially endorsed the new ministry. A sweeping amnesty was immediately granted; a swarm of revolutionaries of all hues came from prison, from Siberia, and from abroad, with little or no gratitude toward the Provisional Government which had authorized their return. Amidst nearly universal rejoicing, the death penalty was abolished (March 25); courts-martial also were done away with (March 26) except at the front, and even there the judges were to include private soldiers. On April 2, "all legal limitations on the rights of Russian citizens, based on faith or nationality," were terminated by government decree.[9] It was with justice that Lenin, immediately on his return from Switzerland (April 16), conceded that "Russia is now the freest of all the belligerent countries of the world." [10]

In other respects, however, it was the Petrograd Soviet, not the Provisional Government, that effected such reforms as were made. As early as March 18, the Soviet called for cessation of all strikes, and most workers returned to the factories the next day. It was the Soviet that stabilized the situation by effecting an agreement with the Petrograd Manufacturers' Association (March 23), which established in the capital an eight-hour day with extra pay for overtime. Attempts of some generals to set the soldiers against the "loafing" workers had little success, and only briefly. The agreement provided also that factory committees, elected without reference to the craft restrictions imposed by the law of 1906, should be recognized as the representatives of the workers in dealings either with the employers or with governmental authorities. The Provisional Government, on its general principle that all disputable questions should be left for decision to the forthcoming Constituent Assembly, took no steps to make the eight-hour day general. In Moscow, the local soviet, finding the employers obstinate, decreed the reform (March 31) on its own authority. In other cities, the eight-hour day was introduced either in the Petrograd or in the Moscow method.

The Petrograd agreement, though not legally sanctioned, was a great gain for the industrial workers, but it could not long satisfy them. Wage rates rose sharply, but galloping inflation prevented a corresponding rise in real wages. Substitution of time rates for piecework, slackening of labor discipline, and the tendency of workers to interrupt work for all sorts of meetings resulted in a great decline in productivity. Shortage of materials and of fuel, aggravated by the spreading breakdown of transportation, added to the human difficulties. Some employers, also, evinced a tendency to close down their plants rather than give in to the demands of their employees. Even during the revolutionary honeymoon, strikes did not cease. The efforts of the Soviet to restrain the workers played into the hands of irresponsible agitators. The mushrooming trade unions tended to coöperate with the Menshevik leadership, but the factory committees, in closer touch with the excited workers and not burdened with over-all responsibilities, like the shop stewards in wartime Britain began to drift ever further leftward.

The problem which Russian revolutionaries had always linked most closely with the demand for freedom—the land—initially caused little trouble and received correspondingly scant attention. Too many of the able-bodied males were in the army, not in the villages, which for some time remained almost completely quiet. Here and there local organizations were set up to arrest a few particularly obnoxious officials, but with hardly any manifestation of bitterness toward noble landowners. Though they might help themselves to privately owned land, the peasants were disposed to be generous in allocating land for personal cultivation by former landholders.

The record of the original negotiations between the Petrograd Soviet and the Duma Provisional Committee includes no mention of the land. Even the Socialist Revolutionaries, in a manifesto pledging conditional support to the Provisional Government (March 15), had made only passing reference to the desirability of organizing peasant unions and of preparing for the Constituent Assembly. The problem was the more easily ignored because men such as Rodzianko solemnly pledged (March 28) that "if the Constituent Assembly should decide that the land should go to all the people, it will be carried out without opposition." [11] On April 8, a meeting of the Peasants' Union, "in which three thousand citizens, peasants, and soldiers participated," expressed its support for continuance of "the war for freedom" on the Soviet basis of no annexations, no indemnities, and the right of self-determination, and it also indicated its preference for "a democratic republic" in Russia. Though the Peasants' Union was more conservative than the peasant soviets which later assumed leadership, its resolution avowed its belief "that the land should be handed over to the toiling people, and that everyone who cultivates the soil with his own hands has the right to the use of it"; in conclusion it recommended that "the landholders immediately be given the possibility of sowing the empty fields, no matter to whom they belong." [12]

The Provisional Government took as little action as possible. On the one hand, fearing famine in the cities, it set up (April 7) a state grain monopoly, to which all surplus grain was to be sold at fixed prices. On the other hand, as agrarian disorders began to increase, it established (May 4) a Main Land Committee, composed partly of appointed members, partly of elected representatives of local land committees, of the Petrograd Soviet and of the Duma Provisional Committee, of peasant soviets and of the Peasants' Union, of the coöperatives and of the several political parties, both socialist and liberal. Its task was to gather information on which legislation might subsequently be based. Shingarev, the Cadet then serving as Minister of Agriculture, issued a series of warnings such as that, in the meantime, "arbitrary [local] action will lead to disaster for the state and will endanger the cause of freedom by provoking discord." [13]

Overshadowing all other problems was one that least of all could wait, the problem of the war. Notwithstanding a considerable amount of demoralization, the front still held, and the rear was still willing to support it. In the soviets, the advocates of continuing the war, whether as "defensists" or as "revolutionary defensists," had an overwhelming majority. Even the Bolsheviks, through Kamenev, took the position (March 28) that:

> Not disorganization of the revolutionary and revolutionizing army and not the empty "Down with the War" is our slogan. Our slogan is pressure on the Provisional Government with the purpose of forcing it openly, before the whole of world democracy, immediately to make an effort to persuade all the countries at war to open negotiations about ways of stopping the world war. Meanwhile everyone remains at his battle station. . . .[14]

This is exactly the spirit in which the Menshevik-led Soviet had already acted. On March 27, it had already broadcast an appeal to "the peoples of the whole world [to] take into their own hands the decision of the question of war and peace"; specifically it called on "our brother-proletarians of the Austro-German coalition [to] throw off the yoke of your semi-autocratic system." [15]

Miliukov, the chief architect of the Provisional Government, had no sympathy with such nonsense. A politician of proven ability, he aspired also to be a statesman. As he later proudly boasted to his party colleagues (May 22), he was determined to realize Russia's historic desire to "secure sovereign rights over the Straits," as promised by the secret treaties of 1915.[16] As Foreign Minister, he was careful to include in his first note to the Allies (March 18) the double-edged assertion that "the Cabinet . . . will remain mindful of the international engagements entered into by the fallen regime and . . . will devote all its energy to bring the war to a victorious conclusion. . . ." [17] Soviet protests induced Prince Lvov to issue (April 9) a reassuring statement that "the Russian people is not working for the increase of its external power at the expense of other nations." [18] An All-Russian Conference of Soviets of Workers' and Soldiers' Deputies, at which for the first time representatives of provincial soviets sat with members of the soviet of the capital, responded approvingly and

> called on all the workers in factories and mills, on the railways, in the mines, and in other enterprises working for the army and for the home front to carry on their work with the utmost intensity. The economic gains of the working class and the striving for further reforms not only must not weaken labor energy but must raise the productivity of labor to the utmost degree in the interests of providing for all the needs of the population and of the army.[19]

In response to anxious inquiries from England and France, Miliukov despatched a new note (May 1), in which, while paying tribute to the consonance between "the general principles enunciated by the Provisional Government" and "the lofty ideas which have been constantly expressed . . . by many eminent statesmen in Allied countries," he reaffirmed that "the Provisional Government, while safeguarding the rights of our country, will fully observe the obligations assumed toward our Allies." [20]

THE MAY CRISIS AND THE COALITION GOVERNMENT

Hostile mass demonstrations and smaller pro-Miliukov demonstrations threatened to clash bloodily in the streets. General Kornilov, whose appointment to command the Petrograd military district had been one of the last acts of Emperor Nicholas II and who, according to General Denikin, at this time advocated "a rigorous clean-up of Petrograd," [21] brought out artillery. Only the vigorous intervention of the Executive Committee of the Soviet, which urgently ordered all troops off the streets, avoided an outbreak (May 4). The Provisional Government hastened to assume collective responsibility for the Miliukov note of May 1 while explaining away its significance.

Hopelessly weakened and resenting the way in which the Soviet Executive Committee, by its unauthorized action, had again proved itself the real government, Lvov's cabinet once more appealed to the Soviet to share formal responsibility (May 11). The first reaction of the Executive Committee, by a vote of 23 to 22, with eight abstentions, was to refuse (May 12). The following day, however, the resignation of the weary Guchkov emphasized the gravity of the crisis. On May 14, in response to an eloquent appeal by Kerensky, the Executive Committee voted, 41-18 with three abstentions, in favor of coalition in principle. Confused negotiations were ended only when Miliukov, who had stubbornly opposed coalition, was told that he must exchange the Foreign Office for the Ministry of Education, more appropriate perhaps for a professor. Announcement of Miliukov's resignation (May 16) opened the way for formation (May 18) of a new Provisional Government. The May crisis was over.

Still headed by Prince Lvov but minus its two strongest figures, the government was increased in size to provide for a substantial minority of socialists. Kerensky moved up to Guchkov's place as Minister of War. Among the new men were: Chernov, the outstanding figure in the Socialist Revolutionary Party, who became Minister of Agriculture; the Menshevik Skobelev, one of the original vice-presidents of the Soviet, who became Minister of Labor; and Tsereteli, a Menshevik returned from Siberia, who, although only Minister of Posts and Telegraphs, became one of the dominant figures. The fact that the socialist members of the new cabinet openly regarded themselves as responsible to the Soviet, while the majority of their colleagues owed their positions to the Duma Provisional Committee, guaranteed continued paralysis of the government, though now from within rather than from without.

The agreed program of the coalition touched, though vaguely, on more questions than had that of its predecessor. It of course committed the government (1) to "peace without annexations, without indemnities, and on the basis of self-determination of peoples." It emphasized (2) the need of "strengthening the beginnings of democratization in our army [and] its fighting strength both for defensive and for offensive operations [as] the most important tasks of the Provisional Government." It promised (3) to "fight economic disruption unflinchingly and decisively" and at the same time (4) to take further measures for "thorough protection of labor." While "leaving to the Constituent Assembly decision of the question of transfer of the land into the hands of the toilers," it proposed (5) in the meantime "to regulate the use of the land in the interests of the national economy and of the toiling population." It advocated (6) fiscal reform by way of "increase of direct taxation of the propertied classes." It promised (7) "democratic organs of self-government" and (8) the speediest possible convocation of a Constituent Assembly. In conclusion, it wistfully declared

> that its fruitful work is possible only on condition of full and unconditional actual implementation of its full power, so necessary for consolidation of the gains of the revolution and for their future development. . . .[22]

The fruits of its work were, however, small, and "the revolutionary people" betrayed rapidly mounting impatience. The new Foreign Minister, Tereshchenko, did politely ask the Allies for a conference "at the earliest moment that conditions become favorable for it" to reconsider their war aims, but was careful to assure them that separate peace was out of the question.[23] Neither England nor France refused, but no definite progress was made. The newly belligerent United States, which had taken the lead in recognizing the first Provisional Government, read Russia friendly but unnecessary lectures on the need to make the world "safe for democracy" by a "partnership of honor in the great struggle for human freedom." [24] To the war-weary Russian masses, hope seemed to center mainly on the International Socialist Congress, to be attended by delegates from all the belligerent countries, which the Petrograd Soviet was trying to organize at neutral Stockholm.

After the abdication of the emperor, the duties of Commander-in-Chief of the armed forces had, despite the protest of Rodzianko, been allowed to devolve on General Alexeiev, former Chief of Staff. Rodzianko was only too well aware that Alexeiev had always resented the attitude of the Duma and "was always of the opinion that the army should give orders to the rear and that the army should give orders to the whole people and that the army should act as if it were itself at the head of the government"; he therefore recommended General Brusilov, who "is the only general who combines brilliant strategic gifts with an understanding of Russia's political problems, and who is capable of quickly evaluating the developing situation." [25] The former energetic War Minister, Guchkov, had retired about a hundred of the most useless generals but had not touched Alexeiev or his new Chief of Staff, General Denikin; Denikin, the able son of a peasant, was later to be the most successful of the "White" generals. Alexeiev, who was to become the first organizer of the "Volunteer Army" against the Bolsheviks, recorded in his diary that he himself always thought of the Soviet of Soldiers' Deputies as the "Soviet of Dogs' Deputies." The new Minister of War, Kerensky, treated both the generals and the army committees elected by the soldiers in more gingerly fashion than had Guchkov. Only after Alexeiev had openly criticized the foreign policy of the coalition did Kerensky venture to replace him with the more amenable Brusilov (June 4).

Encouraged by what seemed signs of better feeling between officers and men, and anxious to give more weight to its negotiations with the Allies for a "democratic" peace, the coalition government ordered an offensive against the Austrians in Galicia (July 1). Demoralization of the army had, however, already gone too far. At the time of the Revolution the troops were already tired by two and a half years of war; the collapse of authority in Petrograd inevitably much increased desertions, cases of refusal of the infantry to allow the artillery to provoke the enemy by firing on him, lynchings of conscientious officers, even instances of fraternization with the Germans. Propaganda to revive the fighting spirit of the men was more vigorous and more intensive than was agitation designed to destroy morale. The newly elected All-Russian Congress of Soviets of Workers' and Soldiers' Deputies and the Executive Committee of the All-Russian Soviets of Peasants' Deputies issued an enthusiastic appeal to the army, including a "call to the country to strain every nerve to help the army." [26] Special shock units, even a Women's Battalion of Death, threw themselves heroically into action, but nothing could compete with the unleashed instinct of survival and with the lure of expropriated land for the peasant recruits in their unfamiliar gray coats. It mattered little whether individual generals won the coöperation of the elected army committees or insisted on ignoring the "democratic" principle. Despite some initial gains, the offensive faltered. On July 19, the

Germans launched a counter-offensive; the Russian retreat approached the proportions of a rout.

The stated domestic objectives of the coalition fared no better. The Ministry of Commerce and Industry had remained in the charge of the Cadet, A. S. Konovalov, a textile manufacturer who had previously served as vice-chairman of the Central War Industry Committee. He now advocated heavy taxation of war profits and government management or even nationalization of plants afflicted by severe labor disputes. When, however, it was proposed that controlled plants be administered through committees elected by the workers, Konovalov resigned (June 2). A simultaneous visit from Arthur Henderson, then leader of the British Labour Party and a member of the War Cabinet, failed to convince the majority of Russian employers that Britain's extensive system of state controls, worked out in collaboration with British labor, was not socialism. The Provisional Government, fearing the consequences if industry should withdraw its support, quietly abandoned its intentions.

Without assuming some measure of control, it was hopeless to prevent wage disputes, inevitable in an inflationary period. Relations between capital and labor therefore steadily deteriorated; while the employers accused the workers of wanting the moon without toil, the workers accused the employers of trying to starve them into submission. The natural sequel was that the influence of the factory committees rose at the expense of that of the trade unions. The All-Russian Conference of Employers' Organizations demanded "the removal of interference by factory committees with the jurisdiction of factory administration." [27] At an All-Russian Conference of Factory Committees, held in June, demands were voiced that the workers "take over control of production and regulation in the plant." As Lenin had foreseen, syndicalist rather than socialist ideas infected the proletariat; for the moment, what mattered was that industry was becoming as disorganized as the army and that old concepts of subordination to properly constituted authority were breaking down all along the line.

The other side of the coin was the "protection of labor." Here, too, the Provisional Government drew a blank, not so much from lack of its own good will as from its general habit of drawing back in the face of any resistance. A "Labor Committee" was set up, composed of equal numbers of representatives of workers' organizations and of industrialists; its "impartial chairman" was the Menshevik Minister of Labor, Skobelev. As one of the employers' members noted,

> The reports which preceded discussion of draft bills were carefully and intelligently prepared, and it was evident that everything had been strictly thought out and coördinated. . . . With their broad erudition, the young Marxist scholars during discussion of draft laws with marked ease supported their arguments with references to the laws and customs of all the countries in the world, to resolutions of congresses, etc., etc.[28]

The employers, unprepared, could only stall and threaten lockouts. Nevertheless, of an imposing program of social reform, all that was enacted were an "absolutely harmless" law on labor exchanges and a health insurance law entailing 50 percent contribution by the insured workers, but with compensation for accidents resting entirely on the employer. All the rest—the "anti-social" unrestricted right to strike, prohibition of child labor ("counter to stern reality"), the eight-hour day, and the like—went back into ministerial pigeonholes.

Most disastrous of all was the inability of the coalition government to grapple with the problem of the land, perhaps the chief factor in the disintegration of the army. Basic though it was, particularly to the problem of the peasants in "gray coats," the land problem was the last to force itself on the attention of the Provisional Government, and already when it was too late. The Socialist Revolutionaries had always demanded "the land for the people," and it was this party which grew most rapidly in membership following the Revolution. In addition, without reference to the Party and its slogans, the peasants tended, as it were instinctively, to feel that the land was theirs, that those who expended their toil on the land had a right to it. Especially with the increasing return of able-bodied men to the village, peasant disorders multiplied, both in violence and in scope.

The Main Land Committee, belatedly set up by the original Provisional Government, bogged down in legalistic discussion; the local land committees, which tended to sympathize strongly with the demands of the peasants, fell foul of restrictive action by the Ministry of the Interior. Chernov, Minister of Agriculture in the coalition government, was the principal intellectual architect of SR policy; he was devoted to the ideal of effecting the promptest possible transfer of landlord land to the peasants. But he was preëminently a theoretician, not a politician, and he allowed himself to be blocked by the exigencies of coalition. It was the socialist minority in the Provisional Government that was now paralyzed, and Chernov's best efforts to solve the land problem were persistently thwarted by the agreement to await decision by the Constituent Assembly. In the meanwhile, overruled by his "bourgeois" colleagues, he could do nothing but prepare for a grand reformation of land tenures in the hope that fresh inequities would not be precipitated by arbitrary seizures on the spot.

The ideal of a democratically elected Constituent Assembly was immensely powerful. Though Russia had never had any experience of democratic action, the concept had captured the allegiance, not only of the bourgeoisie, but also of the masses. Even the soviets were regarded as only an interim regime, which would gladly hand over power to the freely chosen representatives of the whole Russian people. Yet the Constituent Assembly remained a dream. The original Provisional Government, to the chagrin of the Soviet, had suggested the summer as the earliest possible date. Not until June 27 was the date of elections finally set for September 30. The fact of freedom and the aspirations of soldiers, workers, and peasants unleashed by freedom could not be indefinitely restrained. The "revolutionary people" simply would not abide by the timetable set by the revolutionary leaders.

NOTES

1. Shulgin, *Dni,* p. 136.
2. Piontkovskii, *Khrestomatiia po istorii Oktiabr'skoi revoliutsii,* 3rd edition, pp. 37-38.
3. Denikin, *Ocherki russkoi smuty,* Vol. I, Part I, pp. 64-65.
4. Shulgin, *op. cit.,* pp. 142, 157, 134.
5. Kerensky, *Crucifixion of Liberty,* p. 279.
6. Chernov, *Great Russian Revolution,* p. 412; Stalin quotation not included in his *Sochineniia.*
7. *Revoliutsiia 1917 goda . . . ,* I, 190.
8. Sukhanov, *Zapiski o revoliutsii,* II, 278-289 (omitted from English translation).
9. *Revoliutsiia 1917 goda . . . ,* I, 108.
10. Lenin, "April Theses," No. 2, in *Sochineniia,* 3rd edition, XX, 78.
11. Rodzianko to Semenovsky Regiment, *Isvestiia,* No. 13, March 15 (28), 1917.
12. *Izvestiia,* No. 27, March 29 (April 11), 1917.
13. Shingarev on peasant disturbances in Riazan, quoted in Piontkovskii, *op. cit.,* p. 111.
14. "Without Secret Diplomacy," in Lenin, *Sochineniia,* 3rd edition, XX, 602.
15. *Revoliutsiia 1917 goda . . . ,* I, 199.
16. Golder, *Documents of Russian History, 1914-1917,* p. 334.
17. Sack, *Birth of the Russian Democracy,* pp. 246-248.
18. Piontkovskii, *op. cit.,* p. 86.
19. *Revoliutsiia 1917 goda . . . ,* II, 204.
20. Piontkovskii, *op. cit.,* p. 87.
21. Denikin, *op. cit.,* p. 77.
22. Piontkovskii, *op. cit.,* pp. 103-104.
23. *Ibid.,* p. 91.
24. Root, *The United States and the War: The Mission to Russia,* p. 101.
25. *Krasnyi Arkhiv,* II, 284-285.
26. *Izvestiia,* June 20 (July 3), 1917.
27. Pankratova, *Fabzavkomy Rossii . . . ,* p. 202.
28. Auerbach, *"Revoliutsionnoe obshchestvo po lichnym vospominaniiam,"* in *Arkhiv russkoi revoliutsii,* XIV, 14-15.

SUGGESTIONS FOR FURTHER READING

Golder's *Documents* and Chernov's *Great Russian Revolution* continue to be of outstanding value. For this period, see Lenin's *Revolution of 1917* (Vol. XX of the English translation of his *Collected Works*). Trotsky's *History of the Russian Revo-*

lution and Sukhanov's *Russian Revolution* are important afterthoughts by two Social Democrats. Among Kerensky's apologia, his *Crucifixion of Liberty* is the most serviceable. For a bitterly rueful study of the role of the Socialist-Revolutionaries, see Radkey, *The Agrarian Foes of Bolshevism;* Steinberg's *In the Workshop of the Revolution* is a subjective account by a Left SR. Denikin's *Russian Turmoil* contains much valuable material from the standpoint of an able general. For an important extraneous factor affecting the development of the Revolution, see Warth, *The Allies and the Russian Revolution.* Sack's *Birth of Russian Democracy* contains much valuable material, as well as photographs of most of the prominent participants.

Browder and Kerensky, *The Russian Provisional Government, 1917: Documents,* is an indispensable collection of source materials competently selected and arranged.

Chapter

25

Demise of the Revolution: July to November, 1917

THE JULY CRISIS AND THE SOVIETS

By July, the bankruptcy of the Revolution was imminent. Disappointment of the hopes inspired in the anarchic masses was compounded by the disastrous failure of the July offensive against the Germans, which shattered the dream of an early peace. Even before the beginning of the German counter-offensive (July 19), the Cadets had precipitated a fresh ministerial crisis. The only bourgeois party that had maintained a semblance of organization, they had become increasingly convinced that it was folly to continue to accept responsibility for a movement that threatened to swing ever further to the left of anything they desired. Mindful that the French Revolution, after moving irresistibly leftward, had at last swung back and permitted men like Abbé Sieyès to reëmerge as leaders, the Cadets seem to have felt it wise to cease trying to check the swing of the pendulum; by dropping out of the government, they might protect the party's reputation for sanity and be ready to return to the helm after a Russian Thermidor.

The pretext for their escape from the Provisional Government offered itself in the Ukrainian question. The Ukrainians' desire for autonomy had been gathering strength; it fed on the obvious reluctance of the Russian authorities, even after the entry of the socialists into the cabinet, to recognize the "Little Russians" as worthy partners in a federal structure. In June, Kerensky visited Kiev; his emphasis on the need to postpone any decision until the meeting of the Constituent Assembly was ill received. On June 24, Kerensky by telegram forbade the meeting of a Ukrainian Army Congress; the Rada replied with a "Universal" [manifesto], addressed "To the Ukrainian people! To the people of peasants, workers, toilers!" and proclaiming that:

Without separating from Russia, without breaking away from the Russian state, let the Ukrainian people on its own soil have the right itself to regulate its own life. Let order and harmony in the Ukraine be supplied by a People's Ukrainian Assembly [*Seim*] elected by universal, equal, direct, and secret suffrage. All the laws that must supply this harmony here at home, in the Ukraine, may rightfully be issued only by our Ukrainian Assembly.[1]

A delegation from the ministry persuaded the Rada to accept a compromise: provisionally, until the meeting of the All-Russian Constituent Assembly, Ukrainian affairs were to be managed by a General Secretariat, to be set up by the Petrograd government in consultation with the Rada; minority groups in the Ukraine were to be given representation; during the war, the unity of the Russian army was to be preserved, although efforts were to be made to group Ukrainians in special units. Three of the Cadet ministers, emphasizing their sworn duty not to anticipate "the will of the Constituent Assembly and the basic features of the future state structure of Russia" [2] by determining a question to which in principle they took no exception, promptly resigned (July 16).

Their withdrawal raised again the question of direct assumption of power by the soviets, at the head of which now stood the Central Executive Committee of the All-Russian Congress of Soviets of Workers' and Soldiers' Deputies. This July Crisis was sharpened by the spread of Bolshevik influence in the Petrograd garrison, reflected in a disorganized and abortive uprising (July 16-17) against the Provisional Government. A regiment of machine gunners, supported by some other troops and by sailors from Kronstadt, briefly terrorized the capital with indiscriminate shooting in the name of the Bolshevik slogan "All Power to the Soviets." The soviets, however, still did not wish the responsibilities of power, and the July Uprising was suppressed by troops loyal in deed as well as in word to soviet authority.

The First All-Russian Congress of Soviets of Workers' and Soldiers' Deputies (as distinct from the interim All-Russian Conference of Soviets mentioned in the preceding chapter) had held its first meeting at Petrograd on June 14. It was elected by local soviets in rough proportion to their own electorates. Of the 1,090 delegates, only 775 declared any specific party allegiance; the SR's numbered 285, the Mensheviks 248, the Bolsheviks only 105. The main resolution of this Congress, explicitly endorsing the policies of the coalition Provisional Government, was adopted by a vote of 543 to 126, with 52 abstentions. Tsereteli's defense of the need for coalition as being generally recognized was challenged by Lenin, who openly asserted that the Bolsheviks were "ready at any minute" to take all power in their own hands, adding "laugh as much as you like." Kerensky chided Lenin:

The task of . . . the Russian democracy is . . . to consolidate its gains . . . so that Comrade Lenin, who has been abroad, may be able to continue to speak here and not have to go back to Switzerland. . . . You are offering

> childish prescriptions—"arrest, destroy, kill." What are you—Socialists or the police of the old regime?

At this point Lenin demanded that the orator be called to order, but Kerensky continued, with prophetic rhetoric:

> You recommend that we follow the road of the French Revolution of 1792. . . . When by unintentional, reckless alliance with reaction, you destroy our power, then you will open the door for a real dictator. . . .[3]

Leadership remained with the Mensheviks and the SR's. Party labels, however, no longer had great significance, for the socialist organizations, while growing wildly in size, all shared in the general disintegrating processes of the Revolution. The cross-current of ideas arising from the unexpected character of practical developments split old-established ideological unities and led to the formation of new, ephemeral groups. Individual revolutionists floated in and out of these alignments.

Even before the Revolution—indeed, before the war—the Mensheviks had had great difficulty in maintaining the unity of their fraction. One group among them, the "Liquidators," had gone so far, in its Marxist reliance on the spontaneity of the growth of proletarian class-consciousness, as to express the belief that the Party apparatus could be liquidated as unnecessary in view of the overwhelming importance of the material factors making for mass revolution. During the Revolution, the leading group among the Mensheviks remained true to their understanding of Marxism and to the principles of old-fashioned left-wing social democracy. But the headlong current of revolutionary realities in a country where Marxism was necessarily alien left them floundering, fearing Bolshevik anarchy even more than bourgeois liberalism. In the persons of Tsereteli, Chkheidze, Skobelev, and Dan, they continued to dominate the soviets but, unwilling to follow the impatient turbulent masses, which they were increasingly unable to hold in check, their leadership of the Revolution was ever more and more endangered. The man to whose thinking they were most indebted, Plekhanov, had returned to Russia on April 13. Stressing "unity" with Russia's allies, this most famous of Russian Social-Democratic theoreticians and his handful of personal followers exercised no influence at all in the Russian Revolution.

The historic leader of the Mensheviks, Martov, who had been Lenin's co-worker on *Iskra* until the split in 1903, had returned from Switzerland by Lenin's route (May 22). As an orator, as a writer, and as an analytical thinker, Martov towered above all other Russian Social Democrats—Plekhanov, Lenin, and Trotsky not excepted. As a man of action, however, he was hampered by his own intellectual power of seeing clearly all sides of every question. He was unable to engage in that ruthless mouth-to-mouth combat at which Lenin excelled; one of his most ardent admirers has characterized him as a Hamlet. From the moment of his return to Russia until after the Bolshevik seizure of power, Martov remained the leader of a troublesome minority in his Party, which, however, did not dare to expel him. Around him, technically within the Party, gathered a minority group known as the "Menshevik-Internationalists." Opposed from the outset to coalition, Martov in July vainly advocated formation of a new government made up exclusively of soviet elements.

Another, and more definite, split from the Mensheviks was the "Inter-district men" (*Mezhraiontsy*), whose leading figure was Trotsky, who had chosen America as a place of exile. Attempting to return to Russia by way of Canada, he was for a time detained in a prisoner-of-war camp at Halifax; he did not reach Russia until the May crisis had been solved (May 18). A brilliant, though mercurial, orator and writer, he had long since drawn away from the Mensheviks, committing himself to his special "theory of permanent revolution." As early as 1905, Trotsky had discarded the concept that a revolution must have two distinct stages, "bourgeois" and "proletarian." In its stead he had advanced the idea that a "workers' government" should be formed immediately to take charge of the struggle and keep the revolution going "in permanence" through all its stages.

> The Russian democracy can only be revolutionary, else it will not be democratic. . . . This sympathy must be concentrated on the proletariat as the revolutionary force, the début of which at the head of the masses of the people can alone save the future Russia.

He advised efforts to win over the urban petty bourgeoisie and the army, but the factories must be the basic organizing points; demand for a Constituent Assembly would bring in the peasants.

> What is needed for leadership [of the revolution]? A few very simple things: freedom from organizational routine and the petty traditions of the revolutionary underground; a broad view; bold initiative; ability to appraise the situation; once again, bold initiative.[4]

Lenin's retort to the "windbag" Trotsky had been that

> only a revolutionary dictatorship resting on the enormous majority of the people could be at all stable (of course, not absolutely, but relatively). . . . To become the enormous, preponderant majority is possible only by uniting with the mass of the semi-proletarian, semi-proprietorial, i.e., with the mass of the urban petty bourgeoisie and the village poor. . . .[5]

In Russia, said Lenin, this could mean only a "revolutionary dictatorship of the proletariat and of the peasantry." In the heat of controversy with the Mensheviks, among whom Trotsky was then a relatively insignificant, slightly aberrant figure, Lenin had gone further:

> Whoever would advance toward socialism by any road other than political democracy will inevitably reach absurd and reactionary conclusions, both in the economic and in the political sense.[6]

Any notion that Lenin, who consistently endorsed armed uprising, was then advocating democracy should be dispelled by further passages in the same pamphlet such as that the "provisional revolutionary government," participation in which he was advocating, was one "directly replacing the overthrown government and resting on the uprising of the people and not on any sort of representative institutions coming from the people." At that time, Lenin was convinced, Russian workers were themselves not ready for socialism: "The working class is suffering not so much from capitalism as from the lack of development of capitalism. The working class is therefore *unconditionally interested* in the widest, freest, most rapid development of capitalism" —the only road leading to the goal of socialism.

In the fall of 1916 Lenin was still damning Trotsky as a "Kautskyite" [7] and as late as April, 1917, still continued to characterize "Trotskyism" as "wrong." [8] Yet, despite Lenin's repeated rebuffs and despite the scathing criticisms which Trotsky had over the years leveled against Lenin, the practical differences between Trotsky's *Mezhraiontsy* and Lenin's new brand of Bolshevism were confusingly small. For Trotsky, the advocate of "bold initiative," it was no great leap, after the July Uprising, to align himself with his old enemy.

The SR's, never a truly unified party, suffered even more than the Marxists from the influx of new members. Their most popular new spokesman, Kerensky, insisted on regarding himself as above either class or party. Yet the Party did not dare to discipline him. The greatest of its leaders, Victor Chernov, did not return to Russia until April 21, five days after Lenin. Like Martov, however, Chernov was preëminently an intellectual, hesitant and fumbling in action. As leader of his party's "Left Center," he directed his main efforts, not to trying to secure prompt implementation of the policies in which he himself devoutly believed, but to the endeavor to hold together the right wing, which accepted Kerensky and welcomed coalition with the Cadets, and the "Left SR's," who showed increasing tendency to gravitate toward the anarchical policies then advocated by Lenin.

Outright anarchists also maintained an organization, much to Lenin's annoyance, but their contributions to the Revolution were of no account.

THE BOLSHEVIKS PRIOR TO JULY AND THE JULY UPRISING

In striking contrast was the development of the Bolsheviks who, up to July, had exerted no significant influence on the Revolution. Lenin, in Switzerland, had been quite taken aback by the March events and had assumed that the tsarist regime still had dangerous latent strength. Recovering swiftly, he had, in his *Letters from Afar,* interpreted their significance in a way that made no sense to his Party colleagues in Petrograd. While regarding the goals of the Revolution as merely "bread, peace, and freedom," he maintained that they could only be achieved by the triumph of the proletariat, a term which in his mind was identical with its "conscious vanguard," the Bolshevik Party. In the struggle for power on which he insisted, he proposed to rely on two allies, the poorer peasantry in Russia and the international proletariat. The immediate goal should be "a democratic republic and the complete victory of the peasantry over the landlords"; socialism must wait until later.[9]

Through the mediation of Swiss Socialists, at the suggestion of the Menshevik leader Martov, arrangements were made with the German government for the return to Russia of revolutionary exiles in Switzerland; the more confused the situation in Russia, the less the Germans would have to worry about the military position. Accordingly, Lenin and a number of others were permitted to travel on the famous "sealed train" across Germany, forbidden to communicate with anyone en route; from Stockholm they reached Petrograd on April 16. Lenin received a tremendous ovation on his arrival at the Finland Station but replied dryly to Chkheidze's speech of welcome. The next day, at a caucus of the Bolshevik members of the All-Russian Conference of Soviets, held in the palatial former residence of the ballet dancer Ksheshinskaia, Lenin presented his "April Theses":

(1). In place of a "defensist" attitude toward the war, there should be fraternization in the front-line trenches.
(2). The class consciousness of the workers must be aroused.
(3). "No support to the Provisional Government."
(4). Systematic exposure of the errors of the majority of the soviets.
(5). Complete replacement of all old organs of government by the soviets, which alone could call a Constituent Assembly.
(6). Formation of Soviets of Agricultural Laborers' Deputies and nationalization of the land under their communal administration.
(7). Immediate nationalization of the whole banking system.
(8). State capitalism as a transition to socialism.
(9). Revision of the Party program and adoption of the name "Communist."
(10). Creation of a revolutionary International.[10]

This "thunder-like" [11] speech was repeated the same day at a "unity" meeting of Bolsheviks and Mensheviks, and the text of the Theses was published in *Pravda* on April 20.

The April Theses provoked consternation among Social Democrats, who had expected much from Lenin's return. There was widespread feeling that Lenin, so long in isolation, had lost touch with reality, that he had forgotten his Marxism. Plekhanov, the "grandfather of Russian Marxism," characterized Lenin as "delirious." [12] Even among the Bolsheviks, dismay was evident. Goldenberg, a long-time member of the Central Committee, accused Lenin of following in the footsteps of Bakunin. Even the usually docile Kamenev announced in *Pravda* that Lenin's position was "unacceptable." [13]

Lenin was not abashed at rejection of his views; he continued to press them with characteristic urgency, with all the cogency of simplicity. In his *First Letter on Tactics,* he vigorously attacked

> those "old Bolsheviks" who more than once have played a sorry role in the history of our Party, inanely repeating a formula they have learned by heart instead of *studying* the peculiarities of the new living reality.

Dismissing them as "pre-revolutionary antiques," he asserted

> the incontestable truth that a Marxist must pay heed to living life, to the exact facts of *reality,* and not continue to cling to the theory of yesterday, which, like any theory, at best only outlines the basic, the general, and only approximates the complexity of life.

He quoted Mephistopheles: "Theory, my friend, is gray, but green is the eternal tree of life." [14]

Heaping scorn on all those who disagreed with him, Lenin worked indefatigably to popularize the slogan of "All Power to the Soviets." Ready to welcome any manifestation of dissatisfaction with the Provisional Government, whether before or after coalition, Lenin by degrees secured the reversal of his followers' earlier attitude toward subject nationalities such as the Ukrainians, wooed the factory committees while his rivals concentrated on the trade unions, and encouraged the impatience of the peasants for the land. By such tactics he won an ever-increasing number of adherents for his party, though it was the SR's that showed the most phenomenal growth. He was aided by the complete irresponsibility of his faction, which remained a minority in the soviets.

The shock Lenin gave to his adherents by the April Theses drove a number of "old Bolsheviks" permanently out of his party, but his personal ascendancy held together a submissive core, around which gathered a throng of new devotees looking for firm and confident leadership. After all, it was Lenin who had created the Bolshevik fraction; in it he had had subordinates but never equal colleagues. Without Lenin, the Bolshevik party was unthinkable, and it was this fact that principally enabled him by mid-May to recreate a near-monolithic instrument. Its doctrine bore little resemblance to pre-revolutionary Bolshevik teachings; for that matter, its new Bible, Lenin's well-known pamphlet *State and Revolution* (written in September, 1917) was not destined to be its binding and enduring guide. Ever willing to "learn from life," to use one of his favorite phrases, Lenin retained from the past only his basic purpose of establishing socialism in Russia at any cost. His strategy of dividing and confusing his opponents while preserving the fighting unity of his own group remained unchanged; only his tactics were subject to constant revision.

Unimportant in the soviets—or in the trade unions—Bolshevik influence in the street nevertheless grew as the paralysis of the government continued.

Yet the first occasion on which the Bolsheviks' slogans seemed to produce practical results—the July Uprising—also constituted a very great setback for them. The Bolshevik leaders realized that an attempt at that time forcibly to overthrow the Provisional Government was almost certainly foredoomed to failure, for its authority was fully supported by the soviets. They therefore tried to persuade the machine gunners to leave their weapons behind and stage a peaceful demonstration. Stalin apparently acted in good faith when on July 16 he reported to the Soviet Central Executive Committee that the Bolshevik Central Committee was opposed to the uprising. On the other hand, the Bolsheviks could not repudiate their own slogan, now actively supported by some workers, notably from the Putilov plant, as well as by soldiers; they had to put themselves at the head of the demonstration.

On July 17, everything was confusion, most of the garrison refusing to take sides. Small parties of insurgents roved the city, shooting on the slightest provocation and lynching suspected opponents. Armed sailors came from Kronstadt, appealing to the Bolsheviks for leadership. Chernov was roughly handled and rescued only by the personal intervention of Trotsky, who nearly lost his own life in the process. A meeting of the Soviet Executive Committee was invaded by armed Putilov workers. One of them, waving a rifle, hysterically threatened dire action if the Soviet did not take power. Chkheidze, in the chair, calmly handed him a paper, saying, "Here, please take this, Comrade, read it . . . and don't interrupt our business." As Sukhanov records,

> The baffled *sans culotte,* not knowing what else to do, took the appeal and then without much difficulty was got off the platform. . . . This was one of the finest scenes of the Revolution. And with Chkheidze's gesture one of the most dramatic.[15]

On July 18, dependable troops entered the city. With some four hundred casualties (as against fewer than fifteen hundred in the March Revolution), the affair fizzled out. The Bolsheviks, themselves dismayed by this outbreak which Lenin wisely regarded as premature, were discredited and widely believed to be German agents; for the next two months their stock was low. Warrants were issued for the arrest of their leaders, with few protests, except from Trotsky, who asserted that logically he should have been included in the reprisals. "The exception in my favor," Trotsky wrote to the government, "merely emphasizes more vividly the counter-revolutionary arbitrariness with respect to Lenin, Zinoviev, and Kamenev." [16] It was at this moment that, despite Lenin's sharp criticism in April of the ideas that underlay the "theory of permanent revolution," Trotsky concluded that Lenin's ideas were now so close to his own that their differences "have now lost all significance"; he therefore became formally a member of the Bolshevik Party. In August, at the Sixth Congress of the Bolshevik Party (which Lenin, in hiding, was unable to attend), Trotsky was welcomed as a formal member of the Bolshevik organization and, with two other *Mezhraiontsy,* was elected to its new fifteen-member Central Committee.

THE PROVISIONAL GOVERNMENT AND KERENSKY

Suppression of the July Uprising could not solve the crisis created by the resignation of the Cadets. On July 20, the remaining members of the cabinet endorsed their socialist colleagues' proposals, particularly with reference to more vigorous handling of the agrarian question. This was too much for Prince Lvov, who resented any attempt "to confront the Constituent Assembly with an accomplished fact." [17] Nor could he swallow a resolution which the Executive Committees of the All-Russian Congress of Soviets of Workers' and Soldiers' Deputies and of the All-Russian Soviets of Peasants' Deputies had jointly adopted in the excitement of July 17; this had stated that the Provisional Government "should be guided by the resolutions" of those bodies.[18]

Lvov's resignation elevated Kerensky to the office of prime minister. The composition of a new cabinet was, however, more difficult. The Cadets tried to lay down conditions as the price of their participation. After many conferences of all interested parties, a joint meeting of the Soviet Executive Committee (August 4), by a vote of 147 to 45 with 42 abstentions,

> declares that it fully entrusts to Comrade Kerensky formation of a cabinet, made up of representatives of different parties standing on the ground of the program of the Provisional Government, adopted under the presidency of Comrade Kerensky and published on July 21.[19]

The now wholly impotent Duma Provisional Committee echoed this action, which two days later was approved by the Cadet Party also.

So, on August 6, began the "dictatorship" of Kerensky, with a cabinet now made up principally of socialists but including also a few coöperative Cadets. The Menshevik Tsereteli stood aside. Chernov, the SR leader who continued as Minister of Agriculture, alone had the prestige to cope with Kerensky. The prime minister, however, refused to consider himself bound by the instructions of the party to which he professed to belong.

Chernov, anxious to preserve the unity of the SR Party, strove hard to reconcile its right and left wings, but they continued to grow further apart. The left wing ever more insistently demanded immediate transfer of the land to the toiling peasantry in accordance with the Party's principles as understood by its newer recruits; the right wing, impressed with the disorderly and often drunken disputes that characterized much of the peasants' own activity, persisted in believing that only a democratically elected Constituent Assembly could organize transfer of the land on a just and fair basis, without creating new inequities. Chernov, himself "Left Center," was reduced to preparatory work, hampered by Kerensky's desire not to alienate his bourgeois allies in the cabinet. In consequence, little or nothing, save for innumerable carefully worked-out plans, was accomplished on this most vital question. It might have been expected that the land question would most easily have been solved by the SR's, who had so long assumed the role of the intellectual leaders of the peasant masses. Undoubtedly the peasants would have welcomed immediate application of SR ideas, as they would have rejected the nationalization under state control then advocated by the Bolsheviks. But Chernov's inability to carry the new Provisional Government with him made inevitable a steady leftward swing even in the villages.

Matters were not made better by the intransigence of many landlords, who demanded the services of troops to protect their property against the ever more threatening "black partition" (general redistribution), in which not only the land and agricultural inventory were seized, but the libraries, paintings, and wine cellars of the nobles were destroyed by a peasantry incapable of appreciating them. As one progressive liberal, the Octobrist Shidlovsky, later put it:

> I think that the Bolsheviks, without suspecting it, did Russia a colossal service, an unforgettable service, in dispersing the Constituent Assembly, presided over by Chernov. Nothing good could come from it, while it would have done no less harm than the Bolsheviks, though without dictatorship or terrorism; I feel that if the country was doomed to experience a severe crisis, it is better to have all the scorpions at once rather than gradually.[20]

The weakness of the Revolution was that it failed to develop leadership. Able and experienced men, such as Guchkov and Miliukov, lacked the necessary sympathy with the elemental surge of mass sentiment, whether among soldiers, workers, or peasants. They tried in vain to hold the Revolution on the road of constitutional legality and were swept aside by the very forces they had for years been trying to emancipate. In the early stages of the Revolution, Alexander Kerensky had seemed a far more vital force, capable of appreciating the desires of the masses and alive to the need for quick action. For all the sentimentality of his magniloquent oratory, he sincerely believed in democracy and, however vaguely, in socialism. Despite his personal vanity, he gave no evidence of personal cupidity. Though he tended to identify himself as the symbol of all that was fine and noble in the Revolution, he was not cut out to be a dictator. Able to act decisively in small matters, he lacked the ability consistently to pursue an uncompromising policy. The general opinion at the time of the July Crisis that "Sasha" was the only man who could head a new government was fully shared by Kerensky himself. Unlike Lenin, however, he did not have a clear concept of the direction in which he should try to move. His chief concern was to rally all forces, left and right, about his central personality.

Kerensky has been aptly characterized as a bog-jumper. Every morass is dotted with tufts of grasses which can at least briefly support considerable weight. By constantly shifting his footing, a knowledgeable man may remain dry-shod in a marsh. Kerensky displayed considerable talent at constantly shifting his footing, shuffling and reshuffling the composition of his ministries, improvising new forms of government, and trying to make new social combinations. Yet such a policy took no account of the steady deterioration of Russia. After the failure of the July offensive, the disintegration of the army rapidly gathered momentum. The workers, disappointed in their efforts to improve or even maintain their economic position, turned more and more, under the leadership of the factory committees, to demands for outright seizure of the factories and mines. The peasants became increasingly violent, and on an ever-wider scale. Around the periphery, the subject nationalities became more and more restless and prone to self-assertion.

There was one universally recognized symbol of hope, the idea of the Constituent Assembly. It is of course quite possible that even if it had been convened, it might have been unable to bring order out of overwhelming chaos. By deciding issues, it might have driven the minority, which clearly would have meant the propertied classes, into the most desperate resistance. Yet such an outcome could hardly have made matters worse. There already was among generals, industrialists, and landlords a very considerable amount of "Bolshevism of the Right." What might have been avoided was the triumph of "Bolshevism of the Left," which was obviously nourished by the continued inaction of the Provisional Government. On August 22, a decree signed by Kerensky and his Minister of Justice, who was also one of the most determined opponents of Chernov's policies, postponed the date of the election of the Constituent Assembly from September 30 to November 25 and set December 11 for the date of the meeting.

Matters were much complicated by the continuing problem of the war. On the initiative of the Executive Committee of the Petrograd Soviet (May 8), efforts were being made to assemble in Stockholm an International Socialist Congress, to be attended by delegates from the belligerent countries on both sides as well as by neutrals; it was hoped that by joint pressure on their respective governments it would be possible to effect speedy conclusion of a general "democratic" peace. Instead of coöperating, Foreign Minister Tereshchenko, himself a wealthy producer of beet sugar and a dilettante both in politics and in international relations, torpedoed the Stockholm Socialist Congress. On August 21 he advised the British government (which, along with the French and American governments, had refused passports to their citizens) that the Russian government would not officially participate or regard itself as bound by any suggestions for peace that might there be arrived at.

Instead of decisive action to solve pressing problems, Kerensky had preferred to go ahead with his own idea, which he had first advanced on July 25, of convening a "State Conference" at Moscow. He believed that what were then usually called "all the live forces" should rally around the Provisional

Government; as the Government's official journal put it, the Conference was called "for the purpose of uniting the state power and all the organized forces of the country." [21] The Conference opened in the Bolshoi Theater on August 25. Well over two thousand persons had been invited. They included the 488 surviving members of the four successive State Dumas and 265 representatives of zemstvos and city governments; these were only partially balanced by 329 representatives of workers' and soldiers' or peasants' soviets. Capitalist employers' organizations were assigned 150 delegates, the professional intelligentsia and technical organizations 182, the trade unions 176, and the coöperatives 313. The armed forces were allotted 117 delegates, nationality groups 58, and there was considerable representation of governmental and quasi-governmental organizations, such as the food committees, which were allotted 90 delegates. Even the clergy, with 24 delegates, were not forgotten. The total exceeded 2400.

From the outset it was clear that the left viewed the Conference with great suspicion. The Executive Committee of the All-Russian Congress of Soviets, still under Menshevik control, agreed to participate only on the understanding that the Conference was "for the purpose of exchanging opinions" and could take no decisions "of a binding character." [22] The Bolsheviks were openly hostile, though they did not venture to call for a demonstration. Without party leadership, and over the protest of the Moscow Soviet, the local Central Trade Union, said to represent about 400,000 proletarians, voted a strike, with the result that the tramways stopped running and the restaurants were closed. However, despite the obvious hostility of the street crowds, there was no disturbance.

Chkheidze was given the honor of reading a long "Declaration of United Democracy," defending the policies of the Provisional Government.[23] General Kornilov, who on July 31 had succeeded Brusilov as Supreme Commander-in-Chief and who had hesitated to attend, was given a triumphal reception and showered with flowers. By August 28, when the Conference adjourned, it was obvious that the sessions had failed to develop any spirit of unity. As *Izvestiia,* the organ of the Soviet, admitted, Kornilov "was cheered by members of the Dumas, by the representatives of commerce and industry, by all the bourgeoisie groups, and by the representatives of officers." Kerensky received repeated ovations from the soldiers' committees, from the supporters of the soviets, and from the coöperatives, while "the right was motionless." [24] All that the Conference accomplished was to bring out sharply the polarity between the two revolutionary camps.

THE KORNILOV *PUTSCH* AND THE DECLINE OF KERENSKY

A not unnatural sequel was a disastrous personal collision between the head of the Provisional Government and the Supreme Commander-in-Chief.

Kornilov was as devoted to the cause of victory as was Kerensky to the Revolution. On the breakdown of the offensive, Kerensky had authorized reinstatement of the death penalty at the front, and Kornilov was not the man to hesitate to use it. He had accepted the supreme command hesitantly and had asked for a free hand in the restoration of military discipline. This had not been granted, but the general had been encouraged to believe that Kerensky sympathized with his objectives. Though, unlike some of the generals, he had never asked abolition of the army committees, he was anxious that they should be prevented from interfering with military orders. On visits to the capital, the new Supreme Commander urged the need to restore discipline in the rear as well as at the front and asked militarization of the disorganized railways and of the factories producing for the army. He was supported in his attitude by Boris V. Savinkov, formerly a leading SR terrorist and now Deputy Minister of War. Kornilov counted also on the friendly attitude of Rodzianko and other conservative public figures.

Even before the Moscow State Conference, Kornilov had designated General Krymov to command a picked force, including Kornilov's favorite Moslem troops from the Caucasus, which was stationed in readiness to crush any fresh Bolshevik outbreak in Petrograd. It does not appear that Kornilov, who proudly described himself as the "son of a Cossack peasant," distinguished too clearly between the Bolsheviks and their enemy, the Executive Committee of the Congress of Soviets. His reception by "respectable" society at the Moscow State Conference could not fail to influence his self-confidence and his belief that the choice lay between speedy ruin of the army and the country or drastic measures to check decay and to restore Russia's strength. His feelings of desperation were only increased by the Germans' capture of Riga (September 3). Yet it does not appear that Kornilov was deliberately hatching a conspiracy.

What precipitated the denouement was the bumbling efforts of a civilian, V. N. Lvov, to mediate between Kornilov and the government. This Lvov (not to be confused with Prince G. E. Lvov) had served in the first Provisional Government and in its coalition successor in the then unimportant post of Procurator-General of the Holy Synod; he had retired to private life when Kerensky's "dictatorship" was established (August 6). On September 7, on his own initiative, he secured an interview with Kornilov at Headquarters. Representing himself as an emissary of Kerensky, he asked the general to choose one of three possible dictatorships: a new government headed by Kerensky; a committee of three or four men including Kornilov; or Kornilov himself as both civil and military head, with Kerensky serving under him. The bluff general expressed his preference for the third possibility and told Lvov to invite Kerensky to come to Headquarters for his personal safety. The following day, back in Petrograd, Lvov told Kerensky that Kornilov, backed by a number of influential men, asked that Kerensky resign in the general's favor, accepting the Ministry of Justice under him. Calling Kornilov on the direct line, Kerensky asked if what Lvov said was true. Without checking as to what Lvov had said, Kornilov answered in the affirmative and asked when Kerensky could be expected at Headquarters. Replying evasively, Kerensky reverted to his training as a lawyer and busied himself getting witnesses to the unfortunate Lvov's confused account.

On September 9, the rattled Kerensky broadcast an order dismissing Kornilov and placing Petrograd under martial law. An apparently thunderstruck Kornilov denounced Kerensky's version of the affair as a lie. Defiantly refusing to surrender his command, and supported by the other leading generals, though not by Rodzianko and other civilians who had showered him with praise at the Moscow State Conference, Kornilov set General Krymov's force in motion. In the capital, on motion of a Menshevik, the Soviet Executive Committee set up a Military Revolutionary Committee, in which participation even of Bolsheviks was welcomed, to organize resistance. The prompt action of the railwaymen and telegraphers disrupted communications and slowed the advance. As Krymov's Cossacks, and even his "Savage Division," began to realize that there was no Bolshevik uprising in the capital, they became unreliable. Krymov, after an interview with Kerensky, shot himself (September 12). Kornilov and his chief colleagues quietly submitted to arrest by General Alexeiev at Headquarters (September 14).

This strange interlude in the Revolution is in some ways reminiscent of the Decembrist revolt of 1825. Each depended on extraneous and trivial incidents, which might seem insufficient to set off a movement of such serious character. Neither had been adequately prepared, and neither had at its disposal reliable forces for a task of the magnitude it undertook. In both cases, also, failure spelled ruin for the ideals that had motivated them. The differences are apparent, especially the fact that in 1917 the victor was destroyed by his own unedifying role in the victory.

The remaining two months of the Kerensky regime hold little of major interest, unless it be to amateurs of political morphology. Kerensky continued his gyrations, leaping from tussock to tussock in the bog but never recovering his former prestige. On the outbreak of the Kornilov *Putsch* (September 9), the Soviet Central Committee, mistrusting the Cadets, refused further support to Kerensky unless he got rid of his Cadet ministers. Unwilling to put all his weight on "the revolutionary democracy," Kerensky resorted to a curious expedient; he won approval (September 14) for a Directory of Five, made up of Kerensky himself, Foreign Minister Tereshchenko, a Menshevik of doubtful standing (Nikitin), a general, and an admiral. Chernov and a few other ministers resigned, but the majority of his erstwhile colleagues remained, accepting demotion to mere department heads. Kerensky assumed the post of Supreme Commander-in-Chief, recalling General Alexeiev to serve as Chief of Staff. To emphasize its willingness to combat counter-revolution, the Directory simultaneously proclaimed Russia a republic.

This stopgap government could accomplish nothing; it could not even endure. Kerensky had to accept the summons jointly issued (September 16) by the Executive Committee of the Congress of Soviets of Workers' and Soldiers' Deputies and of the Peasant Soviets for the meeting of a "Democratic Conference" on September 25 (postponed to September 27). This body had much the same composition as the Moscow State Conference, except that representatives of the Dumas, of the zemstvos, of the generals, and of the businessmen were not invited. It had no greater success in achieving real unity. At the Democratic Conference, the question of attempting a new coalition was raised (October 2). The delegates of the workers' and soldiers' soviets voted against it, 192-83; those of the peasants approved it, 102-70. The trade unions opposed coalition, 139-32; the coöperatives approved, 140-23. The representatives of the nationalities also opposed coalition, while all other groups favored it. The total vote was 766 for, 688 against, with 38 abstentions. After a recess, however, an amendment was offered, ruling out coalition with the Cadets; it was carried by 595 votes to 493, with 72 abstentions. After a day spent in hectic discussions within the presidium, the snarl was unraveled late that night by a carefully obscure resolution in favor of "appointing a permanent representative organ from among its members" but adding the transfiguring clause that:

> in case propertied elements are also drawn into the composition of the government, this organ may and must be supplemented by delegates from the bourgeois groups. [However,] the preponderance of the democratic elements must be preserved in this organ. The government must be accountable to this organ [the "Pre-Parliament"] and responsible to it.[25]

Armed with this doubtful authorization, Kerensky invited five Moscow industrialists to join a new cabinet (October 4). True to their Cadet principles, however, they refused to accept responsibility to the "Pre-Parliament," which would certainly be dominated by the "democratic" elements. Only after much haggling did they agree to coöperate when Tsereteli, after reaffirming belief in ministerial responsibility, said the socialists would "not insist on this point now." The resultant coalition government was made up of three SR's, four Mensheviks, four Cadets, one Radical Democrat, and five nonparty men; the latter included the vaguely socialist general and admiral who had been members of the Directory.

In the meantime the proposed "Pre-Parliament" had held its first meeting (October 6) and elected to its presidium three Mensheviks, two Bolsheviks, and four SR's. As a result of further negotiations, it was reconstituted as the "Council of the Russian Republic"; it was to have 388 "democratic" representatives and 167 to represent the bourgeoisie, the Cossacks, the nationalities, and other lesser interests. At its first meeting (October 20), under the chairmanship of Catherine Breshkovskaia, "grandmother of the Russian Revolution," it elected a presidium of five. Its chairman, the SR Avksentiev, had been serving as chairman of the Executive Committee of the Peasants' Soviets. The other members were a Menshevik, a Populist-Socialist, and a Cadet; the fifth place, intended for a Bolshevik, was left vacant by that group's withdrawal. Under this doubtful aegis, the last coalition ministry tottered toward its end.

The Soviet Executive Committee had been made very uneasy by the Kornilov episode and its aftermath. It had forced Kerensky to drop the Cadets and had summoned the Democratic Conference. Yet, despite strong opposition, Cadets had been maneuvered back into the government. On the eve of the establishment of Kerensky's last ministry, the Soviet Executive Committee yielded to pressure from provincial soviets and ordered (October 6) election of a new (Second) All-Russian Congress of Soviets of Workers' and Soldiers' Deputies, to meet on November 2. In the subsequent weeks, the army soviets and the Peasants' Executive Committee protested that the summoning of the new Congress would confuse the preparations for the election of the Constituent Assembly scheduled for November 25; they also urged the danger that the Congress, if it should prove to be dominated by the Bolsheviks, might take power, possibly even precipitate civil war.

What would have happened if the Second Congress had met without interference is one of the insoluble problems of history. Until it met and the delegates registered their party affiliations, its composition could not be certainly known. "A preliminary count by officials of the Congress gives a total of 670 members, distributed as follows: Bolsheviks, 300; SR's (Right and Left), 193; . . . Mensheviks, 68; Internationalists, 14; Bund, 10. . . ."[26] Contemporary journalistic versions gave smaller figures, but it seems probable that the Bolsheviks, though having a plurality, would still have been in the minority. Subsequently, however, the Bolshevik official claim of 390 out of some 650 has often been accepted; it is doubtful whether it will ever be possible to establish the facts. In any case, the Bolsheviks had no intention of taking a chance on votes, so much more unreliable than bayonets.

THE BOLSHEVIKS AND THE SEIZURE OF POWER

The most definite result of the Kornilov *Putsch* had been the rapid revival of Bolshevik influence. Kerensky's wild appeals to all to "save the Revolution" had given the Bolsheviks the opportunity to come out of the underground. They had emerged with the frank admission that they were not going to fight for Kerensky but only for the Revolution. Their activity was of no consequence in the collapse of Kornilov's adventure, but in the excited mood of the soldiers and workers it was easy for the Bolsheviks to get the credit for the victory. From this moment they became a force to be reckoned with in the soviets. On September 19, the presidium of the Petrograd Soviet, incensed by passage of a Bolshevik policy resolution at an ill-attended meeting, resigned. The upshot was that Trotsky, who had been released after a brief imprisonment, was installed in place of Chkheidze as chairman of this pivotal, though local, soviet. About the same time, the soviets of Moscow and other important centers passed into Bolshevik hands. Under its new management, the Petrograd Soviet greeted Kerensky's new coalition government with a flat refusal of support (October 8). The Bolsheviks had participated in the Democratic Conference. They attended also the opening of the Pre-Parliament; Trotsky and Kamenev were even elected to the presidium (October 6). On Trotsky's urging, however, they demonstratively walked out (October 7).

Lenin had gone into hiding after the July Uprising; early in September he was smuggled across the border into Finland, where he remained until October 22. It was during this period that he wrote *State and Revolution,* a justification of his current tactics rather than an abstract formulation of permanent theory. Yet he remained the chief directing force of Bolshevik policy, which in these months abandoned the slogan of "All Power to the Soviets" in favor of "Defend the Constituent Assembly," allegedly threatened by Kerensky's continuance in power. During the Kornilov affair, Lenin had remained unusually silent. Only as the *Putsch* collapsed (September 12) did he comment on this "extremely unexpected" turn of events, which he clearly saw brought the Bolsheviks "tremendously nearer" to conquest of power. Now there was no longer need of directly attacking Kerensky; he could now be attacked *"indirectly* [Lenin's italics] by demanding an active and more active, truly revolutionary war against Kornilov." [27] Ironically, it was only after the Bolshevik seizure of power that Kornilov was able to slip away from his place of confinement to help organize the "Volunteer Army."

Lenin had become convinced that the Bolsheviks not only should, but could, overthrow Kerensky. At the end of the month, in a letter to the Central Committee, entitled "The Bolsheviks Must Assume Power," he asserted that "To wait for a 'formal' majority for the Bolsheviks is naïve." [28] At the time of the formation of the new coalition, he argued that the "last chance" for "peaceful development of the Revolution" [29] depended on immediate assumption of power by the soviets. By October 12, arguing that "we are on the threshold of a world proletarian revolution," he rang the changes on the theme that "to 'await' the Congress of Soviets is either *absolute idiocy* or *absolute treason."* Learning that his worried colleagues on the Central Committee had burned his letter, he tendered his resignation, threatening to carry on "propaganda *in the lower ranks* of the Party and at the Party Congress." [30] Thoroughly frightened at finding themselves in opposition to their leader, who continued to insist that "the Bolsheviks have no right to wait for the Congress of Soviets; they must *take power immediately,"* his followers hesitantly accepted his assurance that "victory is assured, and there are nine chances out of ten that it will be bloodless." [31]

On October 23, with Lenin himself present, ten members of the Central Committee committed the Party to an armed uprising, though without setting a date. Zinoviev and Kamenev, insisting that the Bolsheviks needed only to float with the rising tide of their influence over the masses, voted against it; three members were absent. At this same meeting, a new policy organ, the first Politburo, was set up, consisting of Lenin, Zinoviev, Kamenev, Trotsky, Stalin, Sokolnikov, and Bubnov. Three days later (October 26), the Executive Committee of the Petrograd Soviet revived the idea of a Military Revolutionary Committee. As Trotsky recorded its origin:

> At this meeting there was a Left SR named Lazimir. . . . He supported us, and we grabbed him. Thus the demand for creation of a Military Revolutionary Committee seemed to come from a Left SR, not from us. . . . Whether he realized that it was a conspiracy or merely reflected the vague revolutionary mood of the SR left wing, I don't know. . . . When he offered his proposal, we corrected it, concealing as much as possible the revolutionary insurrectionist character of the institution. . . .[32]

While Trotsky was busy with the Soviet, lesser Bolshevik leaders were engaged in stocktaking. On October 28, at a secret meeting of agents of the Party, reports were received on the mood of the workers and soldiers in the several districts of Petrograd; they were almost unanimous:

> We have a large organization of some 50,000 members; 500 will come here. Much drunkenness is to be observed, even amongst our comrades. From a military viewpoint the sailors offer little strength; many of them were sent back from the front for not knowing how to use their weapons. . . .
>
> There is no sentiment for an uprising. . . .
>
> The masses will rise at a call from the Soviet, few will rise at the call of our Party. . . .
>
> There is no fighting spirit, no desire on the part of the workers to come out on the street. . . .
>
> Even if the Soviet should issue a call for an uprising, some plants (ours, for example) will not respond. . . .
>
> If there is an attack by the counter-revolution, we will resist, but if there is a call to take the offensive, I do not think the workers will rise. . . .
>
> The masses will rise at the call of the Soviet. . . .
>
> No definite fighting mood is to be seen among the masses.[33]

These grass-roots reports might seem to make it very clear that the Bolsheviks knew they did not have the active support of the proletariat. This, however, could make no difference to Lenin, steeped in his notion of the Party as the "vanguard of the proletariat." What was more, it was clear that the masses still believed in the soviets. The local soviet had been captured; it was all the more important to take immediate action lest the Second All-

Russian Congress of Soviets escape Bolshevik control. The next day (October 29), at a meeting of the Central Committee with a variety of its subordinate agencies, Lenin rammed home his new slogan: "Either a dictatorship of Kornilov [who was then in prison] or a dictatorship of the proletariat and the poorer strata of the peasantry [i.e., of the Bolsheviks]," and asserted that "the masses have expressed confidence in the Bolsheviks." Minor figures repeated the mournful tale of the lackadaisical sentiment of the workers. For the Military Bureau, Krylenko hopefully reported that "personal observations lead to the conclusion that sentiment in the regiments is entirely with us, but information from our comrades working in the districts differs." Volodarsky, renowned as the most successful of the Bolshevik propagandists among the workers, reported the "general impression that no one is very anxious to go out on the street, but at the call of the soviets all will appear." Shliapnikov added that "in the metal workers' union, the influence of the Bolsheviks prevails, but the Bolshevik uprising is not popular; rumors about it even caused a panic." [34]

Yet the picture was not, from the Bolshevik point of view, utterly dismal. Mass apathy need not be fatal to a Bolshevik adventure. Even at the meeting on October 28, Nevsky, "as a representative of the military organization," had asserted,

> An uprising, an armed outbreak of the proletariat here in Peter [Petrograd], is possible. The whole garrison will follow the Soviet. . . . Will Moscow, and the provinces generally, respond to it? . . . Have we a majority to assure freedom? . . . The military organization will come out whenever you like, but what the result will be I cannot say. The railway organization may play a very important role. Imagine what can happen if the railways do not permit us to bring bread to Peter. In this respect perhaps the peasant masses will play a colossal role. If we can believe that the peasant masses will follow us, then it's alright. . . . The mood of the peasant masses in many parts of Russia hasn't been considered at all. . . . In some districts the peasants are saying that in case of an insurrection they will not give us any bread.[35]

Ominous though the warning was, it could not deter city-bred revolutionists, accustomed to enforced submission of the countryside to the politically ruling centers.

On October 30, the decision of the Soviet Executive Committee to postpone the meeting of the Second All-Russian Congress of Soviets of Workers' and Soldiers' Deputies from November 2 to November 7 gave the Bolsheviks a little more time to perfect their organization. That they were planning an armed uprising was no secret; Zinoviev and Kamenev had leaked the fact to the press (October 31). Yet the Provisional Government was now incapable of taking measures to cope with the menace. It could only repeat the old ideas about the "criminal intentions" of the Bolsheviks against the people's revolution. Effective in July, this sort of talk had lost its force since the Kornilov *Putsch*. To the weary, exhausted masses, whose nerves had been blunted by the constant deluge of agitational propaganda from all sides and who were disheartened by the continued failure to realize the accepted goals of the Revolution, the earlier clarion calls of socialist and democratic orators had lost their appeal. Continued disintegration of the army, accompanied by mass desertions, had imperceptibly been changing the cry for "Bread, Peace, and Freedom" into the far different yearning for "Land, Peace, and Bread." The basis for totalitarianism rather than democracy had been laid, both by the novelty in Russia of libertarian ideals and by the whole course of recent events. The masses, despairing of working out their own salvation, were ready to accept an irresponsible leadership.

For his part, Kerensky remained true to himself, unwilling, if it could possibly be avoided, to admit that the Revolution would "shed blood." He chose to rely on resolutions, on rhetorical exhortations, on anything but the quest for reliable military forces—until it was too late for decisive action. Even the chief gadfly of the Provisional Government, Martov, hesitated: "At the present moment a drift to the Bolsheviks is absolutely out of place. Now the Revolution is endangered not by the Right, but by the Left." [36] Martov was convinced that the fault lay with the inaction of the government which had created the hostile mood of the masses. On November 5, he made what was, philosophically speaking, one of the finest analyses of the course of the Revolution that has ever been made—without, however, indicating a practical solution of the problems it had created. On November 6, he swung the Pre-Parliament away from the course of voting unconditional support to the Provisional Government in favor of a resolution demanding immediate implementation of its own policies, especially with respect to land and peace. Kerensky, nettled, threatened to resign. In panic, many of those who had accepted the force of Martov's reasoning hastened to patch up the situation, while a recalcitrant Kerensky vainly sought concrete support for his regime.

In those last days of the agony of the regime committed to "Bread, Peace, and Freedom," it was Trotsky rather than Lenin who was the shining star. Lenin was still compelled to remain in hiding. In any case, the master strategist was less equipped than Trotsky to function in this sort of crisis. In July, Lenin had been indecisive; Trotsky was completely uninhibited. It was Trotsky who organized the Military Revolutionary Committee and who guided its effective actions. It was Trotsky who visited the key Peter-and-Paul Fortress, with its cannon commanding the heart of the city and its arsenal stocked with a hundred thousand rifles; single-handed, by words alone, he swung its wavering garrison from loyalty to the Provisional Government to the side of the insurrection (November 5).

Incomparable in dealing with tangible enemies, Trotsky could not, however, step into Lenin's shoes as the real mentor of the Bolshevik Revolution. Trotsky still believed that "either the Russian Revolution will lead to a [revolutionary] movement in Europe, or else the surviving powerful countries of the West will crush us."[37] It was a trap that Lenin cautiously skirted. While repeatedly acknowledging the importance of world revolution, Lenin constantly stressed Russia and the paramount significance of the situation there.

Less exuberant than Trotsky, Lenin kept his mind on the immediate situation. In a "Letter to the Comrades," written at the end of October, he had attempted to answer, point for point, all the arguments directed against his policy of immediate seizure of power. The essence of his thinking is, however, best contained in his "Letter to the Members of the Central Committee," written on November 6, the eve of the actual military coup and the night before the Congress of Soviets was to meet:

> With all my power I assure my comrades that now everything hangs on a hair, that on the order of the day are questions that are not solved by conferences, by congresses (even by Congresses of Soviets). . . . If we seize power today, we seize it not against the soviets but for them. Seizure of power is the point of the uprising; its political goal will become clear after the seizure. It would be a disaster or formalism to wait for the uncertain voting of November 7; the people have a right and duty to decide such questions not by voting but by force. . . .[38]

During that night there was nothing left for Lenin to do but to fume against what seemed to him the slowness of Trotsky, who "should be shot." Yet Trotsky was skillfully directing the almost bloodless seizure of practically undefended railway stations and telegraph offices and preparing for the infiltration of the Winter Palace, seat of the Provisional Government and the only seriously defended point in Petrograd. Against the efforts of a handful of military cadets, of a women's battalion, and of reluctant and elusive Cossacks, the persistent pressure of the forces of the Military Revolutionary Committee, threateningly supported by the guns of the cruiser *Aurora* in the Neva, was overwhelming. With less blood than had been shed in the July days, the tired government caved in. Kerensky escaped in a borrowed American legation car, and his colleagues, lucky to escape with their lives, submitted to incarceration in the Peter-and-Paul Fortress.

NOTES

1. Doroshenko, *Istoriia Ukraini 1917-1923,* I, 89; Vinnichenko, *Vidrodzheniia natsii,* I, 219.
2. Piontkovskii, *Khrestomatiia po istorii Oktiabr'skoi revoliutsii,* 3rd edition, p. 126.
3. *Pervyi Vserossiiskii S"ezd sovetov, . . . Stenograficheskii otchet,* in *Tysiacha deviat'sot semnadtsatyi god . . . ,* No. 10, pp. 70, 78, 80.

4. Trotsky, *Do deviatogo ianvaria* and *Poslie peterburgskogo vosstaniia,* in *Sochineniia,* II, i, 3-53 *passim,* 54-57 *passim.*
5. Lenin, "Social Democracy and a Provisional Revolutionary Government" (April, 1905), in *Sochineniia,* 3rd edition, VII, 194, 199.
6. Lenin, "Two Tactics of Social Democracy in a Democratic Revolution" (July, 1905), in *Sochineniia,* 3rd edition, VIII, 41, 51, 57.
7. Lenin, "Imperialism and the Schism in Socialism" (Fall, 1916), in *Sochineniia,* 3rd edition, XIX, 305.
8. Lenin, in "Report on the Current Moment" at Petrograd City Conference of Party (April 27, 1917), in *Sochineniia,* 3rd edition, XX, 182.
9. Lenin, "First Letter from Afar" (March 20, 1917), in *Sochineniia,* 3rd edition, XX, 20.
10. Lenin, *Sochineniia,* 3rd edition, XX, 76-83 *passim,* mainly paraphrased.
11. Sukhanov, *The Russian Revolution* . . . , p. 280.
12. Cf. Lenin, "On the Tasks of the Proletariat in the Present Revolution" (April 20, 1917), in *Sochineniia,* 3rd edition, XX, 90.
13. Lenin, "First Letter on Tactics" (April, 1917), in *Sochineniia,* 3rd edition, XX, 105.
14. *Ibid.,* pp. 101-102. The original of the passage from *Faust* is: *"Grau, teurer Freund, ist alle Theorie, und grün des Lebens goldner Baum"* (from Goethe's *Sämmtliche Werke, Jubiläums-Ausgabe,* XIII, 81.
15. Sukhanov, *op. cit.,* p. 450.
16. Trotsky, *Sochineniia,* III, i, 166.
17. *Izvestiia,* No. 113, July 9 (22), 1917.
18. *Ibid.,* No. 111, July 7 (20), 1917.
19. *Ibid.,* No. 125, July 23 (August 5), 1917.
20. Shidlovskii, *Vospominaniia,* cited in Chernov, *Great Russian Revolution,* p. 257.
21. *Gosudarstvennoe sovieshchanie,* in *Tysiacha deviat'sot semnadtsatyi god* . . . , p. 330.
22. *Izvestiia,* August 11 (24), 1917.
23. For almost complete text, see Golder, *Documents of Russian History, 1914-1917,* pp. 496-504.
24. *Izvestiia,* August 15 (28), 1917.
25. *Piontkovskii, op. cit.,* p. 172.
26. *Vtoroi Vserossiiskii S"ezd Sovetov* . . . p. 171, in *Tysiacha deviat'sot semnadtsatyi god* . . . , VIII.
27. Lenin, Letter to Central Committee, *Sochineniia,* 3rd edition, XXI, 118-119.
28. (September 25, 1917) *Ibid.,* p. 194.
29. "The Tasks of the Revolution" (October 9-10, 1917), *ibid.,* p. 227.
30. "The Crisis has Matured" (October 12, 1917), *ibid.,* pp. 236, 240-241.
31. Letter to Central Committee (October 16-20, 1917), *ibid.,* p. 294.
32. Trotsky, *"Vospominaniia ob oktiabrskom perevote,"* in *Sochineniia,* III, ii, 91.
33. *Krasnaia Letopis',* 1922, Nos. 2-3, pp. 316-332 *passim.*
34. Archives of the Central Committee, in Lenin, *Sochineniia,* 3rd edition, XXI, 331.
35. *Krasnaia Letopis',* 1922, Nos. 2-3, pp. 325-326.

36. Sukhanov, *op. cit.*, p. 531.
37. *Ibid.*, p. 664.
38. Lenin, "Letter to the Members of the Central Committee" (November 6, 1917), in *Sochineniia,* 3rd edition, XXI, 362-363.

SUGGESTIONS FOR FURTHER READING

In addition to works cited in the preceding chapter, mention may be made of Carr's three-volume *Bolshevik Revolution, 1917-1923,* badly organized but including some brilliant chapters, and dominated by near-adoration of Lenin. Deutscher's *The Prophet Armed* is dominated by similar admiration of Trotsky. A more objective discussion is Schapiro's *Origin of the Communist Autocracy,* well equipped with lists of names and dates, which may be used in conjunction with his more recent and comprehensive *Communist Party of the Soviet Union* and Daniels' *Documentary History of Communism,* both previously mentioned. For this period the relevant volume of Lenin's contemporary writings is *Toward the Seizure of Power* (Volume XXI of the English translation of his *Collected Works*). To recapture the idealistic enthusiasm of the Bolshevik upsurge, see *Ten Days That Shook the World,* by John Reed, who lies buried in the Kremlin wall.

Two more recent studies are Rabinowitch's *Prelude to Revolution: The Petrograd Bolsheviks and the July Uprising of 1917* and Daniels' *Red October.*

Chapter

26

The Quest for a Breathing Spell: November, 1917–May, 1918

In a fairy tale, one could at this point record that the fair maiden of the Revolution having been rescued from the evil sorcerer Kerensky by the bold knight Lenin, everyone lived happily ever after. Theoreticians might explain that the "October Revolution" (November 7 was October 25 in the Julian calendar, which the Bolsheviks soon replaced—February, 1918—with the Gregorian) constituted completion of the "February Revolution," transition from the "bourgeois-democratic" to the "proletarian-socialist" phase.

Lenin had no such delusions; the enormous task of "building socialism" still had to be begun. To most socialists and liberals, however, the successful Bolshevik coup simply spelled disaster; the "descent to Bolshevism," as Chernov called it, seemed to spell destruction of all the values of the Revolution. There were, to be sure, those who, hoping for the restoration of the old order, thought the "Bolshevik adventure" held more promise than threat. The American ambassador had not been quite right when, on October 30, he had wired the State Department: "Beginning to think Bolsheviki will make no demonstration; if so, shall regret as believe sentiment turning against them and time opportune moment for giving them wholesome lesson. . . ." [1] Yet many elements in Russia still found comfort in the notion that the fanatical madness of the Bolsheviks and the general unacceptability of their specific program would make their position untenable and soon usher in a Russian Thermidor.

It was a grave error to suppose that the Bolsheviks were fanatically concerned to assure to the Russian people "bread, peace, and land" by way of the immediate triumph of socialism in the guise of nationalization of the land and of industry. Despite their verbal commitments, which included also guarantee of democracy by protection of the Constituent Assembly, the Bolshevik leadership regarded itself as free to plot its course as circumstances might dictate. Their true objective was most succinctly and simply stated by Lenin on November 6: "Seizure of power is the point of the uprising"—seizure of power for the Bolsheviks, that and nothing more. This is not to say that the Bolsheviks were merely power-hungry. Rather, they may properly be viewed as a group of men thoroughly persuaded of the truth of two propositions: (1) that, on the basis of their study of Marx, they knew what would be best for all mankind, both in Russia and in the world at large; (2) that, unlike other Marxists, they alone possessed the integrity and the strength of will to take the measures necessary for the welfare of mankind, whether their fellow-men liked it or not and however much they might resist. If one grants the validity of these two propositions, it follows inexorably that for the welfare of mankind the Bolsheviks had to take power and, having taken it, must retain it.

Fanatical as the Bolsheviks were, Lenin would not permit them prematurely to attempt to put into practice theories not acceptable to those to whom they must be applied; it was necessary to temporize, to weaken by any and all means the position of their enemies, while they consolidated their own strength. Trotsky later pointed out that it is only natural to adjust policies to practical realities; as yet, however, there was no suspicion that Trotsky would in a few years be developing the concept of *The Revolution Betrayed.* For the moment, no sacrifice of theoretical positions mattered; as Lenin had paraphrased Goethe, "Theory, my friend, is gray, but green is the eternal tree of life."

In the background of their thinking was the conviction of the imminence of world revolution. Few supposed that it would be possible for "socialist" revolution to triumph in Russia alone; victory, it was believed, could be achieved only when the more economically advanced countries of the West caught fire from the Russian spark. Lenin, ever skeptical of abstract theory, soon (January 20, 1918) expressed his reservations:

> There is no doubt that the socialist revolution in Europe must begin and is beginning. All our hopes for the *definitive* victory of socialism are based on this conviction and on this scientific prediction. . . . But it would be a mistake to build the tactics of the socialist government of Russia on efforts to determine whether the European, and especially the German, socialist revolution will or will not begin in the next six months (or a similar short period). Since it is nowise possible to determine this, all such attempts, objectively, amount only to a blind gamble.[2]

THE SECOND CONGRESS OF SOVIETS

The most immediately pressing problem was to deal with the Second All-Russian Congress of Soviets, the opening of which was delayed by the Bolsheviks until about 11:00 P.M. on November 7, by which time almost all armed resistance to the uprising had been overcome. Lenin, still mistrusting the "uncertain voting," refused to attend. Amidst scenes of disorder, a presidium of twenty-two members was declared elected by acclamation; fourteen of them were Bolsheviks. Despite his recent treason to the Party by publishing word of the impending uprising, a now penitent Kamenev was put in the chair. Martov demanded immediate measures to stop the bloodshed in the streets and creation of a socialist coalition in place of the Bolshevik dictatorship. Instead of fighting in the Congress, most of the SR's, Mensheviks, and Bund members withdrew; of them only the Left SR's, the Menshevik Internationalists, and Poale Zion (the extreme left Jewish group) remained. About three o'clock in the morning, after a brief recess, Kamenev was able to announce completion of the overthrow of the old government. After a couple more stormy hours, the Bolsheviks were at last able to force adoption of a proclamation that the Congress was assuming power.

After a relatively quiet day, the Congress reconvened at 9:00 P.M. on November 8. Its first action was to abolish the death penalty, which the Kerensky regime had reintroduced at the front; Trotsky later recounted that when Lenin "learned of this first legislative act his anger knew no bounds. 'This is madness,' he repeated. 'How can we accomplish a revolution without shooting?' "[3] The Congress soon turned to more serious business; the three thorniest problems were peace, land, and government.

Enunciation of the Bolshevik attitude toward the war was reserved for Lenin himself. The Bolshevik "Appeal to the peoples and governments of all warring countries" was, to a certain extent, a mere reaffirmation of the demand for immediate peace without annexations and without indemnities which had been the program of the Provisional Government since May. Its futility as a means of achieving peace was implicitly admitted by Lenin, who remarked that "a war cannot be ended by renunciation, a war cannot be ended unilaterally."[4] As critics at the Congress were quick to point out, the peace declaration was not phrased as an ultimatum; Lenin was keeping the door open for negotiations that might lead to a peace on some other basis.

The vital question of land policy was also reserved for presentation by Lenin, whose prestige had never stood higher. Denouncing the late Provisional Government for having contributed to the spread of anarchy and pogroms in the countryside, Lenin proposed a decree which proclaimed the abolition of all landlord rights without compensation, threatened dire punishment to anyone damaging the confiscated property, and left the lands of "rank-and-file peasants and rank-and-file cossacks" in their possession. A long "Peasant Instruction Concerning the Land" still reserved final settlement of the land problem to the Constituent Assembly but gave the force of "temporary law" to a somewhat vague exposition of "the most just solution of the land question." The basic principle was that everyone had the right to work the land by his own or his family's labor (hired labor was prohibited) and to enjoy its fruits. Distribution from the general land fund was to be made periodically "with regard to local conditions, according to a labor or a consumption norm," with compensation for improvements to the former cultivator. In districts where there was insufficient arable land, the State was to assist, and if necessary compel, emigration to less populous regions. Special properties, such as orchards and stud farms, were not to be divided but administered by the State or by communes.[5]

There was immediate protest that these proposals reflected the ideas of the SR's, not of the Marxists. Lenin freely admitted the validity of the comment but retorted:

> We must follow life. . . . Whether the program is in our spirit or in an SR spirit does not matter. What matters is that the peasantry should get the firm conviction that there are no longer landlords in the village, that the peasants themselves may . . . order their own life.[6]

No discussion of the merits of the draft was permitted or even seriously attempted. Instead, spokesmen of the Executive Committee of the All-Russian Soviets of Peasants' Deputies and of the Third Army returned to their demand for immediate release of those of their colleagues who had been arrested with the old Provisional Government in the Winter Palace the night before. In reply, an unidentified peasant from Tver received an ovation for advocating arrest of the whole Peasant Executive Committee, while Trotsky ridiculed the significance of the arrests. After an hour's recess for "study," the land decree and the instruction were adopted in the early morning hours of November 9, amidst stormy enthusiasm, with only one negative vote and eight abstentions recorded.

Formal organization of a new governmental authority caused a little more trouble. From the chair, Kamenev proposed a decree establishing a new Provisional Government, to be known as the Council of People's Commissars (*Sovnarkom*) and to hold power, subject to the Congress of Soviets or its Executive Committee, until the meeting of the Constituent Assembly; a list of commissars, all Bolsheviks and headed by Lenin, was included in the proposal.

Speaking for the Menshevik-Internationalists, B. V. Avilov at once protested that such a government would be no more able to solve the problems of bread and peace than had its predecessor. He predicted that the Bolsheviks —unable to produce manufactured goods to exchange with the peasants; and lacking the support of the upper and middle peasantry, who controlled such food supplies as existed—would be driven to the futile expedient of trying to gather food by force. He foresaw that the only possible peace would be a very grievous one for Russia. He maintained also that it was wrong for the Bolsheviks to monopolize executive power; the only way to save the Revolution from ruin was to base authority on the whole Congress of Soviets, or at the very least on all those groups that had faithfully remained in it.

For the Left SR's, Karelin explained that his fraction had refused to enter the government because their

> entrance into a Bolshevik ministry would have created a gulf between them and the detachments of the revolutionary army that had left the Congress, a gulf which would have precluded the possibility of their mediation between the Bolsheviks and these groups.

He disclaimed any desire to isolate the Bolsheviks, because "with the fate of the Bolsheviks is tied up the fate of the whole revolution; their ruin will be the ruin of the revolution." In this dilemma, he announced that the Left SR's would continue to support the Bolsheviks in their efforts to solve the pressing problems of the day but would vote against the establishment of a purely Bolshevik government, for "the aggressive policy of the Bolsheviks with regard to the other parties is inadmissible." [7]

Trotsky replied intransigently, arguing that the Bolsheviks were interested only in a coalition of classes, not of parties, and that the Bolsheviks alone represented the will of the masses. He evoked tremendous applause by asserting that "there had been needed a party which would snatch power from the hands of the counter-revolutionists and would say to you [the Congress of Soviets]: 'Here is the power, and you must take it.' " [8]

With great difficulty a spokesman of *Vikzhel,* the railwaymen's trade union, got the floor to announce that his organization was opposed to the seizure of power by any one party and that it challenged the legality of this rump of the Congress of Soviets. Pending formation of a broadly based government, the union was taking over operation of the railways. It would not permit the movement of troops against Petrograd, and if the Bolsheviks attempted reprisals, they would cut off the food supply of the capital.

Nevertheless, the proposed decree was adopted "by a preponderant majority," although "in view of the late hour" a roll call was refused.[9] It remained only to confirm the selection of a Central Executive Committee, vested with legislative authority, to which the Council of People's Commissars was to be "responsible." Of its 101 members (soon increased to 110), 62 were Bolsheviks. To the tune of appeals to the front to maintain discipline and to the railwaymen to coöperate in exchange for improved material conditions, the Second All-Russian Congress of Soviets of Workers' and Soldiers' Deputies disbanded just after 5:00 A.M. on November 9. Thus the Bolsheviks had fulfilled Lenin's prediction of November 6: "If we seize power today, we seize it not against the soviets but for them." Garbed in the vestments of the soviets, the Bolsheviks could henceforth deny the nakedness of their actions.

DANGERS AND DIFFICULTIES OF THE NEW REGIME

Outside the precincts of the Smolny Institute, the fashionable school for young ladies which since August had been the Soviet headquarters, matters seemed less promising than within its walls. Most of the other socialist organizations were strongly opposed to a Bolshevik dictatorship. There was still the possibility that Kerensky would succeed in an effort to use the army to crush the new regime. Within the Bolshevik organization itself, there was a lack of experienced personnel, and there were elements not prepared to sacrifice principle to expediency. There was the problem of how to deal with the promised Constituent Assembly. Even assuming that the Bolsheviks could somehow cling to power, current problems must be handled —the press, the courts, the Church, education, social insurance, the direction of industry, the trade unions, the peasants, the transition to a socialist organization of production. Looming over all was the problem of the war, with its danger that the German army might simply overrun Russia and entrust power to its own agents. In the remainder of this chapter, all these problems must be successively considered, for mere decrees in the name of the Second Congress of Soviets could not provide a reliable answer to the very uncertain question of the ultimate outcome.

From a theoretician's standpoint, the almost complete isolation of the Bolsheviks within the ranks of the socialists might have seemed the greatest danger to the permanence of their power. In the early morning of November 8, when the members of the Provisional Government were being arrested in the Winter Palace, a meeting was held to challenge the authority of the Bolshevik-controlled Second Congress of Soviets. In attendance were representatives of the City Duma (the regular municipal government of Petrograd), of the Central Executive Committee of the First (June) Congress of Soviets of Workers' and Soldiers' Deputies, of the Executive Committee of Peasants' Deputies, of the SR and Menshevik delegates who had left the Second Congress at Smolny, of the railwaymen's union, of the post and telegraph union, of the Central Committees of the SR and Menshevik parties, of the Council of the Russian Republic (Kerensky's "Pre-Parliament"), and of various army committees from the front. There was formed an "All-Russian Committee for the Salvation of the Fatherland and the Revolution." It was headed by the SR Gotz, vice-chairman of the Soviet Central Executive Committee, supported by Avksentiev, chairman of the Peasant Soviet and of the Pre-Parliament.

Its efforts to counteract the seizure of power by the Bolsheviks were, however, paralyzed by the same "pacifist illusions," the same reliance on purely moral force and spontaneous voluntarism that had contributed to the downfall of the Kerensky government. It was all very well to cry out: "Do not recognize the authority of violence!" [10] It might be true that "it should be clear to all by now that the Soviet power is nothing but a dictatorship against the will of the proletariat and that counter-revolution can come not only from the Right but also from the Left." But there was no remedy forthcoming from men who, having no organized force of their own, felt:

> It is important . . . to exercise great caution. Already rumors are afloat that certain generals wish to take advantage of the situation. They will at first declare themselves our allies and march under our banners in order that they may overthrow us afterward.[11]

How little the Bolsheviks really had to fear in those critical days from the superficially formidable socialist opposition is perhaps most clearly expressed in a proclamation of the Right SR's, dated November 9:

> The Bolsheviks are doing everything in their power to bring about a bloody civil war. They seized power with the aid of guns, and they now perceive that only by means of guns can they retain power for any length of time. . . . Their power is short-lived. . . . Their creation is a soap bubble. . . . The great Russian Revolution is bigger, more sublime, and on a wider scale than the Petrograd adventure of the Bolsheviks. . . . The toiling masses of Russia *will* secure land, peace, and freedom. . . . But to do this there must be no civil war. The Bolshevik adventure must be brought to an end in a *peaceful manner*. . . . A general strike against the Bolsheviks! Boycott them! . . .[12]

The old-line revolutionaries, who had made so many personal sacrifices in the struggle against tsarism, were unwilling to abandon their principles in the fight against counter-revolutionaries "from the Left." Still intoxicated, perhaps, by the startling and unexpected success of the March Revolution, they looked for a repetition of the miracle, unmindful of the fact that now there sat in the seats of the ministers more than one man "who could bang his fist on the table."

Potentially more formidable were the efforts of Kerensky, who had fled from Petrograd to the front to organize military intervention against the Bolsheviks. These efforts, however, were sabotaged by some of the generals, not from love of the Bolsheviks but from hatred of the Revolution. Kornilov's attempt at direct overthrow of the Revolution in September had failed so miserably that no general would attempt its repetition. Now, however, the Kerensky regime had been assailed in the rear, by professed socialists distinguished by their fanaticism. It was well understood that the Bolsheviks had no significant following, either among the workers or among the peasants. Who on November 7 could foresee that the Bolsheviks would scrap their own land program, known to be wholly unacceptable to the peasantry, in favor of the program of the SR's? Who could foresee that the Bolsheviks would not press nationalization of industry, which could have brought only disorganization and suffering? What reason was there to disagree with revolutionary experts such as the Right SR's: "Their power is short-lived. . . . Their creation is a soap-bubble"? When the bubble burst, who would stand to profit? Not Kerensky, who had fallen so ignominiously. The time would be ripe, without a struggle, for the generals to take over and restore a sane and orderly regime.

Kerensky's order to the Third Cavalry Corps to entrain for Petrograd was countermanded by General Cheremisov, commander-in-chief of the Northern Front. Not until November 9 was General Krasnov able to balance his conflicting loyalties to his superior officers in the chain of command and advance with his Cossacks to attack the revolutionary capital:

> I had at my disposal . . . 480 Cossacks in all. . . . To march with such a force against Tsarskoye Selo, where the garrison consisted of some sixteen thousand soldiers, and on to Petrograd, where there were about two hundred thousand . . . was sheer stupidity. But civil war is not war. Its rules are different, in it resolution and impact are everything. I knew well the habits and the mood of the Petrograd garrison. They go to bed late, after having a good time in the pubs and the cinemas, so that you can't wake them up in the morning; to seize Tsarskoye at dawn, when our strength could not be seen, seemed possible; the taking of Tsarskoye and our approach to Petrograd were bound to influence the morale of the garrison, strengthen the position of those fighting against the Bolsheviks, and make the garrison come over to our side.[13]

Krasnov did take Tsarskoye Selo. What might not have been accomplished if his fellow generals had not dragged their feet?

Anticipating the arrival of Krasnov, the military cadets, still opposed to the Bolsheviks, staged an uprising in Petrograd itself. For a couple of days, the situation was uncertain. As Trotsky has recorded, "The military operations, on both sides, were hidden in a fog." A number of tsarist officers began to aid the Bolsheviks; of one of them Trotsky recalled:

> Colonel Walden commanded at Pulkovaia Gora . . . and this clash decided the fate of Kerensky's offensive. This Walden was a typical colonel, and what his idea was in joining us I still do not understand. The colonel was not young and had been wounded many times. He could not possibly have sympathized with us, for he understood nothing. But evidently he had such a strong hatred for Kerensky that it inspired in him a temporary sympathy for us.[14]

On November 11, the railwaymen's executive committee (*Vikzhel*), proclaiming its neutrality, announced suspension of all rail service if the fighting were not stopped. On the thirteenth, Krasnov proposed a cessation of hostilities; Kerensky found it expedient to disappear. "The Committee for the Salvation of the Revolution" offered the supreme command to General Dukhonin, with Avksentiev as prime minister. Dukhonin accepted but ordered the cessation of all fighting (November 14).

The cessation of fighting confirmed the Bolsheviks in military control at Petrograd. Elsewhere, the situation remained confused. At Moscow, the Bolsheviks had been compelled to evacuate the Kremlin (November 10), but their artillery now brought about the surrender of the local "Committee of Public Safety" (November 15). The same day General Alexeiev began the formation of an anti-Bolshevik Volunteer Army at Novocherkassk, near the mouth of the Don. The Don Cossacks, though threatening no offensive action, had already declared their hostility to the "criminal" action of the Bolsheviks (November 7). A Ukrainian People's Republic was proclaimed at Kiev (November 20).

While the military issue was still in doubt, the Bolsheviks consented to negotiate with the other socialist parties. They insisted, however, that under all circumstances Lenin must head the government; their opponents put forward the candidacy of Chernov. How remote the wrangle was from the sentiment of the Petrograd masses is suggested by the reported remarks of a delegation of workmen who broke into one of the conferences, exclaiming:

> Here's a whole week gone while bloodshed continues between the two revolutionary camps. This criminal civil war! We demand that it be ended immediately! Enough! You've been sitting for two days, discussing the question of an agreement, but it looks as if you weren't in any hurry at all. We cannot permit longer continuance of civil war. To the devil with Lenin and with Chernov! Hang them both! . . .

When both sides insisted that the obstacles were all created by their opponents, the workmen left, exclaiming:

> It's impossible to make head or tail out of which of you is right! The lot of you are not worth having the earth support you! If we were to hang you all on one tree, there would be peace in the country.[15]

It was the old story of tsarist days, when contradictory expositions by the conflicting revolutionary groups had left the masses troubled and confused, with no alternative but to submit to those who directed the bayonets; the only difference was that now armed power was in the hands of the Bolsheviks.

In fact, the external threat to the Bolshevik regime was less serious than were its internal difficulties. For one thing, the Bolsheviks were a party of skilled agitators, but with no experience in administration. The chaotic scenes that had attended the March Revolution seemed a marvel of orderliness compared to the November days. A year later, Larin, who had served as chief of the Bureau of Legislation under the infant Council of People's Commissars, recalled:

> The government held no regular meetings at that time. . . . Of the first fifteen decrees that comprise the present No. 1 of the "Collection of Statutes," only two were actually submitted for consideration by the Sovnarkom. . . . I remember the consternation of Vladimir Ilich [Lenin] when . . . without his

> knowledge but over his name there was published . . . a decree . . . conferring legislative powers on the Sovnarkom. . . .[16]

In the Central Executive Committee of the Second Congress of Soviets, the Left SR's protested bitterly but futilely against abolition of civil liberties by executive decree, never submitted to the responsible Soviet organ. The hit-or-miss methods of the new government in recruiting personnel are startlingly illustrated in Pestkovsky's recollections of how he visited Smolny looking for a minor job and, having mentioned that he had studied banking at the University of London, was told he was to be director of the State Bank. "I was frightened and replied that I had no desire to hold this post, since it was absolutely 'not in my line' ";[17] nevertheless, he was appointed, with Lenin's personal approval.

Another personnel danger was the tendency of some Bolsheviks to gag at the arbitrary line being pursued under Lenin's guidance. Only ten days after the seizure of power (November 17), eleven highly-placed Bolsheviks, including five of the fourteen People's Commissars, protested before the Soviet Central Executive Committee against "preservation of a purely Bolshevik government by means of political terror." [18] Simultaneously, five members of the Party's Central Committee (including Rykov, who, in 1924, was to succeed Lenin as prime minister) resigned in protest against the "ruinous policy of the Central Committee, carried out against the will of a huge part of the proletariat and soldiers who crave the earliest cessation of bloodshed by the separate wings of the democracy." [19] Lozovsky, chief contact man between the Party and the trade unions, published a list of reasons why "I cannot, in the name of Party discipline, be silent," and demanding convocation of a Party congress "to decide whether the Russian Social-Democratic Workers' Party (Bolshevik) shall remain Marxist and the party of the working class or shall follow a course that has nothing in common with revolutionary Marxism." [20]

The Party's only ally, the Left SR's, continued to harass the Bolsheviks with demands for an all-socialist coalition. A Special Congress of Soviets of Peasants' Deputies, completely dominated by the Left SR's, formally demanded (November 26) formation of a new government on a broad base; despite open Bolshevik opposition, the resolution was carried by 175 to 22, with 6 abstaining.

THE CONSTITUENT ASSEMBLY

The Bolsheviks accordingly dared not risk interference with the arrangements for the election of the Constituent Assembly, scheduled for November 25. It was not merely that for months they had been insistently demanding its convocation. Even in its very last proclamation before the uprising, the Military Revolutionary Committee had cited salvation of the Constituent

Assembly as a major reason for the overthrow of Kerensky. So great was the propaganda value of the concept that, even though holding the reins, the Bolsheviks had not claimed to base their power on the soviets alone. The peace declaration of November 8 had specifically promised: "We shall submit [replies] for consideration to the Constituent Assembly, which will then decide, with power, what can and cannot be conceded." [21] The land decree had stated: "The land question in its full scope is to be settled by the All-Russian Constituent Assembly," and had proclaimed only a "temporary law . . . pending the meeting of the Constituent Assembly." [22] Finally, "By decree of the All-Russian Congress of Soviets, a Provisional Workers' and Peasants' Government, to be known as the Council of People's Commissars, is formed to govern the country until the meeting of the Constituent Assembly." [23] Could this admittedly provisional regime risk converting itself into a permanent one without even calling the Constituent Assembly?

No doubt it would have liked to, for the Bolsheviks did not permit themselves even to dream of controlling more than one-third of the Assembly's members. The calculations of the Left SR's that, if they could win the support of the Ukrainian Socialists, the three parties might have a majority, were but cold comfort to Lenin and those who agreed with him on the need for control by a single, compact, rigidly disciplined party. On the eve of the elections, they made it plain in published statements that, after all, they would not regard themselves as bound by the results of "uncertain voting."

As they had anticipated, the outcome of the elections was unsatisfactory. In Petrograd, they had 45 percent of the vote (rising to 77 percent in the wards where the barracks were situated), but in the 54 electoral regions (out of 79) for which the popular vote is available, they polled only 9 million, as against 21 million for the SR's and over 4.5 million for the "bourgeois" parties. The final official figures (omitting a few areas in or near the Caucasus) show 707 deputies, of whom 370 were "Right" and 40 "Left" SR's; the Bolsheviks numbered 175, their Marxist enemies, the Mensheviks, 16; the "bourgeois" Cadets elected only 17.

December 11 had been the day set for the Assembly to meet. On that day, amidst mass demonstrations in the streets of Petrograd, some fifty deputies, mostly SR's but including four Cadets, defiantly met in the old Duma building and elected Chernov temporary chairman. The Sovnarkom at once replied by declaring the Cadet Party the enemy of the people and decreed arrest of its leaders. To protests in the Executive Committee, Trotsky replied:

> At the time of the French Revolution more honest men than the Cadets were guillotined by the Jacobins for opposing the people. We have not executed anyone and do not intend to do so, but there are moments of the people's wrath, and the Cadets are bringing it down on themselves.[24]

Lenin stated flatly: "The soviets are superior to any parliament, to any Constituent Assembly. [Noise; cries of 'Lie.']" [25]

The Left SR's, however, had struck a bargain with the Bolsheviks. Entry of several SR's into the Sovnarkom had for Lenin the immense advantage of further confusing and neutralizing many peasants. Karelin, one of the new Left SR members of the government, defined their purpose in this uneasy alliance:

> Our only point of disagreement is the question of [mass] terror which the Left SR's absolutely condemn. We also think that certain measures though theoretically sound are too daring in practice. On the whole, our party performs the function of regulating and tempering the excessive boldness of the Bolsheviks.[26]

The tempering influence of the junior partner could not prevent the arrest of Avksentiev (December 30) or the issue of orders for the arrest of Chernov and other SR leaders, but it did secure the opening of the Constituent Assembly on January 18, 1918.

Notwithstanding all the pressure the Bolsheviks could bring to bear, Sverdlov, who as chairman of the Soviet Central Executive Committee had insisted on his right to take the chair at the opening of the session, soon had to announce that Victor Chernov had been elected chairman by a vote of 244 to 151. By a similar vote, the Assembly refused to accept a Bolshevik declaration as the basis for discussion. The Bolsheviks, refusing to "shield the enemies of the people in their criminal acts," walked out; the Left SR's followed them. The Assembly then proceeded, before the guards, announcing they were "tired," forced adjournment at 4:40 A.M., to approve a land law similar in principle to the decree of November 8, a declaration favoring a "universal democratic peace" in place of separate negotiations with the Germans, and proclamation of a Russian Democratic Federative Republic.

The Bolsheviks' reply was simple and swift. Backing up Lenin's assertion that "we will not give up the Soviet power for anything in the world," [27] the Central Executive Committee shouted down the protests of the Menshevik-Internationalists and decreed dissolution of the Constituent Assembly. The ease with which the dissolution was accomplished was not wholly a tribute to the efficacy of the Bolsheviks' tactics. It is true that the use of troops to fire on the unarmed crowds that demonstrated enthusiastically for the Constituent Assembly, as well as the murder of two Cadet deputies, helped stifle open protest; only the personal prestige of Maxim Gorky made it possible for him to publish a signed editorial equating the Bolsheviks' action to that of the tsar's soldiers on "Bloody Sunday."

More important, perhaps, was the attitude of the SR majority. Convinced of the moral weight of the Constituent Assembly, they persisted in believing that "the Bolshevik adventure . . . like a soap-bubble, will burst at the first contact with hard facts." They looked forward to a reassembling of the Constituent Assembly at some future date, its honor untarnished by any resort to violence. They had therefore resisted the temptation to reply to provocation and, ignoring the rifles pointed at speakers from the galleries, had concentrated on developing their program for the record. A few, led by Sokolov (probably the author of the famous Order No. 1), privately tried to organize in advance armed resistance to a dissolution order but were discouraged by getting only promises not to march against the Assembly.

No less important than the passivity of the SR majority were the tepid interest of the Cadets and the sullen hostility of monarchist elements, the "Bolsheviks of the Right." After the elections, Lenin had developed an ingenious theory that the single lists offered the voters by the SR's (an arrangement on which the Left had insisted) had given unfair advantage to the Right and Center because, although the peasants were thinking of the Left SR position, the united list made it impossible for the voter to choose between one SR and another. The Cadets offered a different explanation to account for their own poor showing; the results had reflected Bolshevik terrorism, not the free will of the people. They therefore showed little interest in reëstablishing the Constituent Assembly. The extreme Right did not worry about the validity of the election results; as a former colonel of gendarmes is reported to have said: "We are against the Constituent Assembly, we shall so act that the Assembly will not exist, and the Bolsheviks will go along with us." [28]

CONSOLIDATION OF BOLSHEVIK POWER

The suppression of the Constituent Assembly removed the last possibility that the Bolsheviks, who had seized power by force, could be deprived of it by votes. Thenceforth they subjected their policies to scrutiny only by a succession of Congresses of Soviets, the composition of which they were now in a position to control in advance. To signalize the new situation, they made haste to have a Third Congress of Soviets strike the word "Provisional" out of the government's title (January 31). Not until the summer were they faced with serious danger of forcible overthrow. In the meantime, they continued to strengthen the basis of their power and began to shape the lines along which they proposed to "socialize" Russia.

Among the major steps that had immediately been taken to muzzle opposition was a decree of November 9 by which the Sovnarkom authorized itself to shut down all hostile newspapers. A few days later, the Soviet Central Executive Committee broadened this measure by ordering confiscation of all private printing presses and stocks of paper. In reply to objections, Trotsky explained:

> You say that we demanded freedom of the press for *Pravda.* But then we were in such a situation that we were demanding a minimum program. Now we are demanding a maximum.

A Left SR (Karelin) condemned this as "Hottentot morality, under which to steal my wife is wrong, but when I steal it is all right." Lenin curtly said, "Trotsky was right . . . Of course we are offering something new, because we are on the road to socialism. . . ." [29] The opposition was now reduced to the same mouse-and-cat policy that all revolutionaries had pursued in the days of the tsars.

The existing judicial system was abolished, its place being taken by "people's courts," whose proceedings were most informal and arbitrary. As a substitute for the *Okhrana,* the tsarist political police, there was established (December 20) the "All-Russian Extraordinary Commission [*Cheka*] to fight counter-revolution and sabotage"; it was specifically instructed "to turn its attention first of all to the press, Right SR's, saboteurs, and strikers." [30] The Cheka carried on an ever-widening policy of terror, on the explicit principle:

> The foe had to be made to feel that there was an all-seeing eye and a heavy punishing hand that would mercilessly fall on his head as soon as he made an attempt against Soviet power. . . . This is no guillotine cutting off heads in accordance with the decision of a tribunal. No, it destroys him without trial if it catches him on the scene of the offense, isolates him from society by shutting him up in a concentration camp, or hands him over to a tribunal when the case requires detailed investigation and wide publicity.[31]

With increased powers and ever-ramifying organization, the Cheka was to be one of the main props of the Bolshevik dictatorship. Notwithstanding the official abolition of the death penalty, it adopted (February 22) a declaration that

> at the present moment, when the hydra of counter-revolution is becoming every day more insolent, inspired by the treacherous assault of the German counter-revolutionaries, when the world bourgeoisie is trying to stifle the Russian proletariat, the vanguard of the revolutionary international, the All-Russian Extraordinary commission . . . sees no other measures to fight counter-revolutionaries, spies, speculators, ruffians, hooligans, saboteurs and other parasites than *merciless annihilation on the spot of the offense* and therefore declares that all . . . *will be mercilessly shot by the commission's detachments on the spot of the offense.*[32]

As Dzerzhinski, the idealistic Pole whose chief interest was in neglected children, chosen by Lenin to head the Cheka, wrote to his wife: "My thinking compels me to be merciless, and I have the firm will to follow my thinking to the utmost." [33]

The Bolsheviks were slow to interfere in Church affairs. On the one hand, they did not repeal the proclamation of religious freedom made by the

Provisional Government; on the other, they permitted the restoration of the Orthodox Patriarchate, an office that had been in abeyance since the reign of Peter the Great. However, late in December they extended the Provisional Government's interference with Church schools from those receiving State aid to the ecclesiastical seminaries as well. They also decreed civil marriage (December 31) and permitted divorce on the simple affirmation of either party. Provoked by a series of further encroachments on ecclesiastical privilege and outraged by "the frightful and bestial murders of people entirely innocent, even of people lying sick in bed, all done not only under cover of the darkness of night but undertaken with unheard-of insolence and ruthless cruelty, in full daylight, without any trial and in defiance of all justice and legality, . . . the Humble Tikhon, by the Grace of God Patriarch of Moscow and of All Russia" issued a pastoral letter anathematizing the Bolsheviks and calling for the organization of "unions of the spirit" to wage a spiritual struggle against them.[34] The Sovnarkom replied (February 5) with a decree separating the Church from the state, the school from the Church, and the Church from most of its property.

Transfer of Church schools to the state only complicated the chaos in education, for the Bolsheviks had no clear educational policies save destruction of the existing system, staffed principally by their enemies. As late as April 10, Lunarcharsky, People's Commissar of Education, could say only that

> the elementary schools will be reorganized . . . in the spirit of socialist citizenship. . . . The high school is a nursery of counter-revolution. . . . The universities . . . in their present state . . . are of no value whatever.[35]

More attention, naturally, was paid to economic and social questions. Only four days after the seizure of power, a detailed decree established for all Russia a legal eight-hour day and forty-eight-hour week, with elaborate regulations governing overtime and holidays. Two days later, a brief decree promised insurance for all wage-earners without exception, to cover all forms of disability, as well as unemployment. Under the confused circumstances of the times, these decrees could of course have no practical meaning. It may be of interest to note that their authors, Larin and Shliapnikov, were among the Bolsheviks who signed the protest of November 17 against the course then being pursued by their Party as "certain to alienate the proletarian masses . . . and lead to the ruin of the Revolution and the country." [36]

Industry was left in private hands, though the State Bank was taken over at once and a decree of December 27 declared banking a state monopoly. Impatient workers who expelled owners or managers were now told by Lenin that, since they did not know how to run the factories, they must reinstate those who did. To appease them, a Decree on Workers' Control (November 27) nominally gave elected committees of workers the right to supervise production, to fix the minimum of output of the enterprise, and to take measures to establish the cost of production (#6), with right of access to all books and correspondence (#7). "Decisions of the organs of Workers' Control are binding on the owners of enterprises," who might, however, appeal against them within three days to higher organs of workers' control (#8).[37] Regulations attached to the decree expressly forbade the workers' committees to assume functions of executive management. Thus the decree really amounted to the establishment of limited government control over industry, with the threat of nationalization hanging over any employer believed guilty of sabotaging the Revolution by curtailing production. In anticipation of further extension of state direction of the economy, a Supreme Council of People's Economy (often referred to, from its Russian initials, as *Vesenha*) was set up (December 14); on paper it had very wide powers over production, distribution, and state finance; its chairman became a member of the Council of People's Commissars.

Oddly enough, the Bolsheviks destroyed the independence of labor before they gave serious attention to the capitalists. In preparation for the First All-Russian Congress of Trade Unions, Lozovsky, who had become secretary of the All-Russian Central Council of Trade Unions in 1907 and whose boast it was that "after six months of constructive work" (July, 1917 to January, 1918) the number of trade unionists "has passed the 3,000,000 mark,"[38] was publicly expelled from the Party (January 11) for his continued devotion to normal trade-union principles. The Congress, meeting only two days after the dissolution of the Constituent Assembly, dutifully resolved:

> Revolutionary socialists have never regarded trade unions merely as organs of economic struggle of the proletariat for improvement of the condition of the working class within the framework of the capitalist system (#3). . . . The trade unions must wholly and unselfishly support the policy of the socialist Soviet power guided by the Council of People's Commissars (#5). . . . Trade unions must assume the chief work in organizing production and restoring the blasted productive forces of the country (#6). . . . The Congress is convinced that . . . the trade unions will inevitably be converted into organs of the socialist state, membership in which will for all persons engaged in a given [branch of] production be a state obligation.[39]

Gorky's paper continued to publish workers' protests:

> This government which calls itself a Soviet of Workers and Peasants has done everything to oppose the will of the workers. . . . We were promised bread, and were given hunger, civil war. . . . There is unemployment everywhere and . . . no means of fighting it. Our trade unions are crushed, and the factory committees can do nothing for us. [March 20.][40]

> The Soviet Government takes the stand that it alone expresses fully the interests of the working masses and that, therefore, all other organizations

> can exist only in so far as they subscribe without a murmur to the internal and external policies of the Soviet of People's Commissars [Sovnarkom]. Since the November Revolution we have witnessed innumerable instances of how big, small, or even microscopic commissars have used every kind of oppression, including bayonets, in their dealings with recalcitrant proletarian organizations. [April 29.][41]

Nevertheless, the work of coördination went forward. The factory-shop committees, whose independence had once been so useful to the Bolsheviks, were now subjected to the trade unions, the trade unions to the State.

Outstanding among the trade unions was *Vikzhel,* the railwaymen's union, which had been vital in the struggle against Kornilov but had threatened to strike against seizure of power by the Bolsheviks alone. Outmaneuvered then, it had persistently supported the Constituent Assembly. To combat its influence, a rival union was created in January, endowed with special wage arrangements. By March, even Shliapnikov, one of the few proletarians in the Bolshevik high command, had to admit

> the necessity of taking the most rigorous measures in order to reëstablish labor discipline on the railways at any cost and before all else. . . . From the moment the railwaymen were guaranteed a minimum wage they offered no guarantee whatsoever of minimum work on the railways.[42]

The syndicalist regime on the railways was terminated by decree, and the appropriate People's Commissar was given nearly dictatorial powers in matters relating to railway transport.

In the spring of 1918, the Bolsheviks were sufficiently in the saddle to give some thought to the charting of their future course. As Lenin saw it, "We, the party of the Bolsheviks, *convinced* Russia. We *snatched* Russia from the rich for the poor, from the exploiters for the toilers. We must now *govern* Russia." [43] As an expression of the spirit in which Russia must be governed, as well as to distinguish the Party sharply from the Social-Democratic parties of Western Europe, Lenin now renewed his recommendation that the Party change its name. At the first Party Congress after the seizure of power (March, 1918) was adopted the style of "Russian Communist Party (of the Bolsheviks)." Lenin further urged:

> We must clearly set before ourselves the goal . . . of creating a communist society, not limited merely to expropriation of factories, mills, land, and means of production, not limited merely to strict accounting and control over production and distribution, but going on to realization of the principle: from each according to his abilities, to each according to his needs.[44]

What stages must be passed through in the transition, "we do not know and cannot know." [45] Lenin was content to deal with the problems of the moment.

Most difficult to reconcile with Marxist theory was the agrarian situation, for it was clear to all that the peasantry had no stomach for socialism if applied to them. Yet, insisted Lenin, the peasants would support the proletariat, for they themselves wished to "live not by others' toil":

> Right was that old man, a Bolshevik, who explained to a Cossack what Bolshevism is. To the Cossack's question, "Is it true that you Bolsheviks loot?" the old man replied: "Yes, we loot the looted." [46]

Promising to "divide the land justly, from the viewpoint preëminently of petty economy," [47] he secured issue by the Soviet Central Executive Committee of a "Fundamental Law of Land Socialization" (February 19). It reaffirmed and elaborated the principles of the provisional decree of November 8: "The general and basic source of any right to the use of agricultural land is individual labor" [48] (Article 13). The grain trade was to remain a state monopoly (Article 19).

Although the law promised social security (Article 14) and extensive calamity insurance (Article 16) to the peasants, an official of the People's Commissariat of Agriculture was not far wrong in saying "there is not a grain of socialism in it." [49] It is true that the law did anticipate the ultimate establishment of state farms employing hired wage labor. Passing reference was made to the encouragement of collective farming as "leading to socialist economy" (Article 11). One article specified that "surplus income derived from the natural fertility of the best pieces of land and also from a more advantageous situation in relation to the market is to go for social needs at the disposal of organs of the Soviet power" (Article 17). But all this was on paper.

Actually, of course, the peasants continued to carry out seizure and division of the land in their own way, conditioned largely by the traditions of communal land ownership combined with individual economy. In May, Lenin had to recognize that:

> Either we subject this petty bourgeois to *our* control . . . or he will inevitably and unavoidably overthrow our workers' power, as the Napoleons and Cavaignacs overthrew the revolution, precisely on this soil of small ownership. . . . Only Left SR's with their rhetoric about the "toiling" peasantry fail to see this simple and clear truth, but who will take seriously Left SR's drowning in rhetoric? [50]

More than a decade was to pass, however, before it became expedient directly to throw down the gauntlet. For the moment it seemed sufficient to "carry the class war into the villages," organizing "committees of the village poor," themselves individualists, to coöperate with urban "flying columns" sent out to collect the grain needed to feed the cities.

In the realms of industry and trade, the road to socialism seemed clearer. On April 26, Lenin's theses defining "The Immediate Tasks of the Soviet Power" were approved by the Central Committee of the Communist Party.

As the "general slogan of the moment," Lenin advanced: "Keep an accurate and honest account of money, be an economical manager, do not loaf, do not steal, maintain the strictest discipline in labor." [51] To establish "accounting and control" and to guarantee a satisfactory level of technique, the high-priced services of bourgeois specialists must be engaged; however demoralizing to the workers, it was the only way to enable them to learn technique and improve discipline. "The Russian is a bad worker"; he must be taught productivity:

> The last word of capitalism in this respect, the Taylor system—like all capitalist progress—combines the refined brutality of bourgeois exploitation with a number of the richest scientific advances in the matter . . . of elaborating the most correct methods of work. . . . It is necessary to create in Russia the study and teaching of the Taylor system, its systematic trial and adaptation. Along with it it is necessary . . . to lay the foundations of a socialist organization of competition and to call for application of compulsion so that the slogan of the dictatorship of the proletariat may not in practice be profaned by a jelly-like condition of proletarian authority.[52]

In reply to bitter attacks by the "Left Communists," who accused Lenin of leading Russia on the road of state capitalism, Lenin asserted:

> Reality says that for us state capitalism would be a step forward. . . . In the transition from capitalism to socialism . . . our chief enemy is the petty bourgeoisie, its habits, its customs, its economic position. The small owner most of all fears state capitalism, because his one desire is to grab, to get for himself, to destroy the big landlords, the big exploiters, and on this point he supports us. Here he is more revolutionary than the workers . . . but not as a socialist to build discipline and activity of a higher order, merely to grab for himself. . . . Any man who is not out of his mind and who has not stuffed his head with scraps of book truths would have to say that for us state capitalism is salvation. . . . If we had it in Russia, the transition to full socialism would be easy . . . because state capitalism is centralized, subject to accounting and control and collectivized, whereas . . . we are threatened by petty-bourgeois spontaneity. . . . The *declassé* petty-bourgeois intelligentsia does not understand that for socialism the chief difficulty lies in guaranteeing the discipline of labor. . . .[53]

Such was Lenin's blueprint for the "breathing spell" which he thought the end of the war had brought.

BREST-LITOVSK

What Lenin was to call "the greatest difficulty of the Russian Revolution" arose from the fact, in Lenin's words, that "a peaceful domestic animal lay down with a tiger and argued peace without annexations and indemnities." [54] After waiting for two weeks with no reply to the Peace Declaration of November 8, 1917, Trotsky invited the Allies and the Central Powers, separately, to agree to a general armistice. The Allied and Associated Powers merely "were willing to reconsider their war aims in conjunction with Russia . . . as soon as she has a stable government with whom they could act." [55] General Dukhonin, who had refused to transmit the message to the Germans, was murdered; the proposals of his successor, Krylenko, were accepted despite Ludendorff's doubt, "Is it possible to negotiate with these people?" [56]

The separate armistice, effective December 17, was celebrated by Trotsky's promise to aid

> the working class of all countries to overthrow the rule of capital and to seize power for the sake of a democratic peace and a socialist reconstruction of Europe and of all mankind [in which all opposing governments] must be swept away.[57]

With high hopes, Joffe, the chief Soviet representative in the negotiations with the Germans, presented (December 22) at Brest-Litovsk the now-familiar Russian "six points," repeating the established slogan of no annexations, no indemnities, and self-determination for all. The Germans accepted (December 25), though

> only in case all the Powers engaged in the war, without exception and without reservations, by a definite date pledge themselves in the most precise way to observe terms binding on all nations.[58]

The elation inspired by what General Hoffmann, one of the German negotiators, privately said "intrinsically was a lie" [59] was badly shaken, during a recess, by German refusal to transfer negotiations to neutral Stockholm (January 3), by announcement (January 4) of separate peace negotiations with the Ukraine, and by withdrawal, since the Allies had not acted, of Germany's acceptance of a "democratic" peace (January 5).

Belatedly, the Allies sought to capitalize on Russian dismay. Lloyd George, speaking to British trade unionists (January 5), restated Allied war aims in terms of self-determination, at least for areas controlled by the Central Powers. A grander gesture was made by President Wilson (January 8), whose "Fourteen Points" merely echoed and expanded, with certain reservations, the Russian "six points." Unofficial envoys—Raymond Robins for the United States, Bruce Lockhart for the United Kingdom, and Jacques Sadoul for France—were busily trying to arrange for resumption of the war by Russia in exchange for full Allied support of the Bolshevik regime.

Mutual distrust was too deep-rooted. The Allies strongly suspected that the Bolsheviks were the dupes, if not the agents, of the Germans. The Bolsheviks, well aware of their own publicly announced firm intention of supporting "by all possible means" the overthrow of the governments of their allies as well as those of their enemies, could hardly have any confidence in the friendliness of their intended victims. As Sadoul reported:

> Like Trotsky, Lenin is convinced, in spite of Wilson's speech, which nevertheless impresses him favorably, that negotiations have been entered into between Germany and England.[60]

In their self-isolation, the Bolsheviks' only hope seemed to be in the immediate outbreak of revolution in Europe; with this in mind, Trotsky himself had gone to Brest-Litovsk (January 7) to spin out the negotiations.

This hope was frustrated by the German military's desire for a quick settlement. Hoffmann bluntly attacked the Russian insistence on self-determination when their "government is based purely on violence, with which it suppresses anyone who thinks differently." [61] Renewing his theory that Poland and the Baltic states, which had already asserted their independence, might freely decide to unite with Germany, he presented Trotsky with a map (January 18) indicating the territories to be surrendered by Russia.

At a meeting of Bolshevik leaders in Petrograd (January 21) the debate was fiercer than behind the German lines at Brest-Litovsk. Bukharin, the ablest Marxist theoretician and leading "Left Communist," argued for proclaiming a "revolutionary war." Trotsky developed the thesis of "no peace, no war." Lenin was almost beside himself:

> There is no doubt that our army at this moment and for weeks to come (probably for months to come) is absolutely not in condition successfully to repulse a German offensive. . . . By concluding a separate peace we free ourselves as far as *possible at this moment* from both the warring imperialist groups, taking advantage of their enmity, and we use the war—which makes it difficult for them to make a deal against us—getting a certain period with our hands untied to continue and strengthen the socialist revolution. Reorganization of Russia on the basis of the dictatorship of the proletariat, on the basis of nationalization of the banks and of large-scale industry, with barter exchange between the town and rural consumers' societies of petty peasants, is economically entirely possible, given the security of a few months of peaceful work. Such a reorganization will make socialism invincible both in Russia and in the entire world, creating along with it a solid economic base for a mighty worker-peasant Red Army.[62]

Lenin's views won only 15 votes, Trotsky's 16, while the concept of revolutionary war was supported by 32 votes. In the Central Committee, however, a vote of 2-11 for Bukharin's ideal was outbalanced by a vote of 11-2 for Lenin's motion to continue negotiations, while Trotsky won endorsement by 9-7. Trotsky returned to Brest-Litovsk, asserting that "the Allied governments are responsible"; eschewing "idle prophecies," he expressed his trust that

> if German imperialism attempts to crucify us on the wheel of its military machine . . . we shall call to our elder brothers in the West, "Do you hear?" And, we firmly believe, the international proletariat will answer, "We hear!" [63]

It was at this point that the American ambassador, no wiser than he had been in October, telegraphed that he had "absolutely reliable evidence that Lenin, [and] Trotsky accepted German money from June to October professedly for peace propaganda and army demoralization," [64] citing what later became notorious as the "Sisson papers." At Brest meanwhile, the Germans allowed Trotsky to dodge for only ten days more; on February 8, despite Bolshevik capture of Kiev, the Germans signed a separate peace with the Ukrainian Rada. Trotsky played his ace, solemnly announcing (February 10)

> that in refusing to sign the annexationist treaty Russia for her part declares the state of war with Germany [and her allies] terminated. To the Russian troops is simultaneously issued an order for complete demobilization on the whole front.[65]

As Hoffmann reports, "We were all dumfounded." [66] The Bolsheviks were jubilant, confident that if the Germans advanced unopposed, their soldiers would revolt against their red-faced officers and the "permanent" world revolution would begin. Simultaneously, a decree was published at Petrograd declaring:

> All state loans made by the governments of the Russian landowners and of the Russian bourgeoisie . . . are annulled as of December, 1917 [Article 1]. . . . Unconditionally and without any exceptions all foreign loans are annulled [Article 3].[67]

Debt repudiation sharply diminished the chances of effecting an understanding between the Bolsheviks and the Allies, while the Germans quickly recovered their poise. General Hoffmann gave official notice (February 16) of the resumption of hostilities on February 18.

On February 17, the Bolshevik Central Committee rejected (6-5) Lenin's motion that the peace terms be accepted by telegram. The next day, as the German offensive began, Lenin was again voted down (7-6). Later in the day, however, as the smooth rapidity of the German advance became obvious, Lenin made another desperate appeal:

> We cannot joke with war. . . . Had the Germans said that they demanded the overthrow of the Bolsheviks, then we should have had to fight. . . . The revolution in Germany has not begun. . . . All these sacrifices [Latvia, Estonia, Finland, the Ukraine] will not ruin the revolution.[68]

Trotsky shifted his vote, and Lenin's proposal was now carried (7-6). By radiogram to Berlin the German peace terms were accepted.

For five bitterly anxious days no acknowledgment came from the Germans, whose armies were closing in on Petrograd. Trotsky has claimed that "all of us, including Lenin, were of the impression that the Germans had come to an agreement with the Allies about crushing the Soviets, and that a peace on the Western front was to be built on the bones of the Russian revolution."[69] Yet, on February 22, Trotsky reported to the Central Committee what he accepted as a definite offer of aid, made through a French representative; it was voted (6-5) to accept the offer. Bukharin cried out, "We are turning the party into a dung-heap,"[70] but Lenin, though absent, gave his approval. Relief arrived the following day in the form of a delayed message from the Germans, offering for immediate acceptance substantially stiffer terms than those rejected. Even Trotsky now counseled submission, though the Left Communists held out. Lenin showed impatience extreme even for him, threatening to resign if "revolutionary phrases" continued to impede "real work." For him one consideration—the one of which he under no circumstances ever lost sight—was decisive: "These terms do not interfere with the Soviets."[71]

In the Party Central Committee, the final vote was seven (a minority of the fifteen present) for acceptance, four for rejection; the remaining four, including Trotsky, declined to vote. For form's sake, the decision had still to be submitted to the Soviet Central Executive Committee. There, despite violent opposition from the Left SR's and from the Menshevik-Internationalists, the vote was 116-85, with 26 abstentions. On March 3, the treaty was signed at Brest-Litovsk, the Russian delegation openly protesting that they were acting under duress and would not feel bound by their signatures when the international proletariat had gathered its strength. To approve ratification of the treaty, it was deemed necessary to convene a Party Congress. At the Seventh Party Congress (March 6-8), despite all efforts to control its membership, Lenin still had to fight hard against the Left Communists to win endorsement of his policy. The final stage was submission to what was officially the supreme authority, a Congress of Soviets. At the Extraordinary Fourth Congress of Soviets, held for security reasons at Moscow (March 14-18), the Left Communists abstained from voting, and ratification was approved by 784 votes to 261.

The opposition came chiefly from the Left SR's who had loyally supported the Bolsheviks in most of their domestic policies. They now denounced what they regarded as betrayal of the Revolution to "German imperialism" and were specially embittered by the economic provisions, which to them made the notion of a "breathing spell" a mockery. Their break with their Bolshevik allies led to their withdrawal from the government. Martov, veteran leader of the Menshevik-Internationalists, promised: "If this treaty is signed, the Russian proletariat will make war on the government that signed it."[72]

There remained very little chance that Russia, even if fortified by Allied assistance, might renew the war or provoke Germany to renew it. It was true that, even after the signature of the treaty, Trotsky, as Foreign Commissar, welcomed the landing of British forces at Murmansk (March 5). It was true that he continued even after ratification to discuss with Robins, Lockhart, and Sadoul some form of coöperation with their governments. Yet the only hope of renewed struggle that Lenin had held out was that, during the probably brief breathing spell, Russia would prepare, together with "our greatest ally," the international socialist proletariat, to "begin a second socialist-revolution, this time on a world scale." [73] President Wilson's message of greeting to this Fourth Congress of Soviets asserted:

> The whole heart of the people of the United States is with the people of Russia in the attempt to free themselves from autocratic government and become the masters of their own life.[74]

The reply was:

> The happy time is not far distant when the laboring masses of all countries will throw off the yoke of capitalism and will establish a socialistic state of society. . . .[75]

The landing of Japanese forces at Vladivostok (April 5) was taken in Russia as confirmation of the darkest suspicions of capitalist imperialism. Count Mirbach, the first postwar German ambassador, arrived in Moscow on April 23; to many he seemed the real master of the scene. The obvious improvement of Soviet-German relations was convincing proof that to pursue an anti-German policy in Russia entailed also pursuing an anti-Bolshevik policy.

By the terms of the Treaty of Brest-Litovsk, Russia severed all connection with Finland, Estonia, Latvia, Lithuania, Poland, part of White Russia, the Ukraine, Bessarabia, and parts of Transcaucasia.* This amounted to one-fourth of her territory and at least one-third of her population; it meant the loss of her "breadbasket" and of most of her industrialized areas; the loss in heavy industry was particularly severe. In addition to a promise of Russian demobilization (already largely accomplished) and to reciprocal prohibition of agitation and propaganda, the treaty exempted German property in Russia from nationalization. Unquestionably, Russia had lost the peace; it remained to be seen whether she had gained the hoped-for breathing spell.

NOTES

1. U.S. Department of State, *Papers Relating to the Foreign Affairs . . . , 1918, Russia,* I, 216.
2. Lenin, "Theses on the Immediate Conclusion of a Separate and Annexationist Peace" (January 20, 1918), in *Sochineniia,* 3rd edition, XXII, 194.
3. Trotsky, *Lenin,* p. 133.
4. *Vtoroi Vserossiiskii S" ezd . . . ,* p. 62.
5. *Ibid.,* pp. 70-72.
6. *Ibid.,* p. 73.
7. *Ibid.,* p. 83.
8. *Ibid.,* p. 86.
9. *Ibid.,* p. 90.

* See Map VIII.

10. Appeal of "All-Russian Committee for the Salvation of the Fatherland and of the Revolution," in *Revoliutsiia 1917 goda* . . . , I, 293.
11. Skobelev, at meeting (November 9, 1917) of All-Russian Committee for the Salvation of the Fatherland . . . , in Bunyan and Fisher, *The Bolshevik Revolution, 1917-1918* . . . , pp. 146-147.
12. Proclamation of Right Socialist-Revolutionaries (November 9, 1917), in *ibid.*, pp. 147-148.
13. *Arkhiv russkoi revoliutsii,* I (1922), 158-159.
14. Trotsky, at meeting of participants in the seizure of power (November 7, 1920), *"Vospominaniia ob Oktiabr'skom perevote,"* in *Proletarskaia revoliutsiia,* No. 10 (1922), pp. 61-62.
15. S. An-skago, *"Poslie perevorota 25-go Oktiabria 1917 g.,"* in *Arkhiv russkoi revoliutsii,* VIII (1923), p. 49.
16. Larin, "Year of Struggle at the Cradle," in *Narodnoe Khoziaistvo,* No. 11 (November 7, 1918), pp. 16-17.
17. *Proletarskaia revoliutsiia,* 1922, No. 10, pp. 99-100.
18. *Izvestiia Tsentralnogo Ispolnitelnogo Komiteta,* No. 217, November 5 (18), 1917.
19. *Ibid.*
20. Letter to Central Executive Committee (November 17, 1917), in Bunyan and Fisher, *op. cit.*, pp. 204-206.
21. *Vtoroi Vserossiiskii S" ezd* . . . , *loc. cit.*, p. 62.
22. *Ibid.*, p. 72.
23. *Ibid.*, p. 79.
24. Trotsky, at meeting of Petrograd Soviet (December 15, 1917), in *Sochineniia,* III, ii, 138.
25. Lenin, speech at Second All-Russian Congress of Peasants' Deputies (December 15, 1917), *Sochineniia,* 3rd edition, XXII, 113.
26. Newspaper interview (January 2, 1918), in Bunyan and Fisher, *op. cit.*, p. 367.
27. Lenin, speech at a session of the All-Russian Central Executive Committee (January 19, 1918), in *Sochineniia,* 3rd edition, XXII, 187.
28. Vishniak, *Vserossiiskoe Uchreditel'noe Sobranie,* p. 91.
29. Protokol No. 5, November 4 (17), 1917, *Vserossiiskii Tsentral'nyi Ispolnitel'nyi Komitet Sovetov rabochikh i soldatskikh deputatov vtorogo sozyva. Stenograficheskii otchet,* pp. 25-26.
30. *Iz istorii VChK* . . . , p. 79.
31. Latsis (Suarabs), *Chrezvychainye komissii* . . . , p. 8.
32. *Iz istorii VChK* . . . , p. 96.
33. Dzerzhinskii, *Izbrannye stat'i i rechi* . . . , p. 118.
34. Vvedenskii, *Tserkov i gosudarstvo* . . . , pp. 114-116 *passim.*
35. Bunyan and Fisher, *op. cit.*, p. 599.
36. *Izvestiia* . . . , *loc. cit.* (Note 18, *supra*).
37. *Direktivy KPSS i Sovetskogo pravitel'stva po khoziaistvennym voprosam 1917-1957,* I, 26. In *Dekrety sovetskoi vlasti,* I, 84, the word "minimum" is "corrected" to read "norm."
38. *Pervyi Vserossiiskii S" ezd Professionalnykh Soiuzov* . . . , p. 29.
39. *Ibid.*, pp. 119-120.

40. *Novaia Zhizn'*, March 20, 1918.
41. *Ibid.*, April 29, 1918.
42. *Protokoly zasedanii VTsIK 4-go sozyva (Stenograficheskii otchet)*, pp. 44-45.
43. Lenin, "Immediate Tasks of the Soviet Power" (April, 1918), in *Sochineniia*, 3rd edition, XXII, 441.
44. Lenin, "Report on Review of the Program and Name of the Party" at the Seventh Party Congress (March 8, 1918), *op. cit.*, pp. 347-348.
45. *Ibid.*, p. 351.
46. Lenin, speech to agitators being sent to the provinces (February 6, 1918), *op. cit.*, p. 251. This is a garbled version of a report by a Cossack at the Third All-Russian Congress of Soviets of Workers', Soldiers', and Cossacks' Deputies (January, 1918) that a Bolshevik agitator had told an inquisitive old Cossack: "Yes, we are looters, but we loot the looters."
47. Lenin, *op. cit.*, p. 357.
48. *Direktivy . . .* , *op. cit.* (Note 37, *supra*), I, 346.
49. Meshcheriakov, *O selsko-khoziaistvennykh kommunakh.*
50. Lenin, "On 'Leftist' Childishness and on Being Petty-Bourgeois" (May, 1918), *op. cit.*, p. 515.
51. Lenin, *op. cit.*, p. 443.
52. *Ibid.*, pp. 454-455.
53. Lenin, "Report to the All-Russian Central Executive Committee" (April 29, 1918), *op. cit.*, pp. 481-482, 486. For a more extended treatment of the same theme, in which Lenin attacks those who "confine themselves to abstract contrasts between 'capitalism' and 'socialism,' " and asserts that state capitalism "is that rung of the ladder of history between which and the rung called socialism *there are no intervening rungs whatever,*" see the pamphlet cited in Note 50, *supra*, *op. cit.*, pp. 505-528, especially pp. 518-519.
54. Lenin, "Report on War and Peace" (March 7, 1918) at Seventh Party Congress, *op. cit.*, pp. 317, 319.
55. U.S. Department of State, *op. cit.* (Note 1, *supra*), I, 255.
56. Hoffmann, *Der Krieg der versäumten Gelegenheiten*, p. 136.
57. Trotsky, *Sochineniia*, III, ii, 207.
58. *Mirnye peregovory v Brest-Litovske*, I, 9-11.
59. Hoffmann, *op. cit.*, p. 143.
60. Sadoul, *Notes sur la révolution bolchévique*, p. 191.
61. *Mirnye peregovory v Brest-Litovske*, I, 94-95.
62. Lenin, "Theses on the Immediate Conclusion of a Separate and Annexationist Peace," *op. cit.* (Note 2, *supra*), XXII, 197-198.
63. *Tretii Vserossiiskii S"ezd sovetov rabochikh . . .* , pp. 70-71.
64. U.S. Department of State, *op. cit.* (Note 1, *supra*), I, 370-378, 380-381 *passim.*
65. *Mirnye peregovory v Brest-Litovske*, I, 207-208.
66. Hoffmann, *op. cit.*, p. 157.
67. *Direktivy . . .* , *op. cit.* (Note 37, *supra*), I, 33.
68. Lenin, speech at meeting of Central Committee (February 18, 1918), *op. cit.*, pp. 256-257.
69. Trotsky, *My Life*, p. 388.
70. *Ibid.*, p. 389.
71. Lenin, at meeting of Central Committee (February 23, 1918), *op. cit.*, p. 277.

72. *Chetvertyi S" ezd sovetov . . . stenograficheskii otchet,* p. 31.
73. *Ibid.*, p. 22.
74. U.S. Department of State, *op. cit.* (Note 1, *supra*), I, 396.
75. *Ibid.*, pp. 399-400; Lenin's original draft read "all bourgeois countries," *Sochineniia,* 3rd edition, XXII, 387.

SUGGESTIONS FOR FURTHER READING

For a detailed narrative of this whole period by a highly competent journalist (though not an eyewitness), Chamberlin's *Russian Revolution* is very useful. Of the highest value is the comprehensive selection of documents edited by Bunyan and Fisher as *The Bolshevik Revolution, 1917-1918*. Lenin's *Collected Works* continue to be one of the most important sources. Trotsky's *My Life* and his *History of the Russian Revolution* should also be consulted, though they do not reflect his contemporary opinions.

Dobb & Stevens, *Russian Economic Development Since the Revolution,* is a sympathetic penetrating study. As previously mentioned, Carr's first three volumes of *A History of Soviet Russia* are of very uneven value; some of the chapters are outstanding, but as a whole the work cannot be relied on. The reader should consult also the reports of the West's unofficial representatives: Hard's *Raymond Robin's Own Story*. Lockhart's *British Agent,* and Sadoul's *Notes sur la révolution bolchévique*. Radkey's *The Election to the Russian Constituent Assembly of 1917* is the most complete account in English; see also his *The Sickle and the Hammer,* an epilogue to his study on the Socialist Revolutionaries. Daniels' *Conscience of the Revolution* deals with opposition within the Communist Party.

Wheeler-Bennett's *Brest-Litovsk: The Forgotten Peace* is very valuable; a more recent excellent study is Kennan's *Russia Leaves the War*. For the German side, see Hoffman's *War of Lost Opportunities.*

For bibliographies on the Soviet period, see the suggestions at the end of Chapter 1.

Chapter

27

The Crisis of Bolshevism: 1918-1921

ECONOMIC CRISIS AND WAR COMMUNISM

There could be no doubt that, in the spring of 1918, Russia—and the Bolsheviks—needed a breathing spell, for the economic situation was desperate. Politically, the Bolsheviks seemed secure; peace had been made with the Germans, though at the price of the loss of Russia's most productive areas; British troops had landed at Murmansk, but only to keep war supplies accumulated there out of the hands of the Germans; the Japanese landing at Vladivostok was too remote and too limited to have significance; the Volunteer Army being formed by Alexeiev, Kornilov, and other generals behind the shelter of the otherwise neutral Don Cossacks was only a faint cloud on the horizon; throughout Russia, opposition to Bolshevik rule seemed impotent. Yet, in a speech at a congress of Commissars of Labor (May 22, 1918), Lenin frankly summed up the position:

> Now comes the most critical moment, when hunger and unemployment are knocking at the doors of an ever-greater number of workers, when hundreds and thousands of men are suffering the pangs of hunger, when the situation is aggravated by the fact that there is no bread.

His proposed remedy (May 23) was drastic:

> The mass of the workers are living under the impression of older days and hoping that we shall somehow escape from this situation. . . . We need a crusade of the workers against disorganization and against the hiding of grain. . . . There is no other way out.[1]

During the war, industrial production, never high in Russia, had declined fearsomely; even for 1916-17 industrial production has been estimated to have been only about 70 percent of 1913. Revolution, and especially the Bolshevik seizure of power, accompanied by "Red Guard" attacks by workers on factory management, had enormously speeded up the cumulative process of decline. A natural concomitant was the soaring of prices, which even at the time of the Bolshevik coup had reached almost thirteen times the 1913 level. The Bolsheviks made heroic efforts to check inflation by reducing budget deficits. They increased the yield of existing taxes and supplemented them with special levies on the well-to-do, an effort in which the central authorities suffered cruelly from the competitive initiative of local soviets. In the first year of their power, they actually trebled paper receipts and reduced the deficit to two-thirds of total expenditures, as against four-fifths in 1917. Despite their best efforts, however, the currency circulation rose inexorably from 22.5 billion rubles at the beginning of November, 1917, to a little over 40 billion by June 1, 1918. With some reason, a printing press finds an honorable place in many a Soviet "Museum of the Revolution." Strive as they might, largely "due to the rapid decrease in the quantity and turnover of marketable goods and products," the "rate of depreciation of the ruble outstripped the rate of issue." [2] In the spring of 1918, a moneyless economy was rapidly becoming a fact.

To abstract theoreticians this might not be bad. As Bukharin put it:

> "Anarchy" in production . . . is a historically inevitable stage which no amount of lamentation will prevent. . . . The "losses caused by revolution" . . . are the price which human society must pay for the possibility of further development.[3]

Bukharin refused to be seriously worried by the "lowering of productive forces," which was creating a "basis for their tremendous growth, with *reconstruction of relationships of production* on a new footing." He admitted that there was a possibility of society's lapsing back into primitive conditions, but he maintained the risk was worth taking, for in any case the restoration of capitalism would be impossible. Temporary sacrifices, like those made by striking workers, but on a vaster scale, would play the "colossal positive role" of making recovery possible only on the basis of communism.

In May, 1918, it was, however, already clear that peasants were tired of supplying precious grain in return for worthless paper money. The Bolsheviks' substitution of the SR land program for their own Marxist one, their sharing of political power with the Left SR's, their toleration of criticism from these junior partners—all these sacrifices had been made for the sake of necessary food supplies, and still there was not nearly enough food forthcoming. On May 9, therefore, a decree of the Central Executive Committee of the Soviets, published on May 13, resolved:

> 1. In confirming the stability of the grain monopoly and of fixed prices and also the necessity of a ruthless fight against the grain-speculator bagmen, to obligate every possessor of grain within a week . . . to declare for surrender

> his whole surplus above the quantity needed for sowing his fields and for personal consumption at established rates until the next harvest.
>
> 2. To summon all toiling and propertyless peasants to immediate union for a ruthless fight against the kulaks.
>
> 3. To proclaim all those who have excess grain and do not deliver it to the collecting points, and likewise those wasting grain supplies on moonshine, as enemies of the people and to hand them over to the revolutionary tribunal, so that the guilty may be sentenced to imprisonment for a term of not less than ten years, expelled forever from their communes, all their property subjected to confiscation, and moonshiners, in addition, be condemned to compulsory public work.
>
> 4. Half the value of the [unreported and] confiscated grain . . . shall go to the person who supplied the information about the concealed surplus.[4]

This was the basic step in the development of what later came to be called "War Communism." Despite vigorous protests from the Left SR's and the Menshevik-Internationalists, a drive was begun on the kulaks. This old term of personal opprobrium, literally meaning "fists" and equivalent to the English term "tightwads," which had come to be applied to peasants who hired the labor of others to supplement their own, was henceforth to be extended indiscriminately to all peasants who produced more grain than they needed for their own consumption.

In the desperate economic situation, the Council of People's Commissars became as hysterical as Kerensky had been when faced with the Kornilov *Putsch:*

> Petrograd is experiencing an unprecedented catastrophe. There is no bread. . . . The Red capital is on the brink of ruin from starvation. The counterrevolutionists are raising their heads, inciting the dissatisfied, starving masses against the Soviet government. . . . Failure to help is a crime against the Soviet Socialist Republic, against the world socialist revolution.[5]

To the tune of such frantic appeals, the class war was to be carried into the villages, "arming the village poor against the village bourgeoisie." Trotsky, now Commissar of War and Navy, set about organizing regular military expeditions to march from the cities and coöperate with "committees of the village poor." At the First All-Russian Congress of Councils of People's Economy, held at the beginning of June, a nameless objector was shouted down when he protested that in the villages:

> we have bread but are going naked, while here the people are starving. Instead of sending thirty thousand Red Guards our government should send . . . manufactured goods in exchange for bread. As a man of the village I know that you will not succeed in getting bread by bayonets. . . . The peasant works twenty hours a day, and the bread which you intend to seize from him by means of bayonets he gained by hard work.[6]

Six months after the Bolshevik seizure of power, it seemed to many, both within and without the Party, as though the early prediction of the SR's—

"Their power is short-lived. . . . Their creation is a soap-bubble"—was about to come true. Peasant resistance, workers' openly expressed discontent, even a mutiny at Saratov in the new Red Army (May 16-19), seemed to indicate the existence of an abundance of inflammable material. What was lacking was resolute and concerted leadership. Even in January, Jacques Sadoul, then working to keep Russia in the war in the interests of France, had written to his principal in Paris, Albert Thomas, expressing his conviction that

> remarkable as are the aptitudes of the Russians for accommodating themselves to disorder, yet hunger, fear, and wrath may let loose catastrophe. I say catastrophe, for I think more and more that a brutal fall of the Bolsheviks would be a great catastrophe for Russia and for the Allies. We have the rare opportunity of being face to face with Russians who know what they want, who proclaim it brutally, but honestly.[7]

Allowing for the influence of the sympathies that later took Captain Sadoul into the Red Army, it must be recognized that the SR's—both Right and Left—the Mensheviks, and the Cadets all continued to display more talent for oratory and for their several brands of idealism than for practical leadership. As another foreigner, closely connected with the conspiratorial groups that formed in Moscow in the spring of 1918, remarked:

> Unfortunately, the K.D.'s [Cadets] and S.R.'s are Russian, Russian to the core, in their ideas when it comes to programs and phrases. . . . Of all the organizations now in existence, and the Lord knows how many and how loose they are, that which seems to me most likely to make good is the one led by Boris [Savinkov]. . . . He is by far the man who impressed me most; he is endowed with self-possession, clearmindedness, and energy. He does not seem to bother with questions of programs or scruples, a rather exceptional case here, whether this be said to his credit or not.[8]

One grave cause of dissension was whether more coöperation could be had against the Bolshevik dictatorship from the Allies or from the Germans. Miliukov, who in May, 1917, had forfeited his post as Foreign Minister in the Provisional Government for pledging revolutionary Russia's loyalty to the Anglo-French Entente (and to the secret treaties of 1915), was now in Kiev, capital of the German-protected independent Ukraine, negotiating with the Germans for their aid against the Bolsheviks. Most of the surviving liberals and democratic socialists, however, would have no dealings with the ancient Teutonic foe, even though the Allies were too busy with their own problems to have a thought to spare for Russia.

Meanwhile, the Bolsheviks pressed their offensive against the peasantry. Sverdlov, chairman of the Central Executive Committee of the Soviets, announced (May 20):

> Only if we can split the village into two irreconcilably hostile camps, if we can ignite there the same civil war that recently raged in the towns, if we

succeed in rousing the village poor against the village bourgeoisie, only then can we say that with respect to the village we are doing what we were able to do in the cities.[9]

On June 4, at a joint meeting of the Soviet Central Executive Committee, the Moscow Soviet, and the trade unions, Lenin acknowledged:

> We are building a dictatorship. . . . Against the kulaks, the criminals who are torturing the population with the hunger from which tens of millions are suffering, we shall use force. To the village poor we will give all kinds of rewards; they have a right to them. We shall help them if they help us . . . get grain from the kulaks and . . . we must not spare any means.[10]

On June 9, Trotsky, making no reference at all to the fact that on the previous day members of the dispersed Constituent Assembly had established a rival government at Samara on the Volga, dwelt on the theme:

> Among all the questions troubling our hearts there is one simple question which nevertheless weighs more heavily than all the rest. This is the question of our daily bread. Over all our thoughts, over all our ideals, now prevails the one worry, the one fear, how to survive tomorrow. . . . It must be said, every day everything gets more and more difficult. Although it is bad in Petrograd, bad in Moscow, nevertheless there are many places in Russia where they still look at these cities with envy. . . . Here is a telegram: "Give us bread, else we perish." [Another telegram:] "In the factories a tremendous death rate, especially among children." . . . "Absolutely without bread for two weeks. Great starvation and mass illness."

Trotsky canvassed various remedies. To abandon the grain monopoly would be to give a free hand to speculators. To raise prices paid to the peasants would make it necessary to raise workers' wages: "It would be like drinking salt water to quench thirst." To attempt to exchange manufactured goods for grain would be futile; the utmost that could be hoped was to supply the "village poor" gratis with a thin trickle of manufactures through the Commissariat of Food Supply (*Narkomprod*). There remained only one possibility—to enforce the decree of May 9: "This is a correct law, a just law." [11]

A decree of June 11 regularized the establishment and fixed the powers of the "committees of the village poor." In August, a decree provided for food-requisition cordons to cope with the "bagmen," who continued to carry on a small-scale private trade of enormous proportions in foodstuffs. The food-requisition detachments ultimately were placed under a special Food Army Administration, headed by "a committee of three, one member of which must be a military specialist." [12] In 1918, the Food Army came to number 45,000 men; "it resembled the Red Army in its organization and was subject to all decrees affecting the army." [13] It was a bitter jest that "under the tsars the land had been God's and the rye the peasant's, but now the land was the peasant's and the rye was God's."

These desperate hand-to-mouth methods of providing for the food supply were not wholly unsuccessful. In November, 1917, the state supply organizations, inherited from the Provisional Government, had handled 641,000 tons of grain; in December and January the figure had dropped to 136,000 and 46,000 respectively; by June, 1918, the central institutions could get only 2,000 tons of grain. In the succeeding months, notwithstanding the outbreak of civil wars, energetic prosecution of the class war in the villages restored the supply significance of the central agencies. Initial successes (1.5 million tons in 1918-19) were expanded: in 1919-20, the centrally controlled supply of grain was doubled; in 1920-21, it exceeded 5 million tons.

The illicit trade carried on by the "bagmen" was, to be sure, not eliminated. Supplemented by sometimes legally permitted trips to the villages, illegal private trade provided much more than half of the urban food supply throughout the whole period of War Communism. There were other difficulties. The "committees of the village poor" speedily showed a tendency to get out of hand; instead of restricting themselves to coöperating in grain seizures, they too often killed the goose that laid the golden egg, seizing the land and livestock of the "bourgeois" peasants and thus imperiling future production. It was one thing to squeeze the "kulaks"; it was another matter to stop them from producing or, as increasingly happened, to provoke them to open revolt. As early as December 2, 1918, the committees were ordered liquidated.

A policy of coercion, fitful at best, without any economic incentives to production, could not long give even partially successful results. The government had too little power to exert regular control over the villages, even had it clearly envisioned a long-range policy or possessed the material resources to assist in its execution. The land law of February 19, 1918, had called for "distribution of the land among the toilers on equal-labor principles so that the consumption-labor norm . . . should not exceed the labor capacity of the available strength of each individual economy . . ." (Article 12), and had provided for shifting any excess population to other regions (Articles 27-34).[14] In actual practice, the distribution of land confiscated from landlords and often from the more well-to-do peasants was carried out by individual peasant communes with no thought of the interest of neighboring communes. Migration of peasants from one area to another seems not to have taken place at all. No heed was paid to the ideal "consumption-labor norm"; rarely did peasants feel called on for the sake of equality to surrender any land they already held. Addition of a share of the confiscated land therefore gave very different results, not only from region to region, but from commune to neighboring commune and even within the commune. On the whole, the cultivable holdings of the peasants could be increased only by amounts varying from a quarter-acre to about three acres.

The great increase in the percentage of small individual holdings inevitably tended to diminish agricultural production. The law's attempt to salvage something of the higher efficiency of the landlords' estates by creating state farms (*sovkhozy*) and collective farms (*kolkhozy*) failed. Nearly six thousand *sovkhozy* and over ten thousand *kolkhozy* were established; among them, they had been given 6 or 7 percent of the confiscated land. The *kolkhozy* were barely able to support their own members, who were largely urban workers; the *sovkhozy* also produced hardly anything of marketable value. In the general economy, these new forms, however interesting in theory, remained wholly insignificant.

In terms of agriculture, the net results of what came to be known as War Communism were a rapidly accelerated decline in the sown area and a catastrophic fall in gross yields. In the area covered by the Soviet census of 1920, there had before the war (five-year average, 1909-13) been 83 million dessiatines under cultivation; in 1920 the sown area was 63 million, in 1921 only 58.3 million. The gross yield of crops fell from a pre-war average of 3,850 million poods to 2,082 million in 1920 and 1,689 million in 1921. The reduction in number of head of livestock was only somewhat less disastrous. Such was the background of the extremely severe famine of 1920-21 in the Volga region and of a wave of peasant revolts that ranged from Central Russia to Siberia.

CONSTITUTION OF THE R.S.F.S.R.

The attack on peasant producers had been undertaken mainly out of economic despair. Behind it was also the deep-rooted conviction, derived from Marxist teaching, that peasant psychology was inherently petty-bourgeois philosophy, and that a society of small-scale producers was a dangerous breeding ground for Napoleons and Cavaignacs—or Kornilovs—who might rise to crush the "proletarian" regime of the Bolsheviks. This habit of mind found expression also in the first revolutionary constitution, unanimously adopted for the Russian Socialist Federated Soviet Republic (R.S.F.S.R.) by the Fifth All-Russian Congress of Soviets on July 10, 1918.

From the viewpoint of political theory, this constitution holds considerable interest. Its practical significance was so slight that it needs little attention here. Part I was the "Declaration of the Rights of Toiling and Exploited Peoples," which had been rejected by the Constituent Assembly but approved by the Third Congress of Soviets in January. It proclaimed world revolution, overthrow of capitalism and imperialism, and dictatorship of the Soviets. The balance of the constitution reflected a blend of principles derived from the *Communist Manifesto,* from the political practices of pre-war Russia, and from the institutions spontaneously developed during the Revolution. It did not neglect to state that "he who does not work does not eat."

Supreme authority was vested in an All-Russian Congress of Soviets of Workers', Peasants', Cossacks', and Red Army Deputies, which was to meet at least twice (in 1921 changed to once) a year. Numbering over a thousand members, the Congress could not be a deliberative body. Its supposed functions were accordingly delegated to a Central Executive Committee (*Tsik*), originally fixed at two hundred members. Even such a body being somewhat unwieldy, governmental power was actually concentrated in the Council of People's Commissars (*Sovnarkom*), which enjoyed not only executive power but authority to legislate by decree, though technically subject to Tsik's approval.

The word "Federated" in the title meant only that certain fairly compact ethnic groups were allowed a limited amount of cultural autonomy as a function of local government. Real power was actually highly centralized. Not content with listing seventeen types of questions reserved to the Congress of Soviets and its derivative organs, the constitution provided (Article 50) that the central organs might "decide any other question which they deem within their jurisdiction."

Local government was strangely interwoven with the function of choosing national representatives, in a way reminiscent of tsarist practice. The All-Russian Congress of Soviets stood at the apex of a hierarchic pyramid of congresses of soviets of administrative divisions and subdivisions (*oblasti, guberniyas, uiezdy,* and *volosti*) each of which elected its own executive committee to exercise authority locally. At the base of the pyramid stood the soviets of deputies of cities (*gorody*) and villages (*sela*), directly representative of their populations. Each of these congresses of soviets was elected by the local bodies next below it in the chain, the cities being allowed representation at two stages (*guberniya* and *uiezd*) in the complicated process. Distrust of the peasantry found expression in the provision that the cities were entitled to specially weighted representation, one urban elector being equated to five members of the rural population, a ratio which somewhat more than doubled the voting strength of the towns at each of the two stages at which they fed deputies into the congresses of soviets.

A further heritage from tsarist days, though turned inside out in its application, was total exclusion of certain categories from the franchise. Under the new Soviet regime, the disfranchised were: those who hired the labor of others or who lived on interest, dividends, or rents; private businessmen; ecclesiastics; ex-policemen and Romanovs; the mentally unfit; and convicted criminals.

Weighted class representation and partial disfranchisement, which in this inverted sense continued the practices of the tsarist autocracy, were not, however, the principal factors in guaranteeing to the Communist Party full control of the governmental machinery. This resulted chiefly from the more novel features of the electoral process. The outlawing of all other parties, a process not complete when the constitution was drafted in April, made it impossible to organize a legal opposition. Open voting made every elector ponder the advantages of voting for official candidates as against the dangers of voting for independents. Indirect election, at several stages, made it increasingly unlikely that even the stoutest-hearted would vote for alternative candidates whose background they could not know. The higher in the scale the congress of soviets, the more extensive its territory and the less the confidence with which a deputy could vote for other than the official candidate.

In the village soviets, the percentage of Communist deputies might rarely exceed five, but in the township (*volost*) congresses which they elected it was likely to reach ten, while the executive committees of the latter normally ran 40 percent Communist. According to tables published by the People's Commissariat of Internal Affairs (NKVD) in 1926, the percentage of Communists in the county (*uiezd*) congresses fell below fifty only in 1920 and 1921; in their executive committees, there were never less than 74.4 percent of Communists. In the higher (*guberniya*) congresses, Communists regularly numbered at least three-fourths of the deputies; in their executive committees, they numbered from 84 to 91 percent of the members. In the All-Russian Congress, the seats were always virtually monopolized by Party members. It was a system clearly superior to "bourgeois democracy" as a guarantee of the dictatorship established on November 7, 1917.

To the dictatorship of the Party in the country corresponded the dictatorship of the Central Committee within the Party. As noted earlier, this had been the main point of disagreement between Bolsheviks and Mensheviks in 1903. It had led to bitter attacks on Lenin by Trotsky in 1905. Although in the early stages of the "October Revolution" and its aftermath it was still possible for violent wrangles to divide the Bolshevik Central Committee, there was no case in which Lenin's basic principle of a disciplined elite was questioned by the rank and file of the Party.

Party dictatorship was never thought of as purely political; it must as rapidly as possible be extended to control of the whole economic system. For historical semantic reasons, emphasis had to be on the power of the proletariat, which must seem to be the ruling element. In fact, workers supplied less than 20 percent of the deputies even at *guberniya* level. Counting in ex-workers, they constituted less than 40 percent even of the Communist deputies.

WAR COMMUNISM

Lenin had been well aware that the Bolsheviks had no competent personnel to substitute for capitalist managers of enterprises, and no matter what his hopes for the future, he had no confidence in the ability of the workers to take over management in the present. Therefore no wholesale nationalization had been attempted. A few "key" enterprises, such as the electric company at Moscow and the great Putilov plant in Petrograd, were early taken over because of their "importance to the state"; the merchant marine, the sugar and oil industries, and a few branches of commerce, including foreign trade, were nationalized in the spring of 1918. Yet the total number of large factories nationalized by decree of the central authorities in the first eight months of Bolshevik power was only 72; 449 others were seized in spontaneous "Red Guard" attacks, either by local soviets or by their own workers.

Anarcho-syndicalist tendencies, which threatened to increase economic chaos in far greater proportion than could the hostile attitude of the old capitalist class, were strong. The determined group of Bolsheviks, known as Left Communists, who at this time maintained an organized "fraction" within the Party and published their own newspaper (*Kommunist*), feared that Lenin's caution

> will lead to a refusal to continue the destruction of capitalist relationships in production and will be accompanied by their partial restoration. . . . Instead of leading from partial nationalization to complete socialization of large-scale industry, agreements with "captains of industry" would lead to the formation of large trusts controlled by the latter and embracing all basic branches of industry.

They abhorred Lenin's advocacy of state capitalism because it would lead to "labor duty for workers, a piecework system of wages, longer hours of labor, etc." They agreed that the bourgeoisie, its press, and its surviving organizations should be ruthlessly suppressed, but they dreaded a policy under which "government would have to become more bureaucratic and centralized, and individual commissars more dominant":

> The introduction of labor discipline in connection with the restoration of capitalist leadership in production could not materially increase the output of labor, but . . . the Communist Party would . . . ruin itself as the party of the proletariat. . . . Management of enterprises should be handed over to united collegia of workers and technical personnel and placed under the control and leadership of local Councils of People's Economy.[15]

After nearly two months of bitter debate, Lenin took advantage of the First All-Russian Congress of Councils of People's Economy to effect a compromise, without yielding an inch to syndicalists. This Congress decreed (June 3) systematic nationalization of industry on principles which, together with the new policy toward the peasants, later were called War Communism: extreme centralization of industrial administration in the hands of the state, state monopoly over labor, substitution of state-organized barter for trade, a system of distribution based not on the choice of the consumer but on what the state could make available, and increasing meaninglessness of money.

The new industrial policy, sidetracking Lenin's favorite concept of state capitalism, was legally implemented by a decree of June 28, 1918, "nationalizing" all large-scale industry. By this time, Russia was in the throes of civil war, which has enabled the Communists to explain away their action as dictated by "the iron necessities" of the military struggle. At the time, however, no mention was made of "counter-revolutionaries"; the decree justified itself as "for the purpose of a decisive struggle against the economic disorganization and the breakdown of the food supply and of consolidating more firmly the dictatorship of the working class and of the village poor." A contributing factor may well have been desire to forestall possible German acquisition of title to the properties affected, but there can be no real doubt that "War Communism" was deliberately dictated by the exigencies of struggle within the Party itself, not against enemies outside it.

The decree of June 28 applied to over eleven hundred enterprises, the administration of which was supposed to be in the hands of the Supreme Council of People's Economy (*Vesenha*) and its subordinate agencies. Temporarily these enterprises "shall be considered as leased rent-free to their former owners," who were to continue to finance them "and also to receive the income from them on the former basis." [16] A Joint Conference of Factory-Shop Committees and Trade Unions docilely declared (July 1) that under the new conditions "any stoppage of work, or strike, amounts to a betrayal of the proletarian cause." [17] The laws relating to labor, as codified in 1918, included the provisions that:

1. Labor conscription is imposed on all citizens of the R.S.F.S.R., with the exceptions noted in Articles 2 and 3.

2. Not subject to labor conscription are: (a) persons under 16; (b) persons over 50; (c) persons who have permanently lost ability to labor as a result of mutilation or disease.

3. Temporarily free from labor conscription are: (a) persons who have temporarily lost ability to labor as a result of disease or mutilation, for the period needed for recovery; (b) pregnant women, for a period of 8 weeks before delivery and 8 weeks after the birth.

8. The conditions of labor in all Soviet, nationalized, public and private enterprises and economies will be regulated by schedules worked out by the trade unions in agreement with the managers or owners . . . and fixed by . . . the People's Commissariat of Labor.

24. The unemployed have no right to refuse work in their specialty, if the conditions of work do not depart from the norms established by the relevant schedules or, in the absence of a schedule, by the trade union.

27. In case of demand for work in another locality . . . if there are not a sufficient number of volunteers . . . the Department of Distributing Labor will send the needed number of workers. . . .

28. If . . . there are no workers satisfying requirements . . . by agree-

> ment with the relevant trade union, [the Department] has the right . . . to send the unemployed of a different category. . . .
>
> 29. The unemployed, given work not in their specialty, are obligated to take it but may declare their desire to undertake it temporarily. . . .[18]

Labor productivity did not rise. In 1919, absenteeism and delay eliminated almost two-thirds of the possible working days. Hourly productivity declined to 47 percent of 1913; annual productivity dropped to 28 percent. Disorganization; shortages of material, fuel, and tools; lack of material incentives to work; unprecedented hardships—all contributed to a mass flight from the towns. By 1920 there were one-third fewer people in the cities than in 1917; Moscow and Petrograd had lost more than half their population. Unemployment was replaced by labor shortage; the government therefore intensified labor conscription and organized formal "Labor Armies."

The Second All-Russian Congress of Trade Unions, meeting in 1919, advocated "a system of labor remuneration which would inspire competition of the toilers in their effort to raise the productivity of labor" in the form of "piecework and bonus payment of labor, based on a fixed norm of production." [19] In some branches of production, the bonus came to amount to as much as 700 percent of basic wages, but it could not be applied to wages in kind (in the form of food, lodging, and materials for work clothes). In 1920, the total average monthly earnings of an industrial worker were figured as 8.12 rubles (almost the minimum prewar rate for common labor, or about one-third the pre-war average rate for all industrial workers), but the 1920 average money wage was only 0.49 rubles. Any worker was fortunate to receive the bare minimum needed for existence; a Soviet publication of 1939 estimates that in 1920 the real monthly earnings of industrial workers, including food rations, communal services, clothing, and illegal perquisites, were 40.9 percent of 1913 average wages. The necessity of supplementing their income by illegal methods such as production of goods from stolen materials or use of ration cards of the dead—methods that accounted for as much as one-fifth of average earnings—contributed largely to further decline of factory output and all-around worsening of the economic outlook.

The administrative machinery to replace the capitalists developed haphazardly but prolifically, in full accord with "Parkinson's Law." In its fully developed form, Vesenha, which had the status of a People's Commissariat, appointed the members of the chief boards (*glavki*) charged with the administration of the various branches of industry. A hierarchy of lesser boards, based either on subdivision of an industry into its component parts or on geographical division, intervened between the *glavki* and the individual enterprises. The original notion of having a board of managers at the head of each factory had by 1920 been replaced in 85 percent of the cases by the practice of appointing individual managers. Cross-subordination of enterprises to provincial Councils of People's Economy was significant only for enterprises of purely local character.

It was the duty of each manager to report to higher authority how much raw material and fuel he could effectively use, given locally available labor and machines or tools, and to supervise the manufacture, from the supplies allotted to him, of such goods as were specified by his superiors, to whom he was to turn over the finished product; consideration of costs, prices, and profits was not involved. The *glavki* were confronted with the requisitions for raw materials and for fuel made by all the managers under their jurisdiction. To meet this demand, each of them had to apply to whatever other *glavki* were responsible for the enterprises producing the desired commodities. Then they had the problem of trying to match the total supplies reported available against the sum total of requests they had received. Only in this sense could they be said to be "planning" production.

In determining the best allocation of the limited supplies available, it was important to take into account, not only the local possibilities of production, but also the problem of minimizing transportation from the source of supply to the point of manufacture and from the latter to the place of consumption. On all these points, and on many other factors, the central *glavki* could have only the most inadequate information. They could be reasonably certain that each manager, concerned for his own factory and its workers, would pad his requests by more than he could possibly utilize. But by how much? In the absence of financial accounting and control, of profit-and-loss statements, it was impossible to form a serious idea of the relative condition of any enterprise. To check on the managers, it was necessary to employ inspectors, but to check on the inspectors it was soon necessary to employ inspectors to check on the inspectors, and so on *ad infinitum*. The proportion of administrative personnel to total workers rose from 6.4 percent to 13.5 percent; it was said that a quarter of the adult population of Petrograd was made up of officials. Indeed, it was even suggested that the number of clerks, inspectors, and the like sometimes exceeded the number of workers at the bench.

It was small wonder that enterprises ignored Vesenha and its *glavki* as much as possible, manufacturing illegally for a local barter market in order to live. The 1920 census recorded a total of 37,226 state enterprises; only 6,908 were registered by Vesenha. Yet the maw of the state continued to be insatiable, and the process of nationalization was steadily extended. Since small-scale industries sometimes produced goods essential to nationalized industries, Vesenha decided (December 29, 1920) that all enterprises still in private possession and employing more than five workers with any kind of mechanical power or more than ten workers without mechanical power were to be taken over. It was the last gasp of the dragon.

Confusion among the *glavki* themselves was almost as great as between them and their subordinate agencies. Maurice Dobb, a strong sympathizer with the Bolsheviks, notes the story about "the dead mare in the streets of Petrograd surrounded by the representatives of the fifty odd Glavki, disputing within whose sphere the disposal of the carcase came." [20] It is a tale that contrasts strangely with the one long current in Brooklyn of the patrolman who found a dead horse in Kosciuszko Street; unable to fill out a report form because he could not master the spelling, he disposed of the problem by dragging the carcass around the corner into Marcy Avenue.

It would be unjust to suppose that, because of the general hit-or-miss character of Bolshevik economic administration, no attention was paid to the real problems of a socialist planned economy. The basic purpose in establishing Vesenha had been for it to "work out the general norms and the plan for the regulation of the economic life of the country" (Article 2).[21] When it was apparent that Vesenha was swamped by the day-to-day tasks of somehow managing the chaotic economic life of the R.S.F.S.R., the Council of Labor and Defense (STO) was created (March, 1919) to supervise the activity of Regional Economic Councils in planning for the future. Though these organs, too, were unable to raise their heads above the flood tide of current problems, Lenin's personal drive resulted in 1920 in a plan for the electrification of Russia (*Goelro*), which anticipated the reconstruction of industry, agriculture, and transport. Pregnant for the period that was to follow Lenin's death were the comments of Stalin, a then relatively insignificant figure:

> An excellent, well-composed book. A masterly draft of a really *unified* and really *statesmanly* economic plan *without quotation marks*. . . .
>
> You remember Trotsky's "plan" last year (his theses) for the "economic rebirth" of Russia on the basis of mass application to the fragments of pre-war industry of the labor of the unskilled *peasant*-worker masses (the labor army). What poverty, what backwardness compared with the Goelro plan! A medieval craftsman, fancying himself an Ibsen hero, with a calling to "save" Russia by an ancient saga. . . . And what is the value of those tens of "unified plans," every now and then to our shame appearing in our press—the prattle of preparatory-school boys. . . . And another one, Rykov with his philistine "realism," who continues to criticize Goelro, being completely sunk in routine. . . .[22]

Goelro produced no results. Industrial production, already sharply depressed by the war and the March Revolution, had gone into a dizzy tailspin under the Bolsheviks. The indices of production in large-scale industry as later computed by the State Planning Commission (*Gosplan*), with 1913 as a base, show 74.8 for 1917 (the year of revolution), but 33.8 for 1918 (the first year of the Bolshevik regime), 14.9 for 1919, and 12.8 for 1920. Small-scale industry, particularly characteristic of consumer goods over which the Bolsheviks at first made no serious attempts to establish their power, was somewhat less adversely affected; the corresponding indices are 78.4, 73.5, 49, and 44.1. The index for all industry in 1920 was set at 20.4 as against 100 for the same territory in 1913. Per capita production of "goods of prime necessity" declined from 18.2 in 1912 to 2.4 in 1920, both figures expressed in gold rubles.

The Bolsheviks had been slow to attempt to nationalize domestic trade. Foreign trade had been practically annihilated by the closing of the Baltic, Black Sea, and western land frontiers. The decree making foreign trade a state monopoly (April 22, 1918) was therefore of little immediate consequence. The postwar Allied blockade of Russia was lifted on January 16, 1920, though a number of leading Western banks continued unofficially a financial boycott until the middle of 1921. Trade did not revive; in 1920, Russian exports amounted to only one-thousandth of their 1913 value.

At home, the Bolsheviks had from time to time established state monopolies on goods in particularly short supply, notably during the "food dictatorship" established by the decree of May 9, 1918. Conscious of the difficulty of organizing distribution satisfactorily, the state at first kept hands off the consumers' coöperatives, despite the political hostility of their central organ. By the fall of 1918, however, the list of state monopolies had grown so long that the decree of November 21, nationalizing all trade, was almost anticlimactic. Even then, the coöperatives were left in being, though subjected to the Commissariat of Food Supply. What goods were available were furnished to the urban (and in part to the rural) population through an ever more complex rationing system. In place of money receipts, the State Budget relied ever more heavily on *prodrazverstka* (taxation in kind) and on requisitioned foodstuffs and industrial goods; on the expenditure side, it supplied free of charge raw materials and fuel, wages in kind, rations, and lodging. For such few transactions as were still carried out in terms of money, the state attempted to fix prices, which, however, bore no relation to actual prices on the thriving illegal market.

Even this state of affairs did not displease theoreticians. Bukharin's *A.B.C. of Communism* proudly affirmed:

> The Communist mode of production . . . is not production for the market, but for the needs of the community. . . . Consequently there are no *commodities,* but simply *goods.* These goods are not exchanged against one another, they are neither bought nor sold. . . . Under this system money is not necessary.[23]

In retrospect, Communist theory takes a very different view of War Communism. The frightening dip of the Russian economy to unprecedentedly low levels and the staggering burden of human suffering it entailed, far exceeding the most severe depression that ever affected the Western world, could not be admitted to be in any degree the outcome of deliberate Bolshevik policy. It has therefore become orthodox to ascribe War Communism and everything associated with it to the "iron exigencies" of civil war and foreign intervention, which allegedly forced the Bolsheviks onto a road they would not have chosen. It is a fact that for over three years, from the summer of 1918 to the fall of 1921, Soviet Russia was plagued with confused and arduous civil wars, complicated for a time by foreign intervention.

Yet the official theory that writes off War Communism as a phenomenon for which Bolshevism bears no responsibility ignores a number of troublesome facts. Later (October 18, 1921) Lenin himself, with characteristic frankness, admitted:

> Carried away by a wave of enthusiasm . . . we thought . . . or perhaps without adequate consideration we assumed—that by direct orders of the proletarian state we could organize state production and state distribution of products communistically in a land of petty peasants. Life showed us our mistake. . . .[24]

Consideration of chronology bears Lenin out: when the attack on the peasants was begun (May 9), there was no fighting; when Lenin accepted the principle of nationalization (June 3), there was still no domestic civil war. Fighting had begun, but by an odd freak of fate the danger came from a few thousand men who had absolutely no interest in the affairs of Russia.

THE CZECHOSLOVAKS AND CIVIL WAR

Czechoslovak prisoners of war, who had surrendered en masse rather than fight for the hated Hapsburgs, had been armed and formed into a sort of foreign legion, about 45,000 strong, by the Provisional Government. During the armistice they were accepted into the French army, and arrangements were made with the Bolsheviks to evacuate them to France by way of Vladivostok. It was, however, soon realized that the shipping needed to effect the transfer could not then be diverted to the Pacific. Late in April, therefore, in agreement with the French military authorities, Trotsky ordered that all Czech troop trains that had not gone beyond Omsk should be diverted to Murmansk and Archangel. Uninformed of the reasons, the Czechs were suspicious. At this juncture, a brawl between Czech and Hungarian former prisoners of war at Cheliabinsk (May 14-17) took on such proportions that Moscow, which in March had again become the Russian capital, ordered the Czechs disarmed. Their refusal to comply (May 22) provoked a telegram ordering the breakup of their units and their incorporation into the Red Guards or into labor artels (May 23). Trotsky wired the Siberian authorities:

> Every Czechoslovak found armed on the railway line is to be shot on the spot, every detachment in which there is even one armed man is to be detrained and locked up in a war prisoners' camp.[25]

Reacting vigorously, the Czechs seized the Trans-Siberian Railway as far as Irkutsk. A rearguard, about 5,000 strong, established themselves on the middle Volga.

Everywhere under their protection soon blossomed anti-Bolshevik governments, of varying complexions. Most important was the one established by the "Committee of Members of the Constituent Assembly" (*Komuch*) at Samara, which the Czechs had taken on June 8. It declared:

> All limitations and restrictions on freedom introduced by the Bolshevik authorities are abolished, and freedom of speech, of the press, of assembly, and of meetings is restored. . . . United, Independent, Free Russia! All power to the Constituent Assembly! . . .[26]

A decade later, looking back in *My Life,* the exiled Trotsky was to write:

> The spring and summer of 1918 were an exceptionally difficult period. At moments there was the feeling that everything was slipping and crumbling, that there was nothing to hold on to, nothing to depend on. The question arose whether there was in the exhausted, ruined, desperate country enough sap to support the new regime and save its independence. . . . Everywhere conspiracies were festering. . . . The situation seemed irremediable. . . . The fate of the revolution at the most critical moments depended on a single battalion, on a single company, on the steadiness of a single commissar, i.e., it hung on a hair. And so it went from day to day.[27]

The government took desperate measures. On May 29, the Soviet Central Executive Committee decreed conscription in place of voluntary enlistment for the new Red Army. The Cheka redoubled its activities; in the words of its head, Dzerzhinski, "we show no mercy. We terrorize the enemies of the Soviet government in order to stop crime at its inception." [28] At the Fifth Congress of Soviets, Sverdlov boasted: "All of you, I am sure, know that the All-Russian Extraordinary Commission to Fight Counter-revolution has passed and carried out many a death sentence." [29] Its work was supplemented by that of a Supreme Revolutionary Tribunal, instituted on May 29. Martial law was proclaimed; Trotsky ordered:

> If any unit retreats voluntarily, first the commissar shall be shot, then the commander. Courageous, brave soldiers will be rewarded for their services and put in posts of command. Cowards, skin-savers, and traitors will not escape a bullet.[30]

From Samara, a new "People's Army" organized by Komuch pressed the initial successes of the Czechs. Repeating the exploits of Pugachev, its forces took Kazan (August 7), acquiring the Russian gold reserve, estimated at 650 million rubles, and opening the road to Moscow. Acting quite independently, Savinkov seized the opportunity to stage uprisings in several cities of central Russia; the most formidable was at Yaroslavl, on the upper Volga, where the insurrection lasted over two weeks (July 6-23).

No less independently, even the Left SR's attempted a demonstration at Moscow itself. Characteristically, they made no adequate preparations, putting their faith in the proposition that "you cannot stop the march of the revolution" and trusting "the healthy revolutionary psychology of those who . . . are not consecrated to the service of German capital." [31] Maria Spiridonova, the Left SR who had been backed by the Bolsheviks for the presidency of the Constituent Assembly, now denounced their ruthlessness and openly defied them at the Fifth Congress of Soviets (July 4): "You do not have a majority in the country, you do not have a majority among the toiling classes, who are the basic element of our social revolution." [32] Lenin contemptuously replied:

> There has never been a single revolution and period of civil war without executions. . . . Socialism . . . has ceased to be a dogma, as it has perhaps ceased to be a program. Our party has not yet written a new program, and our old one is no good at all. . . . We demand that you look at the matter, not from the standpoint of an exhausted, worried, hungry man . . . but from the standpoint of building a new society. . . . We know it was perhaps a mistake to put your socialization of the land in our law of November 8.[33]

At this Soviet Congress Kamkov bitterly attacked Lenin's "cheap demagogy" and retorted that "the Soviet has become incarnate as the dictatorship of German imperialism, the dictatorship of Mirbach [the German ambassador]." [34] Yet the Left SR's, psychologically unable to adopt new methods of struggle, merely resorted to the tactics that had failed against the tsars. According to the minutes of their Central Committee, as published over Spiridonova's signature by the Cheka, it had already resolved to organize "a series of terroristic acts against the most outstanding representatives of German imperialism";[35] on July 6, two Left SR's, taking advantage of their positions in the Cheka, secured an audience with Ambassador Mirbach and murdered him. That night, instead of attempting to seize the Kremlin, the Left SR's announced their "success" and appealed for the support of the masses. The Bolsheviks, as usual acting decisively, arrested the Left SR delegates to the Congress of Soviets, while a few troops actively loyal to the Bolsheviks, mainly Letts and Hungarians, routed in twenty-four hours the unorganized handful of armed rebels. The most serious sequel, reminiscent of Kurbsky in the days of Ivan the Terrible, was the defection of the Soviet commander-in-chief on the Volga front.

The Fifth Congress proceeded to ratify the new constitution (July 10). The break with the past was given macabre emphasis by the murder of the tsar and his wife and children (July 16). Transferred by Kerensky in August, 1917, to Tobolsk for safekeeping, they had been moved to Yekaterinburg. There, lest they become symbols in the hands of the advancing Czechoslovaks, they were slaughtered by a local commissar, with the approval of Moscow. Yet the Bolsheviks' position continued to seem desperate.

The Germans had attempted to consolidate their position in the Ukraine by overthrowing the democratic and socialist Rada, which had been trying to effect agrarian reforms, and by installing a former tsarist general, Skoropadski, as Hetman. Their anxiety to garner the maximum grain crop, however, provoked peasant uprisings and the murder of the German field marshal at Kiev. The Germans' troubles were small comfort to the Bolsheviks, themselves at war with the Russian peasants and without the consolation of operating in a fertile agricultural area. German penetration of the Crimea led to the scuttling of the Russian Black Sea fleet and aided the growth of German influence in the Caucasus. Establishment of friendly relations with General Krasnov, newly elected Ataman of the Don Cossacks (May 17), promised to make the Donets basin, Russia's chief source of coal and steel, also available to the Germans. On the lower Don, the Volunteer Army, to the command of which General Denikin had succeeded in April, refused to coöperate with the Germans but directed its menace at the Bolsheviks. German military activity in Finland posed a constant threat to the security of Petrograd, and Germany's economic demands on the Bolsheviks were constantly stepped up. Lenin's boast (March 7), "Yes, of course we shall violate the Treaty, we have already violated it thirty or forty times," [36] had not prevented Bolshevik compliance in all matters essential to the Germans.

INTERVENTION AND WITHDRAWAL

Among the advantages the Germans had derived from the Brest-Litovsk Treaty, not the least was the opportunity to withdraw most of their troops from the Eastern front and concentrate them for a formidable drive toward the Channel ports. As General Pershing later reported, "The offensive made such inroads upon the French and British reserves that defeat stared them in the face." [37] It was inevitable that much military opinion on the Allied side should regard prompt restoration of an eastern front as a *sine qua non* for victory. The American chief of staff, General March, records:

> The suggestion was received by the department, from time to time, from many sources, that this country participate in an armed intervention in Russia with the view of restoring order and a strong and stable government and of enabling, by our assistance, the Russian army to be reconstituted and utilized in a renewal of offensive operations on an enlarged scale against the German eastern front.[38]

Foremost among the advocates of intervention were the French authorities, who had been the chief sufferers from repudiation of Russian debts and who had been the earliest to lose faith in the possibility of Bolshevik coöperation. Not unmindful of French investments in Manchuria, they had formally proposed a joint Chinese and French penetration as far as Irkutsk (January 8). Japan, for her own reasons, was obviously ready to act in Siberia and was with difficulty restrained by American opposition (on which Lenin counted heavily) until April 5. Great Britain also had early recommended that Japan be invited to act as mandatory in occupation of the Trans-Siberian Railway (January 28). However, clinging to the belief that the Bolsheviks might yet resume the struggle against the Germans, the British cherished the coöperation of the Murmansk Soviet and, after the unexpected landing of the Japanese at Vladivostok, instructed their agent in Russia to make it plain that "the Allied governments are desirous to do everything they can to afford support and assistance to Trotsky." [39]

The activities of the Czechoslovaks and the establishment of anti-Bolshevik socialist and liberal governments at Samara and elsewhere opened new vistas. The thought of a continuous chain of forces from the Arctic to the Caspian, facing the Germans across the narrow no man's land of Bolshevik Russia, was irresistible. When the chairman of the Murmansk Regional Soviet defied a direct order from Trotsky to attack the British forces there and was declared an outlaw, the opportunity was not allowed to slip by; a formal agreement was entered into (July 6) "for the defense of the Murmansk region against the powers of the German coalition." [40] Already, on July 2, the Supreme War Council of the Allied and Associated Powers had formally resolved on intervention, both in Siberia and in the North; the resolution was based on a memorandum that said:

> There is but the smallest chance of an Allied victory on the western front in 1919 unless Germany is compelled to transfer a considerable amount of her strength back again from west to east. . . . If the Allies are to win the war in 1919, it should be a primary object of their policy to foster and assist the national movement in Russia in order to reform an eastern front.[41]

Even the stubborn opposition of President Wilson collapsed, though he remained adamant in his principles:

> It is the clear and fixed judgment of the Government of the United States arrived at after repeated and very searching reconsiderations of the whole situation in Russia, that military intervention there would add to the present sad confusion in Russia rather than cure it, injure her rather than help her, and that it would be of no advantage in the prosecution of our main design, to win the war against Germany. It cannot, therefore, take part in such intervention or sanction it in principle. Military intervention would, in its judgment, even supposing it to be efficacious in its immediate avowed object of delivering an attack upon Germany from the east, be merely a method of making use of Russia, not a method of serving her. Her people could not profit by it, if they profited by it at all, in time to save them from their present distresses, and their substance would be used to maintain foreign armies, not to reconstitute their own. . . . Whether from Vladivostok or from Murmansk and Archangel, the only legitimate object for which American or Allied troops can be em-

> ployed, it submits, is to guard military stores which may subsequently be needed by Russian forces, and to render such aid as may be acceptable to the Russians in the organization of their own self-defence. . . . Recent developments have made it evident that that is in the interest of what the Russian people themselves desire, and the Government of the United States is glad to contribute the small force at its disposal for that purpose.[42]

Except at Vladivostok, where a substantial American force was landed to prevent the Japanese from making themselves too thoroughly at home, Allied efforts in Russia were carried out by token forces. At Archangel was set up (August 2) a Russian civilian government, formed mainly of members of the Constituent Assembly and headed by an old-time revolutionary, Nikolai V. Chaikovsky, who had spent much of his life in tsarist prisons. It was protected by small British forces detached from Murmansk; American reinforcements, which arrived only on September 4, were made up of a single regiment of infantry, with a few technical troops but no artillery.

Even the French showed extreme caution in extending material aid. A telegram from the French Minister of Foreign Affairs to the Komuch government at Samara promised only:

> As soon as you show us that you have real power in your hands, that you are listened to in Russia, that forces are grouped around you, this will produce an enormous impression. Thus the key to your importance abroad lies rather in real strength than in your legal rights, all the more so since the latter are by no means indubitable. . . . Your origin from the Constituent Assembly . . . has moral rather than legal force. . . . I wish you all success.[43]

The Allies might command the seas, but support of forces in the interioı entailed grave logistical problems. Allied support was therefore of little moment in the Russian civil wars.

The various "White" groups in Russia still could not agree on a common policy. The chief rival of Komuch was a "Western Siberian Commissariat," formed at Tomsk (May 30) but soon moved to Omsk (June 7). It slipped into the hands of more conservative elements, who declared all Soviet decrees annulled (July 4), restored land titles (July 6), and refused to recognize the authority of the Constituent Assembly. Protected by the Volga front, they tried to lure its officers away by offers of higher pay. Under pressure from the Czechs, the two governments combined (September 23), by which time, however, the "Reds" had recovered Kazan. Increasing sentiment in favor of the supposed superior efficiency of a military dictatorship contributed to its overthrow (November 18). The "man on horseback" was Kolchak, a tsarist admiral who had made an excellent record in long postponing mutiny of the Black Sea fleet.

The armistice with Germany (November 11) deprived of its compelling force the primary interest of the Allies in Russian affairs. Yet there remained the possibility that the German revolutionaries, who had replaced the

Kaiser with a soviet regime (November 10), might in desperation make common cause with revolutionary Russia. French troops were therefore landed at Odessa (November 26), British at Batum (December 18), while munitions were sent to "White" elements in Estonia (December 12). The Bolsheviks were in fact aggressively seeking to pit the German revolution against "Anglo-French imperialism." As early as October 3, Lenin had gleefully written:

> The crisis in Germany has only begun. It will inevitably end by political power passing into the hands of the German proletariat. . . . Now even the blindest of the workers of various countries see how right the Bolsheviks were in building their whole tactics on the support of a world workers' revolution. . . . We had decided to have an army of 1,000,000 men by spring; now we need an army of three million men. We can have it. And we shall have it.[44]

At the Sixth Congress of Soviets (November 8), Lenin announced:

> If we have never been so close to international proletarian revolution as now, our position has never been so dangerous as now. . . . The imperialists of the Anglo-French-American group . . . are thinking of building a Chinese wall to protect themselves from Bolshevism, like a quarantine against plague. . . . The bacillus of Bolshevism will pass through the wall and infect the workers of all countries.[45]

The German Social-Democrats, however, put more emphasis on democracy than on socialism. Nor were they pleased with Russia's unilateral repudiation, two days after the armistice, of the Brest-Litovsk Treaty. They refused to readmit the expelled Soviet diplomatic representatives, who now openly boasted that their money and their propaganda had contributed to the "triumph of the German revolution." They quickly replaced their soviets with a democratically elected Constituent Assembly, a "bourgeois parliament."

In considering how to extricate themselves from Russia, the Allies were hampered by the same divided counsels that had made them slow to intervene. Immediate recall of their forces would obviously expose those Russians who had welcomed Allied assistance, and who could not be evacuated wholesale, to savage and bloody reprisals by the Bolsheviks. Keeping troops there obviously invited mutiny among men who had been recruited for the duration of the war against Germany and who expected the armistice of November 11, 1918, to release them to their homes. Low morale was peculiarly evident among the French, on the principle that "no French soldier who had saved his life before Verdun or on the battlefields of the Marne would be willing to lose it on the battlefields of Russia. . . ."[46] By April, 1919, all French forces had been withdrawn from the south. The British, not unconcerned with the possibilities of controlling the oil of the Caucasus, remained in Baku and Tiflis until the summer; at Batum, they clung until July, 1920; soon after, the Menshevik regime in Georgia was overthrown by the Red Army. The British, and to a lesser extent the French, continued to supply arms and funds to Denikin in the south and Yudenich in

Estonia throughout 1919, but the Anglo-American forces were withdrawn from North Russia in the fall of that year. Only Eastern Siberia remained in alien hands; not until October, 1922, did Japan, under persistent American prodding, relinquish Vladivostok.

All efforts to come to an understanding with the Communist regime, and in particular to achieve some settlement of the debt problem, failed completely. The West, unwilling and unable to attempt more direct pressure, relapsed into sullen hostility to the Soviet regime. In the Treaty of Versailles (effective January 10, 1920), they "reserved" the rights of Russia to an indefinite future. In doing so, in lieu of a "Chinese wall" they created a *cordon sanitaire,* a string of small powers—Finland, Estonia, Latvia, Lithuania, Poland, Czechoslovakia, Rumania—designed to prevent future collaboration between defeated Germany and recalcitrant Russia. The blockade, however, was lifted on January 16, 1920.

MILITARY CRISIS AND BOLSHEVIK VICTORY*

Withdrawal of the "interventionist" powers did not at all release the Bolsheviks from their difficulties. On the contrary, concentration of power in the hands of Kolchak in Siberia, Denikin in the south, and Yudenich on the Baltic coast posed graver military danger to the Soviet regime than had the more idealistic efforts of its liberal and socialist enemies. The collapse of Germany had enabled the Bolsheviks to recover Riga, chief seaport on the Baltic, and Kharkov, chief center in the industrial Donets basin, at the beginning of the new year (January 3, 1919). The Ukraine, where the peasant leader Petliura had overthrown the German-supported Hetman Skoropadski, was overrun by the Red Army; Kiev was taken (February 6), while French withdrawal permitted Red occupation of Odessa (April 6). The first Communist republic abroad was established in Hungary by Bela Kun (March 21).

The tide, however, turned rapidly. Failure of the Red Army to take Estonia left it and independent Finland as twin threats to Petrograd. The "Iron Division" of Von der Goltz cleared the Bolsheviks out of the Baltic provinces. Pilsudski's Poland seemed too strong to attack. The Ukraine became a welter of peasant revolts against grain requisitions and of anti-Semitic pogroms. From Siberia, Kolchak launched a drive toward the Volga (March 13). In the southeast, resignation of the pro-German Cossack leader, Krasnov, left all anti-Bolshevik forces in that quarter under the command of Denikin.

Of the anti-Bolshevik military leaders, Kolchak, despite his high-sounding title of Supreme Ruler, proved the least formidable. His best forces, the Czechs, were anxious only to go home; socialists and liberals distrusted the "White" leaders almost as much as they did the "Reds"; inexperience,

* See Maps VIII and IX.

lack of supplies, and conflicting personal ambitions paralyzed the Omsk regime. Before the end of April, the westward advance had been checked; by summer, Kolchak's forces were in full retreat; Omsk itself was taken on November 14, not quite a year after his coup. In the midst of general demoralization, Kolchak was handed over by his Czech guards to a pro-Bolshevik committee in Irkutsk (January 15, 1920), by whose orders he was shot (February 7).

Far more formidable was the advance of Denikin into the Donets basin (May-June, 1919). As the "White" fortunes in Siberia ebbed, Denikin's forces occupied the Ukraine, retaking Odessa (August 23) and Kiev (August 31). By the middle of October, he had taken Orel, little more than two hundred miles south of Moscow. Although his forces numbered little over a hundred thousand, and although his much more numerous enemies had twice as many cannon and machine guns, the superior military skill of his officers, the relatively high discipline of his troops, and the tendency of the population to welcome relief from Bolshevik terror and oppression at first carried all before them. The attempt was, however, overambitious. Westward extension of his lines had been largely dictated by the hope of joining forces with Poland; the Poles, however, were unimpressed with the slogan, "Russia shall be great, united, undivided," and remained quiet. Instead, Denikin fell heir to the problem that had plagued both the Germans and the Bolsheviks, how to deal with the strong nationalist, and at the same time anarchist, sentiments of the Ukrainian peasantry, led by such skilled guerillas as Petliura and Makhno. Even the Cossacks, his most trusted warriors, proved temperamental, far more interested in defending their local privileges than in fighting far from their homes. The monarchist and landlord prejudices of many of his officers, which Denikin was in no position to control, led to widespread sabotage by peasants behind his lines. Failing to smash through to Moscow, Denikin had no alternative but to beat a swift retreat to the Black Sea coast. His army carried off with it everything that could be moved, destroying as much as possible of what it could not take. Budenny, the "Red" cavalry commander, achieved a great reputation because his pursuing horsemen were sometimes able to harry the retreat. Almost at the moment when Kolchak resigned his title of Supreme Ruler to Denikin (January 4, 1920), the seat of Denikin's government was taken by the Red Army (January 8).

Considerably less formidable, though more spectacular, than Denikin's advance was the sudden dash of General Yudenich from Estonia against Petrograd (October, 1919). With less than twenty thousand troops at his disposal, Yudenich drove within thirty miles of the city but, for lack of manpower, was unable to occupy it. His failure removed the threat that the existence of his army had poised over Russia.

In 1920, although the only remaining "White" army was bottled up in the Crimea, a new military danger developed from the West. The Poles suddenly struck into the Ukraine, taking Kiev (May 6). A "Red" force, under Tukhachevsky, promptly struck at Poland, while Budenny's cavalry moved into the rear of the Polish vanguard. If the Poles had hoped to annex the Ukraine, the Russians now set themselves the goal of sovietizing Poland. After a desperate seesaw struggle, in which the Poles were counseled by the French Marshal Weygand, the preliminary Treaty of Riga (October 12, 1920; confirmed March 12, 1921) established the frontier far to the east of the "Curzon line," which the Allies had suggested, although somewhat west of the line the Poles had been holding. The Russians, however, were in no mood to contest continuance of Polish rule over large numbers of Ukrainians and White Russians, or even the Vilna corridor, which prevented direct territorial contact between Russia and Germany.

The Red Army still had to deal with the remnant of the "Whites." Baron Wrangel, the Russian aristocrat who had succeeded the plebeian Denikin (April 4), had taken advantage of the Russo-Polish War to launch a new offensive (June 6). Its objective was not Moscow but control of the most productive area of Russia. Within a few days of the Treaty of Riga, however, Wrangel had been driven back into the Crimea, whence with great difficulty the last of the anti-Bolshevik forces were evacuated on November 14, 1920.

This time the Ukraine remained in the grip of the Soviet forces. Moslem opposition in Central Asia had been beaten down in the summer of 1920. Georgia, the Transcaucasian stronghold of the Mensheviks, was subjected to a Soviet regime early in 1921 (February 27). Though not in Denikin's sense, Russia could again become "great, united, undivided." Finland, the Baltic provinces, and Poland remained independent, actually as well as technically; Bessarabia was retained by Rumania. A Far-Eastern Republic, sympathetic to the Bolsheviks, was a convenient buffer between the R.S.F.S.R. and the area still occupied by Japan. Nor did the R.S.F.S.R. embrace all the remaining territories of the Empire of All the Russias. White Russia, the Ukraine, Georgia, Armenia, and Azerbaijan were officially independent Socialist Soviet Republics, controlled, however, by the Communist Party, the supreme ruler of Russia.

Notwithstanding the open prognostications of most informed observers and the more private beliefs of many participants in both camps, Bolshevism had emerged triumphant from a terrific struggle, unparalleled since the Time of the Troubles three hundred years before. This did not mean that the will of the people had triumphed. The bulk of the population had suffered acutely but passively. The fighting had been done by amazingly small forces; even in 1920, when the Red Army boasted five million soldiers, it had been able to put only sixty thousand in the field. Most of the combatants, on both sides, had been ill-disciplined partisan bands. Many served now on one side, now on the other, as opportunity offered for plunder, rape, and murder with impunity. More than one campaign was lost because of a drunken orgy.

There had, of course, also been much high idealism on both sides. On this score, the Bolsheviks had possessed incalculable advantages, for their future was still a dream scarcely tarnished by waking hours. Moreover, their ideals were directed by a disciplined "monolithic" party, which was able to lay down the shifting principles the rank and file were to embrace. In a territorial as well as in an ideological sense, they had the advantage of interior lines. Their central position, in a vast country with poor means of communication, gave them an enormous superiority. Once the Germans were out of the way, they could rally the forces of Russian nationalism, unimpeded by the presence of foreign uniforms among their advisers or of foreign flags flying over their bases. With respect to the masses, especially the peasant masses, they had the inestimable psychological advantage of being able to preach the destruction of old fetters, no matter what new ones they themselves might be forging.

The principal factor in Bolshevik success, however, was the passivity of the masses, or at least the unorganized character of such spontaneous resistance as could be developed in a predominantly peasant country, a country, as Lenin scornfully expressed it, dominated by a "petty-bourgeois" mentality. The very backwardness of the Russian economy made impossible any rapid progress toward realization of Lenin's dream—"the organization of accounting and control over large-scale enterprises, conversion of the whole state economic mechanism into a single big machine, into a managing organism, so working that hundreds of millions of men are guided by one plan."[47] Economic reorganization on socialist lines, Lenin believed, would be far easier to accomplish in advanced capitalist countries, but the other side of the picture, the conquest of political power, was another matter.

Ever mindful that "seizure of power is the point" of a revolution, Lenin had said at an earlier stage (March 7, 1918):

> History has shown, and it needs to be grasped as a fact, needs to be reckoned with, that world socialist revolution in advanced countries cannot be begun as easily as revolution was begun in Russia, the land of Nicholas and Rasputin, where to a huge part of the population it was absolutely all the same what kind of people lived round about and what they were doing. In such a country beginning a revolution was as easy as lifting a feather.[48]

NOTES

1. Lenin, Speeches at Congress of Commissars of Labor (May 22 and 23, 1918), *Sochineniia,* 3rd edition, XXIII, 32, 34.
2. Baykov, *Development of the Soviet Economic System,* p. 37.
3. Bukharin, *Ekonomika perekhodnogo perioda,* pp. 48-50.
4. *Direktivy KPSS . . . ,* I, 53.
5. Bunyan, *Intervention, Civil War, and Communism in Russia,* p. 463.

6. *Ibid.*, p. 449.
7. Sadoul, *Notes sur la révolution bolchévique*, p. 184.
8. Bunyan, *op. cit.*, pp. 173, 175.
9. *Protokoly zasedanii VTsIK 4-go sozyva* (*Stenograficheskii otchet*), p. 294.
10. Lenin, *op. cit.*, pp. 60-61.
11. Trotsky, *Kak vooruzhalas' revoliutsiia*, I, 74, 82-83.
12. *Sistematicheskii sbornik dekretov i rasporiazheniiakh pravitel'stvennykh po prodovol'stvennomu delu*, I, 54.
13. Report of the Commissariat of Food Supply for 1918-1919, in *Vtoroi god bor'by s golodom*, p. vii.
14. *Direktivy KPSS* . . . , I, 38.
15. "Theses on the Current Moment," reprinted from *Kommunist*, No. 1 (April 20, 1918), as Appendix 12 in Lenin, *op. cit.*, XXII, 561-571, especially 567-569.
16. *Direktivy KPSS* . . . , I, 79.
17. Bunyan, *op. cit.*, p. 402.
18. *Sistematicheskii sbornik vazhneishikh dekretov 1917-1920*, pp. 68-70 *passim*.
19. Lavrent'ev, *Zarabotnaia plata v Rossii prezhde i teper'*, p. 76.
20. Dobb and Stevens, *Russian Economic Development Since the Revolution*, p. 141.
21. *Direktivy KPSS* . . . , I, 27.
22. Stalin, letter to Lenin (March, 1921), *Sochineniia*, V, 50-51; an abridged version appears in *Velikii khoziaistvennyi plan*, p. 16.
23. Bukharin and Preobrazhenskii, *The A B C of Communism*, pp. 57-58.
24. Lenin, "For the Fourth Anniversary of the October Revolution," in *Sochineniia*, 3rd edition, XXVII, 29.
25. Vishniak, *Vserossiiskoe Uchreditel'noe Sobranie*, p. 144.
26. "Order No. 1" (June 8, 1918), in Lelevich, *V dni Samarskoi uchredilki*, pp. 9-10.
27. Trotsky, *Moia zhizn'*, II, 123-126 *passim*. (Cf. also *My Life*, pp. 395 ff.)
28. Newspaper interview, in Bunyan, *op. cit.*, p. 227.
29. *Piatyi Vserossiiskii S"ezd Sovetov, Stenograficheskii otchet*, p. 49.
30. Vishniak, *op. cit.*, p. 159.
31. *Piatyi . . . , op. cit.*, p. 24.
32. *Ibid.*, p. 30.
33. *Ibid.*, pp. 67-72 *passim;* also in Lenin, *Sochineniia*, 3rd edition, XXIII, 124-130 *passim*.
34. *Piatyi . . . , op. cit.*, pp. 73-76.
35. *Krasnaia kniga VChK*, I, 129-130.
36. Lenin, "Report on War and Peace" (March 7, 1918) *op. cit.*, XXII, 327.
37. U.S. War Department, *Annual Reports*, 1919, I, i, 571.
38. *Ibid.*, p. 467.
39. U.S. Department of State, *Papers Relating to Foreign Affairs . . . , 1918, Russia*, II, 109.
40. *Ibid.*, pp. 493-495.
41. *Ibid.*, pp. 243-244.
42. *Ibid.*, pp. 288-289.
43. Vishniak, *op. cit.*, p. 165.

44. Lenin, letter to joint meeting of Soviet Central Executive Committee, the Moscow Soviet, and the Trade Unions, in *Sochineniia,* 3rd edition, XXIII, 215, 217.
45. *Ibid.,* p. 269.
46. Gukovskii, *Frantsuskaia Interventsiia na iuge Rossii, 1918-1919 g.g.,* pp. 122-123.
47. "Report on War and Peace" (March 7, 1918) at Seventh Party Congress, in Lenin, *op. cit.,* XXII, 316.
48. *Ibid.,* p. 322.

SUGGESTIONS FOR FURTHER READING

Among works previously cited, Chamberlin's narrative, the *Collected Works* of Lenin, the writings of Trotsky, and Dobb are of the greatest value.

In addition, the most valuable collection of documentary material is Bunyan's *Intervention, Civil War, and Communism in Russia.* Among monographs, a very important study in English is Kennan's *The Decision to Intervene.* Ullman's *Anglo-Soviet Relations, 1917-1922* parallels Kennan on the British side. For intervention in the North, see Strakhovsky's *Intervention at Archangel* and *The Origins of American Intervention in North Russia, 1918.* Denikin's *White Army* and Wrangel's memoirs tell the story of successive phases of the defeated forces in the south. A very valuable study is Reshetar, *The Ukrainian Revolution, 1917-1920,* which provides also some earlier background and gives the story of the role of the Rada in 1917. On Far Eastern developments, James W. Morley's *Japanese Thrust into Siberia, 1918* and Unterberger's *America's Siberian Expedition, 1918-1920* largely supersede earlier accounts such as General Graves' *America's Siberian Adventure,* which showed little understanding of its purposes.

On the question of revolutionary Russia at the Paris Peace Conference, see Mayer's *Wilson vs. Lenin* and Thompson's thorough and more cautious study, *Russia, Bolshevism, and the Versailles Peace.* Tarulis' *Soviet Policy Toward the Baltic States . . . 1918-1940* and Senn's *Emergence of Modern Lithuania* are useful treatments of the successor states.

On the development of the Russian economy, in addition to Dobb, see Bukharin and Preobrazhenskii, *The A B C of Communism.* Baykov's *Development of the Soviet Economic System* begins to be very useful at this point. Two very helpful studies of the Soviet Army from the time of the Civil War are Erickson's *The Soviet High Command* and Kolkowicz's *The Soviet Military and the Communist Party.* See also Garthoff, *Soviet Military Policy,* and Garder, *A History of the Soviet Army.*

Chapter

28

Launching of the New Economic Policy: 1920-1922

Lenin had early recognized that, "while for us it was immeasurably easier to begin [a revolution], it will be more difficult to continue it than" it would have been in Western Europe. More than three years had passed since the seizure of power, and no constructive work had been accomplished. The ruin of Russia's economy, though it might be blamed on her political difficulties, still did not present a picture in which anyone could really take pride. Recovery of much of her lost territory and lifting of the blockade might offer some hope of a freer flow of raw materials and an increased supply of fuel, but the techniques of War Communism were all too evidently not adapted to the rebuilding of industry. The workers were exceedingly restive, and strikes even against state enterprises were not uncommon. Moreover, the basic occupation of the mass of the Russian people—agriculture—was in a hopeless state. Passive resistance of the peasantry had become massive; agriculture could not be made to function, as Trotsky had made the railways operate, by militarizing the toilers. Worse still, with the counter-irritant of the "Whites" removed, the peasants now concentrated their hatred against their Bolshevik masters in the form of a spreading wave of local revolts, the most serious of which was in the Tambov area.

ORIGINS OF THE THIRD INTERNATIONAL

While conditions within Russia itself were naturally the prime factors in leading to a reorientation of policy, it should not be overlooked that both the world situation and the Bolsheviks' outlook on the world had by 1921 undergone important changes since 1917. When the Bolsheviks had "snatched Russia," they did so in the confident expectation that within a few months at most the proletarian revolution would spread throughout the world, or at least throughout the advanced capitalist portion of it. That this hope had not been fulfilled had not diminished Communist confidence in the "correctness" of their faith. Lenin, to be sure, had cautioned that, although Communist revolution would be easier to complete in countries where economic power was highly developed and highly concentrated, that very concentration, together with emotional "illusions" generated by the war, would make it more difficult to begin the movement in the West. The idea even began to gain ground that the spread of the revolution would be more easily effected in backward colonial areas, which they regarded as suffering from imperialism.

The original thesis, however, that Germany was the most promising ground for promoting revolution had flared anew with the collapse of the Hohenzollern regime in November, 1918. It was with keen disappointment that the Communists, themselves engaged in bitter domestic strife, saw the German Spartacists go down to defeat in January, 1919. Yet they took some comfort from the soviet regime set up in Bavaria by Kurt Eisner, as well as from Bela Kun in Hungary. Encouraging, too, were many evidences of a new temper in certain quarters in the victorious countries of the West.

In 1919, the combined effects of the postwar boom and of the improved position of the industrial workers, relative to other strata of the population, which "war socialism" (i.e., wartime government controls) had brought about, produced in the West phenomenal unrest and enthusiastic activity; even the unromantic British Labour Party had, shortly before the end of the war, adopted an avowedly socialist, though non-Marxist, program. It seemed unthinkable that the masses in Entente countries, which had won the war, should be content to lose the peace by reverting unprotestingly to their pre-war station, while broken-down Russia indulged in the utopian dream of communism, and defeated Germany trod the more orderly path of social democracy. In all Western European countries, apparently animated by revolutionary zeal, strikes for still higher wages and still shorter hours became the order of the day; even the London police and London waiters went on strike, while the English coal miners, railwaymen, and transport workers knit more closely the "Triple Industrial Alliance," with its threat that their joint action would provide the basis for the long-heralded general strike.

This was the atmosphere in which was launched at Moscow the Third International (March, 1919). Ostensibly unconnected with the Soviet government, it was dominated by the Russian Communist Party, which also absolutely controlled the whole Soviet machinery. At its head was placed Zinoviev, who had been closely connected with Lenin in his wartime exile in Geneva and of whom an embittered Trotsky was later to record:

> In favorable periods, when, in Lenin's phrase, "there was nothing to fear," Zinoviev climbed easily to the seventh heaven. But when things took a bad turn, he usually stretched himself out on a sofa—literally, not metaphorically—and sighed.[1]

Although Zinoviev had been bitterly denounced by Lenin for his panicky betrayal of plans for the November uprising, the Third International offered safe scope for his soaring literary and oratorical talents. To be sure, the Third International—a new version of Moscow, the Third Rome—was able to score no major successes, but it fully expressed the Communists' intention of carrying their missionary propaganda throughout the world. At the same time, through the active participation of foreigners in attendance, it gave strong encouragement to the faithful in their desperate struggle against Kolchak, Denikin, and Yudenich.

The First Congress of the new Communist International, held in March, 1919, was necessarily almost wholly a Russian affair. At that time, the chances of survival of Communist Russia against the pressure of "White" armies supported by Allied intervention seemed very slight. Whatever hope there was seemed to depend on outbreak of actual revolution abroad; to save Russia, it was thought, the uprising of organized proletarian masses in capitalist countries must be stimulated by any and all means. Especially because of the disorganization of the old socialist Second International, the prestige of the Bolsheviks then stood highest among European radicals. Practically all of the Italian Socialists promptly joined the Moscow International. So did the German Spartacists, reorganized as the Communist Party of Germany (KPD); the bulk of Germany's Independent Socialist Party (USPD) gravitated in the same direction. Though the British Labour Party held sympathetically aloof and strong syndicalist tendencies prevailed in France, in many countries a Communist Party, of larger or smaller proportions, came into existence and affiliated with the Third International.

The withdrawal of Allied forces and the defeat of Kolchak, Denikin, and Yudenich, although they did not wholly free Communist Russia from military danger, encouraged the Russian Communists to plan a more vigorous offensive to achieve world revolution. Germany, where the monarchist Kapp *Putsch* had shaken the infant democratic republic, and Italy, where the Socialists had scored striking electoral successes, seemed the most promising fields. In the early part of 1920, the danger seemed to be, not that revolution would not break out, but that, if left to develop spontaneously, it might take a Utopian-Radical or a syndicalist direction, instead of following a disciplined Bolshevist path.

Lenin deliberately challenged such tendencies and, in preparation for the Second Congress of the Third International, published a famous pamphlet, translated into English as *Left-Wing Communism, An Infantile Disorder.*[2] Russia's experience, wrote Lenin, has supplied clear evidence that unqualified centralization and the strictest discipline of the proletariat are one of the fundamental conditions for victory over the bourgeoisie. . . . Not a single important political or organizational question is decided by a single state institution in our republic without directives from the Central Committee of the Party.

In its work, the Party rests directly on the *trade unions,* which now number . . . over 4 million members, who are formally *non-Party.* In actual fact, all the directing organs of the huge majority of unions, and first of all, of course, of the All-Russian Trade-Union Center . . . consist of Communists and carry out all the directives of the Party. Thus is secured, all in all and on the whole, a formally non-Communist, flexible, comparatively broad, extremely powerful, proletarian, apparatus, by means of which the Party is closely linked with the *class* and the *mass* and by means of which, under the guidance of the Party, is realized *dictatorship of the class.*

The German and Dutch "Left" Communists, against whom this pamphlet was chiefly directed, were also in error in scornfully pronouncing "parliamentarism 'historically extinct.' This is true as propaganda, but everyone knows that it is very far from having been got rid of in practice." The "Left" Communists were:

doctrinaires of revolution, who never have taken part in a real revolution or pondered the history of revolution, or who naïvely accept subjective "denial" of a given reactionary institution as its real destruction by the united forces of a whole series of objective factors. . . . (It is all right if this is to be explained by their youth: God Himself has ordained that in the course of a certain period the young should talk such nonsense).

Principles were fine things, but Communists should be guided by a sense of realities:

We do not know, and we cannot know, what spark—out of the countless sparks now flying from every quarter in all countries under the influence of the economic and political world crisis—will prove able to light a conflagration . . . and we are therefore obligated with our new Communist principles to set about "cultivation" of any and every field, even the oldest, stalest, and apparently most hopeless. . . .

What did it matter if the trade unions of the West were at that moment dominated by a *"trade-unionist, narrow, egotistical, callous, mercenary, petty-bourgeois, imperialist-minded and imperialist-hired . . . 'aristocracy of labor,'* [by the] Gompers, Hendersons, Messieurs Jouhaux, Mehrheims, Legiens, & Co.?" That was no reason for refusing to work within these "reactionary" institutions; it was no use to "invent a brand-new, tidy 'Workers Union,' innocent of bourgeois-democratic prejudices, untainted by craft- and narrowly trade-unionist sins," but with no roots in the masses.

No doubt, Messieurs the "leaders" of opportunism will resort to all the tricks of bourgeois diplomacy, with the aid of bourgeois governments, priests, policemen,

> and courts in order to deny Communists admittance into the trade unions, to shut them out in every way, to make their work within the trade unions as unpleasant as possible, to insult them, to beat them, to persecute them. It is necessary to know how to withstand all this, to make any and all sacrifices, even—in case of need—to resort to all sorts of stratagems, double-dealing, illegal methods, reticences, concealment of the truth, if only they penetrate the trade unions, stay in them, carry on Communist work in them, come what may.

Similarly, unconditional refusal to participate in bourgeois parliaments is inadmissible, just as harmful to the cause of the revolutionary proletariat as would be participation under the wrong conditions. Revolutionaries must never be afraid of compromise, so long as the compromise brings them nearer to their goal:

> The victory of the Bolsheviks over the Mensheviks required, not only prior to the October Revolution of 1917, *but also after it,* application of the tactics of maneuver, agreement, and compromise—which facilitated, accelerated, and consolidated the Bolsheviks at the expense of the Mensheviks. . . . To tie one's hands in advance, openly to tell an enemy who is at the moment better armed than we are, whether and when we shall fight him, is stupidity and not revolutionism.

Lenin was not dismayed because "in England there is as yet no Communist Party." Nor did he rest his optimism merely on the emergence of people like the young Scot, William Gallacher, who

> splendidly expresses . . . the frame of mind and the viewpoint of young Communists [which] is in the highest degree welcome and valuable [but which] doubtless reveals in the germ *all* the errors being made by the German "Left" Communists. . . . The fundamental law of revolution . . . is: for a revolution it is not enough that the exploited and oppressed masses be conscious of the impossibility of living in the old way and demand changes; for a revolution it is necessary that the exploiters should not be able to live and rule in the old way.

The ruling classes were making blunders; inevitably they would make more. Now was the time, when "the revolution is spreading . . . with such supreme rapidity," to organize a Communist movement "of maximum *flexibility* in tactics," free from any doctrinairism, whether of Right or of Left, to take fullest advantage of the opportunity.

THE THIRD INTERNATIONAL ON THE OFFENSIVE

These were the ideas that underlay the work of the Second Congress of the Third International, held at Moscow in July, 1920, and well attended by international revolutionaries. In a major speech, Lenin argued that imperialism had reached a point at which some 250 million people in the

United States, Japan, Great Britain, and a few smaller countries held 1,500 million people in slavery. The "exploited countries of the East," with India and China in the forefront, were about to rise against the imperialists; since there was no proletariat in these lands, new revolutionary forms—not soviets of workers but soviets of peasants or of toilers—must be devised. Nevertheless, the main hope of world revolution lay not with the oppressed peoples of Asia and Africa; it was the European proletariat—and particularly the German and Italian proletariats—that must be expected to bear the brunt of the effort. For the success of this magnificent movement the most careful preparation was imperative.

The major work of the Second Congress was therefore adoption of twenty-one conditions which must be accepted by any Party desiring membership in the Third International. As the deliberately adopted framework of international Communist organization pending the achievement of world revolution, these "21 Conditions" deserve to be reviewed.[3]

It was hoped to establish in each country a Communist Party affiliated with the Third International (*Comintern*). Each member Party must have organization and rules similar to those of the Russian Communist Party, built on the principle of democratic centralism. Each was to be directed by a "Party Center as the authoritative competent organ with wide powers, enjoying the universal confidence of the members of the Party" (#12). All Party members were to accept "iron discipline." "The Communist cells must be entirely subordinated to the Party as a whole" (#9). "Democratic centralism" required that the rank and file repose full confidence in the Party leadership; the Central Committee was to appoint all Party officials, to give orders to any Communists elected to office or to parliament (#11), to run Party newspapers (#1), and to have power to expel individuals or groups from the Party and to conduct periodic purges (#13); it was to "prepare" Party Congresses in advance so that at them its position could not be challenged.

In its turn, the Central Committee of each Party, which must openly call itself "the Communist Party" of such-and-such a country, was to be absolutely subordinate to the Executive Committee of the International (#17). This Executive Committee was to be elected by the World Congress, and a majority of its members were to come from outside Russia. Nevertheless, there was no question but what the representatives of the Russian Communist Party were to dictate the policies of the Executive Committee, which would be able to prepare the stage at World Congresses just as national Central Committees predetermined the decisions of national Party Congresses.

Communist Parties, thus militarily organized, must pledge themselves to certain lines of strategy and tactics. They must in their respective countries carry on truly Communist propaganda and agitation, with special emphasis on the ideal of the dictatorship of the proletariat as superior to parliamentary or congressional "bourgeois democracy" (#1). They must carry on active propaganda within the armed forces (#4) and eschew "not only social patriotism but also the false and hypocritical social pacifism" (#6) which had helped to destroy the Second International. They must work for the destruction of colonialism in all its forms (#8). They must use the existing parliamentary structure for purposes of revolutionary propaganda and agitation (#1). They must strive to win at least the neutrality of a substantial portion of the peasantry (#5), which should cause less trouble in Western Europe and America because, as Lenin had remarked, "Fortunately there are fewer individual peasants than in Russia." They must devote special zeal to working within the trade unions (#9), and especially those affiliated with the existing Social-Democratic Trade Union International (#10); somewhat contradictorily, as rapidly as possible any captured trade unions were to be transferred to a new Red Trade-Union International, thus splitting the world trade-union movement, on the unity of which effective contact of the Communists with the proletarian masses must rest. In addition to all this activity, which could be legally carried on, each Communist Party was to establish an illegal "apparatus" (#3) in preparation for the civil war that Communism was expected to lead to in almost every country of Europe and America.

Nor was it enough for would-be members of the Comintern to pledge themselves to this type of organization and to all these lines of action. For admission to the International, each Party must also demonstrate the purity of its personnel. It would not suffice to promise to exclude from office all "Reformists" and other moderates. "Parties desiring to belong to the Communist International are pledged to recognize the necessity of a complete break with Reformism and the policy of the Center [i.e., moderate socialism] and to propagate this cleavage as widely as possible among their members" (#7). A number of prominent individuals, including the Italian Turati, the German Kautsky, the American Hillquit, the French Longuet, the British Ramsay MacDonald, were specifically mentioned as untouchables. Here was an open invitation to a Communist witch-hunt against any whose membership would make impossible pursuit of a "consistent" Communist policy. The curious rules for detecting heresy were:

> Those Parties anxious to join the Third International whose policy has not already undergone a radical change must before their entry into the Communist International take measures to see that not less than two-thirds of the members of their Central Committees and all other central executive organs are comrades who unmistakeably and openly advocated entry into the Third International before the assembling of the Second Congress of the Communist International. Exception may be made with the approval of the Executive of the Third International . . . (#20). Members of Parties who refuse in principle to accept the conditions and theses propounded by the Communist International shall be expelled from the Party . . . (#21).

Two well-known Bolsheviks who had successfully purged themselves of the "errors" into which they had fallen in 1917 were placed in the van of the offensive; Zinoviev remained chairman of the Executive Committee of the Comintern, and Lozovsky headed the International of Red Trade Unions. Considerable successes seemed to be in the making. Zinoviev in person, by a four-hour address to a congress at Halle, won acceptance of the 21 Conditions by a majority of the German Independent Socialist Party, which proceeded to merge with the already existing Communist Party of Germany. In France, too, the majority at a Socialist Party Congress decided for affiliation with the Comintern. Even in Great Britain was formed a new-style Communist Party, though an insignificant one. Italy proved disappointing, only a minority of the Socialist Party consenting to accept the 21 Conditions. The general picture seemed very encouraging. A highly organized machinery had been set up to discipline the masses and lead them swiftly and unerringly to the beckoning goal of world revolution and to the shimmering paradise of Communism.

THE THIRD INTERNATIONAL IN RETREAT

This was the achievement of the Second Congress, held in July, 1920. Yet, before the year was out, the whole prospect had changed. The Comintern had been designed to guide the energies of the industrial proletariat, which in 1919 and 1920 had seemed to be approaching fever pitch. Late in 1920, the dream was shattered by the onset of a world depression of unprecedented severity. In the face of sharply dropping production and steeply rising unemployment, strikes lost their point, and labor, chiefly concerned with its own material condition, speedily lost its revolutionary ardor. In France, where the industrial proletariat was proportionately the weakest, reaction came most swiftly; the troublesome Confédération Générale du Travail was ordered dissolved, and its leaders were arrested. In Italy, the occupation of the factories by the workers in the fall of 1920 proved a dismal failure, and there set in that progressive diminution of Socialist prestige which culminated in the political triumph of *Fascismo* in 1922. In Germany the "Red" revolt that had flared up in the Ruhr after the Kapp *Putsch* in the spring of 1920 had been suppressed, and the Communist-led labor disturbances in Thuringia were put down in March, 1921. In Great Britain, where organized labor was strongest, the critical moment was not reached until "Black Friday" (April 5, 1921) when the railwaymen announced that they did not feel bound to support the coal miners, and the threat of a seriously revolutionary general strike passed forever. The international ebb of "direct action" was clearly mirrored in the sobered attitude of the Comintern. The Second Congress had announced: "The world proletariat stands on the eve of decisive battles. We are now living in an age of direct civil war. The final hour is at hand." [4]

The Third Congress, meeting in July, 1921, frankly recognized the change in the world picture produced by the depression of 1920. Communist Russia was no longer engaged in armed warfare and had even begun to conclude trade agreements with capitalist countries, but it was no longer possible for her to expect to compass world revolution within any measurable future. The Congress defined the period from March, 1917, to March, 1921 (from the beginning of the Russian Revolution to the defeat of the German "March Action") as a period of revolutionary flood tide.

> This mighty wave nevertheless did not overturn either world or European capitalism. . . . It was marked by the elemental character of a shock, by a considerable formlessness of methods and aims, and by the excessive panic of the ruling classes. [Now, however,] the leaders of the bourgeoisie . . . in all countries have gone over to the offensive against the working-class masses both on the economic and on the political front.[5]

The Third Congress rebuked the Germans for having undertaken an offensive action when the situation called only for a posture of defense. World revolution was still regarded as inevitable, the recovery of capitalism scientifically impossible. For the moment, however, "in the present defensive struggle of the proletariat," [6] the Comintern must confine itself to more limited objectives. Now it must enter into direct competition with the Socialists, especially in connection with the trade unions, to win the long-range support of the workers. While diligently maintaining an aggressive attitude, Communist parties must, in this period of preparation, abstain from "use of arms and acts of sabotage," [7] save in the most extreme circumstances.

> It is not a question of summoning the proletariat to the attainment of ultimate goals, but of elevating that practical struggle of the proletariat which is alone capable of leading the proletariat towards the battle for the final objectives.[8]

Lenin himself was, as usual, brutally frank in explaining the position as he then saw it. Characteristically, he approached the whole problem of international revolution from the viewpoint of the situation in Russia, lecturing his foreign comrades on the lessons to be derived from Russian experience. Through his speeches at the Third Congress runs one thread, the present interests of the Russian Revolution. In its most summary form, as expressed in his pamphlet, *Theses for a Report on the Tactics of the Russian Communist Party,* his view was:

> The result is an equilibrium, although a very precarious one, a very unstable one, but all the same an equilibrium making it possible for a socialist republic to exist—for a short time, of course—in a capitalist environment.[9]

Lenin went on to explain at some length that "the international bourgeoisie . . . temporarily unable to wage open war against Soviet Russia [was] on the watch for the moment when circumstances permit it to renew the war."

Its position was secured by the support of "petty-bourgeois democracy" and by its influence over the majority of the workers, although "the growing economic crisis is everywhere making the position of the masses worse," a fact which would make necessary "new imperialist wars for the preservation of capitalism." A particularly hopeful sign was colonial unrest, especially in India.

Lenin's new recipe for promotion of Communist victory was therefore organization in preparation for future struggles. To those foreign delegations that argued for utilizing "dynamic tendencies," for "transition from passivity to activity," Lenin countered simply:

> These are phrases which the Left SR's put in circulation against us. Now they are sitting in jail; there they are defending "the aims of communism" and thinking about "transition from passivity to activity."

He challenged the critics:

> Show me a [Communist] Party which has got control of the mass of its working class. . . . Even the German Party—one of the best—even it does not have behind it the majority of the working class. . . . Do you really have the majority of the army? Show me such a country! . . . Will you show me a country in Western Europe, where in the course of a few weeks you could take a majority of the peasantry into your hands? . . . In many countries we have not yet learned even to master leadership.[10]

The late Arthur Rosenberg, himself a member both of the Central Committee of the German Communist Party and of the Executive Committee of the Comintern, subsequently explained the change of front on the question of world revolution on the ground that "a Russia organized on a basis of State Capitalism was no longer dependent upon the irresistible advance of the world revolution." [11] Although this interpretation may be colored by Rosenberg's continuing devotion to Marxist concepts of international communism that led to his break with official Communism, the fact that Russian Communists had shifted their ground is unmistakable. As the principal resolution of the Third Congress baldly put it: "Unreserved support of Soviet Russia was and is the very first duty of Communists of all countries." [12]

Lenin himself, in a report at this same Third Congress of the Comintern, acknowledged that the expectation of immediate world revolution had been a delusion:

> When we [in Russia] began the international revolution . . . we thought: either international revolution will come to our aid and then our victories will be fully assured, or we shall do our modest revolutionary work with the consciousness that, in case of defeat, we shall nevertheless serve the cause of revolution, and that our experience will aid other revolutions. It was clear to us that without the support of international world revolution, the victory of a proletarian revolution was impossible. Even before the revolution and also

> after it, we thought: either immediately or at least very quickly, revolution will begin in other countries, in those capitalistically more advanced, or, otherwise, we must perish. . . . But in actual fact the movement did not go in such a straight line as we had expected. In other large, capitalistically most advanced countries the revolution has not even yet begun. . . . What must we do now? Now we need fundamental preparation of the revolution and deep study of its concrete development in advanced capitalist countries. . . . For our Russian republic we must take advantage of this brief breathing spell to adapt our tactics to the zigzag line of history. . . . I should like also to emphasize the significance of the movement in the colonies. . . . It is absolutely clear that in the coming decisive struggles of the world revolution the movement of the majority of the population of the globe, originally directed at national emancipation, will turn against capitalism and imperialism and perhaps will play a far greater revolutionary role than we expect. It is important to emphasize that for the first time in our International we have approached preparation for this struggle. . . .[13]

DOMESTIC AND INTRA-PARTY TROUBLES

This acceptance of defeat, this groping for new ways of achieving a fixed, though remote, goal, characterized Lenin's approach also to the domestic problems of Russia. The decline of industrial and agricultural production, the ruin and starvation that had attended War Communism, naturally absorbed the main attention of Russian Communists, for they presented immediate problems which must somehow be solved, and at once. World revolution could wait, but Russia could not, if she were to survive, and especially if the Communist dictatorship were to survive in Russia. Even before taking formal stock of the world situation, though strongly under its influence, Lenin had begun to work toward the "New Economic Policy."

More pointed than economic distress, more pointed than the wave of peasant revolts, had been the outbreak, early in March, 1921, of the garrison of the naval base at Kronstadt. Mutiny of the armed forces had been the chief factor in the collapse of the autocracy of the tsars. This mutiny was particularly disturbing for sentimental reasons because "Red Kronstadt" had been regarded as a symbol of Bolshevik victory in the coup of November 7, 1917; if the very "cradle of Bolshevism" now repudiated the Bolsheviks, what could stop the spread of the movement through the Red Army, and what dictatorship can survive if it does not control adequate and wholly reliable military forces?

The program of the "Provisional Revolutionary Committee of Soldiers, Sailors, and Workmen" demanded fresh elections to the soviets, "by secret ballot and with free electioneering facilities for all workers and peasants." Free speech, free press, free parties, free trade unions, equal rations for all workers, freedom for the peasants in their enjoyment of the land—all these demands were subsumed in the slogan, "The Soviets without the Bolsheviks." [14] Naturally the revolt attracted the support of all "counter-revolutionary" elements; even Miliukov became a partisan of soviets as defined by these rebels. It was thus possible for Lenin to condemn the rebels' program as a manifestation of White-Guardism, to dismiss it in a press interview as an "absolutely insignificant incident . . . a much lesser threat than are the Irish troops for the British Empire," and to insist that it merely proved the existence in the world of "two camps: the capitalist outside world and communist Russia." [15] Kronstadt was stormed by loyal troops under Trotsky's command, and the affair was officially treated as a mere link in the long and still-continuing chain of handling all domestic criticism of the dictatorship as a conspiracy hatched by imperialists in capitalist countries.

Its real significance was by no means obscure. Revolts might be crushed, but the disease of which they were symptoms must not be allowed to grow worse. At the Tenth Party Congress, Lenin said on March 15, 1921:

> Classes cannot be deceived. . . . We know that only agreement with the peasantry can save the socialist revolution in Russia, unless revolution begins in other countries. . . . We know that the agreement between the working class and the peasantry is unstable. . . . we must not try to hide anything, but must say plainly that the peasantry is not content with the form of relationships we have established with it, that it does not want this form of relationship, and that it will not go on living this way. This is indisputable. This its will has been definitely expressed. This is the will of the vast masses of the laboring population. We must reckon with it, and we are sober enough politicians to say right out: Let's reconsider our policy in relation to the peasantry. . . .[16]

Such was the basis of the series of measures, introduced piecemeal, which are collectively known as the New Economic Policy. As in the cases of the "April Theses," of the armed uprising, and of the Treaty of Brest-Litovsk, Lenin had a long and arduous fight with his Party colleagues in the process of securing their acceptance.

The ideological difficulties in the way of abandoning War Communism were tremendous. A number of members of the Party had supposed that Russia was making giant strides toward the ultimate goal of communism; if within a mere three years Russia had abolished money and the profit motive, and was operating on the communist principle of "from each according to his abilities, to each according to his needs," how could any devout Communist consider for a moment abandoning the victory so miraculously won? The existence of misery and suffering could not be denied, but surely these were temporary phenomena, arising from the havoc and destruction of prolonged civil wars. Now that Russia was at peace, reconstruction of her shattered economy at Bolshevist tempo must surely depend only on the Communist convictions of the Russian masses, moving steadily forward in the new Eden.

Without disclaiming his own share of responsibility, Lenin later (October 18, 1921) characterized the error of this school of thought:

> Carried away by a wave of enthusiasm, rousing popular enthusiasm at first political and later military, we thought we could achieve directly on the basis of this enthusiasm economic tasks just as great [as the political and military ones]. We thought—or perhaps it would be more accurate to say, we assumed without adequate consideration—that by direct orders of the proletarian state we could set state production and state distribution of products going communistically in a land of petty peasants. Life showed us our mistake. A series of transitional stages were needed: state capitalism and socialism, in order to *prepare*—by the work of a long series of years to prepare—the transition to communism. Not directly on the basis of enthusiasm, but with the aid of the enthusiasm born of a great revolution, on the basis of personal interest, on the basis of personal incentive, on the basis of economic calculation, will you labor to construct the first solid foot-bridge, leading, in a land of petty peasants, by way of state capitalism to socialism; otherwise you will not attain to communism, otherwise you will not lead tens and tens of millions of men to communism. This is what life has told us. This is what the objective course of development of the revolution has told us. . . .
>
> Personal incentive raises production; we need increase in production more than anything and come what may. . . .[17]

More serious was the struggle against prominent members of the Party who, though realizing that drastic reorganization of some kind was necessary, were intoxicated with the concept of the "dictatorship of the proletariat" and had never shared Lenin's realization that in a country such as Russia the relationship of the government to the peasantry was fundamental. The first and most difficult stages of this conflict were fought over a side issue, the role of the trade unions, which then numbered nearly 7 million members (not all industrial workers), only about a half-million of whom were Party members.

Early in November, 1920, Trotsky proposed to "shake up" the existing trade-union administration, headed by Tomsky. The ensuing controversy dragged on within the Party, becoming steadily more embittered, until the Tenth Party Congress in March, 1921. Eight "platforms" were developed by various groups; the two most important were those of Trotsky (who by modifying his original theses won the support of Bukharin, one-time leader of the "Left Communists") and of the "Workers' Opposition," a group which included most of the genuine proletarians who had risen to high position in the Party and was headed by Shliapnikov, a metalworker who had become the first People's Commissar of Labor.

In the background of Trotsky's thinking was the apparent success of the "shock battalions," units of the Red Army which early in 1920 he had employed in the gathering of fuel and in railway-repair work. He now proposed that the trade unions be "stateicized" as rapidly as possible. Accepting perfection of "workers' democracy" and "democratic centralism" in the usual Bolshevik sense that the "selection of the directing personnel of the T.U. movement must proceed under the guiding control of the Party," Trotsky wished these organs of the "organized masses" to take over direction and administration of industry, thus converting them from "trade unions" into "production unions" operating on the basis of what he also called "military democracy." [18]

At the other extreme stood the "Workers' Opposition." They proposed complete transfer of the administration of the whole people's economy from government organs to an "All-Russian Congress of Producers." This was to be freely elected, not controlled by the Party. "All workers and employes, without distinction of duties and occupations, engaged in work in individual economic units, such as factories, mills, mines, transport, and in all forms of rural economy, are the immediate stewards of the property under their direction, responsible . . . to all the toilers of the republic." All wages were to be paid in kind "to guarantee the raising of the productivity of labor and improvement of the life of the producers"; all food rations and "objects of domestic use and wide consumption," all meals, baths, transportation, theaters, and all lodgings were to be furnished to the workers gratis.[19]

LENIN'S INTERVENTION AND ACKNOWLEDGMENT OF ERROR

Lenin had at first remained aloof, but, becoming increasingly alarmed at the harm being done to the Party by the "wide discussion" insisted on by "*such* an authoritative leader as Trotsky," he went patronizingly to the defense of Tomsky and the "state apparatus." "I have never heard that Tomsky claimed the title of theoretician, [but] productive work is more interesting than correction of petty theoretical differences"; the existence of bureaucratic evils must be admitted, but Tomsky was fighting to correct them. Trotsky's arguments were "abstract (and therefore empty) words," which were distracting the Party from real work, "simply politicizing without serious content." The "good Bukharin, [who was] full, of course, of humane feelings and intentions" and among whose "numerous very valuable qualities belongs his theorizing ability," was guilty of eclecticism, resorting to "formal, or scholastic, logic and not to dialectical or Marxist logic." It was foolish and dangerous to prate of "productive democracy."

Trotsky's fundamental mistake was that he supposed the trade unions had "lost the old basis of their existence, the class economic struggle," and must now "organize production." Trotsky misunderstood the real nature of their vital role "as a school for the administrative-technical management of production." His proposal would simply destroy the existing link between the central state administration and the toiling masses and leave them subject to inevitable bureaucratic mistakes, with no intermediate organ to watch out for their economic interests and to make effective "production propaganda" among them. "Productive democracy" was a false slogan: "Production is always necessary, democracy not always."

A special feature of Trotsky's "absolute confusion theoretically" was his forty-first thesis:

> In the field of *consumption,* i.e., of the individual living standards of the toilers, it is necessary to follow the line of equalization. In the field of *production* shock-tactics [bonuses for extra or better work] must still remain decisive for a long time. . . .

How, asked Lenin, is one to give preferential treatment to certain producers without showing a preference to them as consumers? "Otherwise shock-tactics are a dream . . . and we, after all, are materialists. And the workers are materialists; if you talk of shock-tactics, then give bread and clothes and meat." [20] Equality was practicable only among Party members, distinguished from one another "only by the degree of their [class] consciousness, loyalty, endurance, political maturity, revolutionary experience, and readiness for self-sacrifice." [21]

Although Lenin devoted most of his speeches to criticizing the "political immaturity" of Trotsky and Bukharin—the latter for his "eclecticism," the former for his "one-sidedness, enthusiasm, exaggeration, and obstinacy"—his sharpest condemnation was reserved for the "Workers' Opposition." In a final, unusually conciliatory speech (March 14) he gave priority to persuasion over compulsion in correction of his opponents' errors and welcomed what he referred to as "healthy" criticism; "it is true our State is a State with bureaucratic perversions" that must be corrected. Yet the basic syndicalist tendency of Shliapnikov and his associates "must be decisively and definitively condemned." [22] Talk of the supremacy of an "All-Russian Congress of Producers" was "not a Marxist, not a Communist point of view." [23]

Perhaps the clearest expression of Lenin's hostility to "industrial democracy" is found in a report on the role and tasks of trade unions, which he had delivered on January 23 at the Second All-Russian Congress of Miners:

> Is it really true that every worker knows how to administer the state? Practical men know that this is a fable. . . . We have not even liquidated illiteracy. We know how workers, linked with peasants, succumb to non-proletarian slogans. Who among the workers have done any managing? A few thousands in all Russia, not more. If we say that it is not the Party that puts up candidates and runs things, but trade unions themselves, that may sound very democratic, perhaps it may catch votes, but not for long. That would ruin the dictatorship of the proletariat.[24]

At the Tenth Party Congress, meeting while the Kronstadt rebellion was still in progress, the "platform of the ten," endorsed by Lenin, received 336 votes, the "stateicizing" resolution of Trotsky and Bukharin 50, and the program of the "Workers' Opposition" only 18.

With victory in this protracted skirmish behind him, Lenin had little difficulty in persuading the Tenth Party Congress to substitute a fixed tax in kind per acre for compulsory surrender to the state of the peasants' whole surplus product. Lenin's purpose was primarily political, to restore the *smychka* of workers and peasants; *smychka,* it should be noted, was an old sportsman's term meaning a double-leash on which the master could control two dogs at once, slipping either at his pleasure.

This concession to the peasants, or rather this retreat from the effort to "carry the class war into the village," embarked on in May, 1918, was the keystone of the New Economic Policy. Many other bricks remained to be added before the new structure was complete, but none cost as much effort as the preliminary clearing of the ground. The building process was much aided by further measures taken by Lenin at the Tenth Congress, which effectively prevented any subsequent repetition, even after the architect's death, of the sort of dispute that had so shaken Party leadership in the crisis of 1921. Lenin had been much disturbed by the manifest tendency to form "fractions" within the monolithic Party, which, although not a wholly new phenomenon, had given "counterrevolutionary" elements in the country ground to hope for the internal breakup of the dictatorship.

This had been the chief theme of Lenin's speech at the Tenth Party Congress on March 8, 1921, while the Kronstadt rebels were still holding out. Lenin openly admitted a whole series of mistakes made by the Party in the last year: too hasty demobilization, which had given rise to "a new form of war-banditism"; too rapid a military advance on Warsaw, which had cost Russia the most advantageous peace with Poland; too rapid increase in the bread ration, without storing up reserves against a crop failure; too rapid consumption of fuel, reckoning on coal from the Donets and oil from the Caucasus which were not yet available; too much time wasted in the "luxury" of discussing the trade-union question. He pointed to two "lessons" of these mistakes:

> 1. An atmosphere of controversy becomes in the highest degree dangerous and poses a direct threat to the dictatorship of the proletariat.
>
> 2. Spring has brought and will bring grave conditions, such that we shall not be able to act without a maximum closing of ranks.

The following day, stung by continued criticism, he exclaimed:

> We don't now need an opposition, comrades! And I think that the Party Congress will have to draw the conclusion that now there is an end to opposition, a lid, now we have had enough opposition.[25]

The Congress obediently adopted a long and detailed resolution, condemning "the weakening of the spiritual life of the Party" which had produced an "internal Party crisis." There was:

> extreme need [of] enlisting workers and cleansing the Party of non-Communist elements by an accurate check on each individual member of the R.K.P., with respect to his discharge of his official duty and also as a member of the Party.

> In case of a violation of Party discipline, etc., by new members of the Party, the Communists who had recommended them will be subjected to a disciplinary penalty, up to expulsion from the Party for repetition of incautious and frivolous recommendations.[26]

Abuses of position and grafting by Party members were condemned, and detailed provisions were included defining the special duties of all elements in the Party hierarchy, from the local cells to the Central Committee, which must give "real direction" to all Party work. A separate resolution concluded: "The Congress prescribes that all groups basing themselves on this or that platform, without exception, be immediately dissolved. . . ."[27] Another spelled out the errors of the "Workers' Opposition" and provided that "propaganda of these ideas be recognized as incompatible with membership in the R.K.P."[28]

The result was the first major Party purge, carried out "not without certain excesses . . . in the provinces."[29] Of the 730,000 members represented at the Tenth Party Congress, 200,000 were "eliminated from the Party." The strength of the "Workers' Opposition" was broken, so effectively broken that the predominance of "bourgeois" elements in the Party began to alarm even leading Communists. In 1923, at the Thirteenth Party Conference, where Stalin made his first major attack on Trotsky, it was disclosed that only 17 or 18 percent of the Party members, the "vanguard of the proletariat," were actually workers; even including those who had at some time in their lives been workers, the proportion of proletarians among Communists was barely two out of five.

THE NEW ECONOMIC POLICY

Once Lenin had reconsolidated his position and secured a "maximum closing of ranks" by putting a firm "lid" on opposition within the Party, there was no difficulty in rounding out the New Economic Policy by a succession of measures reordering various aspects of Russia's economic life. NEP was less complex—and less fundamental—than Emancipation and Redemption, but it represented a social revolution as far-reaching in its goals as had been the Stolypin reform. On the other hand, it constituted less of a break with the cumulative past; it was merely a retreat from the salient into which the overhasty drive toward communism had tempted the Bolsheviks. The NEP was "one step backward in order to take two steps forward," without specifying how long it would be before one could again move forward.

Only the main features of NEP need be reviewed. Of fundamental importance was the retreat from the agrarian policy adopted in the late spring of 1918. It is true that the basic reason for the about face was, as Lenin acknowledged, the nakedly political purpose to "save the socialist revolution" from a hostile peasantry, which constituted "the vast masses of the laboring population." [30] On purely economic grounds, as a means of increasing agricultural production, the preservation of inefficient small-scale peasant production was indefensible. In fact, the measure initially added to the economic difficulties of the government, for the yield of the fixed tax in kind per acre, even if it had not fallen heavily below estimates, at first gave the government less grain than it had been collecting by forced requisitions.

Only in connection with other measures, themselves necessary in order to give real meaning to the concession to the peasants, could the NEP bring beneficial economic results. Allowing the peasant to retain his surplus over and above the tax could not give him serious incentive to increase the area he cultivated unless he could exchange his own product for other goods he desired. The new policy therefore entailed freedom of exchange, at least within the country. On April 7, the coöperatives were released from official control; on October 21, they were given back their property. Even state industrial enterprises were by degrees given the right to operate freely, in retail as well as in wholesale trade. This legalization of private trade was, of course, not as revolutionary as it might seem on the surface; to assume that it meant reintroduction of something that had not been thriving in Russia would be like assuming that liquor was not sold in America during Prohibition. Legalization meant that private trade, openly conducted, could be subjected to taxation and control.

The activities of the "Nepmen," annoying as they might be to pious Communists who had liked to think that money—the root of all evil—had lost all meaning in Russia, would still have been insufficient to stimulate peasant production. The peasant wanted industrial goods, not money, in exchange for agricultural produce. Moreover, the state was burdened with responsibility for supporting a host of industrial enterprises which it could not supply with raw material and the productivity of which, under War Communism, was in any case exceedingly low. It was therefore necessary drastically to revise the administrative structure of industry, without surrendering control of "the commanding heights." As early as November 23, 1920, the policy of granting concessions to foreign capitalists was approved in principle; Lenin was urging that control of the Caucasus oil industry be handed over to the Deterding interests because "so long as the world revolution keeps us waiting, there is no other way out." [31]

Solution of the problem was sought by dividing industry into two sectors, "private" and "socialist." The former was the less important, and the less successful. Small enterprises were to be leased to private entrepreneurs or even restored to their former owners; by special arrangement, even large enterprises might be handed over to foreigners, with or without state participation. The 1923 census showed that of 165,781 enterprises, 147,471 (88.5 percent) were privately controlled, while 4,613 more (3.1 percent) were held by the coöperatives. The 13,697 state enterprises (8.4 percent) were, however, far more significant; they employed 84.1 percent of the workers.

For a time, individual Nepmen were able to make a good, or at least a flamboyant, living, but the advantages to the state were greater than to these petty entrepreneurs. For one thing, the state escaped the burden of administering and financing these enterprises which, though theoretically nationalized under rigid centralized direction, it had never been able to control. Now the state could concentrate its all-too-scant managerial personnel and its limited fluid capital on the "commanding heights," with more hope of success for "socialist" industry. For another thing, the presumed possibility of making legal use of capital resources that had remained secreted in private hands tended to bring them into active circulation and thus gave a fillip to a stagnating economy. In this connection, the state relied heavily on a resumption, by the road of concessions, of that investment of foreign capital on which Russian industry had depended so heavily before the war.

The "socialist sector" was not organized overnight. For outside observers, its real significance was at first obscured by the green light given to the revival of private capitalism. The interrelated basic principles were twofold: (1) decentralization of administrative direction of state-owned enterprises, and (2) restoration of a market relationship between them. Individual state enterprises were given a complex autonomous administrative structure, in which elected representatives of the workers shared with appointed delegates of the state-operated trade unions and of state organs under the direction of the Supreme Economic Council (*Vesenha*). In fact, the system soon settled down in substance to direction of enterprises by managers, nominally responsible to the factory board, but actually accountable to the central state apparatus. Enterprises were encouraged to combine, ultimately forming "trusts," either vertical or horizontal.

The fixed capital of these organizations was, of course, owned by the state. Their working capital, also, was supplied from the center. By a series of decrees, the decentralized managements were gradually given the power to utilize their resources as they saw fit, operating "on the principle of commercial calculation with the aim of deriving profit." [32] The profit was to be paid into the state coffers, but deductions might be made by management, on a scale annually determined by the Supreme Economic Council, for such purposes as workers' welfare and bonuses for the directing personnel.

This was clearly a peculiar form of "socialism," scarcely recognizable as such by professed socialists. Nor did the fact escape notice by critics within the Communist Party. Quite obviously, the "socialist sector" of Soviet economy simply reflected an advanced stage of monopoly capitalism, which, in Marxian terms, was to "exploit" the workers in order to make profit for the capitalist. True, the capitalist was not a private individual, but the state, allegedly representing the people, and in the first instance the workers. However, given the frankly dictatorial character of the regime, the state was clearly as "soulless" as any capitalist corporation, from which it differed only in two principal ways: (1) the beneficiaries of its profits were not stockholders, free to spend their cash dividends as they individually pleased, but citizens, on whose interests the state might expend as much of the profits—and for whatever purpose—it, not they, might choose; (2) there was no superior authority, such as popular governments in "capitalist" countries, to regulate the capitalist state and compel it to conform to any line of conduct the people might prescribe. The situation was somewhat as though all major corporations in, for example, the United States, should be merged under one board of directors, which at the same time controlled a monopoly labor organization and was vested with the full legislative, executive, and judicial powers of a government not subject to being turned out of office in a free election.

This "leviathan" aspect of the prospect did not trouble Lenin. He had at last arrived at that system of "accounting and control" which he had so long preached and which, reluctantly, he had been compelled temporarily to shelve in the early years of Bolshevik power. Now he could envisage enforcement of that "labor discipline" which in his mind lay at the base of heightened productivity, a productivity which alone could make true communism—as distinct from mere socialism—possible at some unknown date in the remote future. He continued proudly to boast of the establishment of "state capitalism," between which and "socialism" there was no dividing line.

The interests of labor were not overlooked. As one of the last steps in the rounding out of the NEP, a new "Labor Code" was enacted in 1922. It confirmed the eight-hour day for adults, with a six-hour day for persons under eighteen or engaged in specially onerous or difficult work. Child labor was prohibited, and a two-week annual vacation with pay was promised for all workers. Employment was to be through labor exchanges, and rules were laid down governing the right of management to dismiss workers for "criminal" activities, excessive absenteeism, negligence, or incompetence. These regulations were to be enforced by government labor inspectors under the supervision of the trade unions. An extensive system of social insurance, defined by a law of September 15, 1921, covered all workers and their families in almost every conceivable circumstance, including unemployment.

The protection of labor interests was left to the trade unions, which, as the left hand of the state, had the duty of preventing the right hand, the organs directing the economy, from unduly squeezing the workers. Defense of workers against "bureaucratic" abuses was not, however, their sole function. As "schools of communism," they were charged with assisting the workers to increase productivity. Their representatives participated with management in "production conferences" and transmitted to the rank and file both the importance of achieving production goals and the necessity of disciplined effort to increase their individual output. All idea of equal pay was abandoned in favor of the principle, accepted by the Eleventh Party Conference in 1921, that "the direct interest of the worker in production and in raising labor productivity must be made the basis of wage-rate policy and the policy of supplies for the workers." [33]

DEATH OF LENIN

The launching of the New Economic Policy was the last achievement of the Bolsheviks under Lenin's guidance. He was already suffering from the consequences of a neck wound inflicted on August 3, 1918, by Fanny Kaplan, a Left SR would-be assassin. On May 25, 1922, he suffered a paralytic stroke. By October he had recovered sufficiently to participate at important public meetings, but without his customary vigor. It was at this time (December 25, 1922) that he wrote his famous "testament," criticizing all his leading associates, to which ten days later he added a still more famous codicil; these documents were not published in Russia until 1956. On March 23, 1923, came a second severe stroke. Lenin lingered on, conscious but unable to speak or write, until his death on January 21, 1924, a little short of his fifty-fourth birthday.

His place as Chairman of the Council of People's Commissars was taken by Rykov, but there was no possibility of ever filling the gap left by his forceful personality, his genius for political maneuver, and his overwhelming prestige. The fate of the new socio-economic structure he had engineered remained to be tested. The problem of political direction also remained to be settled. Throughout the centuries of monarchic rule in Russia, the problem of the succession had repeatedly created political crises; on Lenin's death, the problem of succession was all the more crucial because the Party, as Lenin had sculpted it, had had no experience in functioning without his guidance from the top and because no provision had been made for determining how the monolith was to be handled without him.

NOTES

1. Trotsky, *My Life,* p. 427.
2. Lenin, "The Childhood Disease of 'Leftism' in Communism" (April 27, 1920), in *Sochineniia,* 3rd edition, XXV, 165-250 *passim.*
3. *Kommunisticheskii Internatsional v dokumentakh . . .* , pp. 101-104 *passim.*
4. *Ibid.,* p. 104.
5. *Ibid.,* p. 166.
6. *Ibid.,* p. 179.
7. *Ibid.,* p. 196.
8. *Ibid.,* p. 191.
9. Lenin, *op. cit.,* XXVI, 427-428.
10. *Ibid.,* pp. 442-446 *passim.*
11. Rosenberg, *History of Bolshevism,* p. 161.
12. *Kommunisticheskii Internatsional v dokumentakh . . .* , p. 199.
13. Lenin, "Report on Tactics of the R.K.P." (July 5, 1921), *op. cit.,* pp. 451-453.
14. "On the Production Tax" (April 21, 1921), *op. cit.,* p. 345.
15. "On the Kronstadt Uprising" (March 26, 1921), *op. cit.,* p. 284.

16. "Report on the Tax in Kind" (March 15, 1921), *op. cit.*, p. 238.
17. "For the Fourth Anniversary of the October Revolution," *op. cit.*, XXVII, 29-30.
18. Theses submitted at Tenth Party Congress; cf. Lenin, *op. cit.*, XXVI, 558.
19. *Op. cit.*, p. 567.
20. Lenin, "On the Trade Unions, On the Current Moment, and On the Mistakes of Comrade Trotsky" (December 30, 1920), and "Once Again on the Trade Unions, On the Current Moment, and on the Mistakes of Comrades Trotsky and Bukharin" (January 25, 1921), *op. cit.*, pp. 61-81 *passim*, 109-145 *passim*.
21. *Kommunisticheskaia Partiia Sovetskogo Soiuza v rezoliutsiiakh* . . . , I, 507.
22. Lenin, speech on trade unions (March 14, 1921), *op. cit.*, p. 236.
23. Cited speech of January 25, 1921, *op. cit.*, p. 139.
24. *Ibid.*, p. 105.
25. *Lenin*, "Account of Political Activity of the C.C. of the R.K.P. (B)" (March 8-9, 1921), *op. cit.*, pp. 202-233, especially 204, 208-210, 228.
26. *Kommunisticheskaia Partiia Sovetskogo Soiuza v rezoliutsiiakh* . . . , I, 507.
27. *Ibid.*, p. 529.
28. *Ibid.*, p. 532.
29. Popov, *Outline History of the C.P.S.U.*, II, 150.
30. Lenin, "Report on the Tax in Kind" (March 15, 1921), *op. cit.*, p. 238.
31. "Account of Political Activity of the C.C. of the R.K.P. (B)" (March 8, 1921), *op. cit.*, p. 213.
32. Decree of VTsIK and SNK (April 10, 1923), "On State Industrial Enterprises Operating on the Principles of Commercial Calculation (Trusts)," in *Sobranie Kodeksov R.S.F.S.R.*, 3rd edition, p. 444.
33. *Kommunisticheskaia Partiia Sovetskogo Soiuza v rezoliutsiiakh* . . . , I, 592.

SUGGESTIONS FOR FURTHER READING

Among works previously cited, Baykov and Dobb are of special value, as are the *Collected Works* of Lenin. Stalin's *Collected Works* were compiled in a spirit very different from that which makes Lenin's so valuable; for what they are worth, they are available also in official English translation. Popov's *Outline History of the C.P.S.U.* is the most factual of Soviet treatments of the subject and was therefore superseded in Stalin's time by the *History of the Communist Party of the Soviet Union (Bolsheviks), Short Course;* Schapiro's *Communist Party of the Soviet Union* is a more recent comprehensive treatment from a Western viewpoint. Rosenberg's *History of Bolshevism* is a very valuable study by a convinced Communist, who played a prominent role in the German Communist Party and in the Third International and later lost faith in Moscow and the Communist Party. Ulam's *The Bolsheviks* is a recent political and ideological study. Schapiro's *Lenin: The Man, the Theorist, the Leader* contains some helpful historiographical and analytical articles.

On early international relations of Soviet Russia, a comprehensive discussion, though with emphasis mainly on the period after 1939, is Rubinstein's *Foreign Policy of the Soviet Union.* Very helpful is *The Communist International, 1919-1943: Documents,* selected and edited by Jane Degras; Volume I covers the crucial years 1919-1922. Michael and Taylor, *The Far East in the Modern World,* is valuable also for earlier and later periods.

Russia Today, the report of a British trade-union delegation in 1924, contains much useful information. Two special studies of Soviet financing, especially in its later development, are Holzman's *Soviet Taxation* and Davies' *Development of the Soviet Budgetary System.* Slusser and Triska, *A Calendar of Soviet Treaties, 1917-1957,* is thoroughly done; see also Triska and Slusser, *The Theory, Law, and Policy of Soviet Treaties.* Dewar's *Labour Policy in the U.S.S.R. 1917-1928* is a most useful compilation. Brown's *Soviet Trade Unions and Labor Relations* is a more recent study.

Chapter

29

The Roaring Twenties: 1922-1928

The history of the Soviet Union after the introduction of the New Economic Policy holds less of novelty than the formative period. The long cumulative process of Russian development from the early days of Kiev, through the formation of Muscovite absolutism and its expansion on an imperial scale, had formulated habits of thought and patterns of action that not even the tremendous upheaval of the Revolution had been able to change. It is true that in the decade following the Bolshevik seizure of power revolutionary impulse remained strong, and that efforts were continued to recast many aspects of Russian life in accordance with preconceived abstract theory. Yet the main lines of development continued in the old ruts, with only relatively minor deviations resulting from the work of Lenin and his associates in their first four years at the helm.

THE NEP AND ECONOMIC RECOVERY

Of major importance was the resumption of the industrial development of Russia on the basis of large-scale capitalist techniques, but economic recovery was not altogether smooth. The famine harvest of 1921 and the failure of the peasantry immediately to respond, by increasing their efforts, to the prospect of being able to purchase industrial goods resulted in a continuing scarcity of agricultural products. At the same time, desperate shortage of working capital impelled manufacturing enterprises to sell their wares as rapidly as possible and even to dispose of their equipment below cost price. This "squandering" of resources created a paradoxical "glut" of scarce goods.

which was made worse by the initially weak development of trade outlets and the paucity of credit facilities.

As the NEP took hold, however, despite difficulties in finding capital, production began to increase. Naturally, the increase was more rapid in agriculture, which required proportionately less investment than did industry. Consequently, prices of farm products tended to fall, while prices of manufactured goods rose. In 1923 there developed the "scissors crisis," so called from the appearance of the graph of agricultural and industrial price indices. By drastic measures, such as reducing costs of industrial production by wholesale dismissal of excess personnel, the most acute phase of the crisis was overcome. Yet the blades of the "scissors" could only partially be closed. As late as 1927, the exchange value of a bushel of rye in terms of cotton goods, sugar, salt, tobacco, kerosene, or nails was barely half of what it had been in 1913.

How to deal with the problem of falling agricultural prices and rising industrial prices was one of the most fruitful sources of argument within the high command of the Party. The direct method of paying higher prices for required deliveries of agricultural produce to the state could not be adopted because it would force increase in the wage levels of industrial labor without regard to incentive bonuses; at the same time, it would militate against serious resumption of export of foodstuffs, without which the government could not afford to import the machinery it so badly needed. It would also benefit the kulaks, the peasants who produced a surplus above their own needs, at the expense of the rest of the population. Yet it was necessary not to destroy the incentive to the peasants to produce.

In its dilemma, the government concluded that private trade constituted a danger to realization of official objectives. Accordingly, it began to take all sorts of measures, including priorities in transport, milling, and credit facilities, to put private traders at a competitive disadvantage with state agencies and especially with the coöperatives. Beginning in 1924, special supplies of scarce industrial goods were made available to the peasants during harvest season. By 1926, of all agricultural products put on the market, half went through the coöperatives and slightly more than a quarter through state organs. Simultaneously, though general retail trade increased to nearly fivefold between 1922 and 1927, the share of private trade was reduced from 75.2 percent in 1922-23 to 22.4 percent in 1927-28.

Foreign trade was throughout retained as a state monopoly, but mixed companies which attracted small amounts of foreign capital were allowed to play a valuable though small specialized role. Without waiting for *de jure* recognition, trade agreements were concluded with a number of countries, the first being with Great Britain (March, 1921). Quasi-official Soviet agencies were set up, such as Amtorg in New York and Arcos in London. In 1922 a general conference, which Lenin himself was too ill to attend and in which the United States refused to participate, was arranged at Genoa to discuss the problem of pre-Bolshevik debts, in the hope that the Entente Powers could be induced to grant recognition and thus facilitate commercial relations. Great Britain and France, however, approached the matter from different angles; Lloyd George was chiefly concerned to secure a trade agreement that might relieve the then pressing problem of unemployment in Britain, but the French, who had to think of their millions of bondholders, were obsessed with the thought of debt repayment. No progress was made at Genoa, but the Russian negotiators took the opportunity of discussing matters with German statesmen, who had thought it might be healthful for them also to visit the Riviera. At Rapallo was concluded a Russo-German treaty, the fruit of the natural affinity felt by two countries still treated as pariahs by the Western Powers.

By the Treaty of Rapallo, Germany became the first major nation to extend *de jure* recognition to Soviet Russia. Germany also accepted Russia's repudiation of prerevolutionary debts to Germany and her nationals, on condition that any subsequent recognition of Russian obligations to other states or their nationals would reinstate German claims. Furthermore, Germany extended to Russia a substantial credit for the purchase of German machinery and equipment. Thus Germany acquired a potentially powerful friend abroad and stimulated her own business activity. Russia acquired immediately sorely needed industrial goods in return for deferred payments, which she was careful to make punctually. Displeased though the rest of Europe was, it could not resist the temptation to follow the German lead. At the beginning of 1924, in a photo-finish race, Labour England and Fascist Italy recognized Russia; France sulked but a few months more. Only the United States could afford officially to ignore the new member of the comity of nations, with which a number of American corporations proved quite willing to deal on their own.

Notwithstanding trade agreements and diplomatic recognition, Russia's foreign trade did not recover to the prewar level. This fact cannot be blamed on the state monopoly, which in its efforts to pay for imports often exported goods at a loss. Soviet Russia, in which large-scale agriculture had been destroyed, simply did not have the prewar surplus of foodstuffs to export. Only in the one year 1926-27 could she export more than one-third the rubles-worth of foodstuffs Russia had exported in 1913. Even in raw materials and semi-manufactured goods she did not quite manage to equal the value of her 1913 exports until the First Five-Year Plan (1928). Exports of manufactures attained the prewar level in 1927-28, but they still constituted only a small proportion of the total.

The principal respect in which the NEP failed was that it did not succeed in stimulating the inflow of capital on which industrial development chiefly seemed to depend. For the most part, applications for concessions had to be rejected, either because "they affected objects which, for one reason or another, we did not wish to concede" [1] or because there was not sufficient capital behind them. Only 163 concessions were granted, less than half of which were still in operation in 1927; many of these were merely agreements providing technical assistance, without actual investment of foreign capital. In this sense, in the hope of reviving under Soviet control the free flow of foreign capital that had been so important in the prewar period, the NEP was a flat failure. No matter what political devices were resorted to, "imperialist" foreign capital, badly burned by the war, remained chary.

In the main, the necessary capital had to be squeezed out of the domestic economy. To the extent that, without provoking indomitable internal resistance, the NEP succeeded in restoring industrial production by 1927-28 to the level of prewar production in the same area, the first stage of the NEP must be recognized as an enormous success. Along with restoration of production went a rise in the material standard of living of the Russian industrial worker, though not of the whole population. By 1927-28, according to certain Soviet official figures, the real wages of the Russian worker had again reached the 1913 level, and in the following year had gone 5 percent beyond it; according to another, later, Soviet computation, the employed workers' standard of living, even without reckoning "socialized wages," had by 1927-28 reached 122.5 percent of 1913 real wages.

As in tsarist days, the industrial boom attracted from the villages many more prospective workers than could immediately be absorbed. The result was industrial unemployment on a huge and continuing scale; as fast as applicants for jobs were absorbed by the expansion of employment, fresh thousands took their places. The official figures reported by the Soviet government to the League of Nations Economic and Financial Section showed nearly 1 million unemployed in 1925, a figure that rose steadily to 1.5 million in 1928. These numbers are much in excess of those then prevailing in smaller, but highly industrialized, countries. This circumstance did not have the same significance as unemployment has in more industrialized countries in time of depression, but unemployment benefits constituted an annoying drain on the state's funds, and the obvious abundance of available labor emphasized the fundamental difficulty of shortage of capital.

Whatever the actual facts as to the material condition of the workers may have been, there can be no doubt that the volume of production had by 1927-28 in most branches of industry reached the prewar level; heavy industry showed a slight lag, reaching the 1913 level only in the following year. The question whether quantity was reflected also in quality may be an open one. Soviet criticisms indicate that in this respect Russian industry, despite its remarkable recovery, fell sadly behind 1913. Will Rogers' jibe at Soviet bathing suits that washed off at the first contact with water was not so fantastic as the uninitiated, bowing to statistics, might assume.

Ignoring such reservations and accepting as a fact that Soviet industry had by 1927-28 practically recovered to the 1913 level, the achievement is no doubt significant. Yet, if one shifts one's eyes from the low level of 1920 and sets Russia's progress against a world perspective, the Russian situation becomes somewhat less creditable. If the Western world had stood still since

1913, it would mean that Russia had resumed her relative place in the world; but, recovering from the extremely severe depression of 1920, the Western world had pushed its production—and consumption—far above pre-war levels. Relatively, then, Russia had lost ground heavily, for the gap between the Russian and Western economies had widened greatly. If the best that could be said was that in absolute, though not in relative, terms, the Russian proletariat in 1927-28 stood where it had been before the war and before the Revolution, while in other countries the masses, along with the classes, had much improved their standard of living, the question arose just what had all its sacrifices been for?

The major difficulty continued to be, as it had been before the Revolution, the problem of agriculture. Elimination, by direct action of the peasants themselves, of large-scale landlord agriculture, which prior to the war had produced a very substantial proportion of the grain that went on the market, had resulted in a very great decrease in agricultural surpluses. Small-scale peasant economy was inherently inefficient. It was hopeless to try to restore the volume of agricultural production without somehow introducing less wasteful agricultural techniques, and the peasants had stubbornly and successfully resisted all attempts to replace their individual economies with state farms (*sovkhozy*) or even collective farms (*kolkhozy*). Determined efforts to stimulate the growth of peasant coöperatives met with only slight success; by 1925 about 38 percent of the peasant households had been linked in agricultural coöperatives, averaging about a hundred member households, but most of these confined themselves to organizing sales of farm products or purchases of manufactures, without affecting producing methods.

Under the circumstances, the Communists had to rely mainly on the kulaks, the more efficient and enterprising peasants who alone produced significant quantities of grain and other crops. Under the NEP, their number increased significantly, as did also that of the "middle" peasants, while the number of "poor" peasants declined and the "agricultural proletariat" increased only very slightly. Initially, the new tax in kind (soon converted into money) had been imposed at a flat rate per acre under cultivation. After the exceptionally good harvest of 1925, which approached the 1913 gross yields (though substantially lower per acre), the latent fear of "peasant capitalists" as a danger to a "socialist" economy again asserted itself. The agricultural tax was made progressive.

As a result, in 1926-27, the 3.9 percent of the peasants classed as kulaks paid 25.9 percent of the total tax; the 62.7 percent of "middle" peasants paid 72.9 percent, and the 22.1 percent rated as "poor" peasants paid only 1.3 percent; the remaining 11.3 percent of the peasants, the agricultural proletariat, paid nothing at all. In fact, the government expended considerable sums in direct subsidies to the weaker peasant households. As a sequel, total crop yields ceased to increase, and the more substantial peasants began to refuse to sell grain at fixed prices to the state. The government retorted by returning to the policy of confiscating hoarded grain and revived committees of the village poor to aid in discovering its hiding places. In their turn, the kulaks replied by curtailing production. Something had evidently gone wrong with the *smychka;* the stubborn disobedience of one of the dogs, which refused to make one-sided sacrifices in the name of "socialism," was threatening to bring back the distressful days of the spring of 1918.

The quest for a "correct" policy seriously disturbed the Fifteenth Party Congress, held late in 1927. The "Right Wing" of the Party was led by the erstwhile "Left Communist" Bukharin, now head of the Comintern, who was supported by Rykov, chairman of the Council of People's Commissars, and by Tomsky, in charge of the trade-union apparatus. It was then advocating giving free play to economic forces, allowing grain prices to rise and, if necessary, buying grain abroad. It revived Guizot's admonition to the restless French bourgeois, bidding the peasants "enrich yourselves," though without the thought that they would thus acquire a share in political power; rather, the implication was that the peasants should be content to improve their material condition and leave politics entirely to the Party. A remnant of the "Left Wing," clinging to Trotsky's old concept of "permanent revolution," was opposed to imperiling further rapid industrialization by yielding to agrarian pressures and advocated an outright decisive struggle to "liquidate" the kulaks. The dominant "Center" group had, for reasons of internal Party politics to be explained presently, been dependent on the support of the "Right Wing" against the "Left." Yet it was now determined to find means to push industrial development at all costs; the result was the Five-Year Plan, announced to begin in 1928. The Party therefore decided to continue and to intensify the pressure on the kulaks. A main objective was to promote the collectivization of agriculture, both in the persistent hope that large-scale agriculture would increase crop yields and in the inherited fear that, if unchecked, "peasant capitalism" would destroy "socialism."

STRUGGLE OVER THE SUCCESSION

A second main problem throughout these years of economic recovery had been the political struggle for power within the Party. This struggle often seemed to involve a conflict of ideologies, but it was essentially a rivalry of personalities, cloaking their ambitions in a shifting argument over tactics. None of the competing individuals had any idea of relaxing the dictatorship or of abandoning the goal of communism. None of them attempted to challenge the authority of the Party. What was taking place within the Party was a truly fratricidal strife among Lenin's old associates. Lenin had been a master impresario; he left a troupe made up of prima donnas and ballerinas, incapable without him of conducting Party business in the old style.

Leon Trotsky was unquestionably the most outstanding man among the

Communists. Next to Lenin—in some respects almost more than Lenin—he had been the chief engineer of the seizure of power. In many ways he seemed the most logical person to assume Lenin's mantle. The fact that he was a Jew did not seem an insuperable obstacle in the new Russia, dominated by a Party in which the percentage of Jews, though small (5.2% in 1922), was very high as compared to the percentage of Jews (1.82%) in the total population. His brilliance, whether of tongue or pen, put him in a class by himself; though he could not match the stubborn intensity and the apt, blunt homeliness of expression with which Lenin had been wont to beat down his opponents, Trotsky had a genius for soaring and persuasive eloquence that not even the most experienced Bolshevik could equal.

Yet Trotsky did not have a good Bolshevik background. Distrusting Lenin's dictatorial tendencies, Trotsky had been a Menshevik, making bitter personal attacks on the Bolshevik leader: "The organization of the Party takes the place of the Party itself; the Central Committee takes the place of the organization; and finally a 'dictator' takes the place of the Central Committee." [2] Wrapped in his "theory of permanent revolution," which he later called the "law of combined development," he had insistently advocated immediate establishment of "a workers' government," which Lenin had condemned as ridiculously impossible in a peasant country.

In the summer of 1917, Trotsky and his followers had been welcomed with open arms by the Sixth Bolshevik Party Congress. He had become chairman of the Petrograd Soviet and later chairman of the Military Revolutionary Committee and had been one of the seven members of the temporary "Politburo" set up to give "political leadership in the uprising." [3] In the original Sovnarkom, he had been Commissar of Foreign Affairs, a post which he had in 1918 exchanged for that of Commissar of War. When the Politburo was permanently established in 1919, he was one of its five members. Yet his violent collisions with Lenin had not ceased, and it was always Lenin who triumphed in the end. Both in the matter of the Treaty of Brest-Litovsk and in the trade-union controversy that had accompanied the introduction of the NEP, Trotsky's ideas had been rejected.

Gregory Zinoviev, the only other Jew in the top flight of Bolsheviks, was of much smaller stature than Trotsky but also had a brilliant tongue and pen. He had been very closely associated with Lenin in the last years before the war; he had returned from Switzerland with Lenin, and he had been one of the three Bolsheviks for whose arrest warrants were issued immediately after the July Uprising. He, too, had been a member of the first (temporary) Politburo, but his record had been badly stained by his betrayal to the press of the impending seizure of power, which he had opposed as constituting an unnecessary risk. He had compounded his offense by being one of the five who had threatened to resign (November 17, 1917) from the Central Committee because of Lenin's refusal even to entertain the idea of a Socialist coalition rather than a solidly Bolshevik Sovnarkom. Yet, although he was not included in the permanent five-member Politburo until 1921, he was serving splendidly as chairman of the Third International.

Leon Kamenev, of a Jewish family that had accepted conversion to Greek Orthodoxy, had a somewhat similar record. At the outbreak of the war, he was editing *Pravda,* a circumstance which soon caused him to be exiled to Siberia. In March, 1917, he had resumed his old role, but he had at first refused to accept Lenin's "April Theses." Yet he was the third, along with Lenin and Zinoviev, whose arrest Kerensky ordered in July. He was another of the members of the original Politburo, but against his record, too, was his coöperation with Zinoviev in opposition to the armed seizure of power and to the establishment of a homogeneous Bolshevik Sovnarkom. However, he had sufficiently recovered standing to be one of the five members in the 1919 Politburo, and he served well and conspicuously in various posts, as vice-chairman of Sovnarkom, as chairman of the Council of Labor and Defense (STO), and as head of the Supreme Council of People's Economy (*Vesenkha*).

Nikolai Bukharin was of a different stamp. Universally acclaimed as the greatest Marxist theoretician in the Party, he was in practical matters, as Lenin put it, "soft wax." During the Brest-Litovsk negotiations he had championed the idea of declaring a "revolutionary war." As leader of the "Left Communists," he had joined forces with Trotsky on the trade-union issue. Not included in the Politburo until Lenin's death in 1924, his principal service was as editor of *Pravda,* a post in which he succeeded Kamenev in 1917.

A. I. Rykov and M. P. Tomsky were much lesser men, but neither of them could be ignored; both were added to an enlarged Politburo in 1922. Rykov had become the first Commissar of the Interior. Although he had stood with Zinoviev and Kamenev against continuance of a purely Bolshevik dictatorship, he had later been designated by the ailing Lenin as his deputy and in 1924 had succeeded him as chairman of Sovnarkom. Almost all his energies were devoted to governmental rather than Party work. Tomsky, originally a worker, had become a trade-union organizer; with Lenin's backing, he headed the central trade-union apparatus.

Joseph V. Dzhugashvili, who had been known as Soso and Koba before he assumed the pseudonym of Stalin, was one of the least conspicuous of Lenin's entourage. Well-known as a strong-arm man, Stalin—perhaps because he was a Georgian, not a Russian—had the rare faculty of saying little or nothing, at least until he had been given a lead by his intellectual superiors. Returning from Siberia very soon after the March Revolution, he had followed Kamenev's line of working for unity with the Mensheviks. On Lenin's return in April, however, he had come obediently to heel. As a loyal and hard-working Bolshevik, he earned inclusion, on the eve of the seizure of power, in the original seven-member Politburo; after the coup he was assigned the relatively unimportant post of Commissar of Nationalities, in which he strove to keep pace with Lenin's shifting attitudes. In 1919 he had the honor of being included, along with Lenin, Trotsky, and Kamenev, in the new permanent Politburo. At the same time he accepted work in the "Orgburo," the significance of which must be explained presently. On April 4, 1922, shortly before Lenin's first stroke, Stalin was appointed to the new office of General Secretary of the Party.

N. M. Krestinsky had been Stalin's immediate predecessor, in fact though not in title. A Bolshevik from the beginning, Krestinsky had in 1917 carried on Party work in the Ural region. In 1919, on the death of Sverdlov, who, besides presiding over the Soviet Executive Committee, had almost without assistance and without records done the secretarial work of the Party, Krestinsky had been put in charge of the newly organized Secretariat. He and Stalin were the only members of the Central Committee who served both on the Politburo and on the Orgburo. Krestinsky, however, was unwise enough to support Trotsky against Lenin in the trade-union controversy; in the purge of 1921 he was relieved of all his offices. Although subsequently he had a distinguished diplomatic career, he never was a serious contender for power.

In the early days of the Party, its supreme governing body had been a small Central Committee. In 1919, on the death of Sverdlov, its informal secretary, the Eighth Congress had created an inner organ, the Politburo. Then consisting of five members only (Lenin, Trotsky, Stalin, Kamenev, and Krestinsky), it was given power to make immediate policy decisions. To meet the charge of oligarchy, all members of the Central Committee were given a voice, though not a vote, at meetings of the Politburo. Though it was not ordinarily true, the Politburo was theoretically—and in rare cases actually—subject to the Central Committee. In matters of high policy, the Politburo was normally the supreme ruling body; the regular governmental organ, the Council of People's Commissars, had but to implement decisions of this top Party organ.

At the same time was established an "Organization Bureau" ("Orgburo"), also consisting of five members of the Central Committee. The Orgburo, which was almost constantly in session, was, like the Politburo, supposed to be responsible to the Central Committee. Instead of dealing with fascinating questions of policy, the Orgburo was charged only "to direct all the organizational work of the Party." [4] This meant scrutinizing the records of rank-and-file Party members and finding among them the persons deemed most capable of filling offices, most of them quite humble, whether in the Party, the government, the diplomatic service, the trade-union apparatus, or any other administrative agency. To the leading Party intellectuals and executives in responsible positions of authority, this seemed very tedious and humdrum work. Of the members of the Politburo only two, Stalin and Krestinsky, had been willing to serve on the Orgburo, the tail that was to wag the dog.

Krestinsky was put in charge also of the Secretariat, which at this time had no clearly defined authority. When Krestinsky was removed from office and even expelled from the Central Committee (1921), three men were named as secretaries; among them were young Molotov and a second Stalin stalwart, Yaroslavsky. Stalin, now the only member of the Orgburo who had the prestige of membership also in the Politburo, began to dominate the Secretariat also; his appointment as General Secretary (April 4, 1922) therefore made no real change in the situation.

Under Stalin's direction, the Secretariat rapidly spread its control downward; by 1923 it controlled all Party appointments even as low as the county (*uiezd*) level. It also managed to transform into agencies of centralized authority the "control commissions" which, to appease "democratic" elements in the Party, had been set up to combat "bureaucratic" abuses; at the Eleventh Party Congress in 1922, further to strengthen the unity and authority of the Party, a Central Control Commission was given complete power over all local organs. In the following year, Stalin managed to have Kuibyshev, one of his most dependable men, made chairman of the Central Control Commission.

Lenin himself had become worried. In his "testament," penned in December, 1922, he had said: "Comrade Stalin, having become General Secretary, has concentrated in his own hands unbounded power, and I am not sure whether he will always know how to use this power cautiously enough." In the codicil, added in January, 1923, Lenin had written:

> Stalin is too rough, and this fault, quite tolerable among ourselves and in dealings between us Communists, becomes intolerable in the office of General Secretary. Therefore I suggest that the comrades think of some means of displacing Stalin from this position and of naming in his stead some other man who will differ from Comrade Stalin only in this dominant characteristic, i.e., will be more tolerant, more loyal, more civil and more considerate toward comrades, less capricious, etc.[5]

During the early stages of Lenin's illness, Trotsky apparently trusted, though with no justification, that Lenin would transfer his authority to him. Conscious of his own personal abilities and of his outstanding record of service to the Party and to the Revolution, Trotsky evidently did not think it necessary to take any organizational precautions to ensure his position. As Commissar of War he had a strong following in the Red Army, but he had established no contacts with the *apparatchiki,* the party secretaries who were in a position to deliver delegates at Party Congresses and Party Conferences. Nor did he, after Lenin's second stroke, take measures to prevent the formation in the Politburo of a coalition against him.

The three other leading members of that body—Stalin, Kamenev, and Zinoviev—all feared Trotsky's prestige and consequently formed an unstable triumvirate to rule Russia; the addition of Rykov and Tomsky to the Politburo in 1922 somewhat strengthened the position of Stalin vis-à-vis the bigger names. Even the most prominent member of the triumvirate, Zinoviev, who had great strength in the Petrograd "apparatus," took alarm at growing evidences of the increase in Stalin's political machine. In September, 1923, he conspired with Bukharin and others, one of whom, Stalin's fellow Georgian Ordzhonikidze, helped to work out an arrangement expected to clip the General Secretary's wings. Trotsky, Bukharin, and Zinoviev were added to the Orgburo. By Zinoviev's own account, however, he attended its boring sessions only once or twice, Trotsky and Bukharin not at all.

Trotsky preferred his own more spectacular method of struggle. He addressed a letter (October 8, 1923) to the Central Committee, complaining:

> The bureaucratization of the party apparatus has developed to unheard-of proportions by means of the method of secretarial selection. There has been created a very broad stratum of party workers, entering into the apparatus of the government of the party, who completely renounce their own party opinion, at least open expression of it, as though assuming that the secretarial hierarchy is the apparatus which creates party opinion and party decisions. Beneath this stratum, abstaining from their own opinions, there lies the broad mass of the party, before whom every decision stands in the form of a summons or a command.[6]

On December 4 he published an open letter to the same effect. It was no way in which to attack the organization, more firmly entrenched and better oiled than any Tammany machine.

Zinoviev, thrown back on his ally, demanded Trotsky's arrest for breach of Party discipline, but Stalin, as he told a Party Congress two years later,

> did not agree with Zinoviev and Kamenev because we knew a policy of lopping off to be fraught with great dangers for the Party, that the method of lopping off, the method of shedding blood (they demanded blood), is dangerous, contagious: today you lop one off, tomorrow another, the next day a third—what will we have left of the Party? [Applause.][7]

At the Thirteenth Party Conference (January, 1924) while Lenin was finally dying, Stalin vigorously accused Trotsky of the factionalism that Lenin had condemned. The Conference condemned Trotsky's "petty-bourgeois deviation," and the Secretariat began to remove his supporters from their posts. At the Thirteenth Congress (May, 1924), Trotsky confessed his sin; though he maintained that his criticisms had in themselves been correct, he acknowledged that it was

> impossible to be correct against the Party. One can be correct only with the Party and through the Party, for history has created no other paths for the realization of correctness. The English have a historical proverb: my country right or wrong. With far more historical truth we can say: right or wrong on individual particular concrete questions, on individual points, it is still my Party.[8]

Stalin, moving warily as always, let matters rest there for the moment. Lenin's "testament" and codicil were reported to the Congress (but not published in Russia until 1956), but Stalin's assurance that he had himself drawn the necessary conclusions was gladly accepted. He secured further increase in the size of the Central Committee and of the Central Control Commission and used the opportunity to pack them with his own devoted adherents. Bukharin succeeded to the vacancy in the Politburo left by Lenin's death.

Stung by the unrestrained attacks of Zinoviev and Kamenev, Trotsky in October, 1924, published a pamphlet, *Lessons of October* (i.e., November, 1917). Intellectually successful in its devastating critique of his enemies, this pamphlet proved politically disastrous to its author. At a plenum of the Central Committee and Central Control Commission (January, 1925), Trotsky was removed from office as Commissar of War. Making no attempt to use his influence in the army against the Party, Trotsky remained as a completely isolated member of the seven-member Politburo.

Stalin was now free to turn against his uncomfortable allies. At the Fourteenth Party Congress (December, 1925), he accused Zinoviev and Kamenev of factionalism. Controlling the Leningrad (formerly Petrograd) delegation, Zinoviev fought back with courage unusual for him. Although he and Kamenev were orators of extraordinary ability, and although Lenin's widow, Krupskaia, defended them, the poison of the recent attack by the now silent Trotsky and, above all, the weight of Stalin's machine crushed them. Kamenev was even demoted from member to alternate in the Politburo, which was again increased by two additional members. The three vacancies were filled by Stalin men—Molotov, Voroshilov, and Kalinin.

Zinoviev and Kamenev in desperation now joined forces with Trotsky. They were the three figures who undoubtedly had the greatest prestige among the surviving heroes of the revolution. Yet the spectacle of these men, who had just been so busily and so eloquently destroying each other's reputations, now trying to act in brotherly fashion while they denigrated recent allies was unedifying, if not ludicrous. Even more importantly, the Leningrad "apparatus" of the Party, formerly Zinoviev's personal stronghold, had been purged. By April, 1926, Zinoviev himself was ousted from the Politburo in favor of another Stalin lieutenant.

Stalin's dictum that the Party was not "a debating society" [9] still could not completely stifle internal criticisms. Early in October, however, Trotsky offered submission; Stalin's terms were outwardly accepted by the opposition, but not without slipping in renewed criticisms of Stalin and Bukharin. The reply of the machine was decisive; Trotsky was dropped from the Politburo, Kamenev lost his place as an alternate, and Zinoviev had to hand headship of the Comintern over to Bukharin. The ideologically strange combination of personalities that has come to be known as the "Left Opposition" was formally condemned as a mere "social-democratic" opposition, unworthy of the name of Communist.[10] Its three chief leaders were still tolerated as members of the Central Committee, by now much enlarged and filled with creatures of Stalin's machine.

In the spring of 1927, the irrepressible Trotsky and his temperamental allies seized a last opportunity to criticize obvious failures of Stalin's foreign policy and to denounce what they condemned as "Thermidorian reaction" at home. In the fall, Stalin counterattacked; Trotsky and Zinoviev were expelled from the Central Committee (October 23) and, soon after, from the Party (November 14). At the Fifteenth Congress (December, 1927), on the heels of wholesale expulsion of "Trotskyites," Zinoviev and Kamenev surrendered ignominiously. Within a few years the groveling members of the "Left Opposition" were readmitted to the Party, though not restored to positions of power.

Trotsky, however, was sent into administrative exile at Alma Ata, in the heart of Asia; he was to be released only to be deported to Turkey (1929) whence he soon went to Norway and thence to Mexico, where in the end he was murdered (August, 1940). Abroad he remained an oracle for those who wished to rekindle the flame of 1917, trying to create a Fourth International, a concept repugnant to Orthodox believers in the mystic number. In Russia his name became a synonym for national treason. For the victorious Stalin, no method of dealing with internal criticism was easier than to condemn his opponents as followers of Trotsky, depicted as the tool of "imperialists" plotting the destruction of the Soviet Union.

The remaining outstanding Communists of the older generation—Bukharin, Rykov, and Tomsky—had been very useful to Stalin in his rise to power. Now they found themselves a helpless minority of three in a nine-member Politburo. As indicated above, the majority faithfully followed Stalin in adopting a line of policy, dictated by current circumstances rather than by abstract considerations and close to that which had been vainly advocated by the now eliminated "Left Opposition." The turn of the "Right Opposition" to suffer the same sort of personal fate that had overtaken their ideological rivals was not far distant.

FORMATION OF THE SOVIET UNION

During the early stages of this struggle, the Union of Soviet Socialist Republics (U.S.S.R.) was brought into existence. The six nominally independent national states then dominated by the Communist Party—the R.S.F.S.R. of 1918, the Ukraine, Byelorussia (White Russia), Georgia, Armenia, and Azerbaijan—were now formally incorporated into a federal union. The title of the new state included no ethnic designation; it was tailored to make possible subsequent inclusion of other nations—Germany, for example—without derogation of their national dignity. At the time, some American critics gibed that Russia had been wiped from the face of the earth; they might have recalled that Virginia and Massachusetts did not cease to exist because of the establishment of the United States of America. Because of her bulk and power, Russia remained dominant within the Union.

The new Constitution was approved by the Party in 1923 and ratified less than a week after Lenin's death (January 21, 1924) by a Congress of Soviets (officially this was the Second All-Union Congress, for the body convened in 1922 as the Tenth All-Russian Congress was converted, even before ratification of the new Constitution, into the First All-Union Congress). The Constitution allowed no play for any serious question of "states' rights." Its centralizing character provoked objections from Ukrainian Communists, but they were overruled by Stalin, who stated flatly:

> We are constructing, not a confederation, but a federation of republics, a single federal state, uniting military, foreign, foreign trade, and other matters, a state the existence of which does not diminish the sovereignty of the individual republics.[11]

The complex governmental structure of the Union was modeled on the original 1918 Constitution of the R.S.F.S.R. and requires little comment. An All-Union Congress of Soviets constituted the new pinnacle of the old pyramid of soviets, ranging downward from provincial to local soviets. Technically, the Congress wielded supreme authority. Out of it was elected an All-Union Central Executive Committee, consisting of two chambers, the Council of the Union and the Council of Nationalities. The former was about the size of the American House of Representatives and, like it, was based on population; the latter, about the size of the American Senate, was made up of delegates to "represent" the several member "sovereign" republics and their principal "federal" subdivisions. Each of these Councils chose its own Presidium, the members of which, together with jointly added members, constituted the Presidium of the Congress. The chairman of this body was officially the highest officer of the united state; this post was assigned to Kalinin, a peasant who had served in the corresponding role under the R.S.F.S.R. and whose practical importance was as a symbol of the peasant-worker *smychka.*

The new All-Union Council of People's Commissars was, in theory, "formed by and responsible to" the Central Executive Committee of the All-Union Congress of Soviets. The previously existing Sovnarkoms of the technically still independent member-states continued to exist, "responsible" to their respective Congresses of Soviets, but they surrendered most of their powers to the new All-Union Sovnarkom. This body included some men with full executive authority in their departments throughout the Union and other men whose central policy decisions were to be executed by the commissars of the six member states. These two categories included all commissariats of major importance, such as foreign affairs, defense, finance, political police, and economic administration. Relatively minor functions, such as justice, education, health, and social welfare, were left entirely to commissars of the "union republics," though the basic principles of their administration in these fields were determined centrally.

The GPU (State Political Administration), which had replaced the Cheka in 1922, now became OGPU (Union State Political Administration). It was directed by the All-Union Council of People's Commissars, with agents attached to the local Councils of People's Commissars. It retained its powers, not merely to arrest, but to try and punish, offenders against the state. As the concept of "counter-revolutionaries" had grown, the activities of GPU had been extended; GPU was actively involved in the fight against "Trotskyites." Most of the organization's attention, however, continued to be given to "former people" (members of the old upper and middle classes) and "politicals" (survivors of the old rival socialist parties); the ordinary population still had little occasion to worry about the political police.

A new feature of the 1924 Constitution of the U.S.S.R., as compared with the 1918 Constitution of the R.S.F.S.R., was the establishment of a Supreme Court. This organ did not have authority to declare U.S.S.R. laws unconstitutional but, in addition to ordinary appellate jurisdiction, it did have the power to make Union laws prevail over conflicting legislation by the member states.

The old method of electing the Congress of Soviets was retained. Prohibition of competitive party organizations, disfranchisement of elements expected to be hostile, weighted representation of the urban population as against the rural, indirect election in a series of states, and open voting continued to guarantee monopoly of power by the Communist Party. In the meantime the tightening of intra-Party dictatorship, spurred by Lenin's 1921 purge and reinforced by successive resolutions during the struggle for leadership, had really made the Party into the monolith of Lenin's early dreams.

EXPERIMENTS WITH THE CHURCH AND EDUCATION

In many directions during those years, Russia undertook experiments. Most of them were ephemeral, and many of them were destructive, dictated by the desire to do away with habits of life that seemed to menace the security of the new regime.

Prominent among them was continued hesitant warfare against religious manifestations, for the Communists shared with tsarist statesmen the belief that "religion is the opiate of the people." Lenin, to be sure, had not wished to become involved in a conflict which to him was a side issue:

> We shall always teach a scientific world outlook; it is necessary for us to fight against the inconsistency of any "Christians," but this does not at all mean that we ought to put the religious question in the forefront, which does not belong to it at all, that we ought to permit splintering of the forces of a really revolutionary economic and political struggle for the sake of third-rate opinions or chimeras which will soon . . . be thrown on the rubbish heap by the mere force of economic development.[12]

Only when Patriarch Tikhon had openly attacked the Bolsheviks (February, 1918) had Lenin struck back; even when Tikhon had persisted in his denunciations, he was only briefly put under house arrest (October, 1918). During the dark days of civil war, Church property was confiscated wholesale, most of the monasteries were suppressed, relic frauds were exposed, a few actively counter-revolutionary ecclesiastics were executed, and "scientific" efforts were made to undermine the prestige of the Church by methods such as placing mummified rats in shrines alongside corpses of saints which millions of pious Orthodox pilgrims were accustomed to kiss. The Church, nourished in the spirit of caesaropapism, tended to turn the other cheek; even while Denikin was still advancing on Moscow, Patriarch Tikhon bade the faithful not "to intervene in the political life of the country, [not] to belong to any party, and above all [not] to make the divine rituals and priestly ministrations a tool of political demonstrations." [13]

Early in the period of the NEP, however, the Communists felt more free to attack an institution which their spiritual father, Karl Marx, had dismissed as a mere rationalization of property relations about to be abolished. In 1922 a special newspaper, *The Godless,* was founded to make open and continuous anti-religious propaganda. Patriarch Tikhon was arrested (May, 1922); after his death in April, 1925, his designated successor, Metropolitan Peter, was also arrested and subsequently exiled to Siberia. In the meantime, a group of "liberal" priests, animated by hostility to the bishops and to the monks from whom the bishops were always drawn, organized a "Living Church." With the permission of the Soviet authorities, the Living Church seemed at first to thrive. Operating on something like the technical status of a commercial concession, it took control of about one-third of all the churches.

Very soon, however, the Orthodox Church itself came to terms with the atheist Soviet regime, much as it had done with the pagan Mongols in the thirteenth century. Metropolitan Sergius, who had been appointed deputy for the exiled Peter, won recognition by the Communists (May, 1927), and the Living Church lapsed into limbo. The relations between Church and State remained undefined. Communists mistrusted the sincerity of the hierarchy in making its submission and were animated by ideological conviction of the pernicious influence of religion. Party members were severely disciplined for errors such as attendance at church services of any kind, and support was given to a League of the Militant Godless, founded in 1925.

At the same time, the Communists began to steal leaves from the Church's book. Lenin's body was mummified and enshrined in a subterranean mausoleum at the edge of the Red Square in the shadow of the Kremlin wall. There the Communist saint entered into direct competition with the older saints whose bodies had long lain on exhibition in sarcophagi in the Vasily Cathedral a few hundred yards across the square. Still not daring to suppress altogether the age-old practice of expressing veneration by kissing the shin of a departed saint, the Bolsheviks simply interposed a plate-glass cover on the sarcophagus and stationed beside it an attendant with an alcohol swab. Himself under glass, Lenin dead continued in the service of the Party as a rival attraction, with the advantage that one might hope a visit to his shrine might bring material advancement in this world instead of waiting for spiritual rewards in the next.

Education was another area in which the Bolsheviks could only fumble. The People's Commissar of Education, Lunacharsky, was one of the most cultured and most unstable men among the Bolsheviks. Continuously entangled in philosophical heresies, he had come into the Party in the summer of 1917, along with Trotsky and the other *Mezhraiontsy*. As an administrator with a difficult problem he was lost. The inherited teaching personnel were either supporters of the old bureaucratic autocracy or partisans of the alien liberalism that had been seeping into the Russian intelligentsia. The latter, because they thought for themselves, were the more dangerous to the new autocracy of the Party and had to be got rid of; it was not easy to replace them. The prewar plans, approved by the Duma, to establish by 1922 a complete system of free elementary schools could not be carried out.

From top to bottom, the Soviet educational system was reduced to reliance on trial and error. Efforts were made to digest the "progressive" ideas of John Dewey and other theorists. The resultant "child-centered" school was characterized by absence of discipline, in both senses of the word as applied to education. The authority of the teachers disappeared; at the same time, such subjects as Latin were eliminated, while history, economics, and political science were replaced by "social science." So far as serious efforts were made to retain standards of instruction, it was with respect to technical subjects; the need for mastery of techniques was too clearly obvious.

Along with disintegration of the school went deliberate efforts to dissolve the "bourgeois family," which Marx had condemned as based "on private gain." Not content with secularizing marriage, the Communists in this period emphasized the "emancipation of woman," as reflected in easy divorce and legalized abortion. At home as in school, the independence of children from their parents was encouraged.

Higher education became the special province of M. N. Pokrovsky. Trained in the best traditions of Russian historical scholarship, under such men as Vinogradov, Pokrovsky had imbibed also the Marxist ideas afloat in the atmosphere of his university generation. In 1905, outraged by Bloody Sunday, he had joined the Bolshevik fraction of the Social-Democratic Party; participation in illegal propaganda work had made it advisable for him to go abroad. While teaching at the Party school on the Isle of Capri, he had written a four-volume *History of Russia from the Earliest Times,* in which he attempted to fit Russian history into the framework of Marxist philosophy. In 1917 he returned to Russia; although he had been guilty of the "Forwardist" heresy, he became chairman of the Moscow Soviet and was appointed Vice-Commissar of Education.

He came to personify the title of the quarterly, *The Marxist Historian,* which he founded and edited. Among many other writings, he revamped his *History* as a *Brief Outline* of strongly propagandistic character. Unable to use "bourgeois" university professors, he organized "workers' faculties" (*rabfaks*) and the Institute of Red Professors. In his hands, the universities were converted from institutions in quest of absolute truth, however hemmed in by bureaucratic restrictions, into seminaries for the study of truth as revealed by Karl Marx and expounded by Lenin.

In addition to embalming his body, Lenin's followers assiduously assembled his words, with certain deliberate exceptions, into a multi-volumed *Collected Works.* Also, they converted Petrograd, which had commemorated the man soon to become known as "the first Bolshevik," into Leningrad. It was the beginning of a practice—which was to grow with time and which makes modern Russian geography as confusing as the British peerage—of renaming Russia's towns in honor of her new lords, in special cases even while they still lived. Thus, Tsaritsyn ultimately became Stalingrad, old Tver became Kalinin, and historic Nizhny Novgorod was renamed to honor Gorky.

EXPERIMENTS IN LITERATURE AND MUSIC

Gorky's name, however, was not in high favor during the early years of the NEP. On his return to Russia in 1917, he had taken a position on the whole favorable to his Bolshevik friends, but a certain fastidious aloofness had from time to time led him to make sharp criticisms of their excesses. During the civil wars he had continued his "autobiographical" writings; his *Recollections of Tolstoy* (1919) constitutes one of the most remarkable, though destructive, appraisals of that outstanding, sometimes sainted, writer. In those years Gorky's intercession saved many a writer from starvation, even though at the price of accepting work as a translator. In 1921, however, Gorky had again abandoned Russia, first for Germany, later for Italy. It was there that he completed his "autobiography," really consisting of sketches of other writers he had known, in *Notes from a Diary* (1924). He returned to Russia only in 1928, for the celebration of his sixtieth birthday, and resumed permanent residence under the Soviets only in 1929.

Along with Gorky, most other Russian writers of significance, including Bunin, Andreev, Kuprin, A. N. Tolstoy, the "modernist" Merezhkovsky, and Alexis Remizov, also abandoned Soviet Russia. Of those who remained, the symbolist Alexander Blok promised to become the greatest Soviet literary figure, but he died in 1921; *The Twelve* (1918), his greatest poem, represented the Bolshevik Revolution as the soul of the Russian blizzard. An offshoot of the symbolists were the "peasant-poets," of whom Serge Esenin (1895-1925), fleetingly married to Isadora Duncan, was the most conspicuous; styling himself the "hooligan poet," he signalized his suicide with the confession that he was "no longer needed here." The man who survived as a sort of poet laureate was the futurist Vladimir Maiakovsky (1894-1930), who had joined the Bolsheviks in 1908. In content, his poems were crudely propagandistic. In style, they bore about the same relation to poetry as formerly understood that the works of Stravinsky and Prokofiev did to nineteenth-century music. Lenin, whose personal tastes ran to Pushkin, suffered acutely through constant repetitions of Maiakovsky's *Left, March* (1919). Although the official darling, Maiakovsky retained a considerable measure of individualism and in the period of the First Five-Year Plan fell into disfavor.

Two other excellent poets continued to live, though in relative silence, under the Bolshevik regime. One of them was Boris Pasternak (1890-1960), whose first important lyrics, *My Sister Life,* written in 1917, circulated only in manuscript copies until 1922; owing to the difficulty of his style, Pasternak's influence remained much greater on other poets than on the general public. The other, whose pen-name was Anna Akhmatova (1889-1966) was the leading "acmeist," a term invented by a contemptuous symbolist for those poets who insisted: "We want to admire a rose because it is beautiful, not because it is a symbol of mystical purity." Her husband, N. S. Gumilev (1886-1921), from whom she was divorced in 1918, was also an able poet but was executed by the Cheka. A poet of deep intensity, Akhmatova was barely tolerated in the new Russia as an old-fashioned reactionary.

In the period of War Communism, a group of writers, centering around the magazine *Proletkult,* attempted, with some assistance from Lunacharsky, to assert its right to be the "culture-creative class organization of the proletariat." The claim was somewhat similar to some of the ideas then becoming current about the role of the trade unions in economic life. Lenin intervened decisively to quash such pretensions; a decree of the Central Committee (December 1, 1920) announced the intention of the Party itself to supervise the direction of literary currents.

The introduction of the NEP initially gave more free rein to "fellow-travelers," though not to anti-Communist writers, as it did also in the field of economic enterprise. Some of the results, such as *Cement* (1924), by Fedor Gladkov (1883-1940), pointed the way for the drab "socialist realism" of the following decade. Yet there appeared a certain amount of good, though undistinguished, prose, dealing mainly with the Revolution and the civil wars. Most notable were: *The Naked Year* (1922) of Boris Pilniak (1894-1946), strongly nationalist in tone; *Red Cavalry* (1926) of Isaac Babel (b. 1894), somewhat suggestive of Gogol's *Taras Bulba;* and some of the stories of Leonid Leonov (b. 1899). Alexei N. Tolstoy (1883-1945) stifled his distaste for Bolshevism and returned to Russia in 1923, along with the noted Ilya Ehrenburg, and began work on *The Road to Calvary*. The first volume of one major novel, *The Silent Don,* by Mikhail Sholokhov (b. 1905) was published in 1928.

In the theater, Vsevolod Meyerhold, a pupil of Stanislavsky, welcomed the Bolshevik regime and tried to develop appropriate new techniques. The ballet was preserved, though it tended to become mummified in traditional forms. In the movies, themselves still a revolutionary art form, Serge Eisenstein won world renown. Painting and sculpture did not flourish; Repin, the patriarch of the old realism, who had made his peace with prewar modernism, now abandoned Russia.

Russian music also stagnated. Rachmaninoff early slipped out of revolutionary Russia, and Stravinsky did not return. Even Prokofiev, though hailed as a cultural revolutionary, secured permission to go abroad. In 1926, influenced by a meeting with Gorky in Italy, he paid a three-month visit to his homeland, where he received a triumphal welcome. Not until 1929, however, did he again revisit Russia and only in 1932, overcome by homesickness, did he return permanently to the land of his birth. The new rising star was Dmitry D. Shostakovich, who entered the Petrograd Conservatory in 1919 at the age of thirteen. His mother's determined sacrifices and a job in a movie theater enabled him, despite ill-health, to continue his studies. His *First Symphony* (1925), though immature, showed enormous facility and met with great success. His *Second Symphony,* in honor of the tenth anniversary of the Revolution, was, because of its deliberate *style mécanique,* utterly incomprehensible to the masses whom it was intended to glorify.

INTERNATIONAL RELATIONS

In diplomacy as in education, literature, and the arts, the early years of the Soviet regime were characterized by experimentation and improvisation. Before the NEP, foreign relations had been almost nonexistent; the Bolsheviks then could think of foreign policy only in terms of world revolution, promoted by the Third International and backed by the Red Army. The about-face of 1921 therefore forced the Soviet Union to grope for a new line.

It was a problem that became entangled in the struggle for power within the Party. The necessity of world revolution if the Russian Revolution were to survive had been a prime article of Bolshevik faith. Even Lenin had in 1918 maintained that for socialism "to triumph definitively is possible only on a world scale and only by the combined forces of the workers of all countries." [14] Yet, in the dark days of 1921 when the prospects of world revolution had so obviously become remote, Lenin, without abandoning the accepted creed, had extended a ray of hope: "a socialist republic can exist—for a short time, of course—in a capitalist environment." [15]

Trotsky had been one of the most emphatic on the score of the imminence of world revolution. Yet, notwithstanding his vanity, which prevented frank admissions of past errors such as Lenin could make, even Trotsky had by 1922 reached the view that "so long as the bourgeoisie remains in power in other European states," agreements with them "at best can help us heal some economic wounds or at least make some step or other forward," though he felt compelled to add: "A genuine rise of socialist economy in Russia will become possible only after the victory of the proletariat in the most important countries of Western Europe." [16]

Stalin, though himself obviously floundering, made shrewd use of this chink in Trotsky's armor. On May 9, 1925, he thrust at Trotsky with the assertion: "Anyone who denies the possibility of building socialism in one country must necessarily deny also that the October [Bolshevik] revolution was justified." [17] Stalin's thesis of "socialism in a single land" was no longer a novel idea; it was merely forthright formulation of the position toward which Lenin —and a more reluctant Trotsky—had been drifting. Nor was it a repudiation of basic principles; in the same speech Stalin included fiery reaffirmation of the inevitability and the desirability of world revolution.

The Treaty of Rapallo (1922), dictated by circumstances rather than premeditated, had represented an astonishing success for the diplomacy of Chicherin, who had succeeded Trotsky as Foreign Commissar in 1918. Friendship with Germany became the sheet anchor of Soviet foreign policy and permitted covert exchange of assistance between the Red Army and the Reichswehr. It suffered ups and downs, becoming noticeably warmer whenever German ministerial coalitions swung rightward and correspondingly cooler when the Social Democrats predominated in the German cabinet. It was affected also by jockeying for position in relations with the West. Although the newly created Soviet Union welcomed recognition by the several Entente Powers (1924), their flirtation with the Germans in the Locarno arrangements (1925) seriously worried the Russians. Particularly disturbing was Germany's admission to the League of Nations (1926), which Soviet Russia was accustomed to denounce as an imperialist conspiracy directed against her. Unable to restrain her partner, Russia had to accept with as good grace as possible the German explanation that, in view of continuing Russo-German friendship, Germany's permanent seat in the Council of the League was the best guarantee that that organization could no longer be used as a weapon against the Soviet Union. Under the new conditions, the old hope that a Communist revolution would soon break out in Germany became a nightmare; German Communists found to their dismay that they were being kept in leash to preserve the democratic Weimar Republic.

Toward England, Russia continued the policy that Lenin had advocated in the days of the Lloyd George coalition government, the policy of supporting the Labour Party "as a rope supports a hanged man." [18] In 1926 Soviet boasts of assistance to the British coal strike caused serious friction, which was embittered by a police raid on Arcos, the Soviet trade agency in London; in 1927 Great Britain broke off diplomatic relations with Russia, which replied with ostentatious preparations for an aerial war; diplomatic relations were not resumed until 1929.

Russia failed to secure recognition by the United States, but she did not in this period display the same hostility toward America as toward the Entente

Powers. At the time of the famine from 1921 to 1923, Russia had gratefully accepted the work of an American Relief Administration, directed by Herbert Hoover. A British "Save the Children Fund" and a League of Nations organization directed by Fridtjof Nansen coöperated, though on a much smaller scale. The A.R.A. organized and supervised the distribution of $60 million worth of food and medical supplies among the famine-stricken villages, of which $24 million was contributed by the United States government; smaller, but very substantial sums were furnished by the Red Cross, the Jewish Joint Distribution Committee, and a number of church organizations. The Russian government was persuaded to buy $12 million worth of seed grain; no payment, however, was ever asked, much less tendered, for the mass humanitarian service rendered by the American people and their government. Transport conditions within Russia made it impossible to deliver all the food donated, and the Relief Administration had to choose between saving all the children, while many of their parents died, or of saving whole families, while letting many children die of starvation. Adoption of the former course left Russia for years after to struggle with the "untended" orphans, who could not be controlled by the peasants to whom they were assigned or by the institutions in which they were placed by the Soviet government. With rapidly fading gratitude for the feeding of some 10 million people, and the concomitant aid given against the spread of disease, the "untended" soon were given the nickname of "Hoover's wolves."

Other factors softened the Russian attitude toward America. The United States had not joined the League of Nations, that "imperialist conspiracy." In particular, Lenin had gloated over the prospect of a mutually destructive war, which he had expected at any moment, between the United States and Japan. In fact, American pressure on Japan had been of much assistance to Russia, which in return had dangled hope of valuable Far-Eastern concessions before the eyes of American capitalists. However, when Japan at length recognized the Soviet Union (1925) and evacuated the last of her troops, the oil concession in Sakhalin went to Japanese interests, not to Sinclair; the principal American prize was the Harriman manganese concession.

The chief sphere of Russia's foreign activity in this period was China, where Sun Yat-sen's continuing revolution seemed to offer most hope for a success of Soviet diplomacy. Bolshevik Russia had promptly renounced her rights under the "imperialist" treaties imposed on China by all the Powers in the nineteenth century, though she did not hand back the territories Muraviev "of the Amur" had seized. In 1924, by treaties with the official Chinese government at Peking and with Chang Tso-lin, who controlled Manchuria, Russia recovered her "imperialist" rights over the Chinese Eastern Railway. Meanwhile, however, she had in 1921 created a Chinese Communist Party. By 1923 it had effected a working alliance with Sun Yat-sen's Kuomintang at Canton; Sun welcomed Russian coöperation, under the direction of Borodin, whom Sun called "Lafayette," against Peking and sent a number of students to Moscow. Sun's successor, however, began in 1926 to turn against his Communist allies; in 1927 Chiang Kai-shek broke openly with them and destroyed their Shanghai organization. A desperate attempt to fight back in December, 1927, brought what seemed to be irretrievable disaster on the cause of Communism in China.

Trotsky, who had vigorously criticized Stalin's policy of coöperation with the Chinese peasantry and nationalist bourgeoisie, attempted to use the fiasco against Stalin; he succeeded only in expediting his own exile to Central Asia, the only area where Soviet foreign policy scored any successes. Although the policy of a "Holy War" against British imperialism, announced at the Baku "Congress of Peoples of the East" in 1920, had to be abandoned, Soviet Russia managed to detach Mongolia from Chinese overlordship and establish there an "independent People's Republic" (1924). More importantly, in this period of weakness she was able to establish good relations with Persia, Afghanistan, and even with Turkey.

Thus, Russia was not yet strong enough to reassume the place in the world she had held before the Revolution or to seize the initiative in international relations. Clinging to her announced policy of working for world revolution, she was not able to give it more reality than, in earlier centuries, the predecessors of the Bolsheviks had given to the concept of "Moscow the Third Rome." Too dependent on her special friendship with the Weimar Republic to desire a Communist revolution in Germany, Russia still showed her historic tendency to bulge wherever external resistance was weak, but she had not yet developed any foreign policy that could have serious effect beyond her immediate borders.

NOTES

1. Butkovskii, *Inostrannye kontsessii v narodnom khoziaistve S.S.S.R.*, p. 44.
2. Trotsky, *Nashi politicheskiia zadachi,* p. 54.
3. *Protokoly TsK R.S.D.R.P., Avgust 1917-Fevral' 1918,* pp. 100-101, cited in Fainsod, *How Russia Is Ruled,* p. 262.
4. *Kommunisticheskaia Partiia Sovetskogo Soiuza v rezoliutsiiakh . . .* , I, 443.
5. *Pravda,* July 3, 1956; full text was published in *Kommunist,* No. 9 (June, 1956), pp. 17-18.
6. Trotsky, *The New Course,* in Shachtman, *The Struggle for the New Course,* p. 154.
7. Stalin, "On the History of Disagreements," speech on report of Central Committee at Fourteenth Party Congress (December 23, 1925), in *Sochineniia,* VII, 380.
8. *Rossiiskaia Kommunisticheskaia Partiia, Trinadtsatyi S"ezd; Stenograficheskii otchet,* pp. 166-167.

9. Stalin, "We Must Preserve the Unity of the Party," report to Leningrad actives (April 13, 1926), *loc. cit.*, VIII, 146.
10. Stalin, "On the Social-Democratic Deviation in Our Party" (November 3, 1926), *loc. cit.*, p. 353.
11. Stalin, at Fourth Conference of Party Central Committee on responsible workers of the national republics and *oblasts* (June 12, 1923), *loc. cit.*, V, 336.
12. Lenin, "Socialism and Religion," published in *Novaia Zhizn'*, November 16, 1905; cf. *Sochineniia*, 3rd edition, VIII, 419-423.
13. Curtiss, *The Russian Church and the Soviet State, 1917-1950,* p. 93. Quoted here and elsewhere in this book by courtesy of Little, Brown and Company.
14. Lenin, "Report on Foreign Policy" to joint meeting of Soviet Central Executive Committee and of Moscow Soviet (May 14, 1918), *loc. cit.*, XXIII, 9.
15. Lenin, "Theses for a Report on Tactics of the RKP at the Third Congress of the Communist International" (June 13, 1921), *loc. cit.*, XXVI, 427.
16. Trotsky, *Sochineniia,* III, i, 93.
17. Stalin, "On the Destiny of Socialism in the Soviet Union" (May 9, 1925), *loc. cit.*, VII, 117.
18. Lenin, "The Childhood Disease of 'Leftism' in Communism" (April 27, 1920), *loc. cit.*, XXV, 226.

SUGGESTIONS FOR FURTHER READING

In addition to works previously cited, Fainsod's *How Russia Is Ruled* is of outstanding value. The fourth volume of Carr's *History of Soviet Russia* (*The Interregnum, 1923-1924*) and the first three volumes of his sequel, *Socialism in One Country, 1924-1926,* contain a mass of valuable detail; though still suffering from compartmentalization of economics and politics, they are free from the hero worship that marred his treatment of Lenin.

In connection with the struggle for power, see Deutscher's hostile *Stalin* and his friendly *Prophet Unarmed: Trotsky, 1921-1929.* Trotsky's *Real Situation in Russia* was published in New York while the author was in exile at Alma Ata.

For details of constitutional changes, see Batsell's *Soviet Rule in Russia.* Harper's *Government of the Soviet Union* is a convenient and not unfriendly summary. Towster's *Political Power in the U.S.S.R., 1917-1947* is a very valuable reference work.

Curtiss, *The Russian Church and the Soviet State, 1917-1950,* is a most thorough study, well presented; Spinka's *Church in Soviet Russia* and Timasheff's *Religion in Soviet Russia* also contain valuable comments. The best treatments of early Soviet literature, in addition to the last part of Mirsky's *Contemporary Russian Literature, 1881-1925,* are Slonim's *Modern Russian Literature* and Gleb Struve's *Soviet Russian Literature;* see also Simmons' chapter "Soviet Russian Literature" in Strakhovsky, *A Handbook of Slavic Studies.* A special approach is Trotsky's *Literature and Revolution.*

Among studies of Soviet foreign policy may be mentioned, in addition to Rubinstein, the very useful Craig and Gilbert, *The Diplomats, 1919-1939.* Kennan's *Russia and the West Under Lenin and Stalin* is also important. Three which take somewhat divergent views of Russo-German relations are: Kochan, *Russia and the Weimar Republic;* Hilger and Mayer, *The Incompatible Allies;* and

Freund, *Unholy Alliance.* Dyck's *Weimar Germany and Soviet Russia, 1926-1933* is more objective and well documented from German sources. For policy toward China in the early period, see Whiting's *Soviet Policies in China, 1917-1924.* Of general reference value is Degras' *Soviet Documents on Foreign Policy, 1917-1941.*

For further details on the famine, see Golder, *On the Trail of the Russian Famine,* and H. H. Fisher, *Famine in Soviet Russia, 1919-1923.*

An excellent study of the ideological aspects of the succession struggle and its effect on economic planning is Erlich's *The Soviet Industrialization Debate, 1924-1928.* See also Spulber's *Foundations of Soviet Strategy for Economic Growth.*

Joravsky's *Soviet Marxism and Natural Science* is an important pioneering study. The gradual reorganization of the leading institutions of all of Russian science is described in Graham's well-organized study, *The Soviet Academy of Sciences and the Communist Party*

Chapter

30

Piatiletka: 1928-1934

The year 1928 has often been characterized as marking the "second revolution." If, however, revolution be understood to mean the transfer of power from one social class to another, nothing of the sort took place at this time. Prior to 1917 it could be said that political power and economic power did not rest in the same hands, and that the consequent disequilibrium had resulted in a revolutionary situation. The success of the Bolshevik coup, which had "snatched" political power and had been followed by absorption of economic power also into the hands of the Communist Party, had removed the possibility of further revolution. There was no longer a situation in which powerful social classes were pitted against one another. There remained only a dictatorship, wielding both political and economic authority over helpless masses. All that happened in 1928 was a change of policy by the ruling group, without reference to the desires of any rival group competing for power.

The policy changes made in 1928 were much less fundamental than those made in 1921. To a limited extent they involved a reversal of that earlier about-face, but without altering the fundamental principles of the NEP. Such reversal as there was lay in the fact that the early stage of the NEP had subordinated the problems of industrial and commercial organization on a new basis to the necessities of coping with the agricultural situation; in considerable measure the new changes reflected subordination of agricultural problems to the interests of industrialization. It is for this reason that the dominant character of the new period is subsumed in the Five-Year Plan, known to Russians by the affectionate feminine diminutive, *piatiletka* ("five-yearie").

PURPOSE AND WORKING OF THE FIVE-YEAR PLAN

The First Five-Year Plan (F.Y.P.) did not represent the beginning of economic planning in Russia. Each year under the NEP, "socialist" production had been planned in advance on the basis of "control figures" accumulated from preceding years and used as the basis for planning the profits of state enterprises. For that matter, "planning" is of the essence of capitalism, which historically is distinguishable from the relatively hand-to-mouth "handicraft" economy or from early medieval speculative enterprise by its rational character—by the deliberate investment of capital, on the basis of a system of financial accounting, with the purposes of attaining definite economic results and thus yielding a calculated profit for the investor. In modern times, no economic enterprise, whether it be a chicken farm or American Telephone and Telegraph, can dispense with economic planning. The size of the enterprise may affect the safe margin of error, but the principle of planning is inescapable for any capitalist enterprise.

Under Russia's state capitalism this was just as true as for small-scale individual or large-scale corporate capitalism. What was new about the Five-Year Plan was not the planning aspect; the F.Y.P. constituted less of a plan, in an economic sense, than had the annual projection of "control figures." In fact, under successive Five-Year Plans, the actual planning continued to be done on an annual basis, subject to intermediate revision. The "Plan" was in essence a prediction, made for psychological reasons, and for the most part without specifying the investment to be made in any particular enterprise or the gains that were to result from any given investment.

The situation that gave rise to the First Five-Year Plan has been suggested in the preceding chapter. The reasons for Russia's lack of industrial progress in the 1920's, as compared to the Western world, were all too obvious. Without a substantial inflow of foreign investment, Russia could not rapidly build up her industrial production. For that purpose she would need heavy import of capital goods; without adequate credit, she would have to pay for them by exports. Apart from export of gold, she would have to balance these imports by sending out agricultural products and raw materials. In order to have a surplus for export she must stimulate peasant production; to do so, she must offer the peasantry industrial goods. These would be available in sufficient quantity only if she could build up imports of capital goods. It was a squirrel cage: to pay for the necessary imports, she must have a surplus of peasant products; to stimulate the peasants, she must produce industrial goods; to this end she needed imports of machinery; and so on, *ad infinitum*. Throughout the period of the struggle for power within the Party, the position had been becoming increasingly clear, overriding all conflicting ideologies.

The only possible solution was manifest: Russia needed capital. But "capital" means simply any form of wealth not used for consumption and therefore available for purposes of production. Each year Russia was producing more wealth; if the balance between production and consumption could be changed, the necessary capital might be found within the Soviet Union. Herein lay the basic idea of the Five-Year Plan. If further increases in consumption were held in check, there would result the needed capital accumulation. In theory, it would not be necessary to stop absolutely a rise in the standard of living; a decline in the rate of the rise of consumption relative to continued increase in production would suffice. If, for example, production of wealth could be doubled while the standard of living was permitted to rise only sixty-odd percent, everyone would be better off than at present, and yet the state would have accumulated a very substantial amount of capital.

The whole problem was to make palatable the prospect of the loss of potential improvement in the material conditions of life in the here-and-now and to stimulate labor to unprecedented efforts. The restriction of the "Plan" to five years held the promise that those who made the sacrifice, rather than their children or grandchildren, would actually benefit. Among other embodiments this idea found expression in the "Loan of the Five-Year Plan"; those who subscribed to state bonds would merely sacrifice purchasing power temporarily for the sake of deferred enjoyment, and with gain to themselves, in a near and measurable future.

In the original draft of the Five-Year Plan, the State Planning Commission (*Gosplan*) took into account the probability of at least one partial crop-failure, the difficulties that had been experienced with foreign trade, and the problem of maintaining the quality of production. The government rejected such caution and demanded preparation of another "plan" assuming "optimal" conditions which no one could rationally expect to be realized. Over a five-year period the enormous sum of 64.5 billion rubles was to be invested in economic expansion; this was almost two and one-half times as much as had been expended for the purpose in the preceding five years. One-quarter of the total, amounting to almost five times the total prewar investment in Russian industry (estimated at 3.5 billion rubles), was to be devoted to construction of new industrial plants; the proportion of new investment in private industry, which even in 1927-1928 had been less than 4 percent of the total, was expected to continue to decline both absolutely and relatively, the great bulk of new investment going into "socialized" industry; 13.5 billion rubles were to be invested in large-scale industrial enterprises controlled by the Supreme Economic Council. This latter share of the investment was to be financed almost entirely out of the profits of industry, old and new.

The "Plan" could not specify the amount of capital to be put at the disposal of individual enterprises or the results that could be achieved by them over a five-year period. It could simply predict that the gross output of industry would increase by a stated percentage, rising each year and adding up to an over-all increase in gross industrial output of 135.9 percent; in the case of large-scale industry controlled by the Supreme Economic Council, the "planned" increase was set at 179 percent. The rise was to be steeper in output of means of production (204%), less in consumer goods (103%). In order to finance new construction from profits, it would be necessary not only to increase output but to reduce costs of production; these were to decrease by 35 percent, though wholesale prices were to decline only 24 percent. To accomplish such results, labor productivity must rise 110 percent, fuel consumption must be cut 30 percent, and construction costs must be halved.

All this would have to be worked out by successive annual plans, subject to frequent "adjustment"; responsibility for their realization must rest on the managements of individual enterprises, trusts, and "combines." Workers must be made to understand the need of stupendous exertions and challenged to improve their work both qualitatively and quantitatively. The only parts of the F.Y.P. that were seriously worked out in advance were those relating to capital construction projects, many of which had been started before the F.Y.P. was formulated. From the outset it was reasonably clear that, if expectations were not realized, the intention was to carry forward construction of new power stations and interrelated chemical and metallurgical "combinats," designed to strengthen the military as well as the civilian productive capacity of the state, if necessary at the expense of works producing "goods of wide consumption." As explained the following year in an official monthly publication,

> The general economic plan and consequently also the financial plan were constructed with the extraordinarily high aim of converting into capital accumulation enormous portions of the national income. This circumstance imposes on the whole plan the clearest imprint and in the most graphic way illustrates its basic intention. Realization of such an intention undoubtedly demands the greatest efforts and sacrifices and first of all enormous restraint in immediate consumption of the annual national-economic income. This is why the financial plan presses like a steel hoop on consumption.[1]

The First F.Y.P., notwithstanding the adoption of Gosplan's "optimal draft," was not a harebrained scheme. Undoubtedly, as an economic plan, it was quite unrealizable. Its essence, however, was that it was a psychological device to accomplish the utmost possible results in the shortest possible time; the government was well aware that the difficulties in the way of fulfillment of the "Plan" were probably insuperable. The emphasis was not on precise statistical achievements but on exciting "the creative efforts of the great mass of the population," of provoking the utmost endeavor and the most tremendous efforts:

> The character of the construction program, the direction of capital investments, the related movement of the basic funds of the country, the tempo of growth of material production, the scope of production in the socialist sector in agriculture, redistribution of national income—all this is incidental and definitely subordinate to the central regulating idea of the Five-Year-Plan,

which charts the course of rapid development of the productive forces of the country by way of industrialization, by way of socialist reconstruction of the village, by way of unflinching socialization of all departments and processes of economic life.[2]

A brief narrative of the industrial results may serve to illuminate the point. In the first year of the F.Y.P., for which the Plan had set a goal of a 21.4 percent increase in production by large-scale industry under the Supreme Economic Council, the increase was 23.7 percent. To be sure, production costs decreased only 4.2 percent instead of the planned 7 percent. Moreover, the Soviet official press complained bitterly of serious decline of qualitative standards, especially in light industry. Nevertheless, the second annual plan under the F.Y.P. stepped up the proposed production increase from the originally "planned" 21.5 percent to 32.1 percent; to make up for the failure of profits to materialize, resort was had to financing through the state budget and by issue of bank notes. At the same time was launched the first campaign for "socialist competition" (which the admiring Sidney and Beatrice Webb, the Fabian Socialists, preferred to call "socialist emulation");[3] the workers of various factories, without expectation of increased wages, were to challenge other factories to increase their output. A continuous "five-day" week was imposed by decree (September, 1929); although each worker was given every fifth day off, the machines were to be kept constantly in operation by other workers. In the second year of the F.Y.P. the gross output of large-scale industry—though not in light industry—did increase by 24.2 percent. Production costs were further reduced, but not in consonance with the "Plan"; Ordzhonikidze, who had become chairman of the Supreme Economic Council, was provoked to complain that "we had to borrow more than a billion rubles from the bank." [4] Quality continued to suffer.

In connection with a change in the fiscal year, the last quarter of 1930 was proclaimed a "shock" quarter; actually production increased by less than half the newly assigned percentage. For 1931, the goal was nevertheless set at a 42.1 percent increase in production; achievement, however, for the first time fell even below the original Plan target (23.8% for the fourth year), though it still showed a substantial rise (20.5%). For the first time, production costs, which had been planned to decrease by 8 percent, showed an absolute rise (6%), and quality continued to deteriorate. The results for 1932 were still less satisfactory. Yet it was officially declared that the F.Y.P. had been "successfully" completed in four and one-half years.

The explanation is not far to seek. The goals set by the F.Y.P. in terms of tons of coal or steel, and still more in terms of yards of cotton goods or pairs of leather boots, were very far from being reached. Yet, in terms of rubles, the objectives had been fulfilled or even overfulfilled. Even if one accepts the Soviet figures, computed in terms of 1926-27 rubles, there were too many articles totally nonexistent in Russia in 1926-27 and therefore not calculable in those terms, for such a comparison to be meaningful. The Soviet claim that the F.Y.P. was fulfilled in four and one-half years is therefore statistically meaningless.

Yet the volume of Soviet output of means of production had been immensely increased beyond the levels of 1927-28. In most cases the increase, in terms of tons, was far below the "Plan" figures, but in terms of rubles, whatever they might mean, the success was up to or ahead of the "Plan." It is therefore impossible to say that the F.Y.P. had failed, especially if one bears in mind that its purposes were fundamentally psychological. It is difficult to see how the Soviet Union could have pulled itself so far upward, industrially speaking, by its bootstraps, without the cover of the F.Y.P. The enormous increase in production, achieved at a time when the "capitalist" world had been experiencing a severe depression, could be touted as a great victory of "socialism."

By 1932, the bottom year of the world depression, Soviet steel production, for example, on which the greatest efforts had been concentrated, stood quantitatively slightly ahead of Germany, France, or Great Britain, though somewhat less than half that of the United States. This had resulted less from increase in Russian output (40% above 1913 production in the same territory) than from the effects of the depression in "capitalist" countries (almost 60% decline in the United States, 54% in Germany, 30% in Great Britain, and 19% in France—all as compared with 1913 production in the same territories). Nevertheless, it naturally excited envy in many quarters abroad.

THE F.Y.P. AND LABOR

The other side of the picture was the material cost to "the great masses of the population" whose "creative efforts" had been called on to make the success possible. In point of fact, the expected increase in production, though it had fallen short of the Plan even in heavy industry, had entailed a great increase in the number of workers above "planned" estimates: in large-scale industry, the excess was 57 percent; in construction, 66 percent. The total wage bill was 108.4 percent above what had been expected; in view, however, of the sharp rise in price levels, this meant depression, rather than improvement, of real wages. Nevertheless, in the interest of "socialist accumulation," nominal wage rates were held down as much as possible, and workers were told that they must subscribe a stated number of weeks' wages toward successive state loans.

Management had its own problems in relation to labor. The seven-hour working day, which had been approved in 1927, was turning out to be a handicap to production, and the "five-day week," introduced in 1929, speedily resulted in "depersonalization," which meant that under the "nonstop week" no individual worker could be held responsible for care of his tools.

Particularly galling to the economic authorities was the continuing shortage of skilled workers, who repeatedly abandoned their jobs in the hope of finding better conditions elsewhere.

A number of measures were taken to stimulate the workers to assist in reducing production costs by raising individual labor productivity. As the head of the trade-union organization, Tomsky had persisted in stressing the continuing duty of the trade unions, even in a "socialist" society, to protect the workers against their employer. In 1929 he was transferred from his old post to the State Printing Office, where his "Right Wing" tendencies could no longer hamper the progress of rapid industrialization. The Sixteenth Party Congress (mid-1930) redefined the functions of the trade unions. Under the direction of his successor, Shvernik, the trade unions abandoned their efforts on behalf of the workers, though continuing to function in handling minor grievances; even the pretense of collective bargaining, which had never been backed up by a recognized right to strike, was allowed to lapse. To guarantee the continued hold of the trade unions over the workers, they retained control of the administration of all forms of social insurance and social welfare.

Their role as "schools of communism" now received increased emphasis. The trade unions were to seek to spread technical knowledge and to secure advancement for the most devoted and energetic workers. By all means at their disposal they were to encourage workers to become "shock workers" (*udarniki*). As "the closest and immediate collaborator of the state," their task "demands more active participation in economic construction, a revolution in their attitude toward production."[5] Sharp distinction was made between the trade union in translation (*profsoiuz*) and the trade union in transliteration (*tred-iunion*). The latter was a "bourgeois" concept, appropriate in a "capitalist" society, where it was the worker's right to demand maximum pay for minimum work. Such *tred-iunionism* must be "rooted out" of the "proletarian" *profsoiuz* movement, the purpose of which was to enable the worker in a "socialist" society to raise his productivity without increasing production costs.

At the end of 1928 was organized the first "shock brigade," a small group of young workers pledged to set an example to their fellow-workers on Lenin's favorite principle of labor discipline. Encouraged by the Communist Party and by its trade-union auxiliary, and backed by grant of special privileges with respect to rations and other forms of "socialized wages," the idea caught on rapidly. "Exemplary workers" were never absent from work, worked even on their rest days, watched their fellow-workers, never left tools idle or allowed them to get into bad condition, attempted to exceed established norms of output, harried indolent managers with suggestions for better technical organization of work, and in every way annoyed ordinary workers who thought only of doing as little work as possible. Official figures indicate that workers actively engaged in "socialist competition" (*udarniki*) amounted in 1930 to 29 percent of all workers and that by 1931 this figure had reached two-thirds. It had to be admitted, however, that many were guilty of "sham adoption of the principles of socialist competition and exemplary work." [6]

The figures officially submitted by the Soviet Union to the League of Nations showed over a million unemployed in 1926 and 1927 (more than Great Britain, then suffering from the effects of the coal strike). One of the most important measures taken to improve this, from the state's viewpoint, undesirable condition of the labor market was the abolition of unemployment. On October 9, 1930, the People's Commissar of Labor simply issued a decree terminating all relief payments to able-bodied persons: "No reasons for refusal of work offered are to be accepted excepting ill-health, confirmed by a hospital certificate." [7] This method of dealing with a problem that was then plaguing all capitalist countries was a logical expansion of the principle advanced a century earlier by English Liberals of the "Manchester School." In 1834, the United Kingdom had sharply reduced poverty, or at least public expenditure on its alleviation, by amending the Poor Law; the preamble of the revised law had stated its purpose as to "make the condition of the able-bodied in receipt of poor relief less eligible than that of the lowest paid laborer not receiving poor relief." [8] Carrying the idea far beyond this limited application, the Soviet authorities could, after 1930, instead of supporting the unemployed in idleness, issue them railway tickets to Magnitogorsk or other remote spots where labor was most needed. It was this fact that enabled the Communists to develop natural resources in the Urals and beyond, which, since the abolition of serfdom, Russian capitalists had had grave difficulty in exploiting.

In June, 1931, Stalin himself vigorously attacked the idea of "wage equalization": in order to reduce labor turnover, which had reached such proportions that there were few factories that did not lose 30-40 percent of their workers every six months or even every quarter, the essential core of skilled workers must be tied to the enterprise; at the same time, "in order to create cadres of skilled workers, it is necessary to give the unskilled workers a stimulus and prospect of advancement, of moving up." [9]

Beginning in coal-mining but soon spreading to other branches of industry, a system was worked out of wage rates elaborately graded according to the worker's degree of skill. To strengthen incentive, the practice of paying piecework wages, which even in 1928 was applied to more than one-half of large-scale industry, was further extended. In 1931 a vigorous attempt was made more fully to shift the task of reducing production costs to the shoulders of the workers; the means adopted was the enforcement of piecework wage rates "in not less than 75% of production." [10] As an added incentive, the rates of pay per piece were set higher the more pieces were turned out above the fixed "norm." In December, 1931, began a vigorous campaign against "depersonalization," which led to replacement of the five-day "continuous week" by a "temporary" six-day week, except for stores, restaurants, and public utilities, which were to retain "the basic form of organization of labor";[11] most enterprises were to shift to a system by which both men and machines were to rest every sixth day, while the normal working day was reduced to six hours.

Inducements to extra effort continued to be supplemented by punishments for slacking. In 1930, the definition of "economic crimes" was widely extended. Though the penalties were heaviest on responsible engineers and "specialists," the rights of workers were seriously curtailed. Toward the end of 1932, exceedingly drastic penalties were imposed for "voluntary absenteeism," up to dismissal for a single day's unexcused absence, together with deprivation of housing privileges. No worker could be hired by any enterprise without a certificate from his former employer. If one keeps in mind the provision in the Constitution that "he who does not work does not eat," [12] the full import of such provisions becomes apparent.

THE SECOND F.Y.P.

All these aspects of Soviet labor policy in the period of the First Five-Year Plan were both symptoms and causes of deep-seated labor discontent. The leadership, committed to the principle of a "Workers' Republic," was well aware of the explosive possibilities of the situation, and *Pravda,* the official organ of the Party, from time to time urged workers to watch their fellow-workers at the bench for signs of "counter-revolutionary" attitudes. In part this consciousness had affected the decision, foreshadowed even at the end of 1930, to announce completion of the Plan before the assigned date. Yet the quantitative results had been so great that the Party leaders were loath to abandon the idea. A Second Five-Year Plan was therefore decided upon at the Seventeenth Party Conference early in 1932, though not publicly announced until two years later, when it was confirmed by the Seventeenth Party Congress at the beginning of 1934.

The greatest weaknesses in industrial development under the First F.Y.P. had been the failure to improve or even to maintain the quality of products and inability to reduce production costs. Because of the emphasis on developing means of production, which could not pay off immediately, rather than on turning out goods of mass consumption, it had not been possible to finance the program out of profits as originally intended. On the contrary, it had been necessary to subsidize much of industry from the state budget. Efforts had been made to improve matters by frequent administrative reorganizations, particularly in 1929. The principle of business accountancy (*khozraschet*) and the principle of managerial responsibility were stressed; the sometimes troublesome relationships between the factory director, the trade union, and the Party cell were defined, and the two latter were forbidden to interfere directly with management, though they might appeal to higher authority against the director's decisions.

At the Seventeenth Party Congress, Stalin acknowledged that

> red-tape bureaucratic methods of management in the People's Commissariats and their organs, including the Peoples Commissariats of Light and Food Industries, are still far from being liquidated.[13]

Accordingly, further administrative reorganization was decreed (1934), involving a considerable measure of local decentralization, on the "productive-territorial principle," for all but the largest enterprises. In the spirit of Stalin's 1931 pronouncement that "technique decides everything," wholesale efforts were made to weed out unqualified persons from managerial positions, a proceeding which paved the way for more efficient direction by responsible managers, operating on the basis of *khozraschet,* during the Second F.Y.P.

The scope of the new Plan differed substantially from that of the first. The original instructions were approved by the Seventeenth Party Conference early in 1932, while the First Plan was still in progress. On the basis of reports from two of Stalin's henchmen—Molotov, who had replaced Rykov as chairman of Sovnarkom in 1930, and Kuibyshev, who had been put at the head of Gosplan—a no less ambitious program was outlined. Nevertheless, in the light of the ill-success of the final year of the First F.Y.P., it was in 1933 decided to substitute a smaller average increase in production. By the time the Second Five-Year Plan was officially approved by the Seventeenth Party Congress (1934), the targets for increased production had been much further reduced: coal output had been cut from 250 million tons to 152.5 (as against 90 million in 1932); the estimated output of electrical energy had been reduced from 100 billion kilowatt-hours to 38 billion (as against 17 billion in 1932).

What remained unchanged was the proposed expenditure on capital investment in large-scale industry, a figure almost three times as great as had been spent, and four times as great as had been "planned" under the First F.Y.P. Of the total, however, just over 40 percent was to be spent on reconstruction and capital repair of existing plants; only 38 billion rubles was to be devoted to new construction, and much of this was inherited from the First F.Y.P. That plan had proposed expenditure of 19.1 billion rubles on all large-scale industry, including electric-power stations; the amount actually expended had been 24.8 billion, including 9 billion on construction not complete at the end of 1932. Whether because their plans were altered or because of higher construction costs, the Second F.Y.P. had to allot 17 billion rubles to complete these unfinished plants. This left only 21 billion rubles to be expended on wholly new enterprises; practically none of these were to be begun until the third year of the Plan period, despite the fact that completion of some of those left over from the First F.Y.P. was to be postponed until after completion of the new Plan.

The high degree of social tension that had attended the stupendous effort at industrialization under the Five-Year Plan induced the planners to make some concessions. Of the 19.1 billion rubles the First Five-Year Plan had expected to invest, 14.7 billion had been allocated to "Group A" (i.e., producers' goods and electric-power development), on which, however, 21.3 billion had actually been spent. Of the 4.4 billion earmarked for investment in plants to produce consumers' goods, only 3.5 billion had been spent. This had been one of a number of factors which, in the period of the First F.Y.P., had caused a sharp drop in the material standard of living of the Russian people. The Second F.Y.P., although still emphasizing the development of heavy industry, therefore attempted to restore the proportionate provision for light industry (23%) that had been envisaged in 1928 but not realized under the First F.Y.P. While 53.4 billion rubles were allotted to "Group A," 16.1 billion were assigned to "Group B."

The early years of the new Plan period did not, however, fulfill the promise of a happier life. In 1933 the growth of industrial production, both for Group A (11.6%) and for Group B (5.5%) was about half what had been planned; in 1934 Group A (20.1%) fell very little short of the target, but Group B (8.8%) still showed barely half of the increase planned for the year. The distinction often made between the First and Second Five-Year Plans on the basis of the larger proportion again allowed by the latter for consumer goods remained on paper.

AGRICULTURE: COLLECTIVIZATION

The urgent tempo of industrialization had a shattering effect on agrarian relations. Even before the F.Y.P., the peasants had been giving the Communists serious worry. Fiscal pressure on the kulaks had not been securing for the state the grain and other products it needed. The old hope of converting small-scale peasant economies into large-scale farms, using machinery and up-to-date techniques, had lingered on, but experience had made the rulers cautious. The F.Y.P. anticipated:

> As the material basis for regulating the whole of agriculture, the socialized sector even in this five-year period will acquire very great significance. But as the mainstay of production individual economy will still play the predominant role.[14]

Once again expressing the intention to prevent the growth of the "exploiting peasant," the Plan warned against confusing the "rich peasant" who "has mastered the methods of agriculture . . . which we plan and preach" with the exploiting kulak. It was planned that the share of gross agricultural production by *sovkhozy* and *kolkhozy* would rise from the 1.8 percent of 1927-28 to 14.7 percent in 1932-33; their share in marketable surplus was to increase from 4.4 percent to 25.3 percent. This would entail a more than ten-fold increase in the output of large-scale farming, but at the same time small-scale peasant production of marketable surplus was expected nearly to double; "stimulation of the middling and poor mass [of peasants] to improvement and intensification of their economies must be one of the bases of the Plan." [15] They must be enlisted in the coöperative movement and given technical instruction and financial assistance. The Plan proposed that a total of 23.2 billion rubles be spent on the development of agriculture; this was a sum substantially larger than that allocated to capital construction in industry but was mainly to be furnished by the peasants themselves.

The poorer peasants, especially those without land, horses, or cows of their own, welcomed state assistance in the formation of collective farms, though these for the most part took the form only of loose associations to cultivate the land. The total number of *kolkhozy* of all types rose from 15,000 at the end of 1927 to 57,000 in the middle of 1929, and the collectivized homesteads increased from 195,000 to 1,003,000. In the fall of 1929, however, only 7 percent of all collectives were complete "communes," while 32 percent were "artels," in which private ownership of dwellings, gardens, and some livestock survived alongside common ownership of the land and productive equipment. Almost 62 percent of the "collectives" were merely associations for joint cultivation, without common ownership of the means of production. Most peasant cultivation remained, however, outside any form of collective, on the old individual basis.

The sown area was somewhat increased, but the gross yield of grain in 1929 was less than for any year since 1924. The difficulty was that, despite the arguments of the "Right Opposition," the state had intensified its tax pressure on the kulaks, who remained the backbone of agricultural production, and they had responded by refusing to cultivate more than a portion of their acres. From the state's point of view, this passive resistance of the most productive portion of the peasantry was intolerable. Without an export surplus, the whole machinery of industrialization would be brought to a standstill. If the kulaks would not coöperate, they must be eliminated as a class. Only large-scale farming could offer any possibility of replacing them as producers. *Sovkhozy,* glowingly described as "grain and meat factories" and operated by hired wage labor, seemed the ideal, but as an intermediate and more quickly attainable device the artel type of *kolkhoz* was deemed a satisfactory substitute.

In the summer of 1929, the original ideas of the 1928 Plan, so far as they related to agriculture, were therefore scrapped, and what is sometimes called the "second agrarian revolution" was energetically begun. Instead of collectivizing only 20 percent of all peasant homesteads during the five-year period, it was now determined to bring the great majority of peasant homesteads into collectives, and without delay. The central authorities announced a whole series of measures, among which the most important were: erection of huge new tractor-building plants; creation of a network of machine-tractor stations, under central direction; suspension of the laws that permitted individual peasants to rent land and hire labor; authorization to local soviets to confiscate kulaks' property and distribute it among collective farms; and redefinition of the artel as the basic form of *kolkhoz,* with collective ownership of all property used for marketable production. Only property used for sustenance of the members was to remain individual.

Although the government warned that, to be effective, collectivization must be voluntary, the poorer peasants and agricultural laborers put their own interpretation on the new policy of eliminating the kulaks as a class. They confiscated not only the land and the barns, the draft animals and productive livestock, the machinery, seed-grain, and fodder supplies, but the whole personal property of relatively well-to-do farmers, often murdering the former owners. No less disastrous was the zeal of the local authorities, reinforced by swarms of Komsomols (members of the Communist Youth organization), who not only used their power to deport kulaks but forced reluctant middle and poor peasants to "socialize" their property. Unwieldy "giant" farms were created, while advance of the necessary credits was delayed; there was also the fact that men elected by their fellows and experienced in agriculture were subjected to much interference in administration of the farms. The statistical results, therefore, exceeded the new pace of collectivization approved by the Party.

This outcome was an enormous "success" for collectivization. In two months the number of *kolkhozy* was almost doubled, and the number of collectivized homesteads soared from 4,393,000 in January, 1930, to 14,264,000 (58% of the total peasant homesteads) by the first of March. This result was achieved only at the price of open mass hostility on the part of the peasants, which made it necessary to employ heavily armed forces under the direction of OGPU. Less spectacularly, but no less dangerously, peasants refused to work the common fields and resorted to wholesale slaughter of livestock rather than surrender it to collectives. In addition, the industrial workers and Komsomols, sent to inspire the peasants, too often attempted to direct operations of which they were fundamentally ignorant, with resultant death of collectivized animals from neglect and other forms of wastage.

Stalin beat a prompt retreat, announcing that the Party was "dizzy with success" (March 2, 1930). New directives reëmphasized that collectivization must be voluntary, that collectivized peasants must be allowed, on a limited basis, to maintain their own individual economies within the artel, and that under certain conditions kulaks and other disfranchised persons could be admitted to membership; the distribution of proceeds among the members of *kolkhozy* was also more carefully regulated, and increased fiscal privileges and credit facilities were extended to them. The immediate consequence, however, was a stampede of peasants to leave the collectives; within two months the number of collectivized peasant households fell from 14,264,000 to 5,778,000.

Relaxation of tension and concessions to the individualist tendencies of the peasant within the collective farms soon brought reversal of this trend. Stalin's promise that "the Soviet Government would give the collective farms privileges and preferences . . . with respect to land, supply of machines, tractors, seed-grain, etc. and with respect to tax alleviation and credits" [16] proved a strong lure, especially as the *kolkhozy* retained the confiscated land of the kulaks. Nor was the policy of eliminating the kulaks as a class abandoned; the remnant of them, now including all peasants who opposed the state's policy, were still subjected to arbitrary pressures and to ruinous taxation. A new surge into the *kolkhozy* took place; by 1931, they already included 13 million peasant homesteads (52.7% of the total), and the figure grew steadily until, by 1938, 18.8 million were members of collectives, constituting 93.5 percent of the then total.

Less successful was the drive to establish huge state farms. Although between 1928 and 1932 the production of grain for the market by *sovkhozy* was quadrupled, official complaints about their inefficiency were numerous and vigorous. Their main value was as agricultural experiment stations and as pioneers in bringing virgin land under cultivation in new areas. In subsequent years many of them were broken up, and their land turned over to *kolkhozy*.

Collectivization had been attended with mass suffering for the peasantry, which took its revenge in continuing wholesale sabotage. Its results in terms of increased yields were therefore disappointing. The harvest of 1930 was good, producing more grain than in any year since the war, more even than in 1913. In 1931 the acreage sown to grain was increased, but the gross yield was less than in any of the six preceding years; 1932 was but very slightly better. Only from 1933 did grain production again attain a satisfactory level. The number of head of livestock continued to decline alarmingly into 1933, and recovery thereafter was slow. In 1931-32 Soviet Russia experienced a second severe famine, particularly in parts of the Ukraine and the Kuban region. Beatrice and Sidney Webb, convinced that "Soviet Communism" spelled "a new civilization," denied in 1935 that a "man-made" phenomenon, which they ascribed to the antisocial obstinacy of the peasants, could properly be classed as a famine, which is an "act of God," [17] but less interpretative writers have been prone to accept a figure of upward of three million deaths from starvation and attendant disease. Among the government's famine-relief measures was deportation to the far north of large numbers of persons regarded as victims of their own obstinacy in resisting collectivization; in remote areas they were given the opportunity at hard labor for subsistence wages to learn the advantages of socialist coöperation.

The shortage of grain in 1928 and still more in 1929 had driven the state to take emergency measures. Grain was high on the list of articles of export which were expected to help balance planned imports of machinery. Unwilling to slacken the proposed pace of industrialization, the government had resorted to confiscation of stocks hoarded by the kulaks. This technique being obviously inadequate, recourse was had to shutting off free trade in agricultural products. By a system of "contracts," the state purchasing organizations increasingly got control of practically all the marketable surplus of agricultural products; these "contracts" were actually a form of compulsory delivery to the state at low fixed prices, somewhat reminiscent of "war communism"; by 1933 even the pretense of negotiation was dropped in favor of tax compulsion.

Agricultural produce, thus acquired, was distributed to the population—or to such part of it as was thought worthy—by a complicated system of rationing, which was soon extended to cover also many industrial "goods of wide consumption." Legal private trade, especially in agricultural products, was by 1931 virtually abolished. State and coöperative trade in rationed commodities, however, faced great difficulties. Especially because the legal ration varied widely with the economic and social status of the recipient, rationed trade could not be expected to absorb the whole purchasing power of the population. The government therefore found it expedient, in order to avoid serious revival of frankly illicit trade, to permit sale of many goods at "commercial prices" substantially above the fixed ration prices.

The difficulties were greatest with agricultural producers, for the low delivery prices, much below the state's resale prices, in effect constituted a tax on the peasants, whether collectivized or not. Realizing that this was one of the main factors in low agricultural yields, the state in 1932 authorized collective farmers to sell on the local free market any surplus above their required deliveries to the state. Although the state attempted, by "decentralized purchase" at rates intermediate between "delivery" prices and free-market prices, to absorb as much as possible of this surplus, the only alternative to substantial revival of a black market was this legalized "*kolkhoz* trade," which, however, affected only about 5 percent of the market for agricultural produce and only on a local basis.

Such a system of gathering virtually all the agricultural surplus into the hands of the state could hardly have been made to function, even if it had been thought necessary, if it had not been preceded and accompanied by wholesale collectivization. An immense aid in controlling the *kolkhozy,* not anticipated by the drafters of the F.Y.P., were the machine-tractor stations (M.T.S.). Even when they had been widely expanded and put under centralized direction in 1929, the M.T.S. had still been thought of only in terms of the economic service they could render by expediting the mechanization of agriculture. Gradually, however, it was realized that if the whole available supply of agricultural machines and of the tractors to draw them (save those needed for *sovkhozy*) were concentrated in the M.T.S., the *kolkhozy* would become subject to their servants. The M.T.S., in making contracts with any individual collective farm, could influence its production program, as well as oversee its punctilious fulfillment. Added to the pressure of a state tax policy adjusted to the type of crop planted, the M.T.S. became a major instrument for directing "socialized" agriculture in the channels the state desired.

In addition to legalizing "*kolkhoz* trade," both by the collectives and by their individual members, the Party under Stalin's guidance also advanced, early in 1933, the new slogan, "Make all collective farmers prosperous." [18] It was a partial reversion to the ideas of Bukharin and the "Right Opposition." To the tune of "every peasant a cow," the state advanced large sums to assist members of collectives to acquire a heifer as their individual property. The theory was developed that the personal consumption of collective farmers could best be provided for by allowing them to carry on their own private economies, while the collective as a whole produced marketable surplus.

The peasants, however, were as easy to spoil as children. They tended to take advantage of every relaxation of "socialist" principles to neglect collective work, to steal what they could from the collective fields, and in general to sabotage *kolkhoz* economy. It was therefore necessary to balance concessions with punitive measures. A force of "15,000 of the best and most proven Bolsheviks" [19] was distributed among the M.T.S. to supervise agricultural work, with authority to summon the peasants to "shock" efforts comparable to those of *udarniki* in industry. *Kolkhoz* property was equated in law to state property; theft of it was to be punished by shooting or, at the very least, by a minimum of ten years' imprisonment. Evasion of collective work or fraudulent accounting were to be punished with appropriate degrees of severity; the enforcement of penalties was not to be left to *kolkhoz* managements but was to be supervised by the local authorities.

THE PARTY AND THE OGPU

The tension to which peasants as well as workers were subjected extended throughout Soviet society. The period of the first F.Y.P. and the early years of the Second did not, to be sure, witness the sort of struggle within the Party that had characterized the years following Lenin's illness. By the time *piatiletka* was launched, Stalin had acquired virtually complete ascendancy. The "Left Opposition" had been wholly eliminated; Trotsky's expulsion from the Soviet Union (January, 1929) was only an echo of an earlier accomplished fact. The "Right Opposition" was headed by a minority of three, boxed in within the nine-member Politburo. Even so, the triumphant Stalin chose to remove them from positions of influence. The first step, in October, 1928, was adoption of the cabinet principle of unanimity; members of the Politburo, whatever their individual opinions, were forbidden to express their disagreement publicly, even within the Party. In January, 1929, Stalin accused Bukharin of "factionalism." In April, at a plenum of the Central Committee and the Central Control Commission, he denounced Bukharin and "his friends" for complaining of "civil execution" in that they were compelled to keep silent when they were criticized; denying that there was any compulsion, Stalin challenged Bukharin to join in condemning "the Right deviation." [20] On April 23, Bukharin was deprived of his post at the head of the Third International; on June 2, Tomsky was demoted from command of the trade-union apparatus. On November 17, the Central Committee accepted removal of Bukharin from the Politburo. Without attempting a futile rear-guard action, Bukharin, Tomsky, and Rykov signed a public declaration:

> We consider it our duty to say that in this dispute the Party and its Central Committee were right. Our views. . . . showed themselves to be mistaken.[21]

Nevertheless, in mid-1930 Tomsky also was dropped from the Politburo. Six months later Rykov followed him out; at the same time he was replaced by Molotov as chairman of the Council of People's Commissars. Four more Stalin *apparatchiki* were added to the Politburo; the personal dictatorship of the Party boss was complete.

Although the Party was scarcely disturbed by this rounding-out of Stalin's control over it, there began at this time at a lower level the policy of savage reprisal that was soon to reach startling proportions in the Party "purge" trials. Even in the middle 1920's, OGPU accumulated some thousands of prisoners, principally at its labor camp on the Solovetsky Islands in the White Sea, but these were mainly "former people" or "politicals." With the coming of *piatiletka,* OGPU's activities were much expanded, embracing the doomed "Nepmen" (private traders), the kulaks and other resistant peasants, and engineers, technicians, and other members of the "bourgeois" intelligentsia. As early as March, 1928, a "show trial" was staged of administrative and technical personnel in the Donets coal mines. This "Shakhty" trial was followed by a long series of prosecutions of "specialists" whenever failures of planned economy became an open scandal. Among them were death sentences on three prominent railway experts (May, 1929) and on forty-eight "counter-revolutionary wreckers" in the food industry (September, 1930). Most conspicuous of all was the show trial (November–December, 1930) of Professor Ramzin and seven other engineers, alleged to have organized an "Industrial Party" in a plot with the French general staff. In March, 1931, Professor Groman, who had insisted that the Plan targets were unrealistic, and thirteen other "specialists" were convicted of conspiring with Mensheviks in exile.

The technique of using scapegoats among the intelligentsia and charging them with collaboration with foreign "imperialist" enemies of the Soviet Union had early proved its value. Yet it had its drawbacks in destroying the morale and paralyzing the initiative of the technical personnel so necessary to the success of industrialization. Even the Webbs later ruefully admitted that, although in their opinion the facts of disloyalty to socialist principles justified the prosecutions, the Ramzin trial

> inaugurated a veritable reign of terror against the intelligentsia. Nobody regarded himself as beyond suspicion. Men and women lived in daily dread of arrest. Thousands were sent on administrative exile to distant parts of the country. Evidence was not necessary. The title of engineer served as sufficient condemnation. The jails were filled. Factories languished from lack of technical leadership. . . .[22]

With characteristic lack of hesitation, Stalin went into reverse (June 23, 1931) and demanded an end to "spetz-baiting." Professor Ramzin was released from prison and restored to duty.

The practice of shifting responsibility, however, was too temptingly easy to be wholly abandoned. The difficult times of 1931-1932 and especially the hardships of the winter of 1932-1933 produced a revival, with even greater emphasis on foreign connivance with the "wreckers." In January, 1933, six British Metro-Vickers engineers and their Russian "accomplices" were subjected to a show trial for alleged sabotage of electric-power stations. Imprisonment of two of the Britons resulted in a British embargo on imports from the Soviet Union; only the change in the international outlook attendant on the rise of Hitler to power in Germany enabled the new Soviet foreign minister, Maxim Litvinov, to secure a resumption of trade relations at the price of release of the convicted engineers. Despite this and other prosecutions, Stalin was, however, moving toward his 1935 substitution of the slogan, "personnel decides everything" for his earlier dictum that "technique decides everything." [23]

The need for a greatly increased supply of personnel with adequate technical training had been becoming ever more obvious. This required thorough overhaul of the educational system and abandonment of Lunacharsky's experimentalism. From 1929, under the direction of Bubnov, who had proved himself as a work horse in organizing the seizure of power and later in managing the Red Army under Voroshilov, discipline was reintroduced. School children were again uniformed, and the "complex" method of education was abandoned. Even in the universities the academic hierarchy reappeared, and traditional subjects of study again began to receive honor. Pokrovsky was given a state funeral, Stalin serving as a pallbearer (1932), but his policies were almost immediately subjected to attack. Major emphasis was placed on technical institutes, though in them accelerated training and narrow subject-matter specialization proved severe handicaps to the students' educational development.

Like the tsars of olden days, from Ivan the Terrible through Peter the Great, the Bolsheviks also drew as heavily as possible on the resources of foreign brains, lured to Russia by promises of golden gains. Americans were on the whole preferred, both because the United States was politically—and militarily—remote and because American industrial "know-how" was most admired. A visitor to Moscow even in 1927 could not fail to be impressed by the lavish display in store windows of Henry Ford's book, and a contract with the Ford Motor Company much assisted the building of the Gorky (formerly Nizhny Novgorod) tractor and automobile plants; the new word "Fordicization" became acclimatized in the Russian language. Among other prominent American advisers were Campbell, a Montana wheat-grower, and Colonel Cooper, who supervised the building of the great Dnieprostroi power station.

Planning brought no benefits to Soviet literature, which went through its shoddiest period. Gorky, to be sure, returned to Russia in 1929 but devoted his energy to assisting others instead of writing himself. Maiakovsky, in spite of Stalin's accolade as "the best and most talented poet of our Soviet period," committed suicide in 1930. From 1928 the literary scene was controlled by the Russian Association of Proletarian Writers (RAPP), which exercised over authors "social command," complete with "shock brigades" patterned on the factories. The mechanically constructed output of these years holds little interest. Exception must be made for occasional lapses by those whom Trotsky had dubbed "fellow-travelers" (*sputniki*) into psychological studies in the Russian tradition of the nineteenth century. Among them were Leonov's *Sot,* in which inner spiritual doubts manage to show through depiction of the technical details of industry, and Boris Pilniak's *The Volga Flows into the Caspian Sea,* in which the industrialization program was even more subordinated to the psychological problems of the engineers.

In 1932, largely because of Gorky's protests, RAPP was ordered dissolved by the Central Committee of the Party, and Russian writers were set comparatively free so long as they observed the canons of an undefined "socialist realism." Taking advantage of the fact that "self-criticism" was permitted and even encouraged so long as it dealt with abuses in practice and not with sacred principles, such writers as Valentin Katayev ventured to resume the sort of satire that had been best embodied in his *Embezzlers* (1927). Still more daring were the deftly humorous short stories of Mikhail Zoshchenko. Among novelists, A. N. Tolstoy interrupted his work on *The Road to Calvary* to write his *Peter I,* in which the tsar was represented as "the first Bolshevik." Sholokhov, interrupting his *Silent Don,* produced (1932-33) *Virgin Soil Upturned,* by far the finest product of Soviet literature in this period. Soviet poetry remained underground, and the drama, though plays were turned out in abundance, failed to shake off its wooden propaganda character.

Russian music in this period also produced little of merit, despite Prokofiev's permanent return in 1932. His activity was mainly confined to composition of ballets, culminating in his *Romeo and Juliet* (1935). Shostakovich's *Third Symphony* (1930) was well described as a "proletarian tract in tones," "raucous and blatant." His ballets were failures, but one of his operas, *Lady Macbeth of Mtsensk,* composed in 1930-32 in the manner of Berg's proto-Nazi *Wozzeck,* achieved a tremendous success in 1934.

INTERNATIONAL RELATIONS

In this period, Soviet diplomacy experienced a "turn" as sharp as those in industry and agriculture. At the time of the launching of the First F.Y.P., Russia still regarded friendship with Germany as the first principle of her foreign policy, a buttress against the much talked-of "imperialist" aggression expected from the former Entente Powers. In 1927 Great Britain had broken off diplomatic relations with the Soviet Union, and France was only less cool, while the United States persisted in ignoring the existence of the Bolsheviks. In 1928 Russia barely managed to get herself included in the Kellogg-Briand Pact "renouncing" war as an instrument of national policy. The following year, however, the second MacDonald government resumed relations with Russia, and in 1930 Litvinov, assuming full charge of Soviet foreign policy, began to proclaim that "peace is indivisible."

The Third International continued to be an obstacle to mutual confidence. Its Sixth Congress (1928) had once more proclaimed the need for world revolution. An extensive program reaffirmed the importance of all means of struggle, whether legal or illegal, and made the direction of Moscow more explicit. Yet the official policy of the Soviet government was assiduously devoted to maintenance of good relations with the "capitalist" world, trade with which was so vital to *piatiletka.*

In this respect, the timing of the Plan proved to have been bad; the world depression, which so seriously affected capitalist industry from the latter part of 1929, was preceded by a great fall on the world market of prices of agricultural products and raw materials. These were precisely the commodities on export of which Russia was relying to pay for imports of machinery. The Soviet Union was caught by the necessity either of pumping out vastly greater quantities of her all too scanty resources or of curtailing her imports and thus sacrificing her program of industrialization. Her choice of the former course naturally made world prices fall all the more precipitately and led to accusations that by deliberate "dumping" she was trying to undermine the stability of the capitalist structure. Onset of the industrial depression, tumbling prices of the goods Russia coveted, brought her some relief and at the same time increased the willingness of capitalist countries, overwhelmed by unemployment, to do business with her.

The increasingly critical situation in Germany, which by 1933 put the Nazis into power, had a profound further effect on Russian foreign policy. Initially, Russia had remained unperturbed by growing Nazi strength, which was accompanied by a sharp rise also in the Communist vote. Apparently the Russian Bolsheviks underestimated the Nazis much as others had underrated the Bolsheviks in 1917; at the moment, they trusted that destruction of the Weimar Republic would permit the Communists to take over in Germany and thus at one stroke vastly increase Soviet power in a perishing capitalist world. Any lingering traces of such a notion were removed by the outlawing of the Communists and by the blood bath of 1934, in which Hitler demonstrated the power of his organization.

The disappearance of Germany as Russia's staunch ally was reinforced by the political overturn at the 1932 elections in the United States. The new American administration, unhampered by traditional policy and in an atmosphere of emergency, was able to come to an understanding with Soviet Russia. In return for Russia's promises of abstention from revolutionary propaganda and even of willingness to discuss a debt settlement, the United States of America at length extended *de jure* recognition to the Union of Soviet Socialist Republics. In Europe good relations between Russia and the West were even more strongly cemented. In 1934, at the moment that Germany officially ceased to be a member of the League of Nations, the Soviet Union stepped into her place; what had been an "imperialist conspiracy" against the Soviet Union now became the main bulwark of the "democratic" world against "Fascism." With France in particular, relations became extremely close; Laval concluded with Russia an agreement (1935) strongly suggestive of the Dual Alliance of 1894. On her other frontier, too, in the Far East, Russia consolidated her position; despite recurrent border clashes and friction over fishing rights, Russia accepted establishment of Japanese control over the newly founded state of Manchukuo (formerly Manchuria) and offered (1933) to sell to this puppet of her old enemy her half-interest in the Chinese Eastern Railway for a minimal sum, an agreement that was consummated early in 1935. Thus Soviet Russia, though still in a defensive rather than an offensive posture, was again taking her place in world politics. If she found herself in friendly alignment with the very countries from which she had expected the worst and to the destruction of whose governments her rulers were committed, it is but an illustration of the truism that "politics makes strange bedfellows."

NOTES

1. Bogolepov, *"Finansy planovogo khoziaistva"* [Finances of planned economy], in *Planovoe khoziaistvo,* 1929, No. 3, p. 283.
2. *Piatiletnyi Plan* . . . , I, 119.
3. Webb, *Soviet Communism: A New Civilization?,* II, 734-740 *passim.*
4. *Za industrializatsiiu,* February 2, 1931.
5. *Kommunisticheskaia Partiia Sovetskogo Soiuza v rezoliutsiiakh* . . . , III, 63.
6. Eskin, *Osnovnye puti razvitiia sotsialisticheskikh form truda,* p. 43.
7. Minute of People's Commissar of Labor (October 9, 1930), published in *Trud,* October 11, 1930, as quoted in Webb, *op. cit.,* II, 665*n.*
8. Poor Law Amendment Act, 4 & 5 William IV, c. 76 (1834).
9. Stalin, "New Setting—New Tasks of Economic Construction," speech at con-

ference of managerial personnel (June 23, 1931), in *Sochineniia,* XIII, 56-58.
10. *Za industrializatsiiu,* June 3, 1931.
11. Decree of the Council of People's Commissars (November 21, 1931), in *Sobranie zakonov i rasporiazhenii SSSR za 1921-1938,* 1931, No. 67 (December 2, 1931), # 448.
12. Article 18 of original (1918) Constitution of R.S.F.S.R.
13. Stalin, *loc. cit.,* p. 315.
14. *Piatiletnyi Plan . . .* , II, i, 285.
15. *Ibid.,* p. 329.
16. *Pravda,* April 3, 1930.
17. Webb, *op. cit.,* I, 258-272 *passim.*
18. Stalin, speech at First Congress of Collective-Farm Shock-Workers (February 19, 1933), *loc. cit.,* p. 247.
19. *Izvestiia,* February 21, 1933.
20. Stalin, "On the Right Deviation in the VKP(b)," June 6, 1929, *loc. cit.,* XII, 103.
21. *Pravda,* November 26, 1929.
22. Webb, *op. cit.,* II, 553.
23. Stalin, speech in Kremlin Palace at graduation of Red Army Cadets (May 4, 1935), in his *Voprosy Leninizma,* 11th edition, p. 490.

SUGGESTIONS FOR FURTHER READING

Among works previously cited, Baykov is of importance for economic developments. Gershenkron's *Economic Backwardness in Historical Perspective* contains some excellent background essays.

Particularly useful also are Bergson's *Real National Income of Soviet Russia Since 1928* and *Economics of Soviet Planning.* Jasny's *Soviet Industrialization* reflects a different interpretation. The studies of Soviet financing by Holzman and by Davies, both previously mentioned, are here very valuable. Dobb's *Soviet Economic Development Since 1917* does not wholly maintain the standard of his earlier work. For a Russian interpretation, to which the Webbs lent the prestige of their names, see *Soviet Communism: A New Civilization?* For an official popularization by the vice-chairman of Gosplan, later People's Commissar of Finance (and ultimately liquidated in the Great Purge), see Grinko, *The Five-Year Plan of the Soviet Union.* Among journalists' accounts, W. H. Chamberlin's *Soviet Russia* and *Russia's Iron Age,* John Scott's *Behind the Urals,* and Maurice Hindus' *Humanity Uprooted* are the best. On collectivization, Volin's *Survey of Soviet Russian Agriculture* and Jasny's *Socialized Agriculture of the U.S.S.R.* should be consulted.

On political developments, Fainsod, already cited, is the most outstanding. Towster continues to be very valuable for reference. Wolin and Slusser, *The Soviet Secret Police,* and D. F. White, *The Growth of the Red Army,* are good on special aspects. Beloff's *Foreign Policy of Soviet Russia* is excellent.

On cultural developments, in addition to works previously cited, may be mentioned Brown's *Proletarian Episode in Russian Literature, 1928-1932,* and Eastman's *Artists in Uniform.*

Chapter

31

Purgatory: 1934-1939

ECONOMIC PROGRESS

With respect to economic conditions, the years 1934-39 were for Russia's rulers much easier than had been the early years of intensive industrialization. It is true that "Bolshevik tempo" had created or exacerbated many difficulties. Hasty absorption of masses of new industrial workers had magnified the problem of an inadequate core of skilled workers, "specialists," and competent managerial personnel. The turnover of workers was extremely rapid; each year the number of new workers hired and of old workers lost both exceeded the average number employed, thus interfering with continuity of production. "Labor discipline" had deteriorated badly; voluntary absenteeism reached 2.5 percent of the possible working days. Average productivity had seriously declined, and huge increases in quantity had been balanced by worsening of the quality of production.

On the other hand, the huge increase in the volume of production, at least of heavy industry, was a fact. No one could deny that Russia's industrial potential had made enormous strides upward. Even in agriculture, once the opposition of the kulaks had been broken by force and collectivization had been made somewhat palatable to the mass of the peasants, production had reached new levels substantially above prewar yields. The good harvest of 1933 was followed by a series of successful years. Even the bad year 1936 gave a yield above 1913, and in 1937 the grain crop was 50 percent above that of 1913.

These circumstances made it possible to contemplate the abolition of rationing, which had been progressively reintroduced from the first years of the Five-Year Plan. The desirability of doing away with rationing was almost as clearly evident as had been the necessity of abandoning War Communism fourteen years earlier. Centralized distribution of marketable products, whether industrial or agricultural, had resulted in great unevenness, with glut at some times and places and extreme scarcity at others. Planning of distribution on the basis of a theoretical "average consumer" meant that the individual had to take what was offered him. Without consumer control it proved impossible to regulate standards of quality. The consumer was treated with contempt and often forced to buy goods he did not want in order to be permitted to buy also what he needed. Despite "planned" prices and officially published check lists, actual prices varied widely. Particular difficulty was caused by the fact that the quantities of goods available at "ration" prices differed with the official status of the individual; consequently, the purchasing power of different categories of the population depended not only on the number of rubles they earned but also on the proportion of their wants they must cover at the higher "commercial" prices. It was a circumstance that made almost impossible the planning of wage rates to achieve the desired incentive effect. Thus, state purposes as well as individual consumer interests demanded derationing.

In the course of 1935, therefore, rationing was gradually abolished. A system of fixed prices was, however, retained, at a level nearer to the old "commercial" prices than to the much lower ration prices. A consequent sharp rise in sale prices of agricultural products entailed substantial increases in industrial wage rates, but increases in industrial prices in consonance with raised production costs were avoided by adjustments in taxation. The "turnover" tax, introduced in 1930, supplied more than half the total receipts of the state budget. Its main purpose, however, was its deliberate use for the purpose of redistributing the national income through the price mechanism; instead of allowing economic enterprises to make whatever profit they individually could on the basis of effective consumer demand, the state siphoned off profits, sometimes exorbitant, for its own purposes. In simplest terms, the turnover tax was set as a percentage of the planned transfer price of any given industrial commodity; it was not calculated on actual cost of production, even including planned profit needed for maintenance of the enterprise. Thus "the difference between the cost of production of a commodity and the price it fetches as an item in the general expenditure on consumption of a society" [1] could be gathered into the State Budget and used for purposes wholly unrelated to the enterprise in question. If the spread between production costs and transfer price increased, the rate of tax was raised; if the spread decreased, the rate of tax was lowered. For most agricultural products the turnover tax was a fixed sum per unit sold. The abolition of rationing much increased the volume of sales of agricultural products subject to turnover tax; at the new fixed price levels for sale of agricultural products, which included specially high rates of turnover tax, there was naturally a great rise (from 4.574 billion rubles in 1934 to 20.729 billion in 1935) in Budget revenues from this source. This quadrupling of tax receipts from agriculture permitted a reduction in rates of turnover tax on industrial products, thus keeping their price down despite rising labor costs.

Retention of fixed prices, which applied generally except in "*kolkhoz* trade," did not, however, alter the fact that freedom of choice, both as to quantity and as to quality, had been restored to the consumer. Notwithstanding the monopolistic character of Soviet trade and industry, the nature of the consumer's response to goods offered for sale could not fail profoundly to affect Soviet planning, however indirectly. Theoretically, in a "planned" as contrasted with a "competitive" productive system, it might be easier to avoid all the problems of stimulating creative initiative instead of stifling it by patent rights and royalties that, by creating monopoly rights, so often hinder, instead of promoting, the wide application of new inventions. Yet the relationship of consumer to producer was fundamentally the same as in any other form of capitalist society. The main difference was that, in a society where production of consumer goods remained quantitatively inadequate, it was more difficult for the consumer to reject goods on account of their poor quality. Whereas the private capitalist, whether individual or corporation, has a direct interest in satisfying the consumer because of the effect on profits, management in the "planned" economy was concerned with fulfilling quantitative plans, even at the price of skimping on quality. To measure quantity was easy, but qualitative results are not readily expressed in any indices which "planning" could take into statistical account. It was quite clear that fixed prices did not reflect and could not guarantee qualitative results. Remedy was sought in prescribing norms of product in terms of quantities of raw material supplied to industry, in the hope that, by strict enforcement coupled with a system of bonuses for management, quality could be linked to quantity.

In the middle of the Second Five-Year Plan, therefore, the quantitative target for 1935, the year of derationing, was cut back from the 19 percent increase the Plan had prescribed for 1934; the new annual plan specified only a 16 percent increase, for emphasis was now to be put on quality. The sequel was remarkable: the actually achieved quantitative increase in 1935 was reckoned at 20 percent (as compared to 8.9% in 1933 and 14.9% in 1934); quality was hailed as substantially improved; and for the first time in the history of Soviet planning, the rise in labor productivity and the reduction of production costs were greater than had been planned for the year.

For 1936 the quantitative goal was again raised (to 23%); a strikingly novel feature was that for this year the percentage increase in light industry was now planned to be greater than that in heavy industry. In part, the results were very encouraging; an increase in production of over 30 percent was achieved, without substantial increase in the size of the labor force. This rise in productivity was, however, balanced by the failure of quality to improve; the proportion of substandard goods turned out was regarded as verv shocking, and a large number of cases of embezzling were announced, with the result that a wave of "wreckers' trials" and a purge of inefficient or corrupt management characterized the succeeding year.

The annual plan for 1937, the last year of the Second F.Y.P., set a 20 percent increase, with the rate for light industry again slightly exceeding that for heavy industry. In an effort to improve quality it was ordered that "*fulfillment of the plan* by an enterprise must be judged not by its gross output, but by the output of finished and perfect production." [2] The stated goals were not achieved, but early in the year it was announced that "the Second F.Y.P. in regard to the most important branches of the national economy has been fulfilled ahead of schedule. . . ." [3] Official figures show that the output of means of production, including armament industries, was in terms of rubles actually well ahead of the official Second F.Y.P (55.2 billion rubles instead of 45.5); in terms of tons of product, the metallurgical industries had done best; coal, however, though the output was quadruple the 1913 figure, had seriously lagged behind the Plan (128 million tons instead of 152.5). The excess of gross output of heavy industry over the target set at the beginning of the Second F.Y.P. was not wholly wiped out by the failure of the output of consumers' goods (40.3 billion rubles instead of a predicted 47.2); in terms of volume, Russia in 1937 produced not quite 3.5 billion meters of cotton textiles instead of an anticipated 5.1 billion (as against 2.25 billion in 1913).

Any attempt to compare accomplishments during the period of the Second F.Y.P. with earlier industrial progress, even under the First F.Y.P., is of course confused by the fact that development of branches of industry previously nonexistent in Russia invalidates comparison in terms of rubles. What can be more confidently stated is, however, the great success of the capital construction program from 1932 to 1937: under the First F.Y.P. estimated costs had been greatly exceeded, but only 60 percent of construction had really gone into production; under the Second F.Y.P., without exceeding anticipated investment, 87 percent of the expenditure was producing results. The tremendous increase in capital equipment was itself one of the major factors in increasing the productivity of labor; instead of the planned increase of 63 percent, Soviet statistics were able to claim an 82 percent actual increase in labor productivity in these five years. In order further to stimulate managerial efficiency by increasing responsibility, a beginning was made in 1936 in withdrawing state subsidies to industries that failed to earn a profit. In turn, it was necessary to overhaul the technique of fixing prices, and the administrative structure of industry was again revised in the direction of greater centralization of authority in Moscow. At the same time, the establishment of a director's fund, receiving a small percentage of planned profits and half of profits beyond the Plan, gave added personal incentive to on-the-spot managers.

The best evidence of the psychological success of the principle of *piatiletka* is the fact that completion of the Second F.Y.P. was immediately followed by announcement of the launching of a Third. The proposed capital investment in industry was doubled, while the 5:1 ratio between investment in heavy industry (Group A) and in production of consumers' goods (Group B) was retained. The 1935-36 pretense that output of consumers' goods would rise faster than output of the means of production was dropped. The percentage goal for rise in gross production was somewhat reduced (from 214.7% approved for the Second F.Y.P. to 192%), but that of Group A was raised (from 197.2% to 207%) and that for Group B lowered (from 233.6% to 172%). The war clouds emanating from Nazi Germany were allowed to obscure Stalin's earlier emphasis on "life is becoming jolly."

In the Third F.Y.P., it was emphasized, new construction in old-established and overconcentrated industrial centers such as Moscow, Leningrad, Kharkov, and Rostov was to be forbidden in favor of development of "economically focal points" such as the Lower Volga region or the Urals, and even of Central Asia and the Far East. In similar spirit, "gigantomania" (i.e., the traditional emphasis on huge "superplants") was vigorously condemned.[4] Completion of the Third F.Y.P. was prevented by the outbreak of war with Germany in 1941. In the three preceding years, output of capital goods, in terms of rubles, increased over 50 percent (one-quarter of the five-year goal) while output of consumer goods increased by less than one-third (under one-fifth of the goal). Thus, throughout the period, production of consumer goods, always subordinated in the Plans, was in practice even further sacrificed to development of the means of production and the growth of the armament industries.

On the eve of World War II, Russia was in some fields of industry one of the world's leading producers, though recovery from depression had on the whole improved the relative position of the Western world. According to the favorite Soviet yardstick, steel production, Russia had slipped back from second to third place; despite Russia's magnificent effort, which had trebled her steel output, simple return of the United States to pre-depression levels had reduced the ratio of Russian to American production from 1:2 to 1:3. The Soviet Union had pulled well ahead of Great Britain as a steel producer but had been unable to keep pace with resurgent Germany. Coal production in the Soviet Union had merely doubled, and Russia held only fourth place in the world. Output of electricity had increased much more rapidly; as also in petroleum production, Russia was second only to the United States. In terms of per capita production, of course, Russia was still not a seriously industrialized country, and in consumers' goods even the absolute figures were not at all impressive.

There were also the problems of poor quality and of high labor cost arising from low output per worker. In the period 1934-39, efforts even more strenuous than before were made to realize Lenin's often stressed ambition to introduce "labor discipline," for no one had ever doubted that he had been right in his insistence that no approach could be made to the achievement of communism, as distinct from "socialism," without a vast increase in individual productivity. The year of derationing was therefore marked also with advancement (May 4, 1935) of Stalin's new slogan, "personnel decides everything."

STAKHANOVISM AND LABOR

On August 30, 1935, it was triumphantly announced that a Donets miner named Stakhanov had, in the presence of official witnesses, hewed 102 tons of coal in a six-hour shift; the average had been six or seven tons a shift, as against ten to seventeen in Ruhr mines; Stakhanov had thus earned for himself 225 rubles, more than a Russian miner's average monthly wage. This feat had been accomplished, not by superhuman physical effort, but by a new division of labor; Stakhanov had concentrated on his own particular job and had left everything else to unskilled workers; at the same time he had studiously avoided all waste motion, thus introducing "rhythm" into his labor. His example was promptly emulated by other highly skilled and specially trained workers, who in some cases even outdid Stakhanov's record.

"Stakhanovism" was at once applied to other occupations; in the Gorky automobile works a forgeman, Busygin, and his brigade turned out 127 crankshafts an hour as against standard American output of 100; in cotton textiles a woman weaver, Vinogradova, successfully tended 144 automatic looms, whereas the very highest American records were stated to be 90 to 100 looms; even agriculture was affected. Every encouragement was given to the widest possible spread of the new device, including specially high piecework wage rates for those who qualified as "Stakhanovites." Workers whose own ambition did not drive them to participate in using the new techniques suffered absolute as well as relative loss of wages. Periodic revision of "production norms," calculated to yield the equivalent of a reasonable time-rate, reduced previously established piecework rates; whenever a visit by Stakhanovites demonstrated the possibility of increasing average individual output, the old "norms" were unceremoniously raised. The consequences were not always what the Party had hoped for; apart from sabotage and even murder of Stakhanovites by ordinary workers, it was officially admitted that "as a reaction there has been a drop in labor productivity, and labor has been leaking away from the Donbas," [5] and that "in the Donbas high individual records and yet a low average standard of work in coal-mining" was the rule.[6]

Yet on the whole the outcome was beneficial to the state as employer. By 1938 it was officially stated that 41.4 percent of all industrial workers had become Stakhanovites. Over-all labor productivity did increase very substantially. In 1937 output per worker employed in heavy industry was more than double what it had been in 1932; in construction and in railway transport the improvement, though less, was substantial. The increase in the number of workers no longer had to keep pace with increase in production. In the period of the First F.Y.P. (1928-1932), the total number of wage-workers in all branches of the national economy had doubled (rising from 11.6 million to 22.9 million); average yearly wages had also doubled (from 703 to 1,427 rubles). From 1932 to 1936, numbers of wage-workers increased only to 27.8 million, permitting average annual wages to be raised to 3,467 rubles without much more than doubling the wages fund. That these figures bore little relation to Plan anticipations (15.7 million to be employed in 1932 and 29.6 million in 1937, at average annual wages of 994 and 1,755 rubles, respectively) is beside the point. Heavy investments in capital construction, aided by Stakhanovism and by the 1937 purge of managers who owed their places to past Party services rather than to their abilities, were at last bearing fruit.

It should be emphasized that Stakhanovism was not simply a continuation of "shock" techniques and "socialist competition." The old incentives had appealed to the morale of workers and had been accompanied by no immediate improvement in the material condition of the participants. It had been a question of extra effort for no extra pay in the hope of more rapid "building of socialism." In contrast, Stakhanovism stressed the material advantage to the individual worker who submitted to the necessary training. As Molotov explained in *What Is Stakhanovism?* (1935):

> Counting minutes and seconds during one's work, introducing a rhythm, observing a definite sequence, and establishing system in all the processes of work, mean putting an end to the indifference to shameful stoppages of machinery and waste of time; it means introducing culture in one's work. It is therefore not a question of *overstrain* on the part of the worker but of a *cultured* attitude toward work.[7]

Molotov, whose position as chairman of Sovnarkom made him in effect chairman of the board of the whole of Soviet industry and trade, added, however:

> One has only to mention that in the case of many Stakhanovites the direct impetus to high productivity of labor is a simple interest in increasing their earnings in order to show that the Stakhanov-Busygin-Vinogradova movement can be understood by the ordinary working man, can be understood by any working woman. . . . The Stakhanovites are not exceptional people, *every worker can become a Stakhanovite.*

As in any other form of capitalist society, differential wage rates and bonuses had always been a major factor in attracting labor to the branches of industry where it was most wanted, in convincing workers of the need to improve their skill, and in stimulating them to greater individual effort. Yet the problem of fixing wage rates was fraught with very great difficulties, and Soviet economists were well aware of the constant recurrence of serious maladjustments. Emergency changes in rates might solve current problems with respect to particular production problems, but they seriously upset calculations of labor costs and thus threw out of balance the planned relationship between production and consumption, disorganizing the whole planning mechanism.

From 1938 on, increased care was given to the fixing of wages and salaries appropriate to the anticipated results. The process was assisted by the fact that as a result of the 1937 management purge the proportion of qualified executives was much increased. As an added inducement to efficient management, there was introduced the practice of allowing "personal salaries . . . up to one and a half times the usual amount for the particular post";[8] the maximum limit for such individualized executive compensation was set at from five to seven times the current average wage, depending on the branch of industry involved.

The new policy of emphasizing individual material rewards did not put an end to the older policy of social incentives. At the end of 1938, a hierarchy of medals was set up. At its pinnacle was the title of "Hero of Socialist Toil," which, as

> the highest degree of distinction in the field of economic and cultural construction is awarded to persons who, by their especially outstanding innovating activity in the field of industry, agriculture, transport, trade, scientific discoveries and technical inventions, have rendered exceptional services to the state, have contributed to the rise of the national economy, culture, or science, and to the growth of the might and glory of the U.S.S.R.[9]

These awards were publicized in the press and were granted without respect to the type of employment; they represented only recognition that the job had been particularly well done, quite independently of the normal value of the task itself. Each grade of award carried material advantages as well as honor. In 1939 "Stalin Prizes," up to 100,000 rubles each, were awarded to specially distinguished workers, whether in the field of production or of culture. Analogous material rewards on a collective basis were given to model enterprises.

In addition to positive incentives, penalties for breach of labor discipline continued to be widely used. Only a week before establishment of the title of "Hero of Socialist Toil," with its automatic membership in the "Order of Lenin," the system of "labor books," containing the full employment record of the individual wage-worker, was tightened up. Eight days later, a decree of the Council of People's Commissars provided that any worker who reported late, took more than the permitted lunch period, quit work early, or loafed on the job was to be reprimanded or even transferred to lower paid work; "those guilty of three such infringements in the course of a month or of four in two consecutive months are to be dismissed for absenteeism."[10] Workers so dismissed could not be taken back for three months; if they found employment with some other enterprise, they lost all rights accruing from previous employment. Any worker wishing to leave his job must give a month's notice. Under an economic system which did not admit of involuntary unemployment, severe penalties were felt to be necessary to ensure labor discipline.

To reduce labor turnover, it was also provided that many of the rights "guaranteed" under the new 1936 Constitution—disability allowances, vacations with pay, admission to rest homes, even old-age pensions and paid maternity leave—became dependent on the length of time the worker had been employed by the particular enterprise. In 1938 official criticism was directed also at procedures in recruiting fresh unskilled workers. The presence in the same district of representatives of a number of recruiting agencies "gives rise to unhealthy competition between different organizations";[11] from 1939 on, labor recruitment in any given area was to be monopolized by a single employing agency.

After the outbreak of war in 1939, though Russia remained at peace until 1941, still more drastic measures were taken. On June 27, 1940, five days after the Vichy government signed an armistice with Germany, a decree of the Presidium of the Supreme Soviet ordered change-over from the seven-hour to an eight-hour day and from the "six-day" to the "seven-day week," with Sunday as a day of rest for all. It also abolished the right of the worker to change his employment; quitting one's job without special authorization became a criminal offense punishable by up to four months in prison. Absenteeism was no longer to lead to dismissal; the new penalty was compulsory labor with one-quarter deduction from wages for six months. Later in the year, a State Labor Reserve scheme authorized conscription annually of 800,000 to 1,000,000 adolescents, aged fourteen to seventeen, to be trained in special schools as industrial workers.

The question whether the substantial wage increases after 1932 raised the standard of living remains moot. Prices also rose, and sharply. In the absence of any possibility of constructing a price index to convert money wages into real wages, no one can speak with assurance. In addition, there is the unresolvable question of the extent to which "socialized wages"—including, along with social insurance, government expenditures on housing, health, education, public libraries, and other "cultural" services—may have raised the standard of living; the obvious gap between theoretical rights of the toilers and their actual realization leaves "socialized wages" a factor of very uncertain value in the case of the "average" worker. Other factors making for uncertainty include the effect of the abolition of unemployment by means of terminating unemployment-relief payments and the rapidly growing proportion of women employed. On the ground of their lack of skill, women were for the most part paid at the lowest wage scales, but the prevalence of family earnings in 1939 obviously makes difficult comparisons with earlier days when wives were not independently employed. On the other hand is the incalculable effect of collectivization and the consequent break between the "average" urban worker and his roots in the peasant village. All that can be said is that, in the opinion of most informed students, it seems probable that the standard of living of the "average" Russian worker did not exceed, if indeed it again reached, the pre-1914 level from which it had been depressed by the launching of the First F.Y.P.

AGRICULTURE

Of agriculture little need be added to what has already been said about its stabilization after 1933 and the increase in crop yields. Even the number of head of livestock began again to increase; it is, however, important to note that, although almost all the peasants were by this time members of collective farms, half the cattle, sheep, and hogs were the personal property of individuals, not of the collectives. Less than two-thirds of gross agricultural production could be attributed to the collectives as such, and less than 10 percent to the state farms; more than one-quarter of all agricultural produce still had to be credited to individual small-scale economies, though most of them were carried on within the framework of the *kolkhozy*.

In February, 1935, detailed statutes were issued governing the "artel," the normal type of collective farm. The *kolkhoz* was confirmed in permanent possession of its land, though without the right to alienate it, even by lease. Within the artel the amount of land that might be allotted to an individual was strictly limited, though his rights to possession of livestock were somewhat extended and the *kolkhoz* was obligated to make adequate provision of communal fodder for individually owned animals. The rights of members and their control over management were emphasized.

The *kolkhoz* was not a state-owned enterprise; it therefore could not expect state subsidies to equalize its receipts with those of neighboring collective farms. About 90 percent of its marketable grain and a still larger proportion of its "technical" crops (sugar beet, flax, etc.) were taken by the state at fixed prices, either as compulsory deliveries or in payments to the M.T.S.; although specified quantities of meat, wool, hides, and milk also had to be delivered to the state, the proportion was much less because so much livestock was individually owned. In addition to sales to the state-controlled agencies, which in 1938 were estimated to constitute nearly 40 percent of the value of the gross yield, a certain share had to be allocated to the collective expenditures and reserve funds.

Something over a quarter of the collective crops, together with an appropriate share of net cash revenues, was distributed among the members on the basis of the number of "labor-days" they had worked. The length of a labor-day depended on the nature of the duties discharged by the individual and accordingly varied from a few hours in the case of highly skilled work to more than one solar day for the least onerous tasks. Compensation for a labor-day varied both from one farm to another and from one season to another, for it represented a proportionate fraction of the total number of labor-days worked by all the members of any given collective farm in any given year. A constant struggle had to be waged against the tendency of the peasants, with the connivance of their fellows, to avoid collective work in order to tend to their own economies. In 1939 it was deemed necessary to set a minimum of labor-days that must be earned by any individual on penalty of being expelled from the collective, with loss of all accumulated rights.

At whatever cost, collectivization and its sequel had by 1939 succeeded in increasing the sown area by one-third as compared to 1913 and had multiplied the marketable crop of grain and sugar beet about three times; the marketable production of milk had been doubled, and that of meat nearly so. An important additional factor in increasing the food supply available to the Russian population was that, with sharply decreasing need for imported machinery, the quantities that had to be exported fell off correspondingly. Disappointing as it was to the United States government, total imports into Russia after American recognition in 1933 never reached half the volume that had prevailed during the world depression; in terms of value, because of depressed prices, they were relatively even smaller.

TENSIONS AND THE PURGE TRIALS

General improvement in economic conditions took time; it could not immediately relax the tensions bequeathed by *piatiletka* and by the varied phenomena concomitant with "five-yearie." Internal tension was enhanced by the ominous fact of Germany's acceptance of Hitler, who in *Mein Kampf* had proposed the acquisition of needed *Lebensraum* from Russia. The consequent danger of foreign war had, however, its compensations for Russia's rulers. It was all the more possible to employ the allegation of foreign conspiracies to justify domestic purges; like medieval physicians with their leeches, like tsarist bureaucrats such as Pleve, Stalin found that the policy of bloodletting had a therapeutic effect on his regime.

There was in truth very considerable danger to its continuance. The mass of the collective farmers lived on the edge of subsistence and almost certainly cherished as deep-seated a hostility toward the government as the peasants ever had toward that of the tsar, however much reverence they had felt toward the concept of their "little father." The mass of the workers, notwithstanding the advantages showered on "exemplary workers" and the vaunted theory of "socialized wages," had little reason to rejoice in the form the promised "workers' republic" had taken; over the majority of them, who did not rise to the bait of honor and rewards in return for extra toil, constantly hung the threat of punitive measures. The old intelligentsia and the remnants of the formerly propertied classes naturally had great nostalgia for the old, relatively freer days of the tsars, when literature, art, and music were not subject to government direction and when the future had held some promise of individual security for those who did not engage in openly revolutionary activity. The subject nationalities continued restive in spite of limited cultural autonomy, which did not permit them to organize their lives in their own way; not only was the percentage of Party membership low in non-Russian areas, but what passed as national Communist parties contained a high percentage of Russian officials and Party workers sent to administer these areas.

None of these hostile currents could, of course, hope to achieve anything by overt hostility to the dictatorship of the Communist Party, any more than their predecessors in the preceding generation had been able successfully to revolt against the autocracy of the tsars. Only internal decay had so weakened the autocracy that, with complete loss of confidence in the person of the ruler, the regime had collapsed under the stress of war. In some ways the new regime was weaker than the old; it lacked the sanctification of centuries of tradition; there could not be the same widespread conviction that, however corrupt, even evil, the administration might be, it was nevertheless legitimate, grounded in something transcending ephemeral human wishes; Stalin might be hailed as a "genius," even greeted as the "little father," and have his name tacked on by a hyphen to the still magic name of Lenin; yet he could not be more than a transient human being, could not confidently project his power into a timeless future.

On the other hand, the Communist Party was more efficient, less inhibited, and more ruthless than had been the tradition-bound tsars. Its very newness still gave some ground to hope that the future would be brighter than the present. Solidly entrenched on "the commanding heights" of industry, it wielded power in every corner of the Russian economy. Monopolizing all the media of propaganda, it could count on mobilizing the youthful aspirations and ideals of each rising generation, even though those it indoctrinated in their youth might all too soon become disillusioned by contact with the realities of life under its aegis. In the police, the army, the trade unions, and the Komsomol—all interlocked with and directed by the Party—it possessed most up-to-date weapons. The position of the new regime was impregnable so long as the Party preserved its unity, but if disputes should arise within the Party, no one could foretell the outcome. The leadership was still officially collegial; if a significant part of it should attempt to capitalize on social or ethnic discontents, it might open a crack that could destroy the whole edifice.

In January, 1934, at the Seventeenth Party Congress, Stalin boasted of the victories won over all deviationist groups: "It must be admitted that the Party today is united as it has never been before. [Stormy, long-continued applause.]" [12] In July, 1934, the political police administration, OGPU, was combined with a newly created All-Union Commissariat of Internal Affairs (NKVD), which also united control of ordinary police functions, theretofore relegated to the several "sovereign" member-republics. At the time it was widely assumed that the intention was to limit the extensive and arbitrary powers of the political police. On December 1 of the same year, Serge Kirov, one of Stalin's most trusted colleagues in the Politburo and head of the

Party apparatus in Leningrad, was assassinated. Murder was a revolutionary technique that had been frequently employed against the tsar's regime. The assassin, Nikolaiev, was himself a member of the Party; he was officially condemned as "belonging to an underground counter-revolutionary terrorist group . . . consisting of former members of the Zinoviev opposition." [13]

Even before the assassination, the doubtful quality of many Party members had been giving some concern. Party membership, which had been less than 25,000 at the beginning of 1917, only 115,000 a year later, and had passed the half-million mark only in 1920, had by the beginning of 1933, including "candidates," reached 3.5 million. In that year a purge, principally of newly-entered collective farmers and workers, had effected a net reduction of nearly 400,000 members and over 450,000 candidates; in 1934 continued examination of qualifications had reduced the total of members and candidates by another 350,000. In this atmosphere the murder of Kirov seemed to require even more drastic purgation of the Party. It was not enough to shoot Nikolaiev and over a hundred "counter-revolutionaries" who had been arrested prior to the murder.

Under Yagoda, an old GPU hand recently promoted to head the NKVD, the full force of that organization was now turned on the Party membership, and most vigorously on those who had the prestige of having joined the Party before 1917. In May, 1935, the Society of Old Bolsheviks was dissolved; a few months later Zinoviev and Kamenev were arrested. A general screening of all Party members resulted in further heavy decline in the number of Party members and candidates. Not until August, 1936, however, did the immensity of the purge become publicly manifest at the first of the show trials of Party members. In open court, sixteen members of the former "Left Opposition," including Zinoviev and Kamenev, confessed their guilt in organizing a terrorist group under the direction of the exiled Trotsky and implicated a number of other Old Bolsheviks, including members of the "Right Opposition"; their reward was prompt execution. A month later Yagoda was replaced as head of NKVD by Yezhov, and the terror-purge entered on a still more violent phase.

The "Yezhovshchina" took on incredibly fantastic proportions. In January, 1937, the "Trial of the 17" officially established the existence of a plot to use the military strength of Germany and Japan for the purpose of destroying the Soviet Union; under the guidance of Trotsky, capitalism was to be restored in Russia. The chief figures in this batch were Austrian-born Karl Radek—who had accompanied Lenin and Zinoviev on the "sealed train" across Germany in 1917, who had played the chief role in organizing the German Communist Party, but who had been made the scapegoat in the Third International for the failure of the German "March Action" in 1921—and Sokolnikov, who had been one of the seven members of the Politburo that had managed the seizure of power in November, 1917. Thirteen of the defendants were shot, but Radek, Sokolnikov, and two others escaped with ten-year prison sentences

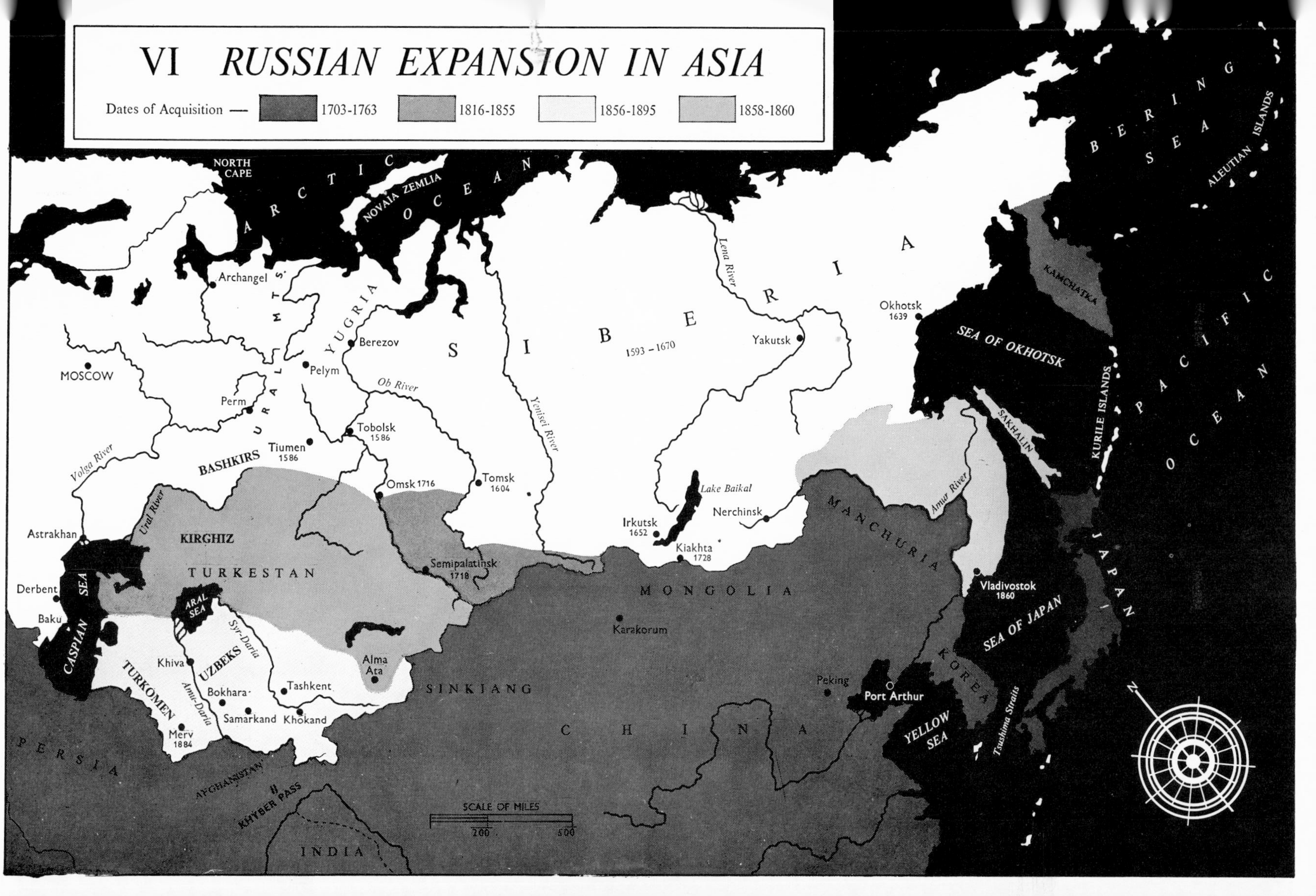
VI RUSSIAN EXPANSION IN ASIA
Dates of Acquisition —
1703-1763
1816-1855
1856-1895
1858-1860
NORTH CAPE
ARCTIC OCEAN
NOVAIA ZEMLIA
BERING SEA
ALEUTIAN ISLANDS
KAMCHATKA
PACIFIC OCEAN
SEA OF OKHOTSK
KURILE ISLANDS
SAKHALIN
JAPAN
SEA OF JAPAN
Tsushima Straits
KOREA
YELLOW SEA
Port Arthur
Peking
Vladivostok 1860
Amur River
MANCHURIA
MONGOLIA
Karakorum
CHINA
SINKIANG
SCALE OF MILES
200
600
INDIA
KHYBER PASS
AFGHANISTAN
PERSIA
SIBERIA
1593 – 1670
Okhotsk 1639
Yakutsk
Lena River
Lake Baikal
Nerchinsk
Irkutsk 1652
Kiakhta 1728
Yenisei River
Tomsk 1604
Ob River
Berezov
YUGRIA
Pelym
Tobolsk 1586
Omsk 1716
Semipalatinsk 1718
Tiumen 1586
URAL MTS.
Archangel
Perm
MOSCOW
Volga River
BASHKIRS
Ural River
KIRGHIZ
TURKESTAN
Astrakhan
Derbent
Baku
CASPIAN SEA
ARAL SEA
Syr-Daria
Amu-Daria
UZBEKS
Khiva
Bokhara
Samarkand
Tashkent
Khokand
Alma Ata
TURKOMEN
Merv 1884

Cossacks
presenting Ivan the Terrible with the booty taken by Yermak from Siberia (1582). From a reproduction of a painting by D. Levitsky.

VII EUROPEAN RUSSIA 1762-1914
Partitions of Poland [Russian shares]
1772
1793
1795
1801-1864 Acquired from native chiefs
1783—Date of acquisition from Turkey
Boundary of Poland before partition
Borders of Russian Empire in 1914
ARCTIC OCEAN
URAL MOUNTAINS
Murmansk
Solovki
Archangel
North Dvina R.
Sukhona R.
FINLAND
Vyborg
Stockholm
Kronstadt
St. Petersburg
Schüsselburg
ESTONIA
Gatchina
Dorpat
Novgorod
LIVONIA
Pskov
BALTIC SEA
COURLAND
Riga
LITHUANIA
West Dvina R.
Tilsit
PRUSSIA
Vilna
Niemen
WHITE RUSSIA
Minsk
Dnieper
Smolensk
BORODINO
Tver
Ivanovo-Voznesensk
Volga R.
Vladimir
Moscow
Oka R.
Nizhny Novgorod
Kazan
Tula
Samara
POZNAN
Vistula
Bialystok
CONGRESS POLAND KINGDOM
Warsaw
Lodz
VOLHYNIA
Kursk
Saratov
KIRGHIZ
Danube R.
Vienna
AUSTRIA
Cracow
GALICIA
Dniester
UKRAINE
PODOLIA
Kiev
Kharkov
Donets R.
Don River
Chigirin
CARPATHIAN MTS.
HUNGARY
BUKOVINA
BESSARABIA
Yelizavetgrad
Yekaterinoslav
DONBAS
1791
Krivoi Rog
Volga River
Jassy
MOLDAVIA
Kishinev
Odessa
1774
Taganrog
Rostov
Astrakhan
1812
1783
Azov
Stavropol
Belgrade
CRIMEA 1783
Kuban R.
Maikop
CASPIAN SEA
WALACHIA
SERBIA
BOSNIA
Shipka Pass
BULGARIA
DOBRUDJA
Sevastopol
Terek R.
Grozny
CAUCASUS MOUNTAINS
DAGHESTAN
Derbent
MONTENEGRO
BALKAN MTS.
RUMELIA
BLACK SEA
1829
GEORGIA
Batum
Adrianople
MACEDONIA
THRACE
Bosporus
Sinope
1878
Kars
Baku
AZERBAIJAN
Constantinople
Trebizond
GREECE
Dardanelles
SEA OF MARMORA
ARMENIA
Erzerum
ASIA MINOR
MOREA
NAVARINO
AEGEAN SEA
PERSIA
MEDITERRANEAN SEA
CRETE
Antioch
SYRIA
CYPRUS
LEBANON
N
PALESTINE
Jerusalem
SCALE OF MILES
100 200
EGYPT

Catherine II, as painted by D. Levitsky (1735–1822), an eighteenth-century court painter, in which, with his customary irony, he brings out some of the characteristics that earned her the name of "the Great."

Pugachev, the cossack leader who, pretending to be Peter III, led the greatest of cossack and peasant revolts, threatening to overthrow the imperial system (1773–1774). Suvorov, the general whose name is attached to the highest military honor conferred by the Soviet Union, was instrumental in his capture.

The Winter Palace barely glimpsed through the archway of the open square, stretches leftward to the Neva, nearly opposite the Peter-and-Paul Fortress. The Ermitage is beyond the right wing of the Winter Palace.

RIGHT
Mussorgsky painted by Repin in 1881 shortly before the composer's death.

The Senate Square in St. Petersburg, scene of the Decembrist uprising in 1825. The statue of Peter the Great is "The Bronze Horseman," which gave its name to one of Pushkin's finest poems. To the right of it is the Admiralty, from which radiate the main boulevards, including the Nevsky Prospekt. At the left, across the Neva, is the spire of the Peter-and-Paul Cathedral, which still dominates the Leningrad skyline.

ВЫСОЧАЙШЕ
УТВЕРЖДЕННЫЯ
ЕГО ИМПЕРАТОРСКИМЪ ВЕЛИЧЕСТВОМЪ
19 ФЕВРАЛЯ 1861 ГОДА
ПОЛОЖЕНІЯ
о
КРЕСТЬЯНАХЪ,
ВЫШЕДШИХЪ ИЗЪ КРѢПОСТНОЙ ЗАВИСИМОСТИ.

САНКТПЕТЕРБУРГЪ.
1861.

На подлинномъ Собственною ЕГО ИМПЕРАТОРСКАГО ВЕЛИЧЕСТВА рукою написано:

«Быть по сему.»

Въ Санктпетербургѣ
19-го Февраля 1861 года.

ОБЩЕЕ ПОЛОЖЕНІЕ
о
КРЕСТЬЯНАХЪ,
ВЫШЕДШИХЪ ИЗЪ КРѢПОСТНОЙ ЗАВИСИМОСТИ.

ВВЕДЕНІЕ.

1. Крѣпостное право на крестьянъ, водворенныхъ въ помѣщичьихъ имѣніяхъ, и на дворовыхъ людей отмѣняется навсегда, въ порядкѣ, указанномъ въ настоящемъ Положеніи и въ другихъ, вмѣстѣ съ онымъ изданныхъ, Положеніяхъ и Правилахъ.

2. На основаніи сего Положенія и общихъ законовъ, крестьянамъ и дворовымъ людямъ, вышедшимъ изъ крѣпостной зависимости, предоставляются права состоянія свободныхъ сельскихъ обывателей, какъ личныя, такъ и по имуществу. Въ пользованіе сими правами они вступаютъ тѣмъ порядкомъ и въ тѣ сроки, какіе указаны въ Правилахъ о приведеніи въ дѣйствіе положеній о крестьянахъ и въ особомъ Положеніи о дворовыхъ людяхъ.

3. Помѣщики, сохраняя право собственности на всѣ принадлежащія имъ земли, предостав-

Emancipation, 1861

LEFT *Title page* of the Manifesto and accompanying decrees, which reads: "Supreme Statutes established by His Imperial Majesty, February 19, 1861, on the peasants emerging from serfdom. St. Petersburg, 1861."

RIGHT *Opening paragraphs* of the printed decree. At the top, "Subscribed on the manuscript by His Imperial Majesty's Own Hand: 'So be it.' " Dated "At St. Petersburg, February 19, 1861." After the heading "General Statute on the Peasants Emerging from Serfdom" comes "Introduction."

"1. Bondage right over the peasants dwelling on landlords' estates and on household people is abolished forever, in the manner indicated in the present Statute and in other Statutes and Regulations published along with it.

"2. On the basis of this Statute and of general laws, the peasants emerging from serfdom are given the rights of the status of free rural inhabitants, both personal and with respect to property. They will enter on the enjoyment of these rights in the manner indicated in the Regulations on implementing the statutes on the peasants and in the special Statute on household people."

Nicholas II and Empress Alexandra (Alix), a photograph which, notwithstanding the unusual ceremonial costumes, strongly suggests their respective characteristics and their mutual relationship.

Rasputin, the Siberian peasant who pretended to be a monk and became the symbol of the "dark forces" that attended the collapse of the autocracy.

LEFT
A Landlord Exchanges Peasants for Dogs, a painting by Taras Shevchenko, the outstanding Ukrainian poet (1814–1861); it is a characteristic specimen of Russian realist painting depicting the iniquities of serfdom.

VIII

EUROPEAN RUSSIA SINCE THE REVOLUTION

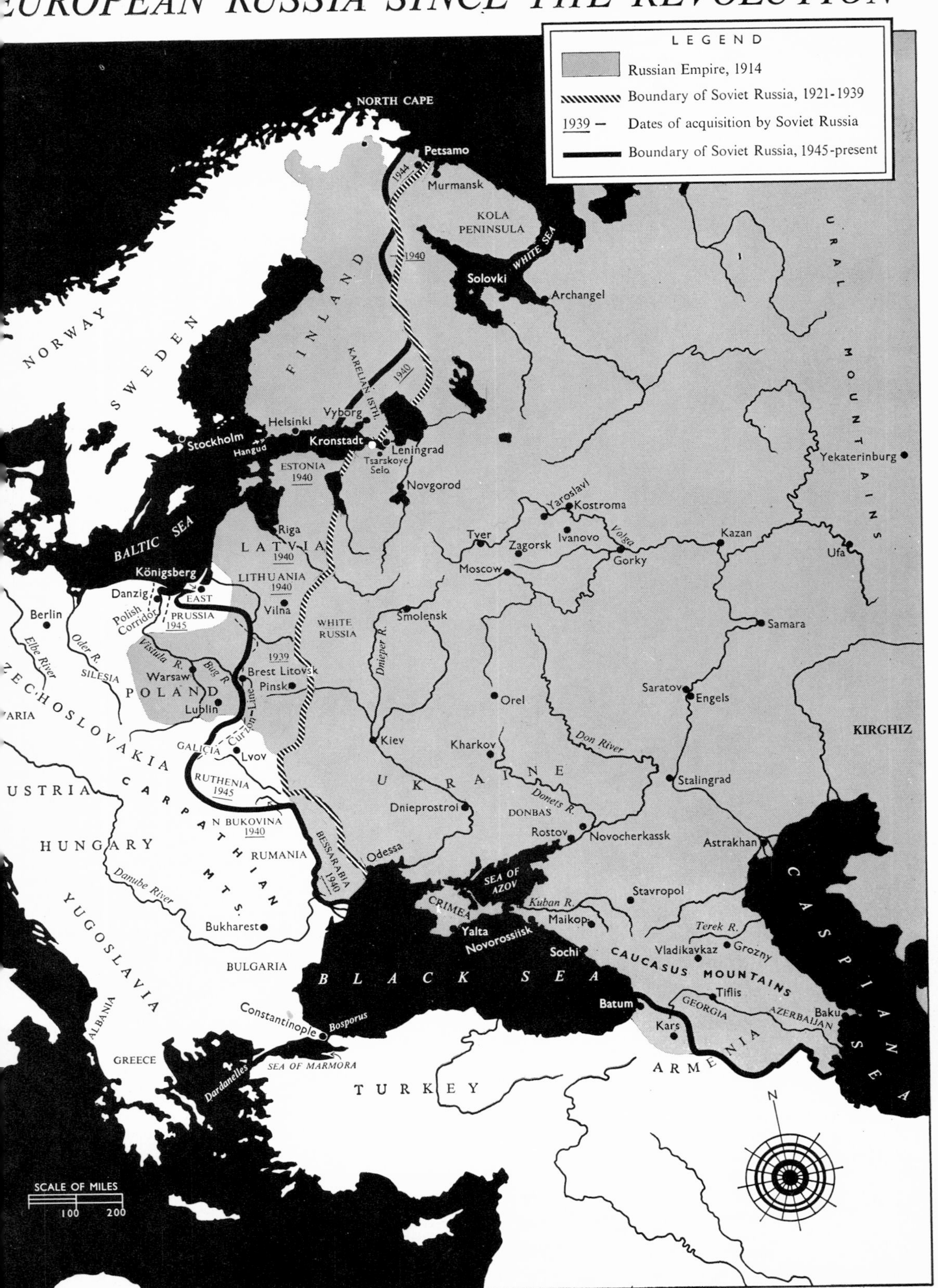

Kerensky,
in his brief military capacity, reviewing Russian troops when they were still subject to discipline.

Lenin addressing the May Day celebration
in the Red Square, with the enormous arcaded stores now known as GUM in the background. His clothing and the thoughtfulness of his attitude are more characteristic than pictures showing him in his demagogic capacity.

XX | XXI

Trotsky
posed for the photographer, apparently in a railway carriage. The affectation of a military uniform is in contrast to Lenin's regular civilian appearance.

The ruins of Stalingrad after the surrender of General Paulus.

RIGHT
One of the "Seven Beauties" the culmination of Russian architecture in the time of Stalin.

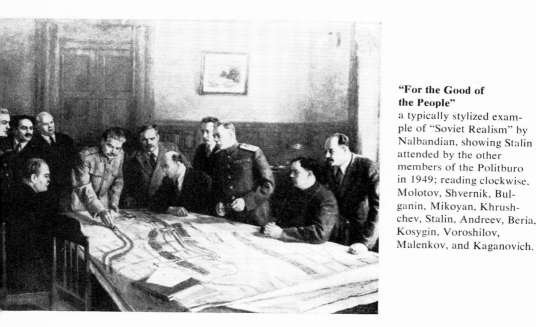

"For the Good of the People" a typically stylized example of "Soviet Realism" by Nalbandian, showing Stalin attended by the other members of the Politburo in 1949; reading clockwise, Molotov, Shvernik, Bulganin, Mikoyan, Khrushchev, Stalin, Andreev, Beria, Kosygin, Voroshilov, Malenkov, and Kaganovich.

De-Stalinization, Hungarian style (1956).

Khrushchev, Major Gagarin, and President Brezhnev on the tribune of the Lenin Mausoleum in the Red Square (1961).

Prague (August, 1968), President Podgorny, Premier Kosygin, General Secretary Brezhnev, Dubcek of Czechoslovakia, and Suslov; in the rear, between Brezhnev and Dubcek, is Shelest, Ukrainian First Secretary.

in return for their publicly sworn detailed accounts of impossible dealings with Trotsky at nonexistent places.

Early in June it was announced that Marshal Tukhachevsky, hero of the Warsaw campaign in 1920 and the most important professional organizer of the Red Army, and seven other of the most highly placed "commanders" had been executed for "espionage and treason to the Fatherland" in the service of an undefined foreign power;[14] since part of the charges had been their alleged willingness to surrender the Ukraine, the implication was that Germany was again meant. Presumably because military men were of tougher fiber than civilian Old Bolsheviks, or perhaps because their lesser degree of loyalty to the Party made them unwilling to sacrifice their reputations for it, the trial had been held in secret. Before the Yezhovshchina was over, the military, naval, and air-force high commands had been decimated; among many others, a second of the five marshals and four hundred officers from colonel up had been liquidated.

In March, 1938, took place the most spectacular of the public trials: the "Trial of the 21" centered on the former "Right Opposition" but included also some of Stalin's most prominent tools. Tomsky had already been removed, officially by suicide (August, 1936). Now Bukharin and Rykov, who as late as 1934 had been permitted to address a Party Congress, lauding Stalin and admitting their own past errors, and who in 1935-1936 had served as members of a special commission to draft a new constitution, were put through the motions of public confession of sins, this time mortal. They admitted a long record of treason and espionage, of "diversionism" and "wrecking," as well as having plotted the murder of Stalin and his colleagues in the Politburo; the effect was somewhat marred by the attempt of Krestinsky, another of the defendants, to repudiate admissions he had made in private examination, but the following day he publicly retracted his retraction. All three of these former members of the Politburo were shot, along with the rest. Among the lesser lights were Christian Rakovsky, the Bulgarian from Rumania who had become the chief Ukrainian Communist but whose career as an ambassador had been cut short by his support of Trotsky, and Grinko, who after serving as vice-chairman of Gosplan at the time of the drafting of the First F.Y.P. had been promoted to be All-Union People's Commissar of Finance.

Most extraordinary of all the confessions was that of Yagoda, under whose auspices as head of NKVD the "Great Purge" had begun. He now said he had murdered his predecessor, Menzhinsky, and had tried to murder his successor, Yezhov. He accepted responsibility for making possible the murder of Kirov and acknowledged the murders of Gorky and of Kuibyshev, the devoted *apparatchik* whom Stalin had raised to the Politburo in 1927. For good measure he added connivance with foreign spies and described his plans for seizing the Kremlin and murdering all the members of the Politburo.

The show trials, with carefully selected and prepared defendants, accounted for only an infinitesimal fraction of the victims of the Yezhovshchina. Among those liquidated were three other members or former members of the Politburo, all of whom had been known as Stalin stalwarts, as well as additional "candidate" members. Out of 71 members and 68 candidates elected to the Party's Central Committee at the Seventeenth ("victory") Congress in 1934, only 16 members and 8 candidates survived to appear on the list unanimously elected to that body at the Eighteenth Congress in 1939. Prominent government personnel, the diplomatic service, the Comintern, the Komsomol, the trade-union apparatus, and every other potential power center suffered along with the top Party leadership and the high command of the armed forces. As in the days of Ivan the Terrible and his destruction of the boyars, the elimination of each high-placed individual was accompanied by liquidation of his personal following.

Many attempts have been made to explain the success of the show trials. At one extreme, some attribute success in securing public confessions of improbable guilt to advanced techniques of mental torture, of "brainwashing" over a prolonged period. Another explanation offered is that, in their despair at Stalin's total domination, many Old Bolsheviks really were guilty of conspiring against him and, when detected, either hoped to escape execution by coöperative admissions requested by the regime or simply decided that they might as well be hanged for sheep as for lambs, even though they were shot. At the other extreme is the version given by Isaac Steinberg, a Left Socialist Revolutionary who had for a few months, until Brest-Litovsk, served as Commissar of Justice; by reason of his strict Jewish orthodoxy, he was known as "the kosher commissar." Personally knowing the individuals involved and the strength of early Bolshevik fanaticism, he in later years stressed the devotion of men like Bukharin to the cause of the Party and maintained that they had willingly sacrificed themselves to it by helping to strengthen the legend of its "correctness," overriding the significance of any individual. Whether one accepts this thesis, so reminiscent of the story of Boris and Gleb in the early eleventh century, or whether one prefers some other explanation more credible to the Western mind and not involving the concept of a "Russian soul," the fact remains that a handful of prominent Bolshevik "has-beens" of varying shades did lend themselves to Stalin's purposes; whatever the motives that activated the defendants, the trials themselves, at which Vyshinsky, who later wrote *The Law of the Soviet State,* acquired his reputation as a prosecutor, were in the opinion of some eminent Western jurists properly conducted, so far as outward appearances go.

In any case, it must be borne in mind that the overwhelming majority of those liquidated were tried in secret, if, indeed, the process of their condemnation can properly be called trials at all. The parallel to the days of the *oprichnina,* which also had claimed many of its own creators as victims, is very striking. It is not surprising that at this time a new Sovkino film was produced in which Ivan the Terrible was represented as a national hero who had struck down the overweening boyars in the interest of the masses they had been oppressing; the part of Prince Kurbsky, Ivan's chief opponent, was even played by an actor with striking physical resemblance to Trotsky. In addition to the large numbers executed, innumerable lesser folk were sent to prisons or to labor camps. Typical of many proud references in the Soviet press is the incidental smug remark included in a *Pravda* item (March 13, 1937) on the construction of the Moscow-Volga Canal:

> There are engaged on the canal a large number of prisoners who, for the first time, are being brought into contact with labor and are attending a good school of labor reëducation.[15]

The most conservative estimates, which of course cannot be proved, put the number of sufferers at at least seven million, if not double that figure.

Though much remains—and probably will long remain—obscure about the "Great Purge," it is reasonably clear that the whole explanation cannot be assigned to the fact that Stalin was "too rough." This phrase of Lenin's, penned in 1923, was very useful to Stalin's successors when, in the years of jockeying with each other for dominance, they admitted that, along with great services to the Soviet Union, he had been guilty also of grave "errors"; rehabilitation of the reputations of some of the victims of the purge helped to tide over difficulties in the "de-Stalinization" process of 1956. Yet it is fairly obvious that Stalin was not a madman and that it was not only Stalin's personal position that was at stake in the 1930's.

POWER AND PERSONALITIES

The security of the regime itself apparently demanded the utmost "monolithic" character of the power structure. No autocracy can function on the basis of the omniscience and omnipresence of one man; it has to depend on a powerful bureaucracy, constructed of specialized segments, which wield the actual power. If the autocrat has hereditary authority, his servants may dominate him but cannot replace him; but when the power is theoretically "collegial," the danger of a schism in the leadership is ever present. Every personal "empire" built up by a powerful official may be used to rally popular discontents and therefore constitutes a threat to every other segment of the bureaucracy. A split at the top threatens not only the dictator but also all his underlings who are not privy to the "deviation." Since a threat to Stalin was also a threat to most of his associates, he was able to rally even his own enemies, actual or potential, against each other and thus in the end to extirpate them wholesale.

Another, though almost certainly unintentional, factor in the purges was the circumstance that liquidation of so many powerful persons gave opportunity of advancement to younger men, who over the bodies of the fallen were able to climb into otherwise inaccessible positions of power. The ancient sacrificial practice of employing scapegoats made such procedures all the easier. In much the same way as overly enthusiastic subordinates had rushed the collectivization program faster than the top leadership had intended, overly ambitious men found it easy in an atmosphere of fear and tension to denounce trusted men in high places and speed them to destruction. As Zhdanov, himself one of the newly risen, reported at the Eighteenth Party Congress in 1939, "slanderers" and "calumniators" were busily at work.

> Experience has shown that in practice the rights of Party members are often violated. There have been frequent cases of bureaucratic and hostile elements hounding and persecuting members for criticism and self-criticism. . . .
>
> The point must be stressed that mass purges [introduced at the beginning of the New Economic Policy] have played a tremendous part in strengthening the Party [but] the method of the mass purge encourages a formal approach. [It permits] a practice which was widely made use of by careerist elements who had made their way into the Party and who tried to distinguish and advance themselves by expelling people from its ranks, as well as by masked enemies within the Party who endeavored, by the wholesale infliction of penalties, to ruin honest Party members and to sow unnecessary suspicion in the Party ranks. . . .

He cited remarks made by Stalin two years earlier that

> "as the result of such a heartless attitude . . . discontent and bitterness are artificially created in a section of the Party, while the Trotskyite double-dealers adroitly seize hold of such embittered comrades and skillfully drag them after themselves into the morass of Trotskyite wrecking."

Zhdanov himself added arguments against "guilt by association":

> A sort of "biological" approach to people, to Party members, has become quite a widespread practice. This is a theory by which Communists are judged, not by their own deeds, but by the deeds of their relatives, near and distant. [Laughter.] . . . We must stop the practice of halfhearted rehabilitation of reinstated members . . . It is wrong to avenge old faults. . . .

He therefore called for a change in the rules to guarantee "an attentive and careful investigation of accusations brought against Party members" in order to "protect the rights of Party members from all arbitrary procedures." [16]

On this note Stalin (of whom Ambassador Davies wrote, "His brown eye is exceedingly kind and gentle. A child would like to sit in his lap and a dog would sidle up to him") [17] called a halt to the purges. In July, 1938, Lavrenty Beria, who had spent ten years (1921-31) as a Chekist and GPU official before he was transferred to Party work, was appointed deputy to Yezhov and took over real control of the NKVD. In December, Beria was formally appointed commissar, and Yezhov soon disappeared without a trace other than another entry on the list of victims of the Yezhovshchina. Before the

"Great Purge" was over, the NKVD itself underwent a vigorous mopping-up, while thousands of its prisoners were released. The speed with which Stalin thus went into reverse was almost more breathtaking than the energy with which the purge had been undertaken. There could be no doubt of its thoroughness. Not only were all positions of trust held by men of his own making; very few of them were men who had joined the Party before 1917.

Among Stalin's eight colleagues in the Politburo were three—Molotov, Voroshilov, and Kalinin—whom Stalin had named to it in 1925. Molotov's whole career was as one of his master's *apparatchiki;* the post of chairman of the Council of People's Commissars, which he had held since 1930, was recognized as that of chief clerk. As Kaganovich had put it on Rykov's removal,

> Can we . . . be satisfied with a Sovnarkom chairman who says that he executes the general line of the Party "as much and as best he can"? We cannot permit the slightest shade of doubt, the slightest cleavage between the Party and the Soviet organs.[18]

Voroshilov was a former tsarist noncommissioned officer who found a marshal's baton in his knapsack. Associated with Stalin in the defense of Tsaritsyn against Krasnov, he had in 1925 been given Trotsky's old office as War Commissar. In that post he had loyally followed all the shifts of policy desired by Stalin; initially he had coöperated in curbing the authority of the political commissars, who had tended to support Trotsky; when in 1937 Marshal Tukhachevsky and so many other high professional officers had been struck down, Voroshilov had readily accepted restoration of the powers of the political commissars, destroying the principle of unity of command by officers. Kalinin had never been more than a symbol of peasant fidelity to Bolshevism. Not one of the three had ever showed signs of independence, either of thought or of action.

Of the seven men added to the Politburo prior to the purge, Kirov had been murdered; according to Yagoda's testimony, Kuibyshev had also been murdered; Ordzhonikidze had died, officially of heart disease, though here, too, murder was suspected; Rudzutak and Kossior had vanished in the purge. Only two survived—Kaganovich and Andreiev. Kaganovich, long an *apparatchik,* had earned the reputation of being Stalin's most efficient and reliable trouble-shooter. As general secretary of the Ukrainian Communist Party, he had repressed Ukrainian efforts to assert themselves against the Muscovites and had pushed the construction of Dnieprostroi; he had been head of the Moscow Party organization (1930-1935) and was responsible for construction of the famous subway; since then he had been striving to bring order into the railway administration, save for an interval when he replaced Ordzhonikidze as Commissar of Heavy Industry. No one could possibly doubt his absolute personal loyalty to Stalin. Andreiev, also an *apparatchik,* had as chairman of the Railway Workers' Union long since erased the stain of his support to Trotsky and Bukharin in the early stages of the trade-union conflict. Since 1930 he had been chairman of the Party Control Commission, a position in which he could be very useful to Stalin without much possibility of personal "empire-building."

Of the two men added to the Politburo shortly after the murder of Kirov, one, Chubar, had disappeared. Mikoyan, an Armenian who had been active at Baku in 1917 and who during the civil wars had been engaged in revolutionary work in the Caucasus, remained. An *apparatchik* for a time, Mikoyan had since 1926 been successively People's Commissar of Trade, of Supplies, and of the Food Industry. Adroit enough not to become involved in political alignments, he had established his ascendancy as a loyal expert in all matters concerned with trade, foreign and domestic.

The other two members of the Politburo—Zhdanov and Khrushchev—were newcomers in 1939. Zhdanov seemed a typical *apparatchik,* enjoying Stalin's special confidence; he had been assigned to replace Kirov in Leningrad. On the Politburo his main assignment was to reorganize the Party Secretariat in the light of conditions at the time the purge was ended. Khrushchev, a former coal miner, had joined the Party in 1918 and had acquired an elementary education with the aid of a "workers' faculty" (*rabfak*); in 1929 he had entered the Industrial Academy to be trained as an executive. Yet he had remained in service as a Party *apparatchik.* In 1934 Kaganovich chose Khrushchev as his assistant; in 1935 he succeeded his patron as head of the Moscow Party organization. In 1938 he was transferred to the troublesome Ukraine in a similar capacity.

One other, also a Stalin man, was assigned to the Politburo, though only as a "candidate" member. This was Shvernik, who had in 1930 been appointed to redeem the trade unions from the false path on which Tomsky had been leading them; his subservience as head of this potentially dangerous power center qualified him later to succeed Kalinin as titular head of the state (1946). The head of the other power center, the NKVD, was not even a candidate member of the Politburo. In this respect, Beria was no exception to the customary rule. Indeed, the record of his predecessors in charge of the political police did not indicate any danger to the regime from this quarter: Dzerzhinsky, a fanatically idealist Pole, had headed the Cheka, the GPU, and OGPU from 1917 to his death in 1926, without ever challenging the Party leadership; Menzhinsky, who had served from 1926 to 1934, had never been a prominent figure; Yagoda (1934-36) and Yezhov (1936-38) had both themselves succumbed in the purge.

Among those on the fringes of power were two who were soon to move into the inner circle. One was a young *apparatchik,* Malenkov, who had joined the Party only in 1920 and had become one of Stalin's personal secretaries in 1925; since 1930 he had held responsible positions, first in the Moscow apparatus and since 1934 in the Secretariat of the Central Committee; in 1939 he was promoted to be one of the Secretaries, still with special responsibility for selection of personnel; only in 1941 was he made a candidate member of the Politburo. Considerably more in the shadow was Bulganin, who had joined the Party in 1917 and become a Chekist; since 1922 he had shown great ability in economic administration and in 1938 had been made chairman of Gosbank.

Such were the chief figures who surrounded "the great Stalin" on his lonely eminence when the purge had done its work. Most of them were to survive their chieftain and engage in a prolonged broil over the succession after 1953. It was a phenomenon sufficiently familiar in Russian history.

NOTES

1. Baykov, *Development of the Soviet Economic System,* p. 367.
2. *Narodno-khoziaistvennyi plan za 1937 g.,* p. 15.
3. *Za industrializatsiiu,* April 29, 1937.
4. *Kommunisticheskaia Partiia Sovetskogo Soiuza v rezoliutsiiakh . . . ,* III, 355, 361.
5. *Za industrializatsiiu,* June 30, 1936.
6. *Pravda,* June 20, 1936.
7. Molotov, *What Is Stakhanovism?* (speech at First All-Union Conference of Stakhanovites, November 16, 1935), pp. 21-22.
8. Decree of Council of People's Commissars (August 29, 1938), in *Sobranie postanovlenii i rasporiazhenii pravitel'stva SSSR,* 1938, No. 39 (September 9, 1938), # 229 (4).
9. Decree of Presidium of Supreme Council (December 27, 1938), in *Sbornik zakonodatel'nykh aktov o trude,* 2nd edition, p. 338.
10. Decree of Council of People's Commissars (January 4, 1939), in *Sobranie postanovlenii . . . , loc. cit.,* 1939, No. 1 (January 7, 1939), # 1.
11. Decree of Council of People's Commissars (August 29, 1938), *loc. cit.,* # 8, p. 537.
12. Stalin, *Sochineniia,* XIII, 348.
13. *History of the Communist Party of the Soviet Union (Bolsheviks), Short Course,* 1952 edition, p. 498.
14. *Pravda,* June 12, 1937.
15. *Ibid.,* March 13, 1937.
16. Zhdanov, *The Communist Party of the Soviet Union,* pp. 19-35 *passim.*
17. Davies, *Mission to Moscow,* p. 357.
18. *Pravda,* December 30, 1930.

SUGGESTIONS FOR FURTHER READING

Among books previously mentioned, Baykov is still valuable on economic phenomena. The four books by Hubbard, though not perfectly accurate in detail, are much easier reading and are very useful surveys. A good introduction is Nove's

The Soviet Economy, which treats structure, theory, and practice. Particularly good special studies are: Bienstock, Schwarz, and Yugow, *Management in Russian Industry and Agriculture*; Brutzkus, *Economic Planning in Soviet Russia*; Bergson, *Structure of Soviet Wages*; and Spulber, *Soviet Strategy for Economic Growth.* See also Nutter's *Growth of Industrial Production in the Soviet Union.*

On labor, in contrast to Molotov's pamphlet *What Is Stakhanovism?,* see Gordon's *Workers Before and After Lenin,* an embittered study by an émigré socialist; a very competent more recent study is S. M. Schwarz, *Labor in the Soviet Union.* Deutscher, *Soviet Trade Unions,* and Dallin and Nikolaievsky, *Forced Labor in Soviet Russia,* are somewhat less impartial.

On the "Great Purge," Fainsod, already mentioned, is by far the most reliable. An interesting contemporary critique is Sir J. Maynard's article, "Light on the Trotskyist Trials." A study of the whole problem is Brzezinski, *The Permanent Purge.* A refutation of the charges, with special reference to Trotsky, is *Not Guilty,* published by an American "Commission of Inquiry into the Charges Made Against Leon Trotsky in the Moscow Trials." Trotsky's own *The Revolution Betrayed* should also be consulted. Deutscher's *The Prophet Outcast* portrays Trotsky in exile.

Works by refugees and by disillusioned Communists or fellow-travelers are numerous and of very uneven value. Particular mention may be made of André Gide's *Return from the U.S.S.R.* and his *Afterthoughts,* as well as of Arthur Koestler's grimly amusing *The Yogi and the Commissar.*

Chapter

32

"Democracy" and Nationalism: 1934-1941

In politics as in economics, Stalin strove for a judicious admixture of encouragement in the midst of a policy of terror. One of his devices to make the population feel closer to its rulers and to give the people a more active sense of participation was the new Constitution of 1936, "the most democratic in the world." It is true that a powerful reason behind the political remodeling of the regime was considerations of foreign policy. At a time when the Soviet Union had lost her basic friendly relations with Germany and was wooing the United States and the former Entente Powers, the Bolsheviks could not well continue to flaunt the superiority of the soviet system over "bourgeois democracy." It seemed expedient now to develop the thesis that there was an impending world struggle to the death between "fascism" and "democracy." Russia must align herself with democracy, even in forms she had previously flouted, and must prove to the peoples who controlled their own governments that the Soviet Union was at least as "democratic" as any bourgeois state. Both at home and abroad there was everything to gain from a change of façade, and nothing to lose so long as the building itself was not altered.

THE STALIN CONSTITUTION

On the surface, the "Stalin Constitution" seemed to betoken a change of tremendous importance, and great precautions were taken to make it seem genuine. On February 6, 1935, two months after the murder of Kirov but before the "Great Purge" was undertaken, a decree of the Seventh Congress of Soviets set up a Constitutional Commission to revise the 1924 Constitution. The instructions to the Commission were interpreted as meaning "taking into account the progress in the life of the U.S.S.R. in the direction of socialism made in the period from 1924 to our days." [1] It is worth noting that this action was taken by the regular governmental machinery, on the proposal of Molotov, chairman of Sovnarkom (i.e., prime minister); Molotov, in his turn, was of course acting on instructions given him a few days earlier by the Central Committee of the Party. Lest there be suspicion that criticism of the Party was involved, Stalin, not then holding a government post, himself accepted the chairmanship of the Commission; as window dressing, Bukharin and Rykov, though not Zinoviev or Kamenev, were also among its members.

Preparation of the draft of the new Constitution was allowed to take almost a year and a half. On June 1, 1936, the draft was approved by the Party Central Committee. It was published on June 12, and with great fanfare all citizens of the Soviet Union were invited to discuss it and to propose modifications. During the time when, as Vyshinsky said, "The draft was read with delight and discussed in all the industrial and transport enterprises, in sovkhozes and kolkhozes, and in government offices," [2] the first great "show trial"—that of Zinoviev and Kamenev—was taking place (August, 1936). A considerable number of amendments were actually suggested. The Constitutional Commission, to which they were referred for study, found that almost all of them were recommendations for legislation, unsuitable in a constitution, or involved merely editorial changes of wording; only eight, two of which Stalin endorsed, were thought worthy of being specifically reported.

The principal change made by the new Constitution was introduction of the democratic principle, which had played so large a role in the Revolution, of election of the supreme legislative body by direct, equal, universal, and secret suffrage. The old Congress of Soviets and its bicameral Central Executive Committee were telescoped into a new bicameral Supreme Council (*Verkhovny Soviet*). The hierarchy of local soviets and congresses of soviets, through which by indirect election at several stages the members of the old All-Union Congress of Soviets had been sifted, retained only the subordinate functions of local administration. Henceforth, every citizen of the Soviet Union, deemed adult at eighteen, was to vote directly for his or her representative in the Supreme Council. There were no longer to be any disfranchised categories, except "the insane and persons sentenced by a court to deprivation of their electoral rights" (Article 135). Nor was there to be any further weighting of urban votes. In addition, balloting was for the first time to be secret. On this basis must rest the proud boast that the "Stalin Constitution" was "the most democratic in the whole world."

There was a joker. Article 141 provided:

> The right to nominate candidates is secured to public organizations and societies of toilers: Communist Party organizations, trade unions, coöperatives, youth organizations, cultural societies.

Fully to appreciate this article, it must be read in conjunction with Article 126:

> In consonance with the interests of the toilers and with the aim of developing organized spontaneous action and political activity of the masses of the people, the citizens of the U.S.S.R. are guaranteed the right of uniting in public organizations: trade unions, coöperative societies, youth organizations, sport and defense organizations, cultural, technical, and scientific societies, while the most active and conscious citizens from the ranks of the working class and other strata of the toilers are united into the All-Union Communist Party (of the Bolsheviks), which is the vanguard of the toilers in their fight to strengthen and develop the socialist structure and which represents the directing kernel of all organizations of the toilers, both public and state.

What the Constitution provided for was democratic election of candidates nominated by organizations in which the Communist Party was "the directing kernel." Stalin made no bones about the meaning of "democracy" under the new Constitution:

> I must admit that the draft of the new Constitution actually leaves in force the regime of the dictatorship of the working class, just as it leaves unchanged the present guiding position of the Communist Party of the U.S.S.R. If our respected critics think this a fault of the draft of the Constitution, then we can only regret it. We Bolsheviks think it a merit of the draft of the Constitution.[3]

At the Extraordinary Eighth Congress of Soviets, which unanimously adopted the new Constitution, Stalin made a long report explaining its significance. This speech is well worth careful reading. In his customary way, with apparent homespun frankness and with subtle illogic, he stressed that the draft was not a blueprint for the future but a record of what had actually been accomplished since 1924. He sketched

> the first period of the NEP, when the Soviet authority permitted a certain revival of capitalism along with the general development of socialism, [when] our industry . . . especially heavy industry . . . had not nearly attained the production of the prewar level [and] was based on old, obsolete, poor technique, [and when] agriculture . . . resembled an immense ocean of petty individual peasant economies with their obsolete medieval technique.

With this "unenviable" picture he contrasted

> industry . . . grown to giant strength . . . based on a new, rich, modern technique with a strongly developed heavy industry and still more developed machine construction [and] the largest mechanized agriculture in the world in the form of an all-embracing system of collective and state farms.

"This means," said Stalin, "that the exploitation of man by man has been abolished, liquidated, and socialist property in the implements and means of production has been established as the unshakeable foundation of our Soviet society." True, the Soviet Union had "not yet attained realization of the higher phase of communism, in which the prevailing principle will be the formula: 'from each according to his abilities, to each according to his needs,' though it aims at future realization of this higher phase of communism." [4] In the meantime, since the Constitution should only mirror existing reality, and since in the Soviet Union reality was socialism, not communism, it was correct to include in Article 12, along with the principle that "he who does not work, does not eat," formulation of "the principle of socialism: 'from each according to his abilities, to each according to his toil.' " It was also in order quietly to drop the old preliminary manifesto, derived from the 1918 "Declaration of the Rights of Toiling and Exploited Peoples," which had in 1923 been thought necessary to explain the formation of the U.S.S.R.

The change in Soviet economics, argued Stalin, had changed its class structure, eliminating all exploiting classes. "There has remained the working class"; freed from exploitation, it was no longer a proletariat (hence Stalin's careful substitution of the phrase "dictatorship of the working class" for the classic "dictatorship of the proletariat"); it was "an absolutely new class." "There has remained the peasant class," also no longer subjected to exploitation, but "an absolutely new peasantry, the like of which the history of mankind has never known." Finally, "There has remained the intelligentsia," which of course cannot itself be a class, but "80-90 percent" of which "has sprung from the working class, the peasantry, and other strata [not "classes"] of the toilers." The intelligentsia "formerly had to serve the wealthy classes. . . . Now it has to serve the people," for it is "an entirely new toiling intelligentsia, the like of which you will not find in any land on the face of the globe."

On the basis of this class analysis, Stalin argued that for the Constitution to have permitted freedom of action for political parties would have been an empty gesture, for parties are merely reflections of the class struggle. They exist to advance the interests of the classes of which they are part against those of other, hostile, classes. In the Soviet Union, as flatly stated in Article 1 of the Constitution, there were only two classes, workers and peasants, and they were mutually friendly. Thus there was no basis in fact for the existence in the Soviet Union of more than one party; the Constitution merely recorded, but did not create, the fact.

In other respects the Stalin Constitution of 1936 did not differ essentially from the original U.S.S.R. constitution of 1924. The Soviet Union remained federal in form, the new Constitution even mentioning the right of free secession; in fact it remained highly centralized, with the new Supreme Council as "the highest organ of state power of the U.S.S.R." (Article 57). Like the old Central Executive Committee, the Supreme Council was made bicameral, consisting of a Council of the Union and a Council of Nationalities; one of the two amendments accepted by Stalin provided that the numbers be equal in both chambers, the other that the upper as well as the lower chamber be directly elected. Executive authority remained, as in 1924, shared at three levels, headed by the All-Union Council of People's Commissars. The theory of parliamentary responsibility of the executive to the legislature was retained. Judges were declared "independent and subject only to the law" (Article 112).

Chapter X, consisting of sixteen articles, defined both the fundamental rights (11 articles) and the fundamental duties (5 articles) of the citizens. The former included: the "right to labor"; the "right to leisure"; the "right to material security in old age and also in case of illness and of loss of ability to work"; the "right to education"; equality of rights irrespective of sex, nationality, or race; "freedom of conscience," with freedom both for performance of religious rites and for anti-religious propaganda; "freedom of speech, freedom of press, freedom of assembly and meetings, freedom of street parades and demonstrations"; the "right of uniting in public organizations" (an exception was made for the Communist Party, which was declared open only to "the most active and conscious citizens from the ranks of the working class and other strata of the toilers"); "inviolability of the person" and of the domicile; "secrecy of correspondence"; and the "right of asylum for foreign citizens persecuted for defending the interests of toilers, for scientific activity, or for fighting for national emancipation." Duties included obedience to the law, preservation of labor discipline, protection of socialist property, and, as especially "honorable," universal military service.

For each of the enumerated rights, the Constitution indicated the "guarantee," but in no one case did it pretend that constitutional rights were enforceable in the courts. As Stalin emphasized, implementation of these rights was a matter for ordinary legislation. So far as the Party did not cause appropriate legislation to be enacted, these rights remained on paper; in any case, even legislated rights could be constricted or abolished by further legislation, which could be adopted at the whim of the Party either by Sovnarkom or by the Presidium of the Soviet, without bothering to convene the official legislature.

According to the Constitution, the "right to labor" required no legislation; beyond abolition of unemployment relief, it was further

> guaranteed by the socialist organization of the people's economy, by the inflexible growth of the productive forces of Soviet society, by the removal of the possibility of economic crises, and by the liquidation of unemployment [Article 118].

The "right to leisure" and the "right to material security" in specified circumstances clearly required legislation, which, as indicated in the preceding chapter, was soon restricted to apply only to those who had served a particular enterprise for a stated number of years. The "right to education" was also hemmed about with limitations, to which further reference will presently be made. The rights accorded to women, equally with men, were guaranteed by equal wage scales, dependent, however, on official evaluation of skill, and by other provisions, including "a broad network of lying-in hospitals, crèches, and kindergartens," dependent on fluctuating appropriations but in which women would at least enjoy "equal rights with men" (Article 122). The equal rights of sundry ethnic groups were protected by condemnation of "any propaganda of racial or national exclusiveness" (Article 123); as things turned out, enforcement was for the most part directed against subject nationalities, especially the Ukrainians, that evinced improper consciousness of difference from and distrust of Great Russians.

Even before adoption of the draft, *Pravda* had, in a series of leading articles, undertaken to extol and explain the special virtues of the civil liberties guaranteed by the Constitution. For example, freedom of speech and of the press differed from their bourgeois counterparts in that the Soviet Union put halls, streets, printing presses, and supplies of paper (all mentioned in Article 125 as "guarantees") freely at the disposition of all citizens. *Pravda's* two-column account concluded, however, with a frank warning:

> He who makes it his task to unsettle the socialist structure, to undermine socialist ownership, who would meditate an attempt on the inviolability of our native country—he is an enemy of the people. He gets not a scrap of paper, he does not set foot over the threshold of the printing press, to realize his base designs. He gets no hall, no room, no cover to inject poison by word of mouth.[5]

How valueless were the constitutional "guarantees" of freedom from arrest and of domiciliary inviolability without a proper warrant was soon made abundantly clear by the "Yezhovshchina."

The aspect of the new "democracy" that most troubled the rulers was the provision for nomination of candidates for the Supreme Council. If anything should go wrong there, the dictatorship of the Party would be jeopardized. The danger was not so much that the population at large might be able to assert its wishes as that "empire-builders" within the Party in the "public organizations and societies of toilers," of which the Party was constitutionally the "directing kernel," might challenge the wishes of the inner circle. This peril was not, of course, great during the Yezhovshchina.

Yet it was thought expedient to prepare for the first election by intensive house-cleaning in accordance with the principle of "intra-Party democracy." It was emphasized that too many of the local Party organizations, to which the right of nominating candidates was officially entrusted, had not been elected in proper form; in many cases, it was said, local organizations had been coöpting new committee members; such organized provinces readily lent themselves to the purposes of larger-scale "empire-builders." Now the rank and file of the Party must be given the opportunity, and by secret ballot, to choose their own local leadership. It soon became apparent that some local Party organizations were misinterpreting this freedom. *Pravda* had to launch a fresh campaign against the "False Concept of Democracy":

> As is well-known, at the time of the electoral assemblies in the primary organizations many Party leaders refrained from guiding the elections and left matters to take their own course. . . . Instead of recommending and actively defending Communists worthy of being elected to Party organs, many Party leaders prefer to preserve at conferences a cowardly neutrality. Such conduct has nothing in common with Bolshevism. Such conduct attests misunderstanding of Party democracy. Abstention from leadership in elections may result in accidental, untested people getting into the Party organs. The task of the Party leader is to assist the assembly or conference to select and to elect by secret ballot the most worthy Communists, those most devoted to the Central Committee.[6]

The mystery of how the centrally appointed Party secretary could influence a secret ballot of the rank and file disappears when it is realized that nominations must be made openly; it would be an inefficient *apparatchik* indeed who could not prevent the names of Tom, Dick, and Harry from being voted on. Thus the old Leninist principle of "democratic centralism" was reinforced. Similar house-cleaning, on identical principles, was put in practice in the trade unions, the coöperatives, the Komsomol, and the "cultural societies." Since failure to cast a ballot in the subsequent "popular election" would be obvious disloyalty, there has never been any difficulty in securing almost 100 percent attendance at the polls; since the officially chosen candidate is the only name on the ballot, the results of "democratic" voting have necessarily been extremely satisfactory to the rulers, while giving the ruled some illusion of determining policy.

As *Pravda* had phrased it on the eve of adoption of the Stalin Constitution,

> The Bolshevist Party has uninterruptedly allied itself with the people, has forever won their love, confidence, and respect. . . . The growing activity of the masses of the people, the introduction of the Stalin Constitution . . . undoubtedly augments the guiding role of the Bolshevist Party. Only a hopeless idiot or a conscious foe of socialism can talk about weakening or diminishing in the new setting the vanguard role of the Party. . . . There is required the most merciless punishment of all the foes of socialist society. . . . Unfailing solicitude for the purity of the Party ranks and for the elevation of the role of the Communist as leader of the toilers is [required]. . . . Monolithic, compact, our Party marches under the leadership of its Central Committee, of the great Stalin. . . .[7]

The image of Lenin, whether bust or picture, remained everywhere on display; his mummy continued to draw huge crowds waiting to file through the mausoleum in the Red Square; his words were still gospel. Yet it was the living figure of Stalin, always scrupulously modest but never shrinking, that naturally loomed largest in Soviet consciousness. Much as he remained ostentatiously in seclusion, his name was constantly in the public press; though he eschewed public office, his appearance on all public occasions was greeted with loud and prolonged "Hails" to the "Leader" (*vozhd*). He was given credit for every desirable result, from extraordinary litters produced by a sow on a collective farm to the most recondite scientific or intellectual achievement. Nothing could be hoped for without the collaboration of the "little father"; nothing was impossible to which he set his mind. The devotion once evoked in the Western world by such magic names as Charlemagne or Frederick Barbarossa was as nothing compared to the abject servility with which the name of Stalin was always, at least officially, greeted. Twenty years later, it is hard to reconstruct the power, for good or for evil, that name commanded; in 1956, in Riga, it was startling to hear Stalin dismissed as merely *"ein böser Mensch"* by a man to whom, incidentally, the name of Khrushchev meant *"Dreck."* In the 1930's, however, the *"cult of the individual,"* as it was later disparagingly called, was in full swing.

THE NATIONALITIES

With the personal adoration Stalin was accorded was coming to be associated the full force of Russian national pride. Explanation of this phenomenon requires a considerable excursus. Stalin himself was not a Russian; his ethnic origin was even more remote from that of the Slavs than had been that of Rurik and his fellow Varangians. Iosif Dzhugashvili was a Georgian, and the Georgians were one of the proudest and most independent peoples of the Transcaucasus. Largely for this very reason, Stalin's official assignment after the seizure of power in 1917 had been as Commissar of Nationalities. In this capacity it was his duty to encourage nationalist sentiments among subject peoples, to direct them against survivals of the imperial regime, and thus to bind them firmly to the internationalist Bolshevik chariot. Non-Russian peoples had indeed played a very important part in the civil wars. It was largely with the aid of Latvian detachments that the uprising of the Left SR's in Moscow had been quelled in 1918. The "White" armies had, by force of circumstances, in the main operated in non-Russian or mixed areas; unable in the minds of their own leaders to substitute the concept of a federal Russian state for that of "Russia great and undivided," they had not only failed to win the coöperation of the subject nationalities but had been hamstrung by the active resistance of the peoples in whose territories their forces were based.

The aspirations of the subject peoples were not all of the same nature. The Ukrainians, who constituted almost one-fifth of the population of the old Russian Empire, were naturally the most powerful. They were, however, Slavs and Orthodox. Although Ukrainian intellectuals resented the ascendancy of what they regarded as upstart Muscovites, the Ukrainian movement was essentially one of the peasantry, dwelling in the most fertile part of

Russia and disliking urban exploitation of their labor; in some parts of the Ukraine the cossack tradition remained strong, and the Ukrainians found it difficult to coöperate with immigrant Great Russian workers. The Ukraine had therefore early split off from Bolshevik Russia and made a separate, though disillusioning, peace with Germany. The national sentiment of "White Russians" (Byelorussians) was much weaker than that of the "Little Russians," and the ethnic composition of their area, poverty-stricken by nature, was very confused, with a large admixture of Poles, Lithuanians, Jews, and Great Russians. Both the Ukraine and White Russia had been resubjugated by Moscow during the civil wars.

In the Baltic provinces, on the other hand, the native and non-Slavic population of Letts, Lithuanians, and Estonians included a large proportion of industrial workers. The German middle class there had welcomed the opportunity of securing independence from their Russian overlords, but the proletariat and peasantry, hating the local German bourgeoisie as much as they did the Russian or Russified landlords, had tended to coöperate heartily with the Bolsheviks. Only German military power had confirmed the independence of the new Baltic states and made it possible for them to continue, under middle-class rule, even after Allied victory. Finland was a special case. Long accustomed to enjoy autonomy as a separate grand duchy under the Russian emperors, she had most easily, though also not without German assistance, won her national independence.

In the Transcaucasus also, the warring nationalist movements had been of fairly conventional type. None of them sought independence from Russia, strongly preferring federal union with her. Georgia gave the Bolsheviks Dzhugashvili (Stalin) and Ordzhonikidze, but she gave the Mensheviks Chkheidze and Tsereteli; it was the Mensheviks who ultimately made Tiflis and Batum their stronghold. The Armenians, many of whom still lived under Turkish rule, were in a most difficult position. The swing of the Armenian nationalist "Dashnak" organization to loyal support of tsarist Russia in the war had provoked a fresh Turkish massacre of Armenians (1915); the collapse of the Russian army on the Caucasus front after the Bolshevik seizure of power and the Brest-Litovsk surrender to Turkey of most of the territory Russia had acquired in 1877-78 forced the Armenians to join the reluctant Georgians in proclaiming the independence of a short-lived Transcaucasian Federative Republic (April 22, 1918) and to compromise with the victorious Turks. Almost immediately (May 26) the federation broke up into its three constituent parts, of which Georgia had the happiest and most democratic existence. The third element, centering in Baku, was that of the Moslem Azerbaijani Turco-Tatars. Even before the war, their principal organization, the *Mussavat,* had sought aid from Constantinople against the "Asiatic bear." They had often engaged in bloody struggles with the Armenians, who were predominantly middle-class. A Bolshevik-dominated Soviet (March-June, 1918) and a brief Turkish occupation (September-November), attended by fresh pogroms against Armenians, had disillusioned the Azerbaijanis of hope of real sympathy from either of these potential friends; British occupation (November, 1918–August, 1919) was unable to restore the oil industry, on which the life of Baku depended, and the situation in Azerbaijan remained very troubled.

The way to restoration of Russian power in the Transcaucasus had been opened by an agreement with Mustapha Kemal, dictator of the new Turkey, who was having difficulties with the Entente Powers similar to those of Soviet Russia. In 1920-21 the whole of the Transcaucasus was brought under Bolshevik military control, though the process was interrupted by Bolshevik preoccupation with the Polish war. Under the guidance of Ordzhonikidze and Kirov, a coup admitted the Red Army to Baku (April 28, 1920); Armenia was overrun in December; Tiflis fell (February 25, 1921) after a heroic defense; despite Turkish intervention, Batum also was soon in Russian hands.

In the North Caucasus, along the Volga, in the southern Urals, and in the steppes of Central Asia, the pattern was quite different. Here the native populations were mainly various admixtures of Turco-Tatar and Mongol stock, with some Finnish survivals. Divided into many ethnic groupings, their chief bond of unity was their common profession of the Moslem faith. The efforts of the largely Westernized Kazan Tatars to put themselves at the head of a Moslem "nationality" were defeated by the need, if such a modern concept were to take hold, fundamentally to alter the habits of thought and ways of life of their fellow Moslems. Most of the Moslem peoples of Russia were still predominantly nomadic, and their nationalism took the largely negative form of opposing invasion of their lands by Russian and Cossack settlers. In 1916 an attempt to draft the Kirghiz for noncombatant service had set off a major rebellion; in one province four-fifths of the innocent settlers were wiped out; the uprising was suppressed only by expulsion of some 300,000 nomads. When in the summer of 1917 the Provisional Government had allowed their return, the Russian settlers had taken matters into their own hands and slaughtered an estimated 83,000 of the returning refugees, even roasting some of them alive. To the Moslem nomads, political coloration made little difference; Russians were enemies whether tsarist, "White," or "Red."

The Bolsheviks, in the steppe as everywhere else, found their main following among the garrisons, but necessarily attracted also much support among the settlers. Soviet-sponsored "Moslem Congresses" were therefore ineffective, and the eastern and southern borderlands for a time passed out of Russian control as completely as those surrendered by the Treaty of Brest-Litovsk or occupied by the Japanese. The Bolsheviks were compelled to abandon their encouragement of a Pan-Islamic movement, even in the shape of a Moslem Communist Party, and to reorganize their efforts in the name of an appeal to the "Peoples of the East." They resorted to dealing, or doubledealing, separately with the Bashkirs, the Kazan Tatars, the Kirghiz, Turkmen, and Uzbeks. In each case, by temporary concession to some elements and by officially setting up "republics" federated within the R.S.F.S.R., the Red Army was by 1920 able to bring the whole area back under Russian control.

Similarly, the Crimean Tatars were reduced and incorporated into the Ukraine. Only slightly different was the story in the North Caucasus. Here there was a three-cornered struggle among the old-established and relatively well-to-do Terek Cossacks, the motley and fiercely resentful "native" populations, mainly Moslem, and immigrant settlers, mainly Russians, who here, however, were chiefly urban workers, not farmers. The shifting division of forces made it fairly simple for the Bolsheviks to establish their authority in Vladikavkaz, even as early as 1918, and to maintain it with the aid of poverty-stricken Moslem mountaineers.

The Bolshevik attitude toward the subject nationalities had originally been based on Western Marxist concepts. Emphasizing the class struggle, they had thought of "national culture" as a figment of bourgeois propagandists, invented to obscure real, fundamental issues. In 1913, however, while an exile in Galicia, Lenin had become much interested in the ideas of Austrian socialists about nonterritorial cultural autonomy. Unable to deny that in Austria-Hungary nationalism was a grave stumbling block to socialist organization, Lenin had gradually arrived at his own theory of national self-determination. The SR's had early (1905) endorsed the principle of federalism, and even the Mensheviks were working toward acceptance in 1917 of the principle of national cultural autonomy as a solution for the problem of nationality. Lenin's idea was quite different. Continuing to believe that nationalism was merely a temporary phenomenon, a by-product of capitalism, he regarded the demand for self-determination as merely a weapon against the Russian Empire, a means of achieving that universal rule of the proletariat that would facilitate the voluntary assimilation of all minor groups into a materially more advantageous unity in the form of a Russian national state, with a single language and a single culture. The future "Left Communists," led by Bukharin and Radek, had vigorously attacked what they called Lenin's attempt to "turn back the wheel of history";[8] the "Forward" (*Vpered*) group, led by Pokrovsky and Lunacharsky, and many, if not most, other Bolsheviks also resisted their leader, just as the majority of the Party was at first to refuse to accept his "April Theses."

Nevertheless, the obvious realism of Lenin's new view of self-determination as a right won it application in the course of 1917 in a considerable number of instances; in particular, it aided in neutralizing the Ukrainian Rada at the moment of the seizure of power. Once in power, the Bolshevik position on the nationalities question had changed as quickly as had all other facets of their program. The Commissar of Nationalities, Stalin, announced (December 12, 1917) the new regime's willingness to recognize the independence of any subject nationality "if the toiling population of the region desires it." [9] In January, 1918, he affirmed:

> All this points to the necessity of interpreting the principle of self-determination as the right to self-determination, not of the bourgeoisie, but of the toiling masses of the given nation. The principle of self-determination must be a means of fighting for socialism and must be subordinated to the principles of socialism.[10]

Although this contradicted Lenin's earlier emphasis on voluntary assimilation of national minorities, it seems probable that the usually silent Stalin was not speaking out of tune with his master's voice. Although Lenin later rebuked Bukharin for applauding Stalin and for trying to formulate a pat distinction between "advanced" nations entitled to "self-determination of the working classes" and backward areas entitled to "national self-determination," [11] the resolution proposed by Lenin at the Eighth Party Congress (March, 1919) was not essentially different. Asserting that every nation must have full rights, including that of secession, and proposing as a "transitional form on the way to full unity . . . a federal union of states, organized on the soviet pattern" (#3), Lenin's resolution stated:

> 4. As to the question who is the carrier of the nation's will to separation, the Russian Communist Party stands on the historico-class point of view, taking into consideration the level of historical development on which a given nation stands: on the road from the Middle Ages to bourgeois democracy, or from bourgeois democracy to Soviet or proletarian democracy, and so forth.[12]

With the subject nationalities, as with Great Russians, Lenin firmly believed in holding a bunch of carrots in front of the donkey's nose in order to make the beast move in the direction he desired. His studies in Austria had convinced him that, with such stubborn animals as national minorities, beating with a stick was of little use. He was therefore seriously worried by the arbitrary way in which Ordzhonikidze overrode the local Communists in Georgia but, due to his illness, was unable to intervene effectively. The further development of Soviet nationality policy remained in the hands of his faithful but "rough" disciple, Stalin. The legal formation of the Soviet Union, begun in 1922, served the double purpose of creating in the outside world the impression that Russia was no longer dominant over the other members and of promoting at home the illusion that each nationality was now self-governing, if not as one of the six sovereign "union-republics," at least as an "autonomous" republic or region within one of them. Further to emphasize this theory, some of the "autonomous republics" in Turkestan were in 1925 detached from the R.S.F.S.R. and reorganized as the independent Turkmen and Uzbek "union republics." A Tadzhik Socialist Soviet Republic was created in 1929, and Kazakh and Kirghiz S.S.R.'s in 1936, bringing the total of "union republics" to eleven (five of them in Central Asia and three in the Transcaucasus).*

* See the map on the inside rear cover.

This apparent decentralization on federal principles was wholly illusory. The real power in the Soviet Union lay in the Communist Party. Although its name was changed in 1925 from "All-Russian" to "All-Union," its unified and centralized structure was not affected. The various "national" Communist Parties were, under the Party statutes, on the same footing as any regional committee; in other words, they were completely subordinate to the authority of the Central Committee and its Politburo. The preponderance of Great Russians in the Party (over 70% of its members, though they constituted little over 50% of the population) was a source of some worry; Lenin, perhaps not unconscious of his own profound conviction of the superiority of Russian culture, had more than once warned against the dangers of "Great Russian chauvinism." Yet continued efforts to recruit an adequate proportion of "natives" into the Party, even at the price of raising the proportion of illiterates, had failed. In Central Asia, and particularly in the Ukraine, the proportion of "natives" remained low, and even so it was repeatedly necessary to purge "nationalists" in local Communist parties.

The growing strength of the Soviet Union and the total centralization of economic authority in Moscow gradually led to greater self-confidence. The Ukraine was continuously subjected to administration by *apparatchiki* such as Kaganovich, whose only interest in Ukrainian feelings was to combat separatism; the purges began earlier and bore more heavily in the Ukraine than anywhere else. Glorification of the achievements of the Great Russian people, always with a nod toward "other peoples of the Soviet Union," became quite open. For example, in greeting the Seventeenth All-Russian Congress of Soviets (January 15, 1937), *Pravda* stressed that the Great Russians constituted about 78 percent of the population of the R.S.F.S.R. (not of the U.S.S.R.) and boasted of their record over the centuries in repelling German aggression. Modestly describing Russians as "first among equals," *Pravda* proudly recited the names of Pushkin, Lermontov, Tolstoy, and Gorky (Dostoevsky, Turgenev, and Chekhov were not mentioned), of Bielinsky, Dobroliubov, and Chernyshevsky (not Herzen, Lavrov, or Bakunin), of Mendeleiev, Sechenov, and Pavlov. It added the names of Lomonosov; the mathematician Lobachevsky; Popov, the inventor of the radio; and other scientists and navigators who "constitute our national glory." Rejoicing that "traces of mistrust on the part of the various nationalities inhabiting the U.S.S.R. toward the Great Russians have vanished," and giving due credit to "the leadership of the Party of Lenin-Stalin," *Pravda* saluted "the Russian people, its language, its culture."

NATIONALISM AND CULTURE

Appreciation of the achievements of the Russians carried with it appreciation of Russia's long and glorious past and of the forerunners of Lenin and Stalin on whose foundations the Party had been building. The new attitude necessitated destruction of the reputation of Pokrovsky, who in his lifetime had been recognized as "the Marxist historian." Scarcely was Pokrovsky dead when the Party Central Committee (August, 1932) took note of "the inadequacy of the historical approach to programs of social studies." In 1934 the Central Committee addressed itself seriously to the problem; jointly with Sovnarkom, it affirmed:

> The textbooks and the very method of instruction bear an abstract, schematic character. Instead of teaching *civic history* in a live, entertaining form with exposition of the most important events and facts in their chronological sequence, with a characterization of historical figures, the pupils are offered abstract definitions of socio-economic formations, thus replacing a connected exposition of civic history with abstract sociological diagrams.

A few months later, Stalin, Zhdanov, and Kirov supplied *Observations* on synopses of textbooks on the history of the U.S.S.R. and on modern history.

Even this produced no satisfactory results. Early in 1937, *Pravda* returned to the attack in a series of signed articles:

> The great Russian thinker, N. G. Chernyshevsky, wrote that it is impossible to be an educated man without knowing history. "It is possible," he wrote, "not to know, not to feel attracted to the study of mathematics, of Greek or Latin, of chemistry, it is possible not to know a thousand sciences and still be an educated man; but not to love history is possible only for a man totally undeveloped intellectually." [13]

Pokrovsky's sin was that he had substituted sociology for history.

> Only mechanists imagine the historical process as a spontaneous process, in which personality is only a straw indicating the direction of movement or, at best, a simple mouthpiece, transmitting the voice of history. The word "mouthpiece" brings to mind the well-known letter of Marx to Lassalle about the latter's drama *Franz von Sickingen*. Marx criticized Lassalle severely for converting his historical heroes into "simple mouthpieces of the spirit of the times." One must not "Schillerize," taught Marx, that is, not portray heroes by diagrammatic declaimers, but "Shakespearize" them, that is, depict them as living men, with all their passions, with individual mind and will through which the times are refracted.[14]

Specifically, Pokrovsky was charged with offering interpretations of history that amounted to treason. In 1930, "when the Finnish Fascists were developing a particularly wide campaign for creation of a 'greater Finland' as far as the Urals," Pokrovsky had printed an article in which he had written that "in the veins of the 'Great Russian people' flows more than 80 percent of Finnish blood." He had never referred to the heroic and successful struggle against the *Drang nach Osten* waged by the Order of Swordbearing Knights (to whom the critic attributed some achievements of the Teutonic

Knights). He had rejected Marx's account of the Mongol-Tatar "regime of systematic terror, with ruin and mass murders as its constant institutions" in favor of the view that—

> the conquest of Rus by the Tatars was by no means an invasion by savage steppe-dwellers of a civilized agricultural land . . . but the collision of two equal cultures, of which it cannot be said which was relatively the higher.

Instead of recognizing the truth of Stalin's explanation that the needs of defense against attacks of Turks, Mongols, and other peoples of the East had led to the formation of centralized states before the formation of nations, Pokrovsky had opposed any such idea of the origin of the multi-national state. Pokrovsky had denied to Minin and Pozharsky credit for saving the national independence of Muscovy from the Poles and had depicted these heroes as counter-revolutionaries. Pokrovsky and his "school" had ignored the long record of brotherly relations between the Russian and Ukrainian peoples and had treated Bogdan Khmelnitsky's leadership of a national uprising against the oppressive Polish magnates as a conflict between the upper crust of cossacks and the peasant masses of the Ukraine. Unlike Marx and Engels, Lenin and Stalin, who had frankly acclaimed Peter as "the Great," Pokrovsky's school had denied that Peter's reforms had had any "progressive significance" and had seen only oppression and ruin of the peasantry. Marx had described Peter's conquest of the Baltic shore line as "absolutely necessary for the development of his country"; Pokrovsky's school had characterized it as only a manifestation of the predatory strivings of serf-owning landlords and of "commercial capital." Pokrovsky's school had denigrated the contributions of the Great Russian people to the civilization of mankind; not one of them had ever mentioned the great Russian scholar Lomonosov. The history of the revolutionary movement had been falsified, and the primary significance of the Decembrists denied, while *narodnichestvo* had been given improper credit.[15]

Before the campaign was over, a whole book had been devoted to his "errors." Survivors of "bourgeois historiography" were encouraged to publish monographs, which were, however, watched with care; their authors, like Tarlé, sometimes found it necessary to go into reverse when their interpretations did not meet with official approval. Some excellent work was done by men such as Grekov, who independently reëxamined the agrarian history of early Russia in the light of comparative scholarship. Yet economic history as a whole developed no one of greater stature than Liashchenko, who was careful in successive editions of his work at least outwardly to conform to Leninist dicta and to shifts in official theory. Pankratova, a woman with no qualifications as a historian save the shamelessness with which she toed the current line, became the leading figure in official historiography, but all attempts to replace the banned Pokrovsky with a general survey of the whole of Russian history were admittedly failures; resort had to be taken to reprinting Kliuchevsky's classic *Course,* the last and finest product of historians in the last days of the tsars.

Much more success was achieved in the field of visual aids, which in any case reached a far wider and more impressionable audience than could books. Reference has already been made to Eisenstein's revised Sovkino version of *Ivan the Terrible.* Among many other films, his *Alexander Nevsky* (1938) was outstanding for its heroic treatment of the historic struggle against the Teutons; to be sure, its ending on the note of Alexander's listening sadly to the sound of Tatar pipes over the hill was romantic rather than historical.

For this and other films, Prokofiev wrote the music, making appropriate "glub-glub" sounds as each slain knight fell through the ice; in fairness, it should be noted that this music was composed after a trip to Hollywood, his last visit to the Western world. For the rest, after his *Peter and the Wolf* (1936) for children, this brilliant composer produced nothing but propaganda pieces. His only possible rival in Russia, Shostakovich, was in 1936 severely chastised by *Pravda* for producing "muddle instead of music." For what had once been proletarianism, he was denounced as "petty bourgeois," "neurotic," "coarse," and "vulgar," and his *Fourth Symphony* (1935-36) was withdrawn. In 1937, however, his *Fifth,* old-fashioned as a Tchaikovsky opera, achieved a magical success.

Despite the generally repressive and terroristic character of this period, during which Gorky died or was murdered (1936), there was no return to the control that RAPP had exercised over literature during the First Five-Year Plan. "Socialist realism" remained the touchstone by which official critics judged Russian authors; though the term was never clearly defined, writers were expected to stress the creative nature of Soviet man and to inspire him to realize his fullest potentialities. The new emphasis on the gloriously heroic character of Russia's past was reflected in a bumper crop of historical novels and plays, thoroughly imbued with patriotic sentiments. The finest of them, Sholokhov's *Silent Don,* completed in 1940, showed remarkable artistic independence, not hesitating to balance human weaknesses against human strength. More acceptable to the critics were a host of other writers who sang the praises of bygone rulers such as Alexander Nevsky, Dmitry Donskoy, and Ivan the Terrible, or of tsarist generals such as Suvorov and Kutuzov. Among them the ablest was A. N. Tolstoy, author of *Peter I,* who carefully concealed his personal distaste for the Soviet regime to which he had returned in order to enjoy the material comforts it afforded him. Any writer who now fell into Pokrovsky's old error of underrating Russian national heroes was called to strict account. Demyan Bedny, once rated in Soviet Russia even higher than Maiakovsky, was sharply reprimanded for his new version of Borodin's *Bogatyri* (1936), in which, it was said, he slandered those fearless defenders of Kiev against the raiding steppe nomads; his operetta was banned from the theater as "alien to Soviet art."

The rising tide of official nationalism brought some amelioration of the position of the Church. The period of *piatiletka* had witnessed an intensification of the campaign against religion. Even in 1927, Stalin, in an interview with a delegation of American workers, had in the name of "science" openly taken a strong stand against "religious prejudice"; referring to "the reactionary clergy, who poison the minds of the laboring masses," he proudly acknowledged, "Yes, we have suppressed [the reactionary clergy]," adding, "the only pity is that they have not been wholly liquidated."[16] In the schools positive "anti-religious instruction" officially superseded (1928) mere "non-religious education." A decree of April 8, 1929, had redefined the legal position of the Church. Although some of its provisions bore much more hardly on sectarians than on the Orthodox Church, all religious organizations alike were forbidden to engage in any activity other than actual performance of their rites. In an intensified campaign, discriminatory taxation, housing, and ration policies had been employed against the clergy. The League of the Militant Godless had increased its membership from 123,000 in 1928 to 2 million at the beginning of 1930. "Anti-religious Museums" had been founded at Moscow (1926) and elsewhere; in Leningrad one was housed in the great Cathedral of the Virgin of Kazan on the former Nevsky Prospekt (1932). Church bells were silenced, if not removed; many churches had been closed altogether.

In the face of difficulties with the collectivized peasants, however, a halt had been called. When Stalin rebuked his ever-zealous agents for being "dizzy with success" (March 2, 1930), Yaroslavsky, who headed the League of the Militant Godless, similarly attacked the "Left deviation" of closing churches and burning icons unless "the predominant majority of the peasants" in the parish ordered it. The campaign against religion continued, but more lamely. By 1932 the League of the Militant Godless numbered more than 5.5 million members, though arrears of dues were alarmingly and increasingly heavy. A "Right deviation" flourished, questioning the need, now that so much progress had been made, of vigorously prosecuting the League's efforts. For its part, the Church had turned the other cheek. Metropolitan Sergius had persisted in his policy of saying prayers for the Soviet authorities. In 1930 he rejected the "warmongering" charges of the pope, backed by the archbishop of Canterbury, against the Soviet regime and denied that the Church was persecuted in Russia. A number of the clergy disturbed their enemies by actively supporting industrialization, collectivization, and village "cultural" activities such as Communist libraries and reading rooms.

From 1934 on, perception of the potential value of the Church to the state increased considerably. The subtle method of combat by taking leaves from its book was not neglected. The Moscow subway, justly famed for its efficiency, was built with the aid of an American engineer, who, incidentally, gives much credit to NKVD supervision of the labor force employed as well as to the method of boring tubes instead of digging ditches. What is here relevant is that the subway was used also in a subordinate way; the gaudy adornment lavished on its station platforms was deliberately calculated to make up to the citizens for the gilt and glitter, though not for the incense, that had made the churches so satisfyingly impressive to souls in need of being awed by material manifestations of a higher power.

Yet the role of the Church as a historic national institution received recognition. Special emphasis was placed on its cultural role. In condemning Demyan Bedny, it was flatly and officially stated that his picture of the forcible conversion of Rus by St. Vladimir was an "unhistorical" travesty; it "was actually a constructive step in the history of the Russian people" and "one of the greatest historic events of Kievan Rus." [17] Alexander Nevsky, who also had been canonized by the Church, was a special favorite of the new Soviet nationalism, mainly directed against Nazi Germany, which was threatening to renew the *Drang nach Osten*.

In an era of wooing the democratic West and of efforts to form "popular fronts" against "fascism," it was not prudent to flout the "prejudices" of bourgeois nations. Along with heavy emphasis on Russian national pride went a drive for the reëstablishment of morality in Russia. The importance of the family, even as a means of disciplining workers, had come to be realized by the Party leaders. Accordingly, divorce was made more difficult, and abortion, unless medically indicated, was made a crime (1936). Even the League of the Militant Godless veered to the position (1939) that: "It would be wrong to think that everything connected with religion is necessarily reactionary." Marxist atheists must not repeat in their propaganda the errors of mere bourgeois atheists:

> Christianity should not be identified with capitalism. . . . Christianity should not be identified with other religions. . . . The beneficial role Christianity played in the development of family relations should not be denied. . . . Christianity has contributed to the improvement of folkways and customs. . . .[18]

Yaroslavsky complained in *The Godless* (1940) that atheists had "not been able to offer the people moral standards for their life." [19]

It should be noted that Christianity was now treated as an exception among religions. The League of the Militant Godless was now inclined to stress that primitive Christianity had arisen among very humble folk, and that at least its original social theories were not irreconcilable with the socio-economic goals of communism. Despite the incrustations of privilege that had grown up over the centuries, this particular "opiate of the people" had persistently retained some of its characteristics as a religion of slaves and freedmen. Insofar as the Orthodox Church was willing to reëmphasize the ideals of the early Church, with its stress on individual morality and its opposition to any form of racial, national, or social discrimination, coexistence with it was entirely possible.

Similar toleration could not, of course, be extended to schismatics and sectarians, whose tradition was too bound up with political opposition to the Russian state. Nor could there be any friendliness toward Roman Catholicism, for it was too well known that the popes had for centuries tried to impose their Latin heresy on the Slavs and were still the archenemies of Russia, whether Orthodox or Communist. Protestant denominations were also dangerous because of their official position in various capitalist states; among them, the Baptists, with no significant connections, might perhaps be allowed to make their relatively harmless emotional appeal.

Non-Christian religions could not be embraced by the new concept. They were officially accorded toleration on the same footing as Christianity, but the pressure on their traditional way of life was heavier. At one stage, the Communist Party had encouraged and tried to lead a Pan-Moslem movement, easily confused with a dangerous Pan-Turanianism. Quite early, however, the anti-religious campaign had set itself the task of undermining Moslem customs, particularly in relation to women. In the mid-twenties, to break the cultural connection with Moslem countries beyond the Soviet border, the Latin alphabet had by decree replaced Arabic characters. In 1938, however, when teaching of the Russian language was made compulsory in all schools throughout the Soviet Union, it was deemed advisable to reform the alphabet once more; Cyrillic letters arbitrarily replaced Latin, thus temporarily further complicating the problem of reducing illiteracy among the subject peoples but facilitating their ultimate assimilation to the culture of their Russian "big brother." An inevitable concomitant of the new religio-national policies was that particularly severe purges were necessary in Moslem Central Asia, which also suffered extremely acute economic dislocations in connection with collectivization and industrialization.

Most of the lesser religious groups, such as Buddhists, caused less trouble; their adherents, scattered in outlying regions, were more afflicted by the colonial than by the religious policies of the Russian government. Most acute became the problem of the Jews, those thorns in the side of the tsars. The Bolsheviks, like other revolutionary parties, had naturally found an unusually high proportion of sympathizers among this peculiarly oppressed people. Yet the Jews were too small a minority in the total population, or even in the urban population, to supply at any time much more than 5 percent of Party membership. As a distinct ethnic group they exercised no influence on Party policy. The Communists persistently refused to recognize the Jews as a "nationality" or to accord them special privileges of any kind. The Party treated Judaism as simply a religion and regarded Jewish Orthodoxy as just as much an "opiate of the people" as any other. Renewed efforts to encourage Jews to settle on the land failed to produce substantial results. Though many of them were exploited workers, the Jews remained largely urban "petty bourgeois" and as such suffered severely from the economic policies of the new regime.

After 1927, as a concession to their nationalist stirrings, some efforts were made to induce Jews to migrate to Biro-Bidzhan, where they could become the majority and thus be entitled to local autonomy; in 1934 Biro-Bidzhan was duly declared an "autonomous" region within the R.S.F.S.R. Situated on the bank of the Amur, across from Japanese-occupied Manchukuo, and with no important natural resources, Biro-Bidzhan seemed a poor joke as a "homeland" and failed to flourish. Unable to establish themselves in the Soviet Union as Jews, they were increasingly inspired by the British-protected "homeland" in Palestine; they were, however, not allowed to emigrate from the Soviet Union. In the purge trials the charge of "Zionism" was equated with Trotskyism as a capital offense, and despite official discouragement, the old Russian anti-Semitism, particularly pronounced among Ukrainians, could not always be prevented from peeking out.

The Party modified but did not abandon its anti-religious position. Yet it was experiencing serious difficulties. By 1937 membership in the League of the Militant Godless had fallen to not more than two million, and their lack of militancy was bitterly criticized. In 1937-1938, at the height of the purge trials, some attempts were made to draw in ecclesiastics as collaborators with Trotsky, but with the sudden termination of the purge in 1939 the position of the Church was again eased. Despite renewed increases in membership of the League, despite renewed efforts to use the schools, the anti-religious museums, books, pamphlets, and the Komsomol, despite Yaroslavsky's insistence as late as 1941 that "we must paralyze all influence of religion upon the rising generation," [20] the issue of the struggle remained doubtful. Though wholly dependent on the contributions of the faithful, the Church still had large revenues. Though the schism created by the Renovationist movement had not been wholly healed, though the Church suffered from a growing shortage of clergy, though outward signs of respect for the Church and its services had declined, there still persisted a very considerable body of strong religious feeling, and not only among the old. This feeling was apparently all the stronger because of the persecution to which it had been subjected. The sloughing off from the Church of the mass of those who had practiced its rites for the sake of expedient outward conformity was more likely to benefit than to injure an organization the purposes of which were purely spiritual.

If in these years the Church gained slightly more freedom of action, the opposite tendency was manifest in the schools. From top to bottom, the educational system was employed in the service of the state. It was not merely that the school provided a means of political indoctrination. Its main purpose was to prepare technically trained personnel for specific jobs, without wasting time and money on "general education." As early as 1933 it was prescribed that every graduate of a university or of a polytechnicum must, as the price of his training, accept the job to which he was assigned, no matter where; evasion was made a criminal offense. In 1938 this practice was tightened up, and its administration entrusted to the appropriate People's Commissariat, which was to keep a careful register of all its specialists with the advantage of higher education and to be continuously responsible for their proper utilization. During the period of the Second F.Y.P. the average number of university graduates was 74,000 a year (as against 34,000 in the period of the First F.Y.P.); the polytechnicums turned out an additional 125,000 a year (as against 58,000). The number of "engineers" graduated was raised from 7,900 in 1933 to 31,300 in 1938; the number of doctors, veterinarians, and pharmacists from 9,400 to 24,200; of teachers from 10,500 to 35,700; while that of other nonmilitary specialists increased only from 6,800 to 15,500.

In the early years of the Soviet regime, children of proletarians or of poor peasants were given stipends to assist them in their schooling. The Stalin Constitution of 1936 guaranteed free instruction, including higher education, to all. In 1940, however, it was announced that youth did not appreciate and fully utilize their educational opportunities unless they had to pay for them. By a decree of October 2, 1940, the date also of the establishment of the State Labor Reserve, tuition fees were introduced for all grades above the seventh. Simultaneously, the system of stipends was altered; instead of social origin, the quality of the student's work was made the determinant for the grant of financial aid. Justification for the new policy might be found in the thought that social classes had virtually disappeared, and that the intelligentsia could not be considered a "class." Nevertheless, the change was an important step in the creation of a new ruling elite, able to escape from manual labor. In view of the great unevennesses in the sprawling, though centrally directed, educational system, a child's chances of moving upward depended very heavily on the particular school he attended. It was only natural that officials, managers, and the new specialists, well able to afford the tuition fees, should also be in the best position to choose the right schools for their children.

Over the whole period, influencing many of its characteristics, hung the threat of approaching war. Its story can best be told connectedly in the next chapter. It may, however, be here observed that in foreign policy, as in domestic, Marxian dialectics did not prove the surest guide.

NOTES

1. Stalin's "Report on the Draft Constitution of the U.S.S.R.," Part I, in *Pravda,* November 26, 1936.
2. Vyshinsky, *Law of the Soviet State,* p. 122.
3. Stalin's "Report . . . ," *op. cit.,* Part IV.

4. *Ibid.*, Part II.
5. *Pravda,* June 2, 1936.
6. *Ibid.*, April 27, 1937.
7. *Ibid.*, November 3, 1936.
8. Radek, in *Berner Tagwacht,* cited in Lenin, "The Revolutionary Proletariat and the Right of Nations to Self-determination" (November 6, 1915), *Sochineniia,* 3rd edition, XVIII, 323.
9. Stalin, "Reply to Ukrainian Comrades in the Rear and at the Front" (December 12, 1917), in *Sochineniia,* IV, 8.
10. Stalin, "Report on the Nationality Question" (January 15, 1918), at the Third All-Russian Congress of Soviets, *loc. cit.*, pp. 31-32.
11. *Leninskii Sbornik,* III (1925), 486-487.
12. *Kommunisticheskaia Partiia Sovetskogo Soiuza v rezoliutsiiakh* . . . , I, 417.
13. V. Zeimal, in *Pravda,* May 11, 1937.
14. F. Rothstein, in *Pravda,* May 18, 1937.
15. P. Drozdov, in *Pravda,* March 28, 1937.
16. Stalin, *Sochineniia,* X, 131-133.
17. All-Union Committee on Matters of Art, "Against Falsification of the People's Past," cited in Curtiss, *The Russian Church and the Soviet State, 1917-1950,* p. 274.
18. Timasheff, *Religion in Soviet Russia,* p. 115.
19. *Ibid.*, p. 130.
20. Yaroslavskii, *Kommunizm i religiia,* p. 32, cited in Curtiss, *op. cit.*, p. 285.

SUGGESTIONS FOR FURTHER READING

The text of the new Constitution and of Stalin's explanatory report should be read carefully. Fainsod's *Smolensk Under Soviet Rule* is a remarkable study, based on records removed by the Germans, of Soviet administration at the local level from 1917 to 1938. In addition to books previously mentioned, Timasheff's *Great Retreat,* though mistitled, contains very much of value. Randall's *Stalin's Russia* attempts an historical reappraisal.

On the problem of nationalities, see particularly: Pipes, *The Formation of the Soviet Union*; Hans Kohn, *Nationalism in the Soviet Union*; Low, *Lenin on the Question of Nationality*; and Barghoorn, *Soviet Russian Nationalism*. For particular ethnic groups, see Kolarz, *Russia and Her Colonies* and *Peoples of the Soviet Far East*; Reshetar, already cited; Kostiuk, *Stalinist Rule in the Ukraine*; and Dmytryshyn, *Moscow and the Ukraine, 1918-1953*; Vakar, *Belorussia . . .*; *Caroe, Soviet Empire: The Turks of Central Asia and Stalinism*; Park, *Bolshevism in Turkestan, 1917-1927*; Hostler, *Turkism and the Soviets*; and Schwarz, *The Jews in the Soviet Union.*

On cultural developments, in addition to books previously cited, see Counts and Lodge, *The Challenge of Soviet Education*; Shore, *Soviet Education: Its Psychology and Philosophy*; Bauer, *The New Man in Soviet Psychology*; and Bauer Inkeles, and Kluckhohn, *How the Soviet System Works.*

Chapter

33

The Road to War: 1934-1941

The foreign policy of any country is the aspect of its activity that most catches the eye of foreign observers. No matter what the social contradictions and crosscurrents that confuse a country's domestic life, its foreign policy is consciously directed by the ruling group; it therefore has a unity and relative simplicity that sometimes make it seem to have a *raison d'être* of its own. One is tempted to forget the fact that no country exists for the primary purpose of having relations with other countries, that its foreign relations, necessary as they are, must always be subordinate to the play of its own domestic interests. This is not to say that an external situation does not often exercise a profound influence on a country's life, for no state exists in a vacuum. What should not be overlooked, however, is that any country's own existence comes first, its contacts with other countries second. The objectives of foreign policy must therefore be subordinate to its domestic objectives, or at least to those of its rulers.

Without reference to these general considerations, Soviet foreign policy is merely a record of unintelligible zigzags, as exciting but as meaningless as a game. If, however, it is realized that Soviet foreign policy, like that of any other land, reflected continuity of domestic purpose in a changing outside world, its seeming contradictions disappear; whatever adjustments had to be made to a shifting international situation which no single country can control, Soviet attitudes and actions at any given moment were determined by the Bolsheviks' concept of Russia's own current needs.

By 1934 Soviet foreign policy had passed through three fairly clearly defined phases. The initial phase, which had lasted until 1920-1921, had been rooted in the conviction that world revolution was about to sweep away all capitalist or imperialist governments; this phase had required no foreign policy in any formal sense and had been characterized by the aggressive attitude of the Third International. The factors that led to the abandonment of "War Communism" in favor of the NEP had shaped Soviet Russia's first real foreign policy. Though the obvious subsidence of revolutionary enthusiasm in the Western world had contributed to the change, the main consideration had been the need of economic reconstruction at home and the hope that this would be facilitated by active economic relations with advanced capitalist countries; Soviet Russia had started to drift away from its pristine pure revolutionary goal to the more modest concept of "socialism in a single land." In this second phase, however, there had been no abatement of political hostility toward the Entente Powers, and Russia had anchored her foreign policy on maintenance of good relations with outcast Germany, no longer the object of immediate revolution. The Soviet Union largely shifted its thoughts to the East, for, particularly in India and China, the revolt of "bourgeois nationalism" seemed to offer valuable allies in the effort to promote the ultimate disintegration of the capitalist world, which, in Leninist theory, had reached the ultimate stage of "imperialism."

The third phase was almost wholly the result of domestic policy. The decision to embark on an all-out drive for rapid industrialization by means of *piatiletka* made peaceful economic relations with the capitalist West even more imperative. Especially when hasty collectivization had thrown Russia into a desperate internal situation, it became necessary to avoid at all costs the possibility of war. Russian policy had made no progress in India and had suffered a disastrous check in China; relations with Japan had become increasingly strained, and Russia's anxiety for American support in the Pacific had become overwhelming. Instead of striving for a coalition with Germany against the Entente Powers, the new Foreign Commissar, Maxim Litvinov, developed the theory that "peace is indivisible." The Soviet Union had subscribed to the Kellogg-Briand Pact (1928) and had taken active, though perhaps not helpful, part in the disarmament conference under the auspices of the League of Nations (1932-1934). The results were mixed. Russia did secure recognition by the United States (1933) but persisted in openly regarding Great Britain as her archenemy. Her policy toward Nazi Germany was at the outset not unfriendly; Russo-German agreements for conciliation and for extension of the neutrality treaty of 1926, both concluded with the Weimar Republic in 1931, were actually ratified (May 5, 1933) after Hitler became chancellor.

THE FIRST PHASE: "COLLECTIVE SECURITY"

Between 1934 and 1941, Soviet foreign policy floundered, passing in rapid succession through three more distinct phases (1934-1936, 1936-1939,

1939-1941). In the first of these, Russia had finally taken alarm at the triumph of Nazism. Not only was the strength of Hitler's power in Germany demonstrated by his crushing of Ernst Röhm; the Nazis' affair with Poland, evident as early as January, 1934, seemed to menace the security of the Ukraine. From the Polish standpoint, this reorientation of Poland's policy may well have been intended merely to make her own position safer; wedged in between a Germany which regarded Danzig and the Polish Corridor as territories to be redeemed and a Russia which had never become reconciled to the boundary drawn by the Treaty of Riga in 1921, Poland, mistrusting the solidity of French support, apparently hoped that the Nazis would be less dangerous to her than had been the old Prussian ascendancy in Germany. In a world of sovereign nations, however, and with live memories of Polish intervention in 1920, Russia could not fail to suspect that Poland might be reviving, on the basis of a deal with Germany, her well-established desire to resubjugate the Ukraine. Notwithstanding renewal (May 5, 1934) of the Soviet-Polish "nonaggression pact" of 1932, Russia remained uneasy. Uppermost in Litvinov's consciousness were the passages in *Mein Kampf* about *Lebensraum* to be secured at Russia's expense.

On a broader scale, the Bolsheviks had never outgrown their belief that the West, aware of the avowed Communist intention to overthrow capitalism throughout the world, might even yet form a coalition, with "fascist" Germany as its spearhead, to destroy the Soviet Union. Scant and scattering as were expressions of such a viewpoint in the West, they sufficed to feed Russian fears. It was clear enough that even moderately "Leftist" sentiment in Great Britain, and even in France, had come to regard the Versailles settlement as unjust and therefore to cherish a guilty sympathy for the Nazis; the Communists tended to mistake the strongly isolationist pacifist sentiment that then dominated the democracies of Britain, France, and the United States for an active opposition to the new Russian concept of "collective security."

In particular, the Russians feared that Nazi Germany, despite its "racist" propaganda, and an expanding Japan—two powers which "have even recognized that they are of common race" [1]—might combine against the Soviet Union. The Communists could not rely on the influence of the Karl Haushofer school of geopolitics, popular in Germany since 1924, especially in the military circles to which he belonged, and which, on the theory of a "Eurasian heartland," urged an alliance of Germany, Russia, Japan, China, and an emancipated India to dominate the world. Nor could they be confident that the Nazi rulers would agree that Oswald Spengler was right when, in 1933, he despondently acknowledged that the Bolsheviks' eastward shift of the center of gravity had made it impossible to conquer Russia by an attack from the west, which "would be a thrust into empty space." [2] Still in the midst of her herculean effort at industrialization, the Soviet Union could not yet with any equanimity contemplate the possibility of war, especially single-handed, even if she had to fight only on one front. For this reason, despite Chinese protest, she abandoned to Manchukuo the Chinese Eastern Railway (March 25, 1933) for a price that represented only one-eighth of its cost. The Japanese military nevertheless posed a new threat to the Russian position in Outer Mongolia, but the Soviet Union was encouraged by a new American naval building program and, despite the vigor of Chiang Kai-shek's current campaign against the Chinese Communists, by its own generally improved relations with China.

Russia's main reliance was now on her strongly argued principle of "collective security," with which France was not at all unwilling to toy. On France's initiative, the Soviet Union was invited (September 10, 1934) to join the League of Nations and to occupy the permanent seat on its Council that Germany was vacating. Thus Russia was enabled to join the Powers, righteously and without risk of commitment to action, in condemning Italy's conquest of Ethiopia (1935). She had the satisfaction also of hearing Great Britain (March 4, 1935) and France (March 5) announce their intention to increase their armaments, with every reason to believe that the move was not directed against the Soviet Union. When Germany (March 16) replied by reintroducing military conscription, Litvinov supported France's appeal to the League. The Anglo-German naval agreement (June 18) was disturbing, however, for it inevitably meant German naval preponderance in the Baltic.

On the other hand, improvement of trade relations with Great Britain was very marked after conclusion of a new trade agreement (February 16, 1934); though Soviet exports to Great Britain substantially exceeded British exports to Russia, the Communists were inclined to feel that, by virtue of invisible exports, Great Britain had the better of the deal. Nazi Germany made a partially successful effort, by fresh extensions of credit in 1935 and 1936, to recover her preponderance in the Russian market, but herself taking only a small proportion of Russian exports, was reduced in 1938 to supplying less than 5 percent of Russia's purchases, as against 17 percent from Great Britain and 28.5 percent from the United States. The phenomenal rise of Russo-American trade following the first trade agreement in 1935 was, however, more apparent than real; the 70 million dollars' worth of goods exported by the United States to Russia in 1938, though a great increase over the 33 million of 1936 or the 43 million of 1937, was only two-thirds of what America had sold to Russia in 1930 or 1931, when she did not even recognize her customer. French trade with Russia was throughout of no significance. The total value of Russian trade, never great, had dwindled rapidly from 1932 on, after the First F.Y.P. had done its work. The carrot of orders to be placed abroad, which Russia had held out to assure a friendly reception by the West, now proved generally disappointing. In the case of the United States, the shining hopes with which the first American ambassador to Soviet Russia, William C.

Bullitt, had gone to Moscow were dashed by the completeness of his failure to get serious debt negotiations even started. In 1936 a soured Bullitt was transferred to Paris, where his influence could hardly be helpful in promoting cordial relations between France and the Soviet Union.

This was particularly unfortunate from the viewpoint of the Russian policy of collective security, which had to hinge on a Franco-Russian understanding. Along with the general idea of collective security to be achieved through the League of Nations, Litvinov had been assiduously working for an "Eastern Locarno" to stabilize the frontiers of the states lying between her borders and Germany. Negotiations to this end had been begun in 1933. Germany, when approached directly, refused (April 14, 1934) to join in a Russo-German guarantee of Finland and the Baltic states; Russia fell back on confirmation of her existing nonaggression pacts with Lithuania, Latvia, and Estonia. A French proposal (June 27) for a general Eastern European mutual-assistance agreement, to include also Poland and Czechoslovakia and which France was prepared to underwrite, was approved by Great Britain; Germany rejected it (September 10), and Poland, who had her own bones to pick with Czechoslovakia, followed suit (September 27). The idea of an "Eastern Locarno" was dead, but Litvinov salvaged what seemed two potentially valuable by-products.

The more important was signature (May 2, 1935) of a Franco-Russian pact, the heart of which was Article 2:

> In the event of France or the U.S.S.R., in the circumstances specified in Article 15, paragraph 7, of the League of Nations Covenant, being the object, in spite of the genuinely peaceful intentions of both countries, of an unprovoked attack on the part of a European State, the U.S.S.R. and, reciprocally, France, shall immediately give each other aid and assistance.[3]

A superficial difference between this and the Franco-Russian agreement of 1891, which had blossomed into the Dual Alliance of 1894, lay in its subordination to the League and, in other provisions, to France's obligations under the Locarno Treaty of 1925. Still other clauses made it clear that its application was limited, not only to Europe, but specifically to Germany as an aggressor. Basically, Europe seemed to be returning to the end of the nineteenth century, with a Franco-Russian agreement threatening Germany with a two-front war, while Great Britain remained on the side lines.

There were, however, certain important differences: Britain gave her blessing to this new arrangement; and it did not harden into an alliance as had the earlier Franco-Russian understanding. Laval did not ask the French president to ratify the pact by decree; there was a consequent delay before the Chamber of Deputies unenthusiastically endorsed it (by a vote of 353 to 164) on February 11, 1936, and the Senate confirmed it (231 to 52) on March 12. Germany's defiant answer, given on March 7, 1936, was military reoccupation of the Rhineland. In view of the state of mind of their own peoples, neither France nor Great Britain took any action in the face of this flagrant breach of the Treaty of Versailles, just as they had not opposed Hitler's threatened occupation of Austria after the murder of dictator Dollfuss in 1934. Most serious of all, the Franco-Russian pact of 1935 was never backed up by supplementary military agreements.

Russia made her own preparations independently. The size of the Russian army was more than doubled, the percentage of regulars as opposed to territorial militia was much increased, and great progress was made with its mechanization. Its administrative organization was unified (1934), and the prestige of the officers enhanced, both by further reducing the powers of political commissars and by reviving all old titles, save those of general and admiral (1935). The French high command, however, had grave doubts of the efficiency and reliability of the Red Army, doubts which were to be strengthened in 1937 by the execution of Marshal Tukhachevsky and his principal associates.

The other by-product of the drive for an Eastern Locarno was a mutual-assistance pact concluded (May 16, 1935) between the Soviet Union and Czechoslovakia. Whereas the Roman Catholic Poles had always regarded their country as the bulwark of a civilized Europe against barbarous Russia, the Czechs, who had never been under Russian rule, tended to share the views of their first president, Tomáš G. Masaryk, that they constituted the necessary link between their fellow Europeans in the West and their fellow Slavs to the east. Apart from other points in dispute, such as Czech possession of Teschen and the harboring in Ruthenia of Ukrainian refugees from Poland, Czechoslovakia resented the interposition of Polish territory between her and Soviet Russia, while Poland resented Czech control of the Carpatho-Ukraine, which cut her off from direct contact with Hungary. The Russo-Czech pact paralleled the Franco-Russian pact and was deliberately geared to it; only if France acted, were Czechoslovakia and the Soviet Union to assist each other. How they could do so, save in the very unlikely event that either Poland or Rumania would permit, or could be forced to permit, the passage of troops, remained a mystery, never to be resolved.

In pursuit of their new policy, the Communists had still a third string to their bow. Never believers in the principle of "off with the old love before you're on with the new," they had kept the Third International in being. As late as the end of 1933, its Executive Committee had remained committed to the theory that the period of temporary capitalist stabilization had ended, and that the world was on the verge of fresh wars and revolutions. In the spring of 1934, however, the "fascist" riots in Paris that followed the Stavisky scandal had alarmed the French Communist Party. Probably not without instruction from Moscow, it signed (July 27) a limited alliance with the French Socialists. This "united front" of "proletarian" elements was soon developed into a "popular front," including groups much further to the "Right";

on Bastille Day, 1935, the Communist, Socialist, and Radical parties jointly demonstrated against "fascism."

The Seventh Congress of the Comintern (July 25-August 21, 1935) fully endorsed the principle of the "popular front." Georgi Dimitrov, a Bulgarian exile who had won fame as the hero of the Reichstag fire trial, was elected General Secretary. The French Maurice Thorez and the American Earl Browder wrapped themselves in the patriotic robes of the revolutionary traditions of their respective countries. Wilhelm Pieck, on his way up among German Communists, was given the honor of making the major "Report on the Activity of the Executive Committee of the Communist International," condemning the "sectarian errors" that had been barring the way to a united "struggle against fascism and war." [4] The Italian Palmiro Togliatti (under his pseudonym of "Ercoli"), in another report on "The Preparation of an Imperialist War and the Tasks of the Communist International," lauded "the peace policy of the U.S.S.R." which had upset the plans of the imperialists and had made it possible for all truly peace-loving governments to support the policy of collective security.[5] Some confusion was left because the Congress could not altogether jettison old slogans; by resolution it still emphasized the principle that "Communist Parties in all capitalist countries must lead the fight: against military expenditures [and] against subsidizing the armament industry. . . ." [6] The United States and Great Britain protested against what they regarded as violation of the no-propaganda provisions of their agreements with the Soviet Union but were reminded that the Comintern was a private affair.

The general effect was doubtless to enhance the prestige of the Soviet Union in those wide circles of the Western world that were then becoming deeply concerned with the menace of "fascism." Yet it was only in France that a "popular front" won an electoral victory. In April, 1935, thanks to preëlection understandings with other groups in the "popular front," Communist representation in the French Chamber of Deputies jumped from 10 to 72. The Blum cabinet, formed June 5, 1936, was dependent on Communist support, though that party refused to accept cabinet portfolios. The world was treated to the spectacle of a millionaire, leader of the Socialist Party, whose tenure as French premier depended on the good will of the Moscow Comintern, pushing desperately forward an ambitious program of rearmament.

THE SECOND PHASE: THE LONE WOLF

The second phase of Soviet foreign policy began to be manifest from 1936. Notwithstanding—perhaps even because of—the intensity of the internal purge, the Communist leadership showed increasing self-confidence, based in part on its economic successes and military reforms. There began to be grounds for some suspicion that the continued emphasis on "collective security" was really designed to embroil the capitalist countries with each other in a fratricidal "imperialist" war from which the Soviet Union might draw profit by abstaining. It was a well-established policy, rooted in Bolshevik realism, and Stalin had expressed it with great clarity:

> Our banner remains as of old the banner of *peace*. But if war sets in, we shall not be able to sit with arms folded—we shall have to take part, but we shall be the last to take part. And we shall take part in order to cast the decisive weight on the scales, the weight able to tip the balance.[7]

In an effort further to strengthen Russia's position, the age of liability to conscription was reduced from 21 to 19 (August 11, 1936), a move promptly countered (August 24) by German lengthening of the period of military service. To guarantee the reliability of the armed forces in face of the purge of high officers, the authority of political commissars was restored (May 10, 1937).

Toward Nazi Germany, the Soviet Union now pursued a policy of carefully patient sympathy, quickened, perhaps, by Germany's fresh extension of trade credits. Although she criticized the Rhineland coup of March 7, 1936, Russia persisted in maintaining that German return to the League would be welcome. In the fall of that year, Hitler unleashed a violent propaganda campaign, not against Russia but specifically against Bolshevism. Its culmination was announcement of the Anti-Comintern Pact with Japan, signed on November 25, 1936. The reply of the Soviet Union was quietly to boast of her own strength: "Just as a pig can never look at the sky, so Hitler will never be able to see our cabbage patch." [8] In an address to the "constituent" Congress of Soviets (November 28), Litvinov, the most ardent champion of collective security, took the isolationist position that it was the West, rather than Russia, that ought to fear Germany:

> We, as a state, are not concerned with the internal Fascist regime of this or that country. Our collaboration with other countries and our participation in the League of Nations are based on the principle of the peaceful coexistence of two systems—the socialist and the capitalist—and we consider that the latter includes the Fascist system. But Fascism is now ceasing to be an internal affair of the countries which preach it.
>
> The Soviet Union . . . will calmly let other states weigh and evaluate the advantages which can be derived for peace from close co-operation with the Soviet Union, and understand that the Soviet Union can give more than receive. . . . Other states, other territories are menaced most. Our security does not depend . . . upon foreign policy combinations. The Soviet Union is sufficiently strong in herself.[9]

That Litvinov was not merely whistling in the dark but counting on the inevitability of a new Anglo-German war is strongly suggested by Russia's increasingly cavalier attitude toward the West. At the Montreux Conference (June 22-July 20, 1936), held to revise the Lausanne Treaty of 1923 governing the regime of the Straits, Russia did not hesitate to clash openly with Great Britain over control of the Bosporus and Dardanelles. The Lausanne arrangements had not conceded Russia's old desire that the Straits be closed to warships of Powers that had no Black Sea coastline. At Montreux, Turkey asked restoration to her of full sovereignty over the Straits, to be coupled with limitations on passage of foreign warships that would in effect give Russia security in the Black Sea without denying her the right of egress for her own warships. Russia supported Turkey, trying only to extend somewhat the arrangements in her favor. Great Britain, backed by Japan, strongly opposed the grant to Russia of the right of egress. In the end, a compromise restored Turkish sovereignty and gave Russia some advantages, though less than originally proposed. Russia's gains were, however, partially nullified by a cooling off of Turkish friendship, for Turkey shifted back to her ancient preference for distant England over neighboring Russia as a protector.

In the 1936 discussions that arose out of the failure of the League to protect Ethiopia, one of its own members, the Soviet Union took a very high line. Western statesmen tended to agree with Neville Chamberlain that "it is time so to limit the functions of the League in future that they may accord with its real powers." [10] Litvinov took the opposite position that what was needed were proposals for "improving the application of the principles of the Covenant." [11] The dispute might seem a renewal of the arguments between President Wilson and his Allied colleagues at Versailles, but to most "practical" statesmen of the 1930's Litvinov's objections appeared rather as evidence that the Soviet Union was artfully endeavoring to force the League Powers into unwanted wars.

Russia's pursuit of an independent policy was even more clearly evident in connection with the Spanish civil war, which broke out in July, 1936. Initially the Soviet Union joined, as did also Germany and Italy, in the non-intervention agreement initiated by Britain and France. When, however, the "fascist" Powers began to give thinly disguised assistance to Franco, the Soviet government felt free to send food and tanks (October, 1936) to the Spanish Loyalists. In November an "International Brigade," recruited by the Comintern but including no Russians, was sent into action. In addition, a few hundred Russians, headed by General Kléber (who was to disappear in the purges after his return), played an important role in saving Madrid for a time. The Spanish gold reserve was welcomed in Moscow, and considerable quantities of arms, mainly foreign, were purchased and transported to Spain.

The motives behind this limited Soviet intervention remain obscure. The Russians ostentatiously made no effort to promote Communist revolution in Spain, an attempt that would in any case certainly have been doomed to failure in view of the preponderantly anarcho-syndicalist traditions of Spanish revolutionaries. The Communists did use the opportunity to assert their own monopoly of revolutionary faith; as *Pravda* reported (December 17, 1936),

> so far as Catalonia is concerned, the cleaning up of the Trotskyist and anarcho-syndicalist elements has already begun and will be carried out with the same energy as in the U.S.S.R.[12]

On the other hand, Dimitrov used the lessons of Spain further to emphasize the need of "united fronts" everywhere. It may well be that Russia's prime interest in the "Spanish labyrinth" was to force the Entente Powers into war with Germany. Alvarez del Vayo, the chief non-Communist supporter of Moscow in Spain, quotes Negrin, Loyalist premier in the latter part of the civil war, as later saying:

> Moscow tried to do for France and England what they should have done for themselves. The promise of Soviet aid to the Spanish Republic was that ultimately Paris and London would awake to the risks involved to themselves in Italo-German victory in Spain and join the U.S.S.R. in supporting us.[13]

If Moscow was really attempting to support "collective security" in this backhanded way, the effect was that of a boomerang. The suspicions of Soviet intentions already cherished by the British and French governments were deepened, and their attitudes toward collaboration with the Soviet Union in international politics hardened. In December, 1937, the French foreign minister visited Poland, Rumania, Yugoslavia, and Czechoslovakia, evidently to check on the strength of French alliances in Germany's rear; it was significant that he did not visit Moscow. In February, 1938, Anthony Eden, who had been sent on a friendly mission to Moscow in 1935 and who was distinguished for his stiff attitude on the need to withdraw Italian "volunteers" from Spain, resigned from the British cabinet. Across the Atlantic, American official policy was still represented by the Neutrality Act of 1935, only slightly amended on May 1, 1937; President Roosevelt's "quarantine the aggressor" speech (October 5, 1937), delivered in the midst of the "recession," was a very small crumb of comfort.

On the other side, notwithstanding the withdrawal of General Kléber (February, 1937) and the drying up of Russian aid to the Spanish Loyalists, the Anti-Comintern Pact was apparently fortified by Italy's adhesion (November 6, 1937); the effect was somewhat diminished by Poland's announcement that she would not join if asked. Japan, taking advantage of the pact, had meanwhile concentrated her attention on China, with which open war was begun in July, 1937. Russia's immediate response was a non-aggression pact with China (August 21), the shipment to her of supplies and "volunteers," and occupation of Sinkiang, the Chinese portion of Turkestan. The Chinese Communist Party, guided by Mao Tse-tung, made an entente with the Kuomintang government, which it faithfully observed; it organized a guerilla operation behind the Japanese lines, but its proposal for organic unity was rejected by the Kuomintang. Despite mastery of most of the important Chinese centers, Japan found herself involved in an immensely difficult and exhausting struggle, which removed her as a serious menace to the Soviet Union. Russia's announcements that the Arctic Sea route had been made "operative" (1935) and that the Trans-Siberian Railway had been double-tracked (1937) were not put to the test. In consequence, the stiffening of the American attitude toward Japan no longer interested the Russians, and the two countries drifted even farther apart. Border clashes between Soviet and Japanese troops, some of them quite serious, continued; but the net effect of Sino-Japanese hostilities was to relieve Russia from pressure in the Far East. In the Middle East, the Soviet Union, hampered by her policies toward her own Moslems in Central Asia, made no headway in extending her influence.

In Europe, Russian isolation, both voluntary and enforced, grew steadily greater. On February 21, 1938, nine days after the inclusion of Austrian Nazis in Schuschnigg's government, the British prime minister publicly stated that "the peace of Europe must depend on the attitude of the four major Powers of Europe: Germany, Italy, France, and ourselves." [14] On March 13, the day of the condemnation of Bukharin and the rest of "The 21" in Moscow, Hitler unilaterally announced *Anschluss* with Austria. Italy, now a member of the Axis, did not repeat her 1934 veto, and Great Britain and France were again acquiescent. Not even Czechoslovakia, clearly next on the list, dared mobilize, but the following day France announced she would stand by her ally. Three days later (March 17), the Soviet Union, which had been waiting to see how the cat would jump, issued through Litvinov a guarded statement to foreign newspaper correspondents in Moscow that "the Soviet Government . . . is ready as before to participate in collective actions . . . decided upon jointly with it. . . ." [15] Immediate action "in the League of Nations or outside of it" was recommended. More informally, Litvinov stated that the Soviet Union would stand by the 1935 agreements if France did; otherwise she would act as she chose. He hinted that Soviet troops would be prepared, if necessary, to force their way across Poland and perhaps Rumania.

How seriously Litvinov's statement to the press can be taken is still an open question. Ambassador Davies recorded in a memorandum to Secretary of State Cordell Hull that six days later (March 23):

> Litvinov stated frankly, "France had no confidence in the Soviet Union and the Soviet Union had no confidence in France. . . ." He expressed the view that if Fascist Germany does become dominant over Europe, the long Russian frontier will have nothing to fear from Germany because she, Germany, will have her hands full in the states bordering it.[16]

Prime Minister Chamberlain expressed (March 24) Great Britain's unwillingness to surrender her right to choose between war and peace by making a definite commitment to support France. Davies warned Washington (March 26):

> England and France . . . have been playing into the hands of the Nazi and the Fascist aims. . . . This may extend to the point where there might be developed a realistic union of these forces with Germany in the not distant future. . . . There is no doubt of the supreme confidence on the part of this regime in their ability to take care of themselves from an attack from either the east or the west.[17]

CZECHOSLOVAKIA

Throughout the crisis, in all pronouncements intended for the public, the Russians asserted their willingness to support French action; late in September, their envoy at Prague is said to have promised that, if the League were to condemn Germany as an aggressor, the Soviet Union would come to the aid of Czechoslovakia, alone if necessary. It is clear that in setting such conditions for their assistance the Russians were committing themselves to nothing. The question of how they could get their forces into the country also remained unanswered; by the beginning of September, Litvinov had ruled out the possibility of forcing a way through Poland or Rumania unless the League approved. It is also noteworthy that at no time did the Soviet Union indicate fear of being involved in war with Germany. From time to time the charge was made that Great Britain and France were trying to encourage Germany to attack Russia, but strong emphasis was constantly put on the danger to the Western Powers themselves if they did not take timely action.

For the British and French governments the crisis presented immense problems, even if they had felt they could count on Russia. That they did not is clear. In a private letter to his sister, Chamberlain acknowledged a year later (March 26, 1939):

> I must confess to the most profound distrust of Russia. I have no belief whatever in her ability to maintain an effective offensive, even if she wanted to. And I distrust her motives, which seem to me to have little connection with our ideas of liberty, and to be concerned only with getting everyone else by the ears. Moreover, she is both hated and suspected by many of the smaller states, notably by Poland, Rumania, and Finland.[18]

Chamberlain was not the only one who regarded Russia as "a very unreliable friend . . . with an enormous irritative power on others." [19] Even his severe critic, Winston Churchill, could not bring himself consistently to advocate joint action with Russia. Similar views were prevalent also in France; while French military opinion of untested Soviet strength, shaken by the Tukhachevsky affair, was very low, Premier Daladier had no intention of allowing France to be drawn into war with Germany without a powerful ally. Charles A. Lindbergh's report (September, 1938) on the vast superiority of the *Luftwaffe* and the demoralized state of the Russian air force struck a responsive chord in many minds.

There were, however, additional paralyzing factors. No one any longer believed that the creation of Czechoslovakia had been a triumph for the principle of national self-determination; it was widely recognized that its existing boundaries, however historic in part, had been accepted in 1919 as a concession to the French craving for the strongest possible ally, to take the place of a collapsed Russia, in Germany's rear. Neither the British people nor the French had yet been sufficiently antagonized by Nazi arrogance and bluster to give wholesale support to a war for the sake of maintaining the injustices of Versailles. The Runciman mission (August-September) was an effort to reach an arrangement by which the German, Slovak, and Ruthenian minorities, benevolently though they had been treated, could be satisfied and yet something of the situation salvaged for the Czechs without a war, which at best could only be a very difficult one.

The road to appeasement, once entered upon, steadily broadened. In May, Great Britain and France had been thinking of constitutional re-arrangements within Czechoslovakia; by September, it was clear that only cession of territory could solve the problem of satisfying Hitler. Chamberlain's visits to Hitler at Berchtesgaden (September 15) and Godesberg (September 22) led straight to the Four-Power meeting at Munich (September 29-30). To the end, however, the British government held firm to its original warning (May 21, 1938) that she would support France if Germany attempted to act unilaterally. For its part, the Soviet Union, furious at not being adequately consulted, made desperate efforts to prevent a settlement; it endorsed Roosevelt's last-minute suggestion to Hitler (September 26) that a "conference of all the nations directly interested in the present controversy" be held in "some neutral spot in Europe."[20] At Geneva, Litvinov had stated (September 23) that the Soviet government, though technically no longer bound, was still willing to act if France would. On this basis the British stated officially (September 26) that if

> a German attack is made upon Czechoslovakia, the immediate result must be that France will be bound to come to her assistance and Great Britain and Russia will certainly stand by France.[21]

This did not of course preclude the possibility that by proper international agreement, accepted, however reluctantly, by Czechoslovakia, German ambitions could not be realized. Hitler refrained from attacking, but, urged by the West, Czechoslovakia yielded (September 30). The notion that Russia was ready to support last-ditch resistance is supported by the final statement of the Czech Minister of Propaganda but contradicted by the whole record of the Soviet position during the crisis, as well as by the hard fact that it evidently would have been futile.

The surrender of Czechoslovakia did not end her troubles, nor those of Europe. Poland seized Teschen but soon found herself faced with German demands for restoration of the Polish Corridor and abandonment of her special position in Danzig. The Carpatho-Ruthenes, temporarily used by the Nazis as bait to detach the Ukraine from Russia, were soon turned over to Hungary (March 16, 1939), three days before the Spanish civil war ended in favor of Franco, who, in Soviet parlance, was a "fascist." On March 15, 1939, the Nazis occupied the remnant of Czechoslovakia. The indications that Poland, notwithstanding her collusion with Germany, would be next were so clear that Prime Minister Chamberlain lost little time in officially announcing (March 31) that Great Britain had given, and Poland had accepted, a British guarantee of her independence.

In this atmosphere of an approaching international showdown, Stalin convened the Eighteenth Party Congress (March, 1939), the first since the "victory" Congress of 1934 before the murder of Kirov and the beginning of the "Great Purge." By this time, under Beria's guidance, the purge had been concluded, and Stalin's control within the Soviet Union was obviously unshakeable. Never before had he been able to speak with such authority as when he personally enunciated (March 10) at the Congress the principles of Soviet Russia's current foreign policy. Stalin returned to the ideological Marxist position that "the new economic crisis [the "recession" that began in 1937] must lead, and is actually leading, to a further sharpening of the imperialist struggle." According to Stalin, the "second imperialist war" was "already in its second year"; yet Great Britain, France, and the United States were not replying vigorously to the aggressions of Germany, Italy, and Japan. The reason for this phenomenon was not their weakness: "The nonaggressive democratic states, taken together, are indisputably stronger than the fascist states, both economically and militarily." Nor was their fear of revolution in the event of war strong enough to account for their passivity. To the ever-suspicious Stalin it was clear that the reason Britain and France, in particular, had decided "on repudiation of the policy of collective security . . . and on a switch to the policy of nonintervention," the reason they talked of the "weakness of the Russian army" and the "demoralization of the Russian air force," was that they were

> pushing the Germans further toward the east, promising them easy booty and repeating: "Just start a war with the Bolsheviks, and then everything will go alright."

Stalin expressed neither moral indignation nor worry over the danger to Russia:

> It would be naive to moralize to people who recognize no human morality. . . . It must be remembered, nevertheless, that the big and dangerous political game started by the advocates of the policy of non-intervention may end in a serious failure for them.

As for the future, Stalin gave a scarcely veiled picture of Soviet policy in the coming crisis. Making no further mention of "collective security," he summed up the Party's foreign policy as:

> 1. To continue to pursue the policy of peace and of strengthening business relations with all countries.
>
> 2. To be cautious and not to allow our country to be drawn into conflicts by war-mongers who are accustomed to use other people's hands to bank the fire.
>
> 3. To strengthen in every possible way the fighting power of our Red Army and Red Navy.
>
> 4. To strengthen the international ties of friendship with the toilers of all countries, who are interested in peace and friendship among peoples.[22]

Russia was on the point of moving into a new phase of her foreign policy.

Stalin's expressed fear that British warmongers would try to involve Russia in a war with Germany while England stayed out was wholly belied by Great Britain's course of action. Chamberlain's guarantee to Poland was quickly followed (April 6) by announcement of an Anglo-Polish mutual-defense agreement which for the moment made Germany pull in her horns. Old British suspicions of Russia's intentions were reinforced by Polish fears that Russian military assistance in the form of sending troops would be as fatal to her as would be a German invasion. In answer to Italy's occupation of Albania (April 7), Great Britain announced (April 13) guarantees to Greece and to Rumania and completed cordial conversations with Turkey leading toward a mutual-assistance pact in that quarter. France followed the British lead but showed some anxiety to secure Soviet coöperation. Throughout subsequent British negotations with the Soviet Union, it was made abundantly clear that the British never asked the Russians to commit themselves to any action that might involve the Soviet Union in war with Germany unless Great Britain and France were already at war with Hitler.

Soviet policy remained equivocal. On the one hand, the Soviet ambassador in Berlin pointedly called German attention (April 17) to the fact that his government was not exploiting the growing tension between Germany and the West. On the other hand, Litvinov replied encouragingly (April 18) to British and French inquiries about the possibility of collective action. The text of these Soviet proposals has not been published but, by collating Soviet, French, Polish, and German accounts, the probable nature of their content has been made reasonably clear. It appears that when the Soviet *History of Diplomacy* speaks of "a military convention which would give the mutual-assistance pact real strength," [23] it refers to a Soviet demand that Russian troops be allowed to enter Polish territory. Molotov is stated to have told the Polish ambassador that the British guarantee must be limited to Poland's western boundaries; in view of Russia's past attitude and of her subsequent conduct, this seems not at all improbable. Ominous also, in view of Russia's persistent claims to Bessarabia, was a reported Russian demand for cancellation of the Polish-Rumanian alliance. A no less difficult point was raised by the admitted demand for "a guarantee by the three Great Powers to all countries between the Baltic and the Black Sea." What this could mean for Finland and the three Baltic states became increasingly clear as the Russians became more insistent on their concept of "indirect aggression" (use of neutral territory through which to launch an attack on the Soviet Union). From the outset these small countries objected to having any Soviet "guarantee" imposed on them.

A British government meditating carrying a united country into war with Germany over an issue that still involved the injustices of Versailles could not possibly meet such Russian terms. In democratic and essentially pacific Britain, the only possibility of mobilizing real enthusiasm for war turned on respect for international morality and the rights of small nations. To go to war on behalf of the sovereign independence and territorial integrity of a small country while simultaneously agreeing to annexation of a large part of its territory by a third power and to sacrifice of the independence of three or four still smaller states would have placed the British government in a ridiculous position before the public. It might be necessary to "stop Hitler" but not by adopting his methods. Even the possibility that the Communists might make a deal with the Nazis seemed a lesser peril than paying so exorbitant a price.

THE THIRD PHASE: COLLABORATION

That a Russo-German deal was even probable was suggested by the resignation (May 3) of Litvinov as Commissar of Foreign Affairs; a Jew, and with an English wife at that, could not be the best intermediary between Stalin and Hitler. His successor, Molotov, who retained his title as chairman of Sovnarkom, soon (May 20) dropped a hint (on which he refused to elaborate) to the German ambassador at Moscow that "the Soviet Government could only agree to a resumption of the [commercial] negotiations if the necessary 'political bases' for them had been created." [24] Russia was in the market but wanted to be courted.

Under the circumstances, the British wasted no vigorous effort on trying to come to an agreement with the Soviet Union. On June 7 a low-level Foreign Office official was sent to Moscow for direct talks; he found the Russians adamant on the question of "indirect aggression" and on the need of forcing "guarantees" on the Baltic states. While Soviet propaganda openly urged the Poles to resist German demands, the Polish ambassador still found that the Russians attached "unacceptable conditions" [25] even to their offers to supply Poland with armaments. No progress could be made, and on June 29 Zhdanov, than regarded as Stalin's chosen heir, published an article in *Pravda* suggesting that

> The English and French desire not a real treaty acceptable to the USSR but only *talks* about a treaty in order to speculate before public opinion in their countries on the allegedly unyielding attitude of the USSR and thus make easier for themselves the road to a deal with the aggressors.[26]

Nevertheless, on August 12 discussions were begun between British and French military missions and their Russian hosts. Voroshilov raised protocol difficulties and expressed dismay at the small military forces at the disposal of the Western Powers. The chief obstacle, however, which led to adjournment of the discussions on August 17, was Russian insistence that the Soviet Union be permitted to send troops into Poland rather than confine itself to furnishing the Polish army with weapons, ammunition, and other war supplies. Despite French entreaties, the Polish attitude continued to be in the spirit of the famous remark attributed to Marshal Smigly-Ridz: "With the Germans we risk losing our liberty, with the Russians our soul." [27] A similar obstacle to the talks was the Russian demand that, because of the danger of "indirect aggression," they must be allowed to occupy the Baltic seaports.

In the meantime the Germans had not been idle. At least as early as July 6, in the course of trade talks at Berlin, a German official had openly suggested the advantages to Moscow that might accrue from her staying out of war. Further conversations, both at Berlin and at Moscow, led to Ribbentrop's suggestion (August 14) that he be invited to visit Moscow for talks with Molotov and Stalin. Coyly yielding to German eagerness, Stalin issued the invitation for August 23. That very night was signed the nonaggression pact by which Germany and Russia openly pledged each other benevolent neutrality in the event either was at war with any third Power. In secret clauses, Germany conceded to the Soviet Union most of what the Western Allies had felt unable to approve. A demarcation line was drawn, leaving to Russia a free hand in Estonia, Latvia, and parts of Finland, Poland, and Rumania; Lithuania and the western portion of Poland were allotted to Germany.[28] The Pact was ratified on August 31. The next day Germany invaded Poland. Another two days later, Great Britain and France declared war on Germany, while Russia remained quiet.

The similarity in principle of the Ribbentrop-Molotov Pact of August 23, 1939, to the Treaty of Tilsit, concluded between Napoleon and Alexander I in 1807, is very striking. Once again a Russian autocracy had given a Western dictator *carte blanche* to deal with his archenemy, England, in return for a free hand for itself to operate east of a defined line. There were, of course, many differences. Prior to 1807, Russia had been at war with Napoleon, as the subsidized ally of England; prior to 1939, Russia had been waging merely a war of words with Hitler, whom Britain was trying to contain by concessions, not yet by blows. In 1807, Russia, accepting the Continental System, had sacrificed her own economic interests for those of France; in 1939, Russia undertook (October 24) to supply Germany with large quantities of grain, oil, manganese, chromium, and other raw materials which the German war machine desperately needed, but only in return for military equipment for her own armed forces. In 1807, there had been between Russia and the Western military dictator a broad belt of territory, ruled by France but awaiting only the opportunity to rise against her; by the fall of 1939, the Russian and German frontiers marched together.

It may well be that even at the last moment Great Britain and France might have put heavy pressure on Poland to concede the most obviously valid of the German demands, and that even Poland's intransigent rulers might have felt compelled to accept a second "Munich." The possibility of such a development was apparently ruled out by Hitler's self-confidence, bred of the extended record of appeasement and nourished by his success in averting by agreement with Stalin the dreaded possibility of a serious two-front war. If it be true that Hitler was surprised when Great Britain and France actually did attack Germany on September 3, Stalin also was in for a no less disturbing shock within a few months after the outbreak of the war which he had predicted and perhaps hoped for.

As of September, 1939, however, it seemed that the Russian leaders had achieved a diplomatic masterpiece. The capitalist world had embarked on what promised to be a long and exhausting struggle which, according to Stalin's calculations, would leave Russia with a defeated neighbor. Even the victors would be too weakened to oppose the will of Socialist Russia, which could utilize the interval enormously to increase her own strength and so at last would be in a position to effect the promised world revolution.

These remoter dreams were not allowed to stand in the way of the practical business of reaping the immediate harvest. On September 16 a truce put an end to border fighting with Japan. On September 17 a note to the Polish ambassador stated that

> The Polish Government has disintegrated and no longer shows any signs of life. . . . In these circumstances, the Soviet Government has directed the High Command of the Red Army to order the troops to cross the frontier and to take under their protection the life and property of the population of Western Ukraine and Western White Russia.[29]

The Soviet troops rushed forward to the agreed demarcation line, the Germans fraternally withdrawing from some areas they had already occupied to the east of it. On September 28 a supplementary treaty with Germany moved the line substantially eastward from the Vistula to the Bug, but eastern Galicia remained in Soviet hands, thus isolating Rumania; in return for Russia's pull-back, most of Lithuania was now transferred to the Russian sphere of interest. The newly acquired territories were duly incorporated into the adjoining Ukrainian and White Russian S.S.R.'s.

The next step was to deal with the Baltic states.* Deprived of any possible protector, they now, one by one, had to accept "mutual assistance" pacts and admit Soviet troops to "protect" them. Estonia was first (September 29), Latvia second (October 5); Lithuania came last (October 10) and was favored by having Vilna, which Poland had occupied since 1920, restored to her. By agreement with Germany, an exchange of populations was begun; all Germans or persons of German descent were permitted, if not encouraged, to return to Germany, while Germany undertook to repatriate all Ukrainians and White Russians in her share of Poland.

Finland offered more difficulty. She was soon served (October 5) with a summons to cede territory on the Karelian isthmus close to Leningrad, for which she was offered in exchange a much larger, but thinly populated territory in the interior, and to lease a naval base on the Hangö peninsula. Finland did not agree to comply. On November 29 the Russians attacked; in order to avoid a "war," they recognized a new Communist "government of Finland," headed by Kuusinen, one-time secretary of the Comintern, whose headquarters were on Soviet territory. Thanks to their spirit and to the narrowness of the isthmus, the Finns were able to hold the Russians back for some months, thus increasing foreign doubts whether the Red Army, like the Soviet economy, did not sacrifice quality for quantity. For a time efforts were made to organize Western intervention in behalf of the Finns, but they were hampered both by the fears of the Scandinavians lest they become involved and by Allied dread of taking on a second enemy while engaged in war with Germany. By March 12, 1940, Finland felt constrained to sign a peace by which she ceded Vyborg to Russia and granted the lease of a naval base; in return for these and other concessions, the Communists abandoned their puppet government. Their Finnish territories, new and old, were made into a Karelian-Finnish S.S.R. within the structure of the Soviet Union.

Russia's relations with the West, never cordial, had been driven to a new low by the master stroke of the Ribbentrop-Molotov Pact. The "Winter War" against Finland and rumors that the Allies were meditating a sudden attack on the oil fields of the Caucasus naturally did nothing to improve them. The attitude of the Comintern and of foreign Communist parties also contributed to make matters worse. On November 7, 1939, a Comintern proclamation had condemned both sides in the new war for world domination but had laid the onus chiefly on the Western Allies. The French Communist Party, caught by surprise, had readjusted quickly; its initial theory that the Communists were ready to resist all acts of aggression and to fulfill their duties as Frenchmen under their country's treaty with Poland had contrasted strangely with the bold headlines in their official paper: "The action of the

* See Map VIII.

Soviet Union in its nonaggression pact with Germany serves to strengthen General Peace."[30] Its leader, Maurice Thorez, had joined his regiment but had soon deserted and fled to Moscow. The relatively insignificant British Communist Party had reacted similarly. In the United States, the Communist Party opposed any aid to the Allies, though, hamstrung by American legislation, it formally withdrew from the Comintern late in 1940. The German Communist Party, more favorably situated, bitterly criticized the new imperialist war being waged by the Allies against Germany.

So long as Germany was tied down by a western front, even under conditions of a mutually defensive "phony war," Russia gave her every appearance of support. On October 6, 1939, with Poland definitely in his pocket, Hitler, disclaiming any desire for further conquests either eastward or westward, launched a "peace offensive," which Molotov supported with seeming conviction. By November, Hitler had abandoned this pretense, but Stalin continued to upbraid the Allies for having refused to listen. Of greater practical value was a new economic agreement (October 24), by which the quantities of raw materials to be delivered to Germany in the next eighteen months were very much increased; delivery of German war materials in exchange was to be staggered over twenty-seven months, though a certain ratio was to be currently maintained. Throughout the winter, despite the reluctance of the German military to part with valuable armaments and despite the strain on Russian resources entailed by large exports of food, oil, and metals, the agreement was scrupulously kept, to the mutual advantage of both parties. A British-Soviet trade agreement (October 11, 1939) seems also to have played into German hands; England did secure needed lumber, but, despite British protests, British rubber, tin, and zinc were evidently passed on by Russia to Germany. In naval matters also, there was coöperation; German vessels found shelter at Murmansk and were given preferential treatment. On the other hand, Hitler could not bring himself to accept Soviet submarines and was reluctant to sell any of his few surface ships to the eager Russians.

On March 29, 1940, Molotov summarized the international situation in a speech before the Supreme Council. He again condemned Great Britain and France for their "imperialist policy toward Germany," which had demonstrated also "the class roots of the hostile policy of the imperialists toward the Socialist state."

> These new, good relations between the U.S.S.R. and Germany have been tested in practice in connection with events in former Poland and their strength has been sufficiently proved. . . . Of the southern neighboring States . . . Rumania is one with which we have no Pact of Non-Aggression . . . although we have never raised the question of recovering Bessarabia by military means. . . . In our relations with Japan we have, not without some difficulty, settled several questions. . . . Nevertheless, we cannot express great satisfaction in regard to our relations with Japan.[31]

THE BREAK WITH GERMANY

At this point the war in the west suddenly came to life. Russia was quite unperturbed by the sudden Nazi invasion of Denmark and Norway (April 9), which in Soviet opinion had been brought on by Allied violations of Norwegian neutrality. Especially in view of German promises to respect Sweden's neutrality, Russia even felt more secure with respect to Finland. However, the German breakthrough on the western front in May, which led to the catastrophe of Dunkirk and to the collapse of the French army, altered the whole situation. The armistice signed (June 22, 1940) by the Vichy government upset the Soviet calculations behind the Pact of August 23, 1939. If Great Britain, whose land forces were now almost wholly disarmed, were also to give in, the security of the Soviet Union would no longer exist. In May the Russians had been very cool to British proposals for new trade talks. On June 5, however, they accepted the nomination of new British and French ambassadors to Moscow. Sir Stafford Cripps, a high-level official, together with his French colleague, reached Moscow on June 12, though, due to delay in transmitting credentials, he was not received by Stalin until July 1.

The details of the way in which the Soviet Union, from a complaisant partner of Germany, was in the course of the following year converted into her principal victim are still shrouded in fog. The evidence later adduced at the Nuremberg "war criminal" trials is illuminating, but there are three main difficulties in relying on it: (1) the purpose of the trials was to prosecute the German leaders, not to establish objective truth; (2) German defendants, fighting for their lives or at least their liberty, had no incentive to tell the truth, the whole truth, and nothing but the truth; and (3) the Soviet authorities repeatedly intervened to cut off lines of testimony not acceptable to them. Any interpretation has therefore to be based largely on guesswork, however fortified by appraisal of what any responsible rulers would be likely to do under the given circumstances and by reference to historical analogy. Some facts are in any case clear.

Russia lost no time in drawing the last ounce of profit from her 1939 pact with Germany. An ultimatum to Lithuania (June 15) resulted in the formation there of a new Communist-controlled government (June 17). Similar action with respect to the other two Baltic states (June 16) produced the same results in Latvia (June 20) and Estonia (June 22). On July 21 all three duly petitioned for incorporation into the Soviet Union, a request graciously granted. Lithuania (August 1), Latvia (August 5), and Estonia (August 8) were declared member states of the Soviet Union. The 1939 Pact had conceded Bessarabia also to Russia, which, however, wanted Bukovina as well, a demand that the Germans hesitated to grant. On June 26 an ultimatum to Rumania demanded immediate cession of Bessarabia and the northern part of Bukovina. Although Rumania had on May

29 put herself under German protection, Germany advised acceptance of the Russian demand. On August 2, Bessarabia, enlarged by some territory formerly included in the Soviet Ukraine, also became a member state of the Soviet Union as the Moldavian S.S.R.; northern Bukovina was allotted to the Ukraine. These four new "independent" but "federated" S.S.R.'s raised the total to sixteen (reduced to fifteen in 1956 when the "Karelian-Finnish S.S.R." was incorporated into the R.S.F.S.R.).

This was the utmost in territorial expansion westward that Germany would allow. Russian interest in the Balkans conflicted with rising German and Italian interests there. Through local Communist parties, Russia tried to work for a Rumanian-Bulgarian-Yugoslav combination, but she dared not oppose decisive German action in that area. On September 27, 1940, Germany, Italy, and Japan signed a Tripartite Pact, one article of which denied that it affected the existing relations of any of them with Soviet Russia. Yet, another article asserted that they would "assist one another with all political, economic, and military means when one of the high contracting parties is attacked by a power at present not involved in the European war or the Sino-Japanese conflict." [32] This could scarcely apply to any state save the United States or the Soviet Union. In which direction the wind was blowing was indicated by the adhesion to the Tripartite Pact of Hungary (November 20), Rumania (November 23), and Slovakia (November 24); Bulgaria, despite heavy Soviet pressure, followed (March 1, 1941). Even in October, 1940, German troops had begun to be posted in Rumania, after her forced surrender of territory to Hungary and Bulgaria; in March, 1941, they were sent also into Bulgaria. In the case of Yugoslavia, German designs hit a snag; on March 25 the Yugoslav Regency reluctantly signed the pact, but within forty-eight hours it had been overthrown by a revolt. On April 6 German troops invaded Yugoslavia, and Greece as well. The Soviet Union, which had promised Yugoslavia a nonaggression pact, promptly tucked in its tail and explained that no military support to Yugoslavia had been intended.

Checkmate by Germany of Russia's forward policy in the Balkans was accompanied by deterioration, from the spring of 1940, of economic relations between the partners in the Moscow Pact. German reluctance to supply the agreed quantities of military equipment, which the German forces wanted for themselves, caused Russia to threaten to stop her supplies of raw materials. This circumstance was evidently an important factor in Hitler's decision, taken perhaps as early as September, 1940, to attack Russia. In November, Molotov visited Berlin in an effort to settle the incipient quarrel; he was told by the Germans to think in terms of Russian expansion by way of the Persian Gulf in the direction of India. Molotov attempted to pin agreement down to withdrawal of German troops that had been sent to Finland after the "Winter War," guarantee of Soviet military power near the Straits, Russian expansion into Iran, and Japanese renunciation of her concessions in northern Sakhalin, but his memorandum of November 25 went unanswered.

In such circumstances it might have been natural to expect that the sequel to the Treaty of Tilsit of 1807 would have been repeated. Just as Napoleon had steadily extended his power over Europe and as England had then stood alone in opposition to his might, so his German successor, Hitler, had now established virtually complete German domination over the Continent; if Great Britain should come to terms, there would be no obstacle to Hitler's complete supremacy in the Old World. Objectively, Russia, if she should have to stand alone, would be in grave danger of being overwhelmed. Common sense clearly indicated that Russia, as in 1812, ought for her own sake to strike some sort of bargain with Great Britain, the only Power offering opposition to the will of the dictator of the Continent. It would not take megalomaniac dreams on the part of Hitler to make Germany realize that Russia's interest now demanded that she attempt to stab her partner in the back and that England could no longer be squeamish about Russia's violations of the principle of maintaining the sovereign independence and territorial integrity of small nations. In much the same way as Napoleon had felt compelled to strike suddenly at Russia before she could complete arrangements with England, so Hitler had no reasonable choice but to try to put Russia out of condition to act before he could dare attempt to invade Britain. Otherwise the colossus might choose its own most opportune moment to hamstring Germany.

How far such considerations influenced the conscious thinking of either Germany or Russia remains "a riddle wrapped in a mystery, inside an enigma." [33] It appears that Sir Stafford Cripps did in October, 1940, indicate British willingness to accept the *fait accompli* in the Baltic area, but no documentary evidence has appeared that the Soviet Union then indicated any interest. Early in 1941, the American government warned the Soviet ambassador that it had information that Germany intended to attack Russia in the spring; the Soviet government later asked for confirmation of this information but apparently gave no further indication of interest. By April the German and Soviet governments were complaining to each other of aircraft flights over their territory; although Russia maintained her deliveries of grain and raw materials, Germany made difficulties about release of aircraft sold to Russia. The German ambassador at Moscow, however, persisted in believing that Stalin would not desert from Germany to the Allies.

Throughout the period of friendship with Germany, Russia had been vigorously striving to increase her own military strength. Evidently dissatisfied with the showing of the Red Army in the war with Finland, the Soviet government had replaced Stalin's intimate, Marshal Voroshilov, with Marshal Timoshenko as Commissar of Defense (March 8, 1940). Under Timoshenko's direction a number of reforms were undertaken, the most sweeping of which was abolition of the political commissars and establishment of unity of military command in the hands of the officers (August 12). Notable efforts were made to shift economic activity "behind the Urals." Troop concentrations on the western frontier, vigorously denied by Soviet sources, evidently were made in 1940-1941. Just as the appeasement policy of Great Britain and France had not prevented them in the late 1930's from pressing forward military preparations, so the manifest desire of the Soviet Union not prematurely to provoke victorious Germany did not prevent her from girding up her loins, diplomatically as well as militarily. When the Japanese foreign minister, Matsuoka, passed through Moscow (March 24, 1941) on his way to Berlin, Stalin seized the opportunity to discuss matters personally with him. On his way home (April 7), further conversations resulted in a Russo-Japanese neutrality pact (April 13). The way to this understanding had been prepared by the serious worsening of relations between the Kuomintang and the Chinese Communist Party, which had led to serious clashes between their respective military forces. After conclusion of the Soviet Union's pact with Japan, Mao Tse-tung insisted that collaboration with the Kuomintang against Japan was still indispensable, but for the Soviet Union the vital fact was that, no matter what happened to the cause of communism in China, Russia's rear was now, notwithstanding the Anti-Comintern Pact of 1936 and the Tripartite Pact of 1940, reasonably secure in case of war with Germany.

The seriousness with which Russia viewed the situation was evidenced by Stalin's personal assumption of the title of chairman of the Council of People's Commissars (May 6). The Soviet Union continued to offer crumbs of appeasement to Germany and publicly denied rumors of impending war. On the German side, it is known, preparations for an attack on Russia went on uninterruptedly; the Russian side of the picture is the uncertain one. Testimony at the Nuremberg trials by highly-placed Germans, such as General Jodl, about their knowledge of Russian war preparations was cut short by Russian protests. The official Soviet position is that the German wolf wantonly attacked the meek Russian lamb. It has, however, to be remembered that Stalin was never given to showing his hand until reasonably certain of the probable outcome. In the face of repeated British and American warnings, he maintained the utmost reserve. Yet he and his advisers could hardly fail to be aware of the balance of forces that made it possible for the American ambassador to tell the British prime minister (June 20) that the American government would, in the event of a Nazi attack on Russia, welcome a British statement declaring the Soviet Union an ally. It is incredible that the rulers of Russia, who so often proved their alertness to *Realpolitik,* were really caught unaware by the German invasion on June 22, 1941.

NOTES

1. Litvinov speech in the Soviet Central Executive Committee (December 29, 1933), *Documents on International Affairs, 1933,* p. 433.
2. Spengler, *Hour of Decision,* p. 61.
3. Great Britain, *Parliamentary Papers,* Cmd. 5143, 27.
4. Pieck, "The Consequences of Sectarian Errors" in principal report (July 26, 1935), *VII Kongress des Kommunistischen Internationale. Gekürztes Stenografisches Protokoll,* pp. 25-28 *passim.*
5. "Ercoli," *ibid.,* pp. 380-445 *passim.*
6. *Ibid.,* p. 583.
7. Stalin, speech at a plenum of the Central Committee (January 19, 1925), *Sochineniia,* VII, 14.
8. Lubchenko, Ukrainian premier, speaking in the All-Union Congress of Soviets (November 26, 1936), *Documents on International Affairs, 1936,* p. 301.
9. Litvinov, *Against Aggression,* pp. 63, 79.
10. Chamberlain, speaking at dinner given him by the Nineteen Hundred Club (June 10, 1936), in Toynbee, *Survey for 1936,* II, 463-464.
11. Litvinov communication to League (August 22, 1936), in *League of Nations Official Journal, Special Supplement 154,* p. 10.
12. *Pravda,* December 17, 1936.
13. Alvarez del Vayo, *Freedom's Battle,* p. 76.
14. Chamberlain, speaking in the House of Commons (February 21, 1938), in *Documents on International Affairs, 1938,* I, 23.
15. Litvinov statement to foreign correspondents in Moscow (March 17, 1938), *loc. cit.,* pp. 314-315.
16. Davies, *Mission to Moscow,* pp. 290-292.
17. *Ibid.,* p. 297.
18. Feiling, *Life of Neville Chamberlain,* pp. 402-403.
19. *Ibid.,* p. 408.
20. *Peace and War . . . ,* pp. 426-429.
21. Communication issued by Foreign Office, circulated in House of Commons by Mr. Butler (September 26, 1938); cf. Hansard, Vol. 344, col. 1230.
22. Stalin, "Report on the International Position of the Soviet Union" (March 10, 1939), at Eighteenth Party Congress, in *Voprosy Leninizma,* 11th edition, pp. 564-575 *passim.*
23. Potemkin (ed.), *Istoriia diplomatii,* III, 674.
24. *Nazi-Soviet Relations . . . ,* p. 6.
25. *Official Documents Concerning Polish-German and Polish-Soviet Relations, 1933-1939,* pp. 208-209.
26. Degras (ed.), *Soviet Documents on Foreign Policy,* III, 354.
27. Reynaud, *La France a sauvé l'Europe,* I, 587; a slightly variant version is given in his *In the Thick of the Fight, 1934-1945,* p. 216.
28. For full text, see Degras, *op. cit.,* pp. 359-361.
29. *Official Documents . . . , op. cit.,* pp. 189-190; for slightly variant translation from the Russian original, cf. Degras, *op. cit.,* p. 374.
30. *L'Humanité,* August 25, 1939; the paper was suppressed by the French government the next day.

31. Molotov, *Soviet Peace Policy,* pp. 50-66 *passim;* extensive excerpts in Degras, *op. cit.,* p. 436-449.
32. U.S. Department of State, *Japan, 1931-1941,* II, 166-168.
33. Churchill broadcast, October 1, 1939.

SUGGESTIONS FOR FURTHER READING

Among books previously mentioned, Beloff is of exceptional value. Dallin, *Soviet Russia's Foreign Policy, 1939-1942,* and Harriet L. Moore, *Soviet Far Eastern Policy, 1931-1945,* are of more limited value. See also, with reservations, Cattell's *Communism and the Spanish Civil War* and his *Soviet Diplomacy and the Spanish Civil War,* which rely rather heavily on the Non-Intervention Committee. Wheeler-Bennett's *Munich: Prologue to Tragedy* presents a special view of that topic. An effort at a general interpretation is Borkenau's *European Communism,* a continuation of his earlier *World Communism.* Taracouzio's *Soviet Union and International Law* and his *War and Peace in Soviet Diplomacy* are excellent studies for the period before World War II. Concerning specifically Finland, see Jakobson's *Diplomacy of the Winter War* and Upton's *Finland in Crisis, 1940-1941.*

For documents, see: Degras (ed.), *Soviet Documents on Foreign Policy, 1917-1941,* Volume III; Shapiro, *Soviet Treaty Series*; Laserson, *Development of Soviet Foreign Policy in Europe, 1917-1942*; *Nazi-Soviet Relations, 1939-1941*; the more complete *Documents on German Foreign Policy, 1918-1945* (especially Series D, Volume VI); and Brandt, Schwartz, and Fairbanks, *Documentary History of Chinese Communism.*

Chapter

34

The Tensions of War: 1941-1945

MILITARY OPERATIONS

Notwithstanding Soviet boasts of the invincibility of the Red Army, notwithstanding the massing of troops on the western border, the initial drive of the German armies pressed forward almost as though no military forces were opposing them. By December, 1941, the front ran irregularly from Lake Ladoga to the mouth of the Don, far to the east of the German positions at the time of Brest-Litovsk. Leningrad had been completely encircled by the enemy, though on the north the blockade was maintained by the Finns, who had entered the war only in the hope of recovering the territories they had lost in the "Winter War" and refused to attack the besieged city. Moscow was threatened by salients both north and south. The most productive agricultural regions were wholly in German hands, and the Donets basin was almost in their grasp.

Utterly unable to withstand the attack, the Russians fell back on their traditional "scorched earth" policy, used by Kutuzov against Napoleon as well as by the Scythians against Darius. The population of the invaded area, or its least trustworthy elements, were rooted up and herded beyond the Urals. All movable industrial equipment was also carried off and, so far as practicable, installed in new areas, remote from the front. In the army, the original commanders, whose reputation dated from the civil wars, were quickly replaced with trained professionals. On the other hand, suspicion of the loyalty of many of the officers led to restoration (July 16, 1941) of the political commissars; one of them, Bulganin, who had behind him a successful career, first as a Chekist, later as an industrial administrator, now made such a brilliant record on the Moscow portion of the front that he was made a lieutenant-general in the following year.

Left to her own devices, the Soviet Union might well have collapsed completely, but Russia was not left to stand alone. Prime Minister Churchill had immediately announced:

> No one has been a more constant opponent of Communism than I have for the last twenty-five years. I will unsay no word that I have spoken about it. But all this fades away before the spectacle which is now unfolding. . . . Any man or state who fights on against Nazidom . . . will have our aid. . . . It follows, therefore, that we shall give whatever help we can to Russia and the Russian people.[1]

Through Sir Stafford Cripps, an Anglo-Soviet mutual-assistance pact was concluded which took the precaution to include guarantees against a separate peace. The United States, though not officially at war until December, 1941, expressed its readiness to extend "Lend-Lease" aid to Russia. By September a joint Anglo-American mission completed arrangements for the supply of more than a billion dollars worth of military supplies within the next year, delivery of which was given the highest priority by the American administration. Stalin "gratefully" acknowledged "the historic utterance of . . . Mr. Churchill . . . and the declaration of the United States government," [2] but did not refrain, even while accepting Lend-Lease aid, from asking Harriman for creation of a "second front." The total value of food, medical supplies, and other military matériel, especially transportation equipment, sent to Russia during the war reached nearly 13 billion dollars.

Since Vladivostok was inaccessible because of Japan's participation in the war, these supplies had to be poured in either through the exceedingly perilous Archangel route or by the roundabout way of Iran, where the Americans constructed a wholly new railway from the Persian Gulf. While it may be argued that, unlike the work of the American Relief Administration of 1921-23, this effort was inspired by self-interest, not by magnanimity, it should also be remembered that the Allies took a tremendous risk that Soviet capitulation, either enforced or voluntary, might make the whole sacrifice go down the drain.

While the Russian defense perforce repeated the pattern of 1812, German strategy differed sharply from that of Napoleon. He had driven straight for Moscow, but its occupation had not broken Russian resistance. The Germans could perhaps have taken both Leningrad and Moscow, but it was clear that the psychological effect on the Russians of their fall would be of little value, and their occupation would have imposed on the conquerors, if only in self-defense against outbreaks of epidemic disease, the necessity of feeding their millions of inhabitants; so long as they were merely under siege, the task of averting starvation of their populations was only a Russian problem which need not worry the invaders. The seat of the Soviet government was, in any case, withdrawn to Kuibyshev (formerly Samara) at the easternmost bend of the Volga. The Nazis' main objective was to secure control of the Ukraine, where the bulk of Russian productive capacity, both agricultural and industrial, was concentrated. Occupation of the Ukraine therefore held dual promise: it would place at the direct disposal of the Germans the materials they had been paying for under their agreements with the Soviet Union; and it would be the most crippling blow that could be struck against this dangerous enemy in their rear.

In the face of a spring counteroffensive by the Russians, the Germans gave ground somewhat on the central front. Their own 1942 offensive wasted little effort on the central front, leaving Moscow in relative security; their main drive carried them to the line of the Don, touching the Volga at Stalingrad; it netted them also the Kuban region, including the ruined Maikop oil fields, while their advanced forces, across the Terek, threatened Grozny as well. This was, however, the peak of their achievement. Dispersion of effort in this two-pronged drive at industrial Stalingrad and into the oil-rich North Caucasus weakened the striking force of both blows. At the same time German air cover in Russia was seriously reduced by the necessity of diverting much of the *Luftwaffe* to the Mediterranean; in October, El Alamein threw Rommel back from Egypt, and in November, Anglo-American forces landed in French North Africa. With much misgiving in some quarters, principally British, and despite the efforts needed to stop the Japanese in the South Pacific and to make the landing at Guadalcanal (August, 1942), military equipment continued to be poured into the Soviet Union across Iran.

The decisive turning point for Russia—the product of all these factors and of the heroic stubbornness of the Russians themselves—was the surrender of the German General Paulus and his Sixth Army amid the ruins of Stalingrad (February 2, 1943). Stalin himself accepted the rank of Marshal (March). In part thanks to Hitler's continued interference with his generals, the Russians during the spring recovered most of the Donbas and cleared the North Caucasus; though the Germans recaptured Kharkov, the main center on the Donets, and held the Black Sea naval base of Novorossiisk, Rostov was again firmly in Soviet hands. On the central front, partisan bands behind the German lines had helped to force the Nazis to pull back somewhat; the complete isolation of Leningrad was ended. In the summer and fall of 1943, while the Allies invaded Sicily (July) and then landed at Salerno (September), bringing about the fall of Mussolini and forcing the Germans to take full responsibility for defending the Italian peninsula, the Russians began to get their own steam roller in motion.

By the time of the Allied landing in Normandy (June 6, 1944), the Germans had evacuated the whole of the Ukraine, and Soviet forces had reoccupied part of their 1939 gains. The Baltic provinces and White Russia were still held by the Nazis. In the remainder of the year, while the Allied forces cleared the whole of France and Belgium and began the penetration of Germany from the west, Russian forces recovered all the territory they had held at the beginning of the "Fatherland War," penetrated Poland as far as the Vistula from just below Warsaw into Galicia, overran most of Hungary, occupied all of Rumania and Bulgaria, and in conjunction with Tito's partisans, a considerable part of Yugoslavia, including Belgrade. Strong Communist organizations seized power in Albania and part of Greece. Finland was compelled to accept an armistice (September 4). The eastern border of Germany still remained almost inviolate, for Russia's rulers preferred the easier pickings of the Balkans. The near approach of the Soviet army to Warsaw set off an uprising there (August 1-October 2, 1944), but the slowness of the Russian advance, probably deliberate, allowed the Nazis to crush it, virtually destroying the city in the process; the Polish-born Russian Marshal Rokossowski entered the suburb of Praga, just across the Vistula, on August 15, but did not move to aid the Poles.

While the Allies were forcing their way across the Rhine (March, 1945), the Russians were completing the occupation of Poland and moving into Silesia and East Prussia. In April, by agreement with the Russians, the Allies limited their advance to the line of the Elbe, except in its lower reaches, while they concentrated on what was expected to be stubborn last-ditch fighting in Bavaria; the Soviet forces were left a free hand to take Vienna (April 13) and to smash their way into Berlin (April 25-May 2). The final armistice of May 8 was almost an anticlimax; only small pockets then remained in Nazi hands, save for Norway, Denmark, part of Holland, most of Bohemia and of Austria, and western Latvia.

Shortly before the German surrender, the Soviet Union, yielding to American blandishments and to the lure of opportunity, gave notice of termination of the Soviet-Japanese nonaggression pact (April 5). Although Russia was pledged not to go to war with Japan for a year after such denunciation, Japanese requests to Stalin to mediate with the United States (July) and the bombing of Hiroshima (August 6) indicated that it was already almost too late. On August 8 the Soviet Union declared war on Japan, in time to share in the spoils without the pains of war in the Far East. On August 15 Japan indicated her willingness to surrender, and the armistice was ceremonially signed aboard the American battleship *Missouri* in Tokyo Bay on September 2.

WARTIME DIPLOMACY

The record of relations between the Allies during the war is a very curious one. The collapse of France in June, 1940, had left Great Britain to bear the whole brunt of the war, though with disguised coöperation from the United States. The German invasion of Russia in June, 1941, initially did nothing to relieve Great Britain; in fact it imposed on her and her secret partner the additional task of supporting the Soviet war effort. The open entry of the United States into the war after Pearl Harbor (December 7, 1941) was not a mere matter of putting at Great Britain's disposal the enormous material resources of America. It meant also a transfer of leadership from the erratic but experienced and knowledgeable Churchill to the cavalier and no less erratic Roosevelt, a novice in international, though not in domestic, politics.

In the early stages of the war, negotiations with Stalin were for the most part carried on at second hand and turned mainly on the question of supplies, though Stalin insisted on his desire for the opening of a "second front." Litvinov, the old advocate of "collective security," was dusted off from retirement to serve as ambassador to Washington, where he signed the United Nations Declaration (January 1, 1942). Molotov, still Commissar of Foreign Affairs, went to London to sign a twenty-year alliance with Britain (May). Churchill himself visited Stalin in Moscow (August) to explain that the obscurely promised second front could not yet be established on the Continent; Stalin declined to accept the invasion of North Africa (November) as a substitute. The Roosevelt-Churchill agreement at Casablanca (January, 1943) on the slogan of "unconditional surrender" of all their enemies was much more satisfying to Stalin, for it seemed to guarantee a bitter-end struggle by Germany and Japan against America and Britain and made it easier for Stalin to reject America's offer of mediation with Finland. On the other hand, disclosure by the Germans of the "Katyn massacre" of Polish officers, allegedly perpetrated by the Russians in 1940, led to a request by the Polish Government-in-exile in London for an International Red Cross investigation (April, 1943); an angered Stalin, more self-reliant since Stalingrad, withdrew his ambassadors from London and Washington.

Nevertheless, in May, 1943, the Comintern was formally dissolved. In August, Stalin sent word of his acceptance of a foreign ministers' meeting, as a sequel to which he agreed to a personal meeting with Roosevelt and Churchill. Yielding to Stalin's reluctance to venture far abroad, the conference was arranged at Teheran, in Iran, for the end of November, 1943. At Stalin's suggestion, Roosevelt acted as chairman. Apparently the American President thought he was dealing with an ordinary, if very successful, machine politician, though perhaps a Chicago-type Fourth-of-July patriot. As Roosevelt later remarked, Stalin was a nationalist but not an "Imperialist" like Churchill. To cajole his new-found friend, and with traditional belief in the value of a "Happy Warrior," Roosevelt permitted himself frequent gibes at his British ally, who was in no position to retaliate. Nothing, of course, was accomplished by such an attitude and such tactics; Churchill's desire for a joint Balkan campaign was shoved aside in favor of a 1944 Channel crossing; Anglo-American forces in the Mediterranean were simultaneously to be employed for a landing in southern France. Stalin also secured Churchill's commitment to acceptance of the "Curzon line" as the future Russo-Polish frontier, on the understanding that Poland would be compensated by being given German territory as far as the Oder; Roosevelt remained aloof, privately explaining to Stalin that he personally agreed with this way of handling the problem but that he did not want at the next election to lose the votes of six or seven million Polish-Americans by publicly accepting the arrangement.[3]

On the way to Teheran, Roosevelt and Churchill had stopped at Cairo for a meeting with Chiang Kai-shek, who had to be kept separate from Stalin because of the latter's still valid nonaggression pact with Japan. At Cairo, it was agreed that Japan was to be demilitarized and confined to her home islands; Manchuria and Formosa were to be restored to China, while Korea was to be once more independent. At Teheran, Stalin, in return for the definite promise of a second front in 1944, agreed to enter the war against Japan when Germany had been defeated; Roosevelt promptly suggested that a warm-water port at Dairen might be just compensation for Russia's aid. At this time, however, the defeat of Germany seemed still so remote that Stalin took no steps to get rid of his obligations under his nonaggression pact with Japan.

In 1944 diplomatic progress toward understanding among the Allies did not keep pace with military successes. At Dumbarton Oaks (July, 1944), Soviet diplomats helped to shape the future United Nations, though the veto problem was vexing. In September, at Quebec, President Roosevelt committed the almost incredible blunder of stiffening German resistance by forcing Churchill to join him in endorsing the utterly ridiculous "Morgenthau Plan" of "converting Germany into a country primarily agricultural and pastoral in its character." [4] In contrast, Soviet propaganda made much of a "Free German" movement, headed by the captive Field Marshal Paulus, designed to convince the German people that the Soviet government had no vengeful designs. Churchill, ignoring Roosevelt, paid another visit to Stalin in Moscow in October and secured agreement to what proved to be a meaningless fractional distribution of influence between Great Britain and the Soviet Union in the several Balkan countries. On the Polish question also, Churchill made no real headway; the best he could accomplish was to arrange for direct conversations between Mikolajczyk, successor of General Sikorski as head of the Polish Government-in-exile, and a Soviet-sponsored "Lublin Committee"; soon afterward (January, 1945), on the eve of another "Big Three" meeting, Russia recognized the Lublin Committee as the government *de jure* of Poland.

At the Yalta Conference (February, 1945), with Stalin playing host in the Crimea and Roosevelt again as chairman, the cards were stacked. Little progress was made on the central problem of how to treat Germany after the war. It had already been agreed that Germany should be divided into three zones of occupation, under the supervision of an Allied Control Council; the boundaries of these zones, originally worked out between the British and the Russians, had been hesitantly accepted by Roosevelt. Now Churchill, fearing

Roosevelt's evident intention promptly to withdraw American troops, secured a modification providing for France a separate zone of occupation and a seat on the Control Council; no serious effort was made to define the terms on which the Western Allies would have access to Berlin, deep within the promised Soviet zone.

Few other definite decisions were taken about what would happen when Germany surrendered. Stalin reminded Roosevelt that he had accepted, "as a basis for discussion," the figure of 20 billion dollars for German reparations. On this point, no definite decision was reached, though it was understood that "50% of it should go to the Union of Soviet Socialist Republics." [5] It was provided that the Russian share should include the "use of German labor," envisaged in the form of employment for ten years in the Soviet Union of two or three million minor German war criminals; if the supply ran out, the deficit could be made up from the ranks of unemployed Germans. Although both Roosevelt and Churchill nourished ideas about permanent partition of Germany, Stalin was unable to secure the definite commitment he pressed for.

As for Poland, Roosevelt's efforts to secure modification of the "Curzon line" so as to give her Lemberg (Lvov) and the oil resources of Galicia were countered by Stalin's suggestion that Poland be compensated with territories long inhabited by Germans on a scale substantially greater than Churchill had proposed at Teheran. What prevailed, without settling anything, was Roosevelt's "compromise" formula that Poland's eastern frontier should approximate to the Curzon line and that "Poland must receive substantial accessions of territory in the North and West." [6] The question of a new Polish government was dismissed in similar fashion, while Roosevelt and Stalin exchanged jokes about Caesar's wife. Despite his apparent growing realization that without military force the Soviet Union could not be prevented from having its way, Churchill continued earnestly to support the original American proposal that both the London and the Lublin "governments" be set aside in favor of a new coalition of democratically minded Poles. A weary Roosevelt, anxious to go home, proposed a new formula which, with slight modification, was gladly accepted by Stalin; pending "free and unfettered elections" based on universal suffrage and secret ballot, to be held as soon as possible, the American President and his disappointed British colleague capitulated, accepting "Uncle Joe's" promise that the

> Provisional Government which is now functioning in Poland should therefore be reorganized on a broader democratic basis with the inclusion of democratic leaders from Poland itself and from Poles abroad.[7]

Although Roosevelt, somewhat distressed by recognition that the British "dominions" were entitled to separate representation, was embarrassed at Stalin's proposal that each of the sixteen S.S.R.'s be given a seat in the Assembly of the United Nations, no objection was made to separate seats for the Ukraine and Byelorussia (White Russia); it was also agreed that in the Security Council there should be no veto on procedural matters.

The Cairo Declaration on the Far East was supplemented at Yalta by a direct Russo-American agreement, which Churchill accepted without discussion: in return for Russian entry into the war against Japan, "the former rights of Russia [i.e., tsarist Russia, once upon a time denounced by the Bolsheviks as "imperialist"] violated by the treacherous attack of Japan in 1904 [when a different Roosevelt had said "Japan is fighting our battle"] shall be restored." On this principle it was specifically provided that the southern portion of Sakhalin (the reader is reminded of the 1905 jeers at "Count Half-Sakhalin") should be returned to Russia; Port Arthur was again to be leased to Russia as a naval base; Dairen was to be put under Russian administration as an "international port"; and the Manchurian railways were to be "jointly" operated with China. With respect to these last two points it was emphasized that "the preeminent interests of the Soviet Union" were to be "safeguarded," though "China shall retain full sovereignty in Manchuria." The official text made the reservation that the agreement "will require concurrence of Generalissimo Chiang Kai-shek," which Roosevelt undertook to obtain; yet the official text also said that "these claims of the Soviet Union should be unquestionably satisfied after Japan has been defeated." [8] Roosevelt blandly accepted what he called "a very reasonable suggestion from our ally . . . to get back that which has been taken from them." [9] In addition, Russia was to retain her position in Outer Mongolia and to receive from Japan, as a sort of bonus, the Kurile Islands. All that remained for Russia was the task of evading her treaty obligations to Japan, a problem solved only by cutting the Gordian knot two days after Hiroshima.

Perhaps sobered by subsequent Soviet actions in dictating the establishment of governments of her own choosing in the newly acquired "satellite states" of Eastern Europe, the American President responded sharply to Stalin's imputation of bad faith in connection with the surrender of German forces in Italy, but a proposed Anglo-American protest concerning Poland was never completed. At the time of the next meeting of the Big Three, at Potsdam (July-August, 1945), Roosevelt was dead, and his successor, President Truman, had not had time to master all the complexities of his office. In the midst of the Conference, Churchill was replaced by Attlee, as head of the new Labour Government resulting from the recent General Election. Only Stalin represented continuity, and continuity was reflected mainly in still avoiding binding decisions. On the negative side, Truman did reject a Soviet proposal that the Ruhr be placed under a special administration with Russian participation in its control; he rejected also a further suggestion that a 10-billion-dollar reparation mortgage be imposed on Germany as a whole.

On the positive side, vital details were left for a Council of Foreign Ministers, which was given the curious task of completing peace treaties with Italy and the Balkan states before dealing with the central problem of Germany, on which everything hinged. For the time being, Germany was simply left divided into four zones of military occupation—American, British, French, and Russian—vaguely subject to an Allied Control Council sitting in Berlin. Though Berlin was a good hundred miles within the Soviet zone, it was to be administered by the four occupying powers. Approval of Stalin's new western boundary for Poland—the Oder-Neisse line, with Stettin thrown in for good measure—was withheld, but no objection was made to wholesale transfer of the German population, whose ancestors had been settled there for centuries, from the areas under Polish "administration" or from Czechoslovakia and Hungary. It was agreed that the Soviet Union might itself annex part of East Prussia, including the old Hohenzollern capital of Königsberg (renamed Kaliningrad). The amount of reparations was not fixed, but it was agreed that the Soviet Union, in addition to milking its own zone of occupation, was entitled to at least 10 percent of the military industrial equipment of the other zones. Japan was not really within the competence of the Potsdam Conference, for the Soviet Union was not yet at war with her. Despite Russia's entry into the Far-Eastern war on August 8, it was the United States that received the Japanese surrender and, under General MacArthur, set up the postwar occupation regime; the Soviet Union was, however, able to salvage occupation of Manchuria, and Korea was divided into two zones.

SOVIET EXPANSION

In this irregular fashion the Soviet Union pushed her power further west and south in Europe than the Russian Empire had ever reached. The territorial gains of the Soviet Union itself were relatively modest. In addition to the territorial acquisitions she had made while still "neutral" in 1939-40 at the expense of Poland, Rumania, Finland, and the Baltic states, the U.S.S.R. acquired the Carpatho-Ukraine, which had formerly been part of Czechoslovakia, part of East Prussia, and additional territory from Finland, the most significant part of which, the Petsamo nickel-mining area, made the Soviet boundary coincide with that of Norway. In addition she had acquired a fifty-year lease on the Porkkala peninsula, ideally situated for a naval base in the Gulf of Finland. In the Far East, besides a lease on Port Arthur, in the Yellow Sea, she had recovered southern Sakhalin and acquired the Kurile Islands.

Her greatest territorial gains, however, were beyond her technical borders. Apart from her occupation zones in Germany and Austria, her troops held and her puppets ruled a Poland with its center of gravity shifted westward, as well as Hungary, Rumania, and Bulgaria. Yugoslavia, though Soviet troops had been withdrawn, seemed secure on the basis of close relations with Tito; a similar situation existed in Albania. Soviet troops received the Japanese surrender in Manchuria; they soon withdrew, but in such fashion as to allow that territory to be taken over by the Chinese Communists rather than by the Nationalist forces of Chiang Kai-shek; nor did the Soviet government neglect, during its brief occupation of Manchuria, to remove to Russia as much as possible of the physical equipment of Japanese-owned plants in that area, as well as to send the Japanese soldiers into Soviet labor camps. In North Korea, occupied by Soviet forces pending establishment of a provisional government for the whole of Korea, a puppet Communist government was promptly set up. Soviet troops remained also in the northwestern corner of Iran, where they had been guarding the American supply line. In addition, the Communists supported strong "underground" movements, sometimes in control of extensive territory, in areas where Stalin had conceded to Churchill a preponderant influence for Britain. Outstanding was the case of Greece, where the "EAM" and its fighting organization, "ELAS," offered strong resistance to British postwar occupation and provoked a civil war. Even in France and Italy, numerically strong Communist parties seemed a threat to the stability of these "liberated" countries.

The Communists made no attempt to incorporate the huge area of Eastern Europe into the Soviet Union or even immediately to introduce the characteristic features of Soviet economy. Even today, what are commonly called the "satellite states" are not rated as "socialist republics" but only as "people's democracies."[10] This was not at all the result of promises made, either at Yalta or elsewhere, nor was it an indication that the Communists had abandoned their dream of world revolution. Rather, it was one more proof of what was already patent enough, namely, that they were principally guided by concern for the interests of the state they ruled as the heirs of the Russian Emperors. Politically they exercised complete control through the handful of adherents (on the style of Germany's Quislings) they attracted in each of the new subject nationalities, backed by their own tested machinery of secret police and arbitrary punishments. In each case they worked through a "front," in which the Communists took key positions in control of the police and the army. With whatever misgivings, leaders of the several national movements agreed to coöperate with their Communist ministerial colleagues; themselves generally believers in genuine democracy, they could not fairly be expected to be more omniscient than the chairman and chief spokesman of the "Big Three" had been. The populations of the several countries, exhausted by their horrifying experiences under Nazi rule and with no possibility of finding aid from the democratic West, had no choice but to submit to the new form of oppression; hating the Russians, but hating also the Germans, and with no love for the other neighbor nations in the same position as themselves, they could only bide their time and hope for a change in the international situation.

There was no possibility that such sullenly hostile peoples could be taken into the structure of the Soviet Union itself. The people whose independent spirit seemed most to be feared were the Poles; but a Poland almost half of whose territories had been forcibly taken from Germany had to depend on Russian support to maintain her national existence, such as it was. The "satellite states," however, served purposes useful to the Soviet Union. For one thing, they constituted a broad belt—a new form of *cordon sanitaire*—which helped to isolate Russia from the "capitalist" West; so long as they could be prevented from establishing independent relations with the West, they constituted a valuable glacis protecting the Russian "socialist" fortress. Economically, too, they were a great advantage to the Soviet Union. The very fact that no attempt was currently being made to extend to them the anticipated blessings of the communism toward which the Soviet Union was striving made it quite unnecessary to promote their rapid economic development. Instead, they could be and were initially used as a sort of colonial empire, the resources of which, in mercantilist spirit, were at the free disposal of their "protector," to aid in the restoration of its own devastated economy.

THE PROBLEM OF THE NATIONALITIES

The appetite of the Soviet Union for swallowing these indigestible nations was also diminished by the grave difficulties it had experienced during the war within its own borders with subject peoples much less developed as nations than were Poles, Magyars, Rumanians, Bulgars, or Yugoslavs. The German invasion had not been entirely unwelcome to very considerable masses among the Soviet peoples. "Great Russians" might for the most part respond to Stalin's proclamation of a "Fatherland War"; even those among them who objected to many features of the Soviet regime were deeply moved by national feeling, a sentiment to be observed also even among anti-Bolshevik scholars "in emigration." Ukrainians, however, and to a less extent White Russians (Byelorussians) and other peoples had, notwithstanding Bolshevik emphasis on "cultural autonomy," so keenly felt the weight of Moscow's hand that many of them were prepared to welcome the Germans as liberators from an oppressive yoke; considerable numbers of them served willingly in the German forces, and there were partisan bands behind the Soviet lines as well as behind the German.

Nazi policy failed to take advantage of such sentiments; Nazi arrogance and brutality revolted their potential friends and undoubtedly constituted a factor of great significance in the ultimate failure of their military effort. Yet Nazi scorn for the "inferior" peoples of Eastern Europe was not the only factor. Any army of occupation in a foreign land is bound to be faced with similar problems; British and American armies have not long been welcome in the lands where they have made a friendly entry. Military operations, whether in the Ukraine or in Normandy, entail great loss of the lives and property of innocent bystanders, to say nothing of the dislocation of their normal lives; military requisitions cannot be avoided, and the rank and file of invading armies tend to feel themselves entitled to take unpleasant liberties among strange peoples. The very fact that they are rescuing people who have not been able to help themselves tends to breed a feeling of contempt for the people they are befriending; innumerable acts of individual kindness—chocolate bars for children and cigarettes for adults—may be welcome, but the irritations on the other side of the ledger tend to sink deeper into the minds of the occupied population. Sooner or later, "Yankee Go Home" or its pertinent equivalent begins to be chalked up on walls even in countries where, in the abstract, the continuing support of the presence of an occupying force is indispensable.

Genuine coöperation between the Germans and the Ukrainians was doomed from the start. The Germans had not invaded the Soviet Union to help Russia's subject peoples to organize their own lives. The German dream of *Lebensraum* for themselves could be achieved only at the expense of the resident population; even their immediate need for grain, oil, metals, and other commodities required it to make sacrifices. Alfred Rosenberg, as Minister for the Eastern Territories, tried in vain to introduce a policy of encouraging nationalist separatism; his directives were sometimes overridden by his more powerful Nazi colleagues, sometimes sabotaged with impunity by his own subordinates on the spot. The Nazis, themselves no great believers in individual enterprise or in religious freedom, did not even embark on a decollectivization program, which indeed might have imperiled their control of peasant production, or on a policy of reopening churches.

In 1942, among their millions of Russian prisoners had been a General Vlasov, of a Great Russian peasant family, who by way of Party membership and service as a Russian adviser in China had risen to a respected position in the Red Army. Although he was willing to be used against his former associates, he was until 1944 employed only for the purpose of making propaganda speeches. After the clumsy and abortive attempt of a few German generals and civilians to murder Hitler, Himmler authorized Vlasov to form a "Committee for the Liberation of the Peoples of Russia" and organized for him a special armed force to fight on the already collapsing front. It was much too late; the chief military service of Vlasov's army was to aid the Czechs against the Germans in Prague. The evident resurgence of Stalin's power and his announcement, which was both promise and threat, that "we shall return" paralyzed his opponents in the Ukraine, who well knew what would happen to anyone who had a record of collaboration with the Germans in occupied territories. Despite the failure of Nazi policy to inflame the whole Ukraine against Russia, large numbers of Ukrainians fled with the retreating Germans. After the war, Vlasov and the remnants of his army, as well as large numbers of other refugees were "repatriated," in accordance with Roosevelt's vague promise at Yalta; back in the Soviet Union, many of them were executed as traitors, but the great majority were isolated in labor camps.

The Ukraine was not the only area in which the wartime attitude of the population called for Muscovite reprisals. Even during the war, suspicion of disloyalty in the "Volga German Autonomous Soviet Socialist Republic" led to extinction of that eighteenth-century settlement, the chief city of which, opposite Saratov, had been renamed Engels; its population was deported to Asia under conditions that practically exterminated this ethnic group. A number of other disloyal nationalities were subjected to similar wholesale annihilating expulsion from their homes; among them were the Crimean Tatars, the Chechen-Ingush of the North Caucasus, and the Kalmyks of the steppe. After the war came the turn of the Letts and others. Less drastic, but vigorous enough, were fresh purges of "nationalists" in local Party leadership.

The Soviet nationality policy did not during the war prove itself the panacea for the evils of nationalism that it was once widely supposed to be. For that matter, in practice it had never corresponded to its theory. Stalin's toast at the end of the war to the health of the Great Russian people was not a new departure, though it was followed by an intensified campaign against "remnants of bourgeois nationalism" as well as, somewhat contradictorily, against "rootless cosmopolitans," among whom Jews were fairly conspicuous. Another sign of increasing intolerance toward nationalism was condemnation of the "lesser evil" theory, which had for a time been advanced in an effort to reconcile Soviet inheritance of the results of tsarist subjugation of alien peoples with the official principle of the rights of nationalities. The "lesser evil" theory was that submission to Russia had saved the subject peoples from even worse foreign conquerors. Now emphasis was placed on the belief that the superior culture of the Great Russian people had brought positive blessings to backward folk.

Perhaps more likely to solve the Soviet Union's perennial nationality problem were the wholesale exchanges of population, in part forcibly carried out, in part the result of industrialization and consequent urbanization, which seem to be making the Soviet Union more of a melting pot and less of an ethnographic museum. The fact that the Russian language is everywhere taught and used, while other languages are really serviceable only in particular areas, promises to promote a certain amount of assimilation. Class interest, cutting across national lines, also tends to weaken nationalist feelings. On the other hand, class grievances as well as local differentiation have in past centuries and may in the future, in the Soviet Union as in other parts of the world, become intertwined with persistent ethnic pride, even where a common language prevails.

RAPPROCHEMENT WITH THE PEOPLE AND THE CHURCH

The "Fatherland War" was accompanied by a deliberate, and apparently successful, effort to bring a rapprochement between the dictatorship and the people. Though feelings of fear were not eradicated, the extreme tension of the purges was largely forgotten. Appeals were directed especially to youth; partly by not insisting overstrictly on payment of dues, Komsomol membership was built up to fifteen million, about half the eligible age group. Marxism was less strictly insisted on, and to such an extent that some worry was caused by the deficiencies of the "political education" of the troops. The proven loyalty of most officers had permitted the office of political commissar to be again abolished (October 9, 1942) and replaced, as in 1940, by *zampolits* (Assistant Commanders for Political Affairs); the *zampolit* worked under a special section of the Commissariat of Defense, which in its turn was directly in contact with the Central Committee of the Party. The *zampolit,* however, was not to interfere with the regular military command in the conduct of operations. As a further sign of the extent to which Marxist internationalism was being superseded by Russian nationalism, a new, patriotic, national anthem was composed to take the place of the *Internationale.*

Perhaps the chief beneficiary of the rapprochement was the Orthodox Church, which earned a greater degree of recognition by its unswerving support of the state. Immediately on the German attack, Metropolitan Sergius instructed all parishes that "The Church of Christ blesses all the Orthodox in defense of the sacred frontiers of our Fatherland." [11] Messages warning against "treason to Church and fatherland," endorsing partisan guerilla activities, and encouraging the faithful to hold out, were matched with very sizable donations of money by the Church to the Red Army. By the end of 1942 the Church had joined in adulation of Stalin, "the divinely anointed leader of the nation." The government reciprocated: the publications of the League of the Militant Godless were shut down, though officially only because of the paper shortage; antireligious museums were closed or made over into "museums of religious history"; in besieged Moscow, the curfew was lifted to permit midnight Easter services; and Metropolitan Nikolai of Kiev was appointed to an official committee to investigate German war crimes. The government consented (September 4, 1943) to the elevation of Sergius to the long-vacant post of Patriarch (September 7); after his death (May 15, 1944) no difficulty was made about the formal installation of Metropolitan Alexius of Leningrad as his successor (February 4, 1945). For the first time in history, an official representative of the Church of England, in the person of the archbishop of York, visited Moscow (September, 1943) to stress the unity of the Anglican and the Orthodox Churches against Nazi Germany; Metropolitan Nikolai paid a return visit to London in the summer of 1945.

Without conceding official reëstablishment of the Church, the government established (October, 1943) a "Council for the Affairs of the Orthodox Church," avowedly to promote good relations with the Church and to facilitate its functioning. Many additional churches were opened, and the law of 1929 was reinterpreted to permit parents to have their children given private religious instruction by priests; in addition, a Theological Institute for the training of Church dignitaries and a Theological Course as a seminary for priests were established in Moscow (June 14, 1944) at the Novodevichy Monastery (to which Boris Godunov had retired prior to his election as tsar in 1598 and where Sophia had been confined by Peter). Medals were freely bestowed on leading ecclesiastics, including Metropolitan Alexius "For the Defense of Leningrad" (October, 1943) and Metropolitan Nikolai "For the Defense of Moscow" (October, 1944). Probably not without assistance from the state, many of the "Renovationists," relics of the "Living Church," were received back into Orthodoxy, and relations with the Orthodox abroad were actively resumed. The *Sobor* that elected Alexius as Patriarch was attended by the Patriarchs of Alexandria and of Antioch and by representatives of those of Constantinople and Jerusalem. The Orthodox Metropolitan of North America was present, along with representatives of the national Orthodox Churches of Rumania and Serbia. Shortly after the capitulation of Germany, Patriarch Alexius made a ceremonial journey through the Near East, though avoiding Constantinople, for Turkey was not at the moment on good terms with the Soviet government. This trip, the first of its kind ever made by a Russian Patriarch, served the dual purpose of enhancing the prestige of the Russian Church and the prestige of the Russian state in that quarter. A critique of the papal claim to be the Vicar of Christ on earth, published by Patriarch Sergius in 1944, was not unwelcome to the Kremlin.

Throughout the war the Church continued to lavish its prayers and blessings on the Soviet government, "headed by its God-given leader." The death of the conciliatory Sergius made no difference; Alexius exhorted Stalin "to trust in the feelings of real love for you and in the gratitude that inspires all those associated with the Church that I shall henceforth head." The Church also voluntarily donated cash, amounting to over 300 million rubles, but the Patriarch stressed (May 12, 1945) that its greatest gift "was to demonstrate to the whole world its complete unity with its government." He added that he would, above all, "always thank God that He sent to us wise leaders of the country and headed it with its chosen leader of genius, Iosif Vissarionovich Stalin." The Party had not abandoned its basically materialist outlook, but a 1944 directive of the Central Committee, "On the Organization of Scientific Education Propaganda" for the purpose of "raising the cultural level of the wide masses of the working people, and the overcoming of survivals of ignorance, superstition, and prejudice," refrained from specifically mentioning the Church as an object of attack.

LITERATURE AND MUSIC

Soviet literature was completely engulfed by the war. Novels, short stories, plays, and poetry became merely different ways of stimulating patriotic enthusiasm by colorful war reporting. Most of the best writers were mobilized in the service of "fighting art." Among the best products of this period were: Leonid Leonov's outstanding plays, *Invasion* (1942) and *Lionushka* (1944), and his very short but excellent story, *The Taking of Velikoshumsk* (1944); Konstantin Simonov's play, *The Russians* (1942), his account of the Stalingrad battle in *Days and Nights* (1944), and his patriotic poems; Korneichuk's play, *The Front* (1942), with its open criticism of commanders who clearly resembled old civil war heroes such as Marshals Budenny and Voroshilov; and Fadeiev's *Young Guard* (1945), a strongly emotional novel of the teen-age resistance movement to the Germans. Among poets, in addition to Simonov, should be mentioned Alexei Surkov, equally patriotic but less individualistic; Olga Bergholz, who served as a radio broadcaster in besieged Leningrad and whose poetry had a classic lyrical quality; Nikolai Tikhonov, who imitated Pushkin; and Vera Inber, whose *Pulkovo Meridian* (1943), also written in besieged Leningrad, won a Stalin Prize. Pasternak and Akhmatova were almost silent, while Zoshchenko and Fedin, who tried to write without reference to war themes, were roughly called to account. Most war literature avoided the psychological analysis of individual human beings to which Soviet criticism had always been opposed; in A. N. Tolstoy's phrase, most of the war heroes were simply so many "leather jackets."

Historical novels dealing with heroic figures of Russia's past continued to be popular. A. N. Tolstoy's *Ivan the Terrible* (1942-43) completely reversed the picture that the nineteenth-century A. K. Tolstoy had painted in his *Prince Serebriany;* his new treatment of "one of the tragic and creative epochs during which the Russian character was formed" [12] was, in the Soviet Union at least, acclaimed because he "for the first time applied the principles of Shakespearean dramaturgy as understood by the founders of Marxism." [13] In other writings, partly autobiographical, A. N. Tolstoy adequately stressed the indignities Russia had long suffered at the hands of Germans. Sergeiev-Tsensky's *Brusilov's Breakthrough* (1943) was at the time welcome for its praise of the general who had shown most sympathy for the Revolution of 1917; later it was to be condemned for its socio-political objectivity. The most prolific writer of the period was Ilya Ehrenburg, whose journalistic facility gave him an immense advantage over slower, though more solid, authors like Sholokhov. Particularly notable was Ehrenburg's *Fall of Paris* (1941), written before the break with Germany and designed to prove that the French Communist worker and peasant would still save their country. Ehrenburg, a "rootless cosmopolitan" with a strong affection for European culture, became the most violent reviler of the Germans. As the war drew to a close, the head of the propaganda section of the Party's Central Committee had to remind him that there were good Germans as well as bad; after all, Russia had launched a "Free German" movement, headed by the captive Field Marshal Paulus.

Russian music at this time was in a still worse state. Prokofiev's *War and Peace* (1941-1942), adapted from Leo Tolstoy's novel, proved a monumental failure; his *Fifth Symphony* (1944) did nothing to restore his earlier reputation. Shostakovich produced three symphonies: his *Seventh,* "The Besieged" (1942), was the purest propaganda, if not music; his *Eighth,* though better, was condemned as "pessimistic, even neurotic"; his *Ninth* (1945) represented a return to his earlier exuberant banter.

MATERIAL DISASTER AND POLITICAL STABILITY

In a material sense, the effects of the war were even more disastrous, and perhaps more long-lasting, than in cultural realms. One of the most obvious was the effect on population. In the Soviet Union, as in tsarist Russia, the relatively short life expectancy of the population permitted few people to survive beyond breeding age, with a naturally resultant high birth rate. Since this birth rate substantially exceeded the normal death rate, and since emigration was held down to negligible proportions, the consequence should have been a continued rapid increase in population. Yet the loss of life during the war had been so stupendous that, even including the 23 million new inhabitants as a result of territorial annexations since 1939, the estimated total population in 1946 was only 193 million, as against the 1939 census figure of 179 million before the annexations.

For the first time since the introduction of the NEP in 1921, industrial production fell off heavily. Coal production in the Donbas, which in 1940 had supplied more than half of the Soviet Union's output, was reduced by more than one-half (from 85.5 million metric tons in 1940 to 36.7 million in 1945). Ural coal production, on the other hand, more than doubled (from 12 to 26.1 million metric tons), and the Karaganda fields did nearly as well (from an estimated 6.5 million to 11 million); the great, but very remote, Kuznetsk basin was estimated to have increased its output from 19 to 27 million. Total production of coal therefore declined apparently only from 166 to 149.3 million metric tons, but the distances from the points of production to possible places of consumption were much increased, thus diminishing its usefulness. Oil production was similarly, but more seriously, affected, falling from 31 to 19.4 million metric tons; the main losses were in Baku and especially in North Caucasian (Maikop and Grozny) output. Electric-power capacity, notwithstanding destruction of the great Dnieprostroi plant, was much less seriously affected.

Iron and steel production suffered very heavily; 50 percent increase in output east of the Urals could not prevent total production of pig iron from falling from 15 to 9.2 million, of steel from 18.3 to 11.2 million metric tons. Production of some nonferrous metals, notably aluminum, zinc, and manganese, largely produced in the occupied areas, also fell heavily, as did that of most chemicals. Much more severe was the drop in production of consumer goods; output of cotton cloth fell off by almost 60 percent, of leather boots and shoes by almost 75 percent. Appalling losses of railway-transport facilities in the first two years of the war were made good by vigorous construction efforts and by Lend-Lease, but remained very inadequate for a country as huge as the Soviet Union. Production of motor vehicles, mainly trucks, was reduced almost by one-half, though here, too, Lend-Lease supplies were of incalculable value. However, the state of Russian roads, normally maintained by forced labor, could not well be improved under war conditions. Housing was subject to an almost incredible strain; it is estimated that in the occupied areas more than half of urban dwelling space and a quarter of rural were destroyed; in the unoccupied areas, where virtually no attention could be devoted to new construction, the swollen refugee population jammed available facilities.

Labor mobilization by conscription had to be intensified, and the military authorities were given a free hand in drafting workers. Because of the huge losses suffered by the armed forces, both by casualties and by capture, a sharply increased proportion of the industrial labor force was made up of women, adolescents, or persons over the age of fifty. Agriculture was afflicted simultaneously by loss of man power, by decline in the numbers of livestock, and by reduction of mechanical equipment. In the unoccupied territories, grain production fell almost 50 percent (from 119 to 66.5 million metric tons), to say nothing of the fact that the most fertile regions were in enemy hands. The reduction in sugar-beet production was even greater (from 20.9 to 8.9 million metric tons); even Central Asian cotton production was more than halved (from 2.7 to 1.2 million metric tons).

The desperate conditions of life in the Soviet Union during the war years are suggested by the difference between ration prices and the free-market prices allowed collective farmers for "surplus" produce beyond required state deliveries; when rye bread was sold for 1 ruble a kilogram on a ration basis, its free price was 130 rubles a kilogram, while sugar, officially rationed at 5 rubles a kilogram, commanded a price of 1,100 rubles a kilogram. In consequence, the structure of the collective farms was much weakened. In the occupied areas, the Germans had not attempted to capitalize on the strong peasant sentiment for the abolition of collectivization, for they, like the Soviet regime, found that collective agriculture made it easier for a central authority to control the product than would be the case with individual farms. In the unoccupied areas, however, the peasants took every advantage of the temporary weakening of central authority to enlarge individual holdings at the expense of the collectives and to concentrate even more on their own economies. The authorities, who had their hands full with the war, were powerless to check these tendencies, which were further stimulated by the high prices prevailing on the legal free market.

The ruling personnel changed little during the war. Malenkov, who since 1939 had been Stalin's chief lieutenant in the Party Secretariat, became a candidate member of the Politburo in 1941, as did Voznesensky, a relative newcomer. Voznesensky's reputation as an economist had led to his transfer in 1935 from the Institute of Red Professors, of which, despite his youth, he had become president in 1934, to the planning commission at Leningrad;

supported by Zhdanov, he had been promoted to chairmanship of the State Planning Commission (*Gosplan*) in 1938.

Almost immediately on the outbreak of the war, a small inner cabinet, called the State Committee of Defense, was formed (June 30, 1941) within the Politburo group. Stalin himself assumed the chairmanship, assigning the vice-chairmanship to his man Friday, Molotov, then serving as Commissar of Foreign Affairs. Stalin's old crony of civil war days, Voroshilov, although he had been relieved as Commissar of Defense after the "Winter War" with Finland, was included. The other two members, Beria and Malenkov, were only "candidates" in the Politburo, but the one headed the NKVD and the other was, under Stalin, chief of the vital Party Secretariat. Early in 1942 (February 3), Mikoyan, the foreign-trade expert, and Voznesensky, the economic planner, were added; Stalin's trusted trouble-shooter, Kaganovich, was added a few days later (February 20). The only subsequent change in its personnel was replacement (November 22, 1944) of Voroshilov, who, however, remained a member of the Politburo, by the rising army politico, General Bulganin, who was not yet even a candidate member of the ruling group. Two days after the formal surrender of Japan, the State Committee of Defense was dissolved (September 4, 1945).

Russia's top rulers at the end of the war were therefore the nine members and four candidate members of the Politburo. Of the men clustered around Stalin, only two—Molotov and Mikoyan—had played a role of any significance at all in the Revolution: Molotov had been a sort of office boy for the Bolsheviks in Petrograd; Mikoyan had been more independently active, but in distant Baku. The others, though several of them had been members of the Party at the time of the seizure of power, had only later come into any sort of prominence. Kalinin, nominal head of the state, had never been more than an innocuous symbol of peasant fidelity to the Bolsheviks. Voroshilov had been a guerilla leader and comrade-in-arms of Stalin. Kaganovich, Andreiev, Zhdanov, and Khrushchev had risen as Party *apparatchiki* in the Leader's service. Each of them had developed his own administrative specialty, and most of them were more or less trusted advisers. None of the candidate members—Shvernik, Beria, Malenkov, and Voznesensky—had been taken into the inner circle before 1939.

Stalin towered above all these, his creatures, much as the architectural monstrosities sometimes mockingly called "The Seven Beauties" were soon to rear themselves above Moscow. Russia was the only one of the "Big Three" powers destined to emerge from the war without a new management.

NOTES

1 Churchill broadcast; cf. his *Grand Alliance,* pp. 371-372.
2. *Pravda,* July 3, 1941.
3. Cf. Feis, *Churchill, Roosevelt, Stalin,* p. 285, citing Bohlen memorandum made at Teheran; cf. also telegram (October 22, 1944) from Roosevelt to Churchill suggesting delay in publication of proposed solution of Polish problem "for about two weeks. You will understand," in U.S. Department of State, *The Conferences at Malta and Yalta, 1945,* p. 207, and Matthews Minutes (Top Secret) made at Yalta (February 6, 1945) in which Roosevelt referred back to his Teheran statement that "there are six or seven million Poles in the United States," *ibid.,* p. 677.
4. The original phrasing was "diverting Germany into largely an agricultural country"; the official version, cited in the text, was the handiwork of an annoyed, apparently puckish, Churchill; cf. Feis, *op. cit.* p. 370.
5. U.S. Department of State, *op. cit.,* p. 920.
6. *Ibid.,* p. 980.
7. *Ibid.,* p. 973.
8. *Ibid.,* pp. 984-987.
9. Leahy, *I Was There,* p. 318.
10. On July 7, 1960, Czechoslovakia was upgraded.
11. All quoted passages in this and the next two paragraphs are cited in Curtiss, *The Russian Church and the Soviet State, 1917-1950,* pp. 290-303 *passim.*
12. A. N. Tolstoi, *"Moi put',"* in *Novy Mir,* No. 1 (1943), p. 108.
13. Veksler, *Aleksandr Nikolaevich Tolstoi,* p. 472.

SUGGESTIONS FOR FURTHER READING

The most specific treatment in English of the Russian share in the war is Liddell Hart (ed.), *The Soviet Army,* which may be supplemented by General Guillaume's *La guerre germano-sovietique.* Werth's *Russia at War, 1914-1945* is extensive but not entirely satisfactory. Gouré's *Siege of Leningrad* concentrates on the hardships undergone. The nature of Gallagher's *Soviet History of World War II: Myths, Memories, and Realities* is suggested by the subtitle. See also Garthoff. *Hitler's Defeat in Russia,* by the Polish General Anders, is an explanation of Russian victory in terms of German blunders. Dallin's *German Rule in Russia, 1941-1945,* and Armstrong's *Ukrainian Nationalism, 1939-1945* are very valuable. Conquest's *Soviet Nationalities Policy in Practice* contains some useful essays.

For a general study of Soviet diplomacy, see Rubinstein, previously cited. Two major presentations of wartime diplomacy may be found in Churchill's *Second World War* and Sherwood's *Roosevelt and Hopkins.* Wilmot's *Struggle for Europe* is an ambitious attempt to reduce the whole military and diplomatic struggle within the confines of one volume. Among more cautious subsequent works, Snell, *The Meaning of Yalta,* and Greenfield (ed.), *Command Decisions,* are specially worthy of attention. Feis, *Churchill, Roosevelt, and Stalin,* and his *Between War and Peace: The Potsdam Conference* are perhaps the most judicious treatments. Kertesz, *The Fate of East Central Europe*; Mikolajczyk, *The Rape of Poland*; and Birke and Neumann, *Die Sowjetisierung Ost-Mitteleuropas,* are excellent studies. On the Finnish episode and its background, see Tanner, *The Winter War;* Lundin, *Finland in the Second World War*; and Wuorinen (ed.), *Finland and World War II.*

Cressey's *Soviet Potentials: A Geographic Appraisal* is very thoughtful. In addition to works previously cited, Albert Rhys Williams, *The Russians . . .* is very suggestive.

Chapter

35

The Tensions of Peace: 1945-1953

THE INTERNATIONAL OUTLOOK AND THE "COLD WAR"

The successive capitulations of Italy, Germany, and Japan brought a cessation of military operations. They did not solve the problems of the shape of the world to be. Of the "Big Three," two—Churchill and Stalin—had during the war given much thought to these problems. The third and most powerful, President Roosevelt, had been content to dream and drift; a man of great personal courage and unsurpassed for political acumen in producing immediate electoral results, he had always shrunk from taking broad decisions of the kind required by statesmanship. At all international conferences he had accepted jovial camaraderie instead of insisting on binding promises and demanding effective guarantees that they would be kept; in the last stages of the war he had tried to evade responsibility for decisions that would determine the relative strength of the wartime allies in their postwar dealings, imposing on his military subordinates the duty of making the decisions on the basis of strictly military rather than widely political considerations. The result was that the Soviet Union found itself, by virtue of the extent of its zone of occupation in Germany, able to play from a position of unexpected strength.

The position of the Soviet Union was all the stronger because Stalin was the only one of the "Big Three" to remain in a position of power. Churchill and the Conservatives were immediately tossed out of office in favor of the Labour Party. The new Prime Minister, Clement Attlee, had, to be sure, been Deputy Prime Minister in the wartime coalition Cabinet, and his new Foreign Secretary, Ernest Bevin, was a hard-headed trade-union leader with no illusions about his new antagonist, so recently a reluctant ally. This element of continuity was outbalanced by the fact that the new Cabinet had been His Majesty's Opposition. Great Britain, with the smallest population and the fewest natural resources among the three victors, was also the one which for the longest period of time had been sustaining the brunt of the war. Her deliberate sacrificial effort, proportionately the greatest of the three, had subjected her to tremendous stresses, both domestic and imperial, that made it impossible for her to play the leading independent role that she might have been able to play if she could, for a time at least, have remained united under the relatively far-seeing leadership of Winston Churchill. Whether such an outcome would in the long run have permitted her to set her own house in order is a different question; what is here relevant is merely that she did not play such a role, leaving the relations between the Soviet Union and the United States as the paramount factor in world politics.

The death of President Roosevelt (April 12, 1945) was not wholly unexpected, but it created a very grave problem of leadership for the world's strongest power. His chosen lieutenant, Vice-President Truman, was known as an experienced politician, with an excellent record as a senator during the early part of the war, but without pretensions as a statesman in the international field. His inexperience was, however, largely compensated by his strong sense of responsibility, his native shrewdness, and his ability to recognize sound advice in split-second decisions. At the Potsdam Conference (July, 1945) there was nothing he could do to alter the *fait accompli* he had inherited, but he did not agree to any further extension of Russia's grip on Germany. His efforts on behalf of Poland, which won Mikolajcyzk nominal participation in its Soviet-controlled government, were necessarily futile. His decision to use the atom bomb against Japan, whether ultimately wise or not, was met by Stalin with studied disinterest but had the effect of persuading Russia to jump into the Far-Eastern situation without further delay.

Probably nothing could have prevented the emergence of the "cold war."* Throughout history the existence of two Powers obviously stronger than the rest has produced a polarity between them and forced the rest of the world to adapt itself as best it can to their inevitable mutual suspicion and consequent hostility. In such situations differences of ideology, whether religious, socio-economic, or political, are purely incidental, but they serve as useful cloaks for the underlying power struggle, inspiring their respective supporters and seeming to give meaning to the conflict. The "cold war" between the United States and the Soviet Union is often idealized, on both sides, as the conflict between "bourgeois" democracy and the dictatorship "of the toilers," between capitalism and communism, between religion and atheism. Yet the nature of a political regime has never stood in the way of friendly relations with other countries, as witness the case of republican France and tsarist Russia, or many other instances throughout history. The facts that there is not a trace of "communism" in the practice of the Soviet Union and that its most devoted champions do not claim for it more than the triumph of a

* For "revisionist" interpretations see p. 721.

"socialism" which is obviously only state capitalism have become obscured by tons of printed words, to say nothing of spoken ones, issued from both camps. Similarly, the evident facts that much of the West's devotion to Christianity is mere lip service and that the "godless" Soviet state reached a *modus vivendi* with the Orthodox Church have not prevented the preponderantly materialist outlook of the modern Western world from taking on a color apparently radically different from that of Russia.

In fact, the essence of the "cold war" is merely the reëmergence of the situation created by the downfall of Napoleon, Hitler's predecessor as dictator of the Continent. When one recalls that in 1814 Great Britain had emerged as definitely the world's greatest power and that Russia then seemed her only possible rival, the "cold war" falls into juster perspective. In those early days of industrialization, with relatively weak development of technology, Russia's size and numbers had made up for little England's commercial and industrial superiority to an extent sometimes forgotten in our day, so much more advanced in science and in economic organization. Today it is only the coupling of industrial and technological progress with size and numbers that makes Russia formidable. Removal of France as the predominant military power had brought to an end the centuries-old Franco-Austrian polarity by land and Anglo-French rivalry by sea. After 1814 Russia was the power most rapidly expanding in all quarters and the dominant factor in the Concert of Europe. England, relying on her own strength, had withdrawn into isolation; the main thread of her foreign policy, until the rise of Germany, had been the effort to block the growth of Russian strength.

Similarly, in 1945, the removal of Germany as the predominant military power shifted the object of fear back to Russia. At the same time, the United States stepped definitely into England's shoes as the leading participant in international politics; there could no longer be the apparent abstention from playing a part in consonance with her might that had largely characterized the period between the great wars of the first half of the twentieth century. It became primarily America's business to "contain" the power of Russia, closely associated in the popular mind with the ogres of communism, atheism, ruthless dictatorship, and, more importantly, the threat posed by the fact that she was the second strongest power in the world. However little the American people and their government might be consciously hostile to their recent ally, their actions, sometimes to their own dismay, spoke louder than words.

On the Soviet side, the hostility fostered by the Party was more deliberate, and for a number of reasons. Stalin's dictatorship permitted striking continuity of policy, not seriously hampered by the sentiments of the Russian people, in pursuit of the interests of the Soviet state. The degree to which this continuity actively depended on lingering faith in the coming world revolution may be somewhat doubtful. There were in any case more immediate considerations that demanded suspicious coldness toward America. A desperate Russia had been well served by lavish American aid, which had been acknowledged as long as it could continue to be useful; gratitude, however, even though it may sometimes count in the relationships of private individuals, has no meaning in the lives of states. While the United States had merely the problem of trying to maintain an existing preponderance of strength, Russia was troubled with the even more uncomfortable consciousness that she must overtake America before she could surpass her. For the postwar Russian state, overshadowed by capitalist America, it was important to consolidate a position of the utmost strength, not in any way dependent on the good will of alien democracies. The added resources gained in the satellite states and through the Soviet zone of occupation in Germany, and her more modest loot in the Far East, were to be made to serve primarily as defensive ramparts but also as jumping-off places for further expansion.

EARLY STAGES IN THE "COLD WAR"

The first case in which the United States challenged Soviet intentions came as early as January, 1946, when the question of Soviet failure to withdraw its troops from Iran was brought up in the United Nations: under persistent American pressure, the Soviet government had to abandon this protoplasmic protrusion. Shortly afterward, the Soviet Union received a second check: during the war, at Yalta, she had raised with her allies the question of revision of the Montreux Convention of 1936; at Potsdam the United States had agreed to an international conference to reëxamine control of the Straits and had later formulated proposals which Great Britain and Turkey were willing to discuss. The Soviet Union, however, had countered (August 7, 1946) by proposing additional clauses which would have left administration and "defense" of the Straits solely in the hands of Turkey and Russia. Flat rejection of this revival of the dream of Catherine the Great, a dream which had led to the Crimean War and had caused the fall of Miliukov in May, 1917, put an end, for the time at least, to Soviet pressure in that quarter. The Soviet Union did continue to push its request for "rectification" of the Soviet-Turkish boundary south of the Caucasus; however, after the announcement of the "Truman Doctrine" in the spring of 1947, Russia shifted her ground to a mere plea for "scientific" examination of the question. Stalin's expression of interest in a Russian trusteeship over Italy's colonies was probably only a trial balloon.

There were also strong internal reasons for reassuming a deliberately hostile attitude toward the outside world. The power of the Soviet government over its citizens rested more on fear than on enthusiasm—but not merely on fear of reprisals from their own rulers. From the outset, the Party had inculcated the idea that the Soviet experiment was being conducted in the midst of a necessarily hostile capitalist world. The concept of a "socialist island" surrounded by a menacing imperialist ocean had been sedulously cultivated; fear of the outside world had been constantly used to justify the dictatorship and to stifle criticisms of its policies. If that fear were suddenly to drop away in an atmosphere of international friendship, Soviet citizens, especially if allowed free contact with the "bourgeois" world and its superior living standards, might become more restive, and the healthy fear they entertained of their own rulers might turn to dangerous hate. The possibility of such a development was not merely theoretical; it had been pointed up during the war by wholesale defections, checked by Nazi brutality more than by patriotic propaganda. Russia might still have been able to live in a genuinely peaceful world, but her rulers could not.

The consequent "cold war" developed gradually on both sides. Perhaps the first indication of what Soviet policy was to be came along the agreed line of demarcation between the armies in Germany; the Russian regiments which had initially fraternized with their allies were after a few days replaced by other troops whose sullen taciturnity puzzled the ingenuous Americans and, though perhaps to a lesser extent, the more sophisticated British. At the termination of hostilities there were in the "pipeline" considerable quantities of supplies already contracted for under Lend-Lease; there was also set up a United Nations organization for relief and rehabilitation of devastated areas (UNRRA). With the cessation of deliveries on these two accounts, the tone of the Soviet press changed markedly. The degree of credit for victory at first given to Russia's allies declined rapidly. As a result, that ablest of phrase-makers, Winston Churchill, aptly remarked in his famous speech (March 5, 1946) at Fulton, Missouri, that an "iron curtain has descended across the continent." Stalin replied by denouncing the "warmonger of a Third World War." A then anonymous American State Department expert on Russia (George F. Kennan) soon publicly advocated the idea of "a long-term, patient but firm and vigilant containment of Russian expansive tendencies." [1]

The rapid cooling-off of Soviet-Western relations of course did not prevent a certain amount of collaboration. All participated, with varying degrees of enthusiasm and in a spirit that could scarcely be called coöperation, in the work of the United Nations and its agencies. The Council of Foreign Ministers of the United States, Great Britain, and the Soviet Union gradually reached agreement on peace treaties (signed February 10, 1947) with Italy, Hungary, Rumania, and Bulgaria; simultaneously the Soviet Union concluded a peace with Finland. So far as the Soviet Union was concerned, these treaties simply confirmed her in possession of what she had chosen to take, together with provisions for reparations to her. No progress, however, was made on a German peace treaty or even on a separate treaty with Austria; nor was agreement reached on the boundaries of the new Poland. "War criminal" trials were held in Nuremberg, but otherwise the Allied Control Council in Berlin was paralyzed. In the Far East the situation remained provisional, with America occupying Japan and southern Korea, while Russia controlled the rest of Japan's mainland holdings.

On the other hand, working through national Communist parties which nominally had no organizational center, Moscow attempted to detach as much as possible of the world from American leadership. In France the Communists exaggerated and attempted to capitalize on their share in the wartime underground "resistance" movement and took the lead in executions of alleged collaborationists. Admitted to De Gaulle's ministry in Algeria, their party, with five million votes, won a plurality, though by no means a majority, in the first postwar French election (October, 1945). Their efforts to recreate a "Popular Front," this time with Communist participation in the Cabinet, were, however, spoiled by De Gaulle's refusal to allot them key ministries; in the spring of 1947 they were expelled altogether from the government. In Italy, by alliance with the Socialists, the Communists won in the parliamentary elections more seats than did the Christian Democrats; in 1947, however, a split in the Socialist Party and Togliatti's attack on the Church enabled De Gasperi to get rid of his unwelcome colleagues.

In their zone of occupation in Germany, the Communists succeeded in forcing the Socialist Party to fuse with them into the Socialist Unity Party, through which the Communists were able to direct the politics of the much more numerous Socialists. The Soviet Union continued to extract everything possible in the form of "reparations," while using Roosevelt's endorsement of the Morgenthau Plan to threaten the Germans with the worse evil that would befall them under American control; this latter line of propaganda, however, lost its efficacy when Secretary of State James F. Byrnes secured authority publicly to repudiate the Morgenthau Plan (September, 1946).

In Poland, lying athwart Soviet lines of military communication with Germany, Mikolajczyk's Polish People's Party, with its roots in the peasantry, was outmaneuvered, by force and by fraud, in the first elections, which were delayed to January, 1947. Mikolajczyk himself was constrained to flee abroad (October, 1947), and by the end of 1948 Poland seemed to be as "monolithic" as Russia itself. In Hungary the dominant Small Farmers' Party was destroyed by methods similar to those employed against Mikolajczyk in Poland. In Rumania and Bulgaria also, Communist monopoly of power was complete by 1948. Albania was in Communist hands. In Yugoslavia, Tito's partisans, closely affiliated with Muscovite Communism, had already established their own monolithic control.

In Czechoslovakia, old pro-Russian sentiment, strengthened by memories of Munich and by agrarian reforms carried out by the occupying forces, gave the Communists 38 percent of the vote in a free election (May, 1946). Gradually inching their way into the most strategic governmental positions, they succeeded under the leadership of Premier Gottwald in driving their non-Communist colleagues to resign without having prepared a serious line of further action. By this coup late in February, 1948, the Communists were able to secure a monopoly of power; their last serious opponent, Jan Masaryk, son of the "father of Czechoslovakia," was removed by a "defenestration" (March 10) more thorough than that of 1618. President Benes resigned (June 7), leaving his country firmly behind the "iron curtain."

In all the satellite countries, nationalization of industry and "planned economy" were soon introduced, but collectivization of agriculture was prudently postponed until division of large estates among the peasants had won their partial acceptance of their new regime and had destroyed the leadership of the older and more powerful nationalist elements.

In Asia, the rapidly rising tide of native hostility to "imperialism" allowed the Communists to make more rapid progress than in Europe. To be sure, some of the areas on which they had set their firmest hopes disappointed them. The Moslem areas in particular showed strong resistance to Communist advances. Turkey continued to prefer the West as against a too-powerful neighbor, and Iran was alienated by Soviet reluctance to abandon her territory. Moscow was only three days behind the United States in recognizing the new state of Israel (May 17, 1948), not from any Soviet love of Zionism but as a means of further stimulating unrest in the Arab world, which at that time it was clearly hopeless for the Communists to approach directly. It should be noted that postwar partition of oil resources in the Middle East among American and British companies, with heavy participation in profits by the Arab rulers, excluded Russian participation.

In India, Britain's voluntary withdrawal (1947) disappointed Soviet hopes of stirring trouble; a Communist uprising in Hyderabad was crushed by Nehru. Similarly, recognition of the independence of the Philippines (1946), of Burma (1948), and Indonesia (1949) prevented full-scale raising of the banner of a crusade against the West, though the Communists were able to cause varying degrees of difficulties throughout southeast Asia. Malaya was a hotbed of jungle warfare, and French efforts to resubjugate Indochina played into the hands of the Communists by giving Ho Chi Minh's government in Vietnam the full force of a struggle against "imperialism."

In China, however, Russia not only legalized the gains Roosevelt had promised to wring from Chiang Kai-shek but, at a price, scored unexpected further triumphs. The Soviet Union had in 1945 concluded a treaty with "Nationalist" China by which all the Yalta concessions were confirmed in return for recognition of Chiang Kai-shek as the legal ruler of all China. Nevertheless, from 1946 on, the rebellious Chinese Communists, led by Mao Tse-tung, Chu Teh, and Chou En-lai, were aided in their civil war against Chiang by supplies furnished by their Russian mentors. The Chinese Communists, though trained in Moscow, had the wit to adapt their tactics to local Chinese conditions, ignoring Stalin's instructions. Their victory, complete on the mainland by the end of 1949, resulted in the establishment of a "People's Republic," with its capital once again at Peking. It promptly concluded (February, 1950) a treaty of alliance with the Soviet Union against potential common enemies; Russia promised to relinquish her rights in Manchuria and the Liaotung peninsula and to aid China with industrial equipment. Red China was both too remote and too powerful to be treated as a satellite, and maintenance of good relations with her imposed on the Soviet Union the need for a good deal of patience. The Soviet Union remained the world's only "socialist" state, but the negative value of bad blood between China and the imperialist world was well worth the sacrifice of any effort at closer integration with Moscow.

To guide the Communist movement outside her borders, whether in the satellite countries or further afield, Russia reëstablished an international organization, theoretically at least less authoritarian than the old Comintern had claimed to be. The headquarters of this new "Communist Information Bureau" (*Cominform*) were set up, not in Moscow, but in Tito's Belgrade (September, 1947). In Yugoslavia, Communism was more home-made than in any other country except Russia or China, and the attempt to bring it into line backfired. Tito's obvious desire to form a confederation of Balkan states under his own leadership worried Moscow, which sought to tie each "Communist" country directly to itself. False charges that Yugoslavia was not pressing collectivization of her peasantry with sufficient vigor were expanded into a curious attack on Tito's regime for being "dictatorial" (June, 1948). Instead of submitting, Yugoslavia pursued a more than ever independent course, developing the Communist heresy of "Titoism."

As a result, Yugoslavia for a time entered into moderately friendly relations with the West. Tito's Minister of Propaganda, Milovan Djilas, attacked Stalin's Russia for its "anti-Leninist" characteristics of bureaucracy and state capitalism (unfortunately for him, he later extended his criticisms to Yugoslavia also, and the chief ideologist of Titoism had to be jailed by Tito). Yugoslavia was protected by its mountainous terrain and by the fierceness of its nationalism, which had been steeled in its violent struggle against the Nazis. Lest its independence be imitated elsewhere, a number of leading Communists in the satellite states were purged in 1949. Among others, the Magyar Laszlo Rajk was executed for "nationalist deviation," the prominent Polish Communist Wladyslaw Gomulka was imprisoned, and the Bulgarian leader Georgi Dimitrov died under surgery in Moscow; simultaneously, the Catholic primate of Hungary, Cardinal Mindszenty, was sentenced to life imprisonment for alleged treason, espionage, and black-market dealings (February 8, 1949).

THE "COLD WAR" IN FULL BLAST

In the meantime the "cold war" had been developing into a system of military and economic alliances. Since 1946 Greek guerillas, operating back and forth across the borders of neighboring and Communist-controlled Albania, Yugoslavia, and Bulgaria, had been waging a war of attrition against the popularly elected government of Greece and the British troops sent to support its authority. In the spring of 1947 the American President announced (March 12) the "Truman Doctrine" of giving aid to countries threatened by "armed minorities or by outside pressures." Congress promptly (May 15) voted the necessary appropriations, and American troops took over from the British the burden of maintaining the principle of free democracy (however undemocratic the Greek and Turkish governments actually were) and of preventing either Greece or Turkey from being forced into the Russian orbit. The civil war in Greece was prolonged and exceedingly bitter, but aided by Tito's quarrel with Stalin and his closing of the frontier to guerillas, had by 1950 obviously saved that strategic area for the West.

The Truman Doctrine had quickly been followed by the even more sweeping "Marshall Plan" (June 5, 1947), in accordance with which an "Organization of European Economic Coöperation" (OEEC) put American resources at the disposal of the overstrained economies of countries staggering under postwar difficulties. The figure of 12 billion dollars to be expended over three and a half years contrasts strangely with the 250 million dollars that is the outside estimate of Soviet aid to China in the three years preceding the nonaggression pact with Japan (1937-40). Welcomed by most Western European countries, the Marshall Plan was rejected by the suspicious Soviet Union, which denounced this new manifestation of American "imperialism." In the face of Russian frowns none of her satellites dared accept the tempting offer. Czechoslovakia, not yet completely in Russia's grip, did indicate her desire to participate in Marshall Plan discussions but, overawed by direct Russian threats, promptly drew back.

The growing unity of the Western world also took a more martial turn. The first sign of changing attitudes was fusion (December, 1946) of the American and British zones of occupation in Germany, though France, fearful of a recrudescence of German power, still held aloof. On March 4, 1947, however, France and Great Britain concluded at Dunkirk a military alliance which, a year later (March 17, 1948) was expanded to include Belgium, the Netherlands, and Luxembourg. At this point (April 1), apparently to test the strength of Western cohesion and to frighten off waverers, the Soviet government ordered a stop put to communications between the West and Berlin, isolated in the midst of the Russian zone of occupation; the blockade became fully effective in June. The prompt and effective reply of the West to the Berlin blockade was organization of an Anglo-American airlift, which at tremendous expense not only preserved contact with its garrisons but enabled the population of democratic West Berlin to survive Russia's economic pressure. On May 12, 1949, the Soviet Union abandoned its effort and lifted the blockade, though the Allies continued the airlift until the end of September. In the meantime (January, 1949) a "Council for Mutual Economic Assistance" was set up in Warsaw as an attempted Soviet answer to the Marshall Plan, but even its propaganda value was very slight; in practice it meant only more effective "integration" of the economies of the satellite states with, and their subordination to, the economic ends of the Soviet Union.

The reaction of the West to Russia's threatening attitude had been strong. Instead of splitting the democracies, the Berlin blockade drove them into closer union. The American Congress immediately completed (April 3, 1948) appropriation of an additional 6 billion dollars in foreign aid. The existing military alliance of Great Britain, France, and the "Benelux" countries was widely expanded. A mutual-defense pact, adopted in March, 1949, led to the creation of a "North Atlantic Treaty Organization" (NATO). A treaty, signed April 4 and ratified by the United States Senate on July 21, provided for combined action of the forces of Great Britain, France, Belgium, the Netherlands, Luxembourg, Italy, Portugal, Norway, Denmark, Iceland, Canada, and the United States. Command was entrusted to General Eisenhower, who had been at the head of Anglo-American forces in the Mediterranean from the time of the landings in Algeria and on the Continent from the Normandy invasion; "Supreme Headquarters, Allied Powers, Europe" (SHAPE) was, however, not formally organized at Paris until April 2, 1951. The organization of NATO was accompanied (April 8, 1949) by a merger of the French zone of occupation in Germany with that jointly administered by her allies, and work was begun by a German representative assembly on a constitution for a Federal Republic of Germany, proclaimed on May 23; on September 21, without a peace treaty, a new democratic Germany came into existence under civilian control, although the "state of war" was not declared ended until 1951 and the independence of the Federal Republic was officially recognized only in 1955. The only answer the Soviet government could make was the lame one of converting its zone of occupation into a "German Democratic Republic" (October 7, 1949) under the presidency of the Comintern veteran, Wilhelm Pieck; the Soviet Union recognized this new East German state as sovereign in 1954.

Five years after the collapse of Germany, the Soviet Union was clearly getting the worst of the "cold war." Her principal triumph, the People's Republic of China, was more of a blow to the West than a positive victory for Russia. Although it immensely increased Communist prestige throughout Asia, it was uncertain how far Chinese Communism, which had relied on its own strategy largely independently of Moscow, could be depended on as a partner. Sino-Russian relations might be those of like-minded friends, but Moscow could not give orders to Peking. Constant negotiation and cajolery would obviously be necessary. An immediate consequence of Mao's victory had been the promise to restore to China the loot Russia had so recently recovered from Japan. In announcing the capitulation of Japan (September 2, 1945), Stalin had referred to the Japanese raid on Port Arthur in 1904 (which he was careful to compare with Pearl Harbor) as something which "lay on our country like a black spot," someday to be wiped out. "For forty years we, the men of the older generation, have waited for this day. Now this day has finally come." [2] One wonders what Stalin's thoughts were when, by treaty with Red China, he again relinquished the Manchurian railways, Port Arthur, and Dairen.

At best, Russia's new link with China was a poor counterpoise to the solidity of the NATO alliance against her in the West. Hope of extending her power throughout Germany became very dim. She could not compete with the advantages the Marshall Plan and subsequent broadening of American foreign aid gave to Russia's opponents in winning over or neutralizing uncommitted or wavering countries. Her break with Yugoslavia had opened a chink in the "iron curtain" and had hampered her penetration of Greece; the loss was not counterbalanced by consolidation of her grip on Czechoslovakia. Almost the only item on the other side of the ledger was official announcement (September 23, 1949) that the Soviet Union had successfully exploded an atom bomb; if there were to be a "push button" war, Russia might not be left at the post.

The Soviet Union had not lost heart, nor had its protozoan tendency to expansion diminished. Soviet agents were all over the world, ready to promote trouble wherever possible. Moscow was constantly alert for signs of weakness, particularly on the part of America. Following withdrawal of Soviet forces from North Korea late in 1948, the American occupation forces had been removed from the South Korean Republic in June, 1949. Early in 1950 an unguarded statement by Secretary of State Dean Acheson spelled out the American "defense perimeter"; omission of mention of Korea from the list of territories, attempts on which would involve the United States in war, could be construed to mean that America no longer had an interest in South Korea. On June 24/25, 1950, the Soviet-trained North Korean army crossed the 38th parallel; officially, and prudently, the Soviet Union was not involved. Within two days the United States had ordered its troops back to Korea. Thanks to a boycott of the United Nations Security Council that Russia had begun in January over refusal of the Council to transfer Nationalist China's seat to the People's Republic, no Soviet veto could prevent that body from promptly calling on all members of the United Nations to coöperate in the intervention. General MacArthur, transferred by the United States from Japan, was given command of a United Nations army, mainly composed of American and South Korean troops, but with larger or smaller token forces supplied by Great Britain, Canada, Australia, New Zealand, South Africa, the Netherlands, Belgium, Luxembourg, France, Greece, Turkey, Ethiopia, Thailand, the Philippines, and Colombia. The North Korean forces were driven back, but penetration of the pursuers as far as the Yalu (November 20) brought an attack of several hundred thousand Chinese "volunteers" from Manchuria (November 26). A disastrous retreat of the United Nations forces went far to reverse the psychological effects throughout Asia that the advance had achieved, although the Chinese offensive was stopped and the front stabilized roughly along the 38th parallel (April, 1951). The General Assembly of the United Nations formally declared Red China an aggressor (February 1, 1952), but General MacArthur, who had wished to carry the war into Manchuria, was recalled, and his successor was instructed not to attempt to advance further, lest what President Truman had termed a "police action" develop into a Third World War. Truce negotiations were begun (July 10) but for long seemed likely to end in a stalemate; not until July 27, 1953, almost three months after Stalin's death, was an armistice signed.

Meanwhile Ho Chi Minh's Communist-backed struggle in Vietnam dragged on, as did the "Huk" revolt in the Philippines and jungle warfare in British Malaya. No serious effort was made to coördinate action against Communist penetration in these areas or elsewhere. On the other hand, a peace treaty was negotiated between Japan and the United States (September 8, 1951), which was accepted by forty-eight other nations. Though the Soviet Union refused to recognize the agreement, Japanese sovereignty was restored in April, 1952.

ECONOMIC RECONSTRUCTION AND EXPANSION

Tension abroad was fully matched by tensions within the Soviet Union. This was not on account of any change in the political structure. The emergency State Committee of Defense was promptly dissolved (September 4, 1945), and there was a complete return to normal administrative procedures; even the special military regime that had been proclaimed in the occupied provinces was speedily liquidated. On February 10, 1946, new elections were held, the first since 1937, to the Supreme Soviet. It should be remembered that in Great Britain, too, no Parliamentary general election was held from 1935 to 1945. The results were very different, however, as is not surprising when one considers the difference in the reality of an election in Great Britain and in the Soviet Union. In the U.S.S.R., where only one party was permitted and where the system of nomination guaranteed only one candidate for each seat, there was nothing phenomenal about the fact that the 1946 election, in which officially 99.7 percent of the registered electors voted, returned a Soviet of the Union in which 84.4 percent of its members were members of the Communist Party; in the Soviet of Nationalities, for propaganda reasons, only 77.4 percent of the members were Communists. Only 819,699 voters (0.8%) ventured to exercise their official privilege of crossing out the name of the sole candidate for office. Similar elections, at the republic level, for local soviets, and for judges, gave corresponding results. In the new Supreme Council there was more discussion than usual, but it turned either on matters of "self-criticism" or of what Americans know as "pork-barrel" legislation rather than on essential principles. The substitution (March 15, 1946) of the Western title of "Minister" for the revolutionary style of "Commissar" had no deep significance. More important were the efforts, not altogether successful, to recombine administrative departments in fewer hands and to transfer more administrative functions from the republics to the Union.

Party membership, swollen by the wartime effort to reëstablish contact between the Party and the masses, had reached a new peak. Malenkov, now the principal *apparatchik* under Stalin, stressed that

> a considerable number of Communists, especially those who have entered the Party in recent years, have not yet succeeded in obtaining the necessary political grounding. . . . For in the final analysis quality is more important than quantity.[3]

The result, coupled with the need of renewed emphasis on "Marxist" education of Party members, was a new purge, which bore with special emphasis on local leaderships, especially in the Ukraine. Khrushchev was temporarily succeeded there by the renowned trouble-shooter, Kaganovich. The new purge, however, was not attended by a recrudescence of the excesses of the Yezhovshchina. In victorious Russia, demotion or transfer took the place of execution or exile. "Self-criticism" by Party members was again invited, notably by Khrushchev in the Ukraine.

Political forms were not the only sense in which the Soviet Union quickly lapsed back into the prewar routine. In the economic field, also, Russia promptly attempted to resume her prewar tempo of industrialization. Here, too, war experience had a certain softening effect. The Fourth Five-Year Plan, launched in 1946, was no doubt ambitious, but it had to reckon with the devastation wreaked by the war. Just how severe the ruin was cannot be statistically supported. The loss of population directly or indirectly traceable to the war has been put at 20 million; considering the Russian rate of reproduction, this is not incompatible with the official figure of a net reduction of 7 million. Voznesensky, then recognized as the leading Soviet economist and a member of the Politburo, put the loss in the occupied area, which had represented about half of the population (45%) and of the cultivated area (47%) and a third of the industrial production, at two-thirds of its capital wealth. The estimate that at least a quarter of the total capital of the Soviet Union was destroyed in the war does not seem exaggerated.

The Fourth F.Y.P. expected not only to make good the war losses but substantially to increase production above 1940 levels. Coal output, which during the war had been reduced by 32 percent, was expected to rise to 50 percent above the prewar level—that is, to double in five years. The figure for oil production (from 63% to 114%) was slightly more modest, but output of electricity, which had suffered less decline (to 89%), was to exceed the 1940 level by 70 percent. Pig iron and steel, which had dropped by almost two-fifths, were to rise by almost one-third. The planned rise in consumption goods was more moderate: for example, manufacture of cotton cloth, which had fallen by almost three-fifths, was expected to exceed 1940 production by only one-fifth—a trebling of the very low rate of production. In agriculture the figure was still more modest; grain production was expected to rise from its actual low of 55 percent of 1940 to only 7 percent above 1940; better things were expected of industrial crops, such as sugar beet, which had fallen to 42 percent but was expected to soar to 124 percent of 1940 output. The number of head of livestock, which had not in prewar years recovered from the disaster of collectivization and which during the war had suffered a further, though lesser, blow, was also expected to show only a moderate increase over 1940.

Available published data are hopelessly inadequate, but it seems evident that the Fourth F.Y.P. and the Fifth, duly launched in 1951, fell far short of their stated goals, as had their predecessors. This does not mean that very substantial increases in production were not achieved and that new resources east of the Urals were not tapped. What seems certain, however, is that the promise made by Stalin in his electoral speech of February, 1946—that Russia would soon overtake America—was an empty dream; even if four more successive F.Y.P.'s were to have turned out as he then predicted, gross Russian production in 1965 would be less than that of the United States in 1947. To "overtake" America at such a rate, it would be necessary not only to assume that American production would stand still but to posit that it would begin to decline.

In the period of the Fourth F.Y.P. and its 1951 successor, as in all their predecessors, emphasis remained on production of the means of production. Scanty as are official Soviet data, it seems beyond doubt that production of consumer goods and the standard of living of the population did not, at least for some years after the war, reach even the low 1940 level. This is, of course, a phenomenon not peculiar to Russia in those years; Great Britain also experienced a period of austerity. In the Soviet Union, however, material discomfort was accompanied by severe repression of labor.

The work of reconstruction and renewed expansion entailed considerable increase in the labor force. To attain this end, rationed prices of food were tripled in September, 1946, without equivalent increases in wage rates; the ration system was modified by reducing the quantities that various kinds of workers, and especially non-workers, could buy at ration prices. In December, 1947, rationing was abolished; although "commercial" prices were much reduced, the economic pressure on the population to find employment was immensely increased. Quite apart from the thousands of prisoners of war, whose release to their home lands was inordinately delayed, and apart from the other thousands still subject to "political reëducation" at the hands of the MVD (formerly NKVD), the effect on productivity was necessarily good, for managers of enterprises were enabled to select from the excess of applicants for jobs those best qualified for higher-paid work. Although compulsory overtime was abolished and vacation privileges were restored, the work week was not again reduced below the eight-hour day, six days a week, to which it had been raised in 1940.

In agriculture the wartime relaxation of the principles underlying collective farming had been accompanied by official encouragement of the "link" (*zveno*) system of organizing labor in place of the older "brigade" system. It had been argued that, particularly in view of the shortage of mechanical equipment, intensive labor of individuals could best be utilized in small groups ("links") responsible for cultivation of particular portions of the collective lands. In 1950 it was suddenly announced that the "link" system, emphasizing the work of individuals, was interfering with large-scale mechanized agriculture and should henceforth be restricted to certain specialized crops.

The attempt to reënlarge the scale of agricultural operations and to prevent possible reëmergence of individual economies was pushed even further. Small collective farms were to be merged into larger units; it was officially reported that in the course of the year 1951 the number of collective farms had been reduced from 252,000 to 123,000. At the beginning of 1951 an even more ambitious program was outlined; *agrigoroda* (farm-cities) were to be organized, in which large centralized settlements, subject to managerial control, were to be surrounded by extensive collective fields. Allotments of plots for individual cultivation, already cut back, were to be reduced to a minimum. Since, however, the basic objective of increasing production was threatened by the probable hostile reaction of the peasantry to such a scheme, the idea of *agrigorody* remained only "a basis for discussion."

In a further effort to increase agricultural production, the government late in 1948 announced a very extensive program of afforestation to provide "shelter-belts" to protect the drought-ridden areas of the eastern Ukraine and lower Volga against desiccating winds. In the 1930's a beginning had been made on this line, but what little had been accomplished had been undone by the war. The new program was on paper ten times more ambitious. It was followed in 1950 by revival of centuries-old schemes of changing the course of the few rivers of Turkestan in connection with a vast irrigation project. It was even suggested that the atomic bomb must be developed by Russia for use on the polar icecap in the hope that northern Siberia, released from the crushing weight of ice, might rise and thus reverse the course of Siberia's mighty rivers, causing them to flow fruitfully in the desert Central Asian steppe instead of wastefully emptying into the frozen Arctic Ocean.

In industry, too, prewar methods of increasing productivity were not abandoned. The State Labor Reserve and concomitant on-the-job training were retained. Stakhanovism, though losing its impetus, was still encouraged. The regulations against voluntary absenteeism in industry were not relaxed, and on the collective farms the rules making a minimum of "labor days" compulsory for every individual were stiffened. Pensions and "fringe benefits" were made ever more strictly dependent on length and continuity of employment.

On the other hand, the unenforcibility of such measures, designed to reduce labor turnover and increase labor output, was clear; management, whether industrial or agricultural, often winked at gross breaches of statute law. The government was compelled to give continued attention also to methods of persuasion to attain "true Bolshevist tempo." The "Director's Fund," suspended during the war, was reinstated, with all its incidental collective benefits for workers in particularly successful enterprises. Individuals continued to be rewarded with bonuses or with higher piecework rates, making for greatly increased inequality of earnings on the basis of the effort and achievement of individual workers. Housing, though it remained hopelessly inadequate, was given special attention as a means of stimulating specially deserving workers. Russia seemed to be moving ever farther from the communist dream of "To each according to his needs" and to be jelling on the basis of the "socialist" slogan of "To each according to his labor."

FAMILY AND CHURCH

The ghost of Karl Marx, though again invoked in a postwar drive properly to educate Party members in the teachings of Marx-Engels-Lenin-Stalin, must have been made very uneasy by the direction that Soviet social theory was taking in his name. In the *Communist Manifesto,* Marx had announced that "the bourgeois family will vanish as a matter of course"; it is true that his objection to the institution was predicated on the thought that "the bourgeoisie has torn away from the family its sentimental veil, and has reduced the family relation to a mere money relation." [4] Marx and Engels had believed in a monogamy, however fleeting, based on "mutual inclination," but as Engels had put it, there was no use in making unhappy couples "wade through the useless mire of a divorce case." [5] Lenin had said that "it is impossible to be a socialist and a democrat without immediately demanding complete freedom of divorce." [6] Mme Kollontai's concept of *Red Love* had been that under capitalism "the family is ceasing to be a necessity for its members as well as for the state." [7]

Reference has already been made to the beginnings in the 1930's of efforts at "strengthening the family," which was, however, treated as a "private matter." A decree of July 8, 1944, ushered in sweeping changes in official attitudes. It was now explained that the family is the basis of society, but for materialist rather than sentimental reasons. The family provides "a real foundation on which [the state] can depend. . . . By strengthening the family the state is strengthening itself, increasing its own might." Accordingly, marriage was declared a solemn procedure, to be attested by official registration, "compulsorily entered in the [domestic] passports" of both parties (Article 22).

In the case of such marriage, the state "with all its power and authority recognizes the given marital relations, approves them, supports them, and takes them under its protection," to the end that the marriage may result in a strong family with many children, and that the children, given a "normal and healthy upbringing," may develop "those qualities and traits . . . which should form the norms of behavior of every citizen of the Soviet Union." Unwed mothers were now forbidden to institute paternity suits (Article 20); they could claim only a small state allowance (Article 3), but might surrender the child to a state institution (Article 4). Unregistered marriage, as "an expression of a thoughtless and flippant attitude," [8] was not to share in the special fiscal privileges accorded to recognized large families unless the unwed mother had at least eight living children. Registered mothers were, among other advantages (including the right of inheritance and of alimony), to receive state payments and monthly maintenance, on a sharply rising scale, for the third and subsequent children (Articles 1-2), while the fifth child would bring even a medal and the tenth would confer the title of "Heroine Mother" (Articles 12-15). On the principle that the stronger the family becomes, the stronger will be society as a whole, divorce was made subject to a two-stage court procedure involving investigation into the reasons and official attempts at reconciliation. Decision was left to the discretion of the higher court; there were set forth no specific grounds, proof of which entitles either party to a verdict (Article 25). In addition, substantial fees were imposed in the event the divorce is granted, while the costs of the procedure must in any event be borne by the litigants (Article 27). Thus, instead of the "sentimental veil" which Marxism wished drawn over marriage and the family, there emerged again what was largely "a mere money relation."

The Church continued to share in the restoration of "bourgeois" relationships. It emerged from the war with a substantially increased number of functioning parishes and a strengthened hierarchy. Church finances were in a healthy state, and even the remaining monasteries were released (1946) from the heavy taxation to which they had been subject. The two theological academies and four seminaries opened during the war were supplemented by additional seminaries. Church attendance was much increased by the popular religious revival that everywhere usually follows a war, and religious education of children by priests, though strictly forbidden in the schools, continued to be privately tolerated by the government's Council on the Affairs of the Orthodox Church, that pale substitute for the tsar's lay Procurator-General of the Holy Synod. In the western provinces, the Church achieved a consolidation of its ecclesiastical jurisdiction it had never won from the tsars;

the Union of Brest of 1596, under which the Orthodox in Poland-Lithuania had accepted the headship of the pope, was annulled. In 1946 the five million Uniates were received back into the Orthodox fold; at the same time the Uniate metropolitan and four Uniate bishops, who resisted the break with Rome, were arrested on charges of collaboration with the Nazi invaders.

The official *Journal of the Patriarchate of Moscow* continued its attacks, not at all unwelcome to the Kremlin, on the Roman Catholic Church. The papacy was alleged to have been the tool of Mussolini and Hitler. It was charged that it had now transferred its affection, through the influence of Cardinal Spellman, to the United States. That country was characterized by Metropolitan Nikolai, the patriarch's right-hand man, as one

> where they lynch people, where they kidnap children, where they throw tear-gas bombs at workers, . . . where they burn grain under the eyes of the starving, where they throw into jail those who try to restore to the word "liberty" its true meaning, where they lavish gold to win foreign countries as accomplices, and cast cannon to flood with human blood the peaceful valleys of Greece, China, Indonesia, and Vietnam. Liberty to plunder, to ravish, to murder—that is their "liberty." [9]

Rome and the United States were said to be actively striving to bring on a third world war in the interest of their ecclesiastical and material domination. The Syllabus of Errors of 1864 was brought up as evidence that the Roman Church was the opponent of all liberalism and progress. The hand of the pope was seen in "fascist" activities in Spain, Greece, and South Korea and in alleged perpetuation of "imperialist" colonialism in Southeast Asia. The hostility of Orthodoxy to the papacy had of course been continuous since the mutual anathema of 1054, but the current political tone of its denunciations differed radically from its language in tsarist days; the Church was still in the service of the state, but service to the Soviet state required a shift in orientation with respect to political details.

In its relations to the rest of the Orthodox world, the Russian Church continued its bid for primacy as "the third [and final] Rome," which necessitated continued cool relations with the Ecumenical Patriarch of Constantinople. In the face of the latter's protest, Patriarch Alexius retreated from his idea of convening an ecumenical council at Moscow and postponed a conference of bishops called to discuss the question "until a more suitable time." [10] In 1948, to celebrate the five hundredth anniversary of Russian autocephaly, a sort of unofficial ecumenical council was held at Moscow with great pomp and ceremony; the Ecumenical Patriarch boycotted the affair, which led one of the Russian metropolitans later to assert, in the official Church journal, that Moscow, not Constantinople, was the real center of Orthodoxy. The 1948 "Conference of Heads of Autocephalous Churches" again roundly condemned the Roman Catholic Church. At the same time, while leaving the door open for establishment of communion with the Church of England, it vigorously refused to have anything to do with the Protestant World Conference of Churches.

The Russian Church continued its adulation of the leaders of the "godless" Communist regime, and of Stalin in particular. On the thirtieth anniversary of the Bolshevik seizure of power, the Patriarch asked God's blessing on the Soviet state:

> Let us intensify our prayers for the divinely protected Russian power and for its Authorities headed by the wise leader, whom the will of God chose and set up to lead our Fatherland along the path of good deeds and glory.

In 1949, in a prepared answer to a question submitted by a foreign newspaper correspondent, Alexius stated:

> No conflict exists or can exist [between loyalty to the Soviet regime and to the Russian Orthodox Church] if the believers follow the teachings of the Gospels and the Apostles.

At a special *Te Deum* to celebrate Stalin's seventieth birthday (December, 1949), Patriarch Alexius went quite as far as any Party sycophant:

> He is the Leader recognized by all peoples of the world, not only of the peoples of the Soviet state, but also of all working people; he is the first in the ranks of proponents and defenders of peace among peoples, peace in the whole world. . . . May the Lord give him long life in health and prosperity to stand at the helm of rule of our native land, and may our country flourish under his wise guidance for many and many years, to the joy and happiness of its peoples. Amen.

The Russian Orthodox Church threw itself energetically into a persistent effort to make Soviet Russia seem the leading proponent and staunchest bulwark of world peace. In 1948 the Moscow Church Conference appealed "To the Christians of the Whole World" against "the aggressiveness of the Western capitalist and imperialist world [that] sharply strikes the eye." In 1950 it refused to "remain indifferent to the sufferings of the Korean people" under "brutal bombing" as a result of "American aggression":

> The Russian Orthodox Church decisively condemns this interference and the resulting inhuman annihilation of the peaceful population of Korea by American aviation.

All its services did not save the Church from a revival of "scientific and enlightening propaganda" to eliminate "remnants of ignorance, superstition, and prejudice." Vipper's *Rise of Christian Literature* (1946) was content to deny the historicity of Jesus and of the Gospels. In 1947, however, the official Komsomol organ once more openly took up the cudgels for an "aggressive ideological struggle" against those who did not recognize "the incompatibility of religious convictions and membership in the Komsomol."

An article in the official *Encyclopedia* emphasized that the Party had "never concealed and does not conceal its negative attitude toward religion"; policies might change at times, but not attitudes. In 1948 the *Teachers' Gazette* joined the chorus, regretting that some teachers were "themselves captives to religious error and at times observe religious rites." By 1950 *Science and Life,* monthly organ of the "Society for the Dissemination of Political and Scientific Knowledge," admitted that religion would not die out of itself under socialism and called for relentless effort:

> Marxism-Leninism and religion are as unreconcilable as materialism and idealism. The struggle between them is particularly acute in our times.

Perhaps believing that barking dogs do not bite, the Church remained imperturbable.

EDUCATION, LITERATURE, AND SCIENCE

The system of public education underwent no major changes in the postwar years. Education was still regarded only as a weapon in the battle to "strengthen the socialist bases of society" and, ultimately, to achieve communism. Since it had long since become obvious that this battle would not be won if left to ordinary human initiative but must be conducted under the direction of the Party, discipline, both moral and intellectual, of the children was further tightened, and the authority over them of the teachers and school officials was correspondingly increased. Officially the curriculum and techniques of instruction remained uniform for all children between the ages of seven and seventeen, but the great variation of material conditions and human resources in various parts of the Soviet Union prevented anything like complete realization of the ideal; differences between urban and rural schools also could not be overcome, and even in the capital, schools actually varied widely in equipment and in the competence of the teachers. The principal exception to the rule of uniform instruction for all children was made during the war when, because of the "necessity of differentiating the military-physical preparation of the youth of the two sexes," [11] coeducation was abolished (July, 23, 1943) in the standard ten-year schools, at least in large centers of population; it was not restored until 1954, after Stalin's death.

The school was by no means the only weapon available for ideological warfare. The adult mind—and, more importantly, adult emotions—could best be kept in line through literature and the arts and by inculcating general appreciation of "culture." Prior to the war Soviet Russia had lived a largely isolated life; after the war it was possible again to drop the "iron curtain." But during the war it had been necessary to pour millions of men across the Soviet borders and to let them be exposed to the "rotten" West. The language barrier between the Russian soldier or officer and those amongst whom he came as conqueror or as liberator tended to keep intellectual contacts to a minimum. Yet the relative magnificence of the architecture of the cities of Western Europe, the superior attractiveness of the clothing, furnishings, and personal property of their inhabitants, and their higher standard of living could not fail to impress the invaders, to stimulate wonder at the reasons why their homeland was so austere and backward, and even to breed doubts about the superiority they had assumed for Soviet "culture."

The Soviet authorities were well aware of the effect of glamour and glitter on the minds of "simple" people and had substituted the splendor of the subways for that of the churches. Even if they were not aware of the Ancient Chronicle's story of how Rus came to be converted to Christianity, they were well aware of the power of attractive women; *Pravda* found it necessary, at the time of the occupation of Bucharest, the "Paris of the East," to warn the troops against the seductions of face paint and powder, silk stockings and other artificial aids; it was thought necessary to point out that if you stripped and bathed these beauties, they would be inferior to Russian women. There was real danger that the experience of Russian armies serving in the heart of the West might turn out in something of the same way as in the days of Napoleon. The Soviet state did not want a new Decembrist movement; it was not prepared to tolerate even the ideological influence of the West that had in the nineteenth century permeated the intelligentsia and had produced Russian writers such as Pushkin, Lermontov, and Turgenev, Bielinsky and Herzen.

The Party did not lose time in taking fiction in hand. On August 14, 1946, the Central Committee condemned two Leningrad literary magazines for having published contributions by Zoshchenko and Akhmatova. Zoshchenko was described as a writer who had

> long since been specializing in writing empty, vapid, trivial things and in preaching a decadent inanity, banality, and apoliticalness, calculated to confuse our youth and to poison its consciousness.

Especially annoying was his *Adventures of a Monkey* (1946), the story of a marmoset set at liberty by a chance bomb, which was regarded as "a banal libel on Soviet life and on Soviet people"; nor was his "sickening" wartime story *Before Sunrise* overlooked. Akhmatova's poetry was "empty, inane, and alien to our people. . . . Her verse, nourished in the spirit of pessimism and decadence . . . cannot be tolerated in Soviet literature." [12]

The attack was based on a report by Zhdanov, who was then regarded as, next to Stalin, the most important member of the Politburo. As early as 1934, at the First Congress of Soviet Writers, Zhdanov had taken the position that

> to be an engineer of human souls means standing with both feet firmly planted on the basis of real life. . . . Soviet literature should be able to portray our heroes, it should be able to glimpse our tomorrow . . . no utopian dream.[13]

He had then expressed pride in the "tendentious" character of Soviet literature. Now he denounced the "rotten" Zoshchenko, the "vulgarian" who had suggested that "life in a zoo is better than life at large and that in a cage one can breathe more freely than among Soviet people." Akhmatova was

> not quite a nun, not quite a wanton, but both a wanton and a nun . . . a relic of the "good old days" of Catherine; [Akhmatova's was the] poetry of an agitated lady, tossing between the boudoir and the chapel. . . .
>
> Some think that if a waste in production is discovered or if some program of production of consumer goods is not fulfilled or if a plan for lumber is not fulfilled, a reprimand is a natural thing, but if a waste in the education of human souls is discovered, if a waste is disclosed in the education of youth, this can be tolerated. Yet is this not a more bitter fault than nonfulfillment of a production program . . . ?
>
> The young Soviet generation must strengthen the power and might of socialist society for a new, unprecedented blossoming of our prosperity and culture. For these great tasks the young generation must be brought up to be steadfast, cheerful, unafraid of obstacles, eager to meet obstacles and able to surmount them. Our people must be high-principled, with high cultural and moral aspirations and tastes. To this end we want our literature and our periodicals not to stand aside from present problems.[14]

The expulsion of the two culprits from the Union of Soviet Writers and their consequent silencing, and promotion of the compliant Fadeiev to be secretary-general of the Union, were only the first small steps in the *Zhdanovshchina*. The Union confessed its sins and those of its members; central was the "un-Soviet spirit of servility before the bourgeois culture of the West." Once launched, the campaign went on, unaffected by Zhdanov's sudden death in 1948. One of its main themes was the "decadence" of the "rotten" West. The specifically anti-American campaign in Soviet literature was more virulent in the postwar years than the one that had been directed against "fascism" in the 1930's. Among a swarm of other novels of this type, the one with the most intrinsic literary merit was Pavlenko's *Happiness* (1947); although it showed some sympathy for Roosevelt as against the "double-dealing" Churchill, its general picture of Americans was that of businessmen, disguised as military officers, in pursuit of the almighty dollar. Surov's *The Ill-Starred Haberdasher* (1948) cast Truman in the role of Hitler. Other writers ridiculed the British as the "errand boys" of their American "bosses" or argued that Hitler had deliberately allowed the British to escape from Dunkirk in order later to enlist them against the Soviet Union.

A more generalized aspect of anti-Westernism in literature was reflected by the bitter assaults on the memory of a nineteenth-century Russian scholar, Alexander Veselovsky (1838-1906), the centenary of whose birth had been celebrated for his "Marxist" ideas about the interdependence of all literatures. In 1947 he was attacked, not without confusing him with his younger brother Alexis (1843-1918), who had written a highly regarded book on *Western Influence on Modern Russian Literature,* for his "cosmopolitan" ideas and particularly for his concept that "literature is only the passive product of the social milieu . . . but does not influence life." [15] Despite—or because of—vigorous attempts to defend his work, it was emphatically stated that the comparative method (which was not in fact alien to Marxism) led to "historical fatalism with all its spiritual diseases—passiveness, contemplativeness, scepticism, 'pure scholarship.' " [16] The denunciation of "rootless cosmopolitanism" (a more literal translation of the Russian phrase is "cosmopolitans without kinsmen") led to a widespread purge of Russian writers who had been unguarded enough to mention Western influence on the great Russian writers of the past. Since Gorky was already dead, he escaped denunciation for his frank acknowledgment of the debt he had owed to certain Western writers. Even the eel-like "historian" Pankratova was chided for mentioning the influence of the *philosophes* on Radishchev. An incidental aspect of the war against "cosmopolitanism" was the apparent care taken to mention the real names of "cosmopolitan" Jewish writers who had used Russian pseudonyms; in view of the lingering latent anti-Semitism of many Russians and Ukrainians, this practice could scarcely fail to have results unfortunate for Soviet Jews.

A complementary theme in the *Zhdanovshchina* was an emphasis on the innate superiority of Russian culture that would have made nineteenth-century Slavophiles squirm. One of its most ridiculous manifestations was the long list of inventions, developed in the West, but now attributed to Russians; in some cases the idea had undoubtedly been conceived quite independently both in Russia and in the West, but the fact that its practical development took place in the West does not in any way justify such fictional titles as *The Story of a Stolen Idea.* Pushkin and Tolstoy, Lermontov and Chekhov, Radishchev, Bielinsky, and Herzen were extolled, not for the spirit or even for the form in which they had written, but because they were precursors of Soviet culture; exceptions, to be sure, were made, for the optimistic creators of the image of a "new Soviet man" could not stomach Dostoevsky, whom Gorky had characterized as dangerously harmful, or muster any enthusiasm for the "aristocratic realism" of Turgenev. The easiest outlet for glorification of Russia was, however, praise of "the leader and father of the peoples," "the Coryphaeus of the sciences," "the great teacher" Stalin.

Emphasis on the belief that "real art teaches and educates" is curiously reminiscent of Leo Tolstoy's dicta in *What Is Art?* Its converse was that any literature that failed to impart proper lessons was to be condemned; even Fadeiev was censured in 1947 for his 1945 *Young Guard,* which had failed to bring out that Party leadership had been more important to the winning of the war than had been the individual qualities of his young heroes.

The general quality of Russian literature under the *Zhdanovshchina,* a more serious version of the days of RAPP, could not be high. The poets, warned by the fate of Akhmatova, were silent or followed the lead of Simonov in toeing the Party line. The drama also languished. Novels, too, were for the most part overwhelmingly and deliberately "tendentious," as prescribed by Zhdanov even in 1934. A welcome exception was the unfinished trilogy of Konstantin Fedin, *First Joys* (1947) and *Unusual Summer* (1948). Politically orthodox, they were well-written, with good character development and human interest. Vera Panova's *Traveling Companions* (1946) and *Kruzhilika* (1948), though centered on the usual themes of constructive service to the state, also had substantial literary merit.

Soviet music shared the fate of Soviet literature. In 1948 Zhdanov held a conference with Soviet musicians, who proceeded to confess their errors in accordance with the new "Decree on Music." Prokofiev, however, still had trouble; his *Story of a Real Man* was condemned as "formalism." In his last years he redeemed himself and won Stalin Prizes. His lyrical *Seventh Symphony* (1952), though musically empty, was officially approved, but his last and melodic ballet, *The Stone Flower,* was performed at the Bolshoi only after his death. Shostakovich, thoroughly chastened, turned out political potboilers in Hollywood vein and was rewarded by being sent to New York in 1949 for the "Congress in Defense of Peace." He nevertheless composed some string quartets of better quality.

Zhdanov had also attacked Soviet philosophers (June, 1947) for timidity, lack of originality, and apathy, and had called for strengthening of the "philosophical front" in the war against capitalist imperialism. With the support of the Academy of Sciences, Leonov attempted to fill the breach with an *Outline of Dialectical Materialism,* carefully fitted together from Marx, Engels, Lenin, and Stalin. It was, however, severely criticized for its failure to realize that the existence of contradictions between supply and demand dooms capitalism to destruction although under socialism it leads to progress. The intellectual front remained unsatisfactory.

Corresponding troubles afflicted some aspects of natural science. Much valuable research, both "pure" and "applied," was carried on, particularly in physics, and Soviet mathematics stood in very high repute. Vavilov, a man of very high caliber in the field of optics, served a term as president of the Academy of Sciences. Under the direction and with the support of the Academy, scientific research, in the social as well as in the physical fields, was planned both on a long-term and a short-term basis. Individual scientists and scholars had to get approval of their research projects from the Academy, much as American scientists and scholars are largely dependent on approval from the foundations whose financial support they need, but with the significant difference that in the Soviet Union there was only one major source of funds to support research. The alternative to approval of individual plans is assignment to scholars on the payroll of the Academy of topics of investigation they have not themselves chosen. The universities, wholly controlled by the All-Union Ministry of Education, and industrial laboratories, under the direction of the several economic ministries, were of subsidiary importance; genuinely independent research, at the personal expense of an individual, was under Soviet conditions extremely difficult.

In those fields of research, such as mathematics, astronomy, and physics, and to a lesser extent chemistry, geology, and geography, science was, on the whole, not excessively hampered by Party interference; the chief difficulty was in establishing and maintaining free contact with researchers in other parts of the world. Soviet scientific publications, though they devoted much attention to summarizing, and even translating, articles in foreign professional journals, could not wholly make up for the absence of direct exchange and discussion of ideas. In those branches of knowledge in which the Party leadership could pretend to understand the ideas and not merely the valuable material results of scholarship, there was much more intervention by the Party. In history, economics, political science, and all those other branches of the study of human relations about which ordinary men tend to think they know as much as specialists can, scholars were regularly told what their findings should be.

Much the same was true of the biological sciences, and it was in this field that the aging Stalin particularly distinguished himself by throwing his support to Lysenko and his claims with respect to the hereditability of acquired characteristics. In contrast to the "bourgeois" theories of Mendel and Weismann, which were supported by most research in "capitalist" countries, the "Marxist" doctrine of Lysenko gave hope of immense practical results for Soviet agriculture and forestry. In consequence his opponents were silenced or demoted, and a theory without the strong support of genuine scientific research was enthroned.

The disaster to the scientific study of genetics in the Soviet Union was, however, partly compensated by Stalin's vigorous attack in 1950 on the linguistic theories of Professor Marr, who had died in 1936. Acknowledging that "I am not a linguist," Stalin admitted that his knowledge of Marxism was sufficient for him to realize that "Marr . . . put linguistics in a muddle." Marr, employing Marxist terminology, had asserted that language is part of the "superstructure" and therefore, having a "class character," must change with the economic "base." Stalin denied this, pointing out that the Revolution had not changed "the basic vocabulary and grammatical structure of the Russian language, which constitute the foundation of the language"; in addition, he suggested that the superstructure "becomes an exceedingly active force, actively assisting its base to take shape and consolidate itself." Stalin's own attitude was lordly:

> It is generally recognized that no science can develop and flourish without a battle of opinions, without freedom of criticism. But this generally recognized rule was ignored and flouted in the most outrageous fashion. A tight group of infallible leaders, having insured themselves against all possible criticism, began to act arbitrarily and highhandedly.[17]

Fortunately, perhaps, he did not have to face the reverse criticism, made after his death, that his new position, as developed by the faithful Aleksandrov, "slurring over the determining role of the [economic] base," meant that the "superstructure" can play an autonomously "creative role" of its own.[18]

THE PARTY LEADERSHIP

The ideological repression of the postwar years was in some ways not dissimilar to the era of the "Great Purge." Yet it was not marked with the same excesses of physical violence. By the same token, the jockeying for position under Stalin's leadership produced no violent convulsions in the ranks of the Politburo. Kalinin died a doubtless natural death in 1946 and was succeeded as chairman of the Presidium of the Supreme Council by Shvernik, another relatively obscure figure, who was not even raised to full membership in the Politburo. The vacant place in that body was instead allotted to Beria, head of the NKVD; an extra tenth place was given to Malenkov. In the same year General Bulganin, who had already (1944) succeeded Voroshilov as civilian administrator of the armed forces, was made a candidate member. So was Kosygin, who at the time of the Revolution had been only a boy of twelve and who later had been trained as an engineer; the purge had opened his way to become People's Commissar of the Textile Industry (1938), from which beginning he had quickly moved up, becoming chairman of the Sovnarkom of the R.S.F.S.R. in 1941. In 1947 Voznesensky was moved up from candidate, making an eleventh full member of the Politburo.

The Orgburo, of less importance than it had been in the days of Stalin's rise, had nevertheless in 1939 included five of the Politburo group. By 1946 three of these had dropped out, leaving only Stalin and Zhdanov as members of both organs. However, one of its three other continuing members, Malenkov, had in the meantime been admitted to the Politburo. The size of the Politburo had been substantially increased and included three more of the Central Committee's secretaries; only one of them was omitted from the Orgburo. In 1947 one of its members, G. F. Aleksandrov, who was also chief of the Agitation and Propaganda Department of the Central Committee and who had ventured to write a *History of Western Philosophy,* was subjected to violent attack by Zhdanov.

The death of Zhdanov (August 31, 1948) resulted in a major shake-up in the top echelons of the Party. As is true of so many other deaths at high levels in the Soviet Union, the suspicion of foul play cannot be excluded. What is certain is that Zhdanov's protégés were soon removed from their posts; among them was Voznesensky, who was dropped from the Politburo in 1949 and soon after completely disappeared. Their places were taken by protégés of Malenkov, who had himself, though remaining in the Politburo, quietly disappeared as a secretary of the Central Committee in 1946, only to be publicly restored on July 21, 1948, little more than a month before Zhdanov's apparently sudden death. It seemed that Stalin had shifted his choice of an heir presumptive.

Zhdanov's place in the Politburo went, not to "President" Shvernik, but to Bulganin; his other fellow-candidate, Kosygin, was next year given Voznesensky's vacant seat. As thus constituted, the Politburo remained unchanged until the Nineteenth Party Congress (October, 1952). Some of its members were relieved of specific ministerial duties in favor of less important men, as in the cases of Molotov and Mikoyan (1949); the Foreign Office was taken over by the renowned prosecutor Vyshinsky, the foreign trade portfolio by Menshikov, but their former holders remained "deputy prime ministers" as well as members of the Politburo. The only serious trouble to befall a member of the Politburo after the death of Zhdanov and the removal of Voznesensky was in the case of Andreiev. He had apparently lived down his 1921 support of Trotsky and Bukharin and, though already a member of the Politburo, had managed to survive the "Great Purge." In 1950, however, he had to confess his error in advocating the "link" system in agriculture; though he retained his place in the ruling group, even retaining his chairmanship of the Party Control Commission, he yielded his role as spokesman of agricultural policy to Khrushchev, who had in 1949 returned to Moscow from his long assignment as boss of the Ukraine.

In October, 1952, was held the Nineteenth Party Congress, the first since before the Ribbentrop-Molotov Pact of 1939. It provided an opportunity, not only for the usual public stocktaking, but for maneuvers to control the succession to Stalin, whose health was obviously failing.

NOTES

1. "The Sources of Soviet Conduct," *Foreign Affairs,* XXV, 4 (July, 1947), p. 575.
2. *"Obrashchenie tov. I. V. Stalina k narodu,"* [Appeal of Comrade I. V. Stalin to the People"] *Bol'shevik,* No. 16 (August, 1945), pp. 1-3.
3. *Informatsionnoie soveshchanie predstavitelii nekotorykh kompartii . . . ,* p. 145.
4. Marx and Engels, *Manifesto of the Communist Party,* 1948 edition, pp. 65, 44.
5. Engels, *Origin of the Family, Private Property, and the State,* 1942 edition, p. 73.
6. Lenin, "On the Caricature of Marxism and on 'Imperialist Economism' " (October, 1916), in *Sochineniia,* 3rd edition, XIX, 232.
7. Kollontai, *Semiia i Kommunisticheskoe Gosudarstvo,* pp. 8-9.
8. Sverdlov, *Legal Rights of the Soviet Family,* pp. 17, 26, text in Appendix; this translation is much less complete than the Russian original.
9. Nikolai, *Slova i rechi,* II, 318.

10. Quoted passages in this and the next three paragraphs are cited in Curtiss, *The Russian Church and the Soviet State, 1917-1950*, pp. 309-324 *passim.*
11. Counts and Lodge, *Challenge of Soviet Education*, p. 80.
12. *Kommunisticheskaia Partiia Sovetskogo Soiuza v rezoliutsiiakh . . .*, III, 485, 486.
13. Zhdanov, *Problems of Soviet Literature*, p. 245.
14. Zhdanov's "Report," in *Zvezda*, 1946, No. 7-8 (July-August), pp. 7-23 *passim.*
15. Kirpotin, "On the Relationship of Russian Literature and of Russian Criticism to the Capitalist West," in *Oktiabr'*, 1947, No. 9 (September), pp. 161-182, especially p. 171.
16. Kirpotin, "On Servility Before the Capitalist West . . . ," in *Oktiabr'*, 1948, No. 1 (January), pp. 3-27, especially pp. 18-19.
17. Stalin, *Marxism and Linguistics*, pp. 9, 31, 10, 29-30.
18. *Kommunist*, 1955, No. 5, p. 15.

SUGGESTIONS FOR FURTHER READING

In addition to works previously mentioned, "X" (George F. Kennan), "The Sources of Soviet Conduct," in *Foreign Affairs* (July, 1947) was an influential analysis. Shulman's *Stalin's Foreign Policy Reappraised* is excellent. Dallin's *New Soviet Empire*, Gurian's *Soviet Imperialism*, Black's *Challenge in Eastern Europe*, and Korbel's *Communist Subversion of Czechoslovakia* all contain valuable material. Bass and Marbury (eds.), *The Soviet-Yugoslav Controversy*, and Benes, *et al., The Second Soviet-Yugoslav Dispute*, are overlapping studies of Russia's main failure. Mousset's *World of the Slavs* emphasizes the "Slav" aspect as a factor in relations between the U.S.S.R. and the satellites. (Further readings on the Soviet bloc may be found at the end of Chapter 37.) Of broader scope is Marguerite Fisher's *Communist Doctrine and the Free World*; Kautsky's *Moscow and the Communist Party of India* may serve as a case study.

A considerable number of so-called "revisionist" books have appeared on the topic of the "cold war." Fleming's *The Cold War and Its Origins* and *The Changing Cold War* reflected serious worry about the absurdities of American public opinion and its lack of understanding of natural Russian motivations. Anxiety to assess "blame" for a clearly unfortunate situation led others, notably Alperowitz in his *Atomic Diplomacy*, to ransack the memoirs of divers American politicians for expressions of hostility to, or at least suspicion of, Russia, without taking into account the Russian side of the picture. The best among other and more valuable studies are LaFeber, *America, Russia, and the Cold War, 1945-1966*, and Halle, *The Cold War as History*.

A worthy collection of articles may be found in *Annals of the American Academy of Political and Social Science*, Volume 271 (September, 1950). The *Annals*, Volume 263 (May, 1949), devoted to a wide range of topics, contains a number of exceedingly valuable articles. Gurian's *The Soviet Union: Background, Ideology, Reality* is a stimulating symposium. Of peculiar interest is Belov's *History of a Soviet Collective Farm*. Monnerot's *Sociology and Psychology of Communism* regards modern Communism as a neurotic religion, rooted in myths rather than in Marxist ideology. Counts and Lodge, *The Country of the Blind,* is a careful presentation of the Party's attitude toward all manifestations of cultural creativity. Simmons' *Continuity and Change in Russian and Soviet Thought* has been summarized as a highly competent, often highly technical, demonstration of the inherited backwardness and irrationality of Russian thought.

Chapter

36

The Changing of the Guard: 1953-1957

THE SUCCESSION

At the Nineteenth Party Congress (October, 1952) it was not Stalin, but Malenkov, who delivered the major political report. This indication of Stalin's choice of an heir was borne out by replacement of the Politburo (and of the Orgburo) by a Presidium of the Central Committee as the highest Party organ. Instead of the eleven members and one candidate who had made up the Politburo, the Presidium included twenty-five members and eleven alternates. Nine of the members of the Politburo were carried over as full members of the Presidium. Only Andreev was dropped, but Kosygin (the most recently promoted) was reduced to candidate, while the former candidate ("President" Shvernik) was at last made a full member. Of the fifteen new members and ten new candidates, only two had been members of the Party at the time of the Revolution; eighteen had joined since Lenin's death. Among the twenty-five, ten were pure *apparatchiki,* seven or eight were distinguished in the field of economic administration, three rated as ideologists, two or three held government positions, and one was the new head of the trade-union apparatus. The general impression was that most of the new men were adherents of Malenkov, who, next to Stalin, had become the principal member of the Party Secretariat.

The enlarged Presidium, however, had not long to live. On March 5, 1953, Stalin died. The next day a new Presidium was announced, consisting of only ten members and four candidates, thus in effect restoring the old Politburo, but with some changes in personnel. Of the ten full members, eight (in order of length of service on the Politburo—Molotov, Voroshilov, Mikoyan, Kaganovich, Khrushchev, Beria, Malenkov, Bulganin) had been full members of the former Politburo. Only two of the fifteen new members of the 1952 Presidium (Pervukhin and Saburov) remained as full members of the new one; all of its candidates, including Kosygin and the ten new ones (of whom Brezhnev had been one), were dropped. Shvernik, relieved of his post as titular head of the state and returned to his old post as head of the trade-union apparatus, was again reduced to candidate membership. The other candidates, also reduced from full membership, were Ponomarenko, former First Secretary in White Russia, and Melnikov, First Secretary in the Ukraine; the latter was soon succeeded in both capacities by Kirichenko. The fourth candidate was Bagirov, First Secretary in Azerbaidjan and the first of Moslem background to appear so near the top; he was soon arrested along with others of Beria's group.

There was also a fresh distribution of key government posts. The two senior members of the old Politburo, Molotov and Voroshilov, were allotted positions of honor rather than of power; the one reassumed office as Minister of Foreign Affairs, the other was made formal head of state as Chairman of the Presidium of the Supreme Council of the U.S.S.R. The able Kaganovich remained a First Deputy Minister, but without portfolio; Mikoyan resumed direction of the Ministry of Trade. The real plums went, however, to the young men whom Stalin had added to the Politburo after the "Great Purge." Khrushchev alone did not claim government office. Beria again took the title of Minister, heading both the Ministry of the Interior (MVD) and the Ministry of State Security (MGB), which had theoretically been separated during the war, though both had in fact remained under Beria's control. Bulganin became again Minister of Defense. Malenkov, perhaps overconfident that he really was Stalin's heir, stepped into the dead Leader's shoes as Chairman of the Council of Ministers; unwisely, but perhaps of necessity, he accepted a bargain (March 14) by which he surrendered the all-important office of First Secretary of the Central Committee of the Party; Khrushchev thus was left as the senior member of the Secretariat, though without the title of First Secretary and giving up his post as secretary of the local Moscow organization, while Malenkov took the post only of Chairman of the Party Presidium. The other two members were of little political importance: Saburov had succeeded Voznesensky (1949) as Chairman of Gosplan, Pervukhin had been serving in important administrative posts in heavy industry; both were important administrators in the economic structure, but neither had been important in the Party.

The situation was strongly reminiscent of that after the death of Peter the Great, when his chief subordinates had, in the guise of the Supreme Privy Council, pursued a policy of collective leadership even while engaged in a dog-eat-dog struggle for individual ascendancy. The figures involved after Stalin's death were less colorful men than those who had survived Lenin, but the factors that determined the outcome of their quarrels were not essentially different; though Malenkov was most featured in the public eye, surface emphasis was once more placed on the principle of "collective leadership."

The hollowness of this ideal was soon revealed. If it was popularly supposed that Malenkov was Number 1 among his colleagues, it was also widely assumed that Beria, heading the police, was Number 2. It is still uncertain whether Beria engaged in an active campaign to seize the primacy or whether his power merely created fear that he might do so. In any case, his Ministry soon found it expedient (April 3) to repudiate the "doctors' plot," which on January 31 had been assigned as the reason for the sudden arrest of the Jewish doctors who had been serving the Kremlin. At that time they had been accused of murdering Zhdanov and others and of conspiring to murder all the top Kremlin leaders. Now, on April 3, it was announced that the whole "plot" had been trumped up and that Ignatiev, as Minister of State Security, had "displayed political blindness and carelessness." [1] His Deputy Minister, Riumin, who had assumed responsibility for exposing the alleged "doctors' plot," was soon (July) shot, thus preventing any further disclosures. The affair was complicated by a vengeful Party purge carried out in Georgia admittedly under Beria's instructions. On July 10, the news was published that Beria had been expelled from the Party because of his "evil scheming to seize power," a charge supported by the usual miscellaneous string of accusations, including the allegation that he had long been "an agent of international imperialism." [2] Direction of the police was entrusted to professionals of no importance in the Party. On December 24, it was announced that Beria and six associates prominent in the MVD or MGB had been shot after a secret trial. Within the year of Stalin's death it was thus already clear that his "colleagues" had been held together only by dread of him.

The death of Stalin, whose personal ascendancy had been so clear, had seemed an earth-shaking event. In the first moments his colleagues were apparently seized with panic as to the possible consequences for themselves; they therefore resorted to measures of domestic appeasement. For one thing, a decree of March 27 granted a sweeping amnesty: all persons sentenced to prison for terms of less than four years were ordered released; all men over fifty-five and all women over fifty (or younger if pregnant or with children under ten) were also to be released; certain categories of offenders were to be freed regardless of age or length of sentence; but no provision was made for those in MVD concentration camps. It was simultaneously promised that the criminal code would be relaxed, a promise which in a more sober sequel it was not felt necessary seriously to honor. Another indication of panic was the holding of two sessions of the Supreme Soviet within the year; apparently the seal of its approval, readily forthcoming, was felt necessary in the absence of the Leader. New elections were held in 1954, at which a further sign of uneasiness was a new procedure that made it virtually necessary for the voter to fold and deposit his ballot without entering the booth, where in privacy he might have ventured to scratch out the name of the sole candidate. The percentage of voters exercising their franchise was happily reported as practically identical (99.98% of those eligible) with that in the election of 1950 (99.7%).

ECONOMIC POLICIES AND PROBLEMS

In the economic field, too, Malenkov announced a policy of appeasement. At the time of Stalin's death the Soviet Union was quantitatively, though not qualitatively, the second greatest industrial producer in the world, but the standard of living, even of the urban population (which then constituted 38% of the total), though it had apparently been rising for two or three years, was in the middle of the Fifth Five-Year Plan apparently no higher than it had been on the eve of the First Five-Year Plan. In an obvious bid to win support on his new eminence, Malenkov promised reversal of the investment policy that his benefactor Stalin had almost unwaveringly pursued. Although the then current Fifth Five-Year Plan could only be fulfilled by continued strenuous concentration on the development of heavy industry, Malenkov on August 8, 1953, at a special session of the Supreme Council, promised an "abundance of food for the population and of raw materials for light industry in two to three years." [3] Caution soon substituted the phrase "a sharp rise" for the word "abundance," but something had to be done quickly to lend some substance to the promise. Since it was obviously impossible in short order to increase in any significant measure the output of consumers' goods by Soviet industry, the Malenkov regime went on what has been aptly characterized as a "shopping spree," which almost doubled Soviet imports at the end of 1953 and in the first half of 1954; simultaneously, the percentage of imports represented by foodstuffs, consumers' goods, and consumer raw materials experienced a very sharp rise, though estimates differ as to the exact figures. This effort to give a modicum of quick satisfaction to the craving of the Soviet population for a better standard of living exceeded the ability of the Soviet Union to balance her imports with exports. In consequence, it became necessary to sell gold in the amount of $150 million between October, 1953, and February, 1954.

The condition of agriculture presented an even greater problem than that of further industrial expansion. The increase in agricultural production had barely kept pace with the increase in population, thus blocking the development of an economy of abundance. The steady increase in the proportion of the urban population (from 18% in 1929 to 38% in 1953), together with its tendency to raise its standard of living, particularly noticeable in the last few years of the Stalin regime, had put an ever heavier burden on agriculture. This was one of the most important factors in keeping Russia's foreign trade to insignificant proportions; while the deliberate policy of autarchy restricted imports, Russia no longer had the agricultural surplus that had formerly enabled her to maintain a considerable flow of exports. It was even becoming necessary for her to import foodstuffs.

Notwithstanding decades of vigorous industrialization, almost half the population was still directly engaged in agriculture. Yet the problem of labor shortage was beginning to be felt on the farms. Instead of the rural population constituting a vast reservoir of surplus labor on which expanding industry had been able freely to draw, it was now the fields that needed manpower; the large proportion of young adult males absorbed by the military forces had tended to throw an undue share of farm work on women, adolescents, and older men, a circumstance which made it difficult to maintain, let alone raise, agricultural productivity. Among the basic difficulties continued to be the unkindness of nature: not more than one-sixth of the total area of the Soviet Union is capable of being used for agricultural purposes; notwithstanding extensive belts of very fertile soil, almost all of Russia lies in such northerly latitudes that the growing season is necessarily short; average rainfall is at best low, and much of the potentially fertile area is subject to frequently recurring droughts, while the flatness of the plain makes difficult retention of melting snows and creates a serious problem for irrigation.

Concentration on capital investment in industry had made it necessary to starve agriculture. In the postwar years the critical situation had led to some diversion of resources, but industry still absorbed about half the new capital investments (about twice the proportion prevailing in the United States). Transport still required about 10 percent (about the same as in America), and the desperate condition of housing attracted about 15 percent (little more than half the proportion of United States expenditures in this field). Of the remaining quarter of the capital available for investment, agriculture received the lion's share (16%, a proportion 50% greater than in the surplus-ridden United States). The Fifth F.Y.P. in 1951 set a goal of a 50 percent increase in agricultural production, but all that was achieved was recovery by the early 1950's to prewar levels, at which point output leveled off. Most of the effort was devoted to ambitious plans to "transform nature" by huge afforestation and irrigation schemes, although the effort to transform man by trying to force him into more scientific crop rotation and into harder work under more careful supervision was not wholly neglected.

Especially in the light of Malenkov's incautious promise of "abundance of food for the population . . . in two to three years" or at least of "a sharp rise" in its production, Stalin's successors had to press vigorously to campaign for heightened agricultural productivity. Great attention was given to production of butter and meat, to be accomplished by "socializing" livestock on the collective farms; efforts to take over privately owned animals, however, were not pressed to the point of altogether discouraging individual ownership of productive livestock. The cows themselves were called on to increase their yield of milk by one-third in the single year 1953-1954. The immediate results were disappointing: state collections of milk, planned to rise by 43 percent between 1952 and 1954, rose only 23 percent; with meat, a similar percentage increase made proportionately better showing as against a planned increase of 37 percent. Although the drought of 1954 was undoubtedly a factor, a more serious problem for the future was posed by the failure of the number of head of livestock to rise as anticipated; only in the case of hogs could success be claimed, but for the reason that they had been miscounted in 1952.

ARCHITECTURE AND OTHER ARTS

Advances in industrial technology had side effects on many aspects of Russian culture. Much of Russia's literary output was reduced to the portrayal of technical accomplishments in industry, but nowhere had the influence of material progress been more evident than on architecture. Building activity over the decades was necessarily tremendous and was largely conditioned by the growth of industry. Side by side with new construction using the most up-to-date electrically operated hoists and other mechanical means, one might see buildings being erected with the aid of old-fashioned scaffolding over which swarming women mounted ladders with hods of bricks over their shoulders. Similarly, architectural designs have represented a mixture of ultramodern techniques with traditional art forms. The lack of experimentation with new architectural ideas has been striking. In part, perhaps, this has reflected the initial predominance among Soviet architects of painters, sculptors, and even movie artists, themselves usually Cubists, Futurists, or Expressionists; very rarely were architects professionals.

The situation in art and architecture in the 1920's had been quite similar to the experimentalism that then afflicted the schools, and its results speedily produced a reaction of disillusionment. "Formalism" in architecture, with its emphasis on the absolute value of abstract forms, was in its pure state of course too "idealistic" for Marxian materialists. It had to be transmuted into the concept that aesthetic forms should be used for the purpose of stimulating the class consciousness of the masses, of providing a dynamic inspiration for their revolutionary zeal. In practice, in the minds of the Soviet authorities, "Formalism" became merely psychotechnical metaphysics, not in consonance with the purposes of Soviet architecture. "Functionalism" had a much stronger appeal, and the thought of beauty in architecture was consciously, and effectively, rejected. In Russia, however, shortage of high-quality building materials and the severity of the weather combined to reduce imposing stucco edifices to drab and positively repellent boxes; violent seasonal extremes of temperature made buildings with large expanses of glass intolerable to the occupants, either in winter or in summer.

By the 1930's, Russian architecture, like so many other aspects of Russia's life, was caught up in "The Great Retreat." Competitive designs for a mammoth Palace of Soviets produced, particularly from foreigners, many modernist projects, but the designs that overwhelmingly won lay approval at exhibitions were those based on traditional Russian versions of classical forms. Much Russian construction has consisted of vast engineering projects —dams, power stations, and canal locks—which necessarily have been basically functional, but there also has been a great amount of building of apartment houses and public edifices, whether schools, hospitals, office buildings, theaters, or stadiums. Predominantly these structures have been built in the traditional spirit, though without slavish imitation, of Russian classicism, and with due reference to the national heritage of the area in which they were erected. As the academician Mordvinov formulated it in 1944:

> The finest specimens of our architectural works glow with a feeling of pride in our country. . . . Too little attention has been paid to the architectural traditions created by the Russian and other peoples of our country. . . .
>
> Russian classicism of the 18th and 19th centuries . . . achieved monumentality and richness of expression with the cheapest of materials. . . .
>
> In selecting the architectural type for public buildings we must make critical studies both of the monumental styles prevalent in our national republics and of the classical heritage. . . .
>
> National forms offer colourful variety. The humanism expressed in classical forms serves to unify the architecture of all the national republics, while yet allowing them to preserve traits peculiarly their own. . . .
>
> Industrial methods of producing suburban homes in nowise run counter to the interests of architecture. . . .[4]

An outstanding characteristic of the new Russian architecture is its massive, monumental appearance. Combined with a great amount of city planning, immense effort has been expended to make Russian cities approach the level of Leningrad with its eighteenth-century grandeur of perspective. This was relatively simple in such a case as the reconstruction of razed Stalingrad, with its magnificent river front. It was most difficult in the case of cluttered Moscow, which had over the centuries gradually swollen from its Kremlin nucleus in topsy-turvy fashion; by ruthless demolitions radial arteries were carved out, connecting the broad ring-boulevards and making some progress toward converting an overgrown village into a modern city. Only a leisurely pedestrian would realize that behind the imposing brick fronts wooden hamlets still huddled in the centers of the long urban blocks. The scattered handful of Stalin's favorite gingerbread structures, the highest of which (the Lomonosov University) rises thirty-two stories, took the place of the dwarfed Kremlin towers as the most conspicuous punctuation marks on the Moscow skyline.

Progressively, creative architecture in Russia had to bow to technical requirements. Technological progress and considerations of cost resulted in deliberate standardization of design and of dimensions, permitting assembly-line manufacture of prefabricated sections, and even of whole buildings. The function of the architect rapidly became the subordinate one of trying to adorn the product of the industrial engineer.

Painters and sculptors did not, in Soviet Russia, enjoy even the limited independence of architects. Lenin's personal taste was strongly opposed to *avant-garde* modernism in the arts as well as in literature. He is quoted by Clara Zetkin as frankly saying:

> We are good revolutionaries, but we feel obliged to point out that we stand at the "height of contemporary culture." I have the courage to show myself a "barbarian." I cannot value the works of expressionism, futurism, cubism, and other "isms" as the highest expressions of artistic genius. I don't understand them. They give me no pleasure. . . .
>
> . . . Art belongs to the people. It must have its deepest roots in the broad mass of workers. It must be understood and loved by them. It must be rooted in and grow with their feelings, thoughts and desires. It must arouse and develop the artist in them. . . .[5]

Lenin's views were later expanded into the repressive concept of "socialist realism." Paintings and sculpture must be realistic enough to be comprehended; they must also convey a dynamic message stressing individual effort and socialist progress. Preference was given to monuments portraying accomplishment of great figures of the past and to no less monumental presentations of modern Soviet man pushing heroically and triumphantly forward to the goal of communism. Socialist realism, however, has not been incompatible with the development of a number of highly competent sculptors and painters, whose work has by no means been frozen in a static mold.

Russian music recovered with difficulty from the *Zhdanovshchina.* Prokofiev died the same day as Stalin. In November, 1953, Khachaturian, next to Shostakovich the leading Soviet musician, published an article "On Creative Boldness and Inspiration"; a second article by him, in March, 1954, somewhat corrected the impression that he was demanding repeal of then existing restrictions on composers. While the issue was still in doubt, the music world was startled by the news that Shostakovich had in the summer and fall of 1953 composed a *Tenth Symphony,* in which he absolutely ignored official instructions to composers. The news was the more surprising in that in April of that year, a month after Stalin's death, he had announced that

> I consider as my most immediate and paramount creative task work on an opera in which will be reflected the great struggle of our people for the building of communism. I shall strive to sing worthily of the men of our heroic Stalinist epoch.[6]

Instead of doing so, he had gone back to the officially proscribed "abstract" form of a programless symphony. What was more, the *Tenth Symphony* was a somber tragedy, suffused with anger and scorn, and it lacked a happy ending. What it was meant to convey was not made clear; Shostakovich refused to go farther than to say that "I tried to communicate human emotions and passions." [7] It has been suggested that another of his articles, on American Negro "Songs of Anger and Struggle," written while he was composing the symphony, was intended as a hint that he was attacking Soviet "slave-labor camps." Musically, the *Tenth* again demonstrated his great technical skill and superb natural talent; yet it was little more than a reversion to the style of Tchaikovsky and Rachmaninoff.

Whatever his purpose, Shostakovich, ever a weather vane, was for the moment "correct." His *Tenth Symphony* was played by the Leningrad Philharmonic Orchestra (December 17, 1953); subsequently, performances were given in Moscow also. The official organ, *Soviet Music,* refrained from mentioning the work until the resignation of Ponomarenko as Minister of Culture; then it invited public discussion by composers and other experts "to assist in the successful solution of the creative problems of the development of Soviet music." [8] The new Minister of Culture, G. F. Aleksandrov, was the man whose *History of Western European Philosophy* had in 1947 been sharply condemned by Zhdanov; though he had been appointed Director of the Institute of Philosophy in the Academy of Sciences, he had obviously not been in favor with Stalin. The official "creative discussion" approved the symphony, but the Union of Soviet Composers still referred to Zhdanov's "historic decree" of 1948 as having opened "the broadest perspectives for the great new upsurge of Soviet music." [9]

Aleksandrov was soon replaced (March 22, 1955) by Mikhailov, who had been a Malenkov *apparatchik.* Khachaturian became again the official commentator on the "wise policies" of the Party,[10] though Shostakovich was allowed to resume work on his *Lady Macbeth of Mtsensk,* so vitriolically attacked in 1936.

LITERATURE, PHILOSOPHY, SCIENCE, AND RELIGION

In literature also, the effects of the *Zhdanovshchina* continued to be felt. A period of intra-Party struggle for power, when rival aspirants were looking for scapegoats to embarrass their opponents, was no time for writers to strike out on new lines. Stalin Prizes continued to be lavished on stereotyped novels, short stories, and poems that reflected the value of the Party in industrial achievements, in improving the work of the collective farms, and in winning the war. Even Leonov, writing his first novel for several years, carefully walked the Party line. One of the best of the postwar writers, Vera Panova, was bold enough, in *Seasons of the Year,* to neglect to show due respect for the Party as the source of all that is fine and noble in human relations; at first enthusiastically received, this new novel by an author whose three previous novels had won Stalin Prizes was soon violently condemned.

In Stalin's last years literary critics had been permitted to attack particularly severe cases of repression. In this respect the boldest position had been taken by Nikolai Virta, one of the ablest playwrights of the period, in an article entitled "Let Us Speak Frankly," published in *Soviet Art* (March 29, 1952). After the dictator's death a genuine critical revolt began to be manifest; the volatile Ilya Ehrenburg, in an article published in October, 1953, asserted:

> A writer is not an apparatus mechanically registering events. A writer writes a book, not because he knows how to write, not because he is a member of the Union of Soviet Writers and they may ask him why for so long he has published nothing. A writer writes a book not because he needs to earn his living. A writer writes a book because he needs to say something of his own to people, because he "aches" with his book, because he has seen people or deeds or feelings that he cannot not describe. . . .[11]

In 1954, Ehrenburg ventured to publish a novel with the symbolic title, *The Thaw*. The new freedom did not go unchallenged. On August 11, 1954, Tvardovsky, whose poem *Space Beyond Space* had shown considerable courage, was dismissed from the editorship of *Novyi Mir*. At the end of 1954, the Second All-Union Congress of Soviet Writers gave complete support to the Party's attitude toward literature. On the other hand, a number of the best Soviet writers, including Sholokhov, joined Ehrenburg in open protest, not against Party authority as such, but against abuses of it by underlings. The strongest plea for the individuality of the writer was made by the poet, Olga Bergholz:

> As you see, from time to time we ourselves have as it were betrayed art, have departed from its great laws. Art begins to lag behind life the moment it ceases to be art. We still, with a certain shyness inspired by the outcries of criticism, have appraised our work and the state of literature, not by criteria of artistic value; yet, you know, without artistic value there exists in art neither content nor Party spirit. To separate one from the other is impossible in art.[12]

In a related field, that of philosophy, the picture remained more dismal. The official journal, *Questions of Philosophy,* preferred to discuss all sorts of issues rather than devote attention to what the outside world understands under that rubric. The study of formal, as contrasted with dialectical, logic, was reintroduced in the secondary schools in 1946, but by 1954 it had again been virtually eliminated. The idea cherished by Stalin, at the height of his interest in Marr, that the "superstructure" may play a significant role independently of the economic base of society, was again abandoned in 1954 in favor of the orthodox Marxist-Leninist formulation of the mainsprings of social and cultural change. Most fields contingent on fundamental philosophical concepts, such as theory of knowledge and philosophy of science, were frankly left to mathematicians, physicists, and others, who perhaps were in any case better equipped to deal with such problems. Ethics made no progress beyond Lenin's views, as succinctly rephrased in the *Great Soviet Encyclopedia* (1954):

> Defense of the interests of the victory of communism—that in our time is the only scientific criterion of morality correctly reflecting the imminent needs of the further development of society.[13]

History of philosophy turned sharply back to interest in Western ideas. For the first time, Francis Bacon and Montaigne were translated into Russian. Discussion of the ideas of Locke, of Kant, and of Hegel was renewed, and the bicentennial of Montesquieu's death was celebrated. Herzen was once more republished in full. Most startling of all, however, was publication of a complete edition of Dostoevsky, begun in 1956. Such shifts could not be made without a scapegoat. Paradoxically, but not surprisingly, it was G. F. Aleksandrov, condemned in 1947 for kowtowing to the West, who was now said to be "nihilistic" toward valid foreign philosophy. In his earlier *History of Western European Philosophy* he had incurred Zhdanov's wrath for denying that Marxist philosophy had represented "a revolutionary leap, a revolution in the world history of philosophic thought";[14] now, in the name of "patriotism," he was making the opposite error of minimizing the significance of Darwinism. It was the same pliancy that brought him condemnation for exaggerating the value of Stalin's intervention in the linguistics controversy over Marr.

Soviet science undoubtedly suffered under the Stalin regime from curtailment of contact with the outside world. Yet its loss was certainly less than popular imagination might lead one to suppose. Cases such as those of Lysenko and Marr were not fairly characteristic of what Soviet science was experiencing. The thaw after 1953 gave Soviet recognition to what informed persons had already realized to be the fact that Soviet science, though largely subordinated to technological purposes, was by no means static. Six months after the death of Stalin, new elections, the first in seven years, to membership in the Academy of Science had no difficulty in finding candidates who already had a reputation in the outside world. In the field of mathematics, in Russia as elsewhere recognized as the "queen of the sciences," two such men, D. S. Aleksandrov and N. N. Bogoliubov, were elected. In physics, a field in which Academician Kapitsa was already clearly predominant, four nuclear physicists and two men working in the realm of solids were found worthy of election. Astronomy, chemistry, and biology were not overlooked, but geology and geography were specially favored. Even more recognition, however, was given to work in development of hydroelectric power, machine design, metallurgy, electronics, and combustion.

Beginning even in the last years of Stalin's life, international contacts in the form of active participation at international scientific congresses were resumed. The Soviet Union has consistently paid careful attention to publication of abstracts, and in many cases of complete translations, of scientific and technological papers published in other countries. The emphasis placed on specialized training in the Soviet Union is common knowledge, but it should be noted that statistics of the number of scientists, engineers, and technicians trained in the Soviet Union, as compared with the numbers similarly trained in Western countries, are largely devoid of meaning. They obscure not only the wide variations in the qualitative value of degrees awarded by different institutions, both in the United States and in the Soviet Union, but they indicate nothing of the comparative value of "average" training in Russia and in the West. It can safely be said that Soviet personnel do not receive anything like the general education afforded to recipients of liberal-arts degrees abroad, but the converse, that narrow specialization produces more competent scientists and technologists, is a complete *non sequitur*.

There is no doubt that Soviet concentration, supported by disproportionate financial expenditures and assisted by captive Germans, helped make possible more rapid production of *sputniki* and of efficient rockets of para-military value, but there is no evidence that the general level of Soviet science and technology was higher than that of the West. Against press alarms should be read the complaints in editions of the Communist Party *Handbook for the Propagandist and Agitator,* intended for domestic consumption, which continued to complain bitterly about the general backwardness and wastefulness of Soviet technology and of Soviet scientific training. If, for reasons of Party policy, the Soviet Union should in the uncertain future throw blocks in the way of the further splendid advances of Soviet mathematics and physics such as it has at times thrown in the path of the "social sciences," of biology, and to a lesser degree, of chemistry, the precarious freedom of science might quickly be set back in the Soviet Union far more than by a Joseph McCarthy-type "security" program in the United States.

The alleged enemy of science, the Orthodox Church, apparently suffered no more than did Western churches from the advance of materialist rationalism. Notwithstanding continued token attacks on religion and official Party demands for "liberation" of the people from "religious prejudices," the relations of Church and state seemingly settled back into the old tsarist rut. In November, 1954, a decree of the Party's Central Committee acknowledged "gross mistakes" in "scientific atheistic propaganda" and condemned attacks on the Church.[15] In the Soviet Union in 1956, the writer was given no pep talk as to the merits of communism at all comparable to that imparted in a two-hour private interview with the bishop of Luga, acting as vicar for the ailing metropolitan of Leningrad. Metropolitan Nikolai, the functioning head of the Church under Patriarch Alexius, was more reserved, but had no complaints to make of the status of the Church under the Soviet regime. Readily admitting that young people, who have very little leisure, preferred to spend their Sundays at sports rather than attend Church services, he emphasized that what is important is that they come to the Church to be married, that they have their children baptized, and that they apply to the Church for last rites for their parents. To him it was a matter of course that the Church should pray for the well-being of the secular authorities, as it has done throughout history, including the period of the "Tatar yoke." Even a stray religious fanatic, whose passport listed him as a "worker" and who showed documentary evidence that he had been imprisoned by the MVD for criticism of Stalin, professed optimistic faith that Bulganin and Zhukov were about to restore the full supremacy of Christianity in Russia; according to him, he depended for food and lodging on the workers, permitting him to spend his time in prayer and agitation. Anyone who has attended the religious celebration at the Troitsa Monastery in Zagorsk on St. Sergius' Day can hardly doubt of the sincerity of widespread religious sentiment, without revolutionary undertones, but with a willingness to make serious sacrifices for the opportunity to participate in religious ceremonies; the driver of the Intourist car, who saw nothing unusual in women performing heavy road repairs, asserted positively that she and almost all Russians are "Orthodox," though she herself, as an Old Ritualist, refused to attend the services because "they make the sign of the Cross with the whole hand."

INTERNATIONAL RELATIONS

The new regime after the death of Stalin proved unsettling also in Russia's new colonial empire. In the unstable equilibrium, the "collective leadership," uncertain of its position at home, had promptly sought to relax tensions in Russia's dependencies as well as in the Soviet Union itself. In April, 1953, serious efforts were begun to woo Yugoslavia back into the fold, but they were long met with cool resistance. In most of the obedient satellites, a certain relaxation, sometimes called the "New Course," was embarked on. In Czechoslovakia, however, the government chose this moment to carry out (June 1, 1953) a currency "reform" which wiped out savings and reduced purchasing power; the result was a serious riot of workers in the Skoda works.

In June, 1953, despite minor concessions by the regime, even more serious riots broke out in the Soviet zone of Germany. President Eisenhower's offer (July 10) of $15 million worth of food to help the hungry population of East Germany was scornfully refused, but it was not possible to prevent shipment of 5,000 tons a week to West Berlin, whose officials set up distribution centers for their countrymen across the line. Forceful repression of the disturbances was followed by more genuine concessions; some thousands of German war prisoners were allowed to return to their homes, reparations were stopped, and occupation charges reduced. Nevertheless, large numbers of refugees from East Germany continued to flee across the border; despite their suspicious and often discouraging reception by the Allied occupation authorities, the number of fugitives from the Communist-controlled areas soon reached two million, a figure comparable to the forced transfer of old-settled residents from regions taken from Germany by Soviet action. On March 25, 1954, the Soviet Union proclaimed the sovereignty of the "German Democratic Republic"; as of September 20, 1955, its "full freedom of action" was officially recognized by Moscow. The practical effect was simply to convert a zone of occupation into a satellite state, easily manipulated to serve Russian purposes.

The Soviet Union had not had influence great enough to prevent Adenauer from winning the West German election in 1953, but it was able to block the reëstablishment of a Germany reunited on the basis of the free will of the German people. The insistence of the Western Powers that the first step toward reunification must be genuinely free elections throughout Germany was—and remains—totally unacceptable to the rulers of Russia. They have persistently countered with a demand for a meeting of delegates of the two existing governments, which would mean that the Soviet puppet must have an equal voice with the people of Western Germany in shaping the future structure of Germany. They couple this proposal with the emotionally more appealing idea of complete demilitarization and neutralization of a reunited Germany. Since it is obvious that the West cannot on any terms sacrifice the principle of democracy, the Soviet position has been a purely negative one. A democratic Germany could only mean Russian withdrawal from an area control of which has been lucrative; it would also bring to the fore the question of Poland's boundaries, which might entail grave embarrassment to the Soviet Union. Russia apparently settled down to wait for what the future might bring, hoping that the stability of the Adenauer regime would give way to divisive party squabbles and that any recession of West German economic prosperity would produce a new crop of Nazis and reckless nationalists. In the meantime it has been simple enough to worry the West, and perhaps to divide it, by posing a new threat to isolate Berlin, for which the Soviet Union need no longer assume direct responsibility; the nominal sovereignty of the "German Democratic Republic" might even confuse enough of the popular mind in Western democracies to make some rattled politicians willing to give way.

Soviet opposition apparently contributed to France's refusal (August 30, 1954) to accept the European Defense Community (EDC), which would have included West Germany. However, the effort to keep France and Germany apart failed, notwithstanding urgent appeals to France by the satellite states and threats by the Soviet Union that she would denounce her existing treaties with France and with England as well. West European Union (WEU) ultimately included (October 23, 1954) a newly sovereign Germany, with permission for her to rearm and to become a member of NATO. Swinging quickly around, the Soviet Union also recognized the sovereignty of the Federal Republic (January 15, 1955) and entertained Adenauer in Moscow (September) for heart-to-heart talks.

In other areas the new Russian regime moved uncertainly. After innumerable conferences of foreign ministers, Russia in 1954 flatly rejected the proposed Austrian peace treaty. On the other hand, Russia lost no time in publicly renouncing her postwar demands on Turkey and tried to improve her relations with Greece also. Neither of these small powers, which had joined NATO at the end of 1951, responded to Russian advances. Even the Cyprus situation did not swing Greece into Russia's arms. Turkey continued to be alarmed by repeated Soviet suggestions that some sort of direct Russo-Turkish agreement be made for control of the Straits.

Of a broader scope was the attempt to sketch out a Soviet "security" system for Europe as an alternative to the alliance of the Western Powers. Before pressing it, however, the Soviet Union was able to announce (August 20, 1953) that it also had exploded a hydrogen bomb. In February, 1954, at the Berlin Conference of foreign ministers for discussion of the Austrian peace treaty, Molotov proposed conclusion of a pact to embrace all European states (including the Soviet Union) "without regard to their social structure" (Article I). Since the United States and the People's Republic of China (*sic*) were members of the United Nations Security Council, they were to be invited to send representatives as "observers" (Article IX). No member of this security organization was to "take part in any coalitions or alliances of whatever sort or to conclude any agreements with purposes contradictory to the purposes of collective security in Europe" (Article VII).[16] The objective of destroying NATO was too clear. Unabashed by his initial failure, Molotov on March 31 proposed to enable NATO to "lose its aggressive character" by admitting to it the Soviet Union and her satellite states. The Soviet Union, "guided by the unchanged principles of its peace-loving foreign policy and striving for diminution of tension in international relations," proposed that NATO include "all the great powers that had made up the anti-Hitler coalition." [17] This friendly gesture, if it had been accepted, would of course have meant that the West's defensive system had crumbled. The attempt to recreate a "spirit of Geneva" by a conference (April 26-July 20, 1954) of the foreign ministers of nineteen states, including Red China, had arranged an interim settlement in Indochina but failed to make any progress toward a real Korean settlement. Failing also to prevent Germany's admission (October, 1954) to WEU and to NATO, the Soviet Union tried a return to threats.

In Asia things looked more promising for the Communist cause. Though recognition of the principle of voluntary repatriation of prisoners was a heavy price to pay, the Korean armistice (1953) at least enabled Asian Communists to claim that they had successfully stood off the armed might of the capitalist West. The settlement with respect to Indochina at Geneva (1954) was a far greater triumph for nationalist Communists. Yet Mao's declaration at the Bandung Conference (April, 1955) that China did not want war with the United States and was prepared to negotiate even about the Formosa Strait seemed to offer hope of peace in that quarter. Russia concluded that she had no choice but to end the state of war with Japan (December 26, 1956) without further insisting that all her demands be met.

The Soviet Union was careful to cultivate by all possible means cordial relations with Red China, without according her recognition as a "socialist" state on a par with Russia. Her efforts included exchanging visits of leaders, welcoming Chinese students in Moscow, trying to improve economic relations, supplying both technical advisers and material aid, and energetically campaigning for transfer to Peking of the Chinese seat in the United Nations Security Council. Russian support was very valuable to China at the Far Eastern Conference held in Geneva in April, 1954; Port Arthur was handed over by Russia to China on May 24, 1955. Yet there remained the facts that the Soviet Union could not begin to satisfy China's needs for imports, that the rapid growth of the Chinese population constituted a potential threat to continued Russian control of her sparsely settled Far Eastern lands, and that if China could succeed in industrializing herself, the shadow of her power might extend over Moscow.

TENSIONS WITHIN THE SOVIET UNION

Within the Soviet Union itself, the political equilibrium remained unstable. On September 13, 1953, it had been announced that Stalin's old post of First Secretary of the Central Committee, which Malenkov had briefly held, had been formally conferred on Khrushchev, already in fact the senior secretary. The quiet sequel was gradual supersession of key Party secretaries in important localities, including Khrushchev's immediate successor at Moscow, by Khrushchev men. In the course of 1954, Khrushchev increasingly shared public honors with Malenkov; it was Khrushchev who headed delegations to visit Poland, Czechoslovakia, and China. By the end of the year he was personally signing Party decrees and, though holding no government post, giving public interviews. It should have come as no surprise when on February 8, 1955, Malenkov, against whom no public charges had been leveled, resigned the chairmanship of the Council of Ministers in a self-abasing letter. Wisely, he stressed that the Party remained "monolithic in its unity and singleness of purpose." [18] He was therefore permitted to slip back into the rank of a Deputy Chairman (though not of a "First Deputy Minister") of the Council of Ministers, while retaining his membership in the Party Presidium. His post as Prime Minister went to "Marshal" Bulganin, who was succeeded as Minister of Defense by a career soldier, Marshal Zhukov, who had earned an outstanding reputation in the war but had subsequently been relegated by Stalin to a minor command; not until the following year, however, was he made even a candidate member of the Presidium. In July, 1955, the vacancies in the Presidium left by the deaths of Stalin and Beria were at last filled. Kirichenko, First Secretary of the Party in the Ukraine, was one of the new members, the other was Suslov, the most experienced of the secretaries of the Central Committee. Among new secretaries named at this time was Shepilov, who also became a candidate member of the Presidium in 1956.

Within the Presidium the power struggle remained unresolved. As shown in the table on pp. 850–852, seven of its eleven members—Molotov, Voroshilov, Kaganovich, Mikoyan, Khrushchev, Malenkov, and Bulganin—had been members of the old Politburo. Three others—Pervukhin, Saburov, and Suslov—had been included by Stalin in his enlarged Presidium. Probably deliberately to obscure their personal rivalries, increased emphasis was placed on the sacred principle of "collective leadership." This entailed a "de-Stalinization" campaign, the extent of which was much exaggerated outside Russia. It was at the Twentieth Party Congress (February, 1956) that Khrushchev made his famous speech, the text of which was not published in the Soviet Union, denouncing certain aspects of the Stalin regime and attributing excesses to Stalin personally. Khrushchev strengthened his position (June 1, 1956) by securing replacement of the stubborn Molotov as Foreign Minister with Shepilov, whom he had so recently added to the Party Secretariat. At the beginning of July, emphasis was placed only on Stalin's degeneration in the last years of his regime.

The effect was to bring into question the credentials of those who had been most closely associated with him toward the end of his life, such as Malenkov, Molotov, and Kaganovich. Malenkov had been permitted to join in the attack on the memory of his master at the Twentieth Congress, but it could not be forgotten that it was during the last phase that Stalin had pushed Malenkov into the limelight; Malenkov also stood self-condemned by his letter of resignation of February 8, 1955. The de-Stalinization campaign was, however, short-lived; within a few months Khrushchev was emphasizing that "I grew up under Stalin," who was "a great fighter against imperialism" and "a great Marxist." At a reception for Chou En-lai (January 17, 1957) he exclaimed, "God grant that every Communist know how to fight as Stalin fought." [19]

It was a matter for no great surprise when, early in July, 1957, a fresh political crisis occurred in Moscow. It is quite uncertain whether or not it had anything to do with Mao's February 27 announcement, published June 18, of a new, though disastrous and short-lived policy:

> Let a hundred flowers blossom and a hundred schools of thought contend. . . . Marxists should not be afraid of criticism from any quarter.[20]

Nor is it entirely clear what actually happened. Apparently the demoted group of leaders, who had been allowed to remain in the Party Presidium, managed to win over enough of Khrushchev's allies to command a majority there. Their effort to oust him while he was away on one of his frequent trips was apparently foiled by his demand, which could not well be denied, that the matter be referred to the whole Central Committee. In that larger body, its First Secretary evidently had little difficulty in whipping his *apparatchiki* into line and turning the tables on his opponents. By vote of the Central Committee, Molotov, Malenkov, and Kaganovich were dismissed from their government posts and dropped, not only from the Presidium but from the

Central Committee as well. The unreliable Shepilov had already been superseded as Foreign Minister by the professional career-man Gromyko but had remained in the circle as a candidate member of the Presidium; he now shared the fate of the bigger men whom he had been imprudent enough to join. Along with them were dropped the two economic advisers, Saburov and Pervukhin, though the latter was allowed to continue as a candidate member of the Presidium.

In true Stalinist style, the accusations against the conspirators turned largely on international questions. Since, however, the Twentieth Congress had endorsed Khrushchev's proposal to "continue the Leninist policy of peaceful coexistence of various states without regard to their social structure," [21] the charge was not of conspiring with foreign enemies but the opposite offense of having obstructed the development of good relations with the outside world, particularly with Yugoslavia and Japan and in the matter of the Austrian peace treaty. Malenkov's 1955 confession of errors was also a convenient stick with which to beat the conspirators for opposing Khrushchev's ideas on economic reorganization. The treatment of the defeated opponents was in the style of the younger and more uncertain Stalin of the 1920's rather than in his full-blown style of the 1930's. Molotov, Malenkov, and Kaganovich were not "liquidated" but merely assigned to minor duties in the depths of Asia.

The expulsion of five members of the Presidium left it with only six full members, not all of whom were trustworthy from Khrushchev's viewpoint. He therefore added nine more, four of whom had not been members or candidates of the enlarged 1952 Presidium elected by the Nineteenth Party Congress shortly before Stalin's death. Only one of them—Marshal Zhukov—seemed to be of any real importance; his inclusion marked the first time that a professional soldier, as distinct from a guerrilla leader such as Marshal Voroshilov or a politician with a military title such as Marshal Bulganin, had been raised to Party eminence. Another "first" was the election of a woman, Furtseva, whose sudden importance to the Party is not clear. Shvernik, who for some time had been nominal head of the state, was again given full membership in the Presidium, as was Kuusinen, once very briefly recognized by Russia as head of its Finnish state. The newest comer, Kozlov, seemed to have the most promising career ahead of him until he was paralyzed by a stroke (April, 1963). Far less conspicuous at the time was Brezhnev, who had served as a candidate in the first, short-lived Presidium and had been restored to that station in 1956. Among the additional nine candidate members of the Presidium no figures were more important than Kosygin and the now demoted Pervukhin. Kosygin had been made a candidate member of the old Politburo as early as 1946 and had been promoted to full membership in 1947; he had, however, been demoted to candidate when the Presidium was established in 1952 and dropped altogether when it was reorganized in 1953. A boy of twelve at the time of the Revolution, he had been trained as an "engineer" and had made his mark not as an *apparatchik* but as an economic administrator, specializing in textiles.

To all outward appearances Russia was now definitely under the collective leadership of a triumvirate—Bulganin, Zhukov, and Khrushchev. Marshal Zhukov, however, was soon relieved (October 26) of his post as Minister of Defense. A few days later (November 2) it was announced that he had also been removed from the Presidium and from the Central Committee because he had "flagrantly violated" the principle of collective leadership by fostering his own "cult of the individual" in the army;[22] it was noted that he had penitently voted for his own ouster. Bulganin's turn was not long in coming. On March 27, 1958, he submitted his resignation as Chairman of the Council of Ministers; for the moment he remained a member of the ministry, resuming his old post as chairman of the State Bank. At the same time, Mikoyan and Kozlov were raised to the rank of "First Deputy Prime Minister." On August 15 Bulganin lost his ministerial rank and was transferred to a minor position at Stavropol in the Caucasus; in the interval two minor figures had been added (June 19) to the Presidium as alternates. On November 14, in the midst of his report on the "control figures" for the new Seven-Year Plan, Khrushchev interpolated a passing reference to the "anti-Party fractional group" which had been "unanimously defeated"; significantly, he included Bulganin among its members, along with Malenkov, Kaganovich, and Molotov, while he mentioned Shepilov only as one who had "sided with them."[23] On December 18 Bulganin himself confessed his guilt, clinching his exclusion from the Presidium. Khrushchev, the civilian who could scarcely be cast in the role of a Bonapartist "man on horseback," had consolidated his power by the methods Stalin had employed in the 1920's. Unlike Stalin, he at once assumed the post of Chairman of the Council of Ministers, a position for which his exuberant personality qualified him far better than did that of the reserved Stalin.

NOTES

1. *Pravda* editorial (April 6, 1953), translated in *Current Digest of the Soviet Press,* V, No. 11 (April 25, 1953), p. 3.
2. *Pravda* editorial (July 10, 1953), translated in *loc. cit.,* No. 24 (July 25, 1953) pp. 9-10.
3. *Pravda,* August 9, 1953.
4. Mordvinov, "Reconstruction of Towns and Art Problems Confronting Soviet Architecture," *VOKS Bulletin,* 1944, No. 9-10, pp. 43-52 *passim.*
5. Zetkin, *Reminiscences of Lenin,* pp. 13-14.
6. *Sovetskaia Muzyka,* XVII, No. 4 (April, 1953), p. 11.
7. *Ibid.,* XVIII, No. 6 (June, 1954), p. 120.
8. *Ibid.,* No. 3 (March, 1954), p. 23

9. *Ibid.*, No. 12 (December, 1954), p. 3.
10. *Ibid.*, XIX, No. 7 (July, 1955), pp. 7-14.
11. Ehrenburg, "On the Work of a Writer," *Znamia,* 1953, No. 10 (October, 1953), pp. 160-183, especially p. 165.
12. Bergholz speech at Congress of Writers, in *Literaturnaia Gazeta,* December 24, 1954, p. 2.
13. "Communist Morality," in *Bol'shaia Sovetskaia Entsiklopedia,* 2nd edition, XXX, 207.
14. "To Raise the Ideological-Theoretical Level of Research on the History of Philosophy," in *Voprosy filosofii,* 1955, No. 3, pp. 3-16, especially pp. 6-7.
15. *Pravda,* November 11, 1954.
16. *Ibid.*, February 11, 1954.
17. *Ibid.*, April 1, 1954.
18. *Ibid.*, February 9, 1955; cf. also *New York Times,* February 9, 1955.
19. *Pravda,* January 19, 1957.
20. *Ibid.*, June 19, 1957.
21. *Ibid.*, February 15, 1956.
22. *Ibid.*, November 3, 1957.
23. *Ibid.*, November 15, 1958.

SUGGESTIONS FOR FURTHER READING

In addition to works previously mentioned, see *The Annals of the American Academy of Political and Social Science,* Vol. 303 (January, 1956), for an excellent collection of articles. Treadgold, previously mentioned, devotes special attention to international relations, to the satellites, and to China. Goodman's *Soviet Design for a World State* is a valiant attempt to project the future on the basis of past statements of Soviet leaders. Wei, *China and Soviet Russia,* is one of the best summaries to 1956.

Jacobson's *The USSR and the UN's Economic and Social Activities* is well documented. See also Nogee's *Soviet Policy Towards International Control of Atomic Energy;* Parry's *Russia's Rockets and Missiles;* and Kramish's *Atomic Energy in the Soviet Union.*

Inkeles and Bauer, *The Soviet Citizen: Daily Life in a Totalitarian Society,* is the product of an eight-year study. Djilas, *The New Class,* is a Yugoslav attack on the Russian regime. Better documented is Parry's *The New Class Divided.* See also Granick's *The Red Executive,* which attempts comparison with the United States. Azrael's *Managerial Power and Soviet Politics* uses a conceptual approach. Grossman's *Soviet Statistics of Physical Output of Industrial Commodities* is somewhat technical.

On legal aspects, especially see Hazard's *Soviet System of Government* and Berman's *Justice in the U.S.S.R. Soviet Education Programs,* by Medlin, *et al.,* supplies translations of some syllabuses. Leyda's *Kino* has some interesting material.

The most reliable way of keeping track of developments in the Soviet Union, as publicly reported there, is provided by the *Current Digest of the Soviet Press.* The Proceedings of Party Congresses since the Nineteenth (1952) are available in the series *Current Soviet Policies,* edited by Gruliow.

Chapter

37

The Khrushchev Interlude: 1957-1964

CONSOLIDATION OF THE NEW REGIME

Changes in the personnel of the Presidium after Khrushchev took over the reins of government were fairly numerous, but few were worthy of special notice. Almost all the newcomers were simply *apparatchiki,* who seemed to be playing a game of musical chairs and who, for the most part, owed their elevation to having served as secretaries of the Central Committee or as First Secretaries in one or the other of the republics or major Russian centers; special emphasis continued to be laid on service in the Ukraine, White Russia, Latvia, the Transcaucasus, or Central Asia. The most significant exception was Kosygin, an economic administrator, once regarded as a protégé of Zhdanov, who had been made chairman of the State Planning Commission in 1959; he was reëlevated to full membership in the Presidium in 1960. In the middle of 1964 Brezhnev was returned to duty as a secretary of the Central Committee; his post as titular head of the state was conferred on the veteran Mikoyan, then sixty-eight years of age, whose membership in the inner circle outdated even Khrushchev's.

Notwithstanding the implicit resumption of the primacy of a single individual, Khrushchev continued to pay lip service to the principle of collective leadership. Party Congresses were held with renewed frequency: the Twentieth (February, 1956), Twenty-first (January-February, 1959), and Twenty-second (October, 1961). De-Stalinization was resumed, and much more openly. At the Twentieth Congress Lenin's "testament," with its characterization of Stalin as "too rough," had been published, but Khrushchev's attack on Stalin at this Congress, with emphasis on his degeneration in his last years, had remained "secret." His fresh denunciation of Stalin's errors, even crimes, at the Twenty-second Congress was published in the Soviet press the following day; an immediate reaction of the Congress was to order the removal of Stalin's body from the Lenin mausoleum in the Red Square. In 1962 the Supreme Council duly elected a commission to revise the "Stalin constitution" of 1936. The work of the Congress was, however, not confined to negative denunciation of bygone mistakes; the Congress enthusiastically endorsed Khrushchev's twenty-year plan for completion of the transition from capitalism to communism, the prospect of banishing war, and the assertion that the dictatorship of the proletariat was no longer indispensable even before the "state" had withered away.

THE CULTURAL "THAW"

In the cultural field the "thaw" announced by Ehrenburg in 1954 continued. Not unnaturally, the West paid most attention to two Soviet novels which definitely would not have passed muster under Zhdanov's criteria. One was Dudintsev's *Not by Bread Alone*. Not very well written, it was sharply critical of bureaucratic abuses which hampered the work of an earnest engineer trying to raise productivity. Yet its criticism of the seamy side of Party authority was obviously not intended to convey any suspicion that the Soviet regime is rotten at the core or any doubt but what, under existing top leadership, virtue will ultimately triumph. The other was the novel *Doctor Zhivago* by the "poet's poet," Boris Pasternak. Awarded the Nobel Prize for literature, acceptance of which Pasternak felt constrained to withdraw, this obscurely written poet's novel makes only silent criticism of the Soviet regime by almost ignoring it.

In a special field overlapping that of literature, historiography seems to have benefited significantly in the period since the death of Stalin. In 1955, for the first time, the Soviet Union sent a delegation to a quinquennial International Historical Congress, held that year in Rome. Although it was obvious that the Soviet scholars were treated by their own authorities as school children, collectively housed in a separate hotel and conveyed *en bloc* to and from the meeting place in special buses, there was the possibility of direct, though limited, individual contact between "socialist" and "bourgeois" historians. The writer recalls the pathetic, but inevitably futile, efforts of one of the Soviet delegates to find out who was the "head" of the American "delegation" and the resultant invitation issued to three Americans to a reception at the Soviet Embassy intended for only one member, the "head," of each national "delegation." In Moscow in 1956 Soviet historians talked quite freely when alone, though a greater degree of caution was obvious in group discussions; even in a group, however, the writer's query why so much Soviet history has been written in the form of sermons expanding cited texts from Marx, Engels, Lenin, and sometimes Stalin, provoked appreciative laughter and assurance that the practice would not continue. Under the auspices of the Academy of Sciences, a multivolume *Outlines of Russian History* was making substantial progress; using a large number of specialized contributors, who did not always give credit to their pre-revolutionary inspiration, these monumental volumes attempted, with considerable success, to present the best of contemporary Soviet historical scholarship.

In 1959 agreements for cultural exchanges were concluded with the United States, the United Kingdom, and France, although they have not always operated without friction. At the Stockholm International Historical Congress (1960) and on subsequent visits to the Soviet Union contacts with Soviet historians and other "intellectuals," were far freer and more outspoken than even in 1956. The quality of Soviet historical research and writing has steadily improved. Among the many discredited historians whose memories have been rehabilitated has even been Pokrovsky, republication of whose works was undertaken in 1962, though not without a properly cautious reserve toward the historical accuracy of his writings.

ECONOMIC PROBLEMS AND POLICIES

In the economic field more difficulties were encountered. With the fall of Malenkov early in 1955, the happy days he had promised were temporarily abandoned. Although there is no reason to believe that the sales of gold made necessary by his "shopping spree" entailed reduction of the Russian gold reserve, these sales violated one of the fundamental principles of Soviet economic thinking and may have played an important role in Malenkov's downfall. Immediately after Malenkov's resignation, his successor Bulganin referred to the "unforgiveable mistake" of "solving special, current tasks at the expense of state reserves." [1] The Soviet Union quickly returned to its policy of autarchy by restricting imports. It did still in emergencies import large quantities of foodstuffs, as it had in the case of sugar after the bad beet harvest of 1954. It was also willing to make new friends, as when it went to the relief of Burma in 1955 by buying her surplus rice, to be paid for in Russian cement.

In the latter case, motives of political policy clearly predominated over the desire to satisfy the Russian consumer, for the Soviet Union was vigorously wooing the "underdeveloped" countries. At what must have been tremendous economic sacrifice, Russia in 1955 underbid the West for a contract to build a million-ton steel mill in India; she undertook to supply $90 million worth of equipment over four to five years, a task the true proportions of which become apparent when it is remembered that her total exports to India in the preceding year had amounted to only $1 million. Subsequent examples of this courtship, sometimes mingled with real economic advantage to the Soviet Union, were the assistance promised to Egypt in the building of the Aswan Dam and Mikoyan's sugar deal with Cuba. It is well to bear in mind the relative insignificance of the Soviet Union in world trade; the large percentage increase therefore represented by even a small absolute rise is best realized in the light of the fact that four-fifths of Russia's foreign trade was with the countries constituting the "Soviet bloc."

The annual targets for 1955 were announced by Marshal Bulganin, the new Premier, with the old emphasis on heavy industry; the planned increase in consumers' goods was set at only half the rise that had been achieved in 1954. Nor was the return to the old policy made surreptitiously; without referring specifically to Malenkov, public attacks were made on the false idea that light industry should now develop faster than production of capital goods. The new F.Y.P., adopted in 1956 but scrapped in 1957 for a similar Seven-Year Plan, was also true to the old pattern. Even during the Malenkov interlude, the annual increase in output of heavy industry had remained almost unaffected in absolute terms, though the rate of increase necessarily slackened; an increase of 2.6 million tons of pig iron from 1948 to 1949 constituted a 19 percent gain, but an increase of 2.5 million from 1953 to 1954 meant a gain of only 9 percent. The reason for high output of pig iron if steel production was to be maintained is clear; save for the first period after the war, Russia was short of scrap metal for the direct production of steel.

The long-term prospects for continuance of a high rate of steel production were beginning to be alarming. Russia had plenty of limestone and could afford to be lavish in use of manganese and chromium, but the supply of the two main necessities, coking coal and iron ore, was less promising. Donbas coke, though the most accessible in Russia, had always had a bad reputation for its high sulfur and ash content; in addition, the Donbas reserves of coking coal had become expensive to mine and were threatened with exhaustion. The huge Kuznetsk coal reserves were of far better quality, but the best coking coal there was already in short supply; moreover, the remoteness of the area and the artificial conditions that must be created if a significant population were to be attracted to the region very seriously impaired the value of the Kuzbas. Karaganda coal, though considerably nearer to the ore deposits of the Urals, has a very high sulfur content and a percentage of ash that makes its use impossible in a blast furnace without admixture of other coke. Other coal deposits have proved to have only a limited value; the best, in the Pechora basin, supplies Leningrad, but to make it of service to the Urals it would be necessary to construct a three-hundred-mile railway over very difficult terrain in a region of exceedingly harsh climate. In the Russian Far East, coal is abundant, but its poor quality has made its use impossible in smelting. The ore reserves also present difficulties. Krivoi Rog, which under the tsars played to the Donbas the role Lorraine played to the Ruhr, is still the main support of the Soviet steel industry, but the quality of the ore has been steadily deteriorating. Magnitogorsk, the famed "iron mountain" in the Urals, on the eve of World War II was supplying one-fourth of Russia's whole output, but it has proved increasingly disappointing both in quality and in quantity. On the other hand, the threat of serious depletion of Russia's natural resources has been counterbalanced by great technological advances, only in part achieved by watching the West. Notable was utilization of a new cheap method of producing oxygen, devised by the renowned Soviet physicist Kapitsa just before World War II. This process gave Russia a great lead in open-hearth steel mills. As a result, Russia could, in 1965, claim an output of 66 million tons of pig-iron and 91 million tons of steel, with hope of raising these figures by 1970 to at least 94 and 124 million tons, respectively. Coal output in 1965 was put at 578 million tons, to be raised to at least 665 million tons by 1970.

The Khrushchev regime announced in 1957 a sweeping reorganization of the administration of the whole economy. Control by ministries in Moscow was to be replaced by transfer of power to regional economic councils, in the hope that these councils would have a better appreciation of local conditions and manpower resources. Particularly in consumer-goods industries, considerable apprehension was caused by accumulation of unsold stocks, for there was no way in which even an authoritarian government could compel the public to buy what they did not want, even though it might have been produced in accordance with the best thinking of an elaborate planning apparatus. In 1962 Liberman, a professor of economics, advanced an idea, by no means new, but now couched in language designed not to repel convinced socialists; its essence was that enterprises for manufacturing "goods of wide consumption" should produce on orders, direct or indirect, from retail outlets and that the success of enterprises should be judged by their profits rather than by quantitative fulfilment of the economic plans.[2] The idea was given qualified approval by Khrushchev and, on an experimental basis, tried out, with success, in a few enterprises.

Agriculture continued to be the most serious problem. Khrushchev attempted to deal with it by the old method of mixing incentives and compulsion in ever-shifting proportions without relaxation of the controls made possible by collectivization. On the one side, what amounts to a subsidy to the peasants has been given by raising prices of compulsory deliveries, which has, however, of course not stimulated the growth of sales on the free market. Similarly, taxes paid by peasant householders were reduced; uncollectible arrears were canceled; and the amounts expected to be subscribed by peasants for state bonds were cut. Progressive rates of taxation, which discouraged efforts at maximum production, were largely abandoned. The *zveno* (link) system, with its larger possibility of rewarding individual effort, was again encouraged. On the other hand, the minimum number of "labor days" the collective farmer must earn in a season was further increased; although noncompliance ceased to be criminally punishable, severe tax penalties were imposed, and not only on the individual delinquent but on the whole household of which he was a member. The administrative grip of the MTS over the collective farms in its area was strengthened, though in 1957 Khrushchev announced that tractors and machinery were to be transferred to individual collective farms. Party members were, even more than formerly, to be installed as chairmen of the *kolkhozy*; regional secretaries who could show a record of agricultural progress in their areas were rewarded, on occasion even with a seat in the Presidium. Yet Khrushchev had good reason to bitterly denounce agricultural "mismanagement" (February, 1961), for little headway was made in inspiring the peasant willingly to coöperate with the regime; he still persisted in his efforts to develop his own individual economy, however backward in its technique, at the expense of the *kolkhoz*. The problem was all the more serious because the Party, in its anxiety to increase the industrial labor supply, had for decades been encouraging a mass movement to the towns. The official estimate of total population as of July 1, 1963, was 225 million, of whom 52 percent were classified as urban. There was much ground for worry lest the agricultural base necessary to an economically independent Russia was about to disappear.

In the effort to increase agricultural output, Khrushchev vigorously pushed the "virgin-soil" program. Over the centuries almost all of the cultivable area had been put under the plow; even before the Revolution attempts further to expand agriculture into the marginal region along the lower Volga had created a "dust-bowl" problem. There remained vast fertile areas, almost uninhabited save for pastoral nomads, in Central Asia, particularly in Kazakhstan, but moisture there was normally inadequate; their remoteness from old centers of population intensified the problem of labor supply. Intensive propaganda campaigns were needed to recruit numbers of urban youth, ostensibly at least on a voluntary basis, from older areas for intensive work in harvest time. The need for housing and extra transportation inevitably raised costs. In the early stages, too, the new-lands program absorbed the bulk of current output of tractors and combines, leaving the older, and most important, agricultural areas to make the best of their inadequate and depreciating equipment.

Notwithstanding all difficulties, in the first years of the program great successes had been achieved, but by 1961 trouble was already evident. In 1963 the once "virgin lands" yielded only 5 million tons of grain, as against their 1958 peak of 14.3 million tons, and the total grain yield for the whole U.S.S.R. was the lowest in a decade. That fall it was necessary to negotiate the purchase of a quarter of a billion dollars worth of wheat from America, to be sold through private channels at world prices.

The difficulties imposed by nature on Russian agriculture have long resulted in human efforts to bend ecology to man's conscious purpose. Soviet Russia has continued the effort of tsarist times to develop new strains of wheat which can be grown in latitudes which had long had to rely on rye. Whereas in the nineteenth century countries such as Canada had drawn great benefit from Russian pioneering in this field, in the twentieth century the trend of emulation has been reversed. Russian plant breeding for a time suffered acutely from the favor shown by Stalin to the genetics theories of Lysenko, which, if sound, promised relatively easy solution to Russia's agricultural problem. In April, 1962, Lysenko resigned as president of the Academy of Agricultural Science, though he was permitted to continue as director of the Institute of Genetics under the Academy of Sciences until January, 1965. In a reversal of old roles, Russia now strove to learn from the United States; a special effort was begun to expand the growing of maize, a project on which Khrushchev in particular pinned most ambitious hopes; enormous quantities of the best hybrid seed were imported into Russia, and the study of Iowa was given top priority. Although admittedly this grain will not ripen properly in the latitudes in which most of Russia lies, reliance has been placed on the quantity of silage the stalks and "milk" ears will yield. Simultaneous increase in the growing of other fodder crops was expected at last to make possible increase in the number and yield of livestock.

EFFORTS AT INTERNATIONAL *DÉTENTE*

Perhaps the most striking aspect of the "thaw" was the fairly consistent effort—pursued particularly by Khrushchev—to effect a *détente* in international relations. Whether from conviction or from policy, the Soviet Union openly embarked on a "peace crusade." This was, to be sure, not a wholly new development; even Lenin, in his last years, had felt constrained to proclaim a truce (his phrase was "breathing spell"), which Stalin speedily developed into "Socialism in a single land." An obviously decisive factor in their desire to stabilize, at least temporarily, relations with the "capitalist" West was the consideration that Russia herself needed an extended period of peace in which to build up her economy on the basis of industrialization; there is also the possibility, as some Soviet economists argued in the past, that they hoped that an international *détente,* by suddenly reducing Western military expenditures, would throw capitalist economies out of gear and plunge the West into a severe economic depression. It is, however, by no means excluded that their successors, for whom the Revolution was at most a memory of their youth, if not merely an inherited legend, have been motivated by a genuine will for a permanent relaxation of international tension, rooted perhaps in the conviction that "socialism" has proved itself and will, without the use of force, everywhere triumph. Whatever the reasons behind it, the present reality of the Soviet "peace offensive" seems clear.

This new "peace crusade" has not, to be sure, been attended by any sign of willingness to abandon positions of strength, nor has it prevented the Soviet Union from encouraging new embarrassments for those whose friendship it cultivates. In 1956, though the Soviet Union was already in the thick of a "peace offensive" beamed at Great Britain and the United States, the Suez crisis offered an overwhelmingly tempting opportunity for Russia to penetrate the Arab world, theretofore closed to her influence. Although Nasser would not accompany his purchases of Czech arms with a friendly gesture toward communism, an opening had been made for Soviet diplomacy in that area. Turkey and Iran, however, which bordered on the Soviet Union, joined forces with Iraq and Pakistan in the Baghdad Pact, of which Great Britain also became a member.

The check to Russia was not of long duration. In August, 1957, a coup in Syria gave pro-Communist elements the upper hand. In an excited aftermath, Turkey, despite a sharp Soviet warning, conducted military maneuvers along the Syrian border; the United States Sixth Fleet was at the ready, and arms were flown to Jordan. The affair passed off mainly to the advantage of Egypt, which, though purchasing Soviet submarines, remained only coolly friendly to the Soviet Union. Russia thus did not succeed in drawing profit to the extent she had when an earlier dictator of Egypt, Mehemet Ali, had absorbed Syria; this time Turkey, instead of throwing herself into Russia's embrace, remained firmly hostile. The United States, playing Great Britain's old role, did not repeat the fumbling mistakes that had preceded the Crimean (and the Korean) War; in clear language she warned Russia that America would support Turkey if she were attacked. Shortly before the Syrian coup, the United States had accepted a seat on the Military Committee of the Baghdad Pact. The value of this instrument was, however, ruined by the Iraqi revolution in July, 1958.

In the sequel, Iraq accepted substantial economic aid from Russia, withdrew from the Baghdad Pact (March, 1959), and refused further military aid from America (June). Another consequence, however, was a worsening of Soviet relations with Nasser's United Arab Republic, which Khrushchev now announced was "bound to fail." [3] By May, Iraq was accepting British arms, while the United States in July resumed its supply to Nasser. Iraq, shaken in March by a revolt apparently inspired by Nasser, found it necessary in July to suppress its own Communists. Despite the crack opened to the Soviet Union in the Near East, Soviet hopes that an "Arab world," supposedly united against an intransigent Israel, might rally against the West remained dim. In the thick of the crisis, neighboring Iran rejected a threatening Soviet offer of a nonaggression pact buttered with economic aid and accepted (February) a new economic and defense agreement with the United States.

In other areas, the Soviet Union had enhanced its reputation as a peace-loving nation at no serious cost. In 1955, she had voluntarily surrendered to Finland her fifty-year lease on the Porkkala naval base, no longer of value in the changed strategic situation in the Baltic; she even offered Finland use of the Saina Canal, which passed through territory annexed by Russia in 1945. She did not, however, make any move to restore to Finland an Arctic port or offer to return the nickel-bearing Petsamo region. In similar spirit Molotov had suddenly offered to sign the Austrian peace treaty on terms

Russia had, after innumerable conferences of foreign ministers, flatly rejected in 1954. Though signature of the treaty necessitated withdrawal of Soviet occupation troops from an advanced, and perhaps untenable, position in the heart of Europe, Russia was able to take the credit for the initiative in finally bringing about a settlement. In addition, she secured a virtual ten-year mortgage on Austria's economy.

Within the Soviet orbit in Eastern Europe the new regime was faced with a number of difficulties. In 1955, Yugoslavia had finally accepted a Soviet apology, delivered by Khrushchev in person and in public at Belgrade. The fact that Khrushchev put all the blame on Beria did not alter the fact that, abandoning the earlier Russian story that resumption of diplomatic relations in 1953 had been made possible by alterations in Yugoslavia's policies, he admitted that the Soviet Union itself had erred. Yugoslavia won a lifting of the Russian economic blockade and was granted both a $54 million credit and a $30 million loan. Although her undertaking to supply Russia with bauxite and other raw materials impaired her newly established good relations with the West, Yugoslavia avoided being wholly sucked back into the Soviet orbit. She had to give up her plans for a Balkan Alliance, which might have greatly strengthened NATO, but this had the compensatory, if perilous, advantage of leaving a neutral Yugoslavia balanced between East and West. Most important of all, although Russia consented to dissolve the Cominform (April 17, 1956), Tito flatly refused to listen to persistent Russian efforts to establish Party unity between his followers and the Soviet Union.

The limited success of Russian policy in its initial rapprochement with Yugoslavia was soon followed by severe blows to Russian prestige in relation to her satellites. On June 28, 1956, Polish workers staged an uprising in Poznan; though the fact was not for some time published in the Soviet press, it immediately became widely known in Russia via the BBC, the principal and most trusted medium of contact between the outside world and the Russian man-in-the-street. The revolt was quickly repressed by Soviet military forces, but the Soviet government found it expedient to withdraw Polish-born Marshal Rokossowski and hand over power (October, 1956) to Gomulka, the Polish Communist imprisoned in 1948 for "nationalist deviationism." The new Polish regime had no possibility of moving out of the Soviet bloc as Yugoslavia had done in 1948; the fact that its new western boundaries rested solely on Russian fiat, not accepted by the Western powers as binding, would in itself have prevented any such development. Yet, with the expressed sympathy of Red China, Poland acquired a limited right to manage her own domestic life. The Roman Catholic Church, though under the necessity of scrupulously avoiding any interference in politics, was one of the chief beneficiaries; Cardinal Wyszinski was at once released from prison (October 29). Poland did not become "Titoist." At home she was now able to set her own pace of progress toward the goal of communism, though riots in Warsaw in October, 1957, suggested that her internal troubles were not over. In international relations, however, Poland remained a subservient mouthpiece advocating Russia's policies.

A still more serious threat to Russian control of her satellites broke out in Hungary on October 23, 1956. After stubborn fighting, in which the Hungarian army and even some Russian units proved unreliable, the revolt was crushed by Soviet troops (November 4). Despite a general strike of Hungarian workers (December 10-17), the Russian victory was far more complete than in Poland; it was followed by ruthless execution of Communist leaders, such as Premier Nagy, who had shown some signs of wavering. The Soviet grip on Hungary emerged unshaken, but the revolt dealt an incalculable blow to Soviet prestige in Eastern Europe and jeopardized the new understanding with Yugoslavia.

Russo-Yugoslav relations remained uncertain, but not unfriendly. In February, 1957, Yugoslavia flared up against the Soviet Union, but in July a promised $250 million credit, which Russia had withheld in anger at Yugoslav sympathy for Hungary, was reinstated. In August, Khrushchev personally assured Tito that relations between their countries must rest "on the basis of equality, mutual assistance and coöperation, respect for sovereignty, and noninterference in internal affairs." [4] In September, however, Tito entertained Gomulka of Poland; at the conclusion of their discussions, they issued a joint statement emphasizing "the diversity of forms and methods of building socialism" and the necessity for socialist "collaboration founded on mutual respect and on the principles of equality and sovereignty." The two countries, with no suggestion that they needed help or even guidance from Moscow, announced their intention of working together in future for the advancement of their common interests.[5] In October, Tito recognized the East German "Democratic Republic," a move which led the West German "Federal Republic of Germany" to break off relations with Yugoslavia. Yet Yugoslavia remained only an uneasy partner of the Soviet Union. In April, 1958, following his unanimous reëlection by parliament as president of Yugoslavia, Tito told (April 22) his Party Congress that the leaders of the U.S.S.R. must abandon their "absurd" ideas of controlling Yugoslav policy; at the same time he praised America's financial aid to his country and the "true internationalism" of her abstention from interference in the domestic policies of Yugoslavia. A year later (April 19, 1959) he repeated his attack on the Russian campaign to force Yugoslavia to become a mere satellite "at any price." Not until 1963 did the Soviet Union finally succeed in greatly improving its relations with Yugoslavia; in the meantime, Khrushchev's 1956 pronouncement of the possibility of "different roads to socialism" had been formally recognized as orthodox doctrine by the Twenty-second Party Congress (October, 1961). By 1963 Rumania also was quietly asserting a limited independence of Russian guidance, particularly in the matter of relations with China.

THE "PEACE CRUSADE" AND THE AMERICAN RESPONSE

A brief return to a threatening posture toward the outside world shortly before Malenkov's resignation had culminated in the announcement that the Soviet Union, East Germany, Czechoslovakia, Poland, Hungary, Rumania, Bulgaria, and Albania had signed at Warsaw (May 14, 1955) a twenty-year treaty of mutual defense, pooling their military power in answer to NATO. The new Bulganin-Khrushchev management soon resumed the propaganda for peace, to be based on a security arrangement embracing all Europe. The Soviet Union took part in the four-power "summit conference" at Geneva in July, 1955, which was followed by a more important foreign ministers' meeting late in the fall. At both these meetings, the Russians again attempted to infiltrate NATO, suggesting that the North Atlantic Pact and the Warsaw Pact be fused into one. Disarmament continued to be a favorite theme of discussion. The Soviet Union made repeated gestures, freely advocating both complete prohibition of the use of nuclear weapons in warfare and total disarmament, but consistently objecting to the establishment of any system of inspection that might guarantee the reality of the agreement. In April, 1956, Bulganin and Khrushchev paid a visit to Great Britain. It was a journey that would have been inconceivable when Lenin or Stalin ruled Russia, though it had a precedent in the time of Nicholas I; yet their efforts to charm the British public, who jeered at them as "Crush and Bulge," failed dismally.

More successful was the opposite and no less novel policy of inviting foreigners to visit Russia. In 1956, the Archbishop of York headed a delegation of Anglican clergymen that went to the Soviet Union and helped officiate at the services in the Troitsa Monastery on St. Sergius' Day. Beginning with a trickle in 1955, and in subsequent years swelling to thousands, American, British, and other tourists were invited to see the Kremlin and the All-Union Agricultural Exhibition, Leningrad and Stalingrad (now Volgograd), Kiev, and Sochi. Most of the Soviet Union for some time remained closed to them officially for the reason that suitable de luxe accommodations were lacking; in 1956 the writer arrived in Riga, en route for Leningrad, on one of the days when the "daily" plane did not connect those cities and found the hotel accommodations in Riga, though supposed to be closed to foreign tourists, much superior to those anywhere else, not excepting Moscow. Tourists generally have been surprised at the warmth of the reception accorded them by the Russian public and by the noninterference of the Soviet authorities in their activities.

After 1956 the Soviet Union persisted in making an obvious bid for cultural contacts capable of fostering a mutually friendly understanding between Soviet Russia and the West. Hordes of foreign tourists have been welcomed and permitted to visit many parts of the Soviet Union from which they were previously debarred, though the letting down of bars has not been extended to wholesale authorization for Soviet citizens to visit the West. Appearances in the Soviet Union of *Porgy and Bess,* Van Cliburn, and Leonard Bernstein were balanced by the Moiseev folk dancers, the tour of the Bolshoi Ballet, and the visit of a delegation of musicians headed by Shostakovich. Notwithstanding these and a number of other cultural exchanges, relations on sociopolitical questions remained cool. Despite the interchange of friendly letters (February-March, 1955) between those old comrades-in-arms, Eisenhower and Zhukov and despite release of American airmen long held by "Red" China (May 31), the "summit conference" held at Geneva in July, 1955, had naturally achieved nothing.

Not until 1959 did it appear that the Arctic wall could be seriously breached. In January of that year Mikoyan, one of the two First Deputy Premiers, made a cautious visit to the United States, the first made by an important Soviet official since Molotov had participated in the organization of the United Nations at San Francisco in 1945. On February 5, at the Twenty-first Party Congress, Khrushchev made a vitriolic speech against the United States and its policy but coupled with it an invitation to President Eisenhower to visit the Soviet Union. Under the circumstances, the invitation was not accepted, though a few weeks later, Harold Macmillan accepted an invitation, differently couched. The British Prime Minister's visit gave Khrushchev a sudden and violent toothache but afforded Macmillan an opportunity to broadcast from Moscow an exceedingly forceful presentation of the views of the West, which he drove home to a convalescent Khrushchev at a farewell reception in the Kremlin. Not to be discouraged, the Soviet Union sent Kozlov, its other First Deputy Premier and a man more important in the Party than was Mikoyan, to open the Soviet Exhibition of Science, Technology, and Culture in New York (June 28). After receiving Eisenhower at the Coliseum (June 29), Kozlov attended an official luncheon tendered him in Washington and took the opportunity of making a two-week tour of the country. In return, Vice-President Nixon flew to Moscow (July 23) to open the American National Exposition with the President's "best wishes for the well-being and prosperity in conditions of peace for the people of the U.S.S.R. from the people of the U.S.A." Cordially received by Khrushchev, who engaged in sharp but not acrimonious public debate with his guest, Nixon was permitted to visit parts of the Soviet Union normally closed to all foreigners; on his way home he spent a few days in Poland, where he conferred with Gomulka.

The apparent success of the thaw encouraged Khrushchev himself to make an unprecedented and much publicized visit to the United States in September. Though he brought with him no notable official retinue, he was accompanied by his own family. In an exuberant effort to win greater friendship for the Soviet Union, Khrushchev was noticeably careful, for the first time in Soviet propaganda, to make no distinction between the plain people of the

United States and their government. While frankly boasting of what he represented as the basic superiority of the Soviet system, he did not hesitate to give credit to American superiority in some respects; evidently relishing hot dogs, he praised American skill in "sausage-making." To cap the climax, President Eisenhower acceded to arrangements for another "summit meeting," to be held in 1960. As a preliminary, the American President undertook to repeat, though under very different circumstances and on a very much extended scale, the visit to the Soviet Union that President Roosevelt had made in 1945.

Despite the attempted thaw, the Soviet Union did not refrain from also rattling the saber. In January, 1957, for instance, the Soviet Union warned that any nation permitting the United States to establish military bases on its soil would expose itself to the peril of retaliatory atomic attacks. In August, it announced that an ICBM had been successfully tested and that the "results obtained show that it is possible to launch a rocket to any region of the globe." [6] In October, the Soviet Union was able to announce that "a mighty hydrogen warhead of a new design" had been successfully tested at "great altitude." [7] On the same day, however, in an interview with James Reston, the able and respected correspondent of the *New York Times,* Khrushchev offered international control of all earth satellites and of pilotless missiles. Cool reception of this idea by the United States Department of State, which rejected any thought of a merely bilateral agreement between the United States and Russia, increased the virulence of Soviet threats. Khrushchev retorted that the United States was seeking war in the Near East. However, his famous remark, "We shall bury you," merely reflected crudely expressed self-confidence rather than acute hostility; certain that communism would outlive capitalism, the ebullient leader of the world's only "socialist" state was promising decent interment to his American friends.

In the meanwhile, on October 4, 1957, the Russians successfully launched the first *sputnik.* A month later, another and larger *sputnik* carried the dog Laika into the wild blue yonder. The propaganda value of these launchings could not be canceled by subsequent United States efforts. Similarly, the first moon rocket (September, 1959) made the United States' reputation for "know-how" seem, at least temporarily, laughable.

The technological triumphs of Soviet science were not allowed to interrupt the Soviet drive for "peaceful coexistence" with the "rotten" West. Yet it failed to achieve its immediate, veiled purposes. Khrushchev had evidently been confident that the projected "summit conference," prepared by a series of jocular personal visits to all the leading countries, would enable him to bring into the open, and drive deeper, the disagreements inevitable among allies and thus give him a chance to win concessions otherwise unattainable. As the time approached, however, evidence accumulated that, despite his camaraderie with individual peoples and their respective responsible leaders, he would in Paris be faced with a united front. It therefore became necessary for him to disrupt the conference in order to avoid a diplomatic defeat which might have shaken even his grip over the Party at home. Among a variety of possibilities, he chose the easiest—the latest of a number of occasions on which a foreign plane had been brought down over, or at least near, Soviet territory; he could do so with all the more relish because U-2's had for at least two years been seriously worrying the Russian military. Significantly, though leaving Paris in an apparent huff, his speech in East Berlin gave no real encouragement to the "East Germans." The ousting of the West from Berlin, which since 1958 he had been making an avowed objective of Soviet foreign policy, was allowed to lapse into temporary oblivion.

Thus, without sacrifice of any position of strength and without creating a situation from which peaceful withdrawal was impossible, Khrushchev was able to retain the posture of injured innocence, obscuring his loss of prestige. He could still hope that electoral excitement might after all give him the negotiating advantage he was seeking. In the meantime, developments in Cuba and in the Congo, with an uneasy Laos in the background, gave him fresh opportunity to fish in troubled waters. With an air of triumph and with seeming ingenuousness, he sought to damage Russia's rivals for world influence. In particular, he made a vigorous attempt to damage the prestige of the United Nations, which since 1950 had been a most serious obstacle to the sort of anarchic nationalism that currently serves the ambitions of Russia. However unsuccessful in the eyes of the West and even of the "neutral" nations his antics may have been, they may have served him well at home. In the form in which they were reported in the Soviet press, their effect could scarcely fail to be enhanced by a Moscow rebroadcast of his farewell television program in New York, on which he was able to pose as bland and friendly under hectoring, except when, as he could pretend, he was called a dog.

The outcome of the American Presidential election gave the Russian leadership the possibility of pretending that more satisfactory improvement in Soviet-American relations had at last become possible. It is unlikely that Khrushchev and his associates really interpreted the closeness of Kennedy's victory as indicating that the American people was deeply and hopelessly divided. Their obvious tactic to greet the new president with kind words was emphasized by the release, early in 1961, of American airmen held by the Soviet Union. In fact, mainly in consequence of Kennedy's initial blundering in the matter of the Bay of Pigs, relations deteriorated rapidly. On April 18, 1961, less than a week after Gagarin had made the first successful human flight in outer space, Khrushchev put the "Truman Doctrine" into reverse and publicly offered assistance to Castro. In May, the Berlin passes dispute raised at the beginning of 1960 was widened by the issue of new East German air-traffic regulations. Nevertheless, Khrushchev and Kennedy had a fruitless personal meeting in Vienna (June 3-4). In August, "Ulbricht's 'Chinese

Wall' " was erected. Vice-President Johnson was rushed to Berlin to view the wall and reassure the West Germans. The united West issued a "solemn warning" (August 26) against unilateral action in the matter of the air corridors, and the Soviet Union announced (August 31) its decision to resume nuclear tests. Neither side, however, proceeded to extremes for over a year.

At the beginning of 1962, when President Kennedy was beginning to show signs of substituting for the Eisenhower policy of sending a few hundred military advisers to South Vietnam the policy of sending auxiliary combat units, the Soviet Union filed with the British government an aide-memoire blaming the United States for "the present worsening of the situation," which was promptly rejected by London; for the moment Khrushchev was content to throw out (May, 1962) a remark that the United States was "acting like a policeman" and that "we are in favor of national liberation wars."

The most dangerous crisis in the history of Soviet-American relations arose in September, 1962, when Khrushchev promised to deliver arms to Castro and warned of the possibility of war, while the American Congress authorized the President to use force, if necessary. On October 22, Kennedy announced the Soviet installation of nuclear missile bases in Cuba and followed with open threats of belligerent action if they were not removed. On October 27, the President, ignoring an offer by Khrushchev to withdraw from Cuba if the United States would withdraw its bases from Turkey, accepted a less conditional promise made by Khrushchev the day before. On October 28, Khrushchev formally agreed to dismantle the bases, which Kennedy aptly characterized as a "statesmanlike decision."

The threatened storm somewhat cleared the atmosphere. Though the two chief protagonists publicly exchanged not altogether complimentary remarks, although friction over Berlin and other problems continued, although Mikoyan was sent on a friendly visit to Cuba (November, 1962), and although Castro was warmly welcomed in Moscow (April, 1963), a nuclear test ban treaty (proposed by President Eisenhower in April, 1959) was finally signed early in August, 1963, closely following the "hot-line" agreement providing for immediate and direct telephone communication between Washington and Moscow.

CHINA

The international *détente* was, however, not worldwide. China, which the Soviet Union had been attempting to treat as a junior partner, was fast becoming a source of great anxiety, reverting to her ancient concept of herself as the "Middle Kingdom." As late as 1959, Chou En-lai, speaking at the Twenty-first Party Congress, had emphasized "the eternal and unbreakable friendship" between China and the Soviet Union, despite the efforts of "United States imperialists" and "Yugoslav revisionists"; later in the year, Khrushchev, visiting China immediately after his return from the United States, was still congratulated by Chou on the "success of his mission to the United States as an envoy of peace." Though he had gone to Peking to help celebrate the tenth anniversary of Red China's triumph, the spokesman of the Russian Revolution chose to remark that "socialism cannot be imposed by force of arms" and to emphasize the already official Russian policy of "peaceful coexistence with states of differing social systems."

In the meantime the quarrel between India, later supplied by Russia with Mig fighting planes, and China, precipitated by Chinese actions in Tibet (March, 1959), clearly was a source of embarrassment to Russia. Although it did not prevent India from once again moving (July 14) recognition of the claim of Red China to be seated in the United Nations, China's "continuing acts of aggression" on the border were vigorously denounced by Nehru (August 29). At the celebration of the tenth anniversary of Communist China (October 1), Khrushchev was almost the only speaker to preach settlement of international problems by peaceful means; at New Delhi, Nehru, despite his continued profound aversion to war in principle, announced (October 24) that India would not "bow down" to Chinese threats, which she was prepared to meet.

Early in 1960 Khrushchev made an extended tour through India and Southeast Asia, lavishing promises of economic aid. At the end of the year he convened in Moscow an exceptionally large conference of world Communist leaders, including the Chinese; it was evident, however, that China would not accept the thesis that war with the capitalist world was not inevitable and that "peaceful coexistence" was desirable. At the Twenty-second Party Congress (October, 1961), Chou, as a guest-speaker, endorsed the principle of peaceful coexistence but gave guarded support to Albanian criticisms of the Soviet Union and its policies. In the course of 1962, however, the divergent views of Russia and China came increasingly to light. At the height of the Sikkim clash between China and India, *Pravda* at first stressed Russian friendship with China and advised India to accept the Chinese proposals for its settlement; eleven days later, however, *Pravda* called for a cease-fire. Nehru was able to announce that Russia would supply the promised Mig's and would help India to build a factory to make them for herself. At the time of the Cuban missile-base crisis (October, 1962), mass meetings in China condemned the United States; they found no echo in Moscow. Instead, in a public address to the Supreme Council (December 12, 1962), Khrushchev taunted China for allowing Macao and Hong-Kong to remain intact as "fragments of colonialism," maliciously adding: "If the Chinese Government tolerates Macao and Hong-Kong, it clearly has good reasons for doing so. It would therefore be ridiculous to levy against it the accusation . . . that this is appeasement." He continued blandly: "Some dogmatists have slithered into Trotskyist positions, and are prodding the Soviet Union and the Socialist countries on to the course of unleashing world war. . . . Clearly the Albanian leaders and those who are goading them on have lost faith in the possibility of the victory of socialism without international war. . . ." The Chinese *People's Daily* retorted that "Russia acquired Vladivostok and 318,000 square miles of territory from China" under the same kind of treaty that accounted for the existence of Hong-Kong and asked whether Russia was ready to revise all such inequitable treaties. There followed a long series of Chinese letters and press attacks and of Russian replies, trading ever more virulent insults. Khrushchev himself, on the eve of the nuclear-test-ban treaty (which the Chinese denounced as "a dirty fraud"), publicly rebuked those who "believed that society could be built upon corpses." Over the year's end Chou visited Africa and Albania in an obvious effort to win support against continued Russian leadership of world Communism. A report by Suslov (February 14, not published in *Pravda* until April 3 in order to give Rumania a chance to mediate) to the Central Committee of the Party accused the Chinese leaders of "steering a course toward a split among the Communist parties and toward the setting up of factions and groups hostile to Marxism-Leninism" and asserted that, because of China's "adventurist" policy, "We consider it inexpedient to help China to produce nuclear weapons." Evidently determined on a showdown with Mao and anxious to stabilize Russia's leadership, Khrushchev pressed for another world Communist conference, not later than December, 1964, even though the outcome might be a complete break with China.

NOTES

1. *Pravda,* February 10, 1955, translated in *New Times,* No. 7 (February 12, 1955).
2. For a statement of his views by Professor Liberman himself, see "The Soviet Economic Reform," *Foreign Affairs,* XLVI, 1 (October, 1967), pp. 53-63.
3. *Pravda,* March 17, 1959.
4. *Ibid.,* August 4, 1957.
5. *Ibid.,* September 18, 1957.
6. *Ibid.,* August 26, 1957.
7. *Ibid.,* October 7, 1957.

SUGGESTIONS FOR FURTHER READING

In addition to works previously cited, Brzezinski's *Soviet Bloc* represents a current attempt at analysis by a political scientist. More narrowly conceived and better documented is Hazard's *Soviet Legal System.* On Khrushchev, see his own *For Victory in Peaceful Competition with Capitalism,* and *The Anti-Stalin Campaign and International Communism,* compiled by the Russian Institute of Columbia University; for his Achilles' heel, see Jasny's *Khrushchev's Crop Policy* and Ploss'

Conflict and Decision-making in Soviet Russia. Current Soviet Policies III and *IV* contain the documentary record of the Twenty-first and Twenty-second Congresses of the CPSU. A recent Party program for domestic and international policy may be found in Ritvo, *The New Soviet Society*.

On literature during the "thaw," see Gibian's *Interval of Freedom,* Ehrenburg's *A Change of Seasons,* and Tertz's *On Socialist Realism.* Ronchey's *Russia in the Thaw* is the best report by a foreign journalist.

Chapter

38

Epilogue

THE FALL OF KHRUSHCHEV

When Khrushchev celebrated his seventieth birthday (April 17, 1964), he had only two associates in the Presidium—Shvernik and Kuusinen (died May 17)—who had been old enough to take any part in the Revolution of 1905; neither had become a regular member of the Presidium until 1957, and neither had ever been of great political weight. Only one other—Mikoyan (who had joined the Party in 1915 at the age of twenty)—was a veteran of the 1917 Revolution; although he had been a member of the Politburo (after 1952 the Presidium) since 1935 and although he had performed great services in connection with Soviet trade, Mikoyan had not been of primary importance in the Party. Khrushchev himself had joined the Party only in 1918; he had been elevated to the Politburo in 1939. None of his other eight colleagues in the Presidium had been even fifteen years old at the time of the "October Revolution." The oldest of them—Suslov—had joined the Party in 1921 (at the age of nineteen), had been elected to the Central Committee only in 1941, and, next to Khrushchev, had the longest record as a member of its Secretariat (from 1947); he had been promoted to the Presidium in 1955, a few months after the fall of Malenkov. Khrushchev's once prominent rivals—Molotov, Malenkov, and Kaganovich—had been expelled even from the Party (February, 1964).

Gifted with the shrewdness, without the mental imbalance, of Hitler (though without the caution of Stalin), Khrushchev had seemed to be in full control of the situation. A visitor to Moscow, however, might hear mutterings about his uncouthness, even "hooliganism." His policy of international *détente* evidently gave great satisfaction, but his tendency to set off occasional fireworks caused alarm. There was also great dissatisfaction with his failure to find a viable agricultural policy. It was therefore a much lesser shock to the Soviet public than to the outside world when, on October 15, 1964, it was announced that on the previous day Khrushchev had been "released," both as First Secretary of the Central Committee of the Party and as Chairman of the Council of Ministers.

His place as First Secretary was taken by Brezhnev (aet. 58); the less important post of Prime Minister went to Kosygin (aet. 60). Brezhnev had been trained as a metallurgist, but he had been an *apparatchik* since 1941; his political work in the armies during the war had won him the rank of Major-General (Lieutenant-General in 1953). He had been a lieutenant of Khrushchev in Party work in the Ukraine; in 1956 the Twentieth Congress had elected him as one of the secretaries of the Central Committee and a candidate member of the Presidium; he became a full member in 1957, just before the majority in that body made its unsuccessful attempt to oust Khrushchev. In 1960 he had succeeded the aging Voroshilov as titular head of the state, but in mid-1964 he had resumed his role in the Secretariat. Kosygin, who had joined the Party in 1927 (four years before Brezhnev), had risen to ministerial rank by service in administering the textile and other light industries. Though raised to the Politburo in 1948, he had been dropped from the Presidium after Stalin's death; not until 1957 was he made even a candidate member, and not until 1960 was he reëlevated to full membership. Never an *apparatchik,* and therefore a rare phenomenon at the highest level, he was obviously well qualified for the highest administrative post in the Soviet Union.

Khrushchev's colleagues lost little time in releasing a statement—apparently a remarkably honest one, though they gave him no opportunity publicly to attempt rebuttal—of the reasons for his removal. Heavy stress was laid on the vital importance of preserving "collective leadership," which Khrushchev had been undermining by promoting a new "cult of the individual"; the former leader was accused also of nepotism (particularly in the case of his son-in-law Adzhubei), of undignified personal behavior, and of making embarrassing impromptu speeches. In general, the victors endorsed his foreign policy, but with several criticisms: among other lesser things, he (1) had engaged in a personal feud with Mao Tse-tung, thus endangering relations with China; (2) had set up missile bases in Cuba, an unwarranted action with an inevitably humiliating sequel; (3) had conducted affairs singlehandedly without consulting his colleagues; (4) had estranged Rumania in the matter of oil production; and (5) had made Nasser a "Hero of the Soviet Union." The major criticisms, however, were in the field of domestic policy: (1) he was blamed for the virgin-lands crisis in agriculture; (2) he had switched to centralization of industry and back again; (3) he had overemphasized light and consumer industry; (4) he had made great errors in the development of economic planning; (5) he had neglected to promote the progress of science; and (6) he had arbitrarily dismissed worthy officials, both in the Party and in the government.

The transfer of power was effected smoothly, with infinitely less commotion than in countries that hold periodic elections, and apparently to the great satisfaction of the population. A month later, Khrushchev's quondam favorite —Kozlov (incapacitated for over a year)—was also "released" from the Presidium. The two vacant places were filled by *apparatchiki*; one of them—Shelepin, formerly chairman of the Control Commission—has been credited with being a prime mover in the fall of Khrushchev. At forty-six, he was the youngest member of the Presidium; he has since been assigned to head the trade-union apparatus, a post which has never been filled by a leader of the first rank. No major changes have since occurred. Mikoyan (aet. 71) and Shvernik (aet. 78) were not reëlected after the Twenty-third Congress (April, 1966), which restored the old name of Politburo and conferred on the First Secretary Stalin's old title of General Secretary. Two more *apparatchiki* were added to the Politburo, and there have been the usual changes among the candidate members and in the Secretariat.

THE ECONOMY

Economic problems, although they had figured largely in the statement of reasons for removing Khrushchev, gave his successors pause. They waited a year before they abolished the regional economic councils that Khrushchev had set up in 1957; on the grounds that "administrative methods have prevailed over economic ones" and that local pride had resulted in detriment to national interests, they reëstablished central ministries and the authority of the State Planning Commission to regulate investment. However, they left the individual enterprises free to decide for themselves how many workers they would employ, the amount and method of payment of wages, and how to employ the total amount of circulating capital supplied by the state. They had already acted more promptly with respect to the basic ideas advanced by Professor Liberman, to which Khrushchev had given limited approval. In January, 1965, it was announced that about one-fourth of the textile, leather, and other consumer-goods factories would by April 1 begin to operate, not on a preconceived "plan," but on the basis of orders received from enterprises that manufactured clothing and footwear; these, in turn, would from July 1 work on orders received from retail outlets. Bonuses for employees were to depend on the profits of the enterprise. It was expected that this practice would be extended, as rapidly as possible, not only to all light industry, but to heavy industry as well. Matskovich, the Minister of Agriculture whom Khrushchev had dismissed in 1960 and who had promptly been reappointed by the new regime, asked that similar principles be applied to agricultural production also. In September Kosygin announced that in the future all enterprises would be judged, not by their overall volume of production, but by the volume of goods actually sold, and that part of the profit would be used as an incentive to the workers. Regardless of the charge that Khrushchev had overemphasized the production of consumer goods, Kosygin had, in March, 1965, told the State Planning Commission that the next Five-Year Plan was to "insure a more rapid rate of improvement of the people's living standard." [1] The new Five-Year Plan for 1966-1970, approved by the Central Committee (February 19, 1966) and enthusiastically adopted by the Twenty-third Congress, still called for an increased production by heavy industry of 49 to 52 percent, but also provided for a rise of 43 to 46 percent in consumers' goods. This plan, however, was subsequently revised several times. By the end of 1967 about 40 percent of industrial production had been affected by the managerial reform; as a result of this and other factors, notably price changes, the Soviet rulers were able to claim a 10 percent increase in gross industrial production. In 1968 it was planned that for the first time light industry would grow faster than heavy industry; by year's end all industry and transport were to be operating on the new system.

Reform of the economy was being pursued with great caution, however, and over the opposition of the Party bureaucracy. In May, 1968, Baibakov, chairman of Gosplan, flatly rejected pressure from advocates of further liberalization who wanted the introduction of a complete market economy. Yet Baibakov did suggest further decentralization of control and more power for managers to regulate wages in the interest of greater productivity by the workers. On December 10 the finance minister announced a further increase in defence spending, but, simultaneously, Baibakov promised, for the second consecutive year, that the production of consumer goods would rise faster than that of capital goods.

The picture in agriculture remained more gloomy. In March, 1965, Brezhnev reported to the Central Committee that, although Khrushchev's Seven-Year Plan for 1959-1965 had called for a 70 percent increase in agricultural production, the actual rise in the first six years had been only 10 percent. He therefore asked for reduction of the target for purchases of grain by the state from the collective farms at fixed prices from 65.5 million tons to 55.7 million tons, a figure to remain unchanged under the forthcoming Five-Year Plan; other agricultural targets were also to be reduced. Prices paid to producers were to be raised, with due regard to local conditions, and bonuses as high as 50 percent were to be paid for surpluses over plans, without, however, raising prices charged to the consumers. Brezhnev also proposed easing of the debt burden on weak collectives and a shift in the income-tax levy from gross profits to net. In 1965 total agricultural production rose, but, because of the weather, grain output fell below that of 1964. It was therefore necessary to continue heavy imports of wheat, principally from Canada, Australia, and Argentina, which entailed sales of gold more than three times greater than those that had played a role in the fall of Malenkov. Fortunately, 1966 yielded a bumper crop. Yet it was deemed wise (April, 1967) to undertake further reform of the operation of state farms, which account for about 40 percent of marketable output. If agricultural production is combined with industrial production, the overall increase in national income in 1967 was only 6.7 percent. The grain crop was 147.6 million tons, whereas 172 million tons had been produced in 1966. From continued high-level discussion of agricultural problems, it is evident that Russia has not overcome her difficulties.

The "race" for the moon continued, with many firsts for the Russians. Major Gagarin's initial flight into space (1961) was speedily followed by that of the American Colonel Glenn (1962); Colonel Leonov's first "walk in space" (1965) was soon emulated—if not exceeded—by American astronauts. In 1966 both powers effected "soft" landings of instruments on the moon, and on January 26, 1967, the United States, the Soviet Union, the United Kingdom, and two lesser states signed a pact agreeing to purely peaceful uses of outer space. The loss in space accidents of three Americans and of a Russian apparently discouraged the Russians from more manned flights. They succeeded with an unmanned orbiting flight, in securing the first pictures of the back side of the moon; it remained for the United States to send the first men to orbit the moon and to report that the moon appeared to be, if not green cheese, something like plaster of Paris. For their part, the Russians have come to stress the greater economy, without risk of valuable human lives, of relying on instrumental shots and have two unmanned spacecraft headed for "soft" landings on Venus by May, 1969. Of four earlier attempts to reach Venus two succeeded, but only one sent back data before landing (October 18, 1967).

Notwithstanding continued heavy expenditures on "space research," which provoke a certain amount of grumbling among the public, and notwithstanding the cost of nuclear-powered submarines, aircraft carriers, and other military gadgets, the standard of living of the Russian people—and the craving of youth for cars of their own—has undoubtedly continued to rise. It was the Party's claim that, in spite of the grave deficiencies of Khrushchev's Seven-Year Plan (1959-1965), the national income had risen 53 percent and industrial output 84 percent—one of the largest increases being that of 150 percent in sea-going merchant tonnage, which has put the Soviet Union in sixth place in the world. Even housing, it was claimed, had markedly improved, with an increase in floor space of 90 percent over the period 1952-1958, almost equaling total construction of new housing from 1917 to 1958.

LITERATURE AND FREEDOM

In the field of literature, writers had taken wide advantage of Khrushchev's "de-Stalinization," a fact which evidently gave concern to some of his successors. Especially galling to the Party leaders was an increasing tendency to smuggle out writings for publication abroad, a procedure that enhanced their sales value in the West, where they "are being actively used in the ideological struggle against the Soviet Union." In September, 1965, a considerable stir was caused by the arrest of two such offenders, a literary critic named Siniavsky ("Abram Tertz") and a professional translator named Daniel ("Nikolai Arzhak"). It must be acknowledged that "Arzhak's" *Moscow Calling* was indeed (to use one of "Tertz's" titles) a "fantastic tale" and, like the other writings of both men, presented a most unflattering picture of the morals and characterlessness of contemporary Russian youth. Nevertheless, a number of other writers publicly rallied to their defense, and in December a student demonstration demanded a public trial. The trial, nominally public, was held in February, 1966; the culprits, who offered a defiant defense, were sentenced to seven and five years, respectively. Knowledgeable Americans, such as Harold Berman and George Kennan, though deploring the severity of the sentences, have characterized the trial as "genuine" and as a "marked improvement of Soviet judicial treatment for individuals accused of political crimes."[2] Oddly, two days before the trial began, Tarsis, a writer who even in Khrushchev's time had been confined for eight months in a mental institution, was allowed to go to London. There he promptly retracted the remarks he had made in Moscow two days earlier that the accused were "cowards, hypocrites, liars" as a "tactless mistake" and declared his solidarity with them in the struggle against "police fascism"; he was simply deprived of his Soviet citizenship. *Izvestiia* commented that he had been mentally ill for twenty years and that, if the West wanted him, it was welcome to him. In Moscow the whole affair provoked further protests from a considerable number of writers; some atomic scientists, including Kapitsa, joined in a warning to the regime against rehabilitating Stalin.

At the Twenty-third Party Congress, early in 1966, Brezhnev, in his four-and-one-half-hour report on the state of the nation, remarked:

> The Party opposes administration by fiat and arbitrary decision on questions of art and literature. At the same time, we are unfailingly guided by the principle of Party spirit in art and a class approach to the evaluation of everything that is done in the sphere of culture. . . . As is known, there are quite a few difficulties and shortcomings in our country, and truthful criticism of them in works of art is useful and necessary and helps the Soviet people overcome these shortcomings.
>
> Unfortunately we also encounter those tradesmen in the arts who, instead of helping the people, select as their specialty the denigration of our system and

> slander against our heroic people. . . . It is perfectly obvious that the Soviet people cannot overlook the disgraceful activity of such individuals. They treat them as they deserve.[3]

In discussion the First Secretary of the Moscow City Communist Party spelled it out: "Unfortunately, there are some individuals who think not so much about their duty to the people as about something else: What will be said about them abroad?"[4] Particularly vigorous was Sholokhov, whose trilogy, *The Silent Don,* has commanded respect both at home and abroad; after praising the progress of Russian letters in recent years, he added: "We get an entirely different picture when a certain writer publishes one thing here and something completely different abroad. . . . I think it is clear to anyone that there is nothing more blasphemous and loathsome than slandering one's own mother, maliciously insulting her and raising one's hand against her! (Strong, prolonged applause.)"[5]

Notwithstanding occasional other arrests and sentences, protests—even public demonstrations—have continued within the Soviet Union. Most arresting in Western eyes has been the flight of Svetlana Alliluevna, but only because she was Stalin's daughter; her confused childhood memories have, however, shed no valuable light on the political forces at work in the U.S.S.R. during her father's regime. More significant have been the protest of Solzhenitsyn—whose *Day in the Life of Ivan Denisov* had the flavor of stark reality and who sent a public letter to the Writers' Union attacking the principle of censorship—and the activities of a number of youths dissatisfied with the gap between constitutional provisions and actual practice, among whom Litvinov's grandson has been particularly conspicuous. In most cases, such protesters have been deprived of their sources of income but not criminally prosecuted.

The growing new freedom of literary expression, which promises to prove invincible (despite the rear-guard activities of the conservative leadership of the Writers' Union), has been shared by the arts and sciences. The cultural landscape has become infinitely less bleak than in the days of the *Zhdanovshchina* in the late 1940's. True, writers whom Zhdanov would have persecuted are not encouraged; Solzhenitsyn is only one of a number of writers critical of various aspects of the Soviet Union who cannot get his works published in the Soviet Union. But in spite of the growth of reaction in 1968, stimulated by events outside Soviet borders, writers have not been personally molested. In January, 1968, it was still possible for Grigory Svirsky to denounce openly not only the repressive censorship but also the positive encouragement given to defenders of Stalin and to call for a return to the principles of the Twentieth Party Congress (held in 1956). Securing positive support of writers for government policy has become difficult, even at critical moments. In October, 1968, when it was believed desirable that the Soviet Writers' Union publish a statement defending the Russian occupation of Czechoslovakia, it was not possible to find any writer who was not a member of the board of the Union's official *Literaturnaia gazeta* who was willing to sign such a statement (and only 39 of the 42 members did, at that).

INTERNATIONAL DEVELOPMENTS

The nervousness of the present leadership and its sensitivity to foreign reactions—especially those of foreign Communists—are by no means wholly unjustified, for the position of Russia as the supreme leader of "the wave of the future" in the shape of the world Communist movement has been gravely compromised. The evident hope that the removal of Khrushchev might make it possible to heal the rift with China while at the same time adhering to the policy of *détente* with the West speedily proved groundless. Chou En-lai did attend the celebration in Moscow of the forty-seventh anniversary of the Bolshevik Revolution (November, 1964), and polemics in the Chinese press did for a time become more mild. The Soviet Union then postponed the projected World Communist Conference, substituting a preparatory drafting commission to meet in March, 1965, but China refused the invitation to participate, as did also the Communist Parties of Albania, Rumania, North Vietnam, Indonesia, North Korea, and Japan. Under the circumstances the meeting (March 1-5) could do little but condemn the American bombing of North Vietnam, against which Kosygin, then in Hanoi, had warned the United States (February 7, 1965) a few hours before it began; on his way to and from Hanoi, Kosygin stopped off in Peking, where he was coolly received. On March 3 a Chinese student demonstration at the American embassy in Moscow was broken up by the police, resulting in a Chinese attack on its "ruthless suppression." In return (March 29) the Soviet Union complained that China was hampering Russia's supply of military equipment to North Vietnam.

After Mao's announcement (April, 1965) of a "Great Proletarian Culture Revolution" Chinese attacks repeatedly rang the changes on the "revisionist" Soviet "alliance" with "United States imperialism." For months *Pravda* was content to "deplore" these attacks and to persist in appeals for unity; by October, however, it felt compelled to point out that it would be wrong to take the Vietnamese struggle for national liberation out of the hands of the Vietnamese themselves, even apart from the danger of a general thermonuclear war. China, which had already made two nuclear tests (October, 1964, and May, 1965), replied (November 11) that the Soviet Union and the United States were "collaborating . . . to dominate the world," that the Soviet Union was not giving real aid to North Vietnam, and that Kosygin's economic policy had put Russia on the road to restoration of capitalism. *Pravda* indignantly commented (November 16) that the Chinese statement was "full of impermissible, utterly groundless, slanderous, provocative fabrications, permeated with a spirit of hostility toward the Soviet people and toward the Communist Party of the Soviet Union."

Among China's grievances were the facts that the Soviet Union, which had been extending substantial aid to India, had welcomed President Shastri to Moscow in May and, in the fall, to China's great annoyance, had helped him and Ayub Khan of Pakistan to settle their grievances at a meeting in Tashkent. Mrs. Gandhi's visit to Moscow in the middle of 1966 was also to be unwelcome to China.

The war of words between Peking and Moscow did not slacken in 1966; reports of troop movements to the frontiers multiplied, and China exploded two more bombs. By the end of November *Pravda* was accusing China of trying to provoke war between the Soviet Union and the United States; the Chinese reply was that the Soviet Union was plotting with the United States to attack China. By January, 1967, Brezhnev felt it necessary to deny rumors of border clashes, though admitting that "minor Chinese provocations may be expected almost any time." Chinese students, recalled home, engaged with the Soviet police in what China insisted was a brutally bloody brawl in the Red Square. At the beginning of February Russia deemed it wise to fly home the wives and children of its embassy staff in Peking; they were jeered, spat on, and otherwise maltreated at the airport. *Pravda,* however, returned to a lofty attitude, asserting that, despite the antics of the "megalomaniac" Mao, who was fearful of his own people and therefore trying to divert them, the Soviet Union would not take the initiative in breaking off relations, coupled with an appeal for a return to friendship, which has not been forthcoming.

The quarrel with China seriously complicated Soviet relations with the United States. No less than the United States, Russia found herself entangled in ideological positions that no longer have a basis in facts, but from which both powers find it difficult to withdraw. Although it may well be that Russia's leaders probably found a malicious pleasure in the spectacle of American ineptitude in its dealings with Saigon—and still more with the Vietnamese people—and although Russia could not well abandon Southeast Asia to the possibility of Chinese dominance in that area, strong indications of an element of truth can be found in Chinese accusations that the Soviet Union has been anxious to try to help the United States to "find a way out of Vietnam." At the beginning of 1966, on an official visit to Hanoi, Shelepin apparently stressed to Ho Chi-minh—whom the Chinese now regard as a Russian puppet—that a guarantee of representation of the National Liberation Front and a cessation of United States bombing of North Vietnam should be the only prerequisites to the opening of peace negotiations. The Soviet Union cannot, of course, refuse assistance to a "war of national liberation"; Vietnam is not Cuba, and China cannot be wholly ignored. Russia's middle-of-the-road policy has resulted in a growing isolation of Red China, whose "adventurist" policy in Indonesia, on the Indian border, and elsewhere had even by the middle of 1966 cost her most of her early sympathizers among Communist Parties in her dispute with Russia.

In 1967 the Israeli-Arab war provided a convenient "red herring" to permit Russia, with minimum risk, to assert her independence of the United States in foreign policy. She has persistently asserted, as Kosygin did at the United Nations on June 19, that Israel had been encouraged in her "aggression" by "United States imperialists." It also enabled Russia to make Egypt more dependent on the Soviet Union. Notwithstanding Egypt's total defeat, Russia promptly supplied Egypt with fresh arms, thus strengthening Soviet influence in a quarter of the world in which she had long been interested but had been able to make only slight headway. Russia, the "bear that cannot swim," took advantage of thé situation to strengthen her naval forces in the Mediterranean and even to send vessels into the Indian Ocean. Instead of trying to secure from friendly Algeria use of the former French base at Mers el Kebir, Russia has freely used Alexandria, giving rise to grumbles that the Russians are getting more value than they are supplying to Egypt in weapons.

For a time the Soviet Union showed no interest in improving relations between Israel and the Arabs, but the multiplying terrorist raids by Palestinian commandos, Israel's retaliations, and the pressure on Nasser of Egyptian students and army officers have increasingly given Russia cause to worry. She would find it hard to stomach a second defeat for her arms—even though they be wielded by Arabs—and has accordingly embarked on approaches to the United States for joint efforts at securing peace in the Near East. In spite of her fulminations against the Israelis as agents of American imperialism, the Soviet Union has never retracted its commitment to Israel's right to exist. Evidently Russia is content with putting pressure on the Arabs, leaving the United States to deal with Israel. Gromyko visited Nasser (Dec. 22, 1968) apparently to warn him that a reckless Egypt could count on no further Rissian support.

Signs of increasing cautious rapprochement between the Soviet Union and the United States have not been lacking. Kosygin's conferences with President Johnson at Glassboro, N.J. (June, 1967), were apparently cordial and took some of the edge off the new outburst of Russo-American hostility, though, having come to New York to present Russia's views on the Near East at the United Nations, Kosygin had no instructions for other negotiations, and therefore nothing concrete could result. In July, Goldberg and Gromyko agreed at the United Nations to a tentative formula for ending the Arab-Israeli deadlock. It was not, however, submitted, both parties leaving the argument to other would-be mediators. It was not until November 22 that the Security Council accepted—and unanimously—a British-sponsored resolution providing a formula for a settlement. It could not, however, be self-implementing, and its chances of success were dimmed by Israel's suspicious intransigence. Israel's raid on Lebanon's airport (Dec. 28, 1968) and France's prompt cancellation of further military aid to Israel encouraged Russia to make new proposals (Dec. 30) to the United States. Viewed with alarm by Israel, the proposals seem to be more acceptable to Washington and to have strong prospects of leading to greater active intervention by the United Nations.

On other fronts, too, there have been signs of easing tension between the two superpowers." On October 7, 1966, President Johnson had made a veiled offer not to press for reunification of Germany as the price for better relations with the Soviet Union, with the implication that the latter should cease supporting North Vietnam. Premier Kosygin still spoke of the "strange and persistent delusion" that closer cooperation with the United States was possible while the Americans continued their effort in Vietnam. However, as the months passed, President Johnson dropped further broad hints, including a warning by McNamara of the escalation of a new arms race. By March 2, Johnson was able to announce he had received from Kosygin a letter—evidently not intended for publication—expressing willingness to discuss the question. From this point on, matters proceeded with what, considering the magnitude and the intricacies of the problem, must be regarded as remarkable rapidity, notwithstanding the subsequent quarrel over Israel and the Arabs. On August 24, the United States and the Soviet Union submitted at Geneva identical rough drafts of a nuclear nonproliferation treaty, which China promptly denounced as "a gigantic fraud" designed to enable its authors to dominate the world. There were also objections for various reasons, but in a more rational spirit, from India, France, Brazil, and several other states.

In spite of the politically motivated decision made in September to emulate the Russians by establishing a "thin" anti-missile screen, ostensibly directed against China, negotiations continued, and Russia gave some ground on the sensitive question of inspection. Ultimately, a nonproliferation treaty was signed (July 1, 1968) by almost sixty governments, with India conspicuous among those refusing to sign. At this time, the Russian ambassador in London offered a list of nine other topics his government wished to discuss. Most significant among them, as reflecting the changed relationships between the Soviet Union and the United States, was the question of limiting —even of reducing—missile stocks. There was also a hint that Russia might offer a proposal to curb the supply of arms to the Near Eastern combatants.

Even the Vietnam problem began to look as though it might be soluble. During the celebrations of the fiftieth anniversary of the Bolshevik seizure of power, Brezhnev, in a carefully balanced major speech (Nov. 3, 1967), reiterated Russia's violent condemnation of American policy in Vietnam, but made no suggestion of further retaliatory measures and emphasized coexistence as the basis of Russian foreign policy. The submission at Geneva (Jan. 18, 1968) of a joint Russo-American nonproliferation treaty draft, which included concessions to states without nuclear power, had done much to clear the air. Despite the annoyance caused by North Korea's seizure of the American ship *Pueblo* and the alarm following the Tet offensive (launched Jan. 30), Johnson announced on March 31 a significant, though partial, cessation of the bombing of North Vietnam, coupled with an offer of negotiations. At the same time, he announced his firm decision not to accept renomination to the Presidency. The Russian press expressed skepticism at this "maneuver"; the government and Party were silent, as was China. Ho Chi Minh, after some days' hesitation, agreed to send a representative to talk with Averell Harriman. Notwithstanding difficulties, cloaked in almost comical procedural disputes reminiscent of the Peace of Westphalia (1648), talks finally got under way in Paris and ultimately led to agreement, at least in principle, to participation by both the Saigon government and Vietcong representatives. Russia's attitude remained ambivalent. On the one hand, Brezhnev continued to stress, in somewhat ridiculous terms, the growth of revolutionary forces in Europe, citing the French Communist Party as "leading this struggle," and even in America, where he thought "the voice of the working class, the future master of the future United States, was becoming stronger and stronger"; on the other hand, in strange contrast to the bluster (voiced largely, no doubt, for Chinese consumption) was the continued collaboration of the Russian government in the matter of limiting the arms race and, perhaps, quiet pressure behind the scenes to modify the North Vietnamese stand and to counter Castro's dreams of Latin American revolution.

The shock of the Russian invasion of Czechoslovakia (August 21, 1968) fluttered Western dovecotes and, in view of the consequent presence on the German border of more Russian divisions than at any time since 1949, led to consultations about the best—and least provocative—way to revivify NATO, which, as one commentator remarked, had come to mean "Not Always Terribly Organized." The most important results have been the apparent decision to press ahead with production of MIRV (Minuteman III and Poseidon) in order to guarantee continued American superiority in readily deliverable nuclear warheads and, in lower key, to advance the date of the planned demonstration of American ability to fly troops en masse across the Atlantic. In 1968, although the Russians manifested a fairly obvious preference for Hubert Humphrey for the American Presidency, their disappointment may in fact have been the prelude to resumption of improved relations between the world's giants.

On other international fronts the chances for Russia to achieve effective cooperation seemed infinitely less promising than in her relations with the United States. Speaking on November 3, 1967, Brezhnev still extolled the "lasting struggle waged by the best sons of the Chinese Communist Party . . . for the preservation of socialist conquests," but also repeated the condemnation of "Mao Tse-tung and his group" adopted by the Central Committee on December 13, 1966. China, for her part, took every opportunity to criticise the Soviet Union. During the Czechoslovak crisis, while roundly condemning the Czechs for their "revisionism," China accused Russia of acting as a colonial power—and a "fascist" one at that. Shortly afterward Albania, China's most faithful echo, announced her intention of quitting the Warsaw Pact. On the other side of the globe, Cuba, the lone Communist country in the America's, went her own way, heaping scorn on both Russia and China. To be sure, after his Glassboro meeting with Johnson (June, 1967) Kosygin had been careful to pay a duty call upon Castro on his way home. Despite Cuba's economic dependence on Russian purchases of sugar, the Soviet leader was coolly received. Russia has consistently refused to endorse Castro's desire to promote revolutions in Latin America and has compounded her offense by seeking to develop friendly economic relations with anti-Communist South American governments. Cuba sent only a delegation of nonentities to help celebrate the fiftieth anniversary of Bolshevik rule; they did not attend the Kremlin reception and rudely went home early.

PROBLEMS IN THE "SOVIET BLOC"

The Soviet Union has also been experiencing difficulties closer to home. Yugoslavia had in 1965 plunged into economic reforms that went far beyond the cautious steps taken in Russia. She had stayed out of the Russian-dominated Comecon (Council for Mutual Economic Aid) and had joined the World Bank and the International Monetary Fund. In April, 1967, Yugoslavia undertook political reforms designed to give voters some choice among candidates at elections, although she by no means permitted democracy. In January, 1968, free, even heated, debate was permitted on the economic problems that plagued her following an adventurous toying with workers' councils and a "private sector" in the economy. She has tried to cope rationally with the nationality problems that have become entangled in her economic reforms. In spite of the official Russian position that each country has a right to find its own road to socialism, these grave deviations could not, as Tito has publicly admitted, be pleasing to the Russians.

Rumania, too, continued to assert its own national sovereignty. On January 31, 1967, she created a sensation with an agreement with the German government at Bonn for resumption of normal diplomatic relations. In December she announced her intention to launch sweeping economic reforms, the implementation of which, however, has been undertaken with no vigor. A member of Comecon, in May, 1968, she undertook exploration of the possibility of entering the World Bank and ultimately the International Monetary Fund. In March, 1968, Rumania had reluctantly attended a meeting in Budapest to prepare a world conference of Communist parties, defiantly asserting that "the idea of a controlling center has long since been rejected." Unable to secure a promise that international Communism would not seek to criticize national parties, the Rumanian delegation demonstratively walked out. Without undertaking general rehabilitation of victims of persecution she published an official report that certain named individuals had been murdered during the Stalinist regime. Rumania, however, attempted no political liberalization, confining her unorthodoxy mainly to the field of foreign relations.

Far more serious were developments in Czechoslovakia, both because the revolutionary nature of the reforms launched there, amidst great popular enthusiasm, ran counter to Russian orthodoxy, and because Czechoslovakia had a common frontier with Russia's chief bugaboo, the German Federal Republic. As an industrial country and as the only "satellite" that Russia had honored with recognition as a "socialist" state, her defection from the official Russian line might even, if it went too far, endanger the grip of the Russian Party bureaucracy on the Russian people. Moreover, development of genuinely friendly economic relations with the West would gravely impair the value of Russia's chief defensive bastion and drive a dangerous wedge between Russia's necessarily loyal "northern tier"—Poland and the "German Democratic Republic"—and the less reliable Russian satellites in the south.

The beginnings were almost imperceptible in Czechoslovakia. In 1962 Ota Sik, an economist and a Communist, began to advocate economic reforms that would go even further than those suggested in Russia by Liberman. Later, a cultural thaw gradually developed, reaching a point where Party Secretary Novotny's efforts to put a lid on it provoked open, angry protests at a meeting of the Writers' Union (June, 1967). Novotny himself, though an old-liner, had compromised by sanctioning experimentation with Sik's ideas (January, 1967). Hamstrung by unsympathetic bureaucrats, the reform led to price rises without increase in productivity. Sik's protests were countered by conservatives who blamed the reforms themselves, not the hesitance with which they were executed. By the end of 1967, such strong dissatisfaction was manifest on the part both of reforming economists and of writers and students, as well as of nationally-minded Slovaks, that a considerable part of the Party leadership revolted against the compromising Novotny and replaced him (Jan. 6, 1968) as Party Secretary by a forty-six year old Slovak, Alexander Dubcek, who had grown up and been educated in the Soviet Union.

Though Dubcek was extremely cautious, evidently anxious to avoid a repetition of the Hungarian debacle of 1956, he was carried along by a wave of popular enthusiasm and jubilation. Without even waiting for legal authorization, censorship collapsed completely. An unprecedented move was launched for general rehabilitation—with financial compensation—of all who had been persecuted since 1948, though in many cases (notably that of Slansky) it was only their memory that could be affected. Although Brezhnev and other notables attended the celebration in February of the twentieth anniversary of the Communist coup in Czechoslovakia, the Czechs had established by May that responsibility for the legal murder of Slansky (1951) could not be placed on Stalin and Beria alone.

The new Czech regime did not merely probe dark corners of the past. It set about preparing electoral reforms that would enable the voters to choose among Communist candidates and even to vote for certain non-Communist parties. This was, of course, very far from democracy. Dubcek was insistent that the Communist Party continue in the "leading role," but he was careful to distinguish between the Party leadership and the government, and there was virtually no overlap in their personnel. Wide discussion was permitted concerning the course and extent of economic reform.

Concerned with giving the Russians no grounds for interference, Dubcek, while standing squarely on the Russian official doctrine that sanctioned different paths to socialism, stressed his loyalty to the Soviet Union in foreign policy. He promised Czechoslovakia's continuing fidelity to its obligations under the Warsaw Pact (from which Hungary in 1956 had proposed to withdraw). He did, however, argue that changes should be made in the pact's organization to reduce Russian dominance and maintained that the Czechoslovakian army could defend its own border with West Germany without the presence of foreign troops on its soil. General Svobodä, who had succeeded Novotny in the Presidency (March 30, 1968), added a hint that Czechoslovakia intended to work for better relations with the European Economic Community, and even with the United States provided it changed its Vietnam policy. The Russian were naturally as well aware as anyone that promises are easier to make than to keep, but for some months they held their peace. What debates were taking place within the Politburo and how fierce they may have been cannot be known; its members are extraordinarily tight-lipped, going far beyond the British principle of cabinet solidarity.

By April 10, however, Brezhnev, in a report to the Central Committee of the Party, called for a "struggle against bourgeois ideology." About the same time, the Czechs published an "action program," stressing personal liberty (including foreign travel), a "socialist federation" to please the Slovaks, and reduction of security police. While the Czech program put persuasion above compulsion, it still insisted on maintaining the "leading role" of the Communist Party. On May 5 Dubcek made a sudden trip to Moscow where he doubtlessly combatted reports in the Russian press of "anti-Communist hysteria in Prague," but on his return had to tell his people that Warsaw Pact maneuvers, even on Czech soil, might be a "necessary precondition" to military preparedness. The maneuvers were duly held (June 20-30), but the Russian troops lingered on.

For some weeks more the Russians seemed willing to gamble on Dubcek's ability to keep Czech "liberalization" under control. On June 27, however, in the midst of elections to a Fourteenth Party Congress scheduled for September 9, a group of seventy-one intellectuals published a 2,000-word manifesto calling for "public criticism, demonstrations, resolutions, strikes and boycotts to bring down people who have misused power and caused public harm." This call to arms by Czech liberals apparently tipped the balance in the Russian Politburo against further toleration of the situation. Despite apparent concessions won by the Czechs in tough debates with the members of the Russian Politburo at Cierna (July 30-August 1), masses of Warsaw Pact troops, principally Russian, were suddenly and efficiently poured into Czechoslovakia on August 21. Especially in view of the presence of the "maneuver" troops already in the country, armed resistance was clearly unthinkable. Dubcek was carried off to Moscow, but the virtually unanimous, heroic passive resistance of both Czechs and Slovaks baffled the Russians. Unable to find the personnel for a regime that could replace Dubcek, the Russians—evidently still rattled—released him, but with a commitment to "normalization."

Although the Russian troops were moved into closed camps (largely for their own protection against infection), their presence could not be ignored. The reform program was gradually, but steadily, eroded. The censorship was restored, although by no means to full effectiveness. The spirit of the Czechs remained unbroken, though somewhat subdued lest mass arrests might after all be made. On October 18 the National Assembly was constrained, not without protests, to ratify a new treaty with the Soviet Union that *ex post facto* legalized the occupation. Although he apparently still hoped to salvage something of his program, Dubcek had to threaten (December 21) "unavoidable measures" if popular opposition continued; a fortnight later this threat took the form of new press and radio controls. Despite Russian displeasure, however, the federalization of Czechia and Slovakia was carried through (January 1, 1969).

PROBLEMS IN WORLD COMMUNISM

The success of the Russians in the unprecedented Czechoslovak crisis—if indeed it proves in the end to have been a success—was won at the price of the apparent destruction of the Russian leadership of world Communism. Khrushchev's desire to assemble a world Communist conference, even at the price of a complete break with China, had been a factor in his downfall. The failure of the efforts of his successors to effect reconciliation had, by the beginning of 1967, made them anxious to take advantage of Mao's alienation of most of his friends and reassert their own unchallengeable world leadership. Preliminary conferences, the most important of which (at Karlovy Vary, April 24-27) was boycotted by both Yugoslavia and Rumania, as well as by the Dutch and Scandinavian Parties, proved discouraging.

Russia had to hold her golden anniversary celebration (November, 1967) without the fillip that a world Communist conference would have given it. Only China and Albania refused to attend the ceremonies, although the Cubans behaved most ungraciously. The main oration by Brezhnev (Nov. 3) had evidently been carefully edited by his colleagues in the Politburo and offered no new blueprint. A Western commentator noted the contrast between the magnificence of the ballet, opera, music, and the lavish restoration of beautiful old buildings; and the drab realities of living conditions which, although much improved, are still far from good. As someone summed up the celebration, "Suddenly nobody burst out singing."

The effort to "stop the rot" in world Communism was not, however, abandoned. On February 26, 1968, the Russians succeeded in assembling at Budapest delegates from sixty-four Communist Parties, a figure which contrasted with the eighty-one represented at the last world conference, held in Moscow in 1960. Among the absentees was not only China but all the Asian Parties (save for a faction of the Indian Party). Castro's Cuba was not in attendance either. To avoid a certain rebuff, Yugoslavia was not even invited. Rumania and Italy accepted with reluctance, and only on the basis of a guarantee that the conference would concern itself only with procedural matters and that Russia would not feel the need to reëstablish a "guiding international center." The conferees did agree to attend an international conference in Moscow at the end of the year, but only after the Rumanians had stalked out; a subsequent meeting at Budapest (April 24-28) set the date of the conference for November 25.

The military occupation of Czechoslovakia (August 21) imperiled the whole project. Not only the Italians reacted strongly; the French Communist Party, with its long record of support for Russian leadership, was shocked into expressing "surprise and disapproval," especially since its leaders had visited both Moscow and Prague in hopes of finding some basis for settlement of the quarrel. Even after the fact, these two major Western Communist Parties, anxious to win new voters at home, called for withdrawal of the occupation forces. Tito had paid a friendly visit to Prague on August 10, and Rumania's premier, who had strongly defended the right of the Czechs to plot their own course (even if wrong) to socialism, was to have followed on August 22. Instead, the Rumanian met for consultation (August 24) with Tito, who had cancelled army leaves. Under the circumstances it was not difficult to secure unanimity at a meeting (September 30) of the preparatory conference in Budapest "temporarily" postponing the world conference scheduled for November 25 and substituting another meeting of the preparatory commission on November 17.

Tito, although alarmed by a press campaign in Russia that spoke of a "socialist commonwealth," which Tito characterised as the "theory of limited sovereignty," could afford to be defiant, confident that the Russians, however rattled, could not seriously consider undertaking military action against Yugoslavia. Rumania, a member of the Warsaw Pact and therefore threatened by the possibility that the Pact's next "maneuvers" might be held on Rumanian soil, stood by her postion, nevertheless, that however wrong the Czechs might be the Soviet Union's violation of Czech sovereignty was to be condemned.

On the eve of the next meeting in Budapest, Brezhnev, speaking at a Polish Party Congress, defended (November 12) the Russian occupation of Czechoslovakia on the basis of the new theory, difficult to reconcile with the still official doctrine of "different roads to socialism," that when a socialist country, abetted by foreign forces, attempted to return to capitalism, the overriding interests of the "socialist commonwealth" demanded defensive action. This concept, the Soviet Union claimed, did not represent a change in policy.

Aided by the passage of time, at Budapest on November 22, the Soviet Union succeeded in beating the opposition of the Western Parties and forcing agreement of all but three of the sixty-six Parties represented to meet at a world conference in Moscow in May, 1969. However, it was promised that all "anti-imperialist forces" would be invited and that on March 17, 1969 there would be another "preparatory" meeting at which a preliminary policy draft would be submitted for consideration. The extent to which the Russians will be able to reform the shattered Communist ranks on a new basis and prevent the dissension apparent within the Politburo from leading to a domestic upset are the outstanding problems of the immediate future.

* * *

Early in the twentieth century it was still possible to suppose that communism—"from each according to his ability, to each according to his needs"—could be achieved, quickly if not immediately, as the result of a seizure of political power by devoted Communists. Therefore, political ideology seemed of primary importance, and the validity of the theory of permanent revolution could be regarded as crucial. The notion that politics determines economics, however contradictory to the basic philosophic principle of Marxism, could be reconciled with some of Marx's expressed ideas. Put in terms of "consciousness versus spontaneity," it had been the mainspring of Lenin's thinking and had been inherited by his immediate successors.

By the middle of the century, however, it had become clear that the political dictatorship of Communists does not presage the introduction of communism. It had always been known that communism cannot exist unless there is economic abundance; this realization had underlain Lenin's demand, once he was in power, for a "crusade" to increase the productivity of labor and had led to the characteristic, but quite uncommunistic, techniques of the carrot and the stick so freely applied to Soviet labor. The triumph of the "socialist" slogan, "From each according to his abilities, to each according to his labor," deliberately embodied in the "Stalin Constitution" of 1936, left Soviet Russia, despite subjective wishful thinking, objectively further from any approach to the communist principle, "to each according to his needs," than is in many aspects the case in the United States, the United Kingdom, or other Western capitalist states.

The concept of world revolution, to be brought about by any and all means, has never been officially repudiated in the Soviet Union. Yet there have been clear indications that the earlier idea of effecting the desired end by force was steadily and rapidly weakening. The ambition to establish communism on a world scale clearly survives, but the strategy has obviously been changing. Though hampered by old slogans and by inherited ways of thinking, the Soviet Union is evidently seeking a new approach to its old problem.

The changes in the regime since the death of Stalin have not yet been as profound as many expected. There has been an apparently basic commitment to the policy of coexistence with the capitalist world. There has also survived a contradictory revolutionary impulse to support "wars of liberation," although only in ways that entail relatively slight involvement in broader conflict and only in areas where national interests of the Soviet Union might be deemed to be at stake. Given the present "collective leadership," it is more difficult to predict specific Societ policies than if a single individual or clearly united element was at the helm. A complicating factor is the rising generation; at least a quarter of the population has reached maturity since Stalin's death. Most of Soviet youth is clearly disillusioned, apolitical, and frankly materialistic, but the future will lie with the earnest minority. Better educated and less timid than their predecessors, it is possible that they will demand vigorous return to the revolutionary myths with which they have no first-hand acquaintance. It is no less possible that their appreciation of the fact that the Soviet Union, lagging in semi-isolation, is in many ways inferior to the West will make them wish closer contact and more intimate relations with the outside world on the basis of a genuine détente.

So far as the "cold war" sprang, not from ideology, but from the sheer polarity of suspicion between two dominant world powers, no "summit conference" could possibly terminate it. More importantly, however, the very growth of the Soviet Union—and of the world at large—has been increasingly outmoding revolutionary Bolshevik theory. Just as Leninism constituted an adaptation, however disguised, of impractical Marxist doctrine to the facts of life, so also has Leninism been undergoing gradual, if almost imperceptible, erosion under the operation of practical realities. It is, of course, too much to expect that Russia will discard the Marxist jargon for Jeffersonian phrases—or for those of Locke—or that the cumulative heritage of Russian history will permit her to embrace "Anglo-Saxon" tradition. Yet diversity of cultures does not need to mean irreconcilable conflict. The obstacles in the way of intelligent understanding and mutual respect are obviously many, and it is not the proper task of history to prophesy the precise shape of things to come.

NOTES

1. *Planovoie Khoziaistvo* (April 19, 1965).
2. *New York Times,* February 16, 1966, p. 8.
3. *Current Digest of the Soviet Press*, XVIII, No. 12, p. 24.
4. *Ibid.,* No. 13, p. 18.
5. *Ibid.,* No. 16, p. 26.

SUGGESTIONS FOR FURTHER READING

In addition to works previously cited, Lowenthal's *World Communism: The Disintegration of a Secular Faith* and Meyer's *Soviet Political System* are outstanding. Ulam's *The Unfinished Revolution* is also very thoughtful. Brzezinski and Huntington, *Political Power: USA/USSR,* is more narrowly conceived. On Soviet attitudes toward war, see General Pokrovsky's *Science and Technology in Contemporary War,* Garthoff's *Soviet Military Policy,* and Wolfe's *Soviet Strategy at the Crossroads.* A valuable collection of documents dealing with the Czechoslovak crisis may be found in *Studies in Comparative Communism,* Vol. I, Nos. 1 and 2 (July-October, 1968.

Bibliography

(*Russian-language books have been included in this Bibliography only if they are cited in the Notes. English translations of titles are provided in brackets. As explained in the "Note on Russian Dates and Names," page ix, the Library of Congress system of transliterating Russian names has been used.*)

ADENEY, W. F., *The Greek and Eastern Churches,* New York, 1908.

AFANAS'EV, A. N., *Russian Fairy Tales,* trans. by Norbert Guterman, commentary by Roman Jakobson, New York, 1945.

AKSAKOV, I. S., *Ivan Sergeevich Aksakov v ego pis'makh* [Ivan S. Aksakov in his Letters], Moscow, 1886-1896.

Akty istoricheskie sobrannye i izdannye Arkheograficheskoiu-Kommissieiu [Documents Collected and Edited by the Archeographic Commission], 2 vols., St. Petersburg, 1841.

Akty otnosiashchiesia k istorii Zapadnoi Rossii, sobrannye i izdannye Arkheograficheskoiu Kommissieiu . . . [Documents Relating to the History of Western Russia, Collected and Edited by the Archeographic Commission], 5 vols., St. Petersburg, 1846-1853.

Akty sobrannye v bibliotekakh i arkhivakh Rossiiskoi Imperii Arkheograficheskoiu ekspeditsieiu imperatorskoi Akademii nauk [Documents Collected in the Libraries and Archives of the Russian Empire by the Archeographical Expedition of the Imperial Academy of Sciences], 4 vols., St. Petersburg, 1836 (5th vol.—Index—1858).

Alexandre Ier et le prince Czartoryski: Correspondance particulière et conversations, 1801-1823, Paris, 1865.

ALLEN, W. E. D., *The Ukraine: A History,* New York, 1941.

ALPEROVITZ, GAR., *Atomic Diplomacy,* New York, 1965.

ALVAREZ DEL VAYO, J., *Freedom's Battle,* trans. from Spanish, New York, 1940.

ANDERS, GENERAL WLADYSLAW, *Hitler's Defeat in Russia,* Chicago, 1953.

Annals of the American Academy of Political and Social Science, Vol. 263 (May, 1949); Vol. 271 (September, 1950); Vol. 303 (January, 1956).

AN–SKII, S., *"Poslie perevorota 25-go Oktiabria 1917 g."* ["After the Coup of November 25, 1917"], in *Arkhiv russkoi revoliutsii,* VIII (1923), 43-55.

ANTHONY, KATHERINE SUSAN, *Catherine the Great,* New York, 1925; Garden City, N.Y., 1927.

ANTSIFEROV, A. N., AND A. D. BILIMOVICH, *Russian Agriculture During the War* (Carnegie Series on Economic and Social History of the World War), New York, 1930.

Arkhiv kniazia F. A. Kurakina, izdavaemyi pod redaktsieiu M. I. Semevskago [Archive of Prince F. A. Kurakin, edited by M. I. Semevskii], 10 vols., St. Petersburg, 1890-1902.

Arkhiv russkoi revoliutsii [Archive of the Russian Revolution], periodical, Berlin, 1921-1937.

ARMSTRONG, JOHN A., *Ideology, Politics, and Government in the Soviet Union,* New York, 1962.

ASTROV, N. I., AND P. P. GRONSKII, *War and the Russian Government* (Carnegie Series on Economic and Social History of the World War), New Haven, 1929.

AUERBACH, V. A., *"Revoliutsionnoe obshchestvo po lichnym vospominaniiam"* ["Revolutionary Society According to Personal Recollections"], in *Arkhiv russkoi revoliutsii,* XIV (1924), 5-38; XVI (1925), 49-99.

AVRICH, PAUL, *The Russian Anarchists,* Princeton, N.J., 1967.

AVTORKHANOV, ABDURAKHMAN, *The Communist Party Apparatus,* Chicago, 1966.

AVVAKUM, *Zhitie protopopa Avvakuma im samim napisannoe i drugie ego sochineniia* [Life of the Archpriest Avvakum, Written by Himself, and Others of His Works], edited with introduction and notes by N. K. Gudzy], Moscow, 1934.

AZRAEL, JEREMY R., *Managerial Power and Soviet Politics,* Cambridge, Mass., 1966.

BABKIN, B. P., *Pavlov,* Chicago, 1949.

BACKUS, OSWALD P., *Motives of West Russian Nobles in Deserting Lithuania for Moscow, 1377-1514,* Lawrence, Kan., 1957.

BADAEV, A. E., *The Bolsheviks in the Tsarist Duma,* New York, 1937.

BADDELEY, JOHN F., *Russia, Mongolia, and China,* 2 vols., London, 1919.

———, *The Russian Conquest of the Caucasus,* London, 1908.

BAIN, ROBERT N., *The Daughter of Peter the Great: A History of Russian Diplomacy and of the Russian Court Under the Empress Elizabeth Petrovna, 1741-1762,* Westminster, 1899.

———, *The First Romanovs (1613-1725). A History of Moscovite Civilization and the Rise of Modern Russia Under Peter the Great and His Forerunners,* London, 1905.

———, *Peter III, Emperor of Russia,* Westminster, 1902.

———, *The Pupils of Peter the Great: A History of the Russian Court and Empire, 1697-1740,* Westminster, 1897.

———, *Slavonic Europe . . . from 1447 to 1796,* Cambridge, 1908.

BAKUNIN, M. A., *Correspondance de Michel Bakounine; lettres à Herzen et à*

Ogareff (1860-1874), edited by Michel Dragomanov, trans. by Marie Stromberg, Paris, 1896.

———, *Discours prononcés au Congrès de la Paix et de la Liberté à Berne (1868)* . . . , Geneva, 1869.

BALABANOFF, ANGELICA, *Impressions of Lenin,* trans. by Isotta Cesari, Ann Arbor, Mich., 1964.

BALZAK, S. S., *et al., Economic Geography of the Soviet Union,* trans. from Russian, New York, 1949.

BARBOUR, PHILIP L., *Dmitry, Called the Pretender: Tsar and Grand Prince of All Russia, 1605-1606,* Boston, 1966.

BARGHOORN, FREDERICK C., *Soviet Russian Nationalism,* New York, 1956.

BARON, SALO W., *The Russian Jew under Tsars and Soviets* (Russian Civilization Series), New York, 1964.

BARON, SAMUEL H., *Plekhanov: The Father of Russian Marxism,* Stanford, Calif., 1963.

BASS, ROBERT H., and ELIZABETH MARBURY (eds.), *The Soviet-Yugoslav Controversy, 1948-1958: A Documentary Record,* introd. by Hans Kohn, New York, 1959.

BATSELL, WALTER R., *Soviet Rule in Russia,* New York, 1929.

BAUER, RAYMOND A., *The New Man in Soviet Psychology,* Cambridge, Mass., 1952.

———, ALEX INKELES, AND CLYDE KLUCKHOHN, *How the Soviet System Works: Cultural, Psychological, and Social Themes,* New York, 1956.

BAYKOV, ALEXANDER, *Development of the Soviet Economic System: An Essay on the Experience of Planning in the U.S.S.R.,* Cambridge, England, 1950.

BELOFF, MAX, *The Foreign Policy of Soviet Russia, 1929-1941,* 2 vols., London, 1949.

BELOV, FEDOR, *History of a Soviet Collective Farm,* New York, 1955.

BENES, V. L., *et al., The Second Soviet-Yugoslav Dispute: Full Text of Main Documents, April-June, 1958, with an Introductory Analysis,* Bloomington, Ind., 1959.

BERDIAEV, N., *The Origins of Russian Communism,* trans. from Russian, London, 1948.

BERG, LEV S., *Natural Regions of the U.S.S.R.* (1937), trans. from Russian, New York, 1950.

BERGSON, ABRAM, *The Economics of Soviet Planning,* New Haven, Conn., 1964.

———, *Economic Trends in the Soviet Union,* Cambridge, Mass., 1963.

———, *The Real National Income of Soviet Russia Since 1928,* Cambridge, Mass., 1961.

———, *Soviet National Income and Product in 1937* (Studies of the Russian Institute, Columbia University), New York, 1953.

———, *Structure of Soviet Wages: A Study in Socialist Economics* (Harvard Economic Studies, Vol. 76), Cambridge, Mass., 1944.

———(ed.), *Soviet Economic Growth; Conditions and Perspectives* (Arden House conference), New York, 1953.

———, AND HANS HEYMANN, *Soviet National Income and Product, 1940–1948,* New York, 1954.

BERLIN, SIR ISAIAH, *The Hedgehog and the Fox: An Essay on Tolstoy's View of History,* New York, 1953.

BERMAN, HAROLD J., *Justice in the U.S.S.R.: An Interpretation of Soviet Law,* Cambridge, Mass., 1963.

BIELINSKII, VISSARION GREGOR'EVICH, *Polnoe sobranie sochinenii* [Complete Collection of Works], 12 vols., Moscow, 1953-1956.

BIENSTOCK, G., S. M. SCHWARZ, AND A. YUGOW, *Management in Russian Industry and Agriculture,* Ithaca, N.Y., 1944.

BILLINGTON, JAMES H., *The Icon and the Axe: An Interpretive History of Russian Culture,* New York, 1966.

———, *Mikhailovsky and Russian Populism,* New York, 1958.

BIRKE, E., AND R. NEUMANN, *Die Sowjetisierung Ost-Mitteleuropas: Untersuchungen ihres Ablaufs in den einzelnen Ländern,* Vol. I, Frankfurt-am-Main, 1959.

BLACK, CYRIL E. (ed.), *Challenge in Eastern Europe: Twelve Essays,* New Brunswick, N.J., 1954.

——— (ed.), *The Transformation of Russian Society: Aspects of Social Change Since 1861,* Cambridge, Mass., 1960.

BLAKE, PATRICIA, AND MAX HAYWARD (eds.), *Dissonant Voices in Soviet Literature,* New York, 1962.

BLEASE, W. L., *Suvorof,* London, 1920.

BLOOMFIELD, LINCOLN P., WALTER C. CLEMENDS, JR., AND FRANKLIN GRIFFITHS, *Khrushchev and the Arms Race; Soviet Interest in Arms Control and Disarmament 1954-1964,* Cambridge, Mass., 1966.

BLUM, JEROME, *Lord and Peasant in Russia from the Ninth to the Nineteenth Century,* Princeton, N.J., 1961.

BOGOLEPOV, M. I., *"Finansy planovogo khoziaistva"* ["The Finances of Planned Economy"], in *Planovoe khoziaistvo,* 1929, No. 3 (March), 263-285.

BOGOSLOVSKII, M. M., *Oblastnaia reforma Petra Velikago* [Provincial Reform of Peter the Great], Moscow, 1902.

Bol'shaia Sovetskaia Entsiklopediia [Greater Soviet Encyclopedia], 2nd edition, 51 vols. plus supplements, Moscow, 1950-1958.

Bol'shevik. See Kommunist.

BOLSOVER, G. H., "Ivan the Terrible in Russian Historiography," in *Transactions of the Royal Historical Society,* 5th series, Vol. 7 (1957), pp. 71-89, London, 1957.

BOND, SIR EDWARD A. (ed.), *Russia at the Close of the Sixteenth Century. Comprising the Treatise "Of the Russe common wealth," by Dr. Giles Fletcher; and the Travels of Sir Jerome Horsey . . . ,* London, 1856.

BORKENAU, FRANZ, *European Communism,* New York, 1953.

———, *World Communism; A History of the Communist International,* New York, 1939.

BORZAKOVSKII, V. S., *Istoriia Tverskogo kniazhestva* [History of the Principality of Tver], St. Petersburg, 1878.

BOWMAN, HERBERT E., *Vissarion Belinski, 1811-1848: A Study in the Origins of Social Criticism in Russia* (Harvard Studies in Comparative Literature, XXI), Cambridge, Mass., 1954.

BRANDT, CONRAD, B. SCHWARTZ, AND J. K. FAIRBANK, *Documentary History of Chinese Communism,* Cambridge, Mass., 1952.

BRIDGE, ADMIRAL SIR CYPRIAN A. G. (ed.), "History of the Russian Fleet During the Reign of Peter the Great," in *Publications of the Navy Records Society,* Vol. XV, London, 1899.

British Trades-Union Delegation to Russia and Caucasia, 1924, *Russia To-day,* New York, 1925.

BROWDER, ROBERT P., *The Origins of Soviet-American Diplomacy,* Princeton, 1953.

———, AND ALEXANDER F. KERENSKY, *The Russian Provisional Government, 1917: Documents,* 3 vols. (Hoover Institute Publications), Stanford, Calif., 1961.

BROWN, EDWARD J., *Proletarian Episode in Russian Literature, 1928-1932* (Studies of the Russian Institute, Columbia University), New York, 1953.

BROWN, EMILY CLARK, *Soviet Trade Unions and Labor Relations,* Cambridge, Mass., 1966.

BRÜCKNER, A., *"Fürst W. W. Golizyn (1643-1714): Eine Biographische Skizze,"* in *Russische Revue,* XIII (1878), 193-223, 289-320.

———, *Das Kupfergeld 1656-1663 in Russland: Ein Beitrag zur Geschichte der Finanzkrisen,* Riga, 1863.

BRUNDAGE, JAMES A. (intro. & notes), *The Chronicle of Henry of Livonia,* Madison, Wisc., 1961.

BRUSILOV, GENERAL A. A., *Mémoires du General Broussilov: Guerre 1914-1918,* Paris, 1929; trans. as *A Soldier's Note-Book, 1914-1918,* New York, 1931.

BRUTZKUS, B. D., *Economic Planning in Soviet Russia,* London, 1935.

BRZEZINSKI, ZBIGNIEW K., *The Permanent Purge: Politics in Soviet Totalitarianism* (Harvard Russian Research Center Studies XX), Cambridge, Mass., 1956.

———, *The Soviet Bloc: Unity and Conflict* (Russian Research Center Studies, No. 37), Cambridge, Mass., 1960, revised edition, 1967.

———, AND SAMUEL P. HUNTINGTON, *Political Power: USA/USSR,* New York, 1964.

BUCHAN, JOHN (ed.), *The Baltic and Caucasian States,* London, 1923.

BUCHANAN, SIR GEORGE W., *My Mission to Russia and Other Diplomatic Memories,* 2 vols., Boston, 1923.

BUKHARIN, NIKOLAI, *Ekonomika perekhodnogo perioda* [Economics of the Transition Period], Moscow, 1920.

———, AND E. PREOBRAZHENSKII, *The A B C of Communism,* trans. of *Azbuka kommunizma,* Detroit, 1921; also trans. by Eden and Cedar Paul, London, 1927.

BUNYAN, JAMES, *Intervention, Civil War, and Communism in Russia, April-December, 1918: Documents and Materials,* Baltimore, 1936.

———, AND H. H. FISHER, *The Bolshevik Revolution, 1917-1918: Documents and Materials* (Hoover War Library Publications No. 3), Stanford, 1934.

BURNET, GILBERT, *Bishop Burnet's History of His Own Time . . . ,* 2nd edition, 6 vols., Oxford, 1733.

BURY, J. B., "Russia 1462-1682," in Vol. V of *Cambridge Modern History,* New York, 1902-1913.

BUTKOVSKII, V., *Inostrannye kontsessii v narodnom khoziaistve S.S.S.R.* [Foreign Concessions in the People's Economy of the U.S.S.R.], Moscow, 1928.

BUXTON, DAVID R., *Russian Mediaeval Architecture,* Cambridge, England, 1934.

CARLGREN, W. M., *Iswolsky und Aehrenthal vor der Bosnischen Annexionskrise: Russische und Österreichisch-Ungarische Balkanpolitik, 1906-1908,* Upsala, 1955.

Carnegie Series on Economic and Social History of the World War, Russian series. *See* ANTSIFEROV, ASTROV, GOLOVIN, KAYDEN, S. KOHN, NOLDE, ODINETZ, POLNER, P. B. STRUVE, ZAGORSKII, ZAITSEV.

CAROE, OLAF, *Soviet Empire: The Turks of Central Asia and Stalinism,* New York, 1953.

CARR, EDWARD H., *A History of Soviet Russia,* 7 vols., New York, 1951-1964.

———, *The Bolshevik Revolution, 1917-1923,* 3 vols., New York, 1951-1953.

———, *The Interregnum, 1923-1924,* New York, 1954.

———, *Socialism in One Country, 1924-1926,* 3 vols., New York, 1958-1964.

———, *Michael Bakunin,* New York, 1937.

CATHERINE II, *Memoirs of Catherine the Great,* edited by Katherine Anthony, New York, 1927.

———, *Memoirs of Catherine the Great,* edited by Dominique Maroger, introd. by G. P. Gooch, trans. from French, New York, 1955.

CATTELL, DAVID T., *Communism and the Spanish Civil War,* Berkeley, 1955.

———, *Soviet Diplomacy and the Spanish Civil War,* Berkeley, 1957.

CHADWICK, N. K., *Russian Heroic Poetry,* Cambridge, England, 1932.

CHAMBERLIN, WILLIAM HENRY, *Russia's Iron Age,* Boston, 1934.

———, *The Russian Revolution, 1917-1921,* 2 vols., New York, 1935.

CHAPMAN, JANET G., *Real Wages in Soviet Russia Since 1928,* Cambridge, Mass., 1963.

CHERNIAVSKY, MICHAEL, *Prologue to Revolution: The Notes of A. N. Iakhontov on the Secret Meetings of the Council of Ministers, 1915,* Englewood Cliffs, N.J., 1967.

———, *Tsar and People: Studies in Russian Myths,* New Haven, Conn., 1961.

CHERNOV, VICTOR M., *Great Russian Revolution,* trans. and abridged by Philip J. Mosely, New Haven, 1936.

CHERNYSHEVSKII, NIKOLAI G., *Polnoe sobranie sochinenii* [Complete Collection of Works], edited by V. Ya. Kiriapin, B. P. Koz′min, and others, 16 vols., Moscow, 1939-1951.

———, *What Is To Be Done?: Tales About New People,* translated and abridged, New York, 1961.

Chetvertyi S″ezd sovetov rabochikh, soldatskikh, krest′ianskikh, i kazach′ikh deputatov: Stenograficheskii otchet [Fourth Congress of Soviets of Workers, Soldiers, Peasants, and Cossacks Deputies: Stenographic Report], Moscow, 1920.

CHEVIGNY, HECTOR, *Russian America: The Great Alaskan Venture, 1741-1867,* New York, 1967.

CHOISEUL-GOUFFIER, COUNTESS SOPHIE DE, *Historical Memoirs of the Emperor Alexander I and the Court of Russia; Memoirs of Prince Adam Czartoryski,* Chicago, 1900.

CHRISTOFF, PETER K., *An Introduction to Nineteenth-Century Russian Slavophilism: A Study in Ideas,* vol. 1, *A. S. Xomjakov,* Hague, 1961.

CHUIKOV, VASILI I., *The Fall of Berlin,* trans. by Ruth Kisch, New York, 1968.

CHURCHILL, SIR WINSTON, *The Second World War,* 6 vols., New York, 1948-1954 (especially *The Grand Alliance,* Vol. 3).

CLARK, C. U., *Bessarabia: Russia and Roumania on the Black Sea,* New York, 1927.

CLYDE, P. H., *International Rivalries in Manchuria, 1689-1922,* Columbus, Ohio, 1922.

COLLINS, SAMUEL, *The Present State of Russia. In a Letter to a Friend at London; Written by an Eminent Person Residing at the Great Tzar's Court at Moscow for the Space of Nine Years,* London, 1671.

Columbia University, Russian Institute, *The Anti-Stalin Campaign and International Communism,* New York, 1956.

Commission of Inquiry [American] into the Charges Made Against Leon Trotsky in the Moscow Trials: *Not Guilty,* New York, 1937.

CONFINO, MICHEL, *Domaines et seigneurs en Russie vers la fin du XVIIIe siècle; étude de structures agraires et de mentalités economiques,* Paris, 1963.

CONQUEST, ROBERT (ed.), *Soviet Nationalities Policy in Practice,* New York, 1967.

CONSTANTINUS PORPHYROGENITUS, *De Administrando Imperio* (Greek and English), Budapest, 1949.

CONYBEARE, F. C., *Russian Dissenters,* Cambridge, Mass., 1921.

COUNTS, GEORGE S., AND NUCIA P. LODGE, *The Challenge of Soviet Education,* New York, 1957.

———, *The Country of the Blind: The Soviet System of Mind Control,* Boston, 1949.

CRAIG, GORDON A., AND FELIX GILBERT (eds.), *The Diplomats, 1919-1939,* Princeton, 1953.

CRESSEY, GEORGE B., *Asia's Lands and Peoples,* 2nd edition, New York, 1951.

———, *The Basis of Soviet Strength,* New York, 1945; revised as *How Strong is Russia? A Geographic Appraisal,* Syracuse, 1954.

———, *Soviet Potentials: A Geographic Appraisal,* Syracuse, N.Y., 1962.

CRESSON, WILLIAM P., *The Cossacks: Their History and Country,* New York, 1919.

CROSS, SAMUEL H., *Mediaeval Russian Churches,* Cambridge, Mass., 1949.

———, *Slavic Civilization Through the Ages,* Cambridge, Mass., 1948.

——— (ed.), *The Russian Primary Chronicle* (Harvard Studies and Notes in Philology and Literature, Vol. XII), pp. 75-320, Cambridge, Mass., 1930; revised edition by Olgerd P. Sherbowitz-Wetzor, Cambridge, Mass., 1953.

Current Digest of the Soviet Union Press, published by Joint Committee on Slavic Studies, appointed by the A.C.L.S. and S.S.R.C., weekly, Washington, 1949——.

Current Soviet Policies, 4 vols., New York, 1953, 1962. See GRUILOW, L.

CURTIN, JEREMIAH, *The Mongols in Russia,* Boston, 1908.

———, *Myths and Folk-Tales of the Russians, Western Slavs and Magyars,* Boston, 1890.

CURTISS, JOHN S., *Church and State in Russia, 1900-1917,* New York, 1940.

———, *The Russian Army under Nicholas I, 1825-1855,* Durham, N.C., 1965.

———, *The Russian Church and the Soviet State, 1917-1950,* Boston, 1953.

CZARTORYSKI, ADAM J., *Memoirs of Prince Adam Czartoryski and His Correspondence with Alexander I,* 2nd edition, London, 1888.

DALLIN, ALEXANDER, *German Rule in Russia, 1941-1945: A Study of Occupation Policies,* New York, 1957.

DALLIN, DAVID J., *The New Soviet Empire,* New Haven, 1951.

———, *The Rise of Russia in Asia,* New Haven, 1949.

———, *Soviet Russia and the Far East,* New Haven, 1948.

———, *Soviet Russia's Foreign Policy, 1939-1942,* trans. from Russian, New Haven, 1942.

———, AND BORIS I. NIKOLAIEVSKY, *Forced Labor in Soviet Russia,* New Haven, 1947.

DAN, THEODORE, *The Origins of Bolshevism,* edit. and trans. by Joel Carmichael, New York, 1964.

DANIELS, ROBERT VINCENT, *The Conscience of the Revolution: Communist Opposition in Soviet Russia* (Russian Research Center Studies, No. 40), Cambridge, Mass., 1960.

———, *Documentary History of Communism,* New York, 1960.

———, *Red October,* New York, 1967.

DARLINGTON, T., *Education in Russia,* London, 1909.

DAVIES, JOSEPH E., *Mission to Moscow,* New York, 1941.

DAVIES, R. W., *The Development of the Soviet Budgetary System,* New York, 1958.

DEGRAS, JANE (ed.), *The Communist International, 1919-1943,* 3 vols., London, 1956-1965.

———, *Soviet Documents on Foreign Policy, 1917-1941,* 3 vols., New York, 1951-1953.

Dekrety sovetskoi vlasti [Decrees of the Soviet Power], Vol. I, Moscow, 1957.

DENIKIN, ANTON I., *Ocherki russkoi smuty,* 2 vols., Brussels, 1921; trans. as *The Russian Turmoil—Memoirs: Military, Social and Political,* New York, 1922.

———, *The White Army,* London, 1930.

DENISOFF, ELIE, *Maxime le Grec et l'Occident, contribution à l'histoire de la pensee religieuse et philosophique de Michel Trivolis,* Paris, 1943.

DE RODES, *Ausführliche Relation der im Ruszlandt umbgehenden Commercien,* 1653.

DERZHAVIN, GAVRIL, *"Mnenie ob otvrashchenii v Bielorussia goloda i ustroistve byta Evreev"* ["Opinion on Combatting the Famine in White Russia and on the Ordering of the Life of the Jews"], in *Sochineniia* [Works], VII, St. Petersburg, 1878.

DEUTSCHER, ISAAC, *The Prophet Armed: Trotsky, 1879-1921,* New York, 1954.

———, *The Prophet Outcast. Trotsky: 1929-1940,* New York, 1963.

———, *The Prophet Unarmed: Trotsky, 1921-1929,* New York, 1959.

———, *Soviet Trade Unions: Their Place in Soviet Labour Policy,* New York, 1950.

———, *Stalin: A Political Biography,* New York, 1949.

DEWAR, MARGARET, *Labour Policy in the U.S.S.R., 1917-1928,* London, 1956.

DEWITT, NICHOLAS, *Education and Professional Employment in the U.S.S.R.,* Washington, D.C., 1961.

Direktivy KPSS i Sovetskogo pravitel'stva po khoziaistvennym voprosam, 1917-1957. Sbornik dokumentov [Directives of the Communist Party of the Soviet Union and of the Soviet Government on Economic Questions, 1917-1957. Collection of Documents], 4 vols., Moscow, 1957.

DJILAS, MILOVAN, *The New Class: An Analysis of the Communist System,* New York, 1957.

DMYTRYSHYN, BASIL, *Moscow and the Ukraine, 1918-1953: A Study of Russian Bolshevik Nationality Policy,* New York, 1956.

DOBB, MAURICE H., *Soviet Economic Development Since 1917,* New York, 1949.

———, AND H. C. STEVENS, *Russian Economic Development Since the Revolution,* New York, 1928.

Documents on German Foreign Policy. See U.S. Department of State.

Documents on International Affairs, edited by John W. Wheeler-Bennett, *et al.,* annual, London, 1928——.

DOROSHENKO, DMITRO, *Istoriia Ukraini 1917-1923* [History of the Ukraine 1917-1923], 2 vols., Uzhgorod, 1930-1932; New York, 1954.

DRAGOMANOV, M. P., *M. A. Bakunin* (Balashov Edition), St. Petersburg, 1906.

———, *Pis'ma M. A. Bakunina* [Letters of M. A. Bakunin], Geneva, 1896.

DUBNOW, S. M., *History of the Jews in Russia and Poland from the Earliest Times to the Present Day,* 3 vols., Philadelphia, 1916.

Dukhovnye i dogovornye gramoty velikikh i udielnikh kniazei XIV-XVI v. [Wills and Treaties of Grand and Appanage Princes of the Fourteenth to the Sixteenth Century], edited by S. S. Bakhrushin and L. V. Cherepnin, Moscow and Leningrad, 1950.

DVORNIK, FRANCIS, *The Making of Central and Eastern Europe,* London, 1949.

———, *The Slavs in European History and Civilization,* New Brunswick, N.J., 1962.

———, *The Slavs: Their Early History and Civilization,* Boston, 1956.

DYCK, HARVEY L., *Weimar Germany and Soviet Russia, 1926-1933: A Study in Diplomatic Instability,* New York, 1966.

DZERZHINSKI, FELIKS E., *Izbrannye stat'i i rechi, 1908-1926* [Selected Articles and Speeches, 1908-1926], Moscow, 1947.

EASTMAN, MAX, *Artists in Uniform: A Study of Literature and Bureaucratism,* New York, 1934.

ECK, A., *Le moyen âge russe,* Paris, 1933.

ECKHARDT, H. VON, *Russia,* New York, 1932.

EFREMOV, SERGII, *Istoriia Ukrains'kogo pis'menstva,* 2 vols., Wetzlar, 1919-1924.

EHRENBURG, ILYA, *A Change of Seasons,* 2 vols., New York, 1962.

———, "O rabote pisatelia" ["On the Work of a Writer"], in *Znamia,* 1953, No. 10 (October, 1953), pp. 160-183.

EINSIEDEL, HEINRICH VON, *I Joined the Russians: A Captured German Flier's Diary of the Communist Temptation,* New Haven, 1953.

ELNETT, E., *Historic Origin and Social Development of Family Life in Russia,* New York, 1927.

ENGELS, FRIEDRICH, *Origin of the Family, Private Property, and the State,* new edition, New York, 1942.

ERICKSON, JOHN, *The Soviet High Command: A Military-Political History, 1918-1941,* New York, 1962.

ERLICH, ALEXANDER, *The Soviet Industrialization Debate, 1924-1928* (Russian Research Center Studies, No. 4.), Cambridge, Mass., 1960.

ERLICH, VICTOR, *The Double Image: Concepts of the Past in Slavic Literature,* Baltimore, Md., 1964.

ERMOLAEV, HERMAN, *Soviet Literary Theories, 1917-1934: The Genesis of Soviet Realism,* Berkeley, Calif., 1963.

ESKIN, M., *Osnovnye puti razvitiia sotsialisticheskikh form truda* [Basic Ways of Developing Socialist Forms of Labor], Moscow, 1936.

EUDIN, XENIA JOUKOFF, AND ROBERT C. NORTH, *Soviet Russia and the East, 1920-1927: A Documentary Survey* (The Hoover Library on War, Revolution, and Peace, No. 25), Stanford, 1957.

———, AND HAROLD H. FISHER, *Soviet Russia and the West, 1920-1927: A Documentary Survey* (The Hoover Library on War, Revolution, and Peace, No. 26), Stanford, 1957.

FAINSOD, MERLE, *How Russia Is Ruled,* Cambridge, Mass., 1953, revised edition, 1963.

———, *Smolensk Under Soviet Rule,* Cambridge, Mass., 1958.

FAL'KOVSKII, N. I., *Moskva v istorii tekniki* [Moscow in the History of Technology], Moscow, 1950.

FEDOTOV, G. R., *The Russian Religious Mind: Kievan Christianity,* Cambridge, Mass., 1946.

———, *The Russian Religious Mind II: The Middle Ages, the Thirteenth to Fifteenth Centuries,* ed. by John Meyendorff, Cambridge, Mass., 1966.

FEILING, K. G., *Life of Neville Chamberlain,* New York, 1946.

FEIS, HERBERT, *Between War and Peace: The Potsdam Conference,* Princeton, N.J., 1960.

———, *Churchill, Roosevelt, Stalin,* Princeton, 1957.

FENNELL, J. L. I. (ed. and trans.), *The Correspondence between Prince A. M. Kurbsky and Tsar Ivan IV of Russia, 1564-1579, with Russian Text,* New York, 1955.

———, *Ivan the Great of Moscow,* New York, 1961.

——— (ed.), *Prince A. M. Kurbsky's History of Ivan IV,* New York, 1965.

FENNO, R. F. (ed.), *The Yalta Conference,* Boston, 1955.

FERGUSON, ALAN D., AND ALFERD LEVIN (eds.), *Essays in Russian History: A Collection Dedicated to George Vernadsky,* Hamden, Conn., 1964.

FIGNER, VERA N., *Memoirs of a Revolutionist,* New York, 1927.

FISCHER, LOUIS, *The Life of Lenin* (Harper Colophon Books), New York, 1964.

FISCHER, RUTH, *Stalin and German Communism: A Study in the Origins of the State Party,* Cambridge, Mass., 1948.

FISHER, H. H., *Famine in Soviet Russia, 1919-1923: The Operations of the American Relief Administration* (Hoover War Library Publications, No. 5), New York, 1927; Stanford, 1935.

FISHER, MARGUERITE, *Communist Doctrine and the Free World: The Ideology of Communism According to Marx, Engels, Lenin and Stalin,* Syracuse, 1952.

FISHER, R. H., *The Russian Fur Trade, 1550-1700,* Berkeley, 1943.

FISHER, RALPH T., *Pattern for Soviet Youth: A Study of the Congresses of the Komsomol, 1918-1954* (Studies of the Russian Institute, Columbia University), New York, 1959.

FLEMING, D. F. (ed.), *The Changing Cold War,* Philadelphia, Pa., 1964.

———, *The Cold War and Its Origins, 1917-1960,* 2 vols., Garden City, N.Y., 1961.

FLETCHER, GILES (Albert J. Schmidt, ed.), *Of the Rus Commonwealth,* Ithaca, N.Y., 1966.

FORSKREUTER, KURT, *Preussen und Russland von den Anfängen des Deutschen Ordens bis zu Peter dem Grossen,* Göttingen, 1955.

FOSTER, SIR WILLIAM, *England's Quest of Eastern Trade,* New York, 1934.

FOY DE LA NEUVILLE, *Relation curieuse, et nouvelle de Moscovie . . . ,* Paris, 1698.

FRÄHN, C. M., *Ibn-Foszlan's und anderer Araber Berichte über die Russen älterer Zeit,* St. Petersburg, 1823.

FREUND, GERALD, *Unholy Alliance: Russian-German Relations from the Treaty of Brest-Litovsk to the Treaty of Berlin,* New York, 1957.

GALLAGHER, MATTHEW P., *The Soviet History of World War II: Myths, Memories, and Realities,* New York, 1965.

GANKIN, OLGA HESS, AND H. H. FISHER, *The Bolsheviks and the World War: The Origins of the Third International* (Hoover Library on War, Revolution, and Peace, No. 15), Stanford, 1940.

GANTENBEIN, JAMES W. (ed.), *Documentary Background of World War II, 1931-1941,* New York, 1948.

GARDER, MICHEL, *A History of the Soviet Army,* trans. from the French, New York, 1966.

GARTHOFF, RAYMOND L., *Soviet Military Policy: A Historical Analysis,* New York, 1966.

GERSCHENKRON, ALEXANDER, *Economic Backwardness in Historical Perspective: A Book of Essays,* Cambridge, Mass., 1962.

GERTSEN. *See* HERZEN.

GETZLER, IZRAEL, *Martov; A Political Biography of a Russian Social Democrat,* Cambridge, Eng., 1967.

GIBIAN, GEORGE, *Interval of Freedom: Soviet Literature during the Thaw, 1954-1957,* Minneapolis, 1960.

GIDE, ANDRÉ, *Afterthoughts: A Sequel to "Back from the U.S.S.R.,"* London, 1937.

———, *Return from the U.S.S.R.,* trans. from French, New York, 1937; also published as *Back from the U.S.S.R.,* London, 1937.

GIMBUTAS, MARIJA, *The Balts,* New York, 1963.

GLEASON, JOHN H., *The Genesis of Russophobia in Great Britain: A Study of the Interaction of Policy and Opinion,* Cambridge, Mass., 1950.

GOELRO. See *Velikii khoziaistvennyi plan. . . .*

GOETHE, *Sämmtliche Werke, Jubiläums-Ausgabe . . . ,* 40 vols., Stuttgart and Berlin, 1902-1907.

GOETZ, L. K., *Deutsch-russische Handelsgeschichte des Mittelalters,* Lübeck, 1922.

———, *Das Russische Recht,* 4 vols., Stuttgart, 1910-1913.

GOLDER, FRANK A., *Bering's Voyages,* 2 vols., New York, 1922-1925.

———, *Documents of Russian History, 1914-1917,* New York, 1927.

———, *On the Trail of the Russian Famine,* Stanford, 1927.

———, *Russian Expansion on the Pacific, 1641-1850,* Cleveland, 1914.

GOLOVIN, GENERAL N. N., *The Russian Army in the World War* (Carnegie Series on Economic and Social History of the World War), New Haven, 1931.

GOLUBINSKII, E. E., *Istoriia russkoi tserkvi* [History of the Russian Church], 2 vols. in 4, Moscow, 1900-1917.

GOOCH, GEORGE P., *Catherine the Great and Other Studies,* New York, 1954.

GOODALL, G., *Soviet Russia in Maps,* London, 1942 (later revisions), distributed in the United States by Stanley Bowmar Co., New York.

GOODMAN, ELLIOTT R., *Soviet Design for a World State* (Studies of the Russian Institute, Columbia University), New York, 1960.

GORDON, MANYA [Mrs. Simeon Strumsky], *Workers Before and After Lenin,* New York, 1941.

GORIAINOV, S., *Le Bosphore et les Dardanelles,* Paris, 1910.

Gosudarstvennaia Duma, Chetvertyi Sozyv . . . Stenograficheskie otchety [Fourth Imperial Duma . . . Stenographic Reports], St. Petersburg, 1912-1917.

Gosudarstvennoe soveshchanie [The State Conference], (*Tysiacha deviat'sot semnadtsatyi god v dokumentakh i materialakh* [The Year 1917 in Documents and Materials], No. 9), Leningrad and Moscow, 1930.

GOT'E [GAUTIER], YU V. (ed.), *Akty, otnosiashchiesia k istorii Zemskikh Soborov* [Documents Relating to the History of the Zemsky Sobors], (*Pamiatniki russkoi istorii* [Monuments of Russian History], No. 3), Moscow, 1909.

GOURÉ, LEON, *The Siege of Leningrad,* Stanford, Calif., 1962.

GRABAR, IGOR E., *Istoriia russkago iskusstva . . .* [History of Russian Art . . .], 6 vols. in 5, Moscow, *c.* 1909.

GRAHAM, LOREN, *The Soviet Academy of Sciences and the Communist Party,* Princeton, N.J., 1967.

GRANICK, DAVID, *Management of the Industrial Firm in the U.S.S.R.: A Study in Soviet Economic Planning* (Studies of the Russian Institute, Columbia University), New York, 1953.

———, *The Red Executive,* New York, 1960.

GRAVE, B., *Burzhuaziia nakanune fevrial'skoi revoliutsii* [The Bourgeoisie on the Eve of the March Revolution], (*Tysiacha deviat'sot semnadtsatyi god v dokumentakh i materialakh* [The Year 1917 in Documents and Materials], No. 6), Leningrad and Moscow, 1927.

GRAVES, GENERAL WILLIAM S., *America's Siberian Adventure, 1918-1920,* New York, 1931.

GREENBERG, LOUIS, *The Jews in Russia,* 2 vols., London, 1944-1945.

GREENFIELD, KENT R. (ed.), *Command Decisions,* New York, 1959.

GREKOV, B. D., *The Culture of Kiev Rus* (in English), Moscow, 1947.

———, *Pravda Russkaia. Teksty i Kommentarii . . . ,* 2 vols., Moscow and Leningrad, 1940-1947.

GRIERSON, P., *Books on Soviet Russia, 1917-1942,* London, 1943.

GRIFFITH, WM. E. (ed.), *Communism in Europe; Continuity, Change, and the Sino-Soviet Dispute,* 2 vols., New York, 1964-1966.

———, *Sino-Soviet Relations 1964-1965, Analysis and Documents,* Cambridge, Mass.

GRINKO, G. T., *The Five-Year Plan of the Soviet Union: A Political Interpretation,* New York, 1930.

GROSSMAN, GREGORY, *Soviet Statistics of Physical Output of Industrial Commodities: Their Compilation and Quality,* Princeton, N.J., 1960.

GRULIOW, LEO (ed.), *Current Soviet Policies*
Vol. I: *The Documentary Record of the 19th Party Congress and the Reorganization After Stalin's Death,* New York, 1953.
Vol. II: *The Documentary Record of the 20th Party Congress and its Aftermath,* New York, 1957.
Vol. III: *Documentary Record of the Extraordinary 21st Congress of the Communist Party,* New York, 1960.
Vol. IV: *Documentary Record of the 22nd Congress of the Communist Party of the Soviet Union,* New York, 1962.

GUDZY, N. K. (ed.), *Zhitie protopopa Avvakuma im samim napisannoe i drugie ego sochineniia* [The Life of the Archpriest Avvakum, Written by Himself, and Others of His Works], with introduction and notes, Moscow, 1934.

GUERNEY, B. G., *A Treasury of Russian Literature,* New York, 1943.

GUILLAUME, GENERAL AUGUSTIN, *La guerre germano-sovietique, 1941-1945,* Paris, 1949.

GUKOVSKII, A. I., *Frantsuskaia Interventsiia na iuge Rossii, 1918-1919 g.g.* [French Intervention in the South of Russia, 1918-1919], Moscow, 1928.

GURIAN, WALDEMAR (ed.), *Soviet Imperialism: Its Origins and Tactics. A Symposium,* Notre Dame, Ind., 1953.

———, *The Soviet Union: Background, Ideology, Reality. A Symposium,* Notre Dame, Ind., 1951.

HAIMSON, LEOPOLD H., "The Problem of Social Stability in Urban Russia, 1905-1917," *Slavic Review,* vol. 23, December, 1964; Vol. 24, March, 1965.

———, *The Russian Marxists and the Origins of Bolshevism,* Cambridge, Mass., 1955.

HAKLUYT, RICHARD, *The Principal Navigations, Voyages, Traffique and Discoveries of the English Nation,* Vol. I, New York, 1903.

HALECKI, O., *History of Poland,* New York, 1943.

HALLE, LOUIS J., *The Cold War as History,* New York, 1967.

HAMMOND, THOMAS T., *Lenin on Trade Unions and Revolution, 1893-1917* (Studies of the Russian Institute, Columbia University), New York, 1957.

——— (ed), *Soviet Foreign Relations and World Communism: A Selected Annotated Bibliography of 7,000 Books in 30 Languages,* Princeton, N.J., 1965.

HANS, N. A., *History of Russian Educational Policy, 1701-1917,* London, 1931.

———, *The Russian Tradition in Education,* New York, 1963.

———, AND S. HESSEN, *Educational Policy in Soviet Russia,* London, 1930.

HARBRON, JOHN D., *Communist Ships and Shipping,* New York, 1963.

HARCAVE, SIDNEY, *First Blood: The Russian Revolution of 1905,* New York, 1964.

HARD, W., *Raymond Robins' Own Story,* New York, 1920.

HARDWICK, CHARLES, *A History of the Articles of Religion,* 3rd edition, London, 1876.

HARE, RICHARD, *Pioneers of Russian Social Thought: Studies of Non-Marxian Formation in Nineteenth-Century Russia and of Its Partial Revival in the Soviet Union,* New York, 1951.

HARPER, SAMUEL N., *Civic Training in Soviet Russia,* Chicago, 1929.

———, *Government of the Soviet Union,* New York, 1938.

———, *New Electoral Law for the Russian Duma,* Chicago, 1908.

HARRISON, J., AND H. MIRLEES, *The Life of the Archpriest Avvakum. By Himself,* London, 1924.

HAUMONT, E., *La Culture française en Russie,* Paris, 1910.

HAVILAND, M. D., *Forest, Steppe and Tundra; Studies in Animal Environment,* New York, 1926.

HAZARD, JOHN N., *The Soviet System of Government,* 3rd. ed. revised, Chicago, 1964.

———, AND ISAAC SHAPIRO, *The Soviet Legal System: Post-Stalin Documentation and Historical Commentary* (Parker School Studies in Foreign and Comparative Law), Dobbs Ferry, N.Y., 1962.

HECKER, JULIUS F., *Russian Sociology,* New York, 1915.

HERBERSTEIN, FREIHERR SIGMUND VON, *Notes upon Russia,* 2 vols., London, 1851-1852.

HERODOTUS, *History,* Rawlinson translation, Everyman edition, I, New York, 1910.

HERZEN, ALEKSANDR I., *From the Other Shore and The Russian People and Socialism,* New York, 1956.

———, *My Past and Thoughts, the Memoirs of Alexander Herzen* . . . authorized trans. by Constance Garnett, 6 vols., New York, 1924-1928.

———, *Polnoe sobranie sochinenii i pisem* [Complete Collection of Works and Letters], Lemke edition, 22 vols., Moscow, 1919-1925.

———, *Sobranie sochinenii v tridsati tomakh* [Collection of Works in Thirty Volumes], Moscow, 1954———. Vol. VII includes *"Le peuple russe et le socialisme."*

HILGER, GUSTAV, AND ALFRED G. MAYER, *The Incompatible Allies: A Memoir-History of German-Soviet Relations, 1918-1941,* New York, 1953.

HILL, CHARLES E., *Danish Sound Dues and the Command of the Baltic: A Study of International Relations,* Durham, N.C., 1926.

HINDUS, MAURICE, *Broken Earth,* New York, 1926.

———, *The Great Offensive,* New York, 1933.

———, *Humanity Uprooted,* New York, 1930.

———, *Red Bread,* New York, 1931.

History of the Communist Party of the Soviet Union (Bolsheviks), Short Course, New York, 1939; new edition (in English), Moscow, 1952.

HODGKINS, JORDAN A., *Soviet Power: Energy Resources, Production and Potentials,* Englewood Cliffs, N.J., 1961.

HOFFMANN, MAX, *Der Krieg der versäumten Gelegenheiten,* Münich, 1924; trans. as *The War of Lost Opportunities,* London, 1924, and included in *War Diaries and Other Papers,* London, 1929.

HOFMANN, R., *Un Siècle d'opéra russe,* Paris, 1946.

HOLZMAN, FRANKLYN D., *Soviet Taxation: The Fiscal and Monetary Problems of a Planned Economy,* Cambridge, Mass., 1955.

HORECKY, PAUL L. (ed.), *Basic Russian Publications: An Annotated Bibliography on Russia and the Soviet Union,* Chicago, 1962.

———, *Russia and the Soviet Union: A Bibliographic Guide to Western-Language Publications,* Chicago, 1965.

HOSTLER, CHARLES W., *Turkism and the Soviets: The Turks of the World and Their Political Objectives,* New York, 1957.

HOWES, ROBERT C., *Testaments of the Grand Princes of Moscow,* Ithaca, N.Y., 1967.

HOWORTH, H. H., *History of the Mongols from the 9th to the 19th Century,* 3 vols., London, 1876-1927.

HRUSHEVSKY, M. S., *A History of the Ukraine,* New Haven, 1941.

———, *A History of Ukraine-Rus,* 10 vols., New York, 1954-1958.

HUBBARD, LEONARD E., *The Economics of Soviet Agriculture,* London, 1939.

———, *Soviet Labour and Industry,* London, 1942.

———, *Soviet Money and Finance,* New York, 1936.

———, *Soviet Trade and Distribution,* New York, 1938.

L'Humanité; organe central du Parti communiste français, daily newspaper, Paris, suppressed after issue of August 25, 1939.

HUNT, R. N. CAREW (ed.), *Books on Communism: A Bibliography,* New York, 1960.

IAKHONTOV. *See* YAKHONTOV.

IAKOVLEV. *See* YAKOVLEV.

IGNATOVICH, I. I., *Pomeshchichi krest'iane nakanune osvobozhdeniia* [The Landlords' Peasants on the Eve of Emancipation], St. Petersburg, 1902.

IKONNIKOV, V. S., *"Blizhnyi boiarin A. L. Ordin-Nashchokin"* ["Privy Boyar A. L. Ordin-Nashchokin"], in *Russkaia Starina,* XL (1883), 17-66, 273-308.

Informatsionnoie soveshchanie predstaviteli nekotorykh kompartii v Polshe v kontse sentiabria 1947 goda [Informational Conference of Representatives of Several Communist Parties in Poland at the End of September, 1947], Moscow, 1948.

INKELES, ALEX AND RAYMOND A. BAUER, *The Soviet Citizen: Daily Life in a Totalitarian Society,* Cambridge, Mass., 1959.

IPATIEFF [IPAT'EV], V. N., *The Life of a Chemist* (Hoover Library on War, Revolution, and Peace, No. 21), Stanford, 1946.

Istorik Marksist: zhurnal [The Marxist Historian: A Journal], edited by M. N. Pokrovskii to 1932; originally quarterly, later bimonthly and monthly; Moscow, 1926-1941.

Iz istorii Vserossiiskoi chrezvychainoi komissii, 1917-1921 gg.: sbornik dokumentov [From the History of the All-Russian Extraordinary Commission, 1917-1921: Collection of Documents], Moscow, 1958.

Izvestiia [News], official daily newspaper founded February 28 (March 13), 1917, as *Izviestiia Petrogradskogo Sovieta rabochikh deputatov* [News of the Petrograd Soviet of Workers' Deputies]; subtitle frequently changed, now *Izvestiia sovetov deputatov trudiashchiksia* [News of the Soviets of Toilers' Deputies]; originally Petrograd, moved to Moscow in March, 1918.

IZVOLSKY, A. P., *Recollections of a Foreign Minister,* Garden City, N.Y., 1921.

JACOBSON, HAROLD KARAN, *The USSR and the UN's Economic and Social Activities,* Notre Dame, Ind., 1963.

JAKOBSON, MAX, *The Diplomacy of the Winter War: An Account of the Russo-Finnish War, 1939-1940,* Cambridge, Mass., 1961.

JASNY, NAUM, *Essays on the Soviet Economy,* New York, 1962.

———, *Khrushchev's Crop Policy,* Glasgow, 1965.

———, *The Socialized Agriculture of the U.S.S.R.: Plans and Performance,* Stanford, Calif., 1949.

———, *Soviet Industrialization, 1928-1952,* Chicago, 1961.

JELAVICH, BARBARA, *A Century of Russian Foreign Policy, 1814-1914* (The Lippincott History Series), Philadelphia, Pa., 1964.

JENKINSON, ANTHONY, *Early Voyages and Travels to Russia and Persia,* 2 vols., London, 1886.

JOHNSON, WILLIAM H. E., *Russia's Educational Heritage: Teacher Education in the Russian Empire, 1600-1917,* Pittsburgh, 1950.

JORAVSKY, DAVID, *Soviet Marxism and Natural Science, 1917-1932* (Studies of the Russian Institute, Columbia University), New York, 1961.

JORDANES, *Gothic History* (Mierow translation), Princeton, 1915.

JUTIKKALA, EINO, *A History of Finland,* trans. by Paul Sjöblon, New York, 1962.

JUVILER, PETER H. (ed.), *Soviet Policy Making: Studies of Communism in Transition,* New York, 1967.

KAMINSKI, HANNS ERICH, *Michel Bakounine, la vie d'un revolutionnaire,* Paris, *c.* 1938.

KAPLAN, HERBERT H., *The First Partition of Poland,* New York, 1962.

———, *Russia and The Outbreak of the Seven Years' War,* Berkeley, Calif., 1968.

KAPTEREV, N. F., *Kharakter otnoshenii Russii k pravoslavnomu Vostoki v XVI i XVII stolietiiakh* [The Character of the Relations of Russia to the Orthodox East in the Sixteenth and Seventeenth Centuries], Sergiev-Posad, 1914.

———, *Patriarkh Nikon i Tsar' Aleksiei Mikhailovich,* 2 vols., Sergiev-Posad, 1909-1912.

KARPOVICH, M., *Imperial Russia, 1801-1917,* New York, 1932.

KATKOV, GEORGE, *Russia 1917: The February Revolution,* New York, 1967.

KATKOV, M. N., *Sobranie peredovykh statei Moskovskikh Viedomostei, 1863-1887 god* [Collection of Leading Articles in the *Moscow Record*], 25 vols., Moscow, 1897-1898.

KAUTSKY, JOHN H., *Moscow and the Communist Party of India: A Study in the Postwar Evolution of International Communist Strategy,* Cambridge, Mass., 1956.

KAYDEN, E. M., *Coöperative Movement in Russia During the War* (Carnegie Series on Economic and Social History of the World War), New Haven, 1929.

KEEP, JOHN L. H., *The Rise of Social Democracy in Russia,* New York, 1963.

KENDRICK, THOMAS D., *A History of the Vikings,* New York, 1930.

KENNAN, GEORGE F., *Russia and The West under Lenin and Stalin,* Boston, 1961.

———, "The Sources of Soviet Conduct," in *Foreign Affairs,* Vol. XXV, No. 4 (July, 1947), pp. 566-582; published under the pseudonym "Mr. X."

———, *Soviet-American Relations, 1917-1920;* Vol. 1, *Russia Leaves the War;* Vol. 2, *The Decision to Intervene;* Princeton, 1956-1958.

KERENSKII, ALEXANDR F., *The Catastrophe: Kerensky's Own Story of the Russian Revolution,* New York, 1927.

———, *Crucifixion of Liberty,* trans. from Russian, New York, 1934.

———, *Russia and History's Turning Point,* New York, 1965.

KERNER, R. J., *Slavic Europe: A Selected Bibliography in the Western European*

Languages, Comprising History, Languages, and Literatures, Cambridge, Mass., 1918.

———, *The Urge to the Sea: The Course of Russian History,* Berkeley, 1942.

KERTESZ, STEPHEN D., *Diplomacy in a Whirlpool: Hungary Between Nazi Germany and Soviet Russia,* Notre Dame, Ind., 1953.

———, *The Fate of East Central Europe: Hopes and Failures of American Foreign Policy* (International Studies of the Committee on International Relations), Notre Dame, Ind., 1956.

KHRUSHCHEV, NIKITA S., *For Victory in Peaceful Competition with Capitalism,* New York, 1960.

"Kilburgers Unterricht von dem russischen Handel, wie solcher mit aus- und eingehenden Waaren 1674 durch ganz Ruszland getrieben worden," in *Büschings Magazin für die Neue Historie und Geographie,* III (1769).

KINDERSLEY, RICHARD, *The First Russian Revisionists: A Study of Legal Marxism in Russia,* New York, 1962.

KINGSBURY, ROBERT C., AND ROBERT N. TAAFFE, *An Atlas of Soviet Affairs,* paper, New York, 1965.

KIRCHNER, WALTHER, *Rise of the Baltic Question,* Newark, Del., 1954.

KIRPOTIN, V., *"O nizkopoklonstve pered kapitalisticheskim zapadom, ob Aleksandre Veselovskom, o ego posledovateliakh i o samon glavnom"* ["On Servility Before the Capitalist West, on Alexander Veselovskii, on His Followers, and on the Main Point"], in *Oktiabr',* January, 1948, pp. 3-27.

———, *"Ob otnoshenii russkoi literatury i russkoi kritiki k kapitalisticheskomu Zapadu"* ["On the Relation of Russian Literature and of Russian Criticism to the Capitalist West"], in *Oktiabr',* September, 1947, pp. 161-182.

KISH, GEORGE, *Economic Atlas of the Soviet Union,* Ann Arbor, Mich., 1960.

KLIUCHEVSKII, V. O., *Kurs russkoi istorii,* 3rd edition, 4 vols., Petrograd and Moscow, 1923, with fifth volume (1762-1855) based on student notes, Petrograd, 1921; also 5 vols. (ACLS Russian Reprint Project Series), Ann Arbor, 1948; trans. (in garbled form) as *A History of Russia,* 5 vols., New York, 1911-1931; new translation of vol. III, with introduction by Alfred J. Rieber (Quadrangle Series in Russian History), Chicago, 1968; portion of Vol. IV available in new translation as *Peter the Great,* New York, 1959.

KLYUCHEVSKY. *See* KLIUCHEVSKII, *above.*

KOCHAN, LIONEL, *Russia and the Weimar Republic,* Cambridge, England, 1954.

KOESTLER, ARTHUR, *The Yogi and the Commissar, and Other Essays,* New York, 1945.

KOHN, HANS, *Nationalism in the Soviet Union,* trans. from German, New York, 1933.

———, *Pan-Slavism: Its History and Ideology,* Notre Dame, Ind., 1953.

——— (ed.), *The Mind of Modern Russia: Historical and Political Thought of Russia's Great Age,* New Brunswick, N.J., 1955.

KOHN, S., AND BARON A. F. MEYENDORFF, *Cost of the War to Russia: The Vital Statistics of European Russia During the World War, 1914-1917,* by Stanislas Kohn; *Social Cost of the War,* by Baron Alexander F. Meyendorff (Carnegie Series on Economic and Social History of the World War), New Haven, 1932.

KOKOVTSOV, V. N., *Out of My Past,* ed. by H. H. Fisher (Hoover War Library Publications, No. 6), Stanford, 1935.

KOLARZ, WALTER (ed.), *Books on Communism: A Bibliography,* New York, 1964.
———, *Peoples of the Soviet Far East,* New York, 1954.
———, *Russia and Her Colonies,* New York, 1953.
KOLKOWICZ, ROMAN, *The Soviet Military and the Communist Party,* Princeton, N.J., 1967.
KOLLONTAI, ALEXANDRA, *Semiia i Kommunisticheskoe Gosudarstvo* [The Family and the Soviet State], Moscow, 1919, trans. as *Communism and the Family.*
Kommunist: teoreticheskii i politicheskii zhurnal TsK Kommunisticheskoi partii SSSR [Communist: Theoretical and Political Journal of the Central Committee of the Communist Party of the U.S.S.R.], semimonthly (under name of *Bol'shevik* 1924 to 1952), 1952——.
Kommunisticheskaia Partiia Sovetskogo Soiuza v rezoliutsiiakh i resheniiakh s''ezdov, konferentsii i plenumov TsK, 1898-1953 [The Communist Party of the Soviet Union in Resolutions and Decisions of Congresses, Conferences, and Plenums of the Central Committee], 7th edition, 3 vols., Moscow, 1954.
Kommunisticheskii Internatsional v dokumentakh: resheniia, tezisy i vozzvaniia kongressov Kominterna i plenumov IKKI, 1919-1932 [The Communist International in Documents: Decisions, Theses, and Appeals of Congresses of the Comintern and of Plenums of the Executive Committee of the Communist International, 1919-1932], edited by Bela Kun, Moscow, 1933.
KOMPANEYETS, A. S., *Physics in the Soviet Union: An Exposition of Theoretical Physics,* trans., New York, 1962.
KOMROFF, MANUEL (ed.), *The Contemporaries of Marco Polo,* New York, 1928.
KONCEVIČIUS, J. B., *Russia's Attitude Towards Union with Rome, Ninth to Sixteenth Centuries,* Washington, 1927.
KONDAKOV, N. P., *The Russian Icon,* trans. by E. H. Minns, Oxford, 1927.
KORBEL, JOSEF, *Communist Subversion of Czechoslovakia, 1938-1948: The Failure of Coexistence,* Princeton, 1959.
KORDT, V. A. (ed.), *"Otchet Al'berta i Iogana van Feltdrilia o posol'stvie ikh v Rossiiu v 1630 i 1631 gg. s prilozheniem Ocherka snoshenii Moskovskogo gosudarstva s respublikoiu Soedinennykh Niderlandov do 1631 g."* ["Report of Albert and John van Feltdril on Their Embassy to Russia in 1630-1631, with an Outline of the Relations of the Muscovite State with the Republic of the United Netherlands to 1631"], in Russkoe Istoricheskoe Obshchestvo, *Sbornik,* Vol. CXVI, St. Petersburg, 1902.
KORNILOV, ALEKSANDER, *Modern Russian History,* 2 vols. in 1, trans. and continued by A. Kaun, New York, 1924.
KOSTIUK, HRYHORY, *Stalinist Rule in the Ukraine: A Study of the Decade of Mass Error, 1929-1939* (Institute for the Study of the USSR, Series I, No. 47), Munich, 1960.
KOTOSHIKHIN, GREGORY KARPOVICH, *O Rossii v tsarstvovanie Aleksieia Mikhailovicha . . .* [On Russia in the Reign of Alexis Mikhailovich . . .], 4th edition, St. Petersburg, 1906.
KOTSEVALOV, A., *Soviet Studies of Ancient Slavery and Slave Uprisings* (in Russian, with English summary), Münich, 1956.
KOVALEVSKY, M. M., *Russian Political Institutions,* Chicago, 1902.
KOVALEVSKY, P. E., *Manuel d'histoire russe: étude critique des sources et exposé historique d'après les recherches les plus récentes,* Paris, 1948.

KRAMISH, ARNOLD, *Atomic Energy in the Soviet Union,* Stanford, Calif., 1959.

Krasnaia Kniga V.Ch.K. [Red Book of the All-Russian Extraordinary Commission], edited by P. Makintsian, Moscow, 1920.

Krasnaia Letopis′: istoricheskii zhurnal [Red Chronicle: A Historical Journal], an official Party periodical, Moscow, 1922-1936.

Krasnaia Nov′: zhurnal khudozhestvennoi literatury, kritiki i publitsistiki. Organ Soiuza sovetskikh pisatelei RSFSR [Red Virgin Soil: Journal of Artistic Literature, Criticism, and Publicism. Organ of the Union of Soviet Writers of the RSFSR], originally bimonthly, monthly from 1926; Moscow, 1921-1942.

KRASNOV, GENERAL P. N., *"Na vnutrennem fronte"* ["On the Home Front"], in *Arkhiv russkoi revoliutsii,* I, 1921.

Krasnyi Arkhiv: istoricheskii zhurnal [Red Archive: An Historical Journal], published irregularly by Tsentral′nyi Arkhiv RSFSR [Central Archive of the RSFSR], Moscow, 1922-1941.

Krasnyi Arkhiv, A Digest of the Krasnyi Arkhiv, compiled, trans., and annotated by Leonid S. Rubinchek. Edited by Louise M. Boutelle and Gordon W. Thayer, Cleveland, 1947.

KRAVCHINSKII, S. M. ["Stepniak"], *Underground Russia: Revolutionary Profiles and Sketches from Life,* preface by P. Lavrov, trans. from Italian, New York, 1883.

KRIZHANICH, YURY, *Russkoe gosudarstvo v polovine XVII vieka. Rukopis′ vremen Tsaria Aleksieia Mikhailovicha* [The Russian State in the Middle of the Seventeenth Century. A Manuscript of the Times of Tsar Alexis], edited by P. Bezsonov, 2 vols. in 1, Moscow, 1859-1860.

KROPOTKIN, PRINCE PETER A., *Memoirs of a Revolutionist,* New York, 1899.

KRYPTON, CONSTANTINE, *The Northern Sea Route: Its Place in Russian Economic History Before 1917,* New York, 1953.

KUBIJOVYC, VOLODYMYR (ed.), *Ukraine: A Concise Encyclopedia* (prepared for the Ukrainian National Association), Toronto, 1963.

KULCZYCKI, L., *Geschichte der russischen Revolution,* trans. from Polish, 3 vols., Gotha, 1910-1914.

KULISCHER, J., *Russische Wirtschaftsgeschichte* [Vol. I, Jena, 1925], translation of KULISHER, IOSIF M., *Istoriia russkogo narodnogo khoziaistva* [History of the Russian People's Economy], 2 vols. in 1, Moscow, 1925.

KURAKIN, B. I., *"Gistoriia o tsarie Petrie Aleksievichie 1682-1694,"* in *Arkhiv kn. F. A. Kurakina,* St. Petersburg, 1890, I, 41-78.

KURBSKII, A. M., *Istoriia o velikom kniazie Moskovskom* [History of the Grand Prince of Moscow], St. Petersburg, 1913; for trans. *see* Fennell.

KUSNIERZ, BRONISLAW, *Stalin and the Poles: An Indictment of the Soviet Leaders,* London, 1949.

LA FEBER, WALTER, *America, Russia and the Cold War, 1949-1960,* New York, 1967.

LAMPERT, E., *Sons Against Fathers: Studies in Russian Radicalism and Revolution,* New York, 1965.

LANG, DAVID M., *The Last Years of the Georgian Monarchy, 1658-1832* (Studies of the Russian Institute, Columbia University), New York, 1957.

LANGER, WILLIAM L., *Franco-Russian Alliance, 1890-1894,* Cambridge, Mass., 1929.

LANTZEFF, G. V., *Siberia in the Seventeenth Century: A Study of Colonial Administration,* Berkeley, 1943.

LARIN [LURIE], YU., *"God bor'by u kolybeli"* ["Year of Struggle at the Cradle"], in *Narodnoe khoziaistvo,* No. 11 (November 7, 1918), pp. 1, 16-23.

LASERSON, MAX M., *The American Impact on Russia: Diplomatic and Ideological, 1784-1917,* New York, 1950.

——— (ed.), *The Development of Soviet Foreign Policy in Europe, 1917-1942: A Selection of Documents,* International Conciliation, January, 1943, No. 386.

LATKIN, V. N. (ed.), *Proekt novago ulozheniia sostavlennyi zakonodatel'noi komissiei 1754-1766 gg.* [Draft of a New Law Code Composed by the Legislative Commission of 1754-1766], St. Petersburg, 1893.

LATSIS [SUARABS], MARTIN I., *Chrezvychainye Komissii po bor'be s kontr-revoliutsiu* [Extraordinary Commissions for the Fight Against Counter-revolution], Moscow, 1921.

LAVRENT'EV, VLADIMIR N., *Zarabotnaia plata v Rossii prezhde i teper'* [Wages in Russia Formerly and Now], 2nd edition, Moscow, 1926.

LAVROV, PETER L. [pseudonym of P. L. Mirtov], *Istoricheskiia pis'ma,* 2nd edition, St. Peterburg, 1905; cf. *Historische Briefe,* Berlin, 1901; *Lettres historiques,* Paris, 1903; and *Historical Letters,* Berkeley, Calif., 1967.

League of Nations Official Journal, Special Supplement 154, Geneva, 1936.

LEAHY, FLEET ADMIRAL WILLIAM D., *I Was There,* New York, 1950.

LEDNICKI, WACLAW, *Russia, Poland and the West: Essays in Literary and Cultural History,* New York, 1954.

LEITES, NATHAN, *A Study of Bolshevism,* Glencoe, Ill., 1953.

LELEVICH, G. [Laborii G. Kalmanson], *V dni Samarskoi uchredilki,* [In the days of the Samara Constitutional Assembly], Moscow, 1921.

LENIN, V. I., *Collected Works,* completely revised, edited, and annotated, New York, 1927-1942. See especially Vol. 4, *The Iskra Period 1900-1902,* 2 vols., 1929; Vol. 13, *Materialism and Empirio-Criticism: Critical Notes Concerning a Reactionary Philosophy, 1927;* Vol. 18, *The Imperialist War: The Struggle Against Social-Chauvinism and Social-Pacifism, 1914-1915, c.* 1930; Vol. 19, *1916-1917;* Vol. 20, *The Revolution of 1917, From the March Revolution to the July Days,* 2 vols., *c.* 1929; Vol. 21, *Toward the Seizure of Power: The Revolution of 1917, from the July Days to the October Revolution,* 2 vols., 1933; Vol. 23, *1918-1919.*

———, *Sobranie sochinenii* [Collected Works], ed. by L. B. Kamenev, 19 vols. in 4, Moscow, 1920-1923.

———, *Sochineniia, Izd. 2* [Works, 2nd edition], 30 vols., Moscow and Leningrad, 1926-1932.

———, *Sochineniia, Izd. 3* [Works, 3rd edition], 30 vols., Moscow and Leningrad, 1928-1937; a reprint of the text of the 2nd edition; this is the edition cited in Notes in this book.

———, *Sochineniia, Izd. 4* [Works, 4th edition], 38 vols., Moscow and Leningrad, 1941-1958.

———, *Polnoe sobranie sochinenii, Izd. 5* [Complete Collection of Works, 5th edition], 56 vols., Moscow, 1958-1966.

Leninskii Sbornik, 35 vols., Moscow, 1924-1945.

LENSEN, GEORGE ALEXANDER, *The Russian Push Toward Japan: Russo-Japanese Relations, 1697-1875,* Princeton, N.J., 1959.

LEONARD, RICHARD A., *A History of Russian Music,* London, 1956.

LEONTOVITSCH, VICTOR, *Geschichte des Liberalismus in Russland,* Frankfurt-am-Main, 1957.

LEROY-BEAULIEU, A., *L'empire des tsars et les russes,* 3 vols., Paris, 1881-1889; trans. by Z. A. Ragozin as *The Empire of the Tsars and the Russians,* 3 vols., New York, 1893-1896.

LEVIN, ALFRED, *The Second Duma: A Study of the Social-Democratic Party and the Russian Constitutional Experiment,* New Haven, 1940, 2nd ed., Hamden, Conn., 1966.

LEVITATS, ISSAC, *The Jewish Community in Russia, 1772-1844,* New York, 1943.

LEYDA, JAN, *Kino: A History of the Russian and Soviet Film,* London, 1964.

LIASHCHENKO, P. I., *History of the National Economy of Russia to the 1917 Revolution,* trans. from Russian, New York, 1949.

LIDDELL HART, B. H. (ed.), *The Soviet Army: The Red Army, 1918-1945; The Soviet Army, 1946 to the Present,* London, 1956; same, under title *The Red Army,* New York, 1956.

LINEFF, E., *The Peasant Songs of Great Russia* (in English and Russian), St. Petersburg and London, 1905.

Literaturnaia Gazeta [Literary Gazette], periodical organ of Pravlenie Soiuza sovetskikh pisatelei [Board of the Union of Soviet Writers], Moscow, January 6, 1942 to November, 1944, when merged with *Sovetskoe iskusstvo* [Soviet Art] to form *Literatura i iskusstvo* [Literature and Art].

LITVINOV, MAXIM, *Against Aggression: Speeches, Together with Texts of Treaties and of the Covenant of the League of Nations,* New York, 1939.

LIUBIMENKO, INNA I., "Letters Illustrating the Relations of England and Russia in the Seventeenth Century," in *English Historical Review,* XXXII (January, 1917), 125.

LOBANOV-ROSTOVSKY, A., *Russia and Asia,* New York, 1933; revised edition, Ann Arbor, 1951.

———, *Russia and Europe, 1789-1825,* Durham, N.C., 1947.

———, *Russia and Europe, 1825-1878,* Ann Arbor, 1954.

LOCKHART, R. H. B., *British Agent,* New York, 1933; originally *Memoirs of a British Agent, Being an Account of the Author's Early Life in Many Lands and of His Official Mission to Moscow in 1918,* New York, 1932.

LONDON, KURT, *The Seven Soviet Arts,* trans. by Eric S. Bensinger, New Haven, 1938.

LORD, ROBERT H., *Second Partition of Poland: A Study in Diplomatic History,* Cambridge, Mass., 1915.

LOSSKY, N. O., *History of Russian Philosophy,* New York, 1951.

LOW, ALFRED D., *Lenin on the Question of Nationality,* New York, 1958.

LOWENTHAL, RICHARD, *World Communism: The Disintegration of a Secular Faith,* New York, 1964.

LUBIMENKO, I., *Les Relations commerciales et politiques de l'Angleterre avec la Russie avant Pierre le Grand,* Paris, 1933.

LUCKYJ, GEORGE S. N., *Literary Politics in the Soviet Ukraine 1917-1934* (Studies of the Russian Institute, Columbia University), New York, 1955.

LUNDIN, C. LEONARD, *Finland in the Second World War,* Bloomington, Ind., 1957.

LUR-SALUCE, *Lomonosov, le prodigieux moujik,* Paris, 1933.

LYASHCHENKO. *See* LIASHCHENKO.

LYDOLPH, PAUL E., *Geography of the U.S.S.R.,* New York, 1964.

MADARIAGA, ISABEL DE, *Britain, Russia, and the Armed Neutrality of 1780: Sir James Harris's Mission to St. Petersburg during the American Revolution,* New Haven, Conn., 1962.

MAGNUS, LEONARD (ed.), *Heroic Ballads of Russia,* London, 1921.

———, *Tale of the Armament of Igor,* London, 1915.

MAICHEL, KAREL, AND J. S. G. SIMMONS, *Guide to Russian Reference Books,* 2 vols., Stanford, Calif., 1962-1964.

MAKARII, MITROPOLIT MOSKOVSKII [Metropolitan of Moscow], *Istoriia russkoi tserkvi* [History of the Russian Church], 12 vols., Moscow, 1868-1883.

MALIA, MARTIN, *Alexander Herzen and the Birth of Russian Socialism, 1812-1855* (Russian Research Center Studies, No. 39), Cambridge, Mass., 1961.

MANDEVILLE, SIR JOHN, *Travels,* London, 1923.

MARRIOTT, J. A. R., *Anglo-Russian Relations, 1689-1943,* London, 1944.

MARTENS, F. F., *Sobranie Traktatov i Konventsii zakliuchennykh Rossieiu s inostrannami derzhavami* (alternative title: *Recueil des Traités et Conventions conclus par la Russie avec les puissances étrangères*), 12 vols., St. Petersburg, 1874-1909; see especially *Tom IX (X) Traktaty c Angleiu 1710-1801,* 1892.

MARTOV [TSEDERBAUM], IULII O., *Geschichte der russischen Sozialdemokratie,* trans. from 3rd edition of *Istoriia rossiiskoi sotsial demokratii* [History of Russian Social Democracy], Berlin, 1926.

MARX, KARL, AND FRIEDRICH ENGELS, *Manifesto of the Communist Party,* new edition (in English), Moscow, 1948.

MASARYK, T. G., *The Spirit of Russia,* 2 vols., London, 1915 (2nd printing, New York, 1955), trans. by Eden and Cedar Paul from *Russland und Europa: Studien über die geistigen Strömungen in Russland, Zur russischen Geschichts- und Religions-philosophie soziologische Skizzen,* 2nd edition, Jena, 1913.

MASSA, ISSAC, *Histoire des guerres de la Muscovie (1601-1610),* written 1610; first published in Brussels, 1866.

MASTERSON, JAMES R., AND HELEN BROWER, *Bering's Successors, 1745-1780: Contributions of Peter Simon Pallas to the History of Russian Exploration Toward Alaska,* Seattle, 1948.

MASUDI, *El-Masudi's Historical Encyclopedia (Meadows of Gold and Mines of Gems),* trans. from the Arabic by Alois Sprenger, Vol. 1, London, 1841.

MATTHEWS, WILLIAM K., *Languages of the U.S.S.R.,* Cambridge, England, 1951.

———, *Structure and Development of Russian,* Cambridge, England, 1953.

MAURICE, MAJOR, chapter on "Russo-Japanese War," in *Cambridge Modern History,* vol. XII, New York, 1910.

MAVOR, JAMES, *An Economic History of Russia,* 2 vols., New York, 1925.

MAYER, ARNO J., *Wilson vs. Lenin: Political Origins of the New Diplomacy, 1917-1918,* Cleveland, 1964.

MAYNARD, SIR J., "Light on the Trotskyist Trials," in *The Political Quarterly*, Vol. VIII, July, 1937.

———, *Russia in Flux: Before October*, London, 1941; abridged as *Russia in Flux*, New York, 1948.

MAZOUR, ANATOL G., *The First Russian Revolution, 1825: The Decembrist Movement, Its Origins, Development, and Significance*, Berkeley, 1937.

———, *Modern Russian Historiography: An Outline of Modern Russian Historiography*, Berkeley, 1939; revised as *Modern Russian Historiography*, Princeton, 1958.

MCCONNELL, ALLEN, *A Russian* Philosophe: *Alexander Radishchev, 1749-1802*, Hague, 1964.

MCGOVERN, W. M., *The Early Empires of Central Asia*, Chapel Hill, N.C., 1939.

MCGREW, RODERICK E., *Russia and the Cholera, 1823-1832*, Madison, Wisc., 1965.

MCLANE, CHARLES B., *Soviet Policy and the Chinese Communists, 1931-1946* (Studies of the Russian Institute, Columbia University), New York, 1958.

MCLEAN, HUGH, MARTIN E. MALIA, AND GEORGE FISHER (eds.), *Russian Thought and Politics* (Harvard Slavic Studies, Vol. IV), Cambridge, Mass., 1957.

MCNEILL, WILLIAM H., *America, Britain, and Russia: Their Co-operation and Conflict, 1941-1946*, New York, 1953.

MEDLIN, WILLIAM K., *Moscow and East Rome: A Political Study of the Relations of Church and State in Muscovite Russia* (*Études d'histoire économique, politique, et sociale*, No. 1), Geneva, 1952.

———, CLARENCE B. LINDQUIST, AND MARSHALL L. SCHMITT, *Soviet Education Programs*, Washington, D.C., 1960.

MEISEL, J. H., AND E. S. KOZERA (eds.), *Materials for the Study of the Soviet System*, 2nd ed., Ann Arbor, 1953.

MEISSNER, BORIS, *The Communist Party of the Soviet Union; party leadership, organization, and ideology*, New York, 1956.

MENDEL, ARTHUR P., *Dilemmas of Progress in Tsarist Russia: Legal Marxism and Legal Populism* (Russian Research Center Studies, No. 43), Cambridge, Mass., 1961.

MESHCHERIAKOV, V. N., *Derevenskaia biednota i put' k cotsializury* (*O selsko-khoziaistvennykh kommunakh*) [On Agricultural Communes], Petrograd, 1918.

MEYENDORFF, JOHN, *The Orthodox Church: Its Past and Its Role in the World Today*, trans. from French by John Chapin, New York, 1962.

MEYER, ALFRED G., *Communism*, New York, 1960.

———, *Leninism* (Harvard Russian Research Center Studies, No. 26), Cambridge, Mass., 1957.

———, *The Soviet Political System: An Interpretation*, New York, 1965.

MICHAEL, F. H., AND G. E. TAYLOR, *The Far East in the Modern World*, New York, 1956.

MICHELL, ROBERT, AND NEVILL FORBES, "The Chronicle of Novgorod," in *Royal Historical Society Publications, Camden Third Series*, Vol. XXV, London, 1914.

MIKOLAJCZYK, STANISLAW, *The Rape of Poland: Pattern of Soviet Aggression*, New York, 1948.

MILIUKOV, P. N., *Essais sur l'histoire de la civilisation russe* [Ocherki po istorii russkoi kul'tury], 3 vols., St. Petersburg, 1904, abridged English translation by M. Karpovich, Philadelphia, Pa., 1942.

———, *Russia and Its Crisis,* Chicago, 1905.

———, C. SEIGNOBOS, AND L. EISERMANN, *Histoire de Russe,* 3 vols., Paris, 1932-1933.

MILLER, MARGARET S., *The Economic Development of Russia, 1905-1914,* London, 1926.

MILLER, WILLIAM, *Ottoman Empire, 1801-1913,* New York, 1913.

MINNS, E. H., *Scythians and Greeks,* New York, 1913.

Mirnye peregovory v Brest-Litovske [Peace Negotiations at Brest-Litovsk], Moscow, 1920.

MIRSKY, D. S., *A History of Russian Literature, Comprising a History of Russian Literature and Contemporary Russian Literature,* New York, 1949.

———, *Russia: A Social History,* London, 1942.

MITCHELL, MAIRIN, *The Maritime History of Russia, 848-1948,* New York, 1950.

MOLOTOV, VIACHISLAV M., *Soviet Peace Policy: Four Speeches,* London, 1941.

———, *What Is Stakhanovism?,* New York, 1936.

MONAS, SIDNEY, *The Third Section: Police and Society in Russia Under Nicholas I* (Russian Research Center Studies, No. 42), Cambridge, Mass., 1961.

MONNEROT, JULES, *Sociology and Psychology of Communism,* trans. from French, Boston, 1953.

MONTAGU-NATHAN, M., *A History of Russian Music,* London, 1918.

MOORE, HARRIET L., *Soviet Far Eastern Policy, 1931-1945,* Princeton, 1945.

MOOSER, R. A., *Annales de la musique et des musiciens en Russie au XVIII siècle,* Geneva, 1948.

MORDVINOV, ACADEMICIAN, "Reconstruction of Towns and Art Problems Confronting Soviet Architecture," in *Voks Bulletin,* 1944, #9-10.

MORLEY, CHARLES, *Guide to Research in Russian History,* Syracuse, 1951.

MORLEY, JAMES W., *The Japanese Thrust into Siberia, 1918* (Studies of the Russian Institute, Columbia University), New York, 1957.

MOSELY, P. E., *Russian Diplomacy and the Opening of the Near Eastern Question in 1838 and 1839,* Cambridge, England, 1934.

——— (ed.), *The Soviet Union, 1922-1962: A Foreign Affairs Reader,* New York, 1963.

MOSSE, W. E., *Alexander II and the Modernization of Russia* ("Teach yourself history," ed. by A. L. Rowse), New York, 1958.

———, "Stolypin's Villages," *Slavonic Review,* vol. 43, London, June, 1965.

MOUSSET, ALBERT, *The World of the Slavs,* trans. from French, revised edition, New York, 1950.

NAGY, FERENC, *The Struggle Behind the Iron Curtain,* trans. from the Magyar, New York, 1948.

Narodno-khoziaistvennyi plan za 1937 g. [The People's Economic Plan for the Year 1937], Moscow, 1937.

Narodnoe khoziaistvo: organ Vyshago soveta narodnago khoziaistva [The People's Economy: Organ of the Supreme Council of People's Economy], Moscow, 1918-1922; continued by *Sotsialisticheskoe khoziaistvo: zhurnal ekonomi-*

cheskoi politiki, finansov i gosudarstvennogo khoziaistva [Socialist Economy: Journal of Economic Policy, Finances, and State Economy], Moscow, to 1930.

Nazi-Soviet Relations, 1939-1941. See U.S. DEPARTMENT OF STATE.

NECHKINA, M. V. (ed.), *Russia in the Nineteenth Century,* trans. from Russian, Ann Arbor, 1952.

NEVSKII, *Istoricheskoe zasedanie peterburgskogo komiteta R.S.-D.R.P.(B) nakanunie oktiabr'skogo vosstaniia* [Historic Meeting of the Petersburg Committee of the R.S.D.W.P.(B) on the Eve of the November Uprising], in *Krasnaia Letopis',* 1922, No. 3, pp. 316-332.

NEWMARCH, R., *The Russian Arts,* London, 1916.

———, *The Russian Opera,* London, 1914.

NIEDERLE, LOUIS, *Manuel de l'Antiquité Slave,* 2 vols., Paris, 1923, 1926.

———, *La Race Slave, Statistique, Démographie, Anthropologie,* trans. from the Czech by Louis Leger, Paris, 1911.

NIKOLAEVSKY, BORIS I., *Power and the Soviet Elite: "The Letter of an Old Bolshevik," and other Essays* (for the Hoover Institution on War, Revolution, and Peace), New York, 1965.

NIKOLAI, MITROPOLIT, *Slova i rechi* [Words and Speeches], Moscow, 1950.

NOGEE, JOSEPH L., *Soviet Policy towards International Control of Atomic Energy,* Notre Dame, Ind., 1961.

NOLDE, B. E., *Russia in the Economic War* (Carnegie Series on Economic and Social History of the World War), New Haven, 1929.

NOLDE, BORIS, *La formation de l'Empire Russe: Études, Notes, et Documents,* 2 vols., Paris, 1952-1953.

Novaia Zhizn' [New Life], daily newspaper edited by Maxim Gorky, Petrograd and later Moscow, 1917-1918.

NOVE, ALEC, *The Soviet Economy: An Introduction* (Minerva Series of Students' Handbooks, No. 5), New York, 1961.

Novyi mir: literaturno-khudozhestvennyi i obshchestvenno-politicheskii zhurnal [New World: Literary-Artistic and Social-Political Journal], monthly, edited originally by A. V. Lunarcharskii, Moscow, from 1925.

NOWAK, F., *Medieval Slavdom and the Rise of Russia,* New York, 1930.

NUTTER, G. WARREN, *Growth of Industrial Production in the Soviet Union,* Princeton, N.J., 1962.

O'BRIEN, C. BICKFORD, *Muscovy and the Ukraine: From the Pereiaslavl Agreement to the Truce of Andrusovo, 1654-1667,* Berkeley, Calif., 1963.

Obshchestvo istorii i drevnostei Rossiiskikh pri moskovskom universitetie [Society of Russian History and Antiquities at the University of Moscow], *Chteniia v imperatorskom obshchestve* [Lectures at the Imperial Society], Moscow, 1845-1918.

Ocherki istorii SSSR: Period feodalizma. Rossiia vo vtoroi polovine XVIII v. [Outlines of the History of the U.S.S.R.: Period of Feudalism. Russia in the Second Half of the Eighteenth Century], Moscow, 1956.

ODINETZ, D. I., AND M. P. NOVGOROTSEV, *Russian Schools and Universities in the World War* (Carnegie Series on Economic and Social History of the World War), New Haven, 1929.

Official Documents Concerning Polish-German and Polish-Soviet Relations, 1933-1939, London, 1940.

Oktiabr': literaturno-khudozhestvennyi i obshchestvenno-politicheskii zhurnal Vsesoiuznoi i Moskovskoi assotsiatsii proletarskikh pisatelei [October (i.e., November, 1917); Literary-Artistic and Socio-Political Journal of the All Union and Moscow Association of Proletarian Writers], Moscow and Leningrad, from 1925.

OKUNE, S. B., *The Russian-American Company,* trans. from Russian (1939), Cambridge, Mass., 1951.

OLEARIUS, ADAM, *The Voyages and Travels of the Ambassadors from the Duke of Holstein, to the Great Duke of Muscovy, and the King of Persia . . . ,* trans. by John Davies, London, 1662.

["Pahlen Report"], *Obshchaia zapiska vysshei komissii dlia peresmotra dieistvuiushchikh o evreiakh v imperii zakonov, 1883-1888* [General Memorandum of the High Commission for Review of the Existing Laws About the Jews in the Empire, 1883-1888], Moscow, 1888.

PALÉOLOGUE, MAURICE, *The Enigmatic Czar: The Life of Alexander I of Russia,* trans. from French, New York, 1938.

———, *La Russie des tsars pendant la grande guerre,* 3 vols., Paris, 1921-1922, trans. as *An Ambassador's Memoirs,* 3 vols., London, 1925.

PALMER, W., *The Patriarch and the Tsar,* 6 vols., London, 1871-1876.

Pamiatniki diplomaticheskikh snoshenii drevnei Rossii s derzhavami inostrannymi [Monuments of the Diplomatic Relations of Ancient Rus with Foreign Powers], 10 vols., St. Petersburg, 1851-1871.

Pamiatniki diplomaticheskikh snoshenii Moskovskago gosudarstva s Angliei [Monuments of Diplomatic Relations of the Muscovite State with England], in Russkoe Istoricheskoe Obshchestvo, *Sbornik,* Vol. 38.

Pamiatniki drevnei russkoi pis'mennosti otnosiashchiesia k smutnomu vremeni [Monuments of Ancient Russian Literacy Relating to the Time of the Troubles], (*Russkaia istoricheskaia biblioteka* [Russian Historical Library] XIII) St. Petersburg, 1891.

PANKRATOVA, A., *Fabzavkomy Rossii v bor'be za sotsialisticheskuiu fabriku* [The Factory-Shop Committees of Russia in the Fight for a Socialist Factory], Moscow, 1923.

PARES, SIR BERNARD, chapters on "Reaction and Revolution in Russia" and "Reform Movement in Russia," in *Cambridge Modern History,* Vol. XII, New York, 1910.

———, *Russia and Reform,* London, 1908.

PARK, ALEXANDER G., *Bolshevism in Turkestan, 1917-1927* (Studies of the Russian Institute, Columbia University), New York, 1957.

PARRY, ALBERT, *The New Class Divided: Science and Technology Versus Communism,* New York, 1966.

———, *Russia's Rockets and Missiles,* Garden City, N.Y., 1960.

PASKIEWICZ, HENRYK, *The Making of the Russian Nation,* London, 1963.

———, *The Origin of Russia,* London, 1954.

PASVOLSKY, LEO, *Russia in the Far East,* New York, 1922.

PAVLOVSKY, G., *Agricultural Russia on the Eve of the Revolution,* London, 1930.

PAVLOVSKY, M. N., *Chinese-Russian Relations,* New York, 1949.

Peace and War. See U.S. DEPARTMENT OF STATE.

PERRY, CAPTAIN JOHN, *The State of Russia Under the Present Czar,* London, 1716.

Pervyi Vserossiiskii S"ezd Professionalnykh Soiuzov, Polnyi stenograficheskii otchet [First All-Russian Congress of Trade Unions: Complete Stenographic Report], preface by M. Tomskii, Moscow, 1918.

Pervyi Vserossiiskii S"ezd sovetov rabochikh i soldatskikh deputatov, Stenograficheskii otchet [First All-Russian Congress of Soviets of Workers' and Soldiers' Deputies, Stenographic Report] (*Tysiacha deviat'sot semnadtsatyi god v dokumentakh i materialakh* [The Year 1917 in Documents and Materials], No. 10), Leningrad and Moscow, 1930-1931.

Petrogradskii sovet rabochikh i soldatskikh deputatov: Protokoly zasedanii [The Petrograd Soviet of Workers' and Soldiers' Deputies: Protocols of Meetings], to June 17 (30) (*Tysiacha deviat'sot semnadtsatyi god v dokumentakh i materialakh* [The Year 1917 in Documents and Materials] 1), Leningrad and Moscow, 1925.

PETROVICH, MICHAEL B., *The Emergence of Russian Panslavism, 1856-1870* (Studies of the Russian Institute, Columbia University), New York, 1956.

PHILIPP, WERNER, *"Ivan Peresvetov und seine Schriften zur Erneuerung des Moskauer Reiches,"* in *Osteuropäische Forschungen,* Vol. XX, Königsberg, 1935.

Piatiletnyi Plan narodnokhoziaistvennogo stroitel'stva SSSR [The Five-Year Plan of Building the People's Economy of the U.S.S.R.], 2nd edition, Moscow, 1929.

Piatyi Vserossiiskii S"ezd Sovetov, Stenograficheskii otchet [Fifth All-Russian Congress of Soviets: Stenographic Report], Moscow, 1918.

PIERCE, RICHARD A., *Russia's Hawaiian Adventure, 1815-1817,* Berkeley, Calif., 1965.

———, *Russian Central Asia, 1867-1917: A Study in Colonial Rule* (Russian and East European Studies), Berkeley, Calif., 1960.

PIONTKOVSKII, S., *Khrestomatiia po istorii Oktiabr'skoi revoliutsii* [Reader on the History of the November Revolution], 3rd edition, Moscow, 1926.

PIPES, RICHARD, *The Formation of the Soviet Union: Communism and Nationalism, 1917-1923,* Cambridge, Mass., 1954.

———, *Social Democracy and the St. Petersburg Labor Movement, 1885-1897,* Cambridge, Mass., 1963.

———, *Karamzin's Memoir on Ancient and Modern Russia. A Translation and Analysis,* Cambridge, Mass., 1959.

PISAREV, DMITRI I., *Sochineniia* [Works], 6 vols., St. Petersburg, 1894; 4 vols., Moscow, 1955.

Planovoe khoziaistvo [Planned Economy], periodical published by Gosplan (State Planning Commission), Moscow, from 1924.

PLATONOV, S. F., *Boris Godunov* (in Russian), Prague, 1924. French translation as *Boris Godounov,* Paris, 1929.

———, *Ivan Groznyi* [Ivan the Terrible], Petrograd, 1923.

———, *K istorii moskovskikh zemskikh soborov* [Toward a History of the Moscow Zemsky Sobors], St. Petersburg, 1905.

———, *Lektsii po russkoi istorii* [Lectures on Russian History], 10th edition, Petrograd, 1917.

———, *Smutnoe vremia* [The Time of the Troubles], St. Petersburg, 1923.

PLOSS, SIDNEY I., *Conflict and Decision-Making in Soviet Russia: A Case Study of Agricultural Policy, 1953-1963* (Sponsored by the Princeton Center of International Studies), Princeton, N.J., 1965.

POBIEDONOSTSEV, K. P., *Reflections of a Russian Statesman,* trans. by R. C. Long, London, 1898.

POKROVSKII, MAJ.-GEN. G. I., *Science and Technology in Contemporary War,* trans. and annotated by R. L. Garthoff, New York, 1959.

POKROVSKII, M. N., *Brief History of Russia from the Earliest Times,* 2 vols., Moscow, 1920; English trans. of 10th (1931) edition, London, 1933.

———, *Russkaia istoriia s drevneishikh vremen* [Russian History from the Earliest Times], 7th edition, 4 vols., Moscow, 1924-1925; first two vols. trans. and ed. by J. D. Clarkson and M. R. M. Griffiths as *History of Russia from the Earliest Times to the Rise of Commercial Capitalism,* New York, 1931.

POLNER, I. I., *et al., Russian Local Government During the War and the Union of Zemstvos* (Carnegie Series on Economic and Social History of the World War), New Haven, 1930.

Polnoe sobranie russkikh lietopisei [Complete Collection of Russian Chronicles], 26 vols., Moscow, 1841-1930, 1949——.

Polnoe sobranie zakonov russkoi imperii . . . 1649-1913 [Complete Collection of the Laws of the Russian Empire . . . 1649-1913], Petrograd, 1830-1916: *Pervoe Polnoe sobranie* [First Complete Collection], *1649-1825,* 46 vols., in 48 and 3 appendixes, 1830-1839; *Vtoroe sobranie* [Second Collection], *1825-1881,* 55 vols., 1830-1884; *Tret'e sobranie* [Third Collection], *1881-1913,* 33 vols., 1885-1916.

POPOV, N. N., *Outline History of the C.P.S.U.,* 2 vols., New York, 1934.

POSIN, DANIEL Q., *Mendeleyev: The Story of a Great Scientist,* New York, 1948.

POSOSHKOV, IVAN T., *Kniga o skudosti i bogatstve i drugie sochineniia* [Book on Poverty and Wealth, and Other Works], Kafengaus edition, Moscow, 1951.

POTEMKIN, VLADIMIR P. (ed.), *Istoriia diplomatii* [History of Diplomacy], 3 vols., Moscow, 1941-1945; trans. as *Histoire de la diplomatie,* 3 vols., Paris, 1946-1947.

Pravda [Truth], daily newspaper published as organ of the Central Committee of the Communist Party of the Soviet Union (or its predecessors) since 1912; when suspended, published under a variety of other titles; moved from Petrograd to Moscow in March, 1918.

PRICE, JACOB M., *The Tobacco Adventure to Russia: Enterprise, Politics, and Diplomacy in the Quest for a Northern Market for English Colonial Tobacco 1676-1722,* Philadelphia, Pa., 1961.

Proletarskaia revoliutsiia [Proletarian Revolution], periodical published by Institute of Marx-Engels-Lenin under the Central Committee of the All-Russian Communist Party (of the Bolsheviks) from 1921.

Protokoly zasedanii VTsIK 4-go sozyva: Stenograficheskii otchet [Protocols of Meetings of the Central Executive Committee of the Fourth Congress of Soviets: Stenographic Report], Moscow, 1920.

PURISHKEVICH, V., *Comment j'ai tué Raspoutine,* Paris, 1924.

PURYEAR, VERNON J., *England, Russia, and the Straits Question,* Berkeley, 1931.

———, *France and the Levant from the Bourbon Restoration to the Peace of Kutiah,* Berkeley, 1941.

PUSHKAREV, SERGEI, *The Emergence of Modern Russia, 1807-1917,* New York, 1963, trans. from *Rossiia v XIX veke,* 1954.

RABINOWITCH, ALEXANDER, *Prelude to Revolution: The Petrograd Bolsheviks and the July Uprising of 1917,* Bloomington, Ind., 1968.

RADISHCHEV, ALEKSANDR N., *A Journey from St. Petersburg to Moscow,* trans. from Russian by Leo Wiener, edited with introduction and notes by R. P. Thaler, Cambridge, Mass., 1958.

RADKEY, OLIVER H., *The Agrarian Foes of Bolshevism: Promise and Default of the Russian Socialist Revolutionaries, February to October, 1917* (Studies of the Russian Institute, Columbia University), New York, 1958.

———, *The Election to the Russian Constituent Assembly of 1917,* Cambridge, Mass., 1950.

———, *The Sickle and the Hammer: The Russian Socialist Revolutionaries in the Early Months of Soviet Rule* (Studies of the Russian Institute, Columbia University), New York, 1963.

RAEFF, MARC, *The Decembrist Movement,* Englewood Cliffs, N.J., 1966.

———, *Michael Speransky: Statesman of Imperial Russia, 1772-1839,* The Hague, 1957.

———, *Origins of the Russian Intelligentsia: The Eighteenth Century Nobility,* New York, 1966.

———, *Plans for Political Reform in Imperial Russia, 1730-1905,* Englewood Cliffs, N.J., 1966.

———, *Siberia and the Reforms of 1822,* Washington, 1956.

RAMBAUD, ALFRED N., *History of Russia: From the Earliest Times to 1882,* trans. by L. B. Lang, 3 vols., New York, 1905.

RANDALL, FRANCIS B., *Stalin's Russia: An Historical Reconsideration,* New York, 1965.

RAUCH, GEORG VON, *Russland: Staatliche Einheit und Nationale Vielfalt,* Munich, 1953.

READING, D. K., *The Anglo-Russian Commercial Treaty of 1734,* New Haven, 1938.

RÉAU, L., *L'Art russe des origines à Pierre le Grand,* Paris, 1921.

———, *L'Art russe de Pierre le Grand à nos jours,* Paris, 1922.

REDMAYNE, W. F. (ed.), *Documents of Catherine the Great,* Cambridge, England, 1931.

REED, JOHN, *Ten Days That Shook the World,* New York, 1919; new edition, New York, 1935.

Relation des particularités de la rébellion de Stenko Razin contre le Grand Duc de Moscovie, Paris, 1672; new edition, Paris, 1856.

RESHETAR, JOHN S., *The Ukrainian Revolution, 1917-1920,* Princeton, 1952.

Revoliutsiia 1917 goda: kronika sobytii [The Revolution of 1917: A Chronicle of Events], by N. Avdeev, *et al.,* 6 vols. in 3, Moscow, 1923——.

REYNAUD, PAUL, *La France a sauvé l'Europe,* 2 vols., Paris, 1947; revised as *Au coeur de la mêlée,* 2 vols., Paris, 1951; latter trans. as *In the Thick of the Fight, 1934-1935,* London, 1955.

RIASANOVSKY, NICHOLAS V., *Nicholas I and Official Nationality in Russia, 1825-1855,* Berkeley, Calif., 1959.

———, *Russia and the West in the Teaching of the Slavophiles: A Study of Romantic Ideology,* Cambridge, Mass., 1952.

RICE, TAMARA TALBOT, *A Concise History of Russian Art,* New York, 1963.

RIEBER, ALFRED J. (ed.), *The Politics of Autocracy: Letters of Alexander II to Prince A. I. Bariatinskii 1857-1864,* Paris, The Hague, 1966.

RIMSKY-KORSAKOV, NIKOLAI A., *My Musical Life,* trans. from revised 2nd Russian edition, New York, 1923; new edition, New York, 1936.

RITVO, HERBERT (ed.), *The New Soviet Society: Final Text of the Program of the Communist Party of the Soviet Union,* paper, New York, 1962.

ROBINSON, GEROID T., *Rural Russia Under the Old Regime: A History of the Landlord-Peasant World and a Prologue to the Peasant Revolution of 1917,* New York, 1932, 1949, 1967.

RODZIANKO, M. V., *Reign of Rasputin: An Empire's Collapse,* New York, 1927.

ROGGER, HANS, *National Consciousness in Eighteenth-Century Russia* (Russian Research Studies, No. 38), Cambridge, Mass., 1960.

ROMANOV, BORIS A., *Russia in Manchuria, 1892-1906* (Russian Translation Project), New York, 1952.

RONCHEY, ALBERTO, *Russia in the Thaw,* New York, 1964.

ROOT, ELIHU, *The United States and the War: The Mission to Russia, Political Addresses,* edited by R. Bacon and J. B. Scott, Cambridge, Mass., 1918.

ROSENBERG, ARTHUR, *History of Bolshevism, from Marx to the First Five Years' Plan,* trans. from German, New York, 1934; paperback, introduction by Samuel J. Hurwitz, Garden City, N.Y., 1967.

Rossiiskaia Kommunisticheskaia Partiia, Trinadtsatyi S"ezd: Stenograficheskii Otchet [Russian Communist Party, Thirteenth Congress, Stenographic Report], Moscow, 1924.

ROSTOVTZEFF, MICHAEL, *Iranians and Greeks in Southern Russia,* Oxford, 1922.

RUBINSTEIN, ALVIN Z. (ed.), *The Foreign Policy of the Soviet Union,* New York, 1960, 2nd ed., New York, 1966.

Russkaia Pravda [Russian Law]. *See* GREKOV, B. D. *and* VERNADSKY, GEORGE.

Russkaia starina . . . istoricheskoe izdanie [Russian Antiquity . . . Historical Edition], monthly, St. Petersburg, 1870-1918.

Russkii arkhiv [Russian Archive], monthly, Moscow, 1863-1917 (except 1881-1884).

Russkoe Istoricheskoe Obshchestvo [Russian Historical Society], *Sbornik Imperatorskogo istoricheskago obshchestva* [Collection of the Imperial Historical Society], 148 vols. in 127, St. Petersburg, 1867-1916.

SACK, A. J. *The Birth of Russian Democracy,* New York, 1918.

SADOUL, JACQUES, *Notes sur la révolution bolchévique,* Paris, 1919.

SAVINKOV, B. V., *Memoirs of a Terrorist,* trans. from Russian, New York, 1931.

SAZONOV, S. D., *Fateful Years, 1909-1916,* New York, 1928.

Sbornik zakonodatel'nykh aktov o trude [Collection of Legislative Documents on Labor], 2nd edition, Moscow, 1958.

SCHAPIRO, LEONARD, *The Communist Party of the Soviet Union,* New York, 1960.

———, *The Government and Politics of the Soviet Union,* New York, 1965.

———, *Origin of the Communist Autocracy: Political Opposition in the Soviet State, First Phase, 1917-1922,* Cambridge, Mass., 1955.

SCHAPIRO, LEONARD B. (ed.), *Lenin; The Man, the Theorist, the Leader, A Reappraisal,* New York, 1967.

SCHEIBERT, PETER, *Von Bakunin zu Lenin,* Vol. I, Leiden, 1956.

SCHELTING, A., *Russland und Europa im russischen Geschichtsdenken,* Bern, 1948.

SCHIEMANN, THEODOR, *Geschichte Ruszlands unter Kaiser Nikolaus I,* 4 vols., Berlin, 1904-1919.

———, *Russland, Polen, und Livland bis ins 17. Jahrhundert* (*Allgemeine Geschichte in Einzeldarstellungen*), 2 vols., Berlin, 1886-1887.

SCHUYLER, E., *Peter the Great,* 2 vols., New York, 1884.

SCHWARTZ, BENJAMIN I., *Chinese Communism and the Rise of Mao* (Russian Research Center Studies, No. 4), Cambridge, Mass., 1951.

SCHWARZ, SOLOMON M., *The Jews in the Soviet Union,* Syracuse, 1951.

———, *Labor in the Soviet Union,* New York, 1951.

———, *The Russian Revolution of 1905: The Workers' Movement and the Formation of Bolshevism and Menshevism,* trans. by Gertrude Vakar, Chicago, 1966.

SCOTT, JOHN, *Behind the Urals: An American Worker in Russia's City of Steel,* New York, 1942.

SCOTT, RICHARDA C., *Quakers in Russia,* London, 1964.

SEBES, JOSEPH, S. J., *The Jesuits and the Sino-Russian Treaty of Nerchinsk (1689): The Diary of Thomas Pereira, S.J.,* Rome, 1961.

SEMENTKOWSKI-KURILO, NIKOLAI, *Alexander I: Rausch und Einkehr einer Seele,* Zurich, 1939.

SEMEVSKII, V. I., *Krest'ianskii vopros v Rossii v pervoi polovinie XIX vieka* [The Peasant Question in Russia in the First Half of the Nineteenth Century], 2 vols., St. Petersburg, 1888.

SENN, ALFRED ERICH, *The Emergence of Modern Lithuania,* New York, 1959.

SERGE, VICTOR, *Memoirs of a Revolutionary, 1901-1941,* trans. by Peter Sedgwick, slightly abridged, New York, 1963.

SHACHTMAN, MAX, *The Struggle for the New Course,* New York, 1943.

SHAPIRO, DAVID (comp.), *A Select Bibliography of Works in English on Russian History, 1801-1917,* New York, 1962.

SHAPIRO, LEONARD, *Soviet Treaty Series:* Vol. 1, *1917-1928,* Washington, 1950; Vol. 2, *1929-1939,* Washington, 1955.

SHERWOOD, ROBERT E., *Roosevelt and Hopkins, An Intimate History,* New York, 1948.

SHOLOKHOV, MIKHAIL A., *The Silent Don: I And quiet flows the Don; II The Don flows home to the sea,* trans. by Stephen Garry, New York, 1942.

———, *Virgin Soil Upturned,* trans. by R. Daglish, Moscow, 1957.

SHORE, MAURICE J., *Soviet Education: Its Psychology and Philosophy,* New York, 1947.

SHTEPPA, KONSTANTIN F., *Russian Historians and the Soviet State,* New Brunswick, N.J., 1962.

SHULGIN, VASILII V., *Dni* [Days], with a preface by S. Piontkovskii, Leningrad, 1927.

SHULMAN, MARSHALL D., *Stalin's Foreign Policy Reappraised* (Russian Research Center Studies, No. 48), Cambridge, Mass., 1963.

VII Kongress der Kommunistischen Internationale Gekürztes Stenografisches Protokoll, Moscow, 1939.

SIENKIEWICZ, HENRYK, *The Deluge,* 2 vols., trans. from Polish by J. Curtin, 9th edition, Boston, 1897.

———, *Pan Michael,* trans. from Polish by J. Curtin, 9th edition, Boston, 1897.

———, *With Fire and Sword,* trans. from Polish by J. Curtin, 9th edition, Boston, 1897.

SIGERIST, H. E., *Socialized Medicine in the Soviet Union,* New York, 1937.

SILVESTER, *Domostroi,* 3rd corrected edition by I. Glazunov, St. Petersburg, 1911.

SIMMONDS, GEORGE W., *Soviet Leaders,* New York, 1967.

SIMMONS, ERNEST J. (ed.), *Continuity and Change in Russian and Soviet Thought* (Arden House Conference), Cambridge, Mass., 1955.

———, "Soviet Russian Literature," in Strakhovsky, *A Handbook of Slavic Studies,* pp. 535-559.

——— (ed.), *Through the Glass of Soviet Literature: Views of Russian Society* (Studies of the Russian Institute, Columbia University), New York, 1953.

Sistematicheskii sbornik dekretov i rasporiazheniiakh pravitelstvennykh po prodovol'stvennomu delu [Systematic Collection of Government Decrees and Orders on Matters of Food Supply], 2 vols., Nizhny-Novgorod, 1919-1920.

Sistematicheskii sbornik vazhneishikh dekretov 1917-1920 [Systematic Collection of the Most Important Decrees, 1917-1920], Moscow, 1921 (under running title *Sobranie uzakonenii i rasporiazhenii rabochego i krest'ianskogo pravitel'stva* [Collection of Statutes and Orders of the Workers' and Peasants' Government]).

SKRINE, F. H. B., AND E. D. ROSS, *The Heart of Asia,* London, 1899.

SLONIM, MARC L., *The Epic of Russian Literature from Its Origins Through Tolstoy,* New York, 1950.

———, *From Chekhov to the Revolution: Russian Literature, 1900-1917,* New York, 1962.

———, *Russian Theater: From the Empire to the Soviets,* Cleveland, and New York, 1961.

———, *Soviet Russian Literature: Writers and Problems,* New York, 1964.

SLUSSER, ROBERT M., AND JAN F. TRISKA, *A Calendar of Soviet Treaties, 1917-1957,* Stanford, Calif., 1959.

SMITH, CLARENCE J., *The Russian Struggle for Power, 1914-1917: A Study of Russian Foreign Policy During the First World War,* New York, 1956.

SMITH, R. E. F., *The Origins of Farming in Russia,* Paris, 1959.

SNELL, JOHN L., *The Meaning of Yalta: Big Three Diplomacy and the New Balance of Power,* Baton Rouge, 1956.

Sobranie gosudarstvennykh gramot i dogorov khraniashchikssia v Gosudarstvennoi kollegii inostrannykh diel' [Collection of State Charters and Treaties Preserved in the State Collegium of Foreign Affairs], 5 vols., Moscow, 1813-1894.

Sobranie Kodeksov R.S.F.S.R. [Collection of Codes of the R.S.F.S.R.], 3rd edition, Moscow, 1925.

Sobranie postanovlenii i rasporiazhenii pravitel'stva S.S.S.R. [Collection of Decrees and Orders of the U.S.S.R.], Moscow, 1939; continuation of *Sobranie uzakonenii i rasporiazhenii rabochego i krest'ianskogo pravitel'stva* [Collection of Statutes and Orders of the Workers' and Peasants' Government], Petrograd and Moscow, 1917-1938.

Sobranie zakonov i rasporiazhenii SSSR za 1921-1938 [Collection of Laws and Orders of the U.S.S.R. for 1921-1938], Moscow, 1939.

SOKOLOV, Y. M., *Russian Folklore,* New York, 1950.

SOLOV'EV, SERGEI M., *Istoriia Rossii s drevnieishikh vremen* [History of Russia from the Earliest Times], 2nd edition, 29 vols. in 6, St. Petersburg, 1894-1895; partial translation as *Histoire de Russie,* Paris, 1879.

SOLOVEYTCHIK, GEORGE, *Potemkin, A Picture of Catherine's Russia,* London, 1939.

Sovetskaia Muzyka [Soviet Music], periodical organ of *Komitet po delam iskusstv S.S.S.R. i Soiuz Sovetskikh kompozitorov* [Committee on Art Matters of the U.S.S.R. and Union of Soviet Composers], Moscow, from 1932, suspended during war.

SPECTOR, IVAR, *The First Russian Revolution: Its Impact on Asia,* Englewood Cliffs, N.J., 1962.

SPENGLER, OSWALD, *Hour of Decision,* trans. from German, New York, 1934.

SPINKA, MATTHEW, *The Church in Soviet Russia,* New York, 1956.

SPULBER, NICHOLAS, *Foundations of Soviet Strategy for Economic Growth,* Bloomington, Ill., 1964.

———, *Soviet Strategy for Economic Growth,* Bloomington, Ill., 1964.

SPULER, B., *Die Goldene Horde,* Leipzig, 1943.

STADEN, HEINRICH VON, *Aufzeichnungen über dem Moskauer Staat,* Hamburg, 1930.

———, *The Land and Government of Muscovy: A Sixteenth Century Account,* trans. and ed. by Thomas Esper, Stanford, Calif., 1967.

STALIN, IOSIF V., *Sochineniia* [Works], 13 vols. (to 1935), Moscow, 1946-1951; official translation, Moscow, 1953-1955.

———, *Marxism and Linguistics,* trans. from Russian, New York, 1951.

———, *Voprosy Leninizma* (Questions of Leninism), 11th ed., Moscow, 1947.

STAVROU, THEOFANIS GEORGE, *Russian Interests in Palestine, 1882-1914: A Study of Religious and Educational Enterprise,* Thessaloniki, Gr., 1963.

STEINBERG, ISAAC NAHUM, *In the Workshop of the Revolution,* New York, 1953.

———, *Spiridonova, Revolutionary Terrorist,* London, 1935.

STEKLOV, YU. M., *Mikhail Aleksandrovich Bakunin: ego zhizn' i deiatel'nost'* [M. A. Bakunin: His Life and Work], *1814-1876,* 2nd edition, 4 vols., Moscow, 1926-1927; especially Vol. III.

STRAKHOVSKY, LEONID I., *Intervention at Archangel,* Princeton, 1944.

———, *The Origins of American Intervention in North Russia, 1918,* Princeton, 1937.

——— (ed.), *A Handbook of Slavic Studies,* Cambridge, Mass., 1949.

STRUVE, GLEB, *Soviet Russian Literature,* Norman, Okla., 1951.

STRUVE, P. B. (ed.), *Food Supply in Russia During the World War* (Carnegie Series on Economic and Social History of the World War), New Haven, 1930.

SUKHANOV [GIMMER], NIKOLAI N., *Zapiski o revoliutsii,* 7 vols., Berlin, 1922-1923, trans. and abridged as *The Russian Revolution, 1917: A Personal Record,* New York, 1955.

SUKHOMLINOV, V. A., *Perepiska V. A. Sukhomlinova c N. N. Yanushkevichem* [Correspondence of V. A. Sukhomlinov with N. N. Yanushkevich], in *Krasnyi Arkhiv,* I, 215-262; II, pp. 130-174; III, pp. 29-74.

Survey of International Affairs, annual, for many years edited by Arnold Toynbee, London, 1920——.

SVERDLOV, G. M., *Legal Rights of the Soviet Family,* London, 1945.

SZCZESNIAK, BOLESLAW (ed. and trans.), *The Russian Revolution and Religion: A Collection of Documents concerning the Suppression of Religion by the Communists, 1917-1920,* Notre Dame, Ind., 1959.

TACITUS, *Complete Works,* Modern Library edition, New York, 1942.

TANNER, VÄINÖ A., *The Winter War, Finland Against Russia, 1939-1940,* Stanford, 1957.

TARACOUZIO, T. A., *The Soviet Union and International Law: A Study Based on the Legislation, Treaties and Foreign Relations of the Union of Socialist Soviet Republics* (Harvard Bureau of International Research), New York, 1935.

———, *War and Peace in Soviet Diplomacy,* Cambridge, Mass., 1940.

TARLE, E. V., *Napoleon's Invasion of Russia, 1812,* New York, 1942; trans. from 1st edition of *Nashestvie Napoleona na Rossiiu 1812 god,* Moscow, 1938.

TARULIS, ALBERT N., *Soviet Policy Toward the Baltic States, Estonia, Latvia, Lithuania, 1918-1940,* Notre Dame, Ind., 1959.

TEMPERLEY, H. W. V., *England and the Near East,* 3 vols. (Vol. 1, *The Crimea*), London, 1936.

TERTZ, ABRAM, *On Socialist Realism,* trans., New York, 1961.

"Tetrad', a v nei imena pisany opal'nvkh pri Tsarie i Vel. Kniazie Ivanie Vasil'evichie vseia Rosii; soobshch. N. Suvorov" ["Notebook in Which Are Written the Names of Those Executed Under Tsar and Grand Prince Ivan the Terrible: Contributed by N. Suvorov"], in Obshchestvo istorii i drevnostei pri moskovskom universitetie [Society of History and Antiquities at Moscow University], *Chteniia* [Lectures], 1859, III, v, *Smies* [Miscellany], 89-100.

THADEN, EDWARD C., *Conservative Nationalism in Nineteenth-Century Russia,* Seattle, 1964.

———, *Russia and the Balkan Alliance of 1912,* University Park, Penn., 1965.

THOMPSON, JOHN M., *Russia, Bolshevism, and the Versailles Peace,* Princeton, N.J., 1967.

THOMSEN, VILHELM, *Relations Between Ancient Russia and Scandinavia and the Origins of the Russian State,* Oxford, 1877.

THOMSON, GLADYS S., *Catherine the Great and the Expansion of Russia,* New York, 1950.

TIMASHEFF, NICHOLAS S., *The Great Retreat: The Growth and Decline of Communism in Russia,* New York, 1946.

———, *Religion in Soviet Russia,* New York, 1942.

TIMOSHENKO, STEPHEN P., *Engineering Education in Russia,* New York, 1959.

TKACHEV, PIOTR NIKITICH, *Izbrannye sochineniia na sotsial'no-politicheskie temy*

[Selected Works on Socio-Political Themes], edited by S. P. Koz′min, 4 vols., Moscow, 1932-1933.

TOLSTOI, ALEKSEI K., *Kniaz Serebrianyi: povest′ vremeni Ivana Groznago* [Prince Serebrianyi: A Tale of the Times of Ivan the Terrible], republished Berlin, 1925; Paris, 1945; Moscow, 1959; trans. as *A Prince of Outlaws*, New York, 1927.

TOLSTOI, ALEXIS N., *"Moia put"* ["My Journey"], in *Novy Mir*, No. 1 (1943).

TOLSTOI, IURII V. [George Tolstoy] (ed.), *The First Forty Years of Intercourse Between England and Russia, 1553-1593* (also titled *Pervyia sorok liet snoshenii mezhdu Rossieiu i Anglieiu*), St. Petersburg, 1875.

TOLSTOI, LEO N., *Chto takoe iskusstvo?*, Moscow, 1898; trans. as *What Is Art?*, London, 1904.

———, *Sevastopol and Other Military Tales*, trans. by L. A. Maude, New York, 1903.

TOMPKINS, PAULINE, *American-Russian Relations in the Far East*, New York, 1949.

TOWSTER, JULIAN, *Political Power in the U.S.S.R., 1917-1947: The Theory and Structure of Government in the Soviet State*, New York, 1948.

TREADGOLD, DONALD W., *The Great Siberian Migration: Government and Peasant in Resettlement from Emancipation to the First World War*, Princeton, 1957.

———, *Lenin and His Rivals: The Struggle for Russia's Future, 1898-1906*, New York, 1955.

———, *Twentieth-Century Russia*, Chicago, 1959.

Tretii Vserossiiskii S″ezd sovetov rabochikh, soldatskikh i krest′ianskikh deputatov. Stenograficheskii otchet [Third All-Russian Congress of Soviets of Workers', Soldiers', and Peasants' Deputies. Stenographic Report], Petrograd, 1918.

TRISKA, JAN F., AND ROBERT M. SLUSSER, *The Theory, Law, and Policy of Soviet Treaties*, Stanford, Calif., 1962.

TROITSKII, P. S., *Tserkov i gosudarstvo v Rossii. Otnoshenie gosudarstva k tserkvi po vozzrieniiam naiboliee vidnykh nashikh pisatelei i obshchestvennykh dieiatelei* [Church and State in Russia. The Relation of the State to the Church According to the Opinions of the Most Outstanding of Our Writers and Public Men], Moscow, 1909.

TROTSKII, LEV [Leon Trotsky], *Do deviatogo ianvaria* [Before the Twenty-Second of January], in *Sochineniia*, II.

———, *Écrits, 1928-1940*, 3 vols., Paris, 1955-1959.

———, *Istoriia russkoi revoliutsii* [History of the Russian Revolution], 3 vols. in 2, Berlin, 1931-1933; English trans. by Max Eastman, New York, 1932, 1957.

———, *Kak vooruzhalas′ revoliutsiia* [How the Revolution Armed Itself], 3 vols., Moscow, 1923.

———, *Lenin*, New York, 1925.

———, *Lessons of October*, New York, 1937; trans. from *Tysiacha deviat′sot semnadtsatyi god, uroki oktiabria* [1917, Lessons of November], Berlin, 1924.

———, *Literature and Revolution*, New York, 1957; original trans. New York, 1925, from *Literatura i revoliutsiia*, 2nd edition, Moscow, 1924.

———, *Moia zhizn′*, trans. as *My Life: An Attempt at an Autobiography*, New York, 1930, and as *My Life: The Rise and Fall of a Dictator*, London, 1930.

———, *Nashi politicheskiia zadachi*, Geneva, 1904.

———, *The New Course. See* SHACHTMAN, MAX, *The Struggle for the New Course.*

———, *Permanent Revolution,* trans. by Max Shachtman from Russian (Berlin, 1930), New York, 1933.

———, *Poslie peterburgskogo vosstaniia* [After the Petersburg Uprising], in *Sochineniia,* III.

———, *The Real Situation in Russia,* trans. by Max Eastman, New York, 1928.

———, *The Revolution Betrayed: What Is the Soviet Union and Where Is It Going?,* trans. by Max Eastman, New York, 1937.

———, *Sochineniia* (*Collected Works*), 21 vols. in 9, Moscow, 1925-1927.

———, *The Suppressed Testament of Lenin: The Complete Original Text, with Two Explanatory Articles by Leon Trotsky,* New York, 1935, 1946.

———, "Vospominaniia ob oktiabrskom perevote" ["Recollections of the November Revolution"], in *Proletarskaia revoliutsiia,* No. 10, (October), 1922.

TUGAN-BARANOVSKII, M. G., *Geschichte der russischen Fabrik,* Berlin, 1900.

TUMANSKII, FEODOR (ed.), *Sobranie raznykh zapisok i sochinenii sluzhashchikh k dostavleniiu polnago sviedeniia o zhizni i dieianiiakh gosudaria imperatora Petra Velikago* [Collection of Divers Memoranda and Writings Serving to Supply Full Information About the Life and Doings of the Lord Emperor Peter the Great], Vol. III, St. Petersburg, 1787.

TURKEVICH, JOHN, *Chemistry in the Soviet Union,* Princeton, N.J., 1965.

Tysiacha deviat'sot piatyi god v Peterburge [The Year 1905 in St. Petersburg], 2 vols. in 1, Leningrad and Moscow, 1925.

ULAM, ADAM B., *The Bolsheviks: The Intellectual and Political History of the Triumph of Communism in Russia,* New York, 1965.

———, *Tito and the Cominform* (Russian Research Center Studies, No. 5), Cambridge, Mass., 1952.

———, *The Unfinished Revolution,* New York, 1960.

ULLMAN, RICHARD H., *Anglo-Soviet Relations, 1917-1921,* vol. I *Intervention and the War,* Princeton, N.J., 1961.

U.S. DEPARTMENT OF STATE, *Documents on German Foreign Policy,* 1918-1945: Series D (1937-1945), Vol. VI: *The Last Months of Peace, March-August, 1939;* from the archives of the German Foreign Office; Washington, 1956.

———, *Nazi-Soviet Relations, 1939-1941,* edited from documents in the archives of the German Foreign Office by R. J. Sontag and J. S. Beddie, Washington, 1948.

———, *Papers Relating to the Foreign Relations of the United States,* Washington. Among the special publications under this series title, the following should be noted: *The Conferences at Malta and Yalta, 1945* (1955); *Japan, 1931-1941* (2 vols., 1943); *Peace and War: United States Foreign Policy, 1931-1941* (1943); *Russia, 1918* (3 vols., 1931-1932), *Russia, 1919* (1937); *The Soviet Union, 1933-1939* (1952).

U.S. WAR DEPARTMENT, *Annual Reports, 1919,* Vol. I, Washington, 1920.

UNTERBERGER, BETTY M., *America's Siberian Expedition, 1918-1920: A Study of National Policy,* Durham, N.C., 1956.

UPTON, ANTHONY F., *Finland in Crisis, 1940-1941: A Study in Small-Power Politics,* Ithaca, N.Y., 1965.

URATADZE, G., *The Founding and Consolidation of the Georgian Democratic Republic* (in Russian with English summary), Munich, 1956.

USTRIALOV, NIKOLAI GERASIMOVICH, *Istoriia tsarstvovaniia Petra Velikogo* [History of the Reign of Peter the Great], 4 vols., St. Petersburg, 1858-1863.

VAKAR, NICHOLAS P., *Belorussia, the Making of a Nation: A Case Study and a Bibliographical Guide to Belorussia* (Russian Research Center Studies, No. 22), Cambridge, Mass., 1956.

VANDAL, ALBERT, *Napoléon et Alexandre Ier. L'alliance russe sous le premier empire,* 3rd edition, 3 vols., Paris, 1893-1896.

VARNEKE, B. V., *History of Russian Theatre,* New York, 1951.

VASILIEV, A. A., *The Byzantine Empire,* Madison, Wis., 1924; 2nd edition, 1952.

———, *The Goths in the Crimea,* Cambridge, Mass., 1936.

VEKSLER, I. I., *Aleksandr Nikolaevich Tolstoi,* Moscow, 1948.

Velikii khoziaistvennyi plan: doklad VIII S"ezdy sovetov gosudarstvennoi komissii po elektrifikatsii Rossii [The Great Economic Plan: Report to the Eighth Congress of Soviets by the State Commission on the Electrification of Russia], 2nd edition, Moscow, 1955. This is a reprint of *Goelro.*

VENTURI, FRANCO, *Roots of Revolution: A History of the Populist and Socialist Movements in Nineteenth-Century Russia,* New York, 1961; translation of *Il Populismo Russo,* 2 vols., Turin, 1952.

VERNADSKY, GEORGE, *Ancient Russia,* New Haven, 1943.

———, *Bohdan, Hetman of Ukraine,* New Haven, 1941.

———, *Kievan Russia,* New Haven, 1948.

———, *The Mongols and Russia,* New Haven, 1953.

———, *The Origins of Russia,* Oxford, 1959.

———, *Political and Diplomatic History of Russia,* Boston, 1936.

———, *Russia at the Dawn of the Modern Age,* New Haven, 1959.

——— (trans. and ed.), *Medieval Russian Laws,* New York, 1947.

VESELOVSKII, BORIS O., *Istoriia zemstva . . .* [History of the Zemstvo], 4 vols., St. Petersburg, 1909-1911.

VILKOV, A. A., *Der Staatshaushalt und das Finanzsystem Russlands vom Beginn des 19 Jahrhunderts bis zur Gegenwart,* 1928.

VINNICHENKO, V., *Vidrodzheniia natsii* [Birth of a Nation], 4 vols., Vienna, 1920.

VINOGRADOFF, PAUL, *Self-Government in Russia,* London, 1915.

———, *Russia: The Psychology of a Nation,* New York, 1914.

VIPPER, ROBERT YU., *Ivan Grozny,* 3rd edition, in English trans., Moscow, 1947.

———, *Vozniknovenie khristianskoi literatury* [Rise of Christian Literature], Moscow, 1946.

VISHNIAK, MARK V., *Vserossiiskoe Uchreditel'noe Sobranie* [The All-Russian Constituent Assembly], Paris, 1932.

VLADIMIRTSOV, B., *The Life of Chingis-Khan,* London, 1930.

———, *Le Régime social des Mongols,* Paris, 1948.

VOKS Bulletin, published in English by the All-Union Society for Cultural Relations with Foreign Countries; succeeded in 1956 by *Culture and Life.*

VOLIN, LAZAR, *A Survey of Soviet Russian Agriculture,* Washington, 1951.

VON LAUE, THEODORE H., *Sergei Witte and the Industrialization of Russia* (Studies of the Russian Institute, Columbia University), New York, 1963.

———, *Why Lenin? Why Stalin? A Reappraisal of the Russian Revolution, 1900-1930* (Critical Periods of History), Philadelphia, Pa., 1964.

Voprosy filosofii [Questions of Philosophy], monthly publication of Academy of Sciences of the U.S.S.R., Institute of Philosophy, Moscow, 1947———.

"Vremennik d' iaka Ivana Timofeeva" ["Chronicle of the Secretary Ivan Timofeev"], in *Pamiatniki drevnei russkoi pis'mennosti otnosiashchiesia k smutnomu vremeni,* Vol. XIII, 3rd edition, Leningrad, 1925.

Vserossiiskaia Kommunisticheskaia Partiia, Trinadtsatyi, S"ezd, Stenograficheskii otchet [All-Russian Communist Party, Thirteenth Congress, Stenographic Report], Moscow, 1924.

Vserossiiskii Tsentral'nyi Ispolnitel'nyi Komitet Sovetov rabochikh i soldatskikh deputatov vtorogo sozyva. Stenograficheskii otchet. [All-Russian Central Executive Committee of Soviets of Workers' and Soldiers' Deputies of the Second Congress, Stenographic Report], Moscow, 1918.

Vtoroi god bor'by s golodom [Second Year of the Fight Against Hunger], Moscow, 1919.

Vtoroi Vserossiiskii S"ezd sovetov rabochikh i soldatskikh deputatov, Stenograficheskii otchet [Second All-Russian Congress of Soviets of Workers' and Soldiers' Deputies, Stenographic Report], (*Tysiacha deviat' sot semnadtsatyi god v dokumentahk i materialakh* [The Year 1917 in Materials and Documents] 8), Leningrad and Moscow, 1928.

VVEDENSKII, ALEKSANDR IVAN, *Tserkov i gosudarstvo: Ocherk vzaimootnoshenii tserkvi i gosudarstva v Rossii* [Church and State: Outline of the Interrelations of Church and State in Russia], *1918-1922,* Moscow, 1923.

VUCINICH, ALEXANDER, *Science in Russian Culture: A History to 1860,* Stanford, Calif., 1963.

VYSHINSKY, ANDREI Y., *The Law of the Soviet State,* New York, 1948.

WALISZEWSKI, K., *Autour d'un trône, Catherine II de Russie; ses collaborateurs; ses amis; ses favoris,* 7th edition, Paris, 1897; trans. as *The Story of a Throne* from 4th edition, London, 1895.

———, *La Dernière des Romanov: Élisabeth Ire, impératrice de Russie, 1741-1762, d'après des documents nouveaux . . . inédits . . . ,* Paris, 1902.

———, *Le Fils de la grande Catherine,* 4th edition, Paris, 1912; trans. as *Paul the First of Russia, The Son of Catherine the Great,* London, 1913.

———, *L'Héritage de Pierre le Grand: règne des femmes, gouvernement des favoris, 1725-1741,* Paris, 1900.

———, *Ivan le Terrible,* 2nd edition, Paris, 1904; trans. by Lady Mary Loyd, Philadelphia, 1904.

———, *Les origines de la Russie moderne. La crise révolutionnaire, 1584-1614* (*smoutnoié vrémia*), 2nd edition, Paris, 1906.

———, *Les origines de la Russie moderne. Le berceau d'une dynastie, les premiers Romanov, 1613-1682,* 3rd edition, Paris, 1909.

———, *Pierre le Grand, l'éducation—l'homme—l'oeuvre d'après des documents nouveaux,* 7th edition, Paris, 1909; trans. from 3rd edition by Lady Mary Loyd, New York, 1897.

———, *Le roman d'une impératrice, Catherine II de Russie; d'après ses mémoires, sa correspondance et les documents inédits des archives d'état,* 4th edition,

Paris, 1902; trans. from 3rd edition, New York, 1894.

———, *La Russie il y a cent ans; le règne d'Alexandre Ier,* Paris, 1923-1925.

WALLACE, SIR DONALD MACKENZIE, *Russia,* New York, 1880; revised edition, New York, 1905, 1912.

WARTH, ROBERT D., *The Allies and the Russian Revolution: From the Fall of the Monarchy to the Peace of Brest-Litovsk,* Durham, N.C., 1954.

WEBB, SIDNEY AND BEATRICE, *Soviet Communism: A New Civilization?,* 2 vols., New York, 1936.

WEI, HENRY, *China and Soviet Russia,* Princeton, 1956.

WEIDLE, WLADIMIR, *Russia: Absent and Present,* trans. by A. Gordon Smith, New York, 1952.

WERTH, ALEXANDER, *Russia at War, 1941-1945,* New York, 1964.

WESTWOOD, J. N., *A History of Russian Railways,* New York, 1964.

WHEELER, GEOFFREY, *The Modern History of Soviet Central Asia* ("Asia-Africa Series of Modern Histories," ed. by Bernard Lewis), New York, 1964.

WHEELER-BENNETT, JOHN W., *Brest-Litovsk: The Forgotten Peace, March 1918,* London, 1938; also as *The Forgotten Peace: Brest-Litovsk, March 1918,* New York, 1939.

———, *Munich: Prologue to Tragedy,* New York, 1948.

WHITE, D. F., *The Growth of the Red Army,* Princeton, 1944.

WHITE, JOHN ALBERT, *The Diplomacy of the Russo-Japanese War,* Princeton, N.J., 1964.

———, *The Siberian Intervention,* Princeton, N.J., 1950.

WHITING, ALLEN S., *Soviet Policies in China, 1917-1924* (Studies of the Russian Institute, Columbia University), New York, 1954.

WIENER, LEO, *Anthology of Russian Literature,* 2 vols., New York, 1902-1903.

———, *An Interpretation of the Russian People,* New York, 1915.

WILDMAN, ALLAN K., *Making of a Workers' Revolution: Russian Social Democracy 1891-1903,* Chicago, 1967.

WILLAN, THOMAS S., *Early History of the Russia Company, 1553-1603,* New York, 1956.

WILLIAMS, ALBERT RHYS, *The Russians: The Land, The People, and Why They Fight,* New York, 1942.

WILLIAMS, H. W., *Russia of the Russians,* New York, 1914.

WILMOT, CHESTER, *The Struggle for Europe,* London, 1952.

WINCKLER, ARTHUR, *Die deutsche Hanse in Russland,* Berlin, 1886.

WISCHNITZER, MARK, *To Dwell in Safety,* Philadelphia, 1948.

WITTE, SERGE, *The Memoirs of Count Witte,* translated by Avrahm Yarmolinsky, Garden City, N.Y., 1921.

WITTRAM, REINHARD, *Baltische Geschichte; die Ostseelande: Livland, Estland, Kurland, 1180-1918. Grundzüge und Durchblicke,* Munich, 1954.

WOLFE, BERTRAM D., *Khrushchev and Stalin's Ghost: Text, Background, and Meaning of Khrushchev's Secret Report to the Twentieth Congress on the Night of February 24-25, 1956,* New York, 1957.

———, *Three Who Made a Revolution: A Biographical History,* New York, 1948.

WOLFE, THOMAS W., *Soviet Strategy at the Crossroads,* Cambridge, Mass., 1964.

WOLIN, SIMON, AND R. M. SLUSSER (eds.), *The Soviet Secret Police,* New York, 1957.

WORTMAN, RICHARD, *The Crisis of Russian Populism,* Cambridge, Mass., 1967.

WOYTINSKY, W. S., *Stormy Passage: A Personal History through two Russian Revolutions to Democracy and Freedom, 1905-1960,* New York, 1961.

WRANGEL, N. E., *From Serfdom to Bolshevism: Memoirs, 1847-1920,* New York, 1927.

WRETT-SMITH, MILDRED, "The English in Russia During the Second Half of the Sixteenth Century," *Transactions of the Royal Historical Society,* Series 4, III, 1920.

WU, AITCHEN K., *China and the Soviet Union: A Study of Sino-Soviet Relations,* New York, 1950.

WUORINEN, JOHN H. (ed. and trans.), *Finland and World War II, 1939-1944,* New York, 1948.

———, *A History of Finland,* New York, 1965.

———, *Nationalism in Modern Finland,* New York, 1931.

YAKHONTOV, "Notes on Meetings of the Council of Ministers," in *Arkhiv russkoi revoliutsii,* XVIII. For trans. *See* Cherniavsky.

YAKOVLEV, *Razlozhenie armii v 1917 godu* (Disintegration of the Army in 1917), (*Tysiacha deviat'sot semnadtsatyi god v dokumentakh i materialkh* [The year 1917 in Documents and Materials], No. 5), Moscow, 1925.

YARMOLINSKY, AVRAHM, *Literature under Communism: The Literary Policy of the CPSU from the End of World War II to the Death of Stalin,* Bloomington, Ill., 1960.

———, *The Memoirs of Count Witte,* Garden City, N.Y., 1921.

———, *Road to Revolution: A Century of Russian Radicalism,* new edition, paper, New York, 1962.

———, *Turgenev,* New York, 1959.

Za industrializatsiiu [For Industrialization], daily newspaper, organ of People's Commissariat of Heavy Industry, Moscow, from January, 1930; name changed to *Industriia* [Industry], September 3, 1937.

ZAGORSKII, S. O., *State Control of Industry in Russia During the War* (Carnegie Series on Economic and Social History of the World War), New Haven, 1928.

ZAITSEV, K. I., AND N. V. DOLINSKII, "Organization and Policy," in Struve, P. B. (ed.), *Food Supply in Russia During the World War.*

ZELENIN, D., *Russische (Ostslavische) Volkskunde,* Berlin and Leipzig, 1927.

ZENKOVSKY, V. V., *A History of Russian Philosophy,* authorized trans., 2 vols., New York, 1953.

ZENKOWSKY, SERGE A., *Pan-Turkism and Islam in Russia,* Cambridge, Mass., 1960.

——— (ed. and trans.), *Medieval Russia's Epics, Chronicles, and Tales,* New York, 1963.

ZERNOV, NICHOLAS, *Moscow, the Third Rome,* New York, 1937; revised edition, 1938.

———, *The Russians and Their Church,* New York, 1945.

ZETKIN, CLARA, *My Reminiscences of Lenin,* London, 1929.

ZHDANOV, ANDREI, *The Communist Party of the Soviet Union,* New York, 1939.

———, *Doklad t. Zhdanova o zhurnalakh "Zvezda" i "Leningrad"* [Report of

Comrade Zhdanov on the Journals *Star* and *Leningrad*], as condensed from *Pravda* in *Zvezda,* 1946 (July-August), pp. 7-22.

———, *Problems of Soviet Literature,* New York, 1935.

ZIMIN, A. A., *I. S. Peresvetov i ego sovremenniki* [I. S. Peresvetov and His Contemporaries], Moscow, 1958.

———, AND D. S. LIKHACHEV (eds.), *Sochineniia I. S. Peresvetova* [Works of I. S. Peresvetov], Moscow and Leningrad, 1956.

Znamia [Banner] (monthly literary-artistic and socio-political journal, organ of the Union of Soviet Writers of the U.S.S.R.), Moscow, from 1942.

ZOLKIEWSKI, STANISLAS, *Expedition to Moscow: A Memoir by Hetman Stanislas Zolkiewski,* London, 1959.

Zvezda [Star] (literary-social and popular-scientific journal), bimonthly, Petrograd, 1924-1925; (literary-artistic and socio-political journal), monthly, Leningrad, from 1927.

Chronology

B.C.

c. 1000 Beginning of Iron Age in steppe
7th century Occupation of steppe by Scythians
Founding of Greek colonies on Black Sea coast
5th century Herodotus describes inhabitants of Scythia and beyond
4th century Sarmatians replace Scythians

CHRISTIAN ERA

1st century Tacitus (and Pliny) describe Veneti and Fenni
3rd century Goths in western steppe
4th century Huns expel Alans and Goths from steppe
5th century Bulgars replace Huns in steppe
6th century Rise of Avars
First known use of term "Slavs"
7th century Varangian trade by Volga
Khazars in control of steppe

9th century Varangian contacts with Constantinople
Rurik established at Novgorod (d. 879)
879 Oleg established at Kiev
Rise of Pecheneg power in steppe

10th century Peak of Varangian robber-trade
Treaties with Greeks (907, 911, 945)
955 Olga baptized
988 Official conversion of Rus under Vladimir

11th century Polovtsy replace Pechenegs in steppe
Cluniac reform in West; Investiture Conflict
1018, 1068 Polish interventions at Kiev
1037 First metropolitan at Kiev
1054 Church schism
Death of Yaroslav the Wise

12th century "Democratic revolution" in Kievan towns
Decline of trade with Constantinople

1113–1125 Vladimir Monomakh

1147 First mention of Moscow (first fortified, 1156)

1169 Sack of Kiev by Andrei Bogoliubsky

1186 Beginnings of German trade and missionary activity in Baltic area

13th century Beginnings of rise of Lithuanian principality

1201 Founding of Riga

1202 Founding of Swordbearing Knights (Livonian Knights)

1204 Fourth Crusade; establishment of Latin Empire at Constantinople (to 1261)

1206 Temuchin (Jinghis Khan) begins career in Mongolia

- *1215* Capture of Peking
- *1219* Overthrow of Khorezm in Central Asia
- *1223* Battle of Kalka; defeat of Polovtsy and Russians

1237 Merger of Swordbearing Knights with Teutonic Knights (of Prussia)

1237–40 Mongol conquest of Rus

1240 Alexander "Nevsky" defeats Swedes on the Neva

1242 Alexander Nevsky defeats Knights on Lake Peipus

1246 Mission of Piano de Carpini to the Mongols

1253–55 Mission of Guillaume de Rubriquis to the Mongols

1259 Alexander Nevsky persuades Novgorod to submit to "Tatar yoke"

1261 Orthodox diocese established at Khanate of the Golden Horde

1263 First permanent local dynasty established at Moscow (without rights to traditional title of "Grand Prince")

14th CENTURY

1309 Metropolitan Peter transfers seat to Vladimir, later (1326) to Moscow

1316–41 Gedimin of Lithuania extends power over Russian princes on upper Dnieper

1319 Yury of Moscow made Grand Prince by Tatars (murdered 1325)

1327 Ivan "Kalita" of Moscow wins title of Grand Prince with aid of Tatars

1340 Poland annexes principality of Galicia

1341–77 Olgerd of Lithuania further extends control in Dnieper basin

1352 First appearance in Russia of Black Death (at Novgorod)

1367 First brick walls built around Moscow Kremlin

1380 Dmitry "Donskoy" wins victory over Tatars at Kulikovo (1382: Tatars win vengeance)

1386 Marriage of Yagailo of Lithuania and Yadwiga of Poland

1392–1430 Partial independence of Lithuania under Vitovt

1397–98 Moscow raids Novgorod's colonial empire

15th CENTURY

1410 Battle of Tannenberg—Teutonic Knights defeated by Poles and Lithuanians

1413 Roman Catholics in Lithuania given special rights, similar to those of Polish Roman Catholics

1420 Khanate of the Crimea separates from Golden Horde

1430–50 "Feud of Shemiaka" between Vasily II and rival princes

1438–39 Council of Florence attempts to heal church schism

c. 1440 Khanate of Kazan separates from Golden Horde

1448 Autocephaly of Russian Church

1453 Constantinople taken by Ottoman Turks (final fall of Byzantine Empire)

1456 Novgorod subordinated to Moscow

1458 Separate metropolitanate at Kiev

1468 Ivan III opens negotiations with

Rome (1472: Ivan's marriage to Sophia Palaeologa)

1471 Ivan III's "crusade" against Novgorod to avenge its acceptance of protection from Roman Catholic Lithuania

1478 Definitive annexation of Novgorod by Moscow

1480 End of "Tatar yoke"

1485 Annexation of Tver by Moscow

1486 Holy Roman Emperor sends envoy to Moscow

1494 Hansa expelled from Novgorod

1497 *Sudebnik* of Ivan III

1498–1502 "Judaizing heresy" and problem of succession

16th CENTURY

1501 Ivan III claims all of former Russian land as patrimony

Poland and Lithuania agree to choose same ruler

1503 Victory of Josephites at Church Council

1510 Annexation of Pskov by Moscow

1514 Annexation of Smolensk from Lithuania

1517 Annexation of Ryazan, last independent principality

1524, 1527 Muscovite envoys visit Spain (via England and Netherlands)

1533 Accession of Ivan the Terrible (at age 3)

1543 Prince Andrei Shuisky given to dogs

1547 Ivan crowned tsar

1549 Peresvietov's first petition to Ivan

1550 *Sudebnik* of Ivan IV

1551 Church Council adopts reforms (*Stoglav sobor*)

1552 Conquest of Khanate of Kazan

1553 Ivan near death

Expedition of Englishmen Willoughby and Chancellor opens trade routes

1556 Conquest of Astrakhan

1558 Beginning of Livonian War

1560 Death of Anastasia, Ivan's first wife

1564 Flight of Prince Kurbsky

1565 Establishment of *oprichnina*

1566 First zemsky sobor

1569 Union of Lublin between Lithuania and Poland

Ivan's overtures to Queen Elizabeth I of England

1570 Murder of Metropolitan Philip

1571 Sack of Moscow by Crimean Tatars

1581 Loss of Narva to Swedes

Ivan courts Lady Mary Hastings

1582 Yermak overthrows Khanate of Sibir

1582–83 Armistices with Poland and Sweden end Livonian War

1584 Death of Ivan the Terrible

1585 Boris Godunov "Lord Protector"

1586 Beginnings of permanent penetration of Siberia

1589 Metropolitan of Moscow raised to rank of patriarch

1590–93 War with Sweden

1591 Report of Giles Fletcher to Queen Elizabeth of England

Failure of last serious raid of Crimean Tatars on Moscow

Death of Tsarevich Dmitry at Uglich

1596 Orthodox clergy of Lithuania accept Brest Union with Rome (Uniate Church)

1597 General registration of *kabalas*

Five-year limitation on recovering fugitive peasants

1598 Extinction of old dynasty; election of Godunov as tsar

1598–1613 Time of the Troubles

17th CENTURY

1601–03 Famine; Khlopka's revolt; appearance of Pretender in Poland

1604 "False Dmitry" invades Russian ukraine

1605 Death of Boris Godunov; enthronement of "False Dmitry"

1606 Murder of "False Dmitry"; Vasily Shuisky tsar

1606–08 Bolotnikov revolt

1608 "Brigand" ("Second False Dmitry") established at Tushino; spread of civil war

1610 Intervention by Poland; Treaty of Smolensk; Poles occupy Moscow

1611 National reaction; Liapunov's march on Moscow; riots

1612 Minin and Pozharsky re-take Moscow from Poles

1613 Election of Michael Romanov by zemsky sobor; beginning of Romanov dynasty

1617 Peace of Stolbovo with Sweden; Swedes evacuate Novgorod

1618 Truce of Deulino with Poland; Poland in possession of Smolensk

1619 Filaret patriarch and co-tsar (died 1633)

1630 Dutch ask grain monopoly

1631 Ecclesiastical Academy founded at Kiev

1632 First Russian ironworks using water power (at Tula)

1632–34 Unsuccessful war with Poland over Smolensk

1637 Russians reach Pacific

1642 Zemsky sobor declines offer of Azov by cossacks

1648 Moscow riots

1649 *Ulozhenie* (code of laws)
Khmelnitsky leads cossacks in revolt against Poles

1652 Founding of "German liberty" settlement at Moscow
Nikon becomes patriarch; launching of reforms (1653)

1653 Alexis extends protection to Zaporogian cossacks; war with Poland (1654–67)

1656–61 War with Sweden

1658 Nikon withdraws from patriarchate

1661 Peace of Kardis with Sweden

1662–63 Riots over copper currency

1665 Founding of Russian foreign post

1666–67 Church Council; deposition of Nikon

1667 Truce of Andrusovo with Poland
Novotorgovyi Ustav (New Trade Statute)

1670–71 Cossack peasant revolt led by Razin

1672 First dramatic troupe

1679 Introduction of household tax

1682 Archpriest Avvakum burned at stake
Abolition of *miestnichestvo*
Accession of Peter I; regency of Sophia (to 1689)

1683 Jan Sobieski of Poland saves Vienna from Turks

1686 Permanent peace with Poland; war with Turks in Crimea

1689 Treaty of Nerchinsk with China
Overthrow of Sophia's regency

1696 Capture of Azov

1697 *Preobrazhensky Prikaz* given wide police powers

1697–98 Peter's first visit to West

1699 Establishment of *Ratusha* and of Privy Chancellery

1700 Lapse of Patriarchate
Reform of calendar (of alphabet, 1708–10)
Peace with Turkey; beginning of Great Northern War against Sweden

18th CENTURY

1701 Pososhkov's *On the Conduct of War*
Revival of Monastery Bureau (founded by Alexis)
Navigation School and Artillery School founded at Moscow

1703 Beginnings of St. Petersburg
Launching of first Russian frigate
Vedomosti ("News"), Peter's newspaper

1705 Beard tax

1707 Charles XII of Sweden defeats Poland, turns on Russia

1708 Administrative decentralization —*guberniyas*

1709 Defeat of Charles XII at Poltava (Lesna, 1708)

1710 Deficit; new census
1711 Pruth campaign against Turks (Russia loses Azov again); beginnings of Senate; "fiscals"
1712 Peter marries Catherine
1714 Naval victory at Hangud over Swedes
Law of *majorat* (repealed 1730)
1715 Naval Academy at St. Petersburg
1715 Birth of grandson (son of Alexis) to Peter
1716 Flight of Tsarevich Alexis
1717 New census
Debacle in Khiva; Khan slaughters Peter's men
1718 Recentralization; the "colleges"; census of "souls" ordered
Trial and death of Tsarevich Alexis
1719 Attempt to reopen negotiations with China
1720 Establishment of Chief Magistracy and of Holy Governing Synod
1721 Peace of Nystadt with Sweden—end of Great Northern War
1721–23 War with Persia
1722 Establishment of lay *Ober-prokuror* of Holy Synod and of Procurator-General of the Senate
Law on Imperial succession
Table of Ranks
1723 Expedition to Madagascar
1724 Captain Bering sent to find limits of America
First (partial) collection of "soul tax"
Russian Academy of Sciences
Pososhkov's *On Poverty and Wealth*
1724 Coronation of Catherine as Empress
1725 Death of Peter I
1726 Formation of Supreme Privy Council
1727 Death of Catherine; accession of Peter II; exile of Menshikov
1730 Death of Peter II; accession of Anna; overthrow of Supreme Privy Council
Return of Bering; second expedition (1733-43)
1731 Establishment of "Cabinet"
1736 Strengthening of nobles' monopoly of ownership of serfs
1740 Working day in "factories" limited to 14 hours
Death of Anna; Münnich conspiracy overthrows Bühren
1741 Accession of Elizabeth—by overthrowing Anna's chosen successor, Ioann Antonovich (Ivan VI)
1742 Elizabeth's heir chosen (Peter III)
1744 Abolition of death penalty
1745 Peter's marriage to Sophia of Anhalt-Zerbst (later Catherine II)
1747 Academy of Sciences (founded 1725) reorganized
1754 Attempted codification of laws; birth of son to Catherine
University of Moscow founded
1756 Entry into Seven Years' War
1758 Academy of Arts founded; Lomonosov in control of Academy of Science
1761 Death of Elizabeth; Peter III withdraws from war with Prussia
1762 Emancipation of nobility from service obligations
Overthrow of Peter III; accession of Catherine II
1763 Senate power destroyed by division into special departments
Poniatowski king of Poland (Russian protectorate by 1767)
1765 Free Economic Society founded
1766 Catherine's "Instruction" to codification Commission charged with preparing new code of laws
1768 Work of Commission turned over to committees
1770–1774 War with Turkey; Treaty of Kuchuk Kainardji (1774)
1772 First Partition of Poland
1773–1774 Pugachev uprising
1775 Break-up of Zaporogian "cossack host"

1775 Reform of local government
1780 "Armed Neutrality of the North"
1783 Legal confirmation of serfdom in Ukraine
Crimea annexed
Reduction of authority of Jewish *kahals*
1785 Charter to the Nobility; Charter to the Towns
1787–1792 War with Turkey; Treaty of Jassy
1790 Radishchev transported to Siberia
1792 Imprisonment of Novikov
1793 Second Partition of Poland
1795 Third Partition of Poland
1796 Death of Catherine; accession of Paul
1798 Suvorov in Italy
1799–1800 Derzhavin Report on policy toward the Jews

19th CENTURY

1801 Murder of Paul; accession of Alexander I
Beginning of conquest of Caucasus
1802 Reorganization of Senate; establishment of Ministries
1803 Decree on "Free Agriculturists"
1804 Statute on the Jews
Founding of universities at Kharkov and Kazan
1805 Entry into coalition against France; Austerlitz (1805), Jena (1806)
1807 Treaty of Tilsit with Napoleon
1808 Attempt at transplantation of Jews
1809 Conquest of Finland
1810 Speransky report
Georgia made a protectorate
1812 Annexation of Bessarabia
Napoleon takes Moscow
1814 Alexander enters Paris in triumph
1814–15 Congress of Vienna
1815 Holy Alliance and Quadruple Alliance
1815 "Military colonies"
1821 Prince Ypsilanti in Rumania; outbreak of Greek revolt
1823 Monroe Doctrine
1825 Death of Alexander I; accession of Nicholas I
Decembrist revolt; aftermath of secret committees to plan reforms
1828–29 War with Turkey; Treaty of Adrianople
1830 July Revolution in France
1831–33 Polish insurrection
1831 Pushkin's *Eugen Onegin* completed
1832 Mehemet Ali attacks Turkey
1833 Treaty of Unkiar-Skelessi with Turkey
Publication of *Full Collection of the Laws*
Pushkin's *The Bronze Horseman*
1834 Pushkin's *The Queen of Spades*
1836 Pushkin's *The Captain's Daughter*
Gogol's *Inspector General*
Glinka's *A Life for the Tsar* (*Ivan Susanin*)
1839 Renewed troubles with Egypt
1840 Permission to emancipate "possessional peasants"
Lermontov's *Hero of Our Times*
1841 London Straits Convention
1842 Gogol's *Dead Souls*
Glinka's *Ruslan and Ludmilla*
1844 Jewish *kahals* abolished
Nicholas revisits London
1847 Bibikov's "Inventory Regulations"
1847–51 Turgenev's *Sportsman's Sketches*
1848 Revolutions in France, Italy, and the Germanies
Death of Bielinsky
1849 Hungary crushed by Russia and restored to Austria
1850 "Humiliation of Olmütz"
1851 Herzen's letter to Michelet, *Russia and Socialism*

1852 Proclamation of Second Empire in France
1853–56 Crimean War; Treaty of Paris
1855 Death of Nicholas I; accession of Alexander II
1856 Turgenev's *Rudin*
1857 Alexander appoints Secret Committee
1858 Publication of Imperial Rescript
1858–59 Chernyshevsky's articles on agrarian problem
1859 Editing Commission appointed
Surrender of Shamil completes conquest of Caucasus
Goncharov's *Oblomov*
First serious project of factory legislation
Russian Musical Society founded by Anton Rubinstein
1860 Founding of State Bank
Founding of Vladivostok
1861 Reëstablishment of local government for Congress Kingdom of Poland
Emancipation Proclamation
1861–62 Flood of revolutionary proclamations and peasant revolts
1861–62 Dostoevsky's *Memoirs from the House of Death*
1861–1876 Activity of Bakunin in Western Europe
1862 Arrest of Chernyshevsky; *What Is to Be Done?* written
1862 Turgenev's *Fathers and Sons*
Petersburg Conservatory founded
1862–68 Activities of Pisarev
1863 Imperial serfs freed
First publication of budget figures
University statutes
1863–64 Polish insurrection
1864 Judicial reform
Dostoevsky's *Memoirs from Underground*
1865–67 Establishment of zemstvos (decreed 1864)
1865–85 Establishment of control over Central Asia
1865 State peasants freed
1866 Dostoevsky's *Crime and Punishment*
Moscow Conservatory founded
Karakozov's attempt on life of Alexander
1867 Katkov turns to Russification
Rimsky-Korsakov's *Sadko*
Sale of Alaska to U.S.
1868 Dostoevsky's *Idiot*
1868–69 Lavrov's *Historical Letters*
1869 Tolstoy's *War and Peace*
1869–70 Nechaiev's "The People's Assize" formed
1870 Repudiation of Black Sea clauses of Treaty of Paris of 1856
Tchaikovsky's *Romeo and Juliet*
Municipal dumas reorganized
1871 Restrictions on Gymnasia
Pogrom at Odessa, first of series
1871–72 Dostoevsky's *The Possessed*
1871–73 Shchedrin-Saltykov's *The Golovlev Family*
1872 Medical schools opened to women
1872–74 Kropotkin's agitation among workers
1874 Army reform on "Prussian system"
Tchaikovsky's *Piano Concerto No. 1*
Mussorgsky's *Boris Godunov* produced
1874–76 "Go to the People" movement
1875 Acquisition of Sakhalin
1876 "Land and Freedom"
Borodin's *Second Symphony*
1877 Tchaikovsky's *Fourth Symphony;* failure of *Swan Lake*
Tolstoy's *Anna Karenina*
1877–78 Russo-Turkish War; Treaty of San Stefano
1878 Congress of Berlin
League of Opposition Elements
Tchaikovsky's *Violin Concerto*
1879 "The People's Will" and "General Redistribution"

1880 Dostoevsky's *Brothers Karamazov*
Leo Tolstoy's "conversion"
1880–81 Loris-Melikov's "dictatorship of the heart"
1881 Assassination of Alexander II; accession of Alexander III
Revival of Three Emperors' League; renewed 1884
1882 Prohibition of child labor in factories
Ignatiev's "Temporary Rules" on the Jews
1883 D. Tolstoy checks pogroms; Pahlen Commission appointed
Peasants Land Bank established
"Emancipation of Labor" formed at Geneva
1884 Railway constructed between Krivoi Rog and Donets basin
1885 Nobles Land Bank established
Tkachev's *Nabat*
Morozov strike; further factory legisolation 1885–86
1886 Abolition of soul tax
1887 "Reinsurance Treaty"
1888 Pahlen Report on government policy toward Jews
1889 Alexander's toast to Montenegro, "Russia's only faithful friend"
Establishment of "land captains"
Chekhov's *Dreary Story*
1891 Trans-Siberian railway begun
1892 Tchaikovsky's *Nutcracker Suite*
1893 Witte appointed Minister of Finance
Death of Tchaikovsky
1894 Dual Alliance with France
Accession of Nicholas II; rejection of zemstvo appeals
1895 Intervention against Japan
1896 Formation of *Bund*
Chinese Eastern Railway begun
St. Petersburg mass strike
1897 Working day limited to 11½ hours
Transition to gold standard begun
1897 Polish National Democratic Party founded
1898 Russian drive for world peace and disarmament launched
Lease on Port Arthur
First Congress of Russian Social Democratic Party at Minsk
Success of Chekhov's *Seagull* under Stanislavsky's direction
1899 First Hague Peace Congress
Curtailment of Finnish autonomy
Hay's "Open Door Policy"
1899–1900 Soloviev's *Three Conversations*
1900 Boxer Rebellion in China

20th CENTURY

1901 Formation of Socialist Revolutionary Party
1902 Wave of peasant disturbances
Anglo-Japanese alliance
Lenin's *What Is to Be Done?*
Gorky's *Lower Depths*
Osvobozhdenie ("Liberation") founded at Stuttgart
1903 "Zemstvo Constitutionalists"
"Second" (Brussels-London) Congress of Russian Social Democratic Workers' Party
Workmen's Compensation Act (broadened 1912)
Witte loses ascendancy to Pleve
Wave of industrial strikes (including Zubatov's at Odessa)
Kishinev pogrom

1904

Jan. Union of Liberation formed
Feb. 9 Japanese attack Port Arthur
July 28 Assassination of Pleve
Oct. Baltic fleet sails for Far East
Nov. Zemstvo meeting at St. Petersburg
Dec. Banquet campaign for constitution

1905

Jan. 1 Surrender of Port Arthur
22 "Bloody Sunday"
Feb. 17 Assassination of Grand Duke Serge
Feb. 26–March 12 Battle of Mukden
March 3 Bulygin promise of consultative Duma
May Formation of Union of Unions
First workers' soviet, at Ivanovo-Voznesensk
May 27 Battle of Tsushima
June Mutiny of the *Potemkin*
Aug. 9 Opening of negotiations at Portsmouth, New Hampshire
14 Defeat of Vladivostok squadron
16 Congress of Peasants' Union
19 Issue of electoral law for Bulygin Duma
Sept. 5 Treaty of Portsmouth signed
Oct. 23 Rail strike becomes general strike
27 Formation of Petersburg Soviet of Workers' Deputies
28 Formation of Constitutional Democratic Party
30 Manifesto promises constitution
Nov. Formation of "Union of 17 October" (Octobrists)
Nov. 1 St. Petersburg Soviet calls off strike
13 Strike renewed for 8-hour day (changed to support of Kronstadt mutiny)
16 Witte's cancellation of redemption dues (halved for 1906)
27–28 Sebastopol mutiny
29 Arrest of committee of Peasants' Union
Dec. 5 Moscow Soviet formed
9 Arrest of chairman of St. Petersburg Soviet, Khrustalev-Nosar; Trotsky succeeds him
15 Attempted fiscal strike

1905 (*cont.*)

15 Mutiny of Moscow garrison
16 Arrest of whole executive committee of Petersburg Soviet
23 Barricades at Moscow (street-fighting Dec. 30-Jan. 1)
24 Publication of new electoral law

1906

Jan. 15 Opening of Algeciras conference
Feb. 19 Limited legalization of trade unions
March 5 New manifesto limits promised concessions
17 Withdrawal of right of free assembly
May 6 Imperial Rescript reaffirms principle of autocracy
10 Meeting of First Duma; dismissal of Witte
July Stolypin prime minister
21 Dissolution of Duma; "Vyborg Manifesto"
Oct. 18–Nov. 22 Stolypin decrees agrarian reform

1907

March 2 Meeting of Second Duma
June 16 Dissolution of Duma; publication of new electoral law
Aug. 31 Conclusion of Triple Entente
Oct. Meeting of Third Duma

1908

Bosnian crisis
Production of Rimsky-Korsakov's *Le Coq d'Or*

1910

Death of Tolstoy
Stravinsky's *Firebird* produced by Diaghilev's *Ballet Russe* in Paris; (*Petrouchka,* 1911; *Sacre du Printemps,* 1913)

1911

Prokofiev's *First Piano Concerto;* (*Love for Three Oranges,* 1918)
Assassination of Stolypin (Sept. 14)

1912

Lena goldfields massacre
National health insurance for workers
Election of Fourth Duma

1913

Gorky's *Childhood*

1914

Aug. 1 Outbreak of war
8 Duma supports government policy
Nov. 1 Arrest of Bolshevik Duma deputies

1915

Formation of War Industry Committees
Sept. Nicholas II assumes Supreme Command
Formation of "Progressive Bloc" in Duma
International socialist meeting at Zimmerwald

1916

Dec. 2 Purishkevich denounces Rasputin in Duma
29 Murder of Rasputin

1917

Jan. Army-Duma discussions of need to remove Empress
March 8 Bread lines in St. Petersburg (Petrograd) lead to general riots
11 Duma prorogued by Imperial edict
12 Collapse of government authority; power vacuum
12 Formation of Provisional Committee of the Duma

1917 (*cont.*)

12 Formation of Petrograd Soviet of Workers' Deputies
12 Emperor orders troops to march against Petrograd
13 Moscow Soviet formed
14 Petrograd Soviet issues Order No. 1
14 Emperor agrees to name Rodzianko premier; he declines
15 Emperor agrees to abdicate
15 Petrograd Soviet ratifies agreement with Provisional Committee of Duma
15 Provisional Government formed, headed by Prince Lvov
15 S.R. Party pledges conditional support to Provisional Government
15 Formation of Ukrainian Rada
16 Grand Duke Michael declines to assume Imperial authority
18 Soviet calls for end of strikes
Miliukov's first note to the Allies
20–April 8 Lenin's *Letters from Afar*
20 Provisional Government orders arrest of Emperor Nicholas II
23 Petrograd Soviet secures employers' agreement to 8-hour day
25 Grand Duke Nicholas relieved of Supreme Command
25 Provisional Government abolishes death penalty
25 Return of Kamenev and Stalin from Siberia
26 Provisional Government abolishes courts martial
27 Soviet broadcasts appeal on war and peace
28 Kamenev's statement on Bolshevik position on war
28 Rodzianko pledge to accept decisions of Constituent Assembly

1917 (*cont.*)

31 Moscow Soviet imposes 8-hour day on employers there

April Lenin's *First Letter on Tactics*

April 2 Provisional Government ends religious and national discrimination

7 Provisional Government establishes state grain monopoly

8 Meeting of Peasants' Union

9 Lvov reassures public on war aims

9 Kamenev explains Bolshevik attitude toward Revolution

11 All-Russian Conference of Soviets meets at Petrograd

13 Return of Plekhanov to Russia

16 Return of Lenin; welcome at Finland Station

17 April Theses announced by Lenin

21 Return of Chernov to Russia

25 Soviet approves Lvov's statement on war aims

May 1 New Miliukov note to Allies

4 Soviet prevents outbreak in streets

4 Main Land Committee appointed

8 Petrograd Soviet calls for international socialist congress at Stockholm

11 Lvov appeals to Soviet for support in crisis

12–16 May crisis

17 Opening of All-Russian Congress of Peasant Deputies

18 Formation of Coalition Provisional Government

Return of Trotsky

22 Return of Martov to Russia

June 2 Resignation of Konovalov

4 Brusilov Commander-in-Chief

4 Opening of First All-Russian Congress of Soviets

24 Kerensky forbids meeting of Ukrainian Army Congress

1917 (*cont.*)

27 Election of Constituent Assembly set for September 30

July 1 July offensive launched by Russian army against Germans in Galicia

16 Resignation of Cadet ministers

16–17 July Uprising against Provisional Government

19 German counter-offensive

20 Provisional Government adopts socialist program

20 Resignation of Prince Lvov; Kerensky premier

25 Kerensky calls for State Conference at Moscow

Aug. 3–16 Sixth Bolshevik Party Congress

4 Soviet entrusts power to Kerensky

6 Kerensky assumes dictatorial power

21 Foreign Minister Tereshchenko torpedoes Stockholm Congress

22 Election of Constituent Assembly postponed to November 25

25–28 Moscow State Conference

Sept. 3 Fall of Riga to Germans

7 Lvov interview with Kornilov

8 Lvov interview with Kerensky

9 Kornilov dismissed—Putsch begins

9 Directory of Five established

14 Kornilov arrested

16 Soviet call for Democratic Conference

19 Resignation of presidium of Petrograd Soviet; Bolsheviks take over

27 Meeting of Democratic Conference

Oct. 4 Kerensky forms new coalition with Cadets

6 Opening of Pre-Parliament

Call for election of Second All-Russian Congress of Soviets

1917 (*cont.*)

8 Petrograd Soviet refuses support to Kerensky

20 Council of Russian Republic meets

22 Lenin returns from Finland to Petrograd

23 Bolshevik Central Committee decides on armed uprising

26 Military Revolutionary Committee set up by Petrograd Soviet

30 Meeting of Second All-Russian Congress of Soviets postponed

Nov. 5 Garrison of Peter-and-Paul Fortress won over by Trotsky

6 Pre-Parliament insists Kerensky initiate reforms at once

6 Beginning of Bolshevik armed uprising

7 Bolshevik seizure of power ("the October Revolution")

7–9 Meeting of Second All-Russian Congress of Soviets

8 Fall of Winter Palace; formation of "Committee to Save the Country and the Revolution" [from the Bolsheviks]; at Moscow, Bolshevik seizure of Kremlin

9 Press decree shuts down hostile newspapers

9–13 Advance of Krasnov on Petrograd

10 Bolsheviks expelled from Kremlin

11 Uprising of cadets in Petrograd; proclamation of 8-hour day

13 Retreat of Krasnov; proclamation of social insurance

15 Bolsheviks recapture Kremlin; beginning of formation of anti-Bolshevik Volunteer Army at Novocherkassk; declaration of self-determination

17 Protest of Bolshevik commissars; resignations from Central Committee

20 Proclamation of Ukrainian National Republic; order to open

1917 (*cont.*)

armistice negotiations ignored by Dukhonin

21 Restoration of Patriarchate

22 Krylenko orders rank-and-file to negotiate with Germans

23–28 Special Congress of Peasants' Deputies

25 Beginning of elections for Constituent Assembly

27 Germans agree to negotiate; "Decree on Workers' Control"

Dec. 1–5 Armistice negotiations at Brest-Litovsk (agreement signed Dec. 15)

11 Demonstration at Petrograd for Constituent Assembly

12 Stalin conditions national independence on demand by workers

14 Supreme Council of People's Economy (*Vesenha*) established

17 Armistice in effect; Bolshevik ultimatum to Ukraine

20 Establishment of *Cheka*

22 Peace negotiations opened at Brest-Litovsk

22 Left SR's enter coalition government with Bolsheviks

25 Germans accept Russian "Six Points" as basis of general peace

27 Nationalization of the banks

31 Civil marriage decreed; independence of Finland conceded

1918

Jan. 4 Germans open negotiations with Ukraine

5 Germans withdraw acceptance of "Six Points"

5 Lloyd George's Mansion House speech

7 Trotsky in person reopens negotiations at Brest

8 Wilson's "Fourteen Points"

11 Lozovsky, trade-union leader, expelled from Bolshevik Party

18 Meeting of Constituent Assembly (dissolved Jan. 19)

1918 (*cont.*)

18 Hoffman ultimatum to Trotsky

21 Bolsheviks decide to stall negotiations pending German revolution

21 Opening of First All-Russian Congress of Trade Unions

22 Ukrainian Rada declares independence

23–31 Third Congress of Soviets

29 Red Army establishes soviet government at Kiev

Feb. 1 Patriarch Tikhon anathematizes Bolsheviks

5 Separation of Church and State

6 Rada signs peace treaty with Germans

9 "Law of land socialization" (published Feb. 19)

10 "No war, no peace"

10 All state loans annulled

16 Germans denounce armistice; hostilties resumed Feb. 18

17 Lenin's plea for acceptance of peace terms rejected (reversal Feb. 18)

22 Trotsky reports Allied offer of aid; accepted

23 New German peace terms accepted

March 3 Treaty signed at Brest-Litovsk

5 British landing at Murmansk

6–8 Seventh Party Congress held at Moscow; adoption of name *Communist*

14–18 Fourth Congress of Soviets; ratification of the peace treaty

16 Occupation of Kiev by Germans

21 Launching of last German offensive in West

26 Agreement for evacuation of Czechoslovak Legion

April 5 Japanese landing at Vladivostok

22 Foreign trade nationalized

1918 (*cont.*)

23 German Ambassador Mirbach arrives in Moscow

26 Lenin's theses on accounting and control approved

May 9 New land decree opens war on "kulaks" (published May 13)

14–17 Brawl at Cheliabinsk (Czech units ordered broken up May 23)

16–19 Mutiny in Red Army at Saratov

17 Krasnov elected ataman of Don Cossacks

30 Establishment of "Western Siberian Commissariat" at Tomsk

June 3 Decision to nationalize industry

8 Establishment of *Komuch* at Samara

11 Law on "committees of the village poor" (ordered liquidated Dec. 2)

28 Decree on nationalization of industry

July 1 Joint Conference of Shop Committees and Trade Unions condemns strikes

2 Allied Supreme War Council decides on intervention

6 British agreement with Murmansk Soviet

6 Murder of Mirbach; Moscow disturbances July 7-8

6–23 Revolt at Yaroslavl

July Fifth Congress of Soviets; constitution of RSFSR adopted July 10

16 Murder of tsar and family

Aug. American and Japanese Troops land in Vladivostok

Aug. 2 Chaikovsky government set up at Archangel

7 People's Army takes Kazan (captures gold reserve)

Sept. 4 American troops land at Archangel

23 "White" coalition government formed at Ufa

1918 (*cont.*)

Oct. Patriarch Tikhon under house arrest

31 General liability to compulsory labor

Nov. 9–10 German revolution; German armistice effective Nov. 11

13 Repudiation of Brest-Litovsk treaty by Sixth Congress of Soviets

18 Kolchak coup at Omsk

21 Nationalization of all trade

26 French landing at Odessa

Dec. 18 British landing at Batum

1919

March 4 Founding of Comintern (Third International), at Moscow

13 Kolchak launches drive against Bolsheviks

18–23 Eighth Party Congress; Politburo and Ogburo established

March Establishment of Council of Labor and Defense (STO)

21 Bela Kun regime set up in Hungary

April Withdrawal of French from Odessa (occupied by Bolsheviks April 6)

May–June Denikin advances into Donbas

Summer Withdrawal of British from Baku

Fall Withdrawal of Allied forces from North Russia

Oct. Yudenich dash on Petrograd

Denikin reaches Orel

Nov. 14 Kolchak loses Omsk

1920

Jan. 15 Kolchak surrendered to Bolsheviks (shot Feb. 7)

8 Denikin's capital taken by Bolsheviks

16 Lifting of blockade by Allies

April 4 Baron Wrangel takes command from Denikin; launches offensive (June 6)

1920 (*cont.*)

27 Lenin's *Left-Wing Communism: An Infantile Disorder*

May 6 Poles take Kiev

July Withdrawal of British from Batum

Second Congress of Comintern, at Moscow (the "21 Conditions")

Oct. 12 Treaty of Riga

Nov. Trotsky proposes shake-up of trade unions

14 Evacuation of Wrangel from Crimea

23 Concessions to foreign capitalists approved in principle

1921

Feb. 27 Soviet regime established in Georgia

March Revolt in Thuringia crushed (The March Action)

March 1–17 Kronstadt mutiny

8–16 Tenth Party Congress (fixed tax on peasants; Party purge ordered)

16 Trade agreement with England

April 5 "Black Friday" in Great Britain

7 Decontrol of coöperatives

July Third Congress of Comintern (announces ebb of revolutionary tide)

Sept. 15 Extension of social insurance

Dec. 19–22 Eleventh Party Conference abandons principle of equal pay

1922

March 27–April 2 Eleventh Party Congress; Cheka replaced by GPU

April 4 Stalin formally Secretary-General

16 Treaty of Rapallo with Germany

May Arrest of Patriarch Tikhon

25 Lenin's first stroke

Oct. Withdrawal of Japanese from Vladivostok

1922 (*cont.*)

Dec. 23 Opening of Tenth Congress of Soviets (First All-Union Congress)

25 Lenin's "testament" written (codicil added in Jan.)

30 Formation of Union of Soviet Socialist Republics announced (Constitution approved by Second Congress on Jan. 31, 1924)

1923

March 23 Lenin's second stroke

April 17–25 Twelfth Party Congress

Oct. 8 Trotsky launches attack on bureaucracy

1924

Peoples Republic established in Mongolia

Jan. 21 Death of Lenin

31 Constitution of U.S.S.R. approved by Second All-Union Congress of Soviets

Feb. Recognition of U.S.S.R. by Great Britain and Italy (by France in Oct., by Japan in following year)

May 23–31 Thirteenth Party Congress; Trotsky confesses errors

Oct. Trotsky publishes *Lessons of October*

1925

Jan. Trotsky removed as War Commissar

Dec. 18–31 Fourteenth Party Congress

1926

April Zinoviev ousted from Politburo

Oct. Trotsky and Kamenev ousted from Politburo

1927

May Recognition of Metropolitan Sergius as head of Church

26 Rupture of diplomatic relations with Great Britain (restored 1929)

1927 (*cont.*)

Nov. 14 Trotsky and Zinoviev expelled from Party

Dec. 2–19 Fifteenth Party Congress

15 Rupture of diplomatic relations with China; Communist revolt in China crushed

1928

Adoption of First Five-Year Plan (*Piatiletka*)

Anti-religious instruction replaces non-religious education

March "Shakhty" trial in Donets coal mines

Aug. 29 Acceptance of Kellogg-Briand Pact

1929

Bubnov in charge of education

Jan. Trotsky deported

April 8 Redefinition of legal position of Church

June Tomsky transferred from trade-union organization

Summer Beginning of "second agrarian revolution"

Nov. 17 Bukharin dropped from Politburo

1930

March 2 Stalin's "dizzy with success" rebuke

March Sergius denies persecution

March Litvinov Foreign Minister

June 26–July 23 Sixteenth Party Congress; Tomsky dropped from Politburo

Oct. 9 Decree abolishing unemployment

Nov.–Dec. Ramzin trial (Ramzin restored June 1931)

Dec. Rykov expelled from Politburo

1931–1932 Famine

1932

Dissolution of RAPP; return of Prokofiev

1932 (*cont.*)

Aug. Opening of attack on Pokrovsky and his educational policies

1933

Jan. Metro-Vickers engineers trial
Japanese control of Manchukuo (Manchuria) accepted

May 5 Ratification of neutrality treaty with Germany

Nov. 17 Agreement on U.S. recognition

1934

Birobidzhan recognized as autonomous Jewish state

Jan. 26–Feb. 10 Seventeenth Party Congress: "victory congress"; Second F.Y.P. endorsed

Feb. Formation of "united front" between Third International and French Socialists

16 New trade agreement with Great Britain

April 14 Germany rejects "Eastern Locarno"

May Unification of army administration

May 5 Renewal of Soviet-Polish nonaggression pact

July OGPU merged into NKVD

Sept. 18 Soviet Union enters League of Nations

Dec. 9 Assassination of Kirov

1935

Feb. 6 Constitutional Commission set up

Feb. New statutes on collective farms

March 23 Sale of Chinese Eastern Railway to Manchukuo completed

March Russian army strengthened; restoration of most military titles

May 2 Mutual assistance pact with France initialed

16 Soviet-Czechoslovak pact

May Society of Old Bolsheviks dissolved

1935 (*cont.*)

June 18 Anglo-German naval agreement

July 25–Aug. 31 Seventh Comintern Congress; "Popular Front" endorsed

Aug. 30 Stakhanovism launched

1936

Death of Gorky
Restrictions on divorce and abortion

March 7 Rhineland coup by Germany

June 5 Formation of Leon Blum's Popular Front cabinet in France

12 Publication of draft constitution

22–July 20 Montreux Conference on Straits

July Outbreak of Spanish civil war

Aug. 11 Conscription age reduced to nineteen

Aug. "Trial of the 16" (Zinoviev, Kamenev, etc.)

23 Suicide of Tomsky

Sept. Yezhov succeeds Yagoda

Nov. 25 Stalin Constitution approved

25 Anti-Comintern Pact formed by Germany and Japan

1937

Jan. "Trial of the 17" (Radek, etc.)

Feb. Withdrawal of Gen. Kleber from Spain

May 10 Authority of political commissars restored in army

June Announcement of execution of Tukhachevsky and other high officers

July Japan openly at war with China

Oct. 5 President Roosevelt's "quarantine the aggressor" speech

Nov. 6 Italy joins Anti-Comintern Pact

1938

Eisenstein's *Alexander Nevsky*
Tightening of control over university and technical graduates

March "Trial of the 21" (Bukharin, Yagoda, etc.)

1938 (*cont.*)

13 Hitler announces *Anschluss* with Austria

July Beria takes over from Yezhov as deputy (commissar in Dec.)

Aug.–Sept. Runciman mission to Czechoslovakia

Sept. 29–30 Munich

1939

League of Militant Godless denounces bourgeois atheism

Minimum number of labor days set on collective farms

Stalin prizes awarded to distinguished workers

March 10 Eighteenth Party Congress; Stalin enunciates Soviet foreign policy

31 British guarantee to Poland

April 7 Italian occupation of Albania

13 British guarantees to Greece and Rumania

May 3 Resignation of Litvinov

Aug. 12–17 Military discussions with Allies at Moscow

23 Ribbentrop-Molotov Pact

Sept. 1 German invasion of Poland

3 England and France declare war on Germany

16 Soviet-Japanese truce

17 Russia declares Polish government at an end

Sept. 29–Oct. 10 Soviet occupation of Estonia, Latvia, Lithuania

Oct. 5 Soviet ultimatum to Finland (war begun Nov. 29)

1940

Completion of Sholokhov's *Silent Don*

March 12 End of "Winter War" with Finland

April 9 German invasion of Denmark and Norway

May German breakthrough in West

June 12 Stafford Cripps arrives in Moscow

1940 (*cont.*)

17–22 Seizure of power in Baltic states

22 Armistice signed with Vichy government

26 Soviet ultimatum to Rumania

27 Return to 8-hour day, normal week

Aug. 1–8 Annexation of Baltic states by Soviet Union

2 Annexation of Bessarabia

20 Trotsky murdered in Mexico

Sept. 27 Formation of Tripartite Pact (Germany, Italy, Japan)

Oct. Introduction of tuition fees for higher education

Rumania occupied by German troops

Oct. 2 Creation of State Labor Reserve

Nov. Hungary, Rumania, Slovakia join Tripartite Pact (Bulgaria and Yugoslavia in March 1941)

1941

March Timoshenko's military reforms

April 6 Germans invade Yugoslavia (and Greece)

13 Russo-Japanese neutrality pact

June 22 German invasion of Russia

July 16 Authority of political commissars again restored

Sept. Completion of arrangements for Anglo-American aid to Russia

Dec. 7 Pearl Harbor

1942

Jan. 1 United Nations declaration

Oct. Authority of political commissars again abolished

Aug. Churchill visit to Moscow

Nov. Landings in North Africa

1943

Jan. Casablanca meeting of Churchill and Roosevelt

Feb. 2 Surrender of German General Paulus at Stalingrad

1943 (*cont.*)

April Poles ask Red Cross investigation of Katyn massacre
May Dissolution of Comintern
July Invasion of Sicily
Sept. 7 Sergius becomes Patriarch; Archbishop of York in Moscow
Oct. Council for the Affairs of the Church established
Sept. Landing at Salerno; followed by fall of Mussolini
Nov. Teheran Conference (following Cairo)

1944

June 6 Allied landings in Normandy
July Dumbarton Oaks
Aug. 1–Oct. 2 Warsaw uprising
Sept. Quebec meeting; Morgenthau Plan adopted
Oct. Churchill revisits Moscow

1945

Jan. Recognition of Lublin Committee by Soviet Union
Feb. Yalta conference
March Allied crossing of the Rhine
April 5 Soviet Union denounces pact with Japan
13 Vienna taken by Russians
25–May 2 Berlin taken by Russians
May 8 Armistice
July Japan requests Stalin to mediate
July–Aug. Potsdam conference
Aug. 6 Hiroshima
8 USSR declares war on Japan
15 Japan offers to surrender (armistice signed Sept. 2)

1946

Jan. Uniates received back into Orthodox Church
Challenge to continued Soviet occupation in Iran
Feb. 10 Elections to Supreme Soviet (first since 1937)

1946 (*cont.*)

March 5 Churchill's "Iron Curtain" speech at Fulton, Mo.
July 4 Independence of Philippines
Aug. Turkey rejects Soviet demands relating to Straits
14 Zhdanov attacks Zoshchenko's *Adventures of a Monkey*
Sept. Morgenthau Plan repudiated

1946

Fourth F.Y.P. announced
Dec. Fusion of American and British zones of occupation in Germany

1947

Feb. 10 Peace treaties with Italy, Hungary, Rumania, Bulgaria (Finland)
March 4 Franco-British alliance
12 Truman Doctrine
June 5 Marshall Plan
July 8 Family declared basis of society
Aug. 15 Independence of India
Sept. Cominform established at Belgrad
Oct. Flight of Mikolajczyk from Poland
Dec. Abolition of rationing in Soviet Union

1948

Celebration of 500 years of autocephaly
Jan. 4 Independence of Burma
March 10 Death of Jan Masaryk
17 Benelux alliance with Great Britain and France
April 1 Beginning of Berlin blockade (effective by June)
May 17 Israel recognized by Moscow
June 7 Resignation of Beneš
June Tito attacked as "dictatorial"

1949

Jan. Council for Mutual Economic Assistance created at Warsaw

1949 (*cont.*)

Feb. Purge of unreliable leaders in the satellites

March 18 Basis of NATO laid

May 23 Work begun on German constitution

Sept. 21 People's Republic of China established at Peiping
German Federal Republic functional (state of war ended 1951; sovereignty 1955)

23 U.S.S.R. announces successful test of atom bomb

Oct. 7 German Democratic Republic set up (sovereign 1954)

Dec. 27 Independence of Indonesia

1950

Attack on theories of Professor Marr

June 25 Outbreak of war in Korea (U.S. troops sent June 27)

Nov. 26 Chinese "volunteers" cross Yalu

1951

April 2 SHAPE set up

July 10 Truce negotiations begun in Korea (armistice July 23, 1953)

Sept. 8 U.S. peace treaty with Japan (sovereignty restored April 1952)

1952

Oct. 5–14 Nineteenth Party Congress; Presidium replaces Politburo

1953

Jan. 31 Announcement of doctors' plot

March 5 Death of Stalin

14 Malenkov resigns as First Secretary, keeping premiership

27 Amnesty decree

April 3 Doctors' plot repudiated

June Riots in Czechoslovakia and East Germany

1953 (*cont.*)

July 10 Beria's expulsion from Party announced

27 Korean armistice

Aug. 8 Malenkov promises "abundance" of food and consumers' goods

20 Explosion of first Soviet hydrogen bomb Aug. 12 announced

Sept. 13 Khrushchev First Secretary of Party Central Committee

Oct. Ehrenburg article on creative literature

Nov. Khachaturian article on creative music

Dec. 17 Shostakovich's Tenth Symphony performed

24 Beria's execution announced

1954

Feb. Berlin Conference of foreign Ministers on Austria; Molotov proposes European security organization

March 25 Soviet recognizes sovereignty of East Germany

31 Molotov proposes world security organization for Europe

April 26–July 20 Far Eastern Conference at Geneva

Aug. 30 France rejects European Defense Community

Sept. Formation of SEATO

Oct. 23 Formation of Western European Union, including sovereignty for West Germany

Nov. Decree condemns gross mistakes in scientific atheist propaganda

1955

Jan. 15 USSR accepts sovereignty of West Germany

Feb. 8 Malenkov letter of resignation; Bulganin premier

Feb.–March Eisenhower-Zhukov correspondence

March 22 Mikhailov Minister of Culture

April Bandung Conference

May 14 Warsaw Pact

1955 (*cont.*)

15 Russian signature of Austrian peace treaty
24 Port Arthur handed over to China
26 Khrushchev arrives in Belgrade with apology
31 China releases detained airmen
July 18–23 Summit conference in Geneva
Sept. Adenauer visits Moscow
20 USSR grants East Germany "full freedom of action"

1956

Jan. 26 Porkkala restored to Finland
Feb. 14–25 Twentieth Party Congress; Khrushchev's "secret speech"; Sixth F.Y.P. adopted
April 17 Dissolution of Cominform
Khrushchev and Bulganin visit Great Britain
June 1 Molotov resigns in favor of Shepilov
28 Poznan riots
30 Central Committee condemns "cult of individual"
July Archbishop of York visits Moscow
Oct. 21 Gomulka takes power in Poland
23 Outbreak of Hungarian revolt (suppressed Nov. 4)
29 Release of Cardinal Wyszinski
31 Beginning of Suez fighting
Dec. 10–17 Strike of Hungarian workers
26 USSR ends state of war with Japan

1957

Jan. Warning *re* U.S. bases on foreign soil
17 Khrushchev praises Stalin as fighter at reception to Chou

1957 (*cont.*)

Feb. Yugoslavia protests Soviet policy
May 7 Decentralization of economic administration announced
June 18 Publication of Mao's "flowers" speech
July USSR credit to Yugoslavia
Ousting of Malenkov, Kaganovich, and Molotov
Aug. USSR tests ICBM
Coup in Syria
Khrushchev reassures Yugoslavia
Sept. Tito entertains Gomulka
Oct. 4 Launching of first *sputnik*
7 Testing of new hydrogen warhead announced
Tito recognizes East Germany
Warsaw riots
26 Zhukov relieved of office
Nov. 2 Zhukov condemned
3 Laika in second *sputnik*

1958

March 27 Bulganin resigns as premier; Khrushchev succeeds
April 19–22 Reëlection of Tito and challenge to USSR
July Iraqi revolution
Aug. 15 Bulganin demoted
Nov. 12 Approval of Seven-Year Plan
14 Khrushchev links Bulganin to Malenkov-Molotov group
Dec. 18 Bulganin confesses guilt

1959

Jan. 4–20 Mikoyan visit to U.S.
Jan. 27–Feb. 5 Twenty-first Party Congress
Feb. 6 Iran rebuffs USSR
21–March 3 Macmillan visits Moscow
March China suppresses Tibet
March 8 Revolt in Iraq
16 Khrushchev rebukes Nasser
24 Iraq withdraws from Baghdad Pact

1959 *(cont.)*

April 13 Eisenhower proposes nuclear test ban treaty

19 Tito criticizes USSR

July U.S. resumes supplies to Nasser Iraq suppresses Communists

14 India again moves admission of China to UN

June 28–July 13 Kozlov visit to U.S.

July 23–Aug. 5 Nixon visit to Moscow and Warsaw

Aug. 29 Nehru denounces Chinese aggression

Sept. Soviet moon rocket

15–27 Khrushchev visit to U.S.

Sept. 29–Oct. 6 Khrushchev in China emphasizes peaceful coexistence

Oct. 24 Nehru threatens resistance to China

Nov.–Dec. Agreements on cultural exchanges

1960

Jan. 29 Beginning of Berlin passes dispute

Feb. 13 Trade agreement concluded between USSR and Cuba for 1960–1964

Feb. 13–March 5 Khrushchev tours Asia

March 1 U-2 shot down

May 15 First unmanned space flight (USSR)

May 16 USSR refusal to participate in Paris summit conference; cancellation of invitation to Eisenhower to visit Soviet Union in June

30 Death of Pasternak

July 1 PB-47 shot down

Aug. 19 Laika in space

Sept. 19–Oct. 13 Khrushchev in New York for U.N. General Assembly

1961

Jan. 25 Release of American airmen

Feb. Khrushchev denounces agricultural "mismanagement"

1961 *(cont.)*

April 12 Gagarin first man into space

May 20 Khrushchev announces shift of emphasis in industrial production to give equal priority to light industry (consumer goods)

June 3–4 Meeting of Khrushchev and Kennedy in Vienna

Aug. 19–20 Vice-President Johnson views "Ulbricht Wall"

Oct. 19–31 Twenty-second Party Congress; "different roads to socialism" made official doctrine

1962

Feb. 8 U.S. "Military Command" established in South Vietnam

May Khrushchev accuses U.S. of "acting like a policeman"

Oct. 13 Liberman proposals partly accepted by Khrushchev

Sept. 3 Khrushchev promises aid to Castro

Oct. 22–27 Cuban crisis

Nov.–Dec. Sino-Indian conflict over Sikkim

1963

July 19 Khrushchev rebukes (Chinese) advocates of war

Aug. 5 Nuclear test ban treaty signed

Fall Agricultural crisis in USSR; import of wheat from U.S.

1964

Feb. 14 Expulsion of Molotov, Malenkov, and Kaganovich from Party

Oct. 14 Dismissal of Khrushchev

Oct. 16 First Chinese nuclear test

Dec. 11 World Communist Conference cancelled

1965

Jan. 13 Liberman ideas to be put widely into effect

Feb. 6 Kosygin in Hanoi warns U.S. against bombing North Vietnam

1965 *(cont.)*

March 1–5 World Communist Consultation held without China and its allies

March Kosygin promises rise in standard of living

March 3 Chinese students demonstrate at American embassy in Moscow

Sept. Soviet Union mediates between India and Pakistan

Sept. Arrest of Siniavsky and Daniel

Nov. 11 Chinese repeat charge of American-Soviet collaboration for world domination

1966

Feb. 19 New Five-Year Plan approved by Central Committee

March 29–Apr. 8 Twenty-third Party Congress

April Mao launches "Great Proletarian Culture Revolution"

Oct. 7 Johnson speech veils offer to USSR of spheres of influences

Dec. 13 Central Committee condemns "Mao Tse-tung and his group"

1967

Jan. Economic reform begins in Czechoslovakia

25 Chinese students clash with police in Red Square

26 Signing of pact on peaceful uses of outer space

31 Rumania recognizes West Germany

Feb. 4–6 Embassy wives and children evacuated from Peking

March 2 Kosygin offers to discuss nuclear arms race

April 14 Yugoslav electoral reforms

24–47 Karlovy Vary conference

May–June Arab-Israeli war

June 10 Soviet Union asks Security Council to condemn Israeli "aggression"

1967 *(cont.)*

23–25 Kosygin and Johnson meet at Glassboro

27–29 Stormy meeting of Czech Writers' Union

28–30 Kosygin visit to Castro

July Golberg-Gromyko draft resolution for UN *re* Middle East

Aug. 24 Joint US-USSR preliminary draft of nonproliferation treaty

Oct. 18 USSR gets data back from Venus shot

Nov. 3–7 Celebration of fiftieth anniversary of Bolshevik Revolution

3 Major speech by Brezhnev

22 *UN* adopts British resolution on Middle East

1968

Jan. 6 Dubcek succeeds Novotny as Party secretary in Czechoslovakia

Jan. Svirsky publicly criticises censorship

18 Complete draft of joint US-USSR nonproliferation treaty

30 Tet offensive begins

Feb. 21 Brezhnev in Prague for celebration of twentieth anniversary of coup

26 Preparatory conference at Budapest to plan world Communist meeting

29 Rumania walks out of Budapest meeting

March 30 Svobodä succeeds Novotny as president

31 Partial bombing halt; Johnson not a candidate for reëlection

April 10 Brezhnev denounces "bourgeois ideology" of Czechs

May 15–18 Gosplan rejects market economy

May 5 Dubcek in Moscow; accepts Warsaw Pact maneuvers

May Rumania investigates World Bank

15–18 Gosplan rejects market economy

1968 *(cont.)*

June 20–30 Warsaw Pact maneuvers in Czechoslovakia

June 27 "2,000-word manifesto" of 71 Czech writers

July 1 Nonproliferation treaty signed

July 30–Aug. 1 Cierna meeting

Aug. 10 Tito visits Prague

21 Soviet invasion of Czechoslovakia

24 Tito consults with Rumanian premier

Sept. 30 Budapest meeting postpones world conference called for Nov. 25

Oct. 18 Czech National Assembly ratifies treaty with USSR

23 Statement of Soviet Writers' Union on Czechoslovakia

Nov. 12 Brezhnev affirms theory of "socialist commonwealth"

22 Budapest meeting sets date of world conference for May 1969

Dec. 10 Further increase in defense spending announced in USSR, but

1968 *(cont.)*

promise production of consumer goods faster than of capital goods

Dec. 21 Dubcek threatens "unavoidable measures" if popular opposition continues

22 Gromyko visits Nasser

21–26 Americans in spacecraft orbit moon

28 Israeli raid on Lebanon airport

30 New Soviet proposals to US for Near East settlement

1969

Jan. 1 Federalization of Czechia and Slovakia

March 17 Final preparatory meeting for world conference to be held

May World Communist conference to meet in Moscow

Soviet spacecraft scheduled to make soft landings on Venus

I. SOME EARLY PRINCES AND GRAND PRINCES OF RUS

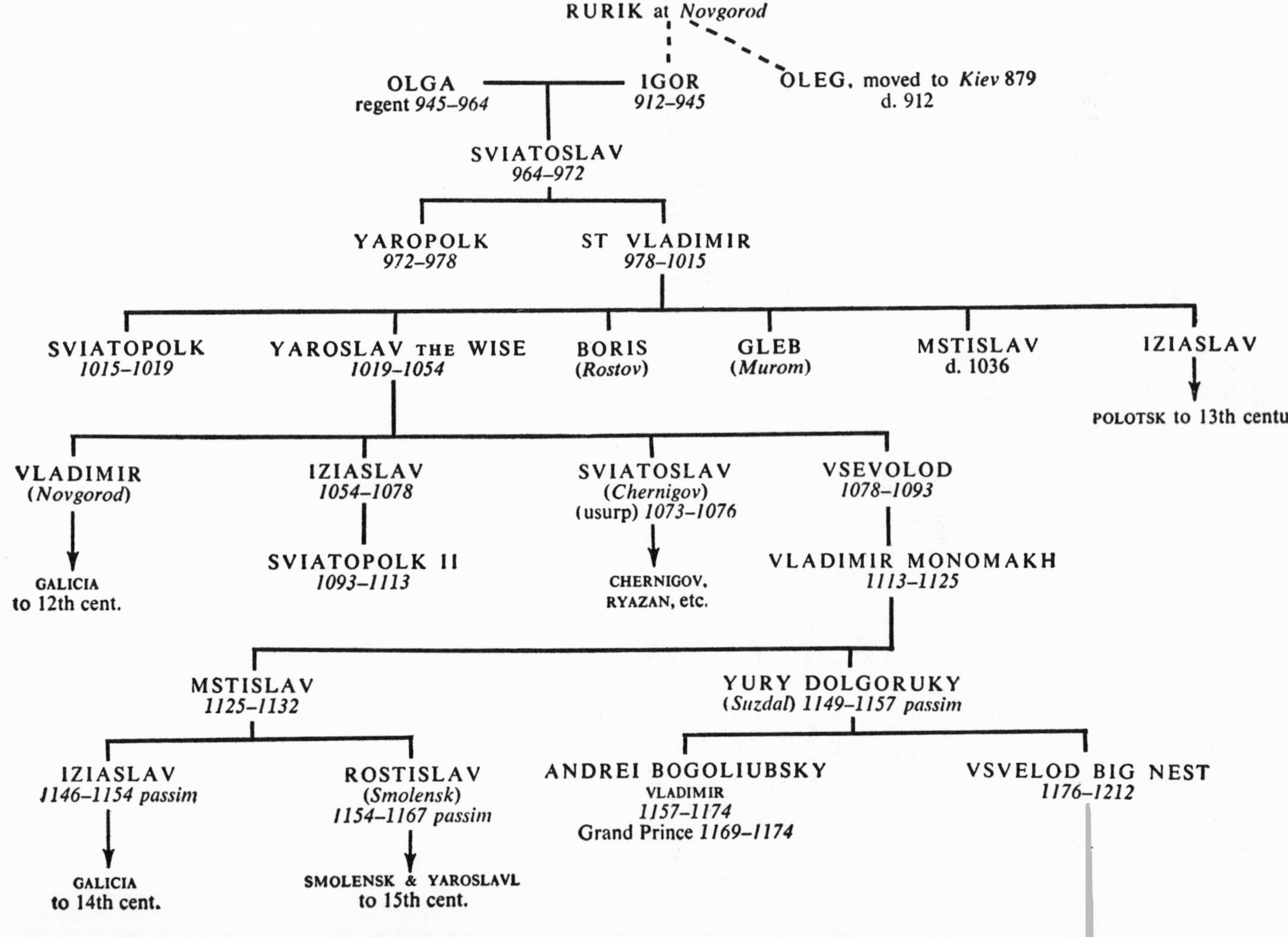

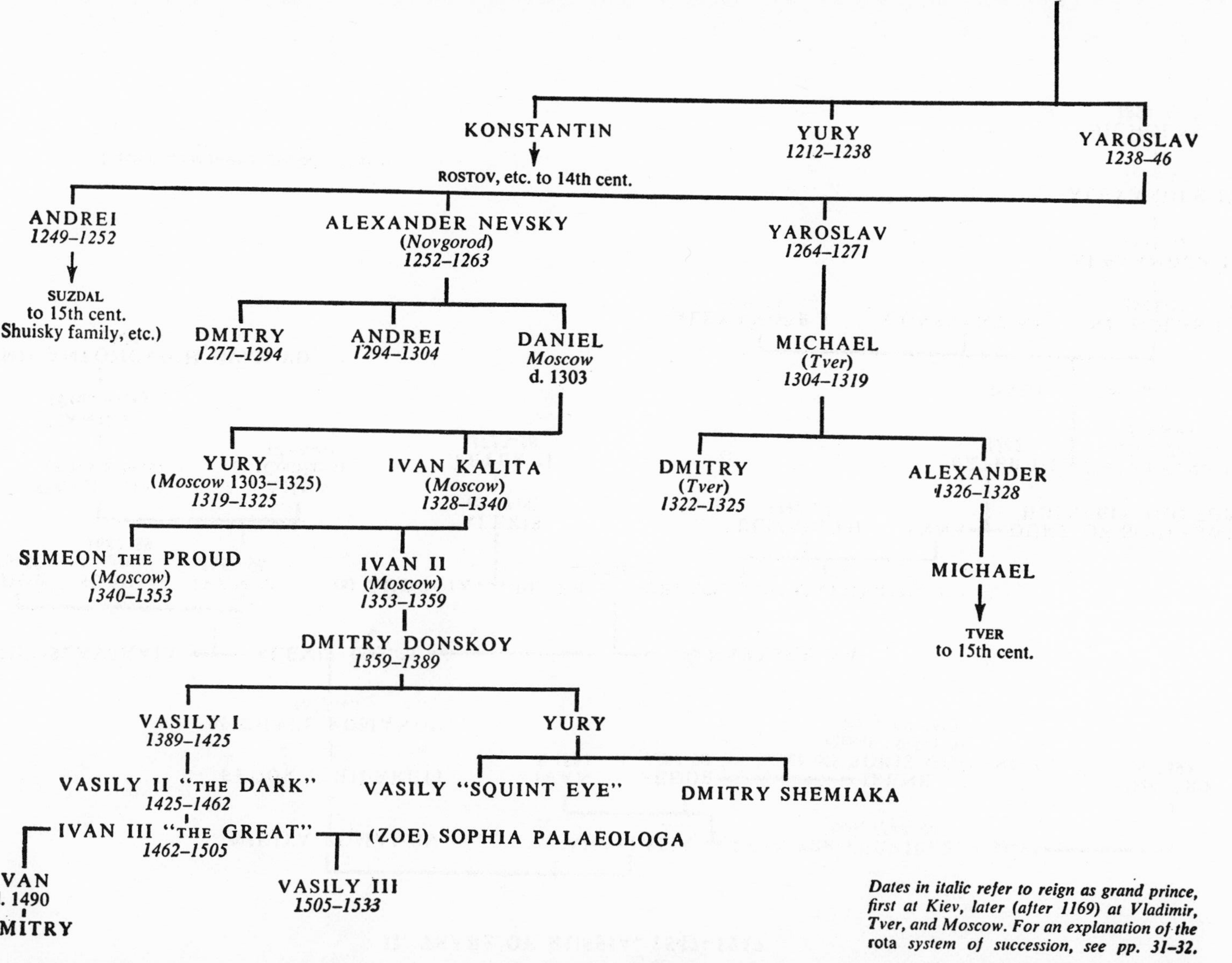

Dates in italic refer to reign as grand prince, first at Kiev, later (after 1169) at Vladimir, Tver, and Moscow. For an explanation of the rota *system of succession, see pp. 31–32.*

(continued on page 848)

II. TSARS OF RUSSIA, 1547–1917

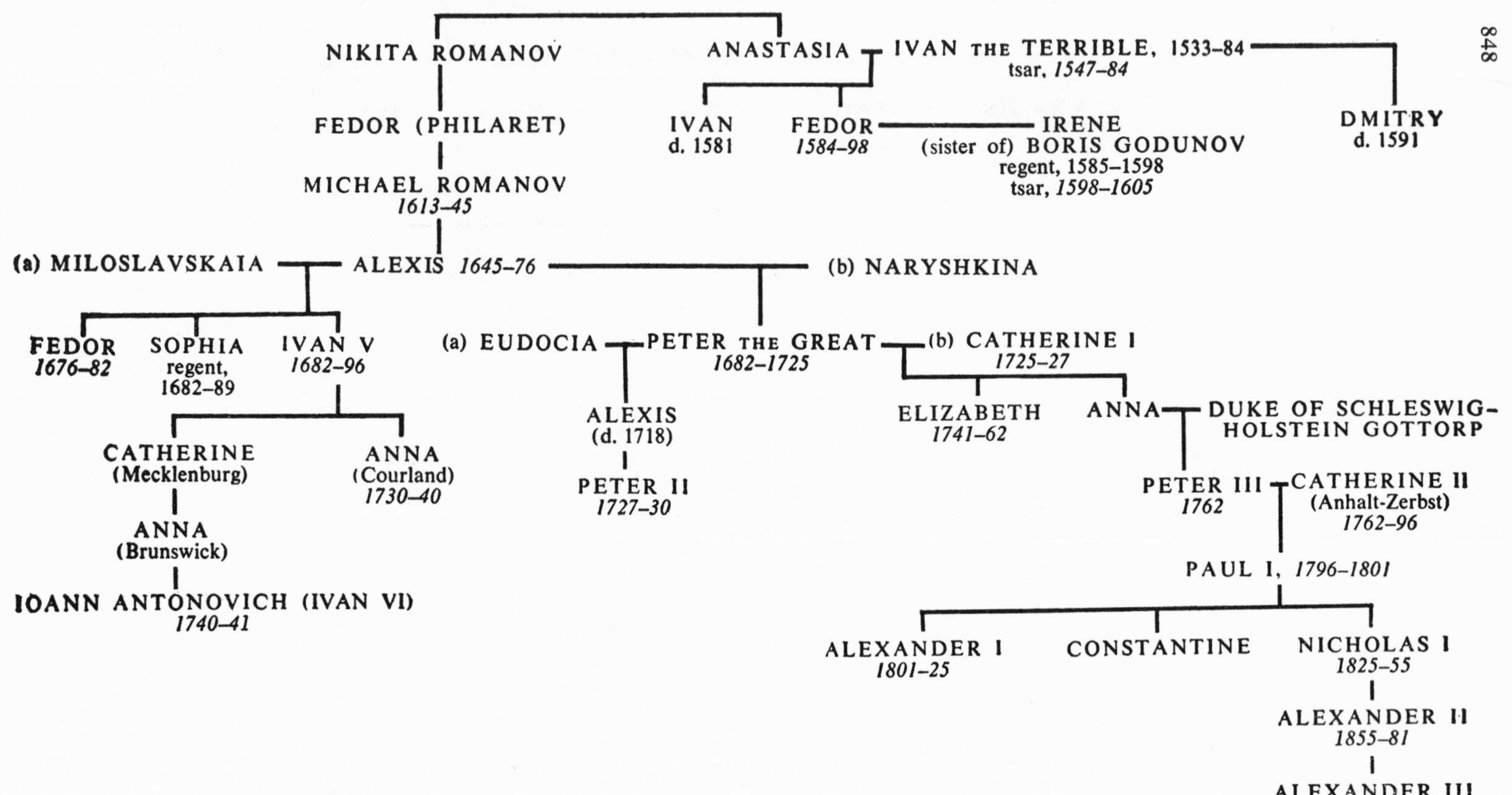

Dates in italic refer to periods of reign.

MEMBERS (M) AND CANDIDATE MEMBERS (C) OF THE POLITBURO AND PRESIDIUM 1917–1968

M and C indicate year of termination. Only years in which changes occurred shown.
Candidate members who never became members omitted.

Ordinal numbers refer to Party Congresses; changes during other years were made at Plenary Sessions of the Central Committee.		*Politburo*																				*Presidium*												*Politburo*		*Notes*
		1917 Temp.	1919–8th	1921–10th	1922–11th	1924–13th	1925–14th	1926	1927–15th	1929	1930–16th	1932	1934–17th	1935	1937	1938	1939–18th	1941	1946	1947	1948	1949	1952–19th	1953	1955	1956–20th	1957	1958	1960	1961–22nd	1962	1964	1965	1966–23rd	1967	
LENIN, V. I.	(1870–1924)	M	M	M	M	~~M~~																														Died; Premier 1917–1924
TROTSKY, L. D.	(1879–1940)	M	M	M	M	M	M	~~M~~																												Expelled; exiled 1929; murdered
STALIN, I. V.	(1879–1953)	M	M	M	M	M	M	M	M	M	M	M	M	M	M	M	M	M	M	M	M	M	M	~~M~~												Died; Premier 1941–1953
KAMENEV, L. B.	(1883–1936)	M	M	M	M	M	M	~~C~~																												Expelled; executed
ZINOVIEV, G. E.	(1883–1936)	M	C	M	M	M	M	~~M~~																												Expelled; executed
SOKOLNIKOV, G. YA.	(1888–)	~~M~~				C	~~C~~																													Imprisoned 1937
BUBNOV, A. S.	(1883–1940)	~~M~~																																		Died
KRESTINSKY, A. N.	(18 ? –1938)		M	~~M~~																																First Secretary 1919–1921; executed
BUKHARIN, N. I.	(1888–1938)		C	C	C	M	M	M	M	~~M~~																										Expelled; executed
MOLOTOV, V. M.	(1890–)			C	C	C	C	M	M	M	M	M	M	M	M	M	M	M	M	M	M	M	M	M	M	~~M~~										Premier 1930–1941; expelled
RYKOV, A. I.	(1881–1938)				M	M	M	M	M	M	~~M~~																									Premier 1924–1930; expelled; executed
TOMSKY, M. P.	(1880–1936)				M	M	M	M	M	M	~~M~~																									Dropped; suicide
RUDZUTAK, YA. E.	(1887–1938)					C	C	M	M	M	M	~~M~~	C	C	C	~~C~~																				Executed
KALININ, M. I.	(1875–1946)					C	C	M	M	M	M	M	M	M	M	M	M	M	~~M~~																	President 1919–1946; died

DZERZHINSKY, F. E.	(1877–1926)					C	C ~~C~~									Died
VOROSHILOV, K. E.	(1881–196?)						M	M M	M M	M M M M	M M M M M M	M M M	M M M ~~M~~			President 1953–1960
ORDZHONIKIDZE, G. K.	(1886–1937)						C	C C	M M	M M ~~M~~						Died
ANDREEV, A. A.	(1895–)						C	C C	C M	M M M M	M M M M M M	~~M~~				Dropped when Presidium established
KIROV, S. M.	(1886–1934)						C	C C	M M	~~M~~						Assassinated
KAGANOVICH, L. M.	(1893–)						C	C C	M M	M M M M	M M M M M M	M M M	M ~~M~~			Expelled
MIKOYAN, A. I.	(1895–)						C	C C	C C	C M M M	M M M M M M	M M M	M M M M	M M M M	~~M~~	President 1964–1965; dropped
KUIBYSHEV, V. V.	(1888–1935)							M M	M M	M ~~M~~						Died
CHUBAR, V. YA.	(1891–1941)							C C	C C	C C M ~~M~~						Purged
KOSSIOR, S. V.	(?)							C	C M	M M M M	~~M~~					Purged
ZHDANOV, A. A.	(1896–1948)									C C C	M M M M ~~M~~					Died
KHRUSHCHEV, N. S.	(1894–)									C	M M M M M M	M M M	M M M M	M M ~~M~~		First Secretary 1953–1964; Premier 1958–1964; dismissed
BERIA, L. P.	(1899–1953)										C C M M M M	M ~~M~~				Expelled; shot
SHVERNIK, N. M.	(1888–)										C C C C C C	M C C	C M M M	M M M M	~~M~~	President 1946–1953; dropped
MALENKOV, G. M.	(1902–)										C M M M M	M M M	M ~~M~~			Premier 1953–1955; expelled
VOZNESENSKY, N. A.	(1903–1950)										C C M M ~~M~~					Arrested
BULGANIN, N. A.	(1895–)										C C M M	M M M	M M ~~M~~			Premier 1955–1958; expelled
KOSYGIN, A. N.	(1904–)										C M M M	C ~~C~~	C C M	M M M M	M M	Premier 1964
ARISTOV, A. B.	(1903–)											M ~~M~~	M M M	~~M~~		Dropped
KOROTCHENKO, D. S.	(1894–)											M ~~M~~	C C C	~~C~~		Dropped
KUUSINEN, O. V.	(1881–1964)											M ~~M~~	M M M	M M ~~M~~		Died
MELNIKOV, L. G.	(?)											M ~~C~~				Dismissed
PERVUKHIN, M. G.	(1904–)											M M M	M C C C	~~C~~		Dropped
PONOMARENKO, P. K.	(?)											M C C	~~C~~			Dropped
SABUROV, M. Z.	(?)											M M M	M ~~M~~			Dropped
SUSLOV, M. A.	(1902–)											M ~~M~~ M	M M M M	M M M M	M M	

(continued on next page)

MEMBERS (M) AND CANDIDATE MEMBERS (C) OF THE POLITBURO AND PRESIDIUM 1917–1968 (*continued*)

M and C indicate year of termination. Only years in which changes occurred shown.
Candidate members who never became members omitted.

Ordinal numbers refer to Party Congresses; changes during other years were made at Plenary Sessions of the Central Committee.		*Politburo* 1917 Temp.	1919–8th	1921–10th	1922–11th	1924–13th	1925–14th	1926	1927–15th	1929	1930–16th	1932	1934–17th	1935	1937	1938	1939–18th	1941	1946	1947	1948	1949	*Presidium* 1952–19th	1953	1955	1956–20th	1957	1958	1960	1961–22nd	1962	1964	1965	*Politburo* 1966–23rd	1967	*Notes*
Other Members																																				
BREZHNEV, L. I.	(1906–)																						7 C	~~7~~ ~~C~~		C	M	M	M	M	M	M	M	M	M	President 1960–1964; First Sec. 1964–1966; General Secretary 1966–
IGNATOV, N. G.	(1901–)																						C	~~C~~			M	M	M	~~M~~						Dropped
KIRICHENKO, A. I.	(1908–)																							C	M	M	M	M	~~M~~							Expelled
ZHUKOV, G. E.	(1896–)																									C	~~M~~									Expelled
MUKHITDINOV, N. A.	(1917–)																										CM	M	M	~~M~~						Dropped
FURTSEVA, E. A.	(1910–)																									C	M	M	M	~~M~~						Dropped
KOZLOV, F. R.	(1908–1965)																										CM	M	M	M	M	~~M~~				Stroke 1963; died
BELIAEV, N. I.	(1903–)																										M	M	~~M~~							Expelled
KIRILENKO, A. P.	(1906–)																										C	C	C	~~C~~	M	M	M	M	M	Dropped; reëlected 1962
MAZUROV, K. I.	(1914–)																										C	C	C	C	C	C	M	M	M	
PODGORNY, N. V.	(1903–)																											C	M	M	M	M	M	M	M	President 1965–
POLIANSKY, D. S.	(1917–)																											C	M	M	M	M	M	M	M	
VORONOV, G.	(?)																													CM	M	M	M	M	M	
SHELEST	(1908–)																															CM	M	M	M	
SHELEPIN, A.	(1918–)																															M	M	M	M	
PELSHE, A.	(1900–)																																	M	M	
Total membership at year's end. Candidate members who never subsequently became Members not listed in table.	MEMBERS	7	5	5	7	7	7	8	9	8	10	10	9	9	9	7	9	9	10	11	12	11	25	9	11	11	15	14	14	11	12	11	12	11	11	
	CANDIDATES	—	2	2	2	6	8	7	8	8	3	3	5	6	5	3	2	5	4	3	1	1	11	13	3	6	8	10	7	5	6	6	7	8	9	

Index

ARCTIC
Murmansk
NOVAIA ZEMLIA
WHITE SEA
Archangel
BALTIC SEA
ESTONIA
LATVIA
LITHUANIA
BYELORUSSIA
Pechora R.
Pechora
Yenisei River
Volga R.
MOSCOW
FEDERATED
Ob River
MOLDAVIA
DATE DUE
GAYLORD
PRINTED IN U.S.A.
Tomsk
Novosibirsk
KUZNETSK BASIN
Irtysh R.
TURKESTAN SIBERIAN RY.
Alma Ata
SINKIANG
TIBET
NEPAL
EAST PAKISTAN
CEYLON
Bosporus Straits
Istanbul
AEGEAN SEA
MEDITERRANEAN SEA
TURKEY
Antioch
CYPRUS
Alexandria
Cairo
ISRAEL
LEB.
SYRIA
Suez Canal
JORDAN
Baghdad
EGYPT
RED SEA
SAUDI ARABIA
ETHIOPIA
IX
THE SOVIET UNION